CANADA

29th Edition

Where to Stay and Eat for All Budgets

Must-See Sights and Local Secrets

Ratings You Can Trust

Portions of this book appear in *Fodor's Montréal & Québec City, Fodor's Nova Scotia & Atlantic Canada, Fodor's Toronto,* and *Fodor's Vancouver & Victoria.*

Fodor's Travel Publications New York, Toronto, London, Sydney, Auckland

www.fodors.com

FODOR'S CANADA

Editors: Joanna Cantor; Rachel Klein; Caroline Trefler

Editorial Production: Tom Holton

Editorial Contributors: Alison Appelbe, Wanita Bates, Bruce Bishop, Jeff Bursey, Teresa Earle, Christine Halon, Carolyn B. Heller, Hélèna Katz, Shannon Kelly, Sue Kernaghan, Chris McBeath, Celeste Moure, Debbie Olsen, Sandra Phinney, Amy Pugsley Fraser, Pat Rediger, Sarah Richards, Amy Rosen, Mary Ann Simpkins, Mark Sullivan, Julie Waters, Paul Waters

Maps & Illustrations: David Lindroth, Ed Jacobus, Mark Stroud, *cartographers*; Bob Blake and Rebecca Baer, *map editors*

Design: Fabrizio LaRocca, *creative director*; Guido Caroti, Siobhan O'Hare, *art directors*; Tina Malaney, Chie Ushio, Ann McBride, *designers*; Melanie Marin, *senior picture editor;* Moon Sun Kim, *cover designer*

Cover Photo (moose, Algonquin Provincial Park, Ontario): John Foster/Masterfile

Production/Manufacturing: Angela L. McLean

COPYRIGHT

29th Edition

ISBN 978–1–4000–0734–9

ISSN 0160–3906

SPECIAL SALES

This book is available at special discounts for bulk purchases for sales promotions or premiums. Special editions, including personalized covers, excerpts of existing books, and corporate imprints, can be created in large quantities for special needs. For more information, write to Special Markets/Premium Sales, 1745 Broadway, MD 6-2, New York, New York 10019, or e-mail specialmarkets@randomhouse.com.

AN IMPORTANT TIP & AN INVITATION

Although all prices, opening times, and other details in this book are based on information supplied to us at press time, changes occur all the time in the travel world, and Fodor's cannot accept responsibility for facts that become outdated or for inadvertent errors or omissions. So **always confirm information when it matters,** especially if you're making a detour to visit a specific place. Your experiences—positive and negative—matter to us. If we have missed or misstated something, **please write to us.** We follow up on all suggestions. Contact the Canada editor at editors@fodors.com or c/o Fodor's at 1745 Broadway, New York, NY 10019.

PRINTED IN THE UNITED STATES OF AMERICA
10 9 8 7 6 5 4 3 2 1

Be a Fodor's Correspondent

Your opinion matters. It matters to us. It matters to your fellow Fodor's travelers, too. And we'd like to hear it. In fact, we need to hear it.

When you share your experiences and opinions, you become an active member of the Fodor's community. That means we'll not only use your feedback to make our books better, but we'll publish your names and comments whenever possible. Throughout our guides, look for "Word of Mouth," excerpts of your unvarnished feedback.

Here's how you can help improve Fodor's for all of us.

Tell us when we're right. We rely on local writers to give you an insider's perspective. But our writers and staff editors—who are the best in the business—depend on you. Your positive feedback is a vote to renew our recommendations for the next edition.

Tell us when we're wrong. We're proud that we update most of our guides every year. But we're not perfect. Things change. Hotels cut services. Museums change hours. Charming cafés lose charm. If our writer didn't quite capture the essence of a place, tell us how you'd do it differently. If any of our descriptions are inaccurate or inadequate, we'll incorporate your changes in the next edition and will correct factual errors at fodors.com immediately.

Tell us what to include. You probably have had fantastic travel experiences that aren't yet in Fodor's. Why not share them with a community of like-minded travelers? Maybe you chanced upon a beach or bistro or B&B that you don't want to keep to yourself. Tell us why we should include it. And share your discoveries and experiences with everyone directly at fodors.com. Your input may lead us to add a new listing or highlight a place we cover with a "Highly Recommended" star or with our highest rating, "Fodor's Choice."

Give us your opinion instantly at our feedback center at www.fodors.com/feedback. You may also e-mail editors@fodors.com with the subject line "Canada Editor." Or send your nominations, comments, and complaints by mail to Canada Editor, Fodor's, 1745 Broadway, New York, NY 10019.

You and travelers like you are the heart of the Fodor's community. Make our community richer by sharing your experiences. Be a Fodor's correspondent.

Happy traveling!

Tim Jarrell, Publisher

CONTENTS

MAPS

CONTENTS

ABOUT THIS BOOK

Our Ratings

Sometimes you find terrific travel experiences and sometimes they just find you. But usually the burden is on you to select the right combination of experiences. That's where our ratings come in.

As travelers we've all discovered a place so wonderful that its worthiness is obvious. And sometimes that place is so unique that superlatives don't do it justice: you just have to be there to know. These sights, properties, and experiences get our highest rating, **Fodor's Choice** indicated by orange stars throughout this book.

Black stars highlight sights and properties we deem **Highly Recommended** places that our writers, editors, and readers praise again and again for consistency and excellence.

By default, there's another category: any place we include in this book is by definition worth your time, unless we say otherwise. And we will.

Disagree with any of our choices? Care to nominate a place or suggest that we rate one more highly? Visit our feedback center at www.fodors.com/feedback.

Budget Well

Hotel and restaurant price categories from ¢ to $$$$ are defined in the opening pages of each chapter. For attractions, we always give standard adult admission fees; reductions are usually available for children, students, and senior citizens. Want to pay with plastic? **AE, D, DC, MC, V** following restaurant and hotel listings indicate whether American Express, Discover, Diners Club, MasterCard, and Visa are accepted.

Restaurants

Unless we state otherwise, restaurants are open for lunch and dinner daily. We mention dress only when there's a specific requirement and reservations only when they're essential or not accepted—it's always best to book ahead.

Hotels

Hotels have private bath, phone, TV, and air-conditioning and operate on the European Plan (aka EP, meaning without meals), unless we specify that they use the Continental Plan (CP, with a Continental breakfast), Breakfast Plan (BP, with a full breakfast), or Modified American Plan (MAP, with breakfast and dinner) or are all-inclusive (including all meals and most activities). We always list facilities but not whether you'll be charged an extra fee to use them, so when pricing accommodations, find out what's included.

Many Listings

- ★ Fodor's Choice
- ★ Highly recommended
- ✉ Physical address
- ✣ Directions
- Mailing address
- ☎ Telephone
- Fax
- On the Web
- E-mail
- Admission fee
- ⌚ Open/closed times
- Ⓜ Metro stations
- Credit cards

Hotels & Restaurants

- Hotel
- Number of rooms
- Facilities
- Meal plans
- ✕ Restaurant
- Reservations
- Smoking
- BYOB
- Hotel with restaurant that warrants a visit

Outdoors

- Golf
- Camping

Other

- Family-friendly
- ⇨ See also
- Branch address
- ☞ Take note

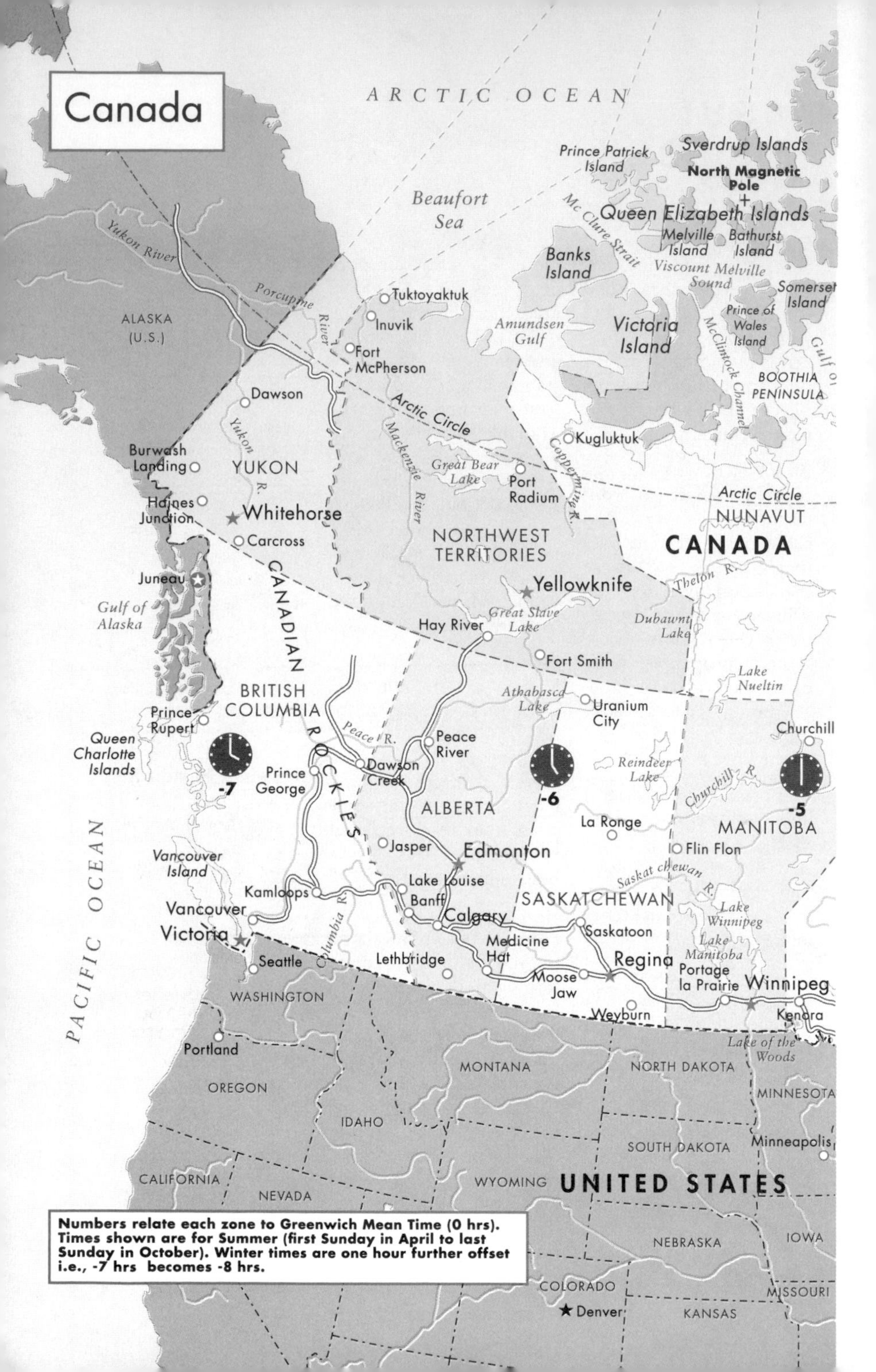

Canada
ARCTIC OCEAN
Beaufort Sea
Prince Patrick Island
Sverdrup Islands
North Magnetic Pole
Queen Elizabeth Islands
Mc Clure Strait
Banks Island
Melville Island
Bathurst Island
Viscount Melville Sound
Somerset Island
Prince of Wales Island
Victoria Island
Amundsen Gulf
McClintock Channel
BOOTHIA PENINSULA
Tuktoyaktuk
Inuvik
Fort McPherson
Porcupine River
Yukon River
ALASKA (U.S.)
Dawson
Arctic Circle
Mackenzie River
Kugluktuk
Great Bear Lake
Port Radium
Coppermine R.
Burwash Landing
YUKON
Yukon R.
Haines Junction
Whitehorse
Carcross
NUNAVUT
CANADA
NORTHWEST TERRITORIES
Juneau
CANADIAN ROCKIES
Yellowknife
Thelon R.
Gulf of Alaska
Hay River
Great Slave Lake
Dubawnt Lake
Fort Smith
Lake Nueltin
BRITISH COLUMBIA
Athabasca Lake
Uranium City
Prince Rupert
Peace R.
Peace River
Churchill
Queen Charlotte Islands
Dawson Creek
Reindeer Lake
Prince George
Churchill R.
-7
-6
-5
ALBERTA
La Ronge
MANITOBA
Jasper
Flin Flon
Edmonton
Vancouver Island
Lake Louise
Saskatchewan R.
Kamloops
Banff
SASKATCHEWAN
Lake Winnipeg
Vancouver
Calgary
Saskatoon
Victoria
Medicine Hat
Lake Manitoba
Columbia R.
Regina
Seattle
Lethbridge
Portage la Prairie
Winnipeg
Moose Jaw
PACIFIC OCEAN
WASHINGTON
Weyburn
Kenora
Portland
Lake of the Woods
MONTANA
NORTH DAKOTA
OREGON
MINNESOTA
IDAHO
SOUTH DAKOTA
Minneapolis
CALIFORNIA
WYOMING
UNITED STATES
NEVADA
NEBRASKA
IOWA
COLORADO
MISSOURI
Denver
KANSAS
Numbers relate each zone to Greenwich Mean Time (0 hrs). Times shown are for Summer (first Sunday in April to last Sunday in October). Winter times are one hour further offset i.e., -7 hrs becomes -8 hrs.

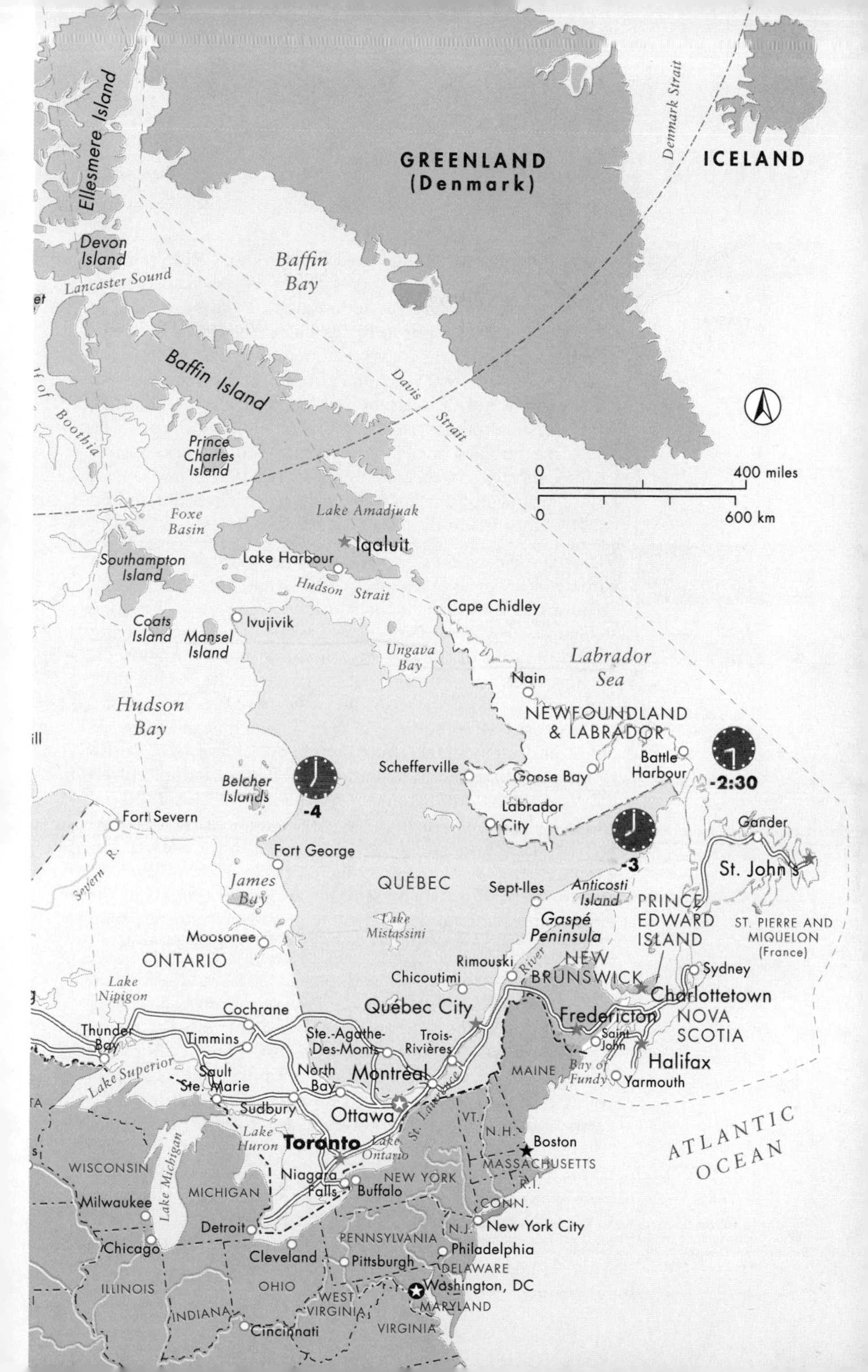

GREENLAND
(Denmark)
ICELAND
Ellesmere Island
Devon Island
Lancaster Sound
Baffin Bay
Denmark Strait
Baffin Island
Davis Strait
Boothia
Prince Charles Island
Foxe Basin
Lake Amadjuak
Iqaluit
Southampton Island
Lake Harbour
Hudson Strait
Cape Chidley
Coats Island
Mansel Island
Ivujivik
Ungava Bay
Labrador Sea
Nain
NEWFOUNDLAND & LABRADOR
Hudson Bay
Schefferville
Goose Bay
Battle Harbour
-2:30
Belcher Islands
-4
Labrador City
Fort Severn
Gander
-3
Fort George
St. John's
Severn R.
James Bay
QUÉBEC
Sept-Iles
Anticosti Island
PRINCE EDWARD ISLAND
Gaspé Peninsula
ST. PIERRE AND MIQUELON (France)
Lake Mistassini
Moosonee
ONTARIO
Rimouski
NEW BRUNSWICK
Sydney
Lake Nipigon
Chicoutimi
Charlottetown
Cochrane
Québec City
Fredericton
NOVA SCOTIA
Thunder Bay
Timmins
Ste.-Agathe-Des-Monts
Trois-Rivières
Saint John
Halifax
Lake Superior
Sault Ste. Marie
North Bay
Montréal
MAINE
Bay of Fundy
Yarmouth
Sudbury
Ottawa
St. Lawrence River
VT.
N.H.
Boston
Lake Huron
Toronto
Lake Ontario
ATLANTIC OCEAN
Lake Michigan
WISCONSIN
MASSACHUSETTS
Niagara Falls
Buffalo
NEW YORK
R.I.
MICHIGAN
Milwaukee
CONN.
Detroit
N.J.
New York City
Chicago
PENNSYLVANIA
Philadelphia
Cleveland
Pittsburgh
DELAWARE
ILLINOIS
OHIO
Washington, DC
WEST VIRGINIA
MARYLAND
INDIANA
Cincinnati
VIRGINIA
0
400 miles
0
600 km

WHAT'S WHERE

VANCOUVER	One of the most beautifully sited cities in the world, Vancouver is much more than a pretty layover for Alaskan cruises. The Pacific Ocean and the mountains of the North Shore form a dramatic backdrop to the gleaming towers of commerce downtown. Vancouver is a new city when compared to others but one that's rich in culture and diversity. Indeed, it's become a hot destination—so hot that it's been chosen, with Whistler, to host the 2010 Winter Olympic Games. The arts scene bubbles in summer, when the city stages most of its film, music, and theater festivals. You'll also find opera, ballet, and symphony, as well as plenty of nightlife and an equally vibrant and diverse cuisine scene.
VICTORIA & VANCOUVER ISLAND	Victoria, the capital of British Colombia, is a stunner. It has a climate like that of Devon in Great Britain, with springs that are glorious with flowers and sunshine, and stately Victorian structures such as the Parliament Buildings, outlined at night with thousands of starry lights. Victoria grew up Anglophile but has been reinventing itself as a city of the Pacific Rim, with due regard for its Asian and native heritage. You can still find a proper afternoon tea, but you'll also find the country's oldest and most intact Chinatown and, at the Royal British Columbia Museum, the definitive First Peoples exhibit. Overall, Vancouver Island stretches northward 483 km (300 mi) end to end—North America's largest Pacific coastal island. At Strathcona Provincial Park, in the middle of the island, stargazers escape the haze of city lights, as do hikers, canoeists, and campers. Whales and seals are among the sights at the Pacific Rim National Park Reserve, but winter storms, symphonic in their grandeur, are the draw for tempest lovers.
BRITISH COLUMBIA	This sprawling province includes some of the last true wilderness in North America—and the chance to enjoy it from a kayak, sailboat, floatplane, or hiking path before bedding down at a high-style lodge or a back-to-nature campsite. In the Lower Mainland, in and around Vancouver, British Columbia appears a brash young province with a population that sees its future in the Pacific Rim. In the north, however, are ancient rain forests, untamed wilderness, and First Nations peoples who have lived on the land for more than 10,000 years. Whistler, a short drive from Vancouver, is on deck to host the 2010 Winter Olympics. Eastward lie the vineyards and orchards of the Okanagan Valley. In the lovely Haida Gwaii, or Queen Charlotte Islands, native Haida culture is undergoing a renaissance.

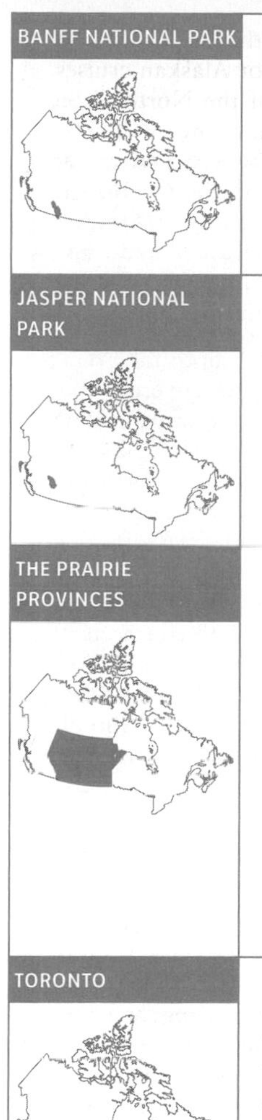

BANFF NATIONAL PARK

Canada's first national park—the third in the world—Banff is located 80 mi (128 km) west of Calgary, Alberta, encompassing 2,564 square mi (6,641 square km) of valleys, mountains, glaciers, forests, meadows, and rivers. Visit during the summer months to see wildlife and hike mountain trails, or come in winter for some of the world's best skiing. When you're done, visit the bustling Banff town site, which is packed with shops and restaurants.

JASPER NATIONAL PARK

Jasper is the largest of the Canadian Rocky Mountain National Parks at 10,878 square km (4,200 square mi), and one of the largest protected mountain ecosystems in the world. It has natural hot springs, rugged terrain, lakes and rivers, glaciers, and plentiful wildlife.

THE PRAIRIE PROVINCES

Fewer than 5 million people live in Alberta, Saskatchewan, and Manitoba, which together fill an area twice the size of France. This makes for a lot of wide and lonely landscapes that have produced people who combine a rugged individualism with a sense of community unrivaled anywhere in the country. The climate is harsh—frigid in winter and hot and dry in summer—but the region is Canada's breadbasket and the source of much of its oil and natural gas. The area's major cities—Calgary, Edmonton, Saskatoon, Regina, and Winnipeg—provide a good base for exploring the area's history: dinosaurs, native sites, frontier forts, and a variety of ethnic communities. National and provincial parks preserve grasslands, badlands, waterways, and forests.

TORONTO

Ethnic diversity is behind much of Toronto's vibrancy. The city encompasses more than 100 ethnic groups speaking more than 100 languages, and its neighborhoods offer a world tour. The mix of cultures can be experienced through the city's myriad attractions, from the world-class theater scene and imposing skyscrapers to the sensual overload of its ethnic markets and abundant nightlife and shopping options. The city's position on the shore of Lake Ontario has brought about a waterfront brimming with opportunities for outdoor and other amusements. A 15-minute ferry ride across Toronto Bay are the breezy Toronto Islands, their more than 550 acres of parkland nearly irresistible, especially in summer.

WHAT'S WHERE

PROVINCE OF ONTARIO

Ontario has both Canada's political capital, Ottawa, and its commercial capital, Toronto. It's also big (four times the size of Great Britain), rich, and growing. You may ice-skate on a canal in Ottawa, ski at first-rate resorts, indulge in Shakespeare in rural Stratford, sail on four of the Great Lakes, or go get lost in a wilderness that stretches all the way to the shores of James Bay. And in the past 20 years or so, Ontario has shuffled off its staid, Scottish ways and learned to eat and drink well and even how to party, thanks largely to an influx of settlers from just about every country on earth.

MONTRÉAL

Montréal and the island on which it stands both take their name from Mont-Royal, a stubby plug of tree-covered igneous rock that rises just 330 feet above the surrounding cityscape. But while its height is unimpressive, "the mountain" forms one of Canada's finest urban parks, and its summit offers visitors a grand overview of what North America's largest French-speaking metropolis has to offer. To the south are the shops, museums, and office towers of the Golden Square Mile and downtown. Beyond them, along the shores of the St. Lawrence River, are the narrow, cobbled streets of Vieux-Montréal, and beyond that are the green sanctuaries of Îles Notre-Dame and Ste-Hélène. Spreading out from Mont-Royal's eastern flank are the polyglot neighborhoods of the Quartier-Latin and Plateau Mont-Royal, abuzz with restaurants, nightclubs, bars, and cafés. Much of the city is easily accessible on foot; the rest can be reached via the métro system.

QUÉBEC CITY

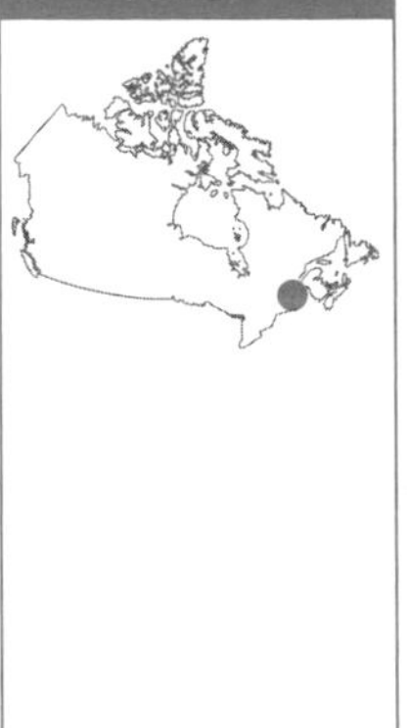

Québec City is widely considered to be the most French city in North America; nearly 95% of the people who live here claim French as their mother tongue. The only walled city north of Mexico is split into two tiers, separated by steep rock against which are more than 25 *escaliers* (staircases). Along the banks of the St. Lawrence River is the Lower Town, or Basse-Ville, the oldest neighborhood in North America. Its time-worn streets brim with up-to-the-minute shops, charming restaurants, and art galleries, as well as touristy stores, all housed in former warehouses and residences. You can see the rooftops of the Lower Town from the Terrasse Dufferin boardwalk in Vieux-Québec's Upper Town, or Haute-Ville. The most prominent buildings of Québec City's earliest European inhabitants stand here. Many of Québec's military sites—fortifications and battlements—and a number of museums and other attractions

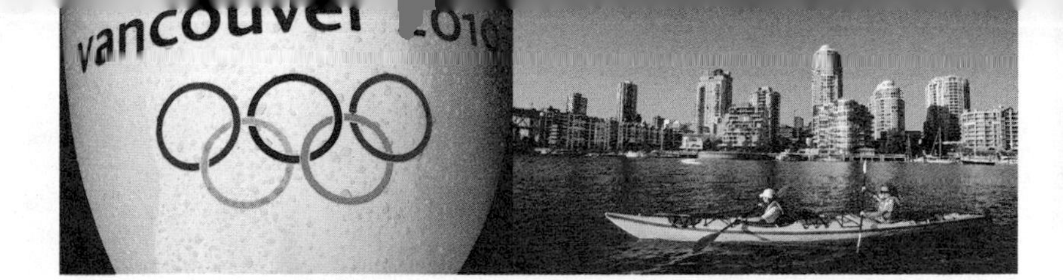

	encircle the city. Beyond the town walls, old and new government buildings intermingle with the structures of a modern metropolis that grew up in the 20th century.
PROVINCE OF QUÉBEC 	Québec is probably what all North America would have been like if the French rather than the English had won the Seven Years' War. This eastern province has always been able to find an excuse for a party. Its historic capital, Québec City, for example, celebrates one of the world's most brutal winters with a carnival that features parades of majorettes and teams who race boats across an ice-choked river. Throughout the province, the rest of the year is full of festivals celebrating jazz, international folklore, film, classical music, fireworks, beer, and hot-air balloons. What really sets Québec apart, of course, is language. French in Québec is more than the language of love—it's the language of law, business, politics, and culture, and of more than 80% of the people.
NEW BRUNSWICK 	New Brunswick is where the great Canadian forest, sliced by sweeping river valleys and modern highways, meets the Atlantic. To the north and east, the gentle, warm Gulf Stream washes more than 90 beaches along 2,000 km (1,240 mi) of coastline. On the Bay of Fundy, four-story sculptures are carved by the tides at Hopewell Cape; you can literally walk along the floor of the ocean during low tide. In addition to the seacoast, pure inland streams, quaint towns with Victorian inns and manicured gardens, and historic cities such as Fredericton and Saint John draw visitors year-round. The province's dual heritage—35% of its population is Acadian French—adds cultural interest.
PRINCE EDWARD ISLAND 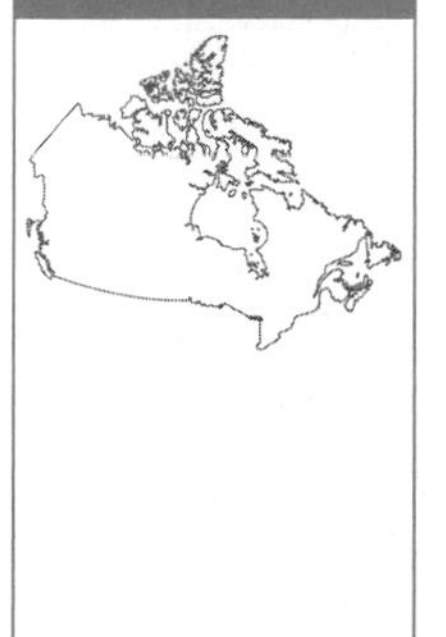	In the Gulf of St. Lawrence north of Nova Scotia and New Brunswick, Canada's smallest province, Prince Edward Island, seems too good to be true, with its crisply painted farmhouses, manicured green fields rolling down to sandy beaches, warm ocean water, and lobster boats in trim little harbors. The vest-pocket capital city, Charlottetown, is packed with architectural heritage and culture. It is here that the Confederation of the Arts hosts the Charlottetown Festival, which features the musical *Anne of Green Gables*. As well as being historically significant as the Cradle of Confederation, PEI is home to some of Atlantic Canada's finest inns, most ornate churches, and much lauded lobster suppers. And thanks to the Confederation Bridge, this Garden of the Gulf is easily accessible from the mainland.

WHAT'S WHERE

NOVA SCOTIA	Almost an island, Nova Scotia is a little province on the Atlantic coast with a long history and a rich culture. Shaped by its rugged coastline and honed by the sea, over the centuries it has served as a haven for blacks arriving as freemen or escaped slaves and for Scots, Germans, and Loyalists from the American Revolution, but its earliest colonial history was enriched by the Acadians and scarred by their brutal deportation. This multicultural mix, dating back 400 years, may account for Nova Scotia's rich musical climate, which includes the Gaelic *ceilidh*—gatherings wild with fiddles and step dancing—and the folk songs of sailors and the sea. Salty ports dot the coastline, and their extravagant Victorian mansions—many of them now bed-and-breakfasts—bespeak the wealth of shipwrights and merchants who traded with the world a century and more ago. Today, Nova Scotia maintains its unique outlook: worldly, warm, and sturdily independent.
NEWFOUNDLAND & LABRADOR	The youngest member of the Canadian family, the province—consisting of Labrador on the mainland and the island of Newfoundland—joined the Confederation in 1949. This is where the New World begins. Norsemen settled in L'Anse aux Meadows around the year 1000, and explorer John Cabot landed on the rocky coast in 1497. The land has a raw beauty, with steep cliffs, roaring salmon rivers, and fishing villages that perch precariously on naked rock. Its people are a rich mix of English, Irish, and Scots who have a colorful grasp of language and a talent for acerbic commentary. St. John's, the capital, is a classic harbor city.
WILDERNESS CANADA	Stretched across the top of Canada above the 60th parallel is the country's last frontier—the Yukon, the Northwest Territories, and Nunavut. Here, tundra plains reach to the Arctic Ocean, remote ice fields engulf the St. Elias Mountains, and white-water rivers snake through mountain ranges and deep canyons. In this thinly populated expanse, native cultures have survived the coming of the white man and are showing signs of new vitality. You can cross the Arctic tundra by dogsled with Inuit hunters or visit native soapstone carvers, painters, printmakers, and clothesmakers.

WHEN TO GO

Many regions in the country are truly year-round destinations. Most travelers plan a trip to Canada for some time in the July–September period. Nevertheless, fall, which paints the trees in vibrant reds, yellows, and golds, is a great time to travel, as the roads are less congested and the scenery is spectacular. May and June also tend to be less crowded. Canada's winter festivals, some of the best in the world, help take the edge off the cold season.

Climate

The following are average daily maximum and minimum temperatures for some major cities.

Forecasts **Weather Channel Connection** (*www.weather.com*).

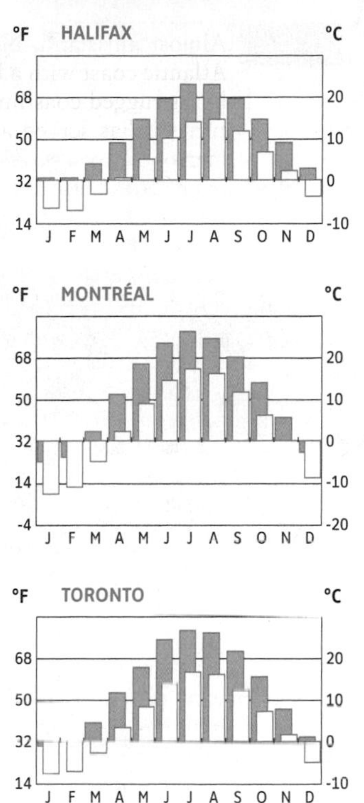

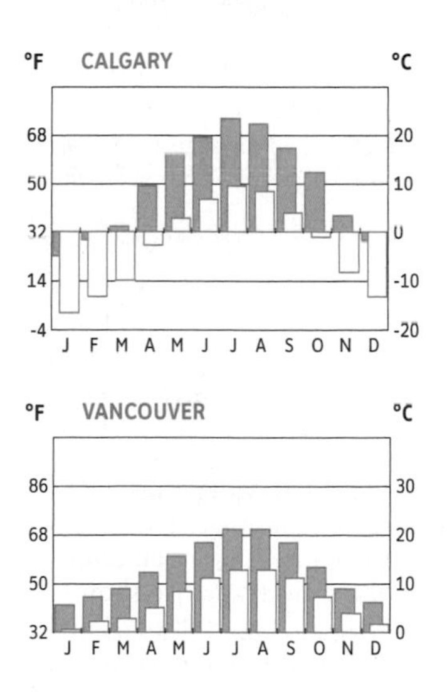

QUINTESSENTIAL CANADA

Learn to Say "Eh"

Canada's "Eh" is like France's "zut, alors," except in Canada, people actually say "eh," and say it all the time. The Canadian Oxford Dictionary says it's most commonly heard in the provinces of Manitoba, Ontario, New Brunswick, but don't worry: Master this verbal tic and you'll fit in anywhere, even French-speaking Quebec. The wonderful thing about "eh" is its versatility. There's the interrogatory "eh" ("You want to go to a movie, eh?"), the consensus-seeking "eh" ("This is good sugar pie, eh?"), the inquisitive "eh" ("She's got a new boyfriend, eh?"), the solo "eh," which means "Repeat please," and the simple punctuation "eh" that can be dropped randomly into long narratives to reassure the listener that it's a dialogue, not a soliloquy. And then there's the conciliatory "eh"—perhaps the oddest one of all. Canadians drop it in at the end of insults to change a command like "Take off" or "Beat it" (or worse) into more of a suggestion than a command. And really, it does take the edge off, eh?

A "Large Double-Double"

Nothing says Canada more clearly than a maple-glazed donut and a "large double-double" (large coffee with two creams and two sugars) at Tim Hortons. Timmy's brown-and-yellow shops line the highways from coast to coast, and are as familiar on the main streets of Vancouver and Toronto as they are in Climax, Saskatchewan, and Come By Chance, Newfounland. Timmy's is Canada's meeting place—despite the fact that the chain is now owned by an American conglomerate and that most people under 40 have forgotten that its founder was hockey great Tim Horton of the Toronto Maple Leafs.

Hockey Night in Canada

Love him or hate him (or love to hate him), there's no question that Don "Grapes" Cherry, the irrepressible hockey commentator, is a Canadian cultural icon. He's an unapologetic exponent of the gritty, rock-em, sock-em version of the sport, and the reason that thousands of fans stay glued to their TV screens at the end of the first period on Hockey Night in Canada instead of running to the bathroom or for more beer: no one wants to miss a second of Cherry's bombast on Coach's Corner. He, like the sport he represents, is the antithesis of everything Canadians are supposed be—rude, opinionated, flamboyant, overbearing, politically incorrect, passionately patriotic, and outrageously partisan. But then again hockey isn't for the faint of heart, or fainthearted commentators. And there's something about both it and Don Cherry that speaks to Canadians.

Cabane à Sucre

It started as a rustic rite of spring. When warm days and chilly nights made the sap in the sugar maples run, farmers would invite friends over to celebrate by pouring freshly boiled maple syrup over snow, where it would harden into strips of sticky taffy. Soon a distinctively Canadian institution was born—the sugar shack, or in French, the *cabane à sucre*. Finding one of these little shacks is easy enough, particularly in the province of Québec, which produces 70 percent of the world's maple syrup. You'll pay for a feast that may include ham and pea soup, syrup-soaked pudding, and maple syrup with beans, eggs, pickles, ham, and little strips of crispy pig skin called "les oreilles du Crisse," or Christ's ears. The resulting sugar rush will keep you wide awake until you get home.

IF YOU LIKE

Visiting National Parks

Yes, Canadians have exciting cities, a vibrant cultural life, and plenty of good food, but what really sets the county apart is an enormous abundance of wild and wide-open spaces. Canadians might be an urban people–more than 70 percent of them live in major population centers–but the wilderness is never far away, either physically or psychologically. And nothing captures the spirit of the Canadian wild better than its system of 43 national parks. Some parks are right on main highways; others are accessible only to those willing to shell out for a charter flight in a float plane. Here are a few you might want to consider:

Banff National Park: Founded in 1885 as a wilderness retreat for the wealthy in Alberta's Rocky Mountains, is the granddaddy of Canada's national-park system. Parts of it are well (even over) developed, but there's still plenty of room in its 6,641 square km (2,564 square mi) for the most intrepid mountain adventurer.

Cape Breton Highlands: One of the most accessible of Canada's national parks offers motorists spectacular mountain and ocean views, right at roadside. But there's nothing to stop you getting out of your car for a walk on the wild side.

Jasper National Park: Wild and untamed, the 10,878 square km (4,200 square mi) of this park encompass rugged mountain terrain, natural hot springs, crystal-clear lakes, rivers, raging waterfalls, glaciers, and an abundance of wildlife.

Point Pelee National Park This park, located in the southernmost tip of mainland Canada in Ontario, is known for an astonishing array of birds, especially during the spring and fall migrations.

Romping in Snow

To really understand Canada and its people, visit in January or February, not June or July. There's a reason this country is nicknamed the Great White North, and sooner or later, every Canadian learns how to come to terms with winter—either that or go cabin crazy. For many, snow is the only solace. If downhill skiing is your passion, Canada has world-class resorts in British Columbia and Alberta in the west and in Québec in the east. If you prefer to trek across country on skis, snowshoes, dogsleds, or snowmobiles, there are thousands of miles of well marked trails, many of them with easy access of the big cities. And if you want to party, Canadians, not surprisingly, pioneered the art of partying in the snow.

Québec Winter Carnival. This classic in one of the coldest capital cities on Earth has been a part of Québec City's calendar since 1894, with parades, fireworks, dog races, concerts, balls, and a boat race across the half-frozen St. Lawrence.

Winterlude. Strap on your skates: the world's longest rink is the focal point of the national capital's annual tribute to winter. Fueled with hot chocolate and beaver tails (fried, sugared dough), Ottawans and visitors alike glide, bogey, and frolic on a frozen 7.8-km (4.8-mi) stretch of Ottawa's Rideau Canal.

Festival du Voyageur. In Winnipeg so cold it's nicknamed "Winterpeg," the Fesitival du Voyageur celebrates the age of the fur trade with music, fireworks, and parades. The heroes of the week are the courreurs des bois, whose backbreaking work paddling canoes thousands of miles into the interior opened the Canadian west.

Wining and Dining in Big Cities

Wide open spaces and the rugged north might be the clichés that spring to mind when Canada is mentioned, but the truth is that Canadians are an overwhelmingly urban people—and if you haven't visited at least one of its three vibrant metropolises, you can't really claim to know the country. Montréal, where French is the mother tongue, has the charm of an old European capital. Toronto, the country's economic capital, blends commercial hustle with a top-notch theater. Laid-back Vancouver reflects the casual, easygoing manners of its Pacific neighbors in Washington and Oregon. The restaurant scene reflects their diverse, cosmopolitan inhabitants. Sample salmon grilled on a plank Native Canadian style in Vancouver, Asian-European fusion in Toronto, and the bold market cuisine of Montréal's innovative young chefs.

C Restaurant. This is one of Vancouver's most innovative seafood restaurants, thanks to executive chef Robert Clark's varied and extensive tasting menus with wine parings. ⊠*2–1600 Howe St., Downtown* ☎*604/681–1164.*

Toqué! A Montréal mainstay, chef Normand Laprise still hasn't lost his touch with his imaginative use of local market cuisine. ⊠*900 pl. Jean-Paul-Riopelle, Vieux-Montréal* ☎*514/499–2084.*

Susur. If you're in the mood for eclectic Asian cuisine, this is the place to come. The country's most renowned chef, Susur Lee, has a unique style and orders his menus with principal courses first and small plates last. ⊠*601 King St. W, Downtown* ☎*416/603–2205.*

Shopping for Furs and Crafts

People have traveled to Canada to look for furs ever since the beginning of the 17th century, and this is still very much the place to come. The fur industry remains an important part of the country's economic picture, contributing about $800 million to the GDP and employing about 60,000 trappers and 5,000 fur farmers, manufacturers, craftspeople, and retailers. Mink, fox, and chinchilla are the most commonly farmed fur-bearing animals, buttrappers supply the market with beaver, raccoon, muskrat, otter, bear, and wolf pelts among others. Note that conservation and humane rules for both farmers and trappers are very strict.

It was the fur trade that allowed many native Canadians—the country's First Nations—to live on the land according to the traditions of their ancestors, which explains why Canada has such a rich heritage of native crafts. Whether it's Inuit soapstone carvings or the wood carvings of British Columbia's Pacific coast nations, Canada is prime territory for arts and crafts. You'll also find Cowichan sweaters and leather goods from the West, Loyalist quilts from Ontario, pine furniture and carvings from Québec, and hooked rugs from the Maritimes.

Coastal Peoples Fine Arts Gallery. ⊠1024 Mainland St., Vancouver, B.C. ☎604/685–9298.

McComber Grosvenor Furs. ⊠402 blvd. de Mainsonneuve Ouest, Montréal, QC ☎514/288–1255.

Galerie Brosseau et Brosseau. ⊠35 rue St-Louis, Québec City, QC ☎418/694–1828.

Vancouver

WORD OF MOUTH

"Vancouver is situated in a gorgeous setting. You need at least one full day in Vancouver. On the other hand, it has so much to offer that you could spend a week there."

—Judy_In_Calgary

Updated by Alison Appelbe, Carolyn B. Heller, Chris McBeath, and Celeste Moure

VANCOUVER IS A YOUNG CITY, even by North American standards, but what it lacks in history, it makes up for with natural beauty and a multicultural vitality that has the readers of *Condé Nast Traveler* (those arbiters of taste) consistently rating it as one of the world's top cities.

The mountains and seascape make Vancouver an outdoor playground for hiking, skiing, kayaking, cycling, and sailing—and so much more—while the cuisine and arts scenes are equally diverse, reflecting the makeup of Vancouver's ethnic (predominantly Asian) mosaic. And despite all this vibrancy, the city exudes an easy West Coast style that can make New York or London feel edgy and claustrophobic to some.

More than 8 million visitors each year come to this, Canada's third-largest metropolitan area, and thousands more are expected as the city gears up to meet the challenges of co-hosting (with Whistler) the Olympic and Paralympic Winter Games in 2010. Because of its peninsula location, traffic flow is a contentious issue, and the construction of new rapid-transit lines and Olympic sites through to 2009 can make getting around by car these days pretty frustrating. Thankfully, Vancouver is deliciously walkable, especially in the downtown core, and the congestion and construction cranes needn't get in the way of enjoying the city and its people.

The mild climate, exquisite natural scenery, and relaxed outdoor lifestyle keep attracting new residents, and the number of visitors is increasing for the same reasons. People often get their first glimpse of Vancouver when catching an Alaskan cruise, and many return at some point to spend more time here.

EXPLORING VANCOUVER

The heart of Vancouver is the city's downtown core: it includes the main business district between Robson Street and the harborfront, Stanley Park, Yaletown, and the West End. It sits on a peninsula bordered by English Bay and the Pacific Ocean to the west; by False Creek (the inlet home to Granville Island) to the south; and by Burrard Inlet, the city's working port, to the north, where the North Shore Mountains loom. The oldest parts of the city, Gastown and Chinatown, lie at the edge of Burrard Inlet, around Main Street, which runs north–south and is roughly the dividing line between the east and west sides. One note about printed Vancouver street addresses: suite numbers often appear *before* the street number, followed by a hyphen.

Elsewhere in the city you'll find other places of interest: the North Shore across Burrard Inlet; Granville Island, south of downtown across English Bay in the West End and the suburb of Richmond, south of the city near the airport.

TOP REASONS TO GO

STANLEY PARK
The views, the activities, the natural wilderness beauty here are quintessential Vancouver.

MUSEUM OF ANTHROPOLOGY AT UBC
The phenomenal collection of art and cultural artifacts and the incredible setting make this Vancouver's must-see museum.

THE SEABUS
The trip across Burrard Inlet is the cheapest cruise around and offers some of the neatest photo angles of Vancouver's working harbor.

KITSILANO BEACHES
Follow the coastline road to the University of British Columbia and you'll travel past a magnificent array of beaches, from grass-edged shores to windswept stretches of sand, to cliff-side coves so private that clothing is optional.

KAYAKING INTO INDIAN ARM
Barely 30 minutes from downtown, the fjordic landscape is stunning *(see Vancouver Outdoors, especially Takaya Tours, for more info).*

DOWNTOWN AND GASTOWN

Museums and buildings of architectural and historical significance are the primary sightseeing draws in this part of downtown Vancouver, but there's also plenty of fine shopping, most notably along Robson Street and in and around Sinclair Centre. The intersection of Granville and Georgia streets is considered the city's epicenter, though it's somewhat disrupted at the moment by the construction of the new SkyTrain line.

The east side of downtown gives way to Gastown, which is touted as an up-and-coming hip neighborhood but is still really geared to tourists, with quaint cobblestone streets, Victorian era–styled streetlamps, and a plethora of souvenir shops from tacky to tasteful. Nevertheless, Vancouverites hold it dear to their hearts. After all, this was the Granville Townsite, where the city originated—albeit around a saloon. In 1867, the garrulous ("Gassy") Jack Deighton opened his saloon on the spot where his statue now stands, in the heart of Gastown, on Maple Tree Square.

At the turn of the century the area became a stopping point for those en route to the Klondike gold rush, and the community continued to thrive. After the Depression, through to the 1950s, commerce shifted elsewhere, hotels were converted into low-rental rooming houses, and the area fell into general neglect. There is little remnant of that neglect today: when Gastown, along with Chinatown, was declared a historic district in 1971, it became the focus of a huge revitalization effort. Warehouses that once lined the shorefront (note some of the "wavy" shapes of the buildings) were remodeled to house boutiques, cafés, loft apartments, and souvenir shops.

GREAT ITINERARIES

IF YOU HAVE 1 OR 2 DAYS

If you don't have a lot of time in Vancouver, you'll probably still want to spend at least a half day in **Stanley Park**: start out early for a walk, bike, or shuttle ride through the park to see the **Vancouver Aquarium Marine Science Centre**, enjoy the views from **Prospect Point**, and stroll along the seawall. If you leave the park at English Bay, you can have lunch on Denman or **Robson Street**, and meander past the trendy shops between Jervis and Burrard streets. Alternatively, you can exit the park at Coal Harbour and follow the Seawall Walk to **Canada Place**, stopping for lunch at a seaside restaurant.

On Day 2, spending a couple hours at the **Granville Island Public Market** on **Granville Island** is a must—plan to have lunch, and, if you have time, check out the multitude of crafts stores. Buses and ferries provide easy transit, and touring the island is best accomplished on foot. (If you drive, parking is available, but traffic to the island can be congested, especially on weekends.)

IF YOU HAVE 3 OR 4 DAYS

On Day 3, spend some time walking the downtown core, which is a great way to get to know the city. Plan a route that starts at **Canada Place** and heads east to **Gastown** and **Chinatown**; that's a good half day. Then, to complete the day, head north to **Yaletown** and travel back via Robson Street, by which time you'll have earned yourself a glass of British Columbia wine at one of Vancouver's excellent restaurants.

On Day 4, spend some time checking out sites beyond downtown Vancouver. A top pick is the Museum of Anthropology the campus of the University of British Columbia, where you can see Northwest Coast First Nations art. If you're traveling with children, and would rather be outside with them, head to the North Shore Mountains to swing high above the Capilano River on the **Capilano Suspension Bridge** and take in the panoramic city views as you ride the Skyride to the top of **Grouse Mountain**.

MAIN ATTRACTIONS

5 **The Bill Reid Gallery of Northwest Coast Art.** Vancouver's new aboriginal art gallery, named after one of B.C.'s pre-eminent artists, Bill Reid (1920–98), is set to open May 10, 2008. Reid's legacy of works includes wood carvings, jewelry, print, and sculpture. ✉ *639 Hornby St., Downtown* ☎ *604/682–3455* 🌐 *www.billreidgallery.com.*

7 **Canada Place.** When Vancouver hosted the Expo '86 world's fair, this former cargo pier was transformed into the Canadian pavilion. Extending four city blocks (about a mile and a half) north into Burrard Inlet, the complex mimics the style and size of a luxury ocean liner, with exterior promenades and open deck space. The Teflon-coated fiberglass roof, shaped like five sails (the material was invented by NASA and once used in astronaut spacesuits!), has become a Vancouver skyline landmark. Home to Vancouver's main cruise-ship terminal, Canada Place can accommodate up to four luxury liners at once. It's also home to the luxurious **Pan Pacific Hotel** and the **Vancouver Convention**

and Exhibition Centre (☎604/647–7390). ✉*999 Canada Place Way, Downtown* ☎*604/775–7200* 🌐*www.canadaplace.ca.*

3 Fairmont Hotel Vancouver. One of the last railway-built hotels in Canada, the Fairmont Hotel Vancouver was designed in the château style, its architectural details reminiscent of a medieval French castle. Construction began in 1929 and wrapped up just in time for King George VI of England's 1939 visit. ✉*900 W. Georgia St., Downtown* ☎*604/684–3131* 🌐*www.fairmont.com.*

1 Robson Street. Robson, Vancouver's busiest shopping street, is lined with see-and-be-seen sidewalk cafés, chain fashion stores, and high-end boutiques. The street, which links downtown to the West End, is particularly lively between Jervis and Burrard streets and stays that way into the evening with buskers and entertainers.

2 Vancouver Art Gallery. Painter Emily Carr's haunting evocations of the British Columbian hinterland are among the attractions at Western Canada's largest art gallery. Carr (1871–1945), a grocer's daughter from Victoria, fell in love with the wilderness around her and shocked middle-class Victorian society by running off to paint it. Her work accentuates the mysticism and the danger of B.C.'s wilderness and records the diminishing presence of native cultures during that era (there's something of a renaissance now). The gallery, which also hosts touring historical and contemporary exhibitions, is housed in a 1911 courthouse that Canadian architect Arthur Erickson redesigned in the early 1980s as part of the Robson Square redevelopment. ✉*750 Hornby St., Downtown* ☎*604/662–4719* 🌐*www.vanartgallery.bc.ca* 🎟*C$19.50; higher for some exhibits; by donation Thurs. 5–9* ⏲*Mon.–Wed. and Fri.–Sun. 10–5:30, Tues. and Thurs. 10–9.*

8 Vancouver Lookout! The lookout looks like a flying saucer stuck atop a high-rise and at 553 feet high, it affords one of the best views of Vancouver. A glass elevator whizzes you up 50 stories to the circular observation deck. On a clear day you can see Vancouver Island and Mount Baker in Washington State. The top-floor restaurant makes one complete revolution per hour; the elevator ride up is free for diners. **■TIP→ Tickets are good all day, so you can visit in daytime and return for another look after dark.** ✉*555 W. Hastings St., Downtown* ☎*604/689–0421* 🌐*www.vancouverlookout.com* 🎟*C$13* ⏲*May–Sept., daily 8:30 AM–10:30 PM; Oct.–Apr., daily 9–9.*

ALSO WORTH SEEING

11 Byrnes Block. George Byrnes constructed Vancouver's oldest brick building on the site of Gassy Jack Deighton's second saloon after the 1886 Great Fire, which wiped out most of the fledgling settlement of Vancouver. For a while this building was Vancouver's top luxury hotel, the Alhambra Hotel, charging a dollar a night. ✉*2 Water St., Gastown.*

4 Christ Church Cathedral. The oldest church in Vancouver was built between 1889 and 1895. Constructed in the Gothic style, this Anglican church looks like the parish church of an English village from the outside, though underneath its sandstone-clad exterior it's made

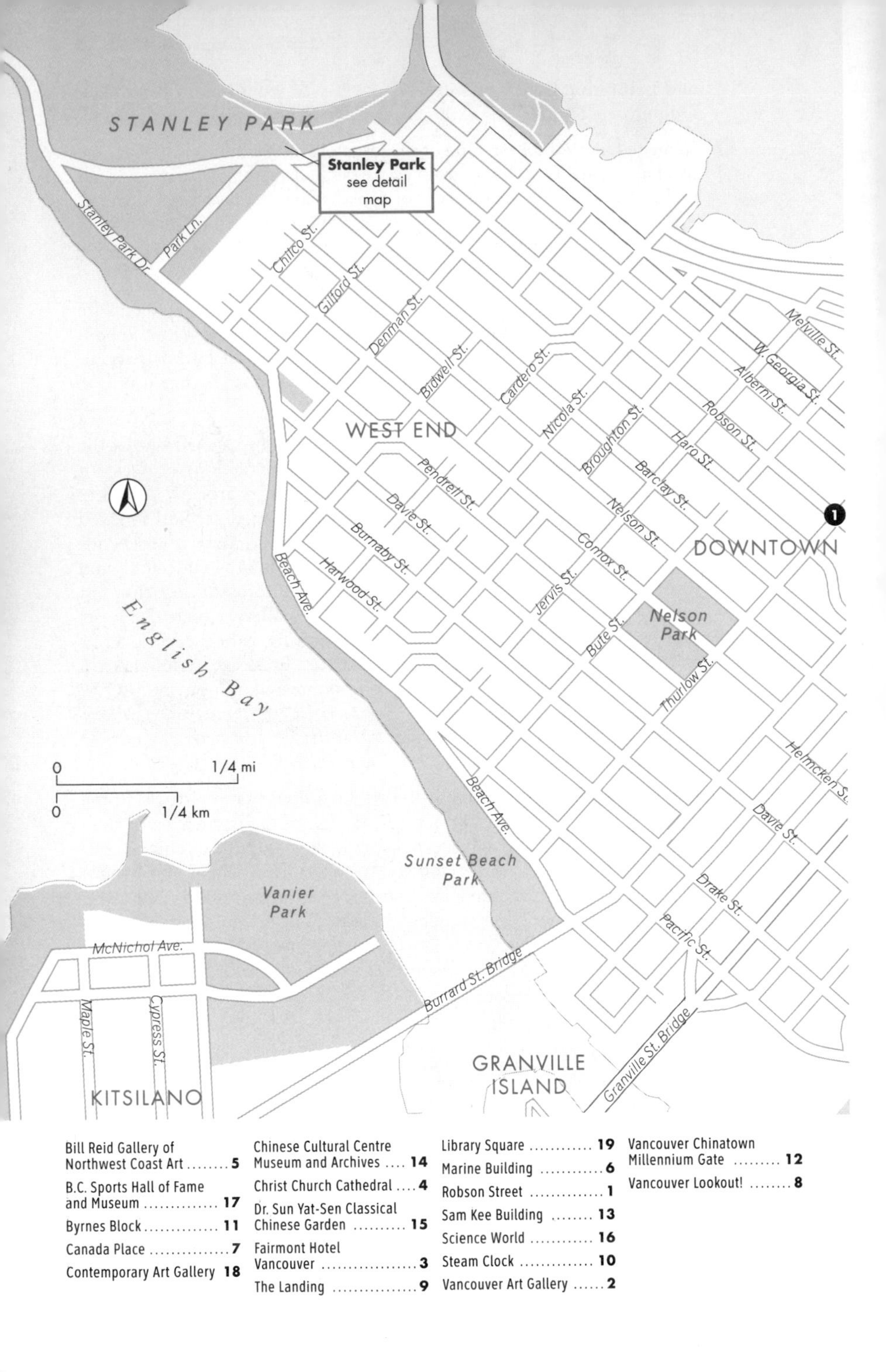
STANLEY PARK
Stanley Park
see detail
map
Stanley Park Dr.
Park Ln.
Chilco St.
Gilford St.
Denman St.
Bidwell St.
Cardero St.
Nicola St.
Broughton St.
Melville St.
W. Georgia St.
Alberni St.
Robson St.
Haro St.
Barclay St.
Nelson St.
Comox St.
Pendrell St.
Davie St.
Burnaby St.
Harwood St.
Beach Ave.
Jervis St.
Bute St.
Thurlow St.
Helmcken St.
Drake St.
Pacific St.
WEST END
DOWNTOWN
1
Nelson
Park
English Bay
0
1/4 mi
0
1/4 km
Sunset Beach
Park
Vanier
Park
McNichol Ave.
Maple St.
Cypress St.
Burrard St. Bridge
Granville St. Bridge
GRANVILLE
ISLAND
KITSILANO
Bill Reid Gallery of Northwest Coast Art 5
B.C. Sports Hall of Fame and Museum 17
Byrnes Block 11
Canada Place 7
Contemporary Art Gallery 18
Chinese Cultural Centre Museum and Archives 14
Christ Church Cathedral 4
Dr. Sun Yat-Sen Classical Chinese Garden 15
Fairmont Hotel Vancouver 3
The Landing 9
Library Square 19
Marine Building 6
Robson Street 1
Sam Kee Building 13
Science World 16
Steam Clock 10
Vancouver Art Gallery 2
Vancouver Chinatown Millennium Gate 12
Vancouver Lookout! 8

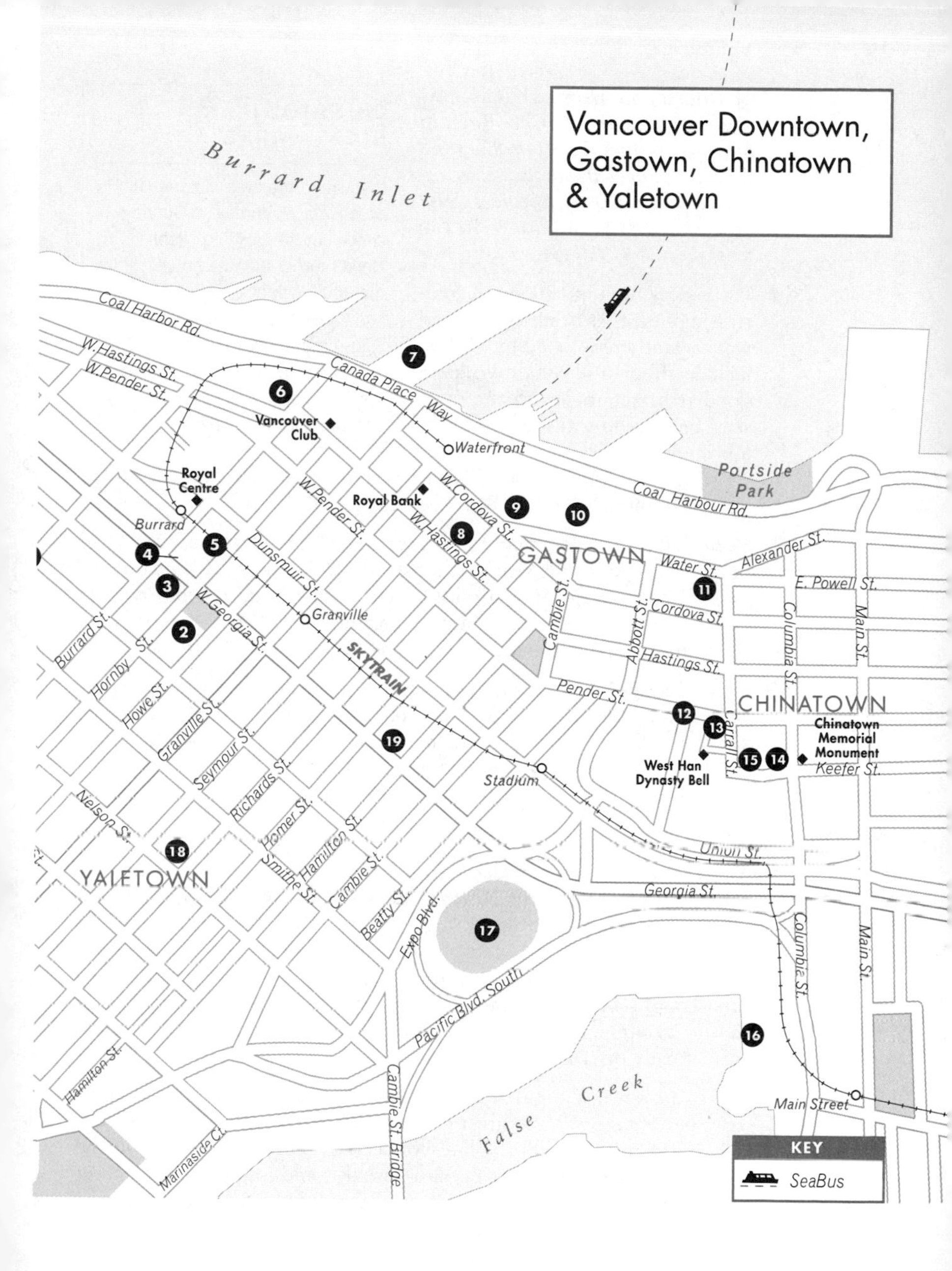

Vancouver Downtown, Gastown, Chinatown & Yaletown
Burrard Inlet
Coal Harbor Rd.
W.Hastings St.
W.Pender St.
Canada Place Way
Vancouver Club
Waterfront
Royal Centre
Royal Bank
Burrard
W.Pender St.
W.Cordova St.
W.Hastings St.
Dunsmuir St.
W.Georgia St.
Granville
SKYTRAIN
Portside Park
Coal Harbour Rd.
GASTOWN
Water St.
Alexander St.
E. Powell St.
Cordova St.
Cambie St.
Abbott St.
Columbia St.
Main St.
Hastings St.
Pender St.
CHINATOWN
Carrall St.
Chinatown Memorial Monument
Keefer St.
West Han Dynasty Bell
Stadium
Burrard St.
Hornby St.
Howe St.
Granville St.
Seymour St.
Richards St.
Homer St.
Hamilton St.
Cambie St.
Smithe St.
Beatty St.
Nelson St.
YALETOWN
Expo Blvd.
Union St.
Georgia St.
Columbia St.
Main St.
Pacific Blvd. South
Hamilton St.
Cambie St. Bridge
False Creek
Main Street
Marinaside Cr.
KEY
SeaBus
1
2
3
4
5
6
7
8
9
10
11
12
13
14
15
16
17
18
19

of Douglas fir from what is now south Vancouver. ✉690 *Burrard St., Downtown* ☎*604/682–3848* 🌐*www.cathedral.vancouver.bc.ca* ⏲*Weekdays 10–4. Services Sun. at 8* AM, *10:30* AM, *and 9:30* PM; *weekdays at 12:10* PM.

> **CHINATOWN NIGHT MARKET**
>
> If you're in the area in summer on a Friday, Saturday, or Sunday, check out the bustling Night Market for food and tchotchkes: the 200 block of East Pender and Keefer are closed to traffic 6:30–11 PM (until midnight on Saturday). For more details check out the Chinatown Web site (🌐*www.vancouver-chinatown.com*).

9 **The Landing.** Built in 1905 with gold-rush money, this brick warehouse was elegantly renovated in 1988 to include shops and Steamworks, a popular brewpub. From the oversized bay window at the rear of the lobby you can appreciate where the shoreline was 100 years ago, as well as enjoy terrific views of the North Shore Mountains. ✉*375 Water St., Gastown.*

10 **Steam clock.** An underground steam system, which also heats many local buildings, supplies the world's first steam clock—possibly Vancouver's most-photographed attraction. On the quarter hour a steam whistle rings out the Westminster chimes, and on the hour a huge cloud of steam spews from the apparatus. ✉ *Water and Cambie Sts., Gastown.*

6 **Marine Building.** Terra-cotta bas-reliefs depicting the history of transportation—airships, steamships, locomotives, and submarines—as well as Maya and Egyptian motifs and images of marine life, adorn this 1930 art deco structure. ✉*355 Burrard St., Downtown.*

CHINATOWN

Vancouver's Chinatown, declared a historic district in 1971, is one of the oldest and largest in North America. Many Chinese immigrants came to British Columbia during the 1850s seeking their fortunes in the Cariboo gold rush that inspired them to name the place Gum-shan, or Gold Mountain. Thousands more arrived in the 1880s, recruited as laborers to build the Canadian Pacific Railway. Despite their willingness to do dangerous work, and their value to the economy, the Chinese were greatly discriminated against.

Today, however, Chinatown is a vital neighborhood and although a large percentage of Vancouver's Chinese community has shifted to suburban Richmond, there's still a wonderful buzz of authenticity in the open-front markets, bakeries, and herbalist and import shops. Street signs are in Chinese lettering, street lights look like lanterns topped with ornamental dragons, and much of the architecture is patterned on that of Guangzhou (Canton).

MAIN ATTRACTION

15 Fodor's Choice ★ **Dr. Sun Yat-Sen Classical Chinese Garden.** The first authentic Ming Dynasty–style garden outside China, this small garden was built in 1986 by 52 artisans from Suzhou, China. It incorporates design elements and traditional materials from several of Suzhou's centuries-old

private gardens. No power tools, screws, or nails were used in the construction. Guided tours (45 minutes long), included in the ticket price, are conducted on the hour between mid-June and the end of August (call ahead for off-season tour times); they are valuable for understanding the philosophy and symbolism that are central to the garden's design. A concert series, including classical, Asian, world, jazz, and sacred music, plays on Friday evenings in July, August, and September. The free public park next door is also designed as a traditional Chinese garden. ■**TIP→ Covered walkways make this a good rainy-day choice.** ✉*578 Carrall St., Chinatown* ☎*604/662–3207* 🌐*www.vancouverchinesegarden.com* 🎫*C$8.75* ⏰*May–mid-June and Sept., daily 10–6; mid-June–Aug., daily 9:30–7; Oct., daily 10–4:30; Nov.–Apr., Tues.–Sun. 10–4:30.*

ALSO WORTH SEEING

⓮ **Chinese Cultural Centre Museum and Archives.** This Ming Dynasty–style facility is dedicated to promoting an understanding of Chinese-Canadian history and culture. A compelling permanent exhibit on the first floor traces the history of Chinese Canadians in British Columbia. The art gallery upstairs hosts traveling exhibits by Chinese and Canadian artists. Across the street is the Chinatown Memorial Monument, commemorating the Chinese-Canadian community's contribution to the city, province, and country. ✉*555 Columbia St., Chinatown* ☎*604/658–8880* 🌐*www.cccvan.com* 🎫*C$4, Tues. by donation* ⏰*Tues.–Sun. 11–5.*

⓭ **Sam Kee Building.** *Ripley's Believe It or Not!* recognizes this 6-foot-wide structure as the narrowest office building in the world. In 1913, after the city confiscated most of the then-owner's land to widen Pender Street, he built a store on what was left, in protest. Customers had to be served through the windows. These days the building houses an insurance agency. ✉*8 W. Pender St., Chinatown.*

⓬ **Vancouver Chinatown Millennium Gate.** This four-pillar, three-story high, brightly painted arch spanning Pender Street was erected in 2002 to mark the millennium and commemorate the Chinese community's role in Vancouver's history.

YALETOWN & FALSE CREEK

In 1985–86 the provincial government cleaned up a derelict industrial site on the north shore of False Creek, built a world's fair, and invited everyone; 20 million people showed up at Expo '86. Now the site of the fair has become one of the largest urban-redevelopment projects in North America as well as the site for the upcoming Winter Olympics Athlete's Village.

Tucked into the forest of green-glass condo towers is the old warehouse district of Yaletown. First settled by railroad workers who followed the newly laid tracks from the town of Yale in the Fraser Canyon, Yaletown in the 1880s and '90s was probably the most lawless place in Canada. It's now one of the city's most fashionable neighborhoods, and the Victorian-brick loading docks have become terraces for cappuccino bars.

MAIN ATTRACTIONS

17 **B.C. Sports Hall of Fame and Museum.** Inside the B.C. Place Stadium complex, this museum celebrates the province's sports achievers in a series of historical displays. You can test your sprinting, climbing, and throwing prowess in the high-tech participation gallery. ✉*B.C. Place, 777 Pacific Blvd. S, Gate A, at Beatty and Robson Sts., Downtown* ☎*604/687–5520* 🌐*www.bcsportshalloffame.com* *C$10* ⏲*Daily 10–5.*

NEED A BREAK?

Urban Fare (✉*177 Davie St., Yaletown* ☎*604/975–7550*) supplies, among other things, truffles, foie gras, and bread air-freighted from France to Yaletown's Francophiles and foodies. It's open daily 6 AM–midnight.

16 **Science World.** In a gigantic, shiny dome built over the Omnimax theater, this hands-on science center encourages children to participate in interactive exhibits and demonstrations. ✉*1455 Québec St., False Creek* ☎*604/443–7443 or 604/443–7440* 🌐*www.scienceworld.bc.ca* *Science World C$16, Science World and Omnimax theater C$18.75* ⏲*July–Labor Day, daily 10–6; Sept.–June, weekdays 10–5, weekends 10–6.*

ALSO WORTH SEEING

18 **Contemporary Art Gallery.** This nonprofit public gallery in a purpose-built modern building has regularly changing exhibits of the latest in contemporary local and international visual art. ✉*555 Nelson St., Downtown* ☎*604/681–2700* 🌐*www.contemporaryartgallery.ca* *By donation* ⏲*Wed. and Fri. noon–6, Thurs. noon–8, weekends noon–5.*

19 **Library Square.** The spiraling library building, open plazas, and lofty atrium of Library Square, completed in the mid-1990s, were built to evoke images of the Colosseum in Rome. A high-tech public library is the core of the structure; the outer edge of the spiral houses cafés and a handful of boutiques. ✉*350 W. Georgia St., Downtown* ☎*604/331–3600* 🌐*www.vpl.vancouver.bc.ca* ⏲*Mon.–Thurs. 10–9, Fri. and Sat. 10–6, Sun. 1–5.*

GRANVILLE ISLAND AND KITSILANO

Fodor'sChoice ★

One of North America's most successful urban-redevelopment schemes was just a sandbar until World War I, when the federal government dredged False Creek for access to the sawmills that lined the shore. The sludge from the creek was heaped onto the sandbar to create the island. In the early '70s, the federal government came up with a creative plan to redevelop the island with a public market, marine activities, and artisans' studios.

Besides the popular public market, the island is home to a marina and boat builders, an art college, theaters, restaurants, pubs, park space, playgrounds, and dozens of crafts shops and artisans' studios.

The nearby beachfront district of Kitsilano (popularly known as Kits), south of downtown Vancouver, is among the trendiest of Canadian neighborhoods. After a period of decline in the mid-20th century, Kits became a haven for hippies and their yuppie offspring who have since restored many of the wood-frame houses, and the neighborhood is once again chic.

WORD OF MOUTH

"What I have enjoyed doing in the past at Granville Market is sampling from the various stalls instead of eating at just one. I'll pick up a couple of slices of meat, a wedge of cheese, some fruit, and a drink then take it outside and sit on the edge of the dock, watching the people and boat traffic as I eat. There are worse ways to spend an hour or two if the weather is good." —dwooddon

Numbers in the text correspond to numbers in the margin and on the Granville Island map.

MAIN ATTRACTIONS

★ **Granville Island Public Market.** Because no chain stores are allowed in this 50,000-square-foot building, each shop here is unique. Dozens of stalls sell locally grown produce direct from the farm; others sell crafts, chocolates, cheese, fish, meat, flowers, and exotic foods. On Thursday in summer, market gardeners sell fruit and vegetables from trucks outside. At the north end of the market you can pick up a snack, lunch, or coffee at one of the many food stalls. ✉ *1689 Johnston St., Granville Island* ☎ *604/666–6477* 🌐 *www.granvilleisland.com* ⏲ *Daily 9–7.*

Kitsilano Beach. Picnic sites, a playground, tennis courts, beach volleyball, a restaurant, take-out concessions, Vancouver's biggest outdoor pool, and some fine people-watching can all be found at Kits Beach. ✉ *2305 Cornwall Ave., Kitsilano* ☎ *604/731–0011 Pool (summer only)* 🌐 *www.vancouver.ca/parks/* 🎫 *Beach free, pool C$4.85* ⏲ *Pool: late May–mid-June, weekdays noon–8:45, weekends 10–8:45; mid-June–Labor Day, weekdays 7 AM–8:45 PM, weekends 10–8:45; Labor Day–mid-Sept., weekdays 7 AM–7:15 PM, weekends 10–7:15.*

H. R. MacMillan Space Centre. The interactive exhibits and high-tech learning systems at this museum include a Virtual Voyages ride, where visitors can take a simulated space journey (definitely not for those afraid of flying); GroundStation Canada, showcasing Canada's achievements in space; and the Cosmic Courtyard, full of hands-on space-oriented exhibits including a moon rock and a computer program that shows what you would look like as an alien. ✉ *Vanier Park, 1100 Chestnut St., Kitsilano* ☎ *604/738–7827* 🌐 *www.hrmacmillanspacecentre.com* 🎫 *C$15* ⏲ *July and Aug., daily 10–5; Sept.–June, Tues.–Sun. 10–5.*

Vancouver Maritime Museum. About a third of this museum has been turned over to kids, with touchable displays offering a chance to drive a tug, maneuver an underwater robot, or dress up as a seafarer. The museum also has an extensive collection of model ships and is the last moorage for the *RCMP Arctic St. Roch,* the first ship to sail in both directions through the treacherous Northwest Passage and the first to circumnavigate North America. ✉ *Vanier Park, 1905 Ogden Ave., north end of Cypress St., Kitsilano* ☎ *604/257–8300* 🌐 *www.vancouvermaritimemuseum.com* 🎫 *C$10* ⏲ *Mid-May–Labor Day, daily 10–5; Labor Day–mid-May, Tues.–Sat. 10–5, Sun. noon–5.*

ALSO WORTH SEEING

Emily Carr Institute of Art and Design. The institute's three main buildings—tin-plated structures formerly used for industrial purposes—were renovated in the 1970s. The **Charles H. Scott Gallery** to the right of the main entrance hosts contemporary exhibitions in various media. Two other galleries showcase student work. ✉ *1399 Johnston St., Granville Island* ☎ *604/844–3811* 🌐 *www.eciad.ca* 🎫 *Free* 🕓 *Weekdays noon–5, weekends 10–5.*

Granville Island Museums. This is two museums under one roof: the collection of the **Model Ships Museum** includes exquisitely detailed early 20th-century military and working vessels, notably a 13-foot replica of the HMS *Hood,* the British Royal Navy ship that was sunk by the German warship *Bismarck* in 1941, and a model of the *Hunley,* an 1863 Confederate submarine that was the first to sink a surface vessel. ✉ *1502 Duranleau St., Granville Island* ☎ *604/683–1939* 🌐 *www.granvilleislandmuseums.com* 🎫 *Both museums C$7.50* 🕓 *Mid-May–mid-Oct., daily 10–5:30; mid-Oct.–mid-May, Tues.–Sun. 10–5:30.*

Vancouver Museum. Vancouver's short but funky history comes to life at this seaside museum. The war-years gallery remembers some poignant episodes involving the Japanese internment, as well as local stories of the war effort. The 1950s Gallery boasts a 1955 Ford Fairlane Victoria and a Seeburg select-o-matic jukebox. ✉ *Vanier Park, 1100 Chestnut St., Kitsilano* ☎ *604/736–4431* 🌐 *www.vanmuseum.bc.ca* 🎫 *C$10* 🕓 *June–Sept., Fri.–Wed. 10–5, Thurs. 10–9; Oct.–June, Tues., Wed., and Fri.–Sun. 10–5, Thurs. 10–9.*

STANLEY PARK

A 1,000-acre wilderness park, only blocks from the downtown section of a major city, is a rare treasure. And it's all thanks to the Americans—sort of! In the 1860s, because of a threat of American invasion, this oceanfront peninsula was designated a military reserve, though it was never needed. When the City of Vancouver was incorporated in 1886, the council's first act was to request the land be set aside as a park. Permission was granted two years later and the grounds were named Stanley Park after Lord Stanley, then governor general of Canada.

Stanley Park is, perhaps, the single most prized possession of Vancouverites, who make use of it fervently to cycle, walk, jog, rollerblade, play cricket and tennis, and enjoy outdoor art shows and theater performances alongside attractions such as the renowned aquarium.

The free **Stanley Park Shuttle** (☎ *604/257–8400* 🌐 *www.vancouver.ca/parks/*) operates mid-June to mid-September between 10 AM and 6:30 PM, providing frequent (every 15 minutes) transportation to 15 major park sights. Pick it up on Pipeline Road, near the Georgia Street park entrance, or at any of the stops in the park.

For information about guided nature walks in the park, contact the **Lost Lagoon Nature House** (☎ *604/257–8544* 🌐 *www.stanleyparkecology.ca*)

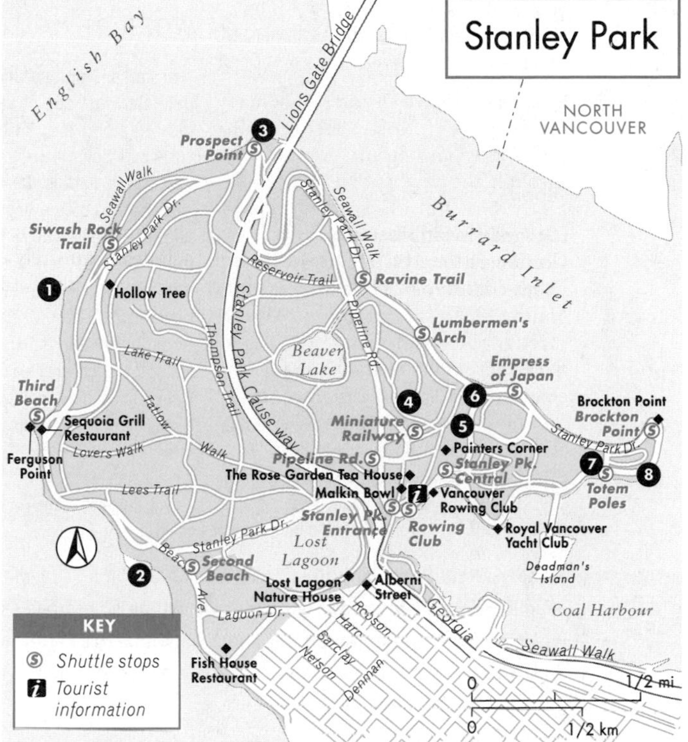

on the south shore of Lost Lagoon, at the foot of Alberni Street. They operate May to September, Tuesday through Sunday, 9–4:30.

THE STANLEY PARK SEA WALL

The seawall path, a 9-km (5½-mi) paved shoreline route popular with walkers, cyclists, and in-line skaters, is one of several car-free zones within the park. If you have the time (about a half day) and the energy, strolling the entire seawall is an exhilarating experience. From the south side of the park, the seawall continues for another 28 km (17 mi) along Vancouver's waterfront, to the University of British Columbia, allowing for a pleasant, if ambitious, day's bike ride.

The seawall can get crowded on summer weekends, but inside the park is a 28-km (17-mi) network of peaceful walking and cycling paths through old- and second-growth forest. The wheelchair-accessible Beaver Lake Interpretive Trail is a good choice if you're interested in park ecology.

WHAT TO SEE

6 **Lumbermen's Arch.** Made of one massive log, this archway, erected in 1952, is dedicated to the workers in Vancouver's first industry. Beside the arch is an asphalt path that leads back to Lost Lagoon and the Van-

couver Aquarium. There's a picnic area, a snack bar, and small beach here, too.

WORD OF MOUTH

"For parks, Stanley Park is the ultimate must-see of Vancouver, located along the northwestern corner of downtown.... My favorite part of the park is the western side, because it's away from traffic and it feels like you're far away from the city. It looks out into the open water and has a few beaches. You can take the seawall from English Bay north toward Second Beach and along to Third Beach for a nice walk in this part of the park." —Judy_in_Calgary

4 **Miniature Railway and Children's Farmyard.** A child-size steam train takes kids and adults on a ride through the woods. Next door is a farmyard full of critters, including goats, rabbits, and pigs. At Christmastime, an elaborate light display illuminates the route, and Halloween displays draw crowds throughout October. **TIP→A family ticket gets everyone in for the child's rate.** *Off Pipeline Rd., Stanley Park 604/257–8531 Each site C$5.50, C$2.75 for adults accompanying children Feb.–May, weekends only, 11–4, weather permitting; June–Sept., daily 10:30–5; call for holiday and off-season hours.*

NEED A BREAK?

Stanley's Park Bar and Grill (*604/602–3088*), in a 1911 manor house, is a family-friendly veranda serving burgers, wraps, soups, and salads. It overlooks the Rose Garden and is very near the Children's Farmyard and Malkin Ball, where outdoor theater and concerts are held in summer. There's also a gift and souvenir shop here.

3 **Prospect Point.** At 211 feet, Prospect Point is the highest point in the park and provides striking views of the Lions Gate Bridge (watch for cruise ships passing below), the North Shore, and Burrard Inlet. There are also a year-round souvenir shop, a snack bar with terrific ice cream, and a restaurant (May–September only). From the seawall, you can see where cormorants build their seaweed nests along the cliff ledges.

2 **Second Beach.** The 50-meter pool, which has lifeguards and waterslides, is a popular spot in summer. The sandy beach has a playground and covered picnic areas. If you like romantic beachside sunsets, this is one for the books. *604/257–8371 summer only www.vancouver.ca/parks/ Beach free, pool C$4.85 Pool mid-May–mid-June, weekdays noon–8:45, weekends 10–8:45; mid-June–late July, daily 10–8:45; late July–Labor Day, Mon., Wed., Fri. 7 AM–8:45 PM, Tues., Thurs., and weekends 10–8:45.*

1 **Siwash Rock.** According to a local First Nations legend, this 50-foot-high offshore promontory is a monument to a man who was turned into stone as a reward for his unselfishness. The rock is visible from the seawall; if you're driving, you need to park and take a short path through the woods. Watch for the Hollow Tree nearby. This 56-foot-wide burnt cedar stump has shrunk over the years but still gives an idea of how large some of the old-growth trees can be.

7 **Totem poles.** Totem poles are an important art form among native peoples along British Columbia's coast. These eight poles, all carved in the latter half of the 20th century, include replicas of poles originally brought to the park from the north coast in the 1920s, as well as poles carved specifically for the park by First Nations artists. The several styles of poles represent a cross section of B.C. native groups, including the Kwakwaka'wakw, Haida, and Nisga'a. An information center near the site has a snack bar, a gift shop, and information about B.C.'s First Nations.

5 ★ **Vancouver Aquarium Marine Science Centre.** Massive pools with windows below water level let you come face to face with beluga whales, sea otters, sea lions, dolphins, and harbor seals at this research and educational facility. In the Amazon rain-forest gallery you can walk through a jungle populated with piranha, caimans, and tropical birds, and in summer, you'll be surrounded by hundreds of free-flying butterflies. Other displays, many with hands-on features for kids, show the underwater life of coastal British Columbia and the Canadian Arctic. A Tropic Zone is home to exotic freshwater and saltwater life, including clownfish, moray eels, and black-tip reef sharks. Beluga whale, sea lion, and dolphin shows, as well as dive shows (where divers swim with aquatic life, including sharks) are held daily. For an extra fee, you can help the trainers feed and train otters, belugas, and sea lions. **■TIP→ The quietest time to visit is before 11 AM or after 2:30 PM.** *604/659–3474 www.vanaqua.org C$19.95 July–Labor Day, daily 9:30–7; Labor Day–June, daily 9:30–5:30.*

GREATER VANCOUVER

Some of Vancouver's best gardens, natural sights, and museums, including the renowned Museum of Anthropology on the campus of the University of British Columbia, are south of downtown Vancouver. In the other direction, cross the Lions Gate Bridge—also known as the Second Narrows Bridge—over Burrard Inlet, or hop onto the SeaBus, and you'll be on the north shore, where the districts of West Vancouver and North Vancouver are found. The Guinness family opened up West Vancouver in the '30s (one of the most prestigious neighborhoods here is called The British Properties—even though the family was Irish) and certainly, West Van, as the locals call it, has retained its well-heeled character and many an English-style, winding country road. North Vancouver lies to the east—a poor relation of sorts and much more commercial in nature. This is where you'll find Capilano Suspension Bridge, Grouse Mountain, Lonsdale Quay, and, farther east, the picturesque hamlet of Deep Cove.

MAIN ATTRACTIONS

Fodor'sChoice ★ **Capilano Suspension Bridge.** At Vancouver's oldest tourist attraction (the original bridge was built in 1889), you can get a taste of rain-forest scenery and test your mettle on the swaying, 450-foot cedar-plank suspension bridge that hangs 230 feet above the rushing Capilano River. Across the bridge is the Treetops Adventure, where you can walk along

650 feet of cable bridges suspended among the trees; there's also a scenic pathway along the canyon's edge, appropriately called Cliff Hanger Walk. Without crossing the bridge, you can enjoy the site's viewing decks, nature trails, totem park, and carving center (where you can watch First Nations carvers at work), as well as history and forestry exhibits, a massive gift shop in the original 1911 teahouse, and a restaurant. May through October, guides in 19th-century costumes conduct free tours on themes related to history, nature, or ecology, while fiddle bands, First Nations dancers, and other entertainers keep things lively. ✉*3735 Capilano Rd., North Vancouver* ☎*604/985–7474* 🌐*www.capbridge.com* 🎟*Mid-May–Oct. C$26.95, Nov.–mid-May C$23.95, plus C$3 for parking* 🕒*May–Labor Day, daily 8:30–8; Nov.–Apr., daily 9–5; Sept., Oct., and Apr.–mid-May call for hrs.*

★ **Grouse Mountain.** North America's largest aerial tramway, the **Skyride** is a great way to take in the city, sea, and mountain vistas (be sure to pick a clear day or evening). The Skyride makes the 2-km (1-mi) climb to the peak of Grouse Mountain every 15 minutes. Once at the top you can watch a half-hour video presentation at the Theatre in the Sky (it's included with your Skyride ticket). Other free mountaintop activities include, in summer, lumberjack shows, chairlift rides, walking tours, hiking, falconry demonstrations, and a chance to visit the grizzly bears and grey wolves in the mountain's wildlife refuge. For an extra fee you can also try tandem paragliding, or take a helicopter tour. In winter you can ski, snowshoe, snowboard, ice-skate on a mountaintop pond, or take Sno-Cat-drawn sleigh rides. A stone-and-cedar lodge is home to a café, a pub-style bistro, and a high-end restaurant, all with expansive city views. ✉*6400 Nancy Greene Way, North Vancouver* ☎*604/980–9311* 🌐*www.grousemountain.com* 🎟*Skyride and most activities C$32.95* 🕒*Daily 9* AM*–10* PM.

OFF THE BEATEN PATH

Lynn Canyon Park. With a steep canyon landscape, a temperate rain forest complete with waterfalls, and a suspension bridge 166½ feet above raging Lynn Creek, this 616-acre park provides thrills to go with its scenic views. The on-site Ecology Centre distributes maps of area hiking trails, waterfalls, and pools as well as information about the local flora and fauna. There's also a gift shop and a café on-site. ✉*3663 Park Rd., at end of Peters Rd., North Vancouver* ☎*604/981–3103 Ecology Centre, 604/984–9311 café* 🌐*www.dnv.org/ecology* 🎟*Ecology Centre by donation, suspension bridge free* 🕒*Park: daily, dawn to dusk; Ecology Centre: June–Sept., daily 10–5; Oct.–May, weekdays 10–5, weekends noon–4.*

Fodor's Choice ★ **Museum of Anthropology.** Part of the University of British Columbia, the MOA has one of the world's leading collections of Northwest Coast First Nations' art. The Great Hall displays dramatic cedar poles, bentwood boxes, and canoes adorned with traditional Northwest Coast painted designs. On clear days, the gallery's 50-foot-tall windows reveal a striking backdrop of mountains and sea. Another highlight is the work of the late Bill Reid, one of Canada's most respected Haida artists. In *The Raven and the First Men* (1980), carved in yellow cedar, he tells a Haida story of creation. Reid's gold-and-silver jewelry work is also on display, as are exquisite carvings of gold, silver, and argillite (a black shale found on Haida Gwaii, also known as the Queen Charlotte Islands) by other First Nations artists. Arthur Erickson designed the cliff-top structure that houses the MOA, which also has a book and fine-art shop and a summertime café. ✉ *University of British Columbia, 6393 N.W. Marine Dr., Point Grey* ☎ *604/822–5087* 🌐 *www.moa.ubc.ca* 🎫 *C$9, free Tues. 5–9* ⏲ *Memorial Day–Labor Day, Tues. 10–9, Wed.–Mon. 10–5; Labor Day–Memorial Day, Tues. 11–9, Wed.–Sun. 11–5.*

ALSO WORTH SEEING

Lonsdale Quay. Of the many public markets in the Greater Vancouver area, this indoor seaside market is one of the most popular. Stalls selling fresh produce, exotic fare, and ready-to-eat food fill the lower level; upstairs are boutiques, toy stores, and a kids' play area. ✉ *123 Carrie Cates Ct., at foot of Lonsdale Ave.* ☎ *604/985–6261* 🌐 *www.lonsdalequay.com* 🎫 *Free* ⏲ *May–Aug., daily 9:30–7; Sept.–Apr., daily 9:30–6:30.*

Nitobe Memorial Garden. Opened in 1960 in memory of Japanese scholar and diplomat Dr. Inazo Nitobe (1862–1933), this 2½-acre walled garden, which includes a pond, a stream with a small waterfall, and a ceremonial teahouse, is considered one of the most authentic Japanese tea and strolling gardens outside Japan. ✉ *University of British Columbia, 1903 West Mall, Point Grey* ☎ *604/822–9666* 🌐 *www.nitobe.org* 🎫 *C$5 mid-Mar.–mid-Oct., C$10 includes admission to the UBC Botanical Gardens; by donation mid-Oct.–mid-Mar.* ⏲ *Mid-Mar.–mid-Oct., daily 10–6; mid-Oct.–mid-Mar., weekdays 10–2:30.*

Queen Elizabeth Park. At the highest point in the city, offering 360-degree views of downtown, this 52-hectare (130-acre) park has lavish sunken gardens (set in a former stone quarry), a rose garden, and an abundance of grassy picnicking spots. In the **Bloedel Floral Conservatory** you can see tropical and desert plants and 100 species of free-flying tropical birds in a glass triodetic dome—the perfect place to be on a rainy day. ✉ *Cambie St. and 33rd Ave., Cambie Corridor* ☎ *604/257–8570* 🌐 *www.vancouver.ca/parks/* 🎫 *Conservatory C$4.50* ⏲ *Apr.–Sept., weekdays 9–8, weekends 10–9; Oct.–Mar., daily 10–5.*

University of British Columbia Botanical Garden. Ten thousand trees, shrubs, and rare plants from around the world thrive on this 70-acre research site on the university campus. The complex includes an Asian garden, a garden of medicinal plants, and an alpine garden with some of the world's rarest plants. A Walk in the Woods is a 20-minute loop that takes you through and past more than 1,000 species of coastal plant life. ✉ *6804 S.W. Marine Dr., Point Grey* ☎ *604/822–9666* 🌐 *www.ubcbotanicalgarden.org* 🎫 *Mid-Mar.–mid-Oct., C$7, C$10 includes admission to Nitobe Memorial Garden; mid-Oct.–mid-Mar. free* ⏲ *Mid-Mar.–mid-Oct., daily 10–5; mid-Oct.–mid-Mar., daily 10–3.*

VanDusen Botanical Garden. An Elizabethan maze, a formal rose garden, a meditation garden, and a collection of Canadian heritage plants are among the many themed displays at this 55-acre site. The collections include flora from every continent and many rare and endangered species. The new Phyllis Bentall Garden area features hybrid water lilies and carnivorous plants (a hit with kids). ✉*5251 Oak St., at W. 37th Ave., Shaughnessy* ☎*604/878–9274 garden, 604/261–0011 restaurant* 🌐*www.vandusengarden.org* *C$8.25 Apr.–Sept., C$6 Oct.–Mar.* ⏲*June–Aug., daily 10–9; Sept.–May, daily (call for hrs).*

WHERE TO EAT

From inventive downtown bistros to waterfront seafood palaces, to Asian restaurants that rival those in Asia, Vancouver has a diverse array of gastronomical options. Many cutting-edge establishments are defining and perfecting Modern Canadian fare, which incorporates Pacific Northwest seafood—notably salmon and halibut—and locally grown produce, often accompanied by British Columbia wines. Small plates are big, too—numerous restaurants offer tapas-style portions designed for sharing.

With at least a third of the city's population of Asian heritage, it's no surprise that Asian eateries abound in Vancouver. From mom-and-pop noodle shops, curry houses, and corner sushi bars to elegant and upscale dining rooms, cuisine from China, Japan, and India (and to a lesser extent, from Taiwan, Korea, Thailand, Vietnam, and Malaysia) can be found all over town. Even in restaurants that are not specifically "Asian," you'll find abundant Asian influences—your grilled salmon may be served with *gai lan* (Chinese broccoli), black rice, or a coconut-milk curry.

British Columbia's wine industry is enjoying great popularity, and many restaurants feature wines from the province's 100-plus wineries. Most B.C. wines come from the Okanagan Valley in the province's interior, but Vancouver Island is another main wine-producing area. Merlot, pinot noir, pinot gris, and chardonnay are among the major varieties; also look for ice wine, a dessert wine made from grapes that are picked while they are frozen on the vines.

If you enjoy strolling to scope out your dining options downtown, try Robson Street for everything from upscale Italian dining rooms to cheap, friendly Asian cafés and noodle shops, or explore Denman and Davie streets for a variety of ethnic eats. In Yaletown, both Hamilton and Mainland streets are full of restaurants and upscale bars, many with outdoor terraces.

WHAT IT COSTS IN CANADIAN DOLLARS

	¢	$	$$	$$$	$$$$
AT DINNER	under C$8	C$8–C$12	C$13–C$20	C$21–C$30	over C$30

Restaurant prices are per person for a main course at dinner.

DOWNTOWN VANCOUVER

BELGIAN

$$–$$$ ✕**Chambar.** Who would have predicted that a hip Belgian eatery in a high-ceiling space on a dreary block between Downtown and Gastown would take Vancouver by storm? A young, smartly dressed crowd hangs out at the bar sipping Belgian beer or funky cocktails such as the "Kissy Suzuki" (vodka infused with jasmine tea and blended with sake, blueberry, and passionfruit), working up their appetites for chef Nico Schuermans's creative cooking, in which classic Belgian dishes are reinvented with flavors from North Africa and beyond. He might rub duck breast with ginger and sumac and serve it with Moroccan-flavored rice pilaf, while *moules* (mussels) might be sauced with smoked chilies, cilantro, and coconut cream. Unusual? Perhaps. Delicious? Definitely. ✉*562 Beatty St., Downtown* ☎*604/879–7119* ▭*AE, MC, V* ⊗*Closed Sun. No lunch.*

CAFÉS

¢–$ ✕**Sciué.** Inspired by the street foods of Rome, this cafeteria-style Italian bakery–café (pronounced "Shoe-eh") starts off the day serving espresso drinks and pastries, then moves on to panini, soups, and pastas. One specialty is the pane romano, essentially a thick-crust pizza, which is sold by weight. There can be lines out the door at noontime, so try to visit early or late (they close at 8 PM weeknights, 6 PM Saturdays). ✉*110–800 W. Pender St., Downtown* ☎*604/602–7263* ✍*Reservations not accepted* ▭*MC, V* ⊗*Closed Sun. No dinner Sat.*

CHINESE

$$–$$$ ✕**Kirin Mandarin Restaurant.** A striking silver mural of a *kirin,* a mythical dragonlike creature, presides over this elegant two-tier restaurant. The specialties here are northern Chinese (Mandarin and Szechuan) dishes, which tend to be richer and spicier than the Cantonese cuisine served at Kirin's other locations. If you're adventurous, start with the spicy jellyfish, redolent with sesame oil. Then try the Peking duck, or the kung pao lobster: sautéed lobster meat served with a deep-fried lobster claw. Dim sum is served daily. ✉*1166 Alberni St., 2nd fl., Downtown* ☎*604/682–8833* ▭*AE, MC, V.*

¢–$ ✕**Legendary Noodle.** Come through the beaded curtains into this sliver of China on Denman Street, decorated with red lanterns and wooden booths. As you'd expect from the name, this compact storefront specializes in noodles, and they're handmade here in the open kitchen. The choices are simple—noodles in soup or stir-fried—but you might also order a plate of garlicky pea shoots or a steamer of dumplings. Despite its plain Formica tables and fluorescent light, the original Mount Pleasant location makes a convenient time-out if you're shopping the Main Street boutiques. ✉*1074 Denman St., West End* ☎*604/669–8551* ✍*Reservations not accepted* ▭*MC, V* ✉*4191 Main St., Main St./Mt. Pleasant* ☎*604/879–8758.*

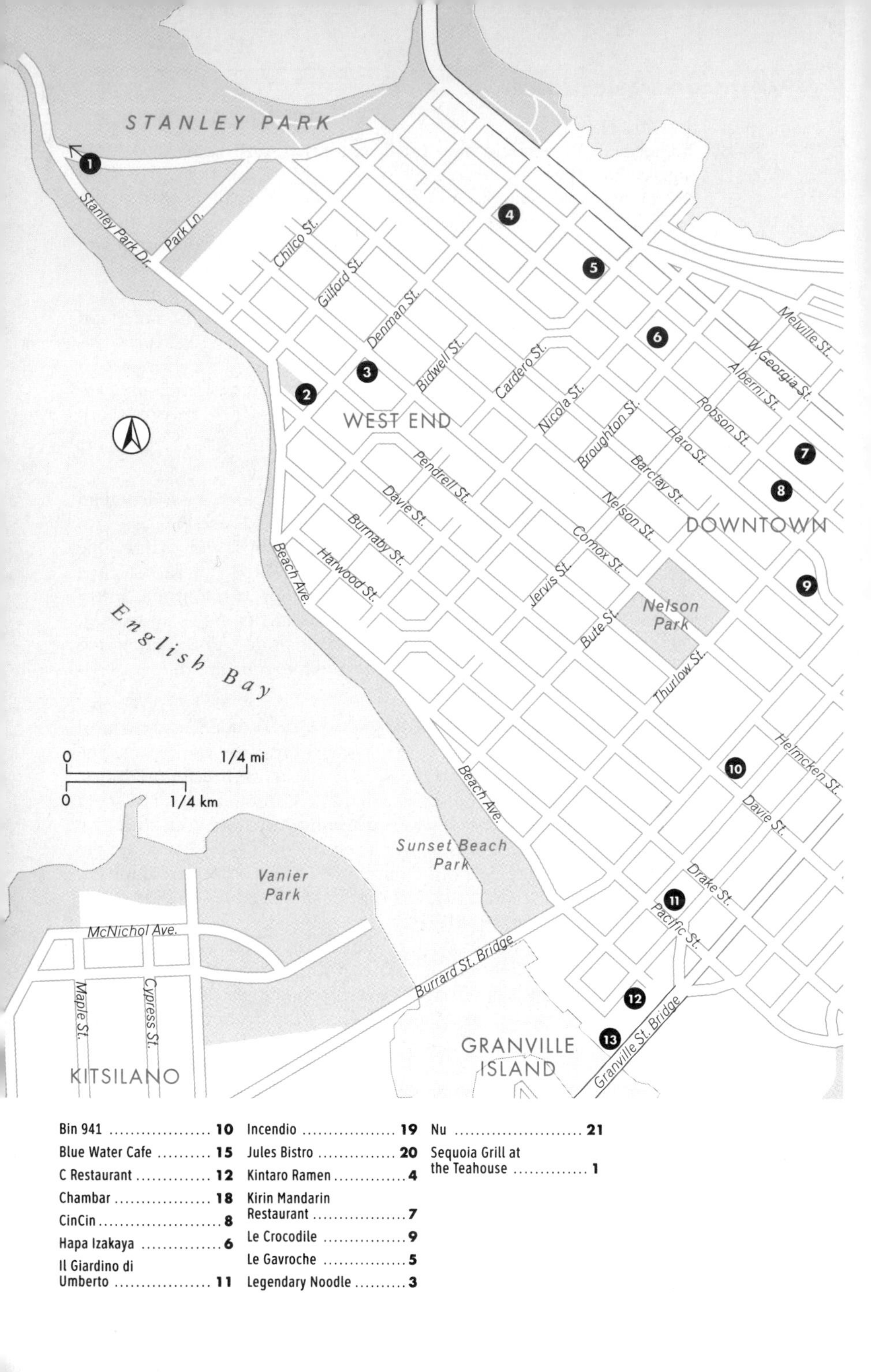

Bin 941 .... **10**
Blue Water Cafe **15**
C Restaurant **12**
Chambar **18**
CinCin **8**
Hapa Izakaya **6**
Il Giardino di Umberto **11**
Incendio **19**
Jules Bistro **20**
Kintaro Ramen **4**
Kirin Mandarin Restaurant **7**
Le Crocodile **9**
Le Gavroche **5**
Legendary Noodle **3**
Nu **21**
Sequoia Grill at the Teahouse **1**

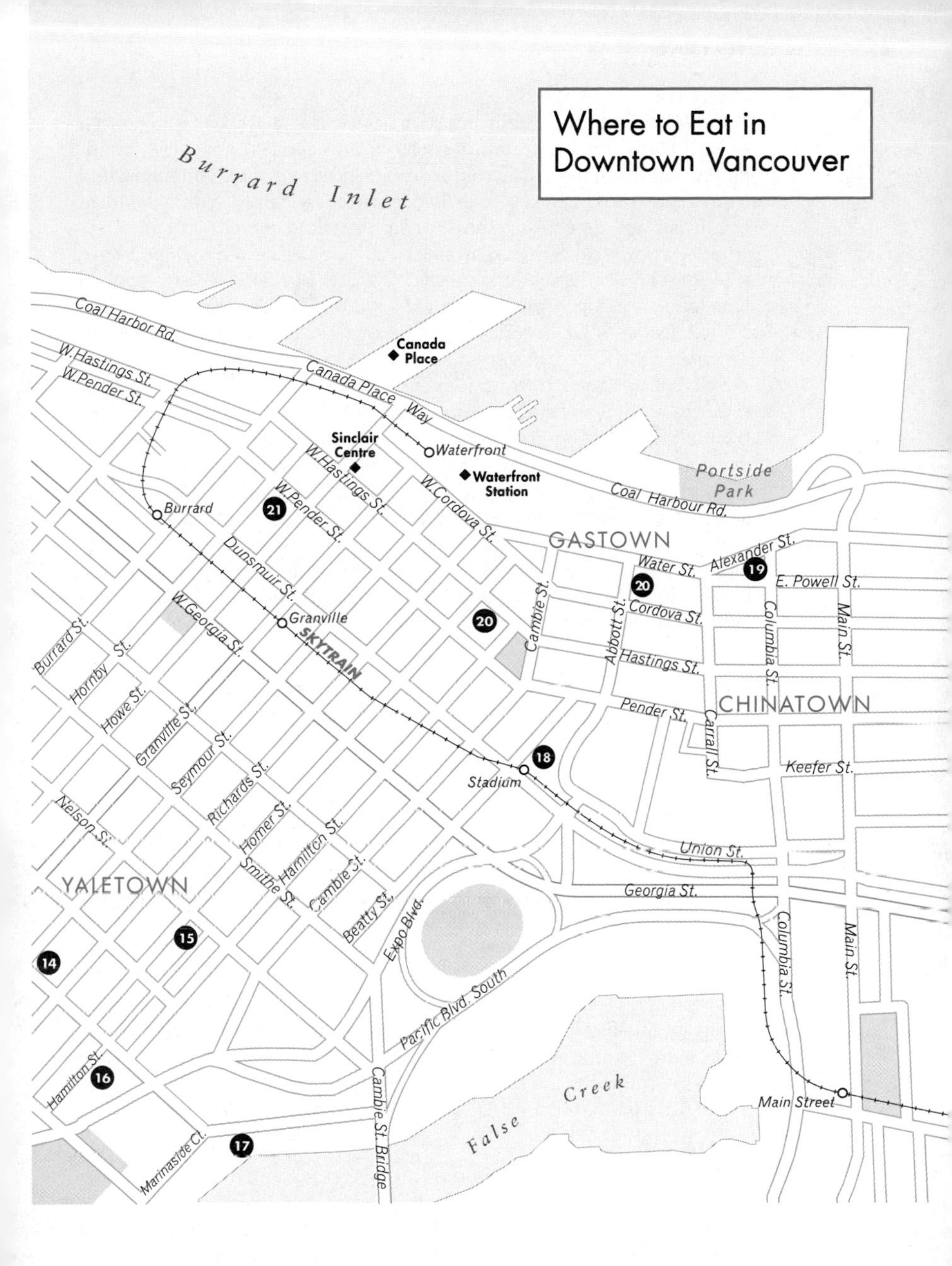

Where to Eat in Downtown Vancouver
Burrard Inlet
Coal Harbor Rd.
W.Hastings St.
W.Pender St.
Canada Place
Canada Place Way
Sinclair Centre
Waterfront
Waterfront Station
Portside Park
Coal Harbour Rd.
Burrard
W.Pender St.
W.Hastings St.
W.Cordova St.
GASTOWN
Water St.
Alexander St.
E. Powell St.
Dunsmuir St.
W.Georgia St.
Granville
SKYTRAIN
Cambie St.
Abbott St.
Cordova St.
Hastings St.
Columbia St.
Main St.
Pender St.
CHINATOWN
Carrall St.
Keefer St.
Burrard St.
Hornby St.
Howe St.
Granville St.
Seymour St.
Richards St.
Homer St.
Hamilton St.
Smithe St.
Cambie St.
Beatty St.
Stadium
Nelson St.
Union St.
Georgia St.
YALETOWN
Expo Blvd.
Columbia St.
Main St.
Pacific Blvd. South
Hamilton St.
False Creek
Main Street
Cambie St. Bridge
Marinaside Ct.
14
15
16
17
18
19
20
20
21

ECLECTIC

$$ ✕ **Bin 941.** Part tapas restaurant, part up-tempo bar, this bustling, often noisy hole in the wall claims to have launched Vancouver's small-plates trend. Among the adventurous snack-size dishes, you might find Moroccan-spiced chicken, a grilled pork chop paired with a salad of nectarines and umeboshi plums, or lamb sirloin served with an olive-studded risotto cake. Snack on one or two, or order a bunch and have a feast. The Bin serves food until 1:30 AM. Bin 942, a sister spot in Kitsilano, is a touch more subdued *(⇨ Dining, Greater Vancouver).* *✉941 Davie St., Downtown ☎604/683–1246 Reservations not accepted ▭MC, V ⏲No lunch.*

$–$$ ✕ **Salt Tasting Room.** If your idea of a perfect lunch or light supper revolves around fine cured meats, artisanal cheeses, and a glass of wine from a wide-ranging list, find your way to this sleek, spare space in a decidedly unsleek Gastown lane. The restaurant has no kitchen and simply assembles its first-quality provisions, perhaps meaty *bunderfleisch* (cured beef), smoked pork chops, or B.C.-made Camembert, with accompanying condiments, into artfully composed grazers' delights—more like an upscale picnic than a full meal. There's no sign out front, so look for the salt-shaker flag in Blood Alley, which is off Abbott Street, half a block south of Water Street. *✉45 Blood Alley, Gastown ☎604/633–1912 ▭AE, MC, V.*

FRENCH

$$$$ ✕ **Le Gavroche.** Classic French cuisine receives contemporary accents at this romantic restaurant, set in an early-20th-century house with mountain views. Seafood entrées range from wild salmon with a carrot-ginger coulis to slow-roasted sablefish with a shellfish ragout; meat options include rich beef tenderloin and mustard-crusted rack of lamb. Vegetarian choices are always available. One of the few places with tableside service of steak tartare and Caesar salad, Le Gavroche also has a 5,000-label wine cellar. *✉1616 Alberni St., West End ☎604/685–3924 ▭AE, DC, MC, V ⏲No lunch weekends.*

$$–$$$ ✕ **Jules Bistro.** From the garlicky escargots and the steak frites to the hearty cassoulet and the lemon tart, traditional French bistro fare is alive and well at this buzzing Gastown spot. You won't find funky fusion creations or east-meets-west innovations here—just the same classic dishes you might see at a neighborhood bistro in Paris. It's cozy inside (some might say cramped), but that's part of the charm. *✉216 Abbott St., Gastown ☎604/669–0033 ▭AE, MC, V ⏲Closed Sun. and Mon.*

ITALIAN

$$$$ ★ ✕ **Il Giardino di Umberto.** The vine-draped terrace with a wood-burning oven or any of the four terra-cotta-tiled rooms inside are attractive places to enjoy this long-established restaurateur's traditional Tuscan cuisine. The frequently changing menu includes a variety of pasta dishes, osso buco Milanese with saffron risotto, grilled salmon with saffron and fennel vinaigrette, and roast reindeer loin with a pink-peppercorn sauce. Dine here with someone special. *✉1382 Hornby St., Downtown ☎604/669–2422 ▭AE, DC, MC, V ⏲Closed Sun. No lunch Sat.*

$$$–$$$$ ✕ **CinCin.** With its gold walls, arched windows, and terra-cotta tiles—and its crowd-pleasing modern Italian menu—this Tuscan-inspired restaurant is appropriate for a business meal, a romantic tête-à-tête, or simply a relaxing dinner at the end of a long day. The heated terrace, shielded with greenery, feels a long way from busy Robson Street below. Inside, there's a lively scene around the hand-carved marble bar. The food, from the open kitchen and the wood-fire grill, oven, and rotisserie, changes seasonally, but might include whole grilled sea bass stuffed with cherry tomatoes, olives, and fennel; beef tenderloin with chanterelles; and thin-crust wood-fired pizza. ✉ *1154 Robson St., upstairs, West End* ☎ *604/688–7338* ▭ *AE, DC, MC, V* ⊙ *No lunch.*

JAPANESE

$–$$ ★ ✕ **Hapa Izakaya.** *Izakayas* are Japanese pubs that serve tapas-style small plates designed for sharing, and they've sprouted up all over Vancouver. One of the best places to sample the izakaya phenomenon is at this sleek pair of pubs popular with festive groups of twenty- and thirty-somethings. Try the mackerel (cooked tableside—with a blowtorch—and served with hot mustard), udon noodles coated with briny cod roe, or the Korean-style stone bowl filled with rice, pork, and vegetables. Sake and Japanese beer are the drinks of choice. If you're dining alone, sit at the counter facing the open kitchen to watch the action. The Robson branch is located city center; the Kitsilano branch is one block from Kits Beach. ✉ *1479 Robson St., West End* ☎ *604/689–4272* ▭ *AE, MC, V* ⊙ *No lunch* ✉ *1516 Yew St., Kitsilano* ☎ *604/738–4272* ▭ *AE, MC, V* ⊙ *No lunch.*

¢–$ ✕ **Kintaro Ramen.** If your only experience with ramen is instant noodles, get thee to this authentic Japanese soup joint. With thin, fresh egg noodles and homemade broth (it's a meat stock, so vegetarians are explicitly not invited), a bowl of noodle soup here is cheap, filling, and ever so tasty. Expect long lines, but you can use the waiting time to decide between lean or fatty pork and miso or soy stock: once you're inside the barebones storefront, the harried staff doesn't tolerate any dithering. ✉ *788 Denman St., West End* ☎ *604/682–7568* ✍ *Reservations not accepted* ▭ *No credit cards* ⊙ *Closed Mon.*

MEDITERRANEAN

$$–$$$$ ✕ **Provence Marinaside.** This airy, modern Mediterranean-style eatery on Yaletown's waterfront presents French and Italian takes on seafood, including a delicious bouillabaisse and lush, garlicky wild prawns, though the rack of lamb and an extensive antipasti selection are also popular. The marina-view patio makes a sunny breakfast or lunch spot, and the take-out counter is a great place to put together a picnic. Under the same ownership, the **Provence Mediterranean Grill** (✉ *4473 W. 10th Ave., Point Grey* ☎ *604/222–1980*) serves a similar menu to West Side denizens. ✉ *1177 Marinaside Crescent, at foot of Davie St., Yaletown* ☎ *604/681–4144* ▭ *AE, DC, MC, V.*

MIDDLE EASTERN

¢–$ ✕**Nuba.** You could make a meal of meze—appetizers like tabbouleh salad, *labneh* (spiced yogurt dip), or crispy cauliflower served with tahini sauce—at this cheap and cheerful duo of Lebanese restaurants. If you're looking for something heartier, try a plate of *mjadra,* a spicy mix of lentils and rice. While they do serve chicken kebabs, lamb *kafta* (patties), and other meat dishes, most of the menu is vegetarian-friendly, and there are plenty of vegan options as well. ⊠*1206 Seymour St., Downtown* ☎*778/371–3266* *Reservations not accepted* ▭*AE, MC, V* ⊠*322 W. Hastings St., Gastown* ☎*604/688–1655* *Reservations not accepted* ▭*AE, MC, V* *Closed weekends.*

MODERN CANADIAN

$$$–$$$$ ★ ✕**Raincity Grill.** One of the best places to try British Columbian food and wine is this pretty candlelit bistro overlooking English Bay. The menu, which owner Harry Kambolis likes to call "stubbornly regional," changes seasonally and relies almost completely on local and regional products, from salmon and shellfish to game and fresh organic vegetables. Vegetarian selections are always on the menu, and the exclusively Pacific Northwest and Californian wine list has at least 40 choices by the glass. The prix-fixe early dinner (C$30), served from 5 to 6 PM is a steal; reservations are required for these early dinners and recommended other times. ⊠*1193 Denman St., West End* ☎*604/685–7337* ▭*AE, DC, MC, V.*

$$$–$$$$ ✕**Sequoia Grill at the Teahouse.** The former officers' mess in Stanley Park is perfectly poised for watching sunsets over the water. The Pacific Northwest menu is not especially innovative, but it includes such specialties as spinach and pear salad, and mushrooms stuffed with crab and mascarpone cheese, as well as seasonally changing treatments of B.C. salmon, ahi tuna, and rack of lamb. In summer you can dine on the patio. ⊠*7501 Stanley Park Dr., Ferguson Point, Stanley Park* ☎*604/669–3281 or 800/280–9893* ▭*AE, MC, V.*

$$–$$$ ✕**Nu.** With its wall of windows overlooking False Creek, this contemporary dining room boasts lovely water views. The name is French for "naked," but that doesn't refer to the patrons' attire (which runs from smart-casual to business suits) or the room's decor (chic Euro style, from the funky bucket seats to the gilded brass ceiling). Instead, it represents the restaurant's philosophy of letting good-quality ingredients shine. You could linger over a cocktail and light bites, perhaps cute mini-burgers or a goat-cheese soufflé, but don't overlook the far more innovative dishes, such as the luxurious seafood salad, the "all-night braised" pork belly paired with yam dumplings, and the caramelized lamb cheeks served with artichokes and saffron-scented couscous. ⊠*1661 Granville St., Yaletown* ☎*604/646–4668* ▭*AE, MC, V.*

PIZZA

$$ ✕**Incendio.** The hand-flipped thin-crust pizzas, with delicious toppings including Gorgonzola, chicken, fresh spinach, and sun-dried tomatoes, and the mix-and-match pastas and sauces (try the hot smoked-duck sausage, artichoke, and tomato combination or the spicy *puttanesca* with anchovies, capers, and olives) draw crowds to this Gastown eat-

ery. The room, in a circa-1900 heritage building, with exposed brick, local artwork, and big curved windows, has plenty of atmosphere. There's a second location in Kitsilano. ✉ *103 Columbia St., Gastown* ☎ *604/688–8694* ▭ *AE, MC, V* ✉ *2118 Burrard St., Kitsilano* ☎ *604/736–2220* ▭ *AE, MC, V* ⊗ *No lunch weekends.*

SEAFOOD

$$$$ ★ ✕**Blue Water Cafe.** Executive chef Frank Pabst features both popular and lesser-known local seafood at this fashionable restaurant; he even offers an appetizer called "Unsung Heroes" that might include such frequently overlooked varieties as mackerel, sardines, and herring. Halibut, which could be paired with roasted cauliflower, and buttery sablefish caramelized with a sake-soy glaze are both excellent options. Ask the staff to recommend wine pairings from the B.C.-focused list. There's a good selection of raw oysters, too, and sushi chef Yoshihiro ("Yoshi") Tabo turns out both classic and new creations. You could dress up a bit, whether you dine in the candlelit interior with exposed beams and brick or outside on the former loading dock that's now an attractive terrace. ✉ *1095 Hamilton St., Yaletown* ☎ *604/688–8078* ▭ *AE, DC, MC, V.*

$$$$ Fodor'sChoice ★ ✕**C Restaurant.** Save your pennies, fish fans—dishes such as pickled sablefish served with mustard sorbet and minty cucumber soup or tuna grilled ultra-rare and dressed with an octopus vinaigrette have established this spot as Vancouver's most innovative seafood restaurant. Start with shucked oysters from the raw bar or perhaps the lavender-cured halibut. The six-course (C$98 per person) and ten-course (C$130 per person) tasting menus with optional wine pairings highlight regional seafood; executive chef Robert Clark is an active promoter of British Columbia's bounty. Both the ultramodern interior and the waterside patio overlook False Creek, but dine before dark to enjoy the view. ✉ *2–1600 Howe St., Downtown* ☎ *604/681–1164* ▭ *AE, DC, MC, V* ⊗ *No lunch weekends or Oct.–Apr.*

$$–$$$ ✕**Rodney's Oyster House.** This fishing-shack look-alike in Yaletown has one of the widest selections of oysters in town (up to 18 varieties), from locally harvested to exotic Japanese kumamotos. You can pick your oysters individually—they're laid out on ice behind the bar and priced at C$1.50 to about C$3 each—or try the clams, scallops, mussels, and other mollusks from the steamer kettles. Oyster lovers can also relax over martinis and appetizers in the attached Mermaid Room lounge. ✉ *1228 Hamilton St., Yaletown* ☎ *604/609–0080* ▭ *AE, DC, MC, V* ⊗ *Restaurant closed Sun., lounge closed Mon.–Wed. No lunch in lounge.*

GREATER VANCOUVER

ASIAN

$–$$ ✕**The Flying Tiger.** Inspired by the street foods of Asia, this laid-back lounge and eatery has a menu that roams from the Philippines to Thailand to Singapore and beyond. Start with a creative cocktail, perhaps the Dragon Slayer (dragon fruit–infused vodka mixed with pomegranate liqueur and fresh lime soda), or a glass of B.C. wine, before sam-

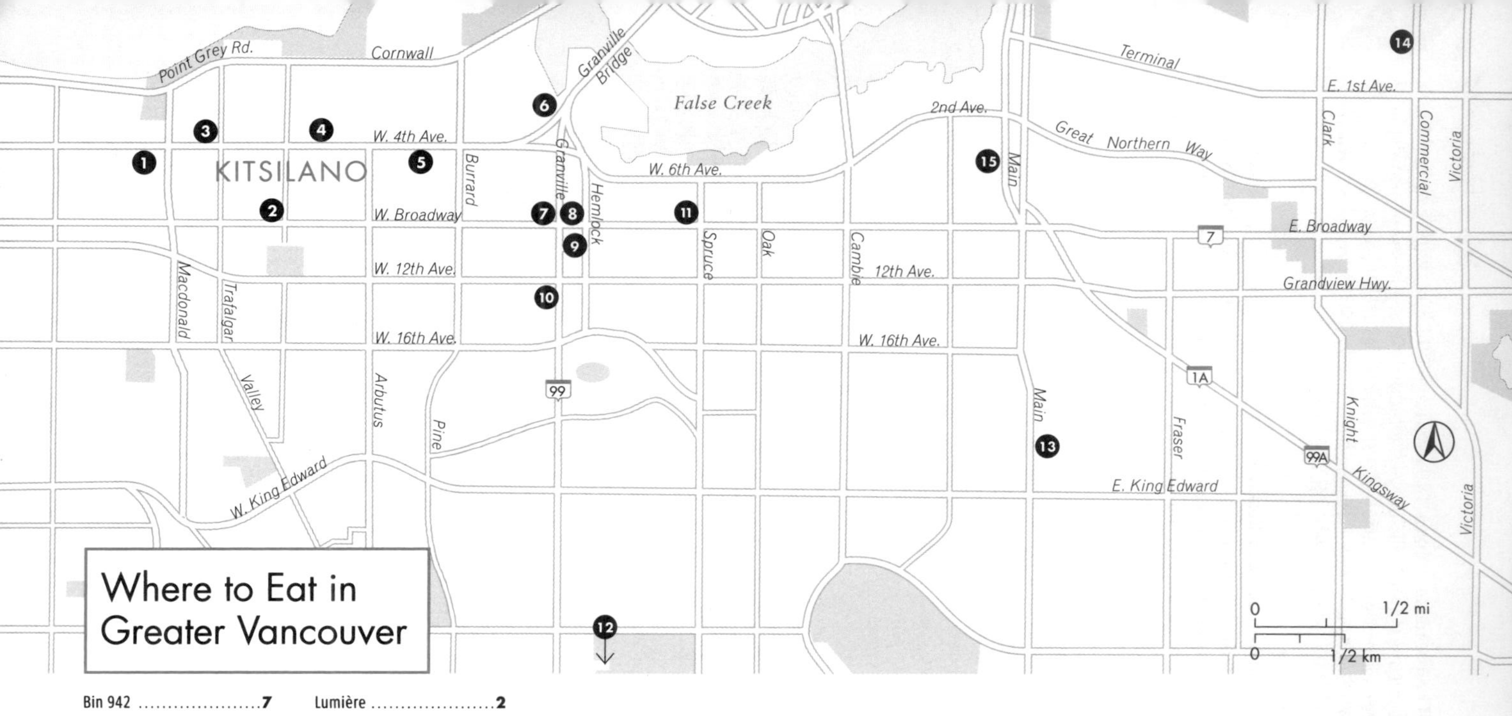

Bin 942 .... **7**	Lumière **2**
Bishop's **4**	Quattro on Fourth **3**
Cru **8**	Stella's Tap & Tapas Bar .. **14**
The Flying Tiger **1**	Sun Sui Wah **12, 13**
Foundation Lodge **15**	Tojo's **11**
Gastropod **5**	Vij's **9**
Go Fish **6**	West **10**

pling a range of small plates, including crisp panko-crusted squid, petite pancakes heaped with duck confit and fresh herbs, or smoked halibut paired with green-papaya salad. Dishes are designed to share, so it's fun with a group. ✉ *2958 West 4th Ave., Kitsilano* ☎ *604/737–7529* ▭ *AE, MC, V* ⊙ *No lunch.*

CHINESE

$$–$$$ ✕ **Sun Sui Wah Seafood Restaurant.** This bright, bustling Cantonese restaurant with locations on the East Side and in suburban Richmond is best known for its excellent dim sum (served 10–3 daily), which ranges from traditional handmade dumplings to some highly adventurous fare. Dinner specialties include roasted squab marinated in the restaurant's secret spice blend and enormous king crab plucked live from the tanks, then steamed with minced garlic. ✉ *3888 Main St., Main St./Mt. Pleasant* ☎ *604/872–8822 or 866/872–8822* ▭ *AE, DC, MC, V* ✉ *4940 No. 3 Rd., Richmond* ☎ *604/273–8208 or 866/683–8208* ▭ *AE, DC, MC, V.*

ECLECTIC

$$ ✕ **Bin 942.** High-energy murals, low lights, and up-tempo (sometimes loud) music draw crowds to this tiny tapas bar. The real star here, though, is the food. From the scallop and tiger-prawn tournedos to the beef tenderloin phyllo Wellington, the chef creates some of the most eclectic small plates in town. Fun is also part of the deal: the chocolate fruit fondue, for example, is designed for two and comes with a paintbrush. Food is served until 1:30 AM (until midnight on Sunday), and the excellent, affordable, wines are all available by the glass. ✉ *1521 W. Broadway, South Granville* ☎ *604/734–9421* ⚠ *Reservations not accepted* ▭ *MC, V* ⊙ *No lunch.*

$ ✕ **Stella's Tap and Tapas Bar.** If you're looking for a bite and a brew while browsing on Commercial Drive, join the locals at this comfortable hangout with burnished wide-plank floors and stone walls. Belgian beers are featured, so be sure to check the "fresh sheet" for current offerings. The menu of eclectic small plates rambles the world, from fried tofu with a sweet soy-sambal sauce, to a grilled veggie antipasto, or a trio of Pacific salmon, so you can pick and choose according to your mood. At midday, the kitchen turns out less exotic but still worthy sandwiches and salads. ✉ *1191 Commercial Dr., East Side* ☎ *604/254–2437* ▭ *MC, V.*

FRENCH

$$$–$$$$ Fodor's Choice ★ ✕ **Lumière.** Chef Robert Feenie is no longer associated with this long-acclaimed restaurant, but the new celebrity chef at the helm is Daniel Boulud, who will be working closely with executive chef Dale MacKay. At press time the restaurant was undergoing renovations to the space and the menu. ✉ *2551 W. Broadway, Kitsilano* ☎ *604/739–8185* ▭ *AE, DC, MC, V* ⊙ *Unknown at press time.*

INDIAN

$$$ ✕ **Vij's.** Vikram Vij, the genial proprietor of Vancouver's most innovative Indian restaurant, uses local ingredients to create exciting takes on South Asian cuisine. The dishes, such as lamb "popsicles" in a creamy

fenugreek-scented curry, or black-eyed peas served on a pilaf of brown basmati rice and vegetables, are far from traditional but are spiced beautifully. Mr. Vij circulates through the room, which is decorated with Indian antiques and whimsical elephant-pattern lanterns, greeting guests and suggesting dishes or cocktail pairings. Expect to cool your heels at the bar sipping chai or a cold beer while you wait for a table (lineups of an hour or more are not uncommon), but if you like creative Indian fare, it's worth it. ⊠*1480 W. 11th Ave., South Granville* ☎*604/736–6664* *Reservations not accepted* ▭*AE, DC, MC, V* ⊙*No lunch.*

ITALIAN

$$$–$$$$ ✕**Quattro on Fourth.** Central Italian cuisine shines at this family-run favorite. The signature Spaghetti Quattro comes with hot chilies, minced chicken, black beans, olive oil, and generous lashings of garlic. Mains include Cornish hen grilled with herbs, garlic, and spicy peppers; rack of lamb with a fig and Dijon demi-glace; and pistachio-crusted black cod with roasted sweet-pepper sauce. Mahogany tables, chandeliers, candlelight, and a hand-painted floor glow indoors; a patio beckons in summer. The cellar has 400 wine varieties and an extensive grappa selection. The same owners also run the similar **Gusto di Quattro** (⊠*1 Lonsdale Ave., next to Lonsdale Quay, North Vancouver* ☎*604/924–4444*) a quick SeaBus ride across the harbor from downtown. ⊠*2611 W. 4th Ave., Kitsilano* ☎*604/734–4444* ▭*AE, DC, MC, V* ⊙*No lunch.*

JAPANESE

$$$–$$$$ ★ ✕**Tojo's.** Hidekazu Tojo is a sushi-making legend in Vancouver, with thousands of special preparations stored in his creative mind. Though the restaurant relocated to a striking modern space in an open high-ceilinged room, complete with a separate sake lounge, Tojo's sushi bar remains a convivial ringside seat for watching the creation of edible art. The best way to experience Tojo's creativity is to reserve a spot at the sushi bar and order *omakase* (chef's choice); chef Tojo will keep offering you wildly more adventurous fare, both raw and cooked, until you cry uncle. Budget a minimum of C$50 per person (before drinks) for the omakase option; tabs topping C$100 per person are routine. ⊠*1133 W. Broadway, Fairview* ☎*604/872–8050* ▭*AE, DC, MC, V* *Reservations essential* ⊙*Closed Sun. No lunch.*

MODERN CANADIAN

$$$$ ★ ✕**Bishop's.** Before "local" and "seasonal" were all the rage, this highly regarded room was serving West Coast cuisine with an emphasis on organic, regional produce. The menu changes weekly, but highlights have included such starters as duck liver terrine and mains like steamed smoked sablefish, Dungeness crab cakes, and locally raised lamb. All are beautifully presented and impeccably served with suggestions from Bishop's extensive local wine list. The split-level room displays elaborate flower arrangements and selections from owner John Bishop's art collection. ⊠*2183 W. 4th Ave., Kitsilano* ☎*604/738–2025* ▭*AE, DC, MC, V* ⊙*Closed 1st wk in Jan. No lunch.*

$$$$ **Fodor'sChoice** ★ ✕**West.** Contemporary regional cuisine is the theme at this chic restaurant, one of the city's most innovative dining rooms. Among the kitchen's creations are fresh tomato jelly with Thai basil, Dungeness crab, and avocado; sablefish with butternut squash puree and white asparagus; and braised pork cheeks served with baby carrots and candied shallots. There's an extensive selection of cheeses and decadent desserts that might include a chocolate-coconut devil's food cake or poached peaches paired with maple ice cream, brioche cinnamon toast, and melted Brie. Marble floors, high ceilings, and warm caramel leather set into red walls make the space feel simultaneously energetic and cozy. Elaborate multicourse tasting menus and a good-value (C$49) early-evening set menu, served before 6 PM, mean plenty of dining options. ✉ *2881 Granville St., South Granville* ☎ *604/738–8938* ▭ *AE, DC, MC, V* ⏲ *No lunch weekends.*

$$$ ★ ✕**Gastropod.** Don't be put off by the name—the first-rate fare coming out of young chef Angus An's kitchen is inventive and grounded in local, organic ingredients. At this Kitsilano bistro, done up with white tablecloths and honey-colored woods, you might find a warm salad of chanterelles, fava beans, and squid; or salmon and pea shoots enlivened with a wasabi sabayon. The chef is a fan of the *sous vide* technique, too, where meat or poultry is sealed in plastic (yes, plastic; it's pretty much a sophisticated version of the boil-in-bag technique) and slow-cooked, creating dishes such as tender chicken breast served with an Asian-flavored pesto. The chocolate fondant with earl grey syrup or lemon tart with fresh basil are sweet endings. ✉ *1938 W. 4th Ave., Kitsilano* ☎ *604/730–5579* ▭ *AE, MC, V* ⏲ *No lunch Sun–Tues.*

$$–$$$ ★ ✕**Cru.** "Small plates and big glasses" is the motto of this tapas- and wine-focused restaurant, stylishly outfitted with tan banquettes and romantic low lighting. More than 35 wines by the glass (plus more by the bottle) complement the inventive designed-to-share dishes. There's a wonderfully crispy duck confit served on a frisée salad with warm bacon dressing, hearty wine-braised short ribs matched with macaroni 'n cheese, and an assortment of cheeses from B.C., Québec, and beyond. Save room for dessert, perhaps the decadent bittersweet chocolate torte or the goat-cheese cake with sour-cherry compote. If you prefer, you can order a three-course prix-fixe meal for C$38. ✉ *1459 W. Broadway, South Granville* ☎ *604/677–4111* ▭ *AE, MC, V* ⏲ *No lunch.*

SEAFOOD

$ ★ ✕**Go Fish.** If the weather's fine, head for this seafood stand on the docks near Granville Island. It's owned by Gord Martin, of Bin 941/942 fame, so it's not your ordinary chippie. The menu is short—highlights include fish-and-chips, grilled salmon or tuna sandwiches, and oyster po' boys—but the quality is first-rate, and the accompanying Asian-flavored slaw leaves ordinary cole slaw in the dust. There are just a few (outdoor) tables, so go early or be prepared to wait. To get here, walk along the waterfront path from Granville Island; by car, drive east from Burrard on 1st Avenue until it ends at the docks. ✉ *1505 W. 1st Ave., Fisherman's Wharf, Kitsilano* ☎ *604/730–5039* ▭ *MC, V* ⏲ *Closed Mon. and Tues. No dinner.*

VEGETARIAN

¢–$ ✕ **Foundation Lounge.** The decor at this East Side vegetarian joint—mismatched Formica tables, 1950s-style vinyl chairs, a cinderblock bar—may not win design prizes, but the bohemian vibe is friendly and the meat-free fare is tasty. Try the satay salad—mixed greens, tofu, and broccoli topped with a warm, tangy peanut sauce—or opt for a hearty veggie burger or the tofu-and-mango scramble. This storefront restaurant is hopping from midday until 1 AM. ✉*2301 Main St., Main St./Mt. Pleasant* ☎*604/708–0881* ▭*MC, V.*

WHERE TO STAY

Accommodations in Vancouver range from luxurious waterfront hotels to neighborhood B&Bs, chain hotels (both luxury and budget), basic European-style pensions, and backpackers' hostels. There are also many top-quality choices that epitomize countryside—within a 30-minute drive of the downtown core.

Although the city is quite compact, each area has its distinct character and accommodation options. All our recommendations are within easy reach of transit that will take you to the major attractions, though if you choose to stay outside of the downtown core, a car will still be the easiest way to tour neighborhoods on the West Side or North Shore.

Be aware that the city is gearing up to host the 2010 Winter Olympics, which means there's a fair amount of construction. This includes the waterfront where there's an expanding convention site and other developments. Most of the heavy machines that go clunk at 7 AM will be long gone by the time you read this, but because work is still in progress, so are some of the photo-perfect views—at least for the time being.

WHAT IT COSTS IN CANADIAN DOLLARS

	¢	$	$$	$$$	$$$$
HOTELS	under C$75	C$75–C$125	C$126–C$175	C$176–C$250	over C$250

Hotel prices are for two people in a standard double room in high season, excluding tax.

DOWNTOWN

$$$$ **Fairmont Hotel Vancouver.** The copper roof of this 1939 château-style hotel dominates Vancouver's skyline, and the hotel itself is considered the city's gracious grand dame. Guest rooms vary in size, but even the standard rooms have an atmosphere of prestige, with high ceilings, lush draperies, and 19th-century-style mahogany furniture. Two friendly dogs (Mavis and Boe) are on hand for petting and walking, and the full-service spa here was Canada's first to cater to men, with big-screen TVs, wireless Internet, and black-leather pedicure chairs. Rooms on the Fairmont Gold floor have access to extra services, including a private lounge and a special concierge. Pros: The male-oriented spa,

great location for shopping, the architecture. Cons: Regal size makes it a shade impersonal, diversity of "standard" room sizes can be irritating for guests expecting a room similar to the one they stayed in before. ✉*900 W. Georgia St., Downtown, V6C 2W6* ☎*604/684–3131* 📠*604/662–1929* 🌐*www.fairmont.com* *556 rooms, 37 suites* *In-room: refrigerator (some), ethernet. In-hotel: 2 restaurants, room service, bar, pool, gym, spa, concierge, laundry service, executive floor, parking (fee), no-smoking rooms, some pets allowed, public Wi-Fi* 💳*AE, D, DC, MC, V.*

$$$$ **Fairmont Waterfront.** This luxuriously modern 23-story hotel is across the street from the Convention and Exhibition Centre and the Canada Place cruise-ship terminal but it's the floor-to-ceiling windows with ocean, park, and mountain views in most of the guest rooms that really make this hotel special. Adorned with blond-wood furniture and contemporary Canadian artwork, each room also has a window that opens. Elevator waits can be frustrating so consider asking for a room on a lower floor, though you'll be sacrificing view for this minor convenience. Next to the mountain-view pool is a rooftop herb garden—an aromatic retreat open to guests. The hotel's canine ambassador, Morgan, is available for petting, pampering, and taking for strolls. Pros: Harbor views, proximity to cruise-ship terminal, the lovely terraced pool near the patio herb garden. Cons: Overlooks the (sometimes noisy) construction of the convention center expansion, the elevator line-ups, the seemingly always busy lobby lounge. ✉*900 Canada Pl. Way, Downtown, V6C 3L5* ☎*604/691–1991* 📠*604/691–1999* 🌐*www.fairmont.com/waterfront* *489 rooms, 29 suites* *In-room: safe (some), kitchen (some), refrigerator, ethernet. In-hotel: restaurant, room service, bar, pool, gym, concierge, laundry service, executive floor, parking (fee), no-smoking rooms, some pets allowed, public Wi-Fi* 💳*AE, D, DC, MC, V.*

$$$$ **Four Seasons.** This 29-story downtown luxury hotel is famous for pampering guests. The lobby, which connects to the Pacific Centre shopping mall, is lavish, with an atrium-style lounge. Standard rooms, with understated color schemes, marble bathroom fixtures, and tall windows with city views, are spacious and traditionally furnished, as are the even more spacious corner rooms with sitting areas. Service at the Four Seasons is top-notch and the many amenities include free evening limousine service. Regular visitors may be saddened to learn that the superlative, long-time signature restaurant is gone, but the new Yew restaurant + bar, serving regional cuisine, is set to takes its place. Pros: Premier location for shopping, Four Seasons service standards. Cons: No on-site spa. ✉*791 W. Georgia St., vehicle entrance on Howe St., Downtown, V6C 2T4* ☎*604/689–9333* 📠*604/684–4555* 🌐*www.fourseasons.com* *306 rooms, 66 suites* *In-room: refrigerator, safe, ethernet. In-hotel: public Wi-Fi, 2 restaurants, room service, bar, pool, gym, concierge, laundry service, parking (fee), no-smoking rooms, some pets allowed* 💳*AE, DC, MC, V.*

$$$$ **Loden Hotel.** Vancouver's newest hotel, this ultra-sophisticated boutique inn has all manner of high-tech amenities such as in-room iPod stations and oversized LCD TV screens. Floor-to-ceiling windows fill

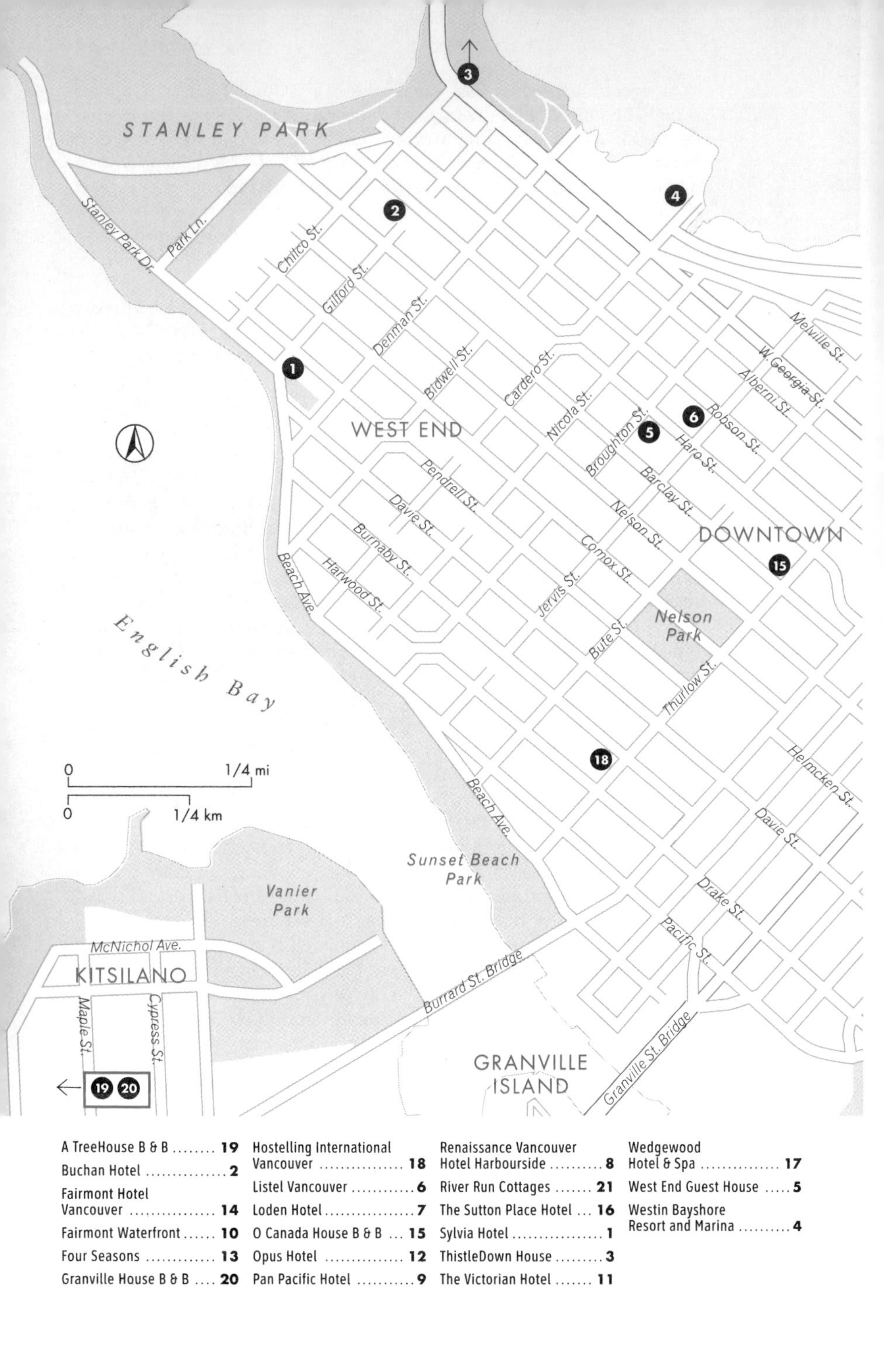

A TreeHouse B & B 19
Buchan Hotel 2
Fairmont Hotel Vancouver 14
Fairmont Waterfront 10
Four Seasons 13
Granville House B & B 20
Hostelling International Vancouver 18
Listel Vancouver 6
Loden Hotel 7
O Canada House B & B ... 15
Opus Hotel 12
Pan Pacific Hotel 9
Renaissance Vancouver Hotel Harbourside 8
River Run Cottages 21
The Sutton Place Hotel ... 16
Sylvia Hotel 1
ThistleDown House 3
The Victorian Hotel 11
Wedgewood Hotel & Spa 17
West End Guest House 5
Westin Bayshore Resort and Marina 4

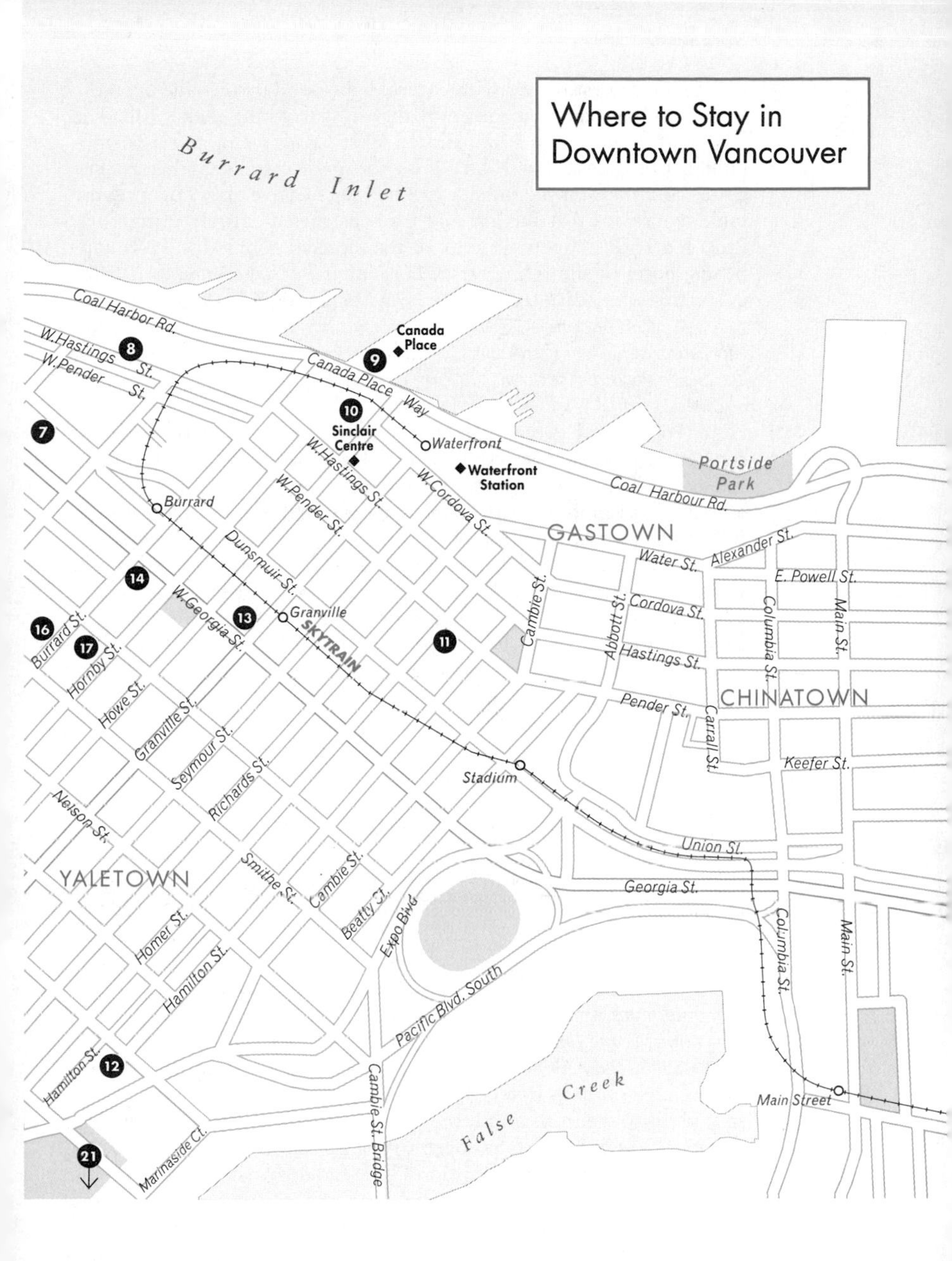
Where to Stay in Downtown Vancouver
Burrard Inlet
Coal Harbor Rd.
W.Hastings St.
W.Pender St.
Canada Place
Canada Place Way
Sinclair Centre
Waterfront
Waterfront Station
Portside Park
Coal Harbour Rd.
Burrard
W.Hastings St.
W.Pender St.
W.Cordova St.
GASTOWN
Dunsmuir St.
W.Georgia St.
Granville
SKYTRAIN
Water St.
Alexander St.
E. Powell St.
Cordova St.
Cambie St.
Abbott St.
Columbia St.
Main St.
Hastings St.
CHINATOWN
Pender St.
Carrall St.
Keefer St.
Burrard St.
Hornby St.
Howe St.
Granville St.
Seymour St.
Richards St.
Stadium
Nelson St.
Union St.
Georgia St.
YALETOWN
Smithe St.
Cambie St.
Beatty St.
Expo Blvd
Homer St.
Hamilton St.
Columbia St.
Main St.
Pacific Blvd. South
Hamilton St.
Cambie St. Bridge
False Creek
Main Street
Marinaside Ct.
7
8
9
10
11
12
13
14
16
17
21

the spacious guest rooms with natural light—and if you slide open the bathroom half-wall you can enjoy the views from the soaker tub. The Voya restaurant has a sophisticated West Coast menu and a cosmopolitan 1940s design with lots of mirrors and crystal chandeliers. The glitter continues on the outside, where the reflective glass covering the building creates the illusion that it's constructed entirely of mirrors. Pros: It's THE happening hotel of the moment. Cons: It's THE happening hotel of the moment. ✉*1177 Melville St., Downtown, V6E 0A3* ☎*604/669–5060 or 877/225–6336* 📠*604/662–8904* 🌐*www.lodenvancouver.com* *70 rooms, 7 suites* *In-room: refrigerator, safe, ethernet, Wi-Fi. In-hotel: restaurant, bar, room service, spa, gym, concierge, laundry service, parking (fee), no-smoking rooms, some pets allowed, public Wi-Fi* 💳*AE, D, DC, MC, V.*

$$$$ ★ **Pan Pacific Hotel.** A centerpiece of waterfront Canada Place, the luxurious Pan Pacific shares a complex with the Vancouver Convention and Exhibition Centre and Vancouver's main cruise-ship terminal. Rooms are large and modern with maplewood throughout, marble vanities, Italian linens, and stunning ocean, mountain, or skyline views, all of which have been enjoyed by a star-studded list of royals, celebs, and well-heeled newsmakers. The high-end suites, some with private steam room, sauna, or baby-grand piano, are popular with visiting VIPs. The 26-room Roman bath–theme Spa Utopia and Salon is a sumptuous experience, and the health and fitness center is state-of-the-art. If you're staying over a Friday or Saturday night, Puccini and pasta were never as good as at the Italian Opera Buffet in the main dining room. Pros: The harbor views, it's only an elevator ride to the cruise-ship terminal (a real plus for heavy baggage transfers), the "go the extra mile" service attitude. Cons: Next door to waterfront construction, the atrium is open to the convention center's main lobby so the hotel foyer, lounge, and entrance fills with delegates bearing conference badges talking shop, nabbing the best seats in the house, and vying for taxis. ✉*999 Canada Pl., Downtown, V6C 3B5* ☎*604/662–8111, 800/663–1515 in Canada, 800/937–1515 in U.S.* 📠*604/685–8690* 🌐*www.panpacific.com* *465 rooms, 39 suites* *In-room: refrigerator, safe, kitchen (some), ethernet, dial-up, Wi-Fi. In-hotel: 2 restaurants, room service, bar, pool, gym, spa, concierge, laundry service, parking (fee), no-smoking rooms, some pets allowed, public Wi-Fi* 💳*AE, DC, MC, V.*

$$$$ ★ **The Sutton Place Hotel.** More like an exclusive European guesthouse than a large modern hotel, the rooms here are furnished in a Parisian style with soft neutrals and lush fabrics, and the service is gracious and attentive. The full spa (also open to nonguests) has a wide menu. La Grande Résidence (part of Sutton Place), an apartment hotel suitable for stays of at least a week, is next door, at 855 Burrard. The hotel's new wine boutique carries a number of hard-to-find specialty labels from all over the world. The Fleuri restaurant serves Continental cuisine and is particularly noted for its late-night chocolate buffet. Pros: Classy, terrific lounge bar for romantic trysts, the chocolate buffet is diet decadence, the spa. Cons: The wide open, nondescript corridor joining restaurant and lounge couldn't be further from the hotel's discreet style: in other words, your tryst better not be clandestine! ✉*845*

Burrard St., Downtown, V6Z 2K6 ☎604/682–5511 or 800/961–7555 📠604/682–5513 🌐www.suttonplace.com 350 rooms, 46 suites, 164 apartments In-room: refrigerator, safe, DVD, ethernet, Wi-Fi. In-hotel: restaurant, room service, bar, pool, gym, spa, concierge, laundry service, parking (fee), no-smoking rooms, some pets allowed, public Wi-Fi ▭AE, D, DC, MC, V.

$$$$ Fodor'sChoice ★ **Wedgewood Hotel & Spa.** The small, lavish Wedgewood has just earned membership to the exclusive Relais & Châteaux Group, and is run by an owner who cares fervently about her guests. The lobby and guest rooms display a flair for old-world Italian luster with original artwork and antiques selected by the proprietor on her European travels. Guest rooms are capacious, and each has a balcony. The four penthouse suites have fireplaces, luxury spa bathrooms, and private garden terraces. All the extra touches are here, too: afternoon ice delivery, dark-out drapes, CD players, robes, and a morning newspaper. The turndown service includes homemade cookies and bottled water. The sophisticated Bacchus restaurant and lounge ($$$–$$$$) is in the lobby; it's also a terrific pit-stop for afternoon tea after shopping along Robson Street. The tiny but luxurious on-site spa is very popular—book ahead for an appointment. Pros: Personalized and attentive service, boutique atmosphere, afternoon tea with flair, great location close to top shops, spa. Cons: The small size means it gets booked quickly. *✉845 Hornby St., Downtown, V6Z 1V1 ☎604/689–7777 or 800/663–0666 📠604/608–5348 🌐www.wedgewoodhotel.com 41 rooms, 43 suites In-room: refrigerator, safe, ethernet, Wi-Fi. In-hotel: restaurant, room service, bar, gym, spa, laundry facilities, laundry service, parking (fee), no-smoking rooms, public Wi-Fi ▭AE, D, DC, MC, V.*

$$$–$$$$ **Renaissance Vancouver Hotel Harbourside.** Like the Vancouver waterfront, this business-district hotel is constantly transforming, though plans for the public areas have been delayed until 2008. Until then, the black marble lobby with its humongous windows is quite spectacular. Rooms are larger than average and have either step out or full-size glassed-in balconies with city or (in the more expensive rooms) partial water and mountain views. There's an indoor pool, a health club, and direct access to a waterside park—take all this and combine it with the "kids under 12 eat free" policy, and you have a good choice for families in an ocean-side high-rise. Pros: At the outer edge of the financial district, waterfront views, revolving restaurant. Cons: Waterfront construction will eventually obstruct some of the views; a 5-block walk to major shopping and Stanley Park (though by 2010 a waterfront path will connect to the park). *✉1133 W. Hastings St., Downtown, V6E 2T3 ☎604/689–9211 or 800/905–8582 📠604/689–4358 🌐www.renaissancevancouver.com 437 rooms, 8 suites In-room: safe (some), ethernet. In-hotel: restaurant, bar, pool, gym, concierge, laundry service, executive floor, parking (fee), no-smoking rooms, some pets allowed, public Wi-Fi ▭AE, D, DC, MC, V.*

$–$$ Fodor'sChoice ★ **The Victorian Hotel.** Budget hotels can be beautiful, as attested by the gleaming hardwood floors, high ceilings, and chandeliers at this prettily restored 1898 European-style pension. This is one of Vancouver's best-value accommodations, and guest rooms in the two connecting three-story buildings have down duvets, oriental rugs atop hardwood floors, lush draperies, and period furniture; a few have bay windows or mountain views. Some of the private bathrooms are outfitted with marble tiles and granite countertops (though some have a shower and no tub). Even the shared baths are spotlessly clean and nicely appointed. With three queen beds, room #15 is a good choice for families. Pros: Great location for the price, helpful staff, clean, comfortable. Cons: Location near the "rummy part of town" a few blocks east. It's relatively safe (honest), but common sense says you would probably take a cab to the door after midnight rather than walk. ✉ *514 Homer St., Downtown, V6B 2V6* ☎ *877/681–6369 or 604/681–6369* 📠 *604/681–8776* 🌐 *www.victorianhotel.ca* *39 rooms, 18 with bath* *In-room: no a/c, refrigerator (some). In-hotel: no elevator, laundry service, parking (fee), no-smoking rooms, public Wi-Fi* 💳 *MC, V* *CP.*

¢–$ **Hostelling International Vancouver.** Vancouver has three Hostelling International locations: a former hotel in the downtown core, above a boisterous bar; a big hostel set in parkland at Jericho Beach in Kitsilano; and a smaller building in a residential neighborhood near English Bay. Each has private rooms for two to four people; bunks in men's, women's, and coed dorms (with bedding and lockers); a shared kitchen, a TV lounge, and a range of free or low-cost tours and activities. The central hostel has rooms with private baths and TVs and is the pricier location; the Jericho, with the cheapest rates, is open only in the summer. Pros: Great staff, cheap and clean but you get what you pay for. Cons: Not for the fussy traveler, lots of students, dorm accommodations can be noisy with snorers and night owls who come in late. ✉ *HI Vancouver Central, 1025 Granville St., Downtown, V6Z 1L4* ☎ *604/685–5335 or 888/203–8333* 📠 *604/685–5351* 🌐 *www.hihostels.ca* *36 rooms, 26 with bath; 41 4-bed dorm rooms* *In-room: no a/c (some), no phone, no TV (some), ethernet. In-hotel: bar, laundry facilities, public Internet, public Wi-Fi, no-smoking rooms* 💳 *MC, V* *CP* ✉ *HI Vancouver Downtown, 1114 Burnaby St., West End, V6E 1P1* ☎ *604/684–4565 or 888/203–4302* 📠 *604/684–4540* 🌐 *www.hihostels.ca* *23 rooms, 44 4-bed dorm rooms* *In-room: no a/c, no phone, no TV. In-hotel: bicycles, laundry facilities, public Internet, public Wi-Fi, parking (no fee), no-smoking rooms* 💳 *MC, V* *CP* ✉ *HI Vancouver Jericho Beach, 1515 Discovery St., Kitsilano, V6R 4K5* ☎ *604/224–3208 or 888/203–4303* 📠 *604/224–4852* 🌐 *www.hihostels.ca* *10 rooms, 9 14-bed dorm rooms* *In-room: no a/c, no phone, no TV. In-hotel: bicycles, laundry facilities, public Internet, parking (fee), no-smoking rooms* 💳 *MC, V* *Closed Oct.–Apr.*

METROPOLITAN VANCOUVER

$$–$$$ ★ **River Run Cottages.** This exceptionally romantic riverside B&B is part of a historic floating-home community, 30 minutes south of downtown. Choose from a little floating house with a loft bed and an antique claw-foot tub; a two-level suite (once a loft for drying fish nets) with a Japanese soaking tub on the deck; or two river's-edge units, each with a woodstove and a waterside deck. Gourmet breakfasts are deliv-

ered to your room and in-room dinners are available with advance notice. Romance packages include champagne and a sprinkling of rose petals. Note that this is tidal country so if you want to explore the area, rubber-soled shoes are recommended. The approach ramps at the marina can get slippery and pitch up to 12 feet. Pros: Unique, on the water, out of town, romantic. Cons: Out of town, need a car to get here and traffic through the tunnel beneath the Fraser River can be painstakingly slow at peak times. ⊠*4551 River Rd. W, Ladner, V4K 1R9* ☎*604/946–7778* 🖷*604/940–1970* 🌐*www.riverruncottages.com* *2 rooms, 2 suites* *In-room: no a/c, refrigerator, no TV. In-hotel: no elevator, bicycles, parking (no fee), no-smoking rooms, some pets allowed* ▭*MC, V* *BP.*

NORTH VANCOUVER

$$–$$$$ ★ **ThistleDown House.** This 1920 Arts and Crafts house with its private, sunny garden, is handy to North Shore hiking and skiing, but just 15 to 30 minutes from downtown. Furnished with a low-key, eclectic arrangement of antiques, art deco touches, local art, and treasures gathered on the hosts' travels, each room has its own charm: Under the Apple Tree, with its private patio, gas fireplace, and air-jet tub, is a romantic choice; Mulberry Peek, an octagonal tower room, has four walls of windows and a private balcony; Pages, the former library, has a cast-iron pedestal tub and book-lined walls. Pros: Personal style of genuine hospitality, attention to detail, free afternoon tea. Cons: Away from the crowds; need a car to get here and to explore. ⊠*3910 Capilano Rd., North Vancouver, V7R 4J2* ☎*604/986–7173 or 888/633–7173* 🖷*604/980–2939* 🌐*www.thistle-down.com* *6 rooms* *In-room: no a/c, no phone. In-hotel: no elevator, laundry service, public Internet, public Wi-Fi, parking (no fee), no kids under 12, no-smoking rooms* ▭*MC, V* *Closed Dec. and Jan.* *BP.*

WEST END

$$$$ ★ **Westin Bayshore Resort and Marina.** Perched on Coal Harbour beside Stanley Park, the Bayshore has a picturesque marina on its doorstep as well as impressive harbor and mountain views. Most rooms take full advantage of this, with floor-to-ceiling windows that open to a railing or a step-out balcony. Interiors are cheery and comfortable, with rich modern blue-and-gold fabrics, plush armchairs, and comfortable beds. The only downtown resort hotel, the Bayshore is also rich with recreational facilities, including fishing charters, sightseeing cruises, and poolside yoga. Vancouver's Seawall Walk connects the resort to Stanley Park and the Vancouver Convention and Exhibition Centre. Pros: Resort amenities within minutes of downtown, the doormen still dress up as Beefeaters, fabulous water views, Stanley Park your next-door neighbor. Cons: Away from the downtown core; the posh new conference space sees a lot of business travelers, which might put families off, and vice versa; the spacious lobby is rather impersonal; tower rooms are a fair walk from registration. ⊠*1601 Bayshore Dr., off Cardero*

St., West End, V6G 2V4 ☎604/682–3377 📠604/687–3102 🌐www.westinbayshore.com 482 rooms, 28 suites In-room: refrigerator, safe (some), ethernet, Wi-Fi (some). In-hotel: 2 restaurants, room service, bar, pools, gym, concierge, laundry service, parking (fee), no-smoking rooms, some pets allowed, public Wi-Fi ▭AE, D, DC, MC, V.

$$$–$$$$ **O Canada House B&B.** This beautifully restored 1897 Victorian, within walking distance of downtown, is where the first version of "O Canada," the national anthem, was written, in 1909. Each bedroom is appointed in late-Victorian antiques, and modern comforts such as bathrobes help make things homey. The top-floor room is enormous, with two king beds and a private sitting/dining area. A separate one-room coach house in the garden is a romantic option though it faces onto the back alley and is a bit cramped. Breakfast, served in the dining room, is a lavish affair. Pros: Gracious service, fantastic breakfast, residential location. Cons: Rooms on the small side (except the top floor). *✉1114 Barclay St., West End, V6E 1H1 ☎604/688–0555 or 877/688–1114 📠604/488–0556 🌐www.ocanadahouse.com 7 rooms In-room: no a/c, refrigerator, VCR, Wi-Fi. In-hotel: parking (no fee), no kids under 12, no-smoking rooms, public Wi-Fi, no elevator ▭MC, V BP.*

$$–$$$$ **West End Guest House.** This Victorian B&B, built in 1906, is painted the deep pink of the fragrant "Painted Lady" variety of Sweet Pea flower that dates back to the 18th century—and the guest house is just as charming inside with a gracious front parlor, cozy fireplace, and early 1900s furniture. Most of the handsome rooms are furnished with antiques; two larger rooms have gas fireplaces and two have brass beds. All the bathrooms have been recently renovated, and each has a mural of one of the heritage homes in the surrounding residential neighborhood. The inn is a two-minute walk from Robson Street and five minutes from Stanley Park. The owners also have a suite in a modern building next door; it's ideal for families and couples looking for weekly rentals. Pros: Great heritage interior, quiet residential location, free use of mountain bikes, private patio garden. Cons: Furnishings a bit precious. *✉1362 Haro St., West End, V6E 1G2 ☎604/681–2889 or 888/546–3327 📠604/688–8812 🌐www.westendguesthouse.com 8 rooms In-room: no a/c, DVD (some), VCR (some), Wi-Fi. In-hotel: no elevator, bicycles, public Internet, public Wi-Fi, parking (no fee), no-smoking rooms ▭AE, D, DC, MC, V BP.*

$$$ **Listel Vancouver.** Art and jazz come together in this stylish hotel on Vancouver's most vibrant shopping street. Gallery-floor guest rooms and suites display original or limited-edition works by Canadian artists like Vancouver's Carmelo Sortino alongside pieces from France, England, the U.S., and Japan. Rooms on the Museum floor are decorated with work from contemporary First Nations artists such as Susan Point and Eugene Alfred. Custom-made furniture in Gallery and Museum rooms complements the art. At time of writing, a Photography floor was in the works. Look to your bedside for *The Vancouver Stories,* a book specially commissioned by the hotel, written by 14 local writers. You can catch live jazz nightly at O'Doul's Restaurant & Bar downstairs. Pros: The art concept offers an eclectic insight into regional

culture, there's quality (local) jazz on your doorstep. Cons: It's a three-block walk from the designer-label area of Robson Street, which can feel like forever if you're laden down with purchases; staff are on the young (inexperienced) side. *⊠1300 Robson St., West End, V6E 1C5 ☎604/684–8461 or 800/663–5491 604/684–7092 ⊕www.listel-vancouver.com 119 rooms, 10 suites In-room: refrigerator, ethernet, Wi-Fi. In-hotel: restaurant, room service, bar, gym, laundry service, parking (fee), no-smoking rooms ▭AE, D, DC, MC, V.*

$–$$$ ★ **Sylvia Hotel.** To stay at the Sylvia in June through August, you must book six months to a year ahead: this Virginia-creeper-covered 1912 building is popular because of its low rates and near-perfect location: about 25 feet from the beach on scenic English Bay, 200 feet from Stanley Park, and a 20-minute walk from Robson Street. The rooms and apartment-style suites vary from tiny to spacious. Many of the basic but comfortable rooms are large enough to sleep four and all have windows that open. The restaurant and bar are popular and its tenure on English Bay has made it a nostalgic haunt for Vancouverites. Pros: Beachfront location, close to restaurants, a good place to mingle with the locals. Cons: Older building, parking can be difficult if the lot is full, the 15-minute walk to the downtown core is slightly uphill. *⊠1154 Gilford St., West End, V6G 2P6 ☎604/681–9321 604/682–3551 ⊕www.sylviahotel.com 97 rooms, 22 suites In-room: no a/c, kitchen (some), dial-up, Wi-Fi. In-hotel: restaurant, room service, bar, laundry service, public Internet, parking (fee), no-smoking rooms, some pets allowed ▭AE, DC, MC, V.*

$–$$ **Buchan Hotel.** On a tree-lined residential street a block from Stanley Park, this 1926 pension-style hotel vies with the Sylvia Hotel as one of Vancouver's best values. Popular with cyclists thanks to its bike storage and low-traffic location, the Buchan also provides free coffee and tea, a lounge with a fireplace, and ski storage, but no elevator. Rooms are simple but comfortable, with checked or floral fabrics and old-fashioned radiators. Rooms without baths have hand basins. Pros: Residential neighborhood, quiet, close proximity to beach and Stanley Park, airport shuttle a five-minute walk away. Cons: Parking either has time limits or is expensive, limited guest-room amenities. *⊠1906 Haro St., West End, V6G 1H7 ☎604/685–5354 or 800/668–6654 604/685–5367 ⊕www.buchanhotel.com 60 rooms, 34 with bath In-room: no a/c, no phone. In-hotel: no elevator, laundry facilities, parking (fee), no-smoking rooms ▭AE, DC, MC, V.*

WEST SIDE

$$$ **Granville House B&B.** At the edge of posh Shaughnessy, this Tudor-revival house exudes a peaceful elegance that belies its address on one of Vancouver's busiest thoroughfares. Triple glazing, radiant floor heat, and electronic locks (which allow you to check-in in advance since there are no keys to exchange) are some of the finishing touches. Trade your shoes for plush slippers (provided) in the front hall and head to one of the five king-size rooms, each with a sitting area and appointed with luxurious linens, spa robes, and amenities made locally on Salt

Spring Island. There's a self-serve refreshment/coffee bar in the inviting modern lounge; Continental breakfast includes one hot dish. Pros: New, on the main drag into/out of town, customized/independent style of check-in. Cons: Granville Street is very busy, everything at this B&B is so new that you might feel hesitant to dirty the linens! ✉ *5050 Granville St., Shaughnessy, V6M 3B4* ☎ *604/307–2300 or 604/733–2963* 🌐 *www.granvillebb.com* *4 rooms* *In-room: refrigerator, Wi-Fi. In-hotel: no elevator, laundry service, parking (no fee), no-smoking rooms, public Wi-Fi* 💳 *AE, DC, MC, V* 🍽 *BP.*

$$–$$$ **A TreeHouse B&B.** Surrounded by tall evergreens, it's easy to see how this Asian-infused, West Coast–style house earned its name. Located on one of Kerrisdale's main thoroughfares, the inn is surprisingly quiet with its small Asian-styled courtyard garden and rooms that mix modern comfort with exotic Eastern influences such as Japanese arts and crafts. All rooms are warm and inviting with swamp coolers taking the place of air-conditioning. At 700 sqare feet, the Tree Top Suite is particularly spacious and private, with a four-poster bed, sitting area, deck, and skylit bathroom complete with 50-air-jet Jacuzzi. In-room spa massages can be arranged. Breakfast is a gourmet affair of four courses, or you can enjoy a self-catered Continental breakfast in your room or a Bag Breakfast to take with you. Pros: You feel like a house guest, personable service. Cons: The sun doesn't always get through all those evergreens so rooms feel a bit dark. ✉ *2490 W. 49th Ave., Kerrisdale, V6M 2V3* ☎ *604/266–2962 or 877/266–2960* 📠 *604/266–2960* 🌐 *www.treehousebb.com* *4 rooms* *In-room: no a/c, refrigerator (some), Wi-Fi. In-hotel: no elevator, no kids under 18, no-smoking rooms, parking (no fee)* 💳 *MC, V.*

YALETOWN

$$$$ ★ **Opus Hotel.** The design team had a good time with this boutique hotel, creating fictitious characters and designing rooms for each. Billy's room is fun and offbeat, with pop art and lime-green accents. Dede's room boasts leopard skin, velveteen, and faux-fur accents, while Bob and Carol's place has softer edges and golden tones. Amenities are fun, too: look for mini-oxygen canisters in the bathrooms—a whiff'll clear your head if you have a hangover, and it'll stimulate blood flow for other pursuits. An interesting note: the nighttime reading by your bed is a hotel murder mystery written by the General Manager himself! Most rooms have a full wall of windows, lots of natural light, and views of the city or the Japanese garden in the courtyard. Two rooms have private access to the garden; seventh-floor rooms have balconies. Other perks include dog-walking if you've brought Fido along, personal shopping, and free car service anywhere downtown. Pros: The central Yaletown location; the hotel is funky and hip the lobby bar is a fashionable meeting spot. Cons: Renovated heritage building has no views surrounding neighborhood is mostly high-rises trendy nightspots nearby can be noisy at night. ✉ *322 Davie St., Yaletown, V6B 5Z6* ☎ *604/642–6787 or 866/642–6787* 📠 *604/642–6780* 🌐 *www.opushotel.com* *85 rooms, 11 suites* *In-room: refrigerator, safe,*

DVD (some), VCR (some), ethernet, Wi-Fi. In-hotel: restaurant, room service, bar, gym, concierge, laundry service, parking (fee), no-smoking rooms, some pets allowed, public Wi-Fi, bicycles ▭*AE, DC, MC, V.*

NIGHTLIFE & THE ARTS

Updated by Celeste Moure

With easy access to the sea and mountains, it's no surprise that Vancouver is such an outdoorsy kind of town but once the sun goes down, the city's dwellers trade in their kayaks, hiking shoes, and North Face windbreakers for something decidedly more chic. There's plenty to choose from in just about every neighborhood: hipster Gastown is the place to go for swanky clubs and trendy wine bars while the gay-friendly West End is all about bumpin' and grindin' in retro bars and clubs. A posh crowd of glitterati flocks to Yaletown's brewpubs and stylish lounges. Meanwhile, Kitsilano (the Venice Beach of Vancouver) attracts a laid-back bunch who like to sip beer and frilly cocktails on cool bar patios with killer views.

This is a city with a rich cultural background and a wide spectrum of nightlife and cultural activities. Galleries, film festivals, cutting-edge theatrical performances, comedy, opera, and ballet await the culture vultures. Note, too, that the art of see-and-be-seen should not be taken lightly here, so put on your sexiest pair of strappy sandals or designer jeans and get ready to discover why Vancouver is the city everybody wants to move to.

BARS, PUBS & LOUNGES

Afterglow. Typically packed by 10 PM, this Yaletown lounge, tucked behind Glowbal restaurant, gets its radiance from the fuchsia lighting on pink and white brick walls (or maybe the fake tans and hairspray have something to do with it). It's a great place to lounge on comfy sofas, sip colorful martinis, and practice the art of see-and-be-seen. ✉*1082 Hamilton St., Yaletown* ☎*604/602–0835.*

Bridges. This Vancouver landmark near the Public Market has the city's biggest marina-side deck and a cozy nautical-theme pub. ✉*1696 Duranleau St., Granville Island* ☎*604/687–4400.*

FodorsChoice ★ **Chill Winston.** Decked out with plush black leather sofas, exposed wood beams, warm lighting, and a view of Gastown's lively square, this restaurant-cum-lounge attracts a well-heeled crowd of jetsetters and urban dwellers. ✉*3 Alexander St., Gastown* ☎*604/288–9575.*

FodorsChoice ★ **Fountainhead Pub.** With one of the largest streetside patios in downtown, you can do as the locals do here: sit back, down a few beers, and watch the passersby. ✉*1025 Davie St.,West End* ☎*604/687–2222.*

Sand Bar. With a highly rated seafood restaurant, a wine bar, and dancing Wednesday to Saturday nights in its **Teredo Bar,** this venue has something for everyone. For dramatic views over False Creek, reserve a table on the rooftop patio. ✉*1535 Johnson St., Granville Island* ☎*604/669–9030.*

★ **The Whip Gallery.** It's a bit out of the way but this lofty space with exposed brick and Douglas fir–beamed ceiling attracts a hip crowd (they wear a lot of black). There's a bar, atrium, and mezzanine with a

DJ. Order what's on tap (Storm Brewing, R&B, Unibroue) or choose from one of seven deadly sin martinis. ✉*209 East 6th Ave., at Main St., East Vancouver* ☎*604/874–4687.*

WINE BARS & BREW PUBS

Dix Barbecue and Brewery. Near Yaletown and B.C. Place Stadium, this relaxed, friendly place has exposed brick and beams, a fireplace, a long mahogany bar, and vats brewing a variety of ales and lagers. Dix also serves a fine southern-style barbecue, slow-smoked in-house in an apple- or cherrywood smoker. Watch out for a testosterone-heavy crowd on hockey and hoops nights. ✉*871 Beatty St., Downtown* ☎*604/682–2739.*

SOMA. Recently reopened in a new location, this stylish café-cum-wine-bar showcases a nice selection of B.C. and New World wines to complement tasty salads, cheeses, and artisanal meats. A free Wi-Fi password is available upon request. ✉*151 E. 8th Ave., Mount Pleasant/SoMa* ☎*604/630–7502.*

COMEDY CLUBS

Vancouver TheatreSports League. A hilarious improv troupe performs four nights a week to an enthusiastic crowd at the New Revue Stage on Granville Island. ✉*Granville Island* ☎*604/738–7013.*

GAY NIGHTLIFE

★ **1181.** This new addition to the gayborhood is all about stylish interior design—plush sofas, glass coffee tables, wood-paneled ceiling—and fancy cocktails (think caipirinhas and mojitos). It gets particularly crowded on Saturdays, when a DJ spins behind the bar. ✉*1181 Davie St., West End* ☎*604/687–3991.*

Celebrities. A recent multimillion-dollar facelift brought the celeb status back to this gay hotspot, which features a scantily clad crowd bumping and grinding to top-40 hits, hip-hop, and R&B on a huge dance floor equipped with the latest in sound, lighting, and visuals. Men and women are welcome. ✉*1022 Davie St., West End* ☎*604/681–6180.*

Lick. Vancouver's most popular lesbian dance bar sizzles as girls who like girls dance to kick-ass electronic, hip-hop, and drum 'n bass beats. A quiet chill-out area in front offers respite from the noise and heat. Two other dance clubs, **Honey** and **Lotus,** at the same site, are open to all. ✉*455 Abbott St., Gastown* ☎*604/685–7777.*

MUSIC CLUBS

Caprice. R&B and Top 40 play to a Britney and Paris wannabe crowd at this two-level former movie theater with a restaurant and lounge. Tag along with a hooked-up local or expect to wait in line, like, forever. ✉*967 Granville St., Downtown* ☎*604/681–2114.*

Cellar Restaurant and Jazz Club. This is the top venue for jazz in Vancouver and the club calendar features a who's who of the Canadian jazz scene. ✉*3611 W. Broadway, Kitsilano* ☎*604/738–1959.*

★ **ginger sixty-two.** This dark, moody '60s-inspired lounge—with its plush carpets, comfy sofas, and black and white retro films projected on the wall—attracts a crowd of beautiful locals and the occasional VIP dressed to the nines. When internationally renowned DJs come to town, this is where they spin. Be prepared to spend at least an hour waiting in line before setting foot inside. ✉ *1219 Granville St., Downtown* ☎ *604/688–5494.*

The Modern. Located in a heritage building and equipped with top-notch sound and light systems, this new addition to the Gastown club scene has a sleek modern (what did you expect?) vibe, including polished concrete floors, dark smoked glass, colored tiling, countless mirrors, and neon lights. House and guest DJs spin an eclectic mix of funk, rock, soul, and top-40 hits to a mostly thirty-something crowd. ✉ *7 Alexander St., Gastown* ☎ *604/647–0121.*

Railway Club. In the early evening, this spot attracts film and media types to its pub-style rooms; after 8 it becomes a venue for local bands. Technically it's a private social club, so patrons must sign in, but everyone of age is welcome. ✉ *579 Dunsmuir St., Downtown* ☎ *604/681–1625.*

THE ARTS

From performing arts to theater, classical music, dance, and a thriving gallery scene, there's much for an art lover to choose from in Vancouver.

CLASSICAL MUSIC

OPERA

Vancouver Opera. The city's opera company stages four productions a year, from October through May, at the Queen Elizabeth Theatre. ☎ *604/682–2871.*

ORCHESTRAS

Vancouver Symphony Orchestra. The resident company at the **Orpheum Theatre** presents classical and popular music performances to a wide variety of audiences. ✉ *601 Smithe St., Downtown* ☎ *604/876–3434.*

DANCE

Ballet British Columbia. Innovative ballet and timeless classics by internationally acclaimed choreographers are presented by this company; most performances are at the Queen Elizabeth Theatre. ☎ *604/732–5003.*

Scotiabank Dance Centre. The hub of dance in British Columbia, this striking building with an art deco facade has performances, studio showings, and other types of events by national and international artists. ✉ *677 Davie St., Downtown* ☎ *604/606–6400.*

MOVIES

Fifth Avenue Cinemas. This small multiplex shows foreign and independent films. ✉ *2110 Burrard St., Kitsilano* ☎ *604/734–7469.*

Ridge Theatre. A long-established art-house cinema, the Ridge is popular with the artsy crowd. ✉ *3131 Arbutus St., Kitsilano* ☎ *604/738–6311.*

THEATER

Arts Club Theatre Company. This company operates two theaters. The **Arts Club Granville Island Stage** (✉ *1585 Johnston St., Granville Island* ☎ *604/687–1644*) is an intimate venue and a good place to catch works by local playwrights. The **Stanley Industrial Alliance Stage** (✉ *2750 Granville St.*) is a lavish former movie palace staging works by such perennial favorites as William Shakespeare and Noel Coward. Both operate year-round.

Chan Centre for the Performing Arts. There's a 1,200-seat concert hall, a theater, and a cinema in the vast performance space. ✉*6265 Crescent Rd., University of British Columbia Campus, Point Grey* ☎*604/822–2697.*

Firehall Arts Centre. Innovative theater and modern dance are the showcase at this intimate downtown east side space. ✉*280 E. Cordova St., Downtown East Side* ☎*604/689–0926.*

Queen Elizabeth Theatre. This is a major venue for ballet, opera, and similar large-scale events. ✉*600 Hamilton St., Downtown* ☎*604/665–3050.*

Vancouver Playhouse. The leading venue in Vancouver for mainstream theater is in the same complex as the Queen Elizabeth Theatre. ✉*649 Cambie St., Downtown* ☎*604/665–3050.*

Vogue Theatre. This former movie palace hosts theater and live music events. ✉*918 Granville St., Downtown* ☎*604/331–7909.*

Theatre Under the Stars. Family-friendly musicals like *The Sound of Music* and *Kiss Me Kate* are the draw at Malkin Bowl, an outdoor amphitheater in Stanley Park, during July and August. You can watch the show from the lawn, or from the Rose Garden Tea House as part of a dinner–theater package. ☎*604/687–0174.*

VANCOUVER OUTDOORS

Blessed with a mild climate, fabulous natural setting, and excellent public facilities, it's not surprising that Vancouverites are an outdoorsy lot. It's not uncommon for locals to commute to work by foot or bike and, after-hours, they're as likely to hit the water, trails, ski slopes, or beach volleyball courts as the bars or nightclubs.

Exceptional for North American cities, the downtown peninsula is almost entirely encircled by a seawall along which you can walk, inline skate, cycle, or otherwise propel yourself. Indeed, it's so popular that it qualifies as an, albeit unofficial, national treasure. There are places along the route where you can hire a bike, Rollerblades, canoe, or kayak, or simply go for a swim or play tennis. Top-rated skiing, snowboarding, mountain biking, fishing, diving, and golf are just minutes away.

The **Mountain Equipment Co-op** is something of a local institution, a veritable outdoors-lovers emporium with every kind of gear imaginable, as well as rentals, books and maps, and information from people in the know. ✉*130 W. Broadway, Fairview* ☎*604/872–7858.*

BEACHES

Greater Vancouver is well endowed with beaches—from the pebbly coves of West Vancouver to a vast tableau of sand at Spanish Banks—but the waters are decidedly cool, even in summer and, aside from the kids and the intrepid, the preferred activity is sun-bathing. That said, the city provides several exceptional outdoor pools—right smack on the ocean. The most spectacular is Kitsilano Pool, where you can gander up at the North Shore Mountains while swimming lengths or lolling in the shallows. At the city's historic beach and round-the-clock social venue, English Bay, you can swim, rent a kayak—or simply stroll and people-watch.

Fodor's Choice ★ **Kitsilano Beach.** To the west of the south end of the Burrard Bridge, this is the city's busiest beach—in-line skaters, volleyball games, and sleek young people are ever present. Facilities include a playground, restaurant and concession stand, and tennis courts. **Kitsilano Pool** is also here: at 137 meters (445 feet), it's the longest pool in Canada and one of the few heated salt-water pools in the world. ✉ *2305 Cornwall Ave., Kitsilano* ☎ *604/731–0011* ⊙ *Late May–mid-Sept.*

Stanley Park beaches. There are several beaches accessed from Stanley Park Drive in Stanley Park. **Second Beach** has a playground, a small sandy area, and a large heated pool with a slide. **Third Beach** has a larger stretch of sand, fairly warm water, and great sunset views. It's a popular evening picnic spot.

West End beaches. English Bay, the city's best known beach, lies just to the east of the south entrance to Stanley Park, at the foot of Denman Street. A waterslide, street performers, and artists keep things interesting all summer. Farther along Beach Drive, **Sunset Beach** is too close to the downtown core for clean, safe swimming, but is a great spot for an evening stroll. You can catch a ferry to Granville Island here, or swim at the **Vancouver Aquatic Centre** (✉ *1050 Beach Ave.* ☎ *604/665–3424*), a public indoor pool and fitness center.

Wreck Beach. Canada's largest clothing-optional beach is reached via a steep trail and flight of stairs from Gate 6, off Marine Drive on the University of British Columbia campus. This 6-km-long (4-mi-long) wildernesslike beach, managed by a team of volunteers, has a delightfully anarchic culture of its own. The driftwood is tangled, bathing suits aren't required, and you can buy a wild array of food, goods, and services: vendors sell pizza, homemade sandwiches, buffalo burgers, and Mexican specialities.

CYCLING

While Vancouver is relatively bike-friendly, its major arteries and busier streets can be uncomfortable and unsafe for all but the experienced cyclist. As a helpful gesture, the city introduced 16 interconnected bikeways, identified by green bicycle signs. Although most of these routes share the road with cars, they're well chosen for safety, and include cyclist-activated signals and other bike-friendly measures.

Fodor's Choice ★ The most popular recreational route, much of it off-road, is the **Seaside route.** It runs about 32 km (20 mi) from the seawall in Coal Harbour, around Stanley Park and False Creek, through Kitsilano to Spanish Banks. For detailed route descriptions and a downloadable map check out 🌐 *www.city.vancouver.bc.ca.*

BIKE RENTALS Most bike-rental outlets also rent Rollerblades and jogging strollers.

Bayshore Bicycles. If you're starting your bike ride near Stanley Park, try this friendly store. It has a range of bikes and Rollerblades as well as baby joggers and bike trailers. ✉*745 Denman St., West End* ☎*604/688–2453.*

Reckless Bike Stores. This outfit rents bikes on the Yaletown section of the bike path. To explore the Granville Island and Kitsilano area, a better bet might be their Kitsilano branch. ✉*110 Davie St., Yaletown* ☎*604/648–2600* ✉*1810 Fir St., at 2nd Ave., Kitsilano* ☎*604/731–2420.*

MOUNTAIN BIKING

Mountain biking may be a worldwide phenom, but its most radical expression, known as free-riding, was born in the 1990s on the steep and rugged North Shore Mountains. Here, the mostly young thrill-seekers ride ultra-heavy-duty bikes through gnarly forest, along log-strewn trails, over rocky precipices, and down stony stream beds (not to mention along self-installed obstacles like planks and teeter-totters)—and live to tell about it. This anarchic culture can be explored at the **North Shore Mountain Biking** Web site, 🌐*www.nsmb.com.*

Lower Seymour Conservation Reserve. Nestled into the precipitous North Shore Mountains, this reserve has 25 km (15.5 mi) of challenging rain-forest trails. ✉*End of Lillooet Rd., North Vancouver* ☎*604/432–6286.*

MOUNTAIN BIKE RENTALS

Cove Bike Shop. In the village of Deep Cove on Indian Arm, the Cove Bike Shop pioneered the design and construction of mountain bikes for this punishing terrain and continues to market them worldwide. Given huge insurance costs, it's also the only bike shop that rents them. Bikes of all types and sizes are available March through October. ✉*4310 Gallant Ave., North Vancouver* ☎*604/929–2222 or 604/985–2222.*

ECO TOURS & WILDLIFE VIEWING

Given a temperate climate and forest, mountain, and marine environments teeming with life, it's no surprise that wildlife watching is an important pastime and growing business in and around Vancouver. Many people walk the ocean foreshores or park and mountain trails, binoculars or scopes in hand, looking for exceptional or rare birds. Others venture onto the water to see seals, sea lions, and whales—as well as the birds that inhabit the maritime world.

Sewell's Marina Horseshoe Bay. This long-time marina at the foot of Howe Sound runs year-round two-hour eco tours of the surrounding marine and coastal mountain habitat. Sightings range from seals to soaring eagles. High-speed rigid inflatable hulls are used. ✉*6409 Bay St., Horseshoe Bay* ☎*604/921–3474.*

BIRD- & EAGLE-WATCHING

Between mid-November and mid-February, the world's largest concentration of bald eagles gathers to feed on salmon at **Brackendale Eagles' Park** (✉*Government Rd. off Hwy. 99, Brackendale*), about an hour north of Vancouver.

George C. Reifel Bird Sanctuary. More than 260 species of migratory birds visit this 850-acre site on Westham Island, about an hour south of Vancouver. A seasonal highlight is the arrival of an estimated 80,000 Lesser Snow Geese in the late fall. ✉*5191 Robertson Rd., Ladner* ☎*604/946–6980* 🎫*C$4* ⏲*Daily 9–4.*

WHALE-WATCHING Between April and October pods of Orca whales travel through the Strait of Georgia, near Vancouver. The area is also home to harbor seals, elephant seals, bald eagles, minke whales, porpoises, and a wealth of birdlife.

Wild Whales Vancouver. Boats leave Granville Island in search of Orca pods in Georgia Strait, traveling as far as Victoria. Rates are C$109 for a three- to seven-hour trip in either an open or glass-domed boat. Each boat leaves once daily, April through October, conditions permitting. ☎ *604/699–2011* 🌐.

GOLF

Vancouver-area golf courses offer challenging golf with great scenery. Most are open year-round.

The Vancouver Park Board operates three public courses, all located on the city's south-facing slope. The most celebrated is the 18-hole, par-72, 6,700-yard **Fraserview Golf Course** (✉ *7800 Vivian Dr., South Vancouver* ☎ *604/257–6923, 604/280–1818 advance bookings*), where facilities include a driving range and a new club house. The green fee is C$55–C$58. The other two, both 18 holes and with slightly lower green fees, are **Langara Golf Course** (✉ *6706 Alberta St.* ☎ *604/713–1816*) and **McCleary Golf Course** (✉ *7188 Macdonald St.* ☎ *604/257–8191*).

Fodor'sChoice ★

Westwood Plateau Golf and Country Club. Westwood is a well-manicured, 18-hole, par-72 course located just east of the city; it's closed November through March. The green fee, which includes a cart, is C$169 and the club also has a restaurant open seasonally. The 9-hole **Academy Course** nearby (604/941–4236) is open year-round. ✉ *3251 Plateau Blvd., Coquitlam* ☎ *604/552–0777 or 800/580–0785.*

HIKING

With its expansive landscape of mountains, inlets, alpine lakes, and approachable glaciers, as well as low-lying rivers, hills, dikes, and meadows, southwestern British Columbia is a hiker's paradise. That said, areas and trails should be approached with physical ability and stamina in mind. If you're heading into the mountains, hike with a companion, pack warm clothes (even in summer), and extra food and water, and leave word of your route and the time you expect to return. Remember that weather can change quickly in the mountains. You can check for a weather forecast with **Environment Canada** (🌐 *http://weatheroffice.ec.gc.ca*).

★ **Lighthouse Park.** This 75-hectare (185-acre) wilderness park wraps around Point Atkinson and its historic lighthouse (of the same name), where Howe Sound meets Burrard Inlet in the municipality of West Vancouver. A bank of soaring granite (popular for picnicking) shapes the foreshore, while the interior is an undulating terrain of mostly Douglas fir, rich undergrowth, birds, and other wildlife. Trails, from easy to challenging, wend throughout. A trail map is downloadable at the municipal Web site. ✉ *Beacon La. off Marine Dr., West Vancouver.*

Fodor'sChoice ★ **Capilano River Regional Park.** This small but spectacular park is where you'll find the Capilano River canyon, several old-growth fir trees approaching 61 meters (200 feet), a salmon hatchery open to the public, and the Cleveland Dam, as well as 26 km (16 mi) of hiking trails. It's at the end of Capilano Park Road, off Capilano Road, North Vancouver. ☎*604/224–5739.*

★ **Grouse Grind.** Vancouver's most famous, or infamous, hiking route, the Grind is a 2.9-km (1.8-mi) climb straight up Grouse Mountain. Thousands do it annually (indeed, it's so popular the name is trademarked), but climbers are advised to be in "excellent physical condition." Those that aren't will suffer (though live to tell about it); it's not for children. The route is open daily, 6:30 AM to 7:30 PM, from spring through autumn (conditions permitting). There is no charge for the climb, but you are charged a small fee (C$5) to ride down the Grouse Mountain Skyride (gondola). A round-trip ticket costs C$32.95. Eco-walks are led along the paths accessed from the Skyride. ✉*6400 Nancy Greene Way, North Vancouver* ☎*604/980–9311 Grouse Mountain, 604/432–6200 Metro Vancouver (formerly GVRD).*

Mount Seymour Provincial Park. Located 30 minutes by car from downtown Vancouver, this historic wilderness park of 3,508 hectares (14,683 acres) offers 14 hiking trails of varying length and difficulty. Some climb into exposed mountainside, and warm clothing—and caution—is advised. They include access to the Baden-Powell Trail, which continues northwest to Horseshoe Bay. Good downloadable maps are available on the Web site. ✉*Mount Seymour Rd. off Seymour Pkwy., North Vancouver.*

Fodor's Choice ★ **Stanley Park.** Stanley Park is well suited for moderate walking and easy hiking. The most obvious and arguably most picturesque route is the 8.8-km (5.5-mi) seawall around its perimeter, but this 1,000-acre park also offers 27 km (16.7 mi) of interior trails through the coniferous forest, including a few small patches of original forest, or old growth. The interior paths are wide and well maintained; here you'll experience something of the true rain forest and spot some of the birds and small mammals that inhabit it. You can download a trail map at the Park Board Web site. ☎*604/257–8400.*

GUIDED HIKES

Heritage Walking Tours. The City of Vancouver provides detailed information on self-guided walking tours of Chinatown, Gastown, Yaletown, and Shaughnessy. Check out their Web site for downloadable brochures and maps.

Rockwood Adventures. This company offers guided walks of rainforest or coastal terrain including Lighthouse Park, Lynn Canyon and Capilano Canyon, and Bowen Island in Howe Sound (including a short flight). They also offer walking tours of Vancouver's Chinatown. ☎*604/980–7749 or 888/236–6606.*

HOCKEY

Although Vancouver's national league hockey team loses more often than it wins, it retains a loyal following. During playoff season in late spring emotions at some games, in sports bars and out on the streets, can run high.

The **Vancouver Canucks** play at **General Motors Place** (✉*800 Griffiths Way, Downtown* ☎*604/899–7400*).

SKIING & SNOWBOARDING

The North Shore Mountains—from Howe Sound in the west to Indian Arm in the east—are made up of dozens of peaks. The most prominent are The Lions, twin granite "ears" visible from around the Lower Mainland. The highest is Brunswick Mountain at 1,788 meters (5,866 feet). Skiing is generally confined to the Cypress Group (Mount Strachan and Hollyburn Mountain), Grouse Mountain, and Mount Seymour; all three have excellent downhill and snowboarding facilities. The ski season generally runs from early December through early spring. Cypress Provincial Park is a major cross-country skiing area.

CROSS-COUNTRY

Cypress Mountain. This private operator within Cypress Provincial Park maintains 19 km (10 mi) of cross-country or "nordic" trails into the undulating, lake-dotted landscape of Hollyburn Mountain. There is a charge for their use. There are also 10 km (6 mi) dedicated to snowshoeing. ✉ *Cypress Bowl Rd., West Vancouver* ✣ *Exit 8 off Hwy. 1 westbound* ☎ *604/419–7669.*

DOWNHILL SKIING & SNOWBOARDING

While Whistler Resort, a two-hour drive from Vancouver, is the top-ranked ski destination in the region, the North Shore Mountains hold three excellent ski and snowboard areas. All have rentals, lessons, night skiing, and a variety of runs suitable for all skill levels. Grouse Mountain can be reached by TransLink buses. Cypress and Seymour each run shuttle buses from Lonsdale Quay and other North Shore stops.

Cypress Mountain. The most recent of three North Shore commercial ski destinations, Cypress is nonetheless well equipped, and will be more so with the completion of freestyle skiing and snowboarding venues being built for the 2010 Winter Olympics. Facilities include five quad or double chairs, 38 downhill runs, and a vertical drop of 1,750 feet. The mountain also has a snow-tubing area and snowshoe tours. ✉ *Cypress Bowl Rd., West Vancouver* ✣ *Exit 8 off Hwy. 1 westbound* ☎ *604/419–7669.*

Grouse Mountain. Reached by gondola (with an entrance fee) from the upper reaches of North Vancouver, much of the Grouse Mountain resort inhabits a slope overlooking the city. Although views are fine on a clear day, at night (the area is known for its night-skiing) they're spectacular. Facilities include two quad chairs, 26 skiing and snowboarding runs, and several all-level freestyle-terrain parks. The vertical drop is 1,210 feet. There's a choice of upscale and casual dining in a good-looking stone-and-timber lodge. ✉ *6400 Nancy Greene Way, North Vancouver* ☎ *604/980–9311, 604/986–6262 snow report.*

Mount Seymour. Described as a full-service winter activity area, the Mount Seymour resort sprawls over 200 acres accessed from eastern North Vancouver. With three chairs for varying abilities; a beginner's rope tow, equipment rentals, and lessons; and toboggan and tubing runs, it's a popular destination for families. Snowboarding is particularly popular. The eateries aren't fancy. ✉ *1700 Mt. Seymour Rd., North Vancouver* ☎ *604/986–2261, 604/718–7771 snow report.*

WATERSPORTS

BOATING & SAILING With an almost limitless number and variety of waterways—from Indian Arm near Vancouver, up Howe Sound and the Sunshine Coast, across Georgia Strait to the Gulf Islands, and on to Vancouver Island—southwestern British Columbia is a boater's paradise. And much of this territory has easy access to marine and public services.

Cooper Boating charters sailboats and cabin cruisers, with or without instructing skippers. ✉ *1620 Duranleau St., Granville Island* ☎ *604/687–4110 or 888/999–6419.*

CANOEING & KAYAKING Kayaking—sea-going and river kayaking—has become something of a lifestyle in Vancouver. While many sea kayakers start out (or remain) in False Creek, others venture into the open ocean and up and down the Pacific Coast. You can white-water kayak or canoe down the Capilano River and several other North Vancouver rivers. And paddling in a traditional, sea-going aboriginal-built canoe is an increasingly popular way to experience the maritime landscape.

Ecomarine Ocean Kayak Centre. Lessons and rentals are offered year-round from Granville Island, and from early May to early September at Jericho Beach and English Bay. ✉ *1668 Duranleau St., Granville Island* ☎ *604/689–7575 or 888/425–2925* ✉ *English Bay* ☎ *604/685–2925* ✉ *Jericho Beach* ☎ *604/222–3565.*

★ **Takaya Tours.** A trip with Takaya is a unique experience: you can paddle a 45-foot Salish ocean-going canoe while First Nations guides relay local legends, sing traditional songs, and point out ancient village sites. The two-hour tours cost C$54 and leave from Cates Park in North Vancouver, and Belcarra Park in Port Moody. They also have trips up Indian Arm on motorized kayaks. Reservations are essential. ☎ *604/904–7410.*

SHOPPING

Updated by Chris McBeath

Unlike many cities where suburban malls have taken over, Vancouver is full of individual boutiques and specialty shops. Antiques stores, ethnic markets, art galleries, gourmet-food shops, and high-fashion outlets abound, and both Asian and First Nations influences in crafts, home furnishings, and foods are quite prevalent.

SHOPPING NEIGHBORHOODS

ROBSON STREET

Stretching from Burrard to Bute, **Robson Street** is the city's main fashion-shopping and people-watching artery. The Gap and Banana Republic have their flagship stores here, as do Canadian fashion outlets Club Monaco and Roots. Souvenir shops and cafés fill the gaps.

ALBERNI STREET

One block north of Robson, Alberni Street is geared to the higher-income visitor and is where you'll find duty-free shopping. At the stores in and around Alberni, and around Burrard, you'll find names such as Tiffany & Co., Louis Vuitton, Gucci, Coach, Hermès, and Betsey Johnson.

GASTOWN & CHINATOWN

Treasure hunters like the 300 block of **West Cordova Street** in Gastown, where offbeat shops sell curios, vintage clothing, and locally designed clothes. It's also the place for souvenirs—both kitschy and expensive. Gastown is becoming the place to be, which means that the hip crowd is starting to move in—restaurateurs, advertising gurus, photographers, etc.—so the boutiques and cafés are getting cooler. Bustling **Chinatown**—centered on Pender and Main streets—is full of Chinese bakeries, restaurants, herbalists, tea merchants, and import shops.

YALETOWN

Frequently described as Vancouver's SoHo, this neighborhood on the north bank of False Creek is home to boutiques, home stores, and restaurants—many in converted warehouses—that cater to a trendy, moneyed crowd.

GRANVILLE ISLAND

On the south side of False Creek, **Granville Island** has a lively food market and a wealth of galleries, crafts shops, and artisans' studios. It gets so busy, especially on the weekends, that the crowds can detract from the pleasure of the place. You're best off getting there before 11 AM.

KITSILANO

West 4th Avenue, between Burrard and Balsam, is the main shopping strip in funky Kitsilano. There are clothing and shoe boutiques, as well as housewares and gift shops. Just east of Burrard, several stores sell ski and snowboard gear.

DEPARTMENT STORES & SHOPPING CENTERS

DEPARTMENT STORES

The Hudson Bay Co. A Canadian institution (even though it's now owned by Americans), The Bay was founded as part of the fur trade in the 17th century. A whole department sells the signature tri-color Bay blankets and other Canadiana. ⊠*674 Granville St., at Georgia St., Downtown* ☎*604/681–6211.*

SHOPPING CENTERS

Chinatown Night Market. Chinatown is at its liveliest when stalls set up shop selling food, T-shirts, and "do I really need this?" bits 'n bobs. It's open from late May to mid-September, 6:30 PM to 11 PM, Friday through Sunday. It's fun to wander. ⊠*Keefer St., between Columbia and Gore Sts., Chinatown* ☎*604/682–8998.*

Pacific Centre Mall. Filling three city blocks in the heart of downtown, this mall has mostly mid-price, mainstream clothing shops on the lower level; chicer, pricier items can be found on the upper floor. There are several street-level entrances as well as access via Holt Renfrew, The Hudson's Bay, and Sears department stores—worth knowing about on rainy days. ⊠*700 W. Georgia St., Downtown* ☎*604/688–7236.*

SPECIALTY STORES

ANTIQUES, AUCTIONS & FLEA MARKETS

Key antiques hunting grounds are Gallery Row on Granville Street and along Main Street from 20th to 30th avenues. There's a small emporium near Gastown that's fun to browse if time is short and you need to stay in the downtown core.

Vancouver Antique Centre. The entrance can be easily missed but once you're inside, you'll find about a dozen antiques and collectibles dealers under one roof. Most are independent, family-run operations, some of which have been in the business for over 50 years. ✉ *422 Richards St., Downtown* ☎ *604/684–9822.*

ART & CRAFTS GALLERIES

Granville Island is a must-do destination for crafts aficionados. Stroll Railspur Alley (off Old Bridge Street), which is lined with working artists' studios; the Net Loft building opposite the Public Market also has several galleries. In the West End, Gallery Row along Granville Street between 5th and 15th avenues is home to about a dozen high-end contemporary-art galleries.

★ **Coastal Peoples Fine Arts Gallery.** The beautiful books and postcards make affordable souvenirs though you could well be tempted by the impressive collection of First Nations jewelry, ceremonial masks, prints, and carvings. ✉ *1024 Mainland St., Yaletown* ☎ *604/685–9298.*

Craft House. Run by the Crafts Association of B.C., this tiny house contains a veritable smorgasbord of works by local artisans. ✉ *1386 Cartwright St., Granville Island* ☎ *604/687–7270.*

Fodor's Choice ★ **Hill's Native Art.** This highly respected store has Vancouver's largest selection of First Nations art. If you think the main level is impressive, try going upstairs where the collector-quality stuff is. ✉ *165 Water St., Gastown* ☎ *604/685–4249.*

Inuit Gallery of Vancouver. In addition to quality Inuit art like the signature carvings in soapstone and antler, there's also an excellent collection of Northwest Coast Native art such as baskets, totems, bentwood boxes, and masks. ✉ *206 Cambie St., Gastown* ☎ *888/615–8399 or 604/688–7323.*

★ **Robert Held Art Glass.** Held is an award-winning glassblower whose work is known world-wide. Located two blocks west of South Granville, you can watch glassblowers in action here, then browse the retail area crammed with one-of-a-kind vases, paperweights, bowls, ornaments, and perfume bottles. Tours are available, too. ✉ *2130 Pine St., between 5th and 6th Aves., South Granville* ☎ *604/737–0020.*

BOOKS

★ **Barbara-Jo's Books to Cooks.** This local chef turned entrepreneur is determined to spread the good-food word with scores of cookbooks, including many by Vancouver- and B.C.-based chefs. The store also hosts special events, recipe demos, and drop-in classes that make for a great rainy-day activity as well as a tasty way to explore local cuisine. ✉ *1740 W. 2nd Ave., Kitsilano* ☎ *604/688–6755* ✉ *11–1666 Johnston St., Net Loft, Granville Island* ☎ *604/684–6788.*

Kidsbooks. Canada's largest selection of books for children, from toddlers to teens, stocks the shelves here—and many of those shelves are kid-friendly low with plenty of reading nooks. ✉*3083 W. Broadway, Kitsilano* ☎*604/738–5335.*

MacLeod's Books. This is one of the city's best antiquarian and used-book stores; it's amazing the titles you'll find. ✉*455 W. Pender St., Downtown* ☎*604/681–7654.*

CLOTHES

Fodor's Choice ★ **Holt Renfrew.** Already high on the ritzy scale, Holts recently refurbished their image and their location: it's the very swanky showcase for international high fashion and accessories for men and women. Think Prada, Dolce & Gabbana, and other designer labels. ✉*Pacific Centre, 737 Dunsmuir St., Downtown* ☎*604/681–3121.*

Hunt and Gather. *Travel & Leisure* magazine bestowed an Honorable Mention for Best Retail Space to this hip clothing store, in its 2007 Best In The World Design Awards. The funky white space is like shopping in Narnia but the locally made clothes provide dramatic splashes of color. ✉*225 Carrall St., Gastown* ☎*604/633–9559.*

John Fluevog. You might've seen these shops in London and New York, but did you know this highly decorative shoeware shop was started by a Vancouverite? ✉*837 Granville St., Downtown* ☎*604/688–2828.*

★ **Leone.** Marble alcoves in an elegantly palatial store set the scene for men's and women's fashions by Jil Sander, Versace, Yves Saint Laurent, Rive Gauche, Dior, Miu Miu, and others. On the lower level is **L-2 Leone,** where you'll find edgier fashions and an Italian café. ✉*350 Howe St., in Sinclair Centre Downtown* ☎*604/685–9327.*

★ **Lululemon Athletica.** This is a real Vancouver success story: everyone from power-yoga devotees to soccer moms covet the fashionable well-constructed workout wear with the stylized "A" insignia. Nike "swoosh" be warned. ✉*1148 Robson St., West End* ☎*604/681–3118* ✉*2113 W. 4th Ave., Kitsilano* ☎*604/732–6111* ✉*Metropolis at Metrotown Centre, Burnaby* ☎*604/430–4659.*

Patricia Fieldwalker. Julia Roberts, Christie Turlington, Kathleen Turner, and Demi Moore have Patricia's lingerie, lounge, and resort wear close to their skin. It sells under the Arabesque label. This is a factory direct showroom. ✉*302–343 Railway St., East Vancouver* ☎*604/689–1210.*

Roots. For outdoorsy clothes that double as souvenirs (many sport maple-leaf logos), check out these Canadian-made sweatshirts, leather jackets, and other comfy casuals. An interesting note: Roots outfits the Canadian Olympic team. ✉*1001 Robson St., West End* ☎*604/683–4305.*

Turnabout. The quality is so good that "used" is almost a misnomer at this long-established vintage-clothing store. The Granville Street location sells upscale women's wear; the Broadway branch sells more casual clothing, as well as men's clothes. ✉*3109 Granville St., South Granville* ☎*604/734–5313* ✉*3112 W. Broadway, Kitsilano* ☎*604/731–7762.*

FOOD

Ganache Patisserie. In true Parisian style, every calorie-laden item is a delicious and decadent work of art. A full cake—maybe chocolate-banana cake or vanilla-chèvre cheesecake—would make a welcome gift but a slice will perk up your shopping day. ✉*1262 Homer St., Yaletown* ☎*604/899–1098.*

Fodor'sChoice ★ **Granville Island Public Market.** All your senses will be exhilarated, though most especially your taste buds. Stalls are packed with fresh produce, meats, just-caught fish, baked goods, and prepared foods from exotic cheeses and hand-made fudge to frothy cappuccinos. If the sun is out, dine on your purchases out on the decks. At the **Salmon Shop** (☎*604/669–3474*), you can pick up fresh or smoked salmon vacuum-packed and wrapped for travel. ✉*1689 Johnston St., Granville Island* ☎*604/666–5784.*

★ **Les Amis du Fromage.** If you love cheese, don't miss the mind-boggling array of selections from B.C., the rest of Canada, France, and elsewhere at this shop of delicacies. The extremely knowledgeable mother-and-daughter owners, Alice and Allison Spurrell, and their staff encourage you to taste before you buy. Yum. ✉*1752 W. 2nd Ave., Kitsilano* ☎*604/732–4218.*

Meinhardt Fine Foods. Pick up fixings for an elegant picnic or find a gift for a foodie friend at this sophisticated neighborhood groceteria. The same owners run a deli-style coffee shop next door; good for sandwiches, wraps, and pastries to eat in or take out. ✉*3002 Granville St., South Granville* ☎*604/732–4405.*

Purdy's. A chocolatier since 1907, Purdy's knows a thing or two about scrumptious chocolates; take special note of their liqueur line which was hawked to the Americans during Prohibition. Purdy's purple-foiled boxes of sweet temptations are *the* special-occasion chocolate gift. Outlets are scattered throughout the city. ✉*Bentall Centre, Burrard at Melville, Downtown* ☎*604/681–6428.*

JEWELRY

Birks. In a neoclassical building that was the former headquarters of the Canadian Imperial Bank of Commerce, this Canada-wide chain has been a national institution since 1879. An impressive staircase connects the main level to the mezzanine floor—descending, it feels as if you're royalty. ✉*698 W. Hastings St., Downtown* ☎*604/669–3333.*

HOUSEWARE

Herzog Crystal. Crystal and elegant giftware for the home are the hallmark of this fun-to-browse store. Items are a good mix of upscale and exclusive alongside fun and affordable choices. ✉*535 Howe St., Downtown* ☎*604/687–7122.*

Doctor Vigari Gallery. In keeping with its offbeat environs on "the Drive" (i.e., Commercial Drive), expect to see a wildly eclectic assortment of jewelry, crafts, paintings, and household items and furniture, most by B.C. artists. ✉*1312 Commercial Dr., Commercial Drive* ☎*604/255–9513.*

SHOES

Dayton Boot Company. These biker boots have a world-wide, cult-like following because they're that enduringly good, and hip, too. Celebrities like Kurt Russell, Harry Connick Jr., Cindy Crawford, and Sharon Stone are wearers. ✉*2250 E. Hastings St., East Side* ☎*604/255–6671.*

VANCOUVER ESSENTIALS

TRANSPORTATION

BY AIR

The major airport is Vancouver International Airport (YVR), located in the suburb of Richmond about 16 km (10 mi) south of downtown Vancouver.

There are many options for getting downtown from Vancouver International Airport, a drive of about 20 to 45 minutes, depending on traffic. If you're driving, go over the Arthur Laing Bridge and north on Granville Street (also sign-posted as Highway 99). Signs direct you to Vancouver City Centre.

The Vancouver Airporter Service bus leaves the international- and domestic-arrivals levels of the terminal building approximately every half hour, stopping at major downtown hotels. The first departure from the airport is 8:30 AM, and the service runs until 9:45 PM. The fare is C$13.50 one-way and C$21 round-trip.

Taxi stands are in front of the terminal building on domestic- and international-arrivals levels. The taxi fare to downtown is about C$30; it's probably the fastest way to downtown. Area cab companies include Black Top and Yellow.

Limousine service from LimoJet Gold costs about C$45 one-way.

For public transportation, catch the #424 bus to Airport Station and transfer to the #98 B-Line express downtown: this takes about 50 minutes. On weekends, holidays, and after 6:30 PM, local bus fare is C$2.50; at other times it's C$3.75. To return to the airport, take a #98 Richmond Centre bus and transfer at Airport Station.

In November 2009, the Canada Line train will offer high-speed service between the airport and downtown.

Contacts **Black Top Cabs** (☎ *604/681–2181*). **LimoJet Gold** (☎ *604/273–1331 or 800/278–8742* 🌐 *www.limojetgold.com*). **TransLink** (☎ *604/953–3333* 🌐 *www.translink.bc.ca*). **Vancouver Airporter Service** (☎ *604/946–8866 or 800/668–3141* 🌐 *www.yvrairporter.com*). **Vancouver International Airport** (☎ *604/207–7077* 🌐 *www.yvr.ca*). **Yellow Cab** (☎ *604/681–1111*).

BY BOAT & FERRY

The British Columbia (BC) Ferry Corporation operates one of the largest ferry fleets in the world, serving about 40 ports of call on B.C.'s west coast. The ferries carry all vehicles as well as bicycles and foot passengers.

Reservations are optional on services between Vancouver and Vancouver Island and on most sailings between Vancouver and the Southern Gulf Islands. Most other services do not accept reservations and load vehicles on a first-come, first-served basis.

BC Ferries operates two major ferry terminals outside Vancouver. From Tsawwassen to the south (an hour's drive from downtown), ferries sail to Swartz Bay near Victoria, to Nanaimo on Vancouver Island, and to the Gulf Islands (the small islands between the mainland and Vancouver Island). From Horseshoe Bay (45 minutes north of downtown), ferries sail to the Sunshine Coast and to Nanaimo on Vancouver Island. Vehicle reservations on Vancouver to Victoria and Nanaimo routes are optional and cost C$15 to C$17.50 in addition to the fare. There's no extra charge for reservations on Gulf Island routes.

The SeaBus is a 400-passenger commuter ferry that crosses Burrard Inlet from Waterfront Station downtown to the foot of Lonsdale Avenue in North Vancouver. Leaving every 15 to 30 minutes, the bus takes 13 minutes and costs the same as the TransLink bus. With a transfer, connection can be made to any TransLink bus or SkyTrain.

Aquabus Ferries connect several stations on False Creek, including Science World, Plaza of Nations, Granville Island, Stamp's Landing, Spyglass Place, Yaletown, and the Hornby Street dock. Some Aquabus ferries take bicycles, and the company also operates two historic wooden boats on some runs.

False Creek Ferries provides foot-passenger service between the Aquatic Centre on Beach Avenue, Granville Island, Science World, Stamp's Landing, and Vanier Park.

False Creek and Aquabus ferries are not part of the TransLink system, so bus transfers aren't accepted.

Contacts Aquabus Ferries (☎ *604/689–5858* 🌐 *www.theaquabus.com*). **BC Ferries** (☎ *250/386–3431, 888/223–3779 in B.C., Alberta, and Washington state* 🌐 *www.bcferries.com*). **False Creek Ferries** (☎ *604/684–7781* 🌐 *www.granvilleislandferries.bc.ca*). **SeaBus** (☎ *604/953–3333* 🌐 *www.translink.bc.ca*).

BUS AND RAPID TRANSIT TRAVEL WITHIN VANCOUVER

TransLink buses provide regular service throughout Vancouver and its suburbs. Exact change is needed to ride TransLink buses: each cash fare offers up to 90 minutes of travel, and fares are based on zones: 1 zone (C$2.50), 2 zones (C$3.75), or 3 zones (C$5). Reduced fares are available for children, students, and seniors. Day passes (C$9) and FareSaver tickets (sold in books of 10) can also be purchased. Transfers (ask for one when you board) are valid for 90 minutes, allow travel in any direction, and are good on buses, SkyTrain, and SeaBus.

A rapid-transit system called SkyTrain travels underground downtown and is elevated for the rest of its route to Coquitlam and Surrey. The system has two lines: the Expo Line and the Millennium Line. These lines stop at the same stations between downtown and Commercial Drive, so unless you're traveling east of Commercial Drive, it doesn't matter which line you use. Trains leave about every two to five minutes. Tickets, sold at each station from machines (correct change is not necessary), must be carried with you as proof of payment. You may use transfers from SkyTrain to SeaBus and TransLink buses and vice versa. SkyTrain is convenient for transit between downtown, B.C. Place Stadium, Pacific Central Station, and Science World.

Contacts **SkyTrain** (☎ *604/953-3333* 🌐 *www.translink.bc.ca*). **Translink** (🌐 *www.translink.bc.ca*).

BY CAR

If you plan to spend most or all your time in downtown Vancouver, you won't need a car: parking can be difficult to secure and most attractions are within walking distance or a short cab or bus ride away. If you do want to rent a car, rates in Vancouver begin at about C$40 a day or C$230 a week, usually including unlimited mileage. Some companies located near Vancouver International Airport offer free customer pick-up and drop-off at the airport, enabling you to avoid the latter fee. Vancouver's airport and downtown locations usually have the best selection.

Local Vancouver Agencies **Lo-Cost Rent A Car** (☎ *888/556-2678* 🌐 *www.locost.com*).

BY TAXI

It can be difficult to hail a cab in Vancouver, especially when it's raining. Unless you're near a hotel, you'll have better luck calling a taxi service. Try Black Top or Yellow.

Contacts **Black Top Cabs** (☎ *604/681-2181*). **Yellow Cab** (☎ *604/681-1111*).

BY TRAIN

Amtrak has service from Seattle to Vancouver, providing connections between Amtrak's U.S.-wide network and VIA Rail's Canadian routes. In B.C. VIA Rail has two routes: Vancouver to Jasper, and Jasper to Prince Rupert with an overnight stop in Prince George. Rocky Mountaineer Vacations operates a variety of spectacular all-daylight rail trips between the Canadian Rockies and the west coast. All trains offer a smoke-free environment.

Reservations are essential on the Rocky Mountaineer and highly recommended on Amtrak and VIA routes. There's no extra charge for reservations on any of the train services listed.

Information **Rocky Mountaineer Vacations** (☎ *800/665-7245* 🌐 *www.rockymountaineer.com*). **VIA Rail Canada** (☎ *888/842-7245* 🌐 *www.viarail.ca*).

CONTACTS & RESOURCES

SPECIAL INTEREST TOURS

BOAT TOURS Aquabus Ferries operates tours of False Creek on small covered boats and vintage wooden ferries. Twenty-five-minute tours cost C$6 and run year-round; 45-minute minicruises are offered May through October and cost C$9. Tours leave every 15 minutes from the Aquabus dock on Granville Island. False Creek Ferries has a 20-minute tour for C$6 and a 40-minute tour for C$9. Both run daily, every 15 minutes from Granville Island. Harbour Cruises, at the north foot of Denman Street on Coal Harbour, operates a 1¼-hour narrated tour of Burrard

Inlet on a paddlewheeler. Tours are given from April through October and cost C$25. Harbour Cruises also offers sunset dinner cruises, four-hour lunch cruises up scenic Indian Arm, and four-hour brunch tours into Howe Sound. Paddlewheeler Riverboat Tours, at the New Westminster Quay, can take you out on the Fraser River in an 1800s-style paddlewheeler. Tours run year-round, and include a variety of sightseeing and evening entertainment options, including cruises to historic Fort Langley.

Fees & Schedules **Aquabus Ferries** (☎ *604/689–5858* ⊕ *www.theaquabus.com*). **False Creek Ferries** (☎ *604/684–7781* ⊕ *www.granvilleislandferries.bc.ca*). **Harbour Cruises** (☎ *604/688–7246 or 800/663–1500* ⊕ *www.boatcruises.com*). **Paddlewheeler Riverboat Tours** (☎ *604/525–4465 or 877/825–1302* ⊕ *www.vancouverpaddlewheeler.com*).

CULINARY Edible British Columbia can arrange short tours of Granville Island, other Vancouver locales, and farther afield.

Contacts **Edible British Columbia** (☎ *888/812–9960* ⊕ *www.edible-britishcolumbia.com*).

MOVIE TOURS If Vancouver looks familiar, chances are you've already seen it on screen, posing as an American city in any of the hundreds of U.S. movies and TV shows filmed here. Vancouver Movie Tours will take you behind the scenes to locations made famous in film and video, including the apartment used by Agent Scully in *The X-Files*. Three-hour tours run daily, year-round, and cost C$35. A tour of Scully's apartment costs about C$15. A combination tour of these two options is about C$42

Fees & Schedules **Vancouver Movie Tours** (☎ *604/609–2770 or 888/250–7211* ⊕ *www.vanmovietours.com*).

ORIENTATION TOURS The Vancouver Trolley Company runs trolley-style buses through Vancouver on a two-hour narrated tour of Stanley Park, Gastown, English Bay, Granville Island, and Chinatown, among other sights. A ticket allows you to use the bus on two consecutive days, getting off and on as often as you like. Start the trip at any of the 23 stops and buy a ticket (C$35) on board. It's a great overview of the city.

Big Bus also offers hop-on, hop-off tours of downtown Vancouver with recorded narration and 20 stops in major tourist areas like Robson Street, Gastown, Chinatown, and Stanley Park. An adult pass valid for two days is C$35. They also have tours of Victoria.

The four-hour City Highlights tour run by West Coast City and Nature Sightseeing is about C$54. A longer tour for C$65 includes a visit to the Capilano Suspension Bridge. Pickup is available from all major hotels downtown.

The one-hour Stanley Park Horse Drawn Tours operate March 1 to the end of October and cost C$25 per person. The tours leave every 20 to 30 minutes from the information booth on Stanley Park Drive. The tours include transport from downtown to Stanley Park.

North Shore tours usually include a gondola ride up Grouse Mountain, a walk across the Capilano Suspension Bridge, a stop at a salmon hatchery, a visit to the Lonsdale Quay Market, and a ride back to town on the SeaBus. North Shore tours are offered early March through late October by Landsea Tours and mid-April through October by West Coast City and Nature Sightseeing. The five-hour tours are about C$89.

Fees & Schedules **Big Bus** (☎ *604/299-0700, 877/299-0701* ⊕ *www.bigbus.ca*). **Landsea Tours** (☎ *604/255-7272 or 877/669-2277* ⊕ *www.vancouvertours.com*). **Stanley Park Horse-Drawn Tours** (☎ *604/681-5115* ⊕ *www.stanleypark.com*). **Vancouver Trolley Company** (☎ *604/801-5515 or 888/451-5581* ⊕ *www.vancouvertrolley.com*). **West Coast City and Nature Sightseeing** (☎ *604/451-1600 or 877/451-1777* ⊕ *www.vancouversightseeing.com*).

WALKING TOURS Students from the Architectural Institute of British Columbia lead 90-minute walking tours of the city's top heritage sites Tuesday to Saturday, mid-June through August. Tours are C$5 per person and meet at 1 PM at various locations. Guides from the Chinese Cultural Centre offer 90-minute walking tours of Chinatown's heritage buildings, clan associations, shops, temples, and other attractions, many of which are not normally open to the public. Tours cost C$10 and run daily at 10 AM and 2 PM between June and September. Reservations are essential. The Gastown Business Improvement Society sponsors free 90-minute historical and architectural walking tours daily June through August. Meet the guide at 2 PM at the statue of "Gassy" Jack in Maple Tree Square. Guides with Walkabout Historic Vancouver dress in 19th-century costume for their two-hour historical walking tours around downtown and Gastown or Granville Island. Tours run March through October and cost C$25.

Fees & Schedules **Architectural Institute of British Columbia** (☎ *604/683-8588, 800/667-0753 in B.C.* ⊕ *www.aibc.ca*). **Chinese Cultural Centre** (☎ *604/658-8883* ⊕ *www.cccvan.com*). **Gastown Business Improvement Society** (☎ *604/683-5650* ⊕ *www.gastown.org*). **Walkabout Historic Vancouver** (☎ *604/720-0006* ⊕ *www.walkabouthistoricvancouver.com*).

VISITOR INFORMATION

Contacts **Downtown Ambassadors** (☎ *604/689-4357* ⊕ *www.downtownvancouver.net*). **Granville Island Information Services** (☎ *604/666-5784* ⊕ *www.granvilleisland.com*). **Vancouver Tourist InfoCentre** (☎ *604/683-2000* ⊕ *www.tourismvancouver.com*).

Victoria & Vancouver Island

WORD OF MOUTH

"The Inner Harbor in Victoria is where 90% of the tourist attractions are located. It's very tine physically—you can walk its entirety in one morning—so having a car is pointless. If you wish to see Butchart Gardens...you can take public transit, or hop on one of the many tour buses that organize packaged trips there."

—Carmanah

www.fodors.com/forums

Updated by Alison Appelbe and Sue Kernaghan

BEACHES, WILDERNESS PARKS, MOUNTAINS, deep temperate rain forests, and a wealth of wildlife have long drawn adventurous visitors to the West Coast's largest island. These days, however, a slew of excellent restaurants, country inns, spas, and ecologically sensitive resorts means you can enjoy all that beauty in comfort—though roughing it is still an option.

Despite its growing popularity, the island rarely feels crowded. Fewer than a million people live here, and virtually all of them cluster on the island's sheltered eastern side, between Victoria and Campbell River; half live in Victoria itself. The island's west coast, facing the open ocean, is wild and often inhospitable, with few roads and only a handful of small settlements. Nevertheless, the old-growth forests, magnificent stretch of beach, and challenging trails of the Pacific Rim National Park Reserve, as well as the chance to see whales offshore, are major draws for campers, hikers, kayakers, and even surfers.

The cultural heritage of the Pacific Coast First Nations peoples is as rich as Vancouver Island's natural bounty. Their art and culture are on display throughout the island, in totems and petroglyphs, in city art galleries, and in the striking collections at the Royal British Columbia Museum in Victoria, the Quw'utsun' Cultural and Conference Centre in Duncan, and the U'mista Cultural Centre in Alert Bay.

EXPLORING VANCOUVER ISLAND

Vancouver Island, touched by Pacific currents, has the mildest climate in Canada. Temperatures are usually above 32°F in winter and below 80°F in summer, although winter brings frequent rains (especially on the west coast). When traveling by car, keep in mind that Vancouver Island's west coast, beyond Port Renfrew, Ucluelet, and Tofino, has very few roads and is accessible mainly by sea or air.

ABOUT THE RESTAURANTS

"Fresh, local, organic" has become a mantra for many Vancouver Island chefs: some have even joined forces with local farmers to ensure supply of the freshest items. Wild salmon, locally made cheeses, Pacific oysters, forest-foraged mushrooms, organic vegetables in season, local microbrews, and even wines from the island's few family-run wineries can all be sampled here. Restaurants in the region are generally casual. Smoking is banned in all public places, including restaurants and bars, in Greater Victoria, and on the Southern Gulf Islands.

ABOUT THE HOTELS

Accommodations on Vancouver Island range from bed-and-breakfasts and country inns to rustic cabins to deluxe ecotourism lodges. Victoria in particular has a great selection of English-style B&Bs. Most small inns and B&Bs ban smoking indoors, and virtually all hotels in the area have no-smoking rooms. Most accommodations lack air-conditioning, as it rarely gets hot enough to need it. Advance reservations are always a good idea, especially in July and August, and in some of the more isolated towns.

TOP REASONS TO GO

CANOE & KAYAK
The island-dotted Strait of Georgia, on the east side of Vancouver Island, provides fairly protected seagoing, stunning scenery, and plenty of opportunities to spot orcas, eagles, and other local fauna. The Broken Group Islands, off the island's west coast, draw kayakers from around the world to their protected, wildlife-rich waters. The mountainous Strathcona Provincial Park offers scenic lake and river paddling.

HIKE THE WEST COAST TRAIL
The West Coast Trail, one of the world's most famous trails, runs along the western side of Vancouver Island. Other trails include the Juan de Fuca Marine Trail and those in Strathcona Provincial Park. But you can find fine hiking-trail networks in almost all of the island's many parks.

SPEND AN AFTERNOON AT BUTCHART GARDENS
A million-and-a-half visitors can't be wrong—these lavish gardens just north of Victoria truly live up to the hype.

TOUR THE ROYAL BRITISH COLUMBIA MUSEUM
One of Canada's best regional museums warrants repeat visits just to take in the myriad displays and exhibits.

TRAVERSE THE INNER HARBOUR VIA A FERRY BOAT
The tiny foot-passenger ferries zipping across the Inner Harbour afford passengers a whole new perspective on the city center.

WHAT IT COSTS IN CANADIAN DOLLARS

	¢	$	$$	$$$	$$$$
RESTAURANTS	under $8	$8–$12	$13–$20	$21–$30	over $30
HOTELS	under $75	$75–$125	$126–$175	$176–$250	over $250

Restaurant prices are for a main course at dinner. Hotel prices are for two people in a standard double room in high season, excluding tax.

VICTORIA

What's not to love about Victoria? The capital of a province whose license plates brazenly label it "The Best Place on Earth" is a walkable, livable seaside town of fragrant gardens, waterfront paths, engaging museums, and beautifully restored 19th-century architecture. In summer, the Inner Harbour—Victoria's social and cultural center—buzzes with visiting yachts, horse-and-carriage rides, street entertainers, and excursion boats heading out to visit pods of friendly, local whales. Yes, it's touristy, but Victoria's good looks, gracious pace, and manageable size are instantly beguiling, especially if you look past the somewhat cheesy mimes and caricature artists, and stand back to admire the mountains and ocean beyond.

GREAT ITINERARIES

IF YOU HAVE 1 TO 3 DAYS

For a short trip, **Victoria** is a fine place to begin. There's plenty to explore, from the flower-fringed Inner Harbour and the museums and attractions nearby to Market Square and the shops and restaurants of Chinatown. World-famous Butchart Gardens on the **Saanich Peninsula** is only a half hour away by car, and you might take a full day to explore the beautiful grounds. On Day 3, head west to **Sooke** or north, over the scenic Malahat region, to **Duncan** or **Chemainus**.

IF YOU HAVE 4 TO 6 DAYS

A brief stay in **Victoria** can be followed by a tour of Vancouver Island. Follow the itinerary above, heading to **Sooke** on Day 3. Day 4 allows time to see the Quw'utsun' Cultural and Conference Centre in Duncan and the murals and restored Victorian buildings of **Chemainus**. On Day 5, one alternative is to trek across the island to the scenic west coast to visit **Ucluelet** and **Tofino** (pick one for your overnight) and spend some time whale-watching or hiking around **Pacific Rim National Park Reserve**. Another choice is to continue up the east coast to visit **Strathcona Provincial Park** or to do some salmon fishing from **Campbell River**. Spend Day 6 retracing your steps to Victoria.

At the southern tip of Vancouver Island, forming the western point of a triangle with Seattle and Vancouver, Victoria dips slightly below the 49th parallel. That puts it farther south than most of Canada, giving it the mildest climate in the country, with virtually no snow and less than half the rain of Vancouver.

The city's geography, or at least its place names, can cause confusion. Just to clarify: the city of Victoria is on Vancouver Island (not Victoria Island). The city of Vancouver is on the British Columbia mainland, not on Vancouver Island, or on Victoria Island (which isn't in British Columbia but rather way up north, spanning parts of Nunavut and the Northwest Territories).

These days, however, Victorians prefer to celebrate their combined indigenous, Asian, and European heritage, and the city's stunning wilderness backdrop. Locals do often venture out for afternoon tea (although typically in a rather informal sense of the tradition), but they're just as likely to nosh on dim sum or tapas. Decades-old shops sell imported linens and tweeds, but newer upstarts offer local designs in hemp and organic cotton. And let's not forget that fabric prevalent among locals: Gortex. The outdoors are ever present here. You can hike, bike, kayak, sail, or whale-watch straight from the city center, and forests, beaches, offshore islands, and wilderness parklands lie just minutes away.

A little farther afield, there's surfing near Sooke, wine touring in the Cowichan Valley, and kayaking among the Gulf Islands. Victoria, however, isn't completely removed from the real world. It's not a theme park. Homelessness and traffic are growing problems (though at relatively insignificant levels that most big cities would envy). And, lest

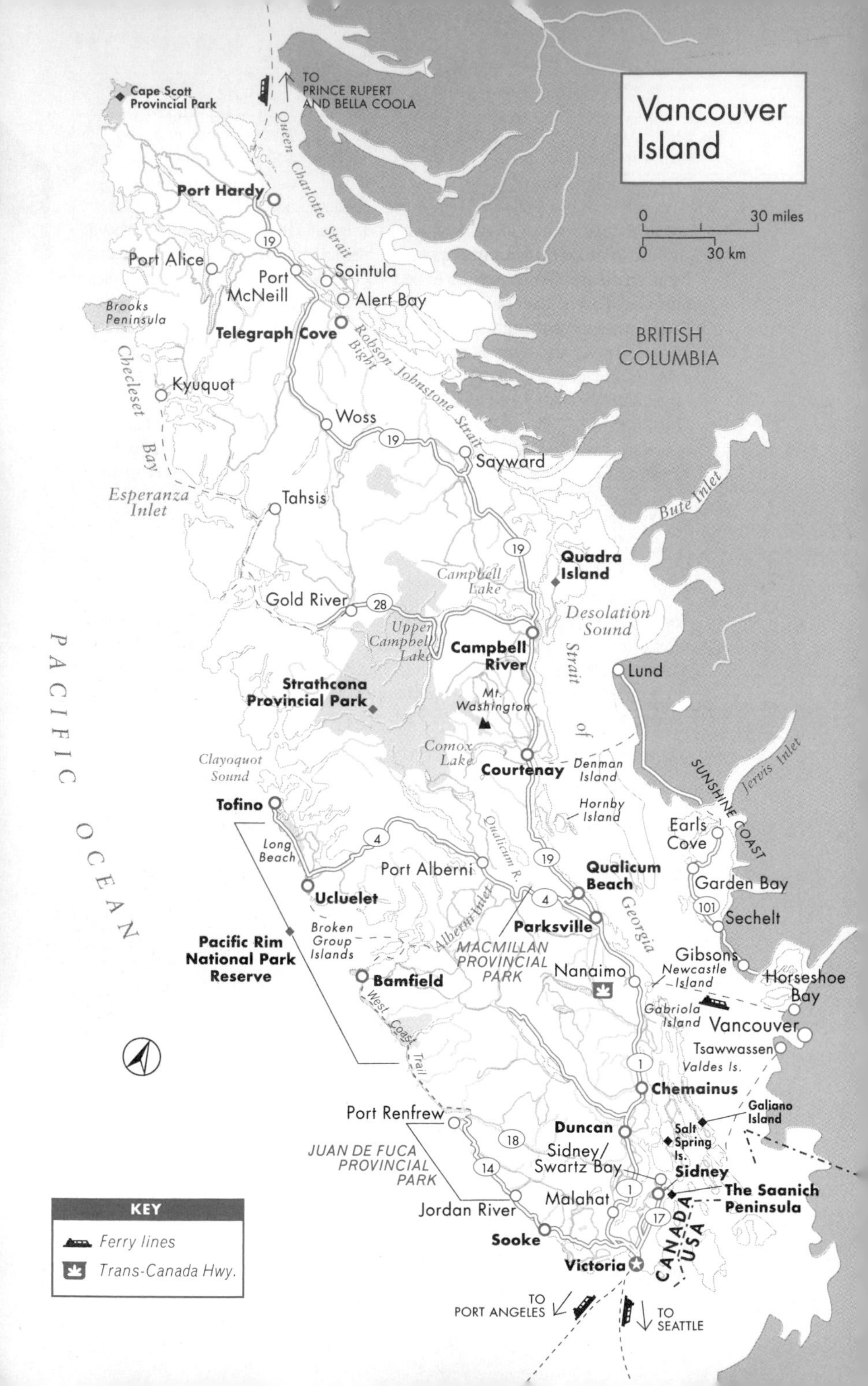

Vancouver Island
0 30 miles
0 30 km
BRITISH COLUMBIA
PACIFIC OCEAN
TO PRINCE RUPERT AND BELLA COOLA
Cape Scott Provincial Park
Queen Charlotte Strait
Port Hardy
19
Port Alice
Port McNeill
Sointula
Alert Bay
Brooks Peninsula
Telegraph Cove
Robson Bight
Johnstone Strait
Checleset Bay
Kyuquot
Woss
Sayward
Esperanza Inlet
Tahsis
Bute Inlet
Quadra Island
Campbell Lake
Gold River
28
Desolation Sound
Upper Campbell Lake
Campbell River
Strait of Georgia
Lund
Strathcona Provincial Park
Mt. Washington
Comox Lake
Courtenay
Denman Island
Hornby Island
Clayoquot Sound
Tofino
Sunshine Coast
Jervis Inlet
Earls Cove
Long Beach
4
Port Alberni
Qualicum R.
Qualicum Beach
Garden Bay
Ucluelet
Alberni Inlet
Parksville
101
Sechelt
Broken Group Islands
Pacific Rim National Park Reserve
MacMillan Provincial Park
Gibsons
Nanaimo
Newcastle Island
Horseshoe Bay
Bamfield
West Coast Trail
Gabriola Island
Vancouver
Tsawwassen
Valdes Is.
1
Chemainus
Galiano Island
Port Renfrew
Duncan
Salt Spring Is.
18
Juan de Fuca Provincial Park
Sidney/ Swartz Bay
Sidney
14
The Saanich Peninsula
Malahat
17
Jordan River
Sooke
Victoria
CANADA
USA
TO PORT ANGELES
TO SEATTLE
KEY
Ferry lines
Trans-Canada Hwy.

those glorious sunsets over the harbor inspire thoughts of moving here, note that Victoria, once a provincial backwater, now boasts the priciest real estate in Canada.

EXPLORING VICTORIA

Exploring Victoria is easy. A walk around downtown, starting with the museums and architectural sights of the Inner Harbour, followed by a stroll up Government Street to the historic areas of Chinatown and Old Town, covers most of the key attractions, though seeing every little interesting thing along the way could easily take two days. Small passenger ferries dart across the Inner and Upper harbours to such waterfront stops as Point Ellice House and Fisherman's Wharf, while several more attractions, including Craigdarroch Castle and the Art Gallery of Greater Victoria, lie about a mile east of downtown in the residential areas of Rockland and Oak Bay. Most visitors also make time for Butchart Gardens, a stunning exhibition garden a 20-minute drive north on the Saanich Peninsula.

DOWNTOWN VICTORIA

WHAT TO SEE

11 **Bastion Square.** James Douglas, the former colonial governor for whom Douglas Street was named, chose this spot for the original Fort Victoria and Hudson's Bay Company trading post in 1843. In summer the square comes alive with street performers and crafts vendors. ✉ *Off Wharf St. at end of View St., Downtown.*

5 ★ **Beacon Hill Park.** The southern lawns and waterfront path of this 154-acre park afford great views of the Olympic Mountains and the Strait of Juan de Fuca. Also here are ponds, jogging and walking paths, abundant flowers and gardens, a petting zoo, a putting green, and a cricket pitch. Music plays in the band shell on summer evenings and, on Friday and Saturday nights in August, the Victoria Film Festival screens free movies in the park. ✉ *East of Douglas St., south of Southgate St., Downtown* ☎ *250/361–0600 City of Victoria Parks Division, 250/381–2532 children's farmyard, 250/389–0444 Victoria Film Festival* 🌐 *www.victoria.ca.*

13 **Chinatown.** Chinese immigrants built much of the Canadian Pacific Railway in the 19th century, and their influence still marks the region. Victoria's Chinatown, founded in 1858, is the oldest and most intact such district in Canada. If you enter Chinatown from Government Street, you'll pass under the elaborate **Gate of Harmonious Interest.** Along Fisgard Street, merchants display paper lanterns, wicker baskets, and exotic produce. Mah-jongg, fan-tan, and dominoes were among the games of chance played along **Fan Tan Alley,** said to be the narrowest street in Canada. Once the gambling and opium center of Chinatown, it's now lined with offbeat shops, few of which sell authentic Chinese goods. ✉ *Fisgard St. between Government and Store Sts., Chinatown.*

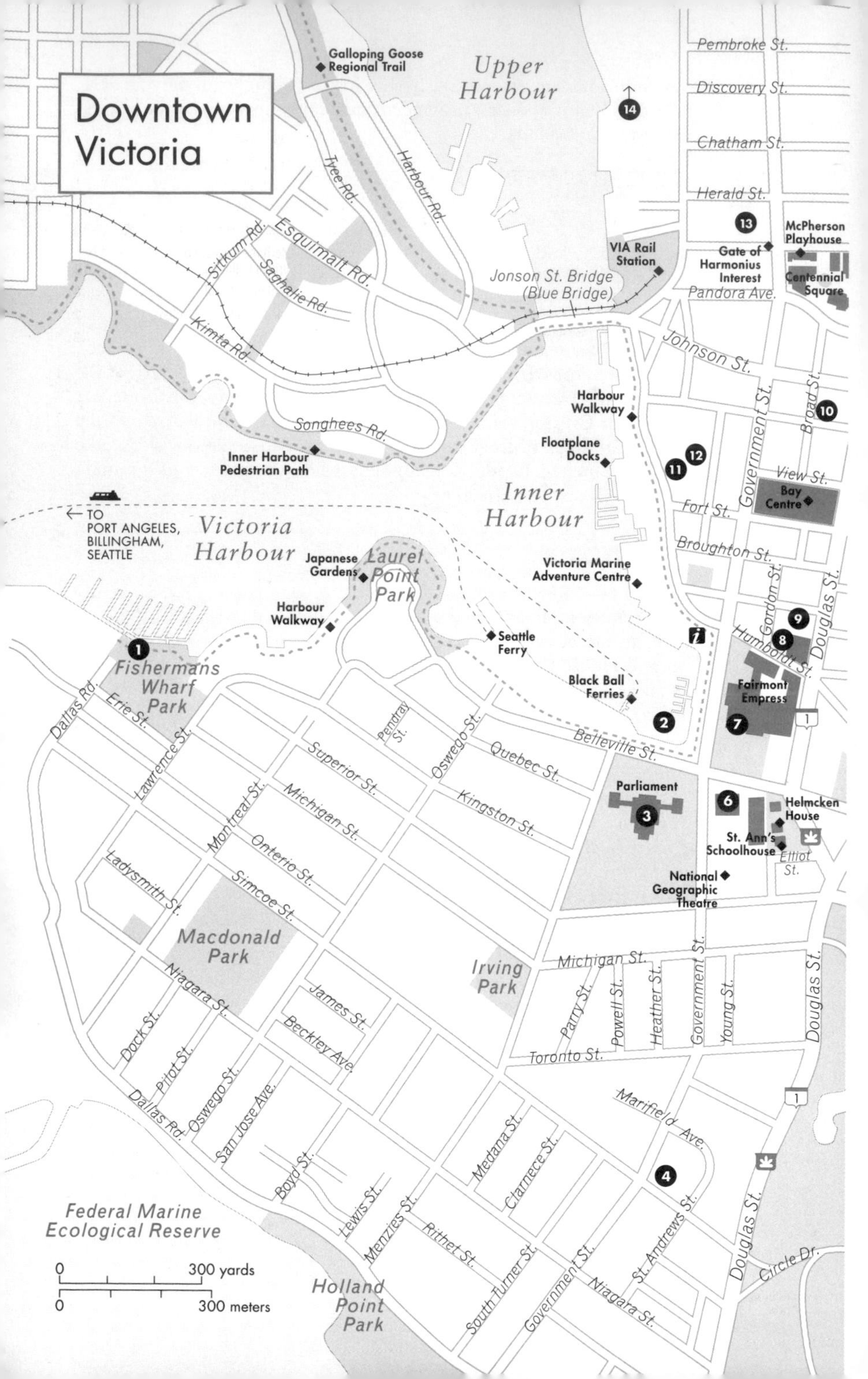

Downtown Victoria
Upper Harbour
Inner Harbour
Victoria Harbour
Galloping Goose Regional Trail
TO PORT ANGELES, BILLINGHAM, SEATTLE
VIA Rail Station
Jonson St. Bridge (Blue Bridge)
Gate of Harmonious Interest
McPherson Playhouse
Centennial Square
Harbour Walkway
Floatplane Docks
Inner Harbour Pedestrian Path
Japanese Gardens
Laurel Point Park
Victoria Marine Adventure Centre
Seattle Ferry
Black Ball Ferries
Bay Centre
Fairmont Empress
Parliament
Helmcken House
St. Ann's Schoolhouse
National Geographic Theatre
Fishermans Wharf Park
Macdonald Park
Irving Park
Holland Point Park
Federal Marine Ecological Reserve
Pembroke St.
Discovery St.
Chatham St.
Herald St.
Pandora Ave.
Johnson St.
Government St.
Broad St.
View St.
Fort St.
Broughton St.
Gordon St.
Douglas St.
Humboldt St.
Belleville St.
Quebec St.
Kingston St.
Superior St.
Michigan St.
Oswego St.
Pendray St.
Ontario St.
Simcoe St.
Montreal St.
Lawrence St.
Erie St.
Dallas Rd.
Ladysmith St.
Niagara St.
Dock St.
Pilot St.
San Jose Ave.
James St.
Beckley Ave.
Boyd St.
Lewis St.
Menzies St.
Rithet St.
Medana St.
Clarnece St.
South Turner St.
Toronto St.
Parry St.
Powell St.
Heather St.
Young St.
Marifield Ave.
St. Andrews St.
Elliot St.
Circle Dr.
Tyee Rd.
Harbour Rd.
Esquimalt Rd.
Sitkum Rd.
Saghalie Rd.
Kimta Rd.
Songhees Rd.
0 300 yards
0 300 meters

Bastion Square	**11**
Beacon Hill Park	**5**
Chinatown	**13**
Emily Carr House	**4**
Fairmont Empress	**7**
Fisherman's Wharf	**1**
Legacy Art Gallery	**10**
Maritime Museum of British Columbia	**12**
Miniature World	**8**
Pacific Undersea Gardens	**2**
Parliament Buildings	**3**
Point Ellice House	**14**
Royal British Columbia Museum	**6**
Victoria Bug Zoo	**9**

4 **Emily Carr House.** One of Canada's most celebrated artists and a respected writer, Emily Carr (1871–1945) was born and raised in this very proper wooden Victorian house before she abandoned her middle-class life to live in, and paint, the wilds of British Columbia. Carr's own descriptions, from her autobiography *Book of Small,* were used to restore the house. Catch, if you can, one of the days when an actress playing Carr tells stories of her life. Art work on display includes work by modern-day B.C. artists and reproductions of Carr's work. You'll need to visit the Art Gallery of Greater Victoria or the Vancouver Art Gallery to see Carr originals. ✉*207 Government St., James Bay* ☎*250/383–5843* 🌐*www.emilycarr.com* 🎫*C$5; C$10 for actress performances and other special events* ⏲*May and Sept., Tues.–Sat. 11–4; July and Aug., daily 11–4; Oct.–Apr. by arrangement or during special events.*

7 **Fairmont Empress.** Opened in 1908 by the Canadian Pacific Railway, the Empress is one of the grand château-style railroad hotels that grace many Canadian cities. Designed by Francis Rattenbury, who also designed the Parliament Buildings across the way, the Empress, with its solid Edwardian grandeur, has become a symbol of the city. ✉*721 Government St., entrance at Belleville and Government, Downtown* ☎*250/384–8111, 250/389–2727 tea reservations* 🌐*www.fairmont.com/empress* 🎫*Free, afternoon tea C$55 July and Aug., C$38–C$49 Sept.–June.*

1 **Fisherman's Wharf.** Harbour Ferries stop at this fun nautical spot, just west of the Inner Harbour. Among the candy-color houseboats bobbing along the dock are several floating shacks selling ice cream, fish-and-chips, live crab, and tickets for whale-watching tours. ✉*At the corner of Superior and St. Lawrence Sts., Downtown* ☎*250/708–0201 Victoria Harbour Ferries* 🌐*www.victoriaharbourferry.com* 🎫*Wharf: free. Ferry: C$4* ⏲*Ferries run May–Sept., daily 9–9; less often Oct.–Apr.*

10 **Legacy Art Gallery and Café.** Victoria's newest art gallery opened in 2007 to display some of the 1,600 paintings, sculptures, and antiques collected by the late Michael Williams, the owner of Swans Hotel. Rotating exhibits in the 3,000-square-foot space comprise mostly Canadian works, including many by First Nations artists, but international painters are represented, too. ✉*630 Yates St., Downtown* ☎*250/381–7670* 🌐*www.maltwood.uvic.ca/legacy_gallery/home.htm* 🎫*Free* ⏲*Wed.–Sun. 10–7:30.*

8 **Miniature World.** Small children and model aficionados adore this charmingly retro attraction, tucked into the side of the Fairmont Empress Hotel. More than 80 miniature dioramas, from space, castle, and fairy-tale scenes to some highly realistic battle reenactments and one of the world's largest model railways, are housed in kid-height glass cases, complete with recorded narration. Most people walk through in 30 minutes, but dollhouse collectors, model-train builders, and preschoolers can be absorbed for hours. ✉*649 Humboldt St., Downtown* ☎*250/385–9731* 🌐*www.miniatureworld.com* 🎫*C$9* ⏲*Mid-May–mid-June and Sept., daily 9-7; mid-June–Labor Day, daily, 8:30 AM–9 PM; Oct.–mid-May, daily 9–5.*

⓬ **Maritime Museum of British Columbia.** The model ships, Royal Navy charts, photographs, uniforms, and ship bells at this museum, in Victoria's original courthouse, chronicle the province's seafaring history. Among the hand-built boats on display is the *Tilikum,* a dugout canoe that sailed from Victoria to England between 1901 and 1904. Kids can climb a crow's nest and learn some scary tales about the pirates of the coast. An 1899 hand-operated cage elevator, believed to be the oldest continuously operating lift in North America, ascends to the third floor, where the original 1888 vice-admiralty courtroom looks ready for a court-martial. *28 Bastion Sq., Downtown* *250/385–4222* *www.mmbc.bc.ca* *C$8* *Daily 9:30–4:30.*

❷ **Pacific Undersea Gardens.** If you want an up-close look at a wolf eel or an octopus, you might check out this underwater sea-life display, housed in and under a barge floating in the Inner Harbour. If you're at all claustrophobic, though, be warned: a dark staircase leads to a dark, narrow tunnel 15 feet below water, where you can see local fish and other marine creatures darting about behind high windows. The U-shaped tunnel opens to an underwater theater, where a 20-minute narrated dive show, run roughly every 45 minutes in summer (less frequently in winter), gives everyone a chance to view the more interesting of the 5,000 or so creatures in the tanks. The biggest room of all is the above-water gift shop, which has a pretty good collection of nautical-theme toys. *490 Belleville St., TK* *250/382–5717* *www.pacificunderseagardens.com* *C$9.50* *Apr.–June, daily 10–6; July and Aug., daily 9–8; Sept.–Mar., daily 10–5.*

❸ **Parliament Buildings.** Officially the British Columbia Provincial Legislative Assembly Buildings, these massive stone structures are more popularly referred to as the Parliament Buildings. Designed by Francis Rattenbury (who also designed the Fairmont Empress Hotel) when he was just 25 years old and completed in 1898, they dominate the Inner Harbour. Atop the central dome is a gilded statue of Captain George Vancouver (1757–98), the first European to sail around Vancouver Island. A statue of Queen Victoria (1819–1901) reigns over the front of the complex. More than 3,000 lights outline the buildings at night. When the legislature is in session, you can sit in the public gallery and watch British Columbia's democracy at work. Free, informative half-hour tours run every 20 minutes during the summer, and hourly in the off-season; they're obligatory on summer weekends (mid-May until Labor Day) and optional the rest of the time. *501 Belleville St., Downtown* *250/387–3046* *www.leg.bc.ca* *Free* *Mid-May–early Sept., weekdays 9–5, weekends 9–7; early Sept.–mid-May, weekdays 9–5 (last tour an hour before closing).*

⓮ **Point Ellice House.** The O'Reilly family home, an 1861 Italianate cottage overlooking the Selkirk Waterway, has been restored to its original splendor, with the largest collection of Victorian furnishings in western Canada. Tea and fresh-baked goodies are served under an awning on the lawn. You can take a half-hour audio tour of the house (presented from a servant's point of view), stroll in the English country garden, or try your hand at croquet. *2616 Pleasant St., Downtown*

CLOSE UP

Victoria's History

Vancouver didn't even exist in 1843 when Victoria, then called Fort Victoria, was founded as the westernmost trading post of the British-owned Hudson's Bay Company. It was the first European settlement on Vancouver Island, and in 1868, it became the capital of British Columbia.

The British weren't here alone, of course. The local First Nations people—the Songhees, the Saanich, and the Sooke—had already lived in the areas for thousands of years before anyone else arrived. Their art and culture—which are currently experiencing a renaissance after decades of enforced decline—are visible throughout southern Vancouver Island. You can see this in private and public galleries, in the totems at Thunderbird Park, in the striking collections at the Royal British Columbia Museum, and at the Quw'utsun'Cultural and Conference Centre in nearby Duncan.

Spanish explorers were the first foreigners to explore the area, although they left little more than place names (Galiano Island and Cordova Bay, for example). The thousands of Chinese immigrants drawn by the gold rushes of the late 19th century had a much greater impact, founding Canada's oldest Chinatown and adding an Asian influence that's still quite pronounced in Victoria's multicultural mix.

Despite its role as the provincial capital, Victoria was largely bypassed, economically, by Vancouver throughout the 20th century. This, as it turns out, was all to the good, helping to preserve Victoria's historic downtown and keeping the city free of skyscrapers and freeways. For much of the 20th century, Victoria was marketed to tourists as "The Most British City in Canada," and it still boasts more than its share of Anglo-themed pubs, tea shops, and double-decker buses.

☎250/380–6506 🌐www.pointellicehouse.ca 🎟C$6, C$22 including tea ⏲May–Sept., daily 11–5; tea daily 11–4; some Christmas and Halloween programs.

❻ **Royal British Columbia Museum.** This excellent museum, one of Victoria's leading attractions, traces several thousand years of British Columbian history. Its First Peoples Gallery, home to a genuine Kwakwaka'wakw big house and a dramatically displayed collection of masks and other artifacts, is especially strong. The Living Land, Living Sea Gallery traces B.C.'s natural heritage, from prehistory to modern-day climate change, in realistic dioramas. An Ocean Station exhibit gets kids involved in running a Jules Verne–style submarine. In the History Gallery, a replica of Captain Vancouver's ship, the HMS *Discovery,* creaks convincingly, and a re-created frontier town comes to life with cobbled streets, silent movies, and the rumble of an arriving train. Also on-site is an IMAX theater showing *National Geographic* films on a six-story-high screen. *✉675 Belleville St., Downtown ☎250/356–7226 or 888/447–7977 🌐www.royalbcmuseum.bc.ca 🎟C$14, IMAX theater C$10.50, combination ticket C$22.50. Rates may be higher during special-exhibit periods ⏲Museum: Mid-Oct.–June, daily 9–5; July–mid-Oct., daily 9–6 (open until 10 PM most Fri. and Sat. early June–mid-Oct.). Theater: daily 10–8; call for show times.*

Fodor's Choice ★

9 **Victoria Bug Zoo.** Local kids clamor to visit this offbeat mini-zoo, home to the largest tropical insect collection in North America. You can even hold many of the 60 or so varieties, which include walking sticks, scorpions, millipedes, and a pharnacia—at 22 inches, the world's longest insect. The staff members know their bug lore and are happy to dispense scientific information. ✉*631 Courtney St., Downtown* ☎*250/384–2847* 🌐*www.bugzoo.bc.ca* *C$8* ⏲*Mid-June–early Sept., daily 10–6; early Sept.–mid-June, Mon.–Sat. 10–5:30, Sun. 11–5:30.*

OAK BAY, ROCKLAND, AND FAIRFIELD

The winding shady streets of Victoria's older residential areas—roughly bordered by Cook Street, Fort Street, and the seaside—are lined with beautifully preserved Victorian and Edwardian homes. These include many stunning old mansions now operating as B&Bs, and Victoria's most elaborate folly: Craigdarroch Castle. With mansions come gardens, and several of the city's best are found here. Clusters of high-end shops include the very British Oak Bay Village, described as a place "behind the Tweed Curtain" for its adherence to Tudor facades and tea shops. Among the lavish waterfront homes are plenty of public parks and beaches offering views across Juan de Fuca Strait to the Olympic Mountains of Washington State.

A car or a bike is handy, but not essential, for exploring this area. For a nice drive or cycling excursion, follow Scenic Marine Drive (also signposted as the Seaside Touring Route for cyclists) along Dallas Road. No wheels? Big Bus, Gray Line, and other tour companies offer Oak Bay and Marine Drive tours.

Art Gallery of Greater Victoria. Attached to an 1889 mansion, this modern building houses one of Canada's largest collections of Chinese and Japanese artifacts. The Japanese garden between the buildings is home to the only authentic Shinto shrine in North America. The gallery, which is a few blocks west of Craigdarroch Castle, off Fort Street, displays a permanent exhibition of works by well-known Canadian artist Emily Carr and regularly changing exhibits of Asian and historical and contemporary Western art. Major touring exhibitions include an Andy Warhol exhibit set for summer 2008. ✉*1040 Moss St., Rockland* ☎*250/384–4101* 🌐*www.aggv.bc.ca* *C$12* ⏲*Mon.–Wed., Fri.–Sun. 10–5, Thurs. 10–9.*

Craigdarroch Castle. This resplendent mansion complete with turrets and Gothic rooflines was built as the home of one of British Columbia's wealthiest men, coal baron Robert Dunsmuir, who died in 1889, just a few months before the castle's completion. Converted into a museum depicting life in the late 1800s, the castle's 39 rooms have ornate Victorian furnishings, stained-glass windows, carved woodwork, displays of the Dunsmuir daughters' party dresses, and a beautifully restored painted ceiling in the drawing room. A winding staircase climbs four floors to a tower overlooking Victoria. In summer, actors playing characters from the era interact with visitors, of which there are many, especially if a tour bus is coming through. Castles run in the family: son

James went on to build the even more lavish Hatley Castle just west of Victoria. ✉ *1050 Joan Crescent, Rockland* ☎ *250/592–5323* 🌐 *www.thecastle.ca* 🎫 *C$11.75* ⏲ *Mid-June–early Sept., daily 9–7:30; early Sept.–mid-June, daily 10–5.*

Government House Gardens. If you're in the area, you might take a stroll through the walled grounds and formal rose garden of Government House, the official residence of British Columbia's Lieutenant Governor, the Queen's representative in B.C. The stately, though modern, house itself isn't open to the public, though the 35 acres of gardens are. ✉ *1401 Rockland Ave., Rockland* 🎫 *Free* ⏲ *Daily dawn–dusk.*

Oak Bay Village. Described as the land "behind the tweed curtain," this self-consciously British area (with its own municipal hall) is home to such theme-y businesses as the Penny Farthing Pub and the Blethering Place tearoom, as well as plenty of sweet shops, bookshops, and antiques stores, most behind mock-Tudor facades. ✉ *Along Oak Bay Ave. roughly between Foul Bay Rd. and Monterey Ave.*

Willows Beach Park. This neighborhood park has a nice sandy beach, a grassy park with a playground, and, this being Oak Bay, a teahouse. ✉ *Along the Esplanade at the foot of Estevan Ave., TK.*

THE SAANICH PENINSULA

30 km (18 mi) north of Victoria on Hwy. 17.

Home to the B.C. and Washington State ferry terminals as well as the Victoria International Airport, the Saanich Peninsula, with its rolling green hills and small family farms, is the first part of Vancouver Island that most visitors see. Here you'll find Butchart Gardens, one of the province's leading attractions.

Fodor's Choice ★

The Butchart Gardens. This stunning 55-acre garden and National Historic Site has been drawing visitors since it was planted in a limestone quarry in 1904. Seven hundred varieties of flowers grow in the site's Japanese, Italian, rose, and sunken gardens. Highlights include the view over the ivy-draped and flower-filled former quarry, the dramatic 21-meter-high (70-foot-high) Ross Fountain, and the formal and intricate Italian garden, complete with a gelato stand. From mid-June to mid-September the gardens are illuminated at night with hundreds of hidden lights. In July and August, kids' entertainers perform Sunday through Friday afternoons; jazz, blues, and classical musicians play at an outdoor stage each evening; and fireworks draw crowds every Saturday night. The wheelchair- and stroller-accessible site is also home to a seed-and-gift shop, a plant identification center, two restaurants (one offering traditional afternoon tea), and a coffee shop; you can even call ahead for a picnic basket. The gardens are about 20 minutes' drive north of downtown; parking is free and plentiful but fills up on fireworks Saturdays. The Butchart Gardens Express Shuttle, run by Grey Line West, runs half-hourly service between downtown Victoria and the Butchart Gardens during peak season. The C$39 round-trip fare includes admission to the gardens. ✉ *800 Benvenuto Ave., Brentwood*

Bay ☎*250/652–5256 or 866/652–4422* ⊕*www.butchartgardens.com* *Mid-June–late Sept. C$25, discounted rates rest of yr* ⊙*Mid-June–Labor Day, daily 9* AM*–10:30* PM*; Sept.–mid-June, daily 9* AM*–dusk; call for exact times.*

> **WORD OF MOUTH**
>
> "Butchart Gardens—beautiful place!! We took the Evening Illuminations tour with Grey Line and got to see the Gardens right before sunset and on into the late night.... Seeing the Gardens lit up at night was unique."
>
> —globetrotterxyz

WHERE TO EAT

Victoria is said to have the second-highest number of restaurants per capita in North America (after San Francisco); this fact, and the glorious pantry that is Vancouver Island, keeps prices down (at least compared to Vancouver) and standards up. Wild salmon, locally made cheeses, Pacific oysters, organic vegetables, local microbrews, and even wines from the island's new farm gate wineries (The B.C. government allows very small wineries to sell their wines "at the farm gate") are tastes to watch for.

Afternoon tea is a Victoria tradition, as is good coffee—despite the Starbucks invasion, there are plenty of fun and funky local caffeine purveyors around town.

DOWNTOWN

ASIAN

$$ ✕**The Mint.** Ever wondered what a Nepalese night club might look like? Well, this subterranean space is as close as it gets, with good, affordable Nepalese and Tibetan dishes, from the traditional—chilies and chicken, spicy lamb curry, and Tibetan dumplings—to the less strictly Himalayan, such as *nan* pizzas and cheese plates. Local vegans swear by the nut burgers and almond-cashew pesto pasta. With DJs playing up-tempo lounge music most nights and both big and small plates offered until 2 AM, the Mint appeals to off-duty restaurant workers, students, and other budget-minded, fun-loving people. ✉*1414 Douglas St., Downtown* ☎*250/386–6468* ▭*AE, MC, V* ⊙*No lunch.*

$–$$ ★ ✕**The Noodle Box.** Noodles, whether Indonesian-style with peanut sauce, thick Japanese Udon in teriyaki, or Thai-style chow mein, are piled straight from steaming woks in the open kitchen to bowls or cardboard take-out boxes at this local answer to fast-food. Malaysian, Singapore, and Cambodian-style curries tempt those who like it hot. The brick, rose, and lime walls keep things modern and high energy. ✉*818 Douglas St., Downtown* ☎*250/384–1314* *Reservations not accepted* ▭*AE, MC, V* ✉*626 Fisgard St., Downtown* ☎*250/360–1312* *Reservations not accepted* ▭*AE, MC, V.*

CAFÉS

¢–$ ✕**Blue Carrot Café.** Tucked off to the north side of Bastion Square, this family-run spot with a few tables on the cobbles outside keeps local office workers in wholesome omelet and benny breakfasts and afford-

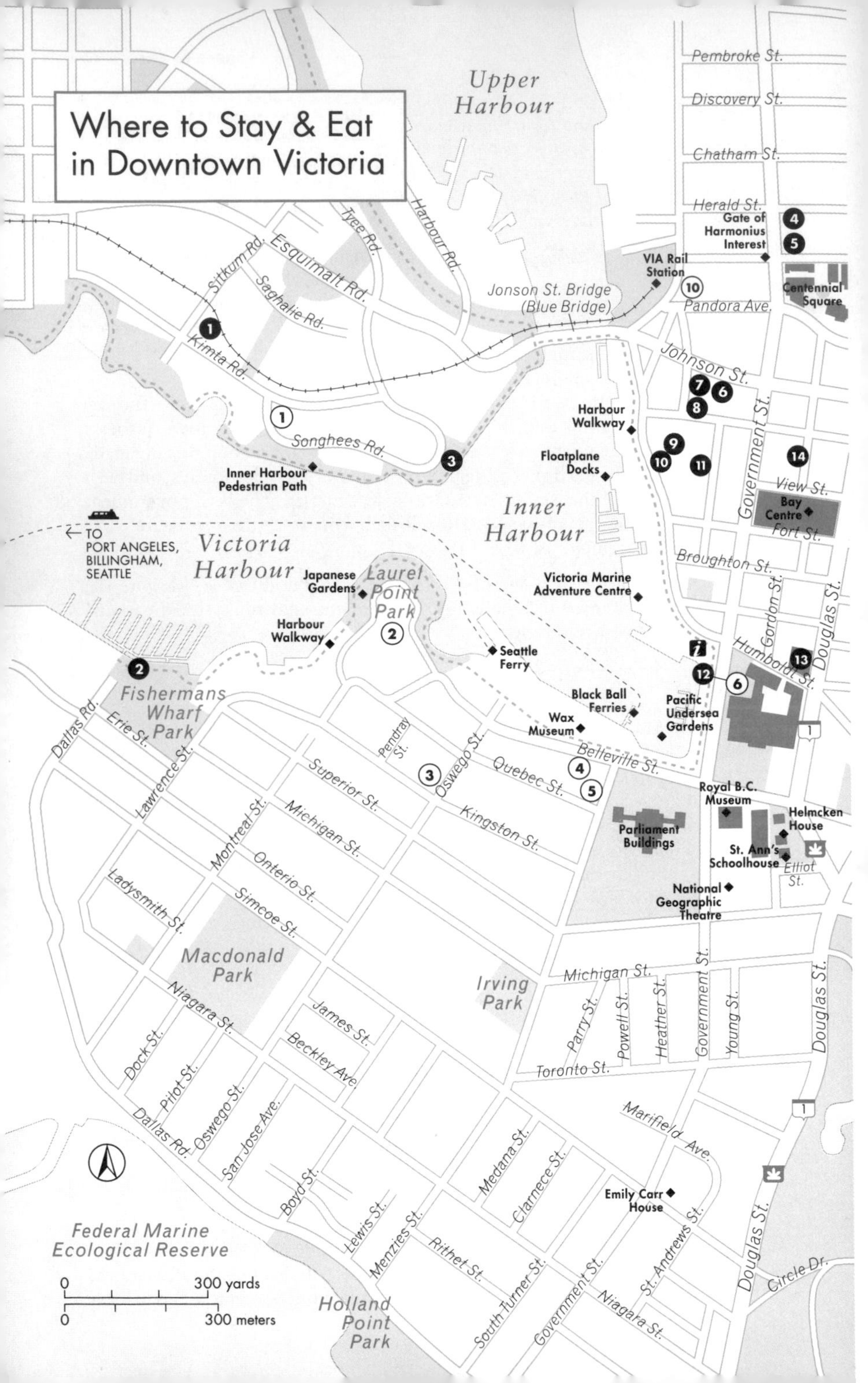

Where to Stay & Eat in Downtown Victoria
Upper Harbour
Inner Harbour
Victoria Harbour
TO PORT ANGELES, BILLINGHAM, SEATTLE
Pembroke St.
Discovery St.
Chatham St.
Herald St.
Gate of Harmonius Interest
VIA Rail Station
Centennial Square
Pandora Ave.
Jonson St. Bridge (Blue Bridge)
Johnson St.
Harbour Walkway
Floatplane Docks
View St.
Bay Centre
Fort St.
Broughton St.
Government St.
Gordon St.
Douglas St.
Humboldt St.
Victoria Marine Adventure Centre
Seattle Ferry
Black Ball Ferries
Pacific Undersea Gardens
Wax Museum
Belleville St.
Quebec St.
Kingston St.
Royal B.C. Museum
Helmcken House
Parliament Buildings
St. Ann's Schoolhouse
Elliot St.
National Geographic Theatre
Tyee Rd.
Harbour Rd.
Esquimalt Rd.
Sitkum Rd.
Saghalie Rd.
Kimta Rd.
Songhees Rd.
Inner Harbour Pedestrian Path
Japanese Gardens
Laurel Point Park
Harbour Walkway
Fishermans Wharf Park
Dallas Rd.
Erie St.
Lawrence St.
Superior St.
Pendray St.
Oswego St.
Michigan St.
Montreal St.
Onterio St.
Simcoe St.
Ladysmith St.
Macdonald Park
Niagara St.
Irving Park
Michigan St.
Parry St.
Powell St.
Heather St.
Government St.
Young St.
Douglas St.
Toronto St.
James St.
Beckley Ave.
Dock St.
Pilot St.
Oswego St.
Dallas Rd.
San Jose Ave.
Marifield Ave.
Medana St.
Clarnece St.
Emily Carr House
Boyd St.
Lewis St.
Menzies St.
Rithet St.
South Turner St.
Government St.
Niagara St.
St. Andrews St.
Douglas St.
Circle Dr.
Federal Marine Ecological Reserve
Holland Point Park
0
300 yards
0
300 meters

Restaurants

- Barb's Place **2**
- Blue Carrot Café **10**
- Brasserie L'école **4**
- Café Brio **16**
- Camille's **11**
- The Empress Room **12**
- Eugene's **14**
- Il Terrazzo **7**
- J&J Won Ton Noodle House **17**
- Lure Seafood Restaurant & Bar **3**
- Matisse **8**
- The Mint **15**
- The Noodle Box, Douglas St. **13**
- The Noodle Box, Fisgard St. **5**
- Re-Bar Modern Food **9**
- Spinnakers Gastro Brewpub **1**
- Willie's Bakery & Café **6**
- Zambri's **18**

Hotels

- Abigail's Hotel **8**
- The Beaconsfield Inn **7**
- The Fairmont Empress **6**
- The Hotel Grand Pacific **4**
- Laurel Point Inn **2**
- Ocean Island Backpackers Inn **9**
- The Oswego Hotel **3**
- Royal Scot Suite Hotel **5**
- Spinnakers Guesthouse **1**
- Swans Suite Hotel **10**

able soup, sandwich, wrap, and burger lunches. Everything, including the Blue Carrot Cake, is homemade: Mom does most of the baking, but grandma makes the chocolate cake. Local art lines the walls. ✉*18B Bastion Sq., Downtown* ☎*250/381–8722* ✍*Reservations not accepted* ▭*MC, V* ⏲*No dinner. Closed Sundays Oct.–Mar.*

¢–$ ✕**Willie's Bakery & Cafe.** Housed in a handsome Victorian building near Market Square, this bakery-café goes organic, free range, and local in its omelets, brioches, French toast, and homemade granola breakfasts and its lunches of homemade soups, thick sandwiches made with house-baked bread, and tasty baked treats. A tiny brick patio with an outdoor fireplace is partially glassed in so you can lunch alfresco even on chilly days. ✉*537 Johnson St., Downtown* ☎*250/381–8414* ✍*Reservations not accepted* ▭*MC, V* ⏲*No dinner.*

CANADIAN

$$$$ ★ ✕**Empress Room.** Candlelight dances on tapestried walls beneath a carved mahogany ceiling at the Fairmont Empress hotel's flagship restaurant where one of the two gracious rooms has an expansive harbour view. The classically influenced Pacific Northwest menu changes frequently, but might start with seared Pacific sea scallops or risotto with local morels, and move to such mains as veal tenderloin with foie gras; local wild salmon; or mustard-crusted rack of lamb. The vegetarian and seafood fare on the spa menu is also tempting. Service is discreet and attentive, and there are more than 800 labels on the wine list. ✉*Fairmont Empress, 721 Government St., Downtown* ☎*250/389–2727* ✍*Reservations not accepted for the Veranda* ▭*AE, D, DC, MC, V.*

$$$ ★ ✕**Cafe Brio.** "Charming, comfortable, and hip with walls of art—all backed by city's best chef and kitchen," is how one fodors.com user describes this bustling Italian villa–style room. The frequently changing menu highlights regional, organic fare and favorites include braised beef short ribs, local wild salmon in season, Cowichan Bay duck breast, local lamb, and housemade charcuterie. Virtually everything, including the bread, pasta, and desserts, as well as some of the cheeses, is made in-house—even the butter is hand churned. ✉*944 Fort St., Downtown* ☎*250/383–0009 or 866/270–5461* ▭*AE, MC, V* ⏲*No lunch.*

$$$ ★ ✕**Camille's.** Working closely with independent farmers, the chef at this long-established favorite concentrates on such locally sourced products as lamb, duck, and seafood; quail, venison, and ostrich often make an appearance, too. The menu changes frequently based on what's fresh from the farms, but might include sea-scallop and rock-prawn cakes, rack of venison with juniper and mustard crust, or a green-curry seafood claypot. The five-course tasting menu, with optional wine matching, is popular. The wine cellar–like setting, on the lower floor of a historic building in Bastion Square, is candlelit and romantic, with exposed brick, local art, low lights, soft music, and lots of intimate nooks and crannies. A well-selected wine list is long on hard-to-find local choices. ✉*45 Bastion Sq., Downtown* ☎*250/381–3433* ▭*AE, MC, V* ⏲*Closed Sun and Mon. No lunch.*

$–$$ ★ ✕**Spinnakers Gastro Brewpub.** Victoria's longest menu of handcrafted beer is just one reason to trek over the Johnson Street Bridge or hop a Harbour Ferry to this Vic West waterfront pub. Canada's oldest licensed brewpub, Spinnakers relies almost exclusively on locally sourced ingredients for its top-notch casual fare. Opt for the pubby adults-only taproom, with its glassed-in waterfront deck, double-sided fireplace, and plethora of paraphernalia-filled rooms; or dine in the all-ages waterfront restaurant. Either way you can enjoy such high-end pub grub as mussels steamed in ale, brewery grain-fed beef burgers, wild salmon fettucine, or fish-and-chips with kennebec fries. ✉*308 Catherine St., Downtown* ☎*250/386–2739 or 877/838–2739* *Reservations not accepted in the Taproom* ▭*AE, MC, V.*

WORD OF MOUTH

"In Victoria, I highly recommend Spinnakers, nice view of harbor and great food for reasonable prices." —bcforlife

CHINESE

$–$$ ✕**J&J Won Ton Noodle House.** Lunchtime queues attest to the popularity of the fresh house-made noodles and won tons at this pan-Chinese spot on antique row. The lines move fast, though, thanks to the efficient service. Szechuan and Shanghai specialities, from shrimp noodle soup to beef with hot chili bean sauce, dominate the long menu, but Singapore-style noodles and Malaysian chow mein appear, too. ✉*1012 Fort St., Downtown* ☎*250/383-0680* ▭*MC, V* ⏲*Closed Sun. and Mon.*

FRENCH

$$$–$$$$ ★ ✕**Matisse.** The gracious owner greets each guest personally at this tiny gem of a traditional French restaurant where white linens, fresh flowers, and candlelight on the dozen or so tables set the stage for meals of such well-executed bistro classics as rack of lamb, bouillabaisse, and filet bordelaise. The primarily French wine list has plenty of affordable options and the crème brûlée and housemade sorbets are much-loved finales. Piaf chansons on the speakers and Matisse prints on the wall add to the pleasing atmosphere. ✉*512 Yates St., Downtown* ☎*250/480–0883* ▭*MC, V* ⏲*No lunch. No dinner Mon. and Tues.*

$$–$$$ ★ ✕**Brasserie L'école.** The French country cooking shines at this informal Chinatown bistro and the historic room—once a schoolhouse for the Chinese community—evokes a timeless brasserie, from the white linens and patina-rich fir floors to the chalkboards above the slate bar listing the day's oyster and mussel options. Sean Brennan, one of the city's better-known chefs, works with local farmers and fishers to source the best seasonal, local, and organic ingredients. The menu changes daily but lists such classic bistro fare as duck confit, steak frites, and trout with chorizo and almonds. The wine list is primarily French and if you order two glasses they'll open any bottle in the house. ✉*1715 Government St., Downtown* ☎*250/475–6260* ▭*AE, MC, V* ⏲*Closed Sun. and Mon. No lunch.*

GREEK

¢–$ ✕ **Eugene's.** Locals flock to this cafeteria-style eatery near Trounce Alley for great cheap eats: souvlaki, in lamb, pork, chicken, and vegetarian versions, is the main event here, but the *spanakopita* (spinach pie), *kalamarakia* (deep-fried squid), and Greek salad are also worthy. Aegean-blue walls, big archways, and Hellenic travel posters add atmosphere to the big bustling room. ✉*1280 Broad St., Downtown* ☎*250/381–5456* *Reservations not accepted* *No credit cards* *No dinner Sun.* ✉*1990 Fort St., Oak Bay* ☎*250/592–7373* *Reservations not accepted* *No credit cards* *No dinner Sun.*

ITALIAN

$$–$$$$ ★ ✕ **Il Terrazzo.** A charming redbrick terrace edged with potted greenery and warmed by fireplaces and overhead heaters makes Il Terrazzo—tucked away off Waddington Alley near Market Square and not visible from the street—the locals' choice for romantic alfresco dining. The menu changes frequently, but starters might include a salad of shredded duck confit and baby spinach, or a dish of roasted artichoke and tiger prawns. Thin-crust pizzas and such traditional Northern Italian mains as Dijon-crusted rack of lamb and osso buco with wild mushrooms come piping hot from the restaurant's wood oven. ✉*555 Johnson St., off Waddington Alley (½ block east of Wharf St.), Downtown* ☎*250/361–0028* *AE, DC, MC, V* *No lunch Sun.*

$$–$$$ ✕ **Zambri's.** The downtown strip-mall setting might not impress, but inside is a lively trattoria warmed by terra-cotta tiles and wood tables. Lunch is busy and casual: order at the counter from a daily changing roster of pastas and hot sandwiches (such as the hot meatball or Italian sausage). Dinner brings table service and a menu of such hearty fare as tagliolini with crab ragù and grappa, and roasted pork loin with salsa pizzaiola and polenta. ✉*110–911 Yates St., Downtown* ☎*250/360–1171* *Reservations not accepted* *AE, MC, V* *Closed Sun. and Mon.*

SEAFOOD

$$$–$$$$ ✕ **Lure Seafood Restaurant and Bar.** Walls of windows embrace Inner Harbour views at the Delta Victoria Ocean Pointe Resort's flagship restaurant. Seafood-loving locals and hotel guests book windowside tables at sunset to watch the lights come on across the water: the large, comfortable, but bland room with upholstered chairs and beige walls doesn't even try to compete with the view. The food puts on a good show, though, with elaborate presentations of locally sourced fare. Sooke trout, wild salmon, and B.C. halibut top a menu that also encompasses Cowichan Valley duck and coriander-crusted lamb loin. ✉*45 Songhees Rd., Downtown* ☎*250/360–5873* *AE, D, DC, MC, V.*

$–$$ ✕ **Barb's Place.** Funky Barb's, a tin-roofed take-out shack, floats on the quay at Fisherman's Wharf, west of the Inner Harbour off St. Lawrence Street. Halibut, salmon, oysters, mussels, crab, burgers, and chowder are all prepared fresh on the premises. The picnic tables on the wharf provide a front-row view of interesting vessels, including a paddle wheeler, houseboats, and some vintage fishing boats, or you can carry your food to the grassy park nearby. Ferries sail to Fisherman's Wharf from the Inner Harbour. ✉*Fisherman's Wharf, St. Lawrence St., Downtown* ☎*250/384–6515* *AE, MC, V* *Closed Nov.–Feb.*

VEGETARIAN

$–$$ ✕ **Re-Bar Modern Food.** Bright and casual, this kid-friendly café in Bastion Square is *the* place for vegetarians in Victoria but don't worry, the almond burgers, enchiladas, decadent baked goodies, and big breakfasts keep omnivores happy, too. An extensive selection of teas and fresh juice shares space on the drinks list with espresso, microbrews, and B.C. wines. ✉ *50 Bastion Sq., Downtown* ☎ *250/361–9223* ▭ *AE, DC, MC, V* ⊙ *No dinner Sun.*

OAK BAY & ROCKLAND

CANADIAN

$$$ ★ ✕ **Paprika Bistro.** Local farmers and fishers and the owners' own garden provide most of the ingredients at this intimate neighborhood bistro where chef George Szasz, together with his wife, Linda, create seasonal menus. He combines his classical French training with some ideas from his Hungarian grandmother and the results might be Cortes Island mussels, a spot prawn bisque, and house-made charcuterie, followed by duck-leg confit with balsamic glaze, organic beef tenderloin with shallot confit, or just-caught local fish. Three small rooms with brocade booths and local art on paprika-and-lemon walls are warm, romantic, and informal. The same owners also run **Stage,** a small-plates and wine bar. ✉ *2524 Estevan Ave., Oak Bay & Rockland* ☎ *250/592–7424* ▭ *AE, MC, V* ⊙ *No lunch, closed Sun.* ✉ *1307 Gladstone Ave.* ☎ *250/388–4222* ▭ *AE, MC, V* ⊙ *No lunch, closed Sun.*

WHERE TO STAY

Victoria has a vast range of accommodation, with what seems like whole neighborhoods dedicated to hotels. Options range from city resorts and full-service business hotels to mid-priced tour-group haunts, family-friendly motels, and backpacker hostels, but the city is especially known for its lavish B&Bs in beautifully restored Victorian and Edwardian mansions.

Downtown hotels are clustered in three main areas: James Bay, on the south side of the Inner Harbour near the Parliament Buildings, is basically a residential and hotel neighborhood. Bordered by the waterfront and Beacon Hill Park, the area is quiet at night and handy for sightseeing by day. It is, however, thin on restaurants and a bit of a hike to the main shopping areas. Hotels in the downtown core, particularly along Government and Douglas streets, are right in the thick of shopping, dining, and nightlife, but do get more traffic noise.

Outside of downtown, Rockland and Oak Bay are lush and peaceful treelined residential districts; the mile or so walk into town is pleasant, but you won't want to do it every day.

DOWNTOWN

$$$$ **Abigail's Hotel.** A Tudor-style inn built in 1930, Abigail's is within walking distance of downtown. The guest rooms are attractively furnished in an English Arts and Crafts style. Down comforters, whirlpool tubs, and wood-burning fireplaces in many rooms add to the luxurious atmosphere, and the six large rooms in the Coach House building are especially lavish. A three-course breakfast is served at a communal table, at tables for two, or on the patio; beer, wine, and appetizers are served each evening in the library. A new spa treatment room adds to the pampering. ✉*906 McClure St., Downtown, V8V 3E7* ☎*250/388–5363 or 800/561–6565* 🖷*250/388–7787* 🌐*www.abigailshotel.com* *23 rooms* *In-room: DVD, Wi-Fi. In-hotel: no elevator, laundry service, concierge, public Internet, parking (no fee), some pets allowed, no-smoking rooms* 💳*AE, MC, V* 🍴*BP.*

$$$$ **The Fairmont Empress.** A hundred years old in 2008, this ivy-draped harborside château and city landmark has aged gracefully, with top-notch service and sympathetically restored Edwardian decor. The 176 different room configurations include standard and harbor-view rooms with 11-foot ceilings, crisp white duvets, and fresh floral drapes. Turret rooms with Jacuzzi tubs are a little-known romantic option. State-of-the-art gym equipment, pillow-top beds, Wi-Fi, and flat-screen TVs are all planned for 2008. The hotel is a tourist attraction, but a guests-only lobby separates hotel guests from the throng. ✉*721 Government St., Downtown, V8W 1W5* ☎*250/384–8111 or 800/257–7544* 🖷*250/381–5959* 🌐*www.fairmont.com/empress* *436 rooms, 41 suites* *In-room: no a/c (some), refrigerator, DVD (some), ethernet (some), Wi-Fi. In-hotel: 2 restaurants, room service, bar, pool, gym, spa, laundry service, concierge, executive floor, public Internet, parking (fee), some pets allowed, no-smoking rooms* 💳*AE, D, DC, MC, V.*

$$$$ ★ **The Oswego Hotel.** Victoria's hip quotient went up a notch with the 2007 opening of this chic all-suites hotel. Just in from the water in quiet but handy James Bay, the unassuming brick building is home to 80 sleek, modern suites. The look—black and white offset with soft neutrals, natural stone floors and countertops, and a wall of windows—is airy, modern, and comfortable with just a touch of West Coast. Full kitchens and balconies, many with sea views, encourage hanging out. The inviting lobby and terrace doubles as a casual bistro ($$). ✉*500 Oswego St., Downtown, V8V 5C1* ☎*250/294–7500 or 877/767–9346* 🖷*250/294–7509* 🌐*www.oswegovictoria.com* *16 studio, 49 one-bedroom suites, 15 two-bedroom suites* *In-room: no a/c, kitchen, ethernet, Wi-Fi. In-hotel: restaurant, bar, gym, laundry facilities, laundry service, public Internet, parking (fee), some pets allowed, no-smoking rooms* 💳*AE, MC, V* 🍴*CP.*

$$–$$$$ ★ **Beaconsfield Inn.** This 1905 registered historic building four blocks from the Inner Harbour is one of Victoria's most faithfully restored Edwardian mansions. Though the rooms and suites all have antique furniture, mahogany floors, stained-glass windows, Ralph Lauren fabrics, and period details, each also has a unique look; one room even includes an Edwardian wooden canopied tub. Three-course breakfasts and afternoon tea and sherry in the conservatory or around the library

fire complete the English country-manor experience. In-room spa services are a nice touch, too. ✉998 *Humboldt St., Downtown, V8V 2Z8* ☎*250/384–4044 or 888/884–4044* 📠*250/384–4052* 🌐*www.beaconsfieldinn.com* *5 rooms, 4 suites* *In-room: no a/c, no phone, no TV, Wi-Fi. In-hotel: no elevator, laundry service, parking (no fee), no kids under 10, no-smoking rooms* 💳*AE, MC, V* *BP.*

2

$$$–$$$$ ★ **Hotel Grand Pacific.** The city's best health club (with yoga classes, an ozone pool, squash courts, and state-of-the-art equipment) and a prime Inner Harbour location appeal to savvy business, government, and leisure regulars, including Seattleites stepping off the ferry across the street. Feng Shui design elements apply throughout, lending a calm energy to the gleaming marble lobby. Rooms are large and surprisingly quiet, with duvets, deep soaker tubs, floor-to-ceiling windows, and a muted, mainstream decor. Upper-floor rooms have views of the harbor, the Parliament Buildings, or distant mountains, which you can admire from your private covered balcony big enough to sit out on. Watch for local politicos plotting in the lounge. ✉*463 Belleville St., Downtown, V8V 1X3* ☎*250/386–0450 or 800/663–7550* 📠*250/380–4475* 🌐*www.hotelgrandpacific.com* *258 rooms, 46 suites* *In-room: safe, refrigerator, DVD (some), VCR (some), ethernet. In-hotel: 3 restaurants, room service, bar, pool, gym, spa, laundry service, concierge, public Internet, public Wi-Fi, parking (fee), some pets allowed, no-smoking rooms* 💳*AE, D, MC, V.*

$$$–$$$$ **Laurel Point Inn.** Set on a peninsula on the Inner Harbour's quiet south shore, this Asian-inspired 1980s-era hotel has harbor views from every room. Some of the public areas might look a bit tired but the sunny decks, Japanese garden, and parklike, harborside setting compensate. Rooms—especially in the Arthur Erickson–designed southern wing—are light and airy, with blonde wood and subtle Asian touches; all have balconies and some suites have large harbor-view decks. In-room spa services, free local calls, and free passes to the downtown Y are all nice touches. ✉*680 Montreal St., Downtown, V8V 1Z8* ☎*250/386–8721 or 800/663–7667* 📠*250/386–9547* 🌐*www.laurelpoint.com* *135 rooms, 65 suites* *In-room: safe, refrigerator, ethernet. In-hotel: restaurant, room service, bar, pool, laundry service, concierge, public Internet, parking (fee), some pets allowed, no-smoking rooms* 💳*AE, D, DC, MC, V.*

$$$–$$$$ **Spinnakers Guesthouse.** Two houses make up the accommodations at this B&B, run by the owner of the popular Spinnakers Gastro Brewpub. The four Garden Suites, each with a separate bed and living room, are the nicest—and priciest: surrounding an ivy-draped courtyard, each has a private entrance and is decorated with Asian antiques, Balinese teak butlers, and other objects gathered during the owner's world travels. Five rooms in the 1884 adults-only Heritage House are smaller (and less expensive) but nicely decorated with local art and English and Welsh antiques. Most of these rooms have fireplaces and double whirlpool tubs with rain showers. Either way, you'll have a breakfast basket delivered in the morning. A self-contained cottage with its own yard is planned for 2008. ✉*308 Catherine St., Downtown, V9A 3S8* ☎*250/386–2739 or 877/838–2739* 📠*250/384–3246* 🌐*www.spinnakers.com* *5 rooms,*

4 suites In-room: no a/c, kitchen (some), Wi-Fi. In-hotel: restaurant, room service, bar, no elevator, laundry service, parking (no fee), some pets allowed, no-smoking rooms AE, MC, V CP.

$$$ **Swans Suite Hotel.** This 1913 former warehouse in Victoria's old town is one of the city's most attractive boutique hotels. The studios and one- and two-bedroom suites, all with full kitchens, are roomy, comfortable, and stylish with rich earth tones, exposed beams, and pieces from the late owner's extensive art collection. Many of the larger units boast 11-foot ceilings, fireplaces, and loft bedrooms. Interior rooms have private courtyard-facing patios or balconies. The art-filled penthouse suite has a private roof-top hot tub. More art—and live music nightly—fills the brewpub on the main floor. *506 Pandora Ave., Downtown, V8W 1N6 250/361–3310 or 800/668–7926 250/361–3491 www.swanshotel.com 30 suites In-room: no a/c, kitchen, DVD, VCR, Wi-Fi. In-hotel: restaurant, room service, bar, laundry facilities, laundry service, public Wi-Fi, parking (fee), no-smoking rooms AE, D, DC, MC, V CP.*

$$–$$$ **Royal Scot Suite Hotel.** Large suites, great rates, a handy location, and friendly staff (some in kilts) keep families, seniors, and bus tours coming back to this well-run James Bay hotel—the games room, pool table, hot tub, laundry room, and even a small grocery store on-site make this an especially good choice. The decor is ordinary, but it's clean, freshly upholstered, and well maintained. The grounds, including a restaurant courtyard, are prettily landscaped with flower beds and hanging baskets, and a shuttle service saves the five-minute walk to the town center. *425 Quebec St., Downtown, V8V 1W7 250/388–5463 or 800/663–7515 250/388–5452 www.royalscot.com 30 rooms, 146 suites in-room: no a/c, safe, kitchen (some), refrigerator, VCR (some), ethernet. In hotel: restaurant, room service, bar, pool, gym, laundry facilities, laundry service, public Internet, parking (no fee), no-smoking rooms AE, D, DC, MC, V.*

¢ ★ **Ocean Island Backpackers Inn.** The backpacker grapevine is full of praise for this fun and friendly downtown hostel. Impeccably managed by a thought-of-everything owner, the historic warren of a building boasts 60 private rooms (three of which have private baths), several 6-bed dorms, secured entry, group daytrips, heaps of travel information, a shared kitchen, and, best of all, an evening snack and beer lounge hopping with planned events—twister tournament anyone? You can even borrow a guitar for open-mike night. **TIP→ Ask for a 3rd- or 4th-floor room if you want an early night.** Seniors and families mix well with the clean-cut young crowd, but ask too about the Ocean Island Suites ($), self-contained accommodations in nearby James Bay. *791 Pandora Ave., Downtown, V8W 1N9 250/385–1785 250/385–1780 www.oceanisland.com 9 6-bed dorms, 60 private rooms In-room: no a/c, no phone, refrigerator (some), no TV, Wi-Fi. In-hotel: bar, laundry facilities, public Internet, parking (fee), no-smoking rooms AE, MC, V.*

OAK BAY & ROCKLAND

$$$–$$$$ **Prior House Bed & Breakfast Inn.** Lush earth tones and brocade bed canopies, ocean-view balconies, wood-burning fireplaces, and down duvets are among the luxurious touches at this beautifully restored 1912 manor home where the Edwardian atmosphere doesn't preclude such modern comforts as large-screen TVs and air-jet tubs. The rooms are big—starting at 750 square feet—all have private balconies or patios, and service standards are top notch. Children and small pets are welcome in the lower-level Hobbit Garden Studios, which have private entrances and sleep four. Lavish breakfasts and afternoon tea are served at tables for two in the dining room; breakfast in bed is always an option. *620 St. Charles St., Rockland V8S 3N7 250/592–8847 or 877/924–3300 250/592–8223 www.priorhouse.com 3 rooms, 3 suites In-room: no a/c, refrigerator, DVD, VCR, ethernet. In-hotel: no elevator, laundry service, public Internet, parking (no fee), some pets allowed, no-smoking rooms MC, V BP.*

$$–$$$ ★ **Abbeymoore Manor Bed & Breakfast Inn.** This 1912 mansion has the wide verandas, dark wainscoting, and high ceilings of its era but the attitude is informal, from the helpful hosts to the free snacks and coffee on tap all day. Two modern, one-bedroom suites on the ground floor have kitchens while five upper-level rooms charm with such period details as claw-foot tubs or sleigh beds, and verandas or antique-tile fireplaces. The Penthouse Suite has a full kitchen and private entrance. Multicourse breakfasts are served family style or at tables for two in the sunroom or on the patio. *1470 Rockland Ave., Rockland V8S 1W2 250/370–1470 or 888/801–1811 www.abbeymoore.com 5 rooms, 3 suites In-room: no a/c, no phone (some), kitchen (some), DVD (some), VCR (some), no TV (some), Wi-Fi. In-hotel: no elevator, public Internet, parking (no fee), some pets allowed, no kids under 12, no-smoking rooms MC, V BP.*

$ **Craigmyle Guest House.** Affordable and historic, this four-story manor near Craigdarroch Castle has been a guest house since 1913. A large, welcoming common room is replete with Victoriana and original stained glass; a traditional English breakfast is served in the garden-view dining room. Rooms are cozy with floral bedspreads and wallpaper; all have private baths though in some cases the baths are across the hall. Two-room units and a guest kitchen appeal to families, and single rooms are offered at a single rate (C$65). A one-bedroom suite, remodeled in 2006, has modern furnishings, a jetted tub, and a rainforest shower; it's the only unit with a phone, TV, and kitchenette. *1037 Craigdarroch Rd., V8S 2A5 250/595–5411 or 888/595–5411 250/370–5276 www.BandBvictoria.com 16 rooms, 1 suite In-room: no a/c, no phone, no TV, Wi-Fi. In-hotel: no elevator, parking (no fee), no-smoking rooms AE, MC, V BP.*

NIGHTLIFE & THE ARTS

For entertainment listings, pick up a free copy of *Monday Magazine* (it comes out every Thursday) or see the listings online at http://web.bcnewsgroup.com/portals/monday/.

NIGHTLIFE

Victoria's nightlife is low-key and casual, with many wonderful pubs, but a limited choice of nightclubs. Several of Victoria's trendier restaurants double as lounges, offering cocktails and small plates well into the night.

BARS AND CLUBS

Bengal Lounge. Deep leather sofas and a Bengal tiger skin help to re-create the days of the British Raj at this iconic lounge in the Fairmont Empress Hotel. Martinis and a curry buffet are the draws through the week. On Friday and Saturday nights a jazz combo takes the stage. ⊠*721 Government St., Downtown* ☎*250/384–8111* *www.fairmont.com/empress.*

Hugo's Brewhouse. Non-pasteurized beers based on traditional Eastern European recipes, such as the signature Hefeweizen, as well as intriguing creations of the brewmaster, are the specialties at this chic and arty downtown brewpub. ⊠*625 Courtney St., Downtown* ☎*250/920–4846.*

Irish Times Pub. Stout on tap, live Celtic music nightly, and a menu of fish-and-chips, shepherd's pie, and Irish stew draw tourists and locals to this former bank building on Victoria's main shopping strip. ⊠*1200 Government St., Downtown* ☎*250/383–7775.*

The Red Jacket. A young crowd lines up to dance to whatever the DJ is spinning at this popular downtown dance club. ⊠*751 View St., Downtown* ☎*250/384–2582.*

Steamers. This downtown bar has live bands every night, ranging from blues to zydeco. ⊠*570 Yates St., Downtown* ☎*250/381–4340.*

Temple. DJs, martinis, and a trendy small-plates menu draw a fashionable late-evening crowd to this downtown restaurant, where a sandstone fireplace warms the cool modernist space. ⊠*525 Fort St, Downtown* ☎*250/383–2313.*

Vista 18. You can take in lofty views of the city at this lounge on the 18th floor of the Chateau Victoria Hotel. ⊠*740 Burdett St., Downtown* ☎*250/382–9258.*

THE ARTS

MUSIC

Summer in the Square. Free jazz, classical, and folk concerts; cultural events; and more run all summer at Centennial Square, next to City Hall at Pandora and Douglas streets. ☎*250/361–0388* *www.victoria.ca/2007summerinthesquare.*

Victoria Jazz Society. Watch for music events hosted by this group, which also organizes the annual JazzFest International in late June. ☎*250/388–4423* *www.vicjazz.bc.ca.*

Victoria Symphony. The Royal Theatre and the University Centre Auditorium are the venues for regular season concerts. Watch, too, for **Symphony Splash** on the first Sunday in August, when the Victoria Symphony plays a free concert from a barge in the Inner Harbour. *Sym-*

phony Information: ☎*250/385–6515.* **Royal Theatre** ✉*805 Broughton St., Downtown* ☎*250/386–6121.* **University Centre Auditorium** ✉*Finnerty Rd., University of Victoria Campus* ☎*250/721–8480.*

OPERA **Pacific Opera Victoria.** Three productions a year are performed at the Royal Theatre. ☎*250/385–0222* 🌐*www.pov.bc.ca.*

THEATER **The Belfry Theatre.** Housed in a former church, the Belfry has a resident company that specializes in contemporary Canadian dramas. ✉*1291 Gladstone Ave., Oak Bay and Rockland* ☎*250/385–6815* 🌐*www.belfry.bc.ca.*

Langham Court Theatre. One of Canada's oldest community theaters, the Langham Court stages the works of internationally known playwrights from September through June. ✉*805 Langham Ct., Oak Bay and Rockland* ☎*250/384–2142* 🌐*www.langhamcourttheatre.bc.ca.*

McPherson Playhouse. This downtown theater hosts touring theater and dance companies. ✉*3 Centennial Sq., Downtown* ☎*250/386–6121* 🌐*www.rmts.bc.ca.*

Theatre Inconnu. Victoria's oldest alternative theater company, housed in a venue across the street from the Belfry Theatre, offers a range of performances at affordable ticket prices. ✉*1923 Fernwood Rd., Oak Bay and Rockland* ☎*250/360–0234* 🌐*www.theatreinconnu.com.*

The Victoria Fringe Festival. Each August a vast menu of offbeat, original, and intriguing performances takes over several venues around town; it's the last stop on a nationwide circuit of fringe-theater events attracting performers—and fans—from around the world. ☎*250/507–2663* 🌐*www.victoriafringe.com.*

SPORTS & THE OUTDOORS

BEACHES

Cadboro Gyro Park. A sandy beach backed by a grassy park with a play area draws families to this sheltered bay, accessible via the Scenic Marine Drive. ✉*Off Cadboro Bay Rd., Oak Bay and Rockland.*

Cordova Bay. A long stretch of sand is the draw at this beach, just north of Mount Douglas Park on the Scenic Marine Drive. ✉*Off Cordova Bay Rd., Sidney and the Saanich Peninsula.*

Juan de Fuca Provincial Park. West of Sooke, this coastal wilderness park comprises a long string of beaches. Tossed with driftwood and backed with old-growth forest, these beaches are wild and beautiful with few services. French Beach and China Beach have campgrounds. French and Sombrio beaches attract surfers; Botanical Beach, near Port Renfrew, has a wonderful array of sea life at low tide. ✉*Off Hwy. 14, Sooke and the West Coast.*

BIKING

Victoria is a bike-friendly town with more bicycle commuters than any other city in Canada. Bike racks on city buses, bike lanes on downtown streets, and tolerant drivers all help, as do the city's three long-distance cycling routes, which mix car-free paths and low-traffic scenic routes.

BIKE ROUTES

Cowichan Valley Trail. A less-known rails-to-trails conversion is this 47-km (29-mi) uncrowded, unpaved path running from Shawnigan Lake to Cowichan Lake in the Cowichan Valley. ⊕*www.trailsbc.ca.*

The Seaside Touring Route. Starting at Victoria's Via Rail Station on Johnson Street, this 11-km (7-mi) route was designed specifically for visitors and takes in most of the city's key sights. Bright-yellow signs lead cyclists around the Inner Harbour, past Fisherman's Wharf, and along the Dallas Road waterfront to Beacon Hill Park. The route follows the seashore to Cordova Bay, where it connects with Victoria's other two long-distance routes: the Lochside and Galloping Goose Trails.

BIKE RENTALS AND TOURS

Cycle BC Rentals. Bicycles, scooters, and motorbikes are for rent at two downtown locations. ✉*747 Douglas St., Downtown* ☎*250/380–2453* ✉*950 Wharf St., Downtown* ☎*250/385–2453.*

GOLF

You can golf year-round in Victoria and southern Vancouver Island, and you almost have to, just to try all the courses.

Olympic View Golf Club. The distant peaks of the Olympic Mountains are the backdrop to this bucolic par-72 course, home to two waterfalls and 12 lakes. The first B.C. course played by Tiger Woods, it's about 20 minutes west of downtown Victoria in the suburb of Colwood. ✉*643 Latoria Rd., The West Shore and the Malahat* ☎*250/474–3673* ⊕*www.olympicviewgolf.com.*

HIKING & WALKING

It's not surprising that Victoria hosts a Walking Festival each spring. It's one of the most pedestrian-friendly cities in North America. Waterfront pathways make it possible to stroll virtually all the way around Victoria's waterfront.

Island Adventure Tours. This company offers guided day hikes in East Sooke Regional Park and Juan de Fuca Marine Park, including hotel pick-up in Victoria and a picnic lunch. They also offer equipment and transport for self-guided multi-day hikes along the Juan de Fuca Marine Trail. ☎*250/812–7103 or 866/812–7103* ⊕*www.islandadventuretours.com.*

★ **Juan de Fuca Marine Trail.** This tough 47-km (30-mi) coastal hike begins at China Beach, near the village of Jordan River, about 48 km (29 mi) west of Victoria. There are three other trailheads, each with a parking lot, at Sombrio Beach, Parkinson Creek, and Botanical Beach (which is 5 km [3 mi] southeast of Port Renfrew), allowing hikers to tackle the trail in day hike sections. ✉*Off Hwy. 14, between Jordan River (southeast end) and Port Renfrew (northwest end)* ☎*800/689–9025 camping reservations* ⊕*www.env.gov.bc.ca/bcparks.*

KAYAKING

The Upper Harbour and the Gorge, the waterways just north of the Inner Harbour, are popular boating spots.

Island Adventure Tours. Based at Sidney's Van Isle Marina, this company offers half- and full-day kayak tours of the Gulf Islands National Park. They also rent kayaks and offer lessons, and will pick you up at your hotel in Victoria or Sidney. ☎*250/812–7103* or *866/812–7103* 🌐*www.islandadventuretours.com*.

SHOPPING

Shopping in Victoria is easy: virtually everything can be found in the downtown area on or near Government Street stretching north from the Fairmont Empress hotel. Victoria stores specializing in English imports are plentiful, though Canadian-made goods are usually a better buy.

SHOPPING DISTRICTS & MALLS

Antique Row. Fort Street between Blanshard and Cook streets is home to dozens of antiques, curio, and collectibles shops.

Chinatown. Exotic fruits and vegetables, toys, wicker fans, fabric slippers, and other Chinese imports fill the shops and the baskets set up in front of them along Fisgard Street. Fan Tan Alley, a narrow lane off Fisgard street, has more nouveau-hippy goods, with a Nepalese import shop and a record store tucked in among its tiny storefronts.

Lower Johnson Street. This row of candy-color Victorian shop-fronts between Government and Store streets is Victoria's hub for independent fashion-designer boutiques. Storefronts—some closet-size—are filled with local designers' wares, funky boutiques, and no fewer than three shops selling ecologically friendly clothes of hemp and organic cotton. ✉*Johnson St. between Government and Store Sts., Downtown.*

Market Square. During the late 19th century, this three-level square, built like an old courtyard, originally provided everything a sailor, miner, or lumberjack could want. It's lined with independent shops selling toys, imports, gifts, souvenirs, jewelry, local art, and even homemade dog treats. ✉*560 Johnson St., Downtown* ☎*250/386–2441*.

Victoria Bay Centre. Downtown Victoria's main department store and mall has about 100 boutiques and restaurants. ✉*1 Victoria Bay Centre, at Government and Fort Sts., Downtown* ☎*250/952–5680*.

SPECIALTY STORES

Artisan Wine Shop. This offshoot of Okanagan winery Mission Hill Family Estate replicates a visit to the winery with a video show and tasting bar. The focus is Okanagan wine, but staff are knowledgeable about Vancouver Island producers as well. ✉*1007 Government St.* ☎*250/384–9994*.

Cowichan Trading Co., Ltd. First Nations jewelry, art, moccasins, and Cowichan sweaters are the focus at this long-established outlet. ✉*1328 Government St., Downtown* ☎*250/383–0321*.

Irish Linen Stores. Since 1917 this tiny shop has kept Victorians in fine linen, lace, and hand-embroidered items. ✉*1019 Government St., Downtown* ☎*250/383–6812*.

Munro's Books. This beautifully restored 1909 building houses one of Canada's prettiest bookstores. ✉*1108 Government St., Downtown* ☎*250/382–2464*.

Murchie's. You can choose from more than 40 varieties of tea, to sip here or take home, plus blended coffees, tarts, and cakes. ✉*1110 Government St., Downtown* ☎*250/383–3112.*

STREET MARKETS

Victorians seem to relish any excuse to head outdoors, which may explain the recent boom in outdoor crafts, farmers', and other open-air markets around town.

Bastion Square Public Market. Crafts vendors and entertainers congregate in this historic square throughout the summer. ✉*Bastion Square, off Government St., Downtown* ☎*250/885–1387* 🌐*www.bastionsquare.ca.*

James Bay Market. Organic food, local produce, crafts, and live music draw shoppers to this summer Saturday market just south of the Inner Harbour. ✉*Superior and Menzies Sts., Downtown* ☎*250/381–5323* 🌐*www.jamesbaymarket.com.*

Inner Harbour Night Market. Local handmade arts and crafts feature at this harbor-side night market, held Friday and Saturday evenings in summer. ✉*Ship Point Pier, Downtown* ☎*250/413–6828* 🌐*www.victoriaharbour.org.*

SIDE TRIPS FROM VICTORIA

A few more days in the area give you time to explore farther afield. Sooke and the Southwest Coast, the Cowichan Valley, or one of the Gulf Islands can make an easy day trip from Victoria, though any of them can warrant a weekend or longer for more serious exploration. These three regions around Victoria can be connected, so you don't have to retrace your steps.

From the Cowichan Valley, BC Ferries sail every hour or so from Crofton, 20 minutes north of Duncan, to Vesuvius, on Salt Spring Island. Ferries also sail from Fulford, at the south end of Salt Spring, to Sidney, on the Saanich Peninsula just north of Victoria. Another BC Ferries route connects Brentwood Bay on the Saanich Peninsula with Mill Bay in the Cowichan Valley.

SOOKE

28 km (17 mi) west of Victoria on Hwy. 14.

The village of Sooke, on the shore of Juan de Fuca Strait about a 30-minute drive west of Victoria, has two claims to fame: it's home to Sooke Harbour House, one of Canada's best-known country inns, and it's the last stop for gas and supplies before heading out to the beaches and hiking trails of the island's wild and scenic southwest coast.

Stop for information at the **Sooke Region Museum and Visitor Information Centre.** Watch for the red-and-white lighthouse lamp at the first traffic light as you arrive from Victoria. It sits in front of the Visitor Information Centre, which is also home to a small museum displaying local

First Nations and pioneer artifacts. ✉ *2070 Phillips Rd., off Hwy. 14* ☎ *250/642–6351* ⏲ *May–Oct., daily 9–5; Nov.–Apr., Tues.–Sun. 9–5.*

★ Extending along the shore from Jordan River to Port Renfrew, **Juan de Fuca Provincial Park** takes in several beaches, including China Beach, which has a campground; Sombrio Beach, a popular surfing spot; and Botanical Beach, with its amazing tidal pools. The **Juan de Fuca Marine Trail** is a tough 47-km (30-mi) hike running along the shore from China Beach, west of Jordan River, to Port Renfrew. Several trailheads along the way—at Sombrio Beach, Parkinson Creek, and Botanical Beach—allow day hikers to walk small stretches of it. ✉ *Off Hwy. 14, between Jordan River (southeast end) and Port Renfrew (northwest end)* ☎ *800/689–9025 camping reservations* 🌐 *www.env.gov.bc.ca/bcparks for park information, www.discovercamping.ca for camping reservations* 🎟 *C$3 per car per day.*

WHERE TO STAY & EAT

$$$ ★ ✕ **Markus' Wharfside Restaurant.** Two art-filled rooms, one with a fireplace, and a small patio overlook Sooke Harbour from this former fisherman's cottage. The European-trained chef-owner makes the most of the local wild seafood and organic produce, with such made-from-scratch dishes as grilled scallops with cherry tomato, cucumber, and mint salsa; grilled lamb sirloin with peppered balsamic glaze; and the signature Tuscan-style seafood soup. ✉ *1831 Maple Ave. S* ☎ *250/642–3596* ▭ *MC, V* ⏲ *Closed Sun. and Mon. No lunch.*

$$$$ Fodor's Choice ★ ✕🏨 **Sooke Harbour House.** Art, food, and gardens work together beautifully at one of Canada's best-loved country inns. Guest rooms, public spaces, and even the outdoors are beautifully decorated with pieces from the owners' vast art collection. The seaside organic garden produces hundreds of herbs, vegetables, and edible flowers destined for the kitchen, and the relaxed, ocean-view dining room is the stage for some of the country's most innovative meals. Nightly four-course menus rely almost entirely on local provisions, and the 15,000-bottle wine cellar is among the country's best. Rooms in the 1929 ocean-front inn, each with a fireplace and most with Japanese soaking tubs on private ocean-view decks, are art-filled, individually themed, and exquisitely comfortable in an informal country-house way. All the romantic requisites, from in-room spa services to breakfast in bed, are offered. TVs and DVDs are available on request. Nonguests can enjoy some of this splendor, too: garden tours, at 10:30 each morning, are open to everyone, as are C$15 picnic lunches (call before 10 AM to order), which you can enjoy on the ocean-front deck or on a quiet beach nearby. ✉ *1528 Whiffen Spit Rd., Sooke V0S 1N0* ☎ *250/642–3421 or 800/889–9688* 📠 *250/642–6988* 🌐 *www.sookeharbourhouse.com* 🛏 *28 rooms* 👍 *In-room: no a/c, refrigerator, no TV, Wi-Fi. In-hotel: restaurant, room service, bar, spa, bicycles, laundry service, concierge, public Internet, parking (no fee), some pets allowed, no-smoking rooms* ▭ *AE, DC, MC, V* ⏲ *Call for weekday closures Dec.–Feb.* 🍽 *BP.*

DUNCAN

60 km (37 mi) north of Victoria on Trans-Canada Hwy., or Hwy. 1.

Duncan, the largest town in the valley, is nicknamed the City of Totems for the more than 40 totem poles that dot the small community. Between May and September, free walking tours of the totems leave hourly from the south end of the train station building on Canada Avenue (contact the Duncan Business Improvement Area Society, at 250/715–1700, for more information). On Saturdays, the city square at the end of Craig Street hosts a farmers market, where you can browse for local produce, crafts, and specialty foods.

The **Cowichan Valley Museum** has local historic artifacts in a still-functioning 1912 train station. ✉ *130 Canada Ave.* ☎ *250/746–6612,* 🌐 *www.cowichanvalleymuseum.bc.ca* 🎫 *C$2* ⏲ *June–Sept., Mon.–Sat. 10–4; Oct.–May, Wed.–Fri. 11–4, Sat. 1–4.*

★ The **Quw'utsun' Cultural and Conference Centre** occupies a parklike setting on 6 acres of shady riverbank. This village of cedar longhouses is one of Canada's leading First Nations cultural and educational facilities. A 20-minute video in a long-house–style theater introduces the history of the Cowichan people, B.C.'s largest aboriginal group, and a 30-minute walking tour reveals the legends behind the site's dozen totem poles. Crafts demonstrations and dance performances run during summer, and the many indigenous plants on-site are labeled with information about their traditional uses. The gift shop stocks, among other things, the hand-knit Cowichan sweaters that the area is known for and the Riverwalk Café offers a rare opportunity to sample First Nations fare. ✉ *200 Cowichan Way* ☎ *250/746–8119 or 877/746–8119* 🌐 *www.quwutsun.ca* 🎫 *Mar.–May C$11, June–Sept. C$13, Oct.–Feb. C$7* ⏲ *June–mid-Oct., weekdays 10–5, weekends 10–4 (tours hourly 11–4); mid-Oct.–May, hrs vary (call ahead).*

Kids and train enthusiasts adore riding the rails at the **British Columbia Forest Discovery Centre,** a 100-acre outdoor museum just north of Duncan. Pulled by a 1910 steam locomotive, a three-carriage train toots through the woods and over a trestle bridge across a lake, stopping at a picnic site and playground on the way. Forestry related exhibits around the site include a 1930s-era logging camp, historic logging equipment and vehicles, and indoor exhibits about the modern science of forestry. Interpretive trails through the forest lead to ancient trees, some dating back more than 500 years. During July and August, the steam train runs every half hour, daily, and guided walking tours of the site are also available. In May, June, and September, the train may be replaced with a gas locomotive and sometimes doesn't run at all, so check ahead. ✉ *2892 Drinkwater Rd., Trans-Canada Hwy.* ☎ *250/715–1113 or 866/715–1113* 🌐 *www.bcforestmuseum.com* 🎫 *C$11; C$14 including train ride* ⏲ *Sept., Apr., and May, Thurs.–Mon. 10–4:30; June–Aug., daily 10–4:30.*

At **Pacific Northwest Raptors,** a conservation center about 10 minutes northeast of Duncan, you can learn about the ecology of raptors, and see owls, hawks, falcons, and eagles in natural settings. Free-flying bird demonstrations are held each day (call for times); you can also join a trainer on a brief falconry course. ✉*1877 Herd Rd.* ☎*250/746–0372* 🌐*www.pnwraptors.com* 🎫*C$9* ⏲*Apr.–Oct., daily 11–4:30.*

CHEMAINUS

25 km (16 mi) north of Duncan.

Chemainus is known for the bold epic murals that decorate its townscape, as well as for its beautifully restored Victorian homes. Once dependent on the lumber industry, the small community began to revitalize itself in the early 1980s when its mill closed down. Since then the town has brought in international artists to paint a total of 38 murals depicting local historical events around town.

WHERE TO STAY & EAT

$$ ★ ✕**Riverwalk Café.** This little riverside café, part of Duncan's Quw'utsun' Cultural and Conference Centre, offers a rare opportunity to try traditional B.C. First Nations fare. All meals start with warm fried bread with blackberry jam and salmon spread. From there, the menu offers both the familiar (salads, burgers, and fish-and-chips made with salmon) and the more unusual: venison in blackberry-mint sauce, elk escalope on baby spinach greens, or a slow-cooked stew of surf clams, salmon, halibut, and vegetables. For a treat, try the Me'Hwulp, a Salish afternoon tea for two, with candied salmon, blue-crab cakes, blackberry tarts, and more—all served on a cedar platter. ✉*200 Cowichan Way, Duncan* ☎*250/746–4370* 💳*MC, V* ⏲*No dinner. Closed Sun. and Oct.–May.*

THE GULF ISLANDS

Of the hundreds of islands sprinkled across Georgia Strait between Vancouver Island and the mainland, the most popular and accessible are Galiano, Mayne, Pender, Saturna, and Salt Spring. A temperate climate, white-shell beaches, rolling pastures, and forests are common to all, but each island has a unique flavor. Though rustic, they're not undiscovered. Writers, artists, and craftspeople as well as weekend cottagers and retirees from Vancouver and Victoria take full advantage of them. Make hotel reservations for summer stays. Ferry service from Vancouver Island is frequent and reservations aren't accepted. If you're bringing a car from the B.C. mainland, though, ferry reservations are highly recommended; for busier sailings, they're required.

The Outer Gulf Islands. Besides Salt Spring, four other islands—Galiano, Mayne, Pender, and Saturna—have ferry service from Swartz Bay, near Victoria, and Tsawwassen, near Vancouver. Marine life, Douglas fir and arbutus forests, shell and pebble beaches, tiny artists' studios, and funky cafés characterize the islands, whose tiny populations are made up largely of craftspeople, retirees, and small-scale organic farmers. None has a town, but food and accommodation are available on all four islands. Mayne, Saturna, and Pender host sections of the Gulf Islands National Park Reserve (☎250/654–4000 🌐www.pc.gc.ca/pn-np/bc/gulf/), Canada's newest national park. Ferry service from Swartz Bay is frequent but sometimes you can't visit more than one island in a day, necessitating overnight stays. It's also possible to visit Mayne and Galiano from Salt Spring via water taxi, which is also the school boat.

SALT SPRING ISLAND

28 nautical mi from Swartz Bay (32 km [20 mi] north of Victoria), 22 nautical mi from Tsawwassen (39 km [24 mi] south of Vancouver).

With its wealth of studios, galleries, restaurants, and B&Bs, Salt Spring is the most developed, and most visited, of the Southern Gulf Islands. It boasts the only town in the archipelago (Ganges) and, although it can get busy on summer weekends, has not yet lost its relaxed rural feel. Outside of Ganges, the rolling landscape is home to small organic farms, wineries, forested hills, quiet white-shell beaches, and several swimming lakes.

What really sets Salt Spring apart is its status as a "little arts town." Island residents include hundreds of artists, writers, craftspeople, and musicians, many of whom open their studios to visitors.

To visit local artists in their studios, pick up a free **Studio Tour** map from the Visitor Information Centre in Ganges.

At the south end of Salt Spring Island, where the ferries from Victoria arrive, is the tiny village of **Fulford,** which has a restaurant, a café, and several offbeat boutiques.

Ferries from Crofton, on Vancouver Island, arrive on the west side of Salt Spring Island at **Vesuvius,** an even smaller community with a restaurant, a tiny grocery store–cum-café, a swimming beach, and crafts studios.

Ganges, a seaside village about 30 km (18 mi) from the Fulford Ferry Terminal, is the main commercial center for Salt Spring Island's 11,000 residents. It has about a dozen art galleries and several restaurants, as well as the essentials: ATMs, gas stations, groceries, and a liquor store.

★ Locals and visitors flock to Ganges on summer Saturdays for the **Salt Spring Island Saturday Market** (☎*250/537–4448* 🌐*www.saltspringmarket.com*), held in Centennial Park every Saturday April through October. Everything sold at this colorful outdoor market is made or grown on the island; the array and quality of crafts, food, and produce is dazzling.

Near the center of Salt Spring Island, the summit of **Mt. Maxwell Provincial Park** (✉*Mt. Maxwell Rd., off Fulford–Ganges Rd.*) has spectacular views of south Salt Spring, Vancouver Island, and other Gulf Islands. The last portion of the drive is steep, winding, and unpaved.

★ **Ruckle Provincial Park** (✉*Beaver Point Rd.* ☎*250/539–2115 or 877/559–2115* 🌐*www.bcparks.ca*) is the site of an 1872 homestead and extensive fields that are still being farmed. Several small sandy beaches and 8 km (5 mi) of trails winding through forests and along the coast make this one of the islands' most attractive parks. Walk-in campsites on a grassy, seaside field, and eight drive-in campsites in the woods, are available on a first-come, first-served basis.

WHERE TO STAY & EAT

$$$–$$$$ ★ ✕ **House Piccolo.** Piccolo Lyytikainen, the Finnish-born chef-owner of this tiny restaurant, serves beautifully prepared and presented European cuisine. Creations include Scandinavian-influenced dishes such as B.C. venison with a rowan- and juniper-berry demi-glace and charbroiled fillet of beef with Gorgonzola sauce. For dessert the vodka-moistened lingonberry crepes are hard to resist. The 250-item wine list includes many hard-to-find vintages. The indoor tables are cozy and candle-lighted; the outdoor patio is a pleasant summer dining spot. ✉ *108 Hereford Ave., Ganges* ☎ *250/537–1844* ▭ *MC, V* ⊙ *No lunch; call ahead for winter hrs.*

$$–$$$ ✕ **Calvin's Bistro.** Seafood—whether in the form of a wild salmon fillet, baby-shrimp linguine, or good old fish-and-chips—tops the menu at this comfortable marina-view bistro in Ganges. A long list of lunch-time sandwiches and burgers includes local lamb, wild salmon, and even wiener schnitzel. Inside booths are cozy, while the big patio has great harbor views. Friendly Swiss owners account for the homemade European desserts and welcoming service. ✉ *133 Lower Ganges Rd., Ganges* ☎ *250/538–5551* ▭ *MC, V* ⊙ *Closed Mon., No lunch Sun. No dinner Sun. Sept.–Apr.*

$–$$$ ✕ **Auntie Pesto's Café & Delicatessen.** Fresh, local ingredients, house-made bread, and Mediterranean flavors keep regulars well fed at this family-run village center spot. From breakfast omelets, enjoyed with fruit salad, good coffee and a stack of British newspapers, to lunches of homemade soup and grilled sandwiches (the Johnny B will feed a hungry teen, though some of the croissant versions are smallish), through to Mediterranean-themed dinners of, say, venison, duck, or big plates of pasta—the bustling interior and marina-view deck stay busy all day. ✉ *2104–115 Fulford Ganges Rd., Ganges* ☎ *250/537–4181* ▭ *MC, V* ⊙ *Closed Sun. No dinner Sat.*

$$$$ Fodor's Choice ★ ✕🏨 **Hastings House Country House Hotel.** The centerpiece of this 22-acre seaside estate—with its gardens, meadows, and harbor views—is a 1939 country house, built in the style of an 11th-century Sussex manor. Guest quarters, which are in the manor, in renovated historic outbuildings, and in a newer addition overlooking Ganges Harbour, are decorated in an English-country style, with antiques, locally crafted woodwork, and fireplaces or woodstoves. The Post, a stand-alone two-room cottage, is a honeymoon favorite; the secluded 3-bedroom Churchill Cottage has a kitchen and a private driveway. Four-course and à la carte dinners in the manor house are open to the public ($$$$; smart casual dress is expected). The excellent cuisine includes local seafood and herbs and produce from the inn's gardens. The two-room spa specializes in massages. A novel activity is a chance to go crab fishing and learn how to catch Dungeness crab. Pros: Wonderful food, top-notch service, historic ambience. Cons: No pool, some rooms overlook a pub next

door, rates are high. ✉*160 Upper Ganges Rd., V8K 2S2* ☎*250/537–2362 or 800/661–9255* 🖷*250/537–5333* 🌐*www.hastingshouse.com* *3 rooms, 14 suites, 1 guesthouse* *In-room: no a/c (some), kitchen (some), refrigerator, no TV, ethernet (some), Wi-Fi (some). In-hotel: restaurant, bar, spa, bicycles, no elevator, public Internet, public Wi-Fi, parking (no fee), no kids under 16, no-smoking rooms* *AE, MC, V* *Closed mid-Nov.–mid-Mar.* *CP.*

GALIANO ISLAND

Galiano, with its 26-km-long (16-mi-long), unbroken eastern shore and cove-dotted western coast is arguably the prettiest of these islands. It's certainly the best for hiking and biking, with miles of trails through the Douglas fir and Garry oak forest. Mt. Galiano and Bodega Ridge are classic walks, with far-reaching views to the mainland.

★ **Montague Harbour Provincial Marine Park** (✉*Montague Park Rd., off Montague Rd.* ☎*800/689–9025 camping reservations* 🌐*www.discovercamping.ca*) has walk-in and drive-in campsites and a long shell beach famed for its sunset views.

You can rent a kayak or moped or take a boat tour at **Montague Harbour Marina** (✉*Montague Park Rd., just east of park* ☎*250/539–5733 marina, 250/539–2442 kayak rentals, 250/539–3443 moped rentals, 250/539–2278 boat tours*).

Harbour Grill (☎*250/539–5733*) at the marina serves burgers, salads, and seafood on its heated outdoor deck May through September.

NEED A BREAK?

The Hummingbird Inn Pub (✉*47 Sturdies Bay Rd.* ☎*250/539–5472*) is a friendly local hangout, with live music on summer weekends. Also in summer, the pub runs a free shuttle bus to the Montague Harbour Marina and campsite.

MAYNE ISLAND

The smallest of the Southern Gulf Islands, Mayne also has the most visible history. The buildings of Miners Bay, the island's tiny commercial center, date to the 1850s, when Mayne was a stopover for prospectors en route to the gold fields.

Plumper Pass Lockup (✉*433 Fernhill Rd.* ☎*No phone*) was built in 1896 as a jail but is now a minuscule museum (open July–Labor Day, hours vary, free) chronicling the island's history.

You can also stop for a drink on the deck at the **Springwater Lodge** (✉*400 Fernhill Rd., Miners Bay* ☎*250/539–5521*), one of the province's oldest hotels. Active Pass Lighthouse, at the end of Georgina Point Road, is part of **Georgina Point Heritage Park.** Built in 1885, it still signals ships into the busy waterway. The grassy grounds are great for picnicking.

Bennett Bay Park, part of the Gulf Islands National Park Reserve, has walking trails and one of the island's most scenic beaches.

A 45-minute hike up **Mt. Parke** leads to the island's highest point and a stunning view of the mainland and other Gulf Islands.

On Saturdays, between July and mid-October, check out the **Farmers Market** outside the Miners Bay Agricultural Hall. Open 10 to 1, it sells produce and crafts while local musicians entertain shoppers.

Built entirely by volunteers, the 1-acre **Japanese Garden** at Dinner Bay Park honors the island's early Japanese settlers. It's about 1 km (½ mi) south of the Village Bay ferry terminal. Admission is free.

PENDER ISLAND

Just a few miles north of the U.S. border, Pender is actually two islands: North Pender and South Pender, divided by a canal and linked by a one-lane bridge. Most of the population of about 2,000 cluster on North Pender, whereas South Pender is largely forested and undeveloped.

★ Both North Pender and South Pender host sections of the **Gulf Islands National Park Reserve** (☎*250/654–4000* 🌐*www.pc.gc.ca/pn-np/bc/gulf/*). On South Pender a steep trail leads to the 244-meter (800-foot) summit of **Mount Norman,** with its expansive ocean and island views. Trails start at Ainslie Road, Canal Road, and the Beaumont section of the park. Even outside the park, the Penders are blessed with beaches, boasting more than 30 public beach-access points.

The small pebble beach at **Gowlland Point Park,** at the end of Gowlland Point Road on South Pender, is one of the prettiest on the islands, with views across to Washington State.

The sandy beach at **Mortimer Spit** is a sheltered spot for swimming and kayaking; it's near the bridge linking the two islands.

There's no town on either island, but you can find groceries and other basics at North Pender's Driftwood Centre. Watch for small crafts shops, studios, and galleries throughout the islands.

Saturna Island. With just 300 residents, remote Saturna Island is taken up largely by a section of the Gulf Islands National Park Reserve and is a prime spot for hiking, kayaking, and beachcombing.

Said to be the only island whose population is campaigning for less ferry service, Saturna usually takes two ferries to reach. It has no bank machine, pharmacy, or campsite, but does have a pub, a general store, and winery—Saturna Island Family Estate Winery—where between May and October, you can lunch on a terrace overlooking the vineyards and the sea. ✉*8 Quarry Trail* ☎*250/539–3521 or 877/918–3388.*

NEED A BREAK?

You can refuel before catching the ferry at the Stand (✉*Otter Bay Ferry terminal, end of Otter Bay Rd.* ☎*250/629–3292*), a rustic take-out shack at the Otter Bay ferry terminal. The burgers—whether beef, venison, oyster, or veggie—are enormous, messy, and delicious.

WHERE TO STAY & EAT

$$$$ **Galiano Oceanfront Inn & Spa.** Lawns, gardens, and waterfalls reach down to the water's edge from this cedar-sided West Coast–style inn. Rooms and suites have a chic West Coast feel with wood-burning fireplaces, balconies or patios, jetted or soaker tubs, and sweeping views of Active Pass. Ten one-bedroom suites, due to open in 2008, will each have a kitchen and private outdoor tub for two. Unique to the inn are the hidden Murphy-style massage tables in each room. The oceanfront restaurant ($$–$$$) serves locally caught seafood and organic produce with selections from an award-winning 250-label wine list; entrées include sandalwood-smoked wild coho salmon and masala-crusted rack of lamb. In summer you can dine alfresco or enjoy a drink at Galiano's only seaside lounge. Hemp-seed rubs and wild-blueberry-smoothie wraps are among the lavish spa's innovative treatments; a fitness room and yoga studio in the garden are planned for 2008. Pros: Adult-oriented, wonderful spa, great views. Cons: Construction should be completed by summer 2008, but delays are possible. ✉ *134 Madrona Dr., Galiano Island V0N 1P0* ☎ *250/539–3388 or 877/530–3939* 📠 *250/539–3338* 🌐 *www.galianoinn.com* *10 rooms, 10 suites* *In-room: no a/c, kitchens (some), refrigerator, DVD, Wi-Fi. In-hotel: restaurant, room service, bar, spa, no elevator, laundry service, public Wi-Fi, no-smoking rooms* 💳 *MC, V* *BP.*

$$$$ **Poets Cove Resort & Spa.** One of the Gulf Islands' most luxurious developments fills a secluded cove on South Pender. A nautical-theme lodge and a scattering of two- and three-bedroom cottages overlook a marina and a forest-framed cove. All units have fireplaces, duvets, and heated bathroom floors, and most have decks or balconies with stunning ocean views. The restaurant ($$$–$$$$) serves top-notch Pacific Northwest fare, and the lounge offers high-end pub meals. A waterfall tumbles over a steam grotto outside the lavish spa. Activities include whale-watching, vineyard tours, deep-sea fishing, yoga classes, kayaking, and scuba diving. A water taxi from Sidney, near Victoria, will pick up car-free guests. Pros: A full range of activities, children's programs (a rarity in B.C.), no need for a car. Cons: Pricey, busy, boaters as well as guests use many of the facilities. ✉ *9801 Spalding Rd., V0N 2M3* ☎ *250/629–2100 or 888/512–7638* 📠 *250/629–2105* 🌐 *www.poetscove.com* *22 rooms, 15 cottages, 9 villas* *In-room: no a/c, kitchen (some), refrigerator, DVD, ethernet. In-hotel: restaurant, room service, bar, tennis courts, pools, gym, spa, diving, water sports, bicycles, concierge, no elevator, children's programs (ages 5–14), laundry facilities, public Internet, public Wi-Fi, some pets allowed, no-smoking rooms* 💳 *AE, MC, V.*

$$$–$$$$ **Oceanwood Country Inn.** From the afternoon tea to the cozy library, wealth of sitting rooms, English-country furnishings, and quiet disregard for modern technology, this Tudor-style seaside house has all the makings of an old-fashioned English country house. Fireplaces, air-jet tubs, and French doors leading to private ocean-view decks are available in several rooms, and some boast Japanese soaking tubs. The waterfront restaurant ($$$$) serves four-course table d'hôte dinners of outstanding regional cuisine. The menu changes daily, but highlights

include slow-roasted wild salmon with Dijon caper sauce, and rosemary-smoked leg of lamb. Phones, guest refrigerators, and satellite TV are available, but are not standard in the rooms. Pros: Lots of common rooms, quiet adults-only vibe. Cons: Few activities. ✉ *630 Dinner Bay Rd., Mayne Island V0N 2J0* ☎ *250/539–5074 or 866/539–5074* 🖷 *250/539–3002* 🌐 *www.oceanwood.com* *12 rooms* *In-room: no a/c, no phone, no TV. In-hotel: restaurant, bar, bicycles, no elevator, no kids under 16, no-smoking rooms* 💳 *MC, V* ⊗ *Closed Nov.–mid-Mar.* 🍽 *BP.*

VICTORIA ESSENTIALS

To research prices, get advice from other travelers, and book travel arrangements, visit www.fodors.com.

TRANSPORTATION

BY AIR

Victoria International Airport is 25 km (15 mi) north of downtown Victoria, off Highway 17. It's served by Horizon, Pacific Coastal, Skywest Airlines, and WestJet airlines. Air Canada and its regional service, Air Canada Jazz, provide frequent airport-to-airport service from Vancouver to Victoria. Flights take about 25 minutes.

You can also fly directly to the Inner Harbour in downtown Victoria. Both West Coast Air and Harbour Air provide daily floatplane service to downtown Victoria from both downtown Vancouver and Vancouver Airport. West Coast Air also flies from Whistler to downtown Victoria between June and September. Kenmore Air operates direct daily floatplane service year round from Seattle to Victoria's Inner Harbour. Helijet has helicopter service from downtown Vancouver and Vancouver International Airport to downtown Victoria. The Vancouver heliport is near Vancouver's SeaBus terminal.

To drive from the airport to downtown, take Highway 17 south. A taxi ride costs about C$40, plus tip. The Airporter bus service drops off passengers at most major hotels. The fare is C$15 one-way. BC Transit bus number 70 runs just six times a day from the airport to downtown Victoria. The one-way fare is C$3.

Contacts and Local Airlines **Airporter** (☎ *250/386–2525 or 877/386–2525* 🌐 *www.victoriaairporter.com*). **BC Transit** (☎ *250/382–6161* 🌐 *www.bctransit.com*). **Harbour Air** (☎ *604/274–1277 or 800/665–0212* 🌐 *www.harbour-air.com*). **Helijet** (☎ *800/665–4354* 🌐 *www.helijet.com*). **Horizon Air** (☎ *800/547–9308* 🌐 *www.horizonair.com*). **Kenmore Air** (☎ *425/486–1257 or 800/543–9595* 🌐 *www.kenmoreair.com*). **Pacific Coastal Airlines** (☎ *250/655–6411 or 800/663–2872* 🌐 *www.pacific-coastal.com*). **Victoria International Airport** (☎ *250/953–7500* 🌐 *www.victoriaairport.com*). **West Coast Air** (☎ *604/606–6888 or 800/347–2222* 🌐 *www.westcoastair.com*).

BY BOAT & FERRY

FROM THE B.C. MAINLAND BC Ferries operates daily service between Tsawwassen, about an hour south of Vancouver, and Swartz Bay, at the end of Highway 17 (the Patricia Bay Highway), about 30 minutes north of downtown Victoria. Sailing time is about 1½ hours. Peak-season weekend fares are C$12 per adult passenger and C$42 per vehicle each way (including taxes and a fuel surcharge). Bicycles are carried for C$2.50. Lower rates apply midweek and in the off-season. Vehicle reservations on Vancouver–Victoria and Nanaimo routes are optional and cost C$15 to C$17.50 in addition to the fare. Reservations, which can be made by phone or online, are recommended if you're traveling with a car on a summer weekend. Reservations are not necessary for foot passengers or cyclists.

BC Transit buses meet the ferries at both ends, but if you're traveling without a car, the easiest option is to take a Pacific Coach Lines bus.

Another option from Vancouver is to travel on the *Ocean Magic II*. Operated by Prince of Whales, this trip combines four hours of whale watching with a trip between Vancouver and Victoria. The 74-passenger boat leaves Waterfront Station in downtown Vancouver daily at 8:15 AM and returns from Victoria at 3:30 PM. Options include returning by floatplane, staying in Victoria and returning on a later date, or adding a trip to the Butchart Gardens. One-way fares start at C$119.

FROM WASHINGTON STATE Black Ball Transport operates the *MV Coho,* a car ferry, daily year-round between Port Angeles, Washington and Victoria's Inner Habour. The car and passenger fare is US$44; bikes are carried for US$5.50.

The *Victoria Clipper* runs daily year-round passenger-only service between downtown Seattle and downtown Victoria. Sailings take about 3 hours, and the one-way fare from mid-May to late September is US$79; bicycles are carried for an extra US$10.

Between late May and late September, the Victoria Express provides daily passenger-only service between Port Angeles, Washington, and downtown Victoria. Sailings cost US$12.50 (US$5.50 for bikes) and take an hour.

Washington State Ferries runs a car ferry daily between mid-March and late December from Anacortes, Washington, to Sidney (some runs make stops at different San Juan Islands), about 30 km (18 mi) north of Victoria. Bikes are welcome and the sailing takes about three hours. One-way high-season fares are US$53.70 for a vehicle and driver.

Between May and September, Victoria San Juan Cruises offer narrated foot-passenger day trips from Bellingham, Washington, to Victoria with a salmon barbecue dinner on the return trip; overnight packages are also an option. One-way high-season fare is US$54.50.

WITHIN VICTORIA Victoria Harbour Ferries serves the Inner Harbour, with stops that include the Fairmont Empress, Chinatown, Point Ellice House, the Delta Victoria Ocean Pointe Resort, and Fisherman's Wharf.

TO AND AROUND THE COWICHAN VALLEY AND THE GULF ISLANDS BC Ferries sails several times a day from Swartz Bay, about 30 minutes north of downtown Victoria, to Salt Spring, Pender, Mayne, Galiano and Saturna islands. Sailings to Salt Spring take 30 minutes. Sailings to the other islands take from 25 minutes to 2 hours, depending on the destination and number of stops. Reservations are not accepted on these routes. You can also sail to three or four different islands directly from Swartz Bay.

BC Ferries also sails to the Southern Gulf Islands (Galiano, Mayne, Pender, Saturna, and Salt Spring) from Tsawwassen, about an hour south of Vancouver. Vehicle reservations, at no extra charge, are recommended and are required on some sailings on these routes.

Boat & Ferry Information **BC Ferries** (☎ *250/386-3431, 888/223-3779 in B.C.* 🌐 *www.bcferries.com*). **Black Ball Transport** (☎ *250/386-2202 or 360/457-4491* 🌐 *www.ferrytovictoria.com*). **Gulf Islands Water Taxi** (☎ *250/537-2510* 🌐 *www.saltspring.com/watertaxi*). *Queen of de Nile* (☎ *Salt Spring Marina: 250/537-5810*). **Prince of Whales** (☎ *888/383-4884* 🌐 *www.princeofwhales.com*). *Victoria Clipper* (☎ *206/448-5000 in Seattle, 250/382-8100 in Victoria, 800/888-2535 elsewhere* 🌐 *www.clippervacations.com/*). **Victoria Express** (☎ *360/452-8088 or 250/361-9144* 🌐 *www.victoriaexpress.com*). **Victoria Harbour Ferries** (☎ *250/708-0201* 🌐 *www.victoriaharbourferry.com*). **Victoria San Juan Cruises** (☎ *360/738-8099 or 800/443-4552* 🌐 *www.whales.com*). **Washington State Ferries** (☎ *206/464-6400 or 888/808-7977* 🌐 *www.wsdot.wa.gov/ferries*).

BY BUS

Pacific Coach Lines operates frequent daily service between downtown Vancouver and downtown Victoria. The bus travels on the ferry, so transfers are seamless. BC Transit serves Victoria and the surrounding areas, including the Swartz Bay ferry terminal, Victoria International Airport, Butchart Gardens, Sidney, and Sooke.

Bus Information **BC Transit** (☎ *Victoria: 250/382-6161. Duncan Transit: 250/746-9899* 🌐 *www.bctransit.com*). **Pacific Coach Lines** (☎ *604/662-8074 in Vancouver, 250/385-4411 in Victoria, 800/661-1725 elsewhere* 🌐 *www.pacificcoach.com*).

TAXIS

Taxi rates in Victoria are C$2.85 for pickup and C$1.64 per km (½ mi). For a cab in Victoria or surrounding area, call Bluebird Taxi, Victoria Taxi, or Yellow Cabs. Salt Spring, Mayne and Galiano also have cab companies.

Contacts **Bluebird Taxi** (☎ *250/382-2222*). **Midas Taxi Company (Mayne Island)** (☎ *250/539-3132 or 250/539-0181*). **Salt Spring Silver Shadow Taxi** (☎ *250/537-3030*). **Taxi Galiano** (☎ *250/539-0202*). **Victoria Taxi** (☎ *250/383-7111*). **Yellow Cabs** (☎ *250/381-2222*).

TOURS

AIR TOURS You can see Victoria and parts of Vancouver Island from the air with Harbour Air Seaplanes. Twenty-minute flight-seeing tours start at C$99 per person.

Fees & Schedules **Harbour Air Seaplanes** (☎ *250/385-9131 or 800/665-0212* 🌐 *www.harbourair.com*).

BOAT TOURS The best way to see the sights of the Inner Harbour, Upper Harbour, and beyond is by Victoria Harbour Ferries; 45- and 50-minute tours cost C$20.

Fees & Schedules **Victoria Harbour Ferries** (☎ *250/708–0201* 🌐 *www.victoria-harbourferry.com*).

BUS TOURS Gray Line West's open-top double-decker buses visit the city center, Chinatown, Antique Row, Oak Bay, and Beacon Hill Park; a combination tour includes the Butchart Gardens. The company also runs a lower-cost shuttle service to Butchart Gardens and Butterfly Gardens.

Fees & Schedules **Gray Line West** (☎ *250/388–6539 or 800/663–8390* 🌐 *www.graylinewest.com*).

VISITOR INFORMATION

Tourist Information **Tourism Cowichan** (☎ *250/746–1099 or 888/303–3337* 🌐 *www.visit.cowichan.net*). **Galiano Island Travel InfoCentre** (☎ *250/539–2233* 🌐 *www.galianoisland.com*). **Hello BC** (☎ *800/435–5622* 🌐 *www.hellobc.com*). **Salt Spring Island Visitor Information Centre** (☎ *250/537–5252 or 866/216–2936* 🌐 *www.saltspringtoday.com*). **Sooke Region Museum and Visitor InfoCentre** (☎ *250/642–6351 or 866/888–4748* 🌐 *www.sooke.museum.bc.ca/srm*). **Tourism Vancouver Island** (☎ *888/655–3483* 🌐 *www.SeeTheIslands.com*). **Tourism Victoria Visitor InfoCentre** (✉ *812 Wharf St.* ☎ *250/953–2033 or 800/663–3883* 🌐 *www.tourismvictoria.com*).

ELSEWHERE ON VANCOUVER ISLAND

Exploring central and northern Vancouver Island will afford you the opportunity to see the quiet seaside towns along the Oceanside Route, such as Parksville and Qualicum Beach; Strathcona Provincial Park; and, for those who love the great outdoors, the rugged wilderness of Campbell River and Quadra Island. At the very top of Vancouver Island is Telegraph Cove, one of the best places in the province to see orca whales, and Port Hardy, a gateway town where you can catch a ferry to British Columbia's vast North Coast

A powerful ocean, stunning wildlife, and one of Canada's premiere national parks, all framed by two rustic but likeable towns, characterize the Pacific Rim region. This stretch of coast on the open Pacific is wild and often inhospitable. And this, of course, is exactly what makes it all the more attractive to surfers drawn to the crashing waves and travelers who come for winter storm watching. Other attractions include the old-growth forests, pristine beaches, and the chance to see whales, bears, eagles, river otters, and other wildlife in a natural setting.

The nearby harbor towns of Ucluelet and Tofino are chock-a-block with character (and characters), funky shops, services, and eateries—and, in Tofino, fine-dining restaurants. Indeed, the burgeoning culinary culture on Vancouver Island definitely extends to the Pacific Rim region. Pacific Rim National Park Reserve (the "reserve" is added because the park is still subject to native land claims) stretches between Ucluelet and Tofino.

PARKSVILLE

38 km (24 mi) northwest of Nanaimo, 154 km (95 mi) north of Victoria.

The resort and retirement town of Parksville marks the start of the Oceanside Route, or Highway 19A (also called the Old Island Highway), which winds along the coast to Campbell River, through woods and past sandy beaches and small seaside settlements. If you're in a hurry, you can travel north on the faster, newer Inland Island Highway (Highway 19).

Forest trails lead to thundering waterfalls at **Englishman River Falls Provincial Park** (✉ *Errington Rd., Exit 51 off Hwy. 19* ☎ *800/689–9025 camping reservations* 🌐 *www.discovercamping.ca*), 13 km (8 mi) southwest of Parksville.

At **Rathtrevor Beach Provincial Park** (✉ *Off Hwy. 19A* ☎ *800/689–9025 camping reservations* 🌐 *www.discovercamping.ca*), 2 km (1 mi) south of Parksville, a 5-km-long (3-mi-long) sandy beach meets the warmest ocean water in British Columbia.

WHERE TO STAY

$–$$$$ ★ **Tigh-Na-Mara Seaside Spa Resort & Conference Centre.** A 2,500-square-foot mineral pool, complete with waterfall and grottolike setting, is the centerpiece of this beachside spa resort. Twenty-two forested seaside acres also include a long, sandy beach, and loads of kids' activities. Rooms in the three waterside lodges all have fireplaces and balconies. Several one- and two-bedroom cottages in a forest setting, and studio cottages near the spa, don't have water views but do have kitchens and fireplaces. ✉ *1155 Resort Dr., off Hwy. 19A, V9P 2E5* ☎ *250/248–2072 or 800/663–7373* 🌐 *www.tigh-na-mara.com* *88 rooms, 67 suites, 37 cottages* *In-room: No a/c, kitchens, Wi-Fi. In-hotel: Restaurant, bar, tennis court, pool, gym, spa, beachfront, no elevator, children's programs (ages 5–16), laundry facilities, concierge (summer only), public Internet, public Wi-Fi, airport shuttle, some pets allowed, no-smoking rooms* *AE, DC, MC, V.*

SPORTS & THE OUTDOORS

With six ocean- and mountain-view courses in the area, Parksville is a major year-round golf destination.

Fairwinds Golf Club (✉ *3730 Fairwinds Dr., Nanoose Bay* ☎ *250/468–7666 or 888/781–2777* 🌐 *www.fairwinds.bc.ca*) is a par-71, 18-hole course designed by Les Furber. **Morningstar Golf Course** (✉ *525 Lowry's Rd.* ☎ *250/248–2244 or 800/567–1320* 🌐 *www.morningstar.bc.ca*) is a par-72, 18-hole course, also designed by Les Furber.

EN ROUTE

The peaks and watersheds inland from Qualicum Beach and Parksville create an environment so distinct the area has been declared a U.N.E.S.C.O Biosphere Reserve (the Mount Arrowsmith Biosphere Reserve). Two provincial parks, both along Highway 4 en route to Port Alberni and the west coast, provide a taste of this unique ecosystem.

At **Little Qualicum Falls Provincial Park** (☎ *800/689–9025 camping reservations*), 15 km (9 mi) west of Qualicum Beach, Cameron Lake empties into Little Qualicum River over a series of waterfalls, and hiking trails lace the woods. The campground is popular with families.

At **Cathedral Grove** in MacMillan Provincial Park, 20 km (12 mi) west of Qualicum Beach, walking trails lead past Douglas fir trees and western red cedars, some as many as 800 years old. Their remarkable height creates a spiritual effect, as though you're gazing at a cathedral ceiling.

EN ROUTE

Highway 4A from Parksville will take you to the offbeat village of Coombs, known for its antique and curio markets, and the goats grazing on the grass-covered roof of the Old Country Market. The **World Parrot Refuge** (✉ *2116 Alberni Hwy., Hwy. 4A* ☎ *250/248–5194* 🌐 *www.worldparrotrefuge.org*) is home to more than 600 free-flying birds. Hundreds of free-flying butterflies, as well as tropical birds and insects, and Canada's largest indoor collection of orchids are on display at **Butterfly World & Gardens** (✉ *1080 Winchester Rd., off Hwy. 4A* ☎ *250/248–7026* 🌐 *www.nature-world.com*). The site is open daily, March to October.

At the **North Island Wildlife Recovery Centre** (✉ *1240 Leffler Rd.* ☎ *250/248–8543* 🌐 *www.niwra.org*) in nearby Errington, you can visit eagles, owls, hawks, deer, and other injured and orphaned wildlife being cared for at the center.

QUALICUM BEACH

10 km (6 mi) north of Parksville.

Qualicum Beach's long stretch of sand has attracted vacationers for more than a century. The pedestrian-friendly village, on a hill above the sea, is full of interesting shops and cafés. From Qualicum Beach, Highway 4 travels to the island's west coast.

At **Milner Gardens and Woodland** (✉ *2179 W. Island Hwy., Hwy. 19A* ☎ *250/752–6153* 🌐 *www.milnergardens.org*) a 1930s tea plantation–style house, where a traditional tea is served each afternoon, and 10 acres of gardens, surrounded by woodlands, are set on a bluff above the sea. The gardens are open Easter to late April and Labor Day to mid-October, Thursday–Sunday 10–5 (last entry at 4). May to Labor Day, daily 10–5 (last entry at 4). Admission is C$10

Guided and self-guided spelunking tours for all levels are conducted year-round at **Horne Lake Caves Provincial Park** (☎ *250/757–8687 information, 250/248–7829 tour reservations* 🌐 *www.hornelake.com*). The park turnoff is about 11 km (7 mi) north of Qualicum Beach off Highway 19 or 19A. From the turnoff, the park is another 13 km (8 mi) along a gravel road.

WHERE TO STAY & EAT

$$–$$$ ✕ **The Beach House Café.** European, Asian, and Canadian dishes highlight this casual, kid-friendly seaside restaurant, where spaetzle and schnitzel share menu space with Thai satay and West Coast bouillabaisse. A local

favorite, though, is roast duckling in blackberry sauce. Sandwiches, burgers, pasta, and pizza fill the lunch menu. Both the beachfront deck and the two-tiered interior have ocean views. ✉ *2775 W. Island Hwy., Hwy. 19A* ☎ *250/752–9626* ▭ *MC, V* ⊗ *Closed Jan.*

$$–$$$ **Ships Point Inn.** Six theme rooms, from the colonial Bombay room to the Mediterranean Rafael room, fill this century-old home 20 km (12 mi) north of Qualicum Bay. Canopy beds, antiques, and lush color schemes make each room unique; seaside gardens include a waterfront walkway and a hot tub in an ocean-view gazebo. The kitchen, deck, sitting room, and several guest rooms also take in sweeping ocean and mountain views. ✉ *7584 Ships Point Rd., Station 39-C27, Fanny Bay, V0R 1W0* ☎ *250/335–1004 or 877/742–1004* ⊕ *www.shipspointinn.com* *6 rooms* *In-room: no a/c, no phone, no TV. In-hotel: Wi-Fi, beachfront, no elevator, laundry service, parking (no fee), no kids under 12, no smoking* ▭ *AE, MC, V* *BP.*

UCLUELET

139 km (87 mi) west of Qualicum Beach, 295 km (183 mi) northwest of Victoria.

Ucluelet, which in the Nuu-chah-nulth First Nations language means "people with a safe landing place," is, along with Bamfield and Tofino, one of the towns serving the Pacific Rim National Park Reserve. A long-time resource industry town, Ucluelet is less visited than Tofino and has a more relaxed pace. Despite a growing number of crafts shops and B&Bs, it still feels more like a fishing village than an ecotourism retreat.

As in Tofino, whale-watching is an important draw, though visitors also come in the off-season to watch the dramatic winter storms that pound the coast here. It's also a regional base for sport fishing and kayaking to the Broken Group Islands.

Various charter companies take boats to greet the 20,000 grey whales that pass close to Ucluelet on their migration to the Bering Sea every March and April. Some grey whales remain in the area year-round, too.

The **Pacific Rim Whale Festival** (⊕ *www.pacificrimwhalefestival.org*) is an event (here and in Tofino) in celebration of the whales, each spring.

Ucluelet is also the starting point for the **Wild Pacific Trail** (⊕ *www.wildpacifictrail.com*), a hiking path that winds along the coast and through the rain forest. Eventually it will link Ucluelet to the Pacific Rim National Park Reserve.

WHERE TO STAY & EAT

$–$$ ✕ **Matterson House.** In a tiny 1931 cottage with seven tables and an outdoor deck in summer, husband-and-wife team Sandy and Jennifer Clark serve up generous portions of seafood, burgers, pasta, and filling standards such as prime rib and veal cutlets. It's simple food, prepared well with fresh local ingredients; everything, including soups, desserts, and the wonderful bread, is homemade. The wine list has local island wines worth trying. ✉*1682 Peninsula Rd.* ☎*250/726–2200* ▭*MC, V.*

$$$–$$$$ ★ **Tauca Lea by the Sea.** This all-suites, family-friendly, waterfront resort of blue-stained cedar lodges combines a variety of facilities with a respect for the natural surroundings. Handcrafted furniture and terra-cotta tiles decorate the spacious one- and two-bedroom suites, which also have fireplaces and ocean-view decks; many with private jetted tubs. The spa provides rain-forest-inspired pampering treatments, and the marina-view Boat Basin restaurant ($$$–$$$$) serves contemporary Pacific Rim fare with fresh, local ingredients—some of them straight from the fishing boats and the resort's own garden. ✉*1971 Harbour Crescent, Box 286, V0R 3A0* ☎*250/726–4625 or 800/979–9303* 🖷*250/726–4663* 🌐*www.taucalearesort.com* *72 suites* *In-room: no a/c, kitchen, dial-up, Wi-Fi. In-hotel: bar, concierge, laundry facilities, no-smoking rooms, some pets allowed, no elevator* ▭*AE, DC, MC, V* *CP.*

$$$–$$$$ **A Snug Harbour Inn.** Set on a cliff above the Pacific, this beach-front couples-oriented B&B has some of the most dramatic views anywhere. The rooms, all with fireplaces, private balconies or decks, and whirlpool baths, are decorated in a highly individual style. The Lighthouse room winds up three levels for great views, the Valhalla has a nautical theme, and the Atlantis room is the largest, with dramatic First Nations art and a Jacuzzi tub for two. Eagles nest nearby, and a staircase leads down to a rocky beach. Two rooms, one of which is wheelchair accessible, in a separate cottage have forest views. ✉*460 Marine Dr., Box 318, V0R 3A0* ☎*250/726–2686 or 888/936–5222* 🖷*250/726–2685* 🌐*www.awesomeview.com* *6 rooms* *In-room: no a/c, phone, refrigerator (some), DVD, TV, Wi-Fi. In-hotel: bicycles, no-smoking rooms, some pets allowed, no kids under 16, no elevator* ▭*MC, V* *BP.*

$–$$$ **Canadian Princess Resort.** You can book a cabin on this 1932 steam-powered survey ship moored at Ucluelet's marina. Though hardly opulent, the staterooms are comfortable, with one to four berths and shared bathrooms. Most guests come here to fish or whale-watch—the resort is home to the area's largest charter company. This place has an ideal downtown Ucluelet location and an attractive laid-back atmosphere, but take note: large fishing cruisers sometimes fire up their engines at quite an early hour. ✉*1943 Peninsula Rd., Box 939, V0R 3A0* ☎*250/726–7771 or 800/663–7090* 🖷*250/726–7121* 🌐*www.canadianprincess.com* *46 shoreside rooms, 27 shipboard cabins without bath, 1 suite* *In-room: no a/c, no phone, no TV (some). In-hotel: restaurant, bar, airport shuttle, parking (no fee), some pets allowed, no-smoking rooms* ▭*AE, DC, MC, V* *Closed mid-Sept.–mid-Mar.*

SPORTS & THE OUTDOORS

ECOTOURS **Long Beach Nature.** A great way to learn about the area's natural history and ecosystems is on a guided walk or hike with this ecotour group. Led by Bill McIntyre, former chief naturalist at Pacific Rim National Park Reserve, and his team of naturalist/biologists, half- and full-day outings range from easy to challenging and include hikes through old-growth forest, beach and headlands, and storm watching during fall and winter. Following safe routes and cliff-top trails, you can experience the fury of winter storms and relive the experience of shipwrecked mariners along this shoreline dubbed "the Graveyard of the Pacific." ☎*250/656–1236* 🌐*www.oceansedge.bc.ca.*

FISHING ★ The **Canadian Princess Resort** has 10 comfortable fishing and whale-watching cruisers with heated cabins and bathrooms. Fishing trips go out several times a day in pursuit of salmon, halibut, and various bottom fish. The relatively inexpensive charters appeal to individuals, groups, and families. ✉*1943 Peninsula Rd.* ☎*250/726–7771 or 800/663–7090* 🌐*www.canadianprincess.com.*

GOLFING **Long Beach Golf Course,** a 9-hole championship course, with 18-hole mini course, is located within the Clayoquot Biosphere Reserve between Tofino and Ucluelet on Highway 4. ✉*1850 Pacific Rim Highway* ☎*250/725–3332* 🌐*www.longbeachgolfcourse.com.*

KAYAKING Experienced guides with **Majestic Ocean Kayaking** can take you out to explore the clear waters surrounding the Broken Group Islands and Barkley Sound, as well as Clayoquot Sound and Deer Group Islands. Trips range from three hours to six days of kayaking and camping. A whale-watching trip for experienced paddlers goes to outside waters. ✉*1167 Helen Rd.* ☎*250/726–2868 or 800/889–7644* 🌐*www.ocean-kayaking.com.*

WHALE-WATCHING **Jamie's Whaling Station** offers guaranteed sightings, so if you don't see a whale on your first trip, you can take another tour at no charge. You can book a whole range of adventures here including kayaking and hot-spring tours. They're open March 15–September 30. ✉*168 Fraser La., on waterfront promenade* ☎*250/726–7444 or 877/726–7444* 🌐*www.jamies.com.*

TOFINO

42 km (26 mi) northwest of Ucluelet, 337 km (209 mi) northwest of Victoria.

The end of the road makes a great stage—and Tofino is certainly that. On a narrow peninsula just beyond the north end of the Pacific Rim National Park Reserve, this is as far west as you can go on Vancouver Island by paved road. One look at the pounding Pacific surf at Long Beach or Chesterman Beach and the old-growth forest along the shoreline convinces many people that they've reached not just the end of the road but the end of the Earth.

Tofino's 1,400 or so permanent residents host about a million visitors every year, but they've made what could have been a tourist trap into a funky little town with several art galleries, good restaurants, and plenty of opportunity to get out to the surrounding wilds. Although many outdoor activities are confined to spring through fall, surfing continues year-round. November through February is devoted to storm watching (most enjoyable from the comfort of a cozy waterfront lodge).

For side trips, boats and floatplanes provide access to the surrounding roadless wilderness. The most popular day trip is to **Hot**

Springs Cove, where you can soak in natural rock pools. On **Meares Island,** an easy 20-minute boardwalk trail leads to trees up to 1,600 years old. The remote sand beaches of Vargas Island are popular in warm weather.

> **WORD OF MOUTH**
>
> "If you are outdoor people I agree strongly with the recommendations on Tofino. Stay at least three or four nights... do as many trails in Pacific Rim National Park as you can. They are all SPECTACULAR." —jimmoi

At the **Tofino Botanical Gardens** trails wind through displays of indigenous plant life. The 12-acre waterfront site about 2 km (1 mi) south of the village on the Pacific Rim Highway is open from 9 AM to dusk daily, and the C$10 admission is good for three days. ✉ *1084 Pacific Rim Hwy.* ☎ *250/725–1220* 🌐 *www.tofinobotanicalgardens.com.*

WHERE TO STAY & EAT

$$$–$$$$ ★ ✕ **The Wickaninnish Restaurant.** Not to be confused with the restaurant at the nearby Wickaninnish Inn, this spectacular wood-beam room is right smack on Long Beach, within Pacific Rim National Park Reserve. Commercial signage is, by park regulation, hugely constrained. All you'll see is the word "restaurant," alongside "Wickaninnish Interpretive Centre," on a green park sign on the Pacific Rim Highway, about 11 km (7 mi) north of Ucluelet; turn onto Wick Road and drive to the ocean. Although the locally caught salmon, halibut, and crab are very good (meat and vegetarian options are available, too), the setting is reason enough to make the trip. The wine list includes a nice selection of B.C. ice wines. Dress is casual. ✉ *Wick Rd., Long Beach, Pacific Rim National Park Reserve* ☎ *250/726–7706* 💳 *DC, MC, AE, V* ⏲ *Closed Oct.–Feb.*

$$–$$$ ★ ✕ **RainCoast Café.** This small and casual yet chic village-center restaurant has a stellar reputation for its Asian take on local seafood and vegetarian options. Sustainably harvested or organic entrées include pan-seared halibut from the coastal waters and duck from B.C.'s Fraser Valley Lower Mainland. ✉ *101–120 4th St.* ☎ *250/725–2215* 💳 *AE, MC, V* ⏲ *No lunch.*

$$–$$$ Fodor'sChoice ★ ✕ **The Schooner on Second.** An institution in downtown Tofino, the main-floor dining room is comfortable and casually upscale. The long-time owner oversees a menu of well-crafted Pacific Rim flavors. The seafood dishes change frequently, but try, if it's available, the halibut Bawden Bay: a halibut fillet stuffed with Brie, crab, pine nuts, and shrimp in an apple-peppercorn brandy sauce. The Schooner is also popular with locals and tourists alike for its hearty breakfasts and lunchtime sandwiches, burgers, and pastas, and the summer patio is a plus. Recently opened, The Schooner Upstairs is both a fine-dining restaurant and a lounge with exceptional views toward Meares Island. ✉ *331 Campbell St.* ☎ *250/725–3444* 💳 *AE, MC, V.*

$$–$$$ Fodor'sChoice ★ ✕ **Sobo.** The name, short for "sophisticated bohemian," sums up the style here: a classically trained chef offering casual fare influenced by international street food. Tapas might be halibut cheeks or sushi rice pockets, forest-mushroom risotto bullets, or carrot-ginger soup. Mains

range from cedar-plank wild salmon to mushroom enchiladas. This popular eatery recently relocated from the Tofino Botanical Gardens into town. There is talk that they'll close Monday or Tuesday in winter, so call first. There's a deli counter, too. ✉ *311 Neil St.* ☎ *250/725–2341* ▭ *AE, MC, V* ⊗ *No dinner Oct.–May.*

2

$$$$ Fodor's Choice ★ **The Wickaninnish Inn.** On a rocky promontory above Chesterman Beach, with open ocean on three sides and old-growth forest as a backdrop, this cedar-sided inn has exceptional First Nations and coastal art, including massive hand-adzed cedar doors inset with abalone shell. Every room in this Relais & Châteaux property has an ocean or beach view, balcony, oversize soaker tub, and fireplace; the Ancient Cedars Spa offers hot-stone massages, Hawaiian treatments, and couples massages in oceanfront treatment rooms; yoga classes run daily. The glass-enclosed Pointe Restaurant ($$$$) has views of the crashing surf and is renowned for its Pacific Northwest cuisine; chef de cuisine Tim Cuff makes the most of such local delicacies as oysters, wild mushrooms, Dungeness crab, Pacific salmon, and regionally sourced farm produce. ✉ *Osprey La., at Chesterman Beach, mailing address: Box 250, Tofino V0R 2Z0* ☎ *250/725–3100 or 800/333–4604* ℻ *250/725–3110* 🌐 *www.wickinn.com* *64 rooms, 11 suites* *In-room: safe, kitchen (some), DVD, ethernet. In-hotel: restaurant, room service, bar, gym, spa, beachfront, concierge, laundry service, public Wi-Fi, no-smoking rooms, some pets allowed* ▭ *AE, DC, MC, V.*

$$$–$$$$ ★ **Long Beach Lodge Resort.** Dramatic First Nations art, a tall granite fireplace, and expansive views of the crashing surf define the striking great room at this luxury lodge, which overlooks the long stretch of sand at Cox Bay. Throughout the lodge and cabins are handcrafted furniture, exposed fir beams, soothing earth tones, and such artful details as handwoven kelp amenities baskets. Accommodations include comfortable lodge rooms and two-bedroom cottages. The chef uses fresh, local, organic ingredients whenever possible for the lunch and dinner menus ($$$$), for the shared plates served in the great room, and even for the picnic lunches. As at other area lodges, winter storms are a major draw (winter rates can be one-third those of summer). Rain wear is provided. ✉ *1441 Pacific Rim Hwy., Box 897, V0R 2Z0* ☎ *250/725–2442 or 877/844–7873* ℻ *250/725–2402* 🌐 *www.longbeachlodgeresort.com* *41 rooms, 20 cottages* *In-room: no a/c, kitchen (some), DVD, Wi-Fi. In-hotel: restaurant, bar, gym, some pets allowed, no-smoking rooms* ▭ *AE, MC, V* *CP.*

$$–$$$$ ★ **Pacific Sands Beach Resort.** On 45 beautiful acres along curvaceous Cox Bay, this long-time resort, with beach villas, a lodge, and waterfront suites and studios, is popular with couples, families, and groups. Cox Bay draws surfers, and the beach and adjacent forest are a walker's and nature-lover's paradise. In winter this is prime storm-watching territory; in summer, resort-planned activities for children may include beach badminton, kite building, and scavenger hunts. There is no on-site dining but the Long Beach Lodge restaurant is a five-minute walk down the beach. Beachfront villas have fully equipped kitchens, fireplaces, and private decks. Raingear, and bookings for regional adventure outings, are available year-round. ✉ *1421 Pacific*

Rim Hwy., Tofino ☎250/725–3322 or 800/565–2322 📠250/725–3155 🌐www.pacificsands.com 22 villas, 57 suites In-room: no a/c, no phone (some), kitchen, DVD, ethernet (some). In-hotel: beachfront, water sports, bicycles, no elevator, children's programs (ages 7 and up), laundry facilities, public Internet, parking (no fee), some pets allowed, no-smoking rooms ▭*AE, DC, MC, V.*

$–$$$ **Inn at Tough City.** Vintage furnishings, a prime location, and First Nations art make this harborside inn funky if a bit cluttered. The name is derived from Tofino's old nickname, from the days before roads, when life here was pretty rough: it certainly isn't anymore. Guest rooms have bold colors, stained-glass windows, hardwood floors, antiques, decks or balconies, and down duvets. Several have views over Tofino Harbour and Clayoquot Sound, fireplaces, and soaking tubs. The hotel's water-view restaurant, Tough City Sushi ($$–$$$), uses fresh local seafood. ✉*350 Main St., Box 8, V0R 2Z0* ☎*250/725–2021 or 877/725–2021* 📠*250/725–2088* 🌐*www.toughcity.com 8 rooms In-room: no a/c. In-hotel: restaurant, bar, no-smoking rooms* ▭*AE, MC, V.*

$$–$$$ ★ **Middle Beach Lodge.** This longtime favorite, set on a bluff over a mile of private beach, has several options: adults-only phone- and TV-free rooms in the Lodge at the Beach; ocean-view rooms and suites, most with kitchenettes, at the Headlands; and self-contained cabins, some with hot tubs, suitable for families. The decor throughout defines West Coast rustic elegance, with recycled timbers, woodsy colors, and a smattering of antiques. Each lodge has an expansive common room with a floor-to-ceiling stone fireplace and far-reaching ocean views. It's truly secluded, with an almost exclusive beach that's ideal for adults seeking peace and privacy, and for families seeking spacious cabins at reasonable prices. ✉*400 MacKenzie Beach Rd., Box 100, V0R 2Z0* ☎*250/725–2900* 📠*250/725–2901* 🌐*www.middlebeach.com 35 rooms, 10 suites, 19 cabins In-room: no a/c, no phone (some), kitchen (some), DVD (some), VCR (some), no TV (some), dial-up (some). In-hotel: restaurant, bar, gym, laundry facilities, public Wi-Fi, no-smoking rooms, some pets allowed* ▭*AE, MC, V Restaurant closed Sun.–Thurs. Nov.–March. No lunch CP.*

¢–$$ Fodor's Choice ★ **Whalers on the Point Guesthouse.** With its hardwood floors, harbor-view picture windows, big stone fireplace, and unbeatable location, this modern seaside hostel looks more like an upscale lodge than a backpackers' haven. It also has pretty much everything a budget traveler could want: a game room and TV lounge, a shared kitchen and living room, even surfboard storage. Accommodation is available in private rooms with shared bathrooms, family rooms (for four) with private bathrooms, and four- and six-bed dorm rooms with shared bathrooms. Advance reservations are highly recommended. ✉*81 West St., Box 296, V0R 2Z0* ☎*250/725–3443* 📠*250/725–3463* 🌐*www.tofinohostel.com 7 rooms, 11 dorm rooms. In-room: no a/c, no phone, no TV* ▭*MC, V.*

SPORTS & THE OUTDOORS

FISHING **Chinook Charters** leads fishing charters in the area. ✉*331 Main St.* ☎*250/725–3431.*

Weigh West Marine Resort Adventure Centre operates a marina and conducts fishing charters, including saltwater fly-fishing. The outfitter can also arrange accommodation, meals, and guides as well as kayaking, whale-watching, hot-springs tours, and surfing trips. ☎*250/725–3277 or 800/665–8922* 🌐*www.weighwest.com.*

KAYAKING ★ **Remote Passages** has easy guided paddles in sheltered waters; no experience is necessary. ✉*71 Wharf St.* ☎*250/725–3330 or 800/666–9833* 🌐*www.remotepassages.com.*

Tofino Sea-Kayaking Company rents kayaks, runs a kayaking school, and offers day and multiday wilderness kayaking trips. No experience is necessary. ✉*320 Main St.* ☎*250/725–4222 or 800/863–4664* 🌐*www.tofino-kayaking.com.*

SURFING The coast from Tofino south to Ucluelet is, despite the chilly waters, an increasingly popular surf destination—year-round.

You can rent boards and other gear at **Live to Surf.** Jean-Paul Froment runs the business (founded in 1984 by his parents) with his sister Pascale, from the funky Outside Break commercial hub south of Tofino, and conveniently close to major surfing spots. The shop sells boards, wetsuits, and accessories, as well as providing rentals and lessons. ✉*1184 Pacific Rim Hwy.* ☎*250/725–4464* 🌐*www.livetosurf.com.*

For surfing lessons at all levels, contact the **Pacific Surf School.** ✉*430 Campbell St.* ☎*250/725–2155 or 888/777–9961* 🌐*www.pacificsurfschool.com.*

Surf Sister has women-only and coed surfing lessons. ✉*1180 Pacific Rim Hwy.* ☎*250/725–4456 or 877/724–7873* 🌐*www.surfsister.com.*

WHALE-WATCHING & MARINE EXCURSIONS In March and April, an estimated 20,000 grey whales migrate along the coast here; resident greys can be seen anytime between March and October. In addition, humpback whales, sea otters, orca, bears, and other wildlife are increasingly seen in the area. Most whale-watching operators lead excursions along the coast and to the region's outlying islands, including Meares Island, Flores Island, and Hot Springs Cove.

Jamie's Whaling Station & Adventure Centre is one of the most established whale-watching operators on the coast. It has both Zodiacs and more comfortable covered 65-foot tour boats. You can book a whole range of adventures here, including kayaking, bear watching, and trips to Meares Island or Hot Springs Cove in Maquinna Marine Provincial Park in Clayoquot Sound. Jamie's operates from February 15 to October 31. ✉*606 Campbell St.* ☎*250/725–3919 or 800/667–9913* 🌐*www.jamies.com.*

★ **Remote Passages Marine Excursions,** a well-established operator, runs whale-watching, bear-watching, and other wildlife-viewing trips with an ecological and educational focus using Zodiacs and covered boats. ✉*71 Wharf St.* ☎*250/725–3330 or 800/666–9833* 🌐*www.remote-passages.com.*

★ With **Tla-ook Cultural Adventures** you can paddle a traditional Nuu-chah-nulth dugout canoe with a First Nations guide. Trips go to traditional native territory on Meares Island and to Echachist Island, an early Nuu-chah-nulth summering territory. The latter is an all-day trip featuring a seafood feast in an old summer village dotted with historic middens. ☎*250/725–2656 or 877/942–2663* 🌐*www.tlaook.com.*

The **Whale Centre** has a maritime museum with a 40-foot whale skeleton you can study while waiting for your boat. The company runs whale-watching, hot springs, and bear- and bird-watching tours, year-round. ✉*411 Campbell St.* ☎*250/725–2132 or 888/474–2288* 🌐*www.tofinowhalecentre.com.*

SHOPPING

In a traditional longhouse, the magnificent **Eagle Aerie Gallery** houses a collection of prints, paintings, and carvings by the renowned B.C. artist Roy Henry Vickers. ✉*350 Campbell St.* ☎*250/725–3235.*

House of Himwitsa sells First Nations crafts, jewelry, and clothing. The complex also has a seafood restaurant and lodge rooms. ✉*300 Main St.* ☎*250/725–2017 or 800/899–1947.*

Wildside Booksellers has an extensive selection of books and kites and houses an espresso bar. ✉*320 Main St.* ☎*250/725–4222.*

PACIFIC RIM NATIONAL PARK RESERVE

105 km (63 mi) west of Port Alberni, 9 km (5 mi) south of Tofino.

This national park has some of Canada's most stunning coastal and rain-forest scenery, abundant wildlife, and a unique marine environment. It comprises three separate units—Long Beach, the Broken Group Islands, and the West Coast Trail—for a combined area of 123,431 acres, and stretches 130 km (81 mi) along Vancouver Island's west coast. The **Pacific Rim Visitor Centre** (✉*Tofino-Ucluelet junction on Hwy. 4* ☎*250/726–4212* 🌐*www.pc.gc.ca/pacificrim*) is open daily mid-March through August, from 9 AM to 7 PM, and until mid-October, 9 AM to 5 PM. Park-use fees apply in all sections of the park: the general adult fee for entry to the park was C$6.90 in 2008. Park users must display a permit, available from the visitor center and valid for 24 hours, in their vehicle.

The **Long Beach** unit gets its name from a 16-km (10-mi) strip of hard-packed sand strewn with driftwood, shells, and the occasional Japanese glass fishing float. Long Beach is the most accessible part of the park and can get busy in summer. A first stop for many Pacific Rim National Park visitors, the **Wickaninnish Interpretive Centre** (✉*Hwy. 4* ☎*250/726–7721*) is on the ocean's edge about 16 km (10 mi) north of Ucluelet. It's a great place to learn about the wilderness; theater programs and exhibits provide information about the park's marine ecology and rain-forest environment. New exhibits are planned for 2010. It's open daily mid-March to mid-October 10 to 6. The fabulous, high-end Wickaninnish Restaurant is next door. The **West Coast Trail,** runs along the coast from Bamfield to Port Renfrew. It's an extremely rugged 75-km (47-mi) trail for experienced hikers; it can be traveled only on foot, takes an average of six days to complete, and is open from May 1 to September 30. A quota system helps the park manage the number of hikers on the trail, and reservations are recommended between mid-June and mid-September, though some spaces are available on a first-come, first-served basis at each end of the trail during this time. A number of fees apply: C$24.75 for a reservation, C$128.75 for a hiker's permit, and C$30 for two ferry crossings. ☎*800/435–5622, 604/435–5622 in Greater Vancouver, 250/387–1642 international* 🌐*www.pc.gc.ca/pacificrim.*

2

COURTENAY

220 km (136 mi) northwest of Victoria, 17 nautical mi west of Powell River, 57 km (34 mi) northwest of Qualicum Beach.

This friendly town makes a good base to enjoy the area's wealth of outdoor activities, including golf, hiking, and skiing at nearby Mount Washington Alpine Resort. Ferries to Powell River on the mainland sail from Little River, 6 km (4 mi) north of Courtenay.

Dinosaur fans should love the **Courtenay and District Museum and Paleontology Centre** (✉*207 4th St.* ☎*250/334–0686* 🌐*www.courtenaymuseum.ca* *By donation* ⏲*Mid-May–Labor Day, Mon.–Sat. 10–5, Sun. noon–4; Sept.–mid-May, Tues.–Sat. 10–5*). It's home to the reconstructed skeleton of a 35-foot elasmosaur—a dinosaur-era sea creature found in the Comox Valley—and a 13-foot mosasaur skeleton. Book ahead for fossil-hunting day trips in the area.

WHERE TO STAY & EAT

$$$ ✕ **Tomāto Tomäto.** Cedar beams, leather armchairs, stone fireplaces, and a summer patio keep things cozy at this 1938 riverside house. Small portions, meant for sharing, are fun: say crispy barbecued duck tacos, taro root chips, or spinach and carrot pakoras. Mains run from local halibut with roasted red pepper jam, to ancho chili rubbed lamb sirloin, and slow-roasted duck with pomegranate glaze. Innovative burgers, sandwiches, and pastas at lunch, house-made desserts, and a decent kids' menu all make this worth a stop. ✉*1760 Riverside La.* ☎*250/338–5406* ▭*AE, DC, MC, V.*

$–$$ ✕ **The Atlas Café.** A vintage map of South America lends an exotic feel to this casual town-center café and local gathering place. The wholesome menu appeals to a globetrotting clientele: nori rolls, falafel, Greek spinach pie, pastas, and vegan dishes appear along with an evening fresh sheet featuring local bounty. The dining room and attached martini bar serve the full menu until 10 PM, and crowds gather at breakfast for huevos rancheros and eggs benny. ✉*250 6th St.* ☎*250/338–9838* ▭*MC, V* ⏲*Closed late Jan. and early Feb. No dinner Mon.*

$$–$$$$ **Kingfisher Oceanside Resort & Spa.** A circuit of massaging waterfalls and mineral pools, called the Pacific Mist Hydropath, is the centerpiece of this adult-oriented spa retreat 7 km (4½ mi) south of Courtenay. Esthetic treatments, aromatherapy, and massage are all available. West Coast fare, using local products, features at the ocean-view restaurant ($$–$$$). Folk art, seashells, and soft earth and sea tones warm the beachfront suites, which all have balconies or patios, kitchenettes, gas fireplaces, and expansive ocean views. Ocean View rooms, set a little farther back from the water, also have views and balconies, and some have kitchenettes. ✉*4330 Island Hwy. S, V9N 9R9* ☎*250/338–1323 or 800/663–7929* 🌐*www.kingfisherspa.com* *28 rooms, 36 suites* *In-room: no a/c, kitchen (some), refrigerator, DVD (some), Wi-Fi. In-hotel: restaurant, room service, bar, tennis court, pool, gym, spa, beachfront, bicycles, laundry service, some pets allowed, no-smoking rooms* *AE, D, DC, MC, V.*

SPORTS & THE OUTDOORS

GOLF The 18-hole, par-72 Championship course at the **Crown Isle Resort & Golf Community** (✉*399 Clubhouse Dr., off Ryan Rd.* ☎*250/703–5050 or 888/338–8439* 🌐*www.crownisle.com*) boasts 11 lakes and mountain views. You can stay here, too, in one of the lavish fairway-view rooms, suites, or kitchen-equipped villas. The clubhouse has a sweeping *Titanic*-style double staircase, classic-car museum, two restaurants, and gym.

SKIING, HIKING & MOUNTAIN BIKING **Mount Washington Alpine Resort** (☎*250/338–1386 or 888/231–1499* 🌐*www.mountwashington.ca*), 30 km (18 mi) from Courtenay via Strathcona Parkway, the island's largest ski area, receives some of North America's biggest snow falls—an average of 9 meters (30 feet) each year. It boasts 60 downhill runs, a 1,657-foot vertical drop, six chairlifts, three surface lifts, and an elevation of 5,200 feet. The resort also has 55 km (33 mi) of track-set cross-country trails, 20 km (12 mi) of snowshoe trails, two snowboard parks, a half pipe (for snowboarding) and snow-tubing chutes. In summer there are miles of alpine hiking and mountain-bike trails accessible by chairlift, as well as minigolf, disc-golf, and a bungee trampoline. The resort has a good selection of restaurants, shops, and ski-in ski-out accommodations.

CAMPBELL RIVER

50 km (31 mi) north of Courtenay, 155 km (96 mi) northwest of Nanaimo, 270 km (167 mi) northwest of Victoria.

Campbell River draws people who want to fish; some of the biggest salmon ever caught on a line have been landed just off the coast here. Cutthroat trout are also plentiful in the river. Other recreational activities include kayaking, whale-watching, and diving in Discovery Passage, where a battleship was sunk for diving purposes. Ferries leave Campbell River for Quadra and Cortes islands, both popular fishing destinations.

The **Campbell River Maritime Heritage Centre** (*621 Island Hwy. 250/286–3161 www.bcp45.org*) has a large range of marine artifacts and marine history displays. It's also home to BCP 45, the little fishing boat that long graced the Canadian $5 bill. Admission is $3. It's open mid-May to mid-October, weekdays 10–3:30; mid-October–mid-May, weekdays noon–3.

On a hill overlooking the sea, the **Museum at Campbell River** (*470 Island Hwy. 250/287–3103 www.crmuseum.ca C$6 Mid-May–Sept., daily 10–5; Oct.–mid-May, Tues.–Sun. noon–5*) has great views, an excellent collection of First Nations artifacts, and some intriguing historical exhibits, including a re-created pioneer cabin and float house, and a dramatic audiovisual retelling of a First Nations legend.

WHERE TO STAY & EAT

$$–$$$$ **Painter's Lodge Holiday & Fishing Resort.** John Wayne and his fishing buddies came to this waterfront lodge to catch salmon in the 1940s and '50s. The attractive, refurbished cedar buildings still draw anglers; the resort's fleet of Boston Whalers runs fishing trips while zodiacs run whale-watching and nature cruises. The rooms, suites, and one- to three-bedroom cabins all have balconies or patios. Some have fireplaces and whirlpool baths and many are on two levels. The resort's ocean-view restaurant ($$–$$$) serves fresh seafood (naturally), and the resort's free water taxi runs to Painter's sister property, April Point Resort & Spa on Quadra Island, where you can dine, kayak, indulge in spa treatments, or explore biking and hiking trails. *1625 McDonald Rd., V9W 5C1 250/286–1102 or 800/663–7090 www.obmg.com 87 rooms, 3 suites, 4 cabins In-room: no a/c, kitchen (some), Wi-Fi (some). In-hotel: 2 restaurants, bar, tennis courts, pool, gym, water sports, no elevator, public Internet, public Wi-Fi, airport shuttle, no-smoking rooms AE, DC, MC, V Closed mid-Oct.–mid-Apr.*

QUADRA ISLAND

10 minutes by ferry from Campbell River.

Quadra is a thickly forested island, rich with wildlife and laced with hiking trails. It's also home to a thriving arts community—the Campbell River Visitor Information Centre has maps of the studios and galleries that are open to the public. At low tide you can spot ancient petroglyphs along the shore at the south end of the island. BC Ferries (⇨ *Vancouver Island Essentials*) runs car ferries here from Campbell River, or you can hop the free foot-passenger ferry run by Painter's Lodge.

Rebecca Spit Provincial Park has pretty pebble beaches and picnic areas.

WHERE TO STAY & EAT

$$–$$$$ **April Point Resort & Spa.** You can try whale-watching, kayaking, fishing, hiking, and biking at this family-oriented, waterfront ecotourism resort. Many rooms have fireplaces, and the three- and four-bedroom guesthouses each have a kitchen, fireplace, hot tub, and sundeck. The window-lined restaurant and sushi bar ($$–$$$) are scenic places to

enjoy fresh seafood. The Japanese-theme spa offers a full range of Aveda treatments and the resort's free water taxi takes you to the tennis courts, pool, and hot tubs at Painter's Lodge in Campbell River. ✉*900 April Point Rd., Quathiaski Cove, V0P 1N0* ☎*250/285–2222 or 800/663–7090* 🌐*www.aprilpoint.com* *43 rooms, 6 cabins, 4 guesthouses* *In-room: no a/c, kitchen (some), refrigerator (some), Wi-Fi (some). In-hotel: restaurant, bar, spa, water sports, bicycles, no elevator, public Wi-Fi, airport shuttle, some pets allowed, no-smoking rooms* *AE, DC, MC, V* *Closed mid-Oct.–mid-Apr.*

$$ **Tsa-Kwa-Luten Lodge.** Set on a bluff amid acres of forest, this lodge, operated by the Cape Mudge First Nations band, has a foyer built in the style of a longhouse and comfortable rooms with Kwagiulth art, balconies, and ocean views. Three two-bedroom beachfront cottages have gas fireplaces, whirlpool tubs, kitchenettes, and private verandas. The four-bedroom guesthouse and the two-bedroom wharf house are great for groups; beachfront RV sites are also available. You can kayak, bike, hike, fish, take a whale- or bear-watching cruise, and even try archery here. The restaurant ($$–$$$) serves cedar-baked salmon and other West Coast seafood dishes. ✉*1 Lighthouse Rd., Box 460, Quathiaski Cove, V0P 1N0* ☎*250/285–2042 or 800/665–7745* 🌐*www.capemudgeresort.bc.ca* *30 rooms, 5 cottages* *In-room: no a/c, kitchen (some), no TV. In-hotel: restaurant, bar, gym, bicycles, laundry service, no-smoking rooms* *AE, DC, MC, V* *Closed mid-Oct.–mid-Apr.*

STRATHCONA PROVINCIAL PARK

40 km (25 mi) west of Campbell River.

The largest provincial park on Vancouver Island, Strathcona Provincial Park encompasses **Mt. Golden Hinde,** at 7,220 feet the island's highest mountain, and **Della Falls,** one of Canada's highest waterfalls, reaching 1,440 feet. This strikingly scenic wilderness park's lakes and 161 campsites attract summer canoeists, hikers, anglers, and campers. The main access is by Highway 28 from Campbell River; Mt. Washington ski area, next to the park, can be reached by roads out of Courtenay. ☎*800/689–9025 camping reservations* 🌐*www.discovercamping.ca.*

WHERE TO STAY

¢–$$ **Strathcona Park Lodge and Outdoor Education Centre.** One of Canada's foremost outdoor education centers, this lakefront resort on the outskirts of Strathcona Provincial Park is a great place for kids and adults to try their hand at rock climbing, hiking, canoeing, kayaking, wilderness camp outs, and more. Family-run and kid-friendly, the resort has comfortable cottages and lodge rooms (some with shared baths), and striking views of the snowcapped mountains behind Upper Campbell Lake. Family activities are designed for parents and kids, ages 6–13, to do together. Beginners of all ages are welcome: the guides here are renowned for their patience and skill. Three wholesome meals are served daily between mid-March and mid-November. ✉*40 km (24 mi) west of Campbell River on Hwy. 28, Box 2160, Campbell River, V9W 5C5* ☎*250/286–3122* 🌐*www.strathcona.bc.ca* *39 rooms, 10* *cottages ♿In-room: no a/c, no phone, kitchen (some), no TV. In-hotel: 2 restaurants, beachfront, water sports, no elevator, laundry facilities, no-smoking rooms ▭MC, V.*

TELEGRAPH COVE

182 km (109 mi) northwest of Campbell River, 56 km (34 mi) southeast of Port Hardy, 16 km (10 mi) off Hwy. 19.

Villages built on pilings over the water were once a common sight on Canada's west coast. Telegraph Cove, with its row of brightly painted shops and houses connected by a boardwalk, is one of the last still standing. It's now home to a pub and restaurant, a general store, a marina, and several bear- and whale-watching and kayaking outfitters. You can see the skeleton of a 60-foot fin whale and other natural artifacts at the **Whale Interpretive Centre** on the boardwalk (☎*250/928–2139* ⏲*Daily mid-May–early Oct.* *By donation*).

Accommodation options include a campground and cabins on the boardwalk run by **Telegraph Cove Resorts** (☎*250/928–3131 or 800/200–4665* 🌐*www.telegraphcoveresort.com*). **Telegraph Cove Venture** offers water-view suites and an RV site (☎*250/928–3163 or 800/835–2683* 🌐*www.telegraphcove.ca*).

WHALE-WATCHING

Telegraph Cove overlooks Johnstone Strait, one of the best places in the province to see orca, or killer, whales especially during the salmon runs of July, August, and September. Between late May and mid-October, **Stubbs Island Whale Watching** (☎*250/928–3185 or 800/665–3066* 🌐*www.stubbs-island.com*), on the boardwalk, runs 3½-hour whale-watching trips on its two 60-foot vessels. A naturalist accompanies the tours, and the boats are equipped with hydrophones for listening to the whales. Reservations are required.

OFF THE BEATEN PATH

From Port McNeill, 26 km (16 mi) north of Telegraph Cove, a 40-minute ferry ride takes you to Alert Bay, home to the **U'Mista Cultural Centre**, with its fascinating collection of First Nations potlatch regalia (✉1 Front St., Alert Bay ☎250/974–5403 🌐www.umista.org). A 20-minute ferry hop from Port McNeill takes you to the village of **Sointula** on Malcolm Island, once home to a Finnish Utopian community.

PORT HARDY

238 km (148 mi) northwest of Campbell River, 499 km (309 mi) northwest of Victoria, 274 nautical mi southeast of Prince Rupert.

Port Hardy is the departure and arrival point for BC Ferries' year-round trips through the scenic Inside Passage to and from Prince Rupert, the coastal port serving the Queen Charlotte Islands and southeast Alaska. In summer ferries sail from Port Hardy to Bella Coola and other small communities along British Columbia's mid-coast. Ferry reservations for the trip between Port Hardy and Prince Rupert or Bella Coola, and hotel reservations in Port Hardy should be made well in advance. **North Island Transportation** (☎*250/949–6300*) runs a shuttle bus between most

Port Hardy hotels and the ferry terminal, which is 10 km (6 mi) from town. The fare is C$6.50.

WHERE TO STAY

$$ **Quarterdeck Inn and Marina Resort.** Most rooms have water views at this hotel on Port Hardy's waterfront. The rooms are bright and spacious with pastel decor. Two rooms have fireplaces and whirlpool tubs. A variety of outdoor activities, wildlife viewing, and First Nations cultural tours can be arranged from the hotel, which is a 10-minute drive from the ferry terminal. ✉*6555 Hardy Bay Rd., V0N 2P0* ☎*250/902–0455 or 877/902–0459* 🌐*www.quarterdeckresort.net* *39 rooms, 1 suite* *In-room: no a/c, kitchen (some), ethernet. In-hotel: restaurant, bar, gym, laundry facilities, some pets allowed, no-smoking rooms* *AE, D, DC, MC, V* *CP.*

$–$$ **Glen Lyon Inn.** You can often spot eagles scouting the water for fish to prey on from this modern hotel next to the marina on Hardy Bay. All rooms have full ocean views, most have balconies and two high-end rooms have king beds, Jacuzzi tubs, a bar, and a fireplace. Diving, wildlife viewing, and chartered fishing can be arranged from here, as well as freezing and storing your catch. The hotel is a 10-minute drive from the ferry terminal. ✉*6435 Hardy Bay Rd., Box 103, V0N 2P0* ☎*250/949–7115 or 877/949–7115* 🌐*www.glenlyoninn.com* *44 rooms* *In-room: no a/c, kitchen (come), refrigerator (some), Wi-Fi. In-hotel: restaurant, bar, gym, laundry facilities, public Internet, some pets allowed, no-smoking rooms* *AE, MC, V.*

VANCOUVER ISLAND ESSENTIALS

To research prices, get advice from other travelers, and book travel arrangements, visit www.fodors.com.

TRANSPORTATION

BY AIR

Kenmore Air operates summer service from Seattle to Nanaimo, which is the gateway for seeing Northern Vancouver Island, as well as Campbell River, Quadra Island, and other North Island and Inside Passage destinations. Northwest Seaplanes operates scheduled summer floatplane service from Seattle to Campbell River, and charter service to Northern Vancouver Island destinations.

Contacts **Kenmore Air** (☎ *425/486-1257 or 800/543-9595* 🌐 *www.kenmoreair.com*).**Northwest Seaplanes** (☎ *800-690-0086* 🌐 *www.nwseaplanes.com*).

BY BOAT & FERRY

BC Ferries operates daily service between Tsawwassen, about an hour south of Vancouver, and Swartz Bay, at the end of Highway 17 (the Patricia Bay Highway), about 30 minutes north of downtown Victoria; a two-hour crossing from Tsawwassen to Duke Point, 15 km (9 mi) south of Nanaimo; a 1½-hour crossing from Horseshoe Bay (a 30-minute drive from Vancouver) to Departure Bay, 3 km (2 mi) north of Nanaimo. Vehicle reservations can be made for any of these routes; a C$15 reservation fee applies if you book more than a week in advance. The fee is C$17.50 for reservations within a week of sailing. Reservations, which can be made by phone or online, are recommended if you're traveling with a car on a summer weekend. Reservations are not necessary for foot passengers or cyclists.

The *Queen of Prince Rupert*, a BC Ferries ship, sails six times a week in July and August, reducing to three times per week in winter. The crossing from Prince Rupert to Skidegate, near Queen Charlotte on Graham Island, takes about seven hours. High-season fares are C$26.25 per adult passenger, C$97.50 per car, and C$159.50 and up for campers (depending on length). Some sailings are overnight; cabins are available for an additional C$45 to C$50.

Information **BC Ferries** (☎ *250/386-3431, 888/223-3779 in B.C., Alberta, and Washington state* 🌐 *www.bcferries.com*).

BY BUS

Gray Line of Victoria provides bus service to most towns on Vancouver Island. From Vancouver, Greyhound serves Nanaimo and Pacific Coach Lines serves Victoria. The Tofino Bus has daily, year-round service from Victoria, and from Nanaimo's Departure Bay ferry terminal and HarbourLynx terminal, to Port Alberni, Tofino, and Ucluelet. One-way fares are C$35 from Nanaimo, C$53 from Victoria

Information **Gray Line of Victoria** (☎ *800/318-0808* 🌐 *www.graylinewest.com.ca*). **Tofino Bus** (☎ *866/986-3466* 🌐 *www.tofinobus.com*).

BY CAR

Major roads on Vancouver Island, and most secondary roads, are paved and well engineered. Many wilderness and park-access roads are unpaved. Inquire locally about logging activity before using logging or forest-service roads.

Highway 17 connects the Swartz Bay ferry terminal on the Saanich Peninsula with downtown Victoria. The Trans-Canada Highway (Highway 1) runs from Victoria to Nanaimo. The Island Highway (Highway 19) connects Nanaimo to Port Hardy. (Highway 19A, the old road, runs parallel as far as Campbell River. It's a slower, seaside option.) Highway 14 connects Victoria to Sooke and Port Renfrew on the west coast. Highway 4 crosses the island from Parksville to Tofino and Pacific Rim National Park Reserve.

BY TRAIN

VIA Rail offers service between Vancouver and Jasper (in Alberta) and from Prince Rupert to Jasper with an overnight stop in Prince George.

Contact **VIA Rail** (☎ *888/842-7245* 🌐 *www.viarail.ca*).

CONTACTS & RESOURCES

TOURS

You can see Victoria and parts of Vancouver Island from the air with Harbour Air Seaplanes. Twenty-minute flight-seeing tours start at C$99 per person.

Contact **Harbour Air Seaplanes** (☎ *250/385-9131 or 800/665-0212* 🌐 *www.harbourair.com*).

VISITOR INFORMATION

Tourist Information **Hello BC** (☎ *800/435-5622* 🌐 *www.hellobc.com*). **Sooke Region Museum and Visitor InfoCentre** (☎ *250/642-6351 or 866/888-4748* 🌐 *www.sooke.museum.bc.ca/srm*). **Tourism Vancouver Island** (☎ *888/655-3483* 🌐 *www.SeeTheIslands.com*).

British Columbia

WORD OF MOUTH

"Whistler . . . SO much to do, and so nice! We go every year now. Usually in January. No rain, and the mountain is so high that you can usually ski ABOVE the clouds and rain if it happens to be a wet day."

—Stephanie_in_Canada

By Chris McBeath & Celeste Moure

BRITISH COLUMBIA'S MAINLAND HARBORS UNTOUCHED FORESTS, snowcapped peaks, powder skiing, and world-class fishing—a wealth of outdoor action and beauty. The citizens are similarly diverse with descendants of original Native American peoples, British, European, and Asian settlers, as well as immigrants from all other corners of the earth.

As Canada's third-largest province (Québec and Ontario are bigger), British Columbia occupies almost 10% of Canada's total area, stretching from the Pacific Ocean eastward to the province of Alberta and from the U.S. border north to the Yukon and Northwest Territories. It spans almost 1 million square km (about 360,000 square mi), making it larger than every American state except Alaska.

EXPLORING BRITISH COLUMBIA

Since most of the province's population is clustered in the Lower Mainland (a region in and around Vancouver) and the provincial capital (Victoria on Vancouver Island), there's plenty of room in B.C. to explore. Two hours north of Vancouver is the popular resort town of Whistler with North America's two biggest ski mountains. The Okanagan Valley in the east, replete with lakes and vineyards, is famous for its wines. To the north lie the ranchlands of the Cariboo-Chilcotin region, beyond which you can discover vast wilderness areas of mountainous and forested terrain, including the mist-shrouded Haida Gwaii, or Queen Charlotte Islands.

The North Coast and the Queen Charlotte Islands can be wet year-round. The interior is drier, with greater extremes, including hot summers and reliably snowy winters. Temperatures here drop below freezing in winter and sometimes reach 90°F in summer.

When you travel by car, keep in mind that more than three-quarters of British Columbia is mountainous terrain. Forest roads cut across the craggy hillsides, which though fun to explore in an all-terrain vehicle are also pretty remote and should be traveled with caution. Many areas, including the North Coast, have no roads at all and are accessible only by air or sea.

ABOUT THE RESTAURANTS

Although Vancouver and Victoria have British Columbia's most varied and cosmopolitan cuisine, smaller communities, particularly Whistler, have garnered a reputation for excellent local cuisine. Regional fare includes seafood, lamb, organic produce, and increasingly good wine. Attire is generally casual, and nearly all restaurants as well as many bars and pubs ban smoking indoors.

ABOUT THE HOTELS

Accommodations range from bed-and-breakfasts and rustic cabins to deluxe chain hotels, country inns, and remote fishing lodges. The cities have an abundance of lodgings, but outside the major centers, especially in summer, it's a good idea to reserve ahead, even for campsites. In winter many backcountry resorts close, and city hotels drop prices

TOP REASONS TO GO

CANOEING & KAYAKING

The Inside Passage, the Strait of Georgia, and the other island-dotted straits and sounds that border the mainland provide fairly protected sea-going from Washington State to the Alaskan border, with numerous marine parks to explore along the way. Two favorites for canoeing are the Powell Forest Canoe Route, an 80-km (50-mi) circuit of seven lakes, and Bowron Lake Park, in the Cariboo region.

FISHING

Miles of coastline and thousands of lakes, rivers, and streams bring more than 750,000 anglers to British Columbia each year. The province's waters hold 74 species of fish (25 of them sport fish), including chinook salmon and rainbow trout.

HIKING THE ROCKIES

Virtually all the national parks have fine hiking-trail networks, and many ski resorts keep their chairlifts running throughout the summer to help hikers and mountain bikers reach trails. Heli-hiking is also very popular; helicopters deliver you to alpine meadows and verdant mountaintops.

SKIING & SNOWBOARDING

With more than half the province higher than 4,200 feet above sea level, more than 60 resorts have downhill skiing and snowboarding facilities. Most of them also offer groomed cross-country (Nordic) ski trails, and many of the provincial parks have cross-country trails as well. The resorts are easy to get to, as several have shuttles from the nearest airport.

3

by as much as 50%. Most small inns and B&Bs ban smoking indoors; almost all hotels have no-smoking rooms.

WHAT IT COSTS IN CANADIAN DOLLARS					
	¢	$	$$	$$$	$$$$
RESTAURANTS	under $8	$8–$12	$13–$20	$21–$30	Over $30
HOTELS	under $75	$75–$125	$126–$175	$176–$250	over $250

Restaurant prices are for a main course at dinner. Hotel prices are for two people in a standard double room in high season.

WHISTLER

Fodor'sChoice ★ With two breathtaking mountains, Whistler and Blackcomb, enviable skiing conditions, championship golf courses, more than 200 shops, 90 restaurants and bars, an array of accommodations, spas, hiking trails, and what may very well be the best mountain bike park in the world, it's no surprise that Whistler consistently ranks as the top ski resort in North America.

Located 75 mi north of Vancouver, Whistler was named in honor of the whistling marmots that lived high in the mountains: the innovative plan for a car-free village was conceived in the mid-1970s and opened for business, along with Blackcomb Mountain, in 1980. Vancouverites as well as adrenaline junkies from around the globe arrived here to enjoy

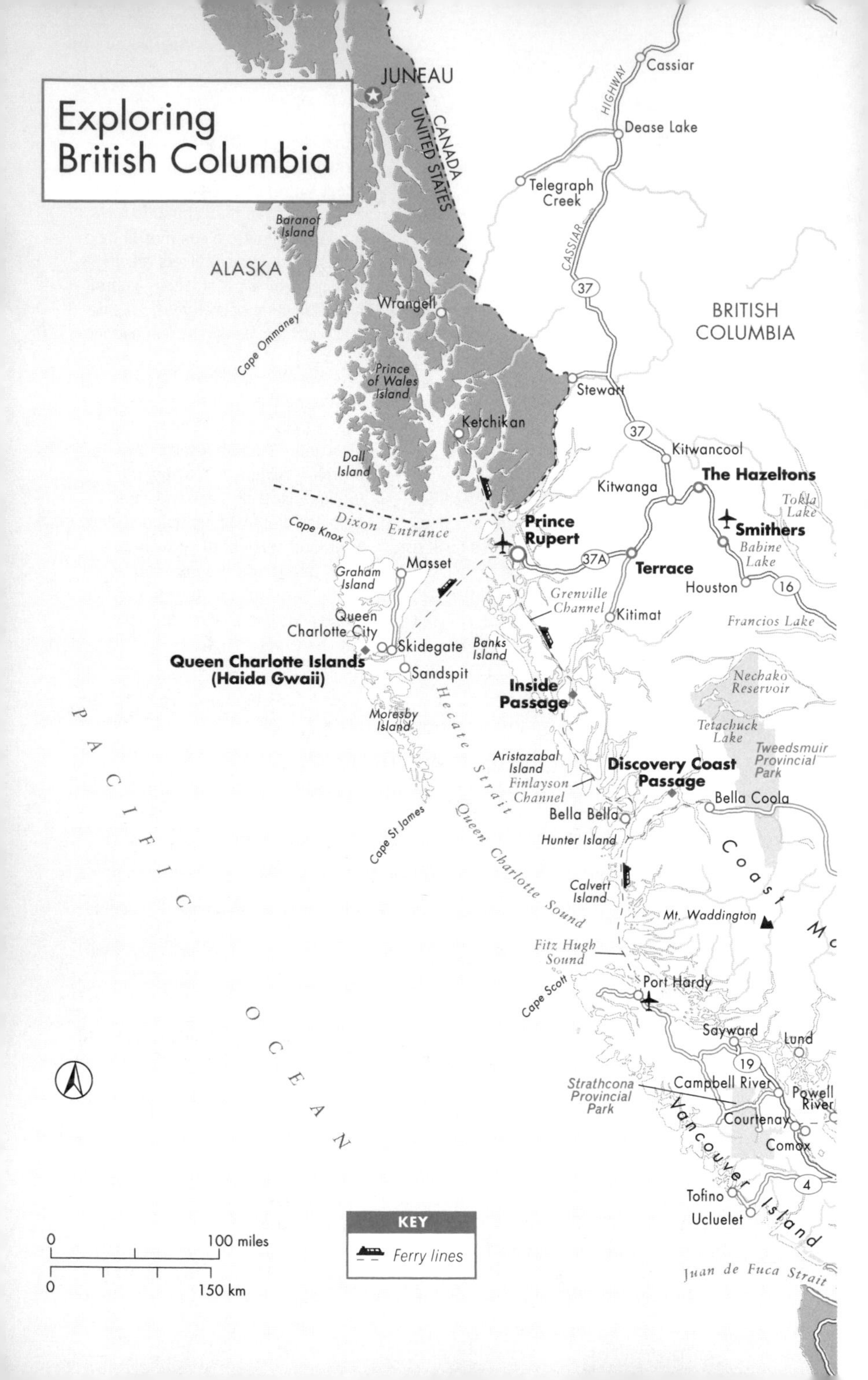

Exploring British Columbia
JUNEAU
CANADA
UNITED STATES
Baranof Island
ALASKA
Wrangell
Cape Ommaney
Prince of Wales Island
Ketchikan
Dall Island
Cassiar
HIGHWAY
Dease Lake
Telegraph Creek
CASSIAR
37
BRITISH COLUMBIA
Stewart
Kitwancool
The Hazeltons
Kitwanga
Tokla Lake
Smithers
Babine Lake
Prince Rupert
Terrace
37A
Houston
16
Dixon Entrance
Cape Knox
Masset
Graham Island
Queen Charlotte City
Skidegate
Sandspit
Queen Charlotte Islands (Haida Gwaii)
Grenville Channel
Kitimat
Francios Lake
Banks Island
Inside Passage
Nechako Reservoir
Tetachuck Lake
Tweedsmuir Provincial Park
Hecate Strait
Moresby Island
Aristazabal Island
Finlayson Channel
Discovery Coast Passage
Bella Coola
Bella Bella
Hunter Island
Cape St James
Queen Charlotte Sound
Coast M
Calvert Island
Mt. Waddington
Fitz Hugh Sound
Cape Scott
Port Hardy
PACIFIC OCEAN
Sayward
Lund
19
Strathcona Provincial Park
Campbell River
Powell River
Courtenay
Comox
Vancouver Island
4
Tofino
Ucluelet
Juan de Fuca Strait
KEY
Ferry lines
0
100 miles
0
150 km

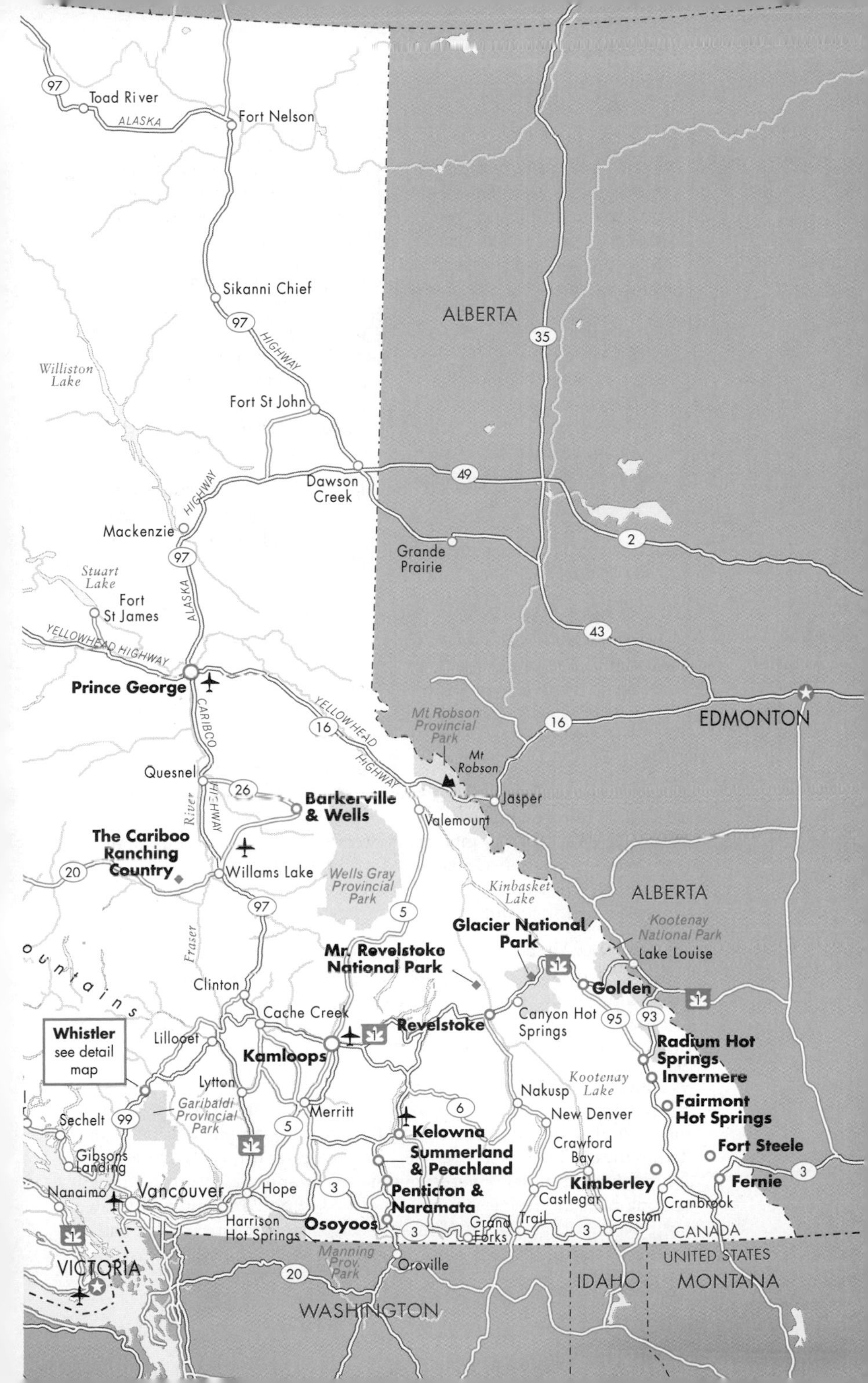
Toad River
ALASKA
Fort Nelson
Sikanni Chief
HIGHWAY
ALBERTA
Williston Lake
Fort St John
Dawson Creek
HIGHWAY
Mackenzie
Grande Prairie
Stuart Lake
Fort St James
ALASKA
YELLOWHEAD HIGHWAY
Prince George
CARIBOO
YELLOWHEAD
HIGHWAY
Mt Robson Provincial Park
Mt Robson
EDMONTON
Quesnel
HIGHWAY
River
Barkerville & Wells
Jasper
Valemount
The Cariboo Ranching Country
Willams Lake
Wells Gray Provincial Park
Kinbasket Lake
ALBERTA
Kootenay National Park
Glacier National Park
Mr. Revelstoke National Park
Lake Louise
Fraser
Mountains
Clinton
Golden
Cache Creek
Revelstoke
Canyon Hot Springs
Whistler see detail map
Lillooet
Kamloops
Radium Hot Springs
Invermere
Lytton
Garibaldi Provincial Park
Kootenay Lake
Nakusp
Merritt
New Denver
Sechelt
Fairmont Hot Springs
Kelowna
Summerland & Peachland
Crawford Bay
Fort Steele
Gibsons Landing
Kimberley
Fernie
Nanaimo
Vancouver
Hope
Penticton & Naramata
Castlegar
Cranbrook
Harrison Hot Springs
Osoyoos
Grand Forks
Trail
Creston
CANADA
UNITED STATES
Manning Prov. Park
Oroville
VICTORIA
IDAHO
MONTANA
WASHINGTON

GREAT ITINERARIES

British Columbia is about the size of Western Europe, with as much geographical variety yet with substantially fewer roads. The good news is that many great sights, stunning scenery, and even wilderness lie within a few days' tour of Vancouver or the U.S. border.

IF YOU HAVE 3 DAYS

If you're based in Vancouver, the perfect three-day excursion is to drive north along the Sea to Sky Highway to **Whistler**, one of the top ski resort destinations in North America. There's plenty to do aside from skiing and snowboarding, from golf to shopping to dining in one of the area's top restaurants.

IF YOU HAVE 6 DAYS

Six days will allow you to stop in **Whistler** as well as take a leisurely drive out to the **Okanagan Valley**. Plan to make stops in **Kelowna**, **Summerland & Peachland**, **Penticton**, and **Oliver & Osoyoos** to relax at a beach or tour a vineyard. Any of these towns is fine for an overnight stay.

IF YOU HAVE 10–12 DAYS

More than a week lets you to get out into the north and western parts of BC. If you're interested in seeing national parks, there are several along the Alberta–British Columbia border, including **Mt. Revelstoke**, **Glacier**, **Kootenay**, and **Yoho**.

Alternatively, you can head up the Cariboo Highway to the **Cariboo-Chilcotin**, where you'll see some of the biggest working ranches in North America. With even more time, you can drive farther north to pick up the **Alaska Highway**, or west to take the BC Ferries to see **Discovery Coast Passage**, **Inside Passage**, and **Queen Charlotte Islands**.

the great outdoors and stayed permanently for the abundant array of everything else—from all-night dance parties to bear-watching, fabulous sandy beaches, and spectator events. Today, Whistler encompasses 100 square mi of land, most of it (92%) zoned for rural use and the rest occupied by tourist, residential, commercial, and municipal buildings. Scattered up and down the valley are a dozen residential areas separated by forest and greenbelts.

As the city of Vancouver prepares to host the 2010 Olympics, Whistler is seeing a bevy of new developments, special events, and darn cool happenings in both hot and cold months. Infused with its own personality, welcoming locals, and gorgeous scenery, Whistler delivers what other resorts only claim to have.

WHERE TO EAT

With a farmers market delivering excellent organic produce—not to mention delicious local jams and baked goods—and increasingly good B.C. wines, Whistler has become a foodie destination of some renown. At many restaurants, award-winning chefs and adventurous up-and-coming ones are fusing regional fare like seafood and lamb with international flavors and styles. Whistler is also home to an excellent annual food and wine festival, Cornucopia, where you'll find all the flavors of the world.

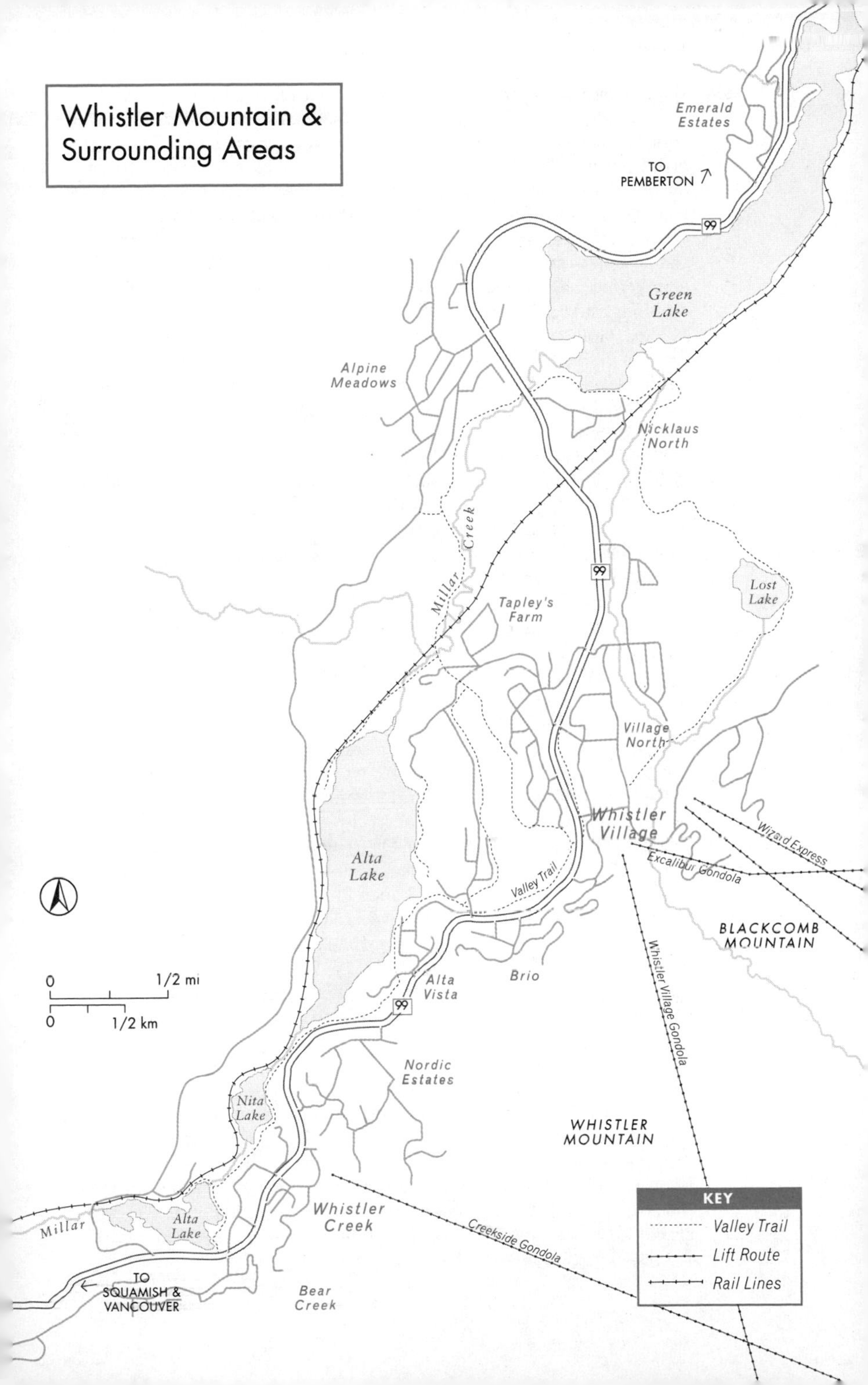

Whistler Mountain & Surrounding Areas
Emerald Estates
TO PEMBERTON
99
Green Lake
Alpine Meadows
Nicklaus North
Millar Creek
Tapley's Farm
Lost Lake
Village North
Whistler Village
Wizard Express
Excalibur Gondola
Alta Lake
Valley Trail
BLACKCOMB MOUNTAIN
Whistler Village Gondola
0
1/2 mi
0
1/2 km
Alta Vista
Brio
Nordic Estates
Nita Lake
WHISTLER MOUNTAIN
Millar
Alta Lake
Whistler Creek
Creekside Gondola
TO SQUAMISH & VANCOUVER
Bear Creek
KEY
Valley Trail
Lift Route
Rail Lines

$$$–$$$$ ✕ **Après Restaurant.** This 50-seat wine bar with frosted-glass accents and '80s retro glass art decorating the walls, consistently draws a crowd. More than 50 wines by the glass are available, as are flights for appropriate pairing. The food, which is more often a hit than a miss, focuses on regional specialties like Cowichan Bay duck and Queen Charlotte Island sable fish. From June through November, the restaurant runs *après gastronomique,* a five-night, six-day cooking school where you can learn all manner of trade secrets from award-winning master chef Eric Vernice. ✉ *103–4338 Main St.* ☎ *604/935–0200* ✍ *Reservations essential* ▭ *AE, DC, MC, V* ⊗ *No lunch.*

$$$–$$$$ ★ ✕ **Araxi.** Golden walls, terra-cotta tiles, antiques, and original artwork create a vibrant backdrop for the French-influenced Pacific Northwest cuisine served here, at one of Whistler's finest restaurants. Local farmers grow produce exclusively for Araxi's chef, who also makes good use of cheese, game, and fish from the province. Breads and pastries are made in-house each morning. The menu changes seasonally, but dishes may include Fraser Valley rabbit and alder-smoked B.C. arctic char with saffron and oyster-mushroom sauce. A heated patio is open in summer, and the lounge is a popular après-ski spot. ✉ *4222 Village Sq.* ☎ *604/932–4540* ✍ *Reservations essential* ▭ *AE, DC, MC, V* ⊗ *No lunch Oct.–May.*

$$$–$$$$ ✕ **Rim Rock Café.** About 2 mi south of the village, this restaurant is a local favorite as much for its cozy, unpretentious dining room (complete with stone fireplace) as for its great seafood. If deciding on only one item is hard, why not go for the samplers: the Rim Rock Trio combines sea bass in an almond-ginger crust, grilled prawns, and rare ahi tuna marinated in soya, sake, and mirin. If you want a booth or a coveted table near the fireplace, make a reservation. ✉ *2117 Whistler Rd.* ☎ *604/932–5565 or 877/932–5589* ▭ *AE, DC, MC, V* ⊗ *No lunch.*

$$–$$$ ✕ **The Mix by Ric's.** Next door to the popular chop house Ric's Grill—which is more expensive and not as hip—is this intimate and upbeat lounge, catering to a young, upbeat crowd as likely to be dressed in Prada as in Diesel jeans and Pumas. The fruity cocktails are delicious, but the food is great, too, and it's open for breakfast, lunch, and dinner. Mouthwatering burgers, innovative tapas, and scrumptious omelets and lattes round out the menu. ✉ *4154 Village Green* ☎ *604/932–6499* ▭ *AE, DC, MC, V.*

$$–$$$ Fodor's Choice ★ ✕ **The Mountain Club.** Hand-crafted cocktails, inspired dishes created with the best local ingredients, a Wine Spectator award of excellence, and a seriously sensual ambience make this Whistler's hottest new restaurant. The menu features "earth" and "ocean" dishes such as seared sockeye salmon with roast turnip, fingerling potatoes, and a spiced carrot reduction, and Fraser Valley pork tenderloin with fig, potato, and chorizo hash. Since it opened in early 2007, this restaurant-cum-lounge—with its warm woods, natural stone, high-back white-leather booths, and excellent down-tempo music selection—has become *the* place to see-and-be-seen come dinnertime. A pretty outdoor patio serves lunch in summer. ✉ *4314 Main St.* ☎ *604/932–6009* ▭ *AE, DC, MC, V* ⊗ *No lunch Dec.–Feb.*

¢–$$ ✕**Hot Buns Bakery.** It's as if this sweet spot had been transported from a rural French town, with its stone floors, vintage skis hanging from the ceiling, and simple wooden tables and chairs. But the reason to come is not the look of the place: they serve the best *pain au chocolat,* lattes, and crepes in town. Choose a savory TexMex crepe for a quick lunch or a decadent pear-and-chocolate crepe to satisfy your après-ski sweet tooth. Not a bad way to start, or end, the day. ✉*4232 Village Stroll* ☎*604/932–6883* ▭*AE, DC, MC, V.*

3

WHERE TO STAY

Price categories are based on January-to-April ski-season rates; prices can be higher during Christmas and spring break, but considerably lower in summer. Many properties require minimum stays, especially during the Christmas season. Also, Whistler Village has some serious nightlife. If peace and quiet are important to you, ask for a room away from the main pedestrian thoroughfares or stay in one of the residential neighborhoods outside the village.

Whistler Central Reservations. Use them to book lodgings, including B&Bs, pensions, and hundreds of time-share condos. They have accommodation information for the 2010 Olympics but note that at this writing, luxury hotels like the Four Seasons already have a waiting list. ☎*604/932–4222, 604/664–5625 in Vancouver, 800/944–7853 in U.S. and Canada* 🌐*www.tourismwhistler.com.*

$$$$ Fodor's Choice ★ **Fairmont Château Whistler Resort.** This family-friendly fortress, just steps from the Blackcomb ski lifts, is a self-contained, ski-in, ski-out resort-within-a-resort with its own shopping arcade, golf course, and an impressive spa with exotic Asian and ayurvedic treatments. The lobby is filled with rustic Canadiana, handmade Mennonite rugs, overstuffed sofas, and a grand fireplace. Standard rooms are comfortably furnished and of average size, and most have mountain views. Rooms and suites on the Entrée Gold floors have fireplaces, whirlpool tubs, and their own concierge and private lounge. Ski and bike storage are convenient. The resort's Wildflower Restaurant serves fine Pacific Northwest fare against stunning mountain views. ✉*4599 Château Blvd., V0N 1B4* ☎*604/938–8000 or 800/606–8244* 📠*604/938–2291* 🌐*www.fairmont.com* *550 rooms, 56 suites* *In-room: safe, ethernet (some). In-hotel: public Wi-Fi, 3 restaurants, room service, bar, golf course, tennis courts, pools, gym, spa, concierge, laundry facilities, laundry service, executive floor, parking (fee), no-smoking rooms, some pets allowed* ▭*AE, D, DC, MC, V.*

$$$$ **Four Seasons Resort Whistler.** This plush nine-story hotel gives alpine chic a new twist with warm earth tones and wood interiors, big leather chairs beside the fireplace in the lobby, and amazingly spacious rooms. The bistro-style restaurant is focused around a central fire pit. The luxurious spa has become a destination in itself with its 15 treatment rooms and wide range of massages. Child-friendly amenities include children's programs and pint-size bathrobes. ✉*Upper Village, 4591 Blackcomb Way, V0N 1B4* ☎*604/935–3400 or 888/935–2460* 📠*604/935–3455* 🌐*www.fourseasons.com* *273 studios and suites, 3 town homes* *In-room: safe, DVD, ethernet, Wi-Fi. In-hotel: public Wi-Fi, restaurant, room ser-*

vice, bar, pool, gym, spa, concierge, children's programs (ages 13 and under), parking (fee), no-smoking rooms ▭*AE, D, DC, MC, V.*

$$$$ **Summit Lodge & Spa.** Service is gracious and attentive at this friendly boutique hotel that is also one of Whistler's best values in the luxury range of hotels. Tucked in a quiet part of the village, the spacious rooms are beautifully decorated with soft neutrals, custom-made cherrywood furnishings, original art, and granite countertops. All units have balconies and fireplaces, and there's a shuttle to whisk guests to the nearby slopes. The full-service spa is among Whistler's most exotic, with a Javanese theme and royal heritage treatments; it claims to be North America's only authentic Indonesian-style spa. ✉*4359 Main St., V0N 1B4* ☎*604/932–2778 or 888/913–8811* 📠*604/932–2716* 🌐*www.summitlodge.com* *75 rooms, 6 suites* *In-room: kitchen, VCR, dial-up. In-hotel: pool, spa, concierge, laundry facilities, laundry service, parking (fee), no-smoking rooms, some pets allowed* ▭*MC, V* 🍽*CP.*

WORD OF MOUTH

"Regardless of whether you love the town of Whistler or hate it, the scenery on the way there and on the way out is gorgeous. And I consider that scenery to be worth seeing even if you have been to the Rockies. The Rockies are impressive, imposing, rugged and . . . well, rocky. But the forests around Whistler are much more lush than those in the Rockies."
—Judy_in_Calgary

$$$$ **Westin Resort & Spa.** This luxury hotel has a prime location on the edge of the village. The dramatic two-story lobby includes elements of stone, slate, pine, and cedar, and rooms are chic and cozy, with moss-green–and-rust color schemes, gas fireplaces, extra-deep tubs, and exceptionally comfortable beds. The 1,400-square-foot, split-level suites are great for families: each has a full kitchen and a loft bedroom with a whirlpool tub. The hotel's large restaurant has an open kitchen and fantastic oversize windows. The spa, with 25 treatment rooms and a mountain-view lounge, offers facials, body wraps, and holistic therapies such as herbology and acupuncture. ✉*4090 Whistler Way, V0N 1B4* ☎*604/905–5000 or 888/634–5577* 📠*604/905–5589* 🌐*www.westinwhistler.com* *204 rooms, 215 suites* *In-room: safe, kitchen (some), ethernet, Wi-Fi. In-hotel: restaurant, room service, public Wi-Fi, bar, pool, gym, spa, concierge, children's programs (ages 18 months–12 yrs), laundry facilities, laundry service, parking (fee), no-smoking rooms* ▭*AE, D, DC, MC, V.*

$$$–$$$$ **Adara Hotel.** Whistler's newest addition and only true boutique hotel is the Adara, sister property to Vancouver's hipster Opus Hotel. With its designer furniture (think curvy white Verner Panton chairs), sheepskin throws, a vibrant color scheme of reds and browns, and unexpected modish touches, like the bright-orange resin antlers that decorate the lobby's wall, the Adara offers a much-needed urban alternative to the typical large ski lodge experience. There are four distinctive room configurations to choose from, all of which feature spacious bathrooms with "rain" shower heads and electric fireplaces, as well as sophisticated surfaces in local wood, stone, and other natural materials. Some

rooms have private terraces. There's an outdoor pool in summer and a year-round hot tub. In winter, a nice spread of complimentary juices, pastries, and coffee is served for breakfast in the lobby. ✉*4122 Village Green, V0N 1B4* ☎*604/905–4009 or 866/502–3272* 🌐*www.adarahotel.com* *20 rooms, 21 suites* *In room: safe, kitchen, ethernet. In-hotel: concierge, pool, parking (fee), some pets allowed (fee)* ▭*AE, D, DC, MC, V.*

$$$ **Edgewater Lodge.** This cedar lodge lies along glacier-fed Green Lake on 45 acres of private forested land, about 3 km (2 mi) north of the village. The rooms and suites are large, with private entrances and window seats set before expansive water and mountain views. The restaurant is a romantic retreat that serves Pacific cuisine including seafood, pasta, steak, and venison. Complimentary Continental breakfast is included. Whistler Outdoor Experience runs an activity center here, providing guests and nonguests with fishing, hiking, canoeing, kayaking, and trail rides in summer, and snowshoeing, sleigh rides, and cross-country skiing in winter. ✉*8841 Hwy. 99, Box 369, V0N 1B0* ☎*604/932–0688 or 888/870–9065* *604/932–0686* 🌐*www.edgewater-lodge.com* *6 rooms, 6 suites* *In-room: no a/c, Wi-Fi (some). In-hotel: restaurant, bar, parking (no fee), no-smoking rooms, some pets allowed, no elevator* ▭*AE, MC, V* *CP.*

3

SPORTS & THE OUTDOORS

There's no getting around the fact that Whistler made its reputation on winter sports, with epic skiing and snowboarding, but there's also tons to do during the summer months. You can explore the mountains by ATV or on horseback; adrenaline junkies can bungee jump or enjoy a white-water rafting trip; and golfers can play a round at any of the four championship golf courses. And don't forget the hundreds of hiking trails, numerous options for kayaking and fishing, glacier tours by helicopter, bear watching opportunities, and a kick-ass bike park. Whistler is an outdoor enthusiast's paradise!

Whistler Activity and Information Center. This is the best first stop for any Whistler outdoor activity: it's the place to pick up hiking, biking, and cross-country maps or find out about equipment rentals, and they can even help you book activities. ✉*4010 Whistler Way* ☎*604/932–2394 or 604/938–2769.*

BIKING & HIKING

The 28-km (45-mi) paved, car-free Valley Trail links the village to lakeside beaches and scenic picnic spots. For more challenging routes, ski lifts whisk hikers and bikers up to the alpine, where marked trails are graded by difficulty. The Peak Chair operates in summer to take hikers to the top of 7,160-foot-high Whistler. The newest addition to the high alpine trail network is the High Note Trail, an intermediate, 5-mi route with an elevation change of 1,132 feet and fabulous coastal mountain views.

Whistler Outdoor Experience. On the shores of Green Lake, the friendly guides at this company lead hikes and mountain-bike tours. ✉*Edgewater Outdoor Centre, 8841 Hwy. 99* ☎*604/932–3389 or 877/386–1888* 🌐*www.whistleroutdoor.com.*

BOATING

Canoe and kayak rentals are available at Alta Lake at both Lakeside Park and Wayside Park. A spot that's perfect for canoeing is the River of Golden Dreams, which connects Alta Lake with Green Lake, both within a couple of miles of the village. If you'd rather leave the planning to others, check out one of the local outfitters.

Canadian Outback Adventure Company. Look these adventure specialists up for guided river-rafting trips in the Whistler area. They have an easy-going trip for families. ☎*604/921–7250 or 800/565–8735* 🌐*www.canadianoutback.com.*

Wedge Rafting. Specializing in rafting adventures, this company features 2-hour to full-day tours on the Green, Birkenhead, or Elaho-Squamish rivers. Tours depart from the village and include all equipment and experienced guides. Adventures are suitable for all levels. ☎*604/932–7171 or 888/932–5899* 🌐*www.wedgerafting.com.*

CROSS-COUNTRY SKIING

The meandering trail around the Whistler Golf Course (🌐*www.whistlergolf.com*) from the village is an ideal beginners' route. The 28 km (17 mi) of track-set trails that wind around scenic Lost Lake, Chateau Whistler Golf Course, the Nicklaus North Golf Course, and Green Lake include routes suitable for all levels; 4 km (2½ mi) of trails around Lost Lake are lighted for night skiing from 4 to 10 each evening.

★ **Whistler Ski Hike.** Operating out of the Whistler Nordic Center right in the village, Whistler Cross Country Ski & Hike and Coast Mountain Guides team up to offer lessons or guided cross-country ski tours at the golf course and other locations ideal for beginners and advanced skiers. ☎*604/932–7711* 🌐*www.whistlerski-hike.com.*

DOWNHILL SKIING & SNOWBOARDING

Blackcomb and Whistler Mountains. The two mountains receive an average of 360 inches of snow a year and feature the longest regular season in Canada, with lifts operating from late November to early June. If that's not enough, Blackcomb's Horstman Glacier is open June to early August for summer glacier skiing. The mountains' statistics are impressive: the resort covers 8,100 acres of skiable terrain in 12 alpine bowls and on three glaciers; it has more than 200 marked trails and is served by the continent's most advanced high-speed lift system. Blackcomb is the steeper of the two mountains and has a 5,280-foot vertical drop—North America's longest—and a top elevation of 7,494 feet. Whistler's drop comes in second at 5,020 feet, and its top elevation is 7,160 feet. Each has its advocates—while some people always head for the Whistler Village Gondola or Creekside Gondola (both serving Whistler Mountain), others prefer Blackcomb's Excalibur Gondola. Expert skiers swear by Whistler Mountain, especially on powder days, while less accomplished skiers might prefer Blackcomb Glacier on powder days because it's an enormous bowl; fresh tracks can be found even a couple of hours after the lift has opened. Meanwhile, snowboarders, especially free riders, prefer the Blackcomb side because of the prevalence of fall-line runs. ☎*604/932–3434 or 800/766–0449* 🌐*www.whistlerblackcomb.com.*

Whistler/Blackcomb Ski and Snowboard School. The school offers lessons for skiers and snowboarders of all levels. ✉*4545 Blackcomb Way* ☎*604/932–3434 or 800/766–0449.*

★ **Whistler Alpine Guides Bureau.** These expert mountain guides offer group tours, instructional clinics, and customized one-on-one trips to get you shredding untouched backcountry powder. ✉*113–4350 Lorimer* 🌐*www.whistlerguides.com* ☎*604/938–9242.*

Whistler/Blackcomb Hi Performance Rentals. They provide equipment rentals at the Whistler gondola base and at several outlets in the village. ✉*3434 Blackcomb Way* ☎*604/905–2252.*

GOLF

Golf season in Whistler runs from May through October; greens fees range from C$159 to C$210. You can arrange advance tee-time bookings through **Last Minute Golf** (☎*604/878–1833 or 800/684–6344* 🌐*www.lastminutegolfbc.com*). The company matches golfers and courses, sometimes at substantial green-fee discounts.

Fodor's Choice ★ **Big Sky Golf and Country Club.** Just 30 minutes north of Whistler in Pemberton is an 18-hole, par-72 course in an idyllic 190-acre location bordered by the emerald Green River, lakes, and creeks. ☎*604/894–6106 or 800/668–7900* 🌐*www.bigskygolf.com.*

★ **Chateau Whistler Golf Club.** Carved from the side of Blackcomb Mountain, this excellent 18-hole, par-72 course was designed by prominent golf-course architect Robert Trent Jones Jr. and features dramatic elevated views of the Whistler valley. ✉*4612 Blackcomb Way* ☎*604/938–2092 or 877/938–2092.*

HELICOPTER ADVENTURES: SKIING, GLACIER WALKING, PICNICS & HIKING

One of the most glaciated regions in the world is in the Coast Mountains of Western Canada, where Whistler is located. The range is approximately 1,600 km long and 200 km wide and is bordered by the Fraser River in the south and the Kelsall River in the north.

Blackcomb Helicopters. Flightseeing tours over Whistler's stunning mountains and glaciers are offered year-round. In summer, it offers heli-hiking, -biking, -fishing, -picnics, and even heli-weddings. ☎*604/938–1700 or 800/330–4354* 🌐*www.blackcombhelicopters.com.*

★ **Whistler Heli-Skiing.** Heli-skiing tours include helicopter-accessed guided day trips with three or more glacier runs for intermediate to expert skiers and snowboarders. The cost starts at C$640 per person. Heli-hiking is available all year long and guided tours can be tailored to your group's abilities, so you can enjoy your specially prepared picnic lunch in an age-old forest, pastoral meadow, or on a 12,000-year-old glacier. ✉*3–4241 Village Stroll* ☎*604/932–4105 or 888/435–4754* 🌐*www.whistlerheliskiing.com.*

OFF-ROAD TOURS

There's no better way to access miles of trails, dirt roads, and backcountry than on an easy-to-maneuver ATV, with a professional guide.

Barely Legal Motorsports. This outfitter offers custom all-terrain hotrod adventure tours though the backcountry to the mountain tops. ✉*1209 Alpha Lake Rd.* ☎*604/932–2222 or 877/932–9800* 🌐*www.blhotrod.com.*

Outdoor Adventures Whistler. This company offers unique ATV outings, like a sunset BBQ at a remote log cabin or an alpine sunrise tour to view resident black bears. ✉*4205 Village Sq.* ☎*604/932–0647* 🌐*www.adventureswhistler.com.*

SNOWMOBILING, SNOWSHOEING & SLEIGH OR SLED RIDES
★

Blackcomb Snowmobiles. Book guided snowmobile trips into the backcountry (from C$119 for two hours) through this company, which has outlets at the Fairmont Chateau Whistler and the Hilton Whistler Resort. ☎*604/932–8484* 🌐*www.blackcombsnowmobile.com.*

Fodor'sChoice ★ **Cougar Mountain Wilderness Adventures.** This outfitter has dogsled trips (from C$140 for 2½ hours) as well as snowmobiling and snowshoeing tours. In summer, dog sleds are equipped with wheels and run like chariots. ✉*36–4314 Main St.* ☎*604/932–4086 or 888/297–2222* 🌐*www.cougarmountain.ca.*

TUBING

Whistler Blackcomb's Coca-Cola Tube Park. Slip and slide in the snow at this family-friendly park which features 1,000 feet of lanes rated green, blue, and black diamond, a magic carpet to get back to the top, a fire pit, play area, and a snack station. There's even a mini zone with minitubes for the little ones. ✉*Excalibur gondola midstation at Blackcomb* ☎*800/944–8537* 🌐*www.whistler.com.*

ZIPLINING & CANOPY TOURS
★

Ziptrek Ecotours. This eco-friendly operator offers two of the newest year-round adventures around Whistler: zip trekking and canopy tours. There are 2½-hour adventures along 10 progressively higher and longer ziplines (one measures 2,000 feet) between Whistler and Blackcomb Mountains. If flying through the air is not your cup of tea, you can sign up for a canopy walk through old-growth treetops via a spectacular network of suspension bridges, boardwalks, and trails. ✉*4282 Mountain Sq.* ☎*604/935–0001 or 866/935–0001* 🌐*www.ziptrek.com.*

APRÈS SKI, NIGHTLIFE & THE ARTS

No Whistler trip would be complete without experiencing the town's après scene—be it after a day of skiing or hiking the trails. With amazing mountain views and ample patio space, Whistler has a surprisingly good choice of nightlife, most of it in the pedestrian-oriented village and within walking distance of the hotels and ski slopes.

For entertainment listings, pick up Whistler's weekly news magazine, the *Pique.*

BARS & CLUBS

Black's Pub. Here you'll find Whistler's largest selection of whiskeys (more than 40 varieties) and 99 beers from around the world. The adjoining restaurant is reasonably priced, offering mainly pizzas and pastas. ✉*4270 Mountain Sq.* ☎*604/932–6945.*

Citta'. The village-center patio is consistently touted as the best outdoor patio–it's *the* hot spot for people-watching and microbrew sipping. The place attracts a ton of late-night partiers. ✉*Whistler Village Sq.* ☎*604/932–4177.*

Garfinkle's. One of Whistler's largest clubs hosts live rock and roll, hiphop, funk, and jazz. It's a hangout for the young and a high point (literally) on any Whistler trip. ✉*1–4308 Main St.* ☎*604/932–2323.*

Fodor'sChoice ★ **Garibaldi Lift Company.** At the Whistler Gondola entrance, overlooking the base of the mountain, this popular joint attracts Whistler's hipsters to its lounge, restaurant, and club. It's a cozy place to relax and watch the latest ski and snowboard videos on the flat-screen TVs during the day; it gets hopping at night with live bands or reggae and house music. Don't miss the fresh-made guac to accompany your pint of imported beer. ✉*2320 London La.* ☎*604/905–2220.*

Tommy Africa's. Guest DJs play alternative and progressive dance music. The trademark shooters (shot glasses of undiluted alcoholic concoctions) make for a lively crowd. ✉*4216 Gateway Dr.* ☎*604/932–6090.*

SHOPPING

Whistler has almost 200 stores, most clustered in the pedestrian-only Whistler Village Centre; more can be found a short stroll away in Village North, Upper Village, and in the shopping concourses of the major hotels. Many goods reflect the tastes (and budgets) of the international moneyed set that vacations here, though savvy shoppers can get good deals on ski gear in spring and on summer clothing in fall.

Can-Ski. Their four locations have a good selection of brand-name ski gear, clothes, and accessories and they also do custom boot fitting and repairs. It's operated by Whistler-Blackcomb Resort. ✉*Crystal Lodge, Village Center* ☎*604/938–7755* ✉*Deer Lodge, Town Plaza* ☎*604/938–7432* ✉*Glacier Lodge, Upper Village* ☎*604/938–7744* ✉*Creekside (winters only)* ☎*604/905–2160.*

Helly Hansen. This is the place for high-quality Norwegian-made skiing, boarding, and other outdoor wear and equipment. ✉*Westin Resort & Spa, 115–4090 Whistler Way* ☎*604/932–0142.*

Rocks & Gems. This interesting shop has an amazing selection of trilobites featuring specimens from around the globe, including rare finds from B.C. This is the shop to go to whether you're searching for a one-of-a-kind collector fossil, an exotic stone like ammolite, or a handcrafted necklace or ring. ✉*4227 Village Stroll* ☎*604/938–3307.*

★ **Roots.** This Canadian-owned enterprise is known for its sweatshirts and cozy casuals, and they're something of a fixture in Whistler, especially since they outfitted both the Canadian and American Olympic teams in 2006. ✉*4229 Village Stroll* ☎*604/938–0058.*

THE OKANAGAN VALLEY

The Okanagan, five hours east of Vancouver by car or one hour by air, contains the largest concentration of people in the "interior"—or, what Vancouverites call South-central British Columbia. The region's sandy lake beaches and hot, dry climate have long made it a family-holiday magnet for Vancouverites and Albertans, and rooms and campsites can be hard to come by in summer.

The Okanagan Valley is the fruit-growing capital of Canada and a major wine-producing area with almost 60 picturesque wineries that welcome visitors with tastings, tours, and restaurants. The Wine Museum in Kelowna and the British Columbia Wine Information Centre in Penticton can help you create a winery tour and can provide details about annual wine festivals. In addition, 25 golf courses and several ski resorts draw sports people to the region year-round.

KELOWNA

390 km (242 mi) northeast of Vancouver, 68 km (42 mi) north of Penticton.

The largest community in the Okanagan Valley, with a regional population of over 160,000, Kelowna makes a good base for exploring the region's beaches, ski hills, wineries, and golf courses. Although its edges are looking untidily urban these days, with strip malls and office parks sprawling everywhere, the town has a convenient location right on Okanagan Lake.

Okanagan Lake splits the Kelowna region in two. On the east side of the lake is Kelowna proper, which includes the city's downtown and the winery district south of the city center that the locals call the Mission. On the west side of the lake is the community of Westbank. Several wineries are on the Westbank side, on and off Boucherie Road.

A good place to start your wine country exploration is at the **Wine Museum,** set in a historic packing house in downtown Kelowna. It's really more of a wine shop than an actual museum, but the staff is knowledgeable and can provide information about local wineries. They host daily wine tastings and occasional wine-related exhibits. ✉*1304 Ellis St.* ☎*250/868–0441* 🌐*www.kelownamuseum.ca* 🎫*By donation* ⏲*Weekdays 10–6, Sat. 10–5, Sun. 11–5.*

Much of the Okanagan valley is still covered with apple orchards, and one of the largest and oldest (dating from 1904) is the **Kelowna Land & Orchard Company,** which you can tour on foot or in a tractor-drawn covered wagon. The farm animals are a hit with kids, but grown-ups might prefer samples from the Raven Ridge Cidery, which turns Fuji, Braeburn, and Granny Smith apples into still wine, sparking cider, and iced ciders. The lake-view **Ridge Restaurant** ($–$$) serves lunch year-round and Sunday brunch from late April through October. ✉*3004 Dunster Rd., 8 km (5 mi) east of Kelowna* ☎*250/763–1091, 250/712–9404 restaurant reservations* 🌐*www.k-l-o.com* 🎫*Site free, tours C$7.50* ⏲*Late Apr.–Oct., daily 9–4:30; tours May–Oct., call for times.*

WINERIES

Almost all of the wineries in and around Kelowna offer tastings and tours throughout the summer and during the Okanagan Wine Festivals held in May and October; several have restaurants and most also have wine shops open year-round. Many wineries charge a nominal fee (C$2–C$5) for tastings.

Cedar Creek Estate Winery, south of Kelowna, has a scenic location overlooking the lake. Recent award-winning wines include several of their 2004 Platinum Reserve reds. Offering wine-friendly salads, cheeses, seafood, and other light contemporary fare, the outdoor **Terrace Restaurant** ($$) serves lunch mid-June through mid-September. ✉*5445 Lakeshore Rd.* ☎*250/764–8866 or 800/730–9463* 🌐*www.cedarcreek.bc.ca* *Tours C$5, tastings C$2–C$5* ⏲*Tours May–Oct., daily 11, 2, and 3. Wine shop May–Oct., daily 10–6; Nov.–Apr., daily 11–5.*

Atop a hill overlooking Okanagan Lake, **Mission Hill Family Estate** produces a wide variety of wines, and several different winery tours are offered, from a basic tour with a tasting of three wines, to a more in-depth visit that includes wine and food pairings. ✉*1730 Mission Hill Rd., Westbank* ☎*250/768–7611 or 800/957–9911* 🌐*www.missionhillwinery.com* *Tours C$5–C$40* ⏲*July–early Sept., daily 9:30–7; Apr.–June and early Sept.–early Oct., daily 10–6; early Oct.–Mar., daily 10–5; call or check the Web site for tour times.*

3

Quails' Gate Estate Winery, on 125 acres above the western edge of Okanagan Lake, gives tours several times daily from May through October. The winery is best known for their chardonnay and pinot noir. ✉*3303 Boucherie Rd.* ☎*250/769–4451 or 800/420–9463* 🌐*www.quailsgate.com* *Tours C$5* ⏲*Tours May–Oct.; call for schedule. Wine shop May and June, daily 10–7; July–early Oct., daily 9:30–7; early Oct.–Apr., daily 10–6.*

Summerhill Estate Winery, south of Kelowna on the east side of the lake, is an organic producer best known for its sparkling and ice wines. What tends to startle visitors, though, is the four-story-high replica of the Great Pyramid of Cheops; it's used to age and store the wine. ✉*4870 Chute Lake Rd.* ☎*250/764–8000 or 800/667–3538* 🌐*www.summerhill.bc.ca* *Tours C$5, tastings C$5* ⏲*Tours daily noon, 2, and 4. Wine shop daily 9–9.*

WHERE TO EAT

$$$–$$$$ ✕**Fresco Restaurant.** Seasonally inspired, locally sourced contemporary cuisine is the theme at this downtown Kelowna restaurant. Chef-owner Rod Butters, one of B.C.'s better-known chefs, prepares creative seafood dishes, such as his signature oat-crusted arctic char. He accents his frequently changing menus with Asian, Italian, and other intriguing touches. The decor is simple, with an open kitchen and exposed brick and beams revealing the historic building's architectural roots. ✉*1560 Water St.* ☎*250/868–8805* *AE, MC, V* *Reservations essential* ⏲*Closed Jan. Closed Sun. and Mon., Feb.–Apr. and Nov.–Dec. Closed Mon. May–Oct. No lunch.*

$$$–$$$$ ★ ✕**The Terrace at Mission Hill.** One of the most romantic of the winery dining rooms, this outdoor restaurant at the Mission Hill Family Estate has panoramic views across the vines and the lake. It's tough to compete with such a classic wine country locale, but the creative kitchen here is up to the task. You might start with a simple salad of perfectly ripe tomatoes and locally made goat cheese, paired with a refreshing tomato sorbet, or venison carpaccio served over arugula, before moving on to pork tenderloin sauced with a warm fig vinaigrette, or seared halibut cheeks. Every menu item is matched with an appropriate wine. Linger over a tasting plate of cheeses (choose an assortment of soft, aged, or

blue) or a trio of lemon or chocolate desserts. Because the restaurant is outdoors, service stops in inclement weather. ✉ *1730 Mission Hill Rd., Westbank* ☎ *250/768–6467* ▭ *AE, MC, V* ⊗ *Closed early Oct.–Apr. No dinner May–mid-June or early Sept.–early Oct.*

$$–$$$ ★ ✕ **Waterfront Wines Wine Bar & Restaurant.** The kind of laid-back place every neighborhood should have, this bistro and wine bar concentrates on small plates paired with local wines (which are also sold in the adjacent shop). They make a first-rate, garlicky Caesar salad, and in the summer, don't miss the juicy fresh tomato plate. Locals rave about the chili-spiced calamari. If you're in the mood for something heartier, you might try the steamed sablefish paired with crab dumplings or a simple roast chicken. The helpful staff know their wines, so you can do well by heeding their suggestions. ✉ *104–1180 Sunset Dr.* ☎ *250/979–1222* ▭ *MC, V* ⊗ *No lunch.*

WHERE TO STAY

$$$$ **Grand Okanagan Resort.** On the shore of Okanagan Lake, this resort is a five-minute stroll from downtown Kelowna, though you may never have to leave the grounds because of all the amenities—there's even a casino on-site. Most standard rooms and suites are spacious, with balconies, sitting areas, and attractive modern furnishings. About half the rooms have views over the lake and the surrounding hills. The two-bedroom waterfront condo suites are a good option for families: suites have two full baths, full kitchens, washer-dryers, and gas fireplaces. The villas in the adjacent Royal Private Residence Club are another option; they have one to three bedrooms, sleeping two to eight people. ✉ *1310 Water St., V1Y 9P3* ☎ *250/763–4500 or 800/465–4651* 🖷 *250/763–4565* 🌐 *www.grandokanagan.com* *261 rooms, 34 suites, 60 condominiums, 70 villas* *In-room: kitchen (some), Wi-Fi. In-hotel: 3 restaurants, room service, bar, 2 pools, gym, spa, bicycles, concierge, laundry service, executive floor, parking (fee), some pets allowed, no-smoking rooms* ▭ *AE, D, DC, MC, V.*

$$$–$$$$ **The Cove Lakeside Resort.** At this all-suites resort hotel on the western shore of Okanagan Lake, the guest suites, done in smart beiges and browns, have all the comforts of home and then some: fully equipped modern kitchens complete with special fridges to chill your wine, 42-inch plasma TVs, and fireplaces. Kids can amuse themselves at the pools, in the game room, or watching a movie in the media center, while active adults gravitate to the small fitness room or take a yoga class. The chic **Bonfire Restaurant & Bar** ($$$), which is run separately from the hotel, is a striking setting for a drink, but give the insipid Southwestern-style dishes a miss. ✉ *4205 Gellatly Rd., Westbank V4T 2K2* ☎ *250/707–1800 or 877/762–2683* 🖷 *250/707–1809* 🌐 *www.covelakeside.com* *150 suites* *In-room: kitchen, DVD, Wi-Fi. In-hotel: restaurant, room service, bar, tennis court, pools, gym, spa, beachfront, water sports, children's programs (ages 5 and up), laundry facilities, public Wi-Fi, no-smoking rooms* ▭ *AE, MC, V.*

$$$ **Hotel El Dorado.** Combining a 1926 building with a modern addition, this boutiquey, adult-oriented, lakeside hotel a short drive south of downtown Kelowna is one of the area's more stylish options. In the older "heritage" wing, the rooms are all different, but done with

1930s-style furniture, vintage radios, and claw-foot tubs. Rooms in the new wing, many of which are quite large, feel more like an upscale summer cottage, with cork floors, refrigerators, and plush furnishings. The traditional **Lakeside Dining Room** ($$–$$$) serves steaks and seafood. *500 Cook Rd., V1W 3G9 250/763–7500 or 866/608–7500 250/861–4779 www.eldoradokelowna.com 49 rooms, 6 suites In-room: refrigerator (some), DVD, Wi-Fi. In-hotel: 2 restaurants, bar, pool, gym, spa, beachfront AE, MC, V.*

$$ **A View of the Lake B&B.** Attention, foodies! Owner Steve Marston and his wife Chrissy run this B&B in their contemporary home; he's a former restaurant chef who whips up elaborate breakfasts and offers periodic cooking demonstrations and dinners in his lavish Food Network–style kitchen. Perched high on a hill, the house has expansive views of the lake and the entire valley, particularly from the huge deck. Inside, you'll find soaring ceilings and bright yellow walls in the living room, and clean, modern furnishings in the guest rooms. *1877 Horizon Dr., Westbank V1Z 3E4 250/769–7854 www.aviewofthelake.com 3 rooms In-room: no TV, Wi-Fi. In-hotel: no elevator, no kids under 12, no-smoking rooms MC, V BP.*

SPORTS & THE OUTDOORS

BIKING & HIKING

Bikers and hikers can follow the **Kettle Valley Rail Trail** between Penticton and Kelowna. Although many of the trail sections and trestle bridges that were destroyed by forest fires several years ago have been restored, be sure you use up-to-date maps and information, available from the visitor center in Kelowna.

GOLF

With four championship golf courses close to town, Kelowna is a major golf destination.

Gallagher's Canyon Golf and Country Club, about 15 km (9 mi) southeast of downtown Kelowna, has an 18-hole, par-72 championship course and a 9-hole, par-32 course; green fees for the 18-hole course are C$110 in high season. *4320 Gallagher's Dr. W 250/861–4240 or 800/446–5322 www.golfbc.com.*

Surrounded by orchards (golfers can pick fruit as they play), **Harvest Golf Club** is an 18-hole championship par-72 course. Green fees in high season are C$110. The Harvest Dining Room ($$$$), in the clubhouse, has lake views and is open to nongolfers for dinner. *2725 KLO Rd. 250/862–3103 or 800/257–8577 www.harvestgolf.com.*

SHOPPING

Carmelis Goat Cheese. If your only experience with "chèvre" is the supermarket cheese logs, you may be surprised by the variety—and the rich flavors—of the goats' milk cheeses that this family-owned artisanal cheese company produces. You can sample many of the cheeses in the shop, which is 12 km (8 mi) south of downtown Kelowna (and you'll likely see Carmelis cheeses on many area menus). To arrange a tour of the cheese production facilities and the goat barns, phone a week in advance. *170 Timberline Rd. 250/470–0341 Tours C$4, tastings free.*

Okanagan Grocery Artisan Breads. A good place to start if you're assembling a picnic, this first-rate bakery sells a variety of hearty loaves. They also offer a selection of local cheeses and other gourmet items. It's located in the Guisachan Village shopping complex, which also houses a produce market, seafood and meat shops, and a chocolate maker. ⊠*2355 Gordon Dr.* ☎*250/862–2811* ⊙*Tues.–Sat. 9:30–5:30.*

SUMMERLAND & PEACHLAND

Summerland is 52 km (31 mi) south of Kelowna, Peachland is 25 km (15 mi) southwest of Kelowna.

Between Kelowna and Penticton, Highway 97 winds along the west side of Okanagan Lake, past vineyards, orchards, fruit stands, beaches, picnic sites, and some of the region's prettiest lake and hill scenery.

WINERIES **Hainle Vineyards Estate Winery,** British Columbia's first organic winery and the first to make ice wines, is a small producer open for tastings (though not tours). The **Vine-Yard Restaurant** ($$–$$$) reopened in 2007 with a new chef and a menu that runs from burgers and steaks to wild sea bass and duck confit. The Trepanier Manor Hotel, a luxury boutique property, is under construction adjacent to the winery, and slated to open in 2008 or 2009. ⊠*5355 Trepanier Bench Rd., Peachland* ☎*250/767–2525 or 800/767–3109* ⊕*www.hainle.com* ⊙*May–Oct., daily 10–5; Nov.–Apr., daily 10–4.*

WHERE TO STAY & EAT

$$–$$$ ✕ **Cellar Door Bistro.** The flavors at this eclectic bistro in the Sumac Ridge Estate Winery ramble the world, drawing inspiration from Europe, Asia, and closer to home. There's a large selection of small plates designed to share, from salads and soups to salt-roasted shrimp or braised beef ribs. If you want a more substantial meal, you might opt for eggplant curry served over quinoa or seared scallops matched with braised greens. And of course, it's all paired with Sumac Ridge wines. ⊠*17403 Hwy. 97 N, Summerland* ☎*250/494–0451* ▭*AE, MC, V* ⊙*Closed Jan. and Feb.*

$$$–$$$$ **Summerland Waterfront Resort.** Designed for families who like the feel of a summer cottage but want the amenities of a resort, the rooms at this modern lakeside hotel are bright and beachy, done in sunny yellows and ocean blues. All have fireplaces and kitchen facilities, and the majority have lake views. A spa is scheduled to open in the spring of 2008. ⊠*13011 Lakeshore Dr. S, Summerland V0H 1Z1* ☎*250/494–8180 or 877/494–8111* 🖷*250/494–8190* ⊕*www.summerlandresorthotel.com* *115 suites* *In-room: kitchen, DVD, ethernet. In-hotel: restaurant, pool, gym, beachfront, water sports, laundry facilities* ▭*AE, MC, V.*

3

PENTICTON & NARAMATA

16 km (10 mi) south of Summerland, 395 km (245 mi) east of Vancouver.

Penticton, with its long, sandy beach backed by motels and cruising pickup trucks, is a nostalgia-inducing family-vacation spot. Drive through the city center to the east side of Okanagan Lake, though, and you'll be in the heart of the burgeoning Naramata wine country. The route along the Naramata Benchlands is peppered with one winery after another, so the seemingly short drive could take all afternoon.

The knowledgeable staff at the **British Columbia Wine Information Centre** will tell you what's new at area wineries and help you plan a self-drive winery tour. The center also stocks more than 500 local wines and offers complimentary tastings daily. They'll pack wine for travel and can arrange shipping within Canada. ✉*553 Railway St., Penticton* ☎*250/490–2006* 🌐*www.bcwineinfo.com* 🕓*May–Oct., daily 9–7; Nov.–Apr., weekdays 9–6, Sat. 10–6, Sun. 10–5.*

WINERIES May through October is high season for the Naramata wineries. Some close or scale back their hours between November and April.

It's hard to miss the 72-foot tower at **Hillside Estate Winery** as you drive along the road between Penticton and Naramata. Their first commercial release was in 1989, and their Old Vines Gamay Noir, Cabernet Franc, Cabernet Merlot, and Hidden Valley Rosé are recent award winners. ✉*1350 Naramata Rd., Penticton* ☎*250/493–6274 or 888/923–9463* 🌐*www.hillsideestate.com* 🕓*Apr. and May, daily 10–5; June–mid-Oct., daily 10–6; mid-Oct.–Mar., weekdays 11–4, weekends by appointment.*

Set on the Naramata Benchlands above Okanagan Lake, **Lake Breeze Vineyards** is one of the region's most attractively located small wineries and their white wines, particularly their gewürztraminer, pinot gris, and pinot blanc, are well regarded. Tastings are available but not tours. The outdoor **Patio Restaurant** ($$) (*see Where to Eat, below*) is open for lunch (weather permitting) between May and the first week of October. ✉*930 Sammet Rd., Naramata* ☎*250/496–5659* 🌐*www.lakebreeze.ca* 🎫*Tastings C$2* 🕓*Apr., Fri.–Sun. 11–5; May–mid-Oct., daily 11–5.*

New owners purchased small producer **Poplar Grove** in 2007 and plan to build a new winery and tasting center. In the meantime, the company is perhaps even better known for its first-rate cheeses. Stop by the cheese shop for the soft and pungent double-cream Camembert or the intense Tiger Blue. ✉*1060 Poplar Grove Rd., Naramata* ☎*250/493–9463 winery, 250/492–4575 cheese shop* 🌐*www.poplargrove.ca* 🕓*Call for winery and cheese shop hours.*

WHERE TO EAT

$$–$$$ **Barrel Room Bistro at Hillside Estate Winery.** The straightforward lunch menu—salads, sandwiches, pizzas, and pastas—brings in the wine tourists, who sip and chew on one of the two patios or in the rustic-style dining room. In the evening, more substantial fare includes grilled steak with a Tiger Blue cheese sauce, duck paired with cherry chutney, and citrus- and honey-glazed salmon. The restaurant can get busy with tour groups. *1350 Naramata Rd., Penticton 250/493–6274 or 888/923–9463 MC, V Closed mid-Oct.–Mar. No dinner Apr. and early Oct. No dinner Mon.–Thurs. May and June.*

¢–$ **The Bench Artisan Food Market.** In the morning, you can pop into this foodie-friendly market and café for coffee and pastries or a bowl of homemade granola. Then at midday, there are soups, salads, sandwiches, and daily specials. They'll make picnic platters to go, or you can assemble your own from the locally made cheeses, fresh-baked breads, and signature molten-chocolate brownies. *368 Vancouver Ave., Penticton 250/492–2222 MC, V No dinner.*

WHERE TO STAY

$$$–$$$$ **Naramata Heritage Inn.** Originally built as a hotel in 1908, this historic structure did time as a girls' school before the current owners converted it back to an inn in 2001. Many of the Mission-style furnishings, wood floors, and claw-foot tubs are original, but plenty of the amenities—heated bathroom floors, fluffy duvets, central air-conditioning—are au courant. The **Cobblestone Wine Bar** ($$–$$$) has a large selection of Okanagan wines, which are paired with contemporary cuisine, including grilled salmon, morel-studded pasta, and top-your-own foccacia; there's a sunny patio for summer lunches. *3625 1st St., Naramata V0H 1N0 250/496–6808 or 866/617–1188 250/496–5001 www.naramatainn.com 11 rooms, 1 suite In-room: no TV (some). In-hotel: restaurant, bar, spa, bicycles, no-smoking rooms AE, MC, V Closed Nov.–Jan. CP.*

$$–$$$ **God's Mountain Estate.** This quirky Mediterranean-style villa sits on 115 acres of sunny hilltop overlooking Skaha Lake, 4 km (2½ mi) south of Penticton, and a stay at this rambling property is a bit like a visit with a gracious, if eccentric, aunt. The three spacious common rooms are filled with an eclectic mix of antiques, plush cushions, and theatrical props, and guests are free to use the large common kitchen. Among the guest rooms, the Roofless Room is the most fun: the four-poster bed is sheltered under a canopy, but the rest of the room, including a fireplace and private hot tub, is open to the stars. Although the other rooms vary, several have expansive lake views. On most Sunday evenings, the inn hosts an elaborate five-course dinner that's open to guests and to the public (C$80 per person, including wine). *4898 Lakeside Rd., Penticton V2A 8W4 250/490–4800 www.godsmountain.com 10 rooms, 4 suites In-room: no a/c (some), no phone, refrigerator (some), no TV. In-hotel: no elevator, pool, public Wi-Fi, no kids under 12, no-smoking rooms MC, V BP.*

OLIVER & OSOYOOS

58 km (36 mi) south of Penticton, 400 km (250 mi) east of Vancouver.

> **WORD OF MOUTH**
>
> "I really think you should stay in Osoyoos.... There are so many wineries between Osoyoos and Penticton you would be hard pressed to see half of them. The area is so pretty." —traveller69

South of Penticton between the southern tip of Lake Okanagan and the U.S. border, Highway 97 runs along a chain of lakes: Skaha, Vaseaux, and Osoyoos, and through Canada's only desert. With a hot, dry climate, the sandy lakeshores can be crowded with families in summer, and it's also a popular winter destination for snowbirds from the Canadian prairies. The climate makes this a prime wine-producing area, and the roads on both sides of Osoyoos Lake between the towns of Oliver and Osoyoos are lined with wineries.

Desert Centre. The northern tip of the Great Basin Desert is home to flora and fauna found nowhere else in the country. You can learn more about the unique local ecology at this interpretive center, where you can take a one-hour guided tour along a boardwalk desert trail. Night tours are offered periodically as well; call for schedule. ✉ *146th St., off Hwy. 97, 4 km (3 mi) north of Osoyoos* ☎ *250/495–2470 or 877/899–0897* 🌐 *www.desert.org* 🎟 *C$6, including tour* 🕘 *May–early Oct., Wed.–Mon. 10–5; guided tours at 10, noon, and 2.*

WINERIES

Wineries line the roads between Osoyoos and Oliver, and continuing north toward the town of Okanagan Falls. Many of these are fairly small operations, but some notable larger producers are here, too. Many wineries close or reduce their operations between November and April, so call first if you're traveling off-season.

From the viewing tower and patio at **Burrowing Owl Estate Winery,** you get sweeping views of the vineyards and Osoyoos Lake. Among their award-winning wines are their 2005 pinot gris and chardonnay, and their 2004 cabernet sauvignon and cabernet franc. Complimentary winery tours are offered on weekends from May through October, and tastings are available year-round. At the 25-foot tasting bar, donations (C$2) for tastings are put toward the Burrowing Oil Recovery Society. Save time for a meal at the terrific **Sonora Room Restaurant.** ✉ *100 Burrowing Owl Pl., off Black Sage Rd., Oliver* ☎ *250/498–0620 or 877/498–0620* 🌐 *www.bovwine.ca* 🕘 *Tours May–Oct., weekends 11* AM *and 2* PM*. Wine shop May–Oct., daily 10–5; call for off-season hrs.*

Just west of downtown Osoyoos lies **The Nk'Mip Cellars,** North America's first aboriginal-owned and -operated winery. On a bench overlooking Osoyoos Lake, this stunningly designed winery is surrounded by both desert and vineyards. In addition to wine, the tasting room sells aboriginal art and gift items. The **Terrace Restaurant** incorporates aboriginal ingredients into the contemporary dishes. ✉ *1400 Rancher Creek Rd., Osoyoos* ☎ *250/495–2985* 🌐 *www.nkmipcellars.com* 🎟 *Tours C$5. Reserve tastings (July and Aug. only) C$15* 🕘 *Tours Jan.–Apr., Nov.,* *and Dec., daily 1 PM; May–Oct., daily 11 AM, 1 PM, and 3 PM. Wine shop Jan.–June and Sept.–Dec., daily 9–5; July and Aug., daily 9–8.*

WHERE TO EAT AND STAY

$$$–$$$$ **Spirit Ridge Vineyard Resort & Spa.** Owned and operated jointly by the Osoyoos Indian Band and Bellstar Hotels & Resorts, this Southwestern-inspired resort on a vine-covered hillside east of downtown Osoyoos is designed for upscale families; all the units, from the one-bedroom suites in the four-story lodge to the one- and two-bedroom "villas" in adjacent townhouses, have kitchens and sleep at least four. Although the hotel is not on the lake, you can rent kayaks, canoes, and motor boats down the hill in the affiliated lakefront campground. The **Passa Tempo Restaurant** ($$–$$$) takes inspiration from native ingredients as well as cuisines from around the world in such dishes as quinoa salad with fried chick peas and feta cheese or grilled bison in a red wine–chocolate sauce. *✉1200 Rancher Creek Rd., Osoyoos V0H 1V0 ☎250/495–5445 or 877/313–9463 250/495–5447 www.spiritridge.ca 94 suites In-room: kitchen, DVD, ethernet. In-hotel: restaurant, bar, golf course, pool, gym, spa, water sports, bicycles, laundry facilities, public Wi-Fi, some pets allowed, no-smoking rooms AE, MC, V.*

THE CANADIAN ROCKIES

Comparing mountains is a subjective and imprecise business. Yet few would deny that the 640-km (397-mi) stretch of the Canadian Rockies that runs along the Alberta–British Columbia border easily ranks as one of the most extravagantly beautiful ranges on earth. It's obvious how the Rockies got their name. Awesome forces of nature combined to thrust wildly folded sedimentary and metamorphic rock up into ragged peaks and high cliffs. Add glaciers and snowfields to the lofty peaks, carpet the valleys with forests, mix in a generous helping of small and large mammals, wildflowers, rivers, and crystal-clear lakes, and you've got the recipe for the Canadian Rockies.

The Columbias and the true Rockies are separated by the Columbia River. "British Columbia Rockies" is in part a misnomer. The term is often used to refer to the Columbia Mountains of southeastern British Columbia, which flank the western slope of the Rockies but are not geologically a part of the Rockies. Four separate ranges form the Columbias themselves. To the north are the Cariboos, west of Jasper and Mt. Robson parks. Reaching south like three long talons from the Cariboos are (west to east) the Monashees, the Selkirks, and the Purcells.

As the first ranges to capture storms moving from the west across the plains of interior British Columbia, the Columbias get much more rain and snow than the Rockies. In the Monashees, the westernmost of the subranges, annual snowfalls can exceed 65 feet. This precipitation has helped create the large, deep glaciers that add to the high-alpine beauty of the Columbias. Lower down, the moist climate creates lusher forests than those in the Rockies to the east. The deep snows in winter make the Columbias a magnet for deep-powder and helicopter skiers.

There are vast stretches of wilderness here that are virtually untouched by man in this part of Canada, the birthplace of Canada's national park system. About 25,000 square km (roughly 10,000 square mi)—an area larger than the state of New Hampshire—are protected in seven national parks in the Rockies and the Columbias. Wildlife is abundant, and from the highway you can see glaciers, lakes, valleys, and snow-capped mountain peaks.

For information on Banff National Park, see Chapter 4; for information on Jasper National Park, see Chapter 5.

GOLDEN

471 km (292 mi) northeast of Osoyoos.

Little more than a truck stop in the early 1990s, Golden, a town of 4,000 residents that serves a regional population of about 7,000 people, today has hotels, restaurants, and tour operators. While the town retains its role as an active service center for the lumber and trucking industries, there's summer sightseeing from the 924-foot gondola ascent and alpine skiing in winter. Many fine alpine lodges, most offering hiking and cross-country skiing right out the door, dot the hills and mountains around Golden, especially at Kicking Horse where resort development can barely keep up with demand as people discover the area's splendor. You still have to scratch below the surface a bit to get past the industrial history of the town, but the effort will be rewarded with some hidden gems, minus the crowds found in the towns of the national parks. 🌐*wwwgo2rockies.com* is a good resource.

The gondola at the **Kicking Horse Mountain Resort** (✉*1500 Kicking Horse Trail* ☎*866/754–5425* 🌐*www.kickinghorseresort.com*), an all-season resort formerly known as Whitetooth, transports eight people per car on the 12-minute ride to the summit of Kicking Horse Mountain. In winter, the ride's part of the skiing experience. In summer the ride up is C$25 and you can zoom down on a mountain bike, sign up for an interpretive hike or choose packages that include a visit to the grizzly bear refuge which opened in 2003 for a transplanted animal from Grouse Mountain in Vancouver. A wildlife ranger will guide you through the bear's wilderness habitat. Hours vary, so call ahead.

For a more indulgent option, consider taking the gondola to Canada's highest restaurant, **Eagle's Eye Restaurant.** At 7,705 feet, the restaurant has an incredible panoramic view of the surrounding mountains and offers a unique fine dining experience. In summer, you can enjoy a gondola ride and brunch for C$36 or a sunset dinner for C$49.95, including gondola transportation. ✉*1500 Kicking Horse Trail* ☎*250/344–2330* 💳*AE, MC, V.*

WHERE TO STAY & EAT

$-$$$ ★ **Eleven 22 Grill & Liquids.** Local artwork (for sale) adorns the walls of this early-20th-century house with numerous cozy dining rooms. The international menu lists appetizers such as Edamame, Beef Satay, and Thai Seafood Soup; entrées are more mainstream and include a daily risotto, Indian curry, pasta, steaks, and seafood. The homemade breads are delectable. Garden seating is available in summer. *1122 10th Ave. S, at Hwy. 95 and 12th St. 250/344–2443 www.eleven22.ca MC, V Closed late Oct.–mid-Nov. and late Apr.–mid-May.*

$$-$$$ **Kicking Horse Grill.** Dark-brown wood dominates this rustic-yet-elegant restaurant with exposed log beams and walls. The cuisine of 18 different countries, including Greece, Japan, Spain, France, Thailand, and Indonesia, gives the restaurant its motto: "taste the world." The menu changes every few months, but could include anything from paella to pasta. The restaurant was selected North American Resort Restaurant of the Year by Good Skiing and Snowboarding's 2005 Guide. *1105 9th St. S 250/344–2330 www.thekickinghorsegrill.ca AE, MC, V.*

$$$-$$$$ **Gondola Plaza.** Situated at the base of the Golden Eagle Express Gondola at Kicking Horse Mountain Resort, these executive-style condos offer ski-on/ski-off access to the hill. Each one-, two-, or three-bedroom condo is privately owned and fully equipped with a kitchen, fireplace, TV, VCR/DVD, and must meet very high standards to be included in the rental pool. Heated parking and ski storage are provided on-site. Rates drop by 60% off-season (spring and summer) *1500 Kicking Horse Trail V0A 1H0 250/439–1160 or 877/754–5486 www.kickinghorsevacations.com 89 rooms In-room: kitchen, DVD. In-hotel: restaurant, pub, pool, sauna, gym, hot tub AE, D, MC, V.*

SPORTS & THE OUTDOORS

HELI-HIKING & SKIING

Golden Alpine Holidays (*250/344–7273 www.goldenalpineholidays.com*) runs three- to seven-day alpine hiking and backcountry ski tours in the Selkirk Mountains, with accommodation in three backcountry mountain huts near the tree line (expect propane lights, woodstoves, saunas, full kitchens, no running water or electricity, and outhouse toilets). For the less hardy, the outfit also operates a comfortable four-bedroom lodge with running water, a sauna and even internet services. You and your gear are helicoptered in to the lodges. You can hire a guide and move between locations or stay at a single lodge. Backcountry skiing season lasts from December through April; hiking is offered from early July to mid-September.

Purcell Heli-Ski/Hiking (*250/344–5410 or 877/435–4754 www.purcellhelicopterskiing.com*) has one- to seven-day heli-skiing-and-snowboarding packages in the Purcell Mountains, with day use of a modern mountain lodge. Overnight accommodations are in Golden. Heli-skiing is available from December to mid-May, and there's also half- or full-day heli-hiking from mid-June to September.

DOWNHILL SKIING

The **Kicking Horse Mountain Resort** (*1500 Kicking Horse Trail 866/754–5425 www.kickinghorseresort.com*) has something for skiers of all levels. There is a year-round express gondola that whisks you to Canada's second highest peak (4,133 feet/1,260 meters) as well as four chair lifts. Together they access 106 ski runs ranging from beginner to expert, and onto snow that is often described as "champagne powder." A day of skiing costs C$62.

RAFTING

With several stretches of Class IV rapids, the Kicking Horse River has excellent white-water rafting. Half-day excursions run about C$65 per person, full-day excursions about C$99–C$150. Rafting season is generally May through September, but high-water conditions, especially in spring, may force cancellation of the wilder trips. **Alpine Rafting** (☎*250/344–6778* 🌐*www.alpinerafting.com*) runs mild to extreme white-water trips on the Kicking Horse. **Glacier Raft Company** (☎*250/344–6521* 🌐*www.glacierraft.com*) specializes in extreme white water (Class IV) but also runs more serene trips. **Wet 'N' Wild Adventures** (☎*250/344–6546 or 800/668–9119* 🌐*www.wetnwild.bc.ca*) conducts moderate to wild half- and full-day trips on Kicking Horse white water.

SPORTING GEAR

Selkirk Source for Sports (✉*504 9th Ave. N* ☎*250/344–2966*) rents and sells bicycles, and cross-country and alpine skis. It also has a large selection of sportswear and accessories. **Summit Cycle** (✉*1007 11th Ave.* ☎*250/344–6600*) also rents bicycles and skis.

SHOPPING

Canyon Creek Pottery (✉*917 10th Ave. N* ☎*250/344–5678*) sells pottery crafted on-site. You can visit the studio and see future gallery items being created.

EN ROUTE

The 105-km (65-mi) drive south from Golden to Radium Hot Springs, where Highway 93 joins Highway 95, is a pleasant excursion, rambling along the rolling floodplain of the Columbia River. To the right are the river and the Purcell Mountains; more immediately to the left are the Rockies, although the major peaks are hidden by the ranges in the foreground. Resorts catering to RVs abound.

GLACIER NATIONAL PARK

58 km (36 mi) west of Golden, 45 km (28 mi) east of Revelstoke.

Glacier National Park, not to be confused with the U.S. park of the same name in Montana, is known for rugged mountains and, not surprisingly, an abundance of glaciers (more than 400). The glaciers result not because of the exceptionally high elevation—although some peaks here do exceed 10,000 feet—but because of the high winter snowfalls in the park. Many of the glaciers can be seen from the highway, but to appreciate Glacier National Park fully, you must take to the trail.

At **Rogers Pass,** near the center of Glacier National Park along Highway 1, the heavy winter snowfalls made rail and road construction exceedingly difficult. Avalanches claimed the lives of hundreds of railway-construction workers in the early 1900s and continued to be a threat during highway construction in the 1950s.

Today, the Rogers Pass war against avalanches is both active and passive. Heavy artillery—105mm howitzers—is used to trigger controlled avalanches before they build up to threaten truly dangerous slides. (If you're traveling in the backcountry, always be alert to unexploded howitzer shells that pose a potential hazard.) On the passive side, train tunnels and long snow sheds along the highway shield travelers from major slide paths.

The **Rogers Pass Centre** documents Glacier National Park's history and is well worth a visit even if you're not stopping long. Exhibits highlight the geology and wildlife of the park, and 30-minute movies focus on such subjects as avalanches and bears. ✉*Hwy. 1* ☎*250/837–7500* *Free with purchase of park pass* ⏲*May–mid-June and Sept.–Nov., daily 8:30–4:30; mid-June–Aug., daily 7:30* AM*–8* PM*; Dec.–Apr., daily 7–5.*

WHERE TO STAY

$$ **Glacier Park Lodge.** The modern, two-story Best Western at the top of Rogers Pass adds wood-veneer tables and chairs and pink carpeting to its familiar chain style as well as six suites ideal for family travel. The steep-sloping A-frame roof is a design concession to the heavy winter snows. The lodge accommodates travelers with its 24-hour service station and 24-hour cafeteria. Rates drop 40% off-season. ✉*Rogers Pass, Glacier National Park, Hwy. 1, V0E 2S0* ☎*250/837–2126 or 800/528–1234* *www.glacierparklodge.ca* *50 rooms* *In-room: no a/c, coffeemaker. In-hotel: restaurant, bar, pool, no elevator* *AE, D, DC, MC, V* *EP.*

SPORTS & THE OUTDOORS

Several trails from the Illecillewaet Campground, a few miles west of the park's Rogers Pass Centre on Highway 1, make good day hikes. One of the best, although fairly strenuous, is the **Asulkan Valley Trail,** a 13-km (8-mi) loop that passes waterfalls and yields views of the Asulkan Glacier and three massifs—the Ramparts, the Dome, and Mt. Jupiter. A much easier hike is the 1½-km (1-mi) **Brook Trail** loop, which starts 6 km (4 mi) west of the Rogers Pass Centre and leads to views of the glaciers of Mt. Bonney.

MT. REVELSTOKE NATIONAL PARK

Eastern border 20 km (12 mi) west of Glacier National Park; western edge is by town of Revelstoke.

This park on the western flanks of the Selkirks has smaller mountains than those in the Rockies to the east, and lusher vegetation, thanks to the additional rain and snow on the west-facing slopes. Conceived primarily as a day-use park, Mt. Revelstoke National Park covers just 260 square km (100 square mi). Its main attraction is the 26-km (16-mi) **Meadows in the Sky Parkway** to the summit of Mt. Revelstoke, at 6,395 feet. As it climbs to the top, the parkway takes you through several different geographical zones, from alpine meadows to tundra. The paved road, which is generally open and snow-free from mid-July to late September, begins from Highway 1, 1½ km (1 mi) before the turnoff to the town of Revelstoke. This is a narrow road with many switchbacks, so trailers are not permitted. From the Balsam Lake parking lot, there's a free shuttle bus for the last 2 km (1 mi) to the summit area daily from 10 to 4:20. Several easy hikes from the Balsam parking lot meander past small lakes and have excellent views of the Selkirk and Monashee ranges.

REVELSTOKE

148 km (92 mi) west of Golden, on western edge of Mt. Revelstoke National Park.

The pretty little town of Revelstoke has both summer and winter activities. The downtown district's spruced-up buildings from the late-19th-century house modern shops, restaurants, and businesses.

The two pools at **Canyon Hot Springs,** tucked between Mt. Revelstoke and Glacier national parks about 35 km (22 mi) east of Revelstoke, make a good rest stop. A 15,000-gallon hot pool is naturally heated to 42°C (108°F), and a 60,000-gallon pool is mixed with cool water to maintain a temperature of 32°C (90°F). Log cabins—with private baths and kitchenettes—and camping are available. **Albert Canyon,** a ghost town that was the site of the original hot-springs complex built by railroad workers in the late 1800s, is a short distance south of the present facility. ✉*Off Hwy. 1* ☎*250/837–2420* 🌐*www.canyonhotsprings.com* *C$8.50* *May–June and Sept., daily 9–9; July and Aug., daily 9 AM–10 PM.*

WHERE TO STAY & EAT

$$–$$$$ ✕**One-Twelve.** Low cedar ceilings and an abundance of historic photos from Canadian Pacific Railway's early years lend warmth to this fine-dining restaurant in the Regent Inn. Fine seafood dishes compose about half the menu; Continental favorites such as chicken *cordon bleu* and top grades of beef complete the choices. The blue-ribbon menu selection is lamb broiled with rosemary and red wine. ✉*112 1st St. E* ☎*250/837–2107* 🌐*www.regentinn.com* *Reservations essential* *AE, MC, V.*

$$ **Regent Inn.** Many styles mix at this Revelstoke landmark in the heart of downtown: colonial, with its brick-arcade facade; true Canadian, in its pine-trimmed lobby area and restaurant; and Scandinavian, in the angular, low-slung wood furnishings of the guest rooms, many with reproduction antiques. Rooms are on the large side but lack views. ✉*112 1st St. E, Box 582, V0E 2S0* ☎*250/837–2107 or 888/245–5523* *250/837–9669* 🌐*www.regentinn.com* *50 rooms* *In-room: Wi-Fi. In-hotel: Wi-Fi, restaurant, bar, gym, Jacuzzi, sauna, no elevator* *AE, D, DC, MC, V* *CP*

SPORTS & THE OUTDOORS

BIKING **Skookum Cycle** (✉*118 Mackenzie Ave.* ☎*250/814–0090*) rents bicycles.

SKIING **Revelstoke Mountain Resort** (☎*800/991–4455* 🌐*www.discoverrevelstoke.com*) took over a local powder and a helicopter skiing outfit to form the base operations for this new resort development which opened in winter 2007 with the longest vertical run in North America—about 7,000 feet. In addition to the new cut and gladed mountain terrain, it organizes two- to five-day all-inclusive packages that run into the Selkirks and on the upper slopes of Mt. MacKenzie in Revelstoke as well as all-inclusive packages in the Selkirk and Monashee mountains near Revelstoke, with accommodations in town.

Revelstoke Snowmobile Tours (☎*250/837–5200* 🌐*www.revelstokecc.bc.ca/rst*) offers half- and full-day tours in the Columbia Mountains that start at C$149; you can also rent snowmobiles here without a guide.

YOHO NATIONAL PARK

57 km (35 mi) northwest of Banff town site, 185 km (115 mi) west of Calgary.

The name *Yoho* is a Cree word that translates, roughly, into "awe inspiring." Indeed, Yoho National Park contains some of the most outstanding scenery in the Canadian Rockies. The park adjoins Banff National Park to the east, but it's quieter than its neighbor. Highway 1 divides Yoho into the northern half, which includes Takakkaw Falls, the Burgess Shale fossil site, the Yoho River valley, and Emerald Lake; and the southern half, of which Lake O'Hara is the center.

23 **Takakkaw Falls** (✉*Yoho Valley Rd., off Hwy. 1, 26 km [16 mi] west of Banff National Park*), in the northern half of Yoho National Park, has a sheer drop of 833 feet—one of the highest waterfalls in Canada. The falls are spectacular in early summer, when melting snow and ice provide ample runoff. The road to the falls is not recommended for vehicles more than 22 feet long; there's a drop-off area for trailers.

24 ★ A World Heritage Site, the **Burgess Shale Site,** on a fossil ridge near Field, British Columbia, was once on the bottom of the ocean and contains the fossilized remains of 120 marine species dating back 515 million years. Guided hikes (maximum 15 people) are the only way to see the actual fossil sites, and they're popular, so make reservations. The hikes are conducted July through September, from Friday to Monday, trail conditions permitting. Groups meet at the Yoho Brothers Trading Post in Field. The going is fairly strenuous; the round-trip distance is 20 km (12 mi). A steeper (3.6 mile round trip) hike leads to the Mt. Stephen trilobite fossil beds. Guided hikes are also offered to extensions of the Burgess Shale fossils in Kootenay and Banff national parks. Allow a full day for any of the hikes. 📫*Yoho-Burgess Shale Foundation, Box 148, Field, BCV0A 1G0* ☎*800/343–3006* 🌐*www.burgess-shale.bc.ca* 🎟*Hikes C$37–C$69.*

25 ★ At **Emerald Lake** (✉*access from 8-km [5-mi] road off Hwy. 1, 19 km [12 mi] west of Banff National Park*), a vivid turquoise shimmer at the base of the President Range, you can rent a canoe, have a cup of tea at the tea house by Emerald Lake Lodge, or take a stroll around the lake. The lake is a trailhead for hikers, cross-country skiers, and snowshoers.

26 ★ **Lake O'Hara,** in Yoho's southern half, is widely regarded as one of the ultimate destinations for outdoor enthusiasts, particularly hikers, in the Canadian Rockies. The scenery here is stunning: mountains surround the small, remote, aquamarine lake. In summer, Lake O'Hara Lodge is booked months in advance. In addition to the lodge, there is a campground operated by Parks Canada (☎250/343–6433) and a backcountry hut operated by the Alpine Club of Canada (☎403/678–3200). To reach the lake, you can hike the forest-lined fire road from Highway 1, but it makes more sense to ride the lodge-run bus (call the lodge for times and space availability). Keep in mind, that to protect the fragile alpine area and to ensure an uncrowded experience, there's a quota on overnight and day use. Only 36 spots are available on the bus, which you must reserve in advance (up to three months). Save your legs for hiking any of several moderately strenuous trails that radiate from the lodge into a high-alpine world of small lakes surrounded by escarpments of rock and patches of year-round snow. Note that there's no fishing or boating on the lake. ✉*Lake O'Hara Fire Rd. off Hwy. 1, 11-km (7-mi) on fire road, 3 km (2 mi) west of Banff National Park western boundary* ☎*250/343–6433* ⊕*www.parkscanada.gc.ca/yoho.*

3

WHERE TO STAY & EAT

$$$$ ★ **Emerald Lake Lodge.** A 20-minute drive from Lake Louise and an hour from Banff, this enchanted place sits at the edge of a glacier-fed lake amid awe-inspiring scenery. The main dining room is a glass-enclosed terrace, with views of the lake through tall stands of evergreens. The menu mixes traditional Canadian and American fare—steaks, game, and fish—with nouvelle sauces like ginger-tangerine glaze. The guest cabins are pleasant, with fireplaces–firewood is supplied daily, and balconies. Be sure to request a lakefront cottage with a balcony overlooking the water. This area also attracts a lot of day visitors and even though the cottages are off limits to non-guests, the time for a more secluded stay is off-season, when room rates drop by 40%. ✉*Off Hwy. 1, Yoho National Park, 9½ km (6 mi) north of Field, Box 10, Field, BC, V0A 1G0* ☎*250/343–6321 or 800/663–6336* 🖷*250/343–6724* ⊕*www.crmr.com* *85 units in 2- and 4-room cottages* *In-room: no a/c, no TV. In-hotel: 2 restaurants, bar, gym, games room, no elevator* *AE, DC, MC, V* *EP.*

$$$$ **Lake O'Hara Lodge.** The historic lodge and lakeside cabins offer luxurious backcountry living with spectacular views. A stay here includes three meals a day, highlighting classic regional cuisine and fresh-baked bread. In summer, a lodge-operated bus shuttles guests along an 11-km (7-mi) fire road between Highway 1 and the grounds. In winter, you have to ski the distance. Reservations for the high summer season (mid-June through September) should be made at least eight months in advance. The minimum stay is two nights. ✉*Off Hwy. 1, Yoho National Park, Box 55, Lake Louise, AB, T0L 1E0* ☎*250/343–6418 in season, 403/678–4110 rest of yr* ⊕*www.lakeohara.com* *23 rooms, 15 with bath* *In-room: no a/c, no phone, no TV* *No credit cards* *Closed mid-Apr.–mid-June and Oct.–mid-Jan.* *FAP.*

SPORTS & THE OUTDOORS

HIKING Yoho is divided into two parts: the popular hiking area around Lake O'Hara, dotted with high-alpine lakes, and the less traveled Yoho River valley, terminating at Yoho Glacier. Entry into the Yoho River valley is from Takakkaw Falls or from Emerald Lake.

BOATING AND FISHING At the **Emerald Lake Lodge** (☎*250/343–6321*), docks, canoe, and fishing equipment rentals can be arranged on Emerald Lake.

KOOTENAY NATIONAL PARK

34 km (21 mi) west of Banff town site, 162 km (100 mi) west of Calgary.

When the tourist population of Banff swells in the busy summer months, Kootenay National Park remains surprisingly quiet, although not for lack of natural beauty—the scenery, including numerous steep rock facades, certainly matches that of Banff and Jasper parks. The park, which is named for the Ktunaxa (or Kootenai) people who have lived in the area for approximately 10,000 years, is just over the Alberta border in British Columbia, adjacent to the west side of Banff National Park and the south end of Yoho National Park. Facilities are few here; most people see the park only as they drive south on busy Highway 93, which traverses the park's length, while on their way to points in British Columbia. Backcountry overnight campers must purchase a wilderness pass, available at any national parks visitor center.

㉑ At 5,416 feet, **Vermilion Pass** (✉*3 km [2 mi] from east boundary of Kootenay National Park on Hwy. 93*) may not be among the highest passes in the Canadian Rockies, but it does mark the boundary between Alberta and British Columbia, as well as the Continental Divide—rivers east of here flow to the Atlantic Ocean, rivers to the west flow to the Pacific. The pass is at the boundary of Banff and Kootenay national parks, on Highway 93.

Just beyond the Vermilion Pass summit is the head of the **Stanley Glacier trail,** a fine choice for a day hike in the park. The trail climbs easily for 5½ km (3½ mi) through fire remnants and new growth, across rock debris and glacial moraine, ending in the giant amphitheater of the Stanley Glacier basin.

㉒ **Floe Lake** (✉*Trailhead: 22 km [14 mi] from east gate of Kootenay National Park on Hwy. 93*), at the base of a 3,300-foot-high cliff called the Rockwall, is one of the most popular hiking destinations in Kootenay. The 10-km (6-mi) trail from the highway passes through characteristic Kootenay backcountry terrain. Plan a full day for this one.

The trail that best characterizes the hiking in Kootenay is the strenuous **Rockwall Trail,** which runs along the series of steep rock facades that are the park's predominant feature. Floe Lake marks the trail's southern terminus; it then runs north for about 29 km (18 mi) to join up with the Helmet Creek Trail, which runs for 15 km (9 mi) back to the highway. The total hiking distance, counting the Floe Lake and

Helmet Creek trails, is almost 56 km (35 mi). Several other long spurs give you the option of doing less than the full distance. ✉ *Trailheads: Floe Lake trailhead for southern end, 22 km (14 mi) from park's east gate; Helmet Creek trailhead for northern end, 9½ km (6 mi) west of park's east gate.*

RADIUM HOT SPRINGS

127 km (79 mi) southwest of Banff, 103 km (64 mi) south of Golden, at junction of Hwys. 93 and 95.

Radium Hot Springs is little more than a service town for the busy highway traffic passing through, but the town makes a convenient access point for Kootenay National Park and has lower prices than the national parks.

Radium Hot Springs, the springs that give the town its name, are the town's longest-standing attraction and the summer lifeblood for the numerous motels in the area. Two outdoor pools are tucked at the bottom of the spectacular Sinclair Canyon. The hot pool is maintained at 41°C (106°F); in a cooler pool, the hot mineral water is diluted to 28°C (82°F). Lockers, towels, and suits (period and modern) can be rented. ✉ *Hwy. 93, 2 km (1 mi) northeast of Hwy. 95* ☎ *250/347–9485 or 800/767–1611* ⊕ *www.parkscanada.gc.ca/hotsprings* *C$6.30 per soak, C$9.55 for day pass* ⊙ *Hot pool: May–mid-Oct., daily 9 AM–11 PM; mid-Oct.–Apr., Fri. noon–9 and Sat. noon–10. Cooler pool: schedule varies with weather.*

WHERE TO STAY & EAT

$$–$$$ ✕ **Black Forest Restaurant.** A Bavarian theme pervades the region, and this is a good place to sample the cuisine. Schnitzels are the specialty, but other options are smoked pork with sauerkraut, bratwurst, seafood, chicken, duck, lamb, and steak. Save room for the elaborate cheesecake desserts. Exposed wood, Bavarian pottery, and big-game trophies decorate the interior, creating something of a cross between a hunting lodge and a Bavarian mountain chalet. ✉ *540 Hwy. 93 (Hwy. 95), 5 km (3 mi) west of town* ☎ *250/342–9417* ▭ *AE, DC, MC, V* ⊙ *No lunch.*

¢–$$$ ✕ **Back Country Jack's.** For all things barbecue, Jack's is the place to go. This fun restaurant has a relaxed and rustic atmosphere and consistently good barbecue ribs, chicken, and steaks. The all-you-can-eat rib or chicken nights are popular with families. ✉ *7555 Main St. W* ☎ *250/347–0097* ▭ *MC, V.*

$$–$$$ **Prestige Inn Radium.** This hotel is a little over 2 km (1 mi) from the Radium Hot Springs. Rooms are spacious and come in a variety of configurations from standard hotel rooms to executive suites to deluxe themed Jacuzzi suites. Theme rooms come in three types: African, Egyptian, and New York City. Ask for an even numbered room; they have the best view and don't cost any more. ✉ *7493 Main St.* ☎ *250/347–2300 or 877/737–8443* ⊕ *www.prestigeinn.com* *In-room: coffeemaker, refrigerator, kitchen (some), Wi-Fi. In-hotel: Wi-Fi, restaurant, bar, pool, gym, spa* ▭ *AE, DC, MC, V.*

$$ **Radium Resort.** Recreational facilities and activities bring this resort to life. Golf is the main attraction (packages are available), along with the proximity to the hot springs. Accommodations are in hotel rooms or one-, two-, or three-bedroom condo units. The rooms are modern, with hardwood furnishings and sponge-painted walls, and each has a sundeck, a mini-refrigerator, and a view overlooking the golf fairways. Condos have full kitchens. Watch for discount golf packages on the Web site to save money. There's a small rate reduction off-season. ✉*8100 Golf Course Rd., Box 310, V0A 1M0* ☎*250/347–9311 or 800/667–6444* 🌐*www.radiumresort.com* *90 rooms, 30 condo units* *In-room: high-speed Internet in rooms, not in condos, coffeemaker, refrigerator, kitchen (some), no a/c in condos. In-hotel: high-speed Internet, no elevator, no pets, golf courses, tennis courts, pool, gym* 💳*AE, D, MC, V.*

SPORTS & THE OUTDOORS

Radium Resort Course (✉*8100 Golf Course Rd.* ☎*250/347–9311 or 800/667–6444* 🌐*www.radiumresort.com*) is an 18-hole, par-69 golf course adjacent to the Radium Resort hotel.

The **Springs Course** (✉*8100 Golf Course Rd.* ☎*250/347–9311 or 800/667–6444* 🌐*www.radiumresort.com*) is an 18-hole par-72 course that is consistently rated as one of the top 100 in Canada. It is home base to a comprehensive golf academy for all skill levels.

INVERMERE

18 km (11 mi) south of Radium Hot Springs.

Invermere, one of the many highway service towns in the British Columbia Rockies, is the central access point for Windermere Lake, the Purcell Wilderness Area, a remote backcountry region encompassing thousands of acres of mountains and forest, and the ever-evolving Panorama Mountain Village Resort.

Panorama Mountain Village (✉*Toby Creek Rd.* ☎*250/342–6941 or 800/663–2929* 🌐*www.panoramaresort.com*) is another resort that Intrawest (owners of Whistler/Blackcomb) is redefining into a more upscale year-round resort. Best known for its terrific skiing in winter, which gets better every year, in summer you can take advantage of an excellent golf course, tennis courts, outdoor pools, water slides, hiking and biking trails, and lift-accessed mountain biking. Yet another new condo development took up residence in 2006 and the alpine village now includes a few outlets such as a specialty art shops and boutiques.

The **Pynelogs Cultural Centre** (✉*1720 4th Ave., at Kinsmen Beach* ☎*250/342–4423*) showcases and sells all types of local crafts: paintings, pottery, photographs, jewelry, and sculptures. This heritage building is also the venue of occasional evening folk or jazz concerts.

For summer water sports, **Windermere Lake**—actually an extra-wide stretch of the Columbia River—is popular among swimmers, boaters, and boardsailors. There's a good beach on the lake.

WHERE TO STAY & EAT

$$–$$$$ **Portabella Restaurant.** Tucked away on a sidestreet in downtown Invermere, Portabella is an intimate little restaurant with a Mediterranean ambience. Local artwork adorns the walls and there is a sunny patio out front. The menu changes regularly and there are two-course dinner specials nightly along with wine features. Expect fine dining with an ethnic flare here. Meals are prepared using fresh organic fruits, vegetables, and meats in season. Fresh fish, AAA beef, and vegetarian dishes are prepared à la minute. Reservations are recommended. ✉722 *13 St.* ☎*250/342–0606* *AE, MC, V* *Closed Mon. No lunch.*

$$–$$$ ★ **Strand's Old House Restaurant.** Strand's is a gem set amid the usual pizza and burger joints in Invermere. The five rooms provide varied levels of coziness; in summer there's seating on a large outdoor patio, and a gazebo opens for additional seating in an attractive courtyard. The menu highlights fresh seafood and a range of tapas-style appetizers such as baked Brie and snails in garlic butter and red wine. Top choices include peppered steak, and rack of lamb flavored with Dijon mustard and herbs. ✉*818 12th St.* ☎*250/342–6344* *Reservations essential* *AE, MC, V* *No lunch.*

$$ **Best Western Invermere Inn.** There are few surprises at this location of the familiar hotel chain, although rooms are on the large side. The hotel is conveniently located at a quiet end of the main shopping and dining area in town. The pub is known for its big screen sports broadcasts during the week and DJ entertainment and dancing at the weekend. It's the nearest major hotel to the town beach, but still about a mile away. Rates drop 20% off-season. ✉*1310 7th Ave., V0A 1K0* ☎*250/342–9246 or 800/661–8911* *250/342–6079* *www.invermereinn.com* *45 rooms* *In-room: coffeemaker, refrigerator, Wi-Fi. In-hotel: restaurant, bar, Wi-Fi, room service, gym, pets allowed (fee)* *AE, D, MC, V* *CP.*

$–$$$ **Panorama Mountain Village.** Accommodations are either in condo villas (many have fireplaces, patios, or balconies) that resemble part of a mountainside suburb, or a choice of lodges, including one at the base of the ski lift that has a college-dorm atmosphere and a lively pub. Depending on the season you can ski, hike, bike, or play golf or tennis. There are two large year-round outdoor heated pools, two hot tubs, and a 4,000-square-foot swimming pool. In summer the water slides are open. Although summer was once regarded as low season, this is no longer the case and best deals have shifted to fall and spring.; rates decrease by 25%. Specialty packages are geared to families such as Kids Under 12 ski for free. ✉ *Toby Creek Rd., 18 km (11 mi) west of Invermere, V0A 1T0* ☎*250/342–6941 or 800/663–2929* *www.panoramaresort.com* *102 hotel rooms, 400 condo units* *In-room: no a/c, ethernet, kitchen (condos), coffeemaker. In-hotel: 3 restaurants, bar, golf course, tennis courts, pools, spa, high-speed Internet, laundry facilities* *AE, D, MC, V.*

SPORTS & THE OUTDOORS

DOWNHILL SKIING **Panorama Mountain Village** (✉*Toby Creek Rd.* ☎*800/663–2929* 🌐*www.panoramaresort.com*) has the second-highest lift-served vertical drop (4,000 feet) in Canada; there are more than 120 runs, two terrain parks, and 9 lifts.

GOLF **Greywolf at Panorama** (✉*Toby Creek Rd.* ☎*800/663–2929* 🌐*www.panoramaresort.com*) has an 18-hole, par-72 course that Golf Digest ranks as one of the best in Canada. The sixth hole requires you to play across "Hopeful Canyon" to a green perched above vertical rock cliffs.

HELI-SKIING **R.K. Heli-Ski** (☎*250/342–3889 or 800/661–6060* 🌐*www.rkheliski.com*), based at the Panorama Mountain Village resort, has daily ski tours in winter.

SPORTING GEAR **Columbia Cycle and Motorsports** (✉*375 Laurier St.* ☎*250/342–6164*) rents bicycles, snowboards, downhill and cross-country skis, and snowshoes. **Invermere Sales & Rentals** (✉*403 7th Ave.* ☎*250/342–6336*) sells and rents canoes, boats, and personal watercraft.

If you're traveling with your own equipment, **D.R. Sports** (✉*2755 13th St.* ☎*250/342–3517*) will sharpen skates, tune up skis, restring racquets, and repair bikes and other sports-relating gear.

EN ROUTE The Columbia River Wetlands are some of the longest wetlands in North America. They stretch for almost 112 mi and provide respite for hundreds of migratory birds including more than 1,000 Tundra Swans in spring, vast flocks of Great Blue Herons, and in autumn, thousands of waterfowl. **Columbia River Outfitters** (✉*Pete's Marina, 25 Laurier St., on the north end of Lake Windermere* ☎*250/342–7397* 🌐*www.adventurevalley.com*) offers guided and self guided tours from C$39.

FAIRMONT HOT SPRINGS

20 km (12 mi) south of Invermere, 94 km (58 mi) north of Fort Steele.

Fairmont Hot Springs is named for the hot springs and the resort that has sprouted around it. The "town" is little more than a service strip along the highway, but turn in at the resort and things become more impressive. The town is also close to Columbia Lake, popular with boaters and boardsailors. Golf is a growing attraction at several fine courses in the area.

WHERE TO STAY

$$$–$$$$ **Fairmont Hot Springs Resort.** The wide selection of activities—from golf to heli-hiking—makes vacationing here feel somewhat like being at camp, only this camp has the luxuries of hot springs and a spa. Inside the attractive, low-slung, bungalow-style structure, rooms are contemporary, many with wood paneling; some are equipped with kitchens and have balconies or patios. The RV sites are popular. Golf, ski, and spa packages are available. Rates decrease by 30% off-season. ✉*Hwy. 93 (Hwy. 95), Box 10, V0B 1L0* ☎*250/345–6311, 800/663–4979 in Canada* 🌐*www.fairmontresort.com* *140 rooms, 311 RV sites* *In-*

room: coffeemaker, high-speed Internet, Wi-Fi (some), kitchens (some). In-hotel: 3 restaurants, bar, golf courses, tennis courts, pools, spa, bicycles, Wi-Fi ▭*AE, D, DC, MC, V.*

SPORTS & THE OUTDOORS

Fairmont Hot Springs Resort (✉*Hwy. 93 [Hwy. 95]* ☎ *800/663–4979* 🌐*www.fairmontresort.com*) has two 18-hole courses: a par-72 course at the resort and a par-71 course along the river in town. There are several hiking trails, including a spectacular trail that leads from the hot-springs waterfall into the canyon.

FORT STEELE

94 km (58 mi) south of Fairmont Hot Springs.

Many German and Swiss immigrants who arrived in the late 19th century settled in Fort Steele and nearby Kimberley to work as miners and loggers. Southeastern British Columbia was not unlike the Tyrol region they had left, so they found it comfortable to settle here. Later, a demand for experienced alpinists to guide and teach hikers, climbers, and skiers brought more settlers from the Alpine countries. Today, a Tyrolean influence is evident throughout southeastern British Columbia, particularly in Fort Steele. Schnitzels and fondues appear on menus as often as burgers and fries.

Fort Steele Heritage Town, a reconstructed 1890s boomtown consisting of more than 60 buildings, is a step back to the silver- and lead-mining days of the 1890s. This living-history museum's theater, period tradespeople, barbershop, and dry-goods store exude the authenticity of a bygone era. Steam-train and wagon rides are available. There's enough here to hold the interest of children and adults alike for a half day or more. ✉*9851 Hwy. 93 (Hwy. 95)* ☎*250/417–6000* 🖷*250/489–2624* 🌐*www.fortsteele.bc.ca* 🎟*July–Sept. C$13; May, June, and Sept.–mid-Oct. C$9.50; mid-Oct.–Apr. free* ⏲*Buildings: July–Sept., daily 9:30–7; May, June, and Sept.–mid-Oct. 9:30–5.*

KIMBERLEY

40 km (25 mi) west of Fort Steele, 98 km (61 mi) south of Fairmont Hot Springs.

A cross between quaint and kitschy, Kimberley is rich with Tyrolean character. The *Platzl* ("small plaza," in German) is a pedestrian mall of shops and restaurants modeled after a Bavarian village. Chalet style buildings are as common here as log cabins are in the national parks. In summer, Kimberley plays its alpine theme to the hilt: merchants dress up in lederhosen, and gimmicks abound—and the promotion works. The Canadian Rockies are a popular destination for German tourists; Kimberley catches their attention, and sometimes there's as much German as English being spoken in the Platzl. Aother key attraction is the Sullivan Mine which, for generations, was the town's backbone industry. It ceased operations in 2001 and has since been transformed into an Intepretive Centre.

WHERE TO STAY & EAT

$$–$$$ ★ **Chef Bernard's Inn and Restaurant.** Eating in this small homey storefront restaurant on the Kimberley pedestrian mall is like dining in someone's pantry. Packed into the shelves of the many small rooms in the dining area are the chef's collection of travel memorabilia—license plates, glass figurines, and much more, including a model train that runs on the ceiling in the restaurant. If things aren't too busy, don't be surprised to see cheery chef Bernard out front in the Platzl, wooing customers inside. The international menu ranges from a Malaysian jambalaya to a spice-as-you-like-it Indian curry to pastas and steaks. Homemade desserts are always popular. There's also an inn upstairs. *170 Spokane St. 250/427–4820 Reservations essential No lunch in winter AE, D, DC, MC, V.*

$$$ **Marriott Trickle Creek Residence Inn.** Lodge pole pine beams and river rock pillars lend an elegant yet rustic feeling to the lobby of this alpine resort. Hotel guests have ski-in, ski-out privileges at the adjacent ski resort and golf privileges at the adjacent Trickle Creek Golf Resort. The studio, one-, two-, and three-bedroom suites have full kichens, fireplaces, and balconies with excellent views of the surrounding mountains. A deluxe Continental breakfast buffet, that includes hot and cold items, is served every morning. This is a non-smoking inn. *500 Stemwinder Dr., V1A2Y6 250/427–5175 or 877/282–1200 250/427–5176 www.marriott.com 80 suites In-room: high-speed Internet, coffeemaker, kitchen, pets (fee). In-hotel: restaurant, bar, golf course, hot tub, pool, gym AE, D, DC, MC, V CP.*

NIGHTLIFE & THE ARTS

In summer, Bavarian bands in Kimberley strike up with oompah music on the Platzl, especially when an event such as the **Old Time Accordion Championships** (*800/667–0871 www.kimberleyvacations.bc.ca*) is in full swing (early July).

SPORTS & THE OUTDOORS

Kimberley Alpine Ski Resort (*Kimberly Ski Area Rd. 250/427–4881 or 800/258–7669 www.skikimberley.com*) has a vertical drop of 2,465 feet, 75 runs (plus tree runs), and 5 lifts, as well as mountain-top accommodations, restaurants, a lounge, and a rental shop. You can go night skiing Thursday to Saturday from late December to mid-March. Lift tickets for the day cost C$55.

GOLF **Trickle Creek Golf Resort** (*250/427–3389 or 888/874–2553 www.tricklecreek.com*) is an 18-hole, par-72 course designed by Les Furber and was rated by readers of *Score Golf* as one of Canada's best.

FERNIE

96 km (60 mi) east of Fort Steele, 331 km (205 mi) southwest of Calgary.

Fernie is primarily a winter destination, serving skiers at the Fernie Alpine Resort ski area, though mountain biking is a popular summer attraction. As one of the largest towns between Cranbrook and Calgary, Fernie has a wider selection of motels and restaurants than other centers along this route. Rather unexpectedly in these mountain landscapes, downtown Fernie exudes a Victorian charm. When a fire devastated the town center in 1908, city forefathers proclaimed that all new buildings had to be built from fireproof materials. Consequently, 100 years later, the main street has several restored brick and stone buildings including the 1911 courthouse, and the former CPR station, now a museum.

WHERE TO STAY & EAT

¢–$$$ ✕**Rip N'Richard's.** Next to the Elk River, this local favorite specializes in Southwestern cuisine, quesadillas, jambalaya, finger foods, calzones, and wood-fired pizza. The restaurant sits right next to the river and has great mountain views from its windows and outdoor decks. ✉*301 Hwy. 3* ☎*250/423–3002* ▭*MC, V.*

$$–$$$ **Fernie Stanford Resort.** There are fully equipped chalets, standard hotel rooms, and theme rooms—including the Greek-inspired Athens Oasis and the Nature's Hotspring room—at this lodge, near the Elk River. The chalets have between one and five bedrooms, kitchens, and gas fireplaces. Nearby are a ski hill and an 18-hole golf course. The swimming pool has a huge water slide. ✉*100 Riverside Way, V0B 1M0* ☎*250/423–5000 or 877/423–5000* 🌐*www.ferniestanfordresort.com* *58 rooms, 75 chalets* *In-room: no a/c in condos, no Wi-Fi in condos. In-hotel: restaurant, bar, pool, gym, hot tub, sauna, spa* ▭*AE, MC, V.*

SPORTS & THE OUTDOORS

Fernie Alpine Resort (✉*Ski Area Rd.* ☎*250/423–4655* 🌐*www.skifernie.com*) has 107 runs, 10 lifts, five bowls, tree skiing, and on-mountain facilities for skiers. In summer a chairlift keeps busy ferrying mountain bikers and their bikes up the slopes. Expansion has increased the vertical drop to 2,816 feet with the addition of two lifts. The resort also has nightclubs, several restaurants and pubs, a grocery, and a liquor store, plus ski-in, ski-out accommodations with hot tubs.

THE CARIBOO-CHILCOTIN

This is British Columbia's Wild West: a vast, thinly populated region stretching from the dense forests of the north to the rolling ranchlands of the south. The Cariboo-Chilcotin covers an area roughly bordered by Bella Coola in the west, Lillooet in the south, Wells Gray Park in the east, and Prince George in the north, though the part most visitors see is along Highway 97, which winds 640 km (397 mi) from Kamloops to Prince George.

In the 19th century thousands followed this route, called the Cariboo Wagon Road or the Gold Rush Trail, looking for—and finding—gold. Those times are remembered throughout the region, most vividly at the re-created gold-rush town of Barkerville. You can still pan for gold here, but these days most folks come for ranch and spa getaways, horseback riding, fly-fishing, mountain biking, and cross-country skiing.

THE CARIBOO RANCHING COUNTRY

73 km (44 mi) west of Kamloops.

The Cariboo is home to some of the biggest working ranches in North America, bucking-bronco rodeos, and a number of guest ranches that provide everything from basic riding holidays (some alongside real-life cowboys) to luxurious full-service spa resorts.

You can tour an 1863 roadhouse, visit a First Nations pit house, and take a stagecoach ride on the old Cariboo Wagon Road at **Historic Hat Creek Ranch** (✉*Hwy. 97, 11 km [7 mi] north of Cache Creek at junction with Hwy. 99* ☎*250/457–9722 or 800/782–0922* 🌐*www.hatcreekranch.com*), once a major stagecoach stop on the Gold Rush Trail. There's also a restaurant, gift shop, and campsite. The ranch is open May to mid-October, daily 9 to 5 with extended hours in July and August; admission is C$8.

WHERE TO STAY

$$$–$$$$ ★ **Echo Valley Ranch & Spa.** The palacelike Baan Thai ("Thai house") is an eye-catching anomaly in the undulating mountain landscapes and sets the stage for an experience that's about as authentically Thai as you can get outside of Thailand—with a Cariboo twist. The fusion of East meets West is what makes this remote luxury resort, 48 km (30 mi) west of Clinton, such an unusual find. The Baan Thai houses yoga classes and a lavishly decorated Thai-style guest suite. The Western spruce-log construction, vaulted ceilings, and expansive-view windows of the resort's main lodge, guest lodges, and cabins are equally beautiful. You can enjoy a Thai massage in the full-service spa; ride horses; hike, bike, fish, or take an all-terrain vehicle safari of the Fraser Canyon; or simply enjoy the fresh mountain air. Meals, taken family-style in the main lodge, make use of the ranch's own organic produce and often include a special Thai night of food and dancing, presented by the resort's Thai staff. Rates include all meals and use of ranch amenities. A three-night stay is required in high season and various custom-designed packages are offered. *Box 16, Jesmond, V0K 1K0* ☎*250/459–2386 or 800/253–8831* 🌐*www.evranch.com* *15 rooms, 1 suite, 3 cabins* *In-room: no phone, no TV, Wi-Fi. In-hotel: dining room, indoor pool, gym, 2 outdoor hot tubs, sauna, spa, fishing, mountain bikes, billiards, hiking, horseback riding, shuffleboard, recreation room, no elevator, shop, laundry service, Wi-Fi, meeting room, airstrip, helipad; no kids under 13, no smoking* *MC, V* *FAP.*

$$$ **The Flying U Ranch.** Founded in 1849, Canada's oldest guest ranch oozes no frills, Wild West charm, right down to the swinging doors at the Longhorn Saloon. Rustic log cabins with a shared bathhouse and hearty, basic meals served family style in the 1880s lodge recall ranch life of a century ago. You can ride all you want through the miles of surrounding ranchland; guides are optional—the horses know their way home. Hayrides and square dances round out the days. A two- to three-day minimum stay applies; rates include meals, riding and most other activities from birding and fishing to canoeing and swimming. ✉*North Green Lake Rd., 33 km (20 mi) south of 100 Mile House*

Box 69, 70 Mile House, V0K 2K0 250/456–7717 www.flyingu.com 25 cabins without bath, 2 tepees, 2 tents In-room: no a/c (fans), no phone, no TV. In-Hotel: dining room, pub, piano, lake, massage, sauna, dock, boating, fishing, hiking, horseshoes, volleyball, no elevator, shop, babysitting, playground, meeting rooms, airstrip MC, V Closed mid-Oct.–mid-May AP.

$$–$$$ **The Hills Health Ranch.** Hiking, horses, hay rides, and line dancing mix with spa treatments, wellness programs, and aerobics classes at this homey, affordable, and long-established health retreat. You can book structured wellness packages such as weight loss, anti-aging, healthy heart, and other medi-oriented programs, or just relax and enjoy the many activities at your own pace. Accommodations include woodsy three-bedroom A-frame chalets (ideal for families) and lodge rooms with standard hotel decor. The spa cuisine is excellent (and calorie counted), but heartier ranch meals and Continental fare are also available. *108 Mile Ranch at Hwy. 97, 60 km (36 mi) south of Williams Lake, 180 km (108 mi) northwest of Kamloops, Box 26, V0K 2Z0 250/791–5225 or 800/668–2233 www.spabc.com 26 rooms, 19 chalets In-room: no a/c (some), no phones (chalets), kitchens (some) In-hotel: 2 restaurants, pub, picnic area, indoor pool, health club, 2 hot tubs, sauna, spa, boating, mountain bikes, billiards, hiking, horseback riding, Ping-Pong, cross-country skiing, downhill skiing, ice-skating, ski shop, sleigh rides, snowmobiling, recreation room, no elevator, shop, playground, laundry service, ethernet, business services, meeting rooms, airstrip, some pets allowed, no smoking AE, MC, V.*

BARKERVILLE & WELLS

80 km (50 mi) east of Quesnel on Hwy. 26.

In 1862, when news of a rich gold strike at this out-of-the-way spot reached the outside world, this tiny settlement rapidly boomed into the biggest town west of Chicago and north of San Francisco.

Fodor's Choice ★ **Barkerville Historic Town,** with 125 original and re-created buildings, is now the largest heritage attraction in western Canada. Actors in period costume, merchants vending 19th-century goods, stagecoach rides, and live musical revues capture the town's heyday. The site is open year-round, but most of the theatrical fun happens in summer. *Hwy. 26, Barkerville 250/994–3332 www.barkerville.ca Mid-May–Sept. 30, C$13 for 1-day pass; 2nd day is C$2; free in winter Daily 8–8.*

Bowron Lake Provincial Park, 30 km (19 mi) east of Barkerville by gravel road, has a 116-km (72-mi) chain of rivers, lakes, and portages that make up a popular canoe route. Canoeists must reserve ahead and pay a fee of C$60 per person, plus C$18 per-boat reservation fee. The west side of the circuit can be paddled in two to four days; the fee is C$30. Note that advance reservations are required; any changes will incur fees, and no date changes are permitted within 14 days of arrival. Tip: A tip-packed pretrip information booklet is available from the Web site. *End of Hwy. 26 604/435–5622, 800/435–5622 canoe trip reservations www.bcparks.ca or www.hellobc.com*

Eight kilometers (5 mi) west of Barkerville, tiny **Wells** is a fascinating stop. A thriving mining town until the 1940s, it's now an atmospheric mountain village of brightly painted false-front buildings. The village, home to a vibrant arts community, has several art galleries and cafés and a summer arts school.

WHERE TO STAY

$-$$$ ★ **Elysia Resort on Quesnel Lake.** Set on the south shore of Quesnel Lake, the deepest fjord lake in the world, this full-service resort offers stunning scenery, terrific fishing, and a location that's just west of three provincial parks: Bowron Lake, Cariboo Mountains, and Wells Gray. All rooms have lake views and private balconies, and are furnished with plush duvets and a decor of rich earth tones to match the cedar trim. The fully licensed dining room has an extensive, ever-changing menu featuring B.C. produce; you can eat beside the fireplace or dine under the stars on the patio. Rates include boat moorage and the resort offers several all-inclusive packages such as photo safaris and fly-fishing. The resort is home-base to the province's only Fly Fishing School for Women. There are 12 full-service RV sites. ✉ *5657 Marshall Creek Rd., Quesnel Lake Junction* *Box 4069, Williams Lake, V2G 2V2* ☎ *250/243–2433* *www.elysiaresort.com* *8 rooms, 11 cabins* *In-room: no phone, no TV, kitchen (some). In-hotel: restaurant, lake, recreation room, marina, hot tub, horseshoes, volleyball, badminton, canoes, guiding services, jet boat excursions, eco-tours, flightseeing, no elevator, airstrip, limited Internet, pets allowed, no smoking* *AE, MC, V.*

$-$$ **Wells Hotel.** The faithfully refurbished 1934 Wells Hotel makes a good base for visiting nearby Barkerville and the Bowron Lake canoeing area and for accessing the 80 km (50 mi) of hiking, biking, and cross-country ski trails nearby. Comfortable rooms and suites are decorated in a 1930s style with hardwood floors, local art, and period photos. Best of all, new management has made sure every room now has a private bathroom. ✉ *2341 Pooley St., Wells* *Box 39, Wells, V0K 2R0* ☎ *250/994–3427 or 800/860–2299* *www.wellshotel.com* *13 rooms* *In-room: no a/c (fans), no phone, no TV. In-hotel: restaurant, pub, outdoor hot tub, no elevator, no Internet, no smoking* *AE, MC, V* *CP.*

NORTHERN BRITISH COLUMBIA

It's a truism that even those well traveled in B.C. rarely use the top half of their maps. The area most British Columbians refer to as "The North" comprises a full half of the province, most of it a little-visited, thinly populated, stunningly beautiful, wildlife-rich wilderness. The north is home to several groups of First Nations peoples who have lived in the regions for thousands of years and compose most of the population in many areas. Insights into these ancient cultures, at 'Ksan, near Hazelton, Kitwanga, and Kitwancool on the Stewart Cassiar Highway, and in other towns and villages throughout the north are, for many, the most rewarding part of a trip north.

Outdoor adventure increasingly draws those seeking out the north's untraveled hiking paths, canoe routes, white-water rivers, freshwater lakes, and backwater channels where exclusive fishing lodges nestle in the wilderness. Traveling the region feels like going on an adventure, as towns are few and far between, and drivers need a good spare tire and a sharp eye on the gas gauge. The rewards, though, are many: snow peaks; hot springs; sightings of bear, moose, and bighorn sheep; long summer days; and occasional glimpses of the northern lights.

Three major highways cross the north. Highway 16, the Yellowhead Highway, runs from Jasper in Alberta via Prince George to Prince Rupert, a route that can also be traveled by train on VIA Rail's Skeena line. Highway 97 heads north from Prince George to Dawson Creek, where it becomes the Alaska Highway. Farther to the west, the little-traveled Stewart-Cassiar Highway links Highway 16 to the Alaska Highway, making it possible to take a multiday circle tour of the region.

PRINCE GEORGE

786 km (487 mi) north of Vancouver, 412 km (247 mi) south of Dawson Creek, 440 mi (273 mi) southeast of Hazelton, 721 km (447 mi) east of Prince Rupert.

At the crossroads of two railways, two highways, and two rivers, Prince George is the province's third-largest city and the commercial center of northern British Columbia.

Century-old cabooses, locomotives, dining cars, and luxury sleeping cars are some of the dozens of restored railcars collected at the **Prince George Railway and Forestry Museum**, an outdoor museum that also displays historic logging and sawmill equipment. ✉ *850 River Rd., next to Cottonwood Park* ☎ *250/563–7351* 🌐 *www.pgrfm.bc.ca* 🎟 *C$6* ⏲ *Mid-May–Oct., daily 10–5; reduced hrs and admissions in winter.*

Logging is one of British Columbia's largest resource industries, and **Canfor** is one of the biggest forestry companies. Every summer, June through August, the company opens its various mill operations to the public. Contact Tourism Prince George for information and tour bookings: ☎ 800/668–7646.

WHERE TO STAY

$$–$$$ **Ramada Hotel.** You can't beat this hotel's central location for shopping, business, and sightseeing. It has a swimming pool, sauna, hot tub, and a popular sports bar (watch for karaoke on Saturday). Rooms are spacious with an upbeat, comfortable ambience; they range from a standard room with two double beds (some have a hide-a-bed sofa) to king size and Jacuzzi suites that are packed with amenities that include warmed bathroom floors, bathrobes, iron, hair dryer, and in-room coffeemakers. The TVs double as video game stations. ✉ *444 George St., V2L 1R6* ☎ *250/563–0055 or 800/830–8830* 🌐 *www.ramadaprince-george.com* *191 rooms, 2 suites* *In-room: safe, refrigerator, DVD (some), Wi-Fi. In-hotel: restaurant, pub, room service, indoor pool,*

gym, hot tub, laundry service, business services, shops, meeting rooms, Wi-Fi, covered parking with plug ins (no fee), some pets allowed (fee), no-smoking rooms ▭*AE, DC, MC, V.*

$-$$$ **Coast Inn of the North.** The rosewood lobby and brass fireplace makes for a striking welcome to this centrally located hotel with its myriad of services, including a gym, a pool, and a day spa in the attached retail concourse. Rooms are attractive, with rosewood furniture and added amenities such as desks, coffeemakers, and cable TV for movies and video games. The standard rooms have two double beds, the premium rooms are corner units with balconies, and the suites have jetted tubs and fireplaces. The two restaurants include a clubby room serving Continental fare and a traditional Japanese steak house. ✉*770 Brunswick St., V2L 2C2* ☎*250/563–0121* 🌐*www.coasthotels.com* *155 rooms, 2 suites* *In-room: safe, minibar (some), dial-up, Wi-Fi. In-hotel: 2 restaurants, coffee shop, pub, room service, indoor pool, gym, tanning salon, hair salon, hot tub, sauna, spa, lounge, shops, laundry service, business services, meeting rooms, Wi-Fi, parking (no fee), some pets allowed (fee), no-smoking rooms* ▭*AE, DC, MC, V.*

OFF THE BEATEN PATH

Fort St. James National Historic Site. This parklike site, 52 km (31 mi) north of Vanderhoof on Highway 27, on the south shore of Stuart Lake, is a former Hudson's Bay Company fur-trading post and the oldest continually inhabited European settlement west of the Rockies. Careful restoration of the original buildings, costumed staff, and demonstrations of aboriginal arts and food preparation help you experience life as a fur trader in 1896. ☎*250/996–7191* 🌐*www.parkscanada.gc.ca* *C$7* *Mid-May–Sept., daily 9–5; reduced hrs in winter.*

SMITHERS

371 km (222 mi) northwest of Prince George, 353 km (211 mi) northeast of Prince Rupert, 1,149 km (689 mi) northwest of Vancouver.

The main town of the Bulkley Valley, Smithers sits under the snowcapped backdrop of 8,700-foot Hudson's Bay Mountain. The Bavarian-theme town center has hotels, restaurants, and several outdoor-equipment outfitters to help visitors explore the surrounding peaks, rivers, and the kind of spectacular landscapes that keep British Columbia top of mind for eco-adventurers and photographers alike.

THE HAZELTONS

293 km (182 mi) northeast of Prince Rupert, 439 km (272 mi) northwest of Prince George, 1,217 km (755 mi) northwest of Vancouver.

Three villages—New, Old, and South Hazelton, each a couple of miles apart—combine to form the Hazeltons, an area rich in the culture of the Gitxsan and Wet'suwet'en peoples. New Hazelton is a modern service strip along Highway 16; South Hazelton is a hamlet just off Highway 16. Old Hazelton is a delightful village of old-fashioned false-front buildings where an old paddle wheeler houses a café and art gallery. It's 4 km (2½ mi) north of New Hazelton, across the Bulkley River by suspension bridge. There are motels in New Hazelton, B&Bs in Old Hazelton, and a campsite and RV park adjacent to 'Ksan Historical Village and Museum.

At **Kispiox,** 11 km (7 mi) north of Old Hazelton on Kispiox Valley Road, you can see 15 intricately carved totems, some more than 100 years old. Guided tours and local crafts are available at the **Kispiox Cultural and Information Centre** (☎*877/842–5911 or 250/842–7057* 🌐*www.kispioxadventures.com*).

★ **'Ksan Historical Village and Museum** is a re-created Gitxsan village. The community of seven longhouses was built in 1965 as a replica of the one that stood on the site, at the confluence of the Skeena and Bulkley rivers, for thousands of years before European contact. Gitxsan guides lead informative tours through three of the longhouses. At the Frog House, artifacts and an audio presentation tell of life in the distant past; at the Wolf House, audiovisual effects re-create the experience of being an honored guest at a feast. The Fireweed House exhibits the elaborate performing regalia of the 'Ksan Performing Arts Group, who reenact ancient songs and dances of the Gitxsan people, Friday evenings in summer. A gift shop sells goods from First Nations groups across the province; a café serves traditional Gitxsan foods. ✉*High Level Rd., Hwy. 62, Old Hazelton* ☎*250/842–5544 or 877/842–5518* 🌐*www.ksan.org* 🎫*C$2, C$10 with tour* ⏲*June–Sept., daily 9–5, tours on the ½ hr; call for winter hrs.*

TERRACE

147 km (88 mi) east of Prince Rupert on Hwy. 16, 577 km (346 mi) northwest of Prince George, 1,355 km (813 mi) northwest of Vancouver.

Terrace is a logging town and the major commercial center for the Skeena Valley. The region is also home to the Tsimchian peoples. The **Terrace Visitor Info Centre** (✉*4511 Keith Rd., Hwy. 16* ☎*250/635–2063* 🌐*www.terracetourism.bc.ca*) has information about area attractions, including Shames Mountain (hiking and skiing) and Skeena River, one of the province's most dynamic waterways for sport fishing (a 99-pound salmon, said to be a world-record catch, was caught in the Skeena).

Heritage Park (✉*4702 Kerby Ave.* ☎*250/635–4546* 🌐*www.heritageparkmuseum.com*) is a re-created turn-of-the-20th-century village, with costumed guides, many original log buildings, and more than 4,000 artifacts. It's open daily 10 to 6, from June to August, with reduced hours September through May. Call ahead to confirm. Admission is C$4.

About 80 km (48 mi) north of Terrace, partly on gravel road, is the **Nisga'a Memorial Lava Bed Park** (☎*250/798–2277*), a dramatic and eerily moonlike landscape that marks the site of Canada's last volcanic eruption, more than 250 years ago.

EN ROUTE

Traveling west toward Prince Rupert (⊕*www.tourismprincerupert.com*), both Highway 16 and the railway line follow the wide Skeena River. The route, which passes under snowcapped mountain peaks and past waterfalls, is one of the most scenic in the province. Prince Rupert is where the ferries depart for the Inside Passage as well as across to the **Queen Charlotte Islands.**

THE ALASKA HIGHWAY

406 km (243 mi) from Prince George to Dawson Creek, 985 km (591 mi) from Dawson Creek to Watson Lake, Yukon.

From Prince George, Highway 97, or the Hart Highway, continues northeast to Dawson Creek, where it becomes the Alaska Highway, the most popular route north for Alaska-bound travelers. It then winds through the foothills and pine forests of the northern Rocky Mountains, past the communities of Fort St. John and Fort Nelson, before crossing the B.C.–Yukon border at Watson Lake and continuing to Delta Junction, near Fairbanks, Alaska.

The Alaska Highway skirts the edges of the Muskwa-Kechika Management Area, a vast, roadless wilderness so rich in wildlife it's been called the Serengeti of the North. Even from the highway, sightings of deer, moose, elk, mountain sheep, and bear are commonplace.

The two-lane highway is paved and open year-round. Communities along the way are small, but basic services (gas, food, lodging) are available at least every few hours en route. Pine Pass, about 200 km (132 mi) north of Prince George, marks the boundary between the Pacific and Mountain time zones. Clocks go forward an hour here.

Dawson Creek, a town of about 11,000, is best known as Mile Zero of the Alaska Highway. The much-photographed signpost is at **Mile Zero Square** (⊠*10th St. and 102nd Ave., Dawson Creek*). Also at the square is **Alaska Highway House** (⊠*10201 10th St., Dawson Creek* ☎*250/782–4714*), which has a small exhibit about the history of the highway. It's open weekdays 8:30–4:30. The **Station Museum** (⊠*900 Alaska Ave., Dawson Creek* ☎*250/782–9595*), in the town's old railway station, has natural-history and railway-history displays and shows a film several times a day about the building of the Alaska Highway. The station is also home to the Dawson Creek Tourist Information Centre, open daily from May to September. ⊠*900 Alaska Ave.* ☎*250/782–9595* ⊕*www.tourismdawsoncreek.com*.

At **Liard River Hotsprings Provincial Park** (⊠*320 km [192 mi] northwest of Fort Nelson* ☎*800/689–9025 camping reservations* ⊕*www.discovercamping.ca*) heat from the springs has generated an oasis of tropical plants, including orchids, in this remote northern spot. Two natural outdoor hot-springs-fed pools are a short walk from the campground; there's a C$5 fee to use the pools. The campsite is popular, and reservations are recommended.

WHERE TO STAY

$ **Northern Rockies Lodge.** As an overnight stop on the Alaska Highway, or as a base camp for exploring the northerly hinterlands, this modern log lodge on Muncho Lake, 30 minutes from Liard River Hot Springs is ideal. It provides comfortable lodge rooms, rustic log cabins, lakefront chalets, a campground with RV hookups, a restaurant, and gas station—registered guests receive a nominal discount on fuel. Boating and outdoor activities are available at the lakeside, and the owner's own bush plane can take you on photo safaris, flightseeing tours, or fishing on a remote mountain lake. You can also stay overnight at one of the lodge's rustic fly-in outpost cabins. All inclusive eco-adventure packages are offered with transport from Vancouver. ✉ *Mi 462, Alaska Hwy., Box 8, Muncho Lake, V0C 1Z0* ☎ *250/776–3481 or 800/663–5269* 🌐 *www.northern-rockies-lodge.com* *21 rooms, 19 cabins, 3 outpost cabins* *In-room: no a/c (fans), refrigerator (some), no phone. In-hotel: restaurant, sauna, boating, fishing, mountain bikes, hiking, laundry facilities, business services, meeting rooms, ethernet (fee), airstrip, helipad, some pets allowed (fee), no-smoking rooms* 💳 *MC, V.*

3

THE STEWART-CASSIAR HIGHWAY

725 km (450 mi) from Kitwanga on Hwy. 16 to Upper Liard, Yukon, on the Alaska Hwy.

Linking Highway 16 to the Alaska Highway (the Yellowhead Highway), Highway 37, also called the Stewart-Cassiar Highway, is the road less traveled between B.C. and the Yukon. Though challenging to drive, it's arguably prettier than the Alaska Highway, with striking mountain views at every turn.

Although most of Highway 37 is paved, there are still some gravel sections. Watch for potholes, logging trucks, single-lane bridges, and low-flying aircraft (parts of the road double as a landing strip). As in all other active logging areas, it's best to drive with your lights on during the day to stay visible to logging trucks. Settlements are small, gas stations and mechanics are few, and snow can fly at any time of year (though it's rare in summer).

The provincial **Ministry of Transportation and Highways** (🌐 *www.drivebc.ca*) has up-to-date road reports.

A couple of miles north of the Yellowhead junction, the village of **Kitwanga** is home to a stunning array of ancient totems. Nearby is the **Battle Hill National Historic Site,** the site of a decisive First Nations battle in about 1600.

One of the largest and oldest collections of totem poles in North America stands at **Kitwancool** (also known as Gitanyow), just 15 km (9 mi) north of the Yellowhead junction.

The 1.6-million-acre **Spatsizi Plateau Wilderness Park** is one of Canada's largest and most remote parks, and one of its richest wildlife reserves. Home to caribou, grizzly bears, black bears, mountain goats, and 140 species of birds, it's virtually untouched wilderness, accessible only by foot, horseback, canoe, or floatplane.

B.C. Parks (☎ *250/847–7320*) in Smithers has information about guides and outfitters.

OFF THE BEATEN PATH

The Glacier Highway. The Glacier Highway (Highway 37A) leaves the Cassiar Highway at **Meziadin Junction,** about 170 km (112 mi) north of the Yellowhead Junction, and travels 65 glacier-lined km (39 mi) west to the oddly paired towns of Stewart, B.C., and Hyder, Alaska. The towns sit about 3 km (2 mi) apart on either side of the international border at the head of the Portland Canal, a 112-km-long (70-mi-long) fjord on the edge of Alaska's Misty Fjords National Monument. **Stewart,** with a population of about 1,000, has a bank, hotels, restaurants, and camping. Across the border, tiny **Hyder,** with a population of about 100, has no road links to the rest of the United States, except the highway through Canada. The few shops here accept Canadian money. It's a tradition for visitors to get "Hyderized": essentially by downing a shot of grain alcohol at the bar.

Telegraph Creek. From Dease Lake, a scenic 115-km (71-mi) gravel road, steep and winding in places, leads to this picturesque ghost town of gold-rush-era buildings on the Stikine River, said to be the oldest community in northern B.C.

WHERE TO STAY

$$ **Bell II Lodge.** Fly-fishing and heli-skiing are the specialties at this riverside resort, though travelers overnighting on the long drive north will also appreciate the comforts here. The guest rooms, in attractive modern log chalets, all have separate entrances, soapstone fireplaces, pine furniture, and down duvets. There are RV and tent sites here, too. ✉ *At Bell II, 250 km (150 mi) north of Hwy. 16 junction* *Box 1118, Vernon, BC, V1T 6N4* ☎ *604/513–5460 or 866/793–2355* *www.bell2lodge.com* *20 rooms* *In-room: no a/c, no TV. In-hotel: 2 restaurants, exercise equipment, outdoor hot tub, sauna, fishing, billiards, Ping-Pong, recreation room, shop, laundry facilities, ethernet, meeting room, parking (no fee), some pets allowed (fee); no smoking* *AE, MC, V.*

NORTH COAST

Gateway to Alaska and the Yukon, this vast, rugged region is marked by soaring snowcapped mountain ranges, scenic fjords, primordial islands, and towering rain forests. Once the center of a vast trading network, the mid- and north coasts are home to First Nations peoples who have lived here for 10,000 years and to immigrants drawn by the natural resources of fur, fish, and forest. The region is thin on roads, but you can travel by ferry, sailboat, cruise ship, plane, or kayak to explore the ancient villages of the coast and the Queen Charlotte Islands. The climate of this mist-shrouded region is one of the world's wettest. Winters see torrential rains, and summers are damp; rain gear is essential year-round.

INSIDE PASSAGE

★ *507 km (314 mi), or 274 nautical mi, between Port Hardy on northern Vancouver Island and Prince Rupert.*

The Inside Passage, a sheltered marine highway, follows a series of natural channels along the green-and-blue-shaded B.C. coast. The undisturbed landscape of rising mountains and humpbacked islands has a striking, prehistoric look. You can take a ferry cruise along the Inside Passage or see it on one of the luxury liners that sail from Vancouver to Alaska.

The comfortable *Northern Adventure,* BC Ferries newest vessel, carries up to 600 passengers and 101 vehicles. It has two- and four-berth cabins (some of them outfitted with flat-screen TVs and DVD players), a cafeteria, buffet, gift shop, elevator, children's play areas, and licensed lounge on board. Between mid-May and late September, sailings from Port Hardy on Vancouver Island to Prince Rupert (or vice versa) are direct and take 15 hours, almost entirely in daylight. Sailings are less frequent and longer the rest of the year, as the ferry makes stops along the way. Reservations are required for vehicles and recommended for foot passengers. You can order meal packages (breakfast and dinner for C$35 per person) when you reserve space. It's also a good idea to make hotel reservations at Port Hardy and Prince Rupert. ✉*BC Ferries, 1112 Fort St., Victoria, V8V 4V2* ☎*250/386–3431, 888/223–3779 in B.C., Alberta, and Washington state* 📠*250/381–5452* 🌐*www.bcferries.com* 🎫*One-way summer passage for car C$300, campers C$480 and up, depending on length, each driver or adult passenger C$125, cabins range C$75–C$200; fares lower Oct.–May when the route is covered by the Queen of Prince Rupert* ⏲*Mid-May–Sept., departing on alternate days from Port Hardy and Prince Rupert at 7:30* AM, *arriving 10:30* PM ☞*Note: Fuel surcharges can add C$16 (passenger only), C$34 (car), and C$95 (camper) to the overall cost of a ticket.*

DISCOVERY COAST PASSAGE

★ *258 km (160 mi), or 138 nautical mi, between Port Hardy on northern Vancouver Island and Bella Coola.*

This BC Ferries summer-only service travels up the Inside Passage to the First Nations community of Bella Bella and then turns up Dean Channel to the mainland town of Bella Coola. The scenery is stunning, and the route allows passengers to visit communities along the way, including Shearwater, Klemtu, and Ocean Falls. It also provides an alternative route into the Cariboo region, via the steep and winding Highway 20 from Bella Coola to Williams Lake. Lodging at ports of call varies from luxury fishing lodges to rough camping, but it's limited and must be booked in advance.

The *Queen of Chilliwack,* carrying up to 389 passengers and 115 vehicles, takes from 13 to 30 hours (depending on the number of stops) to travel from Port Hardy on Vancouver Island to Bella Coola. Reservations are required for vehicles and advised for foot passengers.

There aren't any cabins. ✉ *BC Ferries, 1112 Fort St., Victoria, V8V 4V2* ☎ *250/386–3431, 888/223–3779 in B.C. only* 📠 *250/381–5452* 🌐 *www.bcferries.com* 🎫 *One-way fares between Port Hardy and Bella Coola for each driver or adult traveler C$125, cars C$252, campers C$322 and up. Note: Fuel surcharges can add C$18 (passenger), C$36 (car), and C$50 (camper) to your ticket costs* 🕓 *Mid-June–early Sept., departs Port Hardy Tues., Thurs., and Sat.; leaves Bella Coola Mon., Wed., and Fri.*

PRINCE RUPERT

1,502 km (931 mi) by road and 750 km (465 mi) by air northwest of Vancouver, 15 hrs by ferry northwest of Port Hardy on Vancouver Island.

The port of Prince Rupert is the largest community on British Columbia's north coast. Set on Kaien Island at the mouth of the Skeena River and surrounded by deep green fjords and coastal rain forest, Prince Rupert is rich in the culture of the Tsimshian, people who have been in the area for thousands of years.

As the western terminus of Canada's second transcontinental railroad and blessed with a deep natural harbor, Prince Rupert was, at the time of its incorporation in 1910, poised to rival Vancouver as a center for trans-Pacific trade. This didn't happen, partly because the main visionary behind the scheme, Grand Trunk Pacific Railroad president Charles Hays, went down with the *Titanic* on his way back from a financing trip to England. Prince Rupert turned instead to fishing and forestry. New to tourism, this community of 15,000 retains a laid-back, small-town air.

Prince Rupert is the final stop on the BC Ferries route through the Inside Passage, as well as the base for ferries to the Queen Charlotte Islands and a port of call for Alaska ferries. The terminals for both BC and Alaska ferries and the VIA Rail Station are side by side, about 2 km (1 mi) from town; Farwest Bus Lines (☎ 250/624–3343) has service between the ferry terminals and the city center.

Prince Rupert is also a port of call for a growing number of Alaska-bound cruise ships; the city's two cruise-ship terminals are both near downtown, in the Cow Bay district.

Cow Bay, a 10-minute walk from downtown, is a historic waterfront area of shops, galleries, seafood restaurants, and fishing boats. Cow Bay takes its name seriously: lamp posts, benches, and anything else stationary is painted Holstein-style. Prince Rupert's **Visitor Information Centre** (☎ *250/624–5637 or 800/667–1994* 🕓 *May–Aug., daily 9–7; Sept., weekdays 9–5; Sat. 10–4; Nov–Apr., daily 10–3*) is at the Atlin cruise ship terminal in Cow Bay.

★ The **Museum of Northern British Columbia,** in a longhouse-style facility overlooking the waterfront, has one of the province's finest collections of coastal First Nations art, with artifacts portraying 10,000 years of Northwest Coast history. Artisans work on totem poles in the carving shed nearby and, at the museum's longhouse, you can catch performances of Tsimshian storytelling, song, and dance twice daily between June and September. In summer museum staff also offer a variety of museum and city tours and operate the **Kwinista Railway Museum,** a five-minute walk away on the waterfront. *100 1st Ave. W 250/624–3207 www.museumofnorthernbc.com C$5; additional fees for performances Sept.–May, Mon.–Sat. 9–5; June–Aug., Mon.–Sat. 9–8, Sun. 9–5.*

3

★ In the late 19th century, hundreds of cannery villages, built on pilings on the edge of the wilderness, lined the coast between California and Alaska. Most are gone now, but B.C.'s oldest (it dates to 1889) and most complete is the **North Pacific Historic Fishing Village** in Port Edward, 20 km (12 mi) south of Prince Rupert at the mouth of the Skeena River. Once home to more than 700 people during each canning season, the town, of 28 buildings including managers' houses, the company store, and cannery works, is now a national historic site. Staff members lead tours and demonstrations about the canning process and the unique culture of cannery villages. The site also has a seafood restaurant and overnight accommodation. Farwest Bus Lines (250/624–3343) buses travel here from Cow Bay, though service is infrequent. *Off Hwy. 16, Port Edward 250/628–3538 www.cannery.ca C$12 Mid-May–mid-Sept., daily 9:30–5.*

WHERE TO STAY

$$–$$$$ **Crest Hotel.** On a bluff overlooking the ocean, this full-service hotel has Prince Rupert's best views. The restaurant, lounge, most of the guest rooms, and the outdoor hot tub all command expansive vistas of the harbor and outlying forested islands. The rooms are large, comfortable, and modern; the pricier rooms have double Jacuzzi tubs set before ocean-view windows. The restaurant ($$$–$$$$), decorated with brass rails and beam ceilings, specializes in seafood, particularly salmon. You can also book cruises and fishing charters from here. *222 1st Ave. W, V8J 1A8 250/624–6771 or 800/663–8150 www.cresthotel.bc.ca 100 total rooms, 4 suites In-room: no a/c (fans), safe (some), refrigerator (some), VCR/DVD (some). In-hotel: 2 restaurants, room service, gym, outdoor hot tub, steam room, fishing, lounge, Wi-Fi, shop, babysitting, laundry facilities, laundry service, meeting rooms, parking (no fee), some pets allowed (fee), no-smoking rooms AE, D, DC, MC, V.*

QUEEN CHARLOTTE ISLANDS (HAIDA GWAII)

★ *93 nautical mi southwest of Prince Rupert, 367 nautical mi northwest of Port Hardy.*

The Queen Charlotte Islands, or Haida Gwaii (Islands of the People), have been called the Canadian Galápagos. Their long isolation off the province's North Coast has given rise to subspecies of wildlife found nowhere else in the world. The islands are also the preserve of the

Haida people, who make up about half the population. Their vibrant culture is undergoing a renaissance, evident throughout the islands.

Most of the islands' 5,400 permanent residents live on Graham Island—the northernmost and largest of the group of 150 islands—where 108 km (65 mi) of paved road connects the town of Queen Charlotte in the south to Masset in the north. Moresby Island, to the south, is the second-largest of the islands and is largely taken up by the Gwaii Haanas National Park Reserve and Haida Heritage Site, a roadless ecological reserve with restricted access. The wildlife (including bears, eagles, and otters), old-growth forest, and stunning scenery are like nothing else on earth, and kayaking enthusiasts from around the world are drawn to its waterways. Towns on Graham Island have the most services, including banking, grocery stores, and a range of accommodation and campsites; accommodation is also available in Sandspit, on Moresby Island. In summer it's a good idea to make hotel reservations before arriving.

The **visitor-information center** on Wharf Street in Queen Charlotte has information about area activities, including visits to Gwaii Haanas.

Fodor'sChoice ★ The 1,470-square-km (570-square-mi) **Gwaii Haanas National Park Reserve and Haida Heritage Site,** managed jointly by the Canadian government and the Council of the Haida Nation, protects a vast tract of wilderness, unique flora and fauna, and many historic and cultural sites. These include the island of SGang Gwaay (Anthony Island), a UNESCO World Heritage Site, where SGang Gwaay llnagaay is an excellent example of a traditional Northwest Coast First Nations village site, with 21 standing mortuary and memorial poles and the remains of massive cedar longhouses. The reserve is on Moresby Island and 137 smaller islands at the archipelago's southern end. The protected area, accessible only by air or sea, is both ecologically and culturally sensitive. One way to visit—and highly recommended for those unfamiliar with wilderness travel—is with a licensed operator. Parks Canada and the Queen Charlotte Visitor Information Centre have information about operators. To visit on your own (without a licensed operator), you must make a reservation, register for each trip, and attend a mandatory orientation session. Park-use fees start at C$10 per person per day, plus a C$15 per-person reservation fee. *Parks Canada, Box 37, Queen Charlotte, V0T 1S0 250/559–8818, 800/435–5622 information pack and reservations 250/559–8366 www.pc.gc.ca/gwaiihaanas.*

Fodor'sChoice ★ Just 1 km (½ mi) north of the Skidegate ferry terminal, the **Haida Gwaii Museum at Qay'llnagaay** is set in a striking longhouse-style facility on a bluff overlooking the water. Six totem poles, erected in 2001, stand outside. The museum's collection of Haida masks, totem poles, works by contemporary Haida artists, carvings of silver and argillite (soft black slate), and other artifacts is expanding with the addition of works repatriated from other museums. A gift shop sells Haida art, and a natural-history exhibit gives interesting background on island wildlife. By the summer of 2006, an expanded museum will be part of the **Qay'llnagaay Heritage Centre,** a multifaceted cultural center, which was, at this writing, under construction next to the existing museum. Built in the style of a traditional Haida village on a site once occupied by the old village of Qay'llnagaay, or Sea Lion Town, the center will include a theater, an art school, and a canoe-house sheltering *The Lootaas,* a 50-foot canoe created by renowned Haida artist Bill Reid. ✉*2nd Beach Rd. off Hwy. 16, Skidegate* ☎*250/559–4643* 🌐*www.haidaheritagecentre.com* 🎫*C$5; higher charges once the heritage center opens* 🕒*June–Aug., weekdays 10–5, weekends 1–5; May and Sept., weekdays 10–noon and 1–5, Sat. 1–5; Oct.–Apr., Tues.–Sat. 10–noon and 1–5.*

East Beach, an 80-km (50-mi) stretch of sand, runs the length of **Naikoon Provincial Park** (☎*250/557–4390* 🌐*www.britishcolumbia.com/parks/*), in the northeast corner of Graham Island. Untouched forests, bogs, and wildlife, including some of North America's largest black bears, fill the interior of this vast wilderness preserve. At the south end of the park, in Tlell, are the Park Headquarters and Misty Meadows Campground, which has nonreservable drive-in camping. From the Tlell day-use area nearby, a 10-km (6-mi), three-hour round-trip hike leads onto East Beach and to the wreck of a 1928 logging vessel, the *Pesuta.* At the park's north end, near the town of Masset, Agate Beach has nonreservable drive-in beachfront camping. A one-hour round-trip climb up 400-foot Tow Hill gives stunning views of the wide beach at McIntyre Bay. It's possible to walk along East Beach for days, though hikers planning extended trips in the park are advised to register with B.C. Parks or the Royal Canadian Mounted Police in Masset before setting out, as the area is very remote.

WHERE TO STAY

$ 🏨 **Alaska View B&B Lodge.** On a clear day you can see the mountains of Alaska from the large front deck of this B&B, 13 km (8 mi) east of Masset. A 10-km-long (6-mi-long) sandy beach borders the lodge on one side, and there are woods on the other. Eagles are a familiar sight, and in winter you can often catch glimpses of the northern lights. Common areas are attractively decorated with leather sofas, European antiques, and a hospitable open kitchen–dining area. Two rooms in the main lodge share a bathroom and have easy access to a hot tub; rooms in the guesthouse each have an en suite and a private deck overlooking the wide beach—*the* place to enjoy the delivered-to-your-door breakfast. ✉*12291 Tow Hill Rd., Box 227, Masset, V0T 1M0* ☎*250/626–3333 or 800/661–0019* 🌐*www.alaskaviewlodge.ca* *4 rooms, 2 with bath* *In-room: no a/c. In-hotel: beach, hiking, hot tub, no kids, no smoking* 💳*MC, V* 🍽*BP.*

¢–$ 🏨 **Spruce Point Lodge.** This cedar-sided building, encircled by a balcony, is right on the water's edge at the west end of Queen Charlotte, about 5½ km (3½ mi) from the ferry terminal at Skidegate. Rooms are bright and simple, with modern pine furniture; the suite has a full kitchen. All rooms open onto the veranda, providing views of the water and passing eagles. An on-site tour company, Queen Charlotte Adventures, rents kayaks and offers a range of tours. Note: Street signs are few. Head west from the ferry terminal to Queen Charlotte City and look for the turn off the main drag to Spruce Point Park. The lodge is at the end of the road. ✉ *609 6th St., Box 735, Queen Charlotte, V0T 1S0* ☎📠 *250/559–8234* 🌐 *www.qcislands.net/sprpoint* *6 rooms, 1 suite* *In-room: no a/c, kitchen (some), refrigerator. In-hotel: kayaks, boating, no smoking* *MC, V* *CP.*

BRITISH COLUMBIA ESSENTIALS

TRANSPORTATION

BY AIR

Air Canada subsidiaries connect most major towns in the province.

Northwest Seaplanes offers summer floatplane service between Seattle and fishing lodges in the Inside Passage.

North Pacific Seaplanes runs scheduled floatplane service from Prince Rupert to Queen Charlotte City.

Pacific Coastal Airline has scheduled and charter service from Vancouver International Airport South Terminal to Inside Passage, Cariboo, and Queen Charlotte Islands.

Information **Air Canada Jazz** (☎ *888/247–2262* 🌐 *www.aircanada.ca*). **North Pacific Seaplanes** (☎ *250/627–1341, 800/689–4234 in B.C.* 🌐 *www.northpacific-seaplanes.com*). **Northwest Seaplanes** (☎ *800/690–0086* 🌐 *www.nwseaplanes.com*). **Pacific Coastal Airlines** (☎ *604/273–8666 or 800/663–2872* 🌐 *www.pacific-coastal.com*).

BY BOAT & FERRY

THE NORTH COAST BC Ferries sails along the Inside Passage from Port Hardy to Prince Rupert (year-round) and from Port Hardy to Bella Coola (summer only). Reservations are required for vehicles and recommended for foot-passengers.

QUEEN CHARLOTTE ISLANDS (HAIDA GWAII) The *Queen of Prince Rupert,* a BC Ferries ship, sails six times a week in July and August, reducing to three times per week in winter. The crossing from Prince Rupert to Skidegate, near Queen Charlotte on Graham Island, takes about seven hours. High-season fares are C$26.25 per adult passenger, C$97.50 per car, and C$159.50 and up for campers (depending on length). Some sailings are overnight; cabins are available for an additional C$45 to C$50. Reservations are required for vehicles and recommended for foot-passengers; it's a good idea to book as early as possible, as summer sailings fill quickly. BC Ferries also connects Skidegate Landing to Alliford Bay on Moresby Island (near the airport at Sandspit). Access to smaller islands is by boat or air; make plans in advance through a travel agent.

Information **BC Ferries** (☎ *250/386–3431, 888/223–3779 in B.C., Alberta, and Washington state* 🌐 *www.bcferries.com*).

BY BUS

Greyhound Canada connects destinations throughout British Columbia with cities and towns across Canada and along the Pacific Northwest coast. The company has service to Whistler from the downtown Vancouver depot every few hours; service is also available from Vancouver Airport to Whistler.

The Whistler and Valley Express (WAVE) transit system operates a free public transit system within Whistler village, and paid public transit throughout the Valley and north to Pemberton. BC Transit's Web site has information about local transit in most B.C. communities, including Whistler and Prince Rupert.

Information **BC Transit** (*www.busonline.ca*). **Greyhound Canada** (*604/482–8747 or 800/661–8747* *www.greyhound.ca*). **Whistler and Valley Express** (*604/932–4020*).

BY CAR

Highway 99, also known as the Sea to Sky Highway, connects Vancouver to Whistler. The Trans-Canada Highway (Highway 1) connects Vancouver with Kamloops. highway 3 runs along the province's southern edge and links with highway 95 to the Rockies. Highway 97, the Cariboo Highway, links Kamloops to Dawson Creek, where it becomes the Alaska Highway. Highway 16 cuts east–west across the north, linking Jasper to Prince Rupert. Highway 37, the Stewart Cassiar Highway, travels through the northwest, linking Highway 16 to the Alaska Highway. Highway 20, the Freedom Highway, is a steep, winding, partially paved route linking Williams Lake to Bella Coola on the coast.

ROAD CONDITIONS Major roads, and most secondary roads, are paved and well engineered, although snow tires and chains are needed for winter travel. Many wilderness and park access roads are unpaved, and there are no roads on the mainland coast between Powell River and Bella Coola. Before using logging or forestry-service roads, check with the forest-service office in the area where you plan to travel (Enquiry BC can refer you to the relevant office) about logging activity. You can also check the Ministry of Forests Web site. The Ministry of Transportation's Web site has up-to-date road reports.

Contacts **Enquiry BC** (*800/663–7867 in B.C., 604/660–2421 in Vancouver and outside B.C.* *www.mser.gov.bc.ca/prgs/enquiry_bc.htm*). **Ministry of Forests** (*www.gov.bc.ca/for/cont*). **Ministry of Transportation** (*www.th.gov.bc.ca/bchighways/roadreports*).

BY TRAIN

VIA Rail offers service between Vancouver and Jasper (in Alberta) and from Prince Rupert to Jasper with an overnight stop in Prince George.

Contact **VIA Rail** (*888/842–7245* *www.viarail.ca*).

CONTACTS & RESOURCES

EMERGENCIES

A few areas do not have 911 service, so if you don't get immediate response, dial "0." British Columbia has many hospitals, including Kelowna General Hospital, Prince George Regional Hospital, and Royal Inland Hospital in Kamloops. The Ministry of Forests operates an emergency call service to report forest fires.

Contacts Ambulance, fire, police, poison control (☎ *911 or 0*). **Forest fires** (☎ *800/663–5555, *5555 on a cellular*).

Hospitals Kelowna General Hospital (✉ *2268 Pandosy St., Kelowna* ☎ *250/862–4000*). **Prince George Regional Hospital** (✉ *1475 Edmonton St.* ☎ *250/565–2000*). **Royal Inland Hospital** (✉ *311 Columbia St., Kamloops* ☎ *250/374–5111*).

TOURS

ADVENTURE TRIPS

Bluewater Adventures has 8- to 10-day sailing and natural-history tours of the the Queen Charlotte Islands. Canadian River Expeditions specializes in multiday wilderness rafting expeditions on the Chilcotin. Ecosummer Expeditions has guided multiday sea-kayaking and sailing trips to the Inside Passage and the Queen Charlotte Islands. Some trips involve both sailing and kayaking.

Information Bluewater Adventures (☎ *604/980–3800 or 888/877–1770* 🌐 *www.bluewateradventures.ca*). **Canadian River Expeditions** (☎ *604/270–7238 or 800/898–7238* 🌐 *www.canriver.com*). **Ecosummer Expeditions** (☎ *250/674–0102 or 800/465–8884* 🌐 *www.ecosummer.com*).

CRUISES

Celebrity Cruises offers three- to five-day cruises along B.C.'s coast. The Seattle-based ships sail in September and October and include port calls at Victoria, Vancouver, Nanaimo, Campbell River, and Prince Rupert.

Information Celebrity Cruises (☎ *305/539–6000 or 800/437–3111* 🌐 *www.celebrity.com.*)

HELICOPTER TOURS

Blackcomb Helicopters has year-round flightseeing tours over Whistler's stunning mountains and glaciers. In summer it offers heli-hiking, -biking, -fishing, -picnics, and even heli-weddings.

Information Blackcomb Helicopters (☎ *604/938–1700 or 800/330–4354* 🌐 *www.blackcombhelicopters.com*).

SIGHTSEEING TOURS

In winter Glacier Transportation and Tours runs day trips from Whistler to Vancouver for guided city tours and also offers outings to see NHL ice-hockey games in Vancouver. At this writing, they planned to offer guided trolley tours around the Whistler area in summer 2006.

With Okanagan Limousine you can tour the wine area in chauffeur-driven style. Okanagan Wine Country Tours offer narrated wine-country tours using Ford Expeditions. West Coast Sightseeing offers a sightseeing tour to Whistler that allows you to stay over and return on your date of choice to Vancouver. The tours run year-round; the cost is about C$78 round-trip.

Information **Glacier Transportation and Tours** (*604/932–2705 or 866/905–7779 www.glaciercoachlines.com*). **Okanagan Limousine** (*250/717–5466 or 866/366–3133 www.ok-limo.com*). **Okanagan Wine Country Tours** (*250/868–9463 or 866/689–9463 www.okwinetours.com*). **West Coast Sightseeing** (*877/451–1777, 604/451–1600 in Vancouver www.vancouversightseeing.com*).

VISITOR INFORMATION

Hello BC, run by the provincial ministry of tourism, has information about the province. The principal regional tourist offices are as follows: Cariboo, Chilcotin, Northern British Columbia Tourism Association for information on the Queen Charlotte Islands and northern British Columbia; Thompson Okanagan Tourism Association. Many towns in the region also have visitor-information centers, though not all are open year-round.

Regional Tourist Information **Hello BC** (*888/435–5622 www.hellobc.com*). **Northern British Columbia Tourism Association** (*Box 2373, Prince George, V2N 2S6 250/561–0432 or 800/663–8843 www.northernbctourism.com*). **Thompson Okanagan Tourism Association** (*1332 Water St., Kelowna, V1Y 9P4 250/860–5999 or 800/567–2275 www.thompsonokanagan.com*).

Local Tourist Information **Dawson Creek Visitor Info Centre** (*900 Alaska Ave., off Alaska Hwy. 250/782–9595 or 866/645–3022*). **Kamloops Visitor Info Centre** (*1290 W. Trans-Canada Hwy. 250/374–3377 or 800/662–1994*). **South Cariboo Visitor Info Centre** (*422 Hwy. 97, 100 Mile House 250/395–5353 or 877/511–5353*). **Kootenay National Park** (*250/347–9505 www.pc.gc.ca*). **Prince Rupert Visitor Info Centre** (*100–215 Cow Bay Rd. 250/624–5637 or 800/667–1994*). **Queen Charlotte Island Visitor Information Centre** (*3220 Wharf St., Queen Charlotte 250/559–8316 1 Airport Rd., in airport terminal, Sandspit 250/637–5362*). **Mt. Revelstoke and Glacier National Parks** (*250/837–7500 www.pc.gc.ca*). **Terrace Visitor Information Centre** (*4511 Keith Ave., Hwy. 16 250/635–2063 www.terracetourism.bc.ca*). **Tourism Kelowna** (*544 Harvey Ave. 250/861–1515 or 800/663–4345 www.tourismkelowna.com*). **Tourism Prince George** (*1300 1st Ave. 250/562–3700 or 800/668–7646 www.tourismpg.bc.ca*). **Tourism Whistler** (*4010 Whistler Way 800/944–7853, 604/664–5625 in Vancouver www.mywhistler.com*). **Whistler Activity and Information Center** (*4010 Whistler Way 604/932–2394*).**Yoho National Park** (*250/343–6783 www.pc.gc.ca*).

Banff National Park

WORD OF MOUTH

"A sudden splendour of illumination poured over the field as the sun rose above a mountain, and in a moment, as if by magic, the frost crystals melted away into pendant drops of heaven's own distillation. Beads of clear water dripping from leaves and tinted petals, made tremulous light flashings like the sparkle of diamonds and rubies . . "

—Author Walter D. Wilcox

WELCOME TO BANFF

TO JASPER & JASPER NATIONAL PARK
Columbia Icefield
93
1
11
Saskatchewan Crossing
Mistaya Canyon
Chephren Lake
ALBERTA
BRITISH COLUMBIA

TOP REASONS TO GO

★ **Scenery:** Visitors are often unprepared for the sheer scale of the Canadian Rockies. Scattered between the peaks are glaciers, forests, valleys, meadows, rivers, and the bluest lakes of the planet.

★ **Spectacular ski slopes:** Lake Louise Mountain Resort is Canada's largest single ski area, with skiing on four mountain faces, 4,200 skiable acres, and 113 named trails—and that's only one of the three ski resorts in Banff.

★ **Trails galore:** More than 1,000 mi (1,600 km) of defined hiking trails in the park lead to scenic lakes, alpine meadows, glaciers, forests, and deep canyons.

★ **Banff Upper Hot Springs:** Relax in naturally hot mineral springs as you watch snowflakes swirl around you, or gaze at the stars as you "take the waters" on a cool summer's evening.

★ **Icefields Parkway:** One of the most scenic drives on the continent, this 143-mi (230-km) roadway links Banff and Jasper.

1 Icefields Parkway. There are many sites to be seen along this spectacular 143-mi (230-km) stretch of road. The Crowfoot Glacier, Bow Pass, Mistaya Canyon, Saskatchewan Crossing, and the Columbia Icefield are the primary highlights in the Banff section.

2 Lake Louise, Moraine Lake & the Bow Valley Parkway. Backed by snow-capped mountains, fantastically ice-blue, Lake Louise is one of the most photographed lakes in the world. Lake Louise, Morraine Lake and the Valley of the Ten Peaks, and stunning Johnston Canyon are highlights of this region.

Downhill Skiing, Lake Louise

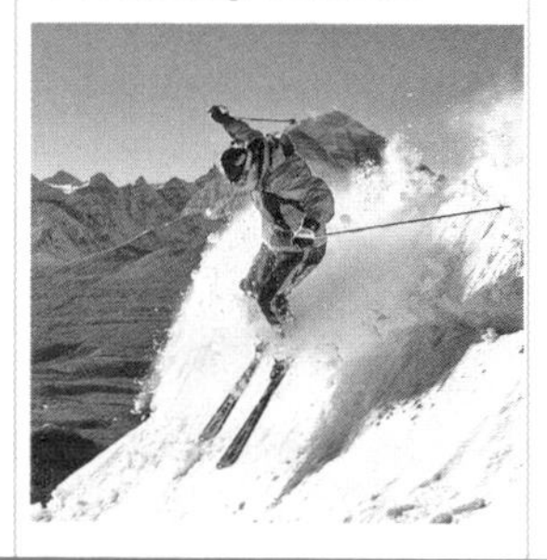

3 Banff Townsite. The Banff Townsite is the hub of the park and is the place to go to find shops, restaurants, hotels, and other facilities. Highlights of the town site: Banff Information Centre, Canada Place, Whyte Museum, Banff Centre, Upper Hot Springs Pool, Sulphur Mountain Gondola, Lake Minnewanka, Vermillion Lakes, and the Hoodoos.

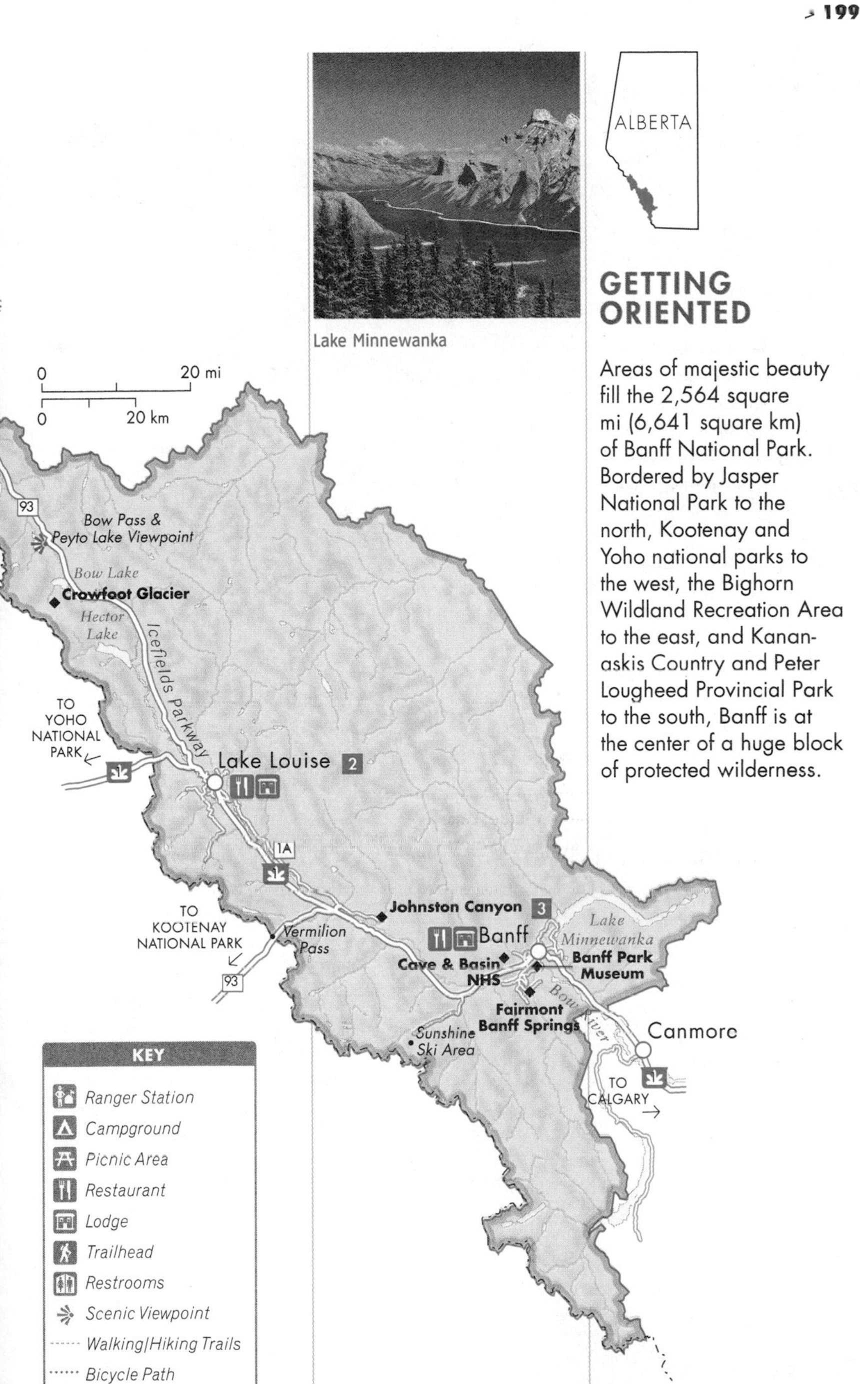

Lake Minnewanka

GETTING ORIENTED

Areas of majestic beauty fill the 2,564 square mi (6,641 square km) of Banff National Park. Bordered by Jasper National Park to the north, Kootenay and Yoho national parks to the west, the Bighorn Wildland Recreation Area to the east, and Kananaskis Country and Peter Lougheed Provincial Park to the south, Banff is at the center of a huge block of protected wilderness.

BANFF NATIONAL PARK PLANNER

When to Go

Banff National Park is an all-season destination. Visit in summer to hike the mountain trails or go in winter to enjoy some of the world's best skiing. Millions of people visit the park every year with the vast majority traveling during July and August, the warmest and driest months in the park. **If you can visit in late spring (May to June) or early fall (September), you will be in shoulder season when prices are lower, crowds are fewer, and the temperatures are usually still comfortable.** The downside to an off-season visit is the fact that you miss the summer interpretive programs and the wildflowers that reach their peak from early July to mid-August.

Both of the park's information centers are open all year, with extended hours during the summer months.

AVG. HIGH/LOW TEMPS

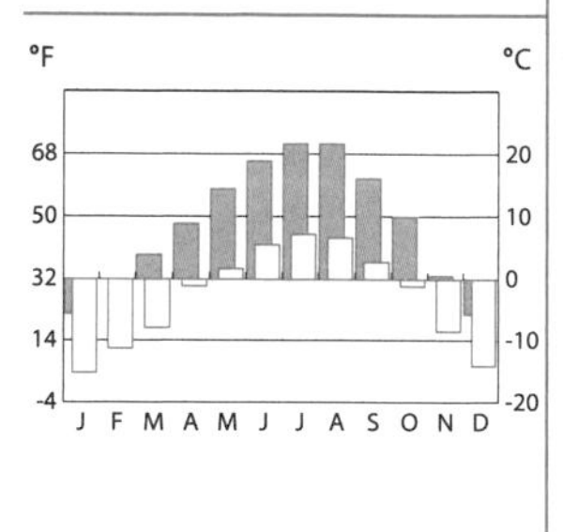

Flora & Fauna

Awesome forces of nature combined to thrust wildly folded sedimentary and metamorphic rock up into ragged peaks and high cliffs. Add glaciers and snowfields to the lofty peaks, carpet the valleys with forests, mix in a generous helping of small and large mammals, wildflowers, rivers, and crystal-clear lakes, and you've got the recipe for Banff National Park.

This diverse topography has resulted in three complex life zones in Banff: montane, subalpine, and alpine. Each zone has characteristic physical environments along with its own species of plants and animals. The montane zone features valleys and grasslands as well as alders, willows, birches, and cottonwoods. The Douglas firs and lodgepole pines that cover the lower slopes of the mountains are also in the montane zone. Subalpine forest extends from the montane to about 6,500 feet and is made up of mostly spruce and pine trees. The fragile alpine zone is found at the highest elevations in the park. The rocky terrain and cold howling winds mean far fewer plants and animals can survive there.

Most of the wildlife is found in the montane life zone where bighorn sheep, deer, elk, and caribou abound. Moose and mountain goats can also be seen, as well as the occasional black bear. Many other animals make their home in the park, including carnivores such as grizzly bears, wolves, coyotes, and cougars. It's common to see smaller mammals such as squirrels, marmots, muskrats, porcupines, and beavers. Birds commonly spotted are grouse, larks, finches, ptarmigans, bald eagles, golden eagles, loons, and Canada geese.

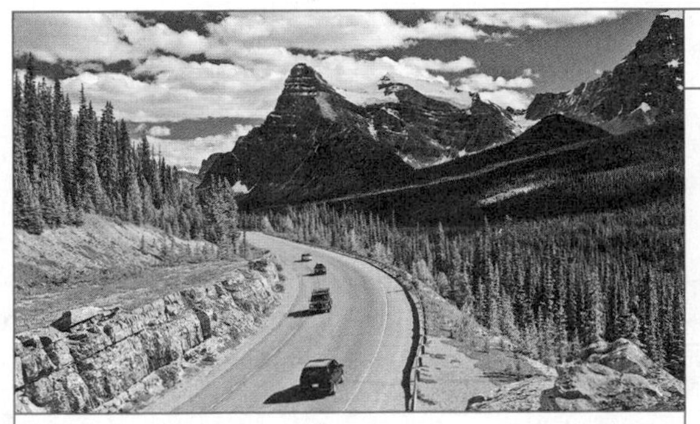

Getting There & Around

Banff National Park, in west-central Alberta, is located 80 mi (128 km) west of Calgary, 250 mi (401 km) southwest of Edmonton, and 530 mi (850 km) east of Vancouver. The closest international airport is in Calgary.

A car allows the most flexible travel in the Canadian Rockies, and the easiest way to get from Calgary to Banff is by car on the Trans-Canada Highway 1. Use Icefields Parkway (Hwy. 93) to get from Jasper to Banff. International car rental agencies are available at Edmonton and Calgary airports and in Banff, Lake Louise, and Jasper.

Greyhound Canada Transportation (☏ *800/661–8747, 800/231–2222 in the U.S.*) provides regular bus service from Calgary, Edmonton, and Vancouver to Banff and Lake Louise. **Brewster Inc.** (☏ *800/661–1152*) provides transportation between Calgary International Airport and Banff.

For travel within the town of Banff, there is a public transit system as well as several local taxi companies to choose from. Greyhound and Brewster offer bus service between Banff and Lake Louise. In the winter, a ski shuttle service picks up guests at most area hotels and transports them to the park's three ski resorts.

Family Picks

Canada Place. At Canada Place you can see what it feels like to step into a real birch-bark canoe or participate in fun games and programs designed to teach you more about Canada. It's free and there are many hands-on activities.

Athabasca Glacier. This glacier is the most accessible one in the park, and a short walk leads you right to its toe. You can explore the free displays at the Icefield Centre and even take an ice explorer vehicle onto the ice. (Note: Do not allow children to venture onto the ice without a trained guide!)

Canoe adventure. Rent a canoe at Lake Minnewanka, Moraine Lake or Lake Louise and learn to paddle like early explorers once did.

Enjoy the view. You can't beat the views from the Banff Gondola during the steep eight-minute ride to the 7,500-foot summit of Sulphur Mountain. From the main deck you can hike the short distance to the summit of Sanson Peak and perhaps catch sight of grazing bighorn sheep.

Adrenaline rush. Try white-water rafting in summer or dog-sledding and skiing in winter. The local ski hills have excellent children's programs.

By Debbie Olsen

COMPARING MOUNTAINS IS A SUBJECTIVE and imprecise business. Yet few would deny that the Canadian Rockies are one of the most extravagantly beautiful ranges on Earth. The mountains and vast stretches of wilderness that make up the birthplace of Canada's first national park offer stunning scenery of glaciers, lakes, valleys, and snowcapped mountain peaks. Large mammals such as deer and elk can be observed in all seasons from the roadside.

You can soak up the rugged alpine scenery, hike on more than 1,000 mi of trails, tour the region by automobile or tour bus, watch wildlife, soak in hot springs, visit historic sites, and enjoy fine dining and shopping in the town sites of Banff or Lake Louise. The winter months are ideal to enjoy outdoor sports like ice-skating, dogsledding, sleigh rides, and cross-country and downhill skiing.

SCENIC DRIVES

Bow Valley Parkway. Formerly known as Highway 1A, this scenic drive between Banff and Lake Louise leads to Hillsdale Meadows, Johnston Canyon, Castle Mountain, and Baker Creek. There are plenty of viewpoints and picnic sites along the way.

Fodor's Choice ★ **Icefields Parkway.** The Icefields Parkway stretches 138 mi (230 km) and connects Banff National Park with Jasper National Park. It is an absolute highlight of the Canadian Rockies.

Lake Minnewanka Loop. It's easy to spend the day along this 15-mi (25-km) loop. Traveling clockwise, you can explore Lower Bankhead and Upper Bankhead, an abandoned coal mine and mining community. Just 2 mi (3 km) farther you come to Lake Minnewanka, the largest lake in the park at 12 mi (20 km). Boat and fishing rentals are available at the lake. Farther along are more lakes and picnic areas.

Mount Noquay Drive. The highlight of this 4-mi (6½-km) route is the viewpoint near the top over the Banff town site. Bighorn sheep and mule deer are often sighted along the twisting road. Trailheads at the top lead to Stoney Squaw Summit and Cascade Amphitheatre.

Tunnel Mountain Drive. On the east side of Banff, Tunnel Mountain Drive makes a scenic 3-mi (5-km) loop. It's closed in winter, but just off the drive, the **hoodoos**—fingerlike, eroded rock formations—are accessible year-round (signs on Banff's main street direct you to the hoodoos).

WHAT TO SEE

HISTORIC SITES

Banff Park Museum. This National Historic Site, made for the 1893 World Exhibition in Chicago, is western Canada's oldest natural-history museum. ✉ *91 Banff Ave., north of the bridge* ☎ *403/762–1558* 🌐 *www.pc.gc.ca* 🎟 *C$4* ⏲ *Mid-May–Sept., daily 10–6; Oct.–mid-May, daily 1–5.*

BANFF IN ONE DAY

Start your day early with a visit to the **Banff Information Centre,** where you can pick up maps and information on the major sites. Buy lunch provisions and drive to beautiful **Lake Louise.** Walk the flat shoreline trail and venture upward along the **Lake Agnes Trail** to the Teahouse (or turn back once you get a satisfyingly lofty view of Lake Louise).

On the drive back to Banff town, stop at Johnston Canyon and allow an hour for the easy round-trip hike to the dramatic waterfall. Have dinner in Banff or at **Fairmont Banff Springs Hotel,** a National Historic Site. After supper, explore the hotel's interior before finishing off the day with an evening dip in the **Banff Upper Hot Springs.**

★ **Banff Upper Hot Springs.** The sulfur pool of hot springwater can be soothing, invigorating, or both. The hot-spring water is especially inviting on a dull, cold day. Lockers, bathing suits (circa 1920s or modern), and towels can be rented, and spa services are available. ✉*Mountain Ave., 2 mi (3 km) south of downtown (or a 20-min hike up a steep trail from the Fairmont Banff Springs parking area)* ☎*403/762–1515, 800/767–1611, 403/760–2500 for spa bookings* 🌐*www.hotspring.ca* 🎟*C$7.50* ⏲*Mid-May–mid-Sept., daily 9 AM–11 PM; mid-Sept.–mid-May, Sun.–Thurs. 10–10, Fri. and Sat. 10 AM–11 PM.*

Cave and Basin National Historic Site. This was given national park protection in 1885, becoming the birthplace of the Canadian Rockies park system. Two interpretive trails explain the area's geology and plant life, while hands-on interpretive displays offer information on the wildlife and history of the national park. You can take a guided tour of the cave daily mid-May through September and weekends throughout the rest of the year. A boardwalk leads to a marsh where the warm springwater supports tropical fish illegally dumped into the waters many years ago. ✉*Cave Ave., 1 mi (2 km) west of downtown* ☎*403/762–1566* 🌐*www.pc.gc.ca* 🎟*C$4* ⏲*Mid-May–Sept., daily 9–6; Oct.–mid-May, weekdays 11–4, weekends 9:30–5.*

★ **Fairmont Banff Springs.** This hotel, 1 mi (2 km) south of downtown Banff, is the town's architectural showpiece and a National Historic Site. Built in 1888, the hotel is easily recognized by its castlelike exterior. Heritage Hall, a small, free museum above the Grand Lobby, has rotating exhibits on the area's history. ✉*405 Spray Ave.* ☎*403/762–2211 or 800/441–1414* 🌐*www.fairmont.com.*

★ **Fairmont Château Lake Louise.** The massive hotel, opened in 1890, overlooks blue-green Lake Louise and the Victoria Glacier. The hotel is also a departure point for several short, moderately strenuous, well-traveled hiking routes. The most popular hike (about 2 mi, or 3 km) is to Lake Agnes. The tiny lake hangs on a mountain-surrounded shelf that opens to the east with a bird's-eye view of the Beehives and Mount Whitehorn. ✉*Lake Louise Dr.* ☎*403/522–3511.*

SCENIC STOPS

Banff Gondola. Views during the steep eight-minute ride to and from the 7,500-foot summit are spectacular. From the upper gondola terminal you can hike the short distance to the summit of Sanson Peak and perhaps catch sight of grazing bighorn sheep, or visit the gift shop or the reasonably priced restaurant. The gondola is south from the center of Banff; you can catch a public Banff transit bus. ✉ *Mountain Ave., 2 mi (3 km) south of downtown (lower terminal next to Upper Hot Springs)* ☎ *403/762–5438 or 403/762–2523* 🌐 *www.banffgondola.com* 🎟 *C$22.50 round-trip* ⏲ *Early May–early Sept., daily 7:30 AM–9 PM; early Sept.–mid-Oct., daily 8:30–6:30; mid-Oct.–early Dec., daily 8:30–4:30; early Dec.–early May, daily 10–4.*

Fodor's Choice ★ **Canada Place.** With its splendid summertime flower gardens, this is a pleasant place for an after-dinner stroll. It stands at the south end of Banff Avenue, across a stone bridge over the Bow River. Inside are interactive activities for children and adults. ✉ *1 Cave Ave.*

Lake Louise Sightseeing Gondola. Ride this to an alpine plateau for a stunning view that includes more than a dozen glaciers. The deck of the Whitehorn Tea House (open June through September for breakfast and lunch) is a good place to eat. In winter, there's a buffet dinner package that includes entertainment and a torchlight ski descent. Free 30- to 90-minute, naturalist-led hikes go to the top of the mountain; schedules vary. ✉ *Hwy. 1 (Lake Louise exit)* ☎ *403/522–3555* 🌐 *www.skilouise.com* 🎟 *C$22* ⏲ *May, daily 9–4; June and Sept., daily 8:30–6; July and Aug., daily 8–6.*

★ **Moraine Lake.** This beauty, 7 mi (11 km) south of Lake Louise, is a photographic highlight of Banff National Park. Set in the Valley of the Ten Peaks, the lake reflects the snow-clad mountaintops that rise abruptly around it. The lake is a major stop for tour buses as well as a popular departure point for hikers. Visit early or late in the day to avoid crowds. Moderate hiking trails lead from the lodge at Moraine Lake into some spectacular alpine country. Call ahead for special trail restrictions.

From June through September, you can rent a canoe from the office of **Moraine Lake Lodge** (☎ *403/522–3733* 🌐 *www.morainelake.com*). ✉ *Moraine Lake Rd. off Great Divide Hwy.* ☎ *403/760–1305 for hiking information.*

VISITOR CENTERS

Banff Information Centre. Park wardens and staff have excellent information on camping, hiking, programs, and sightseeing. ✉ *224 Banff Ave., Banff* ☎ *403/762–1550* 🌐 *www.pc.gc.ca* ⏲ *Jan.–mid-May, daily 9–5; mid-June–Aug., daily 8–8; mid-May–mid-June and Sept., daily 8–6.*

Banff Lake Louise Tourism. Located in the same building as the Banff Information Centre, this information desk can provide you with information on hotels, restaurants, and services in the towns of Banff and Lake Louise. ✉ *224 Banff Ave.* ☎ *403/762–8421* 🌐 *www.BanffLakeLouise.com*

Jan.–mid-May, daily 9–5; mid-June–Aug., daily 8–8; mid-May–mid-June and Sept., daily 8–6.

Lake Louise Visitor Centre. Stop here to get maps and information about area attractions and trails. The Banff Lake Louise Tourism desk can provide information on area accommodations and amenities, and you can purchase educational books and other materials from the Friends of Banff National Park. *Village of Lake Louise next to Samson Mall 403/522–3833 www.pc.gc.ca Jan.–Apr., daily 9–5; mid-June–mid-Sept., daily 8–8; May–mid-June and mid-Sept.–end of Sept., daily 8–6.*

READ ALL ABOUT IT

The Mountain Guide is distributed by parks staff upon entry to Banff National Park. It contains maps and good general park information such as points of interest, safety messages, programs and events, camping information and fees. If you want to use it for advance planning, it is also available on the Parks Canada Web site (*www.pc.gc.ca/jasper*).

4

SPORTS & THE OUTDOORS

AIR TOURS

OUTFITTERS & EXPEDITIONS

Alpine Helicopters. Helicopter sightseeing and heli-hiking in the Canadian Rockies are the specialty for this company. *91 Bow Valley Tr., Canmore 403/678–4802 www.alpinehelicopters.com.*

CMH. This company can arrange heli-hiking, heli-mountaineering, and heli-skiing with accommodation in remote mountain lodges. *Box 1660, Banff 403/762–7100 or 800/661–0252 www.cmhski.com.*

Icefield Helicopter Tours. Located 42 km east of the Icefield Parkway, this company specializes in tours of the Columbia Icefields. They also offer heli-hiking, skiing, and fishing. For something really unique, they can arrange heli-yoga. *Box 146, Lake Louise 403/721–2100 or 888/844–3514 www.icefieldhelicoptertours.com.*

BICYCLING

The biking season typically runs from May through October and the more than 118 mi (189 km) of trails include ones suitable for beginners and advanced bikers. Bikers and hikers often share the trails in the park, with hikers having the right-of-way. Those who wish to enjoy free riding or down-hilling should go to nearby areas like Calgary's Canada Olympic Park, Fernie, or Golden.

OUTFITTERS & EXPEDITIONS

Backtrax Bike Rentals. Backtrax also arranges one- to four-hour guided interpretive bike tours on local Banff trails, which are suitable for any age or physical ability. *225 Bear St., Banff 403/762–8177.*

⇨ *Multisport Outfitters & Expeditions box for additional equipment shops.*

CLOSE UP

Icefields Parkway

Powerfully rugged mountain scenery, glaciers, waterfalls and icefalls, and wildlife: the Icefields Parkway reveals all of these and more as it snakes its way between Lake Louise and Jasper.

There aren't any gas stations along the route, so be sure to check the gas gauge before setting out. Although you could drive this winding road in three to four hours, it's more likely to be a full-day trip when you add in stops. The road rises to near the tree line at several points, and the weather can be chilly and unsettled at these high elevations, even in midsummer, so it's a good idea to bring warm clothing along.

Elk, moose, deer, and bighorn sheep are fairly common along this route, and occasionally you can see bears and mountain goats. In summer, alpine wildflowers carpet Bow Pass and Sunwapta Pass.

The most dramatic scenery is in the north end of Banff National Park and the south end of Jasper National Park, where ice fields and glaciers become common on the high mountains flanking the route (ice fields are massive reservoirs of ice; glaciers are the slow-moving rivers of ice that flow from the ice fields). Scenic overlooks and signposted hiking trails abound along the route.

At 6,787 feet, **Bow Summit** (✉ *25 mi [40 km] north of Lake Louise, 118 mi [190 km] south of Jasper*) is the highest drivable pass in the national parks of the Canadian Rockies. On the south side of the pass is Bow Lake, source of the Bow River, which flows through Banff. You may wish to stop for lunch or supper at **Simpson's Num-Ti-Jah Lodge** (✉ *25 mi [40 km] north of Lake Louise on Hwy. 93* ☎ *403/522–2167* 🌐 *www.num-ti-jah.com*) at Bow Lake. This rustic lodge with simple guest rooms specializes in excellent regional Canadian cuisine. Outside, walking paths circle the lake. Above Bow Lake hangs the Crowfoot Glacier, so named because of its resemblance to a three-toed crow's foot. At least that's how it looked when it was named at the beginning of the 20th century. In the Canadian Rockies, glaciers, including Crowfoot, have been receding. The lowest toe completely melted away 50 years ago, and now only the upper two toes remain. On the north side of Bow Pass is **Peyto Lake**; its startlingly intense aqua-blue color comes from the minerals in glacial runoff. Wildflowers blossom along the pass in summer, but note that it can be covered with snow as late as May and as early as September.

The short (1½ mi [2½ km]), steep **Parker Ridge Trail** is one of the easiest hikes in the national parks to bring you above the tree line. There's an excellent view of the Saskatchewan Glacier, where the river of the same name begins, though you've got to make it to the top of the ridge to get the view. Snowbanks can persist into early summer, but carpets of wildflowers cross the trail in late July and August. Stay on the path to keep erosion to a minimum. The trailhead is about 2½ mi (4 km) south of the boundary between Banff and Jasper parks.

Sunwapta Pass (✉ *76 mi [122 km] north of Lake Louise, 67 mi [108 km] south of Jasper*) marks the border between Banff and Jasper national parks. Wildlife is most visible in spring and autumn after a snowfall, when herds of bighorn sheep come to the road to lick up the salt used to melt snow and ice. At 6,675 feet, Sunwapta is the second-highest drivable pass in the national parks. Be prepared for a series of hairpin turns as you switchback up to the pass summit.

The **Athabasca Glacier** (✉ *79 mi [127 km] north of Lake Louise, 64 mi [103 km] south of Jasper*) is a 4½-mi (7-km) tongue of ice flowing from the immense Columbia Icefield almost to the highway. A century ago the ice flowed over the current location of the highway; signposts depict the gradual retreat of the ice since that time. Several other glaciers are visible from here; they all originate from the Columbia Icefield, a giant alpine lake of ice covering 125 square mi (325 square km), whose edge is visible from the highway. You can hike up to the toe of the glacier, but venturing further without a trained guide is extremely dangerous because of hidden crevasses. **Athabasca Glacier Ice Walks** offers three-, five-, and six-hour guided walks (C$36–C$45), which can be reserved at the Icefield Centre or through Jasper Adventure Centre, in Jasper. You can also take a trip onto the Athabasca Glacier in a specially-designed ice explorer with **Brewster Inc.** (tickets are available at the Icefield Centre for C$35.95).

The Icefield Centre opposite Athabasca Glacier houses interpretive exhibits, a gift shop, and two dining facilities (one cafeteria style, one buffet style). The summer midday rush between 11 and 3 can be intense. There are 32 hotel rooms, available from early May to mid-October. Book through **Brewster's Transport** in Banff. ✉ *Opposite Athabasca Glacier on Hwy. 93, 79 mi (127 km) north of Lake Louise, 64 mi (103 km) south of Jasper* ☎ *877/423–7433* 🌐 *www.brewster.ca* 🎫 *Free* ⏲ *Late May–mid-June and Sept.–early Oct., daily 10–5; mid-June–Aug., daily 10–7.*

As you continue north from the Icefield Centre through Jasper National Park towards the Jasper townsite, you'll see some of the most spectacular scenery in the Canadian Rockies. One of the most stunning sites is the **Stutfield Glacier,** 57 mi (95 km) south of Jasper Townsite. The glacier stretches down 3,000 feet of cliff face, forming a set of double icefalls visible from a roadside viewpoint. Continuing along the parkway, you'll pass the access to spectacular **Sunwapta Falls,** 33 mi (57 km) south of the town of Jasper. You'll also want to stop at **Athabasca Falls,** 19 mi (31 km) south of Jasper Townsite. These powerful falls are created as the Athabasca River is compressed through a narrow gorge, producing a violent torrent of water. The falls are especially dramatic in early summer. Trails and overlooks provide good viewpoints.

BIRD-WATCHING

Birdlife is abundant in the montane and wetland habitats of the lower Bow Valley and more than 260 species of birds have been recorded in the park. Come in the spring to observe the annual migration of waterfowl, including common species of ducks and Canada geese as well as occasional tundra swans, cinnamon teal, Northern shovelers, white-winged and surf scoters, and hooded and common Mergansers. Bald eagles are also seen regularly. Come in mid-October if you want to observe the annual migration of golden eagles along the "super flyway" of the Canadian Rockies. Interpreters and guides are on hand to explain the phenomenon.

BOATING

Lake Minnewanka, near town, is the only place in Banff National Park that allows private motorboats. Aluminum fishing boats with 8-horsepower motors can be rented at the dock (call Lake Minnewanka Boat Tours, *see below*).

Rafting options range from scenic float trips to family-friendly white-water excursions on the Kananaskis River to the intense white water of the Kicking Horse River, with its Class IV rapids.

OUTFITTERS & EXPEDITIONS

Canadian Rockies Rafting. Scenic floats and thrilling white-water rafting tours on the Bow and Kananaskis rivers are available with these local experts. Pickups in Banff and Canmore are included. *Box 8082, Canmore 403/678–6535 or 877/226–7625.*

Hydra River Guides. This is where you want to go for real thrills. The guides here take you through the Class IV rapids on the Kicking Horse River. *211 Bear St., Banff 403/762–4534 or 800/644–8888 www.banffadventures.com.*

Kootenay River Runners. A variety of boating trips, ranging from scenic raft floats on the Toby or Kananaskis rivers to Class IV white-water rafting on the Kicking Horse, are available through this outfitter. A unique Voyageur Canoe Experience is also an option. *110 Banff Ave., Banff 403/762–5385 or 800/599–4399 www.kootenayriverrunners.com.*

Lake Minnewanka Boat Tours. In summer, this operator offers 1½-hour, C$30 tours on the lake. *Box 2189, Banff 403/762–3473 www.minnewankaboattours.com.*

Rocky Mountain Raft Tours. This company specializes in one- and two-hour float trips on the Bow River, starting at $24. They also rent canoes. *Box 1771, Banff 403/762–3632.*

FISHING

You can experience world-class trout fishing on the Bow River in Banff and enjoy fishing for trophy lake trout on Lake Minnewanka and several other mountain lakes. You will need a National Park fishing permit to fish within the park and must follow strict fishing regulations, including no use of live bait. Some waterways are permanently closed to anglers, although others are open only at certain times per year.

Before heading out on your own, read the regulations or speak to the park staff.

OUTFITTERS & EXPEDITIONS

Alpine Anglers. A full-service fly shop, spin- and fly-rod rentals, float trips, and a fly-fishing guide service are available through this company. ✉*208 Bear St., Banff* ☎*403/762–8223* 🌐*www.alpineanglers.com.*

Banff Fishing Unlimited. Bow River floats and walk and wades are available in summer and ice fishing in winter. If you want to go for the big ones, charter a boat on Lake Minnewanka. 📫*Box 8281, Canmore* ☎*403/762–4936* 🌐*www.banff-fishing.com.*

Hawgwild Fly Fishing Guides. Learn how to fly-fish with a local guide. 📫*Box 2534, Banff* ☎*403/760–2446* 🌐*www.flyfishingbanff.com.*

Tightline Adventures. Daylong and multiday fly-fishing trips can be arranged through this company. ✉*129 Banff Ave., Banff* ☎*403/762–4548* 🌐*www.tightlineadventures.com.*

Upper Bow Fly Fishing Company. Enthusiasm is caught not taught at this company where both beginners and advanced fly fishers are catered to. 📫*Box 2772, Banff* ☎*403/762–8263* 🌐*www.upperbowflyfishing.com.*

HIKING

The trail system in Banff National Park allows you to access the heart of the Canadian Rockies. The scenery is spectacular and you can see wildlife such as birds, squirrels, deer, and sheep along many of the trails. Make noise as you travel the trails, so you don't surprise a bear or other large animal. Also, prepare for any and all weather conditions by dressing in layers and bringing at least ½ gallon of drinking water along per person on all full-day hikes. Get a trail map at the information center. Some of the more popular trails have bathrooms or outhouses at the trailhead. Dogs should be leashed at all times.

EASY

Bow River HooDoos Trail. This 3-mi (4.8-km) trail feels as if it is a world away from the busy town site. The trail starts at the Bow Falls Overlook on Tunnel Mountain Drive and leads through meadows and forests and past sheer cliffs until you reach the hoodoos.

Discovery Trail and Marsh Trail. On a hillside above the Cave and Basin Centennial Centre, this ½-mi (.8-km) boardwalk takes you past the vent of the cave to a spring flowing out of the hillside. Interpretive signage explains the geology and history of the Cave and Basin. Follow the Marsh Trail to get a good view of the lush vegetation that is fed by the mineral water and to see the birdlife. Along the boardwalk are telescopes, benches, and interpretive signage as well as a bird blind on the marsh itself. Wheelchairs have limited access to the boardwalk.

Fenland Trail. It will take about an hour round-trip to walk the 1-mi (2-km) trail that slowly changes from marsh to dense forest. Watch for beavers, muskrat, and waterfowl. The trail is popular with joggers and cyclists.

MODERATE

Boom Lake Trail. This 3.2-mi (5-km) hike climbs through a forest of pine, fir, and spruce. Surrounded by mountains and glaciers, the waters of the

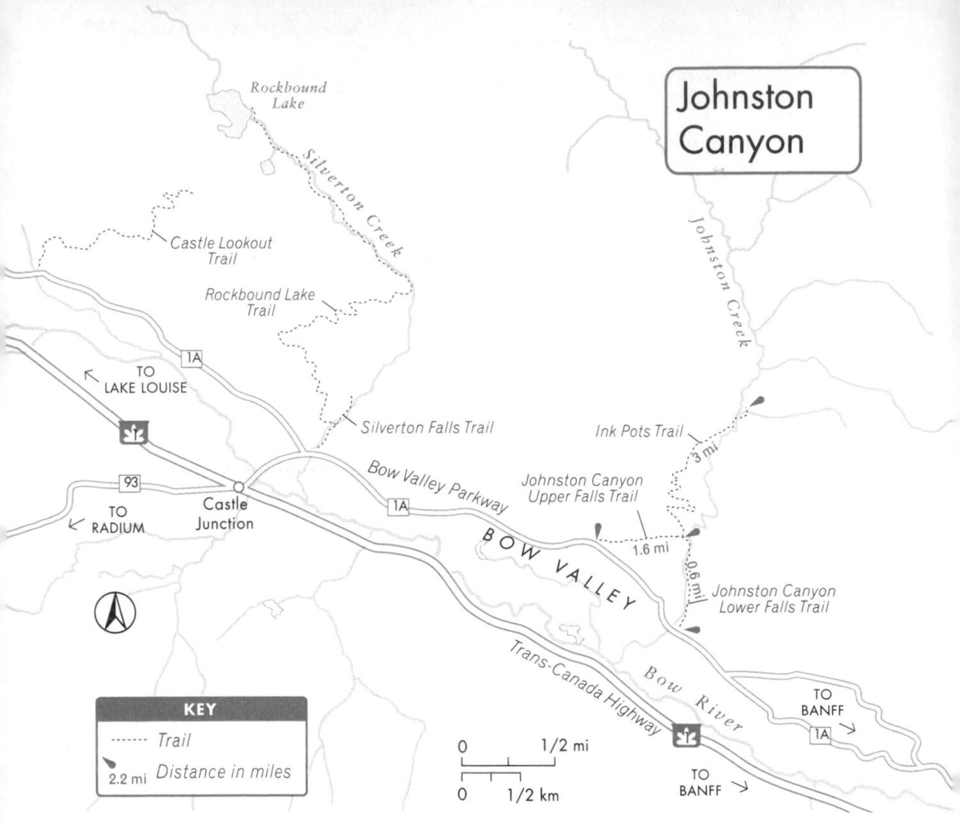

lake are crystal clear. The trail will take a half day round-trip. The trailhead is on Highway 93 South, 4½-mi (7 km) west of Castle Junction.

Castle Lookout Trail. Outstanding views of Castle Mountain and the mountains above the Bow River Valley are the highlight of this 2.3-mi (3.7-km) one-way trail that is somewhat steep.

Fodor'sChoice ★ **Johnston Canyon Trail.** Rushing water has carved a path through this limestone canyon that is a must-see stop. The first .7 mi (1.1 km) is a paved walkway that leads to the 33-foot Lower Falls. From here a slightly more rugged 1¾-mi (2.7-km) trail leads to the almost-100-foot Upper Falls and a 3-mi (5-km) trail to the Ink Pots. The Ink Pots are six green pools filled with springwater. It will take four to five hours to complete the return trip.

★ **Lake Agnes Teahouse Trail.** Off Lake Louise, this 4½-mi (7-km) trail has stunning views of Lake Agnes and Mirror Lake. The trail passes through an old-growth forest and comes up the right side of a waterfall before ending at a teahouse where you can stop for dessert. It will take four hours or more to make the return trip along this trail.

DIFFICULT **Cory Pass Loop Trail.** This six-hour, 8-mi (13-km) hike is one of the most difficult hikes in the park and is only recommended for experienced hikers who are able to trace a difficult route. Hikers are rewarded with awesome views. The return route loops around Mt. Edith and descends the Edith Pass Trail. The trailhead is located at the Fireside picnic area at the eastern end of the Bow Valley Parkway.

Sulphur Mountain Summit Trail. This well-maintained trail crisscrosses underneath the gondola on Sulphur Mountain and climbs from the parking lot to the summit. You may choose to hike up and take the gondola down, but you should check schedules first. A restaurant and cafeteria are located at the summit along with a viewing platform and interpretive signage. It will take four hours to hike the trail round-trip.

HORSEBACK RIDING

Experiencing the Canadian Rockies on horseback takes you back to the era of Banff's early explorers. One-hour, half-day, full-day, and multiday guided trips within the park are offered by several outfitters. Make your reservations well in advance, especially during the peak summer months and for multiday journeys. Hourly rides start at $34 per person. Short-term boarding is available in Canmore and a few other communities outside Banff.

OUTFITTERS & EXPEDITIONS

Brewsters Mountain Pack Tours. Experience the "Cowboy Way of Life" by moving cattle and doing chores on overnight trips. *Box 964, Banff 403/762–3953 or 800/691–5085 www.brewsteradventures.com.*

Holiday on Horseback. Arrangements for hourly or daily rides, as well as lessons, can be made by contacting this company, which operates out of three different locations in Banff (the main stable is located at the Fairmont Banff Springs). They also offer carriage rides in summer and sleigh rides in winter. *132 Banff Ave., Banff 403/762–4551 or 800/661–8352 www.horseback.com.*

Lake Louise Stables. The folks here can arrange trail rides, from one-hour to half- and full day rides. The stables are a five-minute walk from the Fairmont Château Lake Louise. *403/762–5454 www.brewsteradventures.com.*

SWIMMING

Banff Centre. Amenities here include a 25-meter swimming pool, a wading pool, an outdoor sundeck, climbing wall, fitness center, gymnasium, and squash center, as well as fitness classes. *St. Julien Rd. (on Tunnel Mountain), Banff 403/762–6450 www.banffcentre.ca C$4.25 Weekdays 6 PM–9 PM; weekends 11 AM–9 PM.*

Douglas Fir Resort. There are two indoor waterslides, a whirlpool, a steam room, and an indoor pool. *525 Tunnel Mountain Rd., Banff 403/762–5591 or 800/661–9267 www.douglasfir.com C$8 Weekdays 4 PM–9:30 PM; weekends and holidays 10 AM–9:30 PM.*

GOLF

Fairmont Banff Springs Golf Course. This legendary course features 27 holes: the Stanley Thompson 18 and the Tunnel 9. Views are spectacular as the course winds its way along the Bow River under the shadow of Mount Rundle and Sulphur Mountain. A visit to the onsite golf academy and practice facility will ensure that your game is at its best. *405 Spray Ave. 403/762–6801.*

MULTISPORT OUTFITTERS & EXPEDITIONS

Abominable Ski & Sportswear rents and sells ski and snowboarding equipment in winter and bikes and accessories in summer. ✉ *229 Banff Ave., Banff* ☎ *403/762–2905.*

Banff Adventures Unlimited can book you at almost all of the area activities. They also rent bikes. ✉ *211 Bear St., Banff* ☎ *403/762–4554* 🌐 *www.banffadventures.com.*

Canadian Mountain Experience can arrange excursions such as snowmobiling, dog-mushing, and heli-skiing. 📫 *Box 8598, Canmore* ☎ *403/609–3535* 🌐 *www.canadian-mountain.com.*

Chute High Adventures. Mountain climbing, rock climbing, ice climbing, and guided hiking can be arranged through this company. 📫 *Box 1876, Banff* ☎ *403/762–4068.*

Discover Banff Tours Ltd. offers guided sightseeing, wildlife safaris, nature walks, ice walks, and snowshoeing adventures. ✉ *215 Banff Ave, Main Level, Sundance Mall, Banff* ☎ *403/760–5007 or 877/565–9372* 🌐 *www.banfftours.com.*

Great Divide Nature Interpretation. Guided interpretive hikes and snowshoeing trips are the specialty at this outfitter. 📫 *Box 343, Lake Louise* ☎ *403/522–2735* 🌐 *www.greatdivide.ca.*

Mountain Edge stocks equipment and clothing, and you can rent downhill skis, snowboards, and helmets. ✉ *Lake Louise Ski Area, off Lake Louise Dr.* ☎ *403/522–3555.*

Mountain Magic Equipment offers three floors of hiking, climbing, skiing, running, and biking gear and a 30-foot indoor climbing wall for testing equipment. This is Canada's largest independent climbing outfitter. ✉ *224 Bear St.* ☎ *403/762–2591.*

White Mountain Adventures. Daily guided hikes, backpacking, and heli-hiking can be arranged through this company. In winter, you can try snowshoeing, cross-country skiing, or a guided ice walk. ✉ *#7 107 Boulder Crescent, Canmore* ☎ *403/678–4099 or 800/408–0005* 🌐 *www.white-mountainadventures.com.*

Yamnuska Inc. Canada's largest mountain-guide company offers programs for groups and individuals. ✉ *200, 50 Lincoln Park, Canmore* ☎ *403/678–4164* 🌐 *www.yamnuska.com.*

WINTER SPORTS

Whether you're driving a dogsled across a frozen lake, ice climbing, snowshoeing, skiing at one of the world's top mountain ski resorts, or simply taking in the northern lights, there's no shortage of winter activities to choose from.

CROSS-COUNTRY SKIING

Banff Alpine Guides. Ski tours into Banff's backcountry are available with this outfitter. 📫 *Box 1025, Banff* ☎ *403/678–6091.*

White Mountain Adventures. Ski tours and lessons are available throughout the Bow Valley for beginner and intermediate skiers. ✉ *#7 107 Boulder Crescent, Canmore* ☎ *403/678–4099.*

DOWNHILL SKIING

Some of the world's best downhill skiing is found in the Banff area. If you want to try each of the three major hills, a good bargain is the tri-area ski pass from Ski Banff/Lake Louise Sunshine which allows you to ski at Sunshine Village, Ski Norquay, and Lake Louise. It includes free shuttle service to the slopes. Rates start at $231 for three days and you can purchase the pass at the ski areas or at many shops in Banff. ☎403/762–4561 🌐www.skibig3.com.

★ **Lake Louise Mountain Resort.** The downhill terrain is large and varied, with a fairly even spread of novice, intermediate, and expert runs spread across three mountains and north-facing back bowls. The vertical drop is 3,257 feet, there are 105 runs, 11 lifts, and a terrain park. ✉*Off Lake Louise Dr., Lake Louise* ☎*403/522–3555* 🌐*www.skilouise.com.*

Ski Norquay. Just minutes from Banfff, Norquay has been popular with families since it opened in 1926. In addition to a wide variety of runs for all abilities, Norquay has the only night skiing in the bow valley and the only lit terrain park. ✉*Off the Mt. Norquay access road, Banff* ☎*403/762–4421* 🌐*www.banffnorquay.com.*

Sunshine Village. Five miles (8 km) west of the town of Banff, the terrain offers options for all levels of skiers. The vertical drop is 3,514 feet, and there are 103 trails and 12 lifts. ✉*Off Hwy. 1, Banff* ☎*403/762–6500 or 877/542–2633* 🌐*www.skibanff.com.*

SKI & SNOWBOARD EQUIPMENT

Skis and snowboards can be rented on the slopes or at many shops in town, concentrated along Bear Street and Banff Avenue.

Ultimate Banff. Rent ski and snowboard equipment and take advantage of the shop's free hotel delivery. ✉*206 Banff Ave.* ☎*403/762–0547 or 866/754–7433* 🌐*www.ultimatebanff.com.*

For additional equipment shops, ⇨*Multisport Outfitters & Expeditions box.*

EDUCATIONAL OFFERINGS

There are a wide range of park interpretive programs in Banff. At the Banff Information Centre and at Cave and Basin, there are slide shows and presentations throughout the year. In the summer months you can enjoy campground interpretive programs, guided hikes, bicycle tours, film showings, and adventure games at Banff Avenue square.

Fodor's Choice ★ **Canada Place.** This center celebrates Canada's land, people, history, and accomplishments with interactive displays, hands-on activities, interpretive displays, educational games, and programs designed to help children and adults learn more about Canada. ✉*1 Cave Ave.*

Friends of Banff National Park. This nonprofit group provides roving naturalist programs, guided hikes, and junior naturalist programs designed especially for children. The junior naturalist programs take place at Tunnel Mountain Campground, Johnston Canyon Campground, Two Jack Lakeside Campground, and Lake Louise Campground Theatre. ✉*224 Banff Ave., Banff* ☎*403/762–8918* 🎟*Free or nominal fee* 🌐*www.friendsofbanff.com.*

★ **Mountain World Heritage Theatre.** Each summer Parks Canada's troupe of professional actors put on entertaining and educational performances for park guests. Tickets are available at The Friends of Jasper store, DO Travel, and at the door. For showtimes, check at the information center. ✉ *Jasper Heritage Railway Station* ☎ *403/760–1338* *$10* *July and Aug.*

ARTS & ENTERTAINMENT

ARTS VENUES

Most of the cultural activity in the Canadian Rockies takes place in and around Banff, and the hub of that activity is **Banff Centre** (✉ *St. Julien Rd. [on Tunnel Mountain]* ☎ *403/762–6100, 800/413–8368 in Alberta and British Columbia* *www.banffcentre.ca*), which consists of 16 buildings spread across 43 acres. The center presents a performing-arts grab bag throughout the year of pop and classical music, theater, and dance. The season peaks in summer with the monthlong **Banff Arts Festival,** with concerts, performances, films, and discussions. Within the center, the **Walter Phillips Gallery** (☎ *403/762–6281* *Free* *Tues., Wed., and Fri.–Sun. noon–5, Thurs. noon–9*) showcases contemporary artwork by Canadian and international artists.

WHAT'S NEARBY

About 15 mi (24 km) southeast of Banff Townsite, **Canmore** became a modest boomtown with the 1988. It attracts a mix of tourists, residents who seek a mountain lifestyle, and commuters from Calgary who feel the hour-long commute is a fair trade-off for living in the mountains. Canmore makes a good base for exploring both Kananaskis Country and Banff National Park, without the crowds or cost of Banff.

Three provincial parks make up the 1,600-square-mi (4,200-square-km) recreational region known as **Kananaskis Country,** whose northern entrance is 16 mi (26 km) southeast of Canmore. The area includes grand mountain scenery, though perhaps not quite a match for that in the adjacent national parks. You can take part in the same activities you'd find in the national parks, and Kananaskis allows some activities that are prohibited within the national-park system, such as snowmobiling, motorized boating, off-road driving, and mountain biking. The main route through Kananaskis Country is Highway 40, also known as the Kananaskis Trail. It runs north–south through the front ranges of the Rockies. Only the northern 25 mi (40 km) of the road remain open from December 1 through June 15, in part because of the extreme conditions of Highwood Pass (at 7,280 feet, the highest drivable pass in Canada), and in part to protect winter wildlife habitats in Peter Lougheed Provincial Park and southward. Highway 40 continues south to join Highway 541, west of Longview. Access to East Kananaskis Country, a popular area for horseback trips, is on Highway 66, which heads west from the town of Priddis.

4

FESTIVALS & EVENTS

JAN. **Ice Magic ice-sculpting contest.** On weekends, typically beginning the third Friday in January, ice carvers from around the world compete in this annual competition held at various locations in Lake Louise. This free exhibition remains on display until the first of March, weather permitting. ☎ *403/762–8421.*

Banff–Lake Louise Winter Festival. Begins in late November and runs for 10 days. Winter sports are the highlight of the festival that also features outdoor events, nightly bar activities, and a town party. ☎ *403/762–8421.*

APR. **Easter at Sunshine Village.** Easter egg hunts, church service at the top of the strawberry chairlift, and visits by the Easter Bunny. ☎ *403/762–6508.*

JUNE–AUG. **Banff Summer Arts Festival.** Every summer the Banff Centre presents film screenings, visual-art displays, theater, opera, dance, and musical productions. ☎ *403/762–6300.*

JULY **Canada Day Celebration.** Canada Day means free admission to the national park and it means big celebrations in Canmore and Banff including a parade, fireworks, and live music. ☎ *403/762–0285.*

NOV.–DEC. **Santa Claus Parade.** Banff welcomes the Christmas season with a parade, treats, and photos with Santa in Central Park. On Christmas Day Santa skis at the three area ski resorts. ☎ *403/762–8421.*

AREA ACTIVITIES

SPORTS & THE OUTDOORS

Many of the outfitters and operators who run tours in Banff National Park are based in Canmore, so if you're staying here, you can often join the tour from Canmore rather than having to drive to the park. *See the Park section of this chapter for tours and activities within the park.* Equipment for activities can be rented at most sports shops in Canmore.

GOLF **Kananaskis Country Golf Course.** This is one of the premier golf courses in the Canadian Rockies, with two 18-hole, par-72 links. ✉ *Off Hwy. 40* ☎ *403/591–7272 or 877/591–2525.*

Silvertip Golf Course. This 18-hole, par-72 golf course offers spectacular elevation changes and views of the valley and mountains from most holes. ✉ *1000 Silvertip Trail* ☎ *403/678–1600 or 877/877–5444.*

SPELUNKING **Canmore Caverns Ltd.** If you have ever wanted to don a headlamp and explore an undeveloped cave, Canmore Caverns can arrange a suitable caving experience. They supply the equipment and you bring the enthusiasm. Children should be at least nine years of age to participate. ☎ *403/678–8819* 🌐 *www.canadianrockies.net/wildcavetours.*

WATER SPORTS **Blast Adventures.** Unique guided kayak adventures using inflatable kayaks on white water are available with this company. Transportation from Banff or Canmore is included. ✉ *120 B Rundle Dr., Canmore* ☎ *403/609–2009 or 888/802–5278* 🌐 *www.blastadventures.com.*

WINTER SPORTS

★ **Canmore Nordic Centre.** Built for the 1988 Olympic Nordic skiing events, Canmore Nordic Centre has 43 mi (70 km) of groomed cross-country trails in winter that become mountain-biking trails in summer. Some trails are lighted for night skiing, and a 1-mi (1½-km) paved trail is open in summer for roller skiing and rollerblading. This state-of-the-art facility is in the northwest corner of Kananaskis Country, south of Canmore. In late January, the annual **Canmore International Dogsled Race**—a two-day event—takes place here, attracting more than 100 international teams. ✉ *1988 Olympic Way* ☎ *403/678–2400* *Trails free Apr.–Oct., C$7.50 per day Nov.–Mar.* 🌐 *http://tprc.alberta.ca* *Lodge: daily 9–5:30; some trails illuminated until 9* PM.

Nakiska. The site of the 1988 Olympic alpine events, Nakiska is 45 minutes southeast of Banff and has wide-trail intermediate skiing and a sophisticated snowmaking system. The vertical drop is 2,412 feet, and there are four lifts. ✉ *Off Hwy. 40, Kananaskis Village* ☎ *403/591–7777* 🌐 *www.skinakiska.com.*

WHERE TO STAY & EAT

ABOUT THE RESTAURANTS

Eating out is, for the most part, a casual affair with an emphasis on good fresh food served in large quantities. Trout, venison, elk, moose, and bison appear on the menus of even many modest establishments. Prices everywhere are slightly inflated.

ABOUT THE HOTELS

The lodgings in Banff compose an eclectic list that includes backcountry lodges without electricity or running water, campgrounds, hostels with shared bathroom facilities, standard roadside motels, quaint B&B's, supremely luxurious hotels, and historic mountain resorts. Most accommodations do not provide meal plans, but some include breakfast.

With just a few exceptions, room rates are often highest from mid-June to late September and between Christmas and New Year's. In many cases, the best accommodation rates can be found during the months of October to mid-November and May to mid-June when rates can drop by as much as 50%. Lodgings in this chapter are listed with their peak-season rates. Check in advance for off-season rates.

If you want to save money, consider staying in nearby Canmore and in Kananaskis Country.

ABOUT THE CAMPGROUNDS

Parks Canada operates 13 campgrounds in Banff National Park (not including backcountry sites for backpackers and climbers). The camping season generally runs from mid-May through October, although the Tunnel Mountain and Lake Louise campgrounds remain open year-round. Hookups are available at most of the campgrounds and at 4 of the 31 Kananaskis Country campgrounds. Prices for a one-night stay range from C$9 to C$33. A fire permit is required to use a fire pit. In some cases the permit is purchased separately and in others it's included in the rates. Banff and Lake Louise participate in a reservation system that allows visitors to prebook campsites at Tunnel Mountain and Lake Louise campgrounds for a fee of C$11. The other campgrounds in the park operate on a first-come, first-served basis. To reserve a campsite, visit: *www.pc.gc.ca* or call 905/426–4648 or 877/737–3783. For backcountry camping in Banff or Lake Louise, call Lake Louise Backcountry Trails Office at 403/522–1264. Numerous privately run campgrounds can be found outside park boundaries.

	WHAT IT COSTS IN CANADIAN DOLLARS				
	¢	$	$$	$$$	$$$$
RESTAURANTS	under $8	$8–$12	$13–$20	$21–$30	Over $30
HOTELS	under $75	$75–$125	$126–$175	$176–$250	over $250

Restaurant prices are for a main course at dinner. Hotel prices are for two people in a standard double room in high season.

WHERE TO EAT

IN THE PARK

$$$$ ★ **Banffshire Club.** The Scottish influence in the region becomes immediately apparent when you enter the exclusive Banffshire Club, with its vaulted ceilings, oak paneling, tartan drapes, and reproduction Stuart-era furniture. Entrées include roast young partridge with truffles, and pecan-crusted caribou. Staff members are all sommelier trained to help you choose from the extensive wine cellar. A jacket is required; loaners are available from the maître d' if necessary. Fixed-price menus start at C$100 and tasting menus go up to C$310 per person including wine pairings. *Fairmont Banff Springs, 405 Spray Ave., Banff 403/762–6860 www.fairmont.com Reservations essential Jacket required AE, D, DC, MC, V No lunch, Sun and Mon.*

$$$$ Fodor's Choice ★ **Post Hotel.** Here is one of the true epicurean experiences in the Canadian Rockies. A low, exposed-beam ceiling and a stone, wood-burning hearth in the corner lend a warm, in-from-the-cold atmosphere; white tablecloths and fanned napkins provide an elegant touch. The combination of modern and classic dishes leads to daring regionally inspired fresh market cuisine. Look for innovative dishes prepared with fresh fish, game, or Alberta beef. The Post is one of only four restaurants in Canada to receive the *Wine Spectator* Grand Award with a 2,000-label wine list and an incredible cellar that contains more than 30,000 bottles of wine. For a unique dining experience with a group of six or more, ask to dine in the private cellar dining room. There are two sittings for dinner: 6:30 PM and 8:30 PM. *200 Pipestone Rd., Lake Louise 403/522–3989 or 800/661–1586 Reservations essential AE, MC, V.*

$$$–$$$$ **Bow Valley Grill.** Serving breakfast, lunch, and dinner in a relaxed dining room overlooking the Bow Valley, this is one of the most popu-

lar restaurants in the Fairmont Banff Springs hotel. You can choose between à la carte or buffet dining. There's a tantalizing selection of rotisserie-grilled meats, salads, and seafood, plus bread from an on-site bakery. During the summer months, buffet lunch comes with a guided historic hotel tour. ✉ *Fairmont Banff Springs, 405 Spray Ave., Banff* ☎ *403/762–6860* 🌐 *www.fairmont.com* ▭ *AE, D, DC, MC, V.*

$$$–$$$$ ✕ **Fuze Finer Dining.** Voted "Best New Restaurant in the Canadian Rockies" by Where Magazine in 2005, Fuze has been a welcome addition to the Banff dining scene. The chic and modern dining room is set between a wall of display wines and a bar built from wood salvaged from a grain elevator. There is a demonstration kitchen for wine tastings and corporate cooking events, an epicurean boutique to purchase spices and cooking supplies, and a chef's table with dramatic views of the kitchen. Entrées are artfully displayed and signature dishes include such items as roasted tomato soup with double smoked bacon, fruity cream, and pesto oil or herb crusted rack of lamb with tapenade lamb jus. You can't go wrong with the three-course table d'hote menu for $60 per person. There is also an oyster bar and seafood lounge. A Sunday brunch menu is served from 10:30 AM until 2:00 PM on Sundays. ✉ *2nd floor, 110 Banff Ave., Banff* ☎ *403/760–0853* 🌐 *www.fuzedining.com* ▭ *AE, MC, V* ⊗ *No breakfast, no lunch in fall and winter.*

$$$–$$$$ ✕ **Mount Fairview Dining Room.** Set beneath the high ceilings and inside the log-and-stone framework of Deer Lodge, this fine-dining establishment has large picture windows and a rustic look. The specialty is regionally inspired, Rocky Mountain cuisine. Elk, caribou, and bison top out the menu choices. There is an extensive wine list. ✉ *109 Lake Louise Dr., Lake Louise* ☎ *403/522–4202 or 800/661–1595* ▭ *AE, D, DC, MC, V.*

$$$–$$$$ ✕ **Waldhaus.** Fondues are a specialty at this German restaurant. The braised beef short ribs, duck with cider sauce, trout, and Wiener schnitzel are also popular. The downstairs pub serves the same menu items, except for the fondues. In summer, a barbecue lunch is held on the terrace. The savory barbecued entrées—steaks, salmon, or chicken breast on salad—are greatly enhanced by the views. ✉ *Fairmont Banff Springs, 405 Spray Ave., Banff* ☎ *403/762–6860* ✍ *Reservations essential* ▭ *AE, D, DC, MC, V* ⊗ *No lunch Sept.–May.*

$$$–$$$$ ✕ **Walliser Stube.** For something different, try this Swiss wine bar with warm cherrywood and a large selection of fondues. Choose from bison, tuna, or ostrich in broth; classic cheese; beef; and five chocolate dessert fondues. ✉ *Fairmont Château Lake Louise, Lake Louise Dr., Lake Louise* ☎ *403/522–3511 Ext. 1817* ▭ *AE, D, DC, MC, V.*

$$–$$$$ ✕ **Giorgio's Trattoria.** The exotic pizzas are cooked in a wood-burning oven—try the pizza *mare* (of the sea), with tiger shrimp, cilantro, sun-dried tomatoes, and roasted garlic. A popular pasta dish is *roselline di pasta* (ham-and-mozzarella-filled pasta roses in a creamy tomato sauce). Sponge-painted walls, Philippine mahogany tables, and detailed ironwork create an elegant look. ✉ *219 Banff Ave., Banff* ☎ *403/762–5114* ▭ *AE, MC, V* ⊗ *No lunch.*

$$–$$$$ ✕ **Ticino.** The distinctive Swiss dishes of Ticino, the southernmost province of Switzerland, reflect a definite Italian influence, as does the fare at

this eponymous wood-beam and stucco restaurant. Fondue is a house specialty: the *mar-e-mont* (Italian for "ocean and mountain") is a beef-and-shrimp fondue you cook yourself in hot broth. Baked salmon, beef medallions, panfried veal, and lamb are other offerings. For dessert, try the Swiss chocolate dessert fondue. ✉*High Country Inn, 415 Banff Ave., Banff* ☎*403/762–3848* ▭*AE, DC, MC, V* ⊙*No lunch.*

$$–$$$ ✕**Saltlik, A Rare Steakhouse.** AAA steaks are cooked in an infrared oven to preserve flavor and tenderness. Other items include rotisserie grilled chicken, fish, and salads. The atmosphere is fun and casual and the decor is trendy and innovative. The dining room has a vaulted ceiling and a fireplace, and there are eight beers on tap in the lounge. ✉*221 Bear St., Banff* ☎*403/762–2467* ▭*AE, MC, V.*

$$–$$$ ✕**Typhoon.** This intimate, café-style restaurant serves an eclectic mix of Thai, Indian, and other southeast Asian dishes. Always tasty and fresh, the soup of the day—often fragrant with the scent of lemongrass and coconut milk—comes in a huge bowl. The dinner menu includes chicken curry in a green-chili and coconut-milk sauce, tiger prawns with vegetables and noodles, and pot stickers. Dinner is served until 11 PM, appetizers until 1 AM. You can also indulge in a superb martini at the long granite-top bar. ✉*211 Caribou St., Banff* ☎*403/762–2000* ▭*AE, MC, V.*

4

¢–$ ✕**Laggan's Mountain Bakery and Deli.** Local work crews, mountain guides, and park wardens come to this small coffee shop in the Samson Mall for an early-morning muffin and cup of coffee. Laggan's sells excellent baked goods, especially the sweet poppy-seed breads made from organic grains. It's a good place to pick up a sandwich if you're driving north on the Icefields Parkway. ✉*Samson Mall off Hwy. 1, Lake Louise* ☎*403/522–2017* ▭*No credit cards.*

PICNIC AREAS

Bow Lake picnic area. Situated on the shores of stunning Bow Lake, on the Icefields Parkway, this picnic area has a kitchen shelter, five tables, toilets, and fireboxes. ✉*Icefields Pkwy. at the edge of Bow Lake.*

Cascade picnic area. There are 60 tables, flush toilets, a kitchen shelter, and fireplaces at this picnic site, located on Lake Minnewanka Road. ✉*Off Lake Minnewanka Rd.*

Fireside picnic area. Located on the Bow Valley Parkway, this picnic area has picnic tables and toilets nearby. ✉*Off Bow Valley Pkwy.*

★ **Lake Minnewanka picnic area.** This popular picnic area has three picnic shelters, 35 tables, flush toilets, two fire rings, and six fireplaces. Hike, rent a boat or try your luck at fishing. ✉*6 mi (10 km) from Banff on the Minnewanka Loop.*

Moraine Lake picnic area. One of the most beautiful lakes in the Canadian Rockies is the setting for this picnic area located near Lake Louise. There are two kitchen shelters, eight tables, and toilets at this site. ✉*Off Moraine Lake Rd., 3 mi (5 km) from the village of Lake Louise.*

OUTSIDE THE PARK

$–$$ ✕**Grizzly Paw Brewing Company.** A great outdoor patio, a pool table upstairs, and six hand-crafted beers on tap, make this casual restaurant popular with locals and visitors. The menu includes classic burgers, wraps, steaks, and barbecue maple salmon kabobs. There's an excellent children's menu and a selection of hand-crafted sodas with half the sugar and no caffeine. If you dine at the restaurant, you get a discount coupon that is good for merchandise purchased at the Paw Shop located next door. ✉*622 Main St., Canmore* ☎*403/678–0960* 🌐*www.thegrizzlypaw.com* ▭*AE, MC, V.*

WHERE TO STAY

IN THE PARK

$$$$ Fodor'sChoice ★ **Fairmont Banff Springs.** The building of this massive castle-like hotel by the Canadian Pacific Railway in 1888 marked the beginning of Banff's tourism boom. The hotel retains its historic elegance and magnificent views of the Bow River and surrounding peaks, but now includes modern amenities that make for a luxurious lodging experience. Pampering is an art at the world-class Willow Stream spa. Restaurants, bars, and lounges of varying formality and cuisine create a small culinary universe. In summer about 200 rooms per night are reserved for individual travelers on inclusive resort packages. If the hotel is the focus of your visit to Banff, these packages represent good value. Rates decrease substantially off-season. ✉*405 Spray Ave., Box 960, T1L 1J4* ☎*403/762–2211 or 800/441–1414* 🖷*403/762–5755* 🌐*www.fairmont.com* *770 rooms, 70 suites* *In-room: ethernet, Wi-Fi. In-hotel: 10 restaurants, room service, bars, golf course, tennis courts, pools, gym, spa, concierge, some pets allowed* *EP* ▭*AE, D, DC, MC, V.*

$$$$ ★ **Fairmont Château Lake Louise.** There's a good chance that no hotel—anywhere—has a more dramatic view out its back door. Terraces and lawns reach to the famous aquamarine lake, backed by the Victoria Glacier. Guest rooms have neocolonial furnishings, and some have terraces. The hotel began as a wooden chalet in 1890 but was largely destroyed by fire in 1924. It was soon rebuilt into the present grand stone-facade structure. The many dining choices range from family dining in the Brasserie to night-on-the-town elegance in the Fairview Dining Room (jacket required for dinner in summer). ✉*Lake Louise Dr., Lake Louise T0L 1E0* ☎*403/522–3511 or 800/441–1414* 🖷*403/522–3834* 🌐*www.fairmont.com* *433 rooms, 54 suites* *In-room: no a/c (some), ethernet, Wi-Fi. In-hotel: 5 restaurants, pool, gym, spa, laundry service, parking (fee), some pets allowed* ▭*AE, D, DC, MC, V* *EP.*

$$$$ ★ **Post Hotel.** A bright red roof and log construction make this hotel a model of rustic elegance. Rooms come in 15 configurations, from standard doubles to units that have a sleeping loft, balcony, fireplace, and whirlpool tub. The deluxe suites have a king-size bed and a large living room with a river-stone fireplace. For old-fashioned, in-the-mountains romance try one of the three streamside log cabins. Furnishings are solid Canadian pine throughout. The restaurant is regularly rated as one of the best in the Canadian Rockies. Room rates decrease by about 40% off-season. ✉*200 Pipestone Rd., Lake Louise T0L 1E0* ☎*403/522–3989 or 800/661–1586* 🖷*403/522–3966* 🌐*www.postho-*

tel.com 69 rooms, 26 suites, 3 cabins *In-room: no a/c, Wi-Fi. In-hotel: restaurant, pool, gym, spa* *EP* *AE, MC, V.*

$$$$ **Rimrock Resort Hotel.** Luxury and natural splendor coexist in harmony at this 11-story hotel perched on the steep slope of Sulphur Mountain, with a gondola and hot springs nearby. The Grand Lobby has a 25-foot ceiling, giant windows, a balcony facing the Rockies, and an oversize marble fireplace. Nearly all rooms have views of the Bow Valley, though the views from the lower floors are compromised by trees. Off-season rates drop by 50%. You can catch a Banff transit bus or a shuttle to the Banff Townsite. *100 Mountain Ave., Box 1110, T1L 1J2* *403/762–3356 or 800/661–1587* *403/762–4132* *www.rimrockresort.com* *345 rooms, 6 suites* *In-room: no a/c, ethernet. In-hotel: 2 restaurants, pool, gym, spa, concierge* *EP* *AE, D, DC, MC, V.*

$$$–$$$$ **Banff Rocky Mountain Resort.** Numerous outdoor facilities are a draw at this family-friendly resort 3 mi (5 km) east of Banff. Inside the chalet-style building, rooms are bright, with white walls, wall-to-wall carpeting, and blond-wood trim. All have fireplaces and most have kitchenettes with microwave ovens. Off-season rates decrease by 40%. *1029 Banff Ave., at Tunnel Mountain Rd., Box 100, T1L 1A2* *403/762–5531 or 800/661–9563* *403/762–5166* *www.rockymountainresort.com* *171 suites* *In-room: no a/c, kitchen (some), dial-up. In-hotel: tennis courts, pool, gym, bicycles, Internet room* *EP* *AE, D, DC, MC, V.*

$$$–$$$$ **Deer Lodge.** Built in 1921 as a log teahouse, this spot 15 minutes (on foot) from the shores of Lake Louise, has always been a popular destination. Guest rooms were added in 1925, and the frequent renovations since then have preserved most of the original rustic charm of the stone-and-log architecture. Feather comforters and teahouse-era antiques decorate the rooms; the older rooms are small but bright with the most historic charm. Relax around the central fireplace, with a book in one of the hotel's many nooks and crannies, or in the rooftop hot tub, complete with stunning mountain views. Rates decrease off-season. *109 Lake Louise Dr., Box 100, Lake LouiseT0L 1E0* *403/522–3747 or 800/661–1595* *403/522–4222* *www.crmr.com* *73 rooms* *In-room: no a/c, no phone (some), no TV. In-hotel: restaurant* *EP* *AE, DC, MC, V.*

$$$ **High Country Inn.** There's nothing fancy here—just clean, simple, comfortable motel rooms, many with a balcony. Cedar-covered walls give some rooms a touch of regional character. Ask for a room in the back, away from the Banff Avenue traffic. A deluxe Continental breakfast is included in the rate and includes items like pastry, fruit, cereal, and hot waffles. Rates decrease by 50% off-season. *419 Banff Ave., Box 700, T1L 1A7* *403/762–2236, 800/661–1244 in Canada* *403/762–5084* *www.banffhighcountryinn.com* *70 rooms* *In-room: no a/c, VCR. In-hotel: restaurant, pool* *EP* *AE, MC, V* *CP.*

$$$ **Lake Louise Inn.** Five buildings hold a variety of accommodations, from small budget rooms to two-bedroom condo units, some with a balcony, fireplace, and kitchenette. A shuttle to the mountain and mul-

tiday ski packages are winter amenities. Rates decrease by 50% off-season. ✉*210 Village Rd., Lake Louise T0L 1E0* ☎*403/522–3791 or 800/661–9237* 📠*403/522–2018* 🌐*www.lakelouiseinn.com* *232 rooms, 12 suites, 39 condos* *In-room: no a/c, kitchen (some). In-hotel: restaurant, room service, pool* *EP* *AE, DC, MC, V.*

$$–$$$ **Johnston Canyon Resort.** Situated near the trailhead for Johnston Canyon, these rustic cabins have a sense of seclusion you won't find in the busy town site. Several excellent hikes are nearby. There are fireplaces in most cabins. The cabins are also pet-friendly. ✉*Hwy. 1A (halfway between Banff and Lake Louise)* *Box 875, Banff T0L 0C0* ☎*403/762–2971* 📠*403/762–0868* 🌐*www.johnstoncanyon.com* *36 cabins* *In-room: no a/c, no phone, kitchen (some), refrigerator, no TV. In-hotel: restaurant, some pets allowed* *EP* *MC, V.*

$$–$$$ **Skoki Lodge.** A 7-mi (11-km) hike or ski jaunt from the Lake Louise ski area, Skoki is the kind of backcountry lodge you must work to reach. The high-alpine scenery of the valley makes the trek well worth the effort, as does the small lodge itself, built in 1930. The log walls and big stone fireplace epitomize coziness, but don't expect private baths, running water, or electricity. Tasty home-style meals are included; reserve far in advance. There's a minimum two-day stay. *Box 5, Lake Louise T0L 1E0* ☎*403/522–3555* 📠*403/522–2095* 🌐*www.skoki.com* *6 rooms without bath, 3 cabins* *In-room: no a/c, no phone, no TV, no elevator. In-hotel: restaurant* *AE, MC, V* *Closed mid-Sept.–mid-Dec., Jan., mid-Apr.–mid-June* *FAP.*

¢–$ **HI Banff Alpine Centre.** This hostel is one of the best accommodation values in the park. You can purchase packages that include lift tickets in winter or adventure activities in the summer. The hostel has an activities program, but activities are designed for the young adults who tend to stay here and are generally not appropriate for children. The centre also has several new log cabins that can sleep up to five guests with en suite washrooms, TV/telephone, and a living room with a fireplace that are ideal for families. ✉*801 Hidden Ridge Way T1L 1B5* ☎*403/670–7580 or 866/762–4122* 🌐*www.banffvoyagerinn.com* *216 beds, cabins and family rooms* *In-room: no a/c, Wi-Fi. In-hotel: restaurant, kitchen, pub, gamehouse* *EP* *MC, V.*

CAMPGROUNDS & RV PARKS

$$ **Castle Mountain Campground.** This campground is located in a beautiful wooded area close to a small store, a gas bar, and a restaurant. ✉*21 mi (34 km) from Banff on Bow Valley Pkwy.* ☎*403/762–1550* *43 sites* *Flush toilets* *Reservations not accepted* *AE, MC, V* *Open mid-May–early Sept.*

$$ **Johnston Canyon Campground.** This campground is located across from Johnston Canyon. The scenery is spectacular and wildlife is abundant in the area. A small creek flows right by the camping area. ✉*15½ mi (25 km) from Banff on Bow Valley Pkwy.* ☎*403/762–1550* *132 sites* *Flush toilets, showers* *Reservations not accepted* *AE, MC, V* *Open early June–mid-Sept.*

$$ ★ **Lake Louise Campground.** This forested area next to the Bow River is open year-round but in early spring and late fall tents and soft-sided trailers are not permitted in order to protect both people and bears. A protective electrical fence with a Texas gate surrounds the camp-

ground. There are plenty of hiking and biking trails nearby. *½ mi (1 km) from Lake Louise Village and 2½ mi (4 km) from the Lake* *877/737–3783* *399 sites* *Flush toilets, partial hookups (electric), dump station, showers, fire pits* *AE, MC, V.*

$$ **Tunnel Mountain Campground.** Situated close to the town site, this campground has a great view of the valley, hoodoos, and the Banff Springs golf course. There are 321 full-service sites in the trailer court, 188 power-only sites in Village II, and 618 nonserviced sites in Village I. *1½ mi (2½ km) from Banff Townsite on Tunnel Mountain* *877/737–3783* *1,127 sites* *Flush toilets, full hookups, showers, fire pits* *AE, MC, V* *Open mid-May–early Oct.*

$$ **Two Jack Main Campground.** This secluded camp is situated in a beautiful wooded area with lots of wildlife. You can explore the ruins of the coal-mining town of Bankhead, located nearby. If you want showers, stay at Two Jack Lakeside Campground right across the road. *7½ mi (12 km) from Banff on the Minnewanka Loop* *403/762–1550* *380 sites* *Flush toilets* *Reservations not accepted* *AE, MC, V* *Open mid-May–early Sept.*

OUTSIDE THE PARK

$$$–$$$$ **Delta Lodge at Kananaskis.** Now part of the Kananaskis Village built for the 1988 Olympics, this hotel started life as a Canadian Pacific luxury hotel. Rooms are large and lavish—many have fireplaces, hot tubs, and sitting areas. Several restaurants, skewed toward elegance, serve everything from pizza and burgers to haute cuisine. For casual dining, try the Fireweed Grill, which serves a buffet-style breakfast; burgers for lunch; and chicken, salmon, beef tenderloin, and lamb chops for dinner. *Hwy. 40, 17 mi (28 km) south of Hwy. 1, Kananaskis Village T0L 2H0* *403/591–7711 or 888/244–8666* *403/591–7770* *EP.*

$$–$$$ **Rocky Mountain Ski Lodge.** Several motels in Canmore provide lower-price alternatives to Banff. Of these, Rocky Mountain Ski Lodge is a notch above the rest. It's really three separate motel properties rolled into one. Slanting, exposed wood-and-beam ceilings give a chalet-like feel to otherwise simple decor. Rooms in the older section have kitchenettes, but the style is more '60s American than Swiss chalet. Rates drop by 40% off-season. *1711 Bow Valley Tr., at Hwy. 1A, Box 8070, Canmore T1W 2T8* *403/678–5445, 800/665–6111 in Canada* *403/678–6484* *www.rockyski.ca* *82 rooms* *In-room: kitchen (some), VCR (some), Wi-Fi. In-hotel: laundry facilities* *EP* *AE, DC, MC, V.*

CAMPGROUNDS & RV PARKS

$$–$$$$ **Sundance Lodges Campground.** This campground has tent sites, RV sites, tepee camping, and old-fashioned trapper's tents. It's a quiet, secluded campground designed for peace and tranquility. There are no electrical hookups, but there are outlets in the washroom. There is a small fee for pets. *Box 190, Kananaskis VillageT0L 2H0* *www.sundancelodges.com* *403/591–7122* *30 sites, 12 tepees, 18 trapper's tents* *Pit toilets, drinking water, guest laundry, showers, fire pits, public telephone, general store* *MC, V.*

BANFF ESSENTIALS

ACCESSIBILITY

Both visitor information centers are fully accessible and many of the campgrounds are also wheelchair accessible. There are also several trails in the park that are wheelchair accessible and Banff Transit operates one fully accessible shuttle. To find out specifics on accessible campgrounds and trails, call the information center at ☎403/762–1550.

ADMISSION FEES

A park entrance pass is C$8.90 per person or C$17.80 maximum per vehicle per day. An annual pass will cost C$62.40 per adult or C$123.80 per family or group. Larger buses and vans pay a group commercial rate. If you're planning to stay a week or more, your best bet is an annual pass.

ADMISSION HOURS

The park is open 24/7 year-round. It's in the Mountain time zone.

ATMS/BANKS

There are at least a dozen ATMs in Banff Townsite, but only the CIBC or Bank of Montreal ATMs will allow you to withdraw money from a Visa card.

Contacts **CIBC Bank** (✉ *98 Banff Ave., Banff* ☎ *403/762–3317*).

Bank of Montreal (✉ *107 Banff Ave., Banff* ☎ *403/762–2275*).

AUTOMOBILE SERVICE STATIONS

You can buy propane for stoves and barbecues in Lake Louise, but not in Banff. There are two gas stations in Lake Louise and five in Banff. There are also several companies that offer automobile repair service. The Petro-Canada station in Banff is a full-service station with gas sales and automotive repairs.

EMERGENCIES

Contacts **Ambulance, Fire, Police (RCMP)** (☎ *911*). **Banff Mineral Springs Hospital** (☎ *403/762–2222*). **Lake Louise Medical Clinic** (☎ *403/522–2184*). **Park Wardens** (☎ *403/762–4506*).

LOST & FOUND

Contact the Banff National Park Information Centre for information about lost items (☎403/762–1550).

PERMITS

Permits are required for backcountry camping and other activities in the park. Backcountry camping permits ($8.90 per day), day-use permits ($6.90 per day), fire permits ($7.90 per day), dumping station permits ($6.90 per day), and fishing permits ($8.90 per day) are available at the park visitor information center or at some campgrounds. In some cases a fire permit is included in your camping fees. Be sure to check with campground staff.

POST OFFICES

Contacts Banff Post Office (⊠ *204 Buffalo St., Banff* ☎ *403/762–2586*).

PUBLIC TELEPHONES

Public telephones can be found at the information centers, most hotels and bars, and at several key spots around the town site of Banff and the Village of Lake Louise. Cell-phone service is sometimes unpredictable.

RESTROOMS

Public restrooms are located throughout the park at all major day-use areas, in the visitor's center on Banff Avenue, and near the mall in the downtown area. Some day-use areas have flush toilets, while others have public outhouses or dry toilets.

SHOPS & GROCERS

Contacts Canada Safeway (⊠ *318 Marten St., Banff* ☎ *403/762–5378*). **Keller Foods** (⊠ *122 Bear St., Banff* ☎ *403/762–3663*).

NEARBY TOWN INFORMATION

Contacts Tourism Canmore (⊠ *907 7th Ave., Canmore* ✉ *Box 8608, T1W 2V3* ☎ *403/678–1295 or 866/226–6673* 🌐 *www.tourismcanmore.com*).

VISITOR INFORMATION

Contacts Banff National Park (✉ *Box 900, Banff T1L 1K2, Alberta, Canada* ☎ *403/762–1550* 🌐 *www.pc.gc.ca*).

Banff Lake Louise Tourism (✉ *Box 1298, Banff T1L 1B3, Alberta, Canada* ☎ *403/762–8421* 🌐 *www.banfflakelouise.com*).

Jasper National Park

5

WORD OF MOUTH

"The view that lay before us in the evening light was one that does not often fall to the lot of modern mountaineers. A new world was spread at our feet; to the westward stretched a vast ice-field probably never before seen by human eye, and surrounded by entirely unknown, un-named, and unclimbed peaks."

—J. Norman Collie,
British scientist and mountaineer

WELCOME TO JASPER

TOP REASONS TO GO

★ **Larger than life:** Almost as large as the entire state of Connecticut, Jasper is the largest of the Canadian Rocky Mountain national parks, and one of the largest protected mountain ecosystems.

★ **Spectacular scenery:** Jasper's scenery is rugged and mountainous. Within its boundaries are crystal-clear mountain lakes, thundering waterfalls, jagged mountain peaks, and ancient glaciers.

★ **Wonderful wildlife:** The Canadian Rockies provide a diverse habitat for 277 bird species and 69 species of mammals, including deer, elk, moose, sheep, goats, and bears.

★ **Columbia Icefield:** The largest ice field south of Alaska, the Columbia Icefield is also the hydrographic apex of North America, with water flowing to three different oceans from one point.

1 Yellowhead Corridor. Trans-Canada Highway 16 (Yellowhead Highway) travels through the foothills and main ranges of the Canadian Rockies. Highlights are views of the Jasper Lake sand dunes (Km 27), Disaster Point Animal Lick (Km 39.5), Pocahontas Townsite (Km 39.5), the Coal Mine Interpretive Trail (Km 39.5), and Miette Hot Springs (Km 43).

2 Maligne Valley. Highlights of this region include the Athabasca Valley Lookout (Km 5.8), Maligne Canyon (Km 7), Medicine Lake (Km 20.7), and Maligne Lake (Km 45), where the paved road ends.

3 Jasper Townsite. Shops, restaurants, nightclubs, and the main park information center are here. Just outside town are Lac Beauvert, Lake Annette, and Lake Edith, plus Old Fort Point and Whistlers Tramway.

Athabasca Glacier

4 Cavell Road. The road is just past the Astoria River bridge (Km 11.7) on Highway 93A, south of Jasper Townsite. Depending on weather conditions, it's open from early June to mid-October. Highlights include Astoria Valley Viewpoint, Mt. Edith Cavell, and Cavell Meadows.

5 Icefield Parkway. Highway 93 spans 130 mi (210 km) between Jasper Townsite and Lake Louise and is one of the world's most spectacular drives. Highlights include Athabasca Falls (Km 31), Sunwapta Falls (Km 55), Columbia Icefield (Km 103), Sunwapta Pass (Km 108), and the Weeping Wall (Km 125).

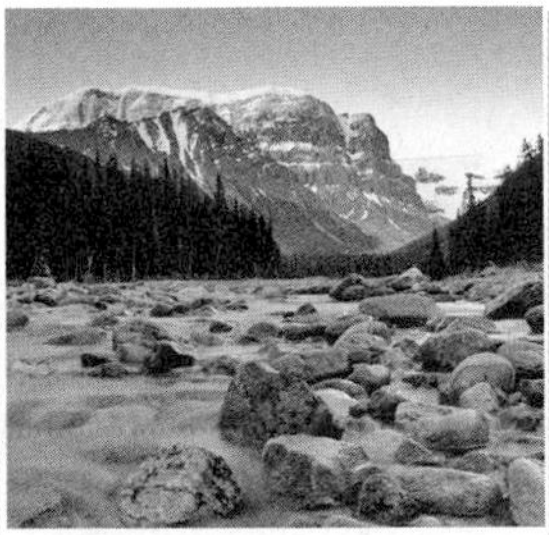

Stuffield Glacier

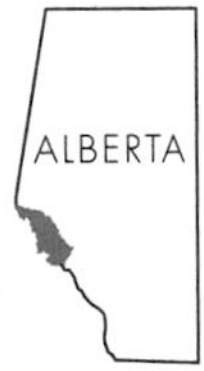
ALBERTA

GETTING ORIENTED

Wild and untamed, the 4,200 square mi (10,878 square km) of Jasper National Park encompasses rugged mountain terrain, natural hot springs, crystal-clear lakes, rivers, raging waterfalls, glaciers, and an abundance of wildlife.

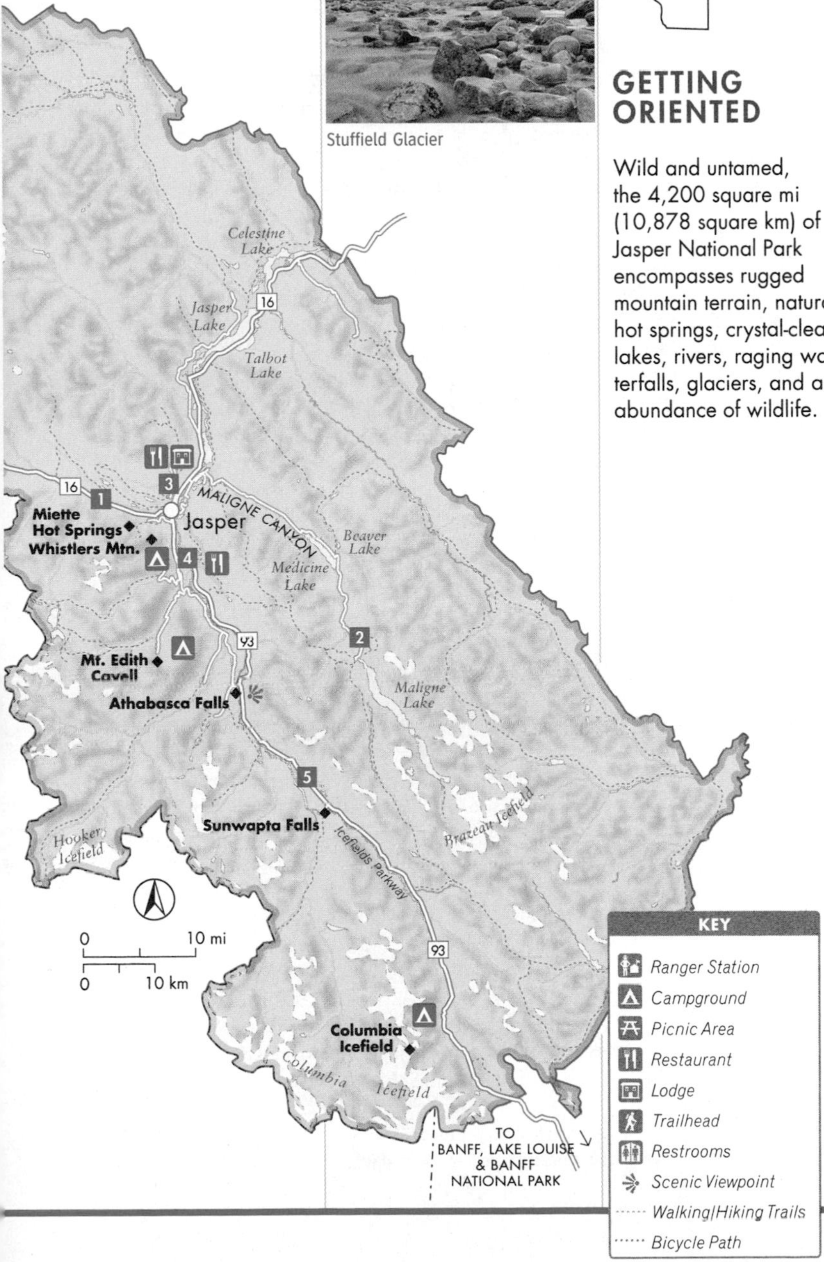
Celestine Lake
Jasper Lake
16
Talbot Lake
16
1
3
Miette Hot Springs
Whistlers Mtn.
Jasper
MALIGNE CANYON
4
Beaver Lake
Medicine Lake
2
93
Mt. Edith Cavell
Athabasca Falls
Maligne Lake
5
Sunwapta Falls
Icefields Parkway
Brazeau Icefield
Hooker Icefield
0
10 mi
0
10 km
93
Columbia Icefield
Columbia Icefield
TO BANFF, LAKE LOUISE & BANFF NATIONAL PARK
KEY
Ranger Station
Campground
Picnic Area
Restaurant
Lodge
Trailhead
Restrooms
Scenic Viewpoint
Walking/Hiking Trails
Bicycle Path

JASPER NATIONAL PARK PLANNER

When to Go

An old saying in the Canadian Rockies states: "If you don't like the weather, just wait a minute." The weather in Jasper National Park is unpredictable and ever changing, so you need to prepare for all weather conditions, especially when hiking. The summer months can be hot enough for swimming in Lake Edith one day and icy cold the next. Temperatures in winter are usually well below freezing, but occasionally warm Chinook winds blow in and begin to melt the snow.

July and August are the peak travel months for visitors and the best time for hiking and viewing wildflowers. If you are traveling then, book accommodations well in advance and expect to pay a bit more.

Temporary road closures may occur due to adverse weather conditions—especially in winter.

AVG. HIGH/LOW TEMPS.

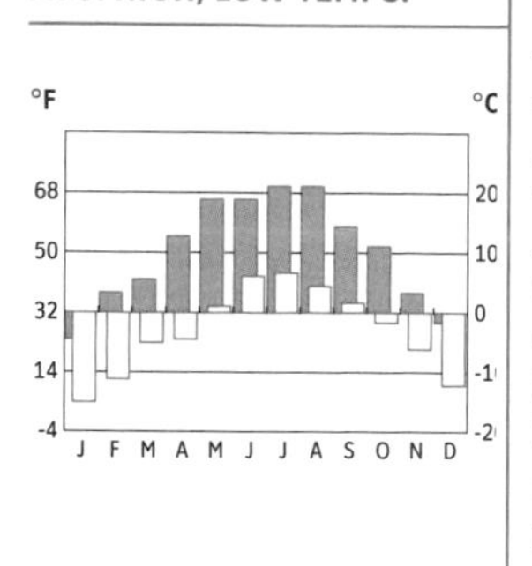

Flora & Fauna

In Jasper it is possible to stand in a field of wildflowers, hike through a thick subalpine forest, and revel in the solitude of the fragile alpine zone all in one day. A wide array of plants occupies the parks' three life zones of montane, alpine, and subalpine. In fact, about 1,300 species of plants and 20,000 types of insects and spiders are part of the complex web of life in the Canadian Rockies.

Jasper's vast wilderness is one of the few remaining places with a full range of carnivores, such as grizzly bears, black bears, wolves, coyotes, cougars, and wolverines. There are also large populations of elk, deer, bighorn sheep, and mountain goats among the park's nearly 53 species of mammals—which are often seen right from the roadsides. Each year hundreds of animals are killed along Jasper's highways, so it is vital to observe all speed limits and especially to slow down in special animal-sighting speed-zone areas. When hiking, keep your distance from wild animals and make a lot of noise as a means of avoiding contact with large mammals, especially bears.

Getting There & Around

Jasper National Park is in central Alberta in the Canadian Rockies. It is 110 mi (178 km) north of Banff Townsite and 31 mi (50 km) east of Jasper Townsite. The closest international airports are in Edmonton, 225 mi (362 km) to the east, and Calgary, 300 mi (480 km) to the southeast. Car rental agencies are available at both airports, as well as in Jasper. Driving is the easiest way to get from Edmonton to Jasper (on Yellowhead Highway 16).

Alternatively, train service is available three times per week (Monday, Thursday, and Saturday) from Edmonton to Jasper with VIA Rail Canada (☎888/842–7245). Also, Greyhound Canada Transportation (☎800/661–8747 or 800/231–2222 in the U.S.) provides regular service to Jasper from Calgary, Edmonton, and Vancouver; and Brewsters Transportation and Tours (☎800/661–1152) provides transportation between Calgary International Airport and Jasper.

By Debbie Olsen

JAGGED MOUNTAIN PEAKS, SHIMMERING GLACIERS, and crystal-clear lakes are just part of the incredible scenery that make up the largest and wildest of Canada's Rocky Mountain parks. Situated along the eastern slopes of the Rockies in west-central Alberta, Jasper National Park encompasses 4,200 square mi (10,878 square km) of land and is home to an astonishing variety of wildlife.

SCENIC DRIVES

Scenic drives skirt the base of glaciers, stunning lakes, and exceptional wildlife-viewing areas. The 142-mi (230-km) **Icefields Parkway** that connects Jasper with Banff provides access to the largest ice field south of Alaska and takes you to the very edge of the treeless alpine tundra. *For more details on the parkway see the Banff National Park chapter.* Within Jasper, **Maligne lake Road** and **Pyramid Lake Road** are good scenic drives, south and north of the town site, respectively.

5

WHAT TO SEE

HISTORIC SITES

There are five National Historic Sites within the boundaries of Jasper National Park: Jasper Information Centre, Athabasca Pass, Yellowhead Pass, Jasper House, and Henry House.

SCENIC STOPS

★ At **Athabasca Falls** (✉*Icefields Pkwy. and Hwy. 93A, 19 mi [31 km] south of Jasper*), the Athabasca River is compressed through a narrow gorge, producing a violent torrent of water. Trails and overlooks provide good viewpoints.

Disaster Point Animal Lick (✉*Hwy. 16, 33 mi [53 km] northeast of Jasper*), less than 3 mi (5 km) before Highway 16 from Jasper reaches the turn for Miette Hot Springs, is the most easily accessible spot in the park for encountering bighorn sheep; it's a rare summer moment when the sheep haven't descended from the adjacent steep slopes to lick up the mineral-rich mud, wandering back and forth across the road. You're likely to see numerous cars stopped by the side of the road.

★ The **Jasper Tramway** whisks you 3,191 vertical feet up the steep flank of Whistlers Mountain to an impressive overlook of the town site and the surrounding mountains. The seven-minute ride takes you to the upper station, above the tree line (be sure to bring warm clothes). A 30- to 45-minute hike from here takes you to the summit, which is 8,085 feet above sea level. Several unmarked trails lead through the alpine meadows beyond. ✉*Whistlers Mountain Rd., 2 mi (3 km) south of Jasper off Hwy. 93* ☎*780/852–3093* 🌐*www.jaspertramway.com* *C$25 round-trip* ⏲*Apr., May, and Oct., daily 9:30–4:30; June–early Sept., daily 8:30 AM–10 PM; rest of Sept., daily 9:30–6:30.*

★ The Maligne River cuts a 165-foot-deep gorge through limestone bedrock at **Maligne Canyon** (✉*Maligne Lake Rd., 7 mi [11 km] south of Jasper*). An interpretive trail winds its way along the river, switching

JASPER IN ONE DAY

Make a stop at the **Jasper Information Centre** to get maps of the park and information about any special activities before driving up to **Mt. Edith Cavell.** The 1 km (½-mi) trail from the parking lot leads to the base of an imposing cliff where you can see the stunning Angel Glacier. If you are feeling energetic, take the steep 3-km (2-mi) trail that climbs up the valley to **Cavell Meadows,** which are carpeted with wildflowers from mid-July to mid-August. Return to the Jasper Townsite for lunch. In the afternoon, take the 45-minute drive southeast of the town site to beautiful **Maligne Lake,** the second-largest glacier-fed lake in the world. Explore the lake and make a stop at **Spirit Island** on a 1½-hour guided boat tour with **Maligne Lake Scenic Cruises.** Return to the town site for supper and end your day by participating in a free ranger-led evening interpretive program at **Whistlers Outdoor Theatre,** south of the Jasper Townsite at Whistlers Campground.

from side to side over six bridges as the canyon progressively deepens. The 2½-mi (4-km) trail along the canyon can be crowded, especially near the trailhead. Just off the path, at the Maligne Canyon teahouse, are a restaurant and a good Native American crafts store.

★ The remarkably blue, 14-mi-long (22-km-long) **Maligne Lake** (✉ *Maligne Lake Rd., 27 mi [44 km] southeast of Jasper* 🌐 *www.malignelake.com*) is one of the largest glacier-fed lakes in the world. The first outsider known to visit the lake was Henry MacLeod, a surveyor looking for a possible route for the Canadian Pacific Railway, in 1875. You can explore the lake on a 1½-hour tour with **Maligne Lake Scenic Cruises** or in a rented canoe. A couple of day hikes (approximately four hours round-trip), with some steep sections, lead to alpine meadows that have panoramic views of the lake and the surrounding mountain ranges. You can also take horseback-riding and fishing trips, and there's an excellent cafeteria. **Tour reservations** ✉ *Maligne Lake Scenic Cruises, 627 Patricia St., Jasper* ☎ *780/852–3370 or 780/852–4803* 🌐 *www.malignelake.com* 🎫 *Boat tour C$43* ⏲ *June and Sept.–early Oct., daily 10–4; July and Aug., daily 10–5; tours every hr on the hr.*

The naturally heated mineral waters of **Miette Hot Springs** originate from three springs and are cooled to 104°F (40°C) to allow bathing in the two hot pools. There's also an adjacent cold pool—especially liked by the younger crowd—which is definitely on the cool side, at about 59°F (15°C). A short walk leads to the remnants of the original hot-springs facility, where several springs still pour hot sulfurous water into the adjacent creek. Day passes and bathing suit, locker, and towel rentals are available. ✉ *Miette Hot Springs Rd., off Hwy. 16, 36 mi (58 km) northeast of Jasper* ☎ *780/866–3939* 🌐 *www.parkscanada.gc.ca/hotsprings* 🎫 *C$6.15* ⏲ *Mid-May–late June and early Sept.–early Oct., daily 10:30–9; late June–early Sept., daily 8:30* AM*–10:30* PM.

Fodor's Choice ★

Mt. Edith Cavelle, the highest mountain in the vicinity of Jasper, towers at 11,033 feet and shows its permanently snow-clad north face to the town. It's named after a World War I British nurse who stayed in Belgium to treat wounded Allied soldiers after Brussels fell to the Germans; she was executed for helping prisoners of war escape. The mountain is arguably the most spectacular site in the park reachable by car. From Highway 93A, a narrow, winding 9-mi (14½-km) road (often closed until the beginning of June) leads to a parking lot at the base of the mountain. Trailers are not permitted on this road, but they can be left at a separate parking lot near the junction with 93A. Several scenic lookouts along the route offer access to trails leading up the **Tonquin Valley,** one of the premier hiking area. ✉ *Off Hwy. 93A, 17 mi (27 km) south of Jasper.*

VISITOR CENTER

Jasper Information Centre. A registered National Historic Site, this information center is in the Jasper Townsite and is worth a stop even if you don't need advice. Completed in 1914, this building was designed by Edmonton A. M. Calderon and is constructed of cobblestone and timber and is one of the finest examples of rustic architecture in Canada's national parks. You can pick up maps, informative brochures, and other materials to help you explore the parks and its trails. A small gift shop and restroom facilities are also inside the building. Parks Canada also operates an information desk at the Icefields Centre 64 mi (103 km) south of Jasper Townsite. ✉ *500 Connaught Dr.* ☎ *780/852–6176, 780/852–6177 (trail office)* ⊕ *www.pc.gc.ca/pn-np/ab/jasper* ⊙ *Apr.–June 14 and Oct., daily 9–5; June 15–Sept. 4, daily 8:30–7; Sept. 5–30, daily 9–6; Nov.–Mar., daily 9–4.*

SPORTS & THE OUTDOORS

In the northern half of the park, backpacking and horse packing trips offer wilderness seclusion, while the park's southern half rewards trekkers with dramatic glacial scenery. Day hikes are popular around Mt. Edith Cavell, Miette Hot Springs, and Maligne Lake; Pyramid Lake and the Fairmont Jasper Park Lodge are destinations for horseback riding.

AIR TOURS

OUTFITTER & EXPEDITIONS

Air Jasper. Aerial small plane tours in the Canadian Rockies, charter flights from Jasper-Hinton Airport to any destination, and air freight services are provided by this local company. ☎ *780/865–3616 or 877/865–3617* *Tours $185–$270 per person* ⊕ *www.airjasper.com.*

High Country Helicopter Tours Ltd. Contact this outfitter to enjoy a helicopter tour of the park, or to arrange heli-hiking or snowshoeing. Flights take off from Jasper Hinton Airport, just outside the park. ☎ *877/777–4354 or 780/852–0125* *Tours $189–$834 per person* ⊕ *www.hcheli.com.*

Icefield Helicopter Tours Inc. Located 42 km (26 mi) east of the Icefield Parkway, this company specializes in tours of the Columbia Icefields, but also offers heli-skiing, hiking, and fishing tours. For something unique try a guided heli-yoga tour. ☎ *403/721–2100 or 888/844–3514* 🎫 *Tours $49–$499 per person* 🌐 *www.icefieldhelicoptertours.com.*

BICYCLING

There are hundreds of miles of mountain bike trails and scenic roadways to enjoy in the park. Riders are expected to stick to designated trails.

See the Multisport Outfitters box for bike rentals and expeditions.

BIRD-WATCHING

An astonishing 277 species of birds make their home in the Canadian Rockies. The golden eagle migration, which occurs in the spring and fall, is the biggest birding event in the park. In late September and early October, you may be able to see more than 200 eagles in one day at the east end of the park (Pocahontas area). At other times of year, the best place to observe birds is at **Cottonwood Slough** along Pyramid Lake Road. This spot is a good place to find Barrow's goldeneye, warblers, snipes, soras and hummingbirds, and red-necked grebe.

OUTFITTER & EXPEDITIONS

On-Line Sport & Tackle. Stop in at this outdoor store to arrange a guided birding trip. ✉ *600 Patricia St.* ☎ *780/852–4245.*

BOATING & RAFTING

Boating in rowboats and canoes is allowed on most of the ponds and lakes in the park. Boats with electric motors without on-board generators are allowed on most road-accessible lakes, but the use of gas-powered motors is restricted. It's always wise to ask park staff about restrictions before launching your boat.

The rafting season runs from May through September and children as young as six years of age can participate on some of the float trips. The Athabasca River has Class II white-water rapids; the Sunwapta and Fraser rivers have Class III rapids.

OUTFITTERS & EXPEDITIONS

Jasper Raft Tours (☎ *780/852–3613* 🌐 *www.jasperrafttours.com*) runs half-day float trips on the Athabasca. **Maligne Tours** (✉ *Maligne Lake* ☎ *780/852–3370 or 866/625–4463* 🌐 *www.mra.ab.ca*) rents boats on beautiful Maligne Lake, and offers rafting on the Athabasca, Sunwapta, and Fraser rivers. **Raven Adventure** (☎ *780/852–4292 or 866/496–RAFT* 🌐 *www.ravenadventure.com*) is a smaller company that conducts a variety of rafting trips in the Jasper area. **Rocky Mountain River Guides** (☎ *780/852–3777* 🌐 *www.rmriverguides.com*) conducts a variety of rafting trips for different levels of rafters. **Whitewater Rafting Jasper Ltd.** (☎ *780/852–7238 or 800/557–7238* 🌐 *www.whitewaterraftingjasper.com*) offers half-day trips on the Athabasca and Sunwapta rivers.

See the Multisport Outfitters box for additional boating outfitters.

GOLF

The **Fairmont Jasper Park Lodge** (✉ *Off Hwy. 16* ☎ *780/852–6090*) has a championship 18-hole, par-71 course that was voted the best golf resort in Canada by *Score Magazine.*

READ ALL ABOUT IT

You will receive **The Mountain Guide** upon entry to the park. This has maps and good general information such as points of interest, safety messages, programs and events, camping information, and fees. It is online at www.pc.gc.ca/jasper.

At the Jasper Information Centre you can pick up a **Points of Interest** map to help you find your way to major points of interest in the park and the town site. A **Summer Trails Guide** contains both maps and details for hiking, mountain biking, and horseback riding trails, while the **Winter Trails Guide** provides maps and details forcross-country skiing and snowshoeing trails. The **Backcountry Visitor's Guide** provides an overview of backcountry options.

HIKING

Long before Jasper was established as a national park, a vast network of trails provided an essential passageway for wildlife, First Nations people, explorers, and fur traders. More than 660 mi (1,060 km) of hiking trails in Jasper provide an opportunity to truly experience wilderness and hardcore backpackers will find multiday loops of more than 100 mi (160 km).

A few of these trails are restricted to pedestrians, but hikers, mountain bikers, and equestrian users may share most of them. There are several paved trails that are suitable for wheelchairs, while others are rugged backcountry trails designed for backpacking trips. Bathrooms are found along the most used day-use trails. You may see elk, bighorn sheep, moose, and mountain goats along the way. It is never a good idea to surprise a large animal such as an elk or bear, so make plenty of noise as you go along, avoid hiking alone, and stick to designated trails. The trails at Mt. Edith Cavell and Maligne Canyon should not be missed.

EASY **Lake Annette Loop.** This short loop trail with interpretive signage is paved and mostly level and was designed especially for wheelchair use. Toilets are at two locations, and there is a shelter halfway around the 1.5-mi (2.4-km) loop that will take an hour to complete.

★ **Maligne Canyon.** This 1.3-mi (2.1-km), one-way trail 5 mi (8 km) east of Jasper Townsite leads to views of Jasper's famous limestone gorge and will take one to two hours to complete. Six bridges stretch across the canyon and a winding trail gains about 328 feet in elevation. Signage lines the trail that leads to a waterfall at the head of the canyon.

Old Fort Point Loop. Shaped by glaciers, Old Fort Point is a bedrock knob that provides an excellent view of Jasper. It will take one to two hours to complete the 2.2-mi (3.5-km) loop trail. There is a wide, easy path that begins behind the trail information kiosk and leads to a sec-

FESTIVALS & EVENTS

JAN. **Jasper in January.** Fun events for the entire family include an ice-sculpting contest, wine tasting, great live music, a chili cook-off, Taste of the Town, outdoor contests, and more. Accommodation deals and reduced ski lift ticket prices are available. ☎ *780/852–3858.*

JULY **Canada Day.** July 1, Canada's birthday, is celebrated with a parade, a full day of activities, and fireworks at dusk. ☎ *780/852–6176.* **Parks Day.** Celebrating national parks, this annual event takes place in mid-July. There are activities for the whole family, a fair on the Information Center lawn in the middle of town and free guided hikes to some of Jasper National Park's most interesting spots. ☎ *780/852–6176.*

NOV.–DEC. **Jasper Welcomes Winter.** Jasper's annual winter kick-off festival marks winter's arrival. Special activities for the entire family include the Santa Claus Parade, the Christmas Craft Fair, and shopping festivities. Special hotel rates are available. Watch for the opening of Jasper's Marmot Basin ski resort in 2007. ☎ *780/852–3858.*

tion of trail that is very steep. The trail passes the oldest rock in Jasper National Park, but the real highlight is the view from the top.

★ **Path of the Glacier Loop.** This short 1-mi (1.6-km) trail only takes about an hour and is a must-do. The start of the trail is paved and runs across a rocky landscape that was once covered in glacial ice. Eventually you come to Cavell pond, which is fed by Cavell Glacier. Small icebergs often float in the water. Across the valley, you will have a good view of the Angel glacier resting her wings between Mt. Edith Cavell and Sorrow Peak. Follow the trail back along Cavell Creek to the parking lot.

Valley of the Five Lakes. It will take two to three hours to complete the 2.3 mi (4.2 km) of this family-friendly hike just 5.6 mi (9 km) south of Jasper Townsite. Five small lakes are the highlight of the trip, which takes you through a lodgepole pine forest, across the Wabasso Creek wetlands, and through a flowery meadow. Watch for birds, beavers, and other wildlife along the way. Note: You can turn this into a moderate hike by continuing another 6.2 mi (10 km) to Old Fort Point.

MODERATE
Fodor's Choice ★
Cavell Meadows Loop. This moderately steep 5-mi (8-km) trail will take four to six hours. The upper section is not recommended in early summer, but from mid-July to mid-August you can enjoy the carpet of wildflowers. There's also an excellent view of the Angel Glacier.

DIFFICULT
Opal Hills Loop. Near Maligne Lake, this 5.1-mi (8.2-km) hike is relatively steep and will take four to six hours to complete. There are excellent views of Maligne Valley on this hike and many opportunities to observe wildlife including moose and bears. Be sure to make noise as you hike and keep your distance from the wildlife. During the summer months, there is often an abundance of wildflowers along the trail.

★ **Wilcox Pass.** Excellent views of the Athabasca Glacier are the highlight of this strenuous 5-mi (8-km) hike near the Icefield Centre. This pass was originally used by explorers and First Nations people and is fairly steep. Keep an eye out for wildflowers and bighorn sheep. Be sure to dress in warm layers, because this pass can be snowy until late July.

WILDERNESS HIKING

The backcountry is some of the wildest and most pristine of any mountain park in the world. For information on overnight camping quotas on the Skyline and Tonquin Valley trails or on any of the hundreds of hiking and mountain-biking trails in the area, contact the park information center. The **Skyline Trail** meanders for 27 mi (44 km) past some of the park's best scenery, at or above the tree line. **Tonquin Valley,** near Mt. Edith Cavell, is one of Canada's classic backpacking areas. Its high mountain lakes, bounded by a series of steep rocky peaks known as the Ramparts, attract many hikers in high summer.

HORSEBACK RIDING

Several outfitters offer one-hour, half-day, full-day, and multiday guided trips within the park. Participants must be at least age 6 to participate in a riding trip, but pony rides are available for younger children. It's wise to make your reservations well in advance, especially during the peak summer months and for multiday journeys. Horses can be boarded at the commercial holding facilities available through the Cottonwood Corral Association at Pyramid Riding Stables.

OUTFITTER & EXPEDITIONS

Pyramid Riding Stables offers rides and full-day excursions in the hills overlooking Jasper; there are also pony and carriage rides. ✉ *Pyramid Resort, Pyramid Lake Rd.* ☎ *780/852–3562.*

Rockin' K Stables can arrange a short ride, a full-day excursion or an all-inclusive five-day pack trip into the Tonquin Valley. Family and group rates are available. ✉ *Pyramid Lake Rd.* ☎ *780/852–8787* 🌐 *www.rockinkstables.com.*

Skyline Trail Rides offers lessons and one-hour to half-day rides. Multi-day trips into the backcountry are also available. ✉ *Fairmont Jasper Park Lodge, off Hwy. 16* ☎ *780/852–4215, 780/852–3301 Ext. 6189, or 888/852–7787.*

Tonquin Valley Adventures is a smaller outfitter that arranges five-day horseback trips into the Tonquin Valley and offers some trail rides. ☎ *780/852–1188* 🌐 *www.tonquinvalleyadventures.com.*

SWIMMING

Lakes Annette and Edith (✉ *Near Fairmont Jasper Park Lodge, off Hwy. 16*) have sandy beaches and water that reaches the low 20s°C/70s°F during warm spells.

Jasper Aquatic Center has a 180-foot indoor waterslide, a kids' pool, and a 25-meter regular pool. A steam room and a hot tub are also on-site, and towel and suit rentals are available. ✉ *401 Pyramid Lake Rd.* ☎ *780/852–3663* *C$6.50* ⏲ *Public swimming daily 2–9.*

WINTER SPORTS

There is a wide choice of groomed and natural trails for skiing and snowshoeing, and equipment and local guides can be arranged through local ski shops. Current cross-country ski information is available at the park visitor center. Snowmobiling is not allowed in the park, but can be experienced in the nearby town of Hinton. **Pyramid and Patricia lakes** (✉ *Pyramid Lake Rd.*) have excellent groomed cross-country trails. **Marmot Basin** (✉ *Off Hwy. 93A* ☎ *780/852–3816*), near Jasper, has a wide mix of downhill skiing terrain (75 runs, 9 lifts, and a snowboard park with all the toys), and the slopes are a little less crowded than those around Banff, especially on weekdays. This area has three day lodges, two of which are at mid-mountain; the vertical drop is 2,944 feet.

OUTFITTER & EXPEDITIONS

You cannot ride a snowmobile through the national park, but **Canadian Rockies Adventures** (☎ *780/865–7380 or 866/666–7823* 🎟 *Tours $95–$300 per person* 🌐 *www.canadianrockiesadvent.com*) has guided tours that take you through stunning scenery just outside the park

For more winter sports outfitters, see the Multisport Outfitters box.

EDUCATIONAL OFFERINGS

INTERPRETIVE PROGRAMS

★ **Jasper Institute.** Seminars and multiday programs, including weekend courses, are offered through the Jasper Institute by the Friends of Jasper National Park. The courses are given by naturalists and other experts; in conjunction with the programs, reasonably priced accommodations and food can be provided. Contact the Friends of Jasper National Park ☎ 780/852–4799 for a list of seminars and programs. ✉ *Jasper Information Centre, 500 Connaught Dr.* ☎ *780/852–4799* 🎟 *C$60–C$150* ⏲ *May–Aug.*

★ **Mountain World Heritage Theatre.** Parks Canada's troupe of professional actors put on entertaining and educational performances for park guests. Tickets are available at The Friends of Jasper Store, DO Travel, and at the door. For show times, check at the information center. ✉ *Jasper Heritage Railway Station* ☎ *780/852–4767* 🎟 *$10* ⏲ *July and Aug.*

★ **Whistlers Outdoor Theatre.** Interpretive programs are offered daily through the summer months at this Whistlers Campground theater. Programs are appropriate for both children and adults, and a schedule of seminars and activities is available at the information center. ✉ *Whistlers Campground* 🎟 *Free* ⏲ *Late June–early Sept.*

TOURS

Currie's Guiding. Currie's offers four- to six-hour driving tours, as well as a "wildlife search" tour. Prices begin around C$59. Fishing tours to Maligne Lake start at C$169. ✉ *406 Patricia St.* ☎ *780/852–5650.*

★ **Friends of Jasper National Park.** This nonprofit organization offers courses on discovering Jasper through guided hikes, nature photography, and wildlife viewing. Local experts lead the sessions at very reasonable prices. Courses also include discount accommodations and meals at the Jasper Palisades Centre, a park facility usually reserved for visiting park wardens and professors. The Friends also loan out free hiking

MULTISPORT OUTFITTERS & EXPEDITIONS

The **Boat House** (✉ *Fairmont Jasper Park Lodge, off Hwy. 16* ☎ *780/852–5708*) rents adult and children's mountain bikes, as well as paddleboats and canoes.

Gravity Gear (✉ *618A Patricia St.* ☎ *780/852–3155 or 888/852–3155*) can arrange for ice climbing, backcountry skiing, and mountaineering trips led by certified guides.

Jasper Source for Sports (✉ *406 Patricia St.* ☎ *780/852–3654* 🌐 *www.jaspersports.com*) rents bikes, fishing and camping equipment, as well as ski and snowboard equipment.

Pyramid Lake Boat Rentals (✉ *Pyramid Lake Resort* ☎ *780/852–4900 or 800/717–1277*) rents canoes, kayaks, electric boats, and paddleboats. They also sell fishing licenses and have rod and reel rentals.

Tonquin Valley Adventures (☎ *780/852–1188*) arranges hiking, skiing, and horseback trips into the Tonquin Valley. In winter there's a private cabin with cooking equipment provided; in the summer there's a cook at the cabin. Reservations for backcountry huts in Tonquin Valley can be made through **Tonquin Valley Pack and Ski Trips** (☎ *780/852–3909* 🌐 *www.tonquinvalley.com*); call well in advance.

Totem Ski Shop (✉ *408 Connaught Dr.* ☎ *780/852–3078 or 800/363–3078*) sells summer and winter sports equipment and clothing.

kits with binoculars, maps, first-aid materials, and other useful items. Kits can be picked up at the Friends store in the information center. ✉ *Jasper Information Centre, 500 Connaught Dr.* ☎ *780/852–4767* 🌐 *www.friendsofjasper.com* *Free or nominal fee.*

Jasper Adventure Centre. Guided tours, birding trips, ice walks, and snowshoeing tours are all available here. Rates start at C$45 per person, with most tours lasting three hours. The center also handles bookings for other adventure companies (canoeing, rafting, and other sports). ✉ *604 Connaught Dr.* ☎ *780/852–5595* 🌐 *www.jasperadventurecentre.com.*

Jasper Motorcycle Tours. For a truly unique perspective on the Canadian Rockies, try riding in the sidecar of a chauffeured Harley-Davidson motorcycle. Personalized tours include full leather and safety gear. Be sure to wear long pants and sturdy footwear. ☎ *780/931–6100* *Tours $30–$140 per person* 🌐 *www.jaspermotorcycletours.com.*

Rocky Mountain Tour Centre. A wide variety of tours are provided by this company including wildlife safaris, train tours, and boat tours. Winter tours are also available including a full day snowmobile tour. ☎ *780/852–1548 or 877/852–7682* *Tours $65–$329 per person* 🌐 *www.tourrockies.com.*

Sun Dog Tours. With offices in Jasper, Banff, and Calgary this company offers a wide range of tours of the Rocky Mountains between Jasper and Banff. ☎ *780/852–4056 or 888/786–3641* *Tours $55–$129 per person* 🌐 *www.sundogtours.com.*

5

MT. ROBSON PROVINCIAL PARK

This provincial park contiguous with Jasper National Park, is a pleasant hour-long drive from Jasper town site on Highway 16. The terrain and scenery are similar to Jasper's, although the vegetation is lusher thanks to the more abundant rainfall on the west side of the Rockies.

At 12,972 feet, towering **Mt. Robson** is the highest mountain in the Canadian Rockies. It was not successfully scaled until 1913, and experienced mountaineers consider certain routes on Robson among the world's most challenging. Mt. Robson's weather is notoriously bad, even when the weather elsewhere is perfectly fine, and it's a rare day that clouds do not encircle the summit. A favorite backpacking trip on the mountain is the strenuous 22-km (14-mi) hike to **Berg Lake** (☎ *800/689–9025 for camping information* 🌐 *www.discovercamping.ca*) through the wonderfully named Valley of a Thousand Falls. Berg Lake is no tranquil body of water; the grunts and splashes as Robson's glaciers calve chunks of ice into the lake are regular sounds in summer. It costs C$6.50 per person to camp overnight at Berg Lake, which operates on a reservations and quota system. The 5-km (3-mi), mostly level hike to **Kinney Lake,** along the Berg Lake trail, is a good option for day hikers. Note that this is a back country trail and hikers would be well advised to register at the Mt. Robson Visitor Centre before setting off.

The **Mt. Robson Visitor Centre** (✉ *Hwy. 16* ☎ *250/566–4325*), open mid-May to early October, has a small restaurant, store, and gas station, as well as a fine view of Mt. Robson.

WHAT'S NEARBY

Jasper National Park is 178 mi (287 km) north of Banff National Park, 248 mi (400 km) northwest of the city of **Calgary,** 224 mi (360 km) west of the city of **Edmonton,** and 34 mi (55 km) west of the town of **Hinton** and the Jasper/Hinton Airport. Most visitors arrive through either Calgary or Edmonton, where the major highway and the two major international airports are located.

WHERE TO STAY & EAT

ABOUT THE RESTAURANTS

Jasper's casual restaurants offer a wide variety of cuisines, including Greek, Italian, Japanese, French, and North American. Regional specialties include Alberta beef, lamb, pheasant, venison, elk, bison, trout, and BC (British Columbia) salmon. For the best views in town, try the cafeteria-style Treeline Restaurant at the top of the Jasper Tramway, 7,500 feet above sea level.

ABOUT THE HOTELS

Accommodations in this area include luxury resorts, fine hotels, reasonably priced motels, rustic cabins, and backcountry lodges. Reserve your accommodations in advance if you are traveling during the peak summer season.

ABOUT THE CAMPGROUNDS

Parks Canada operates 10 campgrounds in Jasper National Park that have a total of 1,772 available sites during the peak season. There is winter camping only at Wapiti campground. Hookup sites are available at Whistlers and Wapiti campgrounds only, so reserve a site in advance if you are traveling during the peak summer season. Reservations can only be made at **Pocahontas, Whistlers, Wapiti, and Wabasso campgrounds** (☎*877/737–3783* 🌐*www.pccamping.ca*), and there is a C$10.90 reservation fee. Other campgrounds work on a first-come, first-served basis and campers line up for sites early in the morning. You can pay using a credit card, but at remote campsites, you may wish to pay cash so that you don't have to wait for the mobile truck to come around to take your credit card payment. If your campsite has a fire pit, you will need to purchase a fire permit for C$7.80 before using it.

If you arrive at the park without a reservation and cannot obtain a serviced (with hookup) site, you may choose to take an unserviced site for the first night; campground staff can advise you on how to go about getting a hookup site for the rest of your stay. Another option is to travel to nearby Hinton, outside the park, where there are a number of serviced campsites and several good campgrounds. For general campground information, call ☎780/852–6176.

5

WHAT IT COSTS IN CANADIAN DOLLARS

	¢	$	$$	$$$	$$$$
RESTAURANTS	under $8	$8–$12	$13–$20	$21–$30	Over $30
HOTELS	under $75	$75–$125	$126–$175	$176–$250	over $250

Restaurant prices are for a main course at dinner. Hotel prices are for two people in a standard double room in high season.

WHERE TO EAT

$$$–$$$$ ✕**Edith Cavell.** This sophisticated restaurant overlooks the impressive mountain of the same name. The menu focuses on fine regional cuisine with local nuances; signature dishes include bison and Alberta rack of lamb. The wine list is extensive. A tasting menu is offered with (C$140) and without (C$90) wine pairings. ✉*Fairmont Jasper Park Lodge, off Hwy. 16, 7 km (4½ mi) northeast of Jasper* ☎*780/852–3301 or 800/441–1414* *Reservations essential* *AE, D, DC, MC, V* ⊙*No lunch.*

$$–$$$$ ★ ✕**Becker's Gourmet Restaurant.** Many visitors to Jasper miss Becker's because of its out-of-town location, but it's a favorite with locals. Spectacular panoramic views of the Athabasca River and Mt. Kerkeslin from a glass-enclosed dining room are a suitable accompaniment to the fine French food. After dinner you can stroll along the upper bank of the Athabasca River. There's a breakfast buffet from 8 to 11. ✉*Beside Becker's Chalets, Hwy. 93, 5 km (3 mi) south of Jasper* ☎*780/852–3535* *AE, MC, V* ⊙*Closed Nov.–Apr. No lunch.*

$$–$$$ ★ ✕ **Andy's Bistro.** This intimate bistro in downtown Jasper is known for its fresh market ingredients. Chef and owner Andy Allenbach is Swiss born and trained and is one of only 700 certified Chefs de Cuisine in Canada. His dishes have a European flare and regional influence, and include in-season organic fruits and vegetables, wild game, and fresh herbs. From November to April enjoy a three-course table d'hôte for $28. ✉ *606 Patricia St., Jasper* ☎ *780/852–4559* ✍ *Reservations essential* ▭ *AE, MC, V.*

$$–$$$ ✕ **Fiddle River.** Candles, dried flowers, and plenty of wood decorate this cozy, second-floor dining room. Seafood is the star and fresh Canadian fish, including salmon, halibut, trout, northern pike, and pickerel, appear on the menu when available. Alberta beef, bison, pork, and chicken are available for landlubbers. ✉ *620 Connaught Dr., Jasper* ☎ *780/852–3032* ▭ *AE, MC, V* ⏲ *No lunch.*

$$–$$$ ✕ **Moose's Nook Northern Grill.** The cuisine is contemporary Canadian at this seasonally open restaurant in the Fairmont Jasper Park Lodge. Live music plays every night during the summer. Wild game, AAA Alberta beef tenderloin, and fresh fish are some of the highlights. ✉ *Fairmont Jasper Park Lodge, off Hwy. 16, 4½ mi (7 km) northeast of Jasper* ☎ *780/852–3301 or 800/441–1414* ✍ *Reservations essential* ▭ *AE, D, DC, MC, V* ⏲ *Closed Nov.–Apr. No lunch.*

$$–$$$ ✕ **Villa Caruso.** Alberta is ranch country and this steak house is a good place to sample the products of the cattle industry. Entrées include flame-grilled grain-fed Alberta AAA Angus beef cuts, such as tenderloin, New York steak, and prime rib. Pasta, fish, chicken, pork tenderloin, lamb, and ribs round out the menu. There's also a children's menu. Cozy up for cocktails next to one of the two fireplaces. ✉ *640 Connaught Dr., Jasper* ☎ *780/852–3920* ▭ *AE, MC, V.*

$ ✕ **Black Sheep Café and Grill.** Internet stations, free wireless, and an espresso bar make this downtown café a popular hangout for locals and visitors. Breakfast is served all day along with homemade burgers, burritos, vegetarian entrées, and yummy baked treats. ✉ *407 Patricia St., Jasper* ☎ *780/852–9788* ✍ *Reservations not accepted* ▭ *MC, V.*

PICNIC AREAS

Airport picnic area. This large area has a shelter and is ideal for family reunions, because it can be reserved in advance. ✉ *Off Hwy. 16 E, 9 mi (15 km) from Jasper Townsite.*

Athabasca Falls picnic area. Dine beside the stunning Athabasca Falls. ✉ *Off Icefields Pkwy., 19 mi (30 km) from Jasper Townsite.*

Lake Annette. Beside Lake Annette, this picnic area has shelters and tables and is a favorite with families who come to the lake to swim. ✉ *Near the junction of Maligne Lake Rd. and Hwy. 16.*

Sixth Bridge. This picnic area is right beside the Maligne River just before it flows into the Athabasca River. There are no shelters, but it is a preferred picnic areas with locals because of the scenic location. ✉ *Off Maligne Lake Rd., 2.2 km (1.3 mi) from the Hwy. 16 junction.*

WHERE TO STAY

IN THE PARK

$$$$ Fodor's Choice ★ **Fairmont Jasper Park Lodge.** With abundant on-site recreational amenities, this lakeside resort, 4½ mi (7 km) northeast of Jasper, is a destination in itself, whether or not you stay overnight. Accommodations vary from cedar chalets and log cabins to specialty cabins with up to eight bedrooms. Rooms include down duvets, and all have either a porch, patio, or balcony. Winter guests love the year-round outdoor swimming pool, which is heated to 86°F /30°C in winter. Canoe rentals and horseback riding are available in the summer months and sleigh rides are offered in the winter. The golf course was voted the "best golf resort in Canada" by readers of *Score Magazine* in 2005, and nearby Marmot Basin has world-class skiing. It's located off Old Fort Point Road, 1½ km (1 mi) from the Highway 93A junction. *Box 40, Jasper T0E 1E0 780/852–3301 or 800/441–1414 780/852–5107 www.fairmont.com 446 rooms, 100 suites In-room: no a/c, ethernet, Wi-Fi. In-hotel: Wi-Fi, 9 restaurants, room service, bar, golf course, tennis courts, pool, gym, bicycles AE, D, DC, MC, V EP.*

$–$$$$ ★ **Patricia Lake Bungalows.** Five minutes north of Jasper, this is one of the few remaining bargain accommodations near Jasper. Though the motel rooms are the least expensive accommodation, the cabins—at a 20% premium over the motel units—are the most popular. Ten new luxury cabins are also available. Rates decrease by up to 50% off-season. *Off Pyramid Lake Rd., Box 657, Jasper T0E 1E0 780/852–3560 or 888/499–6848 780/852–4060 www.patricialakebungalows.com 9 motel rooms, 19 suites, 20 cabins In-room: no a/c, no phone. In-hotel: bicycles, laundry facilities AE, MC, V Closed mid-Oct.–Apr. EP.*

$$–$$$ **Pine Bungalows.** On the banks of the Athabasca River, this property is ideal for families because it has 72 modern cabins with outdoor barbecues, picnic tables, and tubs with showers. Many cabins have fireplaces and most have kitchens; there are laundry facilities on-site. *Approximately 1¼ mi (2 km) east of Jasper Townsite, 2 Cottonwood Creek Rd., Jasper T0E 1E0 780/852–3491 780/852–3432 www.pinebungalows.com 72 cabins In-room: no a/c, no phone, kitchen, no TV. In-hotel: laundry facilities AE, MC, V Closed mid-Oct.–Apr. EP.*

$–$$$ **Becker's Chalets.** On the Icefields Parkway, 3 mi (5 km) south of the town of Jasper, this quaint family-run log cabin resort is set in a picturesque forest glade along the shores of the Athabasca River. Cabins range from one-bedroom cottages to four-room chalets and have fireplaces and kitchenettes. There are also some inexpensive, motel-style rooms. Its restaurant is one of the best in Jasper. *Box 579, Jasper T0E 1E0 780/852–3779 780/852–7202 www.beckerschalets.com 118 rooms In-room: no a/c, no phone, refrigerator. In-hotel: restaurant, laundry facilities AE, MC, V Closed mid-Oct.–May EP.*

¢–$ **HI-Jasper Hostel.** This chalet-style hostel rests at the foot of Whistlers Mountain just 4 mi (7 km) from Jasper. There is an easily accessible trail from the hostel to the summit of Whistlers Mountain. The hostel has mountain-bike rentals, volleyball court, campfire pit, Internet access, and free parking. Linen rentals are $1 per day. There are 74 dorm-style beds and 3 private rooms, including one family room with a queen-size bed and bunk beds. *Box 387, Jasper T0E 1E0 877/852–0781 or 780/852–3215 780/852–5560 www.hihostels.ca/jasper 74 dorm-room beds, 3 private rooms In-room: no a/c, no phone In-hotel: no a/c, no elevator, bicycles, laundry facilities, kitchen, refrigerator, freezer, phone, travel desk, public Internet AE, MC, V EP.*

CAMPGROUNDS & RV PARKS

$$ **Pocahontas Campground.** Near Miette Hot Springs at the park's east end, the campground is close to good hiking trails, including the Pocahontas Mine Trail. *.6 mi (1 km) off Hwy. 16 on Miette Rd. 877/737–3783 140 sites Drinking water, fire pits, picnic tables, public telephone AE, MC, V Closed early Oct. to mid-May.*

$$ **Wabasso Campground.** Families flock to this campground because of its playground and many amenities. *10 mi (16 km) south of Jasper Townsite on Hwy. 93A 877/737–3783 238 sites Flush toilets, dump station, drinking water, public telephone, play area AE, MC, V Closed early Sept. to late June.*

$$ **Whistlers Campground.** This campground is the largest and has the most amenities. It's the number-one choice for families because of the on-site interpretive programs at Whistlers Theatre. *2 mi (3 km) south of Jasper Townsite on Hwy. 93 877/737–3783 781 sites Flush toilets, dump station, drinking water, showers, electricity, public telephone AE, MC, V Closed early Oct to mid-May.*

$–$$ **Wapiti Campground.** Close to Jasper, this campground is near a number of good hiking trails. There are 53 unserviced sites that are open during the winter season. *3 mi (5 km) south of Jasper Townsite on Hwy. 93 877/737–3782 366 sites Flush toilets, dump station, drinking water, showers, electricity, public telephones AE, MC, V.*

$ **Columbia Icefield Campground.** This rustic campground is near a creek and has great views of the Columbia Icefield. Warm camping gear is recommended. *66 mi (106 km) south of Jasper on Hwy. 93 780/852–6176 33 sites Drinking water Reservations not accepted AE, MC, V Closed early Oct.–mid-May.*

$ **Jonas Creek Campground.** This small, primitive campground is in a quiet spot along a creek off the Icefields Parkway. *47 mi (75 km) south of the Jasper Townsite 780/852–6176 25 sites Picnic tables, public telephone Reservations not accepted AE, MC, V Closed early Sept. to mid-May.*

$ **Mt. Kerkeslin Campground.** This is a very basic campground with few facilities. Tent camping is available, and there are fire pits for cooking. *22 mi (35 km) south of Jasper Townsite on Hwy. 93 780/852–6176 45 sites Fire pits Reservations not accepted AE, MC, V Closed early Sept. to early June.*

$ **Snaring River Campground.** This east-side campground on the Snaring River tends to be warmer than many of the park's other campgrounds. *10 mi (16 km) east of Jasper Townsite on Hwy. 16 N*

☎780/852–6176 66 sites (tent only) Picnic tables Reservations not accepted AE, MC, V Closed mid Sept. to mid-May.

$ **Wilcox Creek Campground.** Near the Columbia Icefield, this tent campground is at a high elevation, so bring equipment and clothing suitable for cold weather. *✉69 mi (111 km) south of Jasper Townsite on Hwy. 93 ☎780/852–6176 46 sites Drinking water, picnic tables, public telephone Reservations not accepted AE, MC, V Closed mid Sept. to early June.*

OUTSIDE THE PARK

CAMPGROUNDS & RV PARKS $–$$$

Hinton/Jasper KOA Campground. This campground is 15 minutes from the east entrance of Jasper National Park and about five minutes from the town of Hinton. It's situated in a meadow bordered by three creeks and has many amenities, including 81 fully serviced sites, rustic camping cabins, camper kitchen, and handicap-accessible showers and washrooms. Horseback riding, hayrides, and hiking trails are nearby. *✉Hwy. 16, 2½ mi (4 km) west of Hinton ☎780/865–5061 or 888/562–4714 www.koa.com 106 sites Flush toilets, showers, fire pits, picnic tables, play area MC, V.*

JASPER ESSENTIALS

ACCESSIBILITY

Miette Hot Springs has wheelchair-accessible washrooms and changing rooms and a ramp descending into the pool with a railing. Several trails, scenic viewpoints, and day-use areas are paved. Whistlers Campground has two paved sites, each with adapted picnic tables and fireboxes. Ask for a key at the kiosk for wheelchair-accessible showers. Other campgrounds have various facilities for disabled access.

ADMISSION FEES

A park entrance pass is C$8.90 per person or C$17.80 maximum per vehicle per day. Larger buses and vans pay a group rate. An annual pass costs C$62.40 per adult or C$123.80 per family or group.

ADMISSION HOURS

The park is open 24/7, year-round. It is in the Mountain time zone.

ATMS/BANKS

Contacts **Alberta Treasury Branch** (*✉404 Patricia St., Jasper ☎780/852–3297*). **Canada Trust TD** (*✉606 Patricia St., Jasper ☎780/852–6270*). **CIBC** (*✉416 Connaught Dr., Jasper ☎800/465–2422*).

AUTOMOBILE SERVICE STATIONS

Contacts Licensed technicians offer automobile service and repairs at **Jasper Shell** (*✉638 Connaught Dr., Jasper ☎780/852–3022*). Gas is also available at the following stations: **Avalanche Esso** (*✉702 Connaught Dr., Jasper ☎780/852–4721*). **Jasper Petro Canada** (*✉300 Connaught Dr., Jasper ☎780/852–3366*). **Mountain Esso** (*✉84 Connaught Dr., Jasper ☎780/852–3688*).

EMERGENCIES

For all emergencies dial 911. Call 780/852–6155.

Contacts Cottage Medical Clinic (✉ *505 Turret St., Jasper* ☎ *780/852-4885*). **Seton General Hospital** (✉ *518 Robson St., Jasper* ☎ *780/852-3344*).

LOST & FOUND

Contact (☎ *780/852-6176*).

PERMITS

Permits are required for backcountry camping and certain other activities in the park ☎780/852–6177. Backcountry camping permits (C$8.90 per day), day-use permits (C$6.90 per day), fire permits (C$7.90 per day), dumping station permits (C$6.90 per day), and fishing permits (C$8.90 per day) are available at the information center.

POST OFFICES

Contacts Canada Post Office (✉ *502 Patricia St., Jasper* ☎ *780/852-3041*). **More Than Mail** (✉ *620 Connaught Dr., Jasper* ☎ *780/852-3160*).

PUBLIC TELEPHONES

Look in the Jasper Townsite, at the information center, outside the IGA grocery store, by the Shell gas station, and inside hotels. Also at the Icefields Centre, along some roadways, and at major sites such as Athabasca Falls, Sunwapta Falls, and Mt. Christie picnic area. Cell phones generally only work in and around the town of Jasper.

RELIGIOUS SERVICES

There are seven chapels offering services in the Jasper Townsite. Denominations represented are: Anglican, Baptist, Catholic, Lutheran, Pentecostal, Presbyterian, and United.

RESTROOMS

Restrooms are located throughout the park at all major day-use areas.

SHOPS & GROCERS

Contacts Robinson's IGA (✉ *218 Connaught Dr., Jasper* ☎ *780/852-3195*). **Super A Foods** (✉ *601 Patricia St., Jasper* ☎ *780/852-3200*).

VISITOR INFORMATION

Contacts Jasper National Park (📫 *Box 10, Jasper, AB T0E 1E0* ☎ *780/852-6176* 🌐 *www.pc.gc.ca/pn-np/ab/jasper*).

The Prairie Provinces

ALBERTA, SASKATCHEWAN, MANITOBA

WORD OF MOUTH

"The most important thing to remember about eating in Alberta is that the best beef in the world is raised between Canmore and Calgary, more or less, and smart Alberta ranchers leave the best tasting beef in the province, for their friends and visitors to enjoy."

—BAK

Updated by Christine Hanlon, Debbie, Olsen, Pat Redgier, and Mary Ann Simpkins

ALBERTA, SASKATCHEWAN, AND MANITOBA contain Canada's heartland, the principal source of such solid commodities as wheat, oil, and beef. These provinces are also home to a rich stew of ethnic communities that make the area unexpectedly colorful and cosmopolitan. You'll find exceptional outdoor recreational facilities and a spectrum of historical attractions that focus on Mounties, native peoples, dinosaurs, and railroads; excellent accommodations and cuisine at reasonable prices; and quiet, crowdless wide-open spaces.

The term "prairie provinces" is a bit of a misnomer, as most of this region—the northern half of Alberta and Saskatchewan, and the northern two-thirds of Manitoba—consists of sparsely populated expanses of lakes, rivers, and forests. Most of northern Saskatchewan and Manitoba belongs to the Canadian Shield, the bedrock core of North America, with a foundation of Precambrian rock that is some of the oldest in the world. On the fertile plains of the south, wheat is still king, but other crops, as well as livestock, help boost the economy. The diverse landscape has farms and ranches interspersed with wide river valleys, lakes, rolling hills, badlands, and even dry hills of sand.

The people of the prairie provinces are relaxed, reserved, and fiercely independent. They maintain equal suspicion toward "Ottawa" (big government) and "Toronto" (big media and big business). To visitors, the people of this region convey western openness and Canadian-style courtesy: no fawning, but no rudeness. It's an appealing combination.

EXPLORING THE PRAIRIE PROVINCES

Compared with the Rockies, the prairie provinces' landscape is dramatically flat. From the foothills of Alberta to the Great Lakes, you can explore the prairies from west to east, with visits to the region's five major cities: Calgary, Edmonton, Regina, Saskatoon, and Winnipeg. Traveling by car along Trans-Canada Highway 1 allows convenient access to all the prairie provinces. At 7,821 km (4,860 mi) in length, the Trans-Canada highway system is the longest national highway in the world and joins all 10 provinces of Canada. Provincial highways connect to the Trans-Canada Highway system and provide greater access to each province.

ABOUT THE RESTAURANTS

Restaurants throughout the prairie provinces reflect the region's ethnic makeup and offer a wide variety of cuisines—Ukrainian, Italian, Greek, Chinese, Scandinavian, French, Japanese—to fit every price range. Places specializing in generous helpings of Canadian beef still dominate the scene despite a case of mad cow disease in 2003. Dress in the prairie cities tends toward formality in expensive restaurants but is casual in moderately priced and inexpensive restaurants.

ABOUT THE HOTELS

In the larger metropolitan areas, prices at luxury properties tend to be in line with those in other parts of the country. Smaller centers still offer good value. It's always a good idea to ask about special weekend rates

TOP REASONS TO GO

NATIONAL & PROVINCIAL PARKS
Throughout this vast region, some special places have preserved unique landscapes, from Riding Mountain National Park in the gentle hills of western Manitoba to the barren badlands and eirie hoodoos of Alberta's Waterton Lakes National Park to the vast wilderness and waterways of Prince Albert National Park in Saskatchewan. You can explore grasslands, badlands, lakes, and forests and participate in a number of activities, including fishing, camping, hiking, mountain biking, and cross-country skiing, in national and provincial parks.

REGIONAL HISTORY
The larger history of these provinces encompasses a number of special elements, from the dinosaurs that roamed here to the native peoples and the fur traders and frontier settlers who came from around the world. Each province has highlights, whether it's the dinosaur sites around Drumheller, Alberta; the Wanuskewin Heritage Park in Saskatoon, which interprets native culture; the Mennonite Heritage Village in Steinbach, Manitoba; the Ukrainian Cultural Heritage Village near Edmonton, Alberta; or the Western Development Museum, a re-created 1920s farming village in North Battleford, Saskatchewan. Together, these distinctly different places present an accurate microcosm of how the region was settled.

6

and packages. There's a wide range of lodging options in the prairie provinces ranging from hostels and privately operated B&Bs to chain motels and luxury resorts. Amenities vary depending on the type of accommodation.

WHAT IT COSTS IN CANADIAN DOLLARS

	¢	$	$$	$$$	$$$$
RESTAURANTS	under C$8	C$8–C$12	C$13–C$20	C$21–C$30	over C$30
HOTELS	under C$75	C$75–C$125	C$126–C$175	C$176–C$250	over C$250

Restaurant prices are for a main course at dinner. Hotel prices are for two people in a standard double room in high season, excluding tax.

TIMING

From June through September you're likely to encounter more festivals and the greatest number of open lodgings (some close seasonally). Spring and fall months offer a more tranquil experience for travelers, and September can be particularly rewarding, with a combination of warm weather and some autumn foliage. Although winter can be cold, it's also a magical time to visit, with plenty of fluffy white snow and clear starry night skies that provide good views of the northern lights—visible from mid-August to early April. Winter is also ideal for outdoor sports like skiing, pond skating, or dogsledding.

GREAT ITINERARIES

Enormous distances separate many of the region's major attractions. If you're ambitious and want to include all three prairie provinces, you need considerable time. For a shorter visit, pick a major city and the surrounding area to explore.

IF YOU HAVE 4 DAYS

If you're particularly interested in dinosaurs and fossil hunting, travel from **Calgary**, Alberta, to **Regina**, Saskatchewan, by way of Drumheller, Alberta, and Eastend, Saskatchewan. In Drumheller, just over an hour east of Calgary on the Trans-Canada Highway, you can spend an entire day at the world-class **Royal Tyrrell Museum of Paleontology**. East on the Trans-Canada Highway en route to **Dinosaur Provincial Park**, you pass through unique badlands areas, where rivers flowed more than 70 million years ago. South along the Trans-Canada, the thriving, oil-rich city of **Medicine Hat** is a good choice for an overnight stop. Farther east, south of the Trans-Canada, you come to the small community of **Eastend**, where you can view a fully preserved Tyrannosaurus rex skeleton in a working lab—the T-Rex Discovery Centre.

IF YOU HAVE 12 DAYS

You can choose between two major routes westward from **Winnipeg**: northwest on the Yellowhead (Highway 16) to **Edmonton** via **Saskatoon**, or west on the Trans-Canada to **Calgary** via **Regina**. Either is approximately 1,370 km (850 mi). On the Yellowhead route, you can stop for one or two nights in **Riding Mountain National Park**, a half-hour north of Highway 16 on Highway 10; the town of Wasagaming is inside the park. Here you find forested landscape and sparkling clear lakes, as well as comfortable amenities. Langenburg, just inside the Saskatchewan border, has a provincial tourism-information center. Less than four hours to the northwest you come to **Saskatoon**, Saskatchewan's largest city. Plan on staying at least two nights. Ninety minutes farther west is the historic community of **North Battleford**, where the Western Development Museum and Fort Battleford National Historic Site rate as the two must-see attractions. From here it's four hours to Edmonton.

If you take the more southerly Trans-Canada route, you can stop in such major centers as **Brandon**, **Regina**, **Swift Current**, and **Medicine Hat** en route to Calgary. All offer interesting diversions, and most have adequate facilities for dining and lodging.

CALGARY

With the eastern face of the Rockies as its backdrop, the crisp concrete-and-steel skyline of Calgary, Alberta, seems to rise from the plains as if by sheer force of will. Indeed, all the elements in the great saga of the Canadian West—Mounties, local people, railroads, cowboys, cattle, oil—have converged to create a city with a modern face and a surprisingly traditional soul.

The city supports professional football and hockey teams, and in July the rodeo events of the Calgary Stampede attract visitors from around the world. Calgary hosted the 1988 Winter Olympics, and the downhill slopes and miles of cross-country ski trails are at Kananaskis, less than 90 minutes west of town. The city is also the perfect starting point for one of the preeminent dinosaur-exploration sites in the world, a world-class dinosaur-exploration tour at Dinosaur Provincial Park near Brooks and the Royal Tyrell Museum in Drumheller. The Glenbow Museum is one of the top museums in Canada, and the EPCOR Centre for the Performing Arts showcases theater and musical performances.

Calgary, believed to be derived from the Gaelic phrase meaning "bay farm," was founded in 1875 at the junction of the Bow and Elbow rivers as a North West Mounted Police post. The Canadian Pacific Railway arrived in 1883, and ranchers established major spreads on the plains surrounding the town. Incorporated as a city in 1894, Calgary grew quickly, and by 1911 its population had reached 43,000. More than 40 sandstone buildings constructed during that boom are still in use in the downtown core and the area was recognized as a National Historic District in 2002.

The next major growth came with the oil boom in the 1960s and 1970s, when most Canadian oil companies established their head offices in the city. Today, Calgary is a city of about 933,000 mostly easygoing and downright neighborly people. It's Canada's second-largest center for corporate head offices. Downtown keeps evolving, but Calgary's planners have made life in winter more pleasant by connecting most of the buildings with the Plus 15, a network of enclosed walkways 15 feet (sometimes more) above street level. Among the major cities on the prairies, Calgary usually has the most reasonable winter, thanks to the warm chinook winds that blow in from the nearby Rockies.

DOWNTOWN CALGARY

The soul of Calgary is the bustling, cosmopolitan Stephen Avenue Walk, which was declared a National Historic District in 2002. Shops and restaurants in restored, turn-of-the-20th-century sandstone buildings line the promenade, while shoppers, businesspeople, and street performers pack the street. In warm weather, outdoor patios spill onto the sidewalks and are perfect for people-watching. The residential Eau Claire district, with its high-rise apartments and condominium developments, begins north of 8th Avenue and stretches toward the Bow River, bordering walking, cycling, and running paths. The large and vibrant Chinatown covers several square blocks adjacent to the city core; look for the bright blue cone on top of the spectacular Chinese Cultural Centre, which has its own restaurant. The Kensington district, just north of the city center, has boutique stores and cafés in restored, Victorian-style houses. Beyond the downtown core but still in the heart of the city are 4th Street and Uptown 17th, scenic southwest neighborhoods with thriving shopping and nightlife scenes. The 4th Street dis-

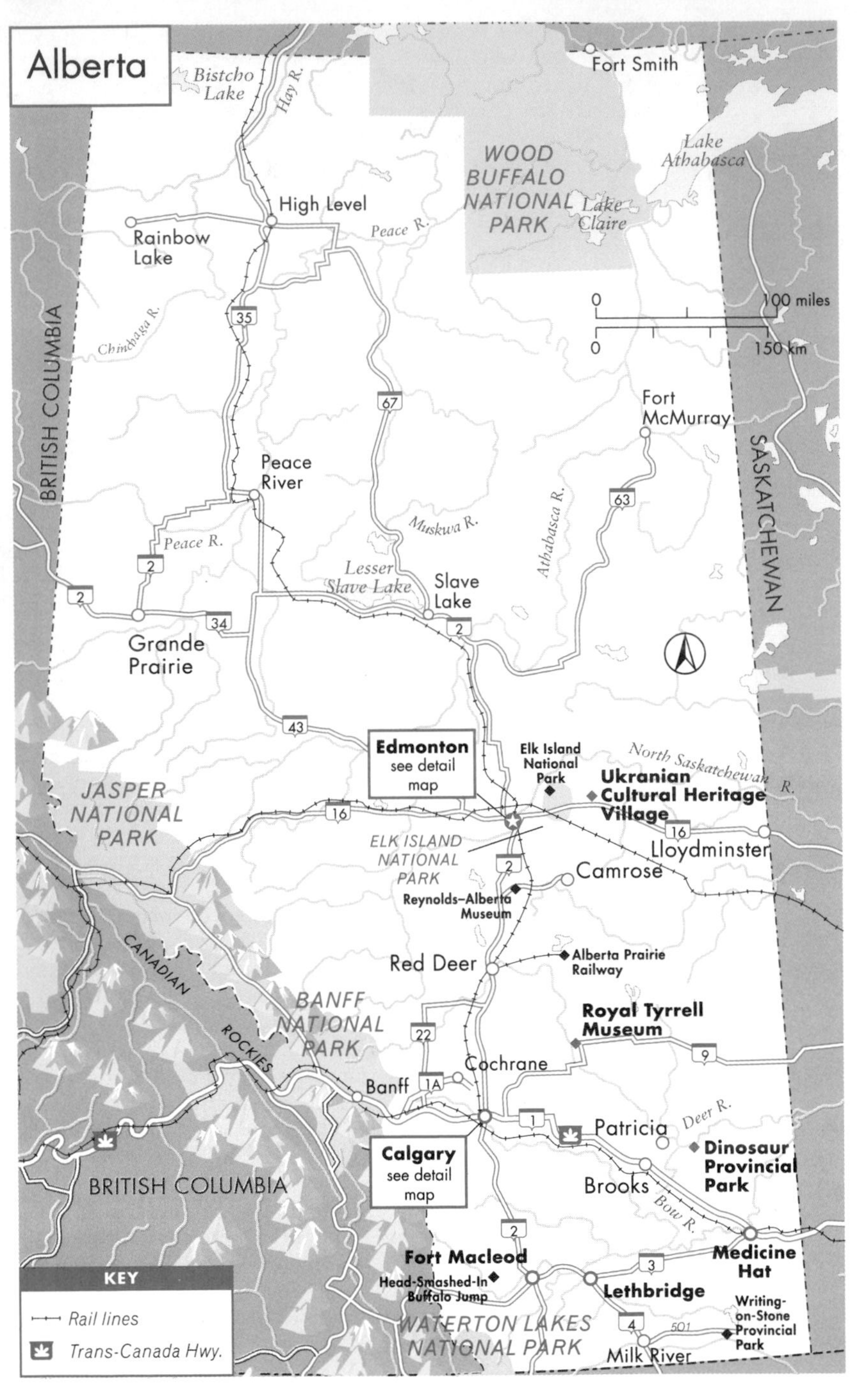
Alberta
Bistcho Lake
Hay R.
Fort Smith
WOOD BUFFALO NATIONAL PARK
Lake Athabasca
Lake Claire
High Level
Rainbow Lake
Peace R.
35
0
100 miles
0
150 km
Chinchaga R.
BRITISH COLUMBIA
67
Fort McMurray
SASKATCHEWAN
Peace River
63
Muskwa R.
Athabasca R.
Peace R.
2
Lesser Slave Lake
Slave Lake
2
34
2
Grande Prairie
43
Edmonton
see detail map
Elk Island National Park
North Saskatchewan R.
Ukranian Cultural Heritage Village
JASPER NATIONAL PARK
16
16
Lloydminster
ELK ISLAND NATIONAL PARK
2
Camrose
Reynolds–Alberta Museum
CANADIAN ROCKIES
Red Deer
Alberta Prairie Railway
BANFF NATIONAL PARK
Royal Tyrrell Museum
22
9
Cochrane
Banff
1A
1
Patricia
Deer R.
Dinosaur Provincial Park
Calgary
see detail map
Brooks
Bow R.
BRITISH COLUMBIA
2
Medicine Hat
Fort Macleod
3
Head-Smashed-In Buffalo Jump
Lethbridge
Writing-on-Stone Provincial Park
WATERTON LAKES NATIONAL PARK
4
501
Milk River
KEY
Rail lines
Trans-Canada Hwy.

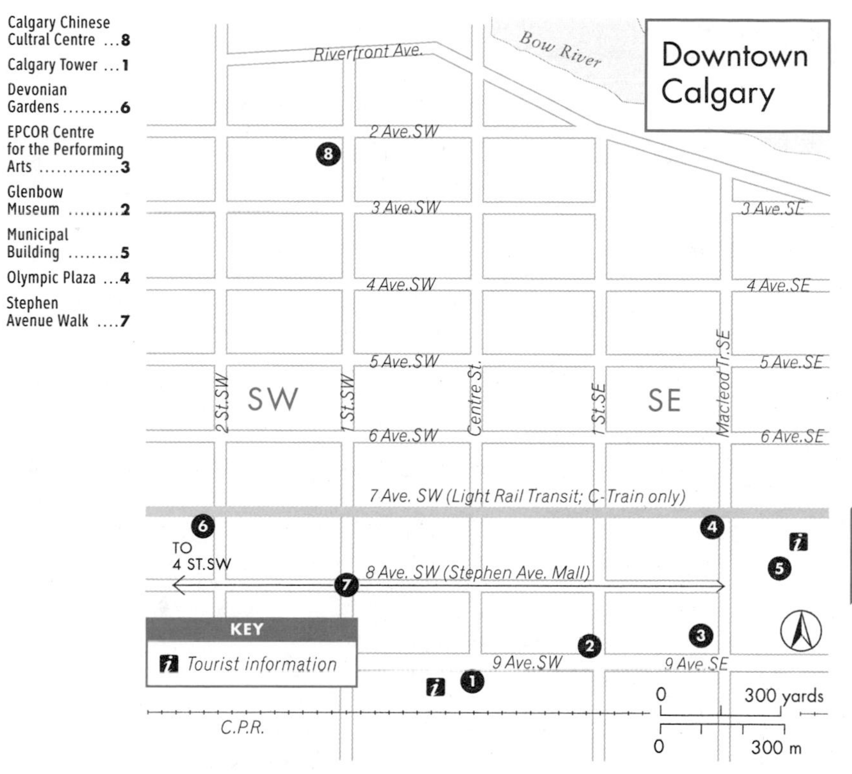

trict extends from the Bow River to 17th Avenue; Uptown 17th runs along 17th Avenue from Macleod Trail to 14th Street Southwest.

Calgary's history as a city began in 1875 when a detachment of North West Mounted police arrived and established Fort Calgary. It wasn't until the Canadian Pacific Railway arrived in 1883 that the population began to climb, and with the establishment of a station in what is now the downtown core, businesses began to gravitate to the area. The city is divided into four quadrants: northwest, northeast, southwest, and southeast. In the Calgary grid pattern, numbered streets run north–south in both directions from Centre Street and numbered avenues run east–west in both directions from Centre Avenue.

WHAT TO SEE

8 **Calgary Chinese Cultural Centre.** The focal point of this ornate building in the heart of Chinatown is the Hall of Prayers of the **Temple of Heaven**; the column details and paintings include 561 dragons and 40 phoenixes. It's modeled after the Temple of Heaven in Beijing. The center houses a cultural museum, an art gallery, a crafts store, an herbal-medicine store, and a 330-seat Chinese restaurant. ✉ *197 1st St. SW, Chinatown* ☎ *403/262–5071* 🌐 *www.culturalcentre.ca* 🎟 *Free, museum C$2* ⏲ *Daily 9:30–9, 11–5 for museum.*

❶ **Calgary Tower.** The views from this 626-foot (191-meter), scepter-shaped edifice take in the city's layout, the surrounding plains, and the face of the Rockies rising 80 km (50 mi) to the west. A "torch" that crowns the tower is lighted for special events and occasions. The tower top also holds the revolving Panorama Room restaurant, which serves all three meals; Tops Grill; and a gift shop. ✉*9th Ave. and Centre St. S, Downtown Commercial Core* ☎*403/266–7171* 🌐*www.calgarytower.com* *C$12.95* ⏲*Daily 7 AM–10:30 PM.*

❻ **Devonian Gardens.** Above Toronto Dominion Square and atop the Toronto Dominion Centre shopping complex, a 2½-acre enclosed roof garden holds 20,000 plants, nearly 2 km (1 mi) of lush walkways, a sculpture court, and a playground. Alberta's largest indoor gardens, which are reached by two glass-enclosed elevators just inside the 7th Avenue light-rail transit (LRT) entrance, have numerous ponds with rainbow trout, koi, goldfish, and turtles. Art exhibitions are held here, and there's a stage for performances. ✉*317 7th Ave. SW, between 2nd and 3rd Sts., Downtown Commercial Core* ☎*403/268–3830* *Free* ⏲*Daily 9–9.*

❸ **EPCOR Centre for the Performing Arts.** The complex of four theater spaces and a state-of-the-art concert hall was pieced together in the 1980s incorporating the historic **Calgary Public Building** (1930) and the **Burns Building** (1913). It's one of the largest arts complexes in Canada. ✉*205 8th Ave. SE, Downtown Commercial Core* ☎*403/294–7455* 🌐*www.epcorcentre.org.*

❷ **Glenbow Museum.** Western Canada's largest museum has three annual special exhibitions and more than 20 permanent galleries chronicling the history of the Canadian West. Don't miss the Mavericks Gallery, which has interactive displays that chronicle the lives of 48 dynamic and incorrigible Alberta natives. Displays of First Nations and pioneer artifacts examine the people, stories, and events that shaped the region. An Asian exhibit has Buddhist and Hindu sculptures dating from the 2nd century to the 18th century, and an extensive military collection includes medieval armor and samurai swords. The Nitsitapiisinni exhibit traces the story of the Blackfoot people in their own words through interactive displays, films, and artifacts. The café serves quick, fresh meals and snacks. ✉*130 9th Ave. SE, Downtown Commercial Core* ☎*403/268–4100 or 403/237–8988* 🌐*www.glenbow.org* *C$14* ⏲*Fri.–Wed. 9–5, Thurs. 9–9.*

Fodor's Choice ★

❺ **Municipal Building.** Reflected in the angular, mirrored walls of this building are several city landmarks, including the stunning City Hall, a stately 1911 sandstone building that houses the mayor's office and other city offices. Self-guided walking tours are available. ✉*800 Macleod Trail SE, East Village* ☎*403/268–2111.*

❹ **Olympic Plaza.** The site of the 1988 Olympic Games medals presentation, the plaza is a popular venue for festivals and entertainment. The wading pool is turned into a skating rink in winter. ✉*7th Ave. SE and Macleod Trail SE, Downtown Commercial Core* ☎*403/268–2300.*

7 ★ **Stephen Avenue Walk.** In this pedestrians-only shopping area, a National Historic District, stores, nightclubs, and restaurants occupy the ground floors of Calgary's oldest structures. The mostly sandstone buildings were erected after an 1886 fire destroyed almost all of the older buildings. ⊠ *8th Ave. between Macleod Trail and 4th St. SW, Downtown Commercial Core.*

GREATER CALGARY

As the railway grew in importance in Calgary, it also established subdivisions aimed at specific income groups. Calgary's emerging elite built palatial homes on large lots in the Mount Royal district while the Ogden subdivision was developed for railway workers. To the east of downtown is Inglewood, the heart of Calgary's first business district. Many of Calgary's first citizens lived here before the Canadian Pacific Railway arrived, forcing business to move to the downtown core. Ninth Avenue Southeast is now lined with antiques stores and home furnishings stores, eateries, and cappuccino bars. As the city grew during the 1950s to the 1970s, suburban neighborhoods were established across sprawling ranch lands following the Northeast, Northwest, Southeast, and Southwest quadrants as they flow out from the downtown core. Most commuters use major arteries such as Crowchild Trail, Deerfoot Trail, Glenmore Trail, and Memorial Drive to enter and exit the downtown core for their workday, so expect traffic on these major routes during morning (7–8:30 AM) and afternoon (4:30–6 PM) rush hours.

WHAT TO SEE

15 **Calaway Park.** Here in the foothills of the Rockies and about 10 km (6 mi) west of Calgary is western Canada's largest outdoor family amusement park. It includes live entertainment, miniature golf, a fishing pond, shops, and an RV park. ⊠ *Hwy. 1, Springbank Rd. Exit, Springbank South* ☎ *403/240–3822* 🌐 *www.calawaypark.com* *C$27* ⏲ *Mid-May–late June, Fri. 5 PM–9 PM, weekends 10–7; late June–Aug., daily 10–7; Sept.–mid-Oct., weekends 11–6.*

10 ★ **Calgary Zoo, Botanical Gardens, and Prehistoric Park.** The zoo, on St. George's Island in the middle of Bow River, is one of Canada's largest, with more than 1,400 animals in natural settings. The Creatures of the Night exhibit contains nocturnal animals and the Canadian Wilds section replicates endangered Canadian ecosystems. Prehistoric Park, a Mesozoic landscape, displays 22 life-size dinosaur replicas. Destination Africa showcases two African ecosystems, the TransAlta Rainforest and the African Savannah, and has mixed-species exhibits of more than 100 animals, the largest indoor hippo immersion habitat in North America, and 84 plant species indigenous to the African continent. ⊠ *1300 Zoo Rd. NE, Inglewood* ☎ *403/232–9372* 🌐 *www.calgaryzoo.org* *Sept.–Apr. C$16; May–Aug. C$18* ⏲ *Daily 9–6.*

14 **Canada Olympic Park.** The site of the 1988 Winter Olympics is a year-round attraction. A one-hour bus tour goes over, under, around, and through the 89- and 114-meter ski jumps and the bobsled and luge tracks (in summer you have the option of walking down the slopes)

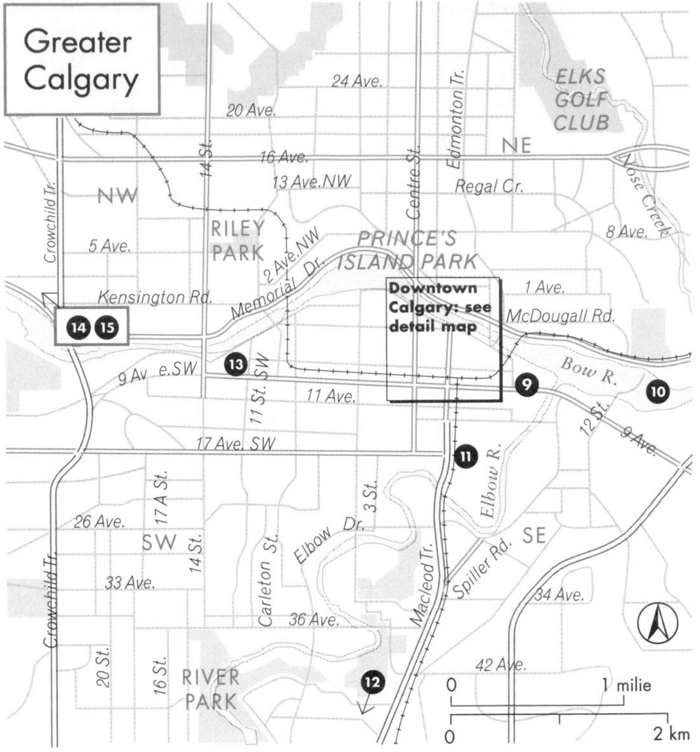

and also takes you to the Ice House, a year-round training facility for world-class competitors. Olympic athletes training at the facility often lead the guided tours. In winter the slopes are open to the public for skiing and snowboarding; lessons are available. A day lodge with a cafeteria and the **Olympic Hall of Fame** are on the premises. ✉ *88 Olympic Rd. SW, Aspen Village* ☎ *403/247–5452* 🌐 *www.canadaolympicpark.ca* 🎫 *Free, excluding activities; tours C$10–C$15* ⏲ *Mid-May–early Nov., daily 8 AM–9 PM; early Nov.–late Mar., weekdays 9–9, weekends 9–5; call for tour, Olympic Hall of Fame, and late Mar.–mid-May hrs.*

9 **Fort Calgary Historic Park.** The fort was established in 1875 at the confluence of the Bow and Elbow rivers by the North West Mounted Police. Designed to stop Montana whiskey traders from selling alcohol to the locals, it remained in operation until 1914. The **Interpretive Centre** here traces the history of the First Nations people, Mounties, and European settlers with the aid of artifacts, audiovisual displays, and interpretive walks. **Deane House Restaurant,** next to Fort Calgary, is a nice place to stop for lunch. It's the restored 1906 fort superintendent's house. The **Hunt House,** directly behind the restaurant, was built in 1876 and is believed to be Calgary's oldest building. ✉ *750 9th Ave. SE, East Village* ☎ *403/290–1875* 🌐 *www.fortcalgary.com* 🎫 *C$10.50* ⏲ *Daily 9–5.*

12 **Heritage Park.** On 66 acres of parkland beside the Glenmore Reservoir, Heritage Park is Canada's largest living-history village. More than 150 exhibits, hundreds of costumed staff and volunteers, and 45,000 artifacts re-create western Canadian life prior to 1914. You can visit an 1850s fur-trading post, a ranch, and an old town; ride on a steam locomotive or horse-drawn wagon; cruise the reservoir on a stern-wheeler; and partake of a free pancake breakfast daily at 9 AM. *1900 Heritage Dr. SW, Eagle Ridge 403/259–1900 www.heritagepark.ca C$13.95, C$22.95 with rides and cruise Mid-May–Labor Day, daily 9–5; early Sept.–mid-Oct., weekends 9–5.*

11 **Stampede Park.** Fodor's Choice ★ International attention focuses on Stampede Park each July for the rodeo events of the **Calgary Stampede** (*403/261–0101 www.calgarystampede.com*). Throughout the year, the Roundup Centre, Big Four Building, and Agriculture Building host trade shows, and the Grandstand hosts Thoroughbred and harness racing. You can wander the park grounds and visit the free **Grain Academy** (*403/263–4594*), an interesting small museum in the Roundup Centre that proclaims itself "Canada's only grain interpretive center." There's a model-train display depicting the movement of grain from the prairies through the Rockies to Vancouver. There's also a working model of a grain elevator. *1410 Olympic Way SE, Victoria Park 403/261–0101 or 800/661–1260 Free Weekdays 10–4, Sat. noon–4.*

13 **TELUS World of Science–Calgary.** Interactive exhibits present the wonders of science in an entertaining way. Shows at the multimedia Discovery Dome, Alberta's largest indoor theater, combine computer graphics, motion-picture images, slides, and a superb sound system. The Children's Discovery Centre is designed for kids three to seven years old. *701 11th St. SW, Downtown West End 403/268–8300 www.calgaryscience.ca C$12 Mon.–Thurs. 9:45–4, Fri. 9:45–5, weekends 10–5.*

WHERE TO EAT

$$$–$$$$ **River Café.** Inspired by the natural surroundings of Prince's Island Park, on Bow River, this restaurant has the look of a fishing lodge. The exquisite regional Canadian cuisine includes Northwest Territories caribou, British Columbia oysters and Pacific salmon, Alberta Black Angus beef, and Alberta lamb. The wine list has earned Wine Spectator's Award of Excellence since 1997. With 24-hours advance notice, the restaurant can prepare you a picnic basket to enjoy in the park. *Prince's Island Park, near Eau Claire Market, Eau Claire 403/261–7670 www.river-cafe.com Reservations essential AE, DC, MC, V.*

$$$ **Catch.** In a historic building, Catch spans three floors and is considered by most to be the best seafood restaurant in the city. Live crab, lobster, fresh oysters, and fish are flown in daily from both Canadian coasts and served with fresh-from-the-field vegetables and fine wines from around the world. The oyster bar, on the main level, is boisterous, but has a greater variety of menu choices at slightly lower prices. If you want a more intimate setting, opt for the dining room on the second floor. ✉ *100 Stephen Ave. SE, Downtown Commercial Core* ☎ *403/206–0000* 🌐 *www.catchrestaurant.ca* ✍ *Reservations essential* ▭ *AE, DC, MC, V* ⏲ *Closed Sun. No lunch Sat. and Sun.*

$$ ✕ **Bistro Twenty Two Ten.** For a taste of France, this sleek and modern bistro in an atmospheric old building is the place to go. You can find bistro classics such as duck confit and moules frites alongside more contemporary fare like butternut squash soup with vanilla beans and maple or braised lamb with fig stuffing and a fragrant pear sauce. The menu features small, medium, and large plates to suit any appetite. ✉ *2210 4th St. W, Mission* ☎ *403/228–4528* 🌐 *www.bistro2210.com* ✍ *Reservations essential* ▭ *AE, DC, MC, V* ⏲ *Closed Sun. No lunch weekends. No dinner Mon.*

$$ ★ ✕ **Buzzard's Cowboy Cuisine.** An authentic cowboy restaurant with great Alberta steaks and terrific burgers, Buzzard's serves up good western food amid rustic country-style decor and cowboy artifacts. If you're feeling brave, this is one of the few places in Calgary where you can sample prairie oysters, otherwise known as bull testicles. The place is renowned for its annual "testicle festival." There's a sunny outdoor patio, and Bottlescrew Bill's Old English Pub next door serves Calgary's largest beer selection, including Buzzard's Breath Ale house brew. ✉ *140 10th Ave. SW, Victoria Park* ☎ *403/264–6959* 🌐 *www.cowboy-cuisine.com* ▭ *AE, DC, MC, V.*

$$ ✕ **Teatro.** The elegant Teatro is in an old bank building on Olympic Plaza, where classical features blend with contemporary decor to create an exquisite setting for fine Italian cuisine. Specialties include numerous antipasti, pizzas from a wood-burning oven, pastas, and risottos. The extensive wine list has earned Wine Spectator's Award of Excellence since 1997. If you're in a hurry, choose the Executive Express set menu for lunch or dinner. ✉ *200 8th Ave. SE, Downtown Commercial Core* ☎ *403/290–1012* 🌐 *www.teatro.ca* ▭ *AE, DC, MC, V.*

$ ✕ **Avenue Diner.** In an old sandstone building on Steven Avenue, this place has the look and feel of a 1930s diner. There's both counter and table service in a casual, relaxed atmosphere. Comfort food is the specialty here, which is why the kitchen serves breakfast all day. The French toast stuffed with Brie is very unique and the mac and cheese may be better than your mom's. ✉ *105 8th Ave. SW, Steven Avenue Walk* ☎ *403/263–2673* 🌐 *www.avenuediner.com* ✍ *Reservations not accepted* ▭ *AE, DC, MC, V* ⏲ *No dinner.*

WHERE TO STAY

If you visit Calgary during the annual Petroleum Convention in early June or during the Calgary Stampede in early July, you should book your accommodations well in advance and expect to pay premium rates.

$$$$ 🏨 **Delta Bow Valley.** This first-class 25-story high-rise is within easy walking distance of the main business district as well as major attrac-

tions. Rooms are decent-size and contemporary, with neutral earth-tone color schemes; those on the upper floors have good views. The sunny lobby with its lush foliage adds to the lively setting. The hotel has many business amenities, including a complimentary sedan for business trips downtown. On weekends the hotel operates a complimentary children's creative center where kids can enjoy games, crafts, and fun activities in a supervised environment. ✉*209 4th Ave. SE, East Village, T2G 0C6* ☎*403/266–1980 or 800/268–1133* 🌐*www.deltahotels.com* *354 rooms, 40 suites* *In-room: ethernet, dial-up. In-hotel: restaurant, lounge, room service, bar, laundry service, pool, gym, concierge, children's programs (ages 1–18), parking (fee), pets (fee), no-smoking rooms* *AE, D, DC, MC, V* *EP.*

$$$$ ★ **Fairmont Palliser.** Built in 1914 as Calgary's grand railroad hotel, the Palliser remains the city's most elegant accommodation. Guest rooms are tastefully appointed with traditional furnishings and have ornate moldings and high ceilings. The Rimrock restaurant is excellent and although the Sunday brunch is a bit pricey it's the best in town. A covered walkway connects the hotel to the performing-arts center and the Glenbow Museum. ✉*133 9th Ave. SW, Downtown Commercial Core, T2P 2M3* ☎*403/262–1234 or 800/441–1414* 🌐*www.fairmont.com* *405 rooms, 17 suites* *In-room: refrigerator, dial-up. In-hotel: restaurant, room service, bar, pool, gym, concierge, laundry service, executive floor, parking (fee), no-smoking rooms* *AE, DC, MC, V* *EP.*

6

$$$$ **Kensington Riverside Inn.** Attention to the smallest detail sets apart this charming inn. Rooms are spacious and have fireplaces, patios, or balconies, and heated towel racks in the bathrooms. Each morning a coffee tray and newspaper appear at your door, and a gourmet breakfast is a short walk away in the dining room. Cookies are served in the lobby all day, and evening hors d'oeuvres are served in the parlor. Callebaut chocolates are part of the turn-down service. Ask for a riverfront room on the second floor if you want to enjoy a nice city view. Heated underground parking is included in the rates. ✉*1126 Memorial Dr. NW, Kensington, T2N3E3* ☎*403/228–4442 or 877/313–3733* 🌐*www.kensingtonriversideinn.com* *19 rooms, 3 suites* *In-room: DVD, VCR, ethernet, Wi-Fi. In-hotel: room service, laundry service, parking (no fee)* *BP* *AE, D, DC, MC, V.*

$$$ **Hyatt Regency Calgary.** Turn-of-the-19th-century buildings combine with a state-of-the-art tower at this 21-story luxury hotel. The collection of paintings, sculptures, and other artwork in the hotel's public areas and guest rooms (a C$1.4 million collection) showcases 50 western Canadian artists. A mahogany canoe hangs from the lobby ceiling, and historical photographs and displays convey the pioneer spirit that helped to settle the West. The hotel is linked to the Telus Convention Centre. ✉*700 Centre St. S, Downtown Commercial Core, T2G 5P6* ☎*403/717–1234* 🌐*www.calgary.hyatt.com* *342 rooms, 13 suites* *In-room: refrigerator, ethernet, Wi-Fi (some). In-hotel: restaurant, room service, bar, pool, gym, spa, parking (fee), no-smoking rooms* *AE, DC, MC, V.*

$$$ ★ **Sheraton Suites Calgary Eau Claire.** Views from this all-suites hotel take in downtown, the river, and the park. An international newsstand and currency exchange are among the amenities. The elegant glass lobby and an outdoor patio adjoin the Eau Claire Market and Prince's Island Park. The Plus 15 indoor walkway leads to downtown, and the nearby outdoor path system follows the Bow River. Suites are plush, with full-size desks and comfortable, duvet-dressed beds. ✉*255 Barclay Parade SW, Eau Claire, T2P 5C2* ☎*403/266–7200 or 888/784–8370* 🌐*www.sheratonsuites.com* *323 suites* *In-room: refrigerator, ethernet, Wi-Fi (some). In-hotel: restaurant, room service, bar, gym, pool, concierge, laundry service, public Wi-Fi, parking (fee), some pets allowed, no-smoking rooms* *AE, DC, MC, V.*

$$ **City View Bed and Breakfast.** This contemporary B&B atop Scotsman's Hill, near downtown, has panoramic views of the city, Bow River, and the Rockies beyond. During the Calgary Stampede you can watch the evening fireworks from the comfort of the living room. The lounge has a fireplace and grand piano. Guest rooms all have large windows; two have fireplaces and private balconies, and one has an old-fashioned claw-foot tub. ✉*2300 6th St. SE, Ramsay, T2G 4S2* ☎*403/870–5640* 🌐*www.calgarycityview.com* *3 rooms* *In-hotel: no elevator, parking (no fee), no kids under 14, no-smoking rooms* *MC, V* *BP.*

$–$$ **Westways Bed and Breakfast.** In a 1912 heritage home, this B&B is near the restaurants, pubs, and shopping venues of Calgary's Mission District and is a 20-minute walk from downtown. Each room is uniquely appointed and has a private bath. Breakfast is a highlight and features such items as eggs prepared to order, homemade pastries, waffles, juice, coffee, and fruit. ✉*216 25 Ave. SW, Mission, T2S 0L1* ☎*403/229–1758 or 866/846–7038* 🌐*www.westways.ab.ca* *5 rooms* *In-room: no a/c, VCR. In-hotel: no elevator, no-smoking rooms* *AE, MC, V* *BP.*

NIGHTLIFE & THE ARTS

THE ARTS

Calgary's premier performing-arts facility is the **EPCOR Centre for the Performing Arts** (✉*205 8th Ave. SE, Downtown Commercial Core* ☎*403/294–7455* 🌐*www.epcorcentre.org*), with four modern theaters and an 1,800-seat concert hall in two contiguous historic buildings. Productions by resident Alberta Theatre Projects (ATP) of works by Canadian playwrights are highly recommended, as are performances by the One Yellow Rabbit Performance Theatre and Theatre Calgary. EPCOR Centre also hosts the **Calgary Philharmonic Orchestra** (☎*403/571–0270* 🌐*www.cpo-live.com*), chamber groups, and a broad spectrum of music shows.

The **Southern Alberta Jubilee Auditorium** (✉*1415 14th Ave. NW, Hillhurst* ☎*403/297–8000* 🌐*www.jubileeauditorium.com/southern*) hosts the Alberta Ballet Company as well as classical music, opera, dance, pop, and rock concerts. Concerts and classic and contemporary theater works are staged at the **University of Calgary Theatre** (✉*2500 University Dr. NW, University Heights* ☎*403/220–4900* 🌐*www.finearts.ucalgary.ca/theatres*).

Tickets for events at the performing arts center and Jubilee Auditorium are available at **Ticketmaster** (☎*403/270–6700 or 403/266–8888* 🌐*www.ticketmaster.ca*) outlets, at the arts center's box office, or can be charged over the phone.

NIGHTLIFE

BARS & CLUBS The **James Joyce Pub** (✉*114 8th Ave. SW, Downtown Commercial Core* ☎*403/262–0708*) is a classic Irish pub where you can have Guinness stout served at three different temperatures at the long antique bar, along with some traditional Irish fare. **Melrose Cafe and Bar** (✉*730 17th Ave. SW, Connaught* ☎*403/228–3566*) is a popular spot that broadcasts the National Trivia Network. A place to see and be seen, **Ming** (✉*520 17th Ave. SW, 17 Avenue*) is a hip martini bar with an exotic understated sophistication. The **Mynt Ultralounge** (✉*516C 9th Ave. SW, 9 Ave South* ☎*403/262–MYNT*) is an edgy night spot with two dance floors that rock until the wee hours of the morning.

MUSIC The **Aussie Rules Foodhouse and Bar** (✉*1002 37 St. SW, Westbrook Mall* ☎*403/249–7933*) is a popular piano bar that features dueling pianos playing a wide variety of musical styles. **Beat Niq Jazz and Social Club** (✉*811 1st St. SW, Downtown Commercial Core* ☎*403/263–1650*) is a sexy New York–style jazz club open Wednesday through Saturday. **Cowboys Dance Hall** (✉*826 5th St. SW, Downtown Commercial Core* ☎*403/265–0699*) includes a bar and a dance hall that plays Top 40 country, dance, and rock tunes, with live entertainment on occasion. It's open Wednesday through Saturday and holds 1,200 people. **Coyotes** (✉*1088 Olympic Way SE, Victoria Park* ☎*403/263–5343*) is a restaurant-nightclub with Top 40 DJ music. **The Ranchman's** (✉*9615 Macleod Trail S, Haysboro* ☎*403/253–1100*) is a legendary honkytonk restaurant-bar frequented by real local cowboys. **Tantra** (✉*355 10th Ave. SW, Victoria Park* ☎*403/264–0202*) plays Top 40 dance music for a mostly under-30 crowd and mixes some of the best martinis around.

6

SPORTS & THE OUTDOORS

The uniquely Canadian **Mountain Equipment Coop** (✉*830 10 Ave. SW, Calgary* ☎*403/269–2420* 🌐*www.mec.ca*) rents and sells outdoor equipment such as backpacks, tents, canoes, skis, and climbing gear. The staff also facilitates annual equipment swaps.

BIKING & JOGGING

Calgary has about 300 km (186 mi) of bicycling and jogging paths, most of which wind along rivers and through city parks. Maps are available at visitor centers and bike shops. You can rent bikes for C$25 to C$45 at **Sports Rent** (✉*4424 16th Ave. NW, Montgomery* ☎*403/292–0077* 🌐*www.sportsrent.ca*).

The **University of Calgary Outdoor Centre** (✉*2500 University Dr. NW, University* ☎*403/220–5038* 🌐*www.calgaryoutdoorcentre.ca*) also has bicycle rentals.

FISHING

The Bow River is an international fly-fishing destination with a self-sustained population of 2,500 trout per mile in some regions. **Fish Tales Fly Shop & Guide Service** (☎*403/640–1273* 🌐*www.fishtales.ca*) is a local fly-fishing shop that also conducts guided fly-fishing trips for trout on the Bow River and other streams.

The **University of Calgary Outdoor Centre** (✉*2500 University Dr. NW, University* ☎*403/220–5038* 🌐*www.calgaryoutdoorcentre.ca*) has equipment rentals and offers beginner and intermediate fly fishing courses during the summer months.

FOOTBALL

The **Calgary Stampeders** (✉*1817 Crowchild Trail NW, University Heights* ☎*403/289–0205* 🌐*www.stampeders.com*) play home games in **McMahon Stadium** from June through November in the Canadian Football league.

HOCKEY

The **Calgary Flames** (✉*555 Saddledome Rise SE, Victoria Park* ☎*403/777–2177* 🌐*flames.nhl.com*) play National Hockey League matches October through April at the **Pengrowth Saddledome** in Stampede Park.

HORSEBACK RIDING

Take advantage of the region's cowboy heritage and go horseback riding. **Saddle Peak Trail Rides** (📫*Box 1463, Cochrane TC4 1B4* ☎*403/932–3299* 🌐*www.saddle-peak.com*) runs assorted horseback trips, from one-hour trail rides around the ranch to four-day wilderness pack excursions. The ranch is about 70 km (44 mi) west of Calgary; check the Web site or call for directions. Reservations are essential.

HORSE RACING

Spruce Meadows (✉*18011 14th St. SW, at corner of Hwy. 22X and Spruce Meadow Trail, Spruce Meadows* ☎*403/974–4200* 🌐*www.sprucemeadows.com*) is one of the world's finest show-jumping facilities, with major competitions held June through September. **Stampede Park** (✉*1410 Olympic Way SE, Victoria Park* ☎*403/261–0214*) includes a track where Thoroughbreds race April through October, trotters July through October.

RODEO

Fodor's Choice ★

For 10 days each July, rodeo events and chuck-wagon races draw the world's top cowboys and plenty of greenhorns to one of Canada's most popular events, the **Calgary Stampede** (☎*800/661–1260* 🌐*www.calgarystampede.com*), held in Stampede Park. In addition to rodeo events, there are livestock shows, concerts, and high-spirited Western-style entertainment. You should make room and ticket reservations well in advance (at least three months) if you plan to attend.

WINTER SPORTS

The primary site for ski jump, bobsled, and luge events for the 1988 Winter Olympics, **Canada Olympic Park** (✉*88 Olympic Rd.* ☎*403/247–5452* 🌐*www.canadaolympicpark.ca*), has downhill skiing, a luge track, and snowboarding, on-site rentals, and first-class instruction.

The ski hill has a racing section, a casual ski area, and an exceptionally good terrain park. A total of six lifts service the hill, including a high-speed chair lift.

The site of the 1988 Olympic alpine events, **Nakiska** (✉*Off Hwy. 40, Kananaskis Village* ☎*403/591–7777* 🌐*www.skinakiska.com*) is less than an hour's drive west of Calgary. The resort has skiing and snowboarding with a sophisticated snowmaking system. There are four lifts.

The sprawling **University of Calgary Outdoor Centre** (✉*2500 University Dr. NW, University* ☎*403/220–5038* 🌐*www.calgaryoutdoorcentre.ca*) rents out more than 10,000 different items, from ski and snowboarding equipment in winter to bikes and camping equipment in summer.

SHOPPING

Calgary's major shopping districts include Kensington at Louise Crossing, Uptown 17, 11th Avenue Southwest, 4th Street Southwest, Inglewood, the Eau Claire Market, and Downtown on 8th. **Bankers Hall** (✉*315 8th Ave. SW, Downtown Commercial Core*) has upscale clothing stores such as Henry Singers and Blu's. **Chinook Centre** (✉*6455 Macleod Trail SW, Chinook* 🌐*www.chinookcentre.com*) completed a $300 million renovation in 2001 and has become a center for flagship stores in western Canada. There are 220 shops, including department stores and restaurants, in the shopping center. **Mount Royal Village** (✉*16th Ave. and 8th St. SW, Connaught*) has mostly upscale and designer shops as well as Oasis, a day spa, on the ground floor. Many large chain clothing stores, such as the Gap, as well as a mixture of jewelry and imported-goods stores are at the **Scotia Centre and TD Square** (✉*7th Ave. and 2nd St. SW, Downtown Commercial Core*). The **Stephen Avenue Walk** is a pedestrian-only stretch of 8th Avenue (between Macleod Trail and 4th Street Southwest), where some of the city's oldest buildings house shops and restaurants.

SPECIALTY STORES

For authentic cowboy boots, there's Alberta's only Western boot manufacturer, **Alberta Boot** (✉*614 10th Ave. SW, Victoria Park* ☎*403/263–4623* 🌐*www.albertaboot.com*). **Art Central** (✉*100 7th Ave. SW, Downtown* ☎*403/543–9900* 🌐*www.artcentral.ca*) brings together art studios, galleries, shops, and small cafés in one locale. **The Bay** (✉*200 8th Ave. SW, Downtown Commercial Core* ☎*403/262–0345*), formerly known as the Hudson's Bay Company, was incorporated in 1670, and is Calgary's—and Canada's—oldest retailer and is a good source for extra-warm clothing. The **Calgary Shoe Hospital and Western Store** (✉*112 8th Ave. SW, Victoria Park* ☎*403/264–4503*) can custom-fit you with cowboy boots.

Livingstone and Cavell Extraordinary Toys (✉*1124 Kensington Rd. NW, Hillhurst* ☎*403/270–4165*) carries unique toys and gifts from around the world, including clockwork toys. **Primitive** (✉*3321 10th St. NW,*

Cambrian Heights ☎*403/270–8490*) stocks contemporary clothing by up-and-coming Canadian designers. **Riley & McCormick** (✉*220 8th Ave. SW, Steven Avenue* ☎*403/228–4024*) is a family-owned Western wear store that has been in business for three generations.

CALGARY ESSENTIALS

TRANSPORTATION

BY AIR

Major airlines serving Calgary include Air Canada, American, British Airways, Continental, Delta, Horizon, Northwest, United, and US Airways.

AIRPORTS & TRANSFERS Calgary International Airport is 20 minutes northeast of the city center. Taxis make the trip between the airport and downtown for C$35 to C$40.

Information **Calgary International Airport** (✉*2000 Airport Rd. NE, McCall North Calgary* ☎*403/735–1372* 🌐*www.calgaryairport.com*).

BY BUS & LIGHT RAIL

Calgary Transit (CT) operates a comprehensive bus and light rail transit system throughout the city. Fares are C$2.25 and you can ask for a free transfer from the driver. Ten-ticket books are C$19.50. A Calgary Transit Day Pass good for unlimited rides costs C$6.75. The C-Train has lines running northwest (Brentwood), northeast (Whitehorn), and south (Fish Creek) from downtown. The C-Train is free within the downtown core.

Information **Calgary Transit** (*CT* ☎*403/262–1000* 🌐*www.calgarytransit.com*).

BY CAR

The Trans-Canada Highway (Highway 1) runs west to southeast across Alberta, through Calgary. Highway 2 passes through Calgary on its way from the U.S. border to Edmonton and points north. Calgary is 690 km (428 mi) northwest of Helena, Montana; it's 670 km (415 mi) northeast of Seattle, via the Trans-Canada Highway. Within Calgary, although many sights are in the downtown area and can be reached on foot, a car is useful for visiting outlying attractions.

TAXIS

Taxis start at C$3 and charge about C$2.50 for each additional 2 km (1 mi).

Information **Associated Cabs** (☎*403/299–1111*). **Checker** (☎*403/299–9999*). **Co-op** (☎*403/531–8294*). **Red Top** (☎*403/974–4444*). **Yellow Cab** (☎*403/974–1111*).

CONTACTS & RESOURCES

EMERGENCIES

Alberta Children's Hospital, Foothills Hospital, Peter Lougheed Hospital, and Rocky View Hospital all have emergency rooms. Super Drug Mart is open daily until midnight.

Emergency Services Ambulance, fire (☎ *911*). Police (☎ *911 or 403/266–1234*). Poison center (☎ *403/670–1414*).

Hospitals Alberta Children's Hospital (✉ *1820 Richmond Rd. SW, Knob Hill* ☎ *403/229–7211*). Foothills Hospital (✉ *1403 29th St. NW, St. Andrews Heights* ☎ *403/670–1110*). Peter Lougheed Hospital (✉ *3500 26th Ave. NE, Sunridge Business Park* ☎ *403/291–8555*). Rocky View Hospital (✉ *7007 14th St. SW, Eagle Ridge* ☎ *403/541–3000*).

Late-Night Pharmacy Super Drug Mart (✉ *504 Elbow Dr. SW, Mission* ☎ *403/228–3338*).

TOURS

Various tour companies run guided city-sightseeing excursions that cover historic and modern Calgary in either vans or buses. A typical three- to four-hour tour includes Fort Calgary and Canada Olympic Park; some include the Stampede Grounds, the Calgary Tower, and the Olympic Speedskating Oval at the University of Calgary. Prices range between C$29 for 1½ hours (without stops) and C$45 for 4 hours, which includes guided tours of Fort Calgary and Canada Olympic Park, as well as an elevation pass for the Calgary Tower. Urban Safari Tours offers culinary tours of Calgary, and New Ming Tours takes you to the heart of Calgary's Chinatown, the third largest in Canada. Some companies operate seasonally; reservations are required for all companies.

6

Day trips to Banff, Lake Louise, and the Columbia Icefields are offered in buses or 15-passenger touring vans. The C$175 Icefields tour is 15 hours round-trip and includes a SnoCoach ride onto the glacier. Banff and Lake Louise tours (C$94–C$107) generally run nine hours and include a driver–guide who explains the history, geology, and ecology of the mountains. Some tours include shopping stops in Banff, a drive around Lake Minnewanka, Moraine Lake, Johnson's Canyon, and the Banff Gondola. A few tours go north to Drumheller and the Royal Tyrrell Museum or south to Head-Smashed-In Buffalo Jump, a UNESCO World Heritage Site.

Information Brewster Tours (✉ *2000 Airport Rd. NE, Box 96, in Calgary International Airport main terminal, McCall North Calgary T2E 6W5* ☎ *403/221–8242* 🌐 *www.brewster.ca*). Hammerhead Scenic Tours (✉ *119 Whiteglen Crescent NE* ☎ *877/260–0940* 🌐 *www.hammerheadtours.com*). New Ming Tours (✉ *323 13th Ave. SW* ☎ *403/554–8687* 🌐 *www.newmingtours.com*). Time Out for Touring (✉ *755 Strathcona Dr. SW* ☎ *403/272–4699* 🌐 *www.tour-time.com*). Urban Safari Tours (✉ *18 Discovery Ridge Gardens SW* ☎ *403/283–3158* 🌐 *www.urbansafaritours.com*).

VISITOR INFORMATION

The main visitor information center, part of the Calgary Convention and Visitors Bureau, is in the Riley McCormick Western Store at 220 8th Street Southwest. There are also walk-in visitor centers on the arrival and departure floors at the airport.

Information Calgary Convention and Visitors Bureau (✉ *238 11th Ave. SE, Suite 200, Victoria Park T2G 0X8* ☎ *403/263–8510 or 800/661–1678* 🌐 *www.tourismcalgary.com*).

ELSEWHERE IN SOUTHERN ALBERTA

Dry, flat prairie wheat fields in the east of this region gradually rise to soft hills and pine forests as you head west toward the Rocky Mountains. Cities and varied sights in the southern part of the province offer a look at key elements of Alberta's history. You can study the world of the dinosaurs at the Royal Tyrrell Museum in Drumheller; learn about the role of the locals, settlers, and the North West Mounted Police in Fort Macleod; and explore prosperous, modern Medicine Hat.

ROYAL TYRRELL MUSEUM OF PALEONTOLOGY

★ *20 km (12 mi) east of Calgary on Trans-Canada Hwy. 1, then 120 km (74 mi) north on Rte. 9, then 6 km (4 mi) northwest on Hwy 838.*

The road to Drumheller and the **Royal Tyrell Museum** is well marked and takes you through the vast flat Canadian prairie. Once a coal-mining area, Drumheller's major industry today is dinosaurs. The museum is in **Midland Provincial Park** and holds one of the world's largest collections of complete dinosaur skeletons with more than 40 full-size animals. The barren lunar terrain of stark badlands and eerie hoodoos that surround the area seem an ideal setting for the dinosaurs that stalked the countryside 75 million years ago; but in fact, when the dinosaurs were here, the area had a semitropical climate and marshlands not unlike those of the Florida Everglades. You can participate in hands-on museum exhibits and meet the first dinosaur discovered here: Albertosaurus, a smaller version of Tyrannosaurus Rex, or travel the 48-km (30-mi) Dinosaur Trail through the Red Deer Valley and surrounding badlands. ✉ *Hwy. 838, 6 km (4 mi) northwest of Drumheller* ☎ *403/823–7707 or 888/440–4240* 🌐 *www.tyrrellmuseum.com* *C$10* ⏲ *Mid-May–early Sept., daily 9–9; early Sept.–early Oct., daily 10–5; early-Oct.–mid-May, Tues.–Sun. 10–5.*

DINOSAUR PROVINCIAL PARK

Fodor's Choice ★ *190 km (118 mi) south of Drumheller, 240 km (149 mi) southeast of Calgary.*

Dinosaur Provincial Park encompasses 73 square km (28 square mi) of Canada's greatest badlands, as well as prairie and riverside habitats. A United Nations World Heritage Site, the park contains some of the world's richest fossil beds—dating as far back as 75 million years—including many kinds of dinosaurs. Much of the area is a nature preserve with restricted public access. Self-guided trails weave through different habitats, and a public loop road leads to two outdoor fossil displays. The **Royal Tyrrell Museum Field Station** has ongoing fossil excavations. Interpretive programs run daily from mid-May to early September and weekends until mid-October, but many require tickets; call for reservations. You should allow at least two full days for an in-depth experience. The campground has a food-service center. To get here from Drumheller, take Route 56 to the Trans-Canada Highway (Highway 1) east, go north at Brooks on Route 873 and then east on

Route 544, and follow the signs. ✉ *Rte. 544, Patricia* ☎ *403/378–4342, 403/378–4344 for interpretive-hike reservations, 403/378–3700 for campground reservations* 🌐 *www.cd.gov.ab.ca* *Park free, C$3 field station, C$8 hikes and bus tours* ⏲ *Field station: mid-May–Aug., daily 8:30 AM–9 PM; Sept.–mid-Oct., daily 9–4; mid-Oct–mid-May, weekdays 9–4.*

MEDICINE HAT

95 km (59 mi) southeast of Patricia (Dinosaur Provincial Park), 293 km (182 mi) southeast of Calgary.

Medicine Hat is a prosperous, scenic city built on high banks overlooking the South Saskatchewan River. Much local lore concerns the origin of its name. One legend tells of a battle between Cree and Blackfoot peoples: the Cree fought bravely until their medicine man deserted, losing his headdress in the South Saskatchewan River. The site's name, Saamis, meaning "medicine man's hat," was later translated by white settlers into Medicine Hat.

6

Originally settled as a tent town for railroad crews in 1883, Alberta's fifth-largest city has derived wealth from vast deposits of natural gas, some of which is piped up to fuel quaint gas lamps in the turn-of-the-19th-century downtown area.

Prosperity is embodied in the striking, glass-sided **Medicine Hat City Hall** (✉ *580 1st St. SE* ☎ *403/529–8115*), which won the Canadian Architectural Award in 1986. Guided group and self-guided tours are available. The building is open weekdays 8:30–4:30.

A nice spot to spend an afternoon is alongside the South Saskatchewan River and Seven Persons Creek, a parkland and environmental preserve interconnected by 15 km (9 mi) of walking, biking, and cross-country ski trails.

The **Tourist Information Centre** (✉ *8 Gehring Rd. SW* ☎ *403/527–6422*) has detailed trail maps of the preserve.

Across the road from the preserve is **Saamis Tepee,** the world's largest tepee built for the 1988 Calgary Winter Olympics in recognition of Alberta's First Nations people.

A dozen water slides add up to 1 km (½ mi) of falling water at **Riverside Amusement Park** (✉ *Hwy. 1 and Power House Rd.* ☎ *403/529–6218*). The park also has go-karts, inner tubing, and an 18-hole championship miniature-golf course.

Echodale Regional Park (✉ *Holsom Rd., off Hwy. 3* ☎ *403/529–8340*) provides a riverside setting for swimming, boating, and fishing; it also has a 1900s farm and a historic coal mine.

Medicine Hat Clay Industries National Historic District Museum. There were many industries that thrived in Medicine Hat prior to World War I, but the manufacture of clay products became a booming industry that still remains today. The historic factories, equipment, and artifacts of this business have been declared one of Canada's national historic treasures, and a tour of the museum will allow you to view historic pottery, stoneware, ceramics, brick, and the equipment that was used to produce it as early as 1885. Guided tours are available. ✉ *713 Medalta Ave. SE* ☎ *403/529–1070* 🌐 *www.medalta.org* 🎫 *C$8* ⏲ *Mid-May–early Sept., daily 10–4.*

WHERE TO STAY

$–$$ **Medicine Hat Lodge.** On the edge of town and adjacent to a shopping mall, this contemporary hotel has several rooms with atrium views of the indoor pool and the two huge water slides. Mamma's Dining Room serves meals with Italian flair. The Lava Lounge, a retro bar, has a varied menu. A variety of guest rooms are available ranging from comfortable rooms with queen-size beds to family suites and luxury suites complete with Jacuzzi tubs. ✉ *1051 Ross Glen Dr. SE, T1B 3T8* ☎ *403/529–2222 or 800/661–8095* 🌐 *www.medhatlodge.com* *222 rooms, 40 suites* *In-room: Wi-Fi. In-hotel: 2 restaurants, room service, bar, pool, spa, bicycles, laundry facilities, laundry service, public Wi-Fi, no-smoking rooms* 💳 *AE, DC, MC, V* *BP.*

LETHBRIDGE

164 km (102 mi) west of Medicine Hat, 217 km (135 mi) south of Calgary.

The main attraction in Lethbridge, **Fort Whoop-Up,** part of the **Indian Battle Park,** is a reconstruction of a southern Alberta whiskey fort established in 1869 by desperadoes from Fort Benton, Montana. It became the largest of many similar forts that sprang up illegally on the Canadian prairies. Along with costumed reenactments, weapons, relics, and a 15-minute audiovisual historical presentation, Fort Whoop-Up has horse-drawn wagon tours of the river valley and other points of historical interest. ✉ *West end of 3rd Ave., off Scenic Dr. S in Indian Battle Park* ☎ *403/329–0444* 🌐 *www.fortwhoopup.com* 🎫 *C$5* ⏲ *Mid-May–Sept., Mon.–Sat. 10–5, Apr.–mid-May and Oct., Wed–Sun. 1–4; Nov.–Mar., weekends 1–4.*

Henderson Lake Park, 3 km (2 mi) east of downtown Lethbridge, is filled with lush trees, a golf course, a baseball stadium, a swimming pool, an artificial lake, a year-round ice-skating rink, and tennis courts. The **Nikka Yuko Japanese Gardens** (☎ *403/328–3511* 🌐 *www.nikkayuko.com*) offer a tranquil setting with manicured trees and shrubs, miniature pools and waterfalls, a teahouse, and pebble designs originally constructed in Japan and reassembled alongside Henderson Lake. Admission to the gardens is C$7. ✉ *Mayor Magrath Dr. and N. Parkside Dr. S* ☎ *403/320–3009* 🎫 *C$7* ⏲ *Mid-May–mid-June and early Sept.–mid-Oct., daily 9–5; mid-June–early Sept., daily 9–8.*

OFF THE BEATEN PATH

Writing-on-Stone Provincial Park. Among rock cliffs and hoodoos alongside the Milk River, this park contains the largest concentration of native petroglyphs on the North American plains. Today a campground and restored Mountie outpost are here. You can explore the *coulées* (gullies) that provided cover for outlaws and illegal whiskey traders.

Guided walks explore some of this history. The park is about 100 km (62 mi) southeast of Lethbridge. ✉*Hwy. 501 about 43 km (26 mi) east of town of Milk River* ☎*403/647–2364* *Free.*

WHERE TO STAY & EAT

$$ ✕ **La Bella Notte.** In the historic fire house in downtown Lethbridge, this is the place to go for a romantic evening out or an important business luncheon. On warm evenings, the old garage doors where the fire trucks once entered are opened wide to let in fresh air. With Lethbridge's most extensive wine list, it has become an established hot spot in the city. Menus feature upscale Italian cuisine as well as steaks and seafood. Try the fresh pastas and sauces made with seasonal ingredients. ✉*402 2nd Ave. S* ⊕*www.labellanotte.com* ☎*403/331–3319* *AE, MC, V.*

$$ ✕ **Guesthouse Restaurant.** This family-run restaurant specializes in home-style Swiss and European cuisine. There are daily supper specials and buffets on weekends. The atmosphere is relaxed and homey. For breakfast try the Danish pancakes with fruit topping. Supper specialties include a wide variety of choices from cabbage rolls to Alberta beef steak. ✉*110 W.T. Hill Blvd.* ☎*403/394–9333* ⊕*www.guesthouse.1ezsite.net* *AE, MC, V.*

$$ ★ **Ramada Hotel & Suites.** This award-winning property has a 12,000-square-foot indoor water park with waterslides, a wave pool, kiddies' water play park, and hot tub. A deluxe Continental breakfast is included in room rates and includes items such as hot freshly baked cinnamon buns. Standard hotel rooms as well as large family suites are available, and there's a free airport shuttle, meeting rooms, and a 24-hour business center on-site. ✉*2375 Mayor Magrath Dr. S, T1K 7M1* ☎*403/380–5050* ⊕*www.ramada.com* *119 rooms* *In-room: refrigerator, ethernet. In-hotel: restaurant, room service, public Internet* *AE, DC, MC, V* *CP.*

$–$$ **Lethbridge Lodge Hotel.** A tropical indoor courtyard with exotic plants and a pool, as well as great views of the Oldman River set this hotel apart. The rooms are fairly spacious and come in five different styles, with good options for business travelers and families. There are two restaurants; at the more formal Anton's, the waiters wear tuxedos, and reservations are required. ✉*320 Scenic Dr., T1J 4B4* ☎*403/328–1123 or 800/661–1232* ⊕*www.lethbridgelodge.com* *154 rooms, 36 suites* *In-room: ethernet. In-hotel: 2 restaurants, bar, pool, no-smoking rooms* *AE, DC, MC, V.*

FORT MACLEOD

50 km (31 mi) west of Lethbridge, 167 km (104 mi) south of Calgary.

The pre-1900 wood-frame buildings and the more recent sandstone-and-brick buildings have established Fort Macleod, southern Alberta's oldest town, as the province's first historic area. It was founded by the North West Mounted Police in 1874 to maintain order among the farmers, local people, whiskey sellers, and ranchers.

6

An authentic reconstruction of the 1874 fort, the **Fort Museum** grants almost equal exhibitory weight to settlers, regional people, the old North West Mounted Police, and today's Royal Canadian Mounted Police. ✉ *219 25th St.* ☎ *403/553–4703* 🌐 *www.nwmpmuseum.com* 🎫 *C$7.50* ⏲ *Mar.–June, daily 9–5; July and Aug., daily 9–6; Sept.–late Dec., daily 9–5.*

A multilevel interpretive center built into the side of a cliff provides information about the lifestyle, legends, and story of the Blackfoot people at **Head-Smashed-In Buffalo Jump,** a UNESCO World Heritage Site. Exhibits describe the history of the buffalo jump, and a film re-creates the event when native peoples herded buffalo over the cliff to their thunderous death. Trails surround the jump, and tours are given by Blackfoot guides. If you visit on Wednesday in summer you can enjoy native dancing, drumming, and singing. During the summer months you can spend the night in a fully equipped Blackfoot tepee. The site is about 18 km (11 mi) west of Fort Macleod. ✉ *Rte. 785 off Hwy. 2* ☎ *403/553–2731* 🌐 *www.head-smashed-in.com* 🎫 *C$9* ⏲ *Mid-May–mid-Sept., daily 9–6; mid-Sept.–mid-May, daily 10–5.*

WATERTON LAKES NATIONAL PARK

106 km (66 mi) south of Fort Macleod, 267 km (166 mi) south of Calgary.

★ The mountains at Waterton Lakes National Park, near the southern end of the Canadian Rockies, seem a bit friendlier than those in the other national parks here—not quite so high, not quite so rugged. A World Heritage Site, Waterton is the meeting of two worlds: the flatlands of the prairie and the abrupt upthrust of the mountains. In this juncture of worlds, the park squeezes into a relatively small area (525 square km or 200 square mi) an unusual mix of wildlife, flora, and climate zones. The town site of Waterton Park is a decidedly low-key community in roughly the geographical center of the park. In summer it swells with tourists, and the restaurants and shops open to serve them. In winter only a few motels are open, and services are largely geared to meet the needs of the several hundred residents.

SCENIC DRIVES

Akamina Parkway. Take this winding 10-mi (16-km) road up to Cameron Lake. A relatively flat, paved, 1-mi (1.6-km) trail hugs the western shore and makes a nice walk. Bring your binoculars, because it's common to see grizzly bears on the lower slopes of the mountains at the far end of the lake.

Red Rock Parkway. The 9-mi (15-km) route takes you from the prairie up the Blakiston Valley to Red Rock Canyon, where water has cut through the earth, exposing red sedimentary rock.

HISTORIC SITES

First Oil Well in Western Canada. Alberta is known worldwide for its oil and gas production and the first oil well in western Canada was established in 1902 in what is now the park. Stop at this National Historic

Site to explore the wellheads, drilling equipment, and remains of the Oil City boomtown. ✉ *Along the Akamina Pkwy.*

★ **Prince of Wales Hotel.** Named for the prince who later became King Edward VIII, this lovely hotel was constructed between 1926 and 1927 and was designated a National Historic Site in 1995. The lobby window affords a pretty view, and afternoon tea is a treat here. ✉ *Waterton Lakes National Park, off Hwy. 5* ☎ *406/756–2444, 403/859–2231 mid-May–late Sept.* 🌐 *www.glacierparkinc.com* ⏲ *Closed late Sept.–mid-May* 🍽 *EP.*

SCENIC STOPS

★ **Cameron Lake.** The jewel of Waterton, Cameron Lake sits in a land of glacially carved cirques (steep-walled basins). In summer, hundreds of varieties of alpine wildflowers fill the area, including 22 kinds of wild orchids. Canoes and pedal boats can be rented here. ✉ *Akamina Pkwy., 13 km (8 mi) southwest of Waterton Park Townsite.*

Goat Haunt. Reached only by foot trail or tour boat from Waterton Townsite, this spot on the U.S. end of Waterton Lake is the stomping ground for mountain goats, moose, grizzlies, and black bears. The ranger posted at this remote station gives thrice-daily 10-minute overviews of Waterton Valley history. ✉ *South end of Waterton Lake* ☎ *406/888–7800 or 403/859–2362* 🎫 *Tour boat $18* ⏲ *Mid-May–Oct.*

★ **Waterton Townsite.** This is a decidedly low-key community in roughly the geographical center of the park. In summer it swells with tourists, and local restaurants and shops open to serve them. In winter only a few motels are open, and services are limited.

WHERE TO STAY & EAT

$$–$$$ ✕ **Prince of Wales Dining Room.** Enjoy upmarket cuisine before a dazzling view of Waterton Lake in the dining room of this century-old chalet high on a hill. Choose from a fine selection of wines to accompany your meal. Every afternoon the lodge's main culinary event unfolds: a British high tea served in Valerie's Tea Room—includes finger sandwiches, scones and other pastries, and chocolate-dipped fruits. ✉ *Waterton Townsite* ☎ *403/859–2231* 🌐 *www.glacierparkinc.com/princeofwaleshotel.htm* 💳 *D, MC, V* ⏲ *Closed Oct.–May.*

$$$$ 🏨 **Prince of Wales Hotel.** Perched between two lakes, with a high mountain backdrop, this hotel has the best view in town. A high steeple crowns the building, which is fantastically ornamented with eaves, balconies, and turrets. Expect creaks and rattles at night—the old hotel, built in the 1920s, is exposed to rough winds. Rates decrease by about 25% off-season. ✉ *Off Hwy. 5, Glacier Park Inc.* 📮 *Box 33, Waterton Park T0K 2M0* ☎ *406/756–2444, 403/859–2231 mid-May–late Sept.* 📠 *406/257–0384* 🌐 *www.glacierparkinc.com* 🛏 *89 rooms* 👍 *In-room: no a/c, no TV. In-hotel: restaurant* 💳 *AE, MC, V* ⏲ *Closed late Sept.–mid-May.*

6

SPORTS & THE OUTDOORS

The park contains numerous short hikes for day-trippers and some longer treks for backpackers. Upper and Middle Waterton and Cameron lakes provide peaceful havens for boaters. A tour boat cruises across Upper Waterton Lake, crossing the U.S.–Canada border, and the winds that rake across that lake create an exciting ride for windsurfers—bring a wet suit, though; the water remains numbingly cold throughout summer.

BICYCLING

Bikes are allowed on some trails, such as the 2-mi (3-km) Townsite Loop Trail. A ride on mildly sloping Red Rock Canyon Road isn't too difficult. Cameron Lake Road is an intermediate route.

OUTFITTER

Pat's Waterton. Choose from surrey bikes, mountain bikes, or motorized scooters. Pat's also rents tennis rackets, strollers, and binoculars. ✉*Corner of Mt. View Rd., Waterton Townsite* ☎*403/859–2266.*

BOATING

Nonmotorized boats can be rented at Cameron Lake in summer; private craft can be used on Upper and Middle Waterton lakes.

OUTFITTERS & EXPEDITIONS

★ **Waterton Inter-Nation Shoreline Cruise Co.** This company's two-hour round-trip boat tour along Upper Waterton Lake from Waterton Townsite to Goat Haunt Ranger Station is one of the most popular activities in Waterton. (*Note that because Goat Haunt is in the United States, you must clear customs.*) The narrated tour passes scenic bays, sheer cliffs, and snow-clad peaks. ✉*Waterton Townsite Marina* ☎*403/859–2362* *403/938-5019* *www.watertoncruise.com* *C$30* *May–early Oct., cruises daily 2–5.*

HIKING

There are 191 mi (225 km) of trails in Waterton Lakes that range in difficulty from short strolls to strenuous treks. Some trails connect with the trail systems of Glacier and British Columbia's Akamina-Kishenina Provincial Park. The wildflowers in June are particularly stunning along most trails.

EASY

★ **Bear's Hump.** This 1.7-mi (2.7-km) trail climbs up the mountainside to an overlook with a great view of Upper Waterton Lake and the town site. ✉*Directly behind the Waterton Information Centre Bldg.*

Cameron Lake Shore Trail. This relatively flat paved 1-mi (1.5-km) trail is a peaceful place for a walk. Look for grizzlies on the lower slopes of the mountains at the far end of the lake. ✉*The trailhead is located at the lakeshore in front of the parking lot, 13 km (8 mi) southwest of Waterton Townsite.*

Crandell Lake Trail. This easy 1.5-mi (2.5-km) trail follows an old wagon road to lead to Oil City. ✉*About halfway up the Akamina Pkwy.*

MODERATE

Bertha Lake Trail. This 8-mi (13-km) trail leads from the Waterton Townsite through a Douglas fir forest to a beautiful overlook of Upper Waterton Lake, then on to Lower Bertha Falls. If you continue on, a

WATERTON ESSENTIALS

ADMISSION FEES
A day pass to Waterton Lakes costs C$7 (C$3.45 per child), and an annual pass costs C$35.

ADMISSION HOURS
The park is open year-round, however, most roads and facilities close October through May due to snow.

PERMITS
Backcountry camping permits are required for the 13 backcountry camp spots, with reservations available up to 90 days in advance. Buy the permit for C$6 per adult per night—reserve for an additional C$11—at the visitor reception center (403/858–5133).

VISITOR INFORMATION
Waterton Lakes National Park (✉ Waterton Park, AB, Canada TOK 2MO ☎ 403/859–2224 or 800/748–7275 📠 403/859–2650 🌐 www.parkscanada.gc.ca/waterton).

steeper climb will take you past Upper Bertha Falls to Bertha Lake. The wildflowers are particularly stunning along this trail in June. ✉ *The trailhead is located on the south end of the townsite. Head towards the lake and you will find a parking lot on the west side of the Rd.*

DIFFICULT
Fodor'sChoice ★

Crypt Lake Trail. This awe-inspiring, strenuous, 5.5-mi (9-km) trail is proclaimed by some to be one of the most stunning hikes in the Canadian Rockies. Conquering the trail involves a boat taxi across Waterton Lake, a climb of 2,300 feet, a crawl through a tunnel that measures almost 100 feet, and a climb along a sheer rock face. The reward is a 600-foot-tall cascading waterfall and the turquoise waters of Crypt Lake. ✉ *Crypt Landing is accessed by ferry from Waterton Townsite.*

HORSEBACK RIDING

Rolling hills, grasslands, and rugged mountains make riding in Waterton Lakes a real pleasure. Scenery, wildlife, and wildflowers are easily viewed from the saddle and many of the park trails allow horses.

OUTFITTERS & EXPEDITIONS

Alpine Stables. You can arrange hourly trail rides and all-day guided excursions within the park as well as multiday pack trips through the foothills of the Rockies. ✉ *Box 53, Waterton Lakes National Park TOK 2M0* ☎ *403/859–2463, 403/653–2449 off-season* 🌐 *www.alpinestables.com* 🕐 *May–Sept.*

SWIMMING

Waterton Lake. It's chilly year-round, but it's still a great place to cool off after a long hot day of hiking. Most visitors wade, but a few join the "polar bear club" and get completely submersed. ✉ *Waterton Townsite.*

EDMONTON

Perched on the steep banks of the North Saskatchewan River, Edmonton is the capital city of Alberta and the sixth-largest city in Canada, with a metro-area population of one million. As the seat of the provincial government and home to the University of Alberta, the city is sophisticated and multiethnic, spawning a thriving arts community and fine restaurants. Known as "Canada's Festival City," this provincial capital plays host to more than 30 annual festivals, celebrating music, dance, visual arts, performing arts, sports, and film. These include the internationally renowned folk, fringe, and children's festivals.

Edmonton is a composite of a handful of major neighborhoods, each with its own mix of personality, history, and culture. The city's street system is a grid with numbered streets running north–south (numbers decrease as you head east) and numbered avenues running east–west (numbers decrease as you head south). Jasper (101) Avenue, the city's main street, runs east–west through the center of downtown. There's also Chinatown, which runs along 102 Avenue between 97 and 95 streets. In Little Italy, you'll find shops and restaurants along 108 Avenue and 95 Street. The Avenue of Nations, northwest of downtown along 107 Avenue from 95 Street to 116 Street, has shops, services, and restaurants with Chinese, Japanese, Vietnamese, Latin American, Polish, and Ukrainian influences. The West End includes West Edmonton Mall, "the greatest indoor show on earth," and the Original West End, with its carefully preserved Edwardian architecture.

This thriving northern city is a boomtown that never seems to go bust. What started as a trading post morphed into a metropolis as a result of three major booms over some 200 years. In 1795 the North West Company and Hudson's Bay Company founded Fort Edmonton as a trading post on the banks of the North Saskatchewan River. Then, during the Klondike Gold Rush in 1897, Edmonton became a starting point for prospectors en route to the Yukon Territory. The annual 10-day Edmonton's Capital EX in July celebrates this aspect of the city's history. Edmonton's third boom gushed from the ground on a cold February morning in 1947, when oil was discovered in Leduc, 40 km (25 mi) to the southwest. More than 10,000 wells were eventually drilled within 100 km (62 mi) of the city, and with them came numerous refineries and supply depots. By 1965 Edmonton had solidified its role as "oil capital of Canada" and today commemorates that role with an NHL hockey team known as the Edmonton Oilers, a Western Hockey League team called the Edmonton Oil Kings, and a Northern League baseball team known as the Edmonton Cracker-Cats.

Edmonton's parks and green spaces aren't typical oil-town scenery. Twenty-two parks along the North Saskatchewan River valley encompass 18,348 acres, have 122 km (76 mi) of trails, and form the largest stretch of urban parkland in North America, known as the river valley parkland.

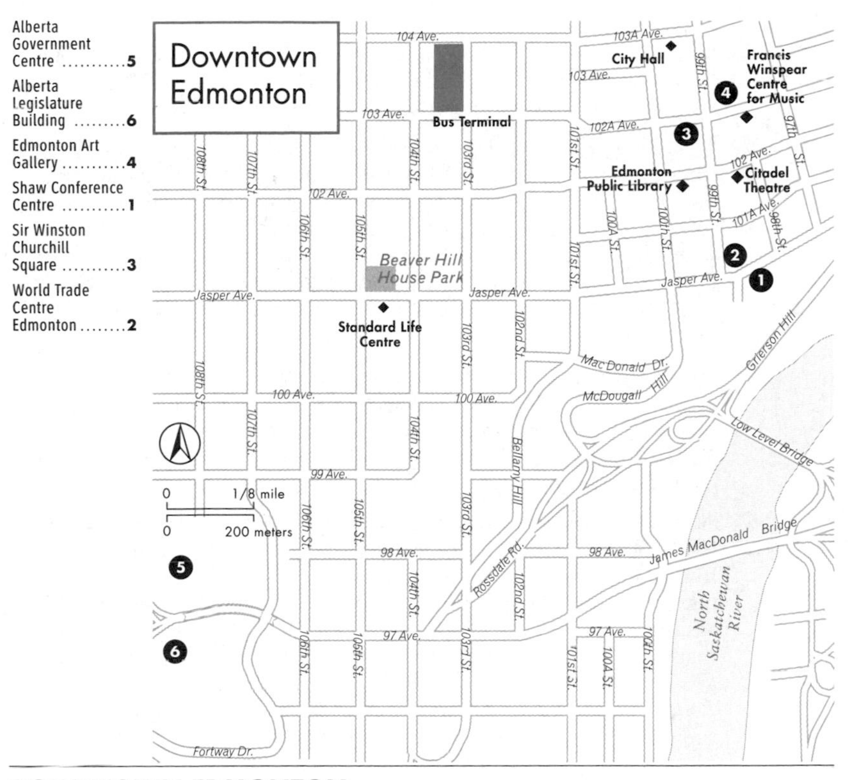

DOWNTOWN EDMONTON

The downtown core lies just north of the river valley, along Jasper (101) Avenue, between 97 and 109 streets. Above ground are shop- and restaurant-lined streets, as well as large malls including Edmonton City Centre, Commerce Place, and ManuLife Place. Beneath the downtown core are a series of Pedways (climate-controlled walkways), which link major hotels, restaurants, and shopping malls with the central Arts District, a four-block area surrounding Sir Winston Churchill Square. At the southern end of the downtown area, near the High Level Bridge on 109 Street and 97 Avenue, stands the Alberta Legislature, seat of the provincial government.

WHAT TO SEE

5 **Alberta Government Centre.** The seat of Alberta's government, this complex encompasses several acres of carefully manicured gardens and fountains. The gardens are open for strolling. ✉ *109 St. and 97 Ave., Downtown* ☎ *780/427–7362.*

6 **Alberta Legislature Building.** The stately 1912 Edwardian structure overlooks the river on the site of an early trading post. Frequent free 40-minute tours of the building and an interpretive center help to explain the intricacies of the Albertan and Canadian systems of government.

⊠109 St. and 97 Ave., Downtown ☎780/427–7362 🌐www.assembly.ab.ca/visitor/tour_info.htm 🎫Free ⏲May–mid-Oct., weekdays 8:30–5, weekends 9–5, last tour at 4; mid-Oct.–Apr., weekdays 9–4:30, last tour at 3, weekends noon–5, last tour at 4.

❹ **Art Gallery of Alberta.** The collection includes paintings, sculptures, prints, installation works, and photographs by national and international artists. The Art Gallery of Alberta has temporarily relocated to 10230 Jasper Avenue during the construction of a new gallery, scheduled to open in late 2009. *⊠2 Sir Winston Churchill Sq., Arts District ☎780/422–6223 🌐www.artgalleryalberta.com 🎫C$10; free Thurs.after 4 ⏲Mon.–Wed. and Fri. 10:30–5, Thurs. 10:30–8, weekends 11–5.*

❶ **Shaw Conference Centre.** This most unconventional structure was built into the banks of the North Saskatchewan River; the terraced levels are reached by glass-enclosed escalators with great views of the river valley. *⊠9797 Jasper Ave., Downtown ☎780/421–9797 🌐www.shawconferencecentre.com.*

❸ **Sir Winston Churchill Square.** The focus of the Arts District is this four-block area that incorporates many of Edmonton's major institutions. It's bordered by 99 and 100 streets and 102 Avenue and 102A Avenue. The **Francis Winspear Centre for Music** (*⊠4 Sir Winston Churchill Sq., Arts District ☎780/428–1414*) has a 1,900-seat concert hall that's home to the Edmonton Symphony Orchestra. The largest theater complex in Canada, the **Citadel Theatre** (*⊠9828 101A Ave., Arts District ☎780/425–1820*) has five venues—plus workshops and classrooms—and an indoor garden with a waterfall. The Edmonton Public Library's **Stanley Milner Library** (*⊠7 Sir Winston Churchill Sq., Arts District ☎780/496–7000*) augments books and art exhibits with a lively round of activities in the Children's Department. The **Chinatown Gate** is a symbol of friendship between Edmonton and its sister city, Harbin, China; the gate spans the portal to Edmonton's Chinatown. **City Hall** (*⊠1 Sir Winston Churchill Sq., Arts District ☎780/496–8200*) is more than a place for civic government. This architectural showcase contains a grand stairway, a large art-exhibition space, and a 200-foot tower with an enormous 23-bell carillon. Self-guided tours are available year-round, and organized tours are available from July through mid-August weekdays at noon and 1.

❷ **World Trade Centre Edmonton.** In a renovated historic bank building, the World Trade Centre Edmonton is home to the Edmonton Chamber of Commerce, Edmonton Economic Development Corporation, Edmonton Tourism Information, and an Edmonton Airports passenger, baggage, and Sky Shuttle facility. While waiting for a connecting flight, you can catch an airport shuttle to the WTCE and make use of luggage storage facilities, Air Canada and Westjet airport check-in kiosks, or visitor information services. Shuttles run every 20-minutes from 6 AM to 9 PM weekdays and cost $25 for a return trip to the Edmonton International Airport. *⊠9990 Jasper Av.e NW, Downtown ☎780/426–4715 or 800/463–4667 🌐www.edmonton.com.*

GREATER EDMONTON

Outside downtown Edmonton are historic sites, museums, and one of the world's largest shopping and entertainment complexes. Jasper Avenue west runs near the Royal Alberta Museum and the Original West End before turning into Stony Plain Road. Farther along it passes near West Edmonton Mall before joining with Highway 16, which leads out of the city toward Jasper National Park.

The University of Alberta has more than 90 buildings on a 217-acre campus, including the Northern Alberta Jubilee Auditorium, the home stage of the Alberta Ballet and the Edmonton Opera Company; the University Hospitals; and Rutherford House, the restored home of Alberta's first premier. Old Strathcona, a favorite haunt of the university crowd, is a historic area of Edmonton that centers on Whyte (82) Avenue, between 99 and 109 streets. Although it was once a separate city across the river from Edmonton, it's grown into a lively area with dozens of bars, restaurants, and chic clubs in historic buildings. This 10-block area also has trendy boutiques, theaters, and the Old Strathcona Farmers' Market. The south-side neighborhood has a number of restaurants, shops, and hotels: South Edmonton Common is the fastest-growing retail area and is located at Gateway Boulevard (Highway 2) and 23 Avenue, and major chain stores like Superstore, Home Depot, Wal-Mart, Ikea, and Cineplex Odeon Cinemas are found in this part of the city.

WHAT TO SEE

★ **Fort Edmonton Park.** Canada's largest living-history park (158 acres) re-creates life in Edmonton during the 19th century using costumed interpreters in a historic setting. The park includes a native settlement; the restored 1846 Hudson's Bay Company fort; a blacksmith shop, a saloon, and a jail along 1885 Street; photo studios and a firehouse on 1905 Street; and relatively modern conveniences on 1920 Street. Horse-drawn wagon, streetcar, stagecoach, and pony rides are available for a small additional fee. A new attraction at the park is a reproduction of a 1920s carnival that includes a carousel with 32 hand-painted horses, a Ferris wheel, and a children's bug ride. You may recognize the park's 1905 steam train from the 2007 film, *The Assassination of Jesse James by the Coward Robert Ford,* starring Brad Pitt and Casey Affleck. ✉ *Whitemud and Fox Drs., River Valley Parkland* ☎ *780/496–8787* 🌐 *www.edmonton.ca/fort* 🎟 *C$13* ⏲ *Late May–June, weekdays 10–4, weekends 10–6; July and Aug., daily 10–6; Sept. and Oct., Tues.–Sun. 10–4; Nov. and Dec., weekends 11–4.*

Muttart Conservatory. The four spectacular glass-pyramid greenhouses that rise up from Edmonton's river valley are home to one of North America's most important botanical facilities, which includes an extensive collection of orchids and bromeliads. Three pyramids contain 700 species of plants in different climates (arid, tropical, and temperate), and a show pyramid has seasonal floral displays. The Muttart has a gift shop, an art gallery, and a fine café. ✉ *9626 96A St., River Valley Parkland* ☎ *780/496–8755* 🌐 *www.edmonton.ca/muttart* 🎟 *C$8.75* ⏲ *Weekdays 9–5:30, weekends 11–5:30.*

> **WORD OF MOUTH**
>
> "The most interesting things about Fort Edmonton are the Fort and the Cree Tipis IMO. In addition, there are three themed streets in different periods showcasing the different periods of development of the city. These streets resemble some historic small town streets. There are also farm buildings (like the round barn), historic homes and the Metis log cabin that will give you a sense of what the pioneer life is like." —Bencito

★ **Old Strathcona Historic Area.** The area surrounding 104 Street and Whyte (82) Avenue on the south side of the river is a district of restored houses and shops built in the 1890s, prior to the amalgamation of Strathcona Town with Edmonton in 1912. Old Strathcona is an attractive shopping district with antiques stores, gift shops, stylish boutiques, music and book stores, theaters, museums, and 75 restaurants and coffeehouses, which provide a vibrant nightlife. **Old Strathcona Farmers' Market** (☒*10330 84 Ave., Old Strathcona* ☎*780/439–1844* 🌐*www.oldstrathcona.ca*) is open Saturday and has fresh produce, baking, and crafts. The **Old Strathcona Foundation** (☎*780/433–5866* 🌐*www.osf.strathcona.org*) can provide information about the Old Strathcona area.

★ **Royal Alberta Museum.** This innovative natural-history museum in a beautiful park includes the Syncrude Gallery of Aboriginal Culture, which spans 11,000 years and 500 generations of native history and displays an impressive collection of artifacts. The Natural History Gallery presents minerals and gems, a "live" bug room, astonishing dinosaur fossils, saber-toothed tigers, and Canada's only complete Columbian mammoth skeleton. The Wild Alberta Gallery contains dioramas of Alberta's wildlife. The museum also has a shop, a café, and an outdoor sculpture park. ☒*12845 102 Ave., West Edmonton* ☎*780/453–9100* 🌐*www.royalalbertamuseum.ca* *C$10; C$5 weekends 9–11* ⏲*Daily 9–5.*

Rutherford House Provincial Historic Site. Built in Jacobean Revival style, the 1911 home of Alberta's first premier, Alexander Cameron Rutherford, has been restored to its elegant post-Edwardian charm. Costumed interpreters give tours (included in admission) detailing life in 1915. The gift shop sells reproductions of Edwardian gifts, cards, linens, and jewelry. Lunch and afternoon tea, which includes freshly baked scones, are served in the Arbour Restaurant. ☒*11153 Saskatchewan Dr., on University of Alberta campus, University District* ☎*780/427–3995* 🌐*www.cd.gov.ab.ca* *C$4* ⏲*Early Sept.–mid-May, Tues.–Sun. noon–5; mid-May–early Sept., daily 9–5.*

TELUS World of Science—Edmonton. The **Margaret Zeidler Star Theatre** has the largest planetarium dome in North America and presents different laser and star shows hourly. There's an amateur ham radio station, an observatory, an IMAX theater, a café, and a gift shop, as well as six interactive exhibit galleries highlighting the human body, the mysteries of forensics, the environment, science, and space. ☒*11211 142 St., West Edmonton* ☎*780/452–9100* 🌐*www.telusworldofscienceedmonton.com* *C$12.95 for museum, C$12.95 for IMAX, C$19.50 for combined ticket* ⏲*July and Aug., daily 10–9; Sept.–June, Sun.–Thurs. 10–5, Fri. and Sat. 10–9.*

★ **West Edmonton Mall.** Alberta's most popular tourist attraction extends over 5.3 million square feet (48 city blocks) and is billed as the "greatest indoor show on earth." There are more than 800 stores and services including more than 100 dining venues. There's a huge emphasis on entertainment and the mall contains the world's largest indoor amusement park, a water park that includes the world's largest indoor wave pool, a NHL-size skating rink, the world's largest indoor artificial lake, an exact replica of Columbus's ship the *Santa Maria,* bumper boats, marine animals, flamingo and penguin colonies, a sea lion enclosure with daily free shows, a 64,000-square-foot Las Vegas–style casino, an 18-hole miniature golf course, bowling, billiards, arcades, go-karts, bungee jumping, and 27 movie theaters. Other interesting shops and services include three radio stations, a dinner theater, a car wash, a post-secondary school, medical services, a youth drop-in center, a daycare facility, six spas, an interdenominational chapel, a post office, and the Fantasyland Hotel. If you don't feel like walking the mall, rent an electric scooter. *⊠8882 170 St., West Edmonton ☎780/444–5200 or 800/661–8890 🌐www.westedmall.com Galaxyland C$29.95; World Waterpark C$29.95; Sea Life Caverns C$4.95 ⊙Mall, daily 24 hrs; shops Mon.–Sat. 10–9, Sun. noon–6.*

6

WHERE TO EAT

$$$ Fodor'sChoice ★ **Characters.** In a historic building in the heart of downtown, this restaurant has coffered ceilings, hardwood floors, and original brick that lend it a relaxed feel. The main dining room's central fireplace certainly makes things homey. From an open kitchen, chef Shonn Oborowsky and his team serve up specialties like Alberta Black Angus beef tenderloin and short rib with morel sauce, hazelnut crusted rack of lamb with apple cider and apricot jus, and glazed ahi tuna with ratatouille and roasted garlic. Be sure to save room for dessert, which includes such items as homemade blackberry ice cream. The restaurant received a Wine Spectator Award of Excellence for the wine list featuring more than 400 labels from around the world. For a more private dining experience, ask for the elevator room, a private table set up in the building's original warehouse elevator. Reservations are recommended. *⊠10257 105 St., Downtown ☎780/421–4100 🌐www.characters.ca ▭AE, DC, MC, V ⊙Closed Sun. No dinner Mon. No lunch Sat.*

$$$ Fodor'sChoice ★ **Hardware Grill.** Casual elegance reigns at this former hardware store, now handsomely refurbished as a well-lighted, spacious restaurant that has received numerous accolades including "Best Restaurant in the Prairies" from *EnRoute Magazine.* From the glassed-in kitchen, chef-owner Larry Stewart prepares progressive Canadian cuisine using fresh local produce, bold flavors, and dramatic presentation. There are no shortcuts here—almost everything is prepared fresh including breads, smoked meats, and homemade sorbets. Applewood-smoked salmon is served with truffled potato pierogi (dumplings); beef tenderloin comes in a goat cheese crust; and the warm gingerbread cake is served with a rhubarb-Saskatoonberry compote. The impressive wine list includes more than 500 choices and has garnered eight con-

secutive Wine Spectator Awards of Excellence. For a quiet dinner, ask for a table with a view of the river valley. If you'd like an interactive experience, ask to sit at the chef's table in the kitchen. Reservations are recommended. ✉ *9698 Jasper Ave., Downtown* ☎ *780/423–0969* 🌐 *www.hardwaregrill.com* 💳 *AE, DC, MC, V* ⏲ *Closed Sun. and 1st wk in July and 1st wk in Jan.*

WORD OF MOUTH

"If you like steak, find yourself a good Edmonton steak house for your dinner, because Alberta has the best beef in Canada, and keeps the finest cuts for themselves and for restaurant eaters."
—BAK

$$$ ★ ✕ **Il Portico.** Whether it be for a business lunch or a romantic dinner, this downtown restaurant is the place to be seen in Edmonton. The interior is decorated in warm sienna hues and you can dine in the main dining room, on the outdoor terrace, or in a private dining room with 2,000 bottles of wine. Highlights of the contemporary Italian cuisine, served from an open kitchen, include an appetizer of grilled radicchio (red cabbage) stuffed with prosciutto-wrapped bocconcini and served with dried cranberries and a sour cherry vinaigrette, or such simple classics as linguini with grilled giant prawns. Reservations are recommended. ✉ *10012 107 St., Downtown* ☎ *780/424–0707* 🌐 *www.ilportico.ca* 💳 *AE, DC, MC, V* ⏲ *Closed Sun. No lunch Sat.*

$$ ✕ **Packrat Louie Kitchen & Bar.** In a historic brick building in the heart of Old Strathcona, this popular Swiss bistro with French, German, and Italian influences serves fresh market cuisine in an open, friendly environment. Favorite dishes include roast pork rib eye topped with blueberry pepper sauce and served with potato gnocchi, and wood-oven-roasted lemon pizza with Edam and mozzarella cheeses. The homemade chocolates and desserts are sensational. Reservations are recommended. ✉ *10335 83 Ave., Old Strathcona* ☎ *780/433–0123* 🌐 *www.packratlouie.ca* 💳 *AE, MC, V* ⏲ *Closed Sun. and Mon.*

$ ✕ **Blue Plate Diner.** Comfort food with a twist is the specialty at this spacious downtown eatery. Red pepper hummus, tandoori chicken, cheese enchiladas, burgers, and sweet potato fries with spicy mayo are mainstays. The atmosphere is relaxed and casual, with simple wooden tables and chairs and exposed brick walls. The lengthy children's menu makes it a popular dining spot for families. A special brunch menu is served on weekends. ✉ *10145 104 St., Downtown* ☎ *780/429–0740* 🌐 *www.blueplatediner.ca* 💳 *MC, V.*

$ ✕ **Flavours Modern Bistro.** This long, narrow dining room was opened where a pancake house once did business, and it makes use of original hardwood flooring and original brick. The eclectic menu, which changes frequently, is a showcase for Alberta staples. Curried lamb dumplings, panko-crusted venison, and braised bison short ribs are served alongside locally grown vegetables. The menu is divided into small and large plate meals, so it's easy to mix and match. A brunch menu is served on Sunday. ✉ *10354 Whyte Ave., Old Strathcona* ☎ *780/439–9604* 💳 *MC, V.*

¢–$ ★ ✕ **Block 1912.** This delightful European-style café is on the bottom floor of a landmark building in the historic Old Strathcona neighborhood. Home-style dishes such as hot blueberry scones, fruit-filled pastries, soups, noodle salads, and grilled sandwiches are specialties. The chicken curry is excellent and the selection of gelati is extensive. There's an impressive selection of organic coffees along with international beer and wine sold by the glass. A collection of Sunday newspapers from around the globe is an added bonus. ✉ *10361 Whyte Ave./82 Ave., Old Strathcona* ☎ *780/433–6575* ▭ *AE, MC, V.*

WHERE TO STAY

$$$$ **Westin Edmonton.** In the heart of downtown and the Arts District sits one of Edmonton's finest hotels. Trees and plants fill the luxurious, comfortable atrium lobby, and bright colors and attractive artwork decorate the spacious rooms. The experienced staff speaks a total of 29 languages. The Pradera Café has excellent food. The Westin is connected to the light rail transit system, downtown theaters, art galleries, shopping, and restaurants via the Pedway system of walkways. For a small extra charge you can rent a room with a treadmill or elliptical trainer. ✉ *10135 100 St., Downtown, T5J 0N7* ☎ *780/426–3636 or 800/937–8461* 🌐 *www.westin.com* *416 rooms, 20 suites* *In-room: ethernet, Wi-Fi. In-hotel: restaurant, room service, bar, pool, spa, public Wi-Fi, parking (fee), some pets allowed, no-smoking rooms* ▭ *AE, DC, MC, V.*

$$$–$$$$ ★ **Fantasyland Hotel at West Edmonton Mall.** A component of the West Edmonton Mall, this deluxe hotel is one of the most unique accommodations in Canada. The hotel contains standard and executive rooms as well as 120 theme rooms. Choose from 12 different themes including Igloo, Western, and Polynesian. All theme rooms have Jacuzzi baths and some have catamaran beds and waterfalls. Add-on packages can save you money on attractions at West Edmonton Mall. ✉ *17700 87 Ave., West Edmonton, T5T 4V4* ☎ *780/444–3000 or 800/737–3783* 🌐 *www.fantasylandhotel.com* *355 rooms, 120 theme rooms* *In room: refrigerator, ethernet, Wi-Fi. In-hotel: 2 restaurants, bar, parking (no fee)* ▭ *AE, DC, MC, V.*

$$$ ★ **Fairmont Hotel Macdonald.** The city's landmark 1915 hotel has maintained its original grandeur and offers first-class modern facilities in both the traditionally furnished guest rooms and the ornate public areas. The Queen Elizabeth II Suite, in the former attic, is spectacular. There's fine dining in the elegant Harvest Room and Sunday brunch in the Empire Ballroom. Some rooms have a sweeping view of the river valley. ✉ *10065 100 St., Downtown, T5J 0N6* ☎ *780/424–5181 or 800/441–1414* 📠 *780/424–8017* 🌐 *www.hotelmacdonald.com* *199 rooms, 16 suites* *In-room: ethernet. In-hotel: restaurant, bar, pool, gym, spa, laundry service, parking (fee), no-smoking rooms, some pets allowed, public Internet* ▭ *AE, D, DC, MC, V.*

$$$ ★ **Union Bank Inn.** A 1911 bank building in the center of downtown now houses an upscale boutique hotel. Showcasing some of Edmonton's finest interior designers, individually decorated rooms range in style from French country to European modern. All rooms have goose-down duvets and fireplaces. Rates include a full breakfast at Maddison's Grill

and evening wine, cheese, and cookies delivered to your room. Fine dining is available throughout the day and evening in the hotel dining room, Maddison's Grill, which is consistently rated as one of the better restaurants in the city. ✉*10053 Jasper Ave., Downtown, T5J 1S5* ☎*780/423–3600 or 888/423–3601* 🌐*www.unionbankinn.com* *34 rooms* *In-room: ethernet. In-hotel: restaurant, gym, parking (no fee)* *AE, DC, MC, V* *BP.*

$$ **Hilton Garden Inn.** Three minutes from West Edmonton Mall and 15 minutes from downtown Edmonton, this hotel has a relaxed atmosphere and light, spacious guestrooms with many well-planned amenities. Rooms have one king- or two queen-size beds as well as microwaves and refrigerators. ✉*17610 Stony Plain Rd., West Edmonton, T5S 1A2* ☎*780/443–2233 or 877/782–9444* 🌐*www.hiltongardeninn.com* *160 rooms, 5 suites* *In-room: refrigerator, ethernet, Wi-Fi. In-hotel: restaurant, room service, pool, public Wi-Fi* *AE, DC, MC, V* *EP.*

$$ **Metterra Hotel on Whyte.** Its excellent location in the Old Strathcona district puts this boutique hotel within walking distance of Edmonton's most interesting shops, bars, and restaurants. The lobby is sleek and modern, and the rooms are comfortable and spacious. There are complimentary wine and cheese in the evenings. The business center and fitness center are both open around the clock. Be sure to give the valet extra time to collect your car when leaving, as the parking lot is several blocks away. ✉*10454 82 Ave., Old Strathcona, T6E 4Z7* ☎*780/465–8150 or 866/465–8150* 🌐*www.metterra.com* *98 rooms, 5 suites* *In-room: ethernet, Wi-Fi. In-hotel: restaurant, room service, bar, public Wi-Fi, some pets allowed (fee), parking (no fee), no-smoking rooms* *AE, DC, MC, V* *CP.*

¢–$ **Lister Centre.** From May to August, 1,800 dorm rooms at the University of Alberta can be rented on a nightly, weekly, or monthly bais. All very basic, some rooms are private and some are meant to be shared. Throughout the rest of the year you can book a hotel-style room at Lister Centre. These rooms are clean and comfortable and include Continental breakfast. Guests staying here can dine in the on-site cafeteria. ✉*8208 106 St., University, T6G 2H6* ☎*780/492–6056* 🌐*www.uofaweb.ualberta.ca/conferenceservices* *1,800 dorm rooms, 20 hotel rooms* *In-room: Wi-Fi. In-hotel: restaurant, no-smoking rooms* *MC, V* *CP.*

NIGHTLIFE & THE ARTS

Tickets for special events and concerts are available from **Ticketmaster** (☎*780/451–8000* 🌐*www.ticketmaster.ca*), which has various locations. **Tix on the Square** (☎*780/420–1757*), across from the Winspear Theatre in Sir Winston Churchill Square, is run by an arts organization and sells theater and music tickets. To find out what's on, log on to 🌐*www.tixonthesquare.ca.*

★ One huge event that encompasses music, shows, and special events is the 10-day **Capital EX** (☎*780/471–7210 or 888/800–7275* 🌐*www.capitalex.ca*) held in late July. The festivities celebrate the prosperity that the Yukon gold rush brought the city, which was a supply route and stopping point for miners.

THE ARTS

Fodor'sChoice ★ In August, Old Strathcona hosts the 11-day **Fringe Theatre Festival** (☎*780/448–9000* ⊕*www.fringetheatreadventures.ca*), the largest fringe festival in North America (second in size only to the Edinburgh Fringe Festival) showcasing alternative theater, dance, and music.

FILM The **Edmonton Film Society** screens eight classic movies per three-month season on Monday evening at a theater in the **Royal Alberta Museum** (✉*12845 102 Ave., West Edmonton* ☎*780/453–9100*). **Metro Cinema** (✉*Zeidler Hall, Citadel Theatre, 9828 101A Ave., Arts District* ☎*780/425–9212*) presents local, alternative, and international films and videos Thursday through Sunday. The **Princess Theatre** (✉*10337 Whyte Ave., Old Strathcona* ☎*780/433–0728*), an old-time movie house in Old Strathcona, shows revivals, experiments, and foreign films.

MUSIC & DANCE The **Brian Webb Dance Company** (☎*780/497–4416* ⊕*www.bwdc.ca*) presents an annual season of contemporary dance at the **John L. Haar Theatre** (✉*10045 156 St., West Edmonton*). The **Edmonton Symphony Orchestra** (☎*780/428–1414* ⊕*www.winspearcentre.com*) performs in the Francis Winspear Centre for Music on Sir Winston Churchill Square. The **Northern Alberta Jubilee Auditorium** (✉*87 Ave. and 114 St., University District* ☎*780/427–2760* ⊕*www.jubileeauditorium.com/northern*), at the University of Alberta, hosts the **Edmonton Opera** (☎*780/424–4040* ⊕*www.edmontonopera.com*) and the **Alberta Ballet Company** (☎*780/428–6839* ⊕*www.albertaballet.com*).

THEATER ★ Edmonton has 13 professional theater companies. The paramount facility is the glass-clad downtown **Citadel Theatre complex** (✉*9828 101A Ave., Arts District* ☎*780/425–1820* ⊕*www.citadeltheatre.com*), where five theaters present a mix of contemporary works and classics. **Northern Light Theatre** (☎*780/471–1586* ⊕*www.northernlighttheatre.com*) stages avant-garde productions at the Third Space Theatre near the Northern Alberta Institute of Technology (NAIT).

NIGHTLIFE

BARS & CLUBS **Ceili's Irish Pub & Restaurant** (✉*2940 Calgary Trail NW, Calgary Trail* ☎*780/430–4567*) serves up a large variety of beers by the glass; complete breakfast, lunch, and dinner menus; and live entertainment in a friendly pub atmosphere. Cocktail bars are the rage, and **Devlin's** (✉*10507 82 Ave., Old Strathcona* ☎*780/437–7489*) has 30 innovative hand-shaken cocktails on the menu. **O'Byrne's Irish Pub** (✉*10616 82 Ave., Old Strathcona* ☎*780/414–6766*) is a great place to grab a couple of pints and hang out with friends or watch the action on Whyte Avenue. **Sapphire** (✉*10416 82 Ave., Old Strathcona* ☎*780/437–0231*) is a martini bar that caters to a young, hip crowd who want to see and be seen.

MUSIC **Cook County Saloon** (✉*8010 103 St., Old Strathcona* ☎*780/432–2665*) repeatedly has been named Canada's best country club by the Cana-

6

dian Country Music Association. **Cowboy's Country Saloon** (⊠*10102 180 St., West Edmonton* ☎*780/481–8739*) holds 1,200 people in the bar and dance hall and plays Top 40 country, dance, and rock Wednesday through Saturday. **Yardbird Suite** (⊠*10203 86 Ave., Old Strathcona* ☎*780/432–0428*) is Edmonton's premier jazz showcase.

SPORTS & THE OUTDOORS

AUTO RACING

Auto Racing is revving its engines with the recent addition of Edmonton to the circuit. The Grand Prix of Edmonton, part of the Champ Car World Series, is a top drawing card. In its inaugural year in 2005, Edmonton set the attendance record with 200,052 spectators. **Castrol Raceway** (⊠*Rte. 19, 2 km [1 mi] west of Hwy. 2 S, on way to Devon* ☎*780/461–5801* 🌐*www.castrolraceway.com*), a multiuse motor-sports complex, has events most weekends from May through October.

BIKING & JOGGING

The North Saskatchewan River valley is a lush park system with 97 km (60 mi) of cycling, jogging, and cross-country ski trails. The **River Valley Centre** (⊠*11240 79 St., River Valley Parkland* ☎*780/496–7275 or 780/496–4999*) can provide information about park activities.

FOOTBALL

From June through November, the Canadian Football League's **Edmonton Eskimos** team plays at **Commonwealth Stadium** (⊠*9022 111 Ave., Northeast Edmonton* ☎*780/448–3757 or 780/448–1525* 🌐*www.esks.com*).

GOLF

More than 70 golf courses are within an hour's drive of the city center. **Victoria Golf Course** (⊠*12130 River Rd., University District* ☎*780/496–4900*) is the oldest municipal golf course in Canada. The par-71, 6,027-yard, 18-hole course is centrally located in the river valley parkland and offers unique views of the Alberta Legislature and the University of Alberta. Green fees are C$22–C$41.

HOCKEY

The **Edmonton Oilers** (⊠*118 Ave. and 74 St., Northeast Edmonton* ☎*780/414–4625* 🌐*oilers.nhl.com*) of the National Hockey League meet their opponents October through April.

New on the scene is a team called the **Edmonton Oil Kings** (☎*780/409–3700* 🌐*www.oilkings.ca*).

HORSE RACING

Northlands Park Spectrum (⊠*116 Ave. and 74 St., Northeast Edmonton* ☎*780/471–7379* 🌐*www.thehorsesatnorthlands.com*) hosts harness racing from early March to mid-June. The Thoroughbred racing season runs from mid-June through October.

SHOPPING

The core of downtown, between 100 and 103 streets, holds a complex of shopping centers and department stores connected by tunnels or second-level walkways. **Commerce Place** (✉ *102 St., Downtown*) is a smaller shopping center with 16 of the city's finest designer shops, such as Plaza Escada for women's fashions, Sam Abouhassan for men, and Diamori for fine jewelry and Rolex watches. **Edmonton City Centre** (✉ *100 St., Downtown*) is the largest downtown shopping center with more than 160 stores and services on four levels and anchor stores like the Bay, Winners, HBC Home Outfitters, and Eddie Bauer. **ManuLife Place** (✉ *102 Ave., Downtown*) has 22 stores and three restaurants and has fashion favorites like Holt Renfrew, Blu's Women's Wear, Birks, and Night Owl Imports.

The area along 124 and 125 streets between Jasper and 109 avenues is full of boutiques, bistros, bookstores, and galleries. There are more than 125 shops, including unique antiques and specialty boutiques, sporting goods stores, furniture design workshops, and a number of art galleries. With its fine restaurants, live theater, specialty shops, and galleries, 124 Street is a must-see. **Old Strathcona Historic Area,** the area surrounding 104 Street and Whyte Avenue on the south side of the river, is a bustling area where you will find locally produced arts and crafts, unique fashions and accessories, interesting antiques, and unusual collectibles. The Saturday farmer's market features local produce.

South Edmonton Common (✉ *23 Ave. and Calgary Trail, South Edmonton*) is a large shopping area that includes stores like Pier 1 Imports, Wal-Mart, Michaels, Indigo Books, Golf Town, and the Brick.

West Edmonton Mall (✉ *8882 170 St., West Edmonton* ☎ *780/444–5200 or 800/661–8890* 🌐 *www.westedmall.com*) is one of the world's largest shopping centers with more than 800 stores and services in 5.3 million square feet of space. The Bay, Club Monaco, Eddie Bauer, Banana Republic, Benetton, Champs, Foot Locker, Guess, Helly Hansen, Gap, Mandarin Duck, H&M, and Roots Canada are but a few of the choices. Outside of shopping, the slew of options includes movie theaters, more than 100 places to eat, an amusement park with a roller coaster, billiards, a bowling center, an ice-skating rink, and an indoor water park and wave pool.

The **Alberta Craft Council** (✉ *10186 106 St., Downtown* ☎ *780/488–5900*) has distinctive Alberta-made items, including pottery and furniture. **The Artworks** (☎ *780/420–6311*), a gift store in Edmonton Centre, has a nice merchandise mix that includes flowers, designer jewelry, and interesting cards.

SIDE TRIPS FROM EDMONTON

Within easy driving distance of Edmonton are beautiful natural areas, national and provincial parks, low-key prairie towns, and historic sites. Several sights near Edmonton relate to Alberta's Ukrainian heritage, and festivals throughout summer celebrate this rich cultural history.

If you travel south, you can ride an authentic steam train or visit a museum that celebrates the history of innovation in Alberta.

The **Reynolds-Alberta Museum** celebrates "the spirit of the machine" in a unique interactive museum of mechanization. Thousands of artifacts and Canada's Aviation Hall of Fame are also on-site. ✉ *89 km (55 mi) SE of Edmonton, 2 km W of Wetaskiwin on Hwy. 13, Box 6360, Wetaskiwin T9A 2G1* ☎ *780/361–1351* 🌐 *www.reynoldsalbertamuseum.com* 🎫 *C$9* ⏲ *Mid-May–June, daily 10–5; July and Aug., daily 10–6; Sept.–mid-May, Tues.–Sun. 10–5.*

Alberta Prairie Railway Excursions, in Stettler, is a bit out of the way, but worth the journey. Ride a vintage train to a small Alberta village and enjoy a buffet supper or participate in a murder mystery dinner on the train. Various excursions are available. Be sure to keep an eye out for train robbers, because the Bolton Gang frequent this part of central Alberta. ✉ *Located in Stettler, 178 km (110 mi) SE of Edmonton, Box 1600, Stettler T0C 2L0* ☎ *403/742–2811, 800/282–3994 in Canada* 🌐 *www.absteamtrain.com* 🎫 *C$65–C$135* ⏲ *Mar.–Oct. and Dec., days and hrs vary, call for schedule.*

ELK ISLAND NATIONAL PARK

★ *48 km (30 mi) east of Edmonton.*

Elk Island was established in 1906 as Canada's first federal wildlife sanctuary. A herd of 600 plains and 350 wood bison roams the park's 194 square km (75 square mi), as do elk, moose, white-tailed deer, and more than 230 species of birds, including herons. The park has more than 90 km (56 mi) of hiking and cross-country-skiing trails, 80 campsites, picnic areas, a 9-hole golf course, and several lakes ideal for canoeing. ✉ *Hwy. 16* ☎ *780/992–2950* 🌐 *www.parcscanada.gc.ca/elk* 🎫 *General entry: C$6.90 May–Oct., C$3.50 Nov.–Apr.*

UKRAINIAN CULTURAL HERITAGE VILLAGE

Fodor's Choice ★ *3 km (2 mi) east of Elk Island National Park, 50 km (31 mi) east of Edmonton.*

The village consists of 34 historic buildings, gathered from around east-central Alberta, which have been assembled in three theme areas to illustrate the culture and lifestyle of pre-1930s Ukrainian settlers. Guides in period dress interpret the displays: the Railway Townsite, Rural Community, and Farmstead. ✉ *Hwy. 16* ☎ *780/662–3640* 🌐 *www.cd.gov.ab.ca/uchv* 🎫 *C$8* ⏲ *May 15–early Sept., daily 10–6; early Sept.–mid-Oct., weekends 10–6.*

The annual **Ukrainian Pysanka Festival** (☎ *780/632–2771* 🌐 *www.vegrevillefestival.ca* 🎫 *C$50*) takes place the first weekend in July in nearby Vegreville, 50 km (31 mi) east of the Ukrainian Cultural Heritage Village. The three-day festival has music, dance, displays, parades, and Ukrainian food. Stop and see the "world's largest Easter egg" (*pysanka*), measuring 31 feet tall, at the east end of the town's main street. The colorfully decorated egg consists of more than 3,500 pieces of aluminum.

EDMONTON ESSENTIALS

TRANSPORTATION

BY AIR

Alaska, Delta, Horizon, Northwest, and United, along with the major Canadian airlines (Air Canada, Air Transat and WestJet), serve Edmonton.

> **WORD OF MOUTH**
>
> "The Ukranian village near Androssen is most interesting, at least it was to me and my wife. We spent a delightful and interesting day there touring the exhibits, the building, tasting the food, and listening to music played by various groups." —bob_brown

AIRPORTS & TRANSFERS Edmonton International Airport, which includes a U.S. Customs preclearance facility, is 29 km (17 mi) south of downtown.

Taxi rides from Edmonton International cost approximately C$30 to South Edmonton Common, C$40 to the downtown city center, and C$46 to West Edmonton Mall. The Sky Shuttle has frequent service between the airport and major hotels; the fare is C$15 one-way, C$25 round-trip.

Information **Edmonton International Airport** (✉ *Hwy. 2, 20 km [12 mi] south of downtown Edmonton, Nisku Industrial Park* ☎ *780/890–8382* 🌐 *www.edmontonairports.com*). **Sky Shuttle** (☎ *780/465–8515* 🌐 *www.edmontontaxiservicegroup.com*).

BY BUS

Greyhound has regular bus service from downtown Edmonton to Jasper, Calgary, Red Deer, and Fort McMurray. Red Arrow has bus service from Edmonton to Red Deer, Calgary, and Fort McMurray.

Information **Greyhound** (☎ *800/661–8747* 🌐 *www.greyhound.ca*). **Red Arrow** (☎ *800/232–1958* 🌐 *www.redarrow.ca*).

WITHIN EDMONTON Edmonton Transit operates a comprehensive system of buses throughout the area, as well as a light-rail transit system (LRT) from downtown to the northeast side of the city. The fare is C$2.50; transfers are free. Buses operate 5:30 AM–2 AM. The Edmonton Transit Information Centre, at Churchill Station, is open weekdays 8–5:30.

Information **Edmonton Transit** (✉ *102A Ave. and 99 St., Downtown* ☎ *780/496–1611*). **Edmonton Transit Information Centre** (✉ *102A Ave. and 99 St., Downtown*).

BY CAR

Edmonton is on the Trans-Canada Highway (Highway 16), which runs from Winnipeg, Manitoba, through the central parts of Saskatchewan and Alberta. This highway has four lanes and is divided through most of Alberta; it intersects with the four-lane divided Queen Elizabeth 2, which runs south to Calgary.

BY TAXI

Taxi meters start at C$2.80 and charge C$1.25 per 2 km (1 mi) thereafter. Of the companies available, Checker cabs are noted for providing upscale cars with uniformed drivers. Cabs may be hailed on the street, but phoning is recommended.

Information **Alberta Co-op Taxi** (☎ *780/425–8310*). **Checker** (☎ *780/484–8888*). **Yellow** (☎ *780/462–3456*).

CONTACTS & RESOURCES

EMERGENCIES

Royal Alexandra Hospital, Misericordia Hospital, Grey Nuns Community Hospital, and University of Alberta Hospital all have emergency rooms. Denta Care offers 24-hour dental care. Some Shopper's Drug Mart branches are open 24 hours.

Dentists **Denta Care** (✉ *464 Southgate Shopping Centre, 10831 51 Ave., South Edmonton* ☎ *780/434–9566*).

Emergency Services **Ambulance, fire, poison center, police** (☎ *911*).

Hospitals **Grey Nuns Community Hospital** (✉ *3015 62 St., South Edmonton* ☎ *780/450–7000*). **Misericordia Hospital** (✉ *16940 87 Ave., West Edmonton* ☎ *780/930–5611*). **Royal Alexandra Hospital** (✉ *10240 Kingsway Ave., Kingsway* ☎ *780/735–4111*). **University of Alberta Hospitals** (✉ *8440 112 St., University District* ☎ *780/407–8822*).

24-Hour Pharmacies **Shopper's Drug Mart** (✉ *11408 Jasper Ave., Downtown* ☎ *780/482–1171* ✉ *8210 109 St., Old Strathcona* ☎ *780/433–3121*).

TOURS

BOAT TOURS The *Edmonton Queen* paddle-wheeler cruises the North Saskatchewan River from May through September. Some excursions include lunch or dinner. Klondike Jet Boats ply the North Saskatchewan River May through October. Edmonton Canoe offers guided and unguided trips on the North Saskatchewan and Athabasca rivers or on a quiet lake in Elk Island National Park.

Information **Edmonton Canoe** (☎ *888/467–9697* 🌐 *www.edmontoncanoe.com*). *Edmonton Queen* (☎ *780/424–2628* 🌐 *www.edmontonqueen.com*). **Klondike Jet Boats** (☎ *780/486–0896*).

SIGHTSEEING TOURS Ride the Eddie, a step-on, step-off tour bus that runs from June to September around Edmonton's major attractions. If you prefer something more magical, join a guided half- or full-day itinerary with Magic Times Tour & Convention Services. For something truly unique, consider a tour with E-Z Air, an Alberta-based helicopter charter company.

Information **Eddie Bus** (☎ *800/463–4667* 🌐 *www.eddiebus.com*). **EZ Air Helicopter Services** (☎ *780/453–2085* 🌐 *www.e-zair.com*). **Magic Times Tour & Convention Services** (☎ *780/940–7479* 🌐 *www.magictimes.ca*).

VISITOR INFORMATION

Edmonton Tourism operates information centers on the south side of the city and in the downtown area. The downtown center, called World Trade Centre Edmonton, operates an Edmonton Airport's passenger, baggage, and Sky Shuttle facility.

If you're visiting Waterton Lakes National Park, stop on the eastern edge of Waterton Townsite to pick up brochures, maps, and books. Park interpreters are on hand to answer questions and give directions.

Information **Edmonton Tourism Information Centre** (*Gateway Park Branch: ✉ Gateway Park, Hwy. 2, South Edmonton; Downtown Branch: ✉ 9990 Jasper Ave. NW, Downtown ☎ 780/496–8400 or 800/463–4667 🌐 www.edmonton.com*). **Waterton Information Centre** (*✉ Waterton Rd. ☎ 403/859–5133 or 403/859–2224 ⏲ Mid-May mid-June, daily 8–6; mid-June–early Sept., daily 8–8; early Sept.–Oct. 8, daily 9–6*).

REGINA

The centerpiece of this city of nearly 202,000 is Wascana Centre, which was created by expanding meager Wascana Creek into the broad Wascana Lake and surrounding it with 2,000 acres of urban parkland. This unique multipurpose site contains the city's major museums, the Saskatchewan provincial legislature, the University of Regina campus, and all the amenities of a big-city park and natural-habitat waterfowl sanctuary.

Regina, Saskatchewan, was originally dubbed Pile O'Bones in reference to the remnants left by hundreds of years of buffalo hunting by native peoples and later European hunters. The city was renamed after the Latin title of Queen Victoria, the reigning monarch in 1883. It was at this time that the railroad arrived and the city became the capital of the Northwest Territories. The Mounties made it their headquarters as they brought peace and stability to the region. When the Province of Saskatchewan was formed in 1905, Regina was chosen as its capital. At the beginning of the 20th century, immigrants from the British Isles, Eastern Europe, and East Asia rushed in to claim parcels of river-fed prairie land for C$1 per lot. Oil and potash were discovered in the 1950s and 1960s, and Regina became a major agricultural and industrial distribution center as well as the head office of the world's largest grain-handling cooperative.

EXPLORING REGINA

Downtown Regina is lively with its boutiques, large mall, and festivals that span all seasons. Just northeast of Downtown is the Old Warehouse District, which has several bars, lounges, and live music venues. Shopping enthusiasts love the locally owned shops in the Cathedral District, southwest of Downtown. The longest urban park in North America and the Saskatchewan Legislature are in Wascana Centre, south of Downtown. Two of the fastest-growing areas of the city are the East End, home to trendy restaurants and several big-box retailers, and North West Regina. South Regina has good shopping and the University of Regina.

Streets in Regina run north–south, avenues east–west. The most important north–south artery is Albert Street (Route 6); Victoria Avenue is the main east–west thoroughfare. The Trans-Canada Highway (Highway 1) bypasses the city to the south and east.

WHAT TO SEE

Casino Regina. The grandeur of a former train station built in 1912 now backdrops Saskatchewan's largest casino, with nearly 800 slot machines and 35 table games including blackjack, baccarat, roulette, Caribbean stud poker, and craps. The private poker room has one-of-a-kind stained-glass windows and hand-carved woodwork. Casual meals, noshes, and drinks are available in the Last Spike restaurant. The attached Show Lounge has live entertainment, ranging from musicals and comedians to classic rock and pop acts. ✉ *1880 Saskatchewan Dr., Downtown* ☎ *306/565–3000 or 800/555–3189* 🌐 *www.casinoregina.com* ⏲ *Daily 9 AM–4 AM.*

6 **Government House Museum and Heritage Property.** Built in 1891, this was the lavish home of Saskatchewan's lieutenant governors until 1945. It now serves as the office of the lieutenant governor and has been restored with period furnishings and mementos of its past residents. Six acres of landscaped grounds include rose and herb gardens. In 2005 Canada's reigning monarch officially opened the "Queen Elizabeth II Wing." The addition includes an interpretive center with interactive multimedia presentations. Tours leave on the half hour. ✉ *4607 Dewdney Ave., Windsor Place* ☎ *306/787–5773* 🌐 *www.gr.gov.sk.ca/govhouse* 🎫 *Free* ⏲ *Tues.–Sun. 10–4.*

2 **Legislative Building.** The dome of this quasi-Versailles–style structure dominates the skyline of the provincial capital. The "Leg" was completed in 1912, with Tyndall stone from Manitoba on the exterior and 34 types of marble from around the world inside. Check out the spectacular rotunda with its three-story-high marble columns, as well as the life-size bronze of Queen Elizabeth II on her favorite horse, Burmese, in the gardens just north of the building. Tours leave on the half hour. ✉ *2405 Legislature Dr., Wascana Centre* ☎ *306/787–5358* 🎫 *Free* ⏲ *Mid-May–Labor Day, daily 8 AM–9 PM; Labor Day–mid-May, daily 8–5.*

3 **MacKenzie Art Gallery.** Named for Norman MacKenzie, an early art collector in western Canada, this museum is known for its research and collections of Saskatchewan art. Exhibits also include 19th- and 20th-century European art and Canadian historical and contemporary works. The diversity of exhibits and free family-friendly programs on Sunday are a big draw, as is the location of the gallery within Wascana Centre. Events such as artists' talks, films, concerts, theater, and other performances are held regularly—call for the current schedule. ✉ *3475 Albert St., Wascana Centre* ☎ *306/584–4250* 🌐 *www.mackenzieartgallery.ca* 🎫 *Free* ⏲ *Mon.–Wed, Sat. 10–5:30, Thurs. and Fri. 10–9, Sun. 11–5:30.*

7 ★ **Royal Canadian Mounted Police Heritage Centre.** Opened in May 2007, this center tells the story of the Royal Canadian Mounted Police (originally the North West Mounted Police). The order's proud history is revealed in exhibits displaying weaponry, uniforms, and photos. The March of

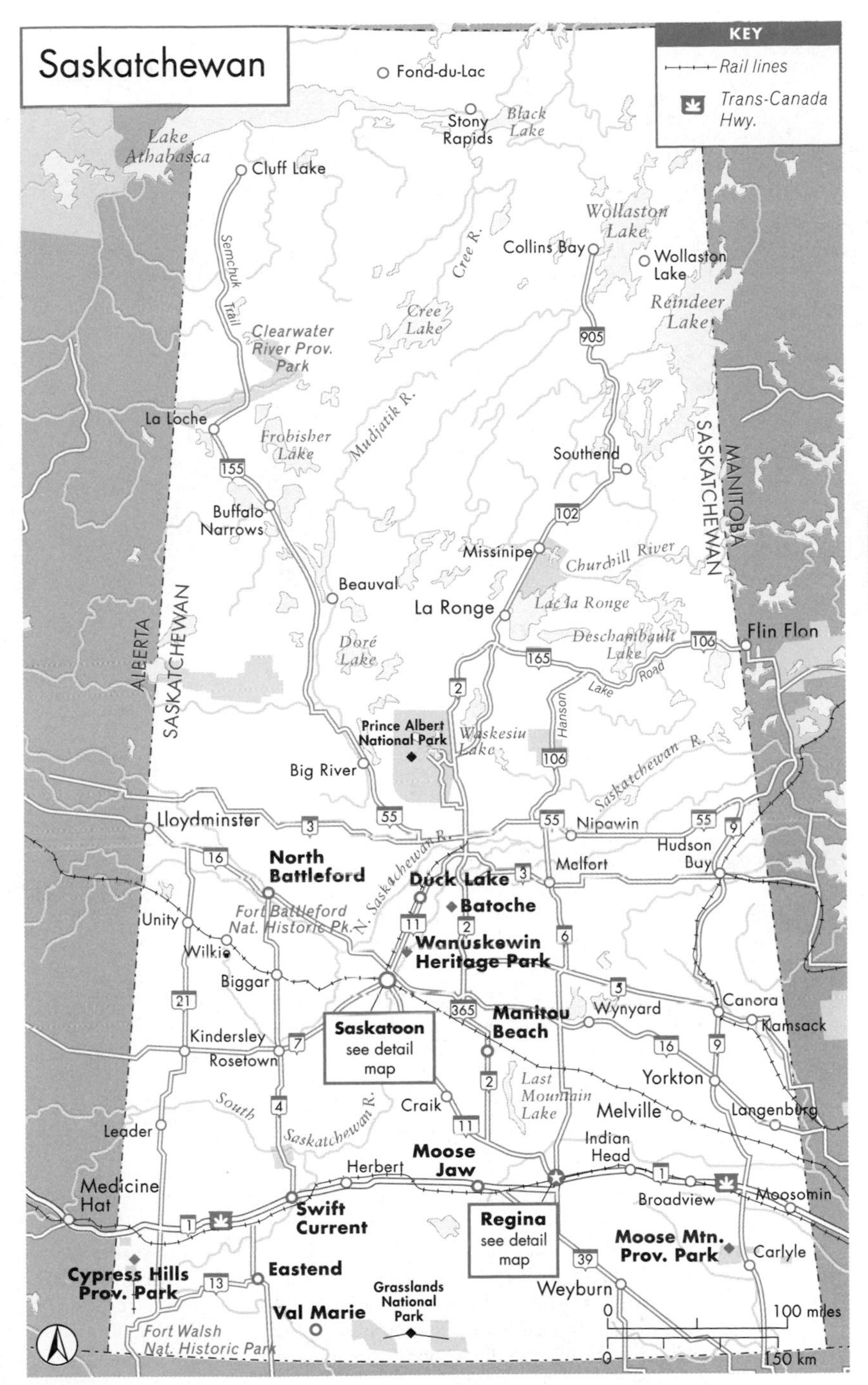
Saskatchewan
KEY
Rail lines
Trans-Canada Hwy.
Fond-du-Lac
Stony Rapids
Black Lake
Lake Athabasca
Cluff Lake
Semchuk Trail
Cree R.
Wollaston Lake
Collins Bay
Wollaston Lake
Reindeer Lake
Cree Lake
Clearwater River Prov. Park
905
Mudjatik R.
La Loche
Frobisher Lake
Southend
155
Buffalo Narrows
102
Missinipe
Churchill River
Beauval
La Ronge
Lac la Ronge
Deschambault Lake
106
Flin Flon
Doré Lake
165
Lake Road
Hanson
2
Prince Albert National Park
Waskesiu Lake
106
Big River
Saskatchewan R.
55
Lloydminster
3
55
Nipawin
55
9
Hudson Bay
N. Saskatchewan R.
16
North Battleford
Duck Lake
3
Malfort
Batoche
Unity
Fort Battleford Nat. Historic Pk.
11
2
6
Wilkie
Wanuskewin Heritage Park
Biggar
3
Canora
21
365
Manitou Beach
Wynyard
Kamsack
Kindersley
7
Saskatoon
see detail map
16
9
Rosetown
Yorkton
South Saskatchewan R.
4
Craik
2
Last Mountain Lake
Melville
Langenburg
Leader
11
Indian Head
Moose Jaw
Herbert
1
Medicine Hat
Broadview
Moosomin
1
Swift Current
Regina
see detail map
Moose Mtn. Prov. Park
Carlyle
39
Cypress Hills Prov. Park
13
Eastend
Weyburn
Grasslands National Park
Val Marie
0
100 miles
Fort Walsh Nat. Historic Park
0
150 km
ALBERTA
SASKATCHEWAN
SASKATCHEWAN
MANITOBA
6

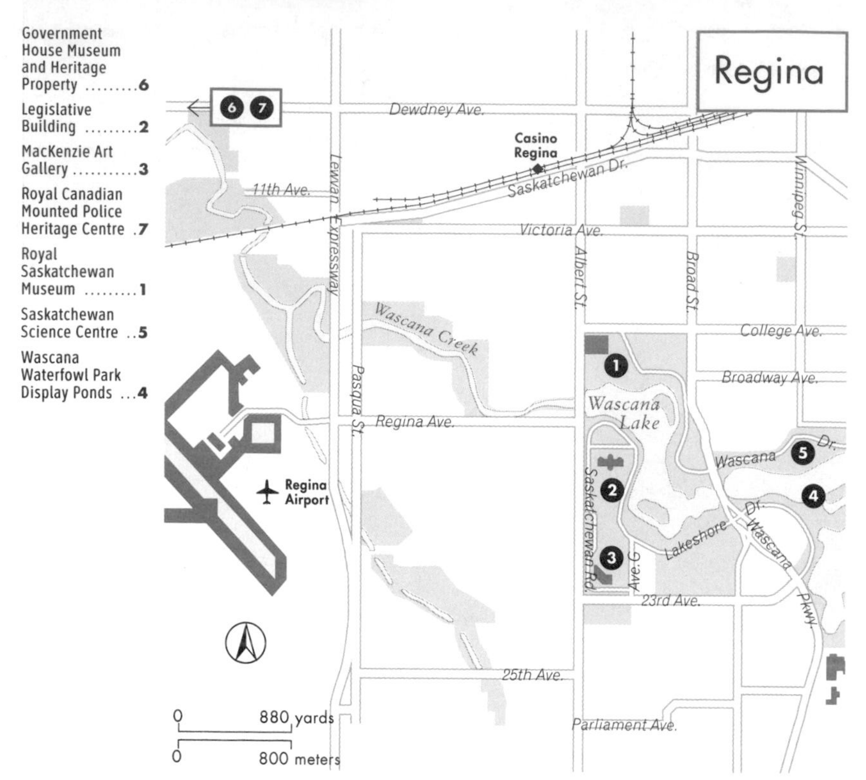

the Mounties, a 30-meter-long display, fills the main hall. A gift shop and food concession round out the offerings. ✉ *5907 Dewdney Ave., Windsor Place* ☎ *800/567–7267* 🌐 *www.rcmpheritagecentre.com* 🎟 *C$12* ⏲ *Tues.–Sun. 10–4:30.*

❶ **Royal Saskatchewan Museum.** At this museum a timeline traces local history from before the dinosaur era to today. The Earth Sciences Gallery depicts 3 billion years of Saskatchewan geological history, and the First Nations Gallery highlights aspects of the life and history of Saskatchewan's native peoples. The Life Sciences Gallery shows the natural history of the province's ecosystems and the impact of humans on them. Kids like the robotized dinosaur, Megamunch, and the Fossil Research Station. ✉ *2445 College Ave. and Albert St., Wascana Centre* ☎ *306/787–2815* 🌐 *www.royalsaskmuseum.ca* 🎟 *C$2* ⏲ *May–Labor Day, daily 9–5:30; rest of yr, daily 9–4:30.*

❺ **Saskatchewan Science Centre.** Housed in the refurbished City of Regina powerhouse, this museum has more than 150 hands-on exhibits and a 60-foot climbing wall, one of the tallest in Canada. Demonstrations of biological, geological, and astronomical phenomena begin on the hour. The permanent exhibit, the Science of Hockey, allows you to test your reaction times and also take slapshots at a virtual goalie. The Kramer IMAX Theatre shows educational films and popular movies on a five-story screen. ✉2903 Powerhouse Dr., Wascana Centre ☎306/522–4629 or 800/667–6300 🌐www.sasksciencecentre.com 🎫C$7, C$12 with IMAX ⏲Mid-May–Labor Day, weekdays 9–6, weekends 10–6; Labor Day–mid-May, hrs vary, call ahead.

4 **Wascana Waterfowl Park Display Ponds.** More than 60 breeds of migratory waterfowl, including geese, swans, and pelicans, thrive at this 640-acre park. Several rare bird species, such as the Arctic loon, black scoter, brant, and Virginia rail, have been observed. Muskrat, mink, jackrabbit, Richardson's ground squirrel, and red fox are also on the grounds. The display ponds feature pinioned geese, swans, and ducks, which roam freely. You can book guided tours of the ponds and adjacent marsh area, which is waterfowl habitat, between 9 and 3, from late May through September. ✉2900 Wascana Dr., Wascana Centre ☎306/522–3661 🌐www.wascana.sk.ca 🎫Free ⏲Daily 9–9.

WHERE TO EAT

$$$ ✕**The Diplomat.** This plain brick building belies its rich oak and burgundy interior, where paintings of Canada's prime ministers adorn the walls. This longstanding and upscale traditional steak house draws business clients and family gatherings alike. It boasts the largest wine collection in Saskatchewan, and extensive offerings of seafood, steaks, and game. Popular entrées include steak with peppercorn sauce, and the rack of lamb encrusted with Greek spices. ✉2032 Broad St., Downtown ☎306/359–3366 🌐www.thediplomatsteakhouse.com 💳AE, D, MC, V.

$$–$$$ ✕**Copper Kettle.** This downtown institution started out some 40 years ago as a simple lunch counter in a drugstore. Today it's packed with office workers who come for the gyros and other Greek items. In warmer months anyone who wants to watch the world go by can snag a spot on the sidewalk patio. If you're looking to sample the best slice in a city known as Canada's pizza capital, try the restaurant's renowned spinach-feta combo. ✉1953 Scarth St., Downtown ☎306/525–3545 💳AE, DC, MC, V.

$$ ✕**Brewsters Brewing Company and Restaurant.** At this full-mash brewery, the fermentation tanks operate right on the premises, so you can find 10 to 12 in-house concoctions on tap. They also offer a large selection of imported and domestic beers, wine, and spirits. The brew even makes it on the menu in dishes such as the house garlic bread made with spent barley. Fare is mostly casual: burgers, wraps, and thin crust pizzas. Some posher options include steelhead trout and steaks. ✉Victoria East Plaza, 1832 Victoria Ave. E (tavern only, must be 19 or older), Glencairn ☎306/761–1500 ✉480 McCarthy Blvd. N, Normanview ☎306/522–2739 ✉4180 Albert St., Parliament Place ☎306/757–2739 💳AE, MC, V.

$$ ✕**Creek in Cathedral Bistro.** Contemporary cuisine and fresh ingredients bring clients back to this charming, intimate bistro. Choose from Kowloon wonton soup (a holdover from when the building housed a popular Chinese restaurant) or modern comfort food such as pork tenderloin stuffed with apricots, or halibut cheeks. Sweet endnotes include

lemon curd tarts, classic crème brûlée, and gingerbread (the owner's grandmother's recipe). On summer evenings, the vine-hidden patio is the place to be. *☒3414 13 Ave., Cathedral District ☎306/352–4448 ▭AE, DC, MC, V.*

$$ ✕**Mediterranean Bistro.** A professional, well-heeled crowd comes to this highly regarded restaurant for executive chef Sandra Watson's fresh seafood, which can include the likes of Hawaiian tuna, marlin, or shark. The international cuisine changes daily, and include monthly world tour specialty menus. The striking color scheme of navy and warm yellows offsets local artists' wares. *☒2589 Quance St. E, River Bend East ☎306/757–1666 ✍Reservations essential ⊕www.medbistro.ca ▭AE, DC, MC, V.*

$$ ✕**Michi Japanese Restaurant.** Kimonoed wait staff, a sushi bar, and blond wood tatami rooms deliver authentic Japanese ambience to this restaurant. Experienced Japanese chefs prepare traditional favorites, as well as more experimental sushi combinations. Noodles and combo meals are a good deal. The dining room is a tad busy and noisy at lunch due to its popularity, but the fare is well worth the wait. The restaurant is highly regarded as authentic and popular with foodies. *☒1943 Scarth St., Downtown ☎306/565–0141 ▭AE, MC, V.*

¢ ✕**The 13th Avenue Coffee House.** Primarily vegetarian, this café draws more than local denizens. The older house has local photography on the walls, and a terrific street corner patio. The morning glory muffins, moist with raisins, cranberries, and pumpkin seeds, sell out fast. Try the rice bowls—brown rice topped with marinated tofu or seasoned chickpeas and loads of fresh veggies. The coffee is organic and fair trade; vegan desserts are available. *☒3136 13th Ave., Cathedral District ☎306/522–3111 ✍Reservations not accepted ▭No credit cards ⊗Closed Sun.*

WHERE TO STAY

$$–$$$ **Delta Regina Hotel.** The tallest building in Saskatchewan, this hotel rises 25 stories and is attached to the Saskatchewan Trade and Convention Centre as well as the Casino Regina. Rooms have calming neutral and earth tones and work desks. The indoor pool has a three-story water slide. *☒1919 Saskatchewan Dr., Downtown, S4P 4H2 ☎306/525–5255 or 888/890–3222 ⊕www.deltahotels.com ⇨251 rooms, 23 suites ♿In-room: ethernet, dial-up. In-hotel: restaurant, bar, pool, gym, public Internet, Wi-Fi, no-smoking rooms ▭AE, DC, MC, V.*

$$ **Radisson Plaza Hotel Saskatchewan.** This former railroad hotel built in 1927 has old-time charm and up-to-date facilities that make it the city's most luxurious lodging. High-ceiling rooms are decorated in grand Victorian style; no two rooms exactly alike. For a light lunch or evening cocktails you can visit the cozy and casually elegant Monarch Lounge; the Cortlandt Hall Dining Room offers superb formal dining in the evenings. *☒2125 Victoria Ave., Downtown, S4P 0S3 ☎306/522–7691 or 800/333–3333 ⊕www.hotelsask.com ⇨224 rooms, 26 suites ♿In-room: ethernet, dial-*

up, Wi-Fi. In-hotel: 2 restaurants, bar, gym, spa, laundry service, public Internet, no-smoking rooms ▭*AE, DC, MC, V.*

$$ **Ramada Hotel and Convention Centre.** A sun-filled lobby is enhanced by abundant foliage at this modern downtown property. A second-floor oasis is the perfect setting for a soothing soak in the whirlpool or a dip in the kids' or standard pool. The modern rooms are airy and furnished in autumny brown and neutral tones. Business-class rooms are available on the 14th and 15th floors. ✉*1818 Victoria Ave., Downtown, S4P 0R1* ☎*306/569–1666 or 800/667–6500* 🌐*www.ramada.ca* *232 rooms, 14 suites* *In-room: ethernet (some), dial-up, Wi-Fi. In-hotel: 2 restaurants, room service, bar, pools, laundry facilities, public Internet, no-smoking rooms* ▭*AE, DC, MC, V.*

$–$$ **Regina Inn Hotel and Conference Centre.** The stonework and serpentine lounge (botaniCa and Vic's Lounge) just off the sunny lobby of this modern downtown hotel is a good, quiet spot for drinks. Each guest room has a balcony overlooking the street, and the room amenities get better the higher up you go in the hotel. A steak house and more casual eatery are on-site, as is Applause! Feast & Folly, a popular dinner theater. ✉*1975 Broad St., at Victoria Ave., Downtown, S4P 1Y2* ☎*306/525-6767 or 800/667–8162* 🌐*www.reginainn.com* *230 rooms, 5 suites* *In-room: Wi-Fi. In-hotel: 2 restaurants, bar, gym, public Internet, no-smoking rooms* ▭*AE, DC, MC, V.*

6

$–$$ **Regina Travelodge Hotel.** This hotel's location, on Regina's main thoroughfare and close to shopping and restaurants, is a big draw. So is Aquaworld, an indoor pool and water-slide complex that has a giant 252-foot water slide, Regina's largest. Guest rooms are spacious—each has two queen beds or a king bed—and are finished in perennially favorite autumn tones. Grab a bite at Johnny Fox's Restaurant & Pub, on the main floor. ✉*4177 Albert St. S, Whitmore Park, S4S 3R6* ☎*306/586–3443 or 800/578–7878* 📠*306/586–9311* 🌐*www.travelodgeregina.com* *194 rooms, 6 suites* *In-room: VCR (some), ethernet, dial-up. In-hotel: restaurant, bar, pool, public Internet, no-smoking rooms* ▭*AE, DC, MC, V.*

¢ **Turgeon International Hostel.** Friendly staff and sunny rooms painted light blue make this quiet hostel a good affordable choice. Housed in a grand, former judge's home built in 1909, the hostel has dorm-style and private rooms, a TV room, guest kitchen, library, travel shop, and lockers. Ideally located adjacent to Wascana Park, it's just a hop, skip, and jump to the Downtown and Cathedral neighborhoods. ✉*2310 McIntyre Street, Downtown, S4P 2S2* ☎*306/791–8165 or 800/467–8357* 🌐*www.hihostels.ca* *28 beds* *In-hotel: laundry facilities, no elevator, public Internet, no-smoking rooms* ▭*MC, V* ⊙*Closed Jan.*

NIGHTLIFE & THE ARTS

THE ARTS

MUSIC & DANCE The **Conexus Arts Centre** (✉*200A Lakeshore Dr., Wascana Centre* ☎*306/525–9999*) is the venue for the Regina Symphony Orchestra, pop concerts, dance performances, and Broadway musicals and plays.

THEATER On a theater-in-the-round stage inside the old City Hall, the **Globe Theatre** (✉*1801 Scarth St., Downtown* ☎*306/525–6400*) shows classic and contemporary works from September through May. **Regina Little Theatre** (✉*Regina Performing Arts Centre, 1077 Angus St., Washington Park* ☎*306/779–2277 or 306/352–5535*) presents lighthearted original productions.

NIGHTLIFE

BARS For nightlife, head for the "strip," a stretch of Dewdney Avenue between Albert and Broad streets, in the revived Warehouse District, just north of downtown. **Bushwakker Brewing Company** (✉*2206 Dewdney Ave.* ☎*306/359–7276*) offers regular and specialty brews, as well as seasonal beers, and good pub food—the crowd is all age ranges here. Check out the pressed-tin ceiling, from 1914, and the photos showing the historic development of Regina. Several other popular nightclubs, bars, taverns, and a pool hall make the "strip" a busy after-hours locale.

SoHo at (✉*2300 Dewdney Ave.* ☎*306/359–7772*) is transformed into a club on weekends, with the resident DJs providing the music.

MUSIC Country and rock bands play **JD's Cafe & Nite Spot** (✉*1055 Park St., Rothwell Place* ☎*306/569–2121*), where the casual, party atmosphere draws twentysomethings and the singles crowd, be they welders or marketing types. The **Pump Roadhouse** (✉*641 Victoria Ave. E, Broders Annex* ☎*306/359–7440*) draws large crowds nightly with live Canadian and American rock and roll, country, and contemporary bands. The **Show Lounge** (✉*1880 Saskatchewan Dr., Downtown* ☎*800/555–3189*), in Casino Regina, offers weekly entertainment including tribute bands, hard rock, musicals, magicians, and comedians.

SPORTS & THE OUTDOORS

BIKING & JOGGING

Wascana Place (✉*2900 Wascana Dr., Wascana Centre* ☎*306/522–3661*) has maps of the many jogging, biking, and hiking trails in Wascana Centre. The Devonian Pathway—8 km (5 mi) of paved trails that follow Wascana Creek and pass through six city parks—is a favorite of both athletes and nature lovers. The Devonian Trail is good for walking, rollerblading, or bicycling and is accessible from many different neighborhoods.

CURLING

You can check out this popular local sport played on ice at the **Caledonian Curling Club** (✉*2225 Sandra Schmirler Way, near airport, South West* ☎*306/525–8171*).

FOOTBALL

The **Saskatchewan Roughriders** (☎*306/525–2181*) of the Canadian Football League play at Mosaic Stadium June through November.

HOCKEY

The **Regina Pats** play other Western Hockey League teams in the **Brandt Centre** (*✉IPSCO Pl., Lewvan Expressway and 11th Ave., Windsor Park ☎306/781–9300 or 800/970–7328*) from September through April.

SHOPPING

Cornwall Centre (*✉2102 11th Ave., Downtown*) is an indoor mall with more than 90 shops. It includes the Bay and Sears department stores, as well as restaurants and coffee shops that are frequented by workers from nearby office towers. **Southland Mall** (*✉2965 Gordon Rd., at Albert St., Albert Park*) is a suburban mall with more than 80 stores. A Chapters bookstore is here, as is a movie theater. The burgeoning retail sector lies in East Regina where new minimalls and retailers are opening at an almost breakneck pace. The area is anchored by **Victoria Square Shopping Centre** (*✉2223 Victoria Ave. E, Gardiner Park*), which has more than 50 stores.

Affinity's Antiques (*✉1178 Albert St., Windsor Place ☎306/757–4265*) sells vintage collectibles including china, glassware, silver jewelry, and clocks as well as some toys. The **Antique Mall** (*✉1175 Rose St., Old Warehouse District ☎306/525–9688*) encompasses 40 antiques, art, and collectibles sellers. **Basket Cases** (*✉103–1275 Broad St., Old Warehouse District ☎306/352–3916*) offers custom-made gift baskets and distinctive home furnishings.

The Cathedral District, orbiting 13th Avenue, has eclectic shops selling wares from vintage clothing to handcrafted candles. **Mysteria Gallery** (*✉2706 13th Ave., Cathedral District ☎306/522–0080*) has earthy accessories, jewelry, and an upstairs art gallery. The **Traditions Handcraft Gallery** (*✉2714 13th Ave., Cathedral District ☎306/569–0199*) carries Saskatchewan artisans—including unique items in pottery, glass, and fiber.

SIDE TRIPS FROM REGINA

In the late 1990s ambitious residents in and around Moose Jaw tapped into forgotten local landmarks to create an ambitious tourism-development project. The city's first venture, a destination spa featuring natural, geothermal mineral pools, spawned several attractions, including a casino, refurbished underground tunnels, and trolley car tours. These successes have drawn tourists from near and far. The Western Development Museum, heritage sites, murals, and artwork also bring prairie history to life.

MOOSE JAW

71 km (44 mi) west of Regina.

Saskatchewan's fourth-largest city, Moose Jaw is a prosperous railroad and industrial center, renowned for its role as a haven for American gangsters in the Roaring '20s. It's said that Al Capone visited here when things got too hot in Chicago. The 39 murals on buildings in the downtown business district bring the town's rich history to life. Today Moose Jaw's most prominent citizen stands right on the Trans-Canada Highway: Mac the Moose, an immense sculpture that greets travelers from beside the visitor-information center.

Casino Moose Jaw has more than 200 slot machines and a variety of table games including blackjack and roulette. The casino celebrates Moose Jaw's colorful history with an art deco–inspired look. Even the walls tell a story with 20 indoor and outdoor murals, each chronicling a moment in Moose Jaw's history. ✉ *21 Fairford St. E* ☎ *306/694–3888* 🌐 *www.casinomoosejaw.com* ⏲ *Sun.–Thurs. 9 AM–2 AM, Fri. and Sat. 9 AM–3 AM.*

The **Moose Jaw Cultural Centre** houses the **Mae Wilson Theatre** and the **Conexus Visual Arts Gallery.** Opened as a cinema in 1916, the Mae Wilson Theatre has been charmingly renovated to highlight its original architecture. Local and national theater and dance productions are held here. Exhibits in the Conexus Visual Arts Centre range from painting to ceramics, display the work of local artists. Tours are C$2 Tuesday–Saturday noon–4. ✉ *217 Main St. N* ☎ *306/693–4700* 🌐 *www.moosejawculture.com* ⏲ *Tues.–Fri. 9–6, Sat. 10–4.*

The **Moose Jaw Museum & Art Gallery** displays regional and national art exhibitions, as well as more than 6,000 artifacts tracing Moose Jaw's colorful history. While you're here, pick up *A Walking Tour of Downtown Moose Jaw* (C$2), a guide to notable and notorious landmarks. ✉ *Crescent Park, 461 Langdon Crescent* ☎ *306/692–4471* 🌐 *www.mjmag.ca* 🎟 *Donation suggested* ⏲ *Daily noon–5.*

The **Moose Jaw Trolley Company** runs one-hour guided tours of Moose Jaw, covering historic homes and businesses, interesting facts and legends, and exquisite parkland. The 34-passenger trolley, with its wide-framed oak windows, curved oak seats, and brass handrails, is a replica of the ones that were used here from 1911 to 1932. Tours are offered several times daily between May and October; phone for schedule. ☎ *306/693–8537* 🌐 *www.moosejaw.ca/tourism* 🎟 *C$12.*

The **Temple Gardens Mineral Spa** has naturally heated indoor and outdoor pools supplied by an artesian well 4,500 feet below the earth's surface. You can take a long soak in the therapeutic mineral waters, or unwind in the spa in the 179-room hotel. Visitors flock here for the face treatments, body wraps, reflexology, and massage. ✉ *24 Fairford St. E* ☎ *306/694–5055 or 800/718–7727* 🌐 *www.templegardens.sk.ca* 🎟 *General admission C$13.50* ⏲ *Sun.–Thurs. 9 AM–11 PM, Fri. and Sat. 9 AM–midnight.*

Fodor'sChoice ★ The **Tunnels of Moose Jaw** is a quirky attraction with good actors and period displays. The tunnels run beneath the streets of Moose Jaw, but their origins are in dispute. By the late 1800s Chinese immigrants were toiling in laundries and burlap factories, and living in the tunnels, which hid them from racist encounters. Later, the tunnels were used by Al Capone to smuggle liquor during Prohibition. One tour focuses on

Canada's early Chinese immigrants and the other on "The Chicago Connection." Tours cost C$13 and depart from 18 Main Street North; call to reserve a space. ☎*306/693–5261* 🌐*www.tunnelsofmoosejaw.com.*

The **Western Development Museum** focuses on air, land, water, and rail transportation. It also houses the **Snowbirds Gallery,** filled with memorabilia (including vintage airplanes) of Canada's air demonstration team, the Snowbirds, who are stationed at the nearby Armed Forces base. ✉*50 Diefenbaker Dr.* ☎*306/693–5989* 🌐*www.wdm.ca* *C$8.50* *Daily 9–5.*

SUKANEN SHIP PIONEER VILLAGE & MUSEUM

13 km (8 mi) south of Moose Jaw, 84 km (52 mi) southwest of Regina.

Besides the old buildings and cars at this offbeat museum, you can see the *Dontianen,* a large, unfinished ship made by a Finnish settler between 1928 and 1941 and patterned after a 17th-century Finnish fishing vessel. The museum site covers 40 acres and includes an old Canadian Pacific Railway caboose, an old village, the Diefenbaker Homestead, and other buildings filled with antiques. ✉*Hwy. 2* ☎*306/693–7315* 🌐*www.sukanenmuseum.ca* *C$6* *Mid-May–mid-Sept., daily 9–5.*

6

REGINA ESSENTIALS

TRANSPORTATION

BY AIR

Regina International Airport is served by Air Canada, Northwest Airlines, WestJet, TransWest Air, and several Canadian commuter airlines.

AIRPORTS & TRANSFERS Regina International Airport is 8 km (5 mi) southwest of downtown within Regina city limits. Taxi cabs charge about C$10 for the 10- to 15-minute ride.

Information **Regina International Airport** (✉*1-5201 Regina Ave., South West* ☎*306/761-7555*).

BY BUS

Regina Transit's 16 bus routes serve the metropolitan area every day, with limited hours on Sunday. The fare is C$2.10.

Information **Regina Transit** (☎*306/777-7433* 🌐*www.reginatransit.com*).

BY CAR

Regina stands at the crossroads of the Trans-Canada Highway (Highway 1) and Highway 11, which goes north to Saskatoon.

BY TAXI

Taxis are easy to find outside major hotels, or they can be summoned by phone.

Information **Capital Cab** (☎*306/791-2222*). **Co-op Taxi** (☎*306/525-2727*). **Regina Cabs** (☎*306/543-3333*).

CONTACTS & RESOURCES

EMERGENCIES

Emergency rooms are at Pasqua Hospital and Regina General Hospital.

Shopper's Drug Marts are usually open until 10 or later. The Albert Street branch is open 24 hours.

Emergency Services Ambulance, fire, police (☎ *911*).

Hospitals Pasqua Hospital (✉ *4101 Dewdney Ave., Windsor Place* ☎ *306/766-2222*). **Regina General Hospital** (✉ *Transition Area, 1440 14th Ave.* ☎ *306/766-4444*).

Late-Night Pharmacies Shopper's Drug Marts (✉ *2202 Broad St.* ☎ *306/777-8166* ✉ *303 Albert St. N* ☎ *306/777-8010* ✉ *2028 Park St.* ☎ *306/777-8030* ✉ *2223 Victoria Ave.* ☎ *306/777-8060* ✉ *380 McCarthy Blvd. N* ☎ *306/777-8070* ✉ *4130 Albert St.* ☎ *306/777-8040* ✉ *5875 Rochdale Blvd.* ☎ *306/949-6616* ✉ *5060 4th Ave.* ☎ *306/777-8181*).

TOURS

Great Excursions runs acclaimed heritage tours based on its archaeological research of Regina. Tours are thematic and include options such as walking the old warehouse district by night; visiting the areas decimated by the 1912 Regina tornado; or exploring the city's history as a railway settlement. CNT Conventions 'N Tours runs tours of Regina in a trolley car; its ghost tour around Halloween is popular.

Information CNT Conventions 'N Tours (☎ *306/584-3524* 🌐 *www.cnttours.ca*). **Great Excursions** (☎ *306/569-1571* 🌐 *www.greatexcursions.com*).

VISITOR INFORMATION

Tourism Regina has an information center on the Trans-Canada Highway (Highway 1) on the eastern approach to the city, open Victoria Day (late May) through Labor Day, weekdays 8:30–7, weekends 10–6; the rest of the year it's open weekdays 8:30–4:30. The Tourism Saskatchewan information center in Regina is open weekdays 8–5, but its call center is open from May to August until 6 on weekdays and from 9 to 4 on weekends.

Information Tourism Regina (📫 *Box 3355, S4P 3H1* ☎ *306/789-5099 or 800/661-5099* 🌐 *www.tourismregina.com*). **Tourism Saskatchewan** (✉ *1922 Park St., Glen Elm Park, Regina S4N 7M4* ☎ *306/787-9600 office, 877/237-2273 call center* 🌐 *www.sasktourism.com*).

AROUND SOUTHERN SASKATCHEWAN

Spread across the southern part of the province are varied attractions, including a fossil research station in Eastend, sites that interpret pioneer and First Nations life, and unique natural areas such as Grasslands National Park near Val Marie.

SWIFT CURRENT

174 km (108 mi) west of Moose Jaw, 245 km (147 mi) west of Regina.

West of Regina, the square townships and straight roads of the grain-belt prairie farms gradually give way to the arid rolling hills of the upland plains ranches. The Trans-Canada Highway skirts the edge of the Missouri Coteau—glacial hills that divide the prairie from the dry western plain—on its way west to Swift Current (population 16,000). The town cultivates its western image during the **Frontier Days Regional Fair** and Rodeo on the July long weekend.

The **Swift Current Museum and Interpretive Centre** focuses on how the geography, climate, and natural resources of southwestern Saskatchewan have influenced human activity. In the museum's brand new facility, visitors see 10,000 years of history in the Southwest, as well as exhibits about endangered plant and animal species. Interactive displays focus on themes such as sustainable resource development, alternate energy resources, and genetically modified organisms. ✉*44 Robert St.* ☎*306/778–2775* 🌐*www.tourismswiftcurrent.ca* *Donation requested* ⏲*June–Aug., weekdays 10–5, weekends 1–5; Sept.–May, weekdays 10–5.*

6

WHERE TO STAY & EAT

$$ ✕ **Wong's Kitchen.** This longtime local favorite, operating since 1964, serves fine Canadian food and an even better Cantonese menu. Dry garlic ribs are the star attraction. Lunch smorgasboard is popular with locals. ✉*Hwy. 1, S. Service Rd. E* ☎*306/773–6244* *Reservations essential* 💳*AE, DC, MC, V.*

$ **Days Inn–Swift Current.** This chain motel property is adjacent to the Trans-Canada Highway and between two major shopping malls. The north rooms have fine views of the surrounding countryside. ✉*905 N. Service Rd. E, S9H 3V1* ☎*306/773–4643* 🌐*www.daysinn.com* *58 rooms, 6 suites* *In-room: Wi-Fi. In-hotel: bar, no elevator, no-smoking rooms* 💳*AE, DC, MC, V* *CP.*

CYPRESS HILLS PROVINCIAL PARK

166 km (103 mi) south of Swift Current, 330 km (205 mi) west of Regina.

Canada's first interprovincial park straddles the Saskatchewan–Alberta border. The Saskatchewan portions of the park consist of two sections, **Centre Block** and the larger **West Block,** which are about 25 km (16 mi) apart and separated by nonparkland; a rough gravel road connects the two.

The West Block of Cypress Hills Provincial Park abuts Alberta's portion of the park and encompasses **Fort Walsh National Historic Park** (✉*Hwy. 271, 55 km [34 mi] southwest of Maple Creek* ☎*306/662–2645*). The fort, built by the Mounties in 1875 to establish order between the "wolfers" (whiskey traders) and the Assiniboine, remained the center of local commerce until its abandonment in 1883. Today, bus service links the Visitor Reception Centre and the fort, which is open mid-May to mid-September, daily 9:30–5:30; admission is C$9.15, including a tour and the bus service. Within the Centre Block, the Cypress Hills plateau, rising more than 4,000 feet above sea level, is covered with spruce, aspen, and lodgepole pines (erroneously identified as cypress by early European explorers). From Lookout Point you have an 80-km (50-mi) view of Maple Creek and the hills beyond. Maps are available at the Park Administrative Office and Nature Centre near the Centre Block park entrance. To get to the West Block in wet weather, take Highway 271 southwest from Maple Creek. ✉ *Hwy. 21, Box 850, Maple Creek S0N 1N0* ☎ *306/662–5411* 🌐 *www.saskparks.net* 🎟 *C$7 per car*. July 2006

WHERE TO STAY

$ **Cypress Park Resort Inn.** This resort is nestled amid a lodgepole-pine forest in the Centre Block of Cypress Hills Provincial Park. Comfortable contemporary rooms are dressed in earth tones. The woodsy restaurant has picture windows that overlook the forest. ✉ *West of Hwy. 21 south of Hwy. 1, Maple Creek S0N 1N0* ☎ *306/662–4477* 🌐 *www.cypressresortinn.com* *33 rooms, 17 cabins, 20 condos* *In-room: refrigerator. In-hotel: restaurant, bar, pool, some pets allowed, no elevator* 💳 *MC, V.*

EASTEND

120 km (74 mi) east of Cypress Hills Provincial Park, 360 km (223 mi) southwest of Regina.

In 1994, in this tiny French River valley town, the fossil of a Tyrannosaurus rex was unearthed, one of only a dozen discovered anywhere in the world. The T. rex, believed to be 65 million years old, is the most complete of any such fossil ever found in Canada.

You can visit the world-class **T-Rex Discovery Centre** and watch paleontologists work on fossils from a unique viewing area. The center is built into the side of a hill and overlooks the beautiful river valley. Ask the center about trips on which you can dig for fossils. ✉ *1 T-Rex Dr. N* ☎ *306/295–4009* 🌐 *www.dinocountry.com* ⏲ *July and Aug., daily 9–9; Sept.–June, daily 9–5* 🎟 *C$7.50.*

VAL MARIE

152 km (94 mi) south of Swift Current, 375 km (233 mi) southwest of Regina.

Val Marie is home to the information center for a unique national park: the 1,554-square-km (600-square-mi) **Grasslands National Park.** Between Val Marie and Killdeer in southwestern Saskatchewan, the park preserves part of the Frenchman River valley. This was the first portion of mixed-grass prairie in North America to be set aside as a park and is marked by strange land formations and badlands. Colonies of black-tailed prairie dogs are the most numerous of the animals here. Interpretive and visitor services are limited, but the center has brochures for self-guided hikes. Tent camping is permitted, and RVs and campers are welcome, but there are no hookups. Tent sites cost C$8.90 per night; RV and camper sites are C$13.85. ✉*Off Hwys. 4 and 18* ☎*306/298–2257* 🌐*www.pc.gc.ca* ⏲*Park open yr-round; information center mid-May–Labor Day, daily 8–5; Labor Day–mid-May, weekdays 8–4:30.*

MOOSE MOUNTAIN PROVINCIAL PARK

478 km (297 mi) east of Val Marie, 220 km (136 mi) southeast of Regina.

Moose Mountain Provincial Park is 401 square km (155 square mi) of rolling poplar and birch forest that forms a natural refuge for moose and elk and a wide variety of birds. A 24-km (15-mi) gravel road leads in to moose and elk grazing areas (best times are early morning and early evening). Beaches, golf, tennis, and horseback riding are also available. More than half of the 330 campsites in the park have electric hookups. The **Kenosee Inn Resort Hotel** (✉*Inside park, off Hwy. 9* ☎*306/577–2099* 🌐*www.kenoseeinn.com*) is a 30-room hotel. There are also cabins available to rent. ✉*Hwy. 9* ☎*306/577–2600 or 800/205–7070* 🌐*www.saskparks.net* 🎫*C$7 per car; camping C$24 per night.*

6

SASKATOON

Saskatchewan's largest city (population 207,700), Saskatoon is nicknamed City of Bridges because it has seven spans across the South Saskatchewan River, which cuts the city in half diagonally. It's considered one of the most beautiful of Canada's midsize cities, in part because a zealous protectionist campaign has allowed the riverbanks to flourish largely in their natural state. The city has a rich cultural life, including a thriving theater scene.

Saskatoon was founded in 1882 when a group of Ontario Methodists was granted 200,000 acres to form a temperance colony. Teetotaling Methodists controlled only half the land, however, and eventually the influence of those who controlled the other half turned the town wet. The coming of the railroad in 1890 made it the major regional transportation hub, but during the 20th century it became known for its three major resources: potash, oil, and wheat. Saskatoon today is the high-tech hub of Saskatchewan's agricultural industry and a hotbed of scientific research. The University of Saskatchewan is a major presence in all aspects of local life; the Canadian Light Source, Canada's only synchrotron and one of the most powerful in the world, is also here.

EXPLORING SASKATOON

Reasonably compact for a western city, Saskatoon proper is easily accessible to drivers and cyclists. Idylwyld Drive divides the city into east and west; 22nd Street divides the city into north and south. The downtown area and Spadina Crescent are on the west side of the South Saskatchewan River.

Running north and south, street names are alphabetized on the west side of the river (for example, Avenue B). On the east side of the river, street names are numbered (for example, 8th Street East). Most sights are concentrated in the Central Business District (more commonly known as the downtown area), close to the river, or on the grounds of the University of Saskatchewan. Others are less than a 15-minute drive away from the center of the city; a good sprinkling of parkland within residential and commercial properties makes driving around the city a delight.

WHAT TO SEE

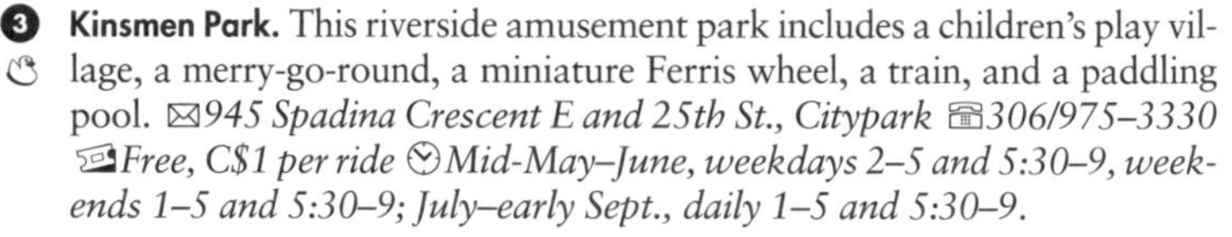

❸ **Kinsmen Park.** This riverside amusement park includes a children's play village, a merry-go-round, a miniature Ferris wheel, a train, and a paddling pool. ✉ *945 Spadina Crescent E and 25th St., Citypark* ☎ *306/975–3330* *Free, C$1 per ride* ⊙ *Mid-May–June, weekdays 2–5 and 5:30–9, weekends 1–5 and 5:30–9; July–early Sept., daily 1–5 and 5:30–9.*

❶ **Meewasin Valley Centre.** The interpretive center traces Saskatoon history back to the city's beginnings as a Methodist temperance colony. The gallery showcases works by local artists. Meewasin is Cree for "beautiful," and this is a fitting description of the **Meewasin Valley Trail,** a 40-km (25-mi) stretch for biking and hiking along the South Saskatchewan River. ✉ *402 3rd Ave. S, Downtown South* ☎ *306/665–6887* *www.meewasin.com* *Donations requested* ⊙ *Weekdays 9–5, weekends noon–5.*

❼ **Prairieland Park.** This 136-acre plot is one of Canada's most prized venues, with more than 180,000 square feet of meeting, trade show, and conference space—the largest in Saskatchewan. Directly south of the park is the **Western Development Museum** (see below). ✉ *503 Ruth St. W and Lorne Ave., Exhibition* ☎ *306/931–7149* *www.saskatoonex.com.*

❺ **Saskatoon Forestry Farm Park and Zoo.** More than 350 animals live in the zoo, which focuses on species native to North America, such as deer, wolf, bison, and fox. The park has barbecue areas, nature displays, fishing, sports fields, and train rides. Regular visiting exhibits include more exotic animals such as snow leopards. ✉ *1903 Forestry Farm Park Dr., off Attridge Dr., Silverspring* ☎ *306/975–3382* *Mid-Apr.–mid-Oct. C$7.10; May–Labor Day, vehicle charge C$2* ⊙ *May–Labor Day, daily 9–9; early Sept.–Apr., daily 10–4.*

❷ **Ukrainian Museum of Canada.** Through photos, costumes, textiles, and of course, the famous *pysanky* (Easter eggs), this collection celebrates the rich history of the Ukrainian people who make up 8% of Saskatchewan's population. ✉ *910 Spadina Crescent E, Downtown* ☎ *306/244–3800* *C$3* ⊙ *Tues.–Sat. 10–5, Sun. 1–5.*

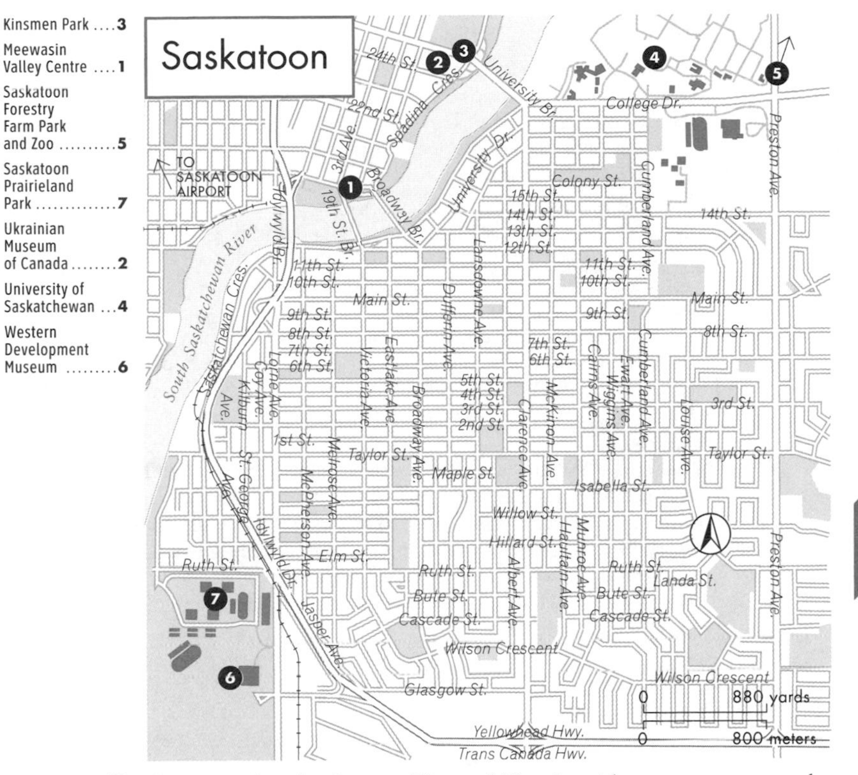

❹ **University of Saskatchewan.** The parklike riverside campus, among the most picturesque in Canada, occupies a 2,425-acre site on the east bank of the river. The university grounds contain several museums and galleries (all free), including the **Museum of Natural Sciences,** the **Little Stone School House,** the **Museum of Antiquities,** the **Kenderine Art Gallery,** and the **Gordon Snelgrove Gallery.** A highlight is the **Diefenbaker Canada Centre,** a museum, archive, gallery, and research center in Canadian studies, commemorating Canada's 13th prime minister. The center explores John Diefenbaker's life and times. Two replica rooms represent the Privy Council Chamber and the prime minister's Ottawa office, where he served in the late 1950s and early 1960s. ✉*Diefenbaker Canada Centre, 101 Diefenbaker Pl., University District* ☎*306/966–8384* 🌐*www.usask.ca* 🎫*C$5* 🕙*Mon., Wed., and Fri. 9:30–4:30, Tues. and Thurs. 9:30–8, weekends noon–4:30.*

❻ **Western Development Museum.** One of four such museums in Saskatchewan, the Saskatoon branch is called 1910 Boomtown and re-creates early-20th-century life in western Canada through a collection of more than 30 full-size buildings filled with artifacts ranging from horse-pulled buggies to clothing and sundries. ✉*2610 Lorne Ave. S, Exhibition* ☎*306/931–1910* 🌐*www.wdm.ca* 🎫*C$8.50* 🕙*Daily 9–5.*

WHERE TO EAT

$$$ ✕ **Samurai Japanese Restaurant.** Excellent food, a tranquil atmosphere, and sheer showmanship are highlights here, and the chef's table-top preparation is a favorite. This restaurant in the Delta Bessborough has a full sushi bar along with less exotic dishes like steak and vegetarian stir-fries. ✉ *601 Spadina Crescent E, Downtown* ☎ *306/683–6926* ▭ *AE, DC, MC, V.*

$$–$$$ ✕ **Calories Bakery and Restaurant.** French chef and owner Remi Cousyn draws raves for his classic cuisine and friendly staff. The "three-course" format is affordable, and fresh mains include a roasted eggplant tower or a leg of duck confit with portobello risotto. The menu changes monthly but always includes seasonal fruits and vegetables and local meats. All baking is done on premises, including Wild Rice Bread and the pleasing Shmoo Torte—a delicate hazelnut chiffon cake with caramel sauce. ✉ *721 Broadway Ave.* ☎ *306/665–7991* ▭ *AE, DC, MC, V.*

$$–$$$ ✕ **Saskatoon Station Place.** The station isn't old, but the vintage railroad cars and decorative antiques are authentic and fascinating. The menu headlines Canadian prime rib and steaks, seafood, and Greek specialties, such as Greek ribs and souvlaki. ✉ *221 Idylwyld Dr. N, Downtown* ☎ *306/244–7777* ▭ *AE, DC, MC, V.*

$$ ✕ **2nd Avenue Grill.** Mahogany wood detailing complements black-and-orange ultramodern and metropolitan furnishings at this casual, fine-dining establishment. Local artwork hangs on the walls and a stylish atrium lets in streams of natural light. The menu is varied, including exotic seafoods imported twice a week, tender Sterling Silver cuts of steak, breast of duck, and tasty burgers. Bananas Foster—bananas sautéed in dark rum, brown sugar, and orange juice and served over ice cream—is a favorite. The restaurant has one of the largest martini lists in Saskatoon. The crowd is sophisticated—no children's menu or high chairs are available. ✉ *10–123 2nd Ave. S, Downtown* ☎ *306/244–9899* ▭ *AE, DC, MC, V.*

$–$$ ✕ **Genesis Family Restaurant.** Authentic Cantonese-style Chinese food is the emphasis here with 120 different items on the menu, including vegetarian dishes. Gingered beef and chicken with black-bean sauce are good choices. Dim sum is a lunchtime and weekend favorite. ✉ *901 22nd St. W, University District* ☎ *306/244–5516* ▭ *AE, MC, V.*

¢–$ ✕ **Taunte Maria's.** Hearty soups, huge farmers' sausages, potato salad, homemade bread, and noodles steeped in gravy are served up at this Mennonite restaurant. The interior, too, reflects the Mennonite tradition: simple, functional, and comfortable. Save room for the Ho-Ho Cake (chocolate cake with cream filling and chocolate icing) or the bread pudding with ice cream. ✉ *212–2750 Faithful Ave., at 51st St., North Industrial* ☎ *306/931–3212* ▭ *AE, MC, V* ⊙ *Closed Sun.*

WHERE TO STAY

$$$ ★ **Delta Bessborough.** Saskatoon's majestic old stone landmark—opened in 1935—looks like a castle, complete with gargoyles, and dominates the skyline from its riverfront setting. The hotel has been upgraded

with modern amenities, but it retains its grand details. Rooms differ in size; all have traditional furniture. The Samurai Japanese Restaurant is excellent. ✉*601 Spadina Crescent E, Downtown, S7K 3G8* ☎*306/244–5521 or 888/890–3222* 🌐*www.deltabessborough.com* *214 rooms, 11 suites* *In-room: ethernet. In-hotel: 2 restaurants, bar, pool, gym, spa, laundry service, public Internet, parking (fee), no-smoking rooms* 💳*AE, DC, MC, V.*

$$ **Saskatoon Inn.** Near the airport, and built around a lush indoor tropical courtyard, this hotel has eight floors of classically styled rooms. Guest rooms are spacious; a mix of earth-tone and spice colors make them bright and inviting. All have large working desks with ergonomic chairs. The botaniCa restaurant has a variety of daily hot entrées, a salad bar, a popular Sunday brunch, and a chocolate buffet on Friday night. ✉*2002 Airport Dr., McNab Park, S7L 6M4* ☎*306/242–1440 or 800/667–8789* 🌐*www.saskatooninn.com* *220 rooms, 30 suites* *In-room: ethernet, Wi-Fi. In-hotel: restaurant, bar, pool, gym, laundry service, public Internet, parking (no fee), no-smoking rooms* 💳*AE, DC, MC, V.*

$$ **Sheraton Cavalier.** Opposite a downtown park and across from the river, this eight-story property has unusually large rooms that face the city or the river, and an elaborate water-sports complex with two giant water slides. Carver's Steak House is the place for elegant dining; Windows restaurant is less formal and has a view of the river from every table. 6Twelve is an upbeat urban lounge serving appetizers and drinks. ✉*612 Spadina Crescent E, Downtown, S7K 3G9* ☎*306/652–6770 or 866/716–8101* 🌐*www.sheratonsaskatoon.com* *238 rooms, 11 suites* *In-room: ethernet, dial-up. In-hotel: 2 restaurants, bar, pools, gym, concierge, laundry service, public Wi-Fi, parking (fee), no-smoking rooms* 💳*AE, DC, MC, V.*

$ **Colonial Square Motel.** This pink-stucco, two-story motel is east of the river, along a busy main thoroughfare. Rooms are furnished in earth-tone colors and have two queen-size beds, a king-size bed and pullout sofa, or a king-size bed. ✉*1301 8th St. E, Varsity View, S7H 0S7* ☎*306/343–1676 or 800/667–3939* 🌐*www.colonialsquaremotel.com* *80 rooms* *In-room: ethernet, Wi-Fi. In-hotel: restaurant, bar, parking (no fee), no-smoking rooms, no elevator* 💳*AE, DC, MC, V.*

$ **Saskatoon Travelodge Hotel.** This sprawling property near the airport has two flora-filled indoor pool complexes and a water slide. Rooms vary in size, and some have balconies overlooking the pool; the executive-style rooms are large, with king-size beds and work areas with desks. The Garden Terrace Restaurant has informal poolside dining. Twice a month, Rodeo's Bar has live entertainment by local and national country-rock groups. ✉*106 Circle Dr. W, Airport District, S7L 4L6* ☎*306/242–8881 or 888/278–4209* 🌐*www.travelodgesaskatoon.com* *268 rooms, 16 suites* *In-room: ethernet, Wi-Fi. In-hotel: restaurant, bar, pools, gym, public Internet, parking (no fee), no-smoking rooms* 💳*AE, DC, MC, V.*

$ **Senator Hotel.** Its location in the heart of downtown makes this European-style hotel appealing, especially if you're looking for an affordable stay. Built in 1908 and last renovated in 2003, it has clean, basic

6

rooms. Authentic ambience can be found on-site in Winston's English Pub and Grill. An ornate dining room is home to a restaurant, Rembrandt's, that serves more elaborate fare such as wild mushroom soup and elk strip loin. ✉*243 21st St. E, Downtown, S7K 0B7* ☎*306/244–6141* 🌐*www.hotelsenator.ca* *36 rooms, 2 suites* *In-room: ethernet, dial-up, Wi-Fi. In-hotel: restaurant, bar, laundry facilities, public Internet, parking (no fee), no-smoking rooms* *AE, MC, V.*

NIGHTLIFE & THE ARTS

THE ARTS

MUSIC & DANCE

When the city symphony isn't in concert, the 2,014-seat **TCU Place** (✉*35 22nd St. E, Downtown* ☎*306/975–7777*) hosts ballet, rock and pop concerts, comedians, musical comedies, and opera. The **Saskatoon Jazz Society** presents local, national, and international jazz performances in the **Bassment** (✉*245 3rd Ave. S, Downtown* ☎*306/683–2277*), its permanent space. The **Saskatoon Symphony** (☎*306/665–6414*) performs September through May at the TCU Place. From late June to early July Saskatoon hosts the popular **SaskTel Saskatchewan Jazz Festival** (☎*306/652–1421*); jazz musicians from around the world play more than 125 performances throughout the province, with most events held in Saskatoon.

THEATER

Gateway Players (☎*306/653–1200*) presents five productions with an emphasis on lighter comedy and period pieces from October through April at **Castle Theater** (✉*1904 Clarence Ave. S, Aden Bowman Collegiate, Saskatoon* ☎*306/653–1200*). **Persephone Theatre** (✉*2802 Rusholme Rd., West End* ☎*306/384–7727*) stages six plays and musicals a year including classic, contemporary, comedy, and drama. **Saskatoon Soaps** has monthly improvisational comedy from September through April at the **Broadway Theatre** (✉*715 Broadway Ave., Nutana* ☎*306/652–6556*). A summer tradition, **Shakespeare on the Saskatchewan** (☎*306/653–2300*) is staged in a riverside tent in July and August. The actors are primarily local. Saskatoon's oldest professional theater, **25th Street Theatre Centre** (✉*400–245 3rd Ave. S, Downtown* ☎*306/664–2239*), produces the Saskatoon International Fringe Festival every summer. Theater companies from around the world bring comedy, drama, and dance performances to the Broadway and Nutana neighborhoods during the 10-day festival.

NIGHTLIFE

BARS & CLUBS

Amigos (✉*632 10th St. E, Broadway District* ☎*306/652–4912*) is a nightclub and Mexican-theme eatery. On weekends, live bands draw a diverse crowd with alternative and reggae music. The **Spadina Freehouse** (✉*608 Spadina Crescent E, Downtown* ☎*306/668–1000*) draws a lively and diverse crowd, with its sophisticated menu and, in summer, a patio that occupies the best spot downtown, across from the castlelike Delta Bessborough. Top local and national blues and rock groups perform at **Bud's on Broadway** (✉*817 Broadway Ave., Nutana* ☎*306/244–4155*). There's live music nightly at **Lydia's Pub** (✉*650 Broadway Ave., Nutana* ☎*306/652–8595*). The neighborhood pub has a wide selection of international beers and a full menu of pub grub.

SPORTS & THE OUTDOORS

BIKING & JOGGING

The **Meewasin Valley Trail** (☎*306/665–6887*) is a gorgeous 40-km (25-mi) biking and jogging trail along both banks of the South Saskatchewan River in Saskatoon.

HOCKEY

The Western Hockey League's **Saskatoon Blades** play major junior hockey at **Credit Union Centre** (✉*3515 Thatcher Ave., Agriplace* ☎*306/938–7800 for information, 306/975–8844 for tickets* 🌐*www.creditunioncentre.com*) from September through March.

HORSE RACING

Marquis Downs Racetrack (✉*Saskatoon Prairieland Park, enter on Ruth St., Lorne Ave., or St. Henry Ave., Exhibition* ☎*306/242–6100* 🌐*www.marquisdowns.com*) has Thoroughbred racing from late May through early September.

SHOPPING

MALLS & SHOPPING DISTRICTS

If you enjoy funkier, smaller boutiques and restaurants, head to **Broadway Avenue** (✉*Between 8th and 12th Sts. east of river, Nutana*), the city's oldest business district and the location of more than 150 shops and restaurants as well as a cinema. The **Midtown Plaza Mall** (✉*201 1st Ave. S, Downtown* ☎*306/653–8844*) is the largest two-level shopping center in Saskatchewan, with 130 stores and services, including such well-known chains as Roots. **Scotia Centre Mall** (✉*123 2nd Ave., Downtown* ☎*306/665–6120*) includes several unique men's and women's clothing stores as well as the popular **2nd Avenue Grill** (☎*306/244–9899*).

SIDE TRIPS FROM SASKATOON

Day trips to a number of sights outside the city can provide an understanding of native and frontier life, including the heritage of the Métis. Prince Albert National Park may be a bit far for a day trip but it's worth an overnight stay.

WANUSKEWIN HERITAGE PARK

Fodor'sChoice ★ *5 km (3 mi) north of Saskatoon.*

The 760-acre park is on the edge of the prairie where Opimihaw Creek flows into the South Saskatchewan River. It portrays 6,000 years of Northern Plains native culture. Wanuskewin, Cree for "seeking peace of mind," includes an interpretive center (fully wheelchair accessible), an exhibit hall with hands-on activities, an archaeological laboratory, and a gift shop. The full-service cafeteria has traditional cuisine such as bison, bannock (First Nations bread), Saskatoon berry pie, and muskeg bush tea. Outside walking trails (some wheelchair accessible) take you to archaeological sites, including a medicine wheel, tepee rings, bison kills, habitation sites, and stone cairns. You can stay overnight in a tepee.

✉Off Hwy. 11 ☎306/931–6767 🌐www.wanuskewin.com 🎫C$8.50 ⏲Mid-May–Labor Day, daily 9–8; Labor Day–mid-May, daily 9–5.

BATOCHE

100 km (62 mi) northeast of Saskatoon.

★ **Batoche National Historic Site** is a center of Métis heritage. It was here that the Métis, under Louis Riel, fought and lost their last battle against the Canadian militia in 1885. The large historical park includes a visitor center, displays, a historic church and rectory, and walking trails that take you by many of the battle sites. Don't miss the award-winning audiovisual presentation about the Métis people. *✉Off Hwy. 11, follow signs ☎306/423–6227 🌐www.pc.gc.ca 🎫C$7.15 ⏲Early May–Sept., daily 9–5.*

DUCK LAKE

20 km (12 mi) northwest of Batoche, 120 km (74 mi) north of Saskatoon.

Duck Lake, which lies along Highway 11 between the North and South Saskatchewan rivers, has a number of buildings decorated with life-size murals depicting the area's history, including the 1885 Northwest Rebellion/Resistance. It's also the site of the first shots fired in the 1885 uprising.

The **Regional Interpretive Centre** has more than 6,000 artifacts from the period between 1870 and 1905, including Gabriel Dumont's gold watch, a letter written by Louis Riel to his mother, and exceptional examples of First Nations beadwork. *✉Hwy. 11 ☎306/467–2057 🌐www.dlric.org 🎫C$4.50 ⏲Mid-May–Labor Day, daily 10–5:30; rest of yr, by appointment.*

OFF THE BEATEN PATH

Fort Carlton Provincial Historic Park. This site, 26 km (16 mi) west of Duck Lake, has a reconstructed stockade and buildings from the mid-1800s fur-trade days. The displays include a tepee encampment depicting Plains Cree culture and a replica of a former Hudson's Bay store. Do a self-guided interpretive hike, or enjoy the river and beautiful setting longer by camping overnight—the sites are basic and inexpensive starting at C$11 a night. *✉Hwy. 212 ☎306/467–5205 🌐www.saskparks.net 🎫C$2.50 ⏲Mid-May–Labor Day, daily 10–6.*

PRINCE ALBERT NATIONAL PARK

Fodor's Choice ★

90 km (56 mi) north of Prince Albert, 229 km (143 mi) north of Saskatoon.

Prince Albert National Park encompasses nearly a million acres of wilderness and waterways, divided into three landscapes: wide-open fescue grassland, wooded parkland, and dense boreal forest. Besides hiking and cycling trails, the park has three major campgrounds with 500 sites, plus rustic campgrounds and primitive sites in the backcountry. Maps and park information are available at the **Prince Albert National Park Information Centre** (*✉Lakeview Dr., Waskesiu ☎306/663–4522*) in Waskesiu, a town with restaurants, motels, a movie theater, stores, and a golf course within the park. It's open May through September, daily 8–8; call ahead for hours the rest of year. The **Interpretive Centre**

(☎306/663–4515), 1½ blocks west of the visitor center, orients you to the plant and animal life of the area. Hiking along the marked trails, you have a good chance of spotting moose, deer, bear, elk, and red fox. The Nature Centre is open late June to September; call ahead for schedule. Across from the visitor center, you can find a replica of Grey Owl's cabin in the bookstore. Canoes, rowboats, and powerboats can be rented from Waskesiu Lake Marina. ✉*Off Hwy. 2* ☎*306/663–4522 or 888/773–8888* 🌐*www.pc.gc.ca* *C$6.90.*

WHERE TO STAY

$$ **Chateau Park Chalets.** Spacious town-house-style chalets each have a full kitchen, two bedrooms with a queen-size bed, two twin beds, a pullout couch, a wood-burning fireplace, and a private deck with barbecue grill. *Box 242, Waskesiu Lake, S0J 2Y0* ☎*306/663–5556* 🌐*www.waskesiu.com* *10 chalets* *In-room: no phone, kitchen* *MC, V.*

$–$$ **Hawood Inn.** Open year-round, this inn has appealing rooms and two rooftop hot tubs. It's across the street from Waskesiu Lake and close to the resort town's attractions: fishing, cycling, tennis, golf, hiking, and beach volleyball in summer; dogsledding, ice-skating, and cross-country skiing in winter. MacKenzie's Dining Room's menu ranges from chicken and steak to seafood and pasta. ✉*850 Lakeview Dr., S0J 2Y0* ☎*306/663–5911 or 877/441–5544* *306/663–5219* 🌐*www.hawood.com* *34 rooms, 7 suites* *In-hotel: restaurant, bar, laundry facilities, no elevator, no-smoking rooms* *AE, MC, V.*

$ **Lakeview Four Seasons Resort Hotel.** Across from Waskesiu Lake, most rooms here have balconies and great sunset views. The highly rated suites, which run from C$120 to C$240, offer patios and BBQs. The Lakeview Pub offers casual fare and pub activities. *Box 26, Waskesiu Lake, S0J 2Y0* ☎*306/663–5311 or 877/331–3302* *306/663–5543* 🌐*www.lakeviewhotel.com* *33 rooms, 13 suites* *In-room: kitchen (some). In-hotel: no-smoking rooms* *AE, MC, V* *Closed mid-Oct.–Apr.*

NORTH BATTLEFORD

139 km (87 mi) northwest of Saskatoon.

North Battleford is the service center to the northwest and is surrounded by fertile farmland, vast forests, and the North Saskatchewan River valley. Four artificial ice rinks, four golf courses, and an indoor swimming pool serve the recreational needs of the 14,000 residents of the city and the adjoining Town of Battleford. The attractions here represent different aspects of the area's history.

The **Western Development Museum Heritage Farm and Village** presents a re-created 1920s farming village, complete with homes, offices, churches, and a Mountie post. The museum also exhibits vintage farming tools and provides demonstrations of agricultural skills during special events. ✉*Hwys. 16 and 40* ☎*306/445–8033* 🌐*www.wdm.ca* *C$8.50* *Mid-May–Labor Day, daily 9–5; rest of yr, weekdays 10–4.*

While you're in town, you can visit the **Allen Sapp Gallery,** which displays the paintings of the Cree artist. Allen Sapp has gained a strong following, both in Canada and abroad, for his images of the Northern Plains Cree, including scenes from his childhood on a reservation. ✉ *1 Railway Ave. E* ☎ *306/445–1760* 🌐 *www.allensapp.com* 🎫 *Donation requested* ⏲ *June–Sept., daily 11–5; Oct.–May, Wed.–Sun. 1–5.*

Fort Battleford National Historic Site pays tribute to the role of mounted police in the development of the Canadian West. The fort was established in 1876 as the territorial headquarters of the North West Mounted Police. Exhibits focus on the history of the mounted police and the lives of natives and settlers. Visitors can explore the interpretive center, meet costumed guides who explain day-to-day life at the post, and watch historic weapons demonstrations. ✉ *Central Ave., Battleford* ☎ *306/937–2621* 🌐 *www.pc.gc.ca* 🎫 *C$7.15* ⏲ *Mid-May–Labor Day, daily 9–5; rest of yr, by appointment.*

MANITOU BEACH

124 km (77 mi) southeast of Saskatoon.

In the 1920s Manitou Beach was a world-famous spa nicknamed the Carlsbad of Canada. The mineral water in Little Manitou Lake is said to be three times saltier than the ocean, similar to the Dead Sea's chemical content, and dense enough to make anyone float. Manitou Beach is 5 km (3 mi) north of the town of Watrous, which has one of the few remaining dance halls with a horsehair-cushioned floor. Today the Manitou Springs spa resort attracts vacationers as well as sufferers from arthritis, rheumatism, and skin disorders.

WHERE TO STAY

$–$$ **Manitou Springs Hotel and Mineral Spa.** The rooms and suites at this lakeshore resort hotel offer private balconies and good views. Guest rooms are comfortable, with either oak or dark cherry furnishings. The mineral pools at the spa contain water drawn from Little Manitou Lake that has been filtered and then heated. Continental cuisine, including some seafood and prairie fare such as steaks and roasts, is served in the light, airy Wellington Dining Room, which overlooks the lake. ✉ *Hwy. 365, Box 610, Watrous, S0K 4T0* ☎ *306/946–2233 or 800/667–7672* 🌐 *www.manitousprings.ca* *97 rooms, 5 suites* *In-room: ethernet (some), dial-up. In-hotel: restaurant, gym, spa, bicycles, no-smoking rooms* 💳 *MC, V.*

SASKATOON ESSENTIALS

TRANSPORTATION

BY AIR

The John G. Diefenbaker International Airport, known as Saskatoon Airport, is served by Air Canada, Air Canada Jazz, Northwest Airlines, WestJet, and Canadian commuter carriers. Regional travel services are provided by Transwest.

AIRPORTS & TRANSFERS Saskatoon Airport is 7 km (4 mi) northwest of downtown. Taxis to downtown cost C$12–C$15.

Information **John G. Diefenbaker International Airport** (*Saskatoon Airport* ✉ *2625 Airport Dr., McNab Park* ☎ *306/975–8900*).

BY BUS

Saskatoon Transit buses offer convenient service to points around the city. Tickets cost C$2.25, a day pass is $5.90.

Information **Saskatoon Transit** (☎ *306/975–3100*).

BY CAR

The two-lane Trans-Canada Yellowhead Highway (Highway 16) passes through Saskatoon on its journey from Winnipeg through to Edmonton and west. There's also access to Saskatoon along Highway 11 from Regina.

BY TAXI

Taxis are plentiful, especially outside downtown hotels, with fares averaging C$10. A ride from the Delta Bessborough Hotel to the trendy shops along Broadway Avenue costs about C$7.

Information **Blue Line Taxi** (☎ *306/653–3333*). **Saskatoon Radio Cab** (☎ *306/242–1221*).

6

CONTACTS & RESOURCES

EMERGENCIES

The Shopper's Drug Mart at Taylor Street East and Broadway Avenue is open daily until midnight; the branch at 2410 22nd Street West is open around the clock.

Emergency Services **Ambulance, fire, poison center, police** (☎ *911*).

Hospitals **City Hospital** (✉ *Queen St. and 5th Ave. N, Citypark* ☎ *306/655–8000*). **Royal University Hospital** (✉ *103 Hospital Dr., University Grounds* ☎ *306/655 1000*). **St. Paul's Hospital** (✉ *1702 20th St. W, Pleasant Hill* ☎ *306/655–5000*).

Late-Night Pharmacies **Shopper's Drug Mart** (✉ *2410 22nd St. W* ☎ *306/382–5005* ✉ *2105 8th St. E* ☎ *306/374–4888*).

TOURS

The *Saskatoon Princess* offers river cruises daily at noon, 1:30, 3, and 4:30 from late May to early September. Boats depart from the Mendel Art Gallery Wharf; the cost is C$15.

Information *Saskatoon Princess* (☎ *306/549–2454 or 888/747–7572*).

VISITOR INFORMATION

Tourism Saskatoon is open mid-May to early September, weekdays 8:15–7 and weekends 10–7, The rest of the year, it's open weekdays 8:15–5. A seasonal information center, at Avenue C and 47th Street, is open mid-May to early September, daily 10–7.

Information **Tourism Saskatoon** (✉ *6–305 Idylwyld Dr. N, Downtown, S7L 0Z1* ☎ *306/242–1206 or 800/567–2444* 🌐 *www.tourismsaskatoon.com*).

WINNIPEG

Winnipeg's geographic isolation and traditionally long, cold winters have fostered an independent spirit among its people. Although its status as a transportation hub and commercial gateway to the West has diminished, the provincial capital of Manitoba has a cultural scene—including a symphony orchestra, a ballet company, two major theaters, and a strong arts community—that is the envy of much larger Canadian cities.

Historically, Winnipeg was the funnel for the first great waves of immigration to the West, and ethnic pride remains strong here. British and French by colonization, with subsequent arrivals of Ukrainians, Italians, members of the Jewish and Mennonite faiths, and many other groups, the city has seen since the 1980s the growing pride of the First Nations and Métis people and the members of newer communities, notably from Portugal, Vietnam, and the Philippines. Population growth is steady, reaching 706,700 in 2007. After years of modest growth since the late 1980s, Winnipeg has rallied since 2003, especially with new business and entertainment developments reviving downtown.

With most of its business activity concentrated in a compact downtown zone, Winnipeg retains much of its historic charm, evidenced in the many edifices from the turn of the 20th century. Because major residential and retail development has been left generally to its fringes, the city still holds many enclaves of older homes on shady lanes, such as the grand, gated residences along Wellington Crescent, often set in surprising contrast to newer structures.

Originally, buffalo-hunting Plains Indians inhabited the area, which was franchised by the British Crown to the Hudson's Bay Company. In 1738 Pierre Gaultier de Varennes established a North West Company fur-trading post at the junction of the Red and Assiniboine rivers. Lord Selkirk, a Scot, brought a permanent agricultural settlement in 1812; Winnipeg was incorporated as a city in 1873; and soon after, in 1886, the Canadian Pacific Railway arrived, bringing a rush of European immigrants. The "Chicago of the North" boomed as a railroad hub, a center of the livestock and grain industries, and a principal market city of western Canada.

EXPLORING WINNIPEG

Neighborhood character in Winnipeg is forged in part by residents' cultural heritage. The Eastern European influence registers strongly in the North End, which begins on Main Street north of downtown and contains onion-domed Ukrainian and Russian Orthodox churches. Turn west from Main down Selkirk Avenue for the shops and restaurants that pay tribute to the roots of late-19th-century European settlement. For a vivid sense of the cultural shift since the 1980s, take Ellice Avenue, into the West End neighborhood, where Portuguese, Indian, and Vietnamese shops and eateries rub shoulders. The St. Boniface area, east of the Red River, honors this region's French heritage, offering historic buildings as well as modern culinary adventures. Street signs in this historically French-speaking community are labeled in both French and English.

Downtown is centered on the intersection of Portage Avenue and Main Street. The nearby Exchange District sets galleries, shops, and beguiling restaurants against a backdrop of the early-20th-century office buildings and warehouses that make this part of Winnipeg a favorite for film shoots. With its downtown core packed close to the junction of the Red and Assiniboine rivers, Winnipeg is an excellent city for walkers. However, the necessity of developing streets against the contours of those rivers makes for many diagonal roads and streets that connect at an angle; a map is recommended.

Paved paths along stretches of both rivers have handsome views of the city. Several overhead enclosed walkways connect parts of the commercial area. A vehicle is necessary for reaching more-distant sites. Portage Avenue (Highway 1) leads west, while Main Street (Route 52) heads north. Pembina Highway (Route 42) is the main artery to the south.

WHAT TO SEE

9 Fodor's Choice ★ **Assiniboine Park.** Hugging the Assiniboine River, the park has 378 acres of rolling fields and dense forest, with picnic areas, a playground, a cricket pitch, and both paved and rugged paths for cyclists. Popular attractions include the **Leo Mol Sculpture Garden,** the only such garden in North America dedicated to a single artist; western Canada's oldest conservatory; a stage for summer music and ballet performances; and the **Assiniboine Park Pavilion,** an art gallery and restaurant. In warm weather, you may visit the English garden and the duck pond. The **Assiniboine Zoo,** also on the grounds, houses more than 1,800 animals (300 species) in reasonably natural settings. ✉ *Park Blvd. and Wellington Crescent, Tuxedo* ☎ *204/986–2327* 🌐 *http://winnipeg.ca/cms* 🎟 *Zoo C$4.25 Mar.–Oct., C$3.75 Nov.–Feb.* ⏲ *Park daily 7 AM–10 PM.*

Opened in 2007 the **Costume Museum of Canada** celebrates fashion, culture, and history with a rotating collection of apparel from various time periods. ✉ *109 Pacific Ave., Downtown* ☎ *204/989–0072* 🌐 *www.costumemuseum.com* 🎟 *C$5* ⏲ *Mon.–Wed., Fri. and Sat. 10–5, Thurs. 10–8, Sun. noon–4.*

2 **Dalnavert Museum.** This finely detailed Victorian house was built in 1895 for Sir Hugh John Macdonald, who became premier of Manitoba. Faithfully restored rooms and many examples of period clothing, furniture, and household devices—all explained vividly by guides—capture the height of elegant living in Winnipeg at the end of the 19th century. ✉ *61 Carlton St., Downtown* ☎ *204/943–2835* 🌐 *www.mhs.mb.ca* 🎟 *C$5* ⏲ *Wed.–Fri. 10–5, Sat. 11–6, Sun. noon–4.*

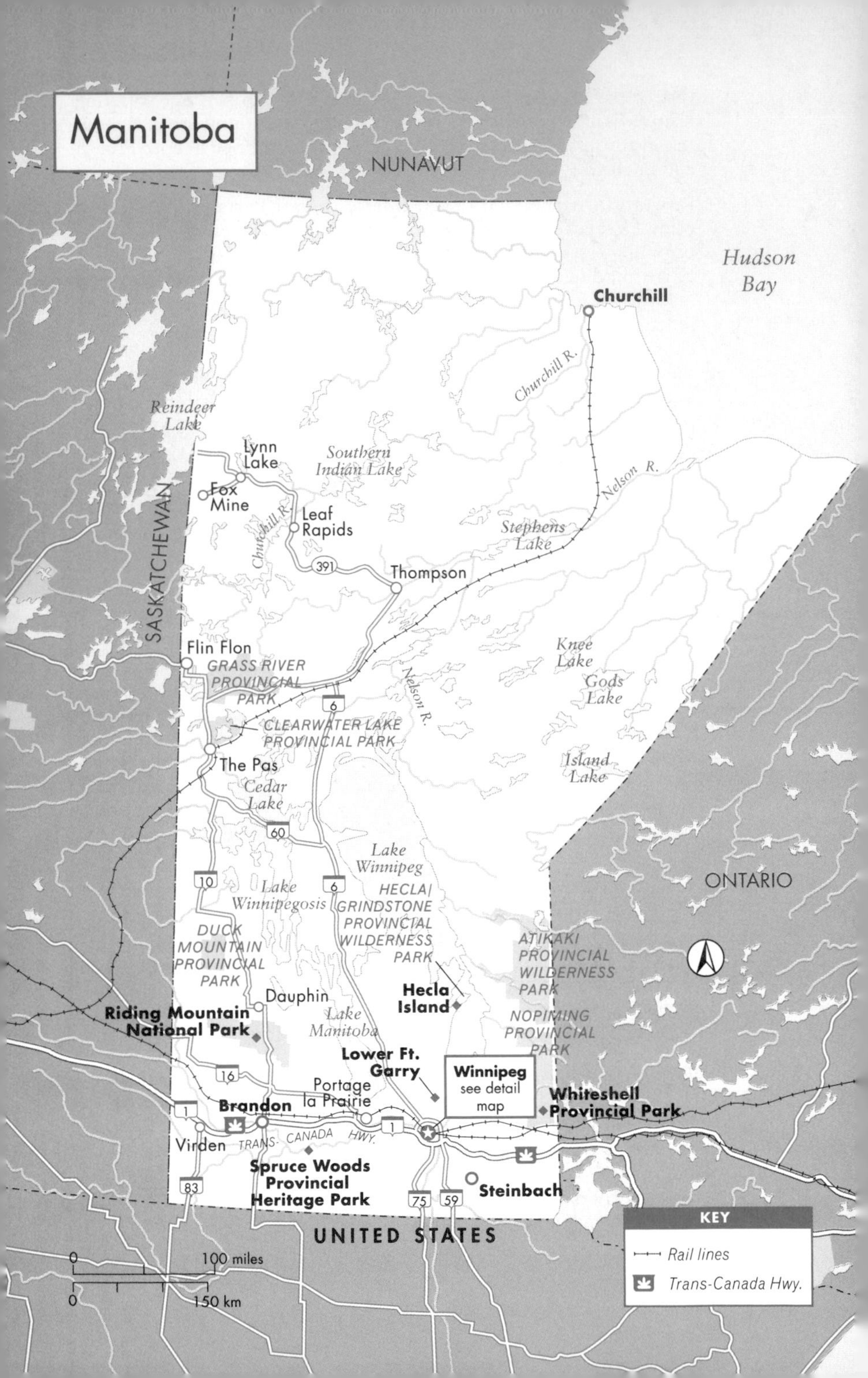

Manitoba
NUNAVUT
Hudson Bay
Churchill
Churchill R.
Reindeer Lake
Lynn Lake
Southern Indian Lake
Fox Mine
Leaf Rapids
Churchill R.
Nelson R.
Stephens Lake
SASKATCHEWAN
391
Thompson
Flin Flon
GRASS RIVER PROVINCIAL PARK
6
Nelson R.
Knee Lake
Gods Lake
CLEARWATER LAKE PROVINCIAL PARK
The Pas
Island Lake
Cedar Lake
60
Lake Winnipeg
10
Lake Winnipegosis
6
HECLA/ GRINDSTONE PROVINCIAL WILDERNESS PARK
ONTARIO
DUCK MOUNTAIN PROVINCIAL PARK
ATIKAKI PROVINCIAL WILDERNESS PARK
Dauphin
Hecla Island
Riding Mountain National Park
Lake Manitoba
NOPIMING PROVINCIAL PARK
Lower Ft. Garry
Winnipeg see detail map
16
Portage la Prairie
Whiteshell Provincial Park
Brandon
1
1
Virden
TRANS-CANADA HWY.
Spruce Woods Provincial Heritage Park
83
75
59
Steinbach
UNITED STATES
0
100 miles
0
150 km
KEY
Rail lines
Trans-Canada Hwy.

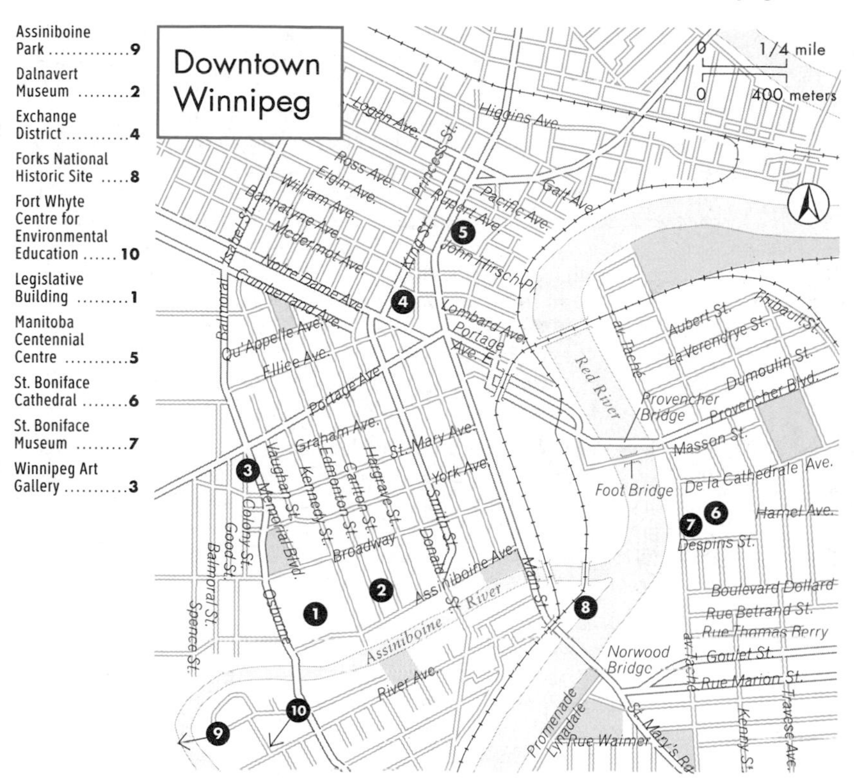

4 **Exchange District.** The original epicenter of Winnipeg's investment and newspaper businesses contains a wealth of architectural history in its surviving offices, warehouses, banks, and hotels. Today entertainment and the arts dominate the area, with many of the city's vital alternative arts galleries within a small radius. **Artspace** (✉ *100 Arthur St.*) includes a gallery and a cinema and is home to many arts organizations. In spring and summer **Old Market Square** (✉ *King St. and Bannatyne Ave.*) is the site of free concerts and the nexus of the popular July **Winnnipeg Fringe Theatre Festival** with performances throughout the neighborhood. ✉ *Between Portage Ave. and Main St., Exchange District* 🌐 *www.exchangedistrict.org.*

8 ★ **Forks National Historic Site.** Winnipeg began here, at the junction of the Red and Assiniboine rivers, with native settlements that date back 6,000 years. You can learn about the region's history through interpretive displays as you stroll the 13 landscaped acres or rest on benches overlooking the river. The Esplanade Riel pedestrian bridge spans the Red river, connecting the site with St. Boniface. The historic site is part of a 56-acre development, **The Forks,** which combines history, commerce, and entertainment. Ice skating is a popular winter activity here. The **Forks Market** (☎ *204/943–7752*) sells fresh produce and specialty foods and contains restaurants in two converted railway buildings. The **Manitoba Children's Museum** (☎ *204/924–4000* 🌐 *www.childrensmuseum.com*) has a delightful range of hands-on activities; kids can check out the working television studio and a vintage diesel train with Pullman car. The museum is open September–June, Sunday–Thursday 9:30–4:30, Friday and Saturday 9:30–6; July and August, daily 9:30–6. Admission is C$6.75. The best in theater for children and teens is found at the **Manitoba Theatre for Young People** (✉ *CanWest Global Performing Arts Centre, 2 Forks Market Rd.* ☎ *204/942–8898* 🌐 *www.mtyp.ca*); the building's bright colors and dramatic courtyard and balcony provide entertainment in themselves. The **Explore Manitoba Centre** (☎ *800/665–0040* ⏲ *Mid-May–Aug., daily 10–6; Sept.–mid-May daily 9–5*) has exhibits about the province and a wealth of information. ✉ *Forks Market Rd. off Main St., The Forks* ☎ *204/983–2007* 🌐 *www.parkscanada.gc.ca/forks* 🎟 *Free.*

⑩ **Fort Whyte Centre for Environmental Education.** The 640-acre center re-creates the natural habitats of Manitoba's lakes and rivers. It's home to bison, white-tailed deer, muskrats, foxes, and numerous species of waterfowl. Self-guided nature trails and an interpretive center explain it all. ✉ *1961 McCreary Rd., Charleswood* ☎ *204/989–8355* 🌐 *www.fortwhyte.org* 🎟 *C$6* ⏲ *Weekdays 9–5, weekends 10–5.*

① **Legislative Building.** This classical structure made of local Tyndall stone contains the offices of Manitoba's premier and members of the cabinet, as well as the chamber where the legislature meets. A 240-foot dome supports Manitoba's symbol, the Golden Boy—a 13½-foot gold-sheathed statue with a sheaf of wheat under his left arm and the torch of progress in his right hand. The beautiful rolling grounds ease down to the Assiniboine River at the south, with a fountain plaza leading to a river walk. Statues around the grounds celebrate Manitoba's ethnic diversity. ✉ *450 Broadway, at Osborne St., Downtown* ☎ *204/945–5813* ⏲ *Daily 8–8; guided tour by appointment.*

⑤ **Manitoba Centennial Centre.** The center includes **Centennial Concert Hall,** home to the Winnipeg Symphony Orchestra and the Royal Winnipeg Ballet. The outstanding **Manitoba Museum,** also here, tracks the province's history back to prehistoric times; galleries include nature dioramas, a miniature prairie town from the 1920s, and a full-size replica of the *Nonesuch,* the ketch that sailed into Hudson's Bay in 1668. Downstairs the **Planetarium** presents a range of stellar shows; the **Science Gallery** offers interactive exhibits. ✉ *190 Rupert Ave., Downtown* ☎ *204/943–3139* 🎟 *Museum C$8; planetarium C$6.50; science gallery C$6.50* ⏲ *Sept.–late May, Tues.–Fri. 10–4, weekends 11–5; late May–Aug., daily 10–5.*

⑥ **St. Boniface Cathedral.** The largest French community in western Canada was founded as Fort Rouge in 1738 and became an important fur-trading outpost for the North West Company. Upon the arrival of Roman Catholic priests, the settlement was renamed St. Boniface. Remnants of a 1908 basilica that survived a 1968 fire can be seen outside the perimeter of the present cathedral, built in 1972. The grave of Louis

Riel, the St. Boniface native son who led the Métis rebellion, is in the churchyard. ✉*Av. de la Cathédrale and Av. Taché, St. Boniface* ☎*204/233–7304* 🎫*Free.*

7 **St. Boniface Museum.** The history of Manitoba's French and Métis people is examined in the oldest structure in Winnipeg, dating to 1846. Artifacts include an altar crafted from papier-mâché and the first church bell in western Canada. ✉*494 Av. Taché, St. Boniface* ☎*204/237–4500* 🌐*www.msbm.mb.ca* 🎫*C$5* ⏲*Mid-May–Sept., Mon.–Wed. and Fri. 9–5, Thurs. 5–8, weekends 10–4; Oct.–mid-May, weekdays 9–5, Sun. noon–4.*

For those traveling by air, the **Western Canada Aviation Museum** is near the airport. The hangar holds numerous historical aircraft as well as a space-flight simulator. It's a fun and fascinating collection for children and adults alike. ✉*958 Ferry Rd.* ☎*204/786–5503* 🌐*www.wcam.mb.ca* 🎫*C$7.50* ⏲*Weekdays 9:30–4:40, Sat. 10–5, Sun. noon–5.*

3 ★ **Winnipeg Art Gallery.** The city's largest art museum is known for one of the world's most extensive collections of Inuit art. The WAG presents a rotating schedule of shows with works from its permanent collection as well as displays of new regional work and traveling exhibitions. Programming also includes music, films, and lectures, and summer concerts on the rooftop plaza. ✉*300 Memorial Blvd., Downtown* ☎*204/786–6641* 🌐*www.wag.mb.ca* 🎫*C$6* ⏲*Tues.–Wed. and Fri.–Sun. 11–5, Thurs. 11–9.*

6

WHERE TO EAT

$$$$ ✕**529 Wellington.** This swank spot, in a renovated old mansion, serves high-quality cuts of prime Canadian beef at pretty posh prices. The wine list, which includes suitably hardy choices, gives you more than 600 options. Imaginative side dishes such as sweet mashed potatoes or sautéed wild mushrooms characterize the à la carte menu. ✉*529 Wellington Crescent, River Heights* ☎*204/487–8325* *Reservations essential* 💳*AE, MC, V* ⏲*No lunch weekends.*

$$$$ ✕**Amici.** The Italian version of nouvelle cuisine extends to lamb, seafood, and imaginative veal dishes—such as a veal scaloppine stuffed with asparagus, portobella mushrooms, and bocconcini cheese—in this elegant and bright restaurant. Pasta preparations are every bit as artful as you would expect. Desserts are heavenly, and include St. Honoré, a cake bedecked with cream-filled pastry puffs. Downstairs is the more casual Bombolini Wine Bar, with a modified version of the menu at lower prices. ✉*326 Broadway, Downtown* ☎*204/943–4997* *Reservations essential* 💳*AE, MC, V* ⏲*Closed Sun.*

$$$$ ★ ✕**Restaurant Dubrovnik.** A charming 1903 home overlooking the Assiniboine River provides the setting for one of Winnipeg's finest restaurants. The menu is all over the map—with dishes such as Dubrovnik's trademark foie gras, chicken stuffed with wild rice and shrimp mousse, and grilled bison fillet with maple-juniper demi-glaze—but the high quality is a constant. The wine list is lengthy.

⊠390 Assiniboine Ave., Downtown ☎204/944–0594 ✍Reservations essential Jacket required ▭AE, MC, V ⊙Closed Sun. No lunch Sat.

$$$ ✕ **Bistro 7¼.** A cool urban vibe sets the tone at this eatery. On any given night chef Alex Svenne whips together any of five moules frites (mussels and fries) options in an open kitchen smack in the middle of the compact space. The counter overlooking the show is perfect for single traveler. An ever-changing seasonal menu continues to create a buzz. *⊠725 Osborne St. S ☎204/777–2525 ✍Reservations essential ▭AE, MC, V ⊙Closed Sun. and Mon.*

$$$ ✕ **Dandelion Eatery.** A decor as fresh at the food attracts people to this funky eatery. The dishes are not only inspired, but also organic. The healthy ingredients include soybeans, brown rice, and buckwheat soba noodles, all draped in delightful sauces with crisp vegetables. Along with free-range chicken, wild salmon, and elk, there are plenty of options for vegeterians and vegans alike. Several dishes are available in two sizes, so you can eat as much (or as little) as you want. *⊠230 Osborne St., Osborne Village ☎204/453–5755 ▭AE, MC, V ⊙No dinner Sun. and Mon.*

$$$ ✕ **Step'N Out.** One the most romantic restaurants in Winnipeg, this enchanting 24-seat hideaway has a veritable foot fetish—shoes of all shapes, sizes, and types dot the claret-color walls in between photos of Bogart and Bacall. Since moving from the Exchange district, the food is more delectable than ever, with a to-die-for pumpkin ravioli in nut butter and a wide selection of impeccably prepared seafood along with a few elegant meat options. Many wines are available by the glass. *⊠157 Provencher Blvd., St. Boniface ☎204/956–7837 ✍Reservations essential ▭AE, MC, V.*

$$ ★ ✕ **Bistro Dansk.** A convivial European atmosphere brings people to this intimate Danish eatery. Portions are so generous, you can easily share one entrée. Specialties such as schnitzel, *frikadeller* (meat patties of ground veal and pork), and the sumptuous hazelnut torte are all made from scratch. A lower-price lunch menu includes a variety of open-face sandwiches. *⊠63 Sherbrook St., West End ☎204/775–5662 ✍Reservations essential ▭AE, MC, V ⊙Closed Sun. and Mon.*

$$ ✕ **BlüFish.** In the evening this place is packed with sushi aficionados enjoying artfully presented dishes bursting with flavor. Tempura and other dishes are good, but the sushi really steals the show. The inside-out rolls are a favorite here. Start with a Japanese beer and relax in the casual burnt orange setting. *⊠179 Bannatyne Ave., Exchange ☎204/779–9888 ▭AE, MC, V.*

$$ ✕ **Ivory.** Indigo walls punctuated by ochre and magenta alcoves filled with Indian artifacts create a soothing ambience at one of the city's most popular buffet restaurants. Here you can enjoy authentically prepared curries, tandoories, and kormas. Renowned for its delicately spiced butter chicken, the kitchen prepares plenty of other temptations ranging from creamy and mild to fiery hot. There are options here for meat-eaters and vegetarians. An à la carte menu is available for those with smaller appetites. *⊠200 Main St., Downtown ☎204/944–1600 ✍Reservations essential ▭AE, MC, V.*

$ ✕ **Baked Expectations.** Towering desserts to break the stoutest willpower are the big draw in this bright and busy Osborne Village eatery. Favorite sweets include a feather-light schmoo torte and a moist, dense banana cake lacquered with butter icing. The menu also includes an ambitious range of omelets, along with giant sandwiches and burgers served with generous side orders of fries. ✉ *161 Osborne St., Osborne Village* ☎ *204/452–5176* ▭ *No credit cards.*

$ ✕ **Elephant and Castle.** A magnet for downtown's after-work crowd, this spot in the Delta Winnipeg hotel combines a British-style pub with an airy, well-lighted restaurant. Pub standbys such as newspaper-wrapped fish-and-chips and steak with thick chips and baked beans share the menu with casual Canadian fare. Many stalwart British ales share the shelf with more familiar North American brands. ✉ *Delta Winnipeg, 350 St. Mary Ave., Downtown* ☎ *204/942–5555* ▭ *AE, MC, V.*

$ ✕ **Kelekis.** A city institution, this North End restaurant—opened in 1931 and still run by the same family—is beloved for its hot dogs, hamburgers, and french fries. Acres of celebrity photos attest to the restaurant's status as a cornerstone of local culture. ✉ *1100 Main St., North End* ☎ *204/582–1786* ✍ *Reservations not accepted* ▭ *No credit cards.*

6

¢ ✕ **Fyxx Espresso Bar.** The popular café offers bold, no-nonsense coffees and huge sandwiches on homemade corn bread. Its Albert Street location is a nerve center for the artistic community in the Exchange District; on Broadway, business types find this the perfect place for sustenance on the go. ✉ *9½ Albert St., Exchange District* ☎ *204/944–0045* ▭ *AE, MC, V* ✉ *101–310 Broadway, Downtown* ☎ *204/989–2470* ▭ *AE, DC, MC, V.*

WHERE TO STAY

$$$ **Delta Winnipeg.** Winnipeg's largest hotel is connected by a walkway to the Winnipeg Convention Centre and is across from the Cityplace mall. Rooms, dressed in neutral tones, are pleasantly modern; some overlook the skylighted pool. A floor of Signature Club rooms includes a private lounge. The hotel's bistro specializes in local ingredients, and the lively British-style pub, Elephant and Castle, is a great place for a drink. ✉ *350 St. Mary Ave., Downtown, R3C 3J2* ☎ *204/942–0551 or 877/814–7706* 🌐 *www.deltahotels.com* *393 rooms, 11 suites* *In-room: refrigerator (some), ethernet. In-hotel: restaurant, room service, bar, pools, gym, laundry service, executive floor, public Internet, parking (fee), some pets allowed, no-smoking rooms* ▭ *AE, MC, V* *CP.*

$$–$$$ **Clarion Hotel & Suites Winnipeg Airport/Polo Park.** A two-story water park with a mineral spa and waterfall reveals the playful side of this full-service hotel. Rooms are contemporary and have large windows. Some suites are themed—Hawaiian, Moroccan, Venetian, etc.—which basically means they have slightly different interior color schemes. The Polo Park mall is a two-minute walk away. ✉ *1445 Portage Ave., St. James, R3G 3P4* ☎ *204/774–5110 or 800/424–6423* 🌐 *www.clarionhotelwinnipeg.*

com *69 rooms, 70 suites* *In-room: refrigerator (some), ethernet. In-hotel: bar, room service, pool, gym, spa, laundry service, public Internet, parking (no fee), no-smoking rooms* *AE, DC, MC, V.*

$$–$$$ **Fort Garry Hotel.** One of Canada's great railway hotels, this building dating from 1913 still holds the charm of a bygone era, down to the marble, brass, and crystal in the grand lobby. Guest rooms are large and still have classic dark-wood furnishings and floral wallpapers. An adjoining complex holds shops and services. *222 Broadway, Downtown, R3C 0R3* *204/942–8251 or 800/665–8088* *www.fortgarryhotel.com* *240 rooms, 15 suites* *In-room: dial-up, Wi-Fi. In-hotel: restaurant, room service, bar, pool, gym, concierge, laundry service, parking (fee), no-smoking rooms* *AE, DC, MC, V* *BP.*

$$–$$$ **Inn at the Forks.** Works by local artists grace every inch of this quiet centrally located hotel. Rooms are luxurious, with great views of the river or the city. Bathrooms have blown-glass sinks and spa showers or soaker tubs. The Inn is also home to the popular Riverstone Spa. *75 Forks Market Rd., R3C 0A2* *204/942–6555* *www.innforks.com* *117 rooms, 7 suites* *In-room: safe, ethernet, Wi-Fi. In hotel: restaurant, room service, bar, gym, spa, laundry service, public Internet, public Wi-Fi, parking (no fee), no-smoking rooms* *AE, MC, V.*

$$ ★ **Fairmont Winnipeg.** Winnipeg's top luxury hotel presides over downtown's central intersection of Portage Avenue and Main Street. Rooms are spacious, with sophisticated furnishings in rich shades of gold and chocolate. The Velvet Glove Dining Room offers elegant dining; lighter meals are served in the Lounge at the Fairmont. An underground complex of shops and restaurants connects the hotel to the Winnipeg Square mall. The Centennial Concert Hall, Manitoba Theatre Centre, and the city's major financial institutions are only a few minutes away.. *2 Lombard Pl., Downtown, R3B 0Y3* *204/957–1350 or 800/441–1414* *www.fairmont.com* *340 rooms, 20 suites* *In-room: refrigerator, ethernet. In-hotel: restaurant, room service, bar, pool, gym, concierge, laundry service, executive floor, public Internet, parking (fee), no-smoking rooms* *AE, DC, MC, V.*

$–$$ **Hampton Inn & Suites, Winnipeg–Manitoba.** This bright, six-story budget-chain hotel opened in 2002. Room options range from double rooms to one-room studio suites; whirlpool suites are equipped with a two-person hot tub. The Forks National Historic Site is a brisk five-minute walk away, as is the central intersection of Portage Avenue and Main Street. *260 Main St., Downtown, R3C 1A9* *204/942–4222 or 800/426–7866* *www.hamptoninn.com* *92 rooms, 36 suites* *In-room: refrigerator, ethernet, Wi-Fi. In-hotel: pool, gym, laundry facilities, parking (no fee), no-smoking rooms* *AE, DC, MC, V* *CP.*

$–$$ **Norwood Hotel.** In the French quarter, this budget-friendly property is close to all the sights but far from the hustle bustle. With a history stretching back to the late 1880s, the hotel exudes the genteel ambience of old-style hospitality while offering all the modern day amenities. *112 Marion St., R2H 0T1* *204/233–4475 or 888/888–1878* *www.norwood-hotel.com* *52 rooms, 4 suites* *In room: refriger-*

ator (some), ethernet, Wi-Fi (some). In hotel: restaurant, room service, bar, parking (no fee), no-smoking rooms ▭*AE, MC, V.*

$–$$ ★ **Place Louis Riel.** This luxury-class lodging is a converted apartment building that has contemporary suites—studios and one or two bedrooms—with living rooms, dining areas, and fully equipped kitchens. Accommodations are being renovated, starting with suites on the upper floors. The downtown location, adjacent to the Cityplace mall and a 10-minute walk from the Forks National Historic Site, is a major advantage. ✉*190 Smith St., Downtown, R3C 1J8* ☎*204/947–6961, 800/665–0569 in Canada* 🌐*www.placelouisriel.com* *294 suites* *In-room: kitchen, ethernet. In-hotel: restaurant, room service, bar, gym, laundry facilities, laundry service, parking (fee), no-smoking rooms* ▭*AE, DC, MC, V.*

$–$$ **Radisson Hotel Winnipeg Downtown.** At the center of Winnipeg's business district and only a few minutes' walk from the Winnipeg Convention Centre, this hotel attracts business travelers. Each guest room has two cordless telephones and a desk with an adjustable chair. A 12th-floor restaurant affords a panoramic view of the city. Now featuring a club floor, the hotel is being progressively renovated from the top down—flat-screen TVs, step-in frameless showers, and all new furnishings—so try to snag a room on one of the top floors. ✉*288 Portage Ave., Downtown, R3C OB8* ☎*204/956–0410 or 800/339–5328* 🌐*www.radisson.com* *261 rooms, 11 suites* *In-room: ethernet, Wi-Fi (some). In-hotel: restaurant, room service, bar, pool, gym, laundry service, concierge, executive floor, public Internet, parking (fee), no-smoking rooms* ▭*AE, DC, MC, V.*

$ **Club Regent Casino Hotel.** Part of the Winnipeg-based Canad Inns chain, this hotel stands proud in the growing northeastern neighborhood of Transcona. The property has a full-scale casino, adorned in a Caribbean theme featuring a shipwreck, waterfall, and walk through saltwater aquarium. The Kildonan Place mall is a two-minute drive away, and the hotel faces Regent Avenue, which is full of restaurants and shops. ✉*1415 Regent Ave. W, Transcona, R2C 3B2* ☎*204/667–5560 or 888/332–2623* 🌐*www.canadinns.com/clubregent* *142 rooms, 4 suites* *In-room: ethernet. In-hotel: restaurant, bar, pool, gym, public Wi-Fi, parking (no fee), no-smoking rooms* ▭*AE, DC, MC, V.*

$ **Holiday Inn Airport/West.** This family-friendly property stands near the Trans-Canada Highway's western approach to Winnipeg, the airport, the racetrack, and shopping areas. Rooms are large and contemporary. Pirate's Cove Playland is a 20-foot-tall interactive play structure complete with cannons and volcano. ✉*2520 Portage Ave., St. James, R3J 3T6* ☎*204/885–4478 or 800/665–0352* 🌐*www.holiday-inn.com/winnipeg-arpt* *226 rooms, 18 suites* *In-room: refrigerator (some), VCR (some), DVD (some), Wi-Fi. In-hotel: restaurant, bar, pool, gym, laundry facilities, laundry service, airport shuttle, parking (no fee), no-smoking rooms* ▭*AE, DC, MC, V.*

NIGHTLIFE & THE ARTS

THE ARTS

FILM A good place to find Canadian independent films as well as imports, art films, oldies, and midnight cult classics is **Cinémathèque** (✉*100 Arthur St., Exchange District* ☎*204/925–3457*). The **Winnipeg Art Gallery** (✉*300 Memorial Blvd., Downtown* ☎*204/786–6641* 🌐*www.wag.mb.ca*) has occasional cinema series.

MUSIC & DANCE Winnipeg's principal venue for orchestral music and dance is the 2,263-seat **Centennial Concert Hall** in the **Manitoba Centennial Centre** (✉*555 Main St., Downtown* ☎*204/956–1360*). Touring rock shows and other big concert productions go to **MTS Centre** (✉*300 Portage Ave.* ☎*204/780–3333*), a state-of-the-art complex that opened downtown in 2004. With maximum seating at 16,800, it's also Winnipeg's main indoor sports arena.

The **Manitoba Opera** (☎*204/942–7479* 🌐*www.manitobaopera.mb.ca*) presents two operas a year—in November and April—at the Centennial Concert Hall. The acclaimed **Royal Winnipeg Ballet** (☎*204/956–2792 or 800/667–4792* 🌐*www.rwb.org*) performs at the Centennial Concert Hall in October, December, March, and May; it's a must for dance fans. From September to mid-May, the Manitoba Centennial Centre is the home of the **Winnipeg Symphony Orchestra** (☎*204/949–3999* 🌐*www.wso.mb.ca*).

Many smaller performing organizations cater to more-specialized interests. **GroundSwell** (☎*204/943–5770* 🌐*www.gswell.ca*) explores the most modern music, with concerts in various locations. The **Manitoba Chamber Orchestra** (☎*204/783–7377* 🌐*www.manitobachamberorchestra.org*) performs eight concerts between September and May at **Westminster Church** (✉*745 Westminster Ave., West End*). Modern dance is championed by several groups, notably **Winnipeg's Contemporary Dancers** (☎*204/452–0229* 🌐*www.winnipegscontemporarydancers.ca*).

THEATER One of Canada's highly acclaimed regional theaters, the **Manitoba Theatre Centre** (✉*174 Market Ave., Downtown* ☎*204/942–6537* 🌐*www.mtc.mb.ca*) produces new plays and classics at the on-site 785-seat Mainstage and more-experimental work in the **MTC Warehouse Theatre** (✉*140 Rupert Ave., Downtown* ☎*204/943–4849*).

The **Manitoba Theatre for Young People** (✉*CanWest Global Performing Arts Centre, 2 Forks Market Rd., The Forks* ☎*204/942–8898* 🌐*www.mtyp.ca*) runs separate seasons for children and teens in its theater at the Forks National Historic Site. The **Prairie Theatre Exchange** (☎*204/942–5483* 🌐*www.pte.mb.ca*) focuses on new Canadian plays in an attractive facility in the Portage Place shopping mall. Musicals the whole family can enjoy are staged outdoors every summer in Kildonan Park at **Rainbow Stage** (✉*2021 Main St., North End* ☎*204/989–0888* 🌐*www.rainbowstage.net*). The company stages winter shows at the beautifully restored Pantages Playhouse, a theater built in 1913 during the vaudeville heyday.

NIGHTLIFE

BARS & CLUBS **Bailey's Restaurant and Bar** (✉*185 Lombard Ave., Downtown* ☎*204/944–1180*) has a plush lounge that's close to the heart of downtown. An oasis for the movers and shakers who work in nearby office towers, the bar is also a magnet for the after-theater crowd. The **Toad in the Hole** (✉*112 Osborne St., Osborne Village* ☎*204/284–7201*) is a chummy English pub well stocked with hearty stouts and ales. The main level teems with raconteurs; the more raucous downstairs room draws a younger clientele.

MUSIC Some of the city's most imaginative jazz players are heard every Tuesday night at the **Franco-Manitoban Cultural Centre** (✉*340 Provencher Blvd., St. Boniface* ☎*204/233–8972*). Classic-rock and country fans kick up their heels at the **Palomino Club** (✉*1133 Portage Ave., West End* ☎*204/772–0454*). The boldest local and visiting rock bands play at the **Pyramid Cabaret** (✉*176 Fort St., Downtown* ☎*204/957–7777*). Established and rising talent perform in the relaxed, cabaret-style **West End Cultural Centre** (✉*586 Ellice Ave., West End* ☎*204/783–6918*). **Windows Sports and Entertainment Lounge** (✉*161 Donald St., Downtown* ☎*204/942–5300*), in the Sheraton Winnipeg hotel, hosts small blues combos on weekends.

6

SPORTS & THE OUTDOORS

BASEBALL

The **Winnipeg Goldeyes** (☎*204/982–2273* 🌐*www.goldeyes.com*) play minor league Class AA baseball in the Northern League. Catch their games at **CanWest Global Park** (✉*1 Portage Ave. E, Downtown*) from April to early September.

HOCKEY

The **Manitoba Moose** (☎*204/987–7825* ✉*260 Hargrave St., Downtown*), of the American Hockey League, hit the ice at the MTS Centre from October through April.

HORSE RACING

Assiniboia Downs (✉*3975 Portage Ave., at Perimeter Hwy. W* ☎*204/885–3330*), on the city's western edge, hosts Thoroughbred racing from May through October.

SHOPPING

ARTS & CRAFTS

Regional artisans are represented at the **Craft Cupboard** (✉*Forks Market, 204-1 Forks Market Rd., The Forks* ☎*204/949–1785*).

Locally made pottery, pewter, and glassware shines at the **Sounding Stone** (✉*519 Osborne* ☎*204/284–2964*).

Stoneware Gallery (✉*778 Corydon Ave.* ☎*204/475–8088*) is one of the longest running artist's cooperatives in Canada. Look for quality pottery and ceramics. **Mayberry Fine Art** (✉*212 McDermot Ave., Exchange*

District ☎*204/255–5690*) has exquisite historical and modern Canadian paintings, prints, and sculptures.

MALLS & SHOPPING DISTRICTS

Winnipeg's own global village is found at the **Forks Market** (✉*201 Forks Market Rd., The Forks* ☎*204/942–6309*), two former railroad buildings beneath a long atrium. Rows of fresh produce mix with exotic fast-food outlets offering a rainbow of delights, from Jamaican roti to Italian gelati. The delicacies at **Fenton's Gourmet Foods–The Cheese Shop** (☎*204/942–8984*) range from massive wheels of imported cheese to local preserves. Specialty shops on the second level of Forks Market include **S. F. Imports** (☎*204/943–8167*), which enchants with traditional Ukrainian collectibles such as the *pysanka* (decorated egg). **Teekca's Aboriginal Boutique** (☎*204/946–0539*) brims with handmade moccasins, dream catchers, and jewelry.

The **Johnston Terminal** (✉*25 Forks Market Rd., The Forks* ☎*204/956–5593*) has three floors of shops and restaurants. Collectors flock to the Johnston Terminal basement, where the **Johnston Terminal Antique Mall** (☎*204/947–3952*) offers an ever-changing range of vintage attractions sold on consignment, from furniture and musical instruments to sports memorabilia. Johnston Terminal's **Global Connections** (☎*204/989–2173*) offers elegant African and Indian clothes and a wide array of ethnic music, resource texts, and ecologically friendly products.

The city's most vivid concentration of boutiques is found in **Osborne Village,** four short blocks of Osborne Street between River and Corydon avenues (near the south end of the Osborne Street bridge). A spray of music, book, and design stores attests to the area's bohemian makeup. Parking here can be difficult, and traffic is heavy on Saturday. The high end of local artistry is honored at **David Rice Jewelry and Objects** (✉*100 Osborne St., Osborne Village* ☎*204/453–6105*). At **Desart** (✉*117 Osborne St., Osborne Village* ☎*204/284–0823*) imaginative gifts that are anything but ordinary. For the latest in independent CDs from Manitoba and beyond, head to **Music Trader** (✉*97 Osborne St., Osborne Village* ☎*204/475–0077*). **Silver Lotus** (✉*111 Osborne St., Osborne Village* ☎*204/452–3648*) sparkles with jewelry from local artisans.

Polo Park (✉*1485 Portage Ave., St. James* ☎*204/784–2523*), the city's most popular shopping mall, has three well-stocked department stores as anchors: The Bay, Sears, and Zellers. **Portage Place** (✉*393 Portage Ave., Downtown* ☎*204/925–4636*) stretches across three downtown blocks and includes more than 120 shops and services. **St. Vital Centre** (✉*1225 St. Mary's Rd., St. Vital* ☎*204/257–5646*) has more than 160 tenants, including the Bay and Wal-Mart, and is a major draw south of the city.

SIDE TRIPS FROM WINNIPEG

Day trips outside the city offer a closer look at Manitoba's cultural heritage. A drive of even an hour beyond city limits reveals fascinating aspects of the region, from delightful beaches to farming towns. Wherever you drive in summer be on the lookout for roadside stands selling fresh produce and homemade delicacies.

STEINBACH

48 km (30 mi) southeast of Winnipeg.

Mennonite Heritage Village is a 40-acre open-air museum that brings to life a village of the late 1800s, when the area was settled by Mennonites fleeing religious persecution in Europe. Guides demonstrate blacksmithing, wheat grinding, and old-time housekeeping. Listen for conversations in the Mennonite German dialect. During the Pioneer Days festival in early August, the staff wears costumes and demonstrates homespun crafts. An authentic and economically priced restaurant serves traditional Mennonite specialties, such as *vereniki* (cheese-filled dumplings) and farmer's sausage. ✉ *Hwy. 12, 2 km (1 mi) north of Steinbach* ☎ *204/326–9661* 🌐 *www.mennoniteheritagevillage.com* *C$8* ⏲ *May, June, and Sept., Mon.–Sat. 10–5, Sun. noon–5; July and Aug., Mon.–Sat. 10–6, Sun. noon–6; Oct.–Apr., weekdays 10–4.*

SELKIRK

32 km (20 mi) north of Winnipeg.

Lower Fort Garry, built in 1830, is the oldest stone fort remaining from the Hudson's Bay Company fur-trading days. Today, costumed employees describe daily tasks and recount thrilling journeys by York boat, the "boat that won the West." ✉ *Hwy. 9 near Hwy. 44* ☎ *204/785–6050* 🌐 *www.pc.gc.ca/lhn-nhs/mb/fortgarry* *C$7.15* ⏲ *Grounds daily dawn–dusk; buildings mid-May–early Sept., daily 9–5.*

WINNIPEG ESSENTIALS

TRANSPORTATION

BY AIR

Winnipeg is served by Air Canada, Bearskin, Calm Air, First Air, Northwest, West Jet, United, and other commuter airlines.

AIRPORTS & TRANSFERS

Winnipeg International Airport is 8 km (5 mi) from the city. Taxi fare between the airport and downtown runs C$15–C$20. Some airport-area hotels have free airport shuttles.

Information **Winnipeg International Airport** (✉ *2000 Wellington Ave., St. James* ☎ *204/987–9402* 🌐 *www.waa.ca*).

BY BUS

Winnipeg Transit spans the city. Adult fare is C$2; exact change is required and transfers are free. Downtown Spirit is a free service that operates in the city center during peak hours. Telebus is an automated service providing arrival times according to bus-stop numbers listed in the Yellow Pages. Some routes operate on limited hours.

Information **Telebus** (☎ *204/287–7433*). **Winnipeg Transit** (☎ *204/986–5700* 🌐 *www.winnipegtransit.com*).

BY CAR

Two main east–west highways link Winnipeg with the prairie provinces. The Trans-Canada Highway (Highway 1) runs through Winnipeg, Regina, and Calgary. West of Winnipeg the Yellowhead Highway (Highway 16) branches off the Trans-Canada and heads northwest toward Saskatoon and Edmonton.

Travelers from the United States can reach the Manitoba capital from Minneapolis along I–94 and I–29, connecting to Highway 75 at the Canadian border. The driving distance between Minneapolis and Winnipeg is 727 km (452 mi).

TAXIS

Taxi service is easily secured with a phone call, although you may quickly catch one in front of a hotel.

Information **Duffy's Taxi** (☎ *204/925–0101*). **Unicity Taxi** (☎ *204/925–3131* 🌐 *www.unicitytaxi.mb.ca*).

CONTACTS & RESOURCES

EMERGENCIES

Many Winnipeg hospitals have emergency rooms, including the Health Sciences Centre and St. Boniface General Hospital. Misericordia Health Centre has a 24-hour urgent-care service for non-life-threatening conditions.

Emergency Services **Ambulance, fire, poison center, police** (☎ *911*). **Misericordia Health Centre** (✉ *99 Cornish Ave., West End* ☎ *204/788–8200* 🌐 *www.misericordia.mb.ca*).

Hospitals **Health Sciences Centre** (✉ *820 Sherbrook St., West End* ☎ *204/774–6511* 🌐 *www.hsc.mb.ca*). **St. Boniface General Hospital** (✉ *409 av. Taché, St. Boniface* ☎ *204/233–8563* 🌐 *www.sbgh.mb.ca*).

24-Hour Pharmacies **Shopper's Drug Mart** (✉ *43 Osborne St., Osborne Village* ☎ *204/958–7000* ✉ *1017 McPhillips St., North End* ☎ *204/586–8091* ✉ *2211 Pembina Hwy., Fort Richmond* ☎ *204/269–8113* 🌐 *www.shoppersdrugmart.ca*).

TOURS

Several boat lines ply the Red and Assiniboine rivers between May and mid-October. The *Paddlewheel River Rouge* has a variety of cruises combining sailings with double-decker bus tours. Exchange District Biz conducts summer walking tours of the Exchange District, offering illuminating descriptions of the region's rich commercial and architectural heritage. In addition to the general, two-hour tour there are shorter, lunch-hour walks devoted to themes, such as theater and journalism history. Cost C$5–C$6.

Information **Exchange District Biz** (✉ *133 Albert St., Exchange District* ☎ *204/942–6716* 🌐 *www.exchangedistrict.org*). *Paddlewheel River Rouge* (☎ *204/942–4500*).

VISITOR INFORMATION

The Government Tourist Reception Office, in the Manitoba Legislative Building, is open mid-May to early September, weekdays 8–5, weekends 9–5; early September to mid-May, weekdays 8:30–4:30. Destination Winnipeg on Portage Avenue is open weekdays 8:30 to 4:30; an airport location is open daily 8 AM to 9:45 PM.

Information **Destination Winnipeg** (✉ *259 Portage Ave., Downtown* ☎ *204/943–1970 or 800/665–0204* ✉ *1800 Wellington Ave., St. James* ☎ *204/982–7543* 🌐 *www.destinationwinnipeg.ca*). **Explore Manitoba Centre** (✉ *21 Forks Market Rd., The Forks* ☎ *204/927–7838 or 800/665–0040* 🌐 *www.travelmanitoba.com*). **Government Tourist Reception Office** (✉ *Broadway and Osborne St., Downtown* ☎ *204/945–5813*).

AROUND MANITOBA

6

A clutch of sites from superb parks and beaches to the Hudson Bay polar-bear mecca of Churchill are among the highlights of this province, which extends from the prairies and deep forests and lakes northward to the arctic tundra.

BRANDON

197 km (122 mi) west of Winnipeg.

Brandon, Manitoba's second-largest city (population about 43,000), lies west of Winnipeg along the Trans-Canada Highway. The city was developed along the 17-km (10½-mi) Assiniboine River corridor, which today links small parks and inviting pathways via a pedestrian bridge. The province's agricultural heritage continues in both industry and crop research, and also in museums and attractions chronicling the development of prairie farming. In early spring the weeklong **Royal Manitoba Winter Fair** (☎ *204/726–3590* 🌐 *www.brandonfairs.com*), one of the largest agricultural shows in Canada, has equestrian events and other family-oriented entertainment.

The **Commonwealth Air Training Plan Museum** honors the days when the Royal Canadian Air Force maintained a crucial training school here. It contains excellent examples of pre–World War II aircraft. ✉ *Brandon Airport, Hangar 1* ☎ *204/727–2444* 🌐 *www.airmuseum.ca* 🎟 *C$5* 🕒 *May–Sept., daily 10–4; Oct.–Apr., daily 1–4.*

WHERE TO EAT

$$$ ✕ **The Keg Steakhouse & Bar.** The thick steaks here—a Brandon tradition—are enjoyed best with a stalwart baked potato. Seafood and chicken are also available, along with a wide range of starters in generous portions, such as bacon-wrapped scallops. ✉ *1836 Brandon Ave.* ☎ *204/725–4223* 💳 *AE, DC, MC, V.*

$$ ✕**Chicago Joe's.** This bright, unpretentious restaurant in the Royal Oak Inn & Suites is big on hearty Canadian beef, chicken, and seafood favorites, including fish-and-chips with Atlantic cod battered in Canadian beer. There are full menus for breakfast and lunch as well, and an adjoining sports bar. ✉*3130 Victoria Ave.* ☎*204/728–5775* ▭*AE, DC, MC, V.*

SPRUCE WOODS PROVINCIAL HERITAGE PARK

180 km (112 mi) west of Winnipeg.

Amid soft hills covered with spruce and basswood is the desertlike **Spirit Sands,** a 16-square-km (6-square-mi) tract of cactus-filled dunes. Walk the self-guided trail through the dunes, home to Manitoba's only lizard, the elusive prairie skink. Your final destination is **Devil's Punch Bowl,** a pit dug out by an underground stream. You can also tour the park in a horse-drawn covered wagon. The nearest town is Carberry, north of the park. ✉*Hwy. 5 south of Hwy. 1 and north of Hwy. 2* ☎*204/827–8850 or 204/834–8800* 🌐*www.gov.mb.ca.*

WHITESHELL PROVINCIAL PARK

125 km (80 mi) east of Winnipeg.

A 2,590-square-km (1,000-square-mi) tract on the edge of the Canadian Shield, Whiteshell Provincial Park encompasses 200 lakes with superb northern-pike, perch, walleye, and lake-trout fishing. West Hawk Lake—formed a few thousand years ago by a falling meteor—is 365 feet deep and full of feisty smallmouth bass; scuba divers love it. Hiking trails for all abilities vein the park. One option for beginners is the Big Whiteshell trail, a one-hour hike on which you might encounter beaver, deer, and other resident critters. Other activities here include mountain biking, cross-country skiing, and snowmobiling.

Main park entry points are Falcon Lake and West Hawk Lake, both towns off Highway 1; Seven Sisters Falls, along Highway 307; and Rennie, along Highway 44. Falcon Lake, at the south end of the park, includes a great beach, a sailing club, an 18-hole golf course, tennis courts, downhill skiing, shops, and the Falcon Lake Resort Hotel. Other lodgings, including cottages and campgrounds, are scattered throughout the park. Entering Whiteshell Provincial Park via Rennie puts you near the **Alfred Hole Goose Sanctuary and Visitor Centre** (✉*Rte. 44* ☎*204/369–5470 June–mid-Oct., 204/369–5246 late Oct.–May* 🎫*Free* ⏲*June–Aug., daily 10:30–6; Sept.–mid-Oct., Fri.–Sun. 10:30–6*), which has an interpretive center. Goslings are abundant from mid-May through June; from late August through September, thousands of geese gather ahead of the fall migration. ☎*204/369–5232* 🌐*www.whiteshell.mb.ca* 🎫*C$5 per car for 3-day pass.*

WHERE TO STAY

$$ **Falcon Lake Resort Hotel.** On the shores of Falcon Lake this hotel makes the most of its splendid hinterland while still offering urban amenities. Room choices include budget-price motel units, more elaborate suites with kitchenettes and patios, and romantic hide-aways with hot tubs and loveseats. A lodge with seven adjoining suites may be rented for executive functions. Nearby facilities include an 18-hole golf course, tennis court, and lawn bowling. *Box 100, Falcon Lake, R0E 0N0 ☎204/349–8400 www.falcon-resort.mb.ca 14 rooms, 25 suites In-room: kitchen (some), DVD, VCR, Wi-Fi. In-hotel: no elevator, restaurant, bar, pool, gym, beach-front, laundry facilities, public Internet AE, MC, V.*

SKIING

Falcon Ridge Ski Recreation Area. Making the most of Manitoba winters, this Falcon Lake site offers 11 runs for downhill skiing; tubing; a detailed terrain designed for snowboarders; and approximately 15 km (9 mi) of cross-country skiing trails for varying skill levels. Equipment rentals and lessons are available. *Box 130, Falcon Lake, R0E 0N0 ☎204/349–8935 www.falcontrails.mb.ca C$18 daily lift rate Winter, weekends 10:30–4:30.*

6

HECLA ISLAND

175 km (109 mi) north of Winnipeg.

The 1,084-square-km (419-square-mi) **Hecla/Grindstone Provincial Park** encompasses a densely wooded archipelago as well as a peninsula that juts into Lake Winnipeg. Hecla Island, the largest island in the park, is about a 2½-hour drive north of Winnipeg and is accessed from the mainland via causeway. It was named for the Icelandic volcano that drove the area's original settlers to Canada in the mid-1870s. **Hecla Village,** an 1880s Icelandic fishing village with several restored buildings, is near **Gull Harbour,** the tourist center of the park and site of the deluxe Gull Harbour Resort. Hiking, cross-country skiing, and snowmobile trails crisscross the island. In winter, ice fishing on the lake is an option. Because the park is on the central North American flyway, some 50,000 waterfowl summer here. The wildlife viewing tower, near the south end of Hecla Island, is a good place from which to spot moose and other animals in early morning and evening. *Rte. 8 ☎204/378–2945 www.gov.mb.ca C$5 per car for 3-day pass.*

WHERE TO STAY

$$$$ **Hecla Oasis Resort.** Opened in late 2007, this impressive resort is part of the Radisson chain. It boasts a family water park, a full-service day spa and mineral pool, and a health and wellness center. Located in Hecla/Grindstone Provincial Park, the resort overlooks Lake Winnipeg and flanks the challenging Hecla Golf Course, ranked first in the province and 26th in Canada. The stunning lobby with its glassed-in atrium is accompanied by posh rooms and loft suites. *Hwy. 8, R0C 2R0 ☎800/267–6700 www.heclaoasis.com 70*

rooms, 22 suites In room: VCR. In hotel: restaurants, room service, golf course, pools, gym, spa, beachfront, bicycles, some pets allowed, no-smoking rooms AE, MC, V.

RIDING MOUNTAIN NATIONAL PARK

Fodor'sChoice ★ *304 km (188 mi) northwest of Winnipeg.*

This park, 3,026 square km (1,168 square mi) in the western part of Manitoba, includes forests and grasslands that support a herd of bison. **Wasagaming,** along Highway 10 at the park's south edge, is the main point of entry. The town is on Clear Lake, which has sand beaches and is popular for fishing (for walleye, perch, and white fish), boating, and swimming. In winter, snowmobile trails crisscross the lake and skirt the park's periphery. In the south-central section of the park are the 18-hole **Clear Lake Golf Course** and six tennis courts.

Hiking, mountain-biking, cross-country-skiing, and skate-skiing trails in the park cover relatively flat terrain to rough, hilly ground; some skiing trails are lighted. A self-guided tour of the bison enclosure is accessible via Lake Audy Road. Camping options are plentiful and range from full-service campgrounds to wilderness tent-only sites. Other lodging, including the Elkhorn Resort Hotel, is available nearby. *204/848–7275 or 800/707–8480 www.pc.gc.ca C$6 daily per person.*

WHERE TO STAY

$$ **Elkhorn Resort Hotel & Conference Centre.** The resort, adjacent to Riding Mountain National Park, combines luxurious facilities with rugged, natural charm. In addition to regular guest rooms—many with fireplaces and private balconies—it offers two-, three-, and four-bedroom chalets with full kitchens. The spa has a mineral pool with water processed from nearby Clear Lake. *Hwy. 10, Onanole R0J 1N0 204/848–2802 www.elkhornresort.mb.ca 57 rooms, 26 chalets In-room: DVD, Wi-Fi. In-hotel: no elevator, restaurant, bar, golf course, pool, gym, spa, public Internet, no-smoking rooms AE, DC, MC, V.*

CHURCHILL

Fodor'sChoice ★ *1,600 km (992 mi) north of Winnipeg by rail.*

Towering grain silos attest to Churchill's history as Canada's northern port for grain shipping. These days, however, this remote town (population about 1,000) on the shore of Hudson Bay is better known as the polar-bear capital of the world. The bears congregate throughout October and early November; it's not unusual to see them foraging on the outskirts of town in summer, too, when special patrols often work overtime to steer the majestic animals back into the wild. Beluga whales, which come to feed in the relatively warm waters of the Churchill River, are another draw, as are the northern lights. The best time to see the whales is usually mid-July through mid-August, when the river's ice has broken up.

You can book day-trip tours or choose a package with accommodations, meals, and transportation to and from Winnipeg. Although Churchill has a local network of roads that stretches some 80 km (50 mi), you can't actually reach it by road; you either have to take a VIA Rail train (about 36 hours) or a plane (about 1,045 km, or 648 mi) from Winnipeg. Avoid the train in summer, when service interruptions are all too common. Polar-bear-tour operators usually employ vehicles equipped to withstand both the winter cold and the rugged subarctic tundra. Some companies focus on whale-watching tours instead. Whenever you choose to visit, book all arrangements—transportation, tours, lodging—well in advance; a year ahead is not too early, especially if you plan to visit during the peak October–November bear-viewing season.

Great White Bear Tours (☎*204/675–2781 or 866/765–8344* 🌐*www.greatwhitebeartours.com*) offers polar-bear-viewing tours for both amateur and professional photographers.

Sea North Tours (☎*204/675–2195 or 888/348–7591* 🌐*www.seanorthtours.com*) runs trips to see beluga whales, seals, and the area's 200 or so bird species. Snorkel with the whales for an experience of a lifetime; the company provides all equipment.

Tundra Buggy Adventure (☎*204/949–2050 or 800/663–9832* 🌐*www.tundrabuggy.com*) uses specially designed vehicles that allow for comfortable polar-bear viewing in summer and fall.

Colorado-based **Natural Habitat Adventures** (☎*303/449–3711 or 800/543–8917* 🌐*www.nathab.com*) runs six- to nine-day excursions that include transportation between Winnipeg and Churchill, tours, accommodations, and most meals.

WHERE TO STAY

$$ **Aurora Inn.** Within walking distance of Churchill's main restaurants and shops, this modern facility has spacious, two-story loft suites with fully equipped kitchens. The inn is open throughout the year. *Box 1030, R0B 0E0* ☎*204/675–2071 or 888/840–1344* 🌐*www.aurora-inn.mb.ca* *22 suites* *In-room: no a/c, kitchen (some), DVD (some), VCR (some). In-hotel: no elevator, laundry service, public Internet, parking (no fee), no-smoking rooms* *AE, MC, V.*

$$ **Lazy Bear Lodge.** This hand-crafted, log-cabin–style hotel has north-country charm in 33 rooms, each equipped with a private bath and shower. The lodge is completely smoke-free, including the restaurant, and is open from late May through November. ✉*Main St., Box 931, R0B 0E0* ☎*204/675–2969 or 866/687–2327* 🌐*www.lazybearlodge.com* *33 rooms* *In-room: Wi-Fi. In-hotel: no elevator, restaurant, parking (no fee), no-smoking rooms* *MC, V.*

6

THE PRAIRIE PROVINCES ESSENTIALS

TRANSPORTATION

BY AIR

Several U.S. airlines serves the prairie provinces. Northwest and Continental fly to Edmonton, Calgary, Saskatoon, Regina, and Winnipeg. Alaska, Delta, and American fly to Calgary and Edmonton. United flies to Winnipeg, Edmonton, and Calgary. Frontier has flights to Calgary.

Air Canada and Air Canada Jazz have direct or connecting flights from many foreign cities to Edmonton, Calgary, Saskatoon, Regina, and Winnipeg, as well as to many smaller prairie cities. Bearskin Airlines, Transwest Air, and Westjet also offer flights to cities throughout the prairie provinces.

BY BUS

Greyhound Lines and local bus companies provide service from the United States, other parts of Canada, and throughout the prairie provinces.

Information **Greyhound Lines** (☎ *800/231–2222* 🌐 *www.greyhound.ca*).

BY CAR

From the United States, interstate highways cross the Canadian border, and two-lane highways continue on to major cities of the prairie provinces. From Minneapolis, I–94 and then I–29 connect to Route 75 at the Manitoba border south of Winnipeg. A main route to Alberta is I–15 north of Helena, Montana, which connects to Highway 2 and routes 3 and 4 to Calgary.

Two main east–west highways link the major cities of the prairie provinces. The Trans-Canada Highway (Highway 1), mostly a four-lane divided freeway, runs through Winnipeg, Regina, and Calgary on its nationwide course. The two-lane Yellowhead Highway (Highway 16) branches off the Trans-Canada Highway west of Winnipeg and heads northwest toward Saskatoon, Saskatchewan, and Edmonton, Alberta. Traveling north–south, four-lane divided freeways connect Saskatoon to Regina (Highway 11) and Edmonton to Calgary (Highway 2).

BY TRAIN

There's no direct rail service between the United States and the prairie provinces. VIA Rail trains connect eastern Canada and the West Coast through Winnipeg–Saskatoon–Edmonton. VIA Rail trains also travel between Winnipeg and Churchill, in Manitoba's northeast corner.

Information **VIA Rail** (☎ *888/842–7245* 🌐 *www.viarail.ca*).

CONTACTS & RESOURCES

VISITOR INFORMATION

Alberta **Travel Alberta** (✉ *Box 2500, Edmonton T5J 2Z4* ☎ *780/427–4321 or 800/252–3782* 🌐 *www.travelalberta.com*).

Manitoba **Explore Manitoba Centre** (✉ *21 Forks Market Rd., Winnipeg R3C 4T7* ☎ *204/927–7800* 🌐 *www.travelmanitoba.com*).

Saskatchewan **Tourism Saskatchewan** (✉ *1922 Park St., Glen Elm Park, Regina S4N 7M4* ☎ *306/787–9600, 306/787–2300 call center, 877/237–2273* 🌐 *www.sasktourism.com*).

Toronto

WORD OF MOUTH

"I definitely have to go back to Toronto, and perhaps next time I will actually be able to look down through the glass floor of the CN Tower while I'm standing on it (just don't hold your breath)."

—toedtoes

"We took the ferry over to one end of the Toronto islands a few weeks ago and walked to the other side of the island. The view back to the city was amazing. Hadn't done that in years and really enjoyed it."

—SusanInToronto

www.fodors.com/forums

Updated by Sarah Richards

"THE WILD AND RABID TORYISM of Toronto, is, I speak seriously, appalling," noted one of Toronto's earliest tourists, writer Charles Dickens back in 1842. Indeed, Canada's largest city has emerged from the dowdy days of muddy York to become the country's epicenter for commerce, culture, and communications.

The city officially became Toronto on March 6, 1834, but its roots are much more ancient. The native Hurons called this place "Toronto," which translates into "meeting place." In the 1600s, the French Jesuit Etienne Brûlé discovered portage routes along the Humber and Don rivers that spill into Lake Ontario. When the British arrived in 1793, they renamed their trading post "York" and locals dubbed the town "Muddy York" for its sloppy road conditions. A steady migration occurred into the 20th century and since World War II, Toronto has attracted residents from around the world.

Over two-thirds of the 4.5 million residents in the Greater Toronto area were born abroad and over 80 ethnic groups are now living in the city. One of the largest Italian communities outside Italy exists in Toronto. It is also home to Canada's largest Chinese community and home to North America's largest Portuguese community. Toronto is home to Canada's largest gay and lesbian community.

Immigration has generated rapid growth resulting in a vibrant mix of cultures that echoes turn-of-the-20th-century New York City—but without slums, crowding, or racial tensions. Torontonians take great pride in their multicultural character, their tolerance, and their tradition of keeping a relatively clean and safe city.

The city that once united Canadians from the Atlantic to the Pacific in a shared hatred of Toronto's sanctimoniousness now tends to draw their collective envy at how well the place works. Some critics insist that Toronto remains too smug (well, yes); too regulated (would they prefer chaos?); too provincial (actually, it's municipal; Ontario is provincial); too prim and proper (would they rather be mugged?); too young (as a major city, perhaps, but it was hardly born yesterday).

That's Toronto, in a nutshell: clean, safe, orderly. Actor Peter Ustinov once famously quipped, "Toronto is like New York run by the Swiss." After New York, it's the second largest destination for live theater on the continent. Mid-2006 saw the creation of the Four Seasons Centre for the Performing Arts, the new 2,000-seat, C$100 million home to both the Canadian Opera Company and the National Ballet of Canada. Toronto is also home to numerous professional sports franchises. First and foremost this is a hockey town, so the Toronto Maple Leafs top the list with baseball's Toronto Blue Jays and basketball's Toronto Raptors to name but a few. And there are year-round festivals, the premiere being the Toronto International Film Festival which occurs every September. And that's just for starters.

TOP REASONS TO GO

WINING & DINING
Those is search of haute cuisine are pampered in Toronto, where some of the world's finest chefs vie for the attention of the city's sizable foodie population. Try Yorkville for grilled meats, King West for bistros, and Bay Street for a power lunch.

PERFORMING ARTS
Toronto has one of North America's most thriving theater scenes. Refurbished theaters such as the Royal Alexandra and the Canon Theatre host a number of big-ticket shows in elegant surroundings.

ARCHITECTURE
Fine examples if architectural variety exist in the Financial District, but single spectacular buildings are sprinkled throughout the city—including lauded Royal Ontario Museum's Michael Lee-Chin Crystal extension.

EXPLORING TORONTO

The boundaries of what Torontonians consider downtown, where most of the city sights are located, are subject to debate, but everyone agrees on the southern cutoff—Lake Ontario and the Toronto Islands. The other coordinates of the rectangle that compose the city core are Bathurst Street to the west, Parliament Street to the east, and Eglinton Avenue to the north. Beyond these borders are numerous Greater Toronto sights that make excellent morning, afternoon, or full-day excursions. An ideal way to get a sense of the city's layout is from one of the observation decks at the CN Tower on a clear day; the view is especially lovely at sunset.

Most streets are organized on a grid system: with some exceptions, street numbers start at zero at the lake and increase as you go north. On the east–west axis, Yonge (pronounced "young") Street, Toronto's main thoroughfare, is the dividing line: You can expect higher numbers the farther away you get from Yonge.

Traffic is dense and parking expensive within the city core. If you have a car with you, leave it at your hotel when exploring the city and use it for excursions to outlying attractions or to towns like Stratford. In the city, take taxis or use the excellent Toronto Transit System (TTC)—it costs C$2.75 a ride, or C$8.50 for an all-day pass (just one pass will cover up to two adults and four children on weekends).

OLD TORONTO

In this district from Yonge Street east to Parliament Street and from King Street south to the lake, Toronto got its municipal start as the village of York in 1793. In 1834, the year the community became a city, the area, described as a ward, was renamed in honor of Canada's patron saint, St. Lawrence. Within blocks you can walk past the huge canopy of the 1960s-era Sony (formerly Hummingbird) Centre to converted late-19th century warehouses housing modern stores.

TIMING If you want to catch the farmers setting out their wares at the St. Lawrence Market, you should arrive as early as 5 AM on Saturday. You could spend anywhere from 30 minutes to two hours in the Hockey Hall of Fame, and it's easy to while away an entire evening having a few pints with dinner in the Historic Distillery District. The remaining sites are scattered throughout the neighborhood and a walking tour would take about an hour.

MAIN ATTRACTIONS

★ **Historic Distillery District.** Under careful restoration, North America's best-preserved collection of Victorian industrial architecture is in this historic enclave in downtown Toronto. Formerly the Gooderham & Worts Distillery (founded in 1832), the Distillery has been developed as a center for arts, culture, and entertainment. This 13-acre cobblestone site includes 45 19th-century buildings and a picturesque pedestrian-only village that houses more than 100 tenants—including galleries, artist studios and workshops, boutiques, retail stores, a brewery, upscale restaurants, bars, cafés, and even a spa. Live music, outdoor exhibitions, fairs, and special events take place year-round, but the summer months are really the best time to visit. ✉ *55 Mill St., south of Front St. and east of Parliament St., Old Toronto* ☎ *416/364–1177* 🌐 *www.thedistillerydistrict.com* 🎫 *Parking C$5* ⏲ *Mon.–Wed. 11–7, Thurs. and Fri. 11–9, Sat. 10–9, Sun. 11–6; individual tenant hrs may vary, including restaurants, cafés, and boutiques* Ⓜ *King, then streetcar east.*

7

❶ ★ **Hockey Hall of Fame and Museum.** Even if you're not a hockey fan, it's worth seeing this shrine to Canada's favorite sport. Exhibits include the original 1893 Stanley Cup, goalie masks, famous hockey jerseys, videos of historic games and more. The former Bank of Montréal building, built in 1885, was designed by architects Darling & Curry. ■ **TIP→Entrance is through BCE Place.** ✉ *30 Yonge St., Old Toronto* ☎ *416/360–7765* 🌐 *www.hhof.com* 🎫 *C$13* ⏲ *Sept.–June, weekdays 10–5, Sat. 9:30–6, Sun. 10:30–5; July and Aug., Mon.–Sat. 9:30–6, Sun. 10–6* Ⓜ *Union.*

❸ Fodor's Choice ★ **St. Lawrence Market.** Built in 1844 as the first true Toronto city hall, the building is now a food market, which began in the early 1900s. Considered by *Food & Wine* magazine to be one of the world's 25 best food markets, it is renowned for its local and imported foods such as fresh shellfish, sausage varieties, and cheeses. Stop and snack on Canadian bacon, also known as "peameal bacon," at the Market's Carousel Bakery. The plain brick building across Front Street, on the north side, is open on Saturday mornings for the 200-year-old farmers' market; it's a cornucopia of fine produce and homemade jams, relishes, and sauces from farms just north of Toronto. On Sunday the wares of more than 80 antiques dealers are on display in the same building. ✉ *Front and Jarvis Sts., Old Toronto* ☎ *416/392–7219* 🌐 *www.stlawrencemarket.com* ⏲ *Tues.–Thurs. 8–6, Fri. 8–7, Sat. 5–5; farmers' market Sat. 5 AM–2 PM; antiques market Sun. 5–5* Ⓜ *Union.*

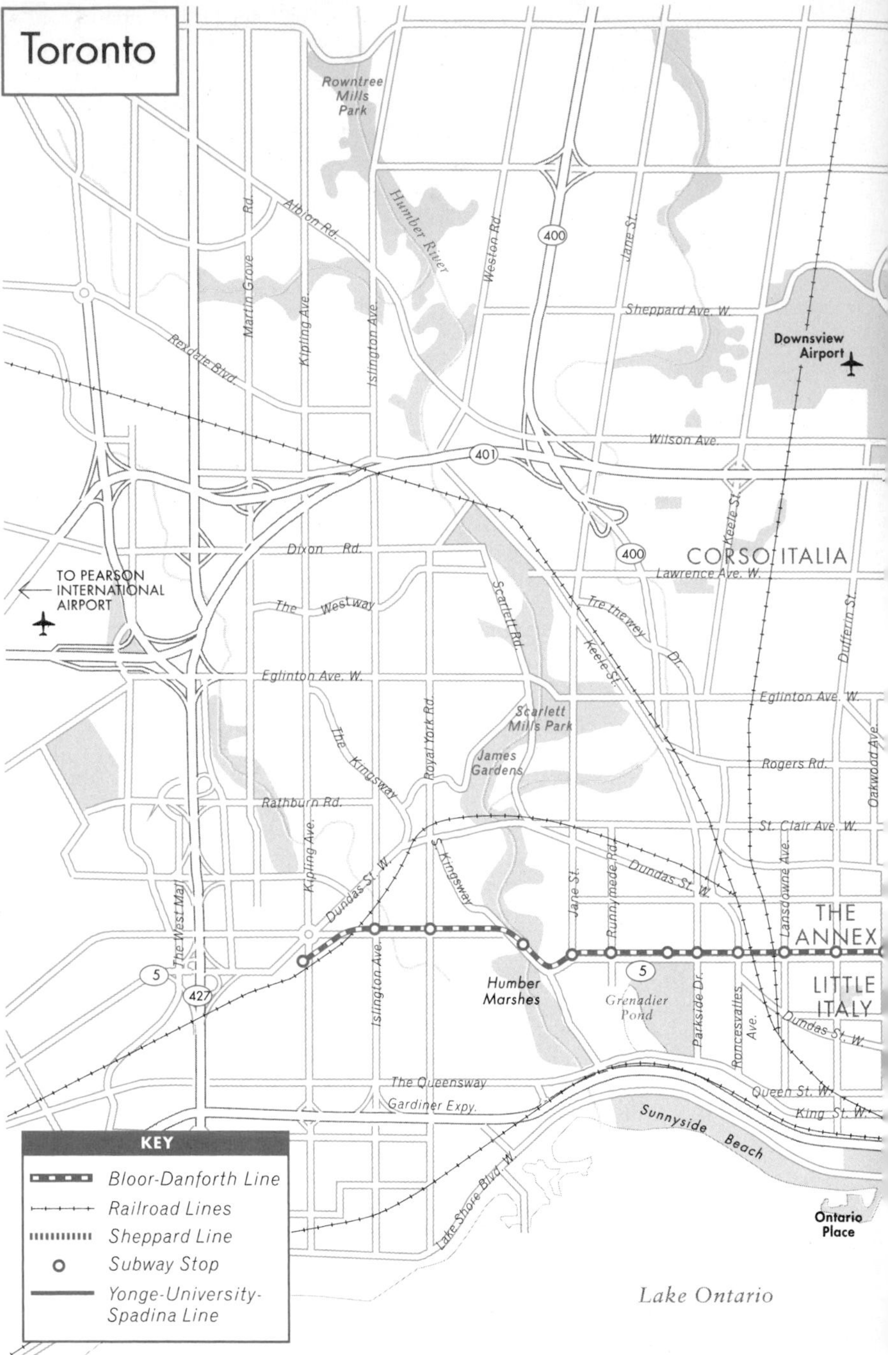
Toronto
Rowntree Mills Park
Humber River
Albion Rd.
Martin Grove Rd.
Kipling Ave.
Islington Ave.
Weston Rd.
400
Jane St.
Sheppard Ave. W.
Downsview Airport
Rexdale Blvd.
Wilson Ave.
401
Keele St.
Dixon Rd.
400
CORSO ITALIA
Lawrence Ave. W.
TO PEARSON INTERNATIONAL AIRPORT
The Westway
Scarlett Rd.
Tretheway Dr.
Dufferin St.
Eglinton Ave. W.
Eglinton Ave. W.
Scarlett Mills Park
The Kingsway
Royal York Rd.
James Gardens
Rogers Rd.
Oakwood Ave.
Rathburn Rd.
St. Clair Ave. W.
Kipling Ave.
S. Kingsway
Runnymede Rd.
Dundas St. W.
Dundas St. W.
Lansdowne Ave.
THE ANNEX
The West Mall
5
427
Islington Ave.
Humber Marshes
5
Grenadier Pond
Parkside Dr.
Roncesvalles Ave.
LITTLE ITALY
Dundas St. W.
The Queensway
Gardiner Expy.
Queen St. W.
King St. W.
Sunnyside Beach
Lake Shore Blvd. W.
Ontario Place
Lake Ontario
KEY
Bloor-Danforth Line
Railroad Lines
Sheppard Line
Subway Stop
Yonge-University-Spadina Line

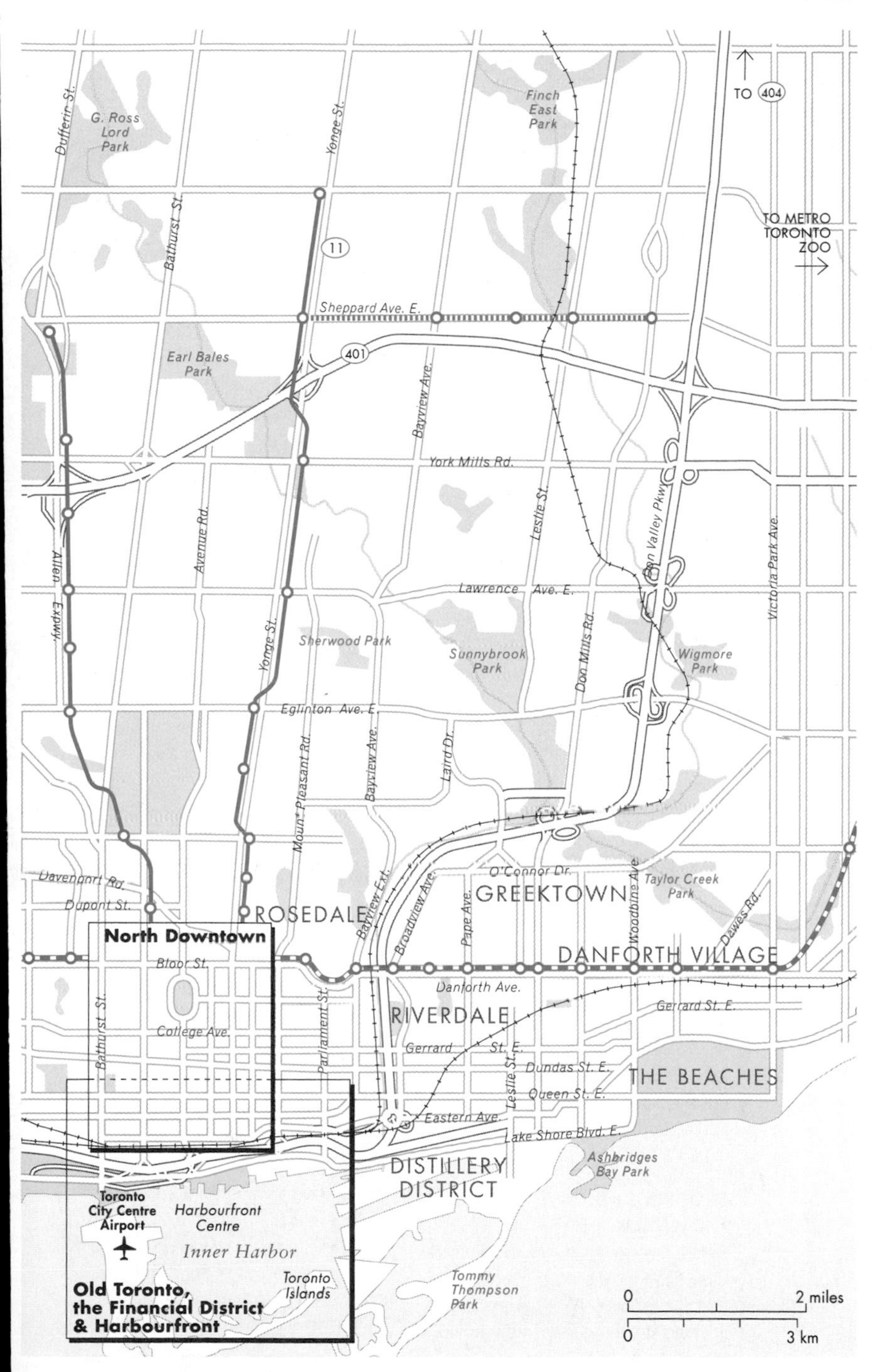

TO 404
TO METRO TORONTO ZOO
Finch East Park
G. Ross Lord Park
Dufferin St.
Yonge St.
Bathurst St.
11
Sheppard Ave. E.
401
Earl Bales Park
Bayview Ave.
York Mills Rd.
Leslie St.
Don Valley Pkwy.
Victoria Park Ave.
Avenue Rd.
Allen Expwy.
Lawrence Ave. E.
Don Mills Rd.
Sherwood Park
Sunnybrook Park
Wigmore Park
Eglinton Ave. E.
Mount Pleasant Rd.
Laird Dr.
Davenport Rd.
Dupont St.
O'Connor Dr.
Taylor Creek Park
ROSEDALE
GREEKTOWN
Broadview Ave.
Bayview Ext.
Pape Ave.
Woodbine Ave.
Dawes Rd.
North Downtown
Bloor St.
DANFORTH VILLAGE
Danforth Ave.
Parliament St.
RIVERDALE
Gerrard St. E.
College Ave.
Gerrard St. E.
Dundas St. E.
THE BEACHES
Queen St. E.
Eastern Ave.
Lake Shore Blvd. E.
Ashbridges Bay Park
DISTILLERY DISTRICT
Toronto City Centre Airport
Harbourfront Centre
Inner Harbor
Toronto Islands
Tommy Thompson Park
Old Toronto, the Financial District & Harbourfront
0
2 miles
0
3 km

GREAT ITINERARIES

To really see Toronto, a stay of at least one week is ideal. However, these great one-day itineraries are designed to inspire thematic tours of some of the city's best sights, whether you're in town for one day or more.

ARCHITECTURE & MUSEUMS

Start at Queen and Bay by pondering Finnish architect Viljo Revell's eye-shaped City Hall and then its regal predecessor, Old City Hall, across the street. From here, head south through the Financial District to admire the historic skyscrapers before swinging west on Front Street to the spectacular CN Tower. It's not hard to find—just look up. Walk up to King and catch a streetcar heading east to the Historic Distillery District. Here cutting-edge design meets restored Victorian industrial architecture—choose any one of the amazing restaurants here for lunch.

If you're still going strong, begin the afternoon at the Royal Ontario Museum. If the steep entrance fee makes you wince, take a minute to admire the fabulous new Michael Lee-Chin Crystal Gallery from outside, before moving on to one of two great alternatives in the immediate vicinity. Pottery devotees will feel at home across the street in the recently expanded Ceramic Museum; fashion enthusiasts will love the quirky Bata Shoe Museum at St. George Street. Breathtaking views from Panorama, in the Manulife Centre at the Bay–Bloor intersection, set the scene for a relaxing drink or dinner.

SHOPPING AROUND THE WORLD

Before the crowds descend at lunchtime, head for the aesthetically chaotic Spadina Avenue–Dundas Street intersection, the core of Chinatown, to browse the stalls overflowing with exotic fruits and vegetables, fragrant herbal tonics, and tons of flashy Chinese baubles. Either pause here for a steaming plate of fried noodles; or for a more unconventional lunch, try one of the many juice bars or vegan restaurants in nearby Kensington Market (head west on Spadina to Augusta and turn right). In the early 1900s this neighborhood housed the first immigrant populations, mostly Jewish and Italian at the time; retail evidence of the later arrival of Eastern European, South American, and Caribbean communities is visible, intermixed with the more modern cafés and funky clothing boutiques. Get the College streetcar east from the northern edge of Kensington Market, to the eastern end of the city (get off at Coxwell Avenue) where the bejeweled saris and bangles of the Indian Bazaar beckon. A fiery madras curry, washed down with a mango lassi or Kingfisher beer is the perfect way to end the day.

WITH KIDS

If the weather is behaving, make an early departure for the Toronto Zoo, where more than seven hundred acres of dense forests and winding creeks offer a lush home for the over 5000 animals and 460 species living here. When the weather isn't cooperating, venture out to the equally enthralling exhibits and demonstrations of the Ontario Science Center. The afternoon is best spent exploring the kid-friendly attractions along the shore of Lake Ontario, starting with the either the water park and IMAX theatre at Ontario Place or a ride up CN Tower to test your nerves on the 1,815-foot-high glass floor and take in a view that extends far enough to let you see the mist from the Falls.

ALSO WORTH SEEING

4 **Flatiron Building.** Similarly shaped relatives live in wedge-shaped lots all over North America. This building, on the triangle of Wellington, Scott, and Front streets, was erected in 1892 as the head office of the Gooderham and Worts distilling company and still hosts important offices. ✉ *Front St. between Church and Scott Sts., Old Toronto* Ⓜ *King.*

2 **Toronto's First Post Office.** Dating from 1833, this working post office continues to use quill pens, ink pots, and sealing wax. Exhibits include reproductions of letters from the 1820s and 1830s. Distinctive cancellation stamps are used on all outgoing cards and letters. ✉ *260 Adelaide St. E, Old Toronto* ☎ *416/865–1833* 🌐 *www.townofyork.com* 🎟 *Free* 🕒 *Weekdays 9–4, weekends 10–4* Ⓜ *King.*

THE FINANCIAL DISTRICT

Those magnificent high-rises that form the greatest part of Toronto's skyline are banks, banks, and more banks. Every one of Canada's major banks is headquartered in downtown Toronto.

The most interesting aspect of a stroll through the Financial District is the architectural variety of the skyscrapers—temples to steel construction that reflect the prosperity of the steel industry in Canada. The towers are connected to the PATH, the underground city of shops, restaurants, and banks.

7

MAIN ATTRACTIONS

Numbers in the margin correspond to numbers on the Old Toronto, the Financial District & Harbourfront map.

6 ★ **Design Exchange.** A delightful example of streamlined modern design, this building is clad in polished pink granite and smooth buff limestone, with stainless-steel doors. Between 1937 and 1983 the DX (as it's now known) was the home of the Toronto Stock Exchange. In the early 1990s, the building reopened as a center devoted to promoting Canadian design. The permanent collection contains examples of contemporary and decorative arts, furniture, and graphic design. The trading floor is used for rotating exhibits. ✉ *234 Bay St., Financial District* ☎ *416/363–6121* 🌐 *www.dx.org* 🎟 *C$5* 🕒 *Weekdays 10–6, weekends noon–5* Ⓜ *St. Andrew.*

5 ★ **Toronto-Dominion Centre (TD Centre).** Mies van der Rohe designed this five-building masterwork, though he died in 1969 before the last building was finished in 1985. As with his Seagram Building in New York, Mies stripped these buildings to their skin and bones of bronze-color glass and black-metal I-beams. The TD Centre's tallest building, the Toronto Dominion Bank Tower, is 56 stories high. Inside the TD Centre's Waterhouse Tower is the **Gallery of Inuit Art** (✉ *79 Wellington St. W* ☎ *416/982–8473* 🎟 *Free* 🕒 *Weekdays 8–6, weekends 10–4* Ⓜ *St. Andrew*). It's one of just a few such galleries in North America. The collection, equal to that of the Smithsonian, focuses on Canada's huge and unexplored northern frontier. ✉ *55 King St. W, Financial District* Ⓜ *St. Andrew.*

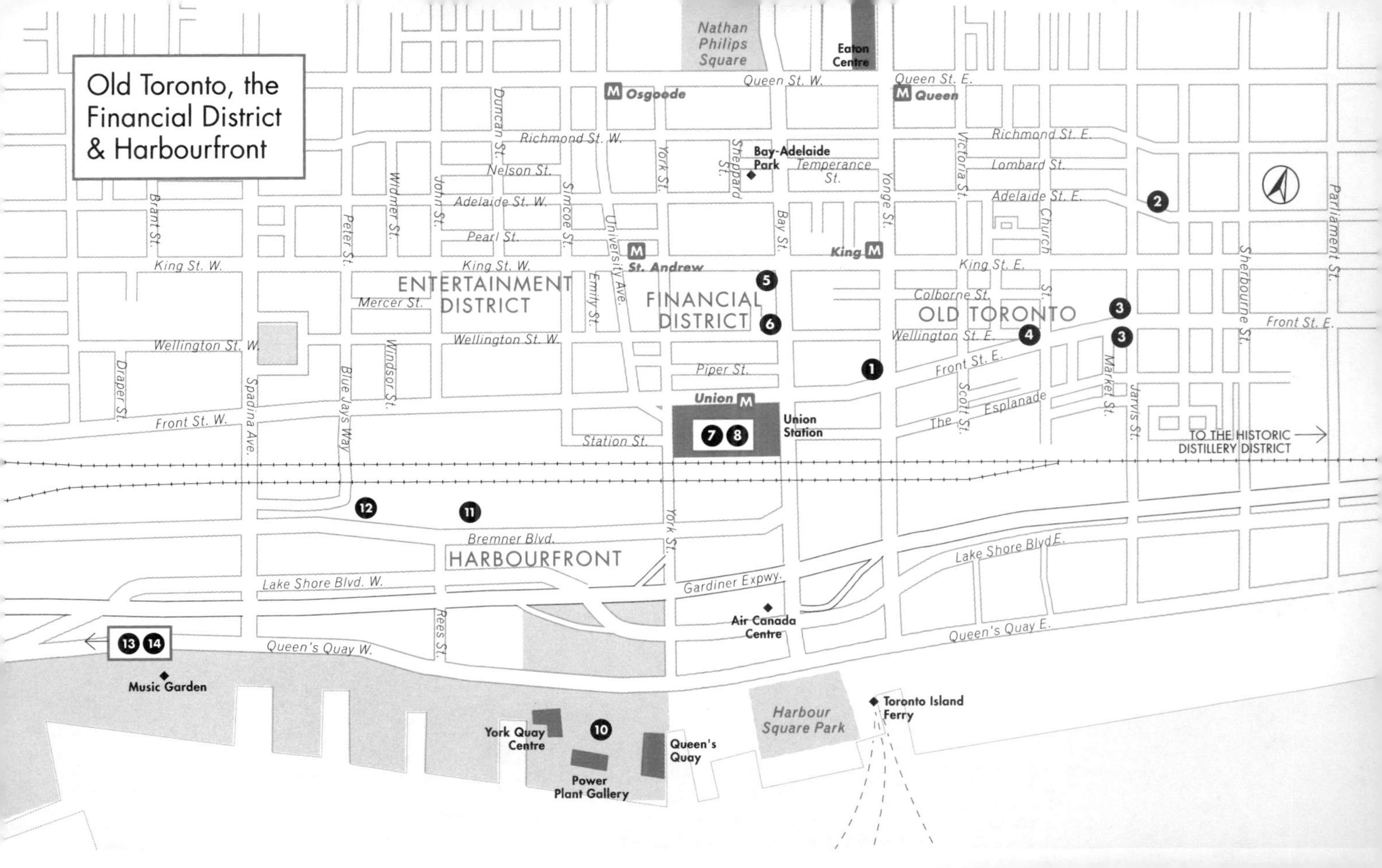
Old Toronto, the Financial District & Harbourfront
Nathan Philips Square
Eaton Centre
Queen St. W.
Queen St. E.
Osgoode
Queen
Richmond St. W.
Richmond St. E.
Duncan St.
Nelson St.
York St.
Sheppard St.
Bay-Adelaide Park
Temperance St.
Yonge St.
Victoria St.
Lombard St.
Adelaide St. E.
Adelaide St. W.
Brant St.
Peter St.
Widmer St.
John St.
Simcoe St.
University Ave.
Pearl St.
Bay St.
Church St.
Parliament St.
Sherbourne St.
King
St. Andrew
King St. W.
King St. E.
ENTERTAINMENT DISTRICT
FINANCIAL DISTRICT
OLD TORONTO
Mercer St.
Emily St.
Colborne St.
Wellington St. W.
Wellington St. E.
Front St. E.
Front St. W.
Piper St.
Draper St.
Spadina Ave.
Blue Jays Way
Windsor St.
Union
Union Station
Station St.
Scott St.
The Esplanade
Market St.
Jarvis St.
TO THE HISTORIC DISTILLERY DISTRICT
Bremner Blvd.
HARBOURFRONT
Lake Shore Blvd. W.
Lake Shore Blvd E.
Gardiner Expwy.
Air Canada Centre
Rees St.
Queen's Quay W.
Queen's Quay E.
Music Garden
York Quay Centre
Queen's Quay
Power Plant Gallery
Harbour Square Park
Toronto Island Ferry

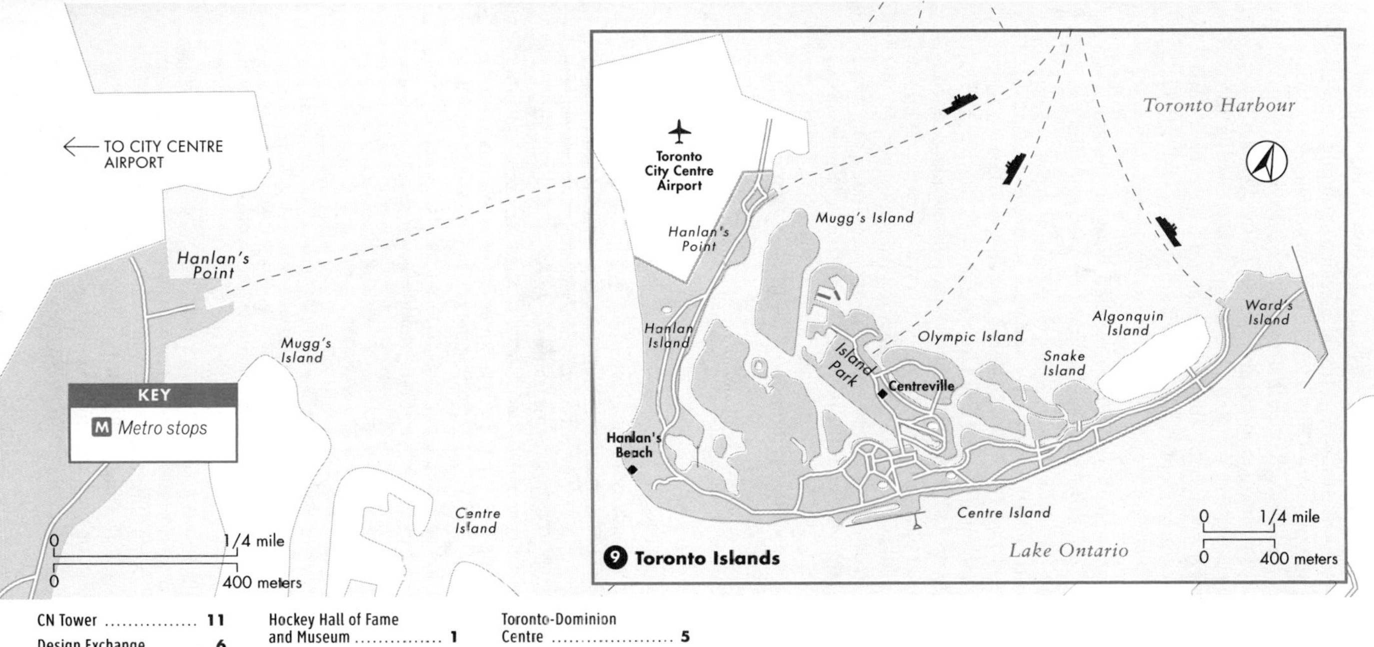

CN Tower **11**
Design Exchange **6**
Flatiron Building **4**
Fort York **13**
Harbourfront Centre **10**
Hockey Hall of Fame and Museum **1**
Ontario Place **14**
PATH **8**
Rogers Centre **12**
St. Lawrence Market **3**
Toronto-Dominion Centre **5**
Toronto's First Post Office **2**
Toronto Islands **9**
Union Station **7**

ALSO WORTH SEEING

8 **PATH.** This subterranean universe, which, according to the *Guinness Book of World Records,* is the biggest underground shopping complex in the world, emerged in the mid-1960s partly to replace the retail services in small buildings that were demolished to make way for the latest round of skyscrapers, and partly to protect office workers from the harsh winter weather. You can walk from Union Station to the Fairmont Royal York hotel, the Toronto-Dominion Centre, First Canadian Place, the Sheraton Centre, The Bay, Eaton Centre, and City Hall without ever surfacing.

7 **Union Station.** Historian Pierre Berton recalled how the planning of Union Station was akin to "the love lavished on medieval churches." Indeed, this train depot, which anchors the financial district, can be regarded as a cathedral built to serve the god of steam. Designed in 1907, and opened in 1927 by the Prince of Wales, it has a 40-foot-high ceiling of Italian tile and 22 pillars weighing 70 tons each. The vast main hall, with its lengthy concourse and light flooding in from arched windows at each end, was designed to evoke the majesty of the country that spread out by rail and imagination from this spot. To this end, too, the names of the towns and cities across Canada that were served by the country's two railway lines, Grand Trunk (which was to become part of today's Canadian National) and Canadian Pacific, are inscribed on a frieze. ✉ *65–75 Front St. W, between Bay and York Sts., Old Toronto* Ⓜ *Union.*

HARBOURFRONT

The new century has brought renewed interest to Toronto's Harbourfront. Cranes dot the skyline as condominium buildings seemingly appear overnight. Pedestrian traffic increases as temperatures rise in spring and summer. Everyone wants to be overlooking, facing, or playing in Lake Ontario. The lakefront is appealing for strolls, and myriad recreational and amusement options make it ideal for those traveling with children. Some of the city's most expensive residential real estate is here, along with shops and parks. A light rapid transit (LRT) line joins Union Station with Harbourfront, and another LT line, the 510 Spadina, stops at numerous locations along Harbourfront and busy Spadina Avenue.

MAIN ATTRACTIONS

Numbers in the margin correspond to numbers on the Old Toronto, the Financial District & Harbourfront map.

11 **CN Tower.** The tallest freestanding tower in the world is 1,815 feet and 5 inches high—and yes, it's listed in the *Guinness Book of World Records*. The CN Tower is tall for a reason: prior to the opening of this telecommunications tower in 1976, so many tall buildings had been built over the previous decades that lower radio and TV transmission towers were having trouble broadcasting. The C$63 million building weighs 130,000 tons and contains enough concrete to build a curb along Highway 401 from Toronto to Kingston, some 262 km (162 mi)

Fodor's Choice ★

to the east. It's worth a visit if the weather is clear, despite the steep fee. Six glass-front elevators zoom up the outside of the tower. The elevators travel at 20 feet per second and the ride takes less than a minute—a rate of ascent similar to that of a jet-plane takeoff. Each elevator has one floor-to-ceiling glass wall—three opaque walls make the trip easier on anyone prone to vertigo. Also, an elevator attendant chatters away during each ride, putting almost everyone at ease.

There are four observation decks to choose from. The **Glass Floor Level** is about 1,122 feet above the ground and is just as the name describes. It's like walking on a cloud. This could well be the most photographed indoor location in the city—lie on the transparent floor and have your picture taken from above like countless before you. **■TIP→ Don't worry, the glass floor has the strength to support 85,000 pounds.** Above is the **Look Out Level,** at 1,136 feet; one floor more, at 1,150 feet, is the excellent **360 Revolving Restaurant.** (If you're here to dine at the restaurant, your elevator fee is waived.) At an elevation of 1,465 feet, the **Sky Pod** is the world's highest public observation gallery. All the levels provide spectacular panoramic views of Toronto, Lake Ontario, and the Toronto Islands. On crystal clear days you can often see Lake Simcoe to the north and the mist rising from Niagara Falls to the south.

On the ground level, the **Marketplace at the Tower** has 12,500 square feet of shopping space with quality Canadian sports and travel items and souvenirs, along with a shop selling Inuit art. There's also the **Fresh Market Cafe,** with seating for 300; the **Maple Leaf Cinema,** which screens the 20-minute documentary *The Height of Excellence,* about the building of the Tower; and the **Themed Arcade,** with the latest in virtual-game experiences, including extreme sports like Alpine Racer and TopSkater. The newest attraction is the Himalamazon motion-picture ride which allows you to experience the travels of the "super-tree," a life-saving, oxygen-dispensing savior from the "super world"—a utopian paradise loosely based on the regions around the Himalayas and Amazon. Feel the spray of water and the rushing wind as you barrel down ravines and through caves.

Peak visiting hours are 11 to 4, particularly on weekends; you may wish to work around them. Hours for rides and attractions vary. ✉ *301 Front St. W, Harbourfront* ☎ *416/868–6937, 416/362–5411 restaurant* 🌐 *www.cntower.ca* 🎫 *First 2 observation levels C$21.49, Sky Pod C$25.99, combined packages start at C$31.99* ⏲ *Sun.–Thurs.* 9 AM–*10* PM, *Fri. and Sat.* 9 AM–*10:30* PM Ⓜ *Union.*

⑬ ★ **Fort York.** The most historic site in Toronto is a must for anyone interested in the origins of the city. The founding of Toronto occurred in 1793 when the British built Fort York to protect the entrance to the harbor during Anglo-American strife. Twenty years later the fort was the scene of the bloody Battle of York, in which explorer and general Zebulon Pike led U.S. forces against the fort's outnumbered British, Canadian, and First Nations defenders. The Americans won this battle—their first major victory in the War of 1812—and burned down the provincial buildings during a six-day occupation. A year later British forces retaliated when they captured Washington and torched its public buildings, including the Executive Mansion. Exhibits include restored barracks, kitchens, and gunpowder magazines, plus changing museum displays. ✉ *100 Garrison Rd., between Bathurst St. and Strachan Ave., Harbourfront* ☎ *416/392–6907* 🌐 *www.toronto.ca/culture/fort_york.htm* 🎟 *C$6* ⏲ *Jan.–late May, weekdays 10–4, weekends 10–5; late May–early Sept., daily 10–5* Ⓜ *Bathurst, then 511 streetcar.*

9 ★ **Toronto Islands.** Though sometimes referred to in the singular, there are actually eight narrow, tree-lined islands plus more than a dozen smaller islets in Lake Ontario just off the city's downtown, providing a welcome touch of greenery. They've been attracting visitors since 1833, and why not? The more than 550 acres of parkland are hard to resist, and it's usually a few degrees cooler than it is in the city.

Sandy beaches fringe the islands, the best ones being those on the southeast tip of Ward's Island, the southernmost edge of Centre Island, and the west side of Hanlan's Island. In 1999 a portion of Hanlan's Beach that had long been used by nude bathers was officially declared "clothing-optional" by Toronto's City Council. The declaration regarding Ontario's only legal nude beach passed without protest or incident—perhaps a testament to the truly international flavor of the city. The section frequented by gays and lesbians is at the easterly end; the "straight" section is more westerly. Overlapping occurs, however, and there is a nice, tolerant attitude here in general. There are free changing rooms near each beach. Lake Ontario's water has at times been declared unfit for swimming, so check reports before you go. Swimming in the lagoons and channels is prohibited. In summer, Centre Island has rowboat and canoe rentals. Pack a cooler with picnic fixings or something you can grill on one of the park's barbecue pits. ■ **TIP→ Note that the consumption of alcohol in a public park is illegal in Toronto**. The winter can be bitter cold on the islands, but snowshoeing and cross-country skiing with downtown Toronto over your shoulder are appealing to many. There are supervised wading pools, baseball diamonds, volleyball nets, and tennis courts—even a Frisbee course.

All transportation on these interconnected islands comes to you compliments of your feet: no cars (except for emergency and work vehicles) are permitted. The boardwalk from Centre Island to Ward's Island is 2½ km (1½ mi) long. Centre Island gets so crowded that no bicycles are allowed on its ferry from the mainland during summer weekends. Consider renting a bike for an hour or so once you get there and working your way across the islands. (Bike rentals can be found south of the Centre Island ferry docks on the Avenue of the Islands.)

There are more than a dozen rides, including a restored 1890s merry-go-round with more than four dozen hand-carved animals, at the children's amusement park **Centreville** (✉ *Centre Island* ☎ *416/203–0405* 🌐 *www.centreisland.ca* ⏲ *June–early Sept., weekdays 10:30–6, weekends 10:30–8; May, mid-Sept.–Oct., weekends 10:30–6*). It's modeled after a late-19th-century village, with shops, a town hall, and a small railroad station. The Far Enough Farm (free) has all kinds of animals to pet and feed, including piglets, geese, and cows. There's no entrance fee to the modest 14-acre park, although there's a charge for rides. ■ **TIP→ Instead of buying tickets, consider a day pass.** You may want to take one of the equally frequent ferries to Ward's or Hanlan's Island. Both islands have tennis courts and picnic and sunbathing spots. Late May through early September, the ferries run between the docks at the bottom of Bay Street and the Ward's Island dock between 6:35 AM and 11:45 AM; for Centre and Hanlan's islands, they begin at 8 AM. Ward's Island Ferries run roughly at half-hour intervals most of the working day and at quarter-hour intervals during peak times such as summer evenings. On Canada Day (July 1) the lines are slow-moving. In winter, the ferries run only to Ward's Island on a limited schedule. ✉ *Ferries at foot of Bay St. and Queen's Quay, Harbourfront* ☎ *416/392–8186 for island information, 416/392–8193 for ferry information* 🎫 *Ferry C$6 round-trip* Ⓜ *Union.*

ALSO WORTH SEEING

10 ★ **Harbourfront Centre.** Stretching from just west of York Street to Spadina Avenue, this culture-and-recreation center is a match for San Francisco's Pier 39 and Baltimore's Inner Harbor and is one of the highlights of a visit to Toronto. The original Harbourfront opened in 1974, rejuvenating more than a mile of city. Today's Harbourfront Center, a streamlined version of the original concept, draws more than 3 million visitors annually.

7

Queen's Quay Terminal (✉ *207 Queen's Quay W* ☎ *416/203–0510* 🌐 *queensquay.sites.toronto.com*) at Harbourfront Centre is a former Terminal Warehouse building, where goods shipped to Toronto were stored before being delivered to shops in the city. In 1983 it was transformed into a magnificent, eight-story building with specialty shops, eateries, the 450-seat Premiere Dance Theatre—and harbor views. Exhibits of contemporary painting, sculpture, architecture, video, photography, and design are mounted at the **Power Plant** (✉ *231 Queen's Quay W* ☎ *416/973–4949* 🌐 *www.thepowerplant.org* 🎫 *C$4* ⏲ *Tues. and Thurs.–Sun. noon–6, Wed. noon–8; tours weekends at 2 and 4, Wed. at 6:30*). It can be spotted by its tall red smokestack. It was built in 1927 as a power station for the Terminal Warehouse's ice-making plant. Wednesday from 5 PM to 8 PM, admission is free. **York Quay Centre** (✉ *235 Queen's Quay W* ☎ *416/973–4000, 416/973–4866 rink info, 416/973–4963 craft studio*) hosts concerts, theater, readings, and even skilled artisans. The Craft Studio, for example, has professional craftspeople working in ceramics, glass, metal, and textiles from February to December (Tuesday through Sunday), in full view of the public. A shallow pond outside is used for canoe lessons in warmer months and as the largest artificial ice-skating rink in North America in more wintry times. At the nearby Nautical Centre, many private firms rent boats and give lessons in sailing and canoeing. Among the seasonal events in Harbourfront Centre are the Ice Canoe Race in late January, Winterfest in February, a jazz festival in June, Canada Day celebrations and the Parade of Lights in July, the Authors' Festival and Harvest Festival in October, and the Swedish Christmas Fair in

November. ✉ *Administrative offices, 410 Queen's Quay W, Harbourfront* ☎ *416/973–4000 event hotline, 416/973–4600 offices* 🌐 *www.harbourfrontcentre.com* Ⓜ *Union.*

⓮ ★ **Ontario Place.** The waterfront entertainment complex stretches along three man-made islands and includes Soak City, downtown Toronto's only water park; pedal boats at Bob's Boat Yard; Wilderness Adventure Ride; and Mars Simulator Ride. The **Cinesphere,** an enclosed dome with a six-story movie screen, uses the world's first IMAX projection system, a Canadian invention. The 16,000-seat outdoor **Molson Amphitheatre** stages performances by singers and rock groups throughout summer, and the **Atlantis Pavilions** is a 32,000-square-foot entertainment and dining facility. Live children's entertainment on two stages is included in the admission price to the park. *The Big Comfy Couch, Toopy and Binoo,* and other children's favorites are featured. **■ TIP→ For the best value, the Play All Day Pass allows unlimited use of most rides and attractions including daytime Cinesphere IMAX films.** Weekends in September bring several annual events to this venue: the Great White North Dragon Boat Challenge, the Toronto In-Water Boat Show, and the Fall Fishing Festival and Kids' Fishing Derby. ✉ *955 Lakeshore Blvd. W, across from Exhibition Place, Harbourfront* ☎ *866/663–4386 recording* 🌐 *www.ontarioplace.com* *Grounds C$15, pass C$39* ⏲ *May, mid-Sept–late Sept., weekends 10–6; June, weekdays 10–5, weekends 10–8; July–early Sept., daily 10–8* Ⓜ *Union, then free shuttle bus.*

⓬ ★ **Rogers Centre.** One of Toronto's most famous landmarks, the Rogers Centre is home to baseball's Blue Jays, and was the world's first stadium with a fully retractable roof. Rogers Communications, the owner of the Blue Jays, bought the stadium, formerly known as the SkyDome, in February 2005 for a mere C$25 million. It has been refurbished with a new playing surface and a state-of-the-art integrated scoring and display system that includes one main screen to replace the existing one, and two color display screens on either side of the outfield wall. One way to see the huge 52,000-seat stadium is to buy tickets for a Blue Jays or Argos game or one of the many other events that take place here. You might watch a cricket match, Wrestlemania, a monster-truck race, a family ice show, or a rock concert—even the large-scale opera *Aida* has been performed here. You can also take a one-hour guided walking tour. There's also a 15-minute film. ✉ *1 Blue Jays Way, tour entrance at Front and John Sts., between gates 1 and 2, Old Toronto* ☎ *416/341–2770 for tours, 416/341–3663 for events and shows, 416/341–1234 for Blue Jays information* 🌐 *www.rogerscentre.com* *Tour C$13.50* ⏲ *Tours daily; times vary based on scheduled events* Ⓜ *Union.*

NORTH DOWNTOWN: ALONG DUNDAS & QUEEN STREETS

The areas along Dundas and Queen streets typify Toronto's ethnic makeup and vibrant youthfulness. To many locals, the Dundas and Spadina intersection means Chinatown and Kensington Market, and Queen West, which was the home of '90s comedy troupe Kids in the Hall and pop-rockers Barenaked Ladies, has always been a haven for shoppers and trend-setters. On the western fringe, the rejuvenated West Queen West neighborhood is quickly becoming Toronto's newest hot spot. Due east, where you find the sprawling town square, two city halls, the two-block-long Eaton Centre, is full of variety in architecture, purpose, and tone.

Numbers in the text and in the margin correspond to points of interest on the North Downtown Toronto map.

TIMING Always a nice stroll in summer, Nathan Phillips Square attracts skaters and Christmas carolers during winter. Chinatown is at its busiest (and most fun) on Sunday. Kensington Market is great any time, though it can feel a bit sketchy at night and it gets mobbed on weekend afternoons. The Campbell and Mackenzie houses merit at least half an hour each, the Art Gallery and the Grange an hour or more. And, of course, Chinatown can gobble up an entire afternoon.

MAIN ATTRACTIONS

9 ★ **Chinatown.** Today, Chinatown—which now has to be described as the main or original Chinatown, as five other areas with large Chinese populations have sprung up elsewhere in metropolitan Toronto—covers much of the area of Spadina Avenue from Queen Street to College Street, running along Dundas Street nearly as far east as Bay Street. ⊠ *Along Dundas St. from Spadina Ave. to Nathan Phillips Sq.* Ⓜ *St. Patrick.*

13 **City Hall.** Toronto's modern city hall was the outgrowth of a 1958 international competition to which some 520 architects from 42 countries submitted designs. The winning presentation by Finnish architect Viljo Revell was controversial—two curved towers of differing height. But there is a logic to it all—an aerial view of City Hall shows a circular council chamber sitting like an eye between the two tower "eyelids" containing offices of 44 municipal wards, with 44 city councillors. A remarkable mural within the main entrance, *Metropolis*, was constructed by sculptor David Partridge from 100,000 common nails. Revell died before his masterwork was opened in 1965, but within months City Hall became a symbol of a thriving metropolis, with a silhouette as recognizable in its own way as the Eiffel Tower. The positive influence that the development of this building has had on Toronto's civic life is detailed in Robert Fulford's book *Accidental City*.

Annual events at City Hall include the Spring Flower Show in late March; the Toronto Outdoor Art Exhibition in early July; and the yearly Cavalcade of Lights from late November through Christmas, when more than 100,000 sparkling lights are illuminated across both new and old city halls.

In front of City Hall, 9-acre **Nathan Phillips Square** (named after the mayor who initiated the City Hall project) has become a gathering place, whether for royal visits, protest rallies, picnic lunches, or concerts. The reflecting pool is a delight in summer, and even more so in winter, when office workers skate at lunchtime. The park also holds a Peace Garden for quiet meditation and Henry Moore's striking bronze sculpture *The*

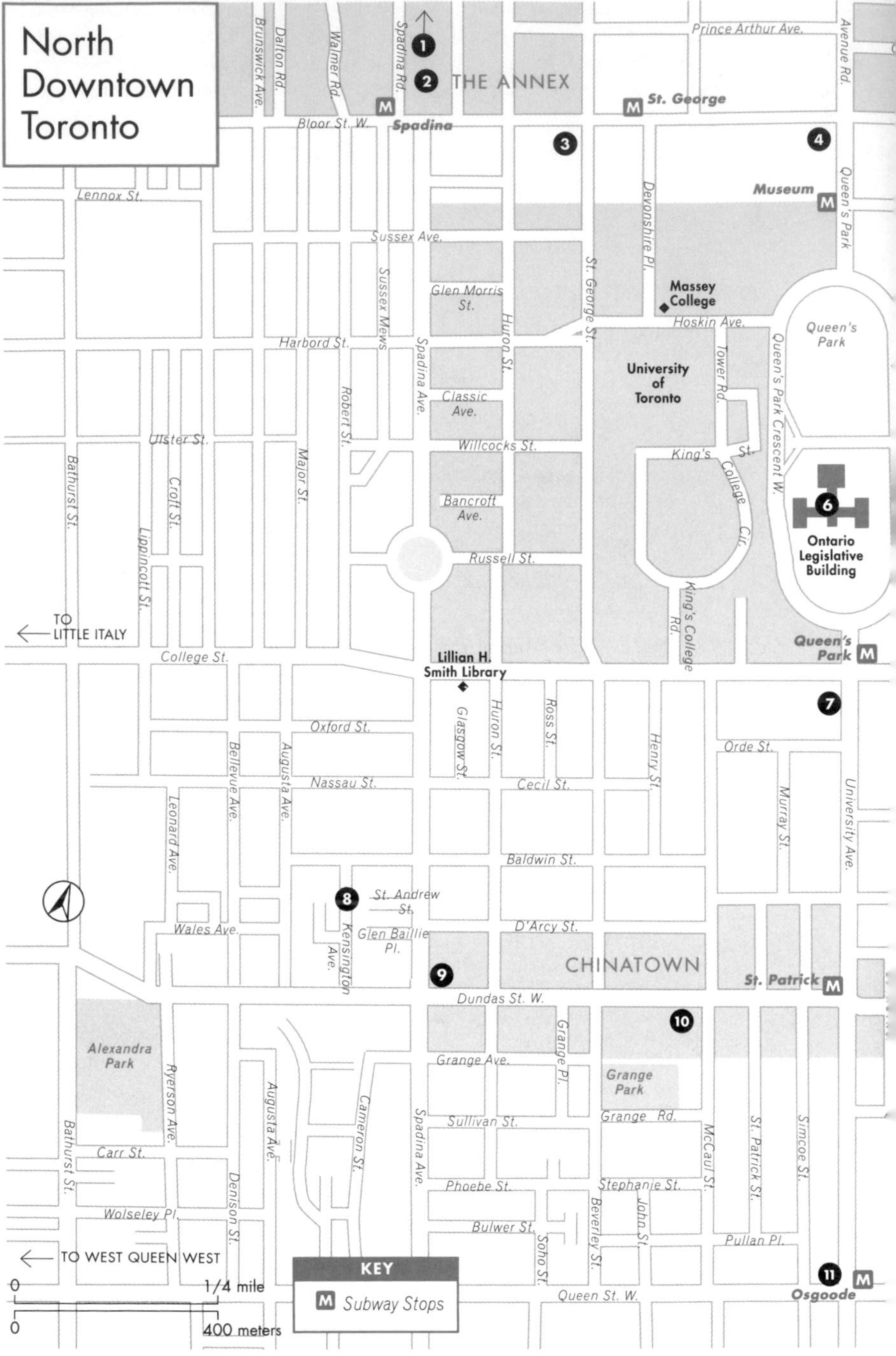
North Downtown Toronto
THE ANNEX
Prince Arthur Ave.
Avenue Rd.
Brunswick Ave.
Dalton Rd.
Walmer Rd.
Spadina Rd.
St. George
Bloor St. W.
Spadina
Museum
Queen's Park
Lennox St.
Sussex Ave.
Sussex Mews
Devonshire Pl.
St. George St.
Massey College
Hoskin Ave.
Glen Morris St.
Huron St.
Harbord St.
Spadina Ave.
Robert St.
Tower Rd.
Queen's Park Crescent W.
University of Toronto
Classic Ave.
Ulster St.
Willcocks St.
King's College Cir.
Bathurst St.
Croft St.
Major St.
Bancroft Ave.
Ontario Legislative Building
Lippincott St.
Russell St.
King's College Rd.
TO LITTLE ITALY
College St.
Lillian H. Smith Library
Oxford St.
Bellevue Ave.
Augusta Ave.
Glasgow St.
Ross St.
Henry St.
Orde St.
Murray St.
University Ave.
Nassau St.
Cecil St.
Leonard Ave.
Baldwin St.
St. Andrew St.
Wales Ave.
Kensington Ave.
Glen Baillie Pl.
D'Arcy St.
CHINATOWN
St. Patrick
Dundas St. W.
Grange Pl.
Alexandra Park
Ryerson Ave.
Grange Ave.
Cameron St.
Grange Park
Grange Rd.
McCaul St.
St. Patrick St.
Simcoe St.
Sullivan St.
Carr St.
Denison St.
Phoebe St.
Stephanie St.
John St.
Beverley St.
Wolseley Pl.
Bulwer St.
Soho St.
Pullan Pl.
TO WEST QUEEN WEST
KEY
Subway Stops
Queen St. W.
Osgoode
0
1/4 mile
0
400 meters
1
2
3
4
6
7
8
9
10
11

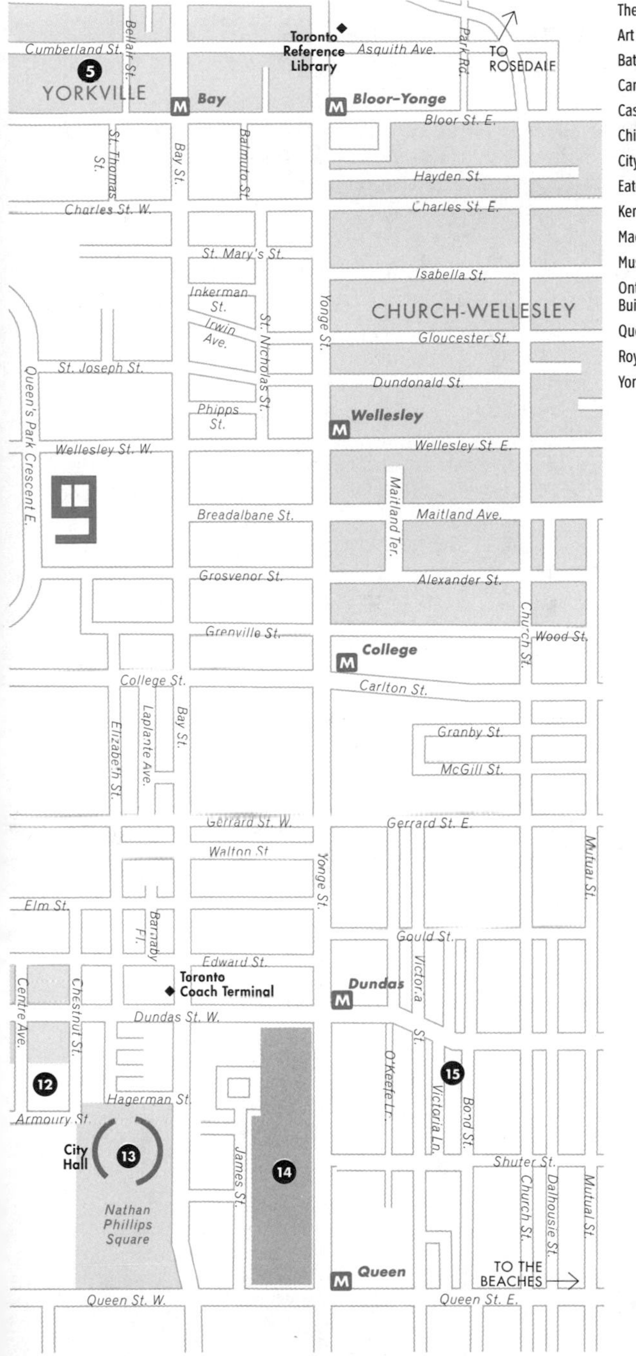

- The Annex 2
- Art Gallery of Ontario 10
- Bata Shoe Museum 3
- Campbell House 11
- Casa Loma 1
- Chinatown 9
- City Hall 13
- Eaton Centre 14
- Kensington Market 8
- Mackenzie House 15
- Museum for Textiles 12
- Ontario Legislative Building 6
- Queen's Park 7
- Royal Ontario Museum 4
- Yorkville 5

7

Archer. On New Year's Eve, crowds gather here for Toronto's answer to New York City's Times Square countdown madness. ✉*100 Queen St. W, Downtown* ☎*416/338–0338, 416/338–0889 TDD* 🌐*www.toronto.ca* ⏲*Weekdays 8:30–4:30* Ⓜ*Queen.*

❽ **Kensington Market.** This raucous, European-style marketplace titillates all the senses. On any given day you can find Russian rye breads, barrels of dill pickles, fresh fish on ice, mountains of cheese, and bushels of ripe fruit. Kensington's collection of vintage-clothing stores is the best in the city.

Kensington Market sprang up in the early 1900s, when Russian, Polish, and Jewish inhabitants set up stalls in front of their houses. Since then, the market—named after the area's major street—has become a United Nations of stores and a microcosm of Toronto's multicultural heritage. Unlike the members of the UN, however, these vendors get along well with one another. Jewish and Eastern European shops sit side by side with Portuguese, Caribbean, and East Indian ones, as well as with a sprinkling of Vietnamese, Japanese, and Chinese establishments. In the late 1970s the market gained national recognition through the long-running hit CBC television sitcom *The King of Kensington,* starring Canadian actor Al Waxman. Saturday is the best day to visit, preferably by public transit; parking is difficult. Note that many stores are closed on Sunday. ✉*Bordered by College St. on the north, Spadina Ave. on the east, Dundas St. on the south, and Augusta Ave. on the west, Kensington Market* ⏲*Daily dawn–dusk* Ⓜ*St. Patrick, then streetcar west.*

ALSO WORTH SEEING

❿ **Art Gallery of Ontario.** From extremely modest beginnings in 1900, the AGO (as it's known) is now in the big leagues in terms of exhibitions and support. In early 2004, "Transformation AGO" was launched—a major expansion designed by world-renowned architect (and Toronto native son) Frank Gehry. With a 20% increase in overall building size, allowing for 97,000 square feet of additional gallery space, completion is expected in late 2008, at a cost of C$254 million. Torontonians will not recognize the new AGO, as Gehry plans a monumental glass and titanium facade to be built over the main building.

Fodor's Choice ★

Temporary exhibits continue to rotate during construction, but the only permanent display open for most of 2008 will be the **Henry Moore Sculpture Centre,** the largest public collection of Moore's sculpture in the world. People of all ages can enjoy climbing in and around Henry Moore's large *Two Forms* sculpture, which is just outside the AGO, on McCaul Street. For a complete list of what's on, check the Web site. ✉*317 Dundas St. W, Chinatown* ☎*416/979–6648* 🌐*www.ago.net* 🎟*C$5; free on Wed. after 6; special exhibitions C$15* PM ⏲*Wed.–Fri. noon–9, weekends 10–5:30* Ⓜ*St. Patrick.*

⓫ **Campbell House.** The stately Georgian mansion of Sir William Campbell, the sixth chief justice of Upper Canada, is now one of Toronto's most charming house museums. Built in 1822 in another part of town, the Campbell House was moved to this site in 1972. It has been tastefully restored with elegant early-19th-century furniture. Costumed guides detail the social life of the upper class. Note the model of the town of York as it was in the 1820s, and the original kitchen. ✉ *160 Queen St. W, Queen West* ☎ *416/597–0227* 🌐 *www.campbellhousemuseum.ca* 🎫 *C$4.50* ⏲ *Oct.–mid-May, Tues–Fri., 9:30–4:30; mid-May–Sept., Tues–Fri., 9:30–4:30, weekends noon–4* Ⓜ *Osgoode.*

⓮ **Eaton Centre.** The 3-million-square-foot Eaton Centre shopping mall has been both praised and vilified since it was built in the 1970s, but it remains incredibly popular. From the graceful glass roof, arching 127 feet above the lowest of the mall levels, to Michael Snow's exquisite flock of fiberglass Canada geese floating poetically in open space, to the glass-enclosed elevators, porthole windows, and nearly two dozen long and graceful escalators, there is plenty to appreciate.

Such a wide selection of shops and eateries can be confusing, so here's a simple guide: Galleria Level 1 contains two food courts; popularly priced fashions; photo, electronics, and music stores; and much "convenience" merchandise. Level 2 is directed to the middle-income shopper; Level 3, suitably, has the highest elevation, fashion, and prices. In the late 1990s a branch of eatons (formerly Eaton's) opened here, even after most of the chain's stores across Canada had closed and the family's merchant dynasty had come to an end. The Centre now retains the famous family's name, but the biggest tenants are Sears and the Canadian flagship store of Swedish retail giant H&M. The southern end of Level 3 has a skywalk that connects the Centre to the seven floors of the Bay (formerly Simpsons) department store, across Queen Street.

Safe, well-lighted parking garages with spaces for some 1,800 cars are sprinkled around Eaton Centre. The building extends along the west side of Yonge Street all the way from Queen Street up to Dundas Street (with subway stops at each end). ✉ *220 Yonge St., Downtown* ☎ *416/598–8560* 🌐 *www.torontoeatoncentre.com* ⏲ *Weekdays 10–9, Sat. 9:30–7, Sun. noon–6* Ⓜ *Dundas.*

⓯ **Mackenzie House.** Once home to journalist William Lyon Mackenzie, who was born in Scotland at the end of the 18th century and emigrated to Canada in 1820, the National Historic Site is now a museum and library. Mackenzie started a newspaper that so enraged the powers that be (a clique known as "the Family Compact") that they dumped all his type into Lake Ontario. An undeterred Mackenzie stayed on to be elected the first mayor of Toronto in 1834 and is said even to have designed the coat of arms of his new city; his grandson, William Lyon Mackenzie King, became the longest-serving prime minister in Canadian history.

Mackenzie served only one year as mayor. Upset with the government big shots in 1837, he gathered some 700 supporters and marched down Yonge Street to try to overthrow the government. His minions were roundly defeated, and Mackenzie fled to the United States with a price on his head. When the Canadian government granted him amnesty years later, he was promptly elected to the legislative assembly and began to publish another newspaper. By this time, though, he was so down on his luck that some friends bought his family this house. Mackenzie enjoyed the place for but a few depressing years and died in 1861. Among the period furnishings and equipment preserved here is the fiery Scot's printing press. ✉ *82 Bond St., Downtown* ☎ *416/392–6915* 🎫 *C$4, holidays C$5.50* ⏲ *Jan.–Apr., weekends noon–5; May–Labor Day, Tues.–Sun. noon–5; Sept.–Dec., Tues.–Fri. noon–4, weekends noon–5* Ⓜ *Dundas.*

⓬ **Museum for Textiles.** Ten galleries showcase cultural displays—men's costumes from northern Nigeria, for example—as well as the latest in contemporary design. Rugs, cloth, and tapestries from around the world are exhibited. Wednesday evenings (5–8) admission is pay-what-you-can. ✉ *55 Centre Ave., Downtown* ☎ *416/599–5321* 🌐 *www.textilemuseum.ca* 🎫 *C$10* ⏲ *Thurs.–Tues. 11–5, Wed. 11–8* Ⓜ *St. Patrick.*

NORTH DOWNTOWN: AROUND QUEEN'S PARK

Bounded by College Street to the south, Church Street to the east, Bloor Street to the north, and Spadina Avenue to the west, this midtown area is a political, cultural, and intellectual feast. Its heart is the large, oval Queen's Park, south of which is the seat of the Ontario Provincial Legislature, and to the east and west the University of Toronto's main campus, which straddles the park and occupies about 160 acres.

MAIN ATTRACTIONS

Numbers in the margin correspond to points of interest on the North Downtown Toronto map.

❷ **The Annex.** Born in 1887, when the burgeoning town of Toronto engulfed the area between Bathurst Street and Avenue Road north from Bloor Street to the Canadian Pacific Railway tracks at what is now Dupont Street, the countrified Annex soon became an enclave for the well-to-do; today it attracts an intellectual set. Timothy Eaton of department-store fame built a handsome structure at 182 Lowther Avenue (since demolished). The prominent Gooderham family, owners of a distillery, erected a lovely red castle at the corner of St. George Street and Bloor Street, now the home of the exclusive York Club.

As Queen Victoria gave way to King Edward, the old rich gave way to the new rich and ethnic groups came and went. Upon the arrival of the ultimate neighborhood wrecker—the developer—many Edwardian mansions were demolished to make room for very ugly 1960s-era apartment buildings.

Still, the Annex, with its hundreds of attractive old homes, can be cited as a prime example of Toronto's success in preserving lovely, safe streets within the downtown area. Examples of late-19th-century architecture can be spotted on Admiral Road, Lowther Avenue, and Bloor Street, west of University Avenue. Round turrets, pyramid-shaped roofs, and conical (some even comical) spires are among the pleasures shared by some 20,000 Torontonians who live in this vibrant community, including professors, students, writers, lawyers, and other professional and artsy types. Bloor Street between Spadina and Palmerston keeps them fed and entertained with its bohemian collection of used-record stores, whole foods shops and juice bars, and restaurants from elegant Italian to hearty Polish and aromatic Indian.

✉*Bordered by Bathurst St. to the west, St. George St. to the east, Bloor St. W to the south, and Dupont St. to the north.*

> **WORD OF MOUTH**
>
> "Your kids might like the Bata Shoe Museum. My dad took my nine-year-old niece there and they both loved it. It is a well-curated museum that does a good job of showing in an interesting way how footwear can tell you something about a culture or a period in history. It's also an interesting building (it looks like a deconstructed shoe box)." —Kate_W

3 ★ **Bata Shoe Museum.** Created by Sonja Bata, wife of the founder of the Bata Shoe Company, the permanent collection contains 10,000 varieties of foot coverings and, through the changing fashions, highlights the craft and sociology of making shoes. Some items date back more than 4,000 years. Pressurized sky-diving boots, iron-spiked shoes used for crushing chestnuts, and smugglers' clogs are among the items on display. Elton John's boots have proved wildly popular, but Marilyn Monroe's red leather pumps give them a run for the money. Admission is free every Thursday from 5 to 8 PM. ✉*327 Bloor St. W, The Annex* ☎*416/979–7799* 🌐*www.batashoemuseum.ca* 🎫*C$12* 🕓*Tues., Wed., Fri., and Sat. 10–5, Thurs. 10–8, Sun. noon–5, Mon. 10–5 (June–Aug. only)* Ⓜ*St. George.*

7

1 **Casa Loma.** A European-style castle, Casa Loma was commissioned by Sir Henry Pellatt, a soldier and financier, who picked up architectural ideas from some of Europe's finest mansions. This grand display of extravagance has 98 rooms, 2 towers, creepy passageways, and lots of secret panels. The home's architect, E. J. Lennox, also designed Toronto's Old City Hall and the King Edward Hotel. Pellatt spent over C$3 million to construct his dream (that's in 1913 dollars), only to lose it to the taxman just over a decade later. Some impressive details are the giant pipe organ; the reproduction of Windsor Castle's Peacock Alley; the majestic, 60-foot-high ceiling of the Great Hall; the mahogany-and-marble stable, reached by a long, underground passage; and the extensive, 5-acre estate gardens (open May–October). The rooms are copies of those in English, Spanish, Scottish, and Austrian castles. This has been the location for many a horror movie and period drama—and for an episode of the BBC's *Antiques Roadshow.* Self-guided audio tours are available in eight languages ($2). The admission price includes a docudrama about Pellatt's life. **TIP→ A tour of Casa Loma is a good 1½-km (1-mi) walk, so wear sensible shoes.** ✉*1 Austin Terr., Forest Hill* ☎*416/923–1171* 🌐*www.casaloma.org* 🎫*C$16* 🕓*Daily 9:30–5, last admission at 4* Ⓜ*Dupont.*

4 ★ **Royal Ontario Museum.** Since its inception in 1912, the ROM, Canada's largest museum, has amassed more than 6 million items. What makes the ROM unique is that science, art, and archaeology exhibits are all appealingly presented in one gigantic complex. The four-year, C$200 million refurbishment project, envisioned by world-renowned architect

Daniel Libeskind (the designer of the Jewish Museum in Berlin) added 40,000 square feet and the ultramodern **Michael Lee-Chin Crystal** gallery—appearing as a series of interlocking prismatic cubes bubbling up from the original Neo-Romanesque home of the museum and spilling out onto Bloor Street.

Highlights include the Learning Centre—a state-of-the-art educational facility for the 220,000 schoolchildren expected annually—and the **Crystal Court,** a four-storied atrium slashed on all sides by sliver-thin windows, through which shards of light and shadows pour into the open space. A look through the windows reveals parts of the treasures inside, such as the frightful creatures from the **Age of Dinosaurs** exhibit standing guard. The **Institute for Contemporary Culture** hangs 110 feet over Bloor Street from its fourth floor perch. The Crystal Five Bistro ("C5" for short) on the fifth floor feels a bit like the Ten-Forward lounge on Star Trek's Enterprise, and after sampling a selection of perfectly presented tapas and the region's finest wines, you may wonder if they're hiding a food "replicator" in the kitchen.

The **Herman Herzog Levy Gallery** exhibits a stunning range of large and colorful textiles, paintings, and prints from the museum's acclaimed Asian collection; the **Chinese Sculpture Gallery** in the Matthews Family Court displays 25 stone Buddhist sculptures dating from the second through 16th centuries; and the **Gallery of Korean Art** is North America's largest permanent gallery devoted to Korean art and culture. The **Patricia Harris Gallery of Textiles and Costume** houses a selection of Chinese imperial court garments, early Canadian quilts and a survey of European fashions from the 18th century to present. ■ **TIP→ Admission is reduced to C$5 on Friday after 4:30 PM.** ✉ *100 Queen's Park, Queen's Park* ☎ *416/586–5549* 🌐 *www.rom.on.ca* 🎫 *C$20* ⏲ *Mon.–Thurs. and weekends 10–6, Fri. 10–9:30* Ⓜ *Museum.*

❺ **Yorkville.** Toronto's equivalent to Rodeo Drive or Madison Avenue is packed with restaurants, galleries, specialty shops, and high-price stores specializing in designer clothes, furs, and jewels. It's also the neighborhood where much of the excitement takes place in September during the annual Toronto International Film Festival. This is said by many to be the world's largest and most people-friendly film festival, where the public actually gets to see premieres and hidden gems and attend industry seminars. Klieg lights shine over skyscrapers, bistros serve alcohol until 2 AM, cafés teem with the well-heeled, and everyone practices air kisses. Yorkville is also home to a unique park on Cumberland Street, designed as a series of gardens along old property lines and reflecting both the history of the Village of Yorkville and the diversity of the Canadian landscape. ✉ *Bordered by Avenue Rd., Yonge and Bloor Sts., and Yorkville Ave., Yorkville* Ⓜ *Bay.*

ALSO WORTH SEEING

❻ **Ontario Legislative Building.** Like City Hall, the home to the provincial parliament was the product of an international contest among architects, in this case won by a young Briton residing in Buffalo, New York. The 1893 Romanesque Revival building, made of pink Ontario sandstone, has a wealth of exterior detail; inside, the huge, lovely halls echo half a millennium of English architecture. The long hallways are hung with hundreds of oils by Canadian artists, most of which capture scenes of the province's natural beauty. Take one of the frequent (on the hour from mid-May to early September, less often the rest of the year) tours to see the chamber where the 130 MPPs (Members of Provincial Parliament) meet. The two heritage rooms—one each for the parliamentary histories of Britain and Ontario—are filled with old newspapers, periodicals, and pictures. These buildings are often referred to simply as Queen's Park, after the park surrounding them, or as the parliament buildings. ✉ *1 Queen's Park, Queen's Park* ☎ *416/325–7500* *Free* *Guided tour mid-May–mid-Sept., weekdays 10–4, weekends 9–4; mid-Sept.–mid-May, weekdays 10–4* Ⓜ *Queen's Park.*

❼ **Queen's Park.** Many visitors consider this to be the heart of Toronto. Surrounding the large oval-shaped patch of land are medical facilities to the south, the University of Toronto to the west and east, and the Royal Ontario Museum to the north. ✉ *Queen's Park Circle between College St. and Bloor St. W, Queen's Park* Ⓜ *Museum.*

GREATER TORONTO

Explore beyond the downtown areas to find the ethnic enclaves, parks, museums, and attractions that make Toronto interesting. The Distillery District is fast becoming a popular destination for tourists as well as the many artists and filmmakers that use the area. High Park is the city's main green space and has Shakespeare productions in summer. The McMichael Canadian Art Collection, north of the city, is an exceptional gallery not to be missed for its Group of Seven pieces.

MAIN ATTRACTIONS

★ **McMichael Canadian Art Collection.** On 100 acres of lovely woodland in Kleinburg, 30 km (19 mi) northwest of downtown, the McMichael is the only major gallery in the country with the mandate to collect Canadian art exclusively. The museum holds impressive works by Tom Thomson, Emily Carr, and the Group of Seven landscape painters, as well as their early-20th-century contemporaries. These artists were inspired by the wilderness and sought to capture it in bold, original styles. First Nations art and prints, drawings, and sculpture by Inuit artists are well represented. Strategically placed windows help you appreciate the scenery as you view art that took its inspiration from the vast outdoors. Inside, wood walls and a fireplace set a country mood. ✉ *10365 Islington Ave., west of Hwy. 400 and north of Major Mackenzie Dr., Kleinburg* ☎ *888/213–1121 or 905/893–1121* *www.mcmichael.com* *C$15, parking C$5* *Daily 10–4.*

★ **Ontario Science Centre.** It has been called a museum of the 21st century, but it's much more than that. Where else can you stand at the edge of a black hole, work hand-in-clamp with a robot, or land on the moon? Even the building itself is extraordinary: three linked pavilions float gracefully down the side of a ravine and overflow with exhibits that make space, technology, and communications fascinating. A dozen theaters show films that bring the natural world to life. Demonstrations of glassblowing, papermaking, lasers, electricity, and more take place regularly throughout the day; check the schedule when you arrive. The museum has a cafeteria, a restaurant, and a gift store with a cornucopia of books and scientific doodads. The 25,000-square-foot Weston Family Innovation Centre, rife with hands-on activities, is all about experience and problem-solving. Make a music soundtrack, take a lie detector test, and measure fluctuations in your own body chemistry as you flirt with a virtual celebrity. ✉ *770 Don Mills Rd., at Eglinton Ave., North York* ☎ *416/696–1000* 🌐 *www.ontariosciencecentre.ca* *C$17, parking C$8* ⏲ *Daily 10–5* Ⓜ *Eglinton, then No. 34 Eglinton East bus to Don Mills Rd. stop; then walk ½ block south.*

> **WORD OF MOUTH**
>
> "Greektown [the Danforth], where much of the movie My Big Fat Greek Wedding was filmed... has lots of restaurants and bistros (and sidewalk cafés in the warmer season). It's particularly lively Saturday nights." —mtjt

★ **Toronto Zoo.** With its varied terrain, from river valley to dense forest, the Rouge Valley was an inspired choice of site for this 710-acre zoo in which mammals, birds, reptiles, and fish are grouped according to their natural habitats. Enclosed, climate-controlled pavilions have botanical exhibits, such as the Africa pavilion's giant baobab tree. A daily program of activities might include chats with animal keepers, and animal and bird demonstrations. Look over an Events Guide, distributed at the main entrance, to help plan your day. An "Around the World Tour" takes approximately three hours and includes the Africa, Americas, Australasia, Indo-Malayan, and the "Canadian Domain" pavilions. From June through early September, the Zoomobile can take you through the outdoor exhibit area.

The African Savanna is the country's finest walking safari, a dynamic reproduction that brings rare and beautiful animals and distinctive geological landscapes to the city's doorstep. You can also dine in the Savanna's Safari Lodge and camp overnight in the Serengeti Bush Camp (reservations required). The zoo is a 30-minute drive east from downtown; parking is free from November through March. ✉ *Meadowvale Rd. (Exit 389 off Hwy. 401), Scarborough* ☎ *416/392–5900, 416/392–9106, 416/392–5947 for camping reservations* 🌐 *www.torontozoo.com* *C$19, parking C$8* ⏲ *Mid-Mar.–late May and early Sept.–mid-Oct., daily 9–6; late May–early Sept., daily 9–7:30; Oct.–mid-Mar., daily 9:30–4:30* Ⓜ *Kennedy, then Bus 86A.*

ALSO WORTH SEEING

The Danforth. This area along Danforth Avenue has a dynamic ethnic mix, although it's primarily a Greek community. Once English-settled (although it was named after Asa Danforth, an American contractor who cut a road into the area in 1799), the neighborhood is now Italian, Greek, South Asian, and, increasingly, Chinese. But a large percentage of the 120,000 Greek Canadians in metropolitan Toronto live here, and the area is still referred to as "Greektown." Late-night taverns, all-night fruit markets, and some of the best ethnic restaurants in Toronto abound. ■ **TIP→ Summer is the best season to visit, since most eateries have patios, most of which are open and busy until the wee hours of morning.**

Every August the local festival, **Taste of the Danforth** (☎ *416/469–5634* 🌐 *www.tasteofthedanforth.com*), pays tribute to this little nook of foodie paradise. More than a million visitors flock to the festival to sample the fare—mainly dolmades, souvlaki, and other Greek specialties—for C$1 to C$5 per taste. The festival motto—"Don't eat for a week before coming"—is helpful advice. ✉ *Bounded by the Don Valley Pkwy. to the west and Warden Ave. to the east, Danforth.*

★ **High Park.** One of North America's loveliest parks, High Park (at one time the privately owned countryside "farm" of John George Howard, Toronto's first city architect) is especially worth visiting in summer, when the many special events include professionally staged Shakespeare productions. Hundreds of Torontonians and guests arrive at dinnertime and picnic on blankets before the show. Admission is by donation. **Grenadier Pond** in the southwest corner of High Park is named after the British soldiers who, it is said, crashed through the soft ice while rushing to defend the town against invading American forces in 1813. You can fish in its well-stocked waters, provided you have a current Ontario Resident's Anglers License. In summer there are concerts on Sunday afternoons, and there is skating in winter.

At the south end of High Park, near Colborne Lodge, is the **High Park Zoo** (☎ *416/392–8186* ⏲ *Daily 7 AM–dusk*). It's more modest than the Toronto Zoo, but a lot closer to downtown and free. Even young children won't tire walking among the deer, Barbary sheep, peacocks, rabbits, and buffalo. **Colborne Lodge** (☎ *416/392–6916* 🎫 *C$4, holidays C$5.50* ⏲ *Jan.–Apr., Fri.–Sun. noon–4; May–Aug., Tues.–Sun. noon–5; Sept., weekends noon–5; Oct.–Dec., Tues.–Sun. noon–4*) was built more than 150 years ago by John George Howard on a hill overlooking Lake Ontario. This Regency-style "cottage" contains its original fireplace, bake oven, and kitchen, as well as many of Howard's own drawings and paintings. From High Park subway station, enter the park and follow signs for the lodge. Other highlights of the 398-acre park are a large swimming pool, tennis courts, fitness trails, and hillside gardens with roses and sculpted hedges. In addition to the TTC, you can also take the College Street streetcar to the eastern end of the park and walk west. There's limited parking along Bloor Street north of the park, and along the side streets on the eastern side. ✉ *Bordered by Bloor St. W, Gardiner Expressway, Parkside Dr., and Ellis Park Rd. Main entrance off Bloor St. W at High Park Ave., Southwest Toronto* ☎ *416/392–1111, 416/392–1748 walking tours* Ⓜ *High Park.*

WHERE TO EAT

Updated by Amy Rosen

Immigration flourishes in Toronto, and no matter if you've come from a far-flung corner of the world, you can often find home cooking here. Multiethnic Little Italy (which has as many French and Chinese restaurants as Italian), a half dozen Chinatowns (urban and suburban), the Greek area of The Danforth, and Little India are just some of the neighborhoods full of restaurants. Southeast Asian cooking—Korean, Vietnamese, Laotian, Thai, and Malaysian—is taking local taste buds by storm with flavors like chili, ginger, lemongrass, coconut, lime, and tamarind. The abundant fresh produce of the province, once exclusively filtered through French, British, and Italian cooking techniques, now benefits from the sweet and pungent flavors of the Middle East and the soulful dishes of Latin America as well. In one short block of Baldwin Street at Kensington Market, there are 23 eateries—you might call it the United Nations of gastronomy.

The Toronto restaurant scene is in a state of perpetual motion. New restaurants open at a vigorous rate to meet the demands of a savvy dining public. Even formal haute-cuisine establishments, which had all but faded into Toronto's gastronomic history, are experiencing a renaissance, joining the ever-swelling ranks of bistros, trattorias, tapas bars, noodle bars, wine bars, and smart cafés. Red meat has made a comeback, but along with steak houses have come more vegetarian-friendly restaurants. The dining-out scene is the most exciting in decades. In fact, a popular TV show, *Opening Soon,* visits new restaurants in the days and weeks before opening, finishing with their premieres.

Recommending restaurants in an up-and-coming foodie destination is a difficult task. There's not enough space to mention many worthy kitchens in the suburbs and outlying areas. Whatever restaurant you choose, it's hard to go wrong in a town where globalization has created a clientele with a sophisticated palate and a demand for high-quality international cuisines.

	WHAT IT COSTS IN CANADIAN DOLLARS				
	¢	$	$$	$$$	$$$$
AT DINNER	under C$8	C$8–C$12	C$13–C$20	C$21–C$30	over C$30

Prices are per person for a main course at dinner.

OLD TORONTO & THE FINANCIAL DISTRICT

AMERICAN

$–$$ **Richtree Market Restaurants.** Herbs grow in pots, fresh fruits and vegetables are piled high, an enormous snowbank holds bright-eyed fish and fresh seafood, and fresh pasta spews from pasta makers, ready to be cooked to order. This old-world market square in a downtown office tower is really a self-service restaurant. A rotisserie roasts lacquer-crisp game birds and European sausages. Bread and croissants are baked before your eyes, and pizza is prepared to order. This high-concept, low-price dining adventure is open daily 7:30 AM–2 AM. Smaller versions are all over town. ✉ *BCE Place, 42 Yonge St., Financial District* ☎ *416/366–8986* ▭ *AE, DC, MC, V* Ⓜ *King.*

CUTTING EDGE

$$$–$$$$ ★ ✕ **Colborne Lane.** Claudio Aprile, heir apparent to the Canadian Molecular Gastronomy throne, eschews loyalty to any single trend or cuisine in his fun and funky scene, housed in a modern room with consciously rough edges. Choose four or five delicious and complex dishes (from a list of two dozen on the à la carte menu) that sound like mains but are appetizer-size, like a bowl of lobster bisque, lobster won ton, and coconut tofu, infused with lime leaves and chili. Lamb rib eye is crusted in pumpernickel and dried olives with a spiced eggplant sidekick; tuna sashimi is accompanied by an intriguing frozen soy sauce powder. Dessert may be a composed chocolate fondue with chocolate sponge and freeze-dried cherries already swimming in the luscious mix. A 15–20 course set menu is only served at an enclosed, semi-private table in the kitchen. ✉ *45 Colborne La., King West* ☎ *416/368–9009* ▭ *AE, DC, MC, V* ⊙ *No lunch. Closed Sun. and Mon.* Ⓜ *King.*

DELICATESSEN

$–$$ ✕ **Shopsy's.** In 1945, when the three Shopsowitz brothers came into the business started by their parents in 1921, you'd pay 8¢ for a corned-beef sandwich. Today Shopsy's belongs to a food conglomerate, and such a sandwich costs C$6.49. The corned beef, always freshly cooked and firm, is piled on fresh rye bread slathered with mustard; there's nothing like it. Soups are satisfying, salads are huge, and hot dogs are legendary. The deli often has a wait at peak hours. ✉ *33 Yonge St., Downtown* ☎ *416/365–3333* ▭ *AE, DC, MC, V* Ⓜ *King* ✉ *1535 Yonge St., Midtown* ☎ *416/967–5252* Ⓜ *St. Clair.*

JAPANESE

$$–$$$ ✕ **Toshi Sushi.** This simple yet well-kept room is where Toshi caters to lovers of both raw and cooked Japanese food. The daily lunch special is an implausibly good deal (C$9.50) for warming miso and a bento box loaded with al dente green beans in luscious sesame-mirin sauce, crunchy shrimp and veg tempura, ginger-tinged green salad, proper sticky rice topped with chicken teriyaki, and happy orange wedges to finish. Don't bypass the stellar sushi lineup, including Westernized riffs like torched foie gras, buttered breadcrumb oysters, and chef's specials such as tuna carpaccio and crispy flounder. The eight-seater bar at the back is where in-the-know Japanese businessmen tuck into the *omakase* menu. ✉ *565 King St. W., Downtown* ☎ *416/260-8588* ▭ *AE, DC, MC, V* ⊙ *Closed Sun.* Ⓜ *King.*

MODERN CANADIAN

$$$$ ★ ✕ **Bymark.** Wood, glass, and water create drama in a space anchored by a 5,000-bottle wine "cellar" inside a two-story glass column. The menu offers delectability and perfection: poached sea scallops with seared foie gras, crème fraîche, and sake beurre blanc; an 8-ounce burger with molten Brie de Meaux and grilled porcini. And there's service to match. The bar one floor up oozes extreme comfort and has a good view

7

KEY
Restaurants
Hotels
Metro stops
0 1/4 mile
0 400 meters
THE ANNEX
Spadina
St. George
Museum
QUEEN'S PARK
Queen's Park
University of Toronto
Ontario Legislative Building
LITTLE ITALY
CHINATOWN
Queen's Park
St. Patrick
Alexandra Park
Grange Park
City Hall
Nathan Phillips Square
Osgoode
QUEEN WEST
ENTERTAINMENT DISTRICT
TO HARBOURFRONT
Lowther Ave.
Hazelton Ave.
Cumberland St.
Bay St.
St. Thomas St.
Avenue Rd.
Bloor St. W.
Spadina Ave.
Madison Ave.
Albany Ave.
Howland Ave.
Lennox St.
Sussex Mews
Sussex Ave.
Brunswick Ave.
Borden St.
Huron St.
St. George St.
Hoskin Ave.
Harbord St.
St. Joseph St.
Queen's Park Cir. W.
Queen's Park Cir. E.
King's College Cir.
Ulster St.
Willcocks St.
Lippincott St.
Croft St.
Major St.
Robert St.
Russell St.
College St.
Oxford St.
Nassau St.
Cecil St.
Beverley St.
Henry St.
University Ave.
Elizabeth St.
Gerrard St. W.
Markham St.
Bathurst St.
Palmerston Blvd.
Bellevue Ave.
Augusta Ave.
Baldwin St.
D'Arcy St.
McCaul St.
Chestnut St.
Dundas St. W.
St. Patrick St.
Simcoe St.
Denison St.
Sullivan St.
Carr St.
Wolseley St.
Bulwer St.
Soho St.
Renfrew Pl.
Pullan Pl.
Queen St. W.
Peter St.
Duncan St.
Richmond St. W.
Tecumseth St.
Nelson St.
York St.
Adelaide St. W.
Widmer St.
John St.
Pearl St.
Portland St.
King St. W.
Mercer St.
Wellington St. W.

Restaurants

- Bar Italia 13
- Bellini's Ristorante 4
- Bistro 990 11
- Boba 1
- Bymark 32
- C5 8
- Canoe 33
- Carman's Club 12
- Chiado 15
- Colborne Lane 29
- Crush Wine Bar 24
- Eggstacy Diner & Grill 5
- The Fifth 25
- Fressen 18
- The Host 2
- Jamie Kennedy at the Gardiner 7
- Jamie Kennedy Wine Bar 28
- Kultura 27
- Lai Wah Heen 17
- Messis 10
- Pangaea 6
- Richtree Market Restaurants 31
- Rodney's Oyster House 23
- Shopsy's 30
- Splendido 9
- Susur 21
- Terroni 19, 26
- Thuet 20
- Toshi Sushi 22
- Truffles 3
- Wah Sing Seafood Restaurant 16
- Xacutti 17

Hotels

- Alan Gardens Bed & Breakfast 9
- Delta Chelsea Hotel 8
- The Drake Hotel 16
- The Fairmont Royal York 11
- Four Seasons Toronto 4
- Global Village Backpackers 15
- Hilton Toronto 12
- Hotel Le Germain Toronto 13
- Hotel Victoria 10
- Howard Johnson Toronto Yorkville 5
- Mulberry Tree Bed & Breakfast 7
- Neill-Wycik College Hotel 6
- Old Mill Inn & Spa 2
- Palmerston Inn Bed & Breakfast 17
- Park Hyatt Toronto 3
- SoHo Metropolitan Hotel 14
- The Westin Bristol Place Toronto Airport 1

of architect Mies van der Rohe's TD Centre Plaza. In summer, sit on the patio. ✉ *66 Wellington St. W, concourse level, Financial District* ☎ *416/777-1144* *Reservations essential* ▭ *AE, DC, MC, V* ⊙ *Closed Sun.* Ⓜ *St. Andrew.*

> **WORD OF MOUTH**
>
> "I LOVED Canoe. I requested a window table when making my reservation, and even though they said they might not be able to accommodate the request, I was pleasantly surprised to have an exceptional window table with a view of the CN tower. Everything about Canoe was beautiful: the room, the food, the service... I would definitely go back." —al

$$$–$$$$ Fodor's Choice ★ ✕ **Canoe.** Look through huge windows on the 54th floor of the Toronto Dominion Bank Tower and enjoy the breathtaking view of the Toronto Islands and the lake while you dine. Classics include foie gras and truffles. A seven-course tasting menu takes you from coast to coast with dishes like roast hind of Yukon caribou with zucchini cornbread cobbler and partridge berry juice. Desserts, such as fireweed honey-butter tart with roasted plum sauce and cream, are quite serious. ✉ *Toronto-Dominion Center, 66 Wellington St. W, 54th fl., Financial District* ☎ *416/364-0054* *Reservations essential* ▭ *AE, DC, MC, V* ⊙ *Closed weekends* Ⓜ *King.*

$$–$$$ ★ ✕ **Jamie Kennedy Wine Bar.** This sleek, spare restaurant–wine bar is amazingly popular, due in part to the charm of Kennedy and key staff. It has dining counters, a few tables, and a wall of the chef's own preserves in gleaming glass jars. Sit on comfy bar stools and watch as Kennedy sautés, grills, seasons, and cooks. From the daily-changing list of 21 items, favorites are an oval scoop of pâté with the chef's own pickled veggies; confit of Cornish hen with cider-poached apples; and tempting artisanal cheeses. Sommeliers offer tasting glasses from a spectacular list to match each dish. There is usually a wait for seating. ✉ *9 Church St., Downtown* ☎ *416/362-1957* *Reservations not accepted* ▭ *AE, DC, MC, V* Ⓜ *Union.*

ALONG DUNDAS, QUEEN & KING STREETS

ASIAN FUSION

$$$$ Fodor's Choice ★ ✕ **Susur.** The country's most renowned chef, Susur Lee, has a unique, eclectic Asian style. His seasonally changing, reverse-set menu begins with the principal course, with subsequent dishes diminishing in size and weight. Appetizers may include braised oxtail and tapioca ravioli; main-course choices might be venison with Italian lentils and currants or fresh fish with black-olive sauce and grapes. Subtle recessed lighting in the square, white room changes from shades of pink to blues and greens. Choose a white leather booth or dining table and prepare for a wait between courses—keeping in mind that the food is worth it. ✉ *601 King St. W, Downtown* ☎ *416/603-2205* *Reservations essential* ▭ *AE, MC, V* ⊙ *Closed Sun. No lunch* Ⓜ *St. Andrew.*

CHINESE

$$$–$$$$ Fodor's Choice ★ **Lai Wah Heen.** In an elegant room with a sculpted ceiling, etched-glass turntables, and silver serving dishes, the service is formal; here mahogany-color Peking duck is wheeled in on a trolley and presented with panache. Excellent choices from the 100-dish inventory include wok-fried shredded beef and vegetables in a crisp potato nest. At lunch, dim sum is divine: baked meat-filled morsels and translucent dumplings burst with juicy fillings of shark's fin sprinkled with bright red lobster roe, and shrimp dumplings with green tops look like baby bok choy. Sister restaurant **Lai Toh Heen,** which opened midtown this year, is also stealing hearts with dishes like fragrant seafood consommé served within a cooked papaya, and tea-smoked duck breast over seaweed salad. *Metropolitan Hotel, 108 Chestnut St., 2nd fl., Chinatown, M5G 1R3 416/977–9899 Reservations essential AE, DC, MC, V St. Patrick 692 Mount Pleasant Rd., Midtown 416 489–8922 Reservations essential AE, DC, MC, V St. Clair Closed Mon. and Tues.*

$–$$ **Wah Sing Seafood Restaurant.** Just one of a jumble of Asian restaurants clustered on a tiny Kensington Market street, this meticulously clean and spacious restaurant has two-for-the-price-of-one lobsters (in season, which is almost always). They're scrumptious and tender, with black-bean sauce or ginger and green onion. You can also choose giant shrimps Szechuan-style or one of the lively queen crabs from the tank. Chicken and vegetarian dishes for landlubbers are good, too. *47 Baldwin St., Kensington Market 416/599–8822 MC, V College.*

7

FRENCH

$$$$ **The Fifth.** Enter through The Easy, a main-floor dance club, and take a freight elevator to The Fifth, a semiprivate dining club and loft space with the right balance of formality and flirtation. The mood is industrial-strength romantic. In winter, sit on a sofa in front of a huge fireplace; in summer, dine on a gazebo terrace. Entrées include steaks, black cod, roasted chicken, and rack of lamb. You could also make a meal of a selection of intriguing sides such as mahogany and basmati rice with caramelized onions. *225 Richmond St. W, Downtown 416/979–3005 Reservations essential AE, DC, MC, V Closed Sun.–Wed. No lunch Osgoode.*

$$$–$$$$ ★ **Thuet.** Classic Alsatian dishes, revved up with over-the-top decadence, are the focus at this fabulous bakery bistro. Chef Marc Thuet has opened his own temple of gastronomy showcasing not only his love of foie gras and bone marrow, but also his deft hand with bread. His artisanal loaves are now sold here and at better retailers across the city. Steak or salmon tartare are done up in clever ways while his beef bourguignonne with mashed potatoes and mushrooms is the closest you can get to the French countryside on a plate. Cassoulet with duck and beans, and saddle of lamb with thyme-flavored sauce have upscale stick-to-your-ribs appeal. Sunday brunch is a pleasure, with the flakiest of pastries and eggs poached in wine sauce. *609 King St. W, Entertainment District, M5V 1M5 416/603–2777 Reservations essential AE, DC, MC, V Closed Sun. and Mon. St. Andrew.*

ITALIAN

$$–$$$ ✕ **Terroni.** This cool pizza joint, whose open shelving is lined with Italian provisions, has a menu to suit one and all. Funghi Assoluti—toasty baked oyster mushrooms with parmigiano on a bed of arugula, dressed to kill in balsamic vinaigrette—is a must. The thin-crust pies, bubbled and blistered, are the best in town, and generous panini are also buono. Daily specials are hit and miss, but desserts (like a flourless wedge of Nutella chocolate cake) are almost universally delicious. Three locations: Queen West (hipsters), Victoria Street (business types), and Yonge-Balmoral (wealthy Rosedalers). ⊠ *720 Queen St. W, Queen West* ☎ *416/504–0320.* ⊠ *1 Balmoral Ave., Midtown* ☎ *416/925–4029* ⊠ *106 Victoria St., Old Toronto* ☎ *416/955–0258* ▭ *AE, DC, MC, V* Ⓜ *Queen.*

MODERN CANADIAN

$$$–$$$$ ✕ **Kultura.** After opening in August of 2006, Kultura instantly became celebrity central during September's International Film Festival. Matt Damon threw a private dinner in the upstairs dining room (where the decor says "NYC loft meets Tibetan rumpus room"), and Vince Vaughn created a self-styled "gangster table" on the second floor. At street level, people sip from a diverse wine card, including 11 types of bubbly, at communal tables with low-slung club chairs. On the menu are small plates for sharing, called "trans-ethnic dishes," like Jamaican chicken risotto and toasted lobster ravioli with lobster saffron bisque. Brunch, also made for sharing, is offered in the renovated 1820s heritage building: eggs Florentine on rounds of puff pastry, and fingers of French toast with caramel brittle, a brunois of candied apple, and spiked whipped cream. ⊠ *169 King St. E., King East* ☎ *416/363–9000* ▭ *AE, DC, MC, V* Ⓜ *King.*

$$$ ✕ **Crush Wine Bar.** They've sandblasted the natural-brick walls and polished the original wood floor in this old building with great results, and an open kitchen lets you see the corps of chefs at work. The four-course prix-fixe menu is a dreamscape of the chef's expertise and might include wild sockeye salmon, black bass with orange crust, oven-roasted squab, and passion-fruit mousse in chocolate puff pastry. A sommelier does wine pairings by the glass with panache and recommends just the right tipple for duck ravioli with roasted garlic or bison steak with red-wine reduction. ⊠ *455 King St. W, Downtown* ☎ *416/977–1234* ✍ *Reservations essential* ▭ *AE, DC, MC, V* ⊙ *Closed Sun.* Ⓜ *St. Andrew.*

SEAFOOD

$$–$$$ Fodor's Choice ★ ✕ **Rodney's Oyster House.** This playful, basement raw bar is a hotbed of bivalve variety frequented by dine-alones and showbiz types. Among the options are soft-shell steamers, quahogs, and "Oyster Slapjack Chowder," plus salty Aspy Bays from Cape Breton or perfect Malpeques from owner Rodney Clark's own oyster beds in Prince Edward Island. A zap of Rodney's own line of condiments or a splash of vodka and freshly grated horseradish are certain eye-openers. Shared meals and half orders are okay. Be sure to ask about the daily white-plate specials. ⊠ *469 King St. W, Downtown* ☎ *416/363–8105* ▭ *AE, DC, MC, V* ⊙ *Closed Sun.* Ⓜ *St. Andrew.*

VEGETARIAN

$$ ✕**Fressen.** A feast of herbivorous cuisine jumps off the page of a menu totally free of meat and dairy, although dishes are designed with eggs. Vegetable soups are silken and perfumed with coconut milk and ginger; pasta dishes are plump with mushrooms and vegetables. Desserts like the chocolate terrine amaze. Sip a groove juice (made from cucumber, celery, kale, and other greens) while you wait for your main course. It's all served in a room decorated by natural materials: ceiling pipes are covered by woven twigs, and piles of rocks and herb-filled jars enhance the environment. ✉*478 Queen St. W, Queen West* ☎*416/504–5127* ▭*MC, V* ⏲*No lunch weekdays* Ⓜ*Osgoode.*

THE ANNEX & LITTLE ITALY

ASIAN

$$–$$$ ✕**Xacutti.** The cliché-free menu is pure joy and the avant-garde decor and table settings are a study in chic minimalism at this modern Indian eatery. The culinary journey begins the moment you're handed a menu, which is divided into small, large, and side dishes. Small dishes include barbecued cinnamon-guava pork ribs with grilled star fruit as well as Mumbai noodles with tiger prawns, vegetables, and toasted cashews in Silk Road Curry. Among the large dishes is a dramatic tandoori salmon in rice paper with curry leaves and tangerine miso. Sunday brunch draws the city's trendsetters. ✉*503 College St., Little Italy, M6G 1A5* ☎*416/323–3957* ✍*Reservations essential* ▭*AE, DC, MC, V* ⏲*No lunch weekdays* Ⓜ*Bathurst, Queen's Park.*

7

ITALIAN

$$–$$$ ✕**Bar Italia.** A fixture in Little Italy, this is where the city's glitterati can be found getting their fix of classic, well-prepared pasta, risotto, fish of the day, and a traditional favorite of sautéed mushroom salad with arugula and Parmesan. In summer, sip a glass of wine on the patio and dig into a specialty, the Cubano sandwich of roasted pork, avocado, pancetta (thick, hand-cut bacon), and garlicky mayo on a huge Italian bun. Close your eyes and pretend you're in Italy; you'll still hear Italian spoken at many tables. ✉*582 College St., Little Italy* ☎*416/535–3621* ▭*AE, DC, MC, V* Ⓜ*Bathurst, Queen's Park.*

MODERN CANADIAN

$$$–$$$$ ★ ✕**Splendido.** Even the most hard to please will thrill to the tasting menus here, which might include poached green and white asparagus with lobster foam, or Alberta lamb rib eye with wild leeks and morel mushrooms. The menu crisscrosses the country, with wood-burning oven-roast whole fish, short ribs of beef, or prime beef strip steak. The kitchen is peerless and the front of the house functions like a fine Swiss watch. Special touches include a champagne trolly and purse stools for the ladies. A huge iron chandelier serves as the focal point in one of the city's most beautifully balanced rooms. ✉*88 Harbord St., The Annex* ☎*416/929–7788* ✍*Reservations essential* ▭*AE, DC, MC, V* ⏲*Closed Mon.* Ⓜ*Spadina.*

$$–$$$ ✕ **Messis.** A skillful chef-owner presents fresh, pretty dishes. Herb-marinated veal loin and a rack of New Zealand lamb with Southern Comfort–rosemary glaze exemplify the inspired comfort food. Enjoy grilled free-range cornish hen with Pommery mustard glaze and a sauté of red potatoes, mushrooms, sundried tomatoes, and red wine. Messis is a favorite for small celebrations because of lovely desserts like a phyllo package of wild blueberries and white chocolate. The summer patio twinkles with lights at night. ✉ *97 Harbord St., The Annex* ☎ *416/920–2186* ▭ *AE, DC, MC, V* ⊙ *No lunch Sat.–Mon.* Ⓜ *Spadina.*

PORTUGUESE

$$$–$$$$ ✕ **Chiado.** It's all relaxed elegance here, beginning with the fine selection of appetizers at Senhor Antonio's tapas bar and continuing through the French doors to the dining room, which has polished wood floors and plum-velvet armchairs. The exquisite fish, which form the menu's basis, are flown in from the Azores and Madeira. You might have bluefin tuna or *peixe espada* (scabbard fish). Traditional Portuguese dishes include *açorda,* in which seafood is folded into a thick, custardlike soup made with bread and eggs. There's much for meat eaters, too—for example, a roasted rack of lamb sparkles with Douro wine sauce. ✉ *864 College St. W, Little Italy* ☎ *416/538–1910* ✍ *Reservations essential* ▭ *AE, DC, MC, V* ⊙ *No lunch weekends* Ⓜ *Bathurst, Queen's Park.*

AROUND QUEEN'S PARK, CHURCH-WELLESLEY & YORKVILLE

AMERICAN

$–$$ ✕ **Eggstacy Diner and Grill.** Stop here for big plates of filling food with diner-friendly service. Eggstacy does a booming egg business: the menu informs that your three extra-larges will be cooked in butter "any way you like them—sunny side up, over easy, over well, scrambled, poached, smashed, squashed, or beaten with a stick." You choose several sides from a list that includes hash browns, baked beans, pancakes, sliced cucumber, toast, and fries. Everything from smoked meat sandwiches to Forest Hill omelettes is on the menu. The pancakes are served with real Canadian maple syrup. ✉ *1255 Bay St., Yorkville* ☎ *416/964–2333* ✍ *Reservations not accepted* ▭ *AE, DC, MC, V* ⊙ *No dinner* Ⓜ *Bay.*

CANADIAN

$$$–$$$$ ✕ **Pangaea.** In this tranquil room with an aura of restrained sophistication, unprocessed seasonal ingredients and the freshest produce are always used. Soups—such as lobster bisque with fiddlehead greens—are unique; salads are creative constructions of organic greens. Soy-honey-glazed quail comes with tempura onion rings; veal, Australian lamb, and caribou are served with truffle-whipped potatoes. Vegetarians can find bliss in this caring kitchen, too. For dessert, seasonal sweets are created by Joanne Yolles, the preeminent pastry chef in the city. ✉ *1221 Bay St., Yorkville* ☎ *416/920–2323* ▭ *AE, DC, MC, V* Ⓜ *Bay.*

FRENCH

$$$$ ★ ✕ **Truffles.** Sophisticated yet warm, this special-occasion eatery serves contemporary cuisine grounded in authentic French flavors. Appetizers include thyme-roasted sweetbreads with lentil ragout, foie-gras torchon, and the signature spaghettini with Perigord Black Gold truffle foam. Entrées such as pepper-seared loin of venison and truffled honey squab breast are pleasures for the palate. Superb wine pairings and an enviable cheese list make for a languid evening of fine dining.. ✉ *Four Seasons Toronto, 21 Avenue Rd., Yorkville* ☎ *416/928–7331* ✍ *Reservations essential* ▭ *AE, D, DC, MC, V* ⊗ *Closed Sun. and Mon. No lunch* Ⓜ *Bay.*

$$$–$$$$ ✕ **Bistro 990.** A superior kitchen is seamlessly paired with bistro informality. Start your experience with traditional pâté de maison, partnered with quince marmalade, wine preserves, and plenty of homemade croutons. Oven-roasted halibut with salsa and feta cheese is a treat, and a roasted half chicken with herb garlic au jus crackles with crispness and Provençal flavor. Ask about the wild-game dish of the day. Faux stone walls stenciled with Cocteau-esque designs, sturdily upholstered chairs, and a tiled floor make the dining area sophisticated but comfortable. ✉ *990 Bay St., Church and Wellesley* ☎ *416/921–9990* ✍ *Reservations essential* ▭ *AE, DC, MC, V* ⊗ *No weekend lunch* Ⓜ *Yonge-Bloor, Wellesley.*

INDIAN

$–$$ ✕ **The Host.** Dine in the garden room among flowering plants or in the handsome main room. Waiters rush around carrying baskets of hot *naan* (a gorgeous, puffy flat bread) from the oven. An excellent dish is tandoori *machi,* whole fish baked in a tandoor oven and served on a sizzling plate with onion and coriander. Sliced tender lamb is enfolded in a curry of cashew nuts and whole cardamom. End your meal with such exotic Indian desserts as *golabjabun,* little round cakes soaking in rosewater-scent honey. ✉ *14 Prince Arthur Ave., Yorkville* ☎ *416/962–4678* ✍ *Reservations essential* ▭ *AE, MC, V* ⊗ *Closed Mon.* Ⓜ *Bay.*

ITALIAN

$$$–$$$$ ✕ **Sotto Sotto.** A coal cellar in a turn-of-the-20th-century home was dug out, its stone walls and floor polished, and a restaurant created in what has become a dining oasis for locals and international jet-setters alike. The menu of more than 20 pasta dishes gives a tantalizing tug at the taste buds. Gnocchi is made daily. Cornish hen is marinated, pressed, and grilled to a juicy brown, and the swordfish and fresh fish of the day are beautifully done on the grill. ✉ *116-A Avenue Rd., Yorkville* ☎ *416/962–0011* ▭ *AE, DC, MC, V* ⊗ *No lunch* Ⓜ *Bay.*

$$–$$$ ✕ **Bellini's Ristorante.** Never wavering from its focus on elegance, good taste, classic food, and professional service, Bellini's has stood the test of time. How can one choose from dishes such as veal agnolotti with grilled oyster mushrooms; roasted pistachio-crusted seabass; the siren call of Provimi veal osso buco with saffron risotto and lemon-thyme jus; or risotto of lobster with honey mushrooms, mascarpone cheese, and chervil? This is an aromatic haven and a quiet oasis for visiting celebs. ✉ *101 Yorkville Ave. W, Yorkville* ☎ *416/929–9111* ▭ *AE, DC, MC, V* ⊗ *No lunch* Ⓜ *Bay.*

7

MODERN CANADIAN

$$$–$$$$ ✕**Boba.** Owners Bob Bermann and Barbara Gordon are a sophisticated culinary couple who cook in a charming brick house personalized with robust and gorgeous color. The seasonal dishes they've dreamed up are original and delicious—grilled fresh Ontario ostrich with herb gnocchi and peppercorn glaze and rare big-eye tuna with coconut noodles, mango and avocado salsa, and black-bean sauce are customer favorites. For a heartier dish, try the traditional grilled Black Angus strip loin with Yukon Gold frites. Vegetarian dinners are spontaneously invented. Boba has one of the city's prettiest patios for summer dining. ✉ *90 Avenue Rd., Yorkville* ☎ *416/961–2622* ▭ *AE, DC, MC, V* ⏲ *No lunch, closed Sun.* Ⓜ *Bay.*

$$–$$$ ✕**C5.** You can't miss the angular, Daniel Libeskind–designed "Crystal" addition to the Royal Ontario Museum as it juts and jabs over Bloor Street, and you shouldn't miss dining at C5, the starkly designed, unapologetically modernist restaurant on the addition's fifth floor. Its regionally focused cuisine is suitably arrayed in five courses, including one of the city's best cheese plates. The menu relies heavily on dishes built in layers, like succulent lobster tail nestled between tender brioche and a crusted poached egg or moist black cod set atop lentil salad and under lobster hollandaise. Visitors also enjoy panoramic city views, while savvy locals know to arrive early for a drink in the stylish lounge. ✉ *100 Queen's Park, 5th floor (enter from Bloor St.), Queen's Park* ☎ *416/586–7928* ▭ *AE, MC, V* ⏲ *No dinner Sun.–Wed.* Ⓜ *Museum.*

$$–$$$ ✕**Jamie Kennedy at the Gardiner.** All limestone, slate, blond oak, and glass, the airy room is a fitting accompaniment to the surrounding ceramics collection. A lunch crowd that has always enjoyed Jamie Kennedy's seasonal starters at his other namesake wine bar will appreciate offerings like a smooth Ontario sweet corn bisque with a plump seared scallop. As always, count on excellent signature frites with lemon mayo, fabulous cheese plates and charcuterie, a great burger, salad niçoise, and innovative Sri Lankan Hoppers complemented by a dazzling array of house-made condiments: lime pickle, coconut-based pol sambol, ghee fried shallots, green mango chutney and more. Wines are matched with each dish, including many from Ontario's Niagara region—home, too, to the berries in the pleasingly retro strawberry shortcake. ✉ *111 Queen's Park, Yorkville* ☎ *416/362–1957* ▭ *AE, MC, V* ⏲ *Open for lunch seven days; dinners on Fri.* Ⓜ *Bay.*

STEAK

$$$$ ✕**Carman's Club.** Arthur Carman opened this steak house in 1959 and nothing has changed except the prices. In a room chockablock with his collection of pewter, copper, porcelain, and paintings he still offers prime steaks with the nine items that make up the package: garlic toast, baked potato with all the trimmings, cottage cheese, olives, peppers, tzatziki, baklava, and coffee or tea. The kitchen has a way with lobster, Dover sole, and garlic shrimp, too. Meander along the hallway and view the photos of stars from the '50s up to now. They all loved the steak. ✉ *26 Alexander St., Church and Wellesley* ☎ *416/924–8697* ✍ *Reservations essential* ▭ *AE, MC, V* ⏲ *Closed Sun. No lunch* Ⓜ *College.*

GREATER TORONTO

FRENCH

$$–$$$ ✕**Pastis Express.** Menu items are etched into the frosted-glass windows, and plastered walls are the color of the morning sun in Provence. Expect pure bistro fare here, like homemade ravioli with snails and garlic herb butter, and fish-and-chips. Thick saffron-flavor fish soup, plump with fish and crustaceans, comes with three tidy add-ons: rouille, croutons, and grated cheese. A tasting plate of three French minidesserts satisfies. The food is good, but this place could run on the Gallic charm of owner George Gurnon alone. ✉*1158 Yonge St., at Summerhill, Midtown* ☎*416/928–2212* ▭*AE, DC, MC, V* ⊙*Closed Sun. and Mon. No lunch* Ⓜ*Summerhill.*

GREEK

$$–$$$ ✕**Christina's.** Who doesn't have a foodie love affair with Greek dips? Here they're served individually or as a large platter combination, *pikilia mezedakia,* that comes with warm pitas. A bottle of Greek wine and specials like *saganaki,* an iron plate of Kefalograviera cheese flamed in brandy, and you may shout "Opa" with the waiters. Order a fish or meat mixed grill and the tray of food almost covers the table. This cheery place, with the colors of the Aegean Sea and sun on the walls, has live music and uninhibited Greek dancing—by patrons and staff alike—on weekends. ✉*492 Danforth Ave., Danforth* ☎*416/463–4418* ▭*AE, DC, MC, V* Ⓜ*Chester.*

INTERNATIONAL

$$$–$$$$ ✕**Centro Restaurant and Lounge.** Showpiece chandeliers and 28-foot ceilings with pillars draped in cream suede to complement brown suede chairs make for a drop-dead gorgeous, totally redone 138 seater with a new focus and attitude. The new American cuisine encompasses Italian, French, Asian but not on one plate. Try pastas such as gnocchi with asparagus pesto or seafood cannelloni in cognac tomato cream sauce. Mains are a global trip: tandoori-spiced pork tenderloin, organic honey-ginger salmon, or pan-roasted veal steak with marsala sauce. Desserts and cheeses are divine. A downstairs lounge has buzz; its own small, less-expensive menu ($$) and live music on weekends. ✉2472 *Yonge St., at Eglinton Ave., Midtown* ☎*416/483–2211* *Reservations essential* ▭*AE, DC, MC, V* ⊙*Closed Sun. No lunch* Ⓜ*Eglinton.*

ITALIAN

$$–$$$$ ✕**Mistura.** Mistura's combination of comfort and casual luxury and its innovative menu make for an ongoing buzz. Choose from one of more than a dozen delectable starters, like savory Maryland crab cakes with lemon aioli on chopped salad, or grilled calamari. Duck two ways—crispy confit and roasted breast with port-infused dried cherries—is a specialty. Balsamic-glazed lamb ribs are always a hit, as are homemade pastas like veal ravioli. Daily whole fish is a carefully thought-out triumph. Vegetarians are given their due with dishes like red-beet risotto. ✉*265 Davenport Rd., ½ block west of Avenue Rd., Midtown* ☎*416/515–0009* ▭*AE, DC, MC, V* ⊙ *Closed Sun. No lunch* Ⓜ*Dupont.*

$$–$$$ ✕**Grano.** What started as a bakery and take-out antipasto bar has grown into a cheerful collage of the Martella family's Italy. Come for animated talk, good food, and great bread in lively rooms with faux-ancient plaster walls, wooden tables, and bright chairs. Choose, if you can, from 40 delectable vegetarian dishes and numerous meat and fish antipasti. Lucia's homemade gnocchi and ravioli are divine, as is the white-chocolate-and-raspberry pie. ✉*2035 Yonge St., between Eglinton and Davisville Aves., Midtown* ☎*416/440–1986* ▭*AE, DC, MC, V* ⊙*Closed Sun.* Ⓜ*Eglinton.*

SEAFOOD

$$$–$$$$ ✕**Joso's.** This two-story seafood institution is decorated with intriguing wall hangings, sensuous paintings of nudes and the sea, and signed celebrity photos. The kitchen prepares dishes from the Dalmatian side of the Adriatic Sea, and members of the international artistic community who frequent the place adore the unusual and healthful array of seafood and fish. ■**TIP→ The black risotto with squid is a must.** A dish of grilled prawns, their charred tails pointing skyward, is often carried aloft by speed-walking servers. ✉*202 Davenport Rd., Midtown* ☎*416/925–1903* ✍*Reservations essential* ▭*AE, DC, MC, V* ⊙*Closed Sun. No lunch Sat.* Ⓜ*Dupont.*

WHERE TO STAY

Updated by Bruce Bishop

Given that more than 100 languages and dialects are spoken in the Greater Toronto area, it's not surprising that much of the downtown hotel market is international-business-traveler savvy. High-speed wireless Internet connections are standard at most high-end properties, and generous work spaces and business services abound. But these same core hotels are close to tourist attractions—the Harbourfront and the Toronto Islands, the cavernous Rogers Centre, the Air Canada Centre, and the Royal Ontario Museum. Not wanting to miss out on potential customers, hotels like the Delta Chelsea have instituted perks for the younger set, like complimentary milk and cookies, kid-size bathrobes, and children's day camp. Another key trend in Toronto's downtown lodgings is the emergence of small, upscale boutique hotels, such as the Hotel Le Germain, the Pantages and Cosmopolitan hotels, and the swank SoHo Metropolitan. There is also a growing number of bed-and-breakfasts and hostels.

Even though the breadth of lodging choices and price ranges is on par with those of other cities of Toronto's size, the attractive exchange rate of the Canadian dollar against most other international currencies really sets this metropolis apart as a lodgings bargain. When booking, remember to first ask about discounts and packages. Even the most expensive properties regularly reduce their rates during low-season lulls and on weekends. Discounts from 20% to 50% are not uncommon. If you're a member of a group (examples: senior citizens, students, auto club, or the military), you may also get a deal. Downtown hotels regularly have specials that include theater tickets, meals, or museum passes. It never hurts to ask for these kinds of perks up front.

	WHAT IT COSTS IN CANADIAN DOLLARS				
	¢	$	$$	$$$	$$$$
FOR TWO PEOPLE	under C$75	C$75–C$125	C$126–C$175	C$176–C$250	over C$250

Prices are for two people in a standard double room in high season, excluding tax.

DOWNTOWN

WORD OF MOUTH

"The Royal York is beautiful. A sight in itself. I often grab a coffee and a book and sit in the lobby waiting for my commuter train to go home. You can certainly still enjoy it without staying there (the rooms are actually quite small, in the old-world Euro way)." —Kaka

$$$$ Fodor'sChoice ★ **The Fairmont Royal York.** Built by Canadian Pacific Railway in 1929 for the convenience of passengers using nearby Union Station, this majestic hotel boasts a lobby with a classic design from the year it was constructed, including travertine walls and columns. Self-check-in kiosks in the lobby are a handy tool for the frequent guest or anybody in a rush. Guest rooms are formal without being stuffy. Comfy beds have ruffled pillows, thick comforters, and classic arched wood headboards. A skylight illuminates a lap pool. The Elizabeth Milan spa offers exceptional treatments, like massage for two in what was once a bank vault, rose petal baths, and other unique experiences. The signature restaurant, Epic, has the city's best Canadian whole lobster (either butter-poached, steamed, grilled, or roasted), and still serves high tea from 2 until 4 in the afternoons. The snug Library Bar just might have Toronto's best martinis. **Pros:** a terrific multipurpose grand hotel, adept at handling large and complex conferences, royalty stays here. **Cons:** some older guestrooms and baths may be smaller than those in newer hotels, some rooms need redecorating, Wi-Fi unreliable in public areas. *100 Front St. W, Financial District, M5J 1E3 416/368–2511 or 800/441–1414 www.fairmont.com 1,304 rooms, 61 suites In-room: ethernet. In-hotel: 5 restaurants, room service, bars, pool, gym, laundry service, concierge, executive floor, public Internet (fee), parking (fee), no-smoking rooms AE, D, DC, MC, V* Ⓜ *Union.*

$$$$ ★ **Four Seasons Toronto.** Some of Toronto's most luxurious guest rooms are here, in fashionable Yorkville. Amenities include antique-style writing desks, comfortable robes and oversize towels. Many of the corner rooms have furnished balconies. Ask for upper rooms to get views facing downtown and the lake. The Studio Café serves modern American dishes and is one of the best places for business breakfasts and lunches in town. The more formal Truffles restaurant has contemporary French cuisine and an acclaimed wine list. **Pros:** movie star hangout, art gallery neighborhood, acclaimed cuisine. **Cons:** movie star hangout, not as lavish as other Four Seasons, a trifle pretentious. *21 Avenue Rd., Yorkville, M5R 2G1 416/964–0411 or 800/819–8053 www.fourseasons.com 230 rooms, 150 suites In-room: ethernet (some), Wi-Fi (some). In-hotel: 2 restaurants, 2 bars, room service,*

pool, gym, laundry service, concierge, parking (fee), no-smoking rooms ▭*AE, D, DC, MC, V* Ⓜ*Bay.*

$$$$ ★ **Hotel Le Germain Toronto.** The Germain Group is known for beautiful, chic, upscale boutique hotels, and the Toronto model is no exception. A retro, redbrick exterior—accented by a soaring glass-and-stainless-steel frontage—works well with the historic architecture of the surrounding theater district. The dazzling lobby contains a library, a cappuccino bar, and a double-side, open-hearth fireplace. Sleek furnishings fill ultramodern rooms, which have plasma-screen televisions. Suites have separate bedrooms and living rooms, wet bars, fireplaces, and private terraces that afford superb views of the skyline. The restaurant, Luce ("light" in Italian), serves first-class cuisine. **Pros:** complimentary breakfast, attentive staff, laptop-sized in-room safes. **Cons:** spotty temperature controls, some guest rooms could use a coat of paint, haughty attitude among some staff. ✉*30 Mercer St., Entertainment District, M5V 1H3* ☎*416/345–9500 or 866/345–9501* 🌐*www.hotelboutique.com* *118 rooms, 4 suites* *In-room: ethernet, Wi-Fi (some). In-hotel: restaurant, gym, laundry service, public Wi-Fi, parking (fee), some pets allowed (fee), no-smoking rooms* ▭*AE, DC, MC, V* *CP* Ⓜ*St. Andrew.*

$$$$ **Park Hyatt Toronto.** The experience here is *très* New York Park Avenue. Elegant guest rooms are a generous 300–400 square feet, with wide windows overlooking Queen's Park and Lake Ontario. Two-level suites have designer kitchenettes, and the 2,500-square-foot Algonquin Suite affords three different skyline views. The Stillwater Spa is one of the city's finest. Check the gift boutique for fine toiletries, soaps, and skin-care items. The Roof Lounge has been a haven for literati for decades, and a retro lunch or drink is not to be missed. The Mezzanine Lounge offers complimentary antipasto at 5–7 PM nightly, and the Annona Dining Room is held in high regard. The steak house Morton's is attached. **Pros:** large marble baths, fast room service, impeccably appointed. **Cons:** inexpensive breakfasts unavailable, locker rooms for paying spa guests only. ✉*4 Avenue Rd., at Bloor St. W, Yorkville, M5R 2E8* ☎*416/925–1234 or 800/778–7477* 🌐*www.parktoronto.hyatt.com* *301 rooms, 45 suites* *In-room: ethernet. In-hotel: 2 restaurants, bar, room service, gym, spa, laundry service, concierge, executive floor, public Internet, parking (fee), no-smoking rooms* ▭*AE, D, DC, MC, V* Ⓜ*Museum.*

$$$$ Fodor's Choice ★ **SoHo Metropolitan Hotel.** Ultraluxury is the only standard at the SoHo Met: Italian Frette linens, European down duvets, walk-in closets, solid marble bathrooms with heated floors, and upmarket bath products. There's even a "sleep concierge" offering amenities such as tea and biscotti, bubble baths, and aromatherapy eye pillows. Glamour begins in the cosmopolitan open-concept lobby, where a stunning glass installation by world-renowned Dale Chihuly is set in the canopy at the front entrance, dazzling guests and passersby. The hotel has the finest amenities, including a state-of-the-art fitness center, lap pool, full-service day spa, and Clefs d'Or concierge services. The hotel's spaciousness and floor-to-ceiling windows create the feeling of luxury, without pretension, throughout. No detail has been left to chance and only the fin-

est materials have been used. The two-level penthouse suite, one of the finest of its kind in the city, has attracted stars like Madonna and film director husband Guy Ritchie. Senses Restaurant is famous for its unique menu, wine cellar, and service. **Pros:** heated bathroom floors, electric "do not disturb" signs and curtains, stylish but not showy. **Cons:** lap pool only three feet deep, toiletries not restocked daily, located slightly away from main streets. ✉*318 Wellington St. W, Entertainment District, M5V 3T4* ☎*416/599–8800 or 800/668–6600* 🌐*www.soho.metropolitan.com* *72 rooms, 22 suites* *In-room: ethernet. In-hotel: restaurant, bar, room service, pool, gym, spa, laundry service, concierge, public Internet, public Wi-Fi, parking (fee), no-smoking* *AE, DC, MC, V* Ⓜ*St. Andrew.*

WORD OF MOUTH

"Yes, the Chelsea is a busy property, and yes, it's very popular with families, but its location can't be beat—you feel like you're in the heart of Toronto. If you want peace and quiet, there's always Deck 27, an adults-only pool/health club/lounge on the roof, with an incredible view of the city." —Bob Sternberg

$$$ **Hilton Toronto.** Golds and browns grace the lobby; guest rooms have wood floors, subtle earth tones, and modern furniture. The indoor-outdoor pool is modest, but there are children's toys and games for kids under 12 that can be borrowed from the front desk. The view of the city from the glass-enclosed elevators is a thrill. The executive-floor lounge has a full-time concierge and complimentary breakfast and cocktails. The Tundra restaurant has stellar Canadian cuisine. The hotel's decor honors Canada's unique history with the Hudson's Bay Company suite, the glamorous Margery Steele suite, the rugged Heritage suite, and the Panorama suite, a one-bedroom hospitality suite with small kitchen for on-site catering. Proximity to the entertainment and financial districts makes the Hilton Toronto a convenient base, and it's across the street from the new Four Seasons Centre for the Performing Arts. **Pros:** on-site steak house very popular, safe and walkable neighborhood, cozy atmosphere. **Cons:** guest rooms generally on the small size, some show signs of wear, may not be as lavish as other Hilton properties. ✉*145 Richmond St. W, Downtown, M5H 2L2* ☎*416/869–3456 or 800/267–2281* 🌐*www.hilton.com* *601 rooms, 47 suites* *In-hotel: 5 restaurants, bars, room service, pool, gym, laundry service, public Internet, parking (fee), no-smoking rooms* *AE, DC, MC, V* Ⓜ*Osgoode.*

$$ **Delta Chelsea Hotel.** Canada's largest hotel has long been popular with families and tour groups, so be prepared for a flurry of activity here. The Family Fun Zone has a children's creative center, the Starcade Games Room, a family pool, and the four-story "Corkscrew"—downtown Toronto's only heated indoor waterslide. Camp Chelsea entertains kids with supervised activities while parents step out (daily from late June to early September, Friday night and Saturday the rest of the year). The Delta Chelsea has standard kitchenettes and deluxe guest rooms, as well as one- and two-bedroom suites. **Pros:** all-inclusive cruise-ship-like atmosphere, excellent service, adults-only floors. **Cons:** many children

7

in public areas, busy and noisy lobby at times, unmemorable guest rooms. ✉ *33 Gerrard St., Downtown, M5G 1Z4* ☎ *416/595–1975 or 800/243–5732* 🌐 *www.deltachelsea.com* *1,590 rooms, 46 suites* *In-hotel: 3 restaurants, bar, room service, pools, gym, children's programs (ages 3–12), laundry facilities, laundry service, executive floor, parking (fee), no-smoking rooms* 💳 *AE, D, DC, MC, V* Ⓜ *College.*

$$ **Howard Johnson Toronto Yorkville.** The rooms are standard fare and the amenities are frugal, but the location is a big asset. The stylish boutiques, antiques shops, and funky eateries of trendy Yorkville are just around the corner, and steps from the lobby door are key public-transit-intersection points. Kids under 12 stay free in their parents' rooms. Ask about discounts for senior citizens and auto-club members. **Pros:** complimentary Continental breakfast, discount parking voucher on request, best value in pricey neighborhood. **Cons:** staff could use some polishing, breakfast not fancy, interiors show some slight wear and tear. ✉ *89 Avenue Rd., Yorkville, M5R 2G3* ☎ *416/964–1220 or 800/446–4656* 🌐 *www.hojo.com* *69 rooms* *In-room: ethernet. In-hotel: laundry service, parking (fee), no-smoking rooms* 💳 *AE, DC, MC, V* *CP* Ⓜ *Bay.*

$$ **Palmerston Inn Bed & Breakfast.** Host Judy Carr has created classic elegance in her 1906, Greek-pillar, Georgian mansion. Period antiques grace each guest room (single or double), and bathrobes and slippers are available. Two rooms have wood-mantled fireplaces. A covered outdoor deck serves as a breakfast room in summer. In winter, breakfast is served in a cozy dining room. There's all-day tea and coffee and afternoon sherry. From here, it's a pleasant stroll on historic, tree-lined Palmerston Boulevard to bustling Bloor Street (north) or to trendy College Street (south). **Pros:** free local phone, air-conditioning, working fireplaces. **Cons:** smokers not welcome at all, bus or subway ride to main shopping and entertainment areas, owner quite particular. ✉ *322 Palmerston Blvd., The Annex, M5G 2N6* ☎ *416/920–7842 or 877/920–7842* 🌐 *www.palmerstoninn.com* *6 rooms* *In-room: Wi-Fi (some). In-hotel: no elevator, parking (no fee), no-smoking rooms* 💳 *MC, V* *BP* Ⓜ *Bathurst.*

$$ **Hotel Victoria.** A local landmark built in 1909, the Vic is Toronto's second-oldest hotel, with a long-standing reputation for service excellence. Architectural traces of the early 20th century are evident in the columned and marbled lobby, stately crown moldings, and floor-to-ceiling windows. Rooms are rather diminutive in size but clean and comfortable. Wingback chairs and quilted bedcovers are nice touches. **Pros:** gym privileges at nearby health club, complimentary newspapers, smoke-free environment. **Cons:** inconvenient, off-site parking, second floor rooms noisy from street, slow elevator. ✉ *56 Yonge St., Old Toronto, M5E 1G5* ☎ *416/363–1666 or 800/363–8228* 🌐 *www.hotelvictoria-toronto.com* *56 rooms* *In-room: ethernet, refrigerator (some). In-hotel: restaurant, laundry services, parking (fee), no-smoking rooms* 💳 *AE, DC, MC, V* Ⓜ *King.*

$ **Alan Gardens Bed & Breakfast.** The mother-daughter team who operate this comfortable B&B have lived in the heart of the city for the past 30-plus years and are excellent ambassadors of all things Toronto.

Their quiet, century-old home is conveniently located, tucked into the city's historical Cabbagetown neighborhood. The high ceilings and elegant, professionally decorated rooms have contemporary, cozy furnishings and include Internet access. The large breakfasts treat guests to home cooking in a luxurious setting. **Pros:** owners very amiable, privacy within intimate surroundings, ideal for architecture buffs. **Cons:** panhandlers prevalent in this neighborhood, streetcar or taxi ride to shopping and entertainment areas, must reserve far in advance due to limited rooms. ✉*106A Pembroke St., Cabbagetown, M5A 2N* ☏*416/967–9614 or 800/215–1937* 🌐*www.alan-gardens-bandb-toronto.ca* *3 rooms, 1 with bath* *In-room: no phone. In-hotel: Wi-Fi (some), parking (no fee), no-smoking rooms, no elevator* *MC, V* *BP* Ⓜ*Dundas.*

$ **Mulberry Tree Bed & Breakfast.** In addition to being a gifted chef (try his signature breakfast of paper-thin Parisian crepes), host Paul Buer is a celebrated photographer, and images from his family's global treks fill the rooms—even the dining room doubles as a kind of gallery. Bedrooms, where antiques and plants abound, are neat as a pin. A small balcony off the guest lounge overlooks an attractive garden. This grand, century-old Heritage home sits on a serene, tree-canopied street. **Pros:** safe neighborhood, in the Church and Wellesley–area "gay village," brightly decorated. **Cons:** no high-speed Internet, owners not prompt in responding to calls or emails, only four rooms. ✉*122 Isabella St., Downtown, M4Y 1P1* ☏*416/960–5249* 🌐*www.bbtoronto.com/mulberrytree* *4 rooms* *In-room: no phone. In-hotel: parking (fee), no-smoking rooms, no elevator* *No credit cards* *BP* Ⓜ*Bloor-Yonge.*

¢ **Global Village Backpackers.** Formerly known as the Spadina Hotel, this hostel is centrally located and filled with international students seeing the world. It's friendly, with a lounge, patio, and bar on premises. Clean linen and towels are supplied at check-in, and the welcoming staff know the city and are great resources. The airport express shuttle drops you two blocks from the hostel. Dorms sleep 6, 10, or 14, but most rooms are quads, sleeping 4, with shared bathrooms. There are six private rooms with double beds in each. **Pros:** weekly and cheaper Internet rates available, bar has live music, free pancake breakfast. **Cons:** some groups may be noisy, on western edge of Entertainment District, must have valid hostelling international ID card for low rates. ✉*460 King St. W, Entertainment District, M5V 1L7* ☏*416/703–8540* 🌐*www.globalbackpackers.com* *30 rooms with 190 beds* *In-hotel: bar, laundry facilities, public Internet* *MC, V* Ⓜ*St. Andrew.*

¢ ★ **Neill-Wycik Summer Hotel.** Fifteen of the 22 floors in this Ryerson University residence become value nonstudent lodging from early May through late August. There are four apartment-style units on each floor; within each unit—equipped with linens, towels, and pillows—are either four or five bedrooms and two bathrooms. Each unit has a common area, a television lounge, and a kitchen (bring your own dishes and utensils). The roof deck has grills for guest use and a great view of the city. The fifth floor has a terrace. Restaurant serves three breakfast specials daily. **Pros:** sauna, rooftop sundeck, barbecues, coin-operated lockers. **Cons:**

no-frills decor, may be noisy, housekeeping may be slack. ✉*96 Gerrard St. E, Downtown, M5B 1G7* ☎*416/977–2320 or 800/268–4358* 🌐*www.neill-wycik.com* *300 rooms without bath* *In-room: no a/c (some), kitchen, no TV. In-hotel: restaurant, laundry facilities, parking (fee)* *MC, V* *CP* *Closed Sept.–Apr.* Ⓜ*Dundas.*

WEST AND SOUTHWEST

$$$ **The Drake Hotel.** Once a notorious flophouse, this 19th-century building is now an off-the-wall boutique hotel. Hanging near the lobby's 110-year-old terrazzo staircase is a Rorschach ink-blot mural that spans the lounge and dining room. Vintage 1950s leather couches, slightly tattered ottomans, art curios, and digital-art projections grace the lobby, while flat-screen TVs, hardwood floors, and transparent shower stalls decorate the guest rooms, which are on the smallish side (150–250 square feet). One interesting feature is that sex toys are for sale from room service. DJs rock and roll in the lounge, the underground bar, and on the rooftop patio nightly, and there are regular art shows and installations by local artists. The on-site Yoga Den has drop-in classes. **Pros:** still attracting the hip downtown crowds, food consistently good, forward-thinking. **Cons:** still attracting the hip downtown crowds, rather seedy neighborhood, service not terribly attentive at times. ✉*1150 Queen St. W, Queen West, M6J 1J3* ☎*416/531–5042 or 866/372–5386* 🌐*www.thedrakehotel.ca* *19 rooms, 1 suite* *In-room: DVD (some), ethernet (some). In-hotel: 3 restaurants, 3 bars, laundry service, public Internet, no-smoking rooms* *AE, MC, V* Ⓜ*Queen streetcar from Osgoode.*

$$$ **The Old Mill Inn & Spa.** Tucked into the Humber River valley, the Old Mill is the only country inn within the city limits of Toronto. Manicured English gardens and a three-arched stone bridge flank the Tudor-style building, constructed in 1914. Burnished mahogany and cherrywood tables, chairs, and beds (some four-poster) grace each guest room. Gas fireplaces, large whirlpool tubs, and down duvets invite romance. Exposed stone walls and a 50-foot-high solid fir cathedral ceiling define the old world–style manor-house restaurant. There's dinner and dancing six nights a week, luncheon buffets, and afternoon tea. It's 15 minutes from downtown and about 25 minutes from the airport. **Pros:** whirlpool tubs, subway and bus stop very close by, live jazz music (Fridays). **Cons:** residential neighborhood which is sometimes too quiet, no shopping nearby, can be very busy with weddings. ✉*21 Old Mill Rd., at Bloor St. W, West Toronto, M8X 1G5* ☎*416/236–2641 or 866/653–6455* 🌐*www.oldmilltoronto.com* *46 rooms, 13 suites* *In-hotel: 2 restaurants, bar, room service, gym, spa, laundry service, concierge, public Internet, parking (no fee), no-smoking rooms.* *AE, DC, MC, V* Ⓜ*Old Mill.*

THE AIRPORT STRIP

$$$ **The Westin Bristol Place Toronto Airport.** This has long been considered one of the ritziest of the airport-strip hotels. It's 100% non-smoking, and bedrooms have plasma TVs, mahogany armoires, tables, and desks with ergonomic chairs. A small waterfall cascades in the lobby. For an airport property, it's fairly quiet—rooms that face east are the quietest of all. **Pros:** safety bars in bathrooms, good restaurant fare, pool has solarium. **Cons:** free Internet only in business center, 14 mi from downtown core, older property. ✉*950 Dixon Rd., Airport West, M9W 5N4* ☎*416/675–9444 or 877/999–3223* 🌐*www.westin.com* *287 rooms, 5 suites* *In-room: Wi-Fi (some). In-hotel: 2 restaurants, bar, pool, gym, public Internet, airport shuttle, parking (fee), some pets allowed, no-smoking rooms* 💳*AE, D, DC, MC, V.*

NIGHTLIFE & THE ARTS

Updated by Shannon Kelly

Toronto's status as one of the most multicultural cities in the world has made its arts and nightlife scene a diverse and exciting one. As the city continues to grow, new venues emerge and some existing venues are magnificently refurbished. Ambitious programs from many of the city's new performance ensembles present a rich variety of entertainment for all tastes and budgets. In the downtown core, the glass-and-steel Four Seasons Centre for the Performing Arts that opened in 2006 is magnificent. The C$181 million venue is home to the Canadian Opera Company and the National Ballet of Canada. The city's glamorous nightlife is maintained thanks in part to the string of celebs and other film and television industry types who paint the town red while on location here. Toronto's "every-city" quality attracts the location scouts, but it's the Torontonians' reputation for being courteous and leaving the stars alone that brings them back again and again. This means it's not uncommon to brush elbows with celebrities while enjoying a night out on the town.

> **WORD OF MOUTH**
>
> "Regarding free entertainment, check out the Harbourfront Centre. It's our lakeshore complex and often has free concerts, movies, opera, ballet, etc. Also check out the Distillery District. There's often free stuff happening there... There are lots of festivals in Toronto in the summer." —hdm

On any night in Toronto, visitors can find a place or entertainment to suit their tastes, from indie rock mash-up nights where arty semiotics majors showcase obscure rock operas and art, to clubs pumping with everything from house to Brit pop, to dark divey clubs where you can hear fancy finger-picking bluegrass musicians. Toronto is known for its many nightclubs—be prepared for long lines on weekends any time of the year as winter draws a lot of university types although summer tends to lure the out-of-towners and regulars. More popular bars and lounges start buzzing around 11 PM with most closing at 3 AM. But don't let that curfew fool you. There are loads of underground parties and several clubs known on the circuit for their all-night scene, finishing up on the weekends at 7 AM.

The best places for information on all the city's cultural events are the free weekly newspapers *NOW* and *Eye Weekly*, which appear on Thursday. Also worth checking are the "What's On" section of the *Toronto Star* (Thursday), the Saturday *Globe and Mail* and *National Post*, and the monthly magazine *Toronto Life*. On the Web, comprehensive and up-to-the-minute listings are available from *Toronto Life* (🌐*www.torontolife.com*), *Eye Weekly* (🌐*www.eye.net*), *NOW* (🌐*www.nowtoronto.com*), and the *Toronto Star* (🌐*www.thestar.com*).

THE ARTS

Toronto is the performing arts capital in English-speaking Canada, but it wasn't always so. Before 1950, Toronto had no opera company, no ballet, and little theater worthy of the title "professional." Then came the Massey Report on the Arts, one of those government-sponsored studies that usually help put sensitive subjects on the back burner for several more years. In this case, however, the heavens broke loose—money began to come in from a variety of government grants; the Canada Council, the Canadian Opera Company, CBC television, and the National Ballet of Canada were born; and a number of small theaters began to pop up, culminating in an artistic explosion throughout the 1970s.

More than money fueled the arts explosion, though. Other factors were a growing sense of independence from the mother country; a recognition that if Canada did not develop its own arts, then the U.S. would do it for them; and, in general, a growing civic and cultural maturity.

Today Toronto is, after New York and London, the largest center for English-speaking theater in the world. The city's smaller theaters have long been filled with interesting classic and contemporary Canadian, English, American, and French drama. Since the 1960s the Sony Centre (formerly the Hummingbird Centre) and Royal Alexandra theaters have provided local and Broadway productions. Restored historic theaters like the Elgin/Winter Garden complex and the Canon Theatre (formerly the Pantages), plus more modern venues explain why it can truly be called "Broadway North."

TICKETS

Full-price theater tickets run from as low as C$20 to as high as C$265. Tickets for pop concerts are usually C$40 to C$100, although at smaller venues the cost may drop to as low as C$20. On certain slow nights and Sunday, many theaters have Pay What You Can (PWYC) entry. Simply phone the venue and ask. Tickets for almost any event in the city can be obtained through **Ticketmaster** (☎*416/870–8000* 🌐*www.ticketmaster.ca*).

Another popular ticket seller is **StubHub** (☎*866/788–2482* 🌐*www.stubhub.com*).

To get half-price tickets—mainly for theater, but also some dance, music, and comedy—on the day of a performance, visit the **T.O. Tix booth** (✉ *Dundas Square, Yonge St. at Dundas St.* ☎ *800/541–0499 or 416/536–6468, Ext. 40* 🌐 *www.totix.ca* Ⓜ *Dundas*), open in good weather Tuesday through Saturday noon to 6:30 PM, and operated by the Toronto Alliance for the Performing Arts. Tickets for Sunday performances are sold on Saturday. In summer, the wait can be 45 minutes or more. ■ **TIP→ If you arrive at around 11:15 you stand the best chance of getting the show you want.** All sales are final, credit cards are accepted (Visa and MasterCard), and a small service charge is added to the price of each ticket.

CLASSICAL MUSIC & OPERA

CLASSICAL MUSIC

Glenn Gould Studio. A variety of classical-, folk-, and world-music companies perform at this 341-seat space named for the famed Canadian (and Torontonian) pianist. Studio recordings are done here as well, a testament to its excellent acoustics. Gould would have expected nothing less. ✉ *250 Front St. W, Entertainment District* ☎ *416/205–5555* 🌐 *glenngouldstudio.cbc.ca* Ⓜ *St. Andrew.*

Tafelmusik. Internationally renowned as one of the world's finest period ensembles, Tafelmusik presents baroque music on original instruments. ✉ *Trinity–St. Paul's United Church, 427 Bloor St. W, The Annex* ☎ *416/964–6337* 🌐 *www.tafelmusik.org* Ⓜ *Spadina.*

The Toronto Mendelssohn Choir. This group of 180 vocalists, which often performs with the Toronto Symphony, was begun in 1894 by Elmer Isler and has since been applauded worldwide. The *Messiah* is performed annually by the choir at Christmastime. Some of the beautiful and heartbreaking music heard in the Academy Award–winning film *Schindler's List* was sung by this choir. ✉ *Roy Thomson Hall, 60 Simcoe St., Entertainment District* ☎ *416/598–0422* 🌐 *www.tmchoir.org* Ⓜ *St. Andrew.*

Toronto Symphony Orchestra. Since 1922 this orchestra has achieved world acclaim with conductors such as Seiji Ozawa, Sir Thomas Beecham, and Andrew Davis. When Canadian-born Peter Oundjian took over as musical director in 2003 it ended several years of instability for the ensemble, and signaled further rejuvenation of an already world-class orchestra. The TSO presents about three concerts weekly at Roy Thomson Hall from September through May when it is not on tour. ✉ *Roy Thomson Hall, 60 Simcoe St., Entertainment District* ☎ *416/593–4828* 🌐 *www.tso.ca* Ⓜ *St. Andrew.*

OPERA

Canadian Opera Company. Founded in 1950, the COC has grown to be the largest producer of opera in Canada and the fifth-largest opera company on the continent. From the most popular operas, such as *Carmen* and *Madame Butterfly,* to more modern or rarer works, such as *The Cunning Little Vixen* and *Hansel and Gretel,* the COC has proven trustworthy and often daring. Recent versions of Verdi's *La Traviata* and Wagner's *The Flying Dutchman* were considered radical by many. The COC often hosts world-renowned performers, and it pioneered the use of scrolling subtitles that appear above the performers, which allow the audience to follow the libretto in English in a capsulized translation. The magnificent Four Seasons Centre opera house opened its doors in 2006. ✉ *Four Seasons Centre, 145 Queen St. W, Entertainment District* ☎ *416/363–6671* 🌐 *www.coc.ca* Ⓜ *Osgoode.*

CONCERT HALLS

★ **Elgin and Winter Garden Theatre Centre.** This jewel in the crown of the Toronto arts scene is composed of two former vaudeville halls, built in 1913, one on top of the other, that together form one of the last operating double-decker theater complexes in the world. From 1913 to 1928, the theaters hosted vaudeville legends like George Burns, Gracie Allen, and Charlie McCarthy. The Elgin's gold-leaf-and-cherub–adorned interior and the Winter Garden's nature-themed decor, complete with hand-painted walls and ceiling hung with beech branches, fell into disrepair. In the 1980s, the Ontario Heritage Foundation completed an admirable C$30 million restoration—showcasing the building's Edwardian charm and reopened the theaters in 1989. The Elgin, downstairs, has about 1,500 seats and is more suited to musicals; Winter Garden, upstairs, is somewhat more intimate, with about 1,000 seats. Both theaters are wheelchair accessible, and both have excellent sight lines. Guided tours (C$7) are given Thursday at 5 PM and Saturday at 11 AM. ✉ *189 Yonge St., Midtown* ☎ *416/872–5555 tickets, 416/314–2901 tours* 🌐 *www.heritagefdn.on.ca* Ⓜ *St. Andrew.*

Sony Centre. When this theater opened in 1960 as the O'Keefe Centre it showcased the world premiere of *Camelot,* starring Julie Andrews, Richard Burton, and Robert Goulet. Renamed in 1996 after major renovations, the theater showcases comedians, rock stars, Broadway shows, and has been the home of the Canadian Opera Company and the National Ballet of Canada. ✉ *1 Front St. E, Old Toronto* ☎ *416/872–2262* 🌐 *www.sonycentre.ca* Ⓜ *King.*

Fodor's Choice ★ **Massey Hall.** It's always been cramped, but Massey Hall's near-perfect acoustics and its handsome, U-shaped tiers sloping down to the stage have made it a great place to enjoy music since 1894, when it opened with a performance of Handel's *Messiah.* The nearly 2,800 seat Massey Hall remains a venerable place to catch the greats of the music world. ✉ *178 Victoria St., Midtown* ☎ *416/872–4255* 🌐 *www.masseyhall.com* Ⓜ *St. Andrew.*

★ **Roy Thomson Hall.** The most important concert hall in Toronto opened in 1982. It was named for the newspaper magnate Lord Thomson of Fleet, after his family donated C$4.5 million in his memory. It is the home of the Toronto Symphony Orchestra and the Toronto Mendelssohn Choir, and also hosts visiting orchestras and entertainers. ✉ *60 Simcoe St., Entertainment District* ☎ *416/872–4255 tickets, 416/593–4822, Ext. 363 tours* 🌐 *www.roythomson.com* Ⓜ *St. Andrew.*

St. Lawrence Centre for the Arts. This center has presented entertainment and public forums since 1970. The two main halls are the luxuriously appointed Bluma Appel Theatre and the Jane Mallett Theatre. ✉ *27 Front St. E, Old Toronto* ☎ *416/366–7723* 🌐 *www.stlc.com* Ⓜ *King.*

DANCE

National Ballet of Canada. Canada's homegrown and internationally recognized classical-ballet company was founded in 1951 by Celia Franca, an English dancer from the Sadler's Wells tradition. The season runs from November through May. A series of outstanding productions, such as John Cranko's *Taming of the Shrew* and *Romeo and Juliet,* and the company's artistic director James Kudelka's *The Nutcracker,* have been performed by the company. The Four Seasons Centre venue opened in 2006. Tickets run C$39–C$133. ■ **TIP→Half-price tickets for students and senior citizens are available at the box office on performance day.** ✉ *Four Seasons Centre for the Performing Arts, 145 Queen St. W., Downtown* ☎ *416/345–9595 information, 866/345–9595 tickets* 🌐 *www.national.ballet.ca* Ⓜ *Osgoode.*

Harbourfront Centre. Two venues for dance are here. The **Premiere Dance Theatre** was built specifically for modern dance in 1983. The proscenium stage hosts some of the best local and Canadian modern and contemporary companies in addition to some international acts. The **Enwave Theatre** welcomes the same types of performances as the Premiere Dance Theatre as well as plays and music performances. Originally designed with music in mind, it has excellent acoustics. Both theaters are small (425 and 450 seats) so you're never far from the stage, and sight lines are great from every seat. ✉ *Harbourfront Centre, 207 Queen's Quay W, 3rd floor, Harbourfront* ☎ *416/973–4000* 🌐 *www.harbourfrontcentre.com* Ⓜ *Union.*

★ **Toronto Dance Theatre.** With roots in the Martha Graham tradition, Toronto Dance Theatre is the city's oldest contemporary dance company. Started in the 1960s with 100 works under its belt, the company tours Canada and has played major festivals worldwide. ✉ *Premiere Dance Theatre, Harbourfront Centre, 207 Queen's Quay W, Harbourfront* ☎ *416/973–4000* 🌐 *www.harbourfrontcentre.com* Ⓜ *Union.*

FILM

Toronto has a devoted film audience and the result is a feast of first- and second-run showings, festivals, and lecture series. A loosely associated group of independent movie theaters also offers low-priced screenings of independent productions, classics, cult films, and new releases.

FIRST-RUN & MAINSTREAM MOVIES

The Docks Drive-in Theatre. For an old-fashioned treat, head to the alfresco Docks Drive-in, open from spring to mid-October, weather permitting. First-run flicks are shown on Friday, Saturday, and Sunday evenings and for half-price on Tuesday evenings, starting at approximately 9 PM. Tickets can be purchased in person at the Docks box office. ✉ *11 Polson St., near harbor, Harbourfront* ☎ *416/461–3625* 🌐 *www.thedocks.com* Ⓜ *St. Andrew.*

Scotiabank Theatre (The Paramount). In the heart of the Entertainment District, this megaplex with 14 screens shows all the latest blockbusters, usually along with a couple of foreign or independent films. For advanced tickets go to their Web site. ✉ *John St. and Richmond St., Downtown* ☎ *416/368–5600* 🌐 *www.famousplayers.com.*

Varsity. The eight screens here show new releases. ■ **TIP→ Smaller VIP screening rooms have seat-side waitstaff ready to take your concession-**

stand orders. VIP tickets are $14.95. ✉55 Bloor St. W, at Bay St., Yorkville ☎416/961–6303 🌐www.cineplex.com Ⓜ Bay.

WORD OF MOUTH

"I live in Toronto and have been to the film festival numerous times over the years. It's really an amazing event that's totally accessible to the public, unlike Cannes." —bittersweet

INDEPENDENT, FOREIGN & REVIVAL FILMS

Cinematheque Ontario. International film programs are presented at the Art Gallery of Ontario year-round. *✉317 Dundas St. W, Midtown ☎416/968–3456 Ⓜ St. Patrick.*

Cumberland 4. An excellent selection of international films is shown here. *✉159 Cumberland St., Yorkville ☎416/646–0444 Ⓜ Bay.*

Film Reference Library. This is the largest collection of English-language Canadian film material in the world. For a small fee, you can view everything. *✉2 Carlton St., Midtown ☎416/967–1517 🌐www.filmreferencelibrary.ca Ⓜ College.*

Harbourfront Centre. Interesting retrospectives are presented here. *✉235 Queen's Quay W, Harbourfront ☎416/973–4000 🌐www.harbourfrontcentre.com Ⓜ Union.*

FILM FESTIVALS & EVENTS

Sprockets: The Toronto International Film Festival for Children. Held yearly at the end of April, this festival features new works and classic films aimed at children ages 4 to 14. Call for times and venues. *☎416/968–3456.*

Toronto International Film Festival. Downtown is dominated by the world's third largest film festival each September. The 10-day event attracts Hollywood celebrities and great international stars. You can get tickets in advance through a balloting process that starts in July; information can be found on the festival's Web site. *☎416/967–7371 or 416/968–3456 🌐www.bell.ca/filmfest.*

THEATER

Some of the most entertaining theater in Toronto is free, though donations are always welcome. Every summer the CanStage theater company presents **Dream in High Park** (*✉High Park, main entrance off Bloor St. W at High Park Ave., West Toronto ☎416/367–8243 information, 416/368–3110 box office 🌐www.canstage.com Ⓜ High Park*), quality productions of Shakespeare, and contemporary works in glorious High Park's outdoor amphitheater.

COMMERCIAL THEATERS

Canon Theatre. This 1920 vaudeville theater, formerly known as the Pantages Theatre, is one of the city's most architecturally and acoustically exciting theaters. The longest running Canadian stage musical, *The Phantom of the Opera,* closed after 10 years on October 31, 1999. The theater was designed by world-renowned theater architect Thomas Lamb. *✉244 Victoria St., Downtown ☎416/872–1212 🌐www.ticketking.com Ⓜ Queen.*

Princess of Wales. State-of-the-art technical facilities and murals by American artist Frank Stella grace this theater. The local producers of *Miss Saigon* built this exquisite 2,000-seat theater in 1991–93 to accommodate the musical when no other venue was available. *✉300*

King St. W, Entertainment District ☎*416/872–1212 or 800/461–3333* 🌐*www.ticketking.com* Ⓜ*St. Andrew.*

Royal Alexandra. Since 1907, this has been the place to be seen in Toronto. The 1,500 plush red seats, gold brocade, and baroque swirls make theatergoing a refined experience. Recent programs have been a mix of blockbuster musicals and a variety of dramatic productions. ✉*260 King St. W, Entertainment District* ☎*416/872–3333 or 800/461–3333* 🌐*www.ticketking.com* Ⓜ*St. Andrew.*

SMALL THEATERS & COMPANIES

Buddies in Bad Times. Local thespians and playwrights present edgy, alternative performances in the country's largest gay-centered multitheater complex. ✉*12 Alexander St., Yonge and College* ☎*416/975–8555* 🌐*buddiesinbadtimestheatre.com* Ⓜ*Wellesley.*

Factory Theatre. This is Canada's largest producer of homegrown theater. Many of the company's plays have toured the country and have won awards. ✉*125 Bathurst St., Entertainment District* ☎*416/504–9971* 🌐*www.factorytheatre.ca* Ⓜ*Bathurst.*

Hart House Theatre. The main theater space of the U of T, since 1919, Hart House mounts four amateur and student productions per season (September–April): two Canadian shows, one musical, and one Shakespeare. Tickets are C$20. ✉*7 Hart House Circle, Queen's Park* ☎*416/978–8668* 🌐*www.harthousetheatre.ca* Ⓜ*Queen's Park.*

Lorraine Kimsa Theatre For Young People. Productions are devoted solely to children, but unlike other traditional children's theater, this place does not condescend, or compromise its dramatic integrity. ✉*165 Front St. E, Old Toronto* ☎*416/862–2222* 🌐*www.lktyp.ca* Ⓜ*King.*

★ **Tarragon Theatre.** The natural habitat for indigenous Canadian theater is in this old warehouse and railroad district. Maverick companies often rent the smaller of the Tarragon's theaters for interesting experimental works. ✉*30 Bridgman Ave., The Annex* ☎*416/531–1827* 🌐*www.tarragontheatre.com* Ⓜ*Dupont.*

Théâtre Passe Muraille. Around Bathurst and Queen streets, this venue has long been the home of fine Canadian collaborative theater. ✉*16 Ryerson Ave., Entertainment District* ☎*416/504–7529* 🌐*www.passemuraille.on.ca* Ⓜ*Osgoode.*

NIGHTLIFE

Toronto has all kinds of music clubs. Downtown, Adelaide Street West from University Avenue to Peter Street has spawned numerous clubs and many don't charge a cover, and those that do rarely ask more than C$10.

BARS, PUBS & LOUNGES

Have a good time in Toronto, but be aware of the strict drinking and driving laws. Police regularly stop cars to check drivers' sobriety with a breath analysis test. If you have a blood-alcohol level higher than .08%, it's the judge or jail, no matter where you're from. Under the city's liquor laws, last call in bars is 2 AM; closing time is 3 AM. The minimum drinking age is 19.

7

Toronto forbids smoking in bars, pool halls, and casinos. Some patios and separate smoking rooms—which are often oppressively smoky—are approved for smokers by the city government, but to avoid hefty fines, check with the venue prior to lighting up.

Allen's. This establishment is a quintessential Irish pub along a mostly Greek avenue. ✉*143 Danforth Ave., East Toronto* ☎*416/463–3086* Ⓜ*Broadview.*

★ **Avenue.** The Four Seasons Toronto hotel's lounge combines New York–style sophistication—pale walls, dark wood—with old-world touches. Beverages are pricey, but what can you expect from this posh hotel? ✉*21 Avenue Rd., Yorkville* ☎*416/964–0411* Ⓜ*Bay.*

Brunswick House. Students from the nearby University of Toronto are the bulk of the crowd here. ✉*481 Bloor St. W, The Annex* ☎*416/964–2242* Ⓜ*Spadina.*

Fodor's Choice ★ **Canoe.** Known for its food and surroundings, this restaurant is on the 54th floor of the Toronto Dominion Centre. The ambience and panoramic view make this spot popular with brokers and financial wizards from the neighboring towers. ✉*66 Wellington St. W, Financial District* ☎*416/364–0054* 🌐*www.canoerestaurant.com* Ⓜ*King.*

Easy and The Fifth. This is what you get when you cross a New York–style loft with a disco playing Top 10 and retro tunes. The dark floors, white walls, and high ceilings give the place height, and the crowd of young professionals provides the scenery. ✉*225 Richmond St. W, Entertainment District* ☎*416/979–3000* 🌐*www.thefifth.com* Ⓜ*Osgoode.*

Hemingway's. One of the most crowded singles bars in Toronto, Hemingway's is cozier than other Yorkville watering holes and attracts many regulars. ✉*142 Cumberland St., Yorkville* ☎*416/968–2828* Ⓜ*Bay.*

★ **Madison Avenue Pub.** On the edge of the U of T campus, the six-storied "Maddy" typifies an English pub, with lots of brass, exposed brick, and dartboards. ✉*14–18 Madison Ave., The Annex* ☎*416/927–1722* Ⓜ*Spadina.*

Fodor's Choice ★ **The Paddock.** Glamorous types pack this art deco–style bar all week to drink specialty cocktails and premium beers and sample the above-average fare, which includes local Ontario produce and game such as bison ribs, elk carpaccio, caribou, and lamb. A capacious dark-wood bar curves along two walls of the room, while high-backed booths offer a little more privacy. CDs of legendary jazz artists play during dinner. ✉*178 Bathurst St., Queen West* ☎*416/504–9997* 🌐*www.thepaddock.ca* Ⓜ*501 Queen West streetcar to Bathurst St.*

Panorama Lounge. Black leather furniture, glamorous chandeliers, and floor-to-ceiling windows combine for a hip, comfortable atmosphere. ■ **TIP→ On the 51st floor, this is the highest outdoor patio in Toronto, and is a great perch to enjoy the nightscape above the city lights.** The southern-facing patio is the choice spot—it has a view of Downtown, the CN Tower, and the lake. It is an ideal spot for celebrity sightings, and there is an excellent selection of cocktails, martinis, and light meals—and a decadent chocolate fondue. A $5 cover charge applies Friday and Saturday nights. ✉*Manulife Centre, 55 Bloor St. W, at Bay, 51st fl., Yorkville* ☎*416/967–0000* 🌐*www.pixelcarve.com/demo/panorama/main.html* Ⓜ*Bay.*

The Roof Lounge. Such Canadian literary luminaries as Margaret Atwood and Mordecai Richler used the 18th-floor Roof Lounge as a setting in their writings. It's a quiet and classy bar with dark-wood and marble accents. Martinis and cosmopolitans are the bar's specialties and go down nicely with selections from the light menu. This remains an important hangout for the upper-middle class. ✉ *Park Hyatt Hotel, 4 Avenue Rd., Yorkville* ☎ *416/925–1234* Ⓜ *Bay.*

★ **Smokeless Joe's.** More than 250 beers from around the world, many of which can't be found anywhere else in Ontario, are served here. ✉ *125 John St., Entertainment District* ☎ *416/591–2221* Ⓜ *St. Andrew.*

Wayne Gretzky's. The pre-game Blue Jays and Maple Leafs fans and the post-theater crowd from Second City comedy club across the street flock to this sports bar and family-style restaurant owned by the hockey icon. ✉ *99 Blue Jays Way, Entertainment District* ☎ *416/979–7825* Ⓜ *Union.*

GAY & LESBIAN

Pegasus on Church. Locals meet, shoot pool, and, above all, play the interactive Internet game NTN Trivia. Pegasus is famous in Toronto for consistently being one of the top scorers on the "wired" trivia game. ✉ *489B Church St., Church and Wellesley* ☎ *416/927–8832* 🌐 *www.pegasusonchurch.com* Ⓜ *Wellesley.*

Slack's. One of the city's oldest gay and lesbian bars, Slack's (formerly Slack Alice) has a great kitchen and provides a friendly atmosphere with nightly events, and contests. ✉ *562 Church St., Church and Wellesley* ☎ *416/969–8742* 🌐 *www.slacks.ca* Ⓜ *Wellesley.*

Woody's. A predominantly upscale male crowd, with lots of professional types, frequents Woody's. ✉ *467 Church St., Church and Wellesley* ☎ *416/972–0887* 🌐 *www.woodystoronto.com* Ⓜ *Wellesley.*

COMEDY CLUBS

The Laugh Resort. Catch stand-up solo acts Wednesday through Saturday night. The cover is C$7 to C$15. Go early for a great seat and enjoy a light preshow dinner. ✉ *370 King St. W, Entertainment District* ☎ *416/364–5233* 🌐 *www.laughresort.com* Ⓜ *King.*

★ **The Rivoli.** Solid up-and-coming acts perform at the Monday ALTdot COMedy Lounge stand-up night or the Tuesday-night Sketch Comedy Lounge. The ratio of chuckles to groans is good. Some later-famous comedians (Mike Myers, Samantha Bee) have performed here. And it's free! ✉ *332 Queen St. W, Queen West* ☎ *416/596–1908 or 416/597–0794* 🌐 *www.rivoli.ca* Ⓜ *Queen.*

Fodor'sChoice ★ **Second City.** Since it opened in 1973, Second City has been providing some of the best comedy in Toronto. Many alumni of this troupe ventured to *Saturday Night Live* and the *SCTV* series. Among those who cut their teeth on the Toronto stage are Mike Myers, Dan Aykroyd, Martin Short, Andrea Martin, and Catherine O'Hara. Tickets are C$20–C$28, or C$45–C$53 for dinner and show. ✉ *56 Blue Jays Way, Entertainment District* ☎ *416/343–0011 or 800/263–4485* 🌐 *www.secondcity.com* Ⓜ *Union.*

DANCE CLUBS

Toronto is a magnet when it comes to attracting large crowds at its countless dance clubs and bars. With two universities, three colleges, and cartloads of tech institutes and other specialty schools, the scene is full of young urbanites who want to get down, chill, and leave the "crib" for a night. Laser shows, dry ice, and "intelligent lights" transform old warehouses into twilight zones of loud music and flashing lights.

★ **The Courthouse Chamber Lounge.** With its lofty ceilings, plush couches, and roaring fireplaces, this club resembles more a 1940s Hollywood mansion than a courthouse. The cocktail crowd is modern and upscale. The Cell Bar cigar bar still shows remnants of the actual holding cells. ✉ *57 Adelaide St. E, Old Toronto* ☎ *416/214–9379* 🌐 *www.liberty-group.com* Ⓜ *Osgoode.*

The Docks. With spectacular views of the city, this enormous lakefront complex provides complete entertainment for partygoers, with video games, beach-volleyball courts, a driving range, a climbing wall, a drive-in movie theater, and more. ✉ *11 Polson St., Harbourfront* ☎ *416/461–3625* 🌐 *www.thedocks.com* Ⓜ *Union.*

Fodor'sChoice ★ **The Guvernment.** Each of the eight lounges and dance clubs in this interlocked complex has its own themed decor and special events. The club gets going after midnight. ✉ *132 Queen's Quay E, Harbourfront* ☎ *416/869–0045* 🌐 *www.theguvernment.com* Ⓜ *Union.*

★ **The Mod Club Theatre.** Britain rules on Saturday nights at this music venue's Anglophile dance night. DJs Bobbi Guy and DJ MRK (aka Mark Holmes, former frontman of '80s new-wave band Platinum Blonde) spin retro and new tunes from across the pond, with the early '60s heavily represented. Go ahead, slip into that A-line minidress—you won't be the only one. ✉ *722 College St., at Ossington St., Little Italy* ☎ *416/588–4663* 🌐 *www.themodclub.com* Ⓜ *501 College streetcar to Grace St.*

System Sound Bar. House, techno, and R&B reverberate throughout this basement-level bar-club. This club is mostly geared to pumped-up electronic-music fans in their early twenties. ✉ *117 Peter St., Entertainment District* ☎ *416/408–3996* 🌐 *www.systemsoundbar.com* Ⓜ *Osgoode.*

Tonic Nightclub. Just above the subterranean System Sound Bar, the sophisticated Tonic attracts an early-twenties to early-thirties crowd. DJs spin house, techno, and R&B. Expect a cover charge of C$10–C$12, depending on the night. Thursdays are free. ✉ *117 Peter St., Entertainment District* ☎ *416/204–9200* 🌐 *www.tonicnightclub.com* Ⓜ *Osgoode.*

GAY & LESBIAN

Free publications for the gay community include *X-Tra,* available at various venues, and *Fab,* a monthly mag distributed at shops and restaurants.

Ciao Edie. Have a colorful cocktail and kick back among the retro furnishings at this laid-back lounge. Girls who just wanna have fun can check out the bar's lesbian Here Kitty Kitty night on Sunday, when DJs spin everything from R&B and Latin to house and hip-hop. ✉ *489 College St. W, Little Italy* ☎ *416/927–7774* Ⓜ *Queen's Park.*

★ **Fly.** Some of the biggest and best DJs from around the world have spun records at the original "Babylon" from television's *Queer as Folk*. An impressive sound system, light show, and 10,000 square feet of excellent vibe have won this queer-positive club several Best Dance Club in Toronto awards. ✉ *8 Gloucester St., between Yonge and Church Sts., Downtown* ☎ *416/410–5426* 🌐 *www.flynightclub.com* Ⓜ *Sherbourne.*

Zipperz–Cell Block. This easygoing gay-and-lesbian bar has a piano bar in front showcasing classic tunes, and the dance club in the back rocks with a DJ on weekends and drag shows weekdays. ✉ *72 Carlton St., Downtown* ☎ *416/921–0066* 🌐 *www.zipperz-cellblock.ca* Ⓜ *College.*

LATIN DANCE CLUBS

Ba-Ba-Lu'U. Truly the best of both worlds, this Yorkville club combines the luxe of a tony lounge with the sizzle of sexy Latin rhythms. Novices can sign up for dance lessons; call for times. ✉ *136 Yorkville Ave., Yorkville* ☎ *416/515–0587* Ⓜ *Bay.*

Lula Lounge. There's no dress code, but Latin-music lovers dress up to get down to bands playing Afro-Cuban and Salsa music. Tasty mint-and-lime-spiked *mojitos* get you in the groove. ✉ *1585 Dundas St. W, West Toronto* ☎ *416/588–0302* 🌐 *www.lula.ca* Ⓜ *Dufferin.*

MUSIC

Most major record companies have offices in Toronto, so the city is a regular stop for top musical celebrities like the Rolling Stones, Shania Twain, and Justin Timberlake. Most clubs have cover charges that range from C$5 to C$10.

LARGE VENUES

The Air Canada Centre. Seating here suits medium and large rock concerts. Recent artists who performed here range from the Red Hot Chili Peppers to the Dixie Chicks to Pavarotti. ✉ *40 Bay St., Downtown* ☎ *416/815–5500* 🌐 *www.theaircanadacentre.com* Ⓜ *Union.*

The Sony Centre. This venue plays host to an eclectic mix of pop and world music. ✉ *1 Front St. E, Old Toronto* ☎ *416/872–2262* 🌐 *www.sonycentre.ca.*

Rogers Centre. This huge venue formerly known as The Skydome can seat 70,000, so it's the stopping place for the biggest shows in town. ✉ *1 Blue Jays Way, Old Toronto* ☎ *416/341–3663* 🌐 *www.skydome.com* Ⓜ *King.*

SMALLER VENUES

The Molson Amphitheatre. Summer concerts occur at this lakefront amphitheater at modest prices. The skyline and the summer breezes make this one of the loveliest places to hear music. ✉ *Ontario Place, 955 Lakeshore Blvd. W, Harbourfront* ☎ *416/870–8000* Ⓜ *Union.*

The Phoenix Concert Theatre. A variety of music is presented at this two-room venue. Many nights, music airs live at local radio stations from the Main Room while in the Parlour, every genre from house to retro-rock and local bands can be enjoyed in an intimate setting. Cover charges range from C$5 to C$8. ✉ *410 Sherbourne St., Cabbagetown* ☎ *416/323–1251* 🌐 *www.libertygroup.com* Ⓜ *Sherbourne.*

FOLK

Free Times Cafe. This restaurant specializes in vegetarian Middle Eastern food and has folk music nightly. ✉ *320 College St., Chinatown* ☎ *416/967–1078* Ⓜ *Queen's Park.*

Hugh's Room. The biggest names in folk music perform at this dinner–folk club. ✉ *2261 Dundas St. W, Downtown* ☎ *416/531–6604* 🌐 *www.hughsroom.com* Ⓜ *Dundas West.*

JAZZ & FUNK

Opal Jazz Lounge. Opened in 2006, this intimate and contemporary-chic venue welcomes performers like pianist Don Glaser and vocalist Arlene Smith. Its restaurant was voted one of the best new restaurants of 2006 by Toronto.com. ✉ *472 Queen St. W, Entertainment District* ☎ *416/646–6725* 🌐 *www.opaljazzlounge.com* Ⓜ *Osgoode.*

The Pilot Tavern. Mainstream jazz is served up Saturday afternoon, along with good burgers. ✉ *22 Cumberland St., Yorkville* ☎ *416/923–5716* 🌐 *www.thepilot.ca* Ⓜ *Bay.*

POP & ROCK

The Cameron Public House. "Alternative" music at this small venue ranges from jazz to hard rock. The crowd gets heavy on weekends. ✉ *408 Queen St. W, Queen West* ☎ *416/703–0811* 🌐 *www.thecameron.com* Ⓜ *Osgoode.*

★ **¿C'est What?** An eclectic mix of local bands plays almost nightly at this downtown club. You'll also find house beers, and good cooking. ✉ *67 Front St. E, Downtown* ☎ *416/867–9499* 🌐 *www.cestwhat.com* Ⓜ *King.*

The Drake Hotel. Talk about so hip it hurts. This is not divey hipster joint, however—it's high-style. The Underground, downstairs, fills up every night with young, artsy types with edgy haircuts here for the indie bands. At the main-floor Drake Lounge, young scenesters sip cocktails and order snacks or dinners from the menu. ✉ *1150 Queen St. W, Queen West* ☎ *416/531–5042* 🌐 *www.thedrakehotel.ca* Ⓜ *501 Queen streetcar to Dufferin St.*

Horseshoe Tavern. Since 1947, this has been known across the city as the tavern with entertainment, especially country music. Charlie Pride, Tex Ritter, Hank Williams, and Loretta Lynn all played here. Now the music is mostly alternative rock, along with some live roots, blues, and rockabilly. Good new bands perform here six nights a week. No food is served, but there's plenty of booze. The place draws a young crowd. ✉ *370 Queen St. W, Queen West* ☎ *416/598–4753* 🌐 *www.horseshoetavern.com* Ⓜ *Osgoode.*

Lee's Palace. Rock-and-roll and punk are served up CBGB style at this club on the edge of the University of Toronto campus. Grab a table or watch the show from the sunken viewing area. ✉ *529 Bloor St. W, The Annex* ☎ *416/532–7383* 🌐 *www.leespalace.com* Ⓜ *Bathurst.*

RHYTHM & BLUES

Grossman's Tavern. Old and raunchy, the setting of Grossman's makes it ideal for the blues. There are R&B bands nightly and jazz on Saturday afternoon. ✉ *379 Spadina Ave., The Annex* ☎ *416/977–7000* 🌐 *www.grossmanstavern.com* Ⓜ *Take the Spadina streetcar from Spadina station.*

The Silver Dollar Room. Some of the top blues acts play here. The bar is long and dark, but the blues-loving clientele are friendly, and you stand a good chance of talking with the musicians. ✉ *486 Spadina Ave., The*

Annex ☎*416/763–9139* 🌐*www.silverdollarroom.com* Ⓜ*Take the Spadina streetcar from Spadina station.*

SUPPER CLUBS The past few years have witnessed the rebirth of the supper club in Toronto. The places listed below also have sit-down bars, for those who prefer to limit the evening to drinks and dancing.

Rosewater Supper Club. Blue velvet banquettes for two fill this lovely place, which is perfect for a festive night on the town. Modern French cuisine is on the menu. One lounge has a baby grand and a torch singer, and a three-piece jazz band performs on Thursday and Saturday, when those so inclined can take a twirl on the dance floor. ✉*19 Toronto St., Old Toronto* ☎*416/214–5888* 🌐*www.libertygroup.com* Ⓜ*King.*

Ultra Supper Club. At this swanky supper club, you can relax in the lounge with a cocktail and later order in the dining room. DJs spin mainstream dance tunes on Thursday, Friday, and Saturday ($C20 cover charge). ✉*314 Queen St. W, Entertainment District* ☎*416/263–0330* 🌐*www.ultrasupperclub.com* Ⓜ*Osgoode.*

SPORTS & THE OUTDOORS

Updated by Shannon Kelly

Toronto enjoys a love-hate relationship with its professional sports teams. Fans can sometimes be accused of being fair-weather—except when it comes to hockey. In Toronto the national sport has always attracted rabid, sell-out crowds, whether the Maple Leafs win, lose, or draw.

For outdoor enthusiasts Toronto has an extensive network of parks and trails available year-round that includes biking, boating, hiking, or cross-country skiing. The parks of the Toronto Islands have spectacular views of the city skyline, and the Don Valley Trail System snakes from north of the city to Lake Ontario.

BEACHES

Lake Ontario is rarely warm enough for sustained swimming, except in late August, and is often too polluted for any kind of dip. Still, it's fun to relax or take a stroll on one of the city's beaches. Once the site of a large, rollicking amusement park, **Sunnyside Beach,** west of downtown, is now a favorite place for a swim in the safe, heated water of the "tank" or a quick snack in the small restaurant inside the handsomely restored 1922 Sunnyside Bathing Pavilion.

★ In the east end, **Beaches Park,** south of Queen Street and east of Coxwell Avenue, has a lengthy boardwalk, local canoe club, and public washrooms. A 20-minute streetcar ride east of downtown, along Queen Street, at Coxwell Avenue, is **Woodbine Beach Park.** The city's most pleasing beaches—and certainly the ones with the best views—are on the **Toronto Islands.** The best ones are those on the southeast tip of Ward's Island, the southernmost edge of Centre Island, and the west side of Hanlan's Island. A portion of Hanlan's Beach is clothing-optional.

PARKS

Fodor's Choice ★ Nearly 400 acres, **High Park** is the city's largest playground; in summer, hordes descend to enjoy the outdoor activities here. Between the manicured rose gardens in the west and the sprawling forest in the east, there are numerous recreational facilities: a large public swimming pool, tennis courts, baseball and soccer fields, fitness trails, and walking paths. In the park's southwest corner is **Grenadier Pond,** home to thousands of migrating birds. You can fish in its well-stocked waters, either from the shore or from a rented rowboat. In winter, you can skate. The modest **High Park Zoo** is free. The park hosts many summer events, including professionally staged Shakespeare productions. To get here, take the TTC to the High Park Station and walk south; you can also take the College Street streetcar to the eastern end of the park and walk west. ✉ *Bordered by Bloor St. W, the Gardiner Expressway, Parkside Dr., and Ellis Park Rd., Southwest Toronto* ☎ *416/392–1111, 416/392–1748 walking tours.*

Along the lakeshore, **Sir Casimir Gzowski Park** has marvelous views of the Toronto Islands, Ontario Place, and the city. There is a paved trail ideal for jogging, biking, and in-line skating. The park is accessible by the 501 Queen and 504 King streetcars and is right next to Sunnyside Park. ✉ *Along Lakeshore Blvd. W, Southwest Toronto.*

SPORTS & FITNESS

BASEBALL

★ The **Toronto Blue Jays** (✉ *Rogers Centre, 1 Blue Jays Way, Old Toronto* ☎ *416/341–1111, 416/341–1234 for ticket information* 🌐 *www.bluejays.com* Ⓜ *Union*) play from April through September. Interest in the team has dropped since their big consecutive World Series championships win in 1992–93. Tickets are C$8 to C$65.

BASKETBALL

The city's NBA franchise, the **Toronto Raptors** (✉ *Air Canada Centre, 40 Bay St., at Lakeshore Blvd., Downtown* ☎ *416/815–5600, 416/872–5000 for tickets* 🌐 *www.raptors.com* Ⓜ *Union*), played its first season in 1995–96. For several years they struggled to win both games and fans in this hockey-mad city, but the Raptors have finally come into their own, and games often sell out. Tickets run from C$14 to C$125 per game for the upper level, lower level, and courtside seats range from C$114 to C$1,560. They are available in July; the season is from October through April.

BICYCLING

More than 29 km (18 mi) of street bike routes cut across the city, and dozens more follow safer paths through Toronto's many parks. Bike rentals are available in Toronto as well as on the Toronto Islands.

The **Don Valley Trail System** begins at Edward's Gardens and runs to the lake. **Humber Valley Parkland** stretches along the Humber River ravine, from north of the city limits (Steeles Avenue) down into Lake Ontario. Its peaceful location away from traffic makes the park ideal for a hiking, jogging, or biking tour. The **Martin Goodman Trail** is a 19-km (12-mi) strip that runs along the waterfront all the way from the Balmy Beach Club in the east end out past the beaches southwest of High Park.

Wheel Excitement (✉ *249 Queens Quay W* ☎ *416/260-9000* 🌐 *www.wheelexcitement.ca*) rents bikes and inline skates. Between York and Spadina, it's as central as you can get and allows you to easily head east or west on the Martin Goodman Trail.

WORD OF MOUTH

"If you are into hockey and the Maple Leafs are in town, try and see a game in Toronto. The arena there is practically brand new and very nice, and as you probably know, hockey in Canada is practically a religion." —Cat123

FOOTBALL

The Canadian Football League (CFL) has a healthy following. In Toronto, the **Toronto Argonauts** (✉ *Rogers Centre, 1 Blue Jays Way, Old Toronto* ☎ *416/341–2746* 🌐 *www.argonauts.on.ca* Ⓜ *Union*) have struggled for fans against the Maple Leafs, Raptors, and Blue Jays. Tickets for home games are a cinch to get. Prices range from C$20 to C$75. The season runs from June to late November.

GOLF

The golf season lasts only from April to late October. The top course in Canada, a real beauty designed by Jack Nicklaus, is the 18-hole, par-73 **Glen Abbey** (✉ *1333 Dorval Dr., Oakville* ☎ *905/844–1800*). The **Canadian Open,** one of golf's Big Five tournaments, is held here in late summer. Cart and green fees are as follows: May 29 to October 6 C$235, May 1 to May 27 and October 9 to season closing C$145.

The **Don Valley Golf Course** (✉ *4200 Yonge St., south of Hwy. 401, North York* ☎ *416/392–2465*) is a par-71, 18-hole municipal course. Green fees are C$50 Monday to Thursday and C$55 Friday to Sunday; twilight rates are available for C$32. You can book up to five days in advance.

The **Flemingdon Park Golf Club** (✉ *155 St. Denis Dr., near Don Mills Rd. and Eglinton Ave., North York* ☎ *416/429–1740* Ⓜ *Eglinton*) is a fairly standard, public, 9-hole course. A round during the week is C$28, and C$30 on weekends and holidays. The course winds along the Don Valley wall and Taylor Creek, making the city seem far away.

HOCKEY

Fodor's Choice ★ Whether the **Toronto Maple Leafs** (✉ *Air Canada Centre, 40 Bay St., at Lakeshore Blvd., Downtown* ☎ *416/870–8000* 🌐 *www.torontomapleleafs.com* Ⓜ *Union*) are on a winning or losing streak, their tickets are the toughest to score. Ticket prices range from C$24 to C$385—scalpers often demand up to three times the face value, so try to buy tickets at least a few months in advance.

ICE-SKATING

★ Toronto operates some 30 outdoor artificial rinks and 100 natural-ice rinks—and all are free. Among the most popular are those in Nathan Phillips Square at Queen and Bay streets; down at Harbourfront Centre (Canada's largest outdoor artificial ice rink); at College Park at Yonge and College streets; on Grenadier Pond within High Park at Bloor and Keele streets; and inside Hazelton Lanes—the classy shopping mall on the edge of Yorkville—on Avenue Road. Rentals are generally available. For details on city ice rinks, call the **Toronto Parks and Recreation Information Line** (☎*416/392–1111*).

JOGGING

Good places to jog are the boardwalk of The Beaches in the city's east end, High Park in the West End, the Toronto Islands, and the ravines or other public parks, many of which have jogging paths and trails. Many hotels now provide printed copies of maps showing interesting routes nearby. Toronto is generally safer than most American cities, but it's still wise to use normal prudence and avoid isolated spots.

★ The **Martin Goodman Trail** (☎*416/338–0338 for a map from Access Toronto*) is a popular 19-km (12-mi) jogging route with incredible views. The dirt and asphalt trails run along the waterfront from the Balmy Beach Club (end of Beech Avenue) past the western beaches and High Park.

SWIMMING

Public swimming is available at 16 indoor pools, 12 outdoor pools, and 15 community recreation centers. For the latest information on city pools, call the **Toronto Parks and Recreation Outdoor Pools Hotline** (☎*416/392–7838*). For information about late-night outdoor swimming, call the **Toronto Late-Night Pool Hotline** (☎*416/392–1899*).

TENNIS

The city has dozens of free courts. Parks with courts open daily from 7 AM to 11 PM May to October, including High Park in the West End; Stanley Park on King Street West, three blocks west of Bathurst Street; and Eglinton Park, on Eglinton Avenue West, just east of Avenue Road. Call the **Toronto Parks & Recreation** (☎*416/392–1111* 🌐*www.toronto.ca/parks*) for information on court times, hours, and locations. The C$45 million **Rexall Centre** (✉*1 Shoreham Dr., Downtown* ☎*416/665–9777, 877/283–6647 for tickets* 🌐*www.rexallcentre.com* Ⓜ*Downsview*) on the York University campus is home to the National Tennis Centre. The 12,500-seat stadium hosts big-name tournaments like the Tennis Masters Canada and the Rogers Cup (alternating years with Montréal; it will be held here in 2009).

SHOPPING

Updated by Sarah Richards

Toronto prides itself on having some of the finest shopping in North America. Indeed, most of the world's name boutiques have branches here, especially in the Yorkville area, where you can find such designer labels as Hermès, Gucci, and Cartier.

For those a little leaner of wallet, join in one of Torontonians' favorite pastimes: bargain hunting. Locals wear discount threads like badges of honor and stretch their dollars at Winner's, whre overstocked and liquidated designer pieces and last-season fashions are slashed to a fraction of their original retail prices.Toronto has a large arts-and-crafts community, with numerous art galleries, custom jewelers, clothing designers, and artisans. Objets d'art like sophisticated glass sculpture and Inuit art are ideal as gifts or for your own home.

Music stores all over Toronto stack shelves with international hits as well as homegrown talent like Alanis Morissette, Nickelback, Avril Lavigne, and a host of lesser-known pop, rap, hip-hop, folk, opera, and country artists. Bookstores such as Indigo have lounge areas where you can sip a coffee from the in-store café while perusing books by Canadian authors such as Barbara Gowdy, Ann-Marie McDonald, and Rohinton Mistry.

When it comes to department stores, all roads lead from Holt Renfrew on Bloor Street West, the epicenter of Toronto's designer mecca. A mere block east is the more mid-price department store The Bay. A second Bay can be found across from Eaton Centre, a sprawling shopping complex with multilevel parking in the heart of the city.

Most stores accept credit cards. U.S. currency generally is accepted, though not always at the most favorable rate of exchange. On Thursday and Friday most stores downtown stay open until 9 PM; on Sunday stores open at noon.

Bear in mind that the national 5% Goods and Services Tax (GST) is added to the cost of your purchases at the cash register, in addition to the 8% Ontario sales tax. You should save receipts from any major purchases and inquire about rebates on the GST. Ask for the latest refund regulations and forms at Lester B. Pearson International Airport, at visitor-information booths like the one outside Eaton Centre, or at stores.

SHOPPING NEIGHBORHOODS

THE ANNEX

The Annex, because of its proximity to the sprawling University of Toronto downtown campus, is home to academics, students, and aging hippies. Many of the houses have been restored to their former glory while others seem a bit seedy and run down. All in all they serve as rooming houses, single-family dwellings, basement apartments, and expensive rent for successful artists and writers. And these are the people who frequent the cafés and bistros, used-book and -CD stores, and the occasional fashion boutique, like Risqué.

At the outer corner of The Annex—Bloor Street West and Bathurst—is Honest Ed's, a tacky discount store. It serves as the gateway to Mirvish Village, a one-block assortment of bookstores, and boutiques on Markham Street south of Bloor Street. Local entrepreneur and theater mogul "Honest" Ed Mirvish is the brain behind the area's development.

THE BEACHES

Queen Street East, starting at Woodbine Avenue, is a great spot for casual-clothing stores, gift and antiques shops, and bars and restaurants, all with a resort atmosphere—a boardwalk along the lake is just to the south. To get to The Beaches, take the Queen Street streetcar to Woodbine and walk east. Parking can be a hassle.

YORKVILLE

In the 1960s Yorkville was Canada's hippie headquarters, a mecca for runaways and folk musicians. Now gentrified, this area is *the* place to find the big fashion names, fine leather goods, upscale shoe stores, important jewelers, some of the top private art galleries, specialty bookstores, and crafts and home-decor shops—as well as eateries, from coffee shops to elegant Italian restaurants. Streets to explore include Cumberland Street, Yorkville Avenue, and Scollard Street, all running parallel to Bloor Street, east of Avenue Road.

Bloor Street West, from Yonge Street to Avenue Road, is a virtual runway for fashionistas. With the world's designer shops on both sides of the street, you might think you're on New York's Fifth Avenue. On the north side you'll find familiar names like Gap, Gap Kids, Banana Republic, the Body Shop, Gucci, Cartier, and Williams-Sonoma. On the south side are Tiffany & Co., Chanel, Prada, Louis Vuitton, and Hermès. These boutiques are worth a visit for their architectural design alone. Several local shops are worth investigating also, including Royal de Versailles Jewelers, Bulgari, and Holt Renfrew, the ultimate designer and haute-couturier mecca. Not to be missed is William Ashley, a china store like no other that ships worldwide. Women should consider parking their guys at Bay Bloor Radio in the Manulife Centre; it's a stereo mecca and only steps from male-fashion bastions like Eddie Bauer for active wear and Harry Rosen for professional attire. Return to the corner of Bellair and Cumberland Street for a snack at MBCo.—a cappuccino, perhaps, or a smoothie, fresh-fruit brioche, or delectable sandwich. Refreshed, walk one block north from Bellair and Cumberland to Yorkville, where you'll find eye-popping shops with unusual accessories—Kumari's has embroidered jackets and shoes, jewelled handbags, and unique shawls and scarves. Gypsy has costume and semiprecious jewelry, and every doorway at Laywines Pens & Organizers holds surprises.

CHINATOWN & KENSINGTON MARKET

While the Chinese have made Spadina Avenue their own from Queen Street north to College Street, Spadina's basic bill of fare is still "bargains galore." The street, and the Kensington Market area tucked behind Spadina west to Bathurst Street, between Dundas and College streets, remains a collection of inexpensive vintage-clothing stores, Chinese clothing stores, Chinese restaurants, ethnic food and fruit shops, and eateries that give you your money's worth. You find gourmet cheeses, fresh ocean fish, yards of fabric remnants piled high in bins, and designer clothes minus the labels. Be warned—this area can be extraordinarily crowded on weekends, when smart suburbanites head here for bargains. Park your car at the lot just west of Spadina Avenue on St. Andrew's Street (a long block north of Dundas Street), or take the College or Queen streetcar to Spadina Avenue.

KING STREET EAST

Furniture heaven is King Street East, beginning at Jarvis Street and continuing almost until the Don River. On King East, sofas and chairs take center stage seducing even the most mildly curious. Punctuated between the furniture stores are custom framing shops, art dealers, and cafés to refresh the weary shopper.

QUEEN STREET EAST

Queen Street East from Pape Street to Jones Avenue is a bustling thoroughfare noted for its antiques and junk shops. Locals endure the crowds who come here for the exceptional assortment of quality reproduction armoires, bureaus, tables, or garden furnishings. Finish a trip to the area at Tango Palace, a hot spot for gourmet coffees and decadent desserts, at the end of the antiques-centered stretch. Parking is at a premium, but the neighborhood is easily accessible via the Queen Street streetcar, which passes through every 20 minutes or so.

QUEEN STREET WEST

If it's funky or fun, it's found on Queen West. The best shops are concentrated on both sides of Queen Street West from University Avenue to Spadina Avenue, with fashionable stores as far west as Bathurst Street and beyond. With its collection of vintage stores, Canadian designer boutiques, and bistros, this strip sets the pace for Toronto's street style. Come summer, street vendors and buskers set up shop and create a carnival atmosphere. On Queen West, the retro stylings of vintage stores like Black Market and Preloved comfortably coexist with Fashion Crimes, which stocks Canadian designs with a bent for the street beat. Even farther west on Queen, around Ossington Avenue, is a relatively new, even hipper area, where boutiques, galleries, and cafés are starting to flourish, called West Queen West.

UNDERGROUND CITY

Downtown Toronto has a vast underground maze of shopping warrens that burrow between and underneath its office towers. The tenants of the Underground City are mostly the usual assortment of chain stores, with an occasional surprise. Marked PATH walkways (the underground street system) make navigating the subterranean mall easy. The network runs roughly from the Fairmont Royal York hotel near Union Station north to the Atrium at Bay and Dundas. Beginning at the Manulife Centre the underground path will take you across Bloor to the Holt Renfrew Centre and east to a vast food court and The Bay.

MIDTOWN

Yonge Street, the longest street in Canada, begins life at Lake Ontario and takes on a multitude of faces before exiting the city. Once you head north from Bloor, you're entering Midtown, which runs approximately from Rosedale to Eglinton. The stretch of Yonge Street that runs from the Rosedale subway stop (at Yonge and Crescent streets) north to just past the Summerhill stop (at Yonge and Shaftesbury streets) is the best place to find the most upscale antiques and interiors shops, such as Absolutely, purveyor of French-provincial wares. If the thought of freight charges dissuades you from serious spending, you can check out the trinkets at tiny shops like French Country and Word of Mouth, which carry every imaginable kitchen device.

DEPARTMENT STORES & SHOPPING CENTERS

The Bay. The modern descendant of the Hudson's Bay Company, which was chartered in 1670 to explore and trade in furs, the Bay carries mid-price clothing, furnishings, housewares, and cosmetics, including designer names as well as the Bay's own lines. The southern end of the Yonge Street store connects to Eaton Centre by a covered skywalk over Queen Street. ☒ *44 Bloor St. E, Yorkville* ☎ *416/972–3333* Ⓜ *Yonge-Bloor* ☒ *176 Yonge St., Downtown* ☎ *416/861–9111* Ⓜ *Queen.*

Fodor'sChoice ★ **Eaton Centre.** The block-long complex with an exposed industrial style is anchored at its northern end (Dundas Street) by the main branch of what used to be eatons and is now Sears, and at its southern end by The Bay. Prices at Eaton Centre increase with altitude—Level 1 offers popularly priced merchandise, Level 2 is directed to the middle-income shopper, and Level 3 sells more expensive fashion and luxury goods. Well-lit parking garages can be found around the center, with spaces for nearly 2,000 cars. The complex is bordered by Yonge Street on the east, and James Street and Trinity Square on the west. At this writing, the Eaton Centre's northern end was undergoing a massive face-lift, culminating in a Times Square–style media tower on top of a gigantic new anchor store, Sweden's popular H&M. ☒ *220 Yonge St., Downtown* ☎ *416/598–8560* Ⓜ *Dundas, Queen.*

Fodor'sChoice ★ **Hazelton Lanes.** With more than 50 stores, a stroll through the two floors of Hazelton Lanes, the country's most upscale shopping mall, is an experience. Stores include Teatro Verde, the garden, home, and tabletop center; fashion-forward TNT Woman and Man (TNT is short for The Next Trend); Hugo Nicholson's exquisite, one-of-a-kind evening wear; Fabrice's unique, semiprecious jewelry, personally chosen and imported from Paris by the owner; as well as a restaurant with seating in an elegant courtyard. ☒ *55 Avenue Rd., Yorkville* ☎ *416/968–8600* Ⓜ *Bay.*

Fodor'sChoice ★ **Holt Renfrew.** This multilevel national retail specialty store is the style leader in Canada. It is the headquarters for Burberry, Canali, Chanel, Karan, Armani, and Gucci as well as cosmetics and fragrances from London, New York, Paris, and Rome. Concierge service and personal shoppers are available, but just browsing makes for a rich experience. ☒ *50 Bloor St. W, Yorkville* ☎ *416/922–2333* Ⓜ *Bay.*

SPECIALTY SHOPS

ANTIQUES & INTERIORS

Absolutely. A mixture of whimsical trinkets as well as English sideboards and tables are sold at this shop. There's also an extensive collection of antique boxes made of materials ranging from horn to shagreen.

⌧*1132 Yonge St., Rosedale* ☎*416/324–8351* Ⓜ*Summerhill* ⌧*1236 Yonge St., Summerhill* ☎*416/922–6784* Ⓜ*Summerhill.*

Belle Époque. Find very French, very *cher* antique and reproduction furnishings here. These days they're featuring what they call an "edgy Paris apartment aesthetic." In addition to home decor and garden ornaments, they also sell fashion accessories. ⌧*1066 Yonge St., Rosedale* ☎*416/925–0066* Ⓜ*Rosedale.*

Howard & Co. Antiques. In this shop renowned for having the best selection of 18th-century English antiques in the city, collectors can find walnut Queen Anne chests, George III bookcases, George II carved mahogany games tables, and more. ⌧*100 Avenue Rd., Yorkville* ☎*416/922–7966* Ⓜ*Rosedale.*

Robert Noakes International. Specializing in 18th-century chests, mirrors, and chairs, this shop has decorated many of the city's finest homes. ⌧*245 Davenport Rd., Yorkville* ☎*416/967–2800* Ⓜ*Dupont.*

Fodor'sChoice ★ **Toronto Antiques On King.** The complex provides a host of choices, including dealers in furniture, dishes, jewelry, art, and carpets. It's open Tuesday through Sunday from 10 to 6, and busiest on days when there are matinees at nearby theaters. ⌧*276 King St. W, Entertainment District* ☎*416/345–9941* Ⓜ*St. Andrew.*

ART & CRAFTS GALLERIES

Toronto is a cosmopolitan art center, with a few hundred commercial art galleries carrying items as varied as glass sculpture, Inuit designs, and contemporary pieces. To find out about special exhibits, check the Saturday edition of the *Globe and Mail* entertainment section, as well as *NOW* and *Eye Weekly*—free weekly local newspapers on culture distributed on Thursday. *Toronto Life* magazine is also a good source of information on gallery happenings. ■ **TIP→ Most galleries are open Tuesday through Saturday from 10 to 5 or 6, but call to confirm.**

★ **Corkin Gallery.** With work by photographers such as André Kertesz and Richard Avedon, this gallery is one of the most fascinating in town. See hand-painted photos, documentary photos, fashion photography, and mixed-media art. ⌧*Tankhouse Lane, Distillery District* ☎*416/304–1050* Ⓜ*King, then streetcar east.*

Gallery Moos. German-born Walter Moos opened his gallery in 1959 to promote Canadian and European art. He's a discerning, reliable dealer who's had Picassos, Chagalls, Mirós, and Dufys, as well as work by such internationally admired Canadians as Gershon Iskowitz, Ken Danby, Sorel Etrog, and Jean-Paul Riopelle. ⌧*622 Richmond St. W, Queen West* ☎*416/504–5445* Ⓜ*Bathurst then streetcar south.*

Olga Korper Gallery. Many important artists, such as Lynne Cohen, Paterson Ewen, John McEwen, and Reinhard Reitzenstein, are represented by this trailblazing yet accessible gallery, which displays art from the 1960s on. It's a good place for beginning contemporary collectors. ⌧*17 Morrow Ave., Dundas West* ☎*416/538–8220* Ⓜ*Dundas West, then streetcar east.*

Fodor'sChoice ★ **Sandra Ainsley Gallery.** The glass-sculpture gallery within the burgeoning Gooderham and Worts complex on Mill Street has large and small pieces. Rotating displays have included artists such as John Kuhn and

Martin Blank. ✉*55 Mill St., Distillery District* ☎*416/214–9490* Ⓜ*King, then streetcar east.*

SPIN Gallery. The trendy latch on to SPIN's innovative sculpture, painting, photography, installation, and new media. ✉*1100 Queen St. W, 2nd fl., Queen West* ☎*416/530–7656* Ⓜ*Osgoode, then streetcar west.*

Stephen Bulger. The photography gallery focuses on historical Canadian work, with Canadian and international artists such as Shelby Lee Adams and Larry Towell. ✉*1026 Queen St. W, Queen West* ☎*416/504–0575* Ⓜ*Osgoode, then streetcar west.*

YYZ Artists' Outlet. There are two exhibition spaces here: one for visual art and one for time-based conceptions. The visual might contain two- and three-dimensional paintings and sculptures, whereas the time-based area might have performances, films, and videos. ✉*401 Richmond St. W, Suite 140, Queen West* ☎*416/598–4546* Ⓜ*Osgoode, then streetcar west.*

CLOTHING

CHILDREN'S CLOTHING

Jacadi. The city's prettiest children's clothes are stocked here, in vibrant colors and fine fabrics from Paris. Three stylish French mothers are the design team. ✉*55 Avenue Rd., in Hazelton Lanes Yorkville* ☎*416/923–1717* Ⓜ*Bay.*

MEN'S CLOTHING

★ **Harry Rosen.** This miniature department store is dedicated to the finest men's fashions, with designers such as Hugo Boss, Armani, and Zegna. The casual section stocks preppy classics. ✉*82 Bloor St. W, Yorkville* ☎*416/972–0556* Ⓜ*Yonge-Bloor.*

Moore's, the Suit People. Browse through thousands of discounted Canadian-made dress pants, sport coats, and suits, including many famous labels. Sizes run from extra short to extra tall and from regular to oversize; the quality is solid and the service is good. ✉*100 Yonge St., Downtown* ☎*416/363–5442* Ⓜ*King.*

Tom's Place. Find bargains aplenty on brand-name suits like Calvin Klein, Armani, and DKNY. Tom Mihalik, the store's owner, keeps his prices low. He carries some women's clothes as well. ✉*190 Baldwin St., Kensington Market* ☎*416/596–0297* Ⓜ*St. Patrick, then streetcar west.*

MEN'S & WOMEN'S CLOTHING

Fodor's Choice ★ **Kama Kazi.** Exclusive collections from Europe and the United Kingdom—including designs by Paris-based Cop-copine, tailored suits by London's Ozwald Boateng, combat military chic from Griffin, and active wear by Kama Kazi and Brazilian Blue Fish—line the shelves of this casually luxurious space. ✉*781 Queen St. W, Queen West* ☎*416/304–0887* Ⓜ*Osgoode, then streetcar west.*

Lileo. Part emporium, part gallery, this is the place to go for forward-looking athletic fashion and lifestyle accessories designed to promote physical and spiritual well-being. ■ **TIP→ Stop by the juice and snack bar to keep your energy up while you shop.** ✉*55 Mill St., No. 35, Distillery District* ☎*416/413–1410* Ⓜ*King, then streetcar east.*

Over the Rainbow. This denim mecca carries every variety of cut and flare: the trendy, the classic, and the questionable fill stacks of shelves. ✉*101 Yorkville Ave., Yorkville* ☎*416/967–7448* Ⓜ*Bay.*

★ **Roots.** Torontonians' favorite leather jackets, bags, and basics come from this flagship store, which also manufactures Olympic uniforms for Canada, the United States, Barbados, and Great Britain. Branches are in several other Toronto neighborhoods. ✉ *100 Bloor St. W, Yorkville* ☎ *416/323–3289* Ⓜ *Bay* ✉ *1485 Yonge St., Midtown* ☎ *416/967–4499* Ⓜ *St. Clair* ✉ *2670 Yonge St., Midtown* ☎ *416/482–6773* Ⓜ *Lawrence* ✉ *356 Queen St. W, Queen West* ☎ *416/977–0409* Ⓜ *Osgoode, then streetcar west* ✉ *Eaton Centre, 220 Yonge St., Downtown* ☎ *416/593–9640* Ⓜ *Queen.*

VINTAGE CLOTHING

Black Market. True vintage buffs hunt through the racks—very thrift shop—to uncover the best bargains. The second-floor shop overlooks Queen Street; a second, larger store across the road houses the biggest discounts. ✉ *319 Queen St. W, Queen West* ☎ *416/591–7945* Ⓜ *Osgoode, then streetcar west* ✉ *256A Queen St. W, Queen West* ☎ *416/599–5858* Ⓜ *Osgoode, then streetcar west.*

★ **Courage My Love.** The best vintage store in Kensington Market is crammed with the coolest retro stuff, from sunglasses to tuxedos. The in-house cat adds a nice touch. ✉ *14 Kensington Ave., Kensington Market* ☎ *416/979–1992* Ⓜ *St. Patrick, then streetcar west.*

Preloved. Former models and fashion insiders stock this shop by combing the vintage market and reconstructing their finds into unique designs. ✉ *613 Queen St. W, Queen West* ☎ *416/504–8704* Ⓜ *Osgoode, then streetcar west.*

WOMEN'S CLOTHING

Comrags. Designers Joyce Gunhouse and Judy Cornish have supplied the city with more than 20 years of sophisticated women's clothing designs. ✉ *654 Queen St. W, Queen West* ☎ *416/360–7249* Ⓜ *Osgoode, then streetcar west.*

Corbò Boutique. Some of the most tasteful designers—Miu Miu, Prada, and Costume National, to name a few—are gathered here under one roof, along with some of the finest footwear in town. Did someone say Jimmy Choo or Ann Demeulemeester? This is upscale one-stop shopping. ✉ *119 Yorkville Ave., Yorkville* ☎ *416/928–0954* Ⓜ *Bay.*

Fashion Crimes. Part old-world romantic, part Queen West funk, this haven of glam party dresses and dreamy designs has a display case packed full of elegant baubles and sparkling tiaras. Designer and owner Pam Chorley also has a pint size label for girls called Misdemeanours. ✉ *322½ Queen St. W, Queen West* ☎ *416/592–9001* Ⓜ *Osgoode, then streetcar west.*

F/X. Some call the crinolined skirts and wild colors here masquerade, but the clothes are undeniably fun, especially for evening wear. There's also a variety of quirky knickknacks, as well as cards and candy. ✉ *515 Queen St. W, Queen West* ☎ *416/504–0888* Ⓜ *Osgoode, then streetcar west.*

★ **Hugo Nicholson.** The selection of evening wear by Oscar, Valentino, Herrera, Lagerfeld, and Galiano is vast and exclusive. The service offered by the owners, the Rosenstein sisters, is old school, with exacting alterations, a selection of accessories, and home delivery. ✉ *55 Avenue Rd., in Hazelton Lanes, Yorkville* ☎ *416/927–7714* Ⓜ *Bay.*

Lululemon. The bright and airy store is a perfect Zen match for items such as specialized yoga sports bras, top-of-the-line yoga mats, and stretchy yoga and gym togs. ✉*342 Queen W, Queen West* ☎*416/703–1399* Ⓜ*Osgoode, then streetcar west* ✉*130 Bloor St. W, Yorkville* ☎*416/964–9544* Ⓜ*Museum* ✉*2558 Yonge St., Midtown* ☎*416/487–1390* Ⓜ*Eglinton.*

WORD OF MOUTH

"Saturday we took the subway to the St. Lawrence Market. It was a great atmosphere; I felt like I was in Europe with all the cheeses and bakery goods. We had our first pea meal bacon sandwich (wonderful)." —Queenie

Mendocino. Score the best of the mid-price, supertrendy lines here—those polished looks you find in *In Style* magazine. Slide on a cute miniskirt or wiggle into a quirky tee. This is a great stop if you have a limited amount of time and want to pack a lot in, since you can peruse the day and evening designs of a number of lines here. ✉*294 Queen St. W, Queen West* ☎*416/593–1011* Ⓜ*Osgoode, then streetcar west.*

★ **Winners.** Toronto's best bargain outlet has designer lines at rock-bottom prices. The Yonge Street branch, below the elegant Carlu event center, is enormous. ✉*57 Spadina Ave., Downtown* ☎*416/585–2052* Ⓜ*Union* ✉*444 Yonge St., Downtown* ☎*416/598–8800* Ⓜ*College* ✉*110 Bloor St. W, Yorkville* ☎*416/920–0193* Ⓜ*Yonge-Bloor.*

FOOD

FOOD MARKETS

Fodor's Choice ★ **Kensington Market.** The outdoor market has a vibrant ethnic mix and charming restaurants, and sells everything from great cheese, coffee, nuts, and spices to natural foods, South American delicacies, and Portuguese baked goods. Vintage-clothing lovers delight in the shops tucked into houses lining the streets. ■**TIP→ Saturday is the best day to go, preferably by public transit; parking is difficult.** ✉*Northwest of Dundas St. and Spadina Ave., Kensington Market* ☎*No phone* Ⓜ*St. Patrick, then streetcar west.*

St. Lawrence Market. Nearly 60 vendors occupy the historic permanent indoor market and sell items such as produce, caviar, and crafts. The building, on the south side of Front Street, was once Toronto's city hall. ■**TIP→ The best time to visit is early (from 5 AM) on Saturday, when there's a farmers' market (in the building on the north side).** ✉*92 Front St. E, at Jarvis St., Downtown* ☎*416/392–7219* ⏲*Tues.–Thurs. 8–6, Fri. 8–7, Sat. 5–5; farmers' market Sat. 5–5* Ⓜ*Union.*

FOOD SHOPS

Pusateri's. From its humble beginnings as a produce stand in Little Italy, Pusateri's has grown into Toronto's deluxe supermarket, with a wide range of in-house prepared foods, local and imported delicacies, and desserts and breads from the city's best bakers. ✉*1539 Avenue Rd., Midtown* ☎*416/785–9100* Ⓜ*Lawrence* ✉*57 Yorkville Ave., Yorkville* ☎*416/785–9100* Ⓜ*Bay.*

Suckers Candy Co. It's like stepping into a comic book. More than 500 different suckers; retro and novelty candy from Canada, the United States, and the United Kingdom; gourmet cotton candy in eight different flavors; and custom-made loot bags and baskets will assuage any sweet tooth.

This place is fun for all ages, and open until midnight on weekends. ✉450 *Danforth Ave., Danforth* ☎*416/405–8946* Ⓜ*Chester.*

JEWELRY

★ **Fabrice.** The owner of this shop has a good eye for pearls, semiprecious stones, and gold and silver designs. She lives in Paris and ships one-of-a-kind pieces from France and other fashion capitals to the delight of discerning Torontonians. ✉*55 Avenue Rd., in Hazelton Lanes* ☎*416/967–6590* Ⓜ*Bay.*

Royal De Versailles. Don't let the front-door security scare you away from some of the most innovatively classic jewelry designs in town. ✉*101 Bloor St. W, Yorkville* ☎*416/967–7201* Ⓜ*Bay.*

SHOES

David's. The collection is always elegant, if somewhat subdued—designers usually include Hugo Boss, Taryn Rose, and Lorenzo Banfi. ✉*66 Bloor St. W, Yorkville* ☎*416/920–1000* Ⓜ*Bay.*

John Fluevog. Fluevog began in Vancouver, infusing good quality with fun, flair, and cutting-edge design, and is now an international shoe star. Stores can be found all over the United States, in Australia, and, luckily, also on Queen Street West. ✉*242 Queen St. W, Queen West* ☎*416/581–1420* Ⓜ*Osgoode, then streetcar west.*

Town Shoes. Shoe-aholics have a field day in this reasonably priced, trendy shop, which carries house brands in everything from flip-flop jellies to suede boots and sports shoes. The styles are cutting-edge for men and women. ✉*131 Bloor St. W, Yorkville* ☎*416/928–5062* Ⓜ*Bay.*

7

SPORTING GOODS

Fodor's Choice ★ **Mountain Equipment Co-op.** MEC, the much-beloved Toronto spot for anyone remotely interested in camping, sells wares for minor and major expeditions. A baffling assortment of backpacks allows you to choose anything from a schoolbag to a globe-trotting sack. ■ **TIP→ Try out the rappelling goods on the climbing wall.** ✉*400 King St. W, Downtown* ☎*416/340–2667* Ⓜ*St. Andrew.*

Sporting Life. The first off the mark with the latest sportswear trends, this is the place to get couture labels like Juicy, La Coste, and Burberry—or to snag snowboard gear and poll the staff for advice on where to go to use it. A second "bikes and boards store" is down Yonge Street. ✉*2665 Yonge St., Midtown* ☎*416/485–1611* Ⓜ*Eglinton* ✉*2454 Yonge St., Midtown* ☎*416/485–4440* Ⓜ*Eglinton.*

TORONTO ESSENTIALS

TRANSPORTATION

BY AIR

Toronto is served by American, Continental, Delta, Northwest, United, US Airways, Alaska Airlines, and Air Canada, as well as more than a dozen European and Asian carriers with easy connections to many U.S. cities. Toronto is also served within Canada by Air Canada Jazz, CanJet, WestJet, Porter, and Air Transat, a charter airline.

Flights into Toronto land at Terminals 1 and 3 of Lester B. Pearson International Airport (airport code YYZ), 32 km (20 mi) northwest of downtown. There are two main terminals, so check in advance which one your flight leaves from to save hassles. The automated LINK cable-line shuttle system (introduced in 2006) moves passengers almost noiselessly between Terminals 1 and 3 and the GTAA Reduced Rate Parking Lot. It has the ability to carry as many as 2,150 people each way every hour.

A handful of provincial flights land at tiny Toronto City Centre Airport in the Toronto Islands.

Information **Lester B. Pearson International Airport** (☎ *416/776–3000* 🌐 *www.torontoairport.ca*). **Toronto City Centre Airport** (☎ *416/203–6942* 🌐 *www.torontoport.com/Airport.asp*).

AIRPORT TRANSFERS Although Pearson International Airport is not far from downtown, the drive can take well over an hour during weekday rush hours (6:30–9:30 AM and 3:30–6:30 PM). Taxis to a hotel or attraction near the lake cost C$45 or more and have fixed rates to different parts of the city. (Check fixed-rate maps at 🌐 *www.gtaa.com/en/travelers*.) You must pay the full fare from the airport, but it's often possible to negotiate a lower fare going to the airport from downtown with regular city cabs. It's illegal for city cabs to pick up passengers at the airport, unless they are called—a time-consuming process, but sometimes worth the wait for the lower fare. Likewise, airport taxis cannot pick up passengers going to the airport.

Pacific Western Transportation offers 24-hour Airport Express coach service daily to several major downtown hotels and the Toronto Coach Terminal (Bay and Dundas streets). It costs C$15.25 one-way, C$26.30 round-trip. Pickups are from the Arrivals levels of the terminals at Pearson. Look for the curbside bus shelter, where tickets are sold.

GO Transit interregional buses transport passengers to the Yorkdale and York Mills subway stations from the arrivals levels. Service can be irregular (once per hour) and luggage space limited, but at C$5.05 it is the least expensive way to get to the city's northern suburbs.

Two Toronto Transit Commission (TTC) buses run from any of the airport terminals to the subway system. Bus 192 (Airport Rocket bus) connects to the Kipling subway station; Bus 58A Malten links to the

Lawrence West station. Luggage space is limited and no assistance is given, but the price is only C$2.75 in exact change.

If you rent a car at the airport, ask for a street map of the city. Highway 427 runs south some 6 km (4 mi) to the lakeshore. Here you pick up the Queen Elizabeth Way (QEW) east to the Gardiner Expressway, which runs east into the heart of downtown. If you take the QEW west, you'll find yourself swinging around Lake Ontario, toward Hamilton, Niagara-on-the-Lake, and Niagara Falls.

Information **Go Transit** (☎ *416/869–3200 or 888/438–6646* ⊕ *www.gotransit.com*). **Pacific Western Transportation Service** (☎ *905/564–6333 or 800/387–6787* ⊕ *www.torontoairportexpress.com*). **Toronto Transit Commission (TTC)** (☎ *416/393–4636 or 416/393–8663 for information, 416/393–4100 for lost and found* ⊕ *www.ttc.ca*).

BY BUS

Most buses arrive at the Toronto Coach Terminal, which serves a number of lines, including Greyhound (which has regular service to Toronto from all over the United States), Coach Canada, Ontario Northland, Penetang-Midland Coach Lines (PMCL), and Can-AR. The trip takes 6 hours from Detroit, 3 hours from Buffalo, and 11 hours from Chicago and New York City.

Information **Can-AR** (☎ *905/564–1242* ⊕ *www.can-arcoach.com.*). **Coach Canada** (☎ *800/461–7661* ⊕ *www.coachcanada.com*). **Greyhound Lines of Canada Ltd.** (☎ *416/594–1010 or 800/661–8747* ⊕ *www.greyhound.ca*). **Ontario Northland** (☎ *705/472–4500 or 800/363–7512* ⊕ *www.ontc.on.ca*). **Penetang-Midland Coach Lines** (☎ *800/461–1767* ⊕ *www.greyhound.ca*). **Toronto Coach Terminal** (✉ *610 Bay St., just north of Dundas St. W, Downtown* ☎ *800/461–8558*).

AROUND TORONTO

Toronto Transit Commission (TTC) buses and streetcars link with every subway station to cover all points of the city. Service is generally excellent, with buses and streetcars covering major city thoroughfares about every 10 minutes; suburban service is less frequent. Although the subway stops running at 2 AM, the bus service operates from 1 to 5:30 AM on Bloor and Yonge streets, and as far north as Steeles. *(⇨ Subway & Streetcar Travel)*

Information **Toronto Transit Commission (TTC)** (☎ *416/393–4636* ⊕ *www.ttc.ca*).

BY CAR

Gas prices in Canada are more expensive than in the U.S. and have been on the rise. At this writing, the per-liter price is between C97¢ and C$1.14 (USD$3.44–$4.04 per gallon). Gas stations are plentiful; many are self-service and part of small convenience stores. Large stations are open 24 hours; smaller ones close after the dinner rush. For up-to-date prices and where to find the cheapest gas in the city (updated daily), go to ⊕ *www.torontogasprices.com.*

Pedestrian crosswalks are sprinkled throughout the city, marked clearly by overhead signs and very large painted yellow Xs. Pedestrians have the right of way in these crosswalks. The speed limit in most areas of the city is 50 kph (30 mph) and usually within the 90–110 kph (50–68 mph) range outside the city.

The Canadian Automobile Association (the Canadian version of AAA and AA) has 24-hour road service; membership benefits are extended to U.S. AAA members.

Contacts Canadian Automobile Association (☎ *416/221–4300 or 800/268–3750* ✉ *info@central.on.caa.ca* 🌐 *www.caa.ca*).

BY SUBWAY & STREETCAR

The Toronto Transit Commission (TTC), which operates the buses, streetcars, and subways, is safe, clean, and reliable. There are two subway lines, with 60 stations along the way: the Bloor/Danforth line, which crosses Toronto about 5 km (3 mi) north of the lakefront, from east to west, and the Yonge/University line, which loops north and south, like a giant "U," with the bottom of the "U" at Union Station. A light rapid transit (LRT) line extends service to Harbourfront along Queen's Quay.

From Union Station you can walk underground (or via the Skywalk) to the Metro Toronto Convention Centre and to many hotels, including the InterContinental Toronto Centre, the Fairmont Royal York, Toronto Hilton, and Sheraton Centre—a real boon in inclement weather.

FARES & SCHEDULES One fare plus a transfer wherever you enter the system permits continuous travel on several vehicles to make a single trip. The fare is C$2.75 in exact change or one ticket/token. Tokens and tickets are sold in each subway station and many convenience stores. All vehicles accept tickets, tokens, or exact change, but you must buy tickets and tokens before you board.

Subway trains stop running at 2 AM, but bus service runs from 1 to 5:30 AM along Bloor and Yonge streets, and as far north on Yonge as Steeles Avenue.

Streetcars that run 24 hours include those on King Street, Queen Street, and College Street. Other streetcar lines run along Queen's Quay and Harbourfront, Spadina Avenue, and Dundas Street. All of them, especially the King line, are interesting rides with frequent service. Riding the city's streetcars is a great way to capture the flavor of the city, since you pass through many neighborhoods.

Information Toronto Transit Commission (TTC) (☎ *416/393–4636 or 416/393–8663 for information, 416/393–4100 for lost and found* 🌐 *www.ttc.ca*).

BY TAXI

Taxi fares cost C$2.75 for the first ⅕ km (roughly ⅒ mi), C$1.37 for each kilometer thereafter, and C$0.25 for each 33 seconds not in motion. A C$0.25 surcharge is added for each passenger in excess of four. The average fare to take a cab across downtown is C$8–C$9. The largest companies are Beck, Co-op, Diamond, Metro, and Royal. For more information, call the Metro Licensing Commission.

Information **Beck** (☎ *416/751-5555*). **Co-op** (☎ *416/504-2667*). **Diamond** (☎ *416/366-6868*). **Metro** (☎ *416/504-8294*). **Royal** (☎ *416/785-3322*). **Metro Licensing Commission** (☎ *416/392-3000*).

BY TRAIN

Amtrak has service from New York and Chicago to Toronto (both 12 hours), providing connections between Amtrak's U.S.-wide network and VIA Rail's Canadian routes. VIA Rail runs trains to most major Canadian cities; travel along the Windsor–Québec City corridor is particularly well served. Amtrak and Via Rail operate from Union Station on Front Street between Bay and York streets. You can walk underground to a number of hotels from the station. There is a cab stand outside the main entrance of the station.

Information **Amtrak** (☎ *800/872-7245* ⊕ *www.amtrak.com*). **Union Station** (✉ *65-75 Front St., between Bay and York Sts.* ☎ *416/366-8411*). **VIA Rail Canada** (✉ *Front St. W at Bay St.* ☎ *888/842-7245 or TTY 888/268-9503* ⊕ *www.viarail.ca*).

CONTACTS & RESOURCES

CONSULATES

United States **Consulate General of the United States** (✉ *360 University Ave., Toronto M5G 1S4* ☎ *416/595-1700* ⊕ *http://toronto.usconsulate.gov* ⊙ *Weekdays 8:30-1*).

VISITOR INFORMATION

Information **Canadian Tourism Commission** (☎ *604/638-8300* ⊕ *www.canadatourism.com*). **Ontario Travel** (☎ *800/668-2746* ⊕ *www.ontariotravel.net*). **Tourism Toronto** (☎ *416/203-2600 or 800/363-1990* ⊕ *www.torontotourism.com*). **Traveller's Aid Society** (✉ *Union Station, arrivals level and departures level, Financial District* ☎ *416/366-7788* ✉ *Pearson Airport, Terminal I, arrivals level, past Customs, near Area B* ☎ *905/676-2868* ✉ *Pearson Airport, Terminal 2, between international and domestic arrivals* ☎ *905/676-2869* ✉ *Pearson Airport, Terminal 3, arrivals level, near international side* ☎ *416/776-5890* ✉ *Toronto Coach Terminal, 610 Bay St., Downtown* ☎ *416/596-8647* ⊕ *http://travellersaid.ca*).

Province of Ontario

WORD OF MOUTH

"I love the lights on the Falls at night when looking at them from above, but Niagara Falls in breathtaking in the daylight too. Even standing nearby and listening to the rush of water and feeling the mist is quite a unique experience."

—TobieT

"...you might want to consider Niagara-on-the-Lake. It's a very charming little town, about an hour and a half's drive from Toronto (and 20 minutes or so from Niagara Falls). It will be beautiful in the spring and the Shaw Festival will be on, if you want to take in some theatre."

—hdm

www.fodors.com/forums

Updated by Sarah Richards

ONTARIO IS AN IROQUOIAN WORD often interpreted as "beautiful lake" or "glittering waters." It's an apt name for a province whose vastness (more than a million square km, or 412,582 square mi) contains 177,388 square km (68,490 square mi) of freshwater—one-fourth of all there is in the world.

More than half of this huge province's population lives in a small fraction of its geographical area: the four cities of the "Golden Horseshoe," at the western end of Lake Ontario. Dominant is the megacity of Toronto, with more than 4.5 million people. Of Ontario's 11.3 million people, 90% live within a narrow strip just north of the U.S. border.

The towns and cities of northern Ontario, on the other hand, are farther apart, strung along the railway lines that first brought them into being. The discovery of gold, silver, uranium, and other minerals by railroad construction gangs sparked mining booms that established such communities as Sudbury, Cobalt, and Timmins.

Ontario has the most varied landscape of any Canadian province. Its most conspicuous topographical feature is the Niagara Escarpment, which runs from Niagara to Tobermory at the tip of the Bruce Peninsula in Lake Huron. The northern 90% of Ontario is part of the Canadian Shield—worn-down mountain ranges of the world's oldest rock, pitted with lakes and cloaked in boreal forest.

The province's climate ranges from subarctic along Hudson and James bays, to humid-continental in its most southerly latitudes. Toward Niagara Falls, in a partial rain shadow of the Escarpment, the gentle climate allows the growing of tender fruits and grapes, making it Canada's largest wine-producing region.

EXPLORING ONTARIO

ABOUT THE RESTAURANTS

Expect a variety of cuisines: fresh-caught fish in Cottage Country to French-influenced dishes in Ottawa; great home-style Canadian fare in small-town inns to haute Canadian in the Niagara Wine Region restaurants. Thanks to a long-standing British influence, there's plenty of roast beef, shepherd's pie, and rice pudding, especially in the English-dominated enclaves of London, Stratford, and Hamilton. Niagara wines make appearances on menus province-wide; try the sweet ice wine with dessert. Reservations at medium-price and upscale restaurants are recommended, particularly during peak season in the ski and festival towns; the same advice applies to Niagara Falls. For a quick snack, try Tim Hortons coffee and doughnuts; the franchise shops are in virtually every city.

ABOUT THE HOTELS

Reservations are strongly recommended everywhere in summer, and most importantly in Ottawa, Toronto, and Niagara Falls. The small inns of Stratford and Niagara-on-the-Lake fill up during the summer cultural festivals here, as well. Prices are comparable to those in the States—although in Canadian dollars. Taxes are seldom included in

TOP REASONS TO GO

MUSEUMS
Ontario's museums document the province's evolution from a pioneer outpost to a lively urban society. Living-history museums, such as Upper Canada Village and Fort Henry, re-create life in earlier centuries. The country's development can also be seen through paintings, carvings, and artifacts—the legacy of European, Canadian, and native artists—displayed at Ottawa's National Gallery of Canada. Contemporary art is regularly unveiled at the Museum London. An ongoing homage to Shania Twain is held at the singer's eponymous center in Timmins, which is connected to the town's historical mining museum.

PERFORMING ARTS FESTIVALS
By combining public and private resources, Ontario has fostered one of North America's most supportive environments for the arts. Each year thousands flock to see great Shakespeare at the Stratford Festival and top-notch plays at Niagara-on-the-Lake's Shaw Festival. Hamilton has Ontario's third-largest art gallery, and Ottawa's National Arts Centre is the biggest performing-arts complex in the country.

SHOPPING
Visitors from the United States often relish Ontario's handsome inventory of things British, scooping up everything from china teacups to crumpet tins. Others marvel at the province's rich handicraft tradition. Ottawa, Sault Ste. Marie, Midland, and Thunder Bay have museum shops and galleries that specialize in First Nations crafts, including Inuit carvings and prints. Antiques stores abound; some of the best are in small towns like Cobourg, Peterborough, and St. Jacobs.

quoted prices, but rates sometimes include food, especially in areas such as Muskoka and Haliburton, where many resorts offer meal plans.

Most major cities have bed-and-breakfast associations. Prices vary according to the location and facilities but are comparable to those found south of the border. All types of accommodations tend to be more expensive in tourist venues. In Niagara Falls, for example, hotel and motel rates are determined by proximity to the famous waterfall.

WHAT IT COSTS IN CANADIAN DOLLARS					
	¢	$	$$	$$$	$$$$
RESTAURANTS	under C$8	C$8–C$12	C$13–C$20	C$21–C$30	over C$30
HOTELS	under C$75	C$75–C$125	C$126–C$175	C$176–C$250	over C$250

Restaurant prices are per person for a main course at dinner. Hotel prices are for two people in a standard double room in high season, excluding tax.

TIMING
In winter Ontario's weather veers toward the severe, making road travel difficult away from major highways, and many museums and attractions are closed or have limited hours. If you like to ski, skate, snowmobile, or ice fish, there's no better time to visit: the province offers some

GREAT ITINERARIES

You could spend several months exploring this enormous province and still not see it all. But if your time is limited, consider one of these itineraries covering the southern part of the province. You might choose one or a combination of these excursions, depending on how many days you have. You can take in most of the major sights in just a few days, plus see some special little corners that even many Ontarians don't know about.

IF YOU HAVE 3 DAYS

Spend two days and nights in Canada's capital city, **Ottawa**, and Gatineau (formerly called Hull). Tour Ottawa's Parliament Buildings and the city's colorful downtown, and take an excursion to neighboring Gatineau, for a panoramic view of Parliament from the excellent Museum of Civilization. On Day 3 drive to Morrisburg and **Upper Canada Village**, a superbly re-created pre-Confederation community of the 1860s. Then set out for **Prescott**, where you can rediscover the War of 1812 at Fort Wellington National Historic Site. You can easily return to Ottawa the same day.

IF YOU HAVE 5 DAYS

Base yourself in the charming town of **Niagara-on-the-Lake**, where you may want to spend at least two days to take in everything. There are historic sites and heritage buildings galore, plus a horde of interesting shops and renowned restaurants. Several of the famous old inns have been renovated to luxury standards, complete with spas and sumptuous cuisine. The Shaw Festival provides excellent entertainment in summer. Spend the evening of Day 1 plus Day 2 in town, enjoy a play, and set out on Day 3 to tour the **Niagara Wine Region** vineyards and wineries of the flourishing Niagara Peninsula. On Day 4 consider an overnight trip to **Stratford**, 160 km (100 mi) from Niagara-on-the-Lake, home of the acclaimed Stratford Festival and terrific restaurants, or head straight on to the hustle and excitement of **Niagara Falls**, a short 15-km (9-mi) drive away. Even if you plan to spend Day 5 at the falls, it's unlikely you can take in all the essentials, but you can come close. Park your car and hop aboard the People Mover, an inexpensive shuttle. It stops where you catch the major tours, from Journey Behind the Falls to the Whirlpool Aerocar and *Maid of the Mist.* You can also fly over the gorge in a helicopter, check out the wax museums on Clifton Hill, and ride to the top of a viewing tower. If you long for respite, drop into the Butterfly Conservatory. On the last night of your five-day tour, fall asleep to the thunder of the falls, knowing you've almost seen it all.

of the world's best winter activities. Otherwise, it's best to visit from April through September, when the Stratford and Shaw festivals are in full swing and most sights are open longer. (Try to avoid the highways over the busy July 1 Canada Day weekend.) The warmer months also bring other outdoor action, such as boating and hiking—or opportunities for resting on a beach or eating at an outdoor café. The increasingly popular Niagara Wine Festival takes place in late September.

OTTAWA

Although Ottawa remains a government town, the growth of the high-tech sector in recent years has given the city, its restaurants, shops, and hotels a modern flavor. The city has festivals, parks, bicycle paths, jogging trails, and the world's longest skating rink, on a 7.8-km (4.6-mi) stretch of the Rideau Canal.

Some of the city's top sites include the Parliament Buildings, the National Arts Centre, home to a fine orchestra plus English and French theater and dance performances, Sparks Street Pedestrian Mall, a shopping and dining strip, and Byward Market, where you can browse through food shops that date back a century, check out unique crafts, or munch on one of Ottawa's famous "beavertail" pastries. There are also two notable museums—the National Gallery of Canada, and the Canadian Museum of Civilization.

Only a few scattered settlers lived in what is now Ottawa in 1826, when Colonel John By and his Royal Engineers arrived to build the Rideau Canal, which links the Ottawa River to Lake Ontario. By's headquarters fast became a rowdy backwoods settlement as hordes arrived seeking employment on the largest construction project on the continent. The canal, completed in 1832, was hacked through 200 km (124 mi) of swamp, rock, and lakes whose different levels were overcome by locks. Bytown, as the settlement was called, officially became a city in 1855, when the population had reached 10,000. It was renamed Ottawa, after the Algonquin-speaking First Nation of the region.

Canadians are taught in school that it was Queen Victoria's fault their capital is inconveniently off the main east–west route along the Great Lakes. From 1841 to 1857 politicians dithered over several towns vying to be the capital of Canada and finally asked Her Majesty to decide. Victoria chose prosperous Ottawa because its beautiful setting—at the confluence of the Ottawa and Rideau rivers—was centrally located between Upper and Lower Canada (present-day Ontario and Québec). It was also reassuringly remote from the hostile United States. (That country had come for land in the war of 1812.) With the big decision finally made, construction began on the magnificent neo-Gothic Parliament Buildings that earned Ottawa the nickname "Westminster in the Wilderness."

DOWNTOWN OTTAWA

Given Ottawa's architectural beauty and the fact that parking is at a premium in the downtown core, one of the best ways to see the city is on foot.

TIMING You'll need at least a day to visit the sights downtown; allow more time if you wish to tour the National Gallery and the other museums.

Many museums are closed Monday, particularly in winter, but across from the Main Gate to the Parliament Buildings, the staff at the **Capital**

Infocentre (☎*613/239–5000 or 800/465–1867*) can help you locate the ones that are open.

WHAT TO SEE

Aboriginal Experiences. A former Algonquin trading post on an island in the middle of the Ottawa River, close to the new War Museum, shows the history of the First Nations people. Tours take visitors through tepees and a longhouse where traditional dances are performed twice daily. An open-air café serves buffalo burgers, venison sausages, and grilled salmon. At the craft workshop, you can make a dream catcher, talking feather, or medicine wheel. ✉ *Victoria Island, off Chaudière Bridge* ☎ *613/564–9494 or 877/811–3233* 🌐 *www.aboriginalexperiences.com* *C$7 and up* ⏲ *Mid-June–early Sept., daily 11–5.*

6 **Bytown Museum.** In the former commissariat used by the Royal Engineers and Colonel John By during the building of the Rideau Canal—the oldest stone masonry building in the city—are exhibits that record the life and times of Bytown and Ottawa. ✉ *1 Canal La., behind Château Laurier hotel* ☎ *613/234–4570* 🌐 *www.bytownmuseum.com* *C$5* ⏲ *Apr.–Victoria Day (mid-May), Thanksgiving (2nd Mon. in Oct.) to Nov., weekdays 10–2; Victoria Day–late June, daily 10–5; late June–Aug., Thurs.–Tues. 10–5, Wed. 10–8; Sept.–Thanksgiving, daily 10–5; Dec.–Mar., by appointment.*

8 ★ **Byward Market.** Excellent fresh produce and maple products have been attracting shoppers to this farmers' market since 1826. Surrounding the market stalls are permanent specialty food shops, some well over 100 years old, as well as restaurants, nightclubs, cafés, and boutiques. ✉ *George and York Sts.* ☎ *613/562–3325* 🌐 *www.byward-market.com* ⏲ *Mon.–Sat. 8–6, Sun. 9–5:30.*

Canadian Museum of Nature. In a castlelike building, the museum and its exhibits explore the earth's evolution, plus the birds, mammals, and plants of Canada. The High Definition Cinema shows nature documentaries that let you dive with whales and sharks or step back to when woolly mammoths roamed North America. The museum is undergoing extensive renovations until 2010, meaning some galleries are closed. Open are the outstanding dinosaur collection, the mammal exhibit with polar bears and grizzlies, and the new bird gallery. ✉ *240 McLeod St., at Metcalfe St.* ☎ *613/566–4700, 800/263–4433 in North America* 🌐 *www.nature.ca* *C$5; free Sat. 9–noon* ⏲ *May–July, Fri.–Tues. 9–6, Wed. and Thurs. 9–8; Sept.–Apr., Tues., Wed., and Fri.–Sun. 9–5, Thurs. 9–8.*

★ **Canadian War Museum.** Emerging from the ground on a slant that reaches a peak of 24.5 meters (80 feet), the dramatic architecture of the new Canadian War Museum echoes the undulating European landscape where Canadians fought in the two World Wars. A path leads onto the grass-covered roof; the greenery symbolizes earth's regeneration over formerly bloody battlefields. The $136 million museum, opened May 2005, traces Canada's military history with artifacts and a re-creation of a walk-through trench, complete with bursting shells, to a replicated Peacekeepers' command post. In one cavernous gallery, you can

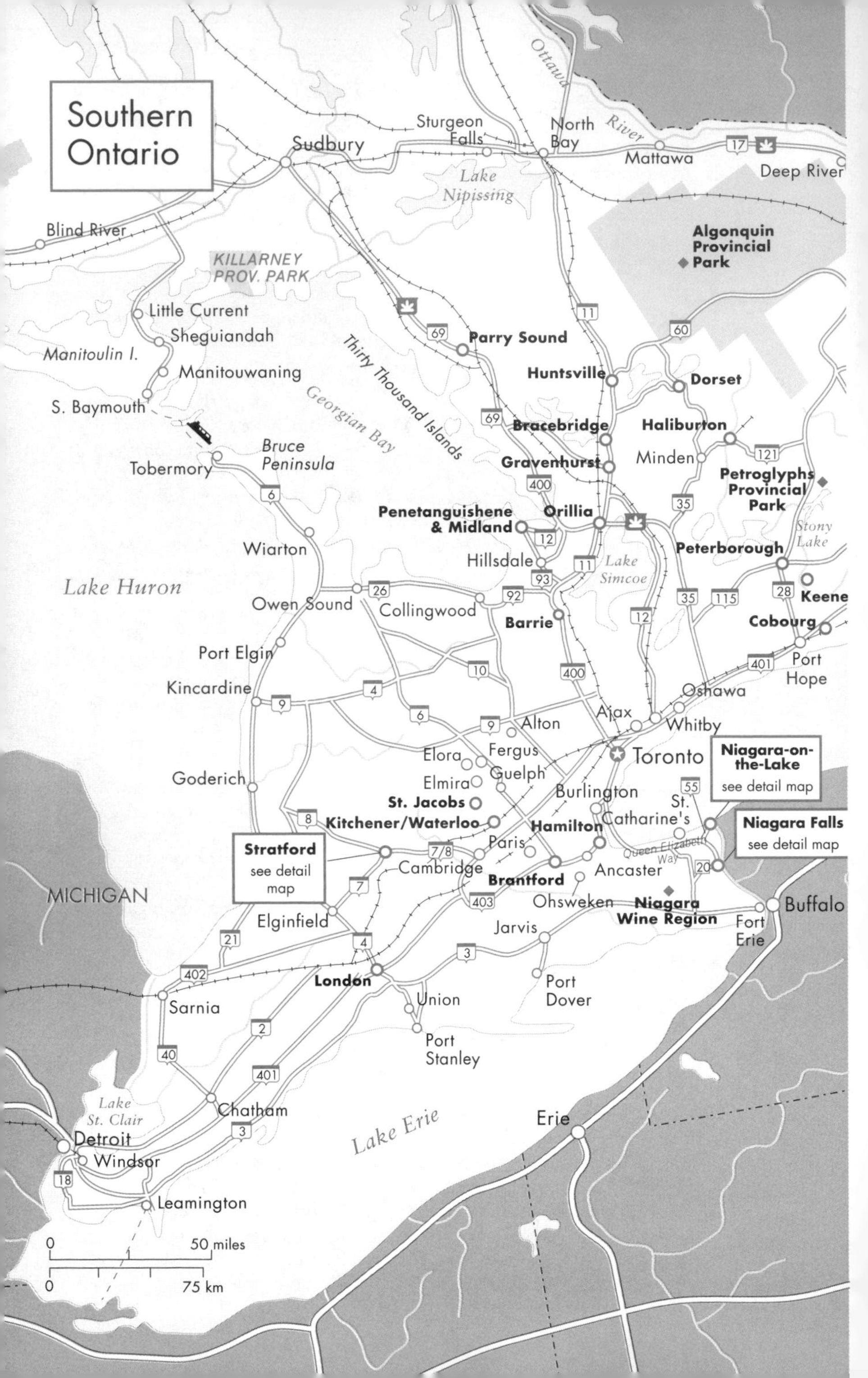

Southern Ontario
Sudbury
Sturgeon Falls
North Bay
Ottawa River
Mattawa
Deep River
Lake Nipissing
Blind River
KILLARNEY PROV. PARK
Algonquin Provincial Park
Little Current
Sheguiandah
Manitoulin I.
Manitouwaning
S. Baymouth
Thirty Thousand Islands
Georgian Bay
Parry Sound
Huntsville
Dorset
Bracebridge
Haliburton
Gravenhurst
Minden
Petroglyphs Provincial Park
Bruce Peninsula
Tobermory
Penetanguishene & Midland
Orillia
Stony Lake
Wiarton
Hillsdale
Lake Simcoe
Peterborough
Keene
Lake Huron
Owen Sound
Collingwood
Barrie
Cobourg
Port Elgin
Port Hope
Kincardine
Oshawa
Ajax
Whitby
Alton
Toronto
Elora
Fergus
Guelph
Niagara-on-the-Lake
see detail map
Goderich
Elmira
Burlington
St. Jacobs
St. Catharine's
Kitchener/Waterloo
Hamilton
Niagara Falls
see detail map
Stratford
see detail map
Paris
Queen Elizabeth Way
Cambridge
Ancaster
Brantford
MICHIGAN
Ohsweken
Niagara Wine Region
Buffalo
Elginfield
Jarvis
Fort Erie
London
Port Dover
Sarnia
Union
Port Stanley
Lake St. Clair
Chatham
Lake Erie
Erie
Detroit
Windsor
Leamington
0
50 miles
0
75 km

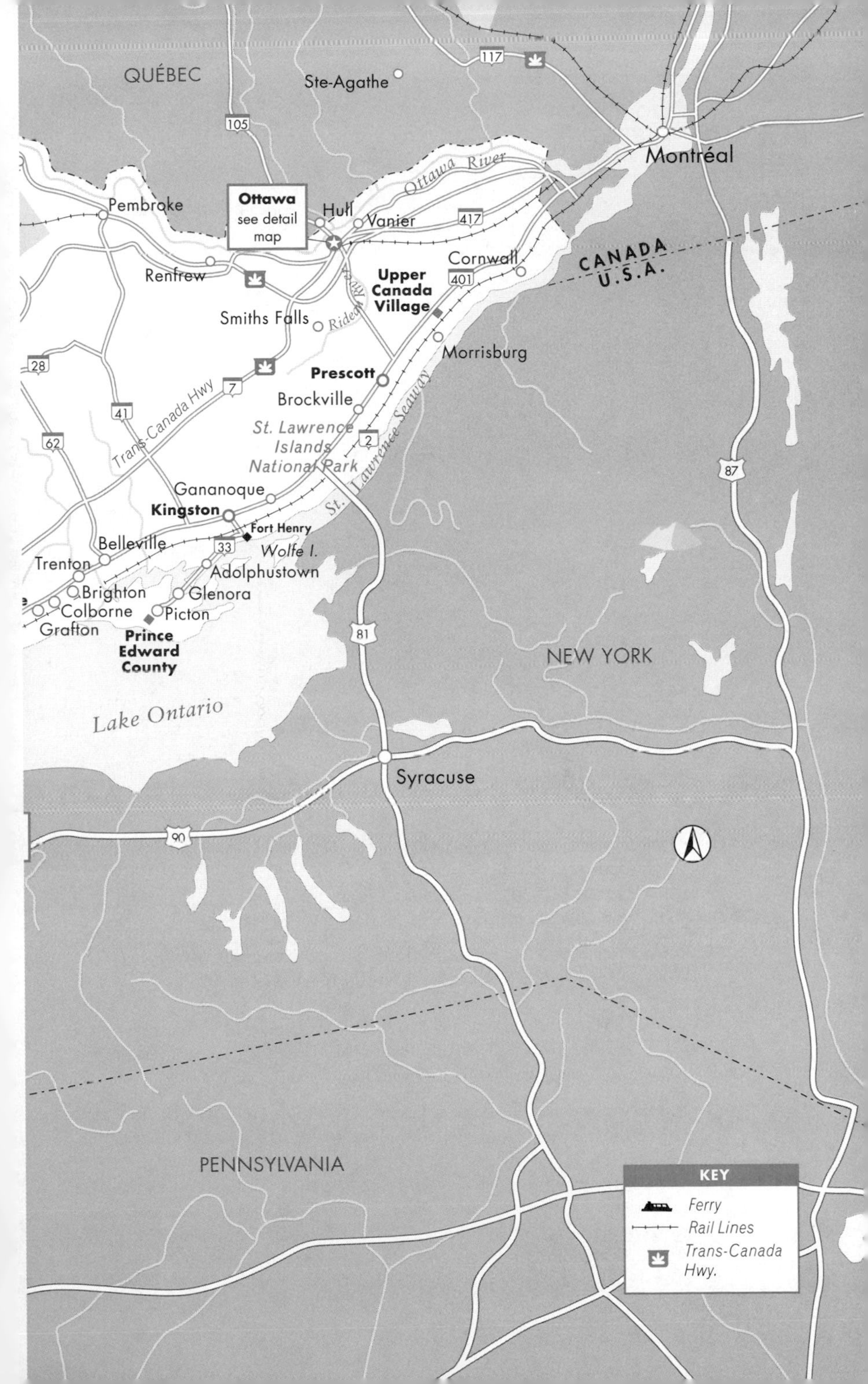
QUÉBEC
Ste-Agathe
117
105
Montréal
Ottawa River
Ottawa
see detail map
Hull
Vanier
417
Pembroke
Renfrew
Cornwall
401
CANADA
U.S.A.
Upper Canada Village
Smiths Falls
Rideau River
Morrisburg
28
Prescott
7
Trans-Canada Hwy
Brockville
41
St. Lawrence Islands National Park
2
St. Lawrence Seaway
62
87
Gananoque
Kingston
Fort Henry
Belleville
33
Wolfe I.
Trenton
Adolphustown
Brighton
Glenora
Colborne
Picton
Grafton
Prince Edward County
81
NEW YORK
Lake Ontario
Syracuse
90
PENNSYLVANIA
KEY
Ferry
Rail Lines
Trans-Canada Hwy.

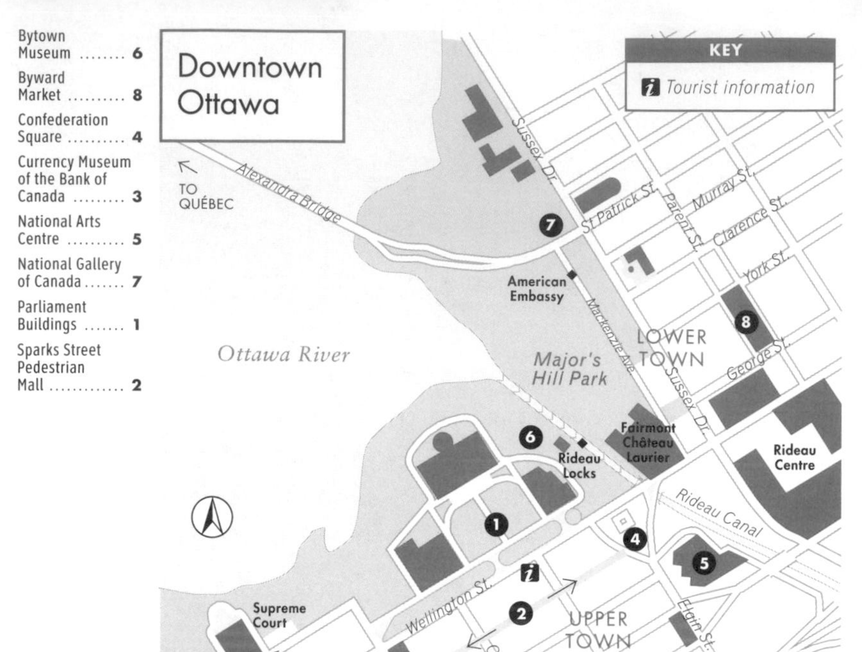

walk around a huge collection of artillery and military vehicles including Hitler's Mercedes-Benz. The restaurant's outdoor patio overlooks the Ottawa River. ✉ *1 Vimy Pl.* ☎ *819/776–8600 or 800/555–5621* 🌐 *www.warmuseum.ca* 🎫 *C$10; free Thurs. 4–9* ⏲ *May, June, and Sept.–mid-Oct., Mon.–Wed. and Fri.–Sun. 9–6, Thurs. 9–9; July and Aug., Mon.–Wed. and weekends 9–6, Thurs. and Fri. 9–9; mid-Oct.–Apr., Tues., Wed., and Fri.–Sun. 9–5, Thurs. 9–9.*

❹ **Confederation Square.** In the center of this triangular junction in the heart of the city stands the **National War Memorial** and the Tomb of the Unknown Soldier, honoring Canada's war dead. To the side is the **Valiants Memorial,** erected in 2006. Statues honor 14 men and women for their roles in Canada's military history over the past four centuries. ✉ *Wellington, Sparks, and Elgin Sts.*

❸ **Currency Museum of the Bank of Canada.** The ancestors of the credit card are all here: bracelets made from elephant hair, cowrie shells, whales' teeth, and what is believed to be the world's largest coin (measuring 6½ feet tall and weighing 3 tons). Here, too, is the country's most complete collection of Canadian notes and coins. ✉ *245 Sparks St.* ☎ *613/782–8852 or 613/782–8914* 🌐 *www.currencymuseum.ca* 🎫 *Free* ⏲ *May–Sept., Mon.–Sat. 10:30–5, Sun. 1–5; Oct.–Apr., Tues.–Sat. 10:30–5, Sun. 1–5.*

Garden of the Provinces and Territories. The floral emblems of Canada's 10 provinces and three territories commemorate Confederation in this park. ✉*Southwest corner of Bay and Wellington Sts.*

Library and Archives Canada. The archives contain more than 60 million manuscripts and government records, 2 million maps, and about 21 million photographs. Genealogists can visit for the parish registers and census returns from across Canada (call ahead). The library collects, preserves, and promotes the published heritage of Canada and exhibits books, paintings, maps, and photographs. Both the library and archives mount exhibitions regularly. ✉*395 Wellington St., at Bay St.* ☎*613/995–5115 or 866/578–7777* 🌐*www.collectionscanada.ca* *Free* 🕓*Genealogy Centre daily 8 AM–11 PM.*

❺ **National Arts Centre.** This complex includes an opera hall, a theater, a studio theater, and a salon for readings and concerts. Inside and outside are sculptures by both Canadian and international artists. The popular canal-side **Le Café** (☎*613/594–5127*) spills outside in warm weather. In winter it's a cozy vantage spot from which to watch skaters on the canal. ✉*53 Elgin St.* ☎*613/947–7000 or 866/850–2787* 🌐*www.nac-cna.ca.*

❼ ★ **National Gallery of Canada.** A magnificent glass-tower structure engineered by Canadian architect Moshe Safdie holds the premier collection of Canadian art in the world. It also houses important European and American art collections and hosts major international traveling exhibits. Inside the National Gallery is the reconstructed **Rideau Convent Chapel,** a classic example of French-Canadian 19th-century architecture with the continent's only neo-Gothic fan-vaulted ceiling. The building also has two restaurants and a large art-focused bookstore. In the **Artissimo** area, children can produce their own masterpieces, which are hung along a corridor for several days, using provided arts-and-crafts materials. ✉*380 Sussex Dr.* ☎*613/990–1985 or 800/319–2787* 🌐*www.national.gallery.ca* *C$6; free Thurs. 5–8* 🕓*May–Sept., Mon.–Wed. and Fri.–Sun. 10–5, Thurs. 10–8; Oct.–Apr., Tues., Wed., and Fri.–Sun. 10–5, Thurs. 10–8.*

❶ Fodor's Choice ★ **Parliament Buildings.** Three beloved neo-Gothic-style buildings with copper roofs dominate the nation's capital from Parliament Hill, overlooking the Ottawa River. Originally built between 1859 and 1877, they were destroyed by fire in 1916. The **Centre Block** was rebuilt by 1920 and is where the two houses of Parliament, the Senate, and the House of Commons work to shape the laws of the land. Masterfully carved stone pillars and provincial emblems in stained glass in the House of Commons are all works of the nationally renowned artist Eleanor Milne. If the House is sitting, be sure to watch Question Period, a lively and at times theatrical 45-minute session during which members of the opposition fire current-events questions at the prime minister and members of the cabinet.

Visitors to the central **Peace Tower,** completed in 1927, often tour the Memorial Chamber's Altars of Sacrifice, with five Books of Remembrance bearing the names of Canadians killed during military service.

Also in the Tower is a 53-bell carillon. From September through June, the Dominion Carillonneur gives 15-minute concerts at noon. In July and August there are one-hour concerts at 2. (All concerts are weekdays only.) Outside on the lawn there's plenty of room to observe the colorful **Changing of the Guard ceremony,** which takes place daily at 10 AM, late June to late August, weather permitting. The Ceremonial Guard brings together two of Canada's most historic regiments, the Canadian Grenadier Guards and the Governor General's Foot Guards.

North of the Centre Block and reached via its corridors is the **Library of Parliament,** the only part of the original Parliament Buildings saved from the fire of 1916. A statue of the young Queen Victoria is the centerpiece of the octagonal chamber, which is surrounded by ornately carved pine galleries lined with books, many of them priceless.

In front of and on either side of the Centre Block are the **East Block** and the **West Block.** The East Block has four historic rooms restored to the period of 1872 and open to the public from July to early September: the original Governor General's office restored to the period of Lord Dufferin, 1872–78; the offices of Sir John A. Macdonald and Sir Georges Étienne Cartier, Fathers of Confederation in 1867; and the Privy Council Chamber. The West Block contains offices for parliamentarians and is not open to the public.

Same-day reservations for 20- to 60-minute tours are available at the Visitor Welcome Centre, inside the entrance to the Centre Block. From mid-May to August, make reservations at the white tent on the lawn. Allow extra time to go through security scanners. A free half-hour **Sound and Light Show** (early July–early September) with highlights of Canada is offered twice nightly. Parliament Hill is also the place to be on Canada Day, July 1, for concerts, fireworks, cultural exhibitions, and free performances by top Canadian entertainers. Note: visiting hours are limited when Parliament is in session, so call ahead. ✉*Parliament Hill* ☎*613/992–4793 or 866/599–4999* 🌐*www.parl.gc.ca* 🎫*Free* 🕒*Late May–Aug., weekdays 9–7:20, weekends 9–4:20; Sept., Mon. and Wed.–Fri. 9–3:20, Tues. 9–7:20; Oct.–late May, daily 9–3:20.*

❷ **Sparks Street Pedestrian Mall.** Here the automobile has been banished, and shoppers and browsers can wander carefree in warm weather among fountains, rock gardens, sculptures, and outdoor cafés. ✉*1 block south of Wellington St. between Confederation Sq. and Kent St.*

Supreme Court. Established in 1875, this body became Canada's ultimate court of appeal in 1949. The nine judges sit in their stately art deco building for three sessions each year. The 10-foot-high statues of Justice and Truth flanking the entranceway were forgotten for 50 years and then rediscovered in 1969, buried in their original shipping crates under a parking lot. ✉*301 Wellington St.* ☎*613/995–5361 or 866/360–1522* 🌐*www.scc-csc.gc.ca* 🎫*Free* 🕒*Tours May–Aug., weekdays 9–5, weekends 9–noon, 1–5; Sept.–Apr., weekdays 9–5 by appointment.*

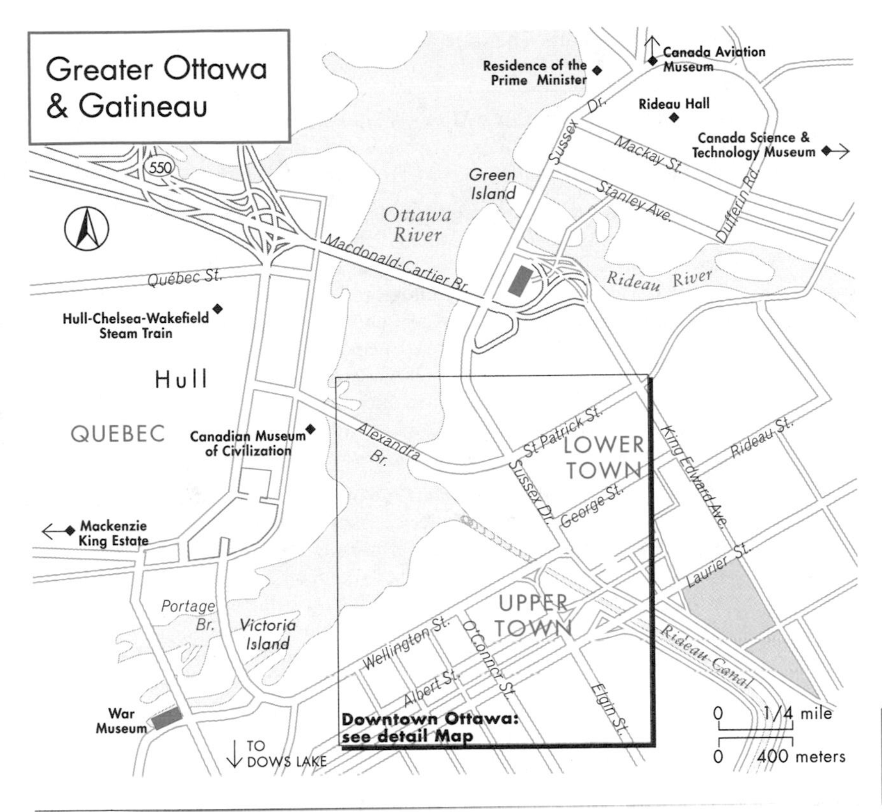

GREATER OTTAWA & GATINEAU

You'll need transportation to see the sights and museums listed below. Note that many museums are closed Monday, particularly in winter. Taxis can take you into Québec and back, but you'll have to get a local taxi to explore within each city. Bus service is limited.

Canada Aviation Museum. Exhibited here is Canada's most comprehensive collection of vintage aircraft, including a replica of the model that made the country's first powered flight, and myriad aeronautical antiques. You can also book a flight over Ottawa in a Cessna 172 or a de Havilland Chipmunk. ✉ *Rockcliffe and Aviation Pkwys., Ottawa* ☎ *613/993–2010 or 800/463–2038* 🌐 *www.aviation.technomuses.ca* *C$6; free 4–5* ⏲ *Sept.–Apr., Wed.–Sun. 10–5; May–Aug., daily 9–5.*

★ **Canadian Museum of Civilization.** Across the Ottawa River in Gatineau, Québec, is one of the area's most architecturally stunning buildings, with striking, curved lines that appear to have been molded more by natural forces than by human design. Exhibits trace Canada's history from prehistoric times to the present. Six west coast longhouses, towering totem poles, and life-size reconstructions of an archaeological dig are in the Grand Hall. Kids can enjoy hands-on activities in the

Children's Museum. The Cineplus holds the larger-than-life IMAX and Omnimax. ✉ *100 Laurier St., Gatineau* ☎ *819/776–7000, 800/555–5621 Cienplus* 🌐 *www.civilization.ca* 🎟 *C$10; Cineplus C$10* ⏲ *May, June, and Sept.–mid-Oct., Mon.–Wed. and Fri.–Sun. 9–6, Thurs. 9–9; July and Aug., Mon.–Wed. and weekends 9–6, Thurs. and Fri. 9–9; mid-Oct.–Apr., Tues., Wed., and Fri.–Sun. 9–5, Thurs. 9–9.*

Canada Science and Technology Museum. Canada's largest science and technology museum has permanent displays of printing presses, antique cars, and steam locomotives, as well as ever-changing exhibits, many of which are hands-on, or "minds-on." The Crazy Kitchen technology is a perennial favorite, as are hair-raising static electricity demonstrations with a Van de Graaff generator. The evening "Discover the Universe" program uses the largest refracting telescope in Canada to stargaze into the world of astronomy. ✉ *1867 St. Laurent Blvd., Ottawa* ☎ *613/991–3044* 🌐 *www.sciencetech.technomuses.ca* 🎟 *C$6* ⏲ *May–Aug., daily 9–5; Sept.–Apr., Tues.–Sun. 9–5.*

Hull-Chelsea–Wakefield Steam Train. One of the last authentic steam trains still in operation in North America plies its way through the scenic Gatineau Hills from the city of Gatineau (formerly Hull) to the town of Wakefield. As you're pulled along by a locomotive built in 1907, the conductor describes the sites and strolling musicians provide entertainment. Once in Wakefield you have two hours to visit the town, dine in one of the restaurants, and watch the train being turned around manually for the return trip. The Sunset Dinner Train serves a four- or five-course meal featuring French cuisine. During fall foliage season, you travel through a world of marvelous colors. ✉ *165 Deveault St., Gatineau* ☎ *819/778–7246 or 800/871–7246* 🌐 *www.steamtrain.ca* 🎟 *C$41 regular, C$65 first class* ⏲ *July and Aug., daily 10 AM departure; call for schedule in May, June, Sept., and Oct.*

Laurier House. This Second Empire–style house built in 1878 was once home to two of Canada's most important prime ministers, Wilfred Laurier and William Lyon Mackenzie King. The original furnishings, including King's crystal ball, give a glimpse into the lives of these two men whose political life spanned the two world wars. A section of the third floor duplicates the basement office in the residence of Lester Pearson. The Nobel Prize winner was prime minister from 1963 to 1968. ✉ *335 Laurier Ave. E, Ottawa* ☎ *613/992–8142* 🌐 *www.parkscanada.gc.ca* 🎟 *C$3.85* ⏲ *Apr.–Victoria Day (mid-May), weekdays 9–5; Victoria Day–Thanksgiving (2nd Mon. in Oct.), daily 9–5; Thanksgiving–Mar., by appointment only.*

Mackenzie King Estate. This sprawling 563-acre estate in Gatineau Park is nearly as eccentric as William Lyon Mackenzie King, the long-serving prime minister who made this his summer home in the early 20th century. Imposing ruins that King collected on his travels adorn part of the grounds; formal gardens or natural woodland occupy the rest. You can tour two of the cottages, Moorside and Kingswood, but the cottage where King died, called the Farm, is now the official residence of the Speaker of the House of Commons and is closed to the public.

⌧Promenade de la Gatineau Pkwy., Gatineau ☎819/827–2020 or 800/465–1867 🌐www.canadascapital.gc.ca/gatineau Parking C$8 ⏲Grounds open daily year-round. Cottages, mid-May–mid-Oct., weekdays 11–5, weekends 11–6.

Residence of the Prime Minister. It has been home to Lester B. Pearson and Pierre Trudeau, among others. Unlike the White House, however, it's not open for public inspection. Lacking an invitation, you can hope only for a drive-by glimpse of a couple of roof gables. Don't even try parking near the mansion; security is tight. *⌧24 Sussex Dr., Ottawa.*

Rideau Hall. The official residence of the Governor General of Canada since 1867 is where the Queen's official representative welcomes visiting heads of state and royalty. The 1838 mansion has a ballroom and, on the grounds, a skating rink and cricket pitch. The Governor General's Foot Guards are posted outside the main gate in summer. Guided and self-guided tours of the public rooms and grounds are available; call ahead for tours of the art collection. *⌧1 Sussex Dr., Ottawa ☎613/991–4422 or 866/842–4422 🌐www.gg.ca ⏲Tours Feb., Sept., and Oct., weekends noon–4; May and June, weekends 10–4; July and Aug., daily 10–4.*

WHERE TO EAT

$$$$ Fodor's Choice ★ ✕ **Beckta Dining & Wine.** With its ever-changing menu and nearly flawless execution, this contemporary Canadian restaurant consistently ranks among Ottawa's top dining spots. It's little wonder it draws everyone from the Rolling Stones to Diana Krall. Begin with sweet-butter poached shrimp on corn cake or tender foie gras topped with black plum caviar and served on cornmeal pancakes. Entrées might include succulent chicken breast on corn risotto, grilled lamb with roasted organic carrots and turnips, and seared scallops with summer succotash, tomato confit, and Serrano ham. Despite its lofty reputation, Beckta has formal but friendly service. *⌧226 Nepean St. ☎613/238–7063 ▭AE, MC, V ⏲No lunch.*

$$$$ ✕ **Domus Café.** Conscientious use of all-Canadian ingredients is a daunting mission, but the Domus Café succeeds. The melt-in-your-mouth foie gras and ostrich come from Québec, the asparagus, tomatoes, and fresh goat cheese from local farms. Ontario wines are offered as a matter of course. And what could be more Canadian than fiddlehead soup, Arctic char, and wild garlic? The menu changes with the seasons, the wild game dishes and root vegetables of winter giving way in summer to pickerel from the Great Lakes with fingerling potatoes, peaches, and cream corn. Organic beef comes with Yukon Gold fries and seasonal market vegetables. *⌧87 Murray St. ☎613/241–6007 ▭AE, DC, MC, V.*

$$$$ ✕ **Empire Grill.** Sunday-evening jazz adds flair to this popular restaurant, and the eclectic menu offers diners a melting pot of New American cuisine: a charred tomato and smoked chili sauce accompanies Brome Lake duck breast; tiger shrimp are sautéed with leeks, garlic, and tomatoes in a Pernod cream sauce; and prosciutto-wrapped Atlantic sea

8

scallops top saffron-infused risotto. In summer you can dine on the patio and enjoy Byward Market's passing parade. ✉*Byward Market, 47 Clarence St.* ☎*613/241–1343* ▭*AE, DC, MC, V.*

$$$$ ★ ✕**Le Baccara.** Nothing is left to chance at this five-star restaurant in the Lake Leamy casino. Service is first class, from the choice of complimentary spring or sparkling water to the fresh linen napkin waiting every time you return to your table. Chef Serge Rourre, in the open kitchen, brings a contemporary twist to classic French cuisine. Rack of caribou is served in a crushed-nut-and-juniper-berry crust. Langoustine tails and seared scallops top an oatmeal galette accompanied by squash puree. The five-course Grand Menu Dégustation du Chef (C$90) and eight-course Menu Gastronomique (C$115) can be paired with wines chosen for each dish. Ask for a window table. The view of the lake makes for a romantic and memorable evening. ✉*1 Blvd. du Casino, Gatineau* ☎*819/772–6210* ▭*AE, DC, MC, V* ⊙*Closed Mon. and Tues. No lunch.*

$$$$ ✕**Signatures.** An 1874 Tudor-style mansion is the showcase for this branch of France's famous Cordon Bleu cooking school. Winning awards for its modern interpretation of French classical cuisine, the restaurant's menu includes lobster medallions with fresh mint oil and venison loin in a spiced bread crust with gratin of fig. Set menus include a four-course Vegetarian Menu (C$48), a three-course Taste of Canada Menu (C$62), a five-course Menu Dégustation (C$81), and a six-course Grand Market Menu (C$101). ✉*453 Laurier Ave. E, Sandy Hill* ☎*613/236–2499 or 888/289–6302* ▭*AE, DC, MC, V* ⊙*Closed Sun. and Mon. No lunch.*

$$$ ✕**Benitz Bistro.** Chef Derek Benitz takes advantage of local ingredients to produce classical but contemporary French cuisine. Inside the cozy dining room or on the outdoor patio of this Victorian-style houses, one of many on Somerset Street, you can opt for the four-course Tasting Plate (C$20). The appetizer-size portions might include pimento-dusted wild prawns with corn salsa, seared foie gras on harvest compote, or braised veal medallion with eryngii mushrooms. In fall, herb-crusted Cornish hen is skillet roasted and served with organic mushroom fricasée, fingerling potatoes, and harvest vegetables. ✉*327 Somerset St. W* ☎*613/567–8100* ▭*AE, MC, V* ⊙*Closed Sun. No lunch Sat.*

$$$ ✕**Trattoria Caffè Italia.** One of more than 15 restaurants in Little Italy, this café with crimson-color walls, ceilings, and tablecloths is known for its more than 5,000-bottle wine cellar and traditional Italian dishes. Chicken Princess, a tender piece of chicken accompanied by asparagus and mozzarella cheese, comes in a white wine sauce. Pasta accompanies every dish or you can opt for potatoes and vegetables. An accordionist plays Friday and Saturday evenings. ✉*254 Preston St.* ☎*613/236–1081* ▭*AE, MC, V.*

$ ✕**Chu Shing.** This large pink-painted restaurant with a wall of windows overlooking Chinatown draws so many dim sum devotees that on weekends and holidays the lines can go down the stairs to the first floor. Waitresses parade with carts bearing everything from shrimp done innumerable ways to sesame balls. Or you can select from the regular Cantonese menu, including shark fin soup with crab (C$30) and Peking duck (C$32). There are also some Szechuan dishes, such as Yu Hsiang scallops in spicy sauce. ✉ *691 Somerset St. W* ☎ *613/233–8818* ▭ *AE, D, DC, MC, V.*

¢ ✕ **Peace Garden.** The bubbling fountain and potted trees reduce the noise of people passing around this vegetarian restaurant in the center of Time Square, a Byward Market office building. For breakfast try waffles with fruit. Later you can opt for an Indian Thali plate of samosa, bottomless dahl, homemade yogurt, and salad. Or pick up a snack such as roll-ups of marinated Italian eggplant or vegan pizza. To wash it all down, try delicious steamed coconut milk or chai tea. ✉ *47 Clarence* ☎ *613/562–2434* ▭ *AE, MC, V.*

¢ ✕ **Richtree.** With its rattan chairs and tropical market atmosphere, this eclectic restaurant is a miracle in the middle of the busy Rideau Centre shopping mall. The morning starts with homemade muesli, fresh fruit, and bowls of steaming hot café au lait. At lunch and dinner you can take a culinary trip around the world, from Swiss rösti, potato pancakes adorned with your choice of topping, to Beni Goreng, an Indonesian noodle dish. Rotisserie chicken and pizzas are also popular. At the adjacent take-out counter and bakery everything from sushi to sandwiches is reduced to half price 30 minutes before the mall closes. ✉ *Rideau Centre, 50 Rideau St.* ☎ *613/569–4934* ▭ *AE, MC, V.*

WHERE TO STAY

Ottawa is very much a government town, and hotel rates are at their highest in spring and fall when the government and conferences are at their busiest. Money-saving packages are available on weekends and during July and August. Be sure to make a reservation if you're coming during Winterlude in mid-February, the Tulip Festival in the first weeks of May, or around Canada Day, July 1.

$$$$ **The Wakefield Mill.** An 1838 converted grist mill houses Gatineau Park's only hotel, a 25-minute drive from Ottawa. Its serene forest setting alongside a waterfall attracts nature lovers, small business groups, and steam train passengers wanting to stay overnight in Wakefield. Inside the thick stone walls is a fine dining restaurant, a spa, and rustic but comfortable guest rooms containing Canadiana or Mission-style furnishings. Some rooms have gas fireplaces. This adults-only inn has no single room rates. Instead, you choose from a variety of packages; the minimum package is a room for two with full breakfast. Pros: Wooded location, peaceful setting, gourmet meals. Cons: Far from downtown Ottawa, limited activities, bathrooms sometimes larger than guest rooms. ✉ *60 Mill Rd., Wakefield, J0X 3G0* ☎ *819/459–1838 or 888/567–1838* 🌐 *www.wakefieldmill.com* *27 rooms* *In-room: Wi-Fi. In-hotel: restaurant, bar, spa, bicycles, parking (no fee), no kids under 12, no-smoking rooms* ▭ *AE, MC, V* *BP.*

$$$$ **Westin Ottawa.** Attached to the Rideau Centre shopping mall and convention center, this 24-story hotel is in the heart of the city. All guest rooms have plush carpeting and elegant furniture. Signature "Heavenly Beds" are topped with fluffy white duvets. Floor-to-ceiling windows provide some of the best views in Ottawa (C$50 extra for rooms facing

8

the Rideau Canal and the Parliament Buildings). Pros: Good location, great views, adjacent to large shopping mall. Cons: Pricy Internet service, tired furnishings, hard-to-find parking lot entrance. ✉ *11 Colonel By Dr., K1N 9H4* ☎ *613/560–7000 or 800/937–8461* 🌐 *www.westin.com/ottawa* *470 rooms, 30 suites* *In-room: safe, refrigerator, ethernet. In-hotel: restaurant, room service, bar, pool, gym, children's program (ages 3–11), laundry service, concierge, executive floor, public Wi-Fi, laundry service, parking (fee), no-smoking rooms, some pets allowed* *AE, D, DC, MC, V.*

$$$–$$$$ **Albert at Bay.** One- and two-bedroom suites with fully equipped kitchens make this 12-story hotel a favorite with those in town for an extended time. The hotel is so popular with families that it offers a children's program in July and August. Most suites have balconies. There are three wheelchair-accessible suites. Pros: Spacious rooms, free Wi-Fi, next to a convenience store. Cons: Not the best location, parking lot entrance too low for some cars, room service ends at 10 PM. ✉ *435 Albert St., at Bay St., K1R 7X4* ☎ *613/238–8858 or 800/267–6644* 🌐 *www.albertatbay.com* *197 suites* *In-room: safe, kitchen, Wi-Fi. In-hotel: restaurant, bar, gym, children's programs (ages 3–12), laundry facilities, laundry service, public Wi-Fi, parking (fee), no-smoking rooms* *AE, D, DC, MC, V.*

$$$–$$$$ **ARC the.hotel.** Luxury and attention to detail are paramount in this ultrahip boutique hotel, from the complimentary daily shoe-shines to personalized business cards. Designed by Yabu Pushelberg, the same firm that redesigned Tiffany's flagship Fifth Avenue store in New York City, the hotel's lean contemporary lines draw entertainers as well as business executives. Cozy gray goose–down duvets cover Egyptian cotton sheets. Guests arriving after 5 PM are greeted with a glass of sparkling wine, while complimentary Starbucks coffee and tea and their signature green apples are available around the clock. Pros: Great location, ultramodern decor, attentive staff. Cons: Small rooms, noisy air-conditioning, no views. ✉ *140 Slater St., K1P 5H6* ☎ *613/238–2888 or 800/699–2516* 🌐 *www.arcthehotel.com* *94 rooms, 8 suites* *In-room: safe, refrigerator, ethernet. In-hotel: restaurant, room service, bar, gym, laundry service, public Internet, parking (fee), no-smoking rooms* *AE, D, DC, MC, V.*

$$$–$$$$ ★ **Fairmont Château Laurier.** This classic hotel's timeless elegance attracts so many celebrities, heads of state, and members of royalty that it has its own protocol manager. The Château was the dream of American Charles Melville Hays, a dream he never saw become reality. Hays perished in April 1912 while sailing back for the hotel's opening aboard the *Titanic.* One of Canada's greatest railroad hotels, it's named for Sir Wilfrid Laurier, prime minister from 1896 to 1911. Rooms are elegant though some standard rooms have only showers. Zoe's, the conservatory lounge, serves afternoon tea. The Terrace restaurant (open summer only) overlooks the Rideau Canal locks. Fairmont Gold Rooms (C$100 extra) offer complimentary Continental breakfast and evening appetizers. Pros: Great location, castlelike building, attentive staff. Cons: Tired-looking furnishings, some cramped-feeling rooms, pricey parking. ✉ *1 Rideau St., K1N 8S7* ☎ *613/241–1414 or 800/257–7544* 🌐 *www.fair-*

mont.com ⇨*396 rooms, 33 suites* ☝*In-room: safe (some), refrigerator, DVD (some), ethernet. In-hotel: restaurant, room service, bar, pool, gym, concierge, laundry service, executive floor, public Internet, parking (fee), no-smoking rooms, some pets allowed* ▭*AE, D, DC, MC, V.*

$$–$$$ **Brookstreet Resort.** The area's only resort hotel, this 18-story tower in Silicon Valley is about a 20-minute drive from Ottawa. Guest rooms have modern furnishings in gray and raspberry and nice touches like coffeemakers and tea kettles. High-tech gadgets include a computerized seesaw in the wading pool. The Executive Health Centre provides medical fitness examinations and the spa has an on-site plastic surgeon. Pros: Adjacent to a golf course, stylish decor, extensive spa treatments. Cons: Far from downtown, expensive restaurants, pools hard to find. ✉*525 Legget Dr., in Kanata, K2K 2W2* ☎*613/271–1800 or 888/826–2220* ⊕*www.brookstreethotel.com* ⇨*241 rooms, 35 suites* ☝*In-room: safe, refrigerator, ethernet, Wi-Fi. In-hotel: 2 restaurants, room service, bars, golf courses, pools, gym, spa, laundry service, public Internet, public Wi-Fi, parking (fee), no-smoking rooms, some pets allowed* ▭*AE, D, DC, MC, V.*

$$–$$$ ★ **Carmichael Inn & Spa.** This hostelry in a century-old brick mansion is particularly popular with women who come to relax at the spa. Treatments include Swedish massage, herbal body wraps, and reflexology. Each guest room is furnished with antiques, and some have fireplaces. A Continental breakfast is included in the rate and complimentary tea, bottled water, and fresh fruit are always available. The inn is near the restaurants and cafés along fashionable Elgin Street. Pros: Elegant decor, good location, peaceful atmosphere. Cons: No elevator, limited number of rooms, spa in basement. ✉*46 Cartier St., K2P 1J3* ☎*613/236–4667 or 877/416–2417* ⊕*www.carmichaelinn.com* ⇨*11 rooms* ☝*In-room: Wi-Fi. In-hotel: spa, no elevator, parking (no fee), no kids under 15, no-smoking rooms* ▭*AE, DC, MC, V* 🍽*CP.*

$$–$$$ **Hilton Lac Leamy.** Three multicolor glass sculptures, composed of individual pieces representing sea creatures, add a whimsical touch to the brown-tone lobby. The quirky works of art amid the conservative decor reflect the hotel's dual appeal. A 10-minute drive from the Parliament, this 23-story hotel has a marina, a spa, a game room for kids, a theater and casino, and other urban resort amenities. Floor-to-ceiling windows in the rooms provide views onto one of two lakes and brighten the otherwise muted decor. Pros: Heated indoor pool, free parking, spacious rooms. Cons: Hard-to-find inexpensive meals, some staff members not very friendly. ✉*3 Blvd. du Casino, Gatineau, J8Y 6X4* ☎*819/790–6444 or 866/488–7888* ⊕*www.hiltonlacleamy.com* ⇨*312 rooms, 37 suites* ☝*In-room: safe, refrigerator, ethernet. In-hotel: restaurant, room service, bar, tennis courts, pool, gym, spa, bicycles, concierge, laundry service, executive floor, public Internet, public Wi-Fi, parking (no fee), no-smoking rooms* ▭*AE, D, DC, MC, V.*

$$ **Auberge McGee's Inn.** Built in 1886 for John McGee, brother of Thomas D'Arcy McGee, a Father of Confederation, this Victorian mansion in the historic Sandy Hill sector is now a cozy B&B. Furnished with antiques, each room has its own distinctive charm and some have working fireplaces. The romantic Egyptian, Windsor, and

Victorian Rose rooms have double whirlpool tubs. For families, there's an extra single bed in some rooms. Pros: Charming atmosphere, good location, friendly staff. Cons: No elevator, cramped rooms, no tub in some bathrooms. ✉*185 Daly Ave., K1N 6E8* ☎*613/237–6089 or 800/262–4337* 🌐*www.mcgeesinn.com* *14 rooms* *In-room: refrigerator, Wi-Fi. In-hotel: no elevator, parking (no fee), no-smoking rooms* *AE, MC, V* *BP.*

¢ **Ottawa International Hostel.** In the former Carleton County Jail, this hostel is certainly the most unique place to stay in Ottawa. You can opt for a bunk behind bars in one of the old prison cells, a bunk in a dorm-style room with a window, or pay a little more for a room of your own. Private rooms on the upper floors have hardwood floors; the nicest are on the ninth floor. The only private bathroom is in the Warden's Apartment, two rooms with a kitchenette suitable for a family. Daily tours visit the original jail cells, death row, and the gallows, the 1869 site of Canada's last public hanging. Try your hand at the interactive exhibits about the history of crime and punishment. Pros: Good location, historic building, friendly staff. Cons: Noisy at times, tiny guest rooms, lots of stairs to climb. ✉*75 Nicholas St., K1N 7B9* ☎*613/235–2595* 🌐*www.hihostels.ca* *125 beds* *In-room: no a/c, no phone, kitchen (some), refrigerator (some), no TV. In-hotel: no elevator, laundry facilities, public Internet, public Wi-Fi, parking (fee), no-smoking rooms* *AE, MC, V.*

NIGHTLIFE & THE ARTS

THE ARTS

Scotiabank Place (✉*1000 Palladium Dr., Kanata* ☎*613/599–0100* 🌐*www.scotiabankplace.com*) is a huge venue where NHL hockey is played—the Ottawa Senators are the home team—and where such big-name acts as Rush perform when in town. It's 20 minutes from downtown, but double that during rush hour or when there is an event.

The **National Arts Centre** (✉*53 Elgin St.* ☎*613/947–7000 or 866/850–2787*) is the home of the National Arts Centre Orchestra, and a top venue for the performing arts, from opera to dance. In summer the center cohosts the Ottawa Dance Festival.

NIGHTLIFE

Casino du Lac-Leamy (✉*1 Blvd. du Casino, Gatineau* ☎*819/772–2100 or 800/665–2274* 🌐*www.casino-du-lac-leamy.com*), five minutes from downtown Ottawa, sits on the shores of Lake Leamy. The upscale casino has more than 1,900 slot machines, 60 gaming tables, and an electronic horse-racing track. The Théatre du Casino attracts a diverse mix of crooners and comedians, mostly popular Québécois performers.

Zaphod Beeblebrox (✉*27 York St.* ☎*613/562–1010*) is Ottawa's finest live music club. The Byward Market institution draws a twenty- to thirtysomething crowd as well as visiting celebrities including Ozzy Osbourne and Drew Barrymore. Musicians and DJs take center stage almost every night.

SPORTS & THE OUTDOORS

BIKING

Ottawa has 150 km (93 mi) of bicycle paths. On Sunday morning Queen Elizabeth Drive, Colonel By Drive, and the Ottawa River Parkway are closed to traffic until noon for cyclists. **Rent A Bike** (☎ *613/241–4140*), across from the National Arts Centre beside the dock for Paul's Boat Line, rents bicycles, including tandems, for riders of all ages.

CROSS-COUNTRY SKIING

Thousands flock to **Gatineau Park** (✉ *33 Scott Rd., Chelsea* ☎ *819/827–2020* 🌐 *www.canadascapital.gc.ca/gatineau*) for the annual Keskinada Loppet, Canada's largest cross-country ski competition held in mid-February. The park offers 200 km (124 mi) of groomed ski trails for all levels. **Gatineau Park Visitors Centre** has trail maps and an area where you can wax your skis.

HIKING

With its rolling hills, scenic lakes, and 165 km (102 mi) of well-maintained trails, **Gatineau Park** is a favorite among hikers in the National Capital Region. For trail maps and information contact the **Gatineau Park Visitor Centre** (✉ *33 Scott Rd., Chelsea* ☎ *819/827–2020* 🌐 *www.canadascapital.gc.ca/gatineau*).

The **Rideau Trail** runs 387 km (241 mi) from Kingston to Ottawa, part of it along the Rideau Canal. Access points from the highway are marked with orange triangles. For information, contact the **Rideau Trail Association** (📫 *Box 15, Kingston K7L 4V6* ☎ *613/545–0823* 🌐 *www.rideautrail.org*).

ICE-SKATING

In winter the **Rideau Canal** (☎ *613/239–5234*) becomes the world's longest skating rink, stretching 7.8 km (4.6 mi) from the National Arts Centre to Dows Lake. Skates can be rented and sharpened across from the National Arts Centre, on the canal by Fifth Avenue. Wooden sleighs can also be rented. Along the route are warm-up shelters and food concessions. Call for a recorded message detailing daily skating conditions.

SHOPPING

Bank Street spans several neighborhoods and has everything from stores offering bargain-basement prices to unique shops, boutiques, and antiques stores farther south in the Glebe and Ottawa South neighborhoods. **Rideau Centre** (✉ *50 Rideau St., between Nicholas and Colonel By Dr.* ☎ *613/236–6565*) is Ottawa's answer to Toronto's Eaton Centre, with more than 200 stores, including Club Monaco, Le Château, and Roots—big Canadian success stories. At **Sparks Street Pedestrian Mall** (✉ *Sparks St.*) you can comb the high-fashion racks at tony Holt Renfrew or browse through some 50 other shops. **Sussex Drive** is the place to go for creations by local designers such as **Richard Robinson** (✉ *447 Sussex Dr.*) or **Justina McCaffrey** (✉ *465 Sussex Dr.*). Outdoor enthusiasts flock to **Westboro Village,** along Richmond Road west of downtown, to pick up everything from camping gear to kayaks at stores like **Mountain Equipment Coop** (✉ *366 Richmond Rd.*) or **Bushtukah Great Outdoor Gear** (✉ *203 Richmond Rd.*).

OTTAWA ESSENTIALS

TRANSPORTATION

BY AIR

Ottawa International Airport, 18 km (11 mi) south of downtown, is served by several major U.S. and Canadian airlines including Air Canada, Air Transat, American, Bearskin, Canadian North, Continental, First Air, Delta, Jazz, Northwest, Porter Airlines, Skyservice Airlines, Sunwing Airlines, United, US Airways, WestJet, and Zoom. Cab fare from the airport to downtown Ottawa is about C$35.

Information **Ottawa International Airport** (✉ *50 Airport Rd., south end of Airport Pkwy.* ☎ *613/248–2000* 🌐 *www.ottawa-airport.ca*).

BY BUS

Voyageur Colonial Bus Lines offers frequent service from Montréal to Ottawa, including some express buses. Greyhound Canada offers regular service between Ottawa and Toronto.

Information **Greyhound Canada & Voyageur Colonial Bus Lines** (✉ *265 Catherine St.* ☎ *613/238–5900* 🌐 *www.greyhound.ca*).

WITHIN OTTAWA OC Transpo serves the Ottawa–Carleton region on the Ontario side of the Ottawa River. It operates buses on city streets and on the Transitway, a system of bus-only roads. All bus routes in downtown Ottawa meet at the Rideau Centre. Adult fare is C$3, exact change required.

Information **OC Transpo** (☎ *613/741–4390* 🌐 *www.octranspo.com*). **Rideau Centre** (✉ *50 Rideau St., between Nicholas and Colonel By Dr.* ☎ *613/236–6565*).

BY CAR

Highway 417 links Ottawa to Québec from the east; Highway 416 connects Ottawa with Highway 401 to the south and Toronto.

BY TAXI

Information **Blue Line** (☎ *613/238–1111*). **Capital Taxi** (☎ *613/744–3333*).

BY TRAIN

Trans-Canada VIA Rail serves the Ottawa rail station, at the southeast end of downtown. A taxi ride to downtown costs about C$18.

Information **VIA Rail** (✉ *200 Tremblay Rd.* ☎ *888/842–7245* 🌐 *www.viarail.ca*).

CONTACTS & RESOURCES

EMERGENCIES

Emergency Services **Ambulance, fire, police** (☎ *911*).

Hospitals **Ottawa Hospital Civic Campus** (✉ *1053 Carling, at Parkdale Ave.* ☎ *613/761–4000*). **Ottawa Hospital General Campus** (✉ *501 Smyth Rd., between St. Laurent Blvd. and Alta Vista* ☎ *613/761–4000*).

24-Hour Pharmacy Shoppers Drug Mart (✉ *1309 Carling, at Westgate Shopping Centre* ☎ *613/722–4277*).

TOURS

BOAT TOURS Paul's Boat Lines Limited offers up to seven 75-minute cruises daily on the Rideau Canal (C$16) and four 90-minute cruises daily on the Ottawa River (C$18) from early May to mid-October. Canal boats dock across from the National Arts Centre; river cruise boats dock at the Bytown Museum at the foot of the Ottawa Locks on the Rideau Canal and at the Hull Marina on the Québec side of the river adjacent to the Museum of Civilization.

Information Paul's Boat Lines Limited (☎ *613/225–6781* 🌐 *www.paulsboat-cruises.com*).

BUS TOURS From April through November, Gray Line has a regular schedule of two-hour tours in double-decker buses and open-air trolleys to Ottawa's major sights. The three-hour Fall Foliage tour, offered mid-September to early October, includes a stop for tea at the Mackenzie King Estate in Gatineau Park.

Information Gray Line (☎ *613/565–5463 or 800/297–6422* 🌐 *www.grayline.ca*).

WALKING TOURS See the last working gallows in Canada or hear about Ottawa's darker side while dropping into various pubs (C$12.50). Haunted Walks offers a choice of six walking tours; some are given year-round. From early May to late October, you can buy tickets at either their booth in the Byward Market building (73 Clarence Street), or on the corner of Sparks and Elgin streets.

Information Haunted Walks (☎ *613/232–0344* 🌐 *www.hauntedwalk.com*).

VISITOR INFORMATION

The Capital Infocentre dispenses detailed information about the city and the Capital Region. The Tourisme Outaouais office across from the Canadian Museum of Civilization has complete information about attractions, restaurants, and hotels on the Québec side of the river.

Information Capital Infocentre (✉ *90 Wellington St.* ☎ *613/239–5000 or 800/465–1867* 🌐 *www.capcan.ca*). **Tourisme Outaouais** (✉ *103 rue Laurier, Gatineau* ☎ *819/778–2222 or 800/265–7822* 🌐 *www.tourisme-outaouais.ca*).

THE HERITAGE HIGHWAYS

Most of Ontario's first French, English, and Loyalist settlers entered the province from the southeast. You can retrace some of their routes on southern Ontario's Heritage Highways. Highway 2, parallel to Highway 401, is smaller than the cross-Ontario freeway and more scenic. It's the original 19th-century route that linked Québec and Kingston to "Muddy York" (Toronto) in the west. With appropriate detours it provides a good glimpse into this area's attractions.

UPPER CANADA VILLAGE

★ *86 km (53 mi) southeast of Ottawa on Hwy. 2.*

Eight villages disappeared under rising waters when the St. Lawrence Seaway opened in 1959, but their best historic buildings were moved to a new site called Upper Canada Village, a re-creation of an Ontario community of the 1860s. The village occupies 66 acres of the 2,000-acre Crysler's Farm Battlefield Park, which figured in the War of 1812. A tour takes three to four hours. Staff members in period costume answer your questions as they work with authentic tools at the mills, craftsmen's shops, and farms. You can take a horse-drawn carriage ride or enjoy lunch or tea at Willard's Hotel (originally built in 1785 by Daniel Mayers, a New York Loyalist whose family came from Germany). ✉ *13740 County Rd. 2, R.R. 1, Morrisburg* ☎ *613/543–4328 or 800/437–2233* 🌐 *www.uppercanadavillage.com* 🎫 *C$16.95* ⏲ *Mid-May–mid-Oct., daily 9:30–5.*

PRESCOTT

★ *35 km (22 mi) west of Morrisburg on Hwy. 2.*

Both Prescott's Fort Wellington and the Windmill Historic Site saw action in the War of 1812, and both have been restored and are open to the public. **Fort Wellington National Historic Site** was built by the British in 1813 to protect goods and troops moving between Montréal and Upper Canada after the outbreak of the War of 1812. The Rideau Canal eliminated the need for the fort, and it was abandoned. In 1837 when rebellion broke out in Upper and Lower Canada, the British built a stronger Fort Wellington on the same site. The restored buildings are furnished in period style. The restored **Battle of the Windmill National Historic Site** is where Canadian rebels and their American allies tried to capture the fort in 1838. ✉ *370 Vankoughnet St.* ☎ *613/925–2896 or 800/230–0016* 🌐 *www.pc.gc.ca/wellington* 🎫 *C$4* ⏲ *Mid-May–Sept., daily 10–5.*

KINGSTON

105 km (65 mi) southwest of Prescott on Hwy. 401.

Kingston's architecture has been amazing visitors since 1673, when Governor Frontenac built a stockaded fort to impress the Iroquois and thus tap into the fur trade. The city occupied a strategic site at the junction of the St. Lawrence River and the Rideau Canal system, making it a major military site. Kingston survived the War of 1812 almost unscathed; many of its beautiful limestone buildings remain in mint condition today. The prestigious Queens University is here and the city's appealing waterfront is filled with sailboats and serves as the jumping-off point for cruises around the scenic Thousand Islands.

From 1841 to 1844, Kingston was the national capital; today the gorgeous, cut-limestone **City Hall** (✉ *216 Ontario St.* ☎ *613/546–4291*) dominates the downtown core, facing a riverfront park. Tours are given weekdays in summer, but you can visit the lobby anytime.

The **Royal Military College of Canada** was founded at Point Frederick in 1876, on the site of the old British Navy dockyard; the dockyard's relics can still be seen on the college grounds. Of particular note is the **Royal Military College Museum,** housed in the largest of four martello towers that guarded the Kingston harbor front. The museum contains the well-known Douglas Arms Collection. ✉ *Off Hwy. 2, east of Kingston* ☎ *613/541–6000 Ext. 6985 or 866/762–2672* 🌐 *www.rmc.ca/other/museum* 🎫 *Free* 🕒 *Last weekend in June–early Sept., daily 10–5.*

★ Massive **Fort Henry** was built between 1832 and 1837 to repel an American invasion that never came. Today it's a living-history museum of early military life with parades and guides in period costume. In a throwback to the era of colonialism, the pomp and pageantry of the 1867 British military is celebrated in the Sunset Ceremony that takes place Wednesday evening in July and August. ✉ *Hwys. 2 and 15* ☎ *613/542–7388* 🌐 *www.forthenry.com* 🎫 *C$11* 🕒 *Late May–early Oct., daily 10–5; early Oct.–late May, by reservation only.*

Locals have nicknamed it "Tea Caddy Castle," but Canada's first prime minister, Sir John A. Macdonald, who lived in the house for a year, called it **Bellevue House** because of its view of Lake Ontario. The 1840 house is now a National Historic Site, restored and furnished in the style of 1848, when Macdonald lived here. ✉ *35 Centre St.* ☎ *613/545–8666* 🌐 *www.pc.gc.ca/lhn-nhs/on/bellevue* 🎫 *C$4* 🕒 *Apr.–May and early Sept.–Oct., daily 10–5; June–early Sept., daily 9–6.*

The **Pump House Steam Museum,** a Victorian-style 1849 municipal water-pumping station, is maintained by the Marine Museum of the Great Lakes. All exhibits run on steam; models displayed might include miniatures and an 1897 engine with a 9-ton flywheel. The discovery center has hands-on displays. ✉ *23 Ontario St.* ☎ *613/542–2261* 🎫 *C$5.25; Pump House and Marine Museum C$6.75* 🕒 *June–Sept., daily 10–4.*

The rambling display area at the **Marine Museum of the Great Lakes,** at the historic former Kingston dry dock, traces Great Lakes shipping since 1678. The *Alexander Henry,* a 3,000-ton, 210-foot retired icebreaker, is open for summer tours; you can even rent a stateroom and sleep aboard. ✉ *55 Ontario St.* ☎ *613/542–2261* 🌐 *www.marmuseum.ca* 🎫 *C$6.50* 🕒 *May–Oct., daily 10–5; Nov.–Apr., Mon.–Sat. 10–4.*

In the former warden's residence of the Kingston Penitentiary, **Canada's Penitentiary Museum** houses a collection of artifacts that trace the history of the federal jail system. The building itself was built by inmates of this Canadian penal landmark between 1870 and 1873. ✉ *555 King St. W* ☎ *613/530–3122* 🌐 *www.penitentiarymuseum.ca* 🎫 *Donations accepted* 🕒 *May–Oct., weekdays 9–4, weekends 10–4; Nov.–Apr., by appointment only.*

8

WHERE TO STAY & EAT

$$–$$$ **Chez Piggy.** An energetic, upbeat kind of place, Piggy's is housed in a string of restored 19th-century buildings. The interior is anchored by a long bar rimmed with slung-back director's chairs. On warm days dining is available in the courtyard. The unusual, but interesting menu makes this a popular spot. Appetizers such as frites mayonnaise, Stilton pâté, and carpaccio with capers share space with Asian delicacies. Entrées might include Mayan chicken with orange and red peppers and black beans, or Monkfish Tajine with charmoula (spicy coriander and parsley sauce). There's also a corn-crusted chicken breast with corn and red bean salsa, and guacamole to remind you of Mexico. For those seeking less exotic fare, a steak is available accompanied by garlicky mashed potatoes. *68-R (rear) Princess St. 613/549–7673 AE, DC, MC, V.*

$$–$$$ **Grizzly Grill.** A log-cabin ambience greets you at this rustic restaurant, which is big on grilled fish and meats. There's a definitely Cajun flair—the most adventurous dish being alligator skewers and blackened potatoes tossed in mayonnaise and spicy salsa. *395 Princess St. 613/544–7566 or 800/336–0891 www.grizzlygrill.on.ca MC, V.*

$$$–$$$$ ★ **Rosemount Bed & Breakfast Inn.** This Tuscan-style villa faithfully recalls its 1850s origins with meticulously selected period room furnishings and colorful, Victorian-inspired decor. The full complimentary breakfast might include the inn's trademark Welsh toast—the owner's unique version of French toast. At teatime the fireplace crackles in the Victorian sitting room. (Some of the guest rooms also have gas fireplaces.) Expanded spa services include massages, facials, and seaweed wraps. The inn, in Kingston's Old Stones neighborhood, is a short walk from the waterfront and downtown shops. *46 Sydenham St. S, K7L 3H1 613/531–8844 or 888/871–8844 www.rosemountinn.com 8 rooms, 1 suite In-room: no a/c (some), no TV (some), dial-up, Wi-Fi. In-hotel: spa, no elevator, parking (no fee), no kids under 14 AE, MC, V Closed mid-Dec.–mid-Jan. BP.*

$$ **Hotel Belvedere.** This Victorian inn, with its mansard roof, airy rooms, and proximity to the waterfront, is steeped in restful charm. Expertly chosen antiques, from plush Persian carpets to Regency tables, furnish the inn's rooms, each of which has a private bath and high ceilings. Breakfast can be served in your room, by the fireplace in the living room, or on the shady terrace in summer. *141 King St. E, K7L 2Z9 613/548–1565 or 800/559–0584 www.hotelbelvedere.com 20 rooms, 1 suite AE, D, DC, MC, V CP.*

PRINCE EDWARD COUNTY

80 km (50 mi) southwest of Kingston on Hwy. 33.

New Englanders wandering the island county of Prince Edward may find themselves wondering if they've ever left home—so similar are the scenery and the pages of history that brought both regions into being. The island was one of the earliest parts of Ontario to be settled after the American Revolution, and a Loyalist influence remained dominant here for generations. The Loyalist church, erected in 1822, is still used as a parish meeting hall. County highlights include such natural wonders as the Lake on the Mountain, situated 200 feet above the level of the Bay of Quinte; more than a dozen nearby conservation parks; miles of quiet sandy beaches; and the famed sandbanks (see *www.ontarioparks.com/english/sand.html*), where some of the constantly shifting dunes can reach 25 meters (82 feet).

Although Prince Edward County can be reached by car via Highway 33, a free 10-minute ride on a car ferry, which departs from Adolphustown every 15 minutes in summer, is another option.

Picton, the island's capital of sorts, is a serene town of 4,300 with fine old buildings and strong associations with Sir John A. Macdonald, Canada's first prime minister, who practiced law at the 1834 county courthouse.

The **Macaulay Heritage Park** is here. It sits on about 15 acres of land and includes picnic facilities, the Neo-Classic **Macaulay House,** built in 1830 by the Reverend William Macaulay, and the **County Museum.** Tours of the park and attractions are available by prior arrangement and may include a visit to the jail, where a double gallows is kept handy (although it hasn't been used since 1884). *1 block south of Hwy. 33 at Union and Church Sts. 613/476–3833 www.pec.on.ca/macaulay C$4 Mid-May–June and Sept.–mid-Oct., Tues.–Sun. 1–4:30; July and Aug., Tues.–Sun. 10–4:30.*

WHERE TO STAY & EAT

$$$ **Isaiah Tubbs Resort and Conference Centre.** A dozen kilometers (about 7 mi) west of Picton, this "country posh" property includes 500 acres of gardens, enchanting ponds filled with ducks, and woodlands on the shore of West Lake. The main inn is a beautifully restored 1820s farmhouse with fireplaces and exposed beam ceilings. Guest rooms at the inn, many with Jacuzzis, look out over the resort's gardens and the surrounding forests. Adjacent to the inn is an annex with 10 contemporary-style guest rooms and suites (two rooms have hot tubs, one room comes with a fireplace), all with private bathrooms, air-conditioning, cable television, and telephone. Two accompanying rustic lodges beside a pond have larger living quarters accommodating up to six people—and for the kids, there's a choice of rooms with bunk beds and play loft. The upscale and romantic two-story Beach House Suites set the mood with an in-room fireplace, scenic vistas of sunsets over the lake, and a private beach. At the casual Restaurant on the Knoll ($$–$$$) you can try innovative dishes such as short back ribs rubbed with pepper and local maple syrup, or Ontario-raised ostrich with portobello mushrooms marinated in rosemary and wine. *1642 County Rd., R.R. 1, K0K 2T0 613/393–2090 or 800/724–2393 www.isaiahtubbs.com 35 rooms, 36 suites In-room: Wi-Fi. In-hotel: no elevator, restaurant, bar, tennis court, pools, gym, bicycles, children's programs (ages 5 and up), parking (no fee) AE, MC, V BP.*

8

$$ **Merrill Inn.** This beautiful, Gothic Italianate–style, redbrick house was built in 1878 for Sir Edwards Merrill, a colleague of Sir John A. Macdonald (Canada's first prime minister). The inn is near the heart of downtown Picton and features a pleasant mix of antique furnishings and modern amenities. It's an excellent example of restored Victorian architecture, with 12 tall gables, iron filigree, and carpenter's gingerbread. Rooms have period furniture and are spacious; many have high ceilings. Chef Michael Sullivan, who received training in some of Toronto's finest restaurants, adds a dash of sophistication and culinary ingenuity to the inn's Restaurant & Wine Bar ($$$). The menu highlights local ingredients in the panfried Lake Ontario yellow perch and the succulent seared mullard duck breast with rhubarb compote. *343 Main St. E, K0K 2T0 613/476–7451 or 866/567–5969 www.merrillinn.com 10 rooms, 3 suites In-room: Wi-Fi. In-hotel: restaurant, bar, no elevator, parking (no fee) AE, DC, MC, V Restaurant closed Sun. and Mon. BP.*

COBOURG

90 km (56 mi) west of Picton on Hwy. 401 or Hwy. 2.

Cobourg once expected to be chosen as the provincial capital but it was passed over. The town nearly went bankrupt building the magnificent **Victoria Hall,** officially opened in 1860 by the young Prince of Wales, later King Edward VII. A courtroom modeled after London's Old Bailey was on the ground floor, and town council meetings and concerts were held on the second floor. Today you can tour some of the 41 rooms. *55 King St. W 905/372–2210 or 888/262–6874 Free Guided tours in summer or by prior arrangement.*

WHERE TO STAY

$$$$ **Ste. Anne's Spa.** Manicured gardens, soothing New Age music, and the scent of eucalyptus greet you at this superbly refurbished, old fieldstone inn, now dedicated to refreshing tired city types. Ste. Anne's, in the gently rolling Northumberland Hills, offers everything from stone massage and hydrotherapy to steamy moor mud baths. Guest rooms allow you to relax in laid-back country comfort, with a mix of Ontario antiques and quality modern furnishings, upscale linens, and Oriental carpets on shiny hardwood floors. Several rooms have fireplaces while others include gas-burning wood stoves and whirlpool baths. Meals—which are focused on healthy fare—are served in the dining room, where the ever-changing menu might include roasted lamb loin with an almond crust and a hint of honey. Prices include spa treatments. *R. R. 1, Grafton, K0K 2G0 905/349–2493 or 888/346–6772 www.spavillage.ca 11 rooms, 4 suites, 6 guesthouses In-room: no TV. In-hotel: tennis courts, pools, gym, spa, parking (no fee) AE, D, DC, MC, V MAP.*

KEENE

67 km (42 mi) north of Cobourg via Hwys. 28 and 2.

Keene's most noteworthy attraction is an unusual grave site. A native burial ground is preserved in **Serpent Mounds Park.** About 2,000 years ago a nomadic tribe buried its dead in nine earth mounds, the largest of which is shaped like a 200-foot-long serpent. An interpretation center explains the site and displays artifacts. ✉*R.R. 2* ☎*705/295–6879 or 866/223–3332* 🌐*www.serpentmoundspark.com* 🎟*C$8 per vehicle* ⏲*May–mid-Nov., daily 8 AM–10 PM.*

The well-signed **Lang Pioneer Village,** about 3 km (2 mi) north of Keene, has a museum and 26 restored and furnished pioneer buildings built between 1820 and 1899, including a working circa 1840s grist mill. In summer you can see displays and demonstrations of pioneer arts and crafts. ✉*104 Lang Rd., off County Rd. 34, Lang* ☎*705/295–6694 or 866/289–5264* 🌐*www.langpioneervillage.ca* 🎟*C$6* ⏲*Mid-May–mid-June, weekdays 10–3; mid-June–early Sept., daily 10–4; early Sept.–mid-Sept., weekdays 10–4.*

PETERBOROUGH

13 km (8 mi) northwest of Keene via Hwys. 34 and 7.

The small city of Peterborough is home to Trent University and a few historical sights.

The lift locks, built in 1904 on the **Trent-Severn Waterway,** are among the world's highest and are in operation mid-May through October. The locks have floated boats straight up 65 feet in less than 10 minutes. Slides and films at the **Peterborough Lift Lock Visitor Centre** can help you learn more about how the locks work. ✉*Hunter St. E* ☎*705/750–4950* 🌐*www.pc.gc.ca* 🎟*C$2 donation, parking C$2* ⏲*Apr.–mid-Oct., daily 10–5.*

The **Canadian Canoe Museum** houses the world's largest collection of canoes, honored here as the greatest gift of the First Nations people. Exhibits, which trace the canoe's impact on history, include kayaks, a Nootka (west coast) whaling dugout, and a huge freighter canoe touted as the world's largest birch-bark vessel at 33 feet long. It takes about an hour to tour the museum. ✉*910 Monaghan Rd.* ☎*705/748–9153* 🌐*www.canoemuseum.net* 🎟*C$7.50* ⏲*Mon–Sat. 10–5, Sun. noon–5.*

WHERE TO STAY

$$ **Holiday Inn Peterborough Waterfront.** Surrounded by a marina in the heart of the downtown area, this four-story Holiday Inn overlooks the Otonabee River, which connects to Trent-Severn Waterway. The location is hard to beat—most hotels here are on the shopping mall strip on the way into town. If you come by boat, which can be reserved through the marina at Del Crary Park, you won't be charged for docking. ✉*150 George St. N, K9J 3G5* ☎*705/743–1144 or 800/465–4329* 🌐*www.holiday-inn.com/waterfront* *153 rooms, 4 suites* *In-room: Wi-Fi. In-hotel: restaurant, pool, gym, parking (free)* *AE, D, DC, MC, V.*

8

$$ **The Village Inn.** About 10 minutes northeast of Peterborough in the village of Lakefield, this modern lodging with a four-story Victorian-style exterior has an up-scale, but decidedly casual, country-inn atmosphere. Spacious guest rooms and suites have wrought-iron, queen-size beds covered in colorful quilts. Bold colors in the decor nicely balance such antique accents as oversized armoires and armchairs. The Thirsty Loon, a dining room and pub, is on-site. ✉*39 Queen St., Lakefield, K0L 2H0* ☎*705/652–1910 or 800/827–5678* 🌐*www.villageinn.ca* *26 rooms, 2 suites* *In-room: dial-up. In-hotel: restaurant, spa, no-smoking rooms* 💳*D, MC, V.*

PETROGLYPHS PROVINCIAL PARK

55 km (34 mi) northeast of Peterborough on Hwy. 28.

Embedded deep within a forest northeast of Peterborough is Canada's largest concentration of native rock carvings. The site, discovered in 1954 at the east end of Stony Lake, is now within Petroglyphs Provincial Park. The well-preserved symbols and figures are carved on a flat expanse of white marble almost 70 feet wide, which is sheltered in a protective building. The more than 900 carvings—depicting turtles, snakes, birds, and humans—are believed to be Algonquin spirit figures. There are a series of well-marked hiking trails that plunge through the thick surrounding woodlands, skirting rocky ridges, and ecologically vital, but fragile, wetlands. ✉*2249 Northey's Bay Rd., east of Hwy. 28, Woodview* ☎*705/877–2552* 🌐*www.ontarioparks.com/english/petr.html* *C$9 per vehicle* *May–mid-Oct., daily 10–5.*

NORTH OF TORONTO TO THE LAKES

Outcroppings of pink-and-gray granite mark the rustic area in the Canadian Shield known to locals as Cottage Country. Drumlins of conifer and deciduous forest punctuate 100,000 freshwater lakes formed from glaciers during the Ice Age. Names of towns and places such as Orillia, the Muskokas, Gravenhurst, Haliburton, and Algonquin reveal the history of the land's inhabitants, from Algonquin tribes to European explorers to fur traders. The area became a haven for the summering rich and famous during the mid-19th century, when lumber barons who were harvesting near port towns set up steamship and rail lines, making travel to the area possible. Since then, Cottage Country has attracted urbanites who make the pilgrimage to hear the call of the loon or swat incessant mosquitoes and blackflies. "Cottages" is a broadly used term that includes log cabins as well as palatial homes that wouldn't look out of place in a wealthy urban neighborhood. For the cottageless, overnight seasonal camping is an option in one of the provincial parks.

To reach this area, take Highway 400 North, which intersects with Cottage Country's highly traveled and often congested Highway 11. Highway 60 is less traveled and cuts across the province through Algonquin Provincial Park.

BARRIE

90 km (56 mi) north of Toronto on Hwy. 400.

Barrie is on the shore of Lake Simcoe and was originally a landing place for the area's aboriginal inhabitants and, later, for fur traders. Today it's an attractive city serving as the gateway to the popular ski resorts and northern Huronia summer vacation lands. Barrie has events year-round.

The town's annual **Winterfest** (☎*705/739–9444 or 800/668–9100* 🌐*www.city.barrie.on.ca*), in early February, has ice fishing, dogsledding, ice sculptures, ice motorcycling, hot-air ballooning, and other colorful activities. From late June through Labor Day, informal drama productions spotlight Canadian playwrights at the **Gryphon Theatre** ✉*Georgian College, Georgian Dr. and Bell Farm Rd.* ☎*705/728–4613* 🌐*www.gryphontheatre.com*). You can watch harness racing at **Georgian Downs Racetrack** (☎*705/726–9400 or 866/915–9400* 🌐*www.georgiandowns.com*).

On the August Simcoe Day long weekend (usually the first full weekend of the month), **Kempenfest Waterfront Festival** (☎*705/739–4216* 🌐*www.kempenfest.com*) transforms about 2½ km (1 mi) of Barrie's waterfront into an arts-and-crafts fair. The event includes live entertainment on two stages, antiques shows, and specialty-food samplings and draws some 200,000 visitors.

WHERE TO STAY & EAT

$$$$ **Blue Mountain Resort.** In addition to being the largest ski resort in Ontario, this acclaimed lodge 71 km (44 mi) outside of Barrie has an outstanding 18-hole golf course and a faux alpine village flanked with shops and restaurants. Rooms are at the **Blue Mountain Inn**; suites have kitchens and fireplaces. The inn's Pottery dining room serves Continental interpretations of Canadian standards. ✉*R.R. 3, Collingwood, L9Y 3Z2* ☎*705/445–0231 or 877/445–0231* 🌐*www.bluemountain.ca* *95 rooms, 2 suites* *In-hotel: 7 restaurants, room service, tennis courts, pool, gym, spa, beachfront, public Internet* *AE, DC, MC, V.*

$$$ Fodor's Choice ★ **Horseshoe Resort.** Modern guest rooms at this top-drawer lodge have down comforters, and many suites have sunken living rooms, fireplaces, and whirlpool baths. Dining options include the distinctive Continental menu of the formal Silks Fine Dining, the casual offerings at the Santa Fe–style Go West Grill, and the hearty bar fare at Crazy Horse Saloon. ✉*Horseshoe Valley Rd., R.R. 1, Box 10, L4M 4Y8* ☎*705/835–2790 or 800/461–5627* 🌐*www.horseshoeresort.com* *54 rooms, 48 suites* *In-hotel: 3 restaurants, bar, golf courses, tennis courts, pools, gym, spa, bicycles* *AE, DC, MC, V.*

$$$ **Talisman Mountain Resort.** Rooms at this year-round resort have views of either the Beaver Valley or Talisman Mountain and are done in floral patterns or warm gold tones. Outdoor hot tubs, a spa, and yoga classes can help you relax after hitting the ski slopes. The Tyrolean Restaurant serves Canadian dishes such as Alberta steak and local trout. ✉*150 Talisman Dr., Kimberley, N0C 1G0* ☎*519/599–2520 or 800/265–3759* 🌐*www.talisman.ca* *85 rooms, 8 suites* *In-hotel: restaurant, golf course, tennis court, pool, spa, bicycles* *AE, D, MC, V.*

8

SKIING & SNOWBOARDING

The province's highest vertical drop, of 720 feet, is at **Blue Mountain Resort** (✉ *R.R. 3, Collingwood* ☎ *705/445–0231, 416/869–3799 from Toronto* 🌐 *www.bluemountain.ca*), 11 km (7 mi) west of Collingwood, off Highway 26. Ontario's most extensively developed and heavily used ski area has 37 trails served by a high-speed quad lift, three triple chairs, four double chairs, and three rope tows.

One of the few resorts to offer snowboarding, tubing, and cross-country and downhill skiing trails and facilities is **Horseshoe Valley Resort** (✉ *Horseshoe Valley Rd., R.R. 1, Box 10* ☎ *705/835–2790 or 800/461–5627* 🌐 *www.horseshoeresort.com*), 50 km (31½ mi) north of Barrie, off Highway 400. The resort has 22 alpine runs, 14 of which are lighted at night, served by seven lifts. The vertical drop is only 308 feet, but several of the runs are rated for advanced skiers.

Skiers and snowboarders can take advantage of 36 runs at **Mount St. Louis Moonstone** (✉ *R.R. 4, Coldwater L0K 1E0* ☎ *705/835–2112 or 416/368–6900* 🌐 *www.mslm.on.ca*), 30 km (18 mi) north of Barrie. The majority of slopes are for beginner and intermediate skiers, though there's a sprinkling of advanced runs. The resort's Kids Camp, a day-care and ski school combination, attracts families. Inexpensive cafeterias within the two chalets serve decent meals. No overnight lodging is available. Nestled at the base of Mt. Talisman in the heart of Beaver Valley is the Tyrolean-inspired **Talisman Mountain Resort** (✉ *150 Talisman Dr., Kimberley* ☎ *519/599–2520 or 800/265–3759* 🌐 *www.talisman.ca*). Families like the resort for its popular Kids Klub, a program in which children are placed into age-based ski groups for daily activities.

PENETANGUISHENE & MIDLAND

47 km (29 mi) north of Barrie on Hwys. 400 and 93.

The quiet towns of Penetanguishene (known locally as Penetang) and Midland occupy a small corner of northern Simcoe County known as Huronia. Both towns sit on a snug harbor at the foot of Georgian Bay's Severn Sound.

★ **Sainte-Marie among the Hurons,** 5 km (3 mi) east of Midland on Highway 12, is a reconstruction of the Jesuit mission that was originally built on this spot in 1639. The village, which was once home to a fifth of the European population of New France, was the site of the European settlers' first hospital, farm, school, and social service center in Ontario. Villagers also constructed a canal from the Wye River. A combination of disease and Iroquois attacks led to the mission's demise. Twenty-two structures, including a native longhouse and wigwam, have been faithfully reproduced from a scientific excavation. The canal is working again, and staff members in period costume saw timber, repair shoes, sew clothes, and grow vegetables—keeping the working village alive. ✉ *Hwy. 12 E* ☎ *705/526–7838* 🌐 *www.saintemarieamongthehurons.on.ca* 🎟 *C$11* ⏲ *Mid-May–mid-Oct., daily 10–5; last entry at 4:45.*

On a hill overlooking Sainte-Marie among the Hurons is the **Martyrs' Shrine,** a twin-spired stone cathedral built in 1926 to honor the eight missionaries who died in Huronia; in 1930, five of the priests were canonized by the Roman Catholic Church. The grounds include a theater, a souvenir shop, a cafeteria, and a picnic area. *Off Hwy. 12 E 705/526–3788 www.martyrs-shrine.com C$3 Mid-May–mid-Oct., daily 8:30 AM–9 PM.*

The best artifacts from several hundred archaeological digs in the area are displayed at the **Huronia Museum** in Little Lake Park, Midland. Behind the museum and gallery building is **Huron-Ouendat Village,** a full-scale replica of a 16th-century Huron settlement. *Little Lake Park 705/526–2844 or 800/263–7745 www.huroniamuseum.com Museum and village C$6 May and June, daily 9–5; July and Aug., daily 9–6; Sept.–Apr., Mon.–Sat. 9–5.*

Cruises leave from the town docks in Midland and Penetang to explore the 30,000 Islands region of Georgian Bay from May through October. The 300-passenger *Miss Midland* (*888/833–2628 www.midlandtours.com*) leaves from the Midland town dock and offers 2½-hour sightseeing cruises daily (C$20) mid-May to mid-October. From the Penetang town dock, the 200-passenger **MS** *Georgian Queen* (*705/549–7795 or 800/363–7447 www.georgianbaycruises.com*) takes passengers on three-hour tours (C$20) of the islands. They depart from one to three times daily; call ahead for times.

WHERE TO STAY

$$ **Best Western Highland Inn and Conference Centre.** An enormous atrium anchors this completely self-contained hotel-motel resort. Honeymoon suites have cherry-red, heart-shaped tubs or fireplace rooms with sunken hot tubs. Sunday brunches by the pool in the Garden Atrium Café are popular; there are two other dining areas (reserve ahead) as well. *924 King St., at Hwy. 12, Midland, L4R 4L3 705/526–9307 or 800/461–4265 www.bestwesternmidland.com 122 rooms, 16 suites In-hotel: 2 restaurants, bar, pool, gym, laundry facilities AE, D, DC, MC, V.*

8

PARRY SOUND

117 km (73 mi) north of Penetanguishene and Midland via Hwy. 400 or 12 and 69.

Parry Sound has two big claims to fame: it's the home of hockey legend Bobby Orr, and it has Canada's largest sightseeing cruise ship, accommodating 550 passengers.

The *Island Queen* offers an extensive three-hour cruise around the narrow channels and shallow waterways known as the 30,000 Islands of Georgian Bay. Tours run once or twice daily, depending on the season. There's free parking at the town dock. *9 Bay St. 705/746–2311 or 800/506–2628 www.island-queen.com C$25 June–mid-Oct., daily; call for cruise times.*

Groove to jazz, folk, and classical music during **Festival of the Sound** (☎705/746–2410 or 866/364–0061 *www.festivalofthesound.on.ca*), which runs from mid-July to mid-August. Performances take place daily at the state-of-the-art Charles W. Stockey Centre for the Performing Arts, the Bobby Orr Hall of Fame & Entertainment Centre, and the decks of the *Island Queen.*

ORILLIA

98 km (61 mi) southeast of Parry Sound on Hwy. 69, 35 km (22 mi) northeast of Barrie on Hwy. 11.

A former lumber town shoehorned between Lake Simcoe and Lake Couchiching in central Ontario, Orillia (which means riverbank in Spanish) developed into a summer-cottage haven at the turn of the 20th century. The year-round cottage town has 30,000 residents and is known for being the hometown of humorist Stephen Leacock.

The redbrick, turreted **Orillia Opera House** was built in 1873 and renovated in 1917 after a fire destroyed much of it. Though some details were changed, such as the design of the roof, the opera house still looks similar to its original design and has been named an Ontario Heritage site. The **Sunshine Festival Theatre Company** (*www.sunshinefestival.ca*) performs classic plays and Broadway shows at the opera house from May through October. ✉ *West St. and Mississaga St.* ☎ *800/683–8747* *www.operahouse.orillia.on.ca.*

★ Readers of Canada's great humorist Stephen Leacock may recognize Orillia as "Mariposa," the town he described in *Sunshine Sketches of a Little Town.* Leacock's former summer home is now the **Stephen Leacock Museum,** a National Historic Site. Among the rotating exhibits are books, manuscripts, and photographs depicting Leacock and the region that inspired his writings. In the Mariposa Room, characters from the book are matched with the Orillia residents who inspired them. ✉ *50 Museum Dr., off Hwy. 12B* ☎ *705/329–1908* *www.leacockmuseum.com* *C$5* *May and Sept., weekdays 10–5; June–Aug., daily 10–5.*

For the past few years, **Casino Rama,** the largest First Nations–run gambling emporium in Canada, has lured thousands of visitors to the Orillia area. The 192,000-square-foot complex 5 km (3 mi) north of town has 2,300 slot machines, more than 120 gambling tables, 9 restaurants, an entertainment lounge, an adjoining 300-room all-suites luxury hotel, and a gift shop. ✉ *R.R. 6, Rama Reserve* ☎ *705/329–3325 or 800/832–7529* *www.casino-rama.com.*

GRAVENHURST

38 km (24 mi) north of Orillia on Hwy. 11.

North along Highway 11, rolling farmland suddenly changes to lakes and pine trees amid granite outcrops of the Canadian Shield. This region, called Muskoka, is a favorite playground of people who live in and around Toronto. Gravenhurst is a town of approximately 10,000 and the birthplace of Norman Bethune, regarded as a Canadian hero.

Bethune Memorial House, an 1880-vintage frame structure, is a National Historic Site that honors the heroic efforts of field surgeon and medical educator Norman Bethune, who worked in China during the Sino-Japanese War in the 1930s and trained thousands to become medics and doctors. There are period rooms and an exhibit tracing the highlights of his life. The house has become a shrine of sorts for Chinese diplomats visiting North America. ✉ *235 John St. N, P1P 1G4* ☎ *705/687–4261* 🌐 *www.parkscanada.gc.ca/bethune* 🎫 *C$3.50* ⏲ *June–Oct., daily 10–4; Nov.–May, weekdays 1–4.*

★ From mid-June to mid-October, the **Muskoka Lakes Navigation and Hotel Company** runs cruises that tour the Muskoka Lakes. Excursions range from 90 minutes to two days in length (passengers dine aboard but sleep in one of Muskoka's grand resorts). Reservations are required. The **RMS** *Segwun* (the initials stand for Royal Mail Ship) is the sole survivor of a fleet of steamships that provided transportation through the Muskoka Lakes. The 128-foot-long, 99-passenger boat was built in 1887 and restored in 1970. The 200-passenger *Wenonah II* is a 1907-inspired vessel with modern technology. The 1915 *Wanda III* steam yacht is available for private cruises only. ✉ *820 Bay St., Gravenhurst* ☎ *705/687–6667* 🌐 *www.segwun.com.*

WHERE TO STAY & EAT

$$$$ Fodor'sChoice ★ **Taboo Resort, Golf and Conference Centre.** A magnificent 1,000-acre landscape of rocky outcrops and windswept trees typical of the Muskoka region surrounds this year-round luxury resort. All kinds of diversions are available, from a highly rated golf course to an outdoor ice-skating rink. The exterior resembles a traditional northern Canadian lodge, but rooms have a sleek design with walnut-wood finishings and crisp, white linens. Lodge rooms offer forest and lake views. At **Elements**, an überchic restaurant and lounge in one, the open-concept Culinary Theatre ($$$) showcases the chef's mastery with plasma TVs running a live feed of him blending Asian influences with local produce. ✉ *Muskoka Beach Rd., P1P 1R1* ☎ *705/687–2233 or 800/461–0236* 🌐 *www.tabooresort.com* *79 rooms, 22 suites, 33 cottages, 15 condos* *In-room: kitchen (some), refrigerator, VCR. In-hotel: 5 restaurants, bars, golf course, tennis courts, pools, gym, spa, bicycles, children's programs (ages 3–12), no-smoking rooms* 💳 *AE, DC, MC, V.*

$$–$$$ **Bayview-Wildwood Resort.** The complex, a 15-minute drive south of Gravenhurst, dates to 1898 and is particularly geared to outdoor types and families. Canoeing and kayaking are popular; floatplane excursions and golf can also be arranged. Some guest rooms have fireplaces, whirlpool baths, and views over the lake. You must book a family vacation, conference package, or weekend package to stay here. ✉ *1500 Port Stanton Pkwy., R.R. 1, Severn Bridge, P0E 1N0* ☎ *705/689–2338 or 800/461–0243* 🌐 *www.bayviewwildwood.com* *34 rooms, 26 suites, 17 cottages* *In-room: kitchen (some). In-hotel: tennis courts, pools, gym, bicycles, no-smoking rooms* 💳 *AE, DC, MC, V* *FAP.*

HALIBURTON

90 km (56 mi) northeast of Gravenhurst via Hwy. 11 and Hwy. 118, 250 km (155 mi) northeast of Toronto.

Pink granite outcroppings left by the Canadian Shield, rushing rivers, groves of sugar maples, and jack pines speckle the topography of Haliburton. Once the stomping ground of the Huron, Mississauga, and Ojibwa tribes, as well as explorers, fur traders, and loggers, Haliburton's rugged environment now attracts snowmobilers, skiers, mountain bikers, canoers, kayakers, and hikers. The all-season destination is close to Algonquin Provincial Park and less congested than its neighbors (the Muskokas and the Kawarthas).

WHERE TO STAY

$$$$ **Domain of Killien.** A haven of year-round relaxation, Killien offers exclusive access to 5,000 acres of private forest, streams, and lakes near Algonquin Provincial Park. Rooms in the main lodge have whirlpool tubs, cedar dressing rooms, and views of the lake. Cabins have fireplaces and decks overlooking the lake. Fine wines are served with sophisticated dishes that showcase local ingredients: wild game in fall, organically grown herbs and vegetables in spring, house-smoked duck and salmon year-round. The trout and bass are fresh from local lakes, and even the maple syrup is homemade. ✉ *Carrol Rd., Box 810, K0M 1S0* ☎ *705/457–1100 or 800/390–0769* 🌐 *www.domainofkillien.com* *5 rooms, 7 cabins* *In-room: no a/c, no TV. In-hotel: restaurant, tennis courts, no-smoking rooms, no elevator* 💳 *AE, DC, MC, V* *MAP.*

$$$$ ★ **Sir Sam's Inn.** The restored inn from 1910 has hints of grandeur, such as a massive stone fireplace, hand-hewn beams, and floor-to-cathedral-ceiling windows overlooking Eagle Lake. Lakeside rooms have wood-burning fireplaces and whirlpool baths. In winter you have access to Sir Sam's ski area, which has 12 runs and 6 lifts, including 2 quad chairs. A nearby pine-and-hardwood forest is inviting for summer strolls. The dining room serves northern specialties—caribou and fresh game hen. *Box 156, Eagle Lake P.O., K0M 1M0* ☎ *705/754–2188 or 800/361–2188* 🌐 *www.sirsamsinn.com* *25 rooms* *In-room: no a/c. In-hotel: restaurant, tennis court, pool, water sports, bicycles, no kids under 12, no-smoking rooms* 💳 *AE, DC, MC, V.*

SPORTS & THE OUTDOORS

SKIING LODGE-TO-LODGE More than 500 km (200 mi) of groomed wilderness trails weave throughout Haliburton County. Three- and four-night guided lodge-to-lodge cross-country ski packages are available along the Haliburton Nordic Ski Trail system. There are groups for skiers of all levels, and the trips cover 8 km to 25 km (5 mi to 16 mi) per day, depending on the group's abilities. Six lodges participate in the program, and skiers stay and dine at a different lodge each night. Packages include all meals, trail passes, and a guide. For information about ski packages, contact **Haliburton Highlands Trails and Tours** (*General Delivery, Carnarvon K0M 1J0* ☎ *705/489–4049* 🌐 *www.trailsandtours.com*).

SNOWMOBILING **C Mac Snow Tours** (*519/887–6686 or 800/225–4258 www.cmacsnowtours.ca*) has five- and six-night all-inclusive snowmobile excursions in Haliburton Highlands–Algonquin Provincial Park. In the 50,000-acre, privately owned **Haliburton Forest** (*R.R. 1, K0M 1S0 705/754–2198 www.haliburtonforest.com*) there are 300 km (186 mi) of snowmobile trails, plus a shelter system. The day-use trail fee is C$30. Machine and cottage rentals are available; call for rates.

BRACEBRIDGE

23 km (14 mi) north of Gravenhurst on Hwy. 11.

Holiday cheer brightens Bracebridge in summer with Christmas-oriented amusements. The Bracebridge Falls on the Muskoka River are a good option for those who prefer a more peaceful excursion.

Youngsters can ride the Kris Kringle River Boat, Rudolph's Sleigh Ride Roller Coaster, the Candy Cane Express Train, bumper boats, paddleboats, ponies, and more at **Santa's Village.** At the same location, **Sportsland** (*C$3 per ticket, rides cost one or two tickets each Mid-June–early Sept., Mon.–Sat. 10–9, Sun. 10–6*), for children 12 and older, has go-karts, batting cages, in-line skating, 18-hole miniature golf, laser tag, and an indoor activity center with video games. *Santa's Village Rd. west of Bracebridge 705/645–2512 www.santasvillage.ca C$20 Mid-June–early Sept., daily 10–6.*

WHERE TO STAY & EAT

$–$$ ★ **Inn at the Falls.** Look out at the magnificent Bracebridge Falls from this Victorian inn, built in 1876, and its annex of motel-style rooms. A few rooms have fireplaces, balconies, and whirlpool tubs, and all are individually decorated in period style. A ghost, said to live in one room, is somewhat of an attraction. The outdoor pool is heated. The main dining room and pub offer food and live entertainment; there's an outdoor patio as well. Try the steak-and-kidney pie. *1 Dominion St., Box 1139, P1L 1V3 705/645–2245 or 877/645–9212 705/645–5093 www.innatthefalls.net 42 rooms, 2 cottages In-room: no a/c (some). In-hotel: restaurant, bar, pool, no-smoking rooms AE, DC, MC, V CP.*

DORSET

48 km (30 mi) northeast of Bracebridge via Hwys. 11 and 117.

Dorset is a handsome village on Lake of Bays.

In summer the self-guided trails at the defunct **Leslie M. Frost Natural Resources Center** (*Hwy. 35 at St. Nora's Lake, Dorset*) are a great way to explore Ontario's wildlife. Though the washroom facilities and information center are closed, the trails are open.

Robinson's General Store (*Main St. 705/766–2415*) has been in business since 1921. Look for the moose-fur hats and pine furniture.

The 82-foot-high **Dorset Tower** (🌐*www.dorset-tower.com*), open mid-May through October, allows you to see across the lake and over the forested landscape from its lookout (C$2 per car or C$10 seasonal pass). You can circle back to Toronto on scenic Highway 35 or make Dorset a stop on a tour from Huntsville around Lake of Bays.

HUNTSVILLE

34 km (21 mi) north of Bracebridge on Hwy. 11, 215 km (133 mi) north of Toronto on Hwys. 400 and 11.

The Huntsville region is filled with lakes and streams, strands of virgin birch and pine, and deer. Because the area is part of Toronto's Muskoka region, there's no shortage of year-round resorts. The area is usually the cross-country skier's best bet for an abundance of natural snow in southern Ontario. All resorts have trails.

WHERE TO STAY & EAT

$$$$ Fodor's Choice ★ **Deerhurst Resort.** The ultraluxe resort spread along Peninsula Lake is an 800-acre, self-contained community. The flavor is largely modern, although the rustic main lodge dates from 1896. The resort's Pavilion wing is four stories high, embellished with an octagonal tower and decorative gables; its rooms are done in a floral-and-stripe combination and have large windows with views of the grounds and lakefront. Steamers restaurant specializes in steaks prepared with a choice of marinades and imaginative sauces. Eclipse Dining Room serves Canadian specialties, such as Ontario lamb, Alberta beef, and rainbow trout. ✉*1235 Deerhurst Dr., P1H 2E8* ☎*705/789–6411 or 800/461–4393* 🌐*www.deerhurstresort.com* *412 rooms* *In-hotel: 3 restaurants, bar, golf courses, tennis court, pool, gym, spa, water sports, no-smoking rooms* *AE, D, DC, MC, V.*

$$$ **Norsemen Restaurant and Resort.** Rustic two- and three-bedroom cottages overlook Walker Lake at this resort. In summer cottages are rented by the week only. Even more famous than the charming lakeside lodgings, however, is the resort's dining room. The Norsemen Restaurant has earned generations of devotees by serving a tempting Canadian harvest—including fresh Atlantic salmon, breast of pheasant, and medallions of caribou—prepared with European flair. It's open for dinner only (seatings from 6 to 8:30) Tuesday through Sunday in summer, and Thursday through Sunday in winter. ✉*1040 Walker Lake Dr., R.R. 4, P1H 2J6* ☎*705/635–2473, 800/565–3856 in Canada* 🌐*www.norsemen.ca* *7 cottages* *In-room: no a/c, no phone, kitchen, no TV. In-hotel: restaurant* *AE, MC, V.*

$–$$ **Portage Inn.** Stay near ski runs and snowmobile trails at this country-style 1889 home, which is open year-round. Rooms have great views of the surrounding forested hills and lake; the king bedroom has an en-suite hot tub. The inn has snowshoeing in winter and canoeing and kayaking in summer. ✉*1563 N. Portage Rd., P1H 2J6* ☎*705/788–7171 or 888/418–5555* 🌐*www.portageinn.com* *6 rooms, 2 cottages* *In-room: no a/c, VCR (some), no TV (some). In-hotel: tennis court, bicycles* *MC, V* *CP.*

ALGONQUIN PROVINCIAL PARK

★ *35 km (23 mi) east of Huntsville on Hwy. 60.*

Algonquin Provincial Park stretches across 7,725 square km (2,983 square mi), containing more than 1,000 lakes and 1,000 species of plants, and encompassing forests, rivers, and cliffs. The typical visitor is a hiker, canoeist, camper—or all three. But don't be put off if you're not the athletic or outdoorsy sort. About a third of Algonquin's visitors come for the day to walk one of the 17 interpretive trails, or enjoy a swim or a picnic. Swimming is especially good at the Lake of Two Rivers, halfway between the west and east gates along Highway 60. A morning drive through the park in May or June is often rewarded by moose and deer sightings. Park naturalists give talks on area wildflowers, animals, and birds, and you can book a guided hike or canoe trip. Expeditions to hear wolf howling take place in late summer and early autumn. The **visitor center,** near the east side of the park, has information on park programs, a bookstore, a restaurant, and a panoramic-viewing deck. The park's **Algonquin Logging Museum** (*Late May–mid-Oct., daily 9–5*) depicts life at an early Canadian logging camp. *Hwy. 60; main and east gate is west of town of Whitney; west gate is east of town of Dwight Box 219, Whitney K0J 2M0 705/633–5572 www.algonquinpark.on.ca C$12 per vehicle Park daily 8 AM–10 PM.*

WHERE TO STAY & EAT

$$$$ Fodor's Choice ★ **Arowhon Pines.** The stuff of local legend, Arowhon is a family-run resort in Algonquin Provincial Park known for unpretentious luxury and superb dining. Two- to 12-bedroom log cabins are decorated with antique pine furnishings. The waterside suites have fireplaces and private decks. Room rates include three daily meals in the tepee-style dining hall overlooking the lake. The fare focuses on Ontario's seasonal ingredients and might include pancakes with maple syrup and Canadian bacon for breakfast. Nonlodgers can reserve prix-fixe meals. If you'd like wine with dinner, bring your own: park restrictions prohibit its sale here. Swimming, sailing, hiking, and birding are all possible. *Off Hwy. 60, Box 10001, Algonquin Park, Huntsville P1H 2G5 705/633–5661 or 416/483–4393 www.arowhonpines.ca 50 rooms in 13 cabins In-room: no a/c, no phone, no TV. In-hotel: restaurant MC, V Closed mid-Oct.–May FAP.*

$$$$ ★ **Bartlett Lodge.** After a short boat ride on Cache Lake, to about halfway through Algonquin Provincial Park, you arrive at this 1917 resort. The immaculate cabins have gleaming hardwood floors and king-size beds or two singles. Quiet reigns: no waterskiing, jet skiing, or motors over 10 horsepower on the lake (but you can take out a canoe); and you won't find radios, phones, or TVs in the cabins. The Algonquin-style dining room offers a choice of traditional Canadian breakfast and table d'hôte menus. Nonlodgers are welcome for dinner. *Box 10004, Algonquin Park, Huntsville P1H 2G8 705/633–5543, 905/338–8908 in winter www.bartlettlodge.com 12 cabins In-room: no a/c, no phone, no TV. In-hotel: restaurant, bicycles MC, V Closed mid-Oct.–May MAP.*

8

CAMPING Camping is available in three categories. Along the Park Corridor, a 56-km (35-mi) stretch of Highway 60, are eight organized campgrounds. Within the park's vast interior, you won't find any organized campsites (and the purists love it that way). In between these extremes are the lesser-known peripheral campgrounds—Kiosk, Brent, and Achray—which you reach by long, dusty roads. These have only firewood and nonflushing pit toilets; the organized campsites have showers, picnic tables, and, in some cases, RV hookups. All organized campsites must be reserved; call **Ontario Parks** (☎ *800/688–7275* 🌐 *www.ontarioparks.com*). You need permits (C$12) for interior camping, available at the Canoe Centre adjacent to the Portage Store or from Ontario Parks.

OUTFITTERS

Algonquin Outfitters (✉ *R.R. 1, Dwight P0A 1H0* ☎ *705/635–2243* 🌐 *www.algonquinoutfitters.com*) has four store locations in and around the park—Oxtongue Lake, Huntsville, Opeongo Lake, and Brent Base on Cedar Lake—specializing in canoe rentals, outfitting and camping services, sea kayaking, and a water-taxi service to the park's central areas. Call to confirm equipment rentals and tour availability.

If you plan to camp in the park, you may want to contact the **Portage Store** (✉ *Hwy. 60, Box 10009, Huntsville P1H 2H4* ☎ *705/663–5622 in summer, 705/789–3645 in winter* 🌐 *www.portagestore.com*), which provides extensive outfitting services. They have packages that might include permits, canoes, and food supplies, as well as maps and detailed information about routes and wildlife.

THE NIAGARA PENINSULA

Within this small expanse of land, bordered by Lake Ontario to the north and Lake Erie to the south, you can stumble across a roadside fruit stand on a tour through rustic vineyards or gamble to your heart's content alongside one of nature's most beautiful displays of water. The Niagara Peninsula's various flavors make it a good place to entertain both high- and low-brow interests. Niagara Falls, with its daring adventure tours, wax museums, and honeymoon certificates—not to mention its wildly popular water attraction—has a certain kitschy-and-glitzy quality. Niagara-on-the-Lake, which draws theatergoers to its annual Shaw Festival, is a more tasteful, serene town. Niagara is also one of Canada's three best regions for wine production (Point Pelee, also in Ontario, and the province of British Columbia are the others). More than 55 small vineyards produce fine wines, and most of them offer tastings and tours.

NIAGARA FALLS

130 km (81 mi) south of Toronto via the Queen Elizabeth Way.

Fodor's Choice ★ Although cynics have had a field day with **Niagara Falls**—calling it everything from "water on the rocks" to "the second major disappointment of American married life" (Oscar Wilde)—most visitors

CLOSE UP

Point Pelee & Pelee Island

The southernmost tip of mainland Canada is along major bird, bat, dragonfly, and butterfly migration routes. This might explain why **Point Pelee National Park** (150 km [93 mi] west of St. Thomas on Hwy. 401 or Hwy. 3, near Leamington), which has the smallest dry land area of any Canadian national park, draws more than a half million visitors every year. The park's visitor center has exhibits, slide shows, and a knowledgeable staff ready to answer questions. A tram operates April through October to "the tip." September is the best time to see monarch butterflies resting in Pelee before they head to Mexico's Sierra Madres. The park is among the world's best vantage points for bird-watching, especially during spring and fall migrations. Camping is not permitted. The park is open year-round. For hours and other information, call ☎519/322–2365, or log on to *www.parkscanada.gc.ca/pelee*.

Pelee Island (25 km [16 mi] and 90 min by ferry from Point Pelee via Hwy. 33 and Leamington ferry) is a small island at the west end of Lake Erie. This is Canada's southernmost inhabited point, on the same latitude as northern California and northern Spain. The island's permanent population is about 275, but in summer it quadruples as vacationers cram into private cottages, small guest inns, and campsites. A big draw is the island's wine. You can visit Pelee Island Winery's Wine Pavillion (open Mon.–Sat. 9–6, Sun. 11–5) or the ruins of Vin Villa winery, which dates from the mid-1800s. Still, Pelee maintains its island pace. On a day trip you might also experience the beaches and wildlife, picnic at the 1833 Pelee Lighthouse, or cycle around the island. There's no bank or ATM here, so exchange currency prior to visiting. In winter there are scheduled flights from Windsor. For more information go to *www.pelee.org*.

are truly impressed. Missionary and explorer Louis Hennepin, whose books were widely read across Europe, described the falls in 1678 as "an incredible Cataract or Waterfall which has no equal." Nearly two centuries later, Charles Dickens declared, "I seemed to be lifted from the earth and to be looking into Heaven." Henry James recorded in 1883 how one stands there "gazing your fill at the most beautiful object in the world."

These rave reviews lured countless daredevils to the falls. In 1859, 100,000 spectators watched as the French tightrope walker Blondin successfully crossed Niagara Gorge, from the American to the Canadian side, on a 3-inch-thick rope. From the early 18th century, dozens went over in boats and barrels. Nobody survived until 1901, when schoolteacher Annie Taylor emerged from her barrel and asked, "Did I go over the falls yet?" The stunts were finally outlawed in 1912.

The waterfall's colorful history began more than 10,000 years ago as a group of glaciers receded, diverting the waters of Lake Erie northward into Lake Ontario. The force and volume of the water as it flowed over the Niagara Escarpment created the thundering cataracts now known so well. The lure of Niagara Falls hasn't dimmed for those who want

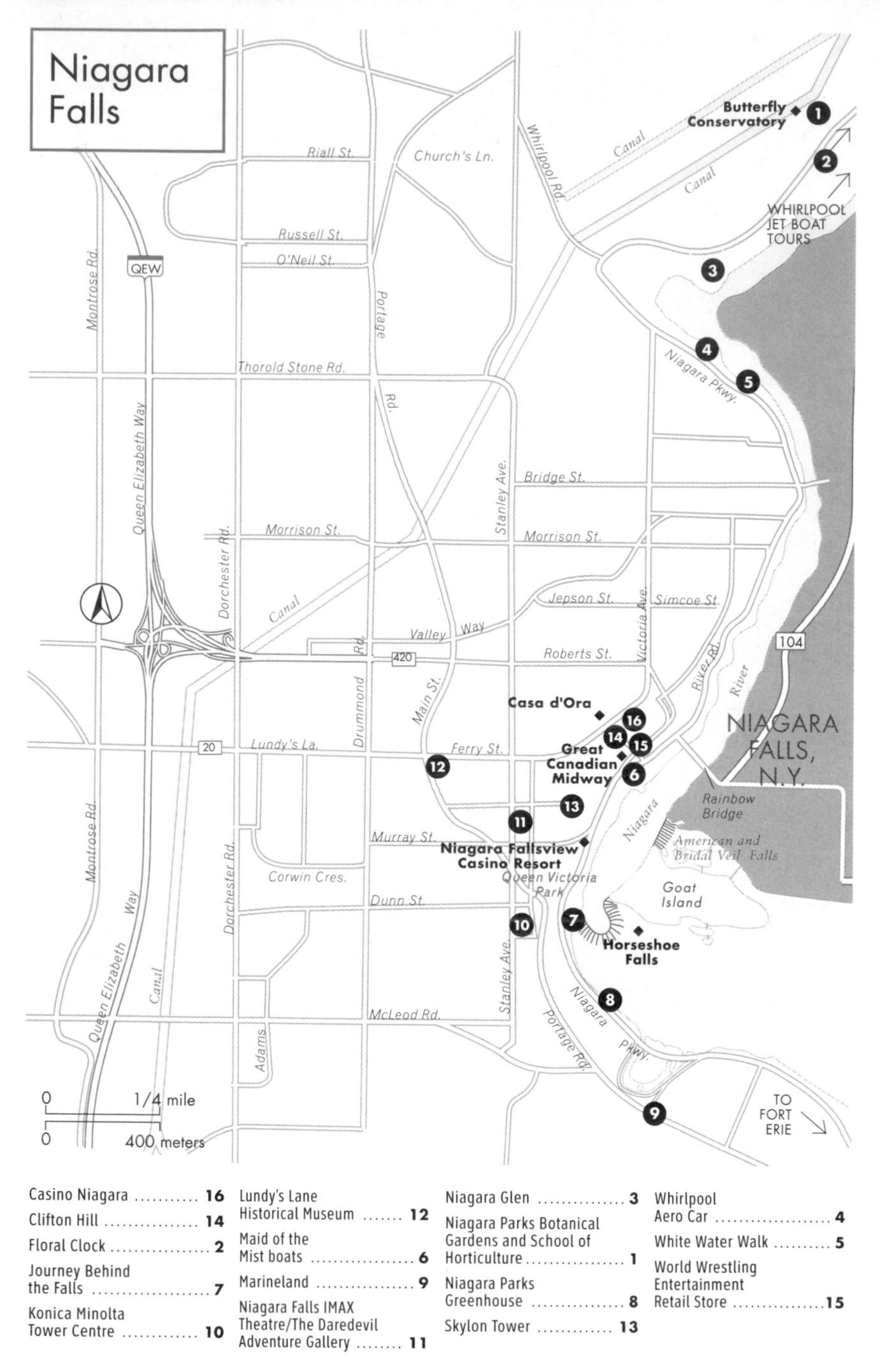
Niagara Falls
Butterfly Conservatory
WHIRLPOOL JET BOAT TOURS
Canal
Riall St.
Church's Ln.
Whirlpool Rd.
Russell St.
O'Neil St.
QEW
Montrose Rd.
Portage Rd.
Thorold Stone Rd.
Niagara Pkwy.
Queen Elizabeth Way
Stanley Ave.
Bridge St.
Morrison St.
Dorchester Rd.
Jepson St.
Simcoe St.
Victoria Ave.
Valley Way
Roberts St.
420
104
River Rd.
River
Drummond Rd.
Main St.
Casa d'Ora
NIAGARA FALLS, N.Y.
20
Lundy's La.
Ferry St.
Great Canadian Midway
Rainbow Bridge
Niagara
Murray St.
Niagara Fallsview Casino Resort
American and Bridal Veil Falls
Corwin Cres.
Queen Victoria Park
Goat Island
Dunn St.
Horseshoe Falls
McLeod Rd.
Adams
TO FORT ERIE
0
1/4 mile
0
400 meters
Casino Niagara 16
Clifton Hill 14
Floral Clock 2
Journey Behind the Falls 7
Konica Minolta Tower Centre 10
Lundy's Lane Historical Museum 12
Maid of the Mist boats 6
Marineland 9
Niagara Falls IMAX Theatre/The Daredevil Adventure Gallery 11
Niagara Glen 3
Niagara Parks Botanical Gardens and School of Horticulture 1
Niagara Parks Greenhouse 8
Skylon Tower 13
Whirlpool Aero Car 4
White Water Walk 5
World Wrestling Entertainment Retail Store 15

to marvel at a premier natural wonder; Niagara Falls, on the border of the United States and Canada, is one of the most famous tourist attractions in the world, and one of the most awe-inspiring.

The falls are actually three cataracts: the American and Bridal Veil Falls in New York State, and the Horseshoe Falls in Ontario. In terms of sheer volume of water—more than 700,000 gallons per second in summer—Niagara is unsurpassed in North America.

On the American side, you can park in the lot on Goat Island near the American Falls and walk along the path beside the Niagara River, which becomes more and more turbulent as it approaches the big drop-off of just over 200 feet.

After experiencing the falls from the U.S. side, you can walk or drive across Rainbow Bridge to the Canadian side, where you can get a far view of the American Falls and a close-up of the Horseshoe Falls. You can also park your car for the day in any of several lots on the Canadian side, and hop onto one of the People Mover buses, which run continuously to all the sights along the river. If you want to get close to the foot of the falls, the *Maid of the Mist* boat takes you close enough to get soaked in the spray.

The amusement parks and tacky souvenir shops that surround the falls attest to the area's history as a major tourist attraction. Most of the gaudiness is contained on Clifton Hill, Niagara Falls's toned-down Times Square. Despite these garish efforts to attract visitors, the landscaped grounds around the falls are lovely and the beauty of the falls remains untouched.

Niagara Falls Tourism (*5515 Stanley Ave., main center 905/356–6061 or 800/563–2557 www.discoverniagara.com*) can help plan your trip and distributes information at its main center. Phone lines are open from 8 to 6 daily.

★ If you're here in winter, the **Winter Festival of Lights** (*www.wfol.com*) is a real stunner. Seventy trees are illuminated with 34,000 lights in the parklands near the Rainbow Bridge. The falls are illuminated nightly from 5 to 11 from late November to mid-January.

The **Niagara Parks Botanical Gardens and School of Horticulture** has been graduating professional gardeners since 1936. The art of horticulture is celebrated by its students with 100 acres of immaculately maintained gardens. Within the Botanical Gardens is the **Niagara Parks Butterfly Conservatory** (*905/356–8119 C$10*), housing one of North America's largest collections of free-flying butterflies—at least 2,000 are protected in a climate-controlled, rain-forest–like conservatory. It's open year-round and houses 50 species from around the world, each with its own colorful markings. *2405 N. Niagara Pkwy. 905/356–8119 or 877/642–7275 www.niagaraparks.com Free Daily 9–6.*

A short distance (downriver) on the Niagara Parkway from the Botanical Gardens and School of Horticulture is a **floral clock,** one of the world's largest, comprising 20,000 small plants. Its "living" face is planted in a different design twice every season.

There are trails maintained by the National Parks Commission (NPC) in the **Niagara Glen** (*www.niagaraparks.com/nature/niagaraglen.php*). A bicycle trail that parallels the Niagara Parkway from Fort Erie to Niagara-on-the-Lake winds between beautiful homes on one side and the river, with its abundant bird life, on the other. The terrain can be steep and rugged, so be sure to pack proper footwear.

4 ★ The **Whirlpool Aero Car,** in operation since 1916, is a cable car that crosses the Whirlpool Basin in the Niagara Gorge. This trip is not for the fainthearted, but there's no better way to get an aerial view of the gorge, the whirlpool, the rapids, and the hydroelectric plants. *Niagara Pkwy., 4½ km (3 mi) north of falls 905/371–0254 or 877/642–7275 www.niagaraparks.com C$10 Mid-June–early Sept., weekdays 10–5, weekends 9–5.*

5 The **White Water Walk** involves taking an elevator to the bottom of the Niagara Gorge, the narrow valley created by the Niagara Falls and River, where you can walk on a boardwalk beside the torrent of the Niagara River. The gorge is rimmed by sheer cliffs as it enters the giant whirlpool. *Niagara Pkwy., 3 km (2 mi) north of falls 905/371–0254 or 877/642–7275 www.niagaraparks.com C$7.50 Mid-Apr.–Oct., daily 9–5.*

6 Fodor'sChoice ★ **Maid of the Mist boats** have been operating since 1846, when they were wooden-hulled, coal-fired steamboats. Today boats tow fun-loving passengers on 30-minute journeys to the foot of the falls, where the spray is so heavy that raincoats must be distributed. From the observation areas along the falls, you can see those boarding the boats in their yellow slickers. *Tickets and entrance at foot of Clifton Hill 905/358–0311 www.maidofthemist.com C$13 May–mid-Oct., daily 9:45–4:45. Call for departure times.*

7 ★ At **Journey Behind the Falls** your admission ticket includes use of rubber boots and a hooded rain slicker. An elevator takes you to an observation deck that provides a fish's-eye view of the Canadian Horseshoe Falls and the Niagara River. From there a walk through three tunnels cut into the rock takes you behind the wall of crashing water. *Tours begin at Table Rock House, Queen Victoria Park 905/371–0254 or 877/642–7275 niagaraparks.com C$10 Mid-June–early Sept., daily 9 AM–11 PM; early Sept.–mid-June, daily 9–5.*

8 **Niagara Parks Greenhouse** houses thousands of living plants, sculpted into life-size creatures, including moose, bears, and geese in flight. *Niagara Pkwy., ½ km (¼ mi) south of the Horseshoe Falls 905/371–0254 or 877/642–7275 www.niagaraparks.com Free Mid-May–Sept., daily 9:30–dusk.*

9 **Marineland,** a theme park with a marine show, wildlife displays, and rides, is 1½ km (1 mi) south of the falls. The daily marine shows includes performing killer whales, dolphins, harbor seals, and sea lions. Three separate aquariums house sharks, an ocean reef, and

freshwater fish from around the world. Children can pet and feed members of a herd of 500 deer and get nose-to-nose with North American freshwater fish. Among the many rides is Dragon Mountain, the world's largest steel roller coaster. Marineland is signposted from Niagara Parkway or reached from the Queen Elizabeth Way by exiting at McLeod Road (Exit 27). *✉8375 Stanley Ave. ☎905/356–9565 🌐www.marinelandcanada.com 🎟C$33.95 ⏲Late June–early Oct., daily 9–6.*

WORD OF MOUTH

"The first time I went to [Niagara Falls], I was fairly certain that I wouldn't enjoy it (I don't care for Las Vegas). I was there only one night and two days. By the second day, I realized that I actually enjoyed it a lot—once I left my 'attitude' out of the equation."
—toedtoes

⑩ **Konica Minolta Tower Centre,** 525 feet above the base of the falls, affords panoramic views of the Horseshoe Falls and the area. *✉6732 Fallsview Blvd. ☎905/356–1501 or 800/461–2492 🌐www.infoniagara.com 🎟C$6.95 ⏲9 AM until lights go off at falls, as late as midnight in summer.*

⑪ **Niagara Falls IMAX Theatre/The Daredevil Adventure Gallery.** You can see the falls up close and travel back in time for a glimpse of its 12,000-year-old history with *Niagara: Miracles, Myths and Magic,* on the six-story IMAX screen. The Daredevil Adventure Gallery chronicles the expeditions of those who have tackled the falls. *✉6170 Fallsview Blvd. ☎905/374–4629 🌐www.imaxniagara.com 🎟C$12 ⏲Daily 9–9; movies run every hr on hr.*

8

⑫ ★ On the site of one of the fiercest battles in the War of 1812 is **Lundy's Lane Historical Museum,** in a limestone building dating to 1874. There are displays of the lives of settlers during the war period, native artifacts, and military attire. *✉5810 Ferry St. ☎905/358–5082 🌐www.lundyslanemuseum.com 🎟C$2 ⏲May–Nov., daily 9–4; Dec.–Apr., weekdays noon–4.*

⑬ ★ Rising 775 feet above the falls, **Skylon Tower** offers the best view of the great Niagara Gorge and the entire city. The indoor-outdoor observation deck has visibility up to 130 km (80 mi) on a clear day. Amusements for children plus a revolving dining room are other reasons to visit. The lower level has a gaming arcade, and there's a 3-D theater within the compound. *✉5200 Robinson St. ☎905/356–2651 or 800/814–9577 🌐www.skylon.com 🎟C$10.50 ⏲Mid-June–early Sept., daily 8 AM–midnight; early Sept.–mid June, daily 10–10.*

⑭ **Clifton Hill** is the most crassly commercial district of Niagara Falls. Sometimes referred to as "Museum Alley," this area includes more wax museums than one usually sees in a lifetime—and a House of Frankenstein Burger King. Attractions are typically open late (11 PM), with admission ranging from C$7 to C$13. They include the **Guinness Museum of World Records** (*☎905/356–2299 🌐www.guinnessniagarafalls.com*); **Ripley's Believe It or Not Museum** and **Ripley's Moving Theatre** (*☎905/356–2261 🌐www.ripleysniagara.com*), a 3-D movie, where you actually move with the picture (seats move in eight directions); and **Movieland Wax Museum** (☎*905/358–3676* 🌐*www.cliftonhill.com/niagara_falls_attractions/movieland_wax_museum*), with such lifelike characters as Indiana Jones and Snow White. A six-story-high chocolate bar, at the base of Clifton Hill, marks the entrance to the **Hershey's World of Chocolate** (✉*5685 Falls Ave.* ☎*800/468–1714* 🌐*www.cliftonhill.com*). Inside are 7,000 square feet of milk shakes, fudge, truffles, cookbooks, and those trademark Kisses. Lots of free samples are doled out and fudge-making demonstrations are held hourly.

⓯ The world's only **World Wrestling Entertainment Retail Store** is filled to its rafters with official WWE clothing, coffee mugs, and memorabilia. You can also take the plunge on the *Pile Driver* (open mid-May through September), a ride that takes you up 220 feet for a seconds-long stomach-dropping plummet. ✉*Clifton Hill and Falls Ave.* ☎*905/354–7526 or 800/263–7135* 🌐*www.wwe.com* *Free, Pile Driver C$10* *Sept.–June, daily 11–11; July and Aug., daily 11 AM–1 AM.*

⓰ **Casino Niagara,** in a setting reminiscent of the 1920s, has slot machines, video poker machines, and gambling tables, where games such as blackjack, roulette, and baccarat are played. Within the casino are several lounges and all-you-can-eat buffet restaurants. Valet parking and shuttle service are available. ✉*5705 Falls Ave.* ☎*905/374–3598 or 888/946–3255* 🌐*www.casinoniagara.com* *Daily 24 hrs.*

Niagara Fallsview Casino Resort, Canada's largest privately funded commercial development, crowns the city's skyline overlooking the Niagara Parks with picture-perfect views of both falls. Within the C$1 billion, 30-story complex is Canada's only casino wedding chapel, a glitzy theater, spa, shops, and, for the gaming enthusiasts, 150 gaming tables, 3,000 slot machines, and plenty of restaurants. ✉*6380 Fallsview Blvd.* ☎*888/325–5788* 🌐*www.fallsviewcasinoresort.com* *Daily 24 hrs.*

WHERE TO STAY & EAT

The walk from most hotels down to the falls is a steep one. You might want to take a taxi back up, or hop aboard the Falls Incline Railway, which operates between Portage Street (at the rear of the **Niagara Fallsview Casino Resort**) and the Niagara Parkway (across from the Canadian Falls). The trip takes about one minute and costs C$3.

$$$$ ✕ **Skylon Tower.** The view from the Revolving Dining Room, perched at 775 feet overlooking the Horseshoe Falls, is breathtaking, and the food is good, too. Traditionally prepared rack of lamb, baked salmon, steak, and chicken make up the list of entrées. The crowd tends toward the eclectic, with people in cocktail wear and casual clothes seated side-by-side. Even with a reservation, there may be a short wait. An "early bird" (4:30 to 6:30) prix-fixe menu is C$35; otherwise, plan on spending at least C$40 per person to dine in the tower. ✉*5200 Robinson St.* ☎*905/356–2651 or 800/814–9577* 🌐*www.skylon.com* *Reservations essential* *AE, DC, MC, V.*

$$$$ ✕ **Table Rock.** The view's the thing here. Table Rock, run by Niagara Parks, serves standard U.S.–Canadian fare, but the setting is extraordinary—you sit perched at the edge of the Horseshoe Falls. The dining

room, in the rear of a two-story souvenir shop, has familiar food, such as Caesar salads and prime rib. Window seats can't be reserved. ✉ *6650 Niagara Pkwy., just above Journey Behind the Falls* ☎ *905/354–3631* 🌐 *www.niagaraparks.com* ▭ *AE, DC, MC, V.*

$$$–$$$$ ★ ✕ **21 Club.** Whether you come to the casino for baccarat or the slots, dining at this elegant restaurant is no gamble. The menu has high-end steak-house fare and some Italian dishes. The insulated dining room is away from the crowds and is a quiet setting in which to appreciate shrimp cocktail or lobster *lasagnetta,* fresh pasta wrapped around sautéed lobster, shallots, and basil. You'd have to search far to find a more delectably grilled 24-ounce Canadian porterhouse steak. ✉ *Casino Niagara, 5705 Falls Ave.* ☎ *905/374–3598* ▭ *AE, DC, MC, V.*

$$$–$$$$ ✕ **Victoria Park.** Inside this former refectory building, which faces the falls, are two restaurants run by Niagara Parks. The upstairs houses the newly opened Edgewaters Tap and Grill, serving burgers and steaks, whereas in the lower level, the Riverview Market Eatery serves fast food from fries to hot dogs. ✉ *River Rd. and Murray St.* ☎ *905/356–2217 or 877/642–7275* ▭ *AE, MC, V.*

$$$ ✕ **Casa d'Oro.** It looks a little like a Disney version of a Venetian castle, but the ornate wall sconces, fireplaces, wine casks, and huge faux-marble and bronze sculptures are somehow not out of place in Niagara Falls. Run by the Roberto family for 30 years, the Italian restaurant draws diners with its gigantic portions of prime rib, T-bones, and the hefty Lasagna Roberto. After dinner, you can cross a painted bridge that spans a water-filled moat to the Rialto nightclub's raised dance floor. ✉ *5875 Victoria Ave.* ☎ *905/356–5646* 🌐 *www.thecasadoro.com* ▭ *AE, D, DC, MC, V.*

$$$ ✕ **Casa Mia.** All the pasta is kitchen-made at this lovely off-the-tourist-track Italian villa, 10 minutes from the falls. Fresh-grated beets impart a shocking pink color to the gnocchi, divine with Gorgonzola sauce. If you've ever wondered what fresh cannelloni is like, try these pasta pancakes, filled with veal and spinach. The veal chop is pan-seared with sage and truffle oil. Heart-smart menu selections are indicated, and even desserts, particularly the *cassata* (a light cake with homemade-ice-cream terrine), are not overly heavy. Weekends bring live music to the piano lounge. ✉ *3518 Portage Rd.* ☎ *905/356–5410* 🌐 *www.casamiaristorante.com* ▭ *AE, MC, V.*

$$ ✕ **Capri.** The family-owned restaurant serves huge, Italian-style platters such as linguine with chicken cacciatore. The three dining rooms, decorated in dark-wood paneling, draw families daily because of the half-dozen specially priced children's dishes and a something-for-everyone menu. ✉ *5438 Ferry St. (Hwy. 20), about 1 km (½ mi) from falls* ☎ *905/354–7519* ▭ *AE, DC, MC, V.*

$–$$ ✕ **Yukiguni.** Reasonable lunch specials, which include miso soup, fresh salad, and such entrées as juicy pepper-flavored chicken skewers, make this a popular spot. Other menu options include tempura soba, thin buckwheat noodles that come with shrimp and vegetable tempura; and steamed smoked eel, served on rice. Chicken and salmon teriyaki leave an aromatic trail as they are carried aloft on sizzling iron plates. ✉ *5980 Fallsview Blvd.* ☎ *905/354–4440* ▭ *AE, DC, MC, V.*

8

$$$$ **Brock Plaza Hotel.** Since its opening in the 1920s, this grande dame of Niagara hotels has hosted royalty, prime ministers, and Hollywood stars. Now completely renovated but with glamorous details intact, the imposing, stone-walled Brock is part of the Casino Niagara complex, with indoor access to gaming facilities, the Hard Rock Cafe, and the Rainbow Grill Restaurant overlooking the falls. White wainscoting and brass fixtures blend with expansive windows that offer views of the falls from nearly every room. *✉5685 Falls Ave., L2E 6W7 ☎905/374–4444 or 800/263–7135 🌐www.niagarafallshotels.com ⇨234 rooms ♿In-hotel: restaurant, bar, pool ▭AE, D, DC, MC, V.*

$$$–$$$$ **Renaissance Fallsview Hotel.** Many rooms overlook the falls at this luxuriously appointed hotel, about ½ km (¼ mi) from the mighty cataracts. The elegant rooms have floor-to-ceiling mirrors and wingback chairs. The Jacuzzi rooms, where bath and bed are separated only by cherry-red drapes, can be romantic. In Mulberry's Dining Room ($–$$), you can sample the artistry of executive chef Michael Heeb. There are recreational facilities on the premises and golf and fishing nearby. *✉6455 Fallsview Blvd., L2G 3V9 ☎905/357–5200 or 800/363–3255 🌐www.renaissancefallsview.com ⇨234 rooms ♿In-hotel: 2 restaurants, bar, pool, gym ▭AE, D, DC, MC, V.*

$$$ **Niagara Fallsview Casino Resort.** The C$1 billion price tag of this casino-resort means there are touches of luxury everywhere: natural light streams through glass domes and floor-to-ceiling windows, chandeliers hang in grand hallways, and frescoes lend an aristocratic feel. All bright and colorful rooms in this 30-story hotel tower overlook the Canadian or American Falls. VIP rooms have extra-large whirlpool tubs. Performers such as Tony Bennett, Cheap Trick, and Smokey Robinson have headlined shows in the performing-arts center. The lavish buffet is excellent and reasonable (C$20 for dinner). *✉6380 Fallsview Blvd., L2G 7X5 ☎905/358–3255 or 888/946–3255 🌐www.fallsviewcasinoresort.com ⇨283 rooms, 85 suites ♿In-room: safe, kitchen (some). In-hotel: 3 restaurants, pool, gym, spa, concierge, laundry service, executive floor, public Internet, no-smoking rooms ▭AE, MC, V.*

$$$ **Quality Inn Clifton Hill.** Very near the falls and not far from a golf course, this chain-run inn is on nicely landscaped grounds, which can be viewed from a pleasant patio. The hotel's basic rooms are clean and comfortable; some suites have hot tubs. The hotel has an eye toward families, with two dragon waterslides, a playground, and rooms with three beds. *✉4946 Clifton Hill, Box 60, L2E 6S8 ☎905/358–3601 or 800/263–7137 🌐www.qualityniagara.com ⇨263 rooms ♿In-hotel: restaurant, bar, pools ▭AE, D, MC, V.*

$$$ ★ **Sheraton Fallsview Hotel and Conference Centre.** Most of the oversize guest rooms and suites in this upscale, high-rise hotel have breathtaking views of the falls, and even basic family suites have wide floor-to-ceiling window bays that overlook the cascades. Loft Suites are spacious, and the Whirlpool Rooms have open whirlpool baths that look out to the bedroom and the falls beyond. The fine dining room offers a C$35 weekend buffet from 5 to 9 PM; à la carte diners can choose from a French menu that might include tournedos with a three-peppercorn

sauce. There's a two-night minimum stay on weekends. ✉*6755 Fallsview Blvd., L2G 3W7* ☎*905/374–1077 or 800/618–9059* 🌐*www.fallsview.com* *295 rooms* *In-hotel: 3 restaurants, bar, pool, spa* ▭*AE, D, DC, MC, V.*

$ **Lincoln Motor Inn.** Don't want much fuss? A pleasant landscaped courtyard gives this motor inn, within walking distance of the falls, an intimate feeling, but otherwise accommodations are plain-Jane. Connecting family suites sleep up to a dozen. The restaurant serves breakfast only. A golf course is nearby. ✉*6417 Main St., L2G 5Y3* ☎*905/356–1748 or 800/263–2575* 🌐*www.LincolnMotorInn.com* *57 rooms* *In-hotel: restaurant, pool* ▭*AE, MC, V.*

$ **Villager Candlelight Inn.** The two-story motel offers good, basic accommodations. Some rooms have whirlpool tubs while others have heart-shape tubs; the two efficiency suites have small kitchens. ✉*7600 Lundy's La., L2H 1H1* ☎*800/572–0308* 🌐*www.candlelightniagara.com* *50 rooms* *In-hotel: restaurant, pool* ▭*AE, DC, MC, V.*

GUIDED TOURS

Double Deck Tours (✉*3957 Bossert Rd.* ☎*905/374–7423* 🌐*www.doubledecktours.com*) operates 4½- to 5-hour tours in double-decker English buses. Tours operate daily from mid-May through October and include most of the major sights of Niagara Falls. The C$56.25 fare includes admission to Journey Behind the Falls, *Maid of the Mist,* and a trip in the Whirlpool Aerocar. Tours depart from the *Maid of the Mist* building at the foot of Clifton Hill.

From late April to mid-October, Niagara Parks operates a **People Mover System** (☎*905/357–9340*) in which air-conditioned buses travel on a loop route between its public parking lot above the falls at Rapids View Terminal (well marked) and the Whirlpool Aerocar parking lot about 8 km (5 mi) downriver. A day pass, which is available at any booth on the system for C$7.50 and includes parking and a People Mover ticket for everyone in the car, allows you to get on and off as many times as you wish at the well-marked stops along the route.

★ **Niagara Helicopters Ltd.** (✉*3731 Victoria Ave.* ☎*905/357–5672 or 800/281–8034* 🌐*www.niagarahelicopters.com* ▭*AE, MC, V*) takes you on a nine-minute flight over the giant whirlpool, up the Niagara Gorge, and past the American Falls, then banks around the curve of the Horseshoe Falls. Daily trips run year-round (weather permitting). It costs C$105 per person; family rates are available. Reservations are not necessary except for large groups.

Wet-and-wild **Whirlpool Jet Boat Tours** (✉*61 Melville St., Niagara-on-the-Lake* ☎*905/468–4800 or 888/438–4444* 🌐*www.whirlpooljet.com*) veer around and hurdle white-water rapids on a one-hour thrill ride that follows Niagara canyons up to the wall of rolling waters, just below the falls. Children under six are not permitted. The tour departs from Niagara-on-the-Lake and Queenston, Canada, and Lewiston, New York. Tours run from May through October, daily, and cost C$54, although discounts are available when you book online.

BIKING & HIKING

The **Niagara Parks Commission** (☎*905/371–0254 or 877/642–7275* 🌐*www.niagaraparks.com*) maintains 56 km (30 mi) of **bicycle trails** along the Niagara River between Fort Erie and Niagara-on-the-Lake. It also has information on nearby hiking trails, local parks, and the Niagara Gorge.

★ The 800-km (496-mi) **Bruce Trail** (✉*Box 857, L8N 3N9* ☎*905/529–6821 or 800/665–4453* 🌐*www.brucetrail.org*) stretches northwest along the Niagara Escarpment from the orchards of the Niagara Peninsula to the craggy cliffs and bluffs at Tobermory, at the end of the Bruce Peninsula. The Escarpment is a UNESCO World Biosphere Reserve (one of 12 in Canada). You can access the hiking trail at just about any point along the route, so your hike can be any length you wish. **Hike Ontario** (☎*416/426–7362* 🌐*www.hikeontario.com*) has information and maps about hikes in the province.

NIAGARA WINE REGION

Niagara Pkwy. between Niagara Falls and Niagara-on-the-Lake and on Hwy. 55.

Some of the Niagara Peninsula's 55 wineries are on the Niagara Parkway between Niagara Falls and Niagara-on-the-Lake, or on Highway 55 from the Queen Elizabeth Way. As the quality of Ontario wines continues to improve and excel in international competitions, winemakers here have caught the attention of a growing number of wine lovers. The majority of area wineries have tastings and tours, in addition to selling their products on-site; call ahead for exact times.

★ The **Niagara Grape & Wine Festival** (☎*905/688–0212* 🌐*www.grapeandwine.com*) celebrates its 55th anniversary in 2006 and oversees several annual festivals and events that honor Niagara's winemaking history. Wine was first produced in the region in 1869 and quality estate wineries started business in 1972. In mid-January the Niagara wine industry celebrates its treasured liquid libation with the **Niagara Ice Wine Festival,** when thousands of visitors take the 10-day Wine Route with a Festival Ice Wine Touring Passport for access to tours, tastings, and winery events. The wine-related event with the biggest buzz is held in late September: the **Niagara Wine Festival** honors the annual grape harvest and is one of Canada's largest annual celebrations, presenting over 100 wine and culinary events, and attracting over 500,000 people to the host city of St. Catharines and the adjoining Niagara Region. Taking place in mid-June, the **Niagara New Vintage Festival** celebrates Ontario's first taste of the previous year's harvest with wine galas. A Festival Touring Pass offers tours, generous samplings, and special events at 35 participating wineries across the Niagara Region.

Fodor's Choice ★ The **Wine Route,** so named for the wineries it passes, takes you on a well-marked strip of highway between Hamilton and Niagara Falls, onto some secondary roads passing the region's attractive scenery, and through postcard-perfect small towns and villages.

From Toronto, take the QEW west and follow the signs for Niagara Falls until just past Hamilton. Exit the QEW at Fifty Road and follow it south, turning east onto Highway 8, which becomes Regional Road 81. This route takes you past wineries, large and small, through the towns of Grimsby, Beamsville, and the appropriately named town of Vineland, as it climbs the Niagara Escarpment past woods and vineyards to the hamlet of Jordan (in addition to the wineries here, there are antiques and specialty shops housed in historic buildings). East of Jordan, the Wine Route turns south on 5th Street and then goes east on 8th Avenue to join Regional Road 89, which goes through the city of St. Catharines before swinging north again on Four Mile Creek toward Niagara-on-the-Lake. There are plenty of wineries to visit here.

Several wineries, including Peller Estates Winery, Hillebrand Estates Winery, and Strewn Winery, have full-service upscale restaurants. Some establishments have patio wine bars and picnic facilities. For a map including locations of wineries and details of summer events, contact the **Wine Council of Ontario** (✉ *110 Hanover Dr., Suite B205, St. Catharines L2W 1A4* ☎ *905/684–8070* 🌐 *www.wineroute.com*).

With more than 300 wine awards, **Hillebrand Estates Winery** is a must-see winery that produces many excellent varieties—small batches of pinot noir, chardonnay, ice wine, and more. After the half-hour cellar and vineyard tour for C$5 are two complimentary tastings of this vintner's latest achievements. The café serves terrific meals ($$$–$$$$). Between May and October you can attend four different themed seminars offered daily (C$8–C$10 per seminar). Daily twilight tours are offered July through September. ✉ *1249 Niagara Stone Rd., Niagara-on-the-Lake L0S 1J0* ☎ *905/468–7123 or 800/582–8412* 🌐 *www.hillebrand.com* ⏲ *Oct.–May, daily 10–7; June–Sept., daily 10–9. Tours every hr on hr until 8* PM.

The visitor center of **Inniskillin Wine** is housed in a restored 1920s barn, among acres of lush vineyards. This large winery specializes in producing premium Vintners Quality Alliance (VQA) wines, including top-notch pinot noir, chardonnay, and cabernet blanc. Be sure to go on the free guided tour, which includes a free tasting of one white variety and one red variety. Additional samplings cost up to C$4. ✉ *Line 3 at Niagara Pkwy., Niagara-on-the-Lake L0S 1J0* ☎ *905/468–2187 or 888/466–4754* 🌐 *www.inniskillin.com* ⏲ *May–Oct., daily 10–6, tasting bar 11–5:30; Nov.–Apr., daily 10–5, tasting bar 11–4:30. Tours May–Oct., daily at 10:30 and 2:30; Nov.–Apr., weekends at 10:30 and 2:30.*

Jackson-Triggs Niagara Estate Winery is an ultramodern facility that blends state-of-the-art winemaking technology with age-old, handcrafted enological savvy. In 2004 the winery received the Best Canadian Winery award at the Vinitaly International Wine competition in Italy, and more accolades at the San Francisco International Wine Competition, including a double gold award for its Grand Reserve Riesling ice wine. Its premium VQA wines can be sipped in the tasting gallery (three complimentary tastings on the winery tour), and purchased in the retail boutique. ✉2145 *Niagara Stone Rd., Niagara-on-the-Lake L0S 1J0* ☎*905/468–4637 or 866/589–4637* 🌐*www.jacksontriggswinery.com* ⏲*May–Oct., daily 10:30–6:30; Nov.–Apr., daily 10:30–5:30. Tours daily 10:30–5:30.*

An ice-wine producer with more than 220 medals in domestic and international competitions, **Pillitteri Estates Winery** is also famous for its wine master, Sue-Ann Staff, who was named Ontario's Winemaker of the Year (2002)—the first woman so honored. The winery's ice wine is unique in that its grapes are harvested far later in winter than those of most other producers. When pressed, these handpicked, frozen grapes yield a juice with an intense concentration of sugars, acids, flavors, and aromas. Tours include two complimentary tastings. ✉*1696 Niagara Stone Rd., Niagara-on-the-Lake L0S 1J0* ☎*905/468–3147* 🌐*www.pillitteri.com* ⏲*May 15–Oct. 15, daily 10–8; Oct. 16–May 14, daily 10–6. Tours daily at noon and 2.*

★ Known as one of Ontario's most beautiful wineries, the 75-acre **Vineland Estates Winery** dates to 1845, when it was a Mennonite homestead. The original buildings have been transformed into the visitor center and production complex. Tours are C$6 and include three free tastings; additional samplings of Vineland's exquisite dry and semidry Rieslings are C$0.50 each. The excellent Italian Vineland Estates Winery Restaurant ($$$–$$$$) serves lunch and dinner, and the patio grill is open July through September. There's also a guesthouse and a one-bedroom B&B on the property. ✉*3620 Moyer Rd., Vineland L0R 2C0* ☎*905/562–7088 or 888/846–3526* 🌐*www.vineland.com* ⏲*June–Oct., daily 10–6; Nov.–May, daily 10–5. Public tours (C$6) June–Oct., daily at 11 and 3; Nov.–May, weekends at 3. Private tours by request.*

WHERE TO STAY & EAT

$$$$ Fodor's Choice ★ ✕ **Vineland Estates Winery Restaurant.** Exquisite Italian food and venerable wines are served by an enthusiastic staff on the wine deck or in the glassed-in restaurant, with a panoramic view of the vineyard and lake. The fresh lemon poppy-seed baguette is served warm, and the pasta is homemade (try the inch-thick pappardelle noodles tossed with Niagara hazelnuts, arugula, cremini mushrooms, and Montasio cheese). Feeling carnivorous? The chef pan-roasts local venison and partners it with parsnip-potato puree, leeks, and blueberry jus. Desserts are a happy marriage of local fruits and an imaginative pastry chef. ✉*3620 Moyer Rd., Vineland* ☎*905/562–7088 or 888/846–3526* 🌐*www.vineland.com* ▭*AE, D, MC, V* ⏲*Closed Mon. and Tues. Nov.–May.*

$$$$ Fodor's Choice ★ 🏨 **Inn on the Twenty.** The inn is part of Leonard Pennachetti's Cave Spring Cellars winery in the village of Jordan, a 30-minute drive from Niagara-on-the-Lake. Rooms have elegant 1920s mahogany headboards, whirlpool baths, and fireplaces. The sophisticated restaurant On the Twenty has top-notch cuisine that emphasizes regional specialties. Dine on signature Shorthills trout in Riesling-rhubarb butter, or partridge in hazelnut-chardonnay sauce. You can tour and sample the wines of Cave Spring Cellars across the street. The restaurant is closed some days in January, so call ahead. ✉*3845 Main St., Jordan, L0R 1S0* ☎*905/562–5336, 905/562–7313 restaurant, 800/701–8074*

⊕www.innonthetwenty.com ⇐29 rooms ♨In-room: refrigerator (some), dial-up. In-hotel: restaurant, no-smoking rooms ▭AE, DC, MC, V 🍴CP.

BICYCLE TOURS

Biking through the Niagara Region in any direction brings a touch of adventure as well as the opportunity to linger a while longer at each stop along the Wine Route. Remember to bring along sunscreen and sunglasses, and always dress for the season. Stiff-sole running shoes for hard pedaling and occasional hiking over rough terrain are recommended.

Niagara Wine Tours International (*⊠92 Picton St., Niagara-on-the-Lake L0S 1J0 ☎905/468–1300 or 800/680-7006 ⊕www.niagaraworldwinetours.com*) leads several daylong, afternoon, and weekend guided bike tours along the Wine Route. A leisurely weekend package with two nights' stay in a local inn includes lunch and four wineries for C$390 per person.

Steve Bauer Bike Tours (*⊠4979 King St., Box 342, Beamsville L0R1B0 ☎905/563–8687 📠905/563–9697 ⊕www.stevebauer.com*) specializes in unique one- or multiday bike tours. Niagara Getaway trips are organized from May through September; the all-inclusive two-night package covers accommodations, full breakfast, lunch, dinner, wine-tasting stops, spa treatments at a local resort, and fruits and snacks en route, and costs C$749. All tours are fully guided with van support.

NIAGARA-ON-THE-LAKE

15 km (9 mi) north of (downriver from) Niagara Falls via the Niagara Pkwy. and Hwy. 55.

Since 1962 Niagara-on-the-Lake has been considered the southern outpost of fine summer theater in Ontario because of its acclaimed Shaw Festival. But it offers far more than Stratford, its older theatrical sister to the west: as one of the country's prettiest and best-preserved Victorian towns, Niagara-on-the-Lake has architectural sights, shops, flower-lined streets in summer, and quality theater nearly year-round. The town of 14,000 is worth a visit at any time of the year for its inns, restaurants, and proximity to the wineries, but the most compelling time to visit is from April through November, during the Shaw Festival.

Niagara-on-the-Lake remained a sleepy town until 1962, when local lawyer Brian Doherty organized eight weekend performances of two George Bernard Shaw plays, *Don Juan in Hell* and *Candida*. The next year he helped found the festival, whose mission is to perform the works of Shaw and his contemporaries.

This is a small town that can easily be explored on foot.

★ **Queen Street** is the core of the commercial portion; walking east along that single street, with Lake Ontario to your north, you get a glimpse of the town's architectural history. At No. 209 is the handsome Charles

Inn, built around 1832 for a member of Parliament, with later additions at the end of the 19th century. No. 187 dates from 1822, with later Greek Revival improvements. No. 165 is an 1820 beauty and No. 157 was built in 1823. McClelland's, a store at No. 106, has been in business in Niagara-on-the-Lake since the War of 1812. The huge "T" sign means "provisioner."

❶ **Grace United Church,** built in 1852, is a collage of architectural styles, including Italianate and Norman. Stained-glass windows dedicated to the memory of Canadians killed in World War I were installed in the 1920s. The church was commissioned by a congregation of "Free Kirk" Presbyterians but was later sold to Methodists and now serves a congregation of the United Church (a merger of Presbyterians, Methodists, and Congregationalists). ✉ *222 Victoria St.* ☎ *905/468–4044.*

❷ The **Niagara Apothecary** was built in 1866 and restored in 1971. The museum has exquisite walnut and butternut fixtures, crystal pieces, and a rare collection of apothecary glasses. ✉ *5 Queen St.* ☎ *905/468–3845* 🎟 *Free* ⏲ *Mid-May–early Sept., daily noon–6.*

❸ The **Niagara Historical Society & Museum,** one of the oldest (established 1895) museums of its kind in Ontario, has an extensive collection relating to the often colorful history of the Niagara Peninsula from earliest times through the 19th century. The museum has a gift shop and offers guided tours of the town. ✉*43 Castlereagh St.* ☎*905/468–3912* 🌐*www.niagarahistorical.museum/home.html* 🎟*C$5* 🕑*May–Oct., daily 10–5:30; Nov.–Apr., daily 1–5.*

WORD OF MOUTH

"Niagara-on-the-Lake is special in its own way. It is like stepping back in history." —prinret

4 Fodor's Choice ★ On a wide stretch of parkland south of town sits **Fort George National Historic Park.** The fort was built in the 1790s but was lost to the Yankees during the War of 1812. It was recaptured after the burning of the town in 1813, and largely survived the war, only to fall into ruins by the 1830s. It was reconstructed a century later, and you can explore the officers' quarters, the barracks rooms of the common soldiers, the kitchen, and more. The town is staffed by people in period uniform who conduct tours and reenact 19th-century infantry and artillery drills. ✉*Queens Parade, Niagara Pkwy.* ☎*905/468–4257* 🌐*www.niagara.com/~parkscan* 🎟*C$8* 🕑*Apr.–Oct., daily 10–5.*

GUIDED TOURS

Queens Royal Tours (✉*128 Anne St., Box 42* ☎*905/468–1008* 🌐*www.queensroyal.com*) conducts year-round tours in and around Niagara-on-the-Lake. Half-hour horse-and-carriage rides are C$50, and one-hour rides are C$90. Wine tours led from a vintage car cost C$50 per person for three wineries, tasting included.

WHERE TO STAY & EAT

The area has some lovely restaurants and inns, both within town and outside it; a number of wineries here have restaurants and inns as well. Especially in summer, make reservations whenever possible.

$$$$ ✕**Buttery Theatre Restaurant.** At Margaret Niemann's authentic British pub–café, the wood-beam ceiling, beaten copper tabletops, and china and pewter all bear the patina of age. Lively Tudor-style banquets and feasts are held every Friday and Saturday (prix fixe C$55), and the tavern menu includes good pâtés and Cornish pasties (beef-filled pastry). The chef bakes chicken with fresh lemons and roasts leg of lamb. The roast duckling on the weekday prix-fixe menu (C$26) is an excellent choice. Afternoon tea is served daily from 2 to 5. ✉*19 Queen St.* ☎*905/468–2564* 🌐*www.thebutteryrestaurant.com* 💳*AE, MC, V.*

$$$$ ★ ✕**Hillebrand Vineyard Café.** After a complimentary winery tour and tasting, you can settle down to a superb meal. Culinary masterpieces include goat cheese truffles on grilled vegetables, and wild mushroom soufflé with foie-gras toast. The tossed salad is a beautiful relationship between organic greens, sun-dried blueberries, and roasted crisp garlic. The pastry chef composes incredible desserts: a bittersweet chocolate cup is filled with vanilla ice cream and topped with candied hazelnuts. ✉*1249 Niagara Stone Rd., at Hwy. 55* ☎*905/468–7123 or 800/582–8412* 🌐*www.hillebrand.com* 💳*AE, D, MC, V.*

$$$$ **Ristorante Giardino.** Italian marble combines with stainless steel and rich colors to create a contemporary Italian setting on 19th-century Queen Street. Chefs recruited from Italy produce antipasti such as Parma ham served with melon, smoked salmon terrine, and marinated swordfish with herbs. There's always grilled fresh fish or oven-roasted chicken and lamb. Make time to indulge in the kitchen's classic Italian desserts and fresh Niagara fruits. The long wine list is worth a careful read. *Gate House Hotel, 142 Queen St. 905/468–3263 www.gatehouse-niagara.com AE, DC, MC, V Closed Jan. and Feb.*

$$ **Fans Court.** Delicate Cantonese cuisine is prepared in a lovely, antiques-filled restaurant in a courtyard between an art gallery and a greenhouse. Mature jade trees in urns stand at the entrance. In summer you can sit outdoors and sample such favorites as lemon chicken, black-pepper-and-garlic beef, and fried rice served in a pineapple. *135 Queen St. 905/468–4511 AE, MC, V.*

$$$$ Fodor's Choice ★ **Harbour House.** A classy nautical theme pervades this Eastern Seaboard–style boutique hotel on the Niagara River. The building's 1880s maritime look is topped off with a cedar shingle roof. Spacious rooms have cozy touches like electric fireplaces, feather-top beds, and Frette robes, as well as DVD and CD players. You can sample local preserves and homemade pastries at breakfast and attend wine and cheese tastings in the afternoon. This is a good alternative to the myriad of B&Bs in town. *85 Melville St., L0S 1J0 905/468–4683 www.harbourhousehotel.ca 29 rooms, 2 suites In-hotel: public Internet, no-smoking rooms, some pets allowed AE, MC, V BP.*

$$$$ **Oban Inn.** Take in views of Lake Ontario at this elegant country inn, which was built in 1869. Each room is distinct, embellished with antiques for a British tone; some have fireplaces. You can while away the day on the inn's broad verandas or in its beautifully manicured gardens. The newly opened Kir Restaurant features organic arctic char, game hen, and beef as well as vegetarian options using seasonal local ingredients. In the lounge you can feast on an all-day menu of traditional fish-and-chips, steak-and-ale pie, sandwiches, and appetizers. On Sunday a brunch of whole turkey, ham, and prime rib attracts the locals. *160 Front St., L0S 1J0 905/468–2165 or 866/359–6226 www.obaninn.ca 25 rooms, 1 suite In-hotel: restaurant, bar, bicycles, concierge, airport shuttle, some pets allowed AE, D, DC, MC, V.*

$$$$ ★ **Pillar and Post.** This hotel, six long blocks from the heart of town, has been a cannery, barracks, and basket factory. Most rooms have handcrafted early-American pine furniture, patchwork quilts, and such modern amenities as hair dryers. The 100 Fountain Spa has soothing body treatments. The casual Vintages Wine Bar and Lounge serves regional cuisine and wines. The Cannery & Carriages Dining Room menu is inspired by what the market has to offer, like pesto-encrusted Atlantic salmon or sea bass with summer squash. *48 John St., L0S 1J0 905/468–2123 or 888/669–5566 www.vintageinns.com 123 rooms In-hotel: 2 restaurants, bar, pools, gym, spa AE, D, DC, MC, V.*

$$$$ **Prince of Wales Hotel.** A visit from the Prince of Wales in the early
Fodor'sChoice ★ 1900s inspired the name of this venerable hostelry. Plenty has changed since then. The improved Prince of Wales has been designed in the style of an upper-crust English manor house, Victorian in flavor and complete with its own tearoom. The Escabèche restaurant serves eclectic cuisine such as arctic char fillet with spinach and artichokes in lemon-caper butter. At the Churchill Lounge, lighter and less-expensive meals such as salads and wild-mushroom risotto are served. ✉ *6 Picton St., Box 46, L0S 1J0* ☎ *905/468–3246 or 888/669–5566* 🌐 *www.vintage-inns.com* *114 rooms* *In-hotel: pool, gym* ▭ *AE, D, DC, MC, V.*

$$$$ ★ **Queen's Landing Inn.** Many rooms at this inn have knockout views of the fields of historic Fort George and the marina—ask for one when making a reservation. A smattering of antiques and canopy beds make rooms elegant; many have working fireplaces and modern whirlpool baths. Overlooking the Niagara River, the Tiara Dining Room has an outstanding regional menu, which combines Asian influences with Niagara produce in a room flattered by stained glass, floor-to-ceiling windows, and rich burgundy hues. *155 Byron St., Box 1180, L0S 1J0* ☎ *905/468–2195 or 888/669–5566* 🌐 *www.vintageinns.com* *144 rooms* *In-hotel: bar, pool, gym* ▭ *AE, D, DC, MC, V.*

$$$$ **Riverbend Inn & Vineyard.** Surrounded by its own private vineyard, this restored palatial 1860s Georgian-style mansion was a local art gallery and still magnificently showcases some artful gems. Fireplaces, dark woods, and rich tones of gold and wine add to the upscale elegance of the suites, which have new bathrooms and plenty of living space. The airy, open restaurant overlooks the vineyard and combines southern staples like pecans with fresh local ingredients. Sit back by the fireside and enjoy the formal but casual setting. Lunch entrées start at C$9. ✉ *16104 Niagara River Pkwy., L0S 1J0* ☎ *905/468–8866 or 888/955–5553* 🌐 *www.riverbendinn.ca* *19 rooms, 2 suites* *In-hotel: restaurant, room service, bar, public Internet, no-smoking rooms* ▭ *AE, DC, MC, V* *MAP.*

$$$$ **White Oaks Conference Resort & Spa.** Though the exterior of this hotel looks rather institutional, the interior is anything but. Sleek, modern room furnishings in woodsy earth tones convey rest and relaxation. The fitness club contains a variety of top-of-the-line equipment. A shuttle bus whisks you from the hotel's front door to the Royal Niagara golf course, a first-class facility across the street. The sleek Liv Restaurant has chic menu items such as grilled sea scallops with crawfish tails accompanied by cilantro and coconut-milk rice. ✉ *253 Taylor Rd., L0S 1J0* ☎ *905/688–2550 or 800/263–5766* 🌐 *www.whiteoaksresort.com* *198 rooms, 22 suites* *In-hotel: 2 restaurants, bar, tennis courts, pool, gym* ▭ *AE, D, MC, V.*

$$$ ★ **The Charles Inn.** An air of old-fashioned civility permeates this 1852 Georgian gem. Spend summer evenings playing board games on the outdoor patio, and then dine on some of the best food to be found in the area. Fireplaces, claw-foot bathtubs, and a mixture of 19th-century antique and reproduction furniture add to the period charm of the large, bright rooms. Many rooms have doors onto the upper veranda. In the Old Towne Dining Room ($$$), chef William Brun-

yansky crafts exquisite dishes. Many, such as pan-seared pickerel with grilled vegetables, draw from the produce of the area. ☒*209 Queen St., L0S 1J0* ☎*905/468–4588* ⊕*www.charlesinn.ca* *10 rooms, 2 suites* *In-hotel: restaurant, room service, laundry service, no-smoking rooms* *AE, MC, V.*

$$$ **Moffat Inn.** Some of the rooms at this charmer have original 1835 fireplaces, outdoor patios, brass beds, and wicker furniture. The independent on-site restaurant, Tetley's ($$–$$$), serves an imaginative variety of dishes including sushi, fondue, and meats cooked on hot granite rocks. ☒*60 Picton St., L0S 1J0* ☎*905/468–4641* ⊕*www.moffatinn.com* *22 rooms* *In-hotel: restaurant, no-smoking rooms* *AE, MC, V.*

$$$ ★ **Olde Angel Inn.** Though established in 1779, the current incarnation of the lemon-yellow, green-shuttered coach house dates to 1816 when a fire swept through during the War of 1812. Rooms have canopy beds. The English-style tavern sets out pub fare such as steak and oyster pie. Entrées on the dining room menu include prime rib of beef au jus and rack of lamb with mint sauce. Even if you don't stay here, be sure to stop in for a meal. ☒*224 Regent St., L0S 1J0* ☎*905/468–3411* ⊕*www.angel-inn.com* *5 rooms, 3 cottages* *In-hotel: restaurant, bar, no-smoking rooms* *AE, D, DC, MC, V.*

NIGHTLIFE & THE ARTS

Fodor's Choice ★ The **Shaw Festival** began modestly in the early 1960s with two plays and a premise: to perform the plays of George Bernard Shaw and his contemporaries, who include Noël Coward, Bertolt Brecht, J.M. Barrie, and J.M. Synge. The season now runs from April through December with close to a dozen plays, in three buildings within a few blocks of one another. The handsome **Festival Theatre,** the largest of the three, stands on Queen's Parade near Wellington Street and houses the box office. The **Court House Theatre,** on Queen Street between King and Regent streets, served as the town's municipal offices until 1969. At the corner of Queen and Victoria streets is the **Royal George Theatre,** the most intimate of the three. Tickets cost C$20 to C$77. *Shaw Festival Box Office, Box 774, 10 Queen's Parade, L0S 1J0* ☎*905/468–2172 or 800/511–7429* ⊕*www.shawfest.com.*

EN ROUTE

The Niagara Peninsula is Ontario's fruit basket. From midsummer to late fall, fruit and vegetable stands proliferate along the highways and byways, and several farmers' markets are scattered along Queen Elizabeth Way (QEW) between Niagara Falls and Hamilton. Some of the best stands are on Highway 55, between Niagara-on-the-Lake and the QEW, as well as along Lakeshore Road, between Niagara-on-the-Lake and St. Catharines.

Harvest Barn Market (☒*Hwy. 55, Niagara-on-the-Lake* ☎*905/468–3224*), marked by a red-and-white-stripe awning, sells regional fruits and vegetables and tempts with its baked goods: sausage rolls, bread, and fruit pies. You can test the market's wares at the picnic tables, where knowledgeable locals have lunch. **Greaves Jams & Marmalades** (☒*55 Queen St.* ☎*905/468–3608 or 800/515–9939* ⊕*www.greaves-jams.com*) makes jams, jellies, and marmalades from mostly local produce using family recipes, some of which have been around since the company began in 1927. The strawberry jam is a favorite, as is grape jelly from local concord grapes. The spreads have no preservatives, pectin, or additives.

HAMILTON & FESTIVAL COUNTRY

Straddling the western end of Lake Ontario, along the area known as the Golden Horseshoe, a combination of rural pleasures and sophisticated theater draws year-round visitors. Nearby, Stratford has made a name for itself with its Shakespeare festival; Kitchener and Waterloo attract thousands with an annual Oktoberfest. Once you're here, you can also enjoy the less famous lures—parks, gardens, and country trails. Hamilton, known for its exceptionally productive iron and steel mills, maintains acre upon acre of lush gardens, and London has handsome riverside parks.

HAMILTON

70 km (43 mi) west of Niagara Falls on the Queen Elizabeth Way.

Hamilton is Canada's steel capital—not exactly the sort of city where you'd expect to find acres of gardens and exotic plants, a symphony orchestra, Ontario's third-largest art gallery, a modern and active theater, 45 parks, and a developed waterfront. But they're all here in the province's second-largest city (population nearly 500,000) and Canada's third-busiest port. Downtown Hamilton, between the harbor and the base of "the mountain" (a 250-foot-high section of the Niagara Escarpment), is a potpourri of glass-walled high-rises, century-old mansions, a convention center, a coliseum, and a shopping complex.

8

With 176 stalls spread over more than 20,000 square feet, **Hamilton Farmers' Market** is Canada's largest. The market, a Hamilton tradition since 1837, is a down-home haven in the very core of the city, with rows of farm fresh produce including tomatoes, fruits, nuts, bright colored flowers, meats, fish, baked goods, zingy cheeses, and ethnic cuisines from all over the world. ✉*55 York Blvd., adjoining Jackson Sq. and Eaton Centre* ☎*905/546–2096* ⏲*Tues. and Thurs. 7–6, Fri. 8–6, Sat. 6–6.*

The **Art Gallery of Hamilton,** in the central business district, is Ontario's third-largest public art gallery, with 8,500 works of Canadian, American, European, and other international art. ✉*123 King St. W* ☎*905/527–6610* 🌐*www.artgalleryofhamilton.com* 🎟*Free; special exhibits C$12* ⏲*Tues.–Wed. noon–7, Thurs. and Fri. noon–9, weekends noon–5.*

Fodor'sChoice ★ The **Royal Botanical Gardens,** Canada's largest botanical garden, opened in 1932 and encompasses five major gardens spread across 2,700 acres. About 50 km (31 mi) of trails wind across marshes and ravines, past the world's largest collection of lilacs, 2 acres of roses, and all manner of shrubs, trees, plants, hedges, and flowers. Two teahouses and a café are open May to mid-October. The Mediterranean Greenhouse, best visited November through May, displays plant species from warm climates. ✉ *680 Plains Rd. W (Hwy. 2), accessible from Queen Elizabeth Way and Hwys. 6 and 403* ☎ *905/527–1158* 🌐 *www.rbg.ca* 🎫 *C$8* 🕓 *Gardens daily 10 AM–dusk; greenhouse daily 9–5.*

At the **Canadian Warplane Heritage Museum,** you can climb into the cockpit of a jet fighter or take a fantasy flight in a T-33 trainer. The museum is home to more than 40 aircraft from World War II to modern jets, including a McDonnell CF-101B Voodoo, a Grumman CSF-2 Submarine Tracker, a North American B25-J Mitchell bomber, and the only flying Avro Lancaster in North America. There are ongoing aircraft restorations to see, military displays, archival photographs, and mountains of memorabilia, almost all of Canadian origin. ✉ *9280 Airport Rd., south of Hamilton on Hwy. 6* ☎ *905/679–4183* 🌐 *www.warplane.com* 🎫 *C$10* 🕓 *Daily 9–5.*

★ Sir Allan Napier MacNab, a War of 1812 hero and a pre-Confederation prime minister of Upper Canada, had **Dundurn Castle** built between 1832 and 1835. The 35-room mansion has been the city's premier landmark ever since. Today it's furnished to reflect the opulence and the Victorian-era decorative sensibilities in which MacNab lived at the height of his political career. ✉ *610 York Blvd., at Dundurn St.* ☎ *905/546–2872* 🎫 *C$10* 🕓 *July–early Sept., daily 10–4; early Sept.–June, Tues.–Sun. noon–4.*

The Canadian Marine Discovery Centre is the city's latest historic addition. The star attraction is a full-scale Great Lakes vessel named the R.V. *Voyageur.* This discovery ship, complete with bridge, is actually a huge interactive exhibit. Anchored at Pier 8, just beside the HMCS *Haida* National Historic Site (a World War II Tribal Class Destroyer—and Canada's most decorated warship), the center explores the storied past and present of Canada's oceans and Great Lakes. A high-definition theater offers presentations and educational programs to illustrate the country's long maritime heritage. ✉ *57 Discovery Dr.* ☎ *905/526–0911* 🌐 *www.pc.gc.ca/decouvertes-discovery* 🎫 *C$7.15* 🕓 *Daily 10–5.*

At **African Lion Safari** there are more than 1,000 exotic birds and animals, comprising 132 different species including lions, cheetahs, rhinos, elephants, and zebras, roaming freely through 5- to 50-acre reserves. You can drive your own car or take an air-conditioned tour bus over a 9-km (6-mi) safari trail through the wildlife park. ✉ *On Safari Rd. between Hwy. 8 and Hwy. 6 north of Hamilton, Cambridge* ☎ *519/623–2620 or 800/461–9453* 🌐 *www.lionsafari.com* 🎫 *C$21.95 from Apr. 30 to late June and from early Sept. to mid-Oct.; C$26.95 from late June to early Sept.; Safari Tour bus fare not included* 🕓 *Late Apr.–June and Sept.–mid-Oct., weekdays 10–4, weekends 10–5; July and Aug., daily 10–5:30.*

WHERE TO STAY & EAT

$$$ ★ ✕ **Ancaster Old Mill.** Just outside Hamilton, this historic mill is worth the trip if only to sample the bread, baked daily with flour ground on millstones installed in 1863. Main dishes include grilled Atlantic lobster served with fresh cut fries and pork loin stuffed with creamy

goat cheese and rosemary apple fritters. The dining rooms are light and bright with hanging plants. Try to get a table overlooking the mill stream and waterfall. ✉ *548 Old Dundas Rd., Ancaster* ☎ *905/648–1827* 🌐 *www.ancasteroldmill.com* *Reservations essential* 💳 *AE, DC, MC, V.*

$$ **Staybridge Suites.** Downtown Hamilton's best lodging option, this modern hotel is all about convenience and comfort. Laundry facilities, a heated pool, and an ample breakfast buffet are some of the amenities; the great central location on the city's main commercial strip speaks for itself. All rooms come with complete kitchens and sofas. ✉ *118 Market St., L8R 3P9* ☎ *905/577–9000 or 877/238–8889* 🌐 *www.ichotelsgroup.com* *108 suites* *In-room: kitchen, refrigerator, ethernet, dial-up, Wi-Fi. In hotel: pool, gym, laundry facilities, public Wi-Fi, some pets allowed (fee)* 💳 *AE, D, DC, MC, V.*

$ **Admiral Inn.** Clean and modern, and just around the corner from famed Dundurn Castle, this comfortable inn offers an ideal starting point to reach most of the city's main shopping areas and tourist sites. The carpeted rooms have matching floral bedspreads and curtains. Satellite TV and local phone calls are included in the rate. The dining room, called Reflections ($–$$), is a popular gathering spot for locals—everyone loves the hearty, homemade soups. ✉ *149 Dundurn St. N, L8R 3E7* ☎ *905/529–2311 or 866/236–4662* 🌐 *www.admiralinn.com* *58 rooms, 4 suites* *In-room: dial-up, Wi-Fi. In-hotel: restaurant, parking (no fee)* 💳 *AE, DC, MC, V.*

NIGHTLIFE & THE ARTS

The Great Hall at **Hamilton Place** (✉ *10 MacNab St.* ☎ *905/546–3100* 🌐 *www.hecfi.on.ca*) can accommodate more than 2,100 people. It's the city's focal point for live entertainment, ranging from comedy to country music and rock concerts. Opera Hamilton also holds performances here from October through April. Its repertoire includes works such as *La Bohème* and *The Daughter of the Regiment.*

SPORTS & THE OUTDOORS

Fodor's Choice ★ The 850-km (about 530-mi) **Bruce Trail** (*Box 857, L8N 3N9* ☎ *905/529–6821 or 800/665–4453* 🌐 *www.brucetrail.org*) stretches northwest along the Niagara Escarpment from the orchards of the Niagara Peninsula to the cliffs and bluffs at Tobermory, at the end of the Bruce Peninsula. You can access the hiking trail at just about any point along the route, so your hike can be any length you wish. **Hike Ontario** (☎ *905/833–1787 or 800/894–7249* *905/833–8379* ✉ *165 Dundas St. W, Mississauga L5B 2N6* 🌐 *www.hikeontario.com*) has information and maps about hikes in the province.

BRANTFORD

40 km (25 mi) west of Hamilton on Hwy. 403.

Brantford is named for Captain Joseph Brant, the Loyalist Mohawk chief who brought members of the Six Nations Confederacy into Canada after the American Revolution.

In 1785, King George III showed gratitude to Chief Brant by building the **Mohawk Chapel.** In 1904, by royal assent, it was given the name "His Majesty's Chapel of the Mohawks" (now, of course, changed to "Her Majesty's"). This simple, white-painted frame building with eight stained-glass windows depicting the colorful history of the Six Nations people is the oldest Protestant church in Ontario. ✉ *301 Mohawk St.* ☎ *519/756–0240* 🌐 *www.mohawkchapel.ca* 🎟 *Donations requested for individual visitors, C$3 per person for groups* ⏲ *May–early Sept., daily 10–5:30; early Sept.–mid-Oct., Wed.–Sun. 10–5.*

Fodor's Choice ★ **Woodland Cultural Centre** aims to preserve and promote the culture and heritage of First Nations people of the Eastern Woodland area. The modern complex contains a resource library, prehistoric artifacts, historic and contemporary native arts and crafts, and exhibits showing early Woodland Native American culture. Be sure to take the museum's two-hour guided tour. ✉ *184 Mohawk St., near Mohawk Chapel* ☎ *519/759–2650* 🌐 *www.woodland-centre.on.ca* 🎟 *C$5* ⏲ *Weekdays 9–4, weekends 10–5.*

Although Brantford is the hometown of hockey star Wayne Gretzky, it's better known as the Telephone City—Alexander Graham Bell invented the device here and made the first long-distance call from his parents' home to nearby Paris, Ontario, in 1874. The **Bell Homestead,** where Bell spent his early years before moving to the United States, is now a National Historic Site. Also part of the site is the house of the Reverend Thomas Henderson, who left his Baptist church when he recognized the profit potential in telephones. His home served as the first telephone office and is now a museum of telephone artifacts and displays. Guided tours can be arranged. ✉ *94 Tutela Heights Rd.* ☎ *519/756–6220* 🌐 *www.bellhomestead.ca* 🎟 *C$5* ⏲ *Tues.–Sun. 9:30–4:30.*

WHERE TO STAY & EAT

$$$–$$$$ ★ ✕ **The Olde School Restaurant.** Queen Elizabeth II once dined in this dazzlingly restored circa 1870s school house. The seven private dining rooms are all brimming with nostalgia and school-day memorabilia. Highly recommended is the chef's signature boneless breast of pheasant in a raspberry sauce, and the medallions of venison tenderloin drizzled in a port wine sauce. Before or after your meal, you can relax in the piano bar or cigar lounge. ✉ *687 Powerline Rd., Hwy. 2 W at Paris Rd.* ☎ *519/753–3131 or 888/448–3131* 🌐 *www.theoldeschoolrestaurant.ca* ✍ *Reservations essential* 💳 *AE, D, DC, MC, V.*

¢ 🏨 **The Bear's Inn.** Iroquois history and culture are built into the design and spirit of this fascinating inn, in the heart of the Six Nations Reserve, about 25-minutes from downtown Brantford. The inn comprises two log buildings made of white pine logs (the traditional tree of peace for the Iroquois). Each room has a different story to tell: the Brant Suite has solid oak furnishings and a portrait of Mohawk leader Joseph Brant gracing the wall; the Poet Suite has a remake of an 18th-century four-poster bed with a drawing of poet Pauline Johnson and her homestead; and the Wampum Suite features a sleigh bed, accompanied by drawings of wampum belts. ✉ *1979–4th Line Rd., Ohsweken N0A*

1M0 ☎519/445–4133 🌐www.thebearsinn.com ⇨14 rooms ♿In-room: Wi-Fi. In-hotel: parking (no fee) ▭AE, MC, V 🍽CP.

SPORTS & THE OUTDOORS

BICYCLING Part of the coast-to-coast Trans Canada Trail, the 40-km (about 25-mi) **Gordon Glaves Memorial Pathway** (*🌐www.city.brantford.on.ca/gordonglaves*) locally links Brantford to both Hamilton and Cambridge. Most sections of the trail parallel the Grand River as it meanders through town.

HIKING The **Grand Valley Trail** is really a series of trail linkages running 128 km (79 mi) between Elora and Brantford. For information, contact the **Grand River Conservation Authority** (*✉400 Clyde Rd., Box 729, Cambridge N1R 5W6 ☎519/621–2761 🌐www.grandriver.ca*), which is responsible for stewardship of the 47,000 acres of fragile lands and watershed.

KITCHENER & WATERLOO

40 km (25 mi) north of Brantford on Hwy. 24.

Kitchener and Waterloo, which merge into one another for a combined population of 300,000, are usually referred to as K–W. Swiss-German Mennonites journeying from Pennsylvania in covered Conestoga wagons settled here around 1800, and the region's German origins remain obvious: there's a huge glockenspiel in downtown Kitchener by Speakers' Corner, and each October since 1967 the city has hosted Oktoberfest. The event now draws more than 700,000 people, who swarm to more than a dozen festival halls where they dance late into the evening, gorge on German-style food, and listen to oompah bands.

8

Farm-fresh produce sellers mingle with modern shops and clothing boutiques at ★ **Your Kitchener Market,** renowned in the region for its adjoining farmers' market, ranking as one of the oldest and most popular food-gathering hubs in the province. After more than 130 years of selling the gamut of goods from bushels bursting with fruits and vegetables, to seasoning herbs and multigrain baked goods, it's a tasty tradition that brings in visitors from miles around, from as far away as Toronto and Detroit. Buyers and browsers alike are drawn here to squeeze the ripe tomatoes, or take home a jar of pure Canadian maple syrup, and sample hand-prepared cold-cut meats and tangy cheeses. The Market Shops are open Tuesday through Thursday 8 AM–4 PM, and Saturday 7 AM–2 PM; and the farmers' market is open June through September on Wednesday 8 AM–2 PM; year-round Saturday 7 AM–2 PM. *✉300 King St. E ☎519/741–2287 🌐www.kitchenermarket.ca.*

William Lyon Mackenzie King, prime minister of Canada for almost 22 years between 1921 and 1948, spent part of his childhood living in a rented 10-room house, now **Woodside National Historic Site.** There's no particular imprint here of the bachelor prime minister, whose diaries reveal his belief in mysticism, portents, and communications with the dead, but the house has been furnished to reflect the Victorian period of the King family's occupancy. *✉528 Wellington St. N ☎519/571–*

5684, 800/839–8221 Parks Canada general inquiry line ⊕www.pc.gc.ca C$4 ⊙Late May–mid-Dec., daily 10–5.

Doon Heritage Crossroads is a complete living-history site with a restored 1914 village and two farms. The village recalls the tranquillity of rural lifestyles in the early 1900s. You can cross a covered bridge and wander tree-shaded roads to visit with costumed staff members who perform authentic period trades and activities. ✉*10 Huron Rd. at Homer Watson Blvd., north of Hwy. 401* ☎*519/748–1914* ⊕*www.region.waterloo.on.ca* *C$6* ⊙*Early May–early Sept., daily 10–4:30; early Sept.–late Dec., weekdays 10–4:30.*

WHERE TO STAY & EAT

$$$$ Fodor's Choice ★ **Langdon Hall Country House Hotel & Spa.** This magnificent Colonial Revival–style mansion on 200 acres of gardens and woodlands has grand public rooms and huge fireplaces. Built in 1898 as a summer home for a great-granddaughter of legendary financier John Jacob Astor, the Relais & Châteaux property has 12 guest rooms in the original building and 40 in two modern annexes. The restaurant, where reservations are essential, specializes in regional cuisine such as Ontario milk-fed veal chop, Québec foie gras, and vegetables from Langdon's own gardens. ✉*R.R. 33, Cambridge N3H 4R8* ☎*519/740–2100 or 800/268–1898* ⊕*www.langdonhall.ca* *52 rooms* *In-room: Wi-Fi. In-hotel: restaurant, room service, tennis court, pool, gym, spa, parking (no fee)* *AE, DC, MC, V.*

$$ **Hillcrest Bed & Breakfast.** This quintessential Victorian home, on a quiet residential street in the city center, is a Waterloo historic landmark. It has grand ceilings, antique furnishing, and touches of Italianate architecture. On-site Swedish massage and aesthetic services are available. ✉*73 George St., Waterloo N2J 1K8* ☎*519/744–3534* ⊕*www.hillcresthouse.ca* *3 rooms with private baths* *In-room: no a/c, DVD, dial-up. In-hotel: public Internet, parking (no fee)* *AE, MC, V* *CP.*

$$ Fodor's Choice ★ **Waterloo Hotel.** This intimate, historic hotel has been lovingly restored and filled with antique furniture. The lobby, with its oak-paneled staircase, soft blue and brown period wallpaper, and sofas with rich fabrics and colors, all complement the 1890 period of the building. Guest rooms are Victorian-era in inspiration with faux paint finishes, hardwood floors, high ceilings, six-foot-tall windows, fireplaces, and carved walnut beds with feather duvets. The inn partners with Gina's Health and Beauty Spa across the street which offers specialized facials, mud wraps, and a Vichy rain shower massage. Centrally located in the Waterloo business district, the inn is close to universities, shops, and restaurants, and within a 10-minute drive of spots for canoeing, biking trails, golf courses, horseback riding, and in the winter, cross-country skiing, ice-skating, ski shops, and country sleigh rides. ✉*2 King St. N, Waterloo N2J 2W7* ☎*519/885–2626 or 877/885–1890* ⊕*www.waterloohotel.net* *14 rooms* *In-room: Wi-Fi. In-hotel: room service, bar, laundry service, airport shuttle, parking (no fee)* *AE, DC, MC, V* *CP.*

$ **Comfort Inn Kitchener.** It's no frills here, but neat as a pin and comfortably appointed. Themed whirlpool suites—the Country Suite, Roman Suite, Safari Suite, and Feng Shui Suite—are a step up. The hotel serves as a good central base from which to conduct day trips to local tourist attractions and shopping areas, most within a few minutes' drive. In winter, at Chicopee Ski Hill about 5 km (3 mi) away, there are cross-country skiing, downhill skiing, a ski shop, snowmobiling, and tobogganing. *2899 King St. E, Kitchener N2A 1A6 519/894–3500 or 877/270–9434 www.choicehotels.com/ires/hotel/cn275 100 rooms, 4 suites In-room: refrigerator, dial-up, Wi-Fi. In-hotel: gym, laundry service, public Wi-Fi, parking (no fee) AE, MC, V CP.*

ST. JACOBS

★ *12 km (7 mi) north of Kitchener and Waterloo on Hwy. 8.*

The nostalgic charm of a bygone era and the flair of contemporary style blend gracefully in the villages of St. Jacobs and Elmira (10 km, or 6 mi, north of St. Jacobs via Route 86 and County Road 21) in the heart of Mennonite country.

Stop by the **Mennonite Story Visitor Centre** (*1408 King St. N, N0B 2N0 519/664–3518 www.stjacobs.com*) in St. Jacobs to learn more about the area's Old Order Mennonite community.

St. Jacobs is also a lively and unique shopping destination with more than 100 shops that run the gamut from antiques to high-end home decor and contemporary clothing boutiques. The St. Jacobs **Farmers' Market and Flea Market** (*www.stjacobs.com*) is known as one of the best in Canada for its 600 vendors selling fresh farm produce and Mennonite crafts. The market is open year-round on Thursday and Saturday from 7 to 3:30, and Sunday from 10 to 4; from June through late September it's also open Tuesdays from 8 to 3.

WHERE TO STAY & EAT

$$$$ Fodor's Choice ★ **Millcroft Inn.** This 19th-century stone knitting mill has been converted to an exquisite full-service country inn with a health and beauty spa. About 40 km (25 mi) northeast of Elmira (80 km [50 mi] northwest of Toronto) in Alton, it's on 100 acres of rolling woodland and meadows, most of which you can ride through on horseback. Some larger rooms have fireplaces. Rooms are available in both the older inn and a more modern annex, where they tend to be more spacious. The dining room, where reservations are essentials, uses Canadian and imported ingredients to create such imaginative dishes as vanilla poached tuna loin and roasted wild mushrooms in tarragon foam. *55 John St., Alton L7K 0C4 519/941–8111 or 800/383–3976 519/941–9192 www.millcroft.com 52 rooms In-room: DVD, ethernet. In-hotel: restaurant, tennis courts, pool, gym, spa, parking (no fee) AE, DC, MC, V CP.*

8

$$$ Fodor'sChoice ★ **Elora Mill.** One of Canada's few remaining five-story gristmills has been converted to luxury accommodations and a superb restaurant. Many of the furnishings and fixtures here are reproductions of historic mill machinery. Wide windows provide spectacular vistas over Elora Gorge below. There are 22 guest rooms in the main building, an 1859 mill, and 10 more in three other historic stone buildings near the mill. Its location in Elora village, which is full of European-inspired stone buildings, is about 15 km (9 mi) north of Guelph. The restaurant, where reservations are essentials, serves such sumptuous dishes as pistachio-crusted rack of New Zealand lamb; oven-roasted breast of capon with wild mushroom risotto in a smoked chicken broth emulsion; and the signature entrée, Chateaubriand for two. ✉ *77 Mill St. W, Elora N0B 1S0* ☎ *519/846–9118 or 866/713–5672* 🌐 *www.eloramill.com* *32 rooms* *In-room: ethernet. In-hotel: restaurant* *AE, MC, V.*

$ **Benjamin's.** This is a lovely re-creation of the original 1852 Farmer's Inn. Nine guest rooms on the second floor are furnished with antiques, and every bed is covered with a locally made Mennonite quilt. The 120-seat restaurant is open for lunch and dinner, and in keeping with the inn's country roots is pleasingly appointed with pine ceiling beams and an open-hearth fireplace. The dinner menu includes Kobe beef burgers with sweet-potato fries and brandy-roasted Atlantic lobster, as well as Moroccan-inspired roasted lamb with couscous. From May until the weather turns too chilly, "alfresco" dining is available for afternoon and evening repasts on the covered patio. ✉ *1430 King St. N, N0B 2N0* ☎ *519/664–3731* 🌐 *www.stjacobs.com/benjamins* *9 rooms* *In-hotel: restaurant, parking (no fee)* *AE, DC, MC, V* *CP.*

SPORTS & THE OUTDOORS

BIKING Two popular **bike routes** can be reached from Fergus, 18 km (11 mi) northwest of Elmira: one is a 32-km (20-mi) tour around Lake Belwood, the other a 40-km (25-mi) loop around Eramosa Township. There is little traffic on these scenic routes. Restaurants are few and far between, so take a picnic lunch.

Many of the roads in and around St. Jacobs are great choices for cycling excursions, with a mix of flatlands and gently rolling hills. Communities with restaurants (or where refreshments can be purchased) are 3 km–4 km (2 mi–2½ mi) apart. For guided tours, contact **Green Valley Bicycle Adventures** (☎ *519/669–9067*).

HIKING In St. Jacobs the **Health Valley Trail** is a colorful 5-km (3-mi) walking trail with boardwalks over wetlands beside the Conestoga River. A 1½-km (about 1-mi) minihike can be enjoyed even by parents with babies in strollers on the generations-old **Mill Race Trail.** The 5-km (3-mi) **pathway** along the Elora Gorge between Fergus and Elora, 15 km (9 mi) north of Elmira, is another great minihike. Landmarks on the path include a whirlpool at Templin Gardens, a restored English garden, and a bridge, which hikers cross at Mirror Basin.

STRATFORD

45 km (28 mi) west of Kitchener on Hwys. 7 and 8.

In July 1953, Alec Guinness, one of the world's greatest actors, joined with Tyrone Guthrie, probably the world's greatest Shakespearean director, beneath a hot, stuffy tent in a backward little town about 145 km (90 mi) and 90 minutes from Toronto. This was the birth of the Stratford Festival of Canada, which now runs from April to early November and is one of the most successful and admired festivals of its kind.

The origins of Ontario's Stratford are modest. After the War of 1812, the British government granted a million acres of land along Lake Huron to the Canada Company, headed by a Scottish businessman. When the surveyors came to a marshy creek surrounded by a thick forest, they named it "Little Thames" and noted that it might make "a good mill-site." It was Thomas Mercer Jones, a director of the Canada Company, who decided to rename the river the Avon and the town Stratford. The year was 1832, 121 years before the concept of a theater festival would take flight and change Canadian culture.

For many years Stratford was considered a backwoods hamlet. Then came the first of two saviors of the city, both of them (undoubting) Thomases. In 1904 an insurance broker named Tom Orr transformed Stratford's riverfront into a park. He also built a formal English garden, where every flower mentioned in the plays of Shakespeare—monkshood to sneezewort, bee balm to bachelor's button—blooms grandly to this day.

8

Next, Tom Patterson, a fourth-generation Stratfordian born in 1920, looked around; saw that the town wards and schools had names like Hamlet, Falstaff, and Romeo; and felt that some kind of drama festival might save his community from becoming a ghost town. The astonishing story of how he began in 1952 with C$125 (a "generous" grant from the Stratford City Council), tracked down Tyrone Guthrie and Alec Guinness, and somehow, in little more than a year, pasted together a long-standing theater festival is recounted in Patterson's memoirs, *First Stage—The Making of the Stratford Festival.*

Soon after the festival opened, it wowed critics from around the world with its professionalism, costumes, and daring thrust stage. The early years brought giants of world theater to the tiny town of some 20,000: James Mason, Alan Bates, Christopher Plummer, Jason Robards Jr., and Maggie Smith. But the years also saw an unevenness in productions and a tendency to go for flash over substance. Many never lost faith in the festival; others, such as Canada's greatest theater critic, the late Nathan Cohen of the *Toronto Star,* have bemoaned the fact that Stratford has become Canada's most sacred cow.

Sacred or not, Stratford's offerings are still among the best of their kind in the world, with at least a handful of productions every year that put most other summer arts festivals to shame. The secret to deciding which ones to see is to try to catch the reviews of the plays. The *New*

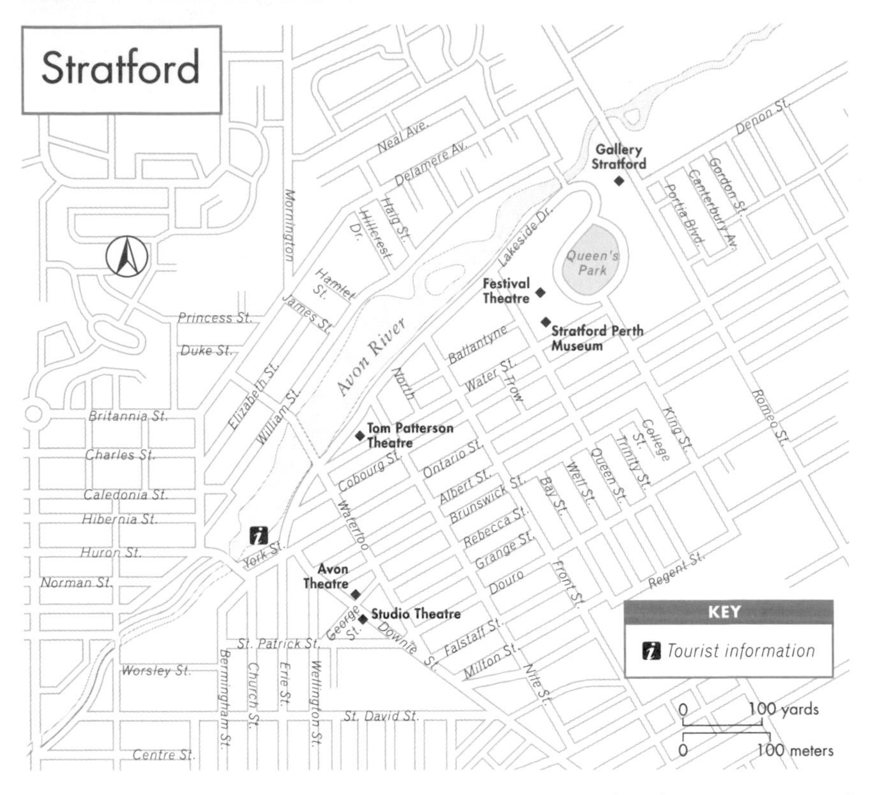

York Times always runs major write-ups, as do other newspapers and magazines in many American and Canadian cities.

Today Stratford is a city of 30,000 that welcomes over 550,000 annual visitors. There are quieter things to do in Stratford when the theaters close. Art galleries remain open throughout winter. Shopping is good off-season, and those who love peaceful walks can stroll along the Avon. Many concerts are scheduled in the off-season, too.

Gallery Stratford has regular exhibits of Canadian visual art (some for sale) and, in summer, of theater arts. ✉ *54 Romeo St.* ☎ *519/271–5271* 🌐 *www.gallerystratford.on.ca* 🎟 *May–early Sept., C$8; mid-Sept.–Apr., C$5* 🕒 *Tues.–Fri. and Sun. 1–4, Sat. 10–4.*

★ You can brush up on Stratford and Perth County history at the **Stratford Perth Museum.** Watch demonstrators crank the working printing press from 1827, or browse through the other displays, which cover such topics as hockey in Stratford, the city's railroad, and the settlement of the area in the early 1800s. An exhibit on some of Canada's firsts includes the story of Dr. Jenny Trout, Canada's first female physician. ✉ *270 Water St.* ☎ *519/271–5311* 🌐 *www.stratfordperthmuseum.ca* 🎟 *Donation* 🕒 *May–Oct., Tues.–Sat. 10–5, Sun. and Mon. noon–5; call for reduced hrs Nov.–Apr.*

WHERE TO STAY & EAT

$$$$ Fodor's Choice ★ **Rundles Restaurant.** The look is Venetian, in a theatrical Stratford way. Flowing white silk scarves hang from primitive stone masks in this sophisticated, calm space. Several three-course prix-fixe menus and a wine-with-dinner menu offer plenty of choices. The Tasmanian ocean trout, flavored with lemongrass and served with sliced fingerling potatoes and a delicately balanced lobster bouillon, is an example of the considerable artistry lavished on both the preparation and presentation. ✉ *9 Cobourg St.* ☎ *519/271–6442* 🌐 *www.rundlesrestaurant.com* ▭ *AE, DC, MC, V* ⊙ *Closed mid-Oct.–mid-May.*

$$$ **Bijou.** Stratford residents flock to this small, self-professed "culinary gem," whose menu changes seasonally. Five-spiced quail with organic shiitake mushrooms in a honey, lime, and ginger sauce may be an option for your main course. For dessert, there might be a banana terrine with caramelized banana, crème fraîche, and caramel. ✉ *105 Erie St.* ☎ *519/273–5000* 🌐 *www.bijourestaurant.com* ✍ *Reservations essential* ▭ *AE, MC, V* ⊙ *Closed Mon. No lunch Tues.–Thurs.*

$$$ ★ **Church Restaurant and Belfry.** It was constructed in 1873 as a Congregational church, but today white tablecloths gleam in the afternoon light that pours through the stained-glass windows. Meals here, whether prix fixe or à la carte, are production numbers. Licorice-dusted diver scallops are topped with candied fennel and citrus, and elk strip steak is pan-roasted. The roast Ontario lamb with garlic custard and eggplant flan is outstanding. Upstairs the Belfry uses the same excellent kitchen, but the setting is casual, and the dishes are lighter. ✉ *70 Brunswick St.* ☎ *519/273–3424* 🌐 *www.churchrestaurant.com* ✍ *Reservations essential* ▭ *AE, DC, MC, V* ⊙ *Closed Mon. and Jan.–Mar.*

$$$ **Old Prune.** A converted Victorian house holds a number of charming dining rooms and a glass-enclosed conservatory surrounded by a tidy sunken garden. Chef Bryan Steele coaxes fresh local ingredients into innovative dishes: smoked rainbow trout with apple radish and curry oil, vegetable lasagna with roasted tomato sauce, or, with a nod to the East, chicken seasoned with coriander and cumin. Desserts are baked fresh for each meal and come straight from the oven. ✉ *151 Albert St.* ☎ *519/271–5052* 🌐 *www.oldprune.on.ca* ▭ *AE, MC, V* ⊙ *Closed Mon. and Nov.–mid-May. No lunch Tues.*

$$ **Bentley's.** The well-stocked bar at this long and narrow British-style pub divides the room into two equal halves. There's an unspoken tradition: the actors have claimed one side, and the locals the other. The pub fare has staples such as good fish-and-chips, grilled steak and fries, and steak-and-mushroom pie. Regulars to this watering hole say they come for the imported, domestic, and microbrew beers, 15 of which are draft—the easygoing clientele and camaraderie are bonuses. ✉ *99 Ontario St.* ☎ *519/271–1121* 🌐 *www.bentleys-annex.com* ▭ *AE, MC, V.*

$$ **Down the Street Bar and Café.** Funky and informal, this bistro with live jazz and food by Stratford Chefs School graduates is the hottest place in town. Thrilling grills of Thai chicken, Moroccan lamb, and Black Angus sirloin make for delicious casual dining. An inspirational late-night menu includes options such as spicy spring rolls, steamed Prince

Edward Island mussels, and a classic cheeseburger with the works. A comprehensive selection of imported and microbrew beers is on tap. ✉30 *Ontario St.* ☎*519/273–5886* ▭*AE, MC, V* ⊗*No lunch Mon.*

$ ✕ **Boomer's Gourmet Fries.** No time for leisurely dining? Boomer's quickly serves fries of every ilk (no preservatives, cooked in canola oil) and scrumptious fish-and-chips year-round. Try *poutine,* a Canadian pairing of fries, cheese curds, and gravy. ✉*26 Erie St.* ☎*519/275–3147* 🌐*www.boomersgourmetfries.ca/* ▭*MC, V.*

$ ★ ✕ **York Street Kitchen.** Locals favor the signature thick and juicy sandwiches and homemade comfort dishes, such as meat loaf and mashed potatoes or sweet-and-sour beef short ribs. You can visit the takeout window for lunch and dinner express service or eat in the funky dining room, with exposed-brick walls painted an eye-popping green, for breakfast, lunch, and dinner. During festival season the lines form early. ✉*41 York St.* ☎*519/273–7041* 🌐*www.yorkstreetkitchen.com* ▭*MC, V.*

¢ ✕ **Principal's Pantry.** Generously sized sandwiches and a selection of gluten-free, lactose-free, vegan, and organic foods are served at this unpretentious, cafeteria-style eatery. You can also select one of the Ontario wines and beers listed on the menu board. Although the restaurant is in an industrial-looking Victorian building, the interior is bright and cheerful. ✉*Discovery Centre, 270 Water St.* ☎*519/272–9914* 🌐*www.principalspantry.com* ▭*AE, MC, V* ⊗*Closed Sun. and Mon.*

$$$$ Fodor's Choice ★ **XIS.** A married couple whose backgrounds are in accounting and pharmacy transformed this former downtown bank building into an exquisite, ultra-hic inn (XIS is pronounced *zees*). White leather chairs and sleek, shojilike wood-and-glass panels in the rooms might help you sink into a Zen-like mood. You can pamper yourself with Bulgari bath products and Frette linens or treat yourself to cashews, Evian water, and crisp green apples. Coffee, tea, and ice are delivered upon request. ✉*6 Wellington St., N5A 2L2* ☎*519/273–9248* 🌐*www.xis-stratford.com* *6 rooms* *In-room: safe. In-hotel: bar, no-smoking rooms* ▭*AE, MC, V* ⊗*Closed mid-Nov.–mid-Apr.* *CP.*

$$$–$$$$ **Stewart House Inn.** The interior of this elegant 1870s home draws on the Victorian period but with a modern touch. Each of the six guest rooms has a Victorian-inspired theme, from the soft green Georgian Room with Egyptian linens to the China Trade Room with pearl shades and black lacquered furnishings. All the bathrooms have heated tiles and some have soaker tubs. You can start the day on the right foot with a grand complimentary breakfast. The hotel does not permit children or pets, either of which might clash with the owner's two miniature schnauzers. ✉*62 John St. N, N5A 6K7* ☎*519/271–4576 or 866/826–7772* 🌐*www.stewarthouseinn.com* *6 rooms* *In-room: refrigerator. In-hotel: pool, no-smoking rooms, no kids* ▭*MC, V* *BP.*

$$ **Deacon House.** Dianna Hrysko and Mary Allen are the well-traveled hosts of this elegant, Edwardian-style home built in 1907. They have created a pleasant, cheery setting in a central location; the long porch is perfect for lounging with a book. Lots of antique country Canadiana fills the guest rooms and the two sitting rooms, and most rooms run to floral patterns and shades of pinks. The full buffet break-

fast includes scrumptious scones and muffins and homemade sausages. ✉101 Brunswick St., N5A 3L9 ☎519/273–2052 🌐www.bbcanada.com/1152.html 6 rooms In-hotel: no-smoking rooms, no kids ▭MC, V BP.

$$ ★ **Foster's Inn.** The hotel's bar and restaurant, two doors away from the Avon Theatre, attract a lively mix of patrons. The brick building dates to 1906 and has a bit of history—it once housed the International Order of Odd Fellows, a fraternal organization that started in the United Kingdom. Brightly painted rooms, on the second and third floors, are comfortable if basic, with queen-size beds and wood floors. Though they're above the bar and restaurant, noise isn't a problem. The dining room's artsy waitstaff deliver good-size portions from an open kitchen. Room rates are discounted substantially in winter. ✉111 Downie St., N5A 6S3 ☎888/728–5555 🌐www.fostersinn.com 9 rooms In-hotel: restaurant, bar, no-smoking rooms ▭AE, D, DC, MC, V.

$$ ★ **Queen's Inn at Stratford.** The hotel dates to 1858, though a 1905 remodeling gave it its present-day stone facings and exterior ornamental tinwork. It retains a small-town feel and is still family owned and operated. The restaurant, Henry's ($$–$$$), serves such traditional English fare as beef tenderloin and rack of lamb, at reasonable prices. The Boar's Head is a popular pub-lounge with light snacks and great brews. ✉161 Ontario St., N5A 3H3 ☎519/271–1400 or 800/461–6450 www.queensinnstratford.ca 32 rooms, 3 suites In-hotel: restaurant, bar, no-smoking rooms ▭AE, MC, V CP.

$$ **The River Garden Inn.** Tucked among the pines and towering century-old maples along the Avon River, this year-round inn has some suites with Jacuzzi tubs and fireplaces to take the chill out of the fresh countryside air. Many rooms have balconies. The garden patio is also a good place to breathe in some of that fresh air. The walk to the theaters and restaurants in town takes 15 minutes, but the inn's Sawyers on the River restaurant has a reputation for the juiciest Canadian beef served in the area. Packages with room, breakfast, and dinner are a good deal. ✉10 Romeo St. N, N5A 5M7 ☎519/271–4650 or 800/741–2135 🌐www.rivergardeninn.com 115 rooms In-room: refrigerator (some). In hotel: restaurant, bar, pool, no-smoking rooms ▭AE, D, DC, MC, V.

$ **23 Albert Place.** Since this three-story, brick-front building was opened in 1876 as the Windsor Arms, it has been refurbished a few times; no elevator was ever installed, however, so prepare to walk up one or two flights to your room. The hotel is at the heart of the downtown shopping area, close to the Avon Theatre. Some suites have mini-refrigerators and VCRs. ✉23 Albert St., N5A 3K2 ☎519/273–5800 519/273–5008 29 rooms, 5 suites In-room: refrigerator (some), VCR (some). In-hotel: restaurant, bar ▭AE, MC, V.

$ **Festival Inn.** The old-English atmosphere has survived modernization at this fairly large hotel on the eastern outskirts of town, only a short drive from the theaters. All rooms at this year-round inn have refrigerators and coffeemakers, and four have double whirlpool baths. ✉1144 Ontario St., Box 811, N5A 6W1 ☎519/273–1150 or 800/463–3581

8

www.festivalinnstratford.com *182 rooms* *In-room: refrigerator. In-hotel: restaurant, bar, pool, no-smoking rooms* *AE, MC, V.*

$ **Swan Motel.** This unassuming brick motel, 3 km (2 mi) south of the Avon Theatre, is known for the flower beds on its generous grounds. Free coffee and muffins await guests in the morning. The Swan can book guests at nearby golf courses. *959 Downie St. S, N5A 6S3* *519/271–6376* *www.swanmotel.on.ca* *24 rooms* *In-room: refrigerator, dial-up. In-hotel: pool, no-smoking rooms* *MC, V* *Closed Dec.–late Apr.* *CP.*

THE ARTS

Fodor'sChoice ★ The **Stratford Festival** performances—now a mix of Shakespeare, works by other dramatists, and popular musicals—take place in four theaters, each in its own building and each with particular physical aspects (size, stage configuration, technical support) that favor different types of productions. This means that at the height of the season (July and August) you may be able to choose among four simultaneous performances, and weekend options might include up to 12 different productions.

The Festival Theatre (*55 Queen St.*), the original and the largest, has a thrust stage that brings the action deep into the audience space. Try for fairly central seats in this theater. **The Avon** (*100 Downie St.*) has a traditional proscenium stage, good sight lines, elevators to each level, and a theater store. The **Tom Patterson Theatre** (*111 Lakeside Dr.*) is the most intimate of the festival venues. It has a modified thrust stage. The **Studio Theatre** (*George St. and Waterloo St.*) specializes in experimental and new works. The Festival and the Avon theaters are open from late April to early November. The Tom Patterson and Studio productions start in May and close by the end of September. Matinee and evening performances run Tuesday through Saturday; Sunday has regular matinee and occasional evening shows. Theaters are closed Monday.

Regular tickets are C$50 to C$110, but there are many ways to pay less. Spring previews and select fall performances are discounted 30%. Tickets for designated student and senior matinees and performances can run 50% lower than normal prices; these shows require advance booking. Theatergoers aged 18 to 29 can buy seats online for C$20 for selected performances two weeks prior to performances.

For tickets, information, and accommodations, contact the **Stratford Festival** (*Box Office, Box 520, N5A 6V2* *519/273–1600 or 800/567–1600* *www.stratfordfestival.ca*).

SHOPPING

Stratford's downtown area invites browsing with numerous clothing boutiques, antiques stores, garden shops, music stores, fine furniture and tableware shops, arts-and-crafts studios, galleries, and bookshops. The Theatre Stores, in the lobbies of the Festival and Avon theaters and at 100 Downie Street, offer exclusive festival-related gifts, original costume sketches, and play-related books and music, plus art books, literature, and children's classics.

VISITOR INFORMATION

The **Stratford Festival** (☎ *519/273–1600 or 800/567–1600* 🌐 *www.stratfordfestival.ca*) has an accommodations bureau that can help you book a room if you're buying tickets, and lots of festival-related information. **Tourism Stratford** (✉ *47 Downie St., N5A 1W7* ☎ *519/271–5140 or 800/561–7926* 🌐 *www.city.stratford.on.ca*) has information on all area goings-on.

LONDON

60 km (37 mi) southwest of Stratford on Hwys. 7 and 4.

Nicknamed Forest City, quiet and provincial London has more than 50,000 trees and 1,500 acres of parks. London is notable as one of the country's oldest cities. More than 200 years ago British officer John Graves Simcoe was scouting a location to establish a capital for Upper Canada. Apparently he liked this densely forested point at the bend of a river in what is now the city's downtown core. Although London eventually lost out to Toronto, the groundwork was laid for a flourishing city.

The easiest way to get an overview of the town is to take a two-hour **Double-Decker bus tour** on a big, red London-style bus. Buses leave daily from the Tourism London office on Wellington Street, July through Labor Day at 10 AM. ✉ *391 Wellington St., at Dundas* ☎ *800/265–2602* 🎫 *C$12.*

Labatt Brewery offers two-hour tours, including a sampling session, that take place at the Simcoe Street Brewery. Founder and master brewer John Kinder Labatt started making beer here more than 150 years ago. ✉ *150 Simcoe St.* ☎ *519/850–8687* 🌐 *www.labatt.com* 🎫 *C$5.*

8

London Regional Children's Museum uses a hands-on approach to learning. Theme rooms focus on space and dinosaurs, and crafts projects are always in the works, particularly around holidays. ✉ *21 Wharncliffe Rd. S* ☎ *519/434–5726* 🌐 *www.londonchildrensmuseum.ca* 🎫 *C$5* ⏲ *Sept.–June, Tues.–Sun. 10–5; July and Aug., daily 10–5.*

Because **Storybook Gardens** is owned and operated by the city of London, it's one of the country's least expensive children's theme parks. The Gardens are on the Thames River in the 281-acre Springbank Park and include a castle, nursery rhyme characters, and a variety of animals. There's also an old-fashioned merry-go-round, a miniature train, and a large children's playground and spray pad. ✉ *929 Springbank Dr. W* ☎ *519/661–5770* 🌐 *www.storybook.london.ca* 🎫 *C$8.25* ⏲ *May–mid-Oct. and Dec.–mid-Mar., daily 10–8; mid-Oct.–early Dec. and mid-Mar.–end of Apr., daily 10–4.*

The **Museum London** consists of six joined, glass-covered structures whose ends are the shape of croquet hoops. Its exhibits are as interesting as its architecture and include an impressive collection of regional historical art and contemporary art, plus regularly changing exhibitions, complemented by films and lectures. (A half-block north of the museum is

Eldon House, the city's oldest residence, built in 1834, elegantly and lavishly furnished to re-create high-style living in 19th-century Canada.) ✉*Forks of the Thames, 421 Ridout St. N* ☎*519/661–0333* 🌐*www.museumlondon.ca* 🎫*Free* ⏲*Tues.–Sun. and holidays noon–5.*

★ The **London Museum of Archaeology** maintains more than 40,000 native artifacts plus a gallery of artists' conceptions of the lives of the Attawandaron native people who inhabited the Lawson site, a nearby archaeological dig, 500 years ago. Nearby is a reconstructed multifamily longhouse on its original site. ✉*1600 Attawandaron Rd., south of Hwy. 22* ☎*519/473–1360* 🌐*www.uwo.ca/museum* 🎫*C$3.50* ⏲*May–Labor Day, daily 10–4:30; Sept. 3–Dec., Wed.–Sun. 10–4:30; Jan.–Apr., weekends 1–4.*

WHERE TO STAY & EAT

$$ ✕**Joe Kool's.** Unusual decor items such as Elvis in his coffin and a 1,000-plus beer can collection make this one of the city's most popular eateries. Its varied menu includes deep-dough kitchen-sink pizza, Mom's meat-loaf sandwich, potato-crusted whitefish, and panfried lake perch fillet with sweet potato fries. Kool's is also a sports lover's gathering spot with sports memorabilia on the walls and big-screen TVs showing all the games. ✉*595 Richmond St., N6A3G2* ☎*519/663–5665* 📠*519/846–9911* 🌐*www.joekoolslondon.com* 💳*AE, DC, MC, V.*

$$ ✕**Marienbad and Chaucer's Pub.** The reasonably priced Czech fare served here includes popular favorites such as goulash, schnitzel, chicken paprika, and Carlsbad roulade (rolled beef stuffed with ham and egg). Forget the diet: most dishes come with rib-sticking dumplings. ✉*122 Carling St.* ☎*519/679–9940* 🌐*www.londonsource.com* 💳*AE, MC, V.*

$$ ✕**Michael's on the Thames.** Wood-beam decor, a large stone fireplace, and a nice view overlooking the scenic Thames River make this upscale restaurant one of the most popular for beef and seafood lovers in the region. Many of the entrées are prepared tableside, including the flambéed desserts. The menu encompasses Canadian steak, a daily choice of farmed game dishes, and pasta-perfect cuisines. Highly recommended are the Brome Lake duckling à l'orange, and panfried whole Dover sole (delicately filleted at your table). Exquisitely decadent are the fresh strawberries—sautéed in brown sugar, brandy, and orange liqueur, and served on strawberry ice cream. A pianist entertains most evenings. ✉*1 York St., at Thames River* ☎*519/672–0111* 🌐*www.michaelsonthethames.com* ✍*Reservations essential* 💳*AE, MC, V.*

$$$ 🏨**Delta London Armouries Hotel.** This 20-story, silver-mirrored tower rises from the center of the 1905 London Armoury. The lobby is a greenhouse of vines, trees, plants, and fountains, wrapped in marble and accented by rich woods and old yellow brick. The architects left as much of the original armory intact as possible. A set of steps through manicured jungle takes you to the indoor pool, sauna, and whirlpool. Guest rooms are spacious and decorated in pastel shades. Suites vary in size and grandeur: the Middlesex Suite has a wet bar, fireplace, and Jacuzzi tub. This hotel also provides a Creative Centre for youngsters 12 years and under (check for times when supervised play is avail-

able), where the kids can make crafts, use the play equipment, watch movies, and play games including minigolf. ✉ *325 Dundas St., N6B 1T9* ☎ *519/679–6111 or 877/814–7706* ℻ *519/679–3957* 🌐 *www.deltahotels.com* *245 rooms, 3 suites* *In-room: dial-up. In-hotel: restaurant, bar, pool* *AE, D, DC, MC, V.*

$$ **Idlewyld Inn.** Although an elevator was installed in this converted 1878 mansion, the architects succeeded in preserving the house's original details. Rooms are furnished with antiques; suites have a whirlpool tub. Many rooms have large windows with original detailing and shutters. Breakfast, snacks, and parking are included in the rate. Golf, spa, and theater packages are available. ✉ *36 Grand Ave., N6C 1K8* ☎℻ *519/433–2891 or 877/435–3466* 🌐 *www.idlewyldinn.com* *20 rooms, 7 suites* *In-room: Wi-Fi. In-hotel: parking (no fee)* *AE, D, DC, MC, V* *CP.*

SAULT STE. MARIE & WEST TO THUNDER BAY

Trans-Canada Highway 17 hugs the northeastern shore of Lake Superior as it connects the towns of this region. Several provincial parks and the amazing Ouimet Canyon are here.

SAULT STE. MARIE

690 km (428 mi) northwest of Toronto via Trans-Canada Hwy. 69 and Hwy. 17.

The history of Sault Ste. Marie largely stems from its location on the banks of the St. Mary's River and its rapids. The river was a natural east–west conduit from Lake Huron to Lake Superior and westward, but the rapids seriously impeded the flow of water traffic. As a result, Sault Ste. Marie has always been a natural meeting place. Long before Étienne Brûlé "discovered" the rapids in 1622, Ojibwa tribes gathered here. Whitefish, their staple food, could easily be caught year-round, and in winter the rapids were often the only sources of open water for miles. When Father Jacques Marquette opened a mission in 1668, he named it Sainte Marie de Sault. *Sault* is French for "rapids." Today locals call the city simply "the Sault," pronounced "the Soo."

Fodor'sChoice ★ **Agawa Canyon Train Tours** runs day trips to and from scenic Agawa Canyon, a deep river valley with 800-foot-high cliff walls. In summer the train makes a two-hour stopover in the canyon. From here, you can lunch in a park, hike one of three waterfalls, or climb the 300 stairs to a lookout platform 250 feet up. In colder months the Snow Train makes the same trip, minus the layover. ✉ *129 Bay St.* ☎ *705/946–7300 or 800/242–9287* 🌐 *www.agawacanyontourtrain.com* *C$65–C$85* *Mid-June–mid-Oct., daily; Snow Train late-Jan.–mid-Mar., Sat. only; trains depart at 8 AM and return at about 5:30 PM.*

★ Lock Tours Canada runs two-hour excursions through the 21-foot-high **Soo Locks**, the 16th and final lift for ships bound for Lake Superior from the St. Lawrence River and the Atlantic Ocean 3,200 km (2,000 mi) away. Tours aboard the 200-passenger MV *Chief Shingwauk,* a double-deck vessel with a viewing lounge and food service, leave twice a day from late May through mid-October. ✉*Roberta Bondar Park dock off Foster Dr.* ☎*705/253–9850 or 877/226–3665* 🌐*www.lock-tours.com* 🎫*C$26.*

WHERE TO STAY & EAT

$$ **Bay Front Quality Inn.** Across the street from the Algoma Central railroad station, this comfortable hotel is the one most conveniently located if you're planning to take the Agawa Canyon Train Tour. The train leaves at 8 AM, so making it there by 7:30 AM is easy from here. Rooms and suites are basic and functional. Some rooms include a hot tub and in-room TVs with video games and movies. This is also a good winter base from which to access cross-country- and downhill-skiing facilities, an ice-skating arena, and snowmobiling and tobogganing trails, all within a 10- to 30-minute drive. When you return from your day trip, the hotel's indoor swimming pool and dining room await you. An overhead skylight makes the Gran Festa Ristorante ($–$$$) a bright and airy spot to savor its signature Italian pasta and carne dishes as well as its steaks, veal, and fresh fish. ✉*180 Bay St., P6A 6S2* ☎*705/945–9264 or 800/228–5151* 🌐*www.qualityinnssm.com* *110 rooms, 13 suites* *In-room: dial-up. In-hotel: restaurant, room service, bar, pool, gym, bicycles, laundry service, parking (no fee)* *AE, DC, MC, V.*

NIGHTLIFE

Casino Sault Ste. Marie (✉*30 Bay St. W* ☎*705/759–0100 or 800/826–8946* 🌐*www.sault-canada.com/tourism*) has 450 slot machines and 16 tables and is open year-round.

EN ROUTE

Wawa, 225 km (140 mi) north of Sault Ste. Marie on Trans-Canada Highway 17, is the first town north of Lake Superior Provincial Park. Its name is derived from the Ojibwa word meaning "wild goose." Accordingly, a 30-foot-tall Canada goose stands guard at the entrance to town, next door to the log-cabin tourist information office.

WHITE RIVER

93 km (58 mi) northwest of Wawa on Trans-Canada Hwy. 17.

This town is marked by a huge thermometer indicating 22°C (72°F) below zero and a sign that advises: "White River—coldest place in Canada." But it has another claim to fame as the actual birthplace of the bear cub that went to England to become immortalized as Winnie-the-Pooh in the children's stories by A. A. Milne. A 25-foot-tall statue honors Pooh, and each August the town holds a three-day Winnie's Hometown Festival, with parades, street dances, and a community barbecue.

WHERE TO STAY & EAT

$ ★ **Rossport Inn.** The hamlet of Rossport, about 175 km (110 mi) east of Thunder Bay on a harbor off Lake Superior, is about as close as you can get to an unspoiled outpost on the Great Lakes. Built in 1884 as a

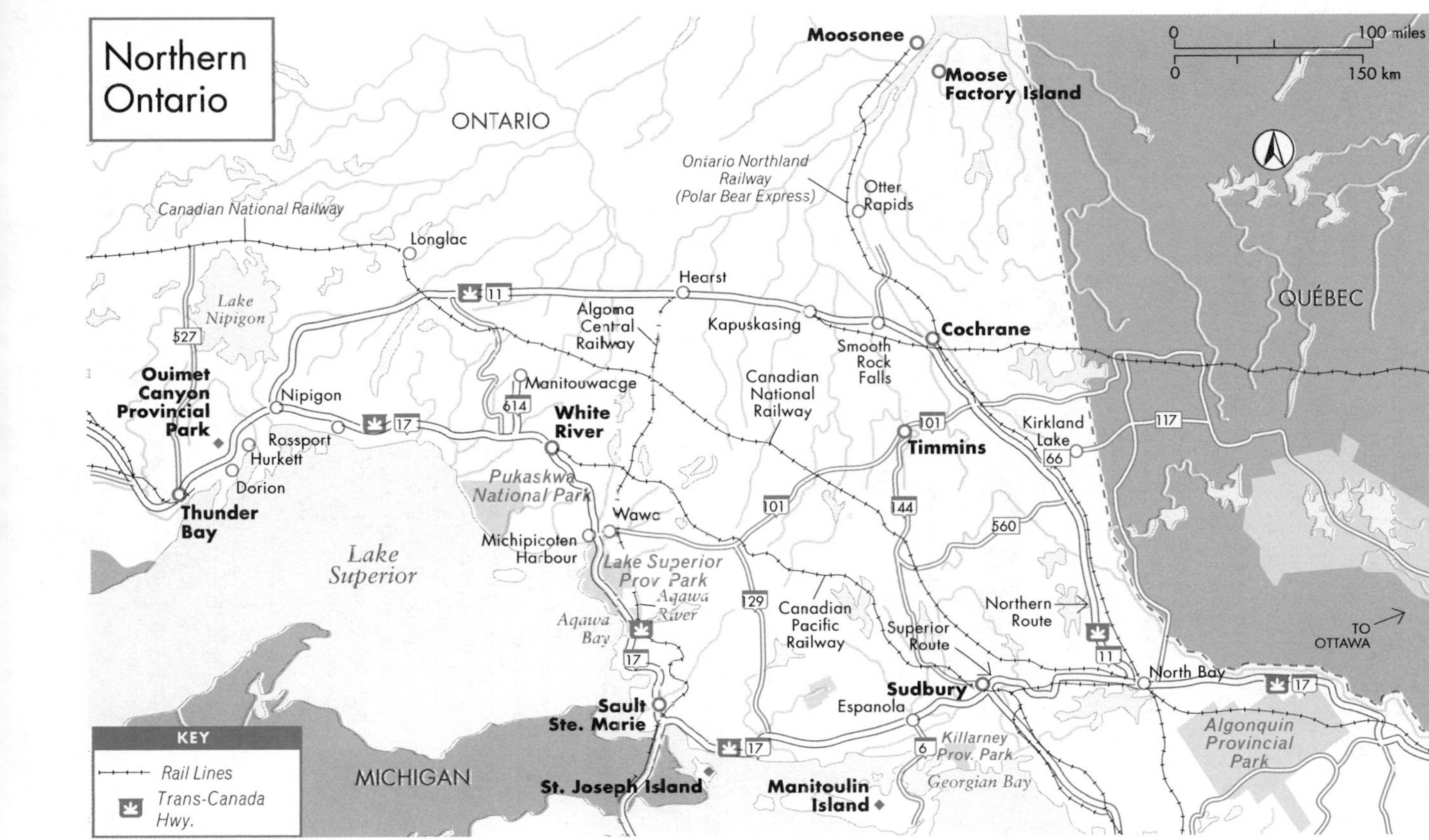
Northern Ontario
ONTARIO
QUÉBEC
MICHIGAN
0
100 miles
0
150 km
Moosonee
Moose Factory Island
Ontario Northland Railway (Polar Bear Express)
Otter Rapids
Canadian National Railway
Longlac
Hearst
Kapuskasing
Smooth Rock Falls
Cochrane
Algoma Central Railway
Canadian National Railway
Lake Nipigon
527
11
Ouimet Canyon Provincial Park
Nipigon
Rossport
Hurkett
Dorion
Thunder Bay
17
Manitouwacge
614
White River
Pukaskwa National Park
Wawa
Michipicoten Harbour
Lake Superior
Lake Superior Prov Park
Agawa River
Agawa Bay
Sault Ste. Marie
St. Joseph Island
101
Timmins
144
560
Kirkland Lake
66
117
129
Canadian Pacific Railway
Superior Route
Northern Route
Sudbury
Espanola
6
Killarney Prov. Park
Georgian Bay
Manitoulin Island
North Bay
TO OTTAWA
Algonquin Provincial Park
KEY
Rail Lines
Trans-Canada Hwy.

railroad hotel, the cozy, down-home inn is now one of the province's nicest, with hardwood floors and quilts on the comfy beds. The dining room's ($$) home-style cuisine, which includes Lake Superior trout and whitefish, as well as steak, chicken, pork chops, and lobster, is irresistible. Reservations are essential. ✉ *Rossport Loop, 1 km (½ mi) from Trans-Canada Hwy. 17, 6 Bowman St., P0T 2R0* ☎ *807/824–3213 or 877/824–4032* 🌐 *www.rossportinn.on.ca* *7 rooms, 1 with bath; 7 cottages* *In-room: no TV. In-hotel: restaurant* *AE, MC, V* *Closed Nov.–Apr.* *BP.*

OUIMET CANYON PROVINCIAL PARK

Fodor'sChoice ★ *315 km (195 mi) west of White River on Trans-Canada Hwy. 17.*

Steep, narrow Ouimet Canyon cuts so deeply into the volcanic rock of Lake Superior's north shore that botanists have discovered Arctic plants growing on its sunless floor. A walking path stops short at the edge of the 2½-km-long (1½-mi-long) chasm, where viewing platforms allow you to look 350 feet straight down; the far wall is only 492 feet away. Geologists believe the canyon could be a gigantic fault in the earth's surface or the result of glacial action. (Note: access to the canyon floor is restricted due to its fragile nature.) To get here, watch for signs to Ouimet Canyon, just past the town of Hurkett, west of Nipigon. ✉ *11 km (7 mi) off Trans-Canada Hwy. 17, 10 km (6 mi) west of Hurkett* ☎ *807/977–2526 or 888/668–7275* 🌐 *www.ontarioparks.com/english/ouim.html* *Day use C$8 per vehicle* *Mid-May–mid-Oct., daily 9–5.*

EN ROUTE

Eagle Canyon Adventures offers one of Ontario's newest park attractions: an opportunity to walk across two of Canada's longest foot suspension bridges, each spanning about 300 feet of gaping canyon. The bridges sway 150 feet off the canyon floor and afford unparalleled vistas of the surrounding northern Ontario ecology: tall pines, streams that meander through acres of dense forests, and eagles soaring atop air currents wafting overhead. For anglers, the park has a spring-fed lake that comes well stocked with brook trout. Hikers can explore the woods on a gravel path that leads up to the sheer walls of the canyon face. For campers and RVers, there are 30 full-service RV hookups, hot showers, picnic tables, laundry facilities, and a convenience store on-site. Camping/RV fees are C$25 per night, which includes access and use of the entire park and bridge walks. The park is about 40 mi (65 km) northeast of Thunder Bay, off Highway 11 on Ouimet Canyon Road; follow the signs. ✉ *275 Valley Rd., Dorion* ☎ *807/857–1475* 🌐 *www.eaglecanyonadventures.ca* *C$11 for day-swingers only for access to bridges* *Daily 9–9.*

Ontario's official mineral is amethyst, an imperfect quartz tinted violet or purple. There are five amethyst mines and an agate mine between Sleeping Giant Provincial Park and Ouimet Canyon, a distance of 50 km (31 mi) along highways 11 and 17 east of Thunder Bay. All are signposted from the highway, and each offers the opportunity to hand-pick some samples (paid for by the pound). The **Amethyst Mine Pan-**

orama is closest to Thunder Bay. Mine tours run daily, at 11, 12:30, and 3 (and during July and August only, another tour leaves at 5). Follow East Loon Road from highways 11 and 17; the mine is 40 km (25 mi) east of Thunder Bay. ✉*400 Victoria Ave. E* ☎*807/622–6908* 🌐*www.amethystmine.com* 🎫*C$3* ⏲*Mid-May–June and Sept.–mid-Oct., daily 10–5; July and Aug., daily 10–6.*

THUNDER BAY

65 km (40 mi) southwest of Ouimet Canyon on Trans-Canada Hwy. 17.

Thunder Bay, the world's biggest freshwater port, has an extraordinary ethnic mix of 42 nationalities, including the largest Finnish population outside Finland. Gateway to the fabled country north of Lake Superior and within easy reach of four provincial parks, Thunder Bay has Ontario's best alpine and cross-country skiing (and the longest ski season), superb fishing, great camping and hiking, unlimited canoe and boating routes, and even ice climbing. Several amethyst mines have shops in the city. There are also dozens of good restaurants, a growing number of B&Bs, an art gallery, golf courses galore, and nine shopping malls.

At **Old Fort William,** one of the largest living-history sites in North America with 42 historic buildings on a 25-acre site, interpreters recreate an early 1800s fur-trading fort. ✉*Broadway Ave. to King Rd.* ☎*807/473–2344* 🌐*www.fwhp.ca* 🎫*C$14 mid-June to early Sept., C$12 at other times* ⏲*Mid-May–mid-Oct., daily 10–5.*

8

The **Thunder Bay Museum** exhibits some of the best prehistoric artifacts and historical restorations in Ontario. The Peter McKellar Gallery has a long-term exhibit tracing the 10,000-year-old history of people in this region. There's a 1928 vintage theater showing old movies, and a wonderful replica of a 19th-century Thunder Bay street where you can drop in at an old tavern, a doctor's office, and a photographer's shop. You can also view a selection of HAM radios made by telecommunications pioneer Charles McDonald in his re-created studio. ✉*425 Donald St. E* ☎*807/623–0801* 🌐*www.thunderbaymuseum.com* 🎫*C$3* ⏲*June 15–Labor Day, daily 11–5; after Labor Day–mid-June 14, Tues.–Sun. 1–5.*

WHERE TO STAY & EAT

$$ **Valhalla Inn.** The warm lobby is based on an old Scandinavian design and has plenty of wood and brass. Guest rooms are large, with queen-size beds and local art. The Nordic dining room serves set menu dinners featuring high-quality fare, from fettuccini with prosciutto ham and cream to grilled medallions of pork tenderloin with spicy Jamaican-style pimentos. ✉*1 Valhalla Inn Rd., P7E 6J1* ☎*807/577–1121 or 800/964–1121* 📠*807/475–4723* 🌐*www.valhallainn.com* *267 rooms* *In-room: ethernet, dial-up. In-hotel: 2 restaurants, pool, gym, Wi-Fi* 💳*AE, D, DC, MC, V* *CP.*

SPORTS & THE OUTDOORS

North of Superior Climbing Company (✉ *Batchawana Island View Resort, Batchawana Bay, P0S 1A0* ☎ *705/946–6054 or 877/877–7385* 🌐 *www.northofsuperiorclimbing.com*) offers ice-climbing lessons, professionally led climbs, and two-day packages. Accommodations in condos or small cottages are provided, and there's a casual diner-style restaurant on the premises.

At **Kakabeka Falls Provincial Park** (✉ *32 km (20 mi) west of Thunder Bay off Hwys. 11 and 17* ☎ *807/473–9231* 🌐 *www.ontarioparks.com/english/kaka.html*), Kakabeka Falls on the Kaministiquia River drops 128 feet over a limestone ledge. Paths lead around the falls, and there are large, free parking lots.

EAST ALONG GEORGIAN BAY & SOUTH TO MANITOULIN ISLAND

On a half-day journey by car from Sault Ste. Marie you can see the stunning beauty of Georgian Bay. Highlights include the wildflowers of St. Joseph Island, the rugged simplicity of Manitoulin Island, and educational fun at Science North in Sudbury.

ST. JOSEPH ISLAND

45 km (28 mi) southeast of Sault Ste. Marie on Hwy. 17.

St. Joseph Island is a sparsely settled bit of land about 24 km by 30 km (15 mi by 19 mi) in the mouth of the St. Mary's River, connected by causeway and bridge to the mainland. In spring the island is a scented riot of wild lilac, and you're likely to see moose and deer along the quiet side roads.

★ In fur-trading days **Fort St. Joseph,** established by the British at the southeast tip of the island, guarded the trade route from Montréal to the upper Great Lakes. Today you can wander through this National Historic Site where the fort once stood and see the outlines and a few aboveground stone ruins of the 42 building sites that have been identified. Free walking tours and a documentary-style orientation movie are offered at the visitor center, about 30 minutes by car southeast of the Gilbertson Bridge. Call ahead for directions. ✉ *Richards Landing* ☎ *705/246–2664* 🌐 *www.pc.gc.ca* 🎟 *C$4* ⏲ *June–mid-Oct., daily 9:30–5.*

MANITOULIN ISLAND

235 km (146 mi) east of St. Joseph Island and south of Espanola via Trans-Canada Hwy. 17 and Hwy. 6.

Manitoulin, the world's largest freshwater island, sits at the top of Lake Huron. The island, with a total area of 2,800 square km (1,081 square mi), is ruggedly handsome, with granite outcrops, forests, meadows, rivers, and rolling countryside. Yachters rate these waters among the best in the world, and anglers have taken advantage of the island's riches for generations. Hikes and exploration could easily turn this "side trip" into a weeklong stay. Winter is a snow-lover's dream, with plenty of trails for snowmobiling, cross-country skiing, skating, and great ice fishing. For the most part, the island has not been ravaged by time and human incursions. Archaeological digs have unearthed traces of human habitation more than 30,000 years old. There is no interim record of people living here until explorer Samuel de Champlain met some island residents in 1650. Island towns such as Little Current (closest to the mainland), Sheguiandah, and Wikwemikong are simple and sweet.

★ The **MS *Chi-Cheemaun*** connects the town of Tobermory, at the northern tip of the Bruce Peninsula, with South Baymouth on Manitoulin Island. The ferry's a good alternative to driving if you're heading to the island from southern Ontario (rather than from Sault Ste. Marie). The trip takes an hour and 45 minutes each way. There are four sailings in each direction daily between late June and Labor Day, and three during spring and fall. Sunset dinner cruises are also available (C$46 per person, including the four-hour round-trip ferry ride to the island). Reservations are advised. ✉ *Owen Sound Transportation Company, 343 8th St. E, Owen Sound N4K 1L3* ☎ *519/376–6601 or 800/265–3163* 🌐 *www.ontarioferries.com* 🎫 *One-way C$14.20, plus C$30.95 and up per vehicle.*

Little Current–Howland Centennial Museum, in the village of Sheguiandah about 11 km (7 mi) south of Little Current, displays local native and pioneer artifacts. ✉ *Hwy. 6* ☎ *705/368–2367* 🌐 *www.manitoulin-island.com/museums* 🎫 *C$3* ⏲ *Apr.–mid-May and mid-Sept.–mid-Oct., Tues.–Sun. 12:30–4:30; mid-May–mid-Sept., daily 10–4:30.*

Wikwemikong Unceded Indian Reserve (☎ *705/859–2385 Wikwemikong Heritage Organization* 🌐 *www.wiky.net*) encompasses the entire southeastern peninsula of Manitoulin Island. This reserve is unceded—it's the only one in Canada—meaning the Wikwemikong (translated as: "Bay of the Beaver") never relinquished its land title to the government by treaty or any other means. One of Manitoulin's most colorful events is the Wikwemikong Pow Wow, the oldest in central Canada; it's held on Civic Holiday (the first weekend in August). Dancers accompanied by drummers and singers compete while performing the steps of their ancestors.

WHERE TO STAY

$ **Southbay Gallery and Guesthouse.** Tastefully decorated rooms adorned with quilts, interesting trinkets, and paintings by local artists await you in this B&B near the ferry terminal. Breakfasts go cosmopolitan with organic cereals, juice smoothies, and espresso drinks. There's a comfortable veranda for whiling away the afternoon. For the budget-conscious traveler, a few rooms with shared bath are available at C$60 per night. If you're adventurous, you can experience a night in a Tipi, the traditional home of the Ojibwa people. The on-site sauna and outdoor hot tub are perfect for relaxing after a long day of sightseeing. ✉ *14–15 Given Rd., South Baymouth P0P 1Z0* ☎ *705/859–2363 or 877/656–8324* 🌐 *www.southbayguesthouse.com* *7 rooms* *In-room: Wi-Fi. In-hotel: spa* *MC, V* *CP.*

SUDBURY

70 km (43 mi) east of Espanola on Trans-Canada Hwy. 17.

The mining town of Sudbury used to bear the brunt of frequent unkind jokes. After all, didn't the U.S. astronauts go there to train in the type of terrain they were likely to encounter on the moon? Today, the greening of Sudbury, an ongoing reclamation project, has revived much of the landscape that suffered from years of logging, smelter emissions, and soil erosion. The town has earned numerous international environmental awards for its reclamation efforts—to date more than 8 million trees have been planted. What you see now is typical Canadian Shield country, with more than 330 beautiful lakes, rocky outcroppings, and sprawling provincial forests all within 100 km (60 mi) of Sudbury. The town has outdoor concerts, art centers, museums, and cruises on Ramsey Lake, the largest freshwater lake inside city limits in North America.

Fodor'sChoice ★ **Science North** is northern Ontario's largest tourist attraction, encompassing a science museum, a giant-screen IMAX theater, and the Inco Cavern Theatre, which shows "Wings over the North"—a breathtaking 4-D cinematic adventure over and across Canada's rugged northern landscape. The museum explores science in the everyday world; you can touch live animals, gaze at the stars, test your senses, play with technology, and more. Friendly staff scientists are available to share their knowledge. The museum's frequent special events may affect ticket prices. ✉ *100 Ramsey Lake Rd.* ☎ *705/523–4629 or 800/461–4898* 🌐 *www.sciencenorth.ca* *Museum C$18 May–Aug., C$13 Sept.–Apr.; IMAX theater C$9* *Daily 10–4.*

Fodor'sChoice ★ **Dynamic Earth** is on the west side of Sudbury at the site of the Big Nickel monument, a local landmark. There's an underground tour (45 minutes) through hard rock tunnels that accurately depict mining in the early 1900s, 1950s, and today. Other "subterranean" exhibits include the geological Earth Gallery, Mining Command Centre, and the Explora-Mine for kids. ✉ *Big Nickel Rd.* ☎ *705/523–4629 or 800/461–4898* 🌐 *www.dynamicearth.ca* *Museum C$16 May–Aug., C$13 Sept.–Apr.; IMAX theater C$9, double bill C$13.50* *Daily 10–4.*

WHERE TO STAY

$$ **Auberge-sur-lac.** Sunsets sparkling over tranquil McFarlane Lake (a 13-minute drive south from downtown Sudbury) help ignite the senses for this romantic 1½-acre lakefront estate that's rimmed with a blueberry patch. Relaxation comes easy on the home's upper or lower decks, or in a hilltop swing with an unobstructed view of the lake. There's also a double Jacuzzi overlooking the lake in the aptly named Sunset Suite. The breakfast specialty is the host's homemade country

apple berry crisp tinged with brown sugar and cinnamon. In winter well-marked trails that wind into the bush begin at this B&B's front door for cross-country skiing, snowshoeing, and snowmobiling. After January, thick ice forms on the lake, ideal for long, leisurely skating. ✉*1672 S. Lane Rd., P3G 1N8* ☎*705/522–5010 or 888/535–6727* 🌐*www.cyberbeach.net/asl* *3 rooms* *In-room: no a/c, no phone, no TV. In-hotel: bicycles, public Internet, parking (no fee)* *AE, DC, MC, V* *CP.*

FROM COCHRANE TO MOOSONEE & MOOSE FACTORY ISLAND

This far northeastern region is called the James Bay Frontier. It runs from the tall pine forests north of Temagami to the lowlands of James and Hudson bays, then onward to the southern tip of the Arctic Ocean.

The land is part of the great northern Boreal forest and the massive rock formation known as the Canadian Shield. Mining and forestry are the kings of this land.

The James Bay Frontier is also a favorite for hunters and anglers who know that the remote forests and lakes are teeming with fish and wild game. Many take part in popular fly-in adventures that make this huge area more accessible.

COCHRANE

380 km (236 mi) north of Sudbury via Trans-Canada Hwys. 17 E and 11 N.

Cochrane is Ontario's gateway to the Arctic: all rivers from here flow north into James Bay and eventually into the Arctic Ocean. It's also the way to Moose Factory and Moosonee at the southern end of James Bay, but don't expect a road to the Far North—you need to take a train or fly to those areas. There's train service to Cochrane from Toronto and North Bay, contact **Ontario Northland Information and Reservations** (☎*800/461–8558* 🌐*www.ontc.ca*).

Cochrane's newest attraction is the **Polar Bear Conservation and Education Habitat and Heritage Village.** Visitors who are brave enough can swim with the bears ... well, sort of. A special glass barrier separates the bear pool from the people pool. Aurora, Nikita, and Nanook are the current resident bears. The facility has also re-created a heritage village depicting the lives of the first European farmers and homesteaders in this part of Canada. ☎*705/272–2327 or 800/354–9948* 🌐*www.polarbearhabitat.ca.*

You can fly to Moosonee from Timmins via **Air Creebec** (✉*Timmins Airport, R.R. 2, P4N 7C3* ☎*705/264–9521 or 800/567–6567* 🌐*www.aircreebec.ca*), a 100% Cree Indian–owned airline.

8

Fodor'sChoice ★ Ontario Northland's famous *Polar Bear Express* (✉*555 Oak St. E, North Bay P1B 8L3* ☎*705/472–4500 or 800/268–9281* 🌐*www.polarbearexpress.ca*) is the most memorable way to go. Every weekday from late June through Labor Day the *Polar Bear* leaves Cochrane at 9 AM for the 300-km (186-mi) journey across the James Bay lowlands to the Arctic tidewater, arriving at Moosonee just before 2 PM. It departs Moosonee at 5 PM and returns to Cochrane by 9:42 PM. The fare is C$89.50. Meals, light lunches, and snacks are available in the snack car.

WHERE TO STAY

If you plan to take the *Polar Bear Express* train, consider overnighting in Cochrane. There are 10 motels in and around town. Not all have restaurant facilities but they are geared to early wake-up calls for guests taking the train and late check-ins for those returning from the excursion. All are reasonably priced.

$ **Station Inn.** This inn is at the center of town beside Ontario Northland's century-old railway station. Rooms are compact but comfortable. The interior walls are bedecked with old photos and paintings depicting the history of the railroad—a suitable theme for a town that once lived and breathed by the train schedule. This is an ideal spot for those wishing to take the *Polar Bear Express*. The solarium-enclosed restaurant offers a basic menu of pastas and burgers. In winter, there's well-groomed snowmobiling trails right outside the inn's front door. ✉*200 Railway St., P0L 1C0* ☎*705/272–3500 or 800/265–2356* 📠*705/272–5713* *23 rooms* *In-room: ethernet. In-hotel: restaurant, gym, laundry service, parking (no fee)* 💳*AE, DC, MC, V.*

MOOSONEE

300 km (186 mi) north of Cochrane by train.

Moosonee, Ontario's only tidal port, came into existence in 1903 when Revillon Frères Trading Company established a post to compete with the Hudson's Bay Company in Moose Factory. A local museum details their exploits. It wasn't until the Ontario Northland Railway arrived in 1932 that the region's population began to catch up to that of Moose Factory. Now about 2,500 people live here, many of them Mushkegowuk Cree, whose ancestors lived in the region for centuries before fur traders created settlements. During tourist season locals open stalls on Revillon Road to sell First Nations handicrafts ranging from moccasins and buckskin vests to jewelry, beadwork, and wood and stone carvings.

The **Moosonee visitor center** (✉*Ferguson Rd. at 1st St.* ☎*705/336–2238* 📠*705/336–3899* 🌐*www.moosonee.ca*) is in a small, one-story office building.

In the modern **James Bay Education Centre** (✉*1st Ave., Box 130, P0L 1Y0* ☎*705/336–2913*) Northern College operates interpretive programs where you can see exhibits of regional wildlife and the area's geological and geographical history.

MOOSE FACTORY ISLAND

2½ km (1½ mi) from Moosonee by boat.

One of a number of islands in the delta of the Moose River, historic Moose Factory Island was the site of the Hudson's Bay Company's second trading post, established in 1673. The puzzling place name is derived from its location on the Moose River as well as from the fur trade era: the officer in charge of the fur-trading post was referred to as the "factor."

You can reach the island by water taxi—a freighter canoe from Moosonee (C$6 each way; canoes line up at the Moosonee dock)—or take a 20-minute boat ride on a 100-passenger cruise vessel operated by **TwoBay Tours** (*Box 280* *16 Ferguson Rd., P0L 1Y0* *705/336–2944* *www.twobay.com*), aboard the *Polar Princess.* The best way to experience this part of Canada is by taking the Frontier Package (5 days/4 nights), which begins in Cochrane (on Saturday in July and August only), and includes a tour of Fossil Island, a hike out to the Muskeg lands that stretch to the horizon along a 4-km (2½-mi) trail, and a tour of Moose Factory Island. The Frontier Package starts at C$590 per person, meals and lodgings included, and is offered in conjunction with the Polar Bear Express (reservations must be made directly through Ontario Northland: 800/268–9281). The company's C$24.50 day-trip fare includes a bus tour of the island with stops at historic sites. The *Polar Princess* gets back to Moosonee in time for day-trippers to board the *Polar Bear Express* for the return journey to Cochrane.

Contrary to popular myth, **St. Thomas Anglican Church** (*Front Rd.* *705/658–4800*) never floated away. Holes in the 1850 edifice's floor are to let floodwater out and to ventilate the foundation. When the church was being built in 1864, the foundation floated a short distance in a spring flood, but the church itself has never floated anywhere. The altar cloths and lectern hangings are of moose hide decorated with beads.

The Hudson's Bay post now known as the North West Company is a modern building, but beside it is the 1850 **Hudson's Bay Staff House** (*River Rd.* *705/272–5338*), in which animal pelts, carvings, snowshoes, gloves, slippers, and beadwork are sold.

The **Blacksmith's Shop** in Moose Factory Centennial Park Museum isn't the oldest wooden building in Ontario, but the stone forge inside it may be the province's oldest "structure." The original shop was built in the late 1600s but moved back from the riverbank in 1820. The forge stones had to be transported a long distance and were disassembled and rebuilt at the present location. In summer an apprentice smith runs the forge.

WHERE TO STAY

$$ **Cree Village Ecolodge.** Canada's first indigenously owned lodge focuses on the traditional values of Cree cultural and ecological sustainability, manifest in low-noise ceiling fans, no-odor compost toilets, and bio-

degradable toiletries. This little piece of paradise is great for hikers, with trails leading out from the lodge's front door. Across the river is Tidewater Provincial Park, which is popular with outdoorsy types who come here for the cross-country skiing and bird-watching. For the less athletically inclined, star gazing, whale-watching, or educational river tours by nature experts can make any stay delightful. ✉*Box 730, P0L 1W0* ☎*705/658–6400 or 888/273–3929* 🌐*www.creevillage.com* *20 rooms* *In-hotel: public Wi-Fi* *MC, V* *CP.*

TIMMINS

90 km (56 mi) southwest of Cochrane on Hwys. 11 and 101.

The mining center of Timmins prides itself on being the largest city in Canada—geographically, that is. Timmins gained size when it amalgamated with neighboring townships a few decades ago, but its population is a modest 43,000. Because of its unspoiled vastness, there's plenty to see and do here for those interested in off-the-beaten-track adventures. In summer the city boasts excellent hiking and cycling trails. In winter this region is a world-class snowmobiling destination.

From Timmins you can fly to Moosonee via **Air Creebec** (✉*Timmins Airport, R.R. 2, P4N 7C3* ☎*705/264–9521 or 800/567–6567* 🌐*www.aircreebec.ca*).

★ At the **Timmins Gold Mine Tour and Museum** visitors dress in full mining attire for the 2½-hour tour of the old Hollinger gold workings. Surface attractions include a prospector's trail with a view of mineral outcrops and a refurbished miner's house. (The road to the tour site near downtown Timmins is well marked.) At the same site is the **Shania Twain Centre** (🌐*www.shaniatwaincentre.com* *C$9* *Daily 10–5*) devoted to the country superstar, whose hometown is Timmins. The center contains interactive multimedia displays, live concert simulations, and some of Twain's own memorabilia. ✉*220 Algonquin Blvd. E* ☎*705/360–2619 or 800/387–8466* 🌐*www.timminsgoldminetour.com* *Tour C$19* *Gold Mine tours: mid-May–June, Sept. and Oct., Wed.–Sun. at 10:30 and 1:30; July and Aug., daily at 9:30, 11:30, noon, 1:30, and 3.*

WHERE TO STAY & EAT

$ **Cedar Meadows Resort.** Close to town, this year-round resort in a 224-acre wilderness park overlooking the mighty Mattagami River offers a true taste of northern ecology, with guided wilderness hikes and tours, canoeing, and camping. The rustic Voyageur Restaurant serves sizzling steaks of elk and bison as well as Black Angus seasoned with vine-ripened vegetables and fresh herbs grown in the resort's own greenhouse. ✉*1000 Norman St., P4N 8R2* ☎*705/268–5800 or 877/207–6123* *705/268–1336* 🌐*www.cedarmeadows.com* *49 rooms* *In-hotel: restaurants* *AE, D, MC, V.*

PROVINCE OF ONTARIO ESSENTIALS

TRANSPORTATION

BY AIR

Toronto, the province's largest city, serves most major airlines at Pearson International Airport. Ottawa International Airport is the gateway to Ontario's Capital Region. The Niagara Falls International Airport in Niagara Falls, New York, is the closest air link to Niagara Falls, Ontario, and its popular attractions.

Information **Niagara Falls International Airport** (☏ *716/855-7300* 🌐 *www.nfta.com*). **Ottawa International Airport** (✉ *50 Airport Rd., south end of Airport Pkwy.* ☏ *613/248-2000* 🌐 *www.ottawa-airport.ca*). **Toronto Pearson International Airport** (☏ *416/247-7678 Terminals 1 and 2, 416/776-5100 Terminal 3, 866/207-1690 toll-free* 🌐 *www.gtaa.com*).

BY BUS

About 20 intercity bus lines connect communities all over Ontario; many are run by Greyhound Canada and its affiliates. Ontario Northland serves Toronto, Central Ontario, and Northern Ontario. Penetang-Midland Coach Lines serves Toronto and Central Ontario. Trentway-Wagar Coach Canada serves Niagara Falls, Hamilton, Toronto, and Kingston. Ontario Tourism can provide details on intercity bus routes, contacts, and schedules.

Information **Greyhound Canada & Voyageur Colonial Bus Lines** (☏ *416/367-8747 in Toronto, 800/661-8747 across Canada and U.S.* 🌐 *www.greyhound.ca*). **Ontario Northland** (☏ *705/670-2455 or 800/449-3393* 🌐 *www.webusit.com*). **Penetang-Midland Coach Lines** (☏ *800/461-1767* 🌐 *www.greyhoundtravel.com/charter/pmcl*). **Trentway-Wagar Coach Canada** (☏ *416/961-9666 or 800/461-7661*). **Ontario Travel Information Centre** (✉ *Atrium on Bay, street level, 595 Bay St., Toronto M7A 2E1* ☏ *905/282-1721 or 800/668-2746*).

BY CAR

The Macdonald-Cartier Freeway, known as Highway 401, is Ontario's major highway link. It runs from Windsor in the southwest through Toronto, along the north shore of Lake Ontario, and along the north shore of the St. Lawrence River to the Québec border west of Montréal.

The Queen Elizabeth Way (QEW), named for the late Queen Mother, who was the wife of King George VI, runs from the U.S. border through the Niagara Region to Toronto. The four- to eight-lane freeway traverses Fort Erie, Niagara Falls, St. Catharines, Hamilton, Burlington, Oakville, Mississauga, and ends in Toronto. Highway 400 is the main north–south route between Toronto and the Cottage Country (Muskoka Region).

The Trans-Canada Highway follows the west bank of the Ottawa River from Montréal to Ottawa and on to the town of North Bay. From here there are two branches of the Trans-Canada (Highways 11 and 17): one is from North Bay to Nipigon at the northern tip of Lake Superior; another is just west of Thunder Bay to Kenora, near the Manitoba border.

CANADIAN AUTOMOBILE ASSOCIATION (CAA) The CAA is affiliated with several international automobile clubs, including the American Automobile Association (AAA), and members are entitled to reciprocal benefits.

Information Canadian Automobile Association (☎ *416/221–4300 in Toronto, 416/222–5222, 800/268–3750 elsewhere in Ontario* 🌐 *www.caa.ca*).

ROAD CONDITIONS Information on highway conditions (winter) and construction (summer) in the province is available all year from the Ministry of Transportation regional offices.

Information Road-condition information (☎ *800/268–4686* 🌐 *www.mto.gov.on.ca*).

RULES OF THE ROAD Ontario is a no-fault province and minimum liability insurance is C$200,000. If you're driving across the Ontario border, bring the policy or the vehicle registration forms and a free Canadian Non-Resident Insurance Card from your insurance agent. If you're driving a borrowed car, also bring a letter of permission signed by the owner.

Driving motorized vehicles while impaired by alcohol is taken seriously and results in heavy fines, imprisonment, or both. You can be convicted for refusing to take a Breathalyzer test. Radar warning devices are not permitted in Ontario even if they are turned off. Police can seize them on the spot, and heavy fines may be imposed.

Studded tires and window coatings that do not allow a clear view of the vehicle interior are forbidden. Right turns on red lights are permitted unless otherwise noted. Pedestrians crossing at designated crosswalks have the right of way.

TRAIN TRAVEL

Ontario is served by cross-Canada VIA Rail, which stops in towns and cities across the southern sector of the province. VIA Rail connects with Amtrak service at Niagara Falls (New York) and Fort Erie (Buffalo, New York). Ontario Northland Rail Services provides four different routes throughout Ontario, with service to and from Toronto.

Information Amtrak (☎ *800/872–7245* 🌐 *www.amtrak.com*). **Ontario Northland Rail Services** (☎ *705/472–4500 or 800/363–7512* 🌐 *www.ontc.on.ca*). **VIA Rail** (☎ *416/366–8411 or 888/842–7245* 🌐 *www.viarail.ca*).

CONTACTS & RESOURCES

SPORTS & THE OUTDOORS

CAMPING Peak season in Ontario parks is June through August, and it is advised that you reserve a campsite if reservations are accepted; sites can be guaranteed by phone, by mail, or in person by using a Visa or MasterCard. All provincial parks that offer organized camping have some sites available on a first-come, first-served basis. In an effort to avoid overcrowding on canoe routes and hiking or backpacking trails, daily quotas have been established governing the number of people permitted in the parks. Permits can be reserved ahead of time. For detailed information on all parks and campgrounds province-wide, contact Ontario Parks for the *Ontario Parks Guidebook* or Ontario Tourism for a free outdoor-adventure guide.

Information Ontario Parks (*888/668-7275 www.ontarioparks.com*). **Ontario Travel Information Centre** (*Atrium on Bay, street level, 595 Bay St., Toronto M7A 2E1 905/282-1721 or 800/668-2746 www.ontariotravel.net*).

DOGSLEDDING Burton Penner of Vermilion Bay, 91 km (56 mi) east of Kenora (480 km, or 298 mi, west of Thunder Bay), offers guided dogsled tours into the wilderness, overnighting in an outpost cabin or heated wall tent. Winterdance Dogsled Tours take you on afternoon or multiday adventures in Haliburton and Algonquin Park. Voyageur Quest provides Canadian wilderness trips year-round in Algonquin Park and throughout northern Ontario.

Information Burton Penner (*888/240-3739*). **Voyageur Quest** (*416/486-3605 or 800/794-9660 www.voyageurquest.com*). **Winterdance Dogsled Tours** (*705/457-5281 www.winterdance.com*).

8

FISHING Licenses are required for fishing in Ontario and may be purchased from Ministry of Natural Resources offices and from most sporting goods stores, outfitters, and resorts. Seasons and catch limits change annually, and some districts impose closed seasons. Restrictions are published in *Recreational Fishing Regulations Summary*, free from the Ministry.

There are about 500 fishing resorts and lodges listed in the catalog of fishing packages available free from Ontario Tourism. The establishments are not hotels near bodies of water that contain fish but businesses designed to make sportfishing available to their guests. Each offers all the accoutrements, including boats, motors, guides, floatplanes, and freezers. Rates at these lodges are hefty.

Information Ministry of Natural Resources (*300 Water St., Peterborough K9J 8M5 705/755-2001 or 800/667-1940 www.mnr.gov.on.ca/mnr/fishing*). **Ontario Travel Information Centre** (*Atrium on Bay, street level, 595 Bay St., Toronto M7A 2E1 905/282-1721 or 800/668-2746 www.ontariotravel.net*).

MULTIACTIVITY SPORTS Call of the Wild offers guided trips of different lengths—dogsledding and cross-country skiing in winter, canoeing and hiking in summer—in Algonquin Provincial Park and other areas in southern Ontario. Prices include transportation from Toronto.

Information **Call of the Wild** (☎ *905/471–9453 or 800/776–9453* 🌐 *www.callofthewild.ca*).

RAFTING A growing number of companies in eastern Ontario offer packages ranging from half-day to weeklong trips from May through September. Esprit Rafting Adventures offers trips on the Ottawa River, canoeing in Algonquin Provincial Park, or mountain biking in the Upper Ottawa Valley. Owl Rafting conducts half-day excursions on the nearby Ottawa and Madawaska rivers. RiverRun, in Beachburg, a 90-minute drive north of Ottawa, has a one-day tour on the Ottawa River.

Information **Esprit Rafting Adventures** (☎ *819/683–3241 or 800/596–7238* 🌐 *www.espritrafting.com*). **Owl Rafting** (☎ *613/646–2263 summer, 613/238–7238 winter, 800/461–7238* 🌐 *www.owl-mkc.ca*). **RiverRun** (☎ *613/646–2501 or 800/267–8504* 🌐 *www.riverrunners.com*).

SKIING Ski Ontario and snow report have information on the condition of slopes across the province.

Information **Ski Ontario** (☎ *705/443–5450* 🌐 *www.skiontario.on.ca*). **Snow report** (☎ *905/282–1721 or 800/668–2746*).

SNOWMOBILING Ontario has 49,000 km (30,380 mi) of trails, and many outfitters and guided excursions are available from Haliburton Highlands–Algonquin Provincial Park to Kenora in the province's far northwest. Halley's Camps has guided excursions on wilderness trails to outpost camps for three to six nights.

Information **Halley's Camps** (☎ *807/224–6531, 800/465–3325 in Ontario* 🌐 *www.halleyscamps.com*).

VISITOR INFORMATION

Ontario has a wealth of excellent and free tourist information. Ontario Tourism provides detailed guides about a variety of travel interests, from cruising rivers and lakes to big-city adventures, and can help you find information about nearly every corner of the province.

Information **Algoma Country Travel Association** (✉ *485 Queen St. E, Suite 204, Sault Ste. Marie P6A 1Z9* ☎ *705/254–4293 or 800/263–2546* 🌐 *www.algomacountry.com*). **Brantford Tourism** (✉ *399 Wayne Gretzky Pkwy., Brantford N3R 8B4* ☎ *519/751–9900 or 800/265–6299* 🌐 *www.visitbrantford.ca*). **Cobourg Tourism** (✉ *212 King St. W, Cobourg K9A 2N1* ☎ *905/372–5481 or 888/262–6874* 🌐 *www.cobourgtourism.ca*). **Convention and Visitors Bureau of Windsor, Essex County, and Pelee Island** (✉ *333 Riverside Dr. W, Suite 103, Windsor N9A 5K4* ☎ *519/253–3616 or 800/265–3633* 🌐 *www.visitwindsor.com*). **Hamilton Tourism** (✉ *34 James St. S, Hamilton L8P 2X8* ☎ *905/546–2666 or 800/263–8590* 🌐 *www.hamiltonundiscovered.com*). **James Bay Frontier Travel Association** (📭 *Bag 920, 76 McIntyre Rd., Schumacher P0N 1G0* ☎ *705/360–1989 or 800/461–3766* 🌐 *www.jamesbayfrontier.com*). **Kingston Tourism** (✉ *216 Ontario St., Kingston K7L 2Z3* ☎ *613/544–2725* 🌐 *www.kingstoncanada.com*). **London Tourism** (✉ *696 Wellington St. S, London N6C 4R2* ☎ *519/661–6157* 🌐 *www.londontourism.ca*). **Manitoulin Island Tourism** (☎ *705/377–5845* 🌐 *www.manitoulin-island.com*). **Midland-Penetanguishene Tourism** (✉ *208 King St., Midland L4R 3L9* ☎ *705/526–*

7884 or 800/263–7745 ⊕ www.georgianbaytourism.on.ca). **Muskoka Tourism** (*✉ 1342 Hwy. 11 N, R.R. 2, Kilworthy P0E 1G0 ☎ 705/689–0660 or 800/267–9700 ⊕ discovermuskoka.ca).* **Niagara Economic and Tourism Corp** (*✉ 424 S. Service Rd., Grimsby L3M 5A5 ☎ 905/945–5444 or 800/263–2988 ⊕ www.tourismniagara.com).* **North of Superior Tourism** (*✉ Maata's Rd., R.R. 1, Box 5, Nipigon P0T 2J0 ☎ 807/887–3333 or 800/265–3951 ⊕ www.nosta.on.ca).* **Ontario East Tourism Corp** (*✉ 104 St. Lawrence St., Merrickville K0G 1S0 ☎ 613/269–2777 or 800/576–3278 ⊕ www.ontarioeast.com).* **Ontario Travel Information Centre** (*✉ Atrium on Bay, street level, 595 Bay St., Toronto M7A 2E1 ☎ 905/282–1721 or 800/668–2746 ⊕ www.ontariotravel.net).* **Peterborough and the Kawarthas Tourism** (*✉ 175 George St. N, Peterborough K9J 3G6 ☎ 705/742–2201 or 800/461–6424 ⊕ www.thekawarthas.net).* **Prince Edward County Chamber of Tourism & Commerce Office** (*✉ 116 Main St., Picton K0K 2T0 ☎ 613/476–2421 or 800/640–4717 ⊕ www.pecchamber.com).* **Sault Ste. Marie** (*✉ 99 Foster Dr., Sault Ste. Marie P6A 5X6 ☎ 705/759–5432 or 800/461–6020 🖷 705/759–2185 ⊕ www.sault-canada.com)* **St. Jacobs Country** (*✉ 1386 King St., St. Jacobs N0B 2N0 ☎ 800/265–3353 🖷 519/664–2218 ⊕ www.stjacobs.com).*

Montréal

WORD OF MOUTH

"Montréal . . . is not about attractions as it is about its neighborhoods, and strolling around trying different cafés, browsing into shops, admiring the architecture, strolling through the parks. It's not what's inside, but what's on the outside."

—Carmanah

"You must go to the Jazz Festival—it is a superb, world-class event. Lots of outdoor concerts, music is not all jazz (if you are not a fan). Held on St. Catherine St. East, they block off the streets around the multiple stages. Easy access by Metro."

—Michel_Paris

www.fodors.com/forums

By Paul and Julie Waters, and Brandon Presser

CANADA'S MOST ROMANTIC METROPOLIS, MONTRÉAL is an island city that favors grace and elegance over order and even prosperity, a city where past and present intrude on each other daily. In some ways it resembles Vienna—well beyond its peak of power and glory, perhaps, yet still vibrant and beautiful.

But don't get the wrong idea. Montréal's always had a bit of an edge. During Prohibition, thirsty Americans headed north to the city on the St. Lawrence for booze, jazz, and a good time, and people still come for the same things. Festivals all summer long celebrate everything from comedy and French songs to beer and fireworks, and, of course, jazz. Clubs and sidewalk cafés are abuzz from late afternoon to the early hours of the morning and all year long. Rue St-Denis is almost as lively on a Saturday night in January as it is in July.

Montréal is the only French-speaking city in North America and the second-largest French-speaking city in the Western world, but about 14% of the 3.3 million people who call Montréal home claim English as their mother tongue. Chatter in the bars and bistros of rue St-Denis east of boulevard St-Laurent still tends to be French, and crowds in clubs and restaurants on rue Crescent downtown speak, argue, and court in English. But the lines have definitely blurred.

Both major linguistic groups have had to come to grips with no longer being the only players on the field. So called *allophones*—people whose mother tongue is neither French nor English—make up fully 19% of the city's population, and to them the old, French–English quarrels are close to meaningless. Some—Jews, Italians, Greeks, and Portuguese—have been here for generations, while others—Arabs, Haitians, Vietnamese, and Latin Americans—are more recent arrivals. But together they've changed the very nature of the city, and are still doing so.

EXPLORING MONTRÉAL

The best way to see Montréal is to walk and take public transportation. Streets, subways (Métro), and bus lines are clearly marked. The city is divided by a grid of streets roughly aligned east–west and north–south. North–south street numbers begin at the St. Lawrence River and increase as you head north; east–west street numbers begin at boulevard St-Laurent, which divides Montréal into east and west halves.

VIEUX-MONTRÉAL

A walk through the cobbled streets of Vieux-Montréal is a lot more than a privileged stroll through history; it's also an encounter with a very lively present—especially in summer, when the restaurants and bistros spill out onto the sidewalks; jugglers, musicians, and magicians jostle for performance space on the public squares and along the riverfront in the Vieux-Port; and visitors and locals alike crowd the district to drink, to dine, to party, take in a show, and maybe even go to church. To get around, you can rent a bike or in-line skates (murder

TOP REASONS TO GO

GET TO CHURCH
The Basilique Notre-Dame-de-Montréal is not to be missed, and there are several smaller ones sprinkled throughout the city, including Chapelle Notre-Dame-de-Bon-Secours.

INDULGE IN ART
Montréal has a flurry of fabulous museums and galleries, including the Musée des Beaux-Arts and the McCord Museum.

PARTY TILL DAWN
There's a strong history of late-night revelry in this city. Stroll along rue St-Denis or rue Crescent at about 10:30 pm and look for the place with the longest line and the rudest doorman.

SAMPLE WORLD CUISINE
Swoon over culinary innovations at Toqué! and Globe, but don't leave without trying the local eats: smoked meat, barbecued chicken, and soggy stimés (steamed hot dogs).

SHOP TILL YOU DROP
Thanks to Cité Souterraine (the Underground City), shopping is a year-round sport. Add in the trendy boutiques on avenue Monkland, boulevard St-Laurent, and rue St-Denis, and your Visa will get a workout.

on cobblestones but fine along the waterfront), hire a horse-drawn calèche, or simply walk. But however you travel, you can't escape the history. Vieux-Montréal, once enclosed by stone walls, is the oldest part of the city. It runs roughly from the waterfront in the south to ruelle des-Fortifications in the north and from rue McGill in the west to rue Berri in the east. The churches and chapels stand testament to the religious fervor that inspired the French settlers who landed here in 1642 to build a "Christian commonwealth." Stone warehouses and residences are reminders of how quickly the fur trade commercialized that lofty ideal and made the city one of the most prosperous in 18th-century Nouvelle France. And finally, the financial houses along rue St-Jacques, bristling with Victorian ornamentation, recall the days when Montrealers controlled virtually all the wealth of the young Dominion of Canada. History and good looks aside, however, Vieux-Montréal still works for a living. Stock brokers and shipping companies continue to operate out of the old financial district. The city's largest newspaper, La Presse, has its offices here. Lawyers in black gowns hurry through the streets to plead cases at the Palais de Justice or the Cour d'Appel, the City Council meets in the Second Empire City Hall on rue Notre-Dame, and local shoppers hunt for deals in the bargain clothing stores just off rue McGill.

MAIN ATTRACTIONS

❸ Fodor'sChoice ★ **Basilique Notre-Dame-de-Montréal** *(Our Lady of Montréal Basilica)*. Few churches in North America are as wow-inducing as Notre Dame. Everything about the place, which opened in 1829, seems designed to make you gasp—from the 228-foot twin towers out front to the tens of thousands of 24-karat gold stars that stud the soaring blue ceiling. Nothing in a city renowned for churches matches Notre-Dame for sheer grandeur—or noisemaking capacity: its 12-ton bass bell is the largest in North America and its 7,000-pipe Cassavant organ can make the walls tremble. The pulpit is a work of art in itself, with an intricately curving staircase and fierce figures of Ezekiel and Jeremiah crouching at its base. Every year dozens of brides march up the aisle of **Chapelle Notre-Dame-du-Sacré-Coeur** (Our Lady of the Sacred Heart Chapel), behind the main altar, to exchange vows with their grooms before a huge modern bronze sculpture that you either love or hate.

In the evening, the nave of the main church is darkened for "La Lumière Fut" ("There Was Light"), a light-and-sound show that depicts the history of Montréal and showcases the church's extraordinary art.

Notre-Dame is an active house of worship, so dress accordingly (i.e., no shorts or bare midriffs). The main church is closed to tours on Sunday during the 9:30 AM, 11 AM, and 5 PM masses. The chapel can't be viewed weekdays during the 12:15 PM and 5 PM masses, and is often closed Saturday for weddings. ⊠ *110 rue Notre-Dame Ouest, Vieux-Montréal* ☎ *514/842–2925 or 866/842–2925* 🌐 *www.basiliquenddm.org* *C$4, including guided tour; La Lumière Fut C$10* ⏲ *Daily 7–5; 20-min tours in French and English every ½ hr July–Sept., weekdays 8–4:30, Sat. 8–3:15, Sun. 12:30–3:15; every 2 hrs (or by prior arrangement) Oct.–June* Ⓜ *Place-d'Armes.*

★ ⓫ **Chapelle Notre-Dame-de-Bon-Secours** *(Our Lady of Perpetual Help Chapel).* Mariners have been popping into Notre-Dame-de-Bon-Secours for centuries to pray for a safe passage—or give thanks for one. Often, they've expressed their gratitude by leaving votive lamps in the shape of small ships, many of which still hang from the barrel-vaulted ceiling. This is why most Montrealers call the chapel the Église des Matelots (the Sailors' Church), and why many still stop by to say a prayer and light a candle before leaving on a long trip. St. Marguerite Bourgeoys, entombed in the side altar on the east side of the chapel, had the original chapel built in 1657. The current chapel dates from 1771; a renovation project in 1998 revealed some beautiful 18th-century murals that had been hidden under layers of paint. The steep climb to the top of the steeple is worth the effort for the glorious view of the harbor, as is the equally steep climb down to the archaeological excavations under the chapel for a glimpse into the chapel's history and the neighborhood. The chapel is closed mid-January through February except for the 10:30 AM mass on Sunday. ⊠ *400 rue St-Paul Est, Vieux-Montréal* ☎ *514/282–8670* 🌐 *www.marguerite-bourgeoys.com* *Museum C$6, museum plus archaeology site with guide C$8* ⏲ *May–Oct., Tues.–Sun. 10–5:30; Nov–mid-Jan., Tues.–Sun. 11–3:30; Mar. and Apr., Tues.–Sun. 11–3:30* Ⓜ *Champ-de-Mars.*

9

OFF THE BEATEN PATH

Fodor's Choice ★

Maison St-Gabriel. Walk into the big, low-ceiling kitchen of the Maison St-Gabriel, close your eyes, and you can almost hear the squeals and giggles of the *filles du roy* (king's daughters) as they learn the niceties of 17th-century home management. The filles du roy were young women who crossed the Atlantic to become the wives and mothers of New France. At the Maison, they learned from St. Marguerite Bourgeoys and her religious order how to cook and clean, how to pray

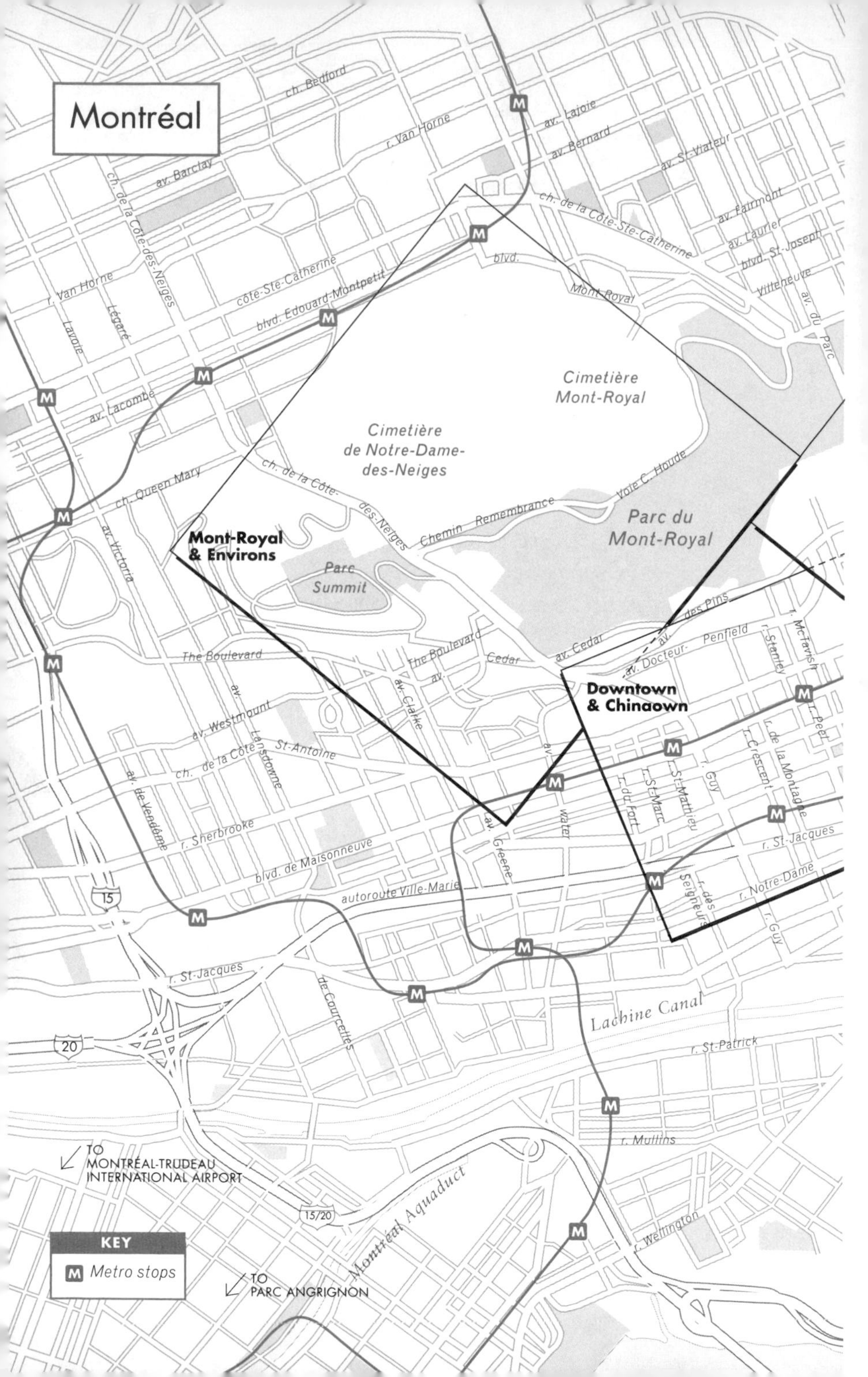

Montréal
Mont-Royal & Environs
Downtown & Chinaown
Cimetière Mont-Royal
Cimetière de Notre-Dame-des-Neiges
Parc du Mont-Royal
Parc Summit
Lachine Canal
Montréal Aquaduct
TO MONTRÉAL-TRUDEAU INTERNATIONAL AIRPORT
TO PARC ANGRIGNON
KEY
Metro stops
ch. Bedford
r. Van Horne
av. Lajoie
av. Bernard
av. St-Viateur
av. Barclay
ch. de la Côte-des-Neiges
ch. de la Côte-Ste-Catherine
av. Fairmont
av. Laurier
blvd. St-Joseph
Villeneuve
av. du Parc
blvd. Mont Royal
côte-Ste-Catherine
blvd. Edouard-Montpetit
Lavoie
Légaré
av. Lacombe
ch. Queen Mary
av. Victoria
Chemin Remembrance
Voie C. Houde
The Boulevard
av. Cedar
av. des Pins
av. Docteur-Penfield
r. McTavish
r. Stanley
r. Peel
av. Clarke
av. Westmount
ch. de la Côte St-Antoine
av. Lansdowne
av. de Vendôme
r. Sherbrooke
blvd. de Maisonneuve
av. Greene
av. Atwater
r. St-Marc
r. du Fort
r. St-Mathieu
r. Guy
r. Crescent
r. de la Montagne
r. St-Jacques
r. des Seigneurs
r. Notre-Dame
autoroute Ville-Marie
15
20
15/20
de Courcelles
r. St-Patrick
r. Mullins
r. Wellington

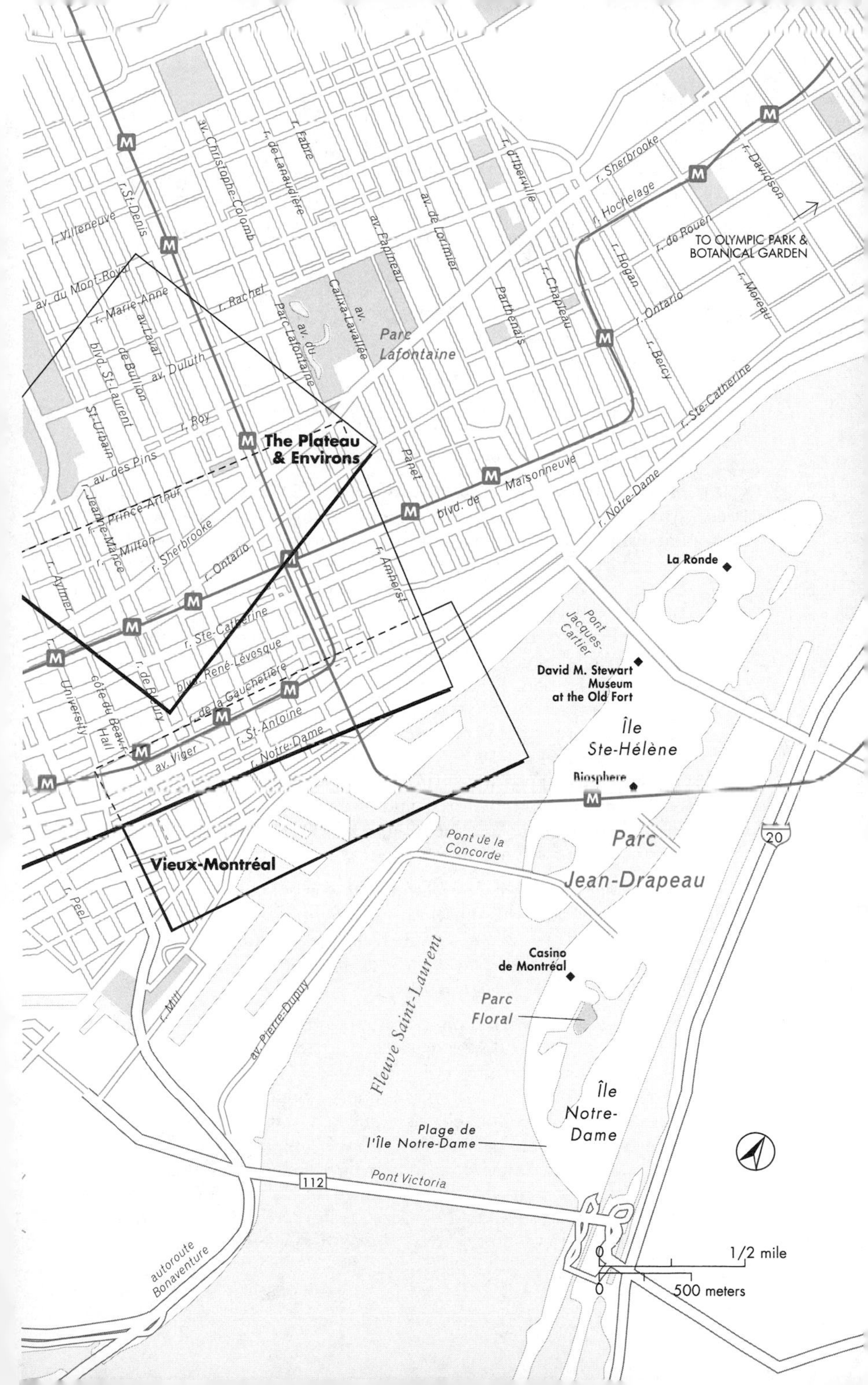

The Plateau & Environs
Vieux-Montréal
TO OLYMPIC PARK & BOTANICAL GARDEN
Parc Lafontaine
La Ronde
Pont Jacques-Cartier
David M. Stewart Museum at the Old Fort
Île Ste-Hélène
Biosphere
Parc Jean-Drapeau
Pont de la Concorde
Casino de Montréal
Parc Floral
Fleuve Saint-Laurent
Île Notre-Dame
Plage de l'Île Notre-Dame
Pont Victoria
112
20
autoroute Bonaventure
av. Pierre-Dupuy
r. Mill
r. Peel
University
côte-du Beaver-Hall
av. Viger
r. St-Antoine
r. Notre-Dame
r. de la Gauchetière
blvd. René-Lévesque
r. Ste-Catherine
r. de Bleury
r. Ontario
r. Sherbrooke
r. Milton
r. Aylmer
r. Jeanne-Mance
r. Prince-Arthur
av. des Pins
St-Urbain
blvd. St-Laurent
de Bullion
av. Laval
r. Marie-Anne
av. Duluth
r. Roy
r. Rachel
av. du Mont-Royal
r. Villeneuve
r. St-Denis
av. Christophe-Colomb
r. de Lanaudière
r. Fabre
av. Papineau
av. de Lorimier
av. Calixa-Lavallée
av. du Parc-Lafontaine
r. Amherst
Papinet
blvd. de Maisonneuve
r. Notre-Dame
r. Ste-Catherine
Parthenais
r. Chapleau
r. d'Iberville
r. Sherbrooke
r. Hochelage
r. de Rouen
r. Hogan
r. Ontario
r. Bercy
r. Davidson
r. Moreau
0
1/2 mile
0
500 meters

and read, and how to survive the rigors of colonial life. St. Marguerite, however, did have the latest in looms and butter churns, laborsaving spit turners for roasting meat, and an ingenious granite sink with a drainage system that piped water straight out to the garden. Well off the beaten path, this little island of New France is certainly worth the 10-minute taxi ride from Vieux-Montréal. ✉*2146 pl. Dublin, Pointe St-Charles* ☎*514/935–8136* 🌐*www.maisonsaint-gabriel.qc.ca* 🎫*C$8* ⏲*June 25–early Sept., Tues.–Sun. 11–6 (guided tours every hr); early-Sept.–mid-Dec. and late Apr.–June 24, Tues.–Sun. 1–5* Ⓜ*Charlevoix, 57 bus.*

WORD OF MOUTH

"While in Montreal, spend some time in Old Montreal where you'll discover several tourists sites, including the Old Port, monuments, religious and government buildings, tourist shops, and a host of good French restaurants, distinctly Quebecois in flavor."

—zola

❹ Fodor's Choice ★ **Musée d'Archéologie et d'Histoire Pointe-à-Callière** *(Pointe-à-Callière Archaeology and History Museum)*. The modern glass building is impressive and the audiovisual show is a breezy romp through Montréal's history from the Ice Age to the present, but the real reason to visit the city's most ambitious archaeological museum is to take the elevator ride down to the 17th century. It's dark down there, and just a little creepy thanks to the 350-year-old tombstones teetering in the gloom, but the trip takes you to the very foundations of the city on the banks of the long-vanished Rivière St-Pierre, where the first settlers built their homes and traded with the Native Canadian inhabitants. From there you climb up toward the present, past the stone foundations of an 18th-century tavern and a 19th-century insurance building. Along the way, filmed figures representing past inhabitants appear on ghostly screens to chat to you about their lives and times. For a spectacular view of the Vieux-Port, the river, and the islands, ride the elevator to the top of the tower, or stop for lunch in the museum's glass-fronted café.

In summer there are re-creations of period fairs and festivals on the grounds near the museum. ✉*350 pl. Royale, Vieux-Montréal* ☎*514/872–9150* 🌐*www.pacmuseum.qc.ca* 🎫*C$12* ⏲*July and Aug., weekdays 10–6, weekends 11–6; Sept.–June, Tues.–Fri. 10–5, weekends 11–5* Ⓜ*Place-d'Armes.*

★ ❼ **Place Jacques-Cartier.** The cobbled square at the heart of Vieux-Montréal is part carnival, part flower market, and part sheer fun. You can pause here to have your portrait painted or to buy an ice cream or to watch the street performers. The 1809 monument honoring Lord Nelson's victory over Napoléon Bonaparte's French navy at Trafalgar angers some modern-day Québec nationalists, but the campaign to raise money for it was led by the Sulpician priests, who were engaged in delicate land negotiations with the British government at the time and were eager to show what good subjects they were. ✉*Bordered by rues Notre-Dame Est and de la Commune, Vieux-Montréal* Ⓜ*Champ-de-Mars.*

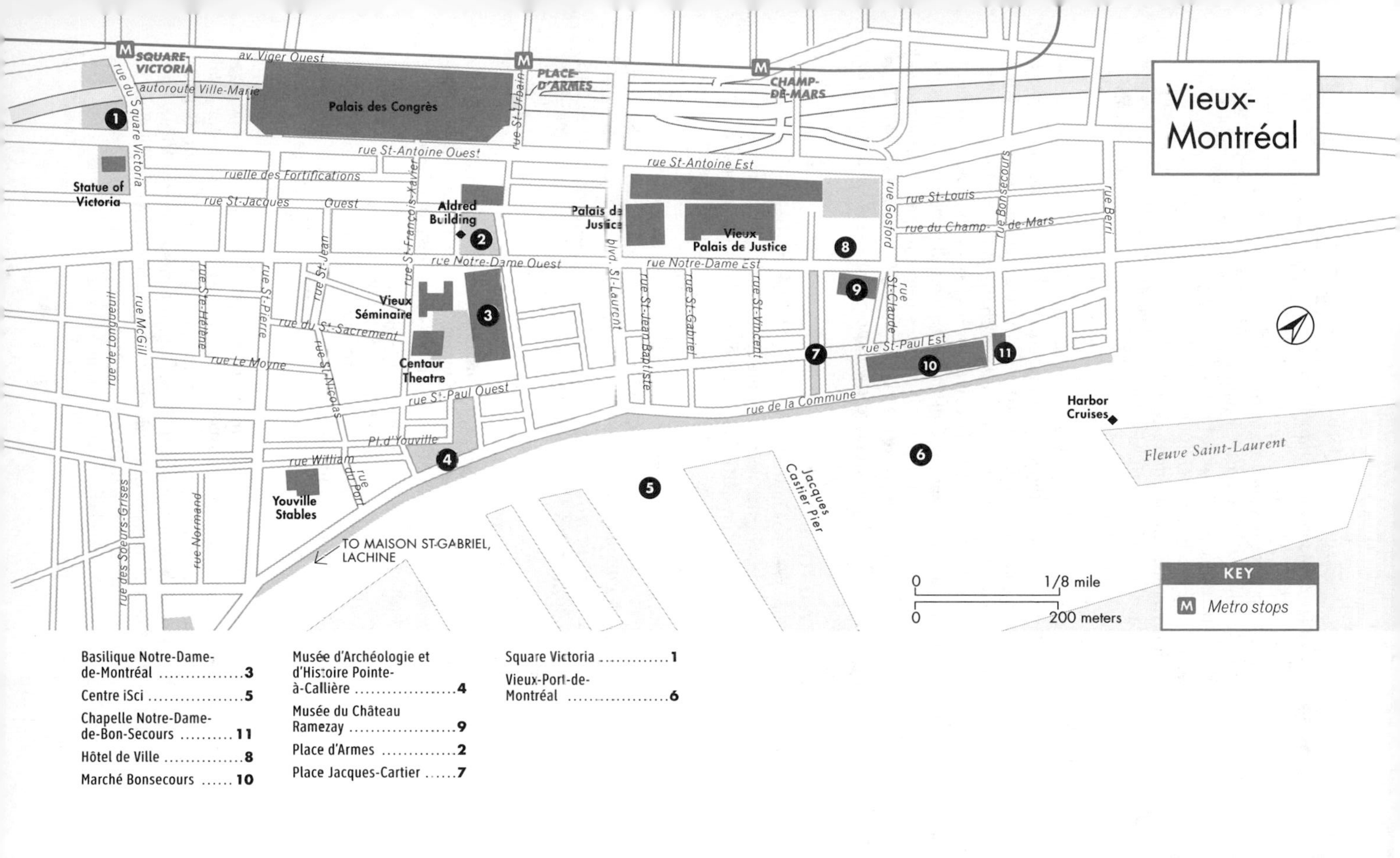
Vieux-Montréal
SQUARE-VICTORIA
PLACE-D'ARMES
CHAMP-DE-MARS
av. Viger Ouest
autoroute Ville-Marie
Palais des Congrès
rue du Square Victoria
Statue of Victoria
rue St-Antoine Ouest
ruelle des Fortifications
rue St-Jacques Ouest
Aldred Building
rue St-François-Xavier
rue St-Urbain
Palais de Justice
Vieux Palais de Justice
rue St-Antoine Est
rue Notre-Dame Ouest
rue Notre-Dame Est
blvd. St-Laurent
rue St-Jean-Baptiste
rue St-Gabriel
rue St-Vincent
rue Gosford
rue St-Louis
rue du Champ-de-Mars
rue Bonsecours
rue Berri
rue St-Claude
rue St-Paul Est
rue St-Paul Ouest
rue de la Commune
Vieux Séminaire
Centaur Theatre
rue du St-Sacrement
rue St-Jean
rue St-Nicolas
rue Le Moyne
rue St-Pierre
rue Ste-Hélène
rue McGill
rue de Longueuil
rue des Soeurs-Grises
rue Normand
Pl. d'Youville
rue William
rue du Port
Youville Stables
TO MAISON ST-GABRIEL, LACHINE
Jacques Castier Pier
Harbor Cruises
Fleuve Saint-Laurent
0 1/8 mile
0 200 meters
KEY
Metro stops
Basilique Notre-Dame-de-Montréal 3
Centre iSci 5
Chapelle Notre-Dame-de-Bon-Secours 11
Hôtel de Ville 8
Marché Bonsecours 10
Musée d'Archéologie et d'Histoire Pointe-à-Callière 4
Musée du Château Ramezay 9
Place d'Armes 2
Place Jacques-Cartier 7
Square Victoria 1
Vieux-Port-de-Montréal 6

WORD OF MOUTH

"We visited both St Joseph's and The Basilica in Montréal. The Basilica Notre Dame is stunning. I did gasp a bit at its sheer beauty when we entered."

—PamSF

★ 6 **Vieux-Port-de-Montréal** *(Old Port of Montréal).* Montréal's favorite waterfront park is your ideal gateway to the St. Lawrence River. You can rent a pedal boat, take a ferry to **Île Ste-Hélène,** sign up for a dinner cruise, or, if you're really adventurous, ride a raft through the turbulent Lachine Rapids. If you're determined to stay ashore, however, there's still plenty do. You can rent a bicycle or a pair of in-line skates at one of the shops along rue de la Commune and explore the waterfront at your leisure or visit the iSci science center on **King Edward Pier.** If your lungs are in good shape you can climb the 192 steps to the top of the **Clock Tower** for a view of the waterfront and the islands at the eastern end of the waterfront. Every couple of years or so, Montréal's Cirque du Soleil comes home to pitch its blue-and-yellow tent in the Vieux-Port. ⊠ *Vieux-Montréal* ☎ *514/496–7678 or 800/971–7678* 🌐 *www.quaysoftheoldport.com* Ⓜ *Place-d'Armes or Champ-de-Mars.*

ALSO WORTH SEEING

5 **Centre iSci.** You—or more likely, your kids—can design an energy-efficient bike, decode an electronic message, analyze data from satellite photos, try using an MRI image to make a diagnosis, or just watch an IMAX movie on a giant screen at Montréal's interactive science center. Games, puzzles, and hands-on experiments make it an ideal place for rainy days or even fair ones. ⊠ *Quai King Edward, Vieux-Montréal* ☎ *514/496–4724 or 877/496–4724* 🌐 *www.isci.ca* 🎫 *Exhibit halls C$10, IMAX C$12, combined ticket C$17* ⏲ *May 10–Sept. 16, daily 9 AM–9 PM; Sept. 16 to May 10, weekdays 8:30–4, weekends 9:30–5* Ⓜ *Place-d'Armes.*

8 **Hôtel de Ville** *(City Hall).* President Charles de Gaulle of France marked Canada's centennial celebrations in 1967 by standing on the central balcony of Montréal's ornate city hall on July 24 and shouting "*Vive le Québec libre*" ("Long live free Québec"), much to the delight of the separatist movement, and to the horror of of the federal government that had invited him over in the first place. Perhaps he got carried away because he felt so at home: the Second Empire–style city hall, built in 1878, is modeled after the one in Tours, France. Free guided tours are available daily 9–5 in June, July, and August. ⊠ *275 rue Notre-Dame Est, Vieux-Montréal* ☎ *514/872–3355* 🎫 *Free* ⏲ *Daily 9–5* Ⓜ *Champ-de-Mars.*

10 **Marché Bonsecours** *(Bonsecours Market).* You can't buy fruits and vegetables in the Marché Bonsecours anymore, but you can shop for local fashions and crafts in the row of upscale boutiques that fill its main hall, or lunch in one of several restaurants opening onto the Vieux-Port or rue St-Paul. But the Marché is best admired from the outside. Built in the 1840s as the city's main market, it is possibly the most beautifully proportioned neoclassical building in Montréal, with its six cast-iron

GREAT ITINERARIES

Getting a real feel for this bilingual, multicultural city takes some time. An ideal stay is five days, but even three days of walking and soaking up the atmosphere is enough time to visit Mont-Royal, explore Vieux-Montréal, do some shopping, and perhaps visit the Stade Olympique (recommended for children). It also includes enough nights for an evening of bar-hopping on rue St-Denis or rue Crescent and another for enjoying a long, luxurious dinner at one of the city's excellent restaurants.

IF YOU HAVE 3 DAYS

Any visit to Montréal should start with the peak of Mont-Royal, the city's most enduring symbol. Afterward wander down to avenue des Pins and then through McGill University to downtown. Make an effort to stop at the Musée des Beaux-Arts de Montréal and St. Patrick's Basilica. On Day 2, explore Vieux-Montréal, with special emphasis on the Basilique Notre-Dame-de-Montréal, the Chapelle Notre-Dame-de-Bon-Secours, and the Musée d'Archéologie et d'Histoire Pointe-à-Callière. On Day 3 you can either visit the Stade Olympique or stroll through the Quartier Latin.

IF YOU HAVE 5 DAYS

Start with a visit to Parc du Mont-Royal. After viewing the city from the Chalet du Mont-Royal, visit the Oratoire St-Joseph. You should still have enough time to visit the Musée des Beaux-Arts before dinner. On Day 2, get in some shopping as you explore downtown, with perhaps a visit to the Centre Canadien d'Architecture. Spend all of Day 3 in Vieux-Montréal, and on Day 4 stroll through the Quartier Latin. On Day 5, visit the Stade Olympique and then do one of three things: visit the islands, take a ride on the Lachine Rapids, or revisit some of the sights you missed in Vieux-Montréal or downtown.

Doric columns and two rows of meticulously even sashed windows, all topped with a silvery dome. The parliament of Canada met briefly in the market's upper hall in the late 1800s. ✉*350 rue St-Paul Est, Vieux-Montréal* ☎*514/872–7730* 🌐*www.marchebonsecours.qc.ca* Ⓜ*Champ-de-Mars.*

★ ❾ **Musée du Château Ramezay.** Claude de Ramezay, the city's 11th governor, was probably daydreaming of home when he built his Montréal residence. Its thick stone walls, dormer windows, and steeply pitched roof make it look like a little bit of 18th-century Normandy dropped into the middle of North America—although the round, squat tower is a 19th-century addition. The extravagant mahogany paneling in the Salon de Nantes was installed when Louis XV was still king of France. Most of the exhibits are a little staid—guns, uniforms, and documents on the main floor and tableaux depicting colonial life in the cellars—but they include some unexpected eccentricities, such as the bright-red automobile the De Dion-Bouton Co. produced at the turn of the 20th century for the city's first motorist. ✉*280 rue Notre-Dame Est, Vieux-Montréal* ☎*514/861–3708* 🌐*www.chateauramezay.qc.ca* 🎟*C$8* ⏲*June–mid-Oct., daily 10–6; Oct.–May, Tues.–Sun. 10–4:30* Ⓜ*Champ-de-Mars.*

CLOSE UP

Montréal History

The first European settlement on Montréal island was Ville-Marie, founded in 1642 by 54 pious men and women under the leadership of Paul de Chomedey, sieur de Maisonneuve, and Jeanne Mance, a French noblewoman, who hoped to create a new Christian society.

But piety wasn't Ville-Marie's only raison d'être. The settlement's location on the banks of the St. Lawrence and Ottawa rivers meant a lucrative trade in beaver pelts, as the fur was a staple of European hat fashion for nearly a century.

The French regime in Canada ended with the Seven Years' War—what Americans call the French and Indian War. The Treaty of Paris ceded all of New France to Britain in 1763. American troops under Generals Richard Montgomery and Benedict Arnold occupied the city during their 1775–76 campaign to conquer Canada, but their efforts failed and the troops withdrew. Soon invaders of another kind—English and Scottish settlers, traders, and merchants—poured into Montréal. By 1832 the city became a leading colonial capital. But 1837 brought anti-British rebellions, and the unrest led to Canada's becoming a self-governing dominion in 1867.

The city's ports continued to bustle until the St. Lawrence Seaway opened in 1957, allowing ships to sail from the Atlantic to the Great Lakes without having to stop in Montréal to transfer cargo.

The opening of the Métro in 1966 changed the way Montrealers lived, and the next year the city hosted the World's Fair. But the rise of Québec separatism in the late 1960s under the charismatic René Lévesque created political uncertainty, and many major businesses moved to Toronto. By the time Lévesque's separatist Parti Québécois won power in Québec in 1976—the same year the summer Olympics came to the city—Montréal was clearly No. 2.

Uncertainty continued through the 1980s and '90s, with the separatist Parti Québécois and the federalist Liberals alternating in power in Québec City. Since 1980 the city has endured four referenda on the future of Québec and Canada. In the most recent—the cliff-hanger of 1995—just 50.58% of Québécois voted to remain part of Canada. Montréal bucked the separatist trend and voted nearly 70% against independence.

❷ **Place d'Armes.** The pigeons are particularly fond of the triumphant statue of Montréal's founder, Paul de Chomedey, with his lance upraised, perched above the fountain in the middle of this cobblestone square. He slew an Iroquois chief in a battle here in 1644 and was wounded in return. ✉ *Bordered by rues Notre-Dame Ouest, St-Jacques, and St-Sulpice, Vieux-Montréal* Ⓜ *Place-d'Armes.*

❶ **Square Victoria.** The perfect Montréal mix: an 1872 statue of Queen Victoria on one side and an authentic Parisian Métro entrance on the other. Both are framed by a two-block stretch of trees, benches, and fountains that makes a great place to relax and admire the handsome 1920s business buildings on the east side. The art nouveau Métro entrance, incidentally, was a gift from the French capital's transit commission. ✉ *Rue Square Victoria, between rues Viger and St-Jacques, Vieux-Montréal* Ⓜ *Square-Victoria.*

DOWNTOWN & CHINATOWN

> **WORD OF MOUTH**
>
> "In Old Montréal there is a strip of nice galleries between St. Sulpice and St. Laurent Street."
>
> —mitchdesi

Rue Ste-Catherine—and the Métro line that runs under it—is the main cord that binds together the disparate, sprawling neighborhoods that comprise Montréal's **downtown,** or *centre-ville.* It's a long, boisterous, sometimes seedy, and sometimes elegant street that runs from rue Claremont in Westmount to rue d'Iberville in the east end. The downtown stretch—usually clogged with traffic and lined with department stores, boutiques, bars, restaurants, strip clubs, amusement arcades, theaters, cinemas, art galleries, bookstores, and even a few churches—is considerably shorter, running from avenue Atwater to boulevard St-Laurent, where downtown morphs into the Quartier Latin and the Village, the center of Montréal's gay and lesbian community.

Much of the real action, however, happens on such cross streets as Crescent, Bishop, de la Montagne, and Peel, which are packed with some of the district's best clubs, restaurants, and boutiques. One of the livliest blocks in the city than is the stretch of rue Crescent between rue Ste-Catherine and boulevard de Maisonneuve.

A little farther north on the lower slopes of Mont-Royal is what used to be the most exclusive neighborhood in Canada—the Golden Square Mile. During the boom years of the mid-1800s, the families who lived in the area—most of them Scottish and Protestant—controlled about 70% of the country's wealth. Their baronial homes and handsome churches covered the mountain north of rue Sherbrooke roughly between avenue Côte-des-Neiges and rue University. Many of the old homes are gone—replaced by high-rises or modern town houses—but there are still plenty of architectural treasures for you to admire, even if most of them are now foreign consulates or university institutes.

At the other end of the downtown area is **Chinatown,** an 18-block area between boulevard René-Lévesque and avenue Viger to the north and south, and near rue de Bleury and avenue Hôtel de Ville on the west and east. Chinese people first came to Montréal in large numbers after 1880, following the construction of the transcontinental railroad. Their legacy is a shrinking but lively neighborhood of mainly Chinese and Southeast Asian restaurants, food stores, and gift shops.

MAIN ATTRACTIONS

7 **Cathédrale Marie-Reine-du-Monde** *(Mary Queen of the World Cathedral).* The best reason to visit this cathedral is that it's a quarter-scale replica of St. Peter's Basilica, complete with a magnificent reproduction of Bernini's ornate baldachin (canopy) over the main altar and an ornately

CLOSE UP

Art in the Métro

Operating since 1966, the Métro is among the most architecturally distinctive subway systems in the world, with each of its 65 stations individually designed and decorated. The largest of these is Berri-UQAM, a cross-shaped station with many corridors filled with artworks. The most memorable pieces include a huge black granite bench; three Expo '67 murals depicting science, culture, and recreation; a 25th-anniversary plaque and time capsule; a statue of Montréal heroine Mother Émilie Gamelin, a 19th-century nun who worked with the poor; and a vibrant red-and-blue stained-glass mural depicting three founders of Montréal.

The newer stations along the Blue Line are all worth a visit as well, particularly Outremont, with a glass-block design from 1988. Even Place-d'Armes, one of the least visually remarkable stations in the system, includes a treasure: look for the small exhibit of archaeological artifacts representing each of Montréal's four historical eras (Aboriginal, French, English, and multicultural).

coffered ceiling. ✉ *1085 rue de la Cathédrale (enter through main doors on blvd. René-Lévesque), Downtown* ☎ *514/866–1661* 🌐 *www.cathedralecatholiquedemontreal.org* *Free* ⏲ *Weekdays 6:30 AM–6:30 PM, Sat. 7 AM–6:30 PM, Sun. 7 AM–6:30 PM* Ⓜ *Bonaventure or Peel.*

❸ **Christ Church Cathedral.** This cathedral offers a series of free noontime concerts and organ recitals that are very popular with downtowners and visitors alike, and offers a bit of a respite from Ste-Catherine's crowds. Built in 1859, the cathedral is modeled on Snettisham Parish Church in Norfolk, England, with some distinctly Canadian touches. The steeple, for example, is made with aluminum plates molded to simulate stone, and inside, the Gothic arches are crowned with carvings of the types of foliage growing on Mont-Royal when the church was built. ✉ *635 rue Ste-Catherine Ouest, Downtown* ☎ *514/843–6577* 🌐 *www.montreal.anglican.org/cathedral* *Free* ⏲ *Daily 10–6* Ⓜ *McGill.*

★ ❶ **Musée d'Art Contemporain** *(Museum of Contemporary Art).* If you have a taste for pastoral landscapes and formal portraits, you might want to stick with the Musée des Beaux-Arts. But for a walk on the wild side of art, see what you can make of the jagged splashes of color that cover the canvases of the "Automatistes," as Québec's rebellious artists of the 1930s styled themselves. Their works form the core of this museum's collection of 5,000 pieces. One of the leaders of the movement, Jean-Paul Riopelle (1923–2002), often tossed his brushes and palette knives aside and just squeezed the paint directly on to the canvas—sometimes several tubes at a time. Hours for guided tours vary. ✉ *185 rue Ste-Catherine Ouest, Downtown* ☎ *514/847–6226* 🌐 *www.macm.org* *C$8, free Wed. after 6 PM* ⏲ *Mid-June–Labor Day, Mon.–Tues. 11–6, Wed. 11–9, Thurs.–Sun. 11–6; closed Mondays the rest of the year* Ⓜ *Place-des-Arts.*

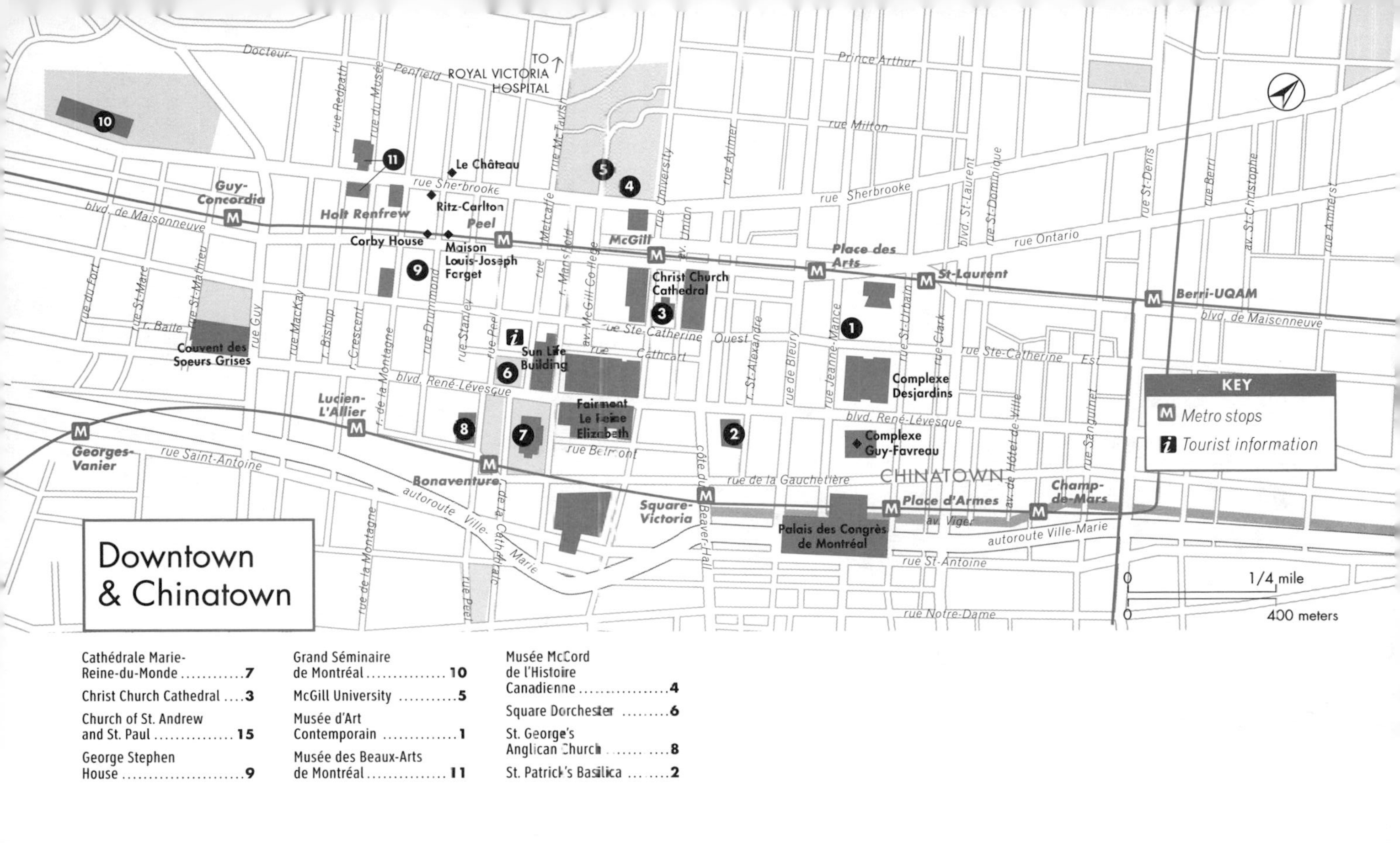
Downtown
& Chinatown
KEY
Metro stops
Tourist information
0
1/4 mile
0
400 meters
Cathédrale Marie-Reine-du-Monde 7
Christ Church Cathedral 3
Church of St. Andrew and St. Paul 15
George Stephen House 9
Grand Séminaire de Montréal 10
McGill University 5
Musée d'Art Contemporain 1
Musée des Beaux-Arts de Montréal 11
Musée McCord de l'Histoire Canadienne 4
Square Dorchester 6
St. George's Anglican Church 8
St. Patrick's Basilica 2
TO ROYAL VICTORIA HOSPITAL
Guy-Concordia
Peel
McGill
Place des Arts
St-Laurent
Berri-UQAM
Lucien-L'Allier
Georges-Vanier
Bonaventure
Square-Victoria
Place d'Armes
Champ-de-Mars
Le Château
Ritz-Carlton
Holt Renfrew
Corby House
Maison Louis-Joseph Forget
Christ Church Cathedral
Sun Life Building
Fairmont Le Reine Elizabeth
Couvent des Soeurs Grises
Complexe Desjardins
Complexe Guy-Favreau
CHINATOWN
Palais des Congrès de Montréal
Docteur-Penfield
Prince Arthur
rue Milton
rue Sherbrooke
rue Ontario
blvd. de Maisonneuve
rue Ste-Catherine Ouest
rue Ste-Catherine Est
rue Cathcart
blvd. René-Lévesque
rue Belmont
rue de la Gauchetière
rue Saint-Antoine
rue St-Antoine
autoroute Ville-Marie
av. Viger
rue Notre-Dame
rue du Fort
rue St-Marc
rue St-Mathieu
r. Baile
rue Guy
rue MacKay
r. Bishop
r. Crescent
r. de la Montagne
rue de la Montagne
rue Drummond
rue Stanley
rue Peel
rue Metcalfe
r. Mansfield
av. McGill College
rue University
av. Union
rue Aylmer
r. St-Alexandre
rue de Bleury
rue Jeanne-Mance
rue St-Urbain
rue Clark
blvd. St-Laurent
rue St-Dominique
av. de l'Hôtel de Ville
rue Sanguinet
rue St-Denis
rue Berri
av. St-Christophe
rue Amherst
rue Redpath
rue du Musée
rue McTavish
côte du Beaver-Hall
de la Cathédrale

CLOSE UP

The Other "Downtown"

When Place Ville-Marie, the cruciform skyscraper designed by I. M. Pei, opened in the heart of downtown in 1962, the tallest structure of the time also signaled the beginning of Montréal's subterranean city. Montrealers were skeptical that anyone would want to shop or even walk around in the new "down" town, but more than four decades later they can't live without it. About half a million people use the 30-km (19-mi) underground pedestrian network daily. The tunnels link 10 Métro stations, 7 hotels, 200 restaurants, 1,700 boutiques, and 60 office buildings—not to mention movie theaters, concert halls, convention complexes, the Bell Centre, two universities and a college, and subway, commuter rail, and bus stations. Montrealers who live in one of more than 2,000 apartments connected to the Underground City can pop out to buy a liter of milk on a February day and never have to change out of shirtsleeves and house slippers.

Most of the Underground City parallels the Métro lines. The six-block sector of continuous shopping between La Baie (east of the McGill station) and Les Cours Montréal (west of the Peel station) is perhaps the densest portion of the network. Montréal was ahead of the curve in requiring all construction in the Métro system to include an art component, resulting in such dramatic works as Frédéric Back's mural of the history of music in Place-des-Arts and the dramatically swirling stained-glass windows by Marcelle Ferron in Champs-de-Mars. The art nouveau entrance to the Square Victoria station, a gift from the city of Paris, is the only original piece of Hector Guimard's architectural-design work outside the City of Light.

—By Patricia Harris and David Lyon

⓫ Fodor's Choice ★ **Musée des Beaux-Arts de Montréal** *(Montréal Museum of Fine Arts)*. Canada's oldest museum has been accumulating art from all over the world since 1860. If landscapes are your thing, the collected works of Québec artist Marc-Aurèle Fortin were acquired by the museum in 2007. The museum's permanent collection includes everyone from Rembrandt to Renoir, and not surprisingly, one of the best assemblies of Canadian art anywhere, with works by such luminaries as Paul Kane, the Group of Seven, and Paul-Émile Borduas.You can trace the country's history from New France to New Age through the museum's decorative art, painting, and sculpture. But it's not all serious: in 2001 the museum absorbed the Musée des Arts Décoratifs, so you can also take a look at bentwood furniture designed by Frank Gehry, 18th-century English porcelain, and 3,000—count 'em—Japanese snuffboxes collected by, of all people, Georges Clémenceau, France's prime minister during World War I. All this is housed in two buildings linked by an underground tunnel—the neoclassical **Michal and Renata Hornstein Pavilion,** on the north side of rue Sherbrooke, and the glass-fronted **Jean-Noël-Desmarais Pavilion,** across the street. The museum also has a gift shop, a bookstore, a restaurant, a cafeteria, and a gallery where you can buy or even rent paintings by local artists. ✉ *1380 rue Sherbrooke Ouest, Square Mile* ☎ *514/285–2000* 🌐 *www.mmfa.qc.ca* 🎟 *Permanent collection* *free, special exhibits C$15, C$7.50 Wed. ⏲Tues.–Fri. 11–9, weekends 10–6 Ⓜ Guy-Concordia.*

WORD OF MOUTH

"The Métro is really easy to navigate in Montréal. You will be able to get a map at all Métro booths."
—Jojonana

★ 4 **Musée McCord de l'Histoire Canadienne** *(McCord Museum of Canadian History)*. David Ross McCord (1844–1930) was a wealthy pack rat with a passion for anything that had to do with Montréal and its history. His collection of paintings, costumes, toys, tools, drawings, and housewares provides a glimpse of what city life was like for all classes in the 19th century. If you're interested in the lifestyles of the elite, however, you'll love the photographs that William Notman (1826–91) took of the rich at play. One series portrays members of the posh Montréal Athletic Association posing in snowshoes on the slopes of Mont-Royal. There are guided tours (call for schedule), a reading room, a documentation center, a gift shop, a bookstore, and a café. ✉*690 rue Sherbrooke Ouest, Square Mile* ☎*514/398–7100* 🌐*www.mccord-museum.qc.ca* *C$12* ⏲*June 25–early Sept., Mon. and weekends 10–5, Tues.–Fri. 10–6; early Sept.–June 24, Tues.–Fri. 10–6, weekends 10–5* Ⓜ *McGill.*

★ 2 **St. Patrick's Basilica.** St. Pat's—as most of its parishioners call it—is the mother church the Montréal's Anglophone Catholics. Built in 1847, it is one of the purest examples of the Gothic Revival style in Canada, with a high vaulted ceiling glowing with green and gold mosaics. The tall, slender columns made of pine logs are decorated to look like marble. One of the joys of visiting the place is that you'll probably be the only tourist there, so you'll have plenty of time to check out the old pulpit and the huge lamp decorated with six 6-foot-tall angels hanging over the main altar. ✉*454 blvd. René Lévesque Ouest, Downtown* ☎*514/866–7379* 🌐*www.stpatricksmtl.ca* *Free* ⏲*Daily 8:30–6* Ⓜ *Square-Victoria.*

ALSO WORTH SEEING

9 **George Stephen House.** Sir George Stephen (1829–1921) the Scottish-born founder of the Canadian Pacific Railway, was the Donald Trump of his day. In 1882 he spent C$600,000—an almost unimaginable sum at the time—to build a home for himself and his family. Artisans from all over the world paneled its ceilings with Cuban mahogany, Indian lemon tree, and English oak and covered its walls in marble, onyx, and gold. It's now a private club, but you can get a glimpse of all this grandeur on Saturday evening when the dining room welcomes the public for dinner (C$40 for three courses, C$70 for seven) and on Sunday for brunch and music (C$42, including a guided tour). ✉*1440 rue Drummond, Square Mile* ☎*514/849–7338* 🌐*www.clubmountstephen.net* *Reservations essential* Ⓜ *Peel or Guy-Concordia.*

10 **Grand Séminaire de Montréal.** Education goes way back at the Grand Séminaire. In the mid-1600s, St. Marguerite Bourgeoys used one of the two stone towers in the garden as a school for First Nations (Native Canadian) girls while she and her nuns lived in the other. The 1860

CLOSE UP

Underground City Know-How

To get the optimum use of the whole network of tunnels, shops, and Métro lines that make up the Underground City, buy a Métro pass. Daily and weekly passes are available. Start at Place Ville-Marie. This was the first link in the system and is still part of the main hub. From here you could cover most of the main sites—from the Centre Bell to Place des Arts—without ever coming up and without having to take the Métro. But the network is so large, you'll want to use the subway system to save time, energy, and wear and tear on your feet. You might also want to explore some of the Underground City's more remote centers—the Grande Bibliothèque or Westmount Square, for example. Remember: it's easy to get lost. There are no landmarks and routes are seldom direct, so keep your eyes on the signs (a Métro map helps), and if you start to feel panicky, come up for air.

seminary buildings behind the towers are now used by men studying for the priesthood. In summer there are free guided tours of the towers, the extensive gardens, and the college's beautiful Romanesque chapel. *✉2065 rue Sherbrooke Ouest, Square Mile ☎514/935–7775 Ext. 239 📠514/935–5497 🌐www.gsdm.qc.ca 🎟By donation ⏲Guided tours June–Aug., Tues.–Sat. at 1 and 3* PM*; mass Sept.–June, Sun. at 10:30* AM *Ⓜ Guy-Concordia.*

5 **McGill University.** Merchant James McGill would probably be horrified to know that the university that he helped found in 1828 has developed an international reputation as one of North America's best party schools. The administration isn't too happy about it, either. But McGill is also one of the English-language universities in Canada, and certainly one of the prettiest. Its campus is an island of grass and trees in a sea of traffic and skyscrapers. If you take the time to stroll up the drive that leads from the Greek Revival Roddick Gates to the austere neoclassical Arts Building, keep an eye out to your right for the life-size statue of McGill himself, hurrying across campus clutching his tricorn hat. If you have an hour or so, drop into the templelike **Redpath Museum of Natural History** to browse its eclectic collection of dinosaur bones, old coins, African art, and shrunken heads. *✉859 rue Sherbrooke Ouest, Square Mile ☎514/398–4455, 514/398–4094 tours, 514/398–4086 museum 🌐www.mcgill.ca 🎟Free ⏲Museum weekdays 9–5, Sun. 1–5 (June–Aug., closed Fri.) Ⓜ McGill.*

NEED A BREAK?

Sit in the shade of one of the 100-year-old maples at McGill University (*✉859 rue Sherbrooke Ouest, Square Mile ☎514/398–4455 Ⓜ McGill*) and read a chapter or two of a Montréal classic like Hugh MacLennan's *Two Solitudes*, or just let the world drift by.

 **Square Dorchester.** On sunny summer days you can join the office workers, store clerks, and downtown shoppers who gather in Square Dorchester to eat lunch under the trees and perhaps listen to an open-air concert. If there are no vacant benches or picnic tables, you can

still find a place to sit on the steps at the base of the dramatic monument to the dead of the Boer War. Other statues honor Scottish poet Robert Burns (1759–96) and Sir Wilfrid Laurier (1841–1919), Canada's first French-speaking prime minister. ✉ *Bordered by blvd. René-Lévesque and rues Peel, Metcalfe, and McTavish, Downtown* Ⓜ *Bonaventure or Peel.*

CALÈCHE-CATCHING?

The best place to find a calèche for a horse-drawn tour of the old city is on the south side of Place d'Armes. And be careful what you pay. Fares are set by the city. In 2007 they were C$45 for a 30-minute ride and C$75 for an hour.

8 **St. George's Anglican Church.** St. George's is possibly the prettiest Anglican (Episcopalian) church in Montréal. Step into its dim, candle-scented interior and you'll feel you've been transported to some prosperous market town in East Anglia. The double hammer-beam roof, the rich stained-glass windows, and the Lady Chapel on the east side of the main altar all add to the effect. ✉ *1101 rue Stanley, Downtown* ☎ *514/866–7113* 🌐 *www.st-georges.org* 🎫 *Free* ⏲ *Tues.–Sun. 9–4; Sun. services at 9 and 10:30* AM Ⓜ *Bonaventure.*

THE PLATEAU & ENVIRONS

Plateau Mont-Royal—or simply The Plateau—is still home to a vibrant Portuguese community, but much of the housing originally built for factory workers has been bought up and renovated by artists, professionals, and academics eager to find houses that are also close to all the action. The **Quartier Latin** or the **Quartier Latin** just south of the Plateau has been drawing the young since the 1700s, when Université de Montréal students gave the area its name. Both the Quartier Latin and the Plateau have rows of French and ethnic restaurants, bistros, coffee shops, designer boutiques, antiques shops, and art galleries.

The gentrification of the Plateau inevitably pushed up rents and drove students, immigrant families, and single young graduates out farther north to **Mile-End,** an old working-class neighborhood that is now full of inexpensive restaurants and funky little shops selling handicrafts and secondhand clothes. Farther north is **Little Italy,** which is still home base to Montréal's enormous Italian community.

The lively strip of rue Ste-Catherine running east of the Quartier Latin is the backbone of the **Village**—Montréal's main gay community. Its restaurants, antiques shops (on rue Amherst), and bars make it a popular destination for visitors of all persuasions.

Many of the older residences in these neighborhoods have the wrought-iron balconies and twisting staircases typical of Montréal. To save interior space, the stairs leading to the upper floors or working-class tenements were placed outside. In summer, the stairs and balconies are often full of families and couples gossiping, picnicking, and partying. If Montrealers tell you they spend the summer in Balconville, they mean

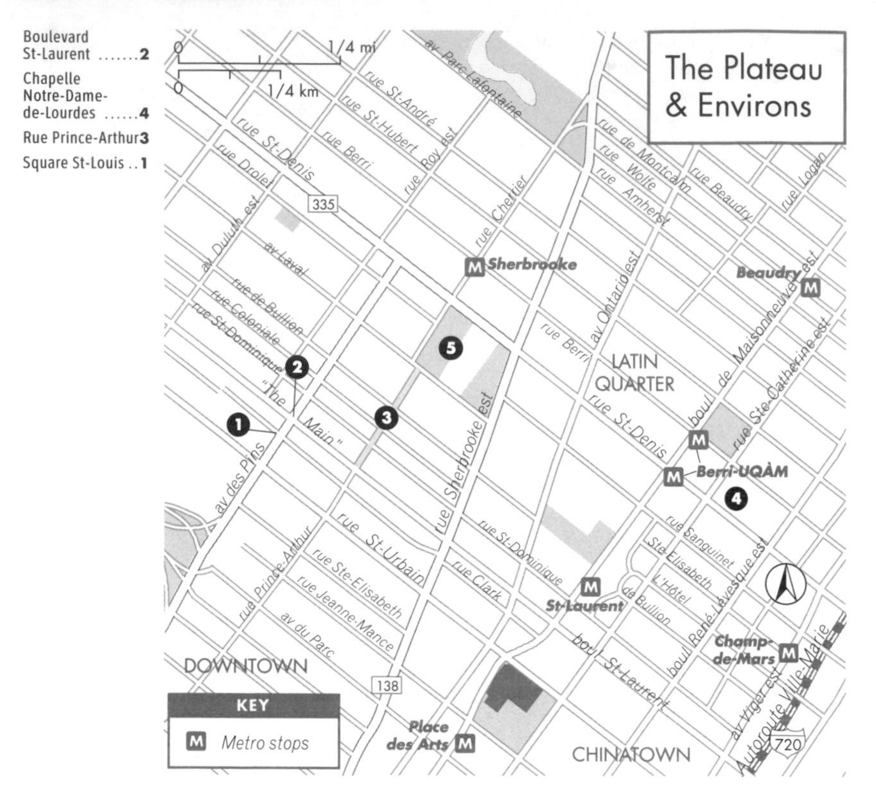

they don't have the money or the time to leave town and won't get any farther than their balconies.

MAIN ATTRACTIONS

❷ **Boulevard St-Laurent.** A walk along boulevard St-Laurent is like a walk through Montréal's cultural history. The shops and restaurants, synagogues and churches, that line the 10-block stretch north of rue Sherbrooke reflect the various waves of immigrants that have called it home. Keep your eyes open and you'll see Jewish delis, Hungarian sausage shops, Chinese grocery stores, Portuguese favelas, Italian coffee bars, Greek restaurants, Vietnamese sandwich shops, and Peruvian snack bars. You'll also spot some of the city's trendiest restaurants and nightclubs. It was Jewish refugees fleeing pogroms in Eastern Europe who first called the street "the Main," as in Main Street—a nickname that endures to this day. Ⓜ *St-Laurent, Sherbrooke, or Mont-Royal.*

NEED A BREAK?

Wilensky's Light Lunch (✉ *34 av. Fairmount Ouest, Plateau Mont-Royal* ☎ *514/271-0247* Ⓜ *Laurier*) hasn't changed its decor, menu, or 'tude since 1932. Stop in for the infamous special—grilled salami or bologna on an onion roll with a splash of mustard and a cherry Coke, or maybe an egg cream. The food's cheap and the nostalgia's free.

❹ **Chapelle Notre-Dame-de-Lourdes** *(Our Lady of Lourdes Chapel).* Artist and architect Napoléon Bourassa called the Chapelle Notre-Dame-des-Lourdes *l'oeuvre de mes amours,* or a labor of love—and it shows. He designed the little Byzantine-style building himself and set about decorating it with the exuberance of an eight-year-old making a Mother's Day card. He covered the walls with murals and encrusted the altar and pillars with gilt and ornamental carving. ✉ *430 rue Ste-Catherine Est, Quartier Latin* 🎟 *Free* ⏲ *Mon.–Sat. 7:30–6, Sun. 9–6:30* Ⓜ *Berri-UQAM.*

> **WORD OF MOUTH**
>
> "The Plateau/Quartier Latin—to me this is the 'real' Montreal. Very French, very lively. Lots of outdoor cafés, small shops, byob restaurants, ethnic neighborhoods. It gets a bit run down as you get into the lower end, near St. Catherine, but much of it is quiet tree-lined streets." —zootsi

❸ **Rue Prince-Arthur.** In the 1960s rue Prince-Arthur was the Haight-Ashbury of Montréal, full of shops selling leather vests, tie-dyed T-shirts, recycled clothes, and drug paraphernalia. It still retains a little of that raffish attitude, but it's much tamer and more commercial these days. The blocks between avenue Laval and boulevard St-Laurent are a pedestrian mall, and the hippie shops have metamorphosed into inexpensive Greek, Vietnamese, Italian, Polish, and Chinese restaurants and neighborhood bars. So grab a table, order a coffee or an *apéro,* and watch the passing parade. Ⓜ *Sherbrooke.*

❶ **Square St-Louis.** The prosperous bourgeois families who built their comfortable homes around Square St-Louis's fountain and trees in the late 1870s would probably be dismayed to see the kind of people who congregate in their little park these days. It's difficult to walk through the place without dodging a skateboarder or a panhandler. But the square is still worth a visit just to see the elegant Second Empire–style homes that surround it. ✉ *Bordered by av. Laval and rue St-Denis between rue Sherbrooke Est and av. des Pins Est, Quartier Latin* Ⓜ *Sherbrooke.*

9

MONT-ROYAL & ENVIRONS

Fodor'sChoice ★ In geological terms, Mont-Royal is a mere bump—a plug of basaltlike rock that has been worn down by several ice ages to a mere 760 feet. But in the affections of Montrealers it's a Matterhorn. Without a trace of irony, they call it simply *la Montagne* or "the Mountain." It's where Montrealers go to get away from it all—to walk, to jog, to ski, to feed the squirrels, and to admire the view—and sometimes to fall in love. And even when they can't get away, they can see the mountain glimmering beyond the skyscrapers and the high-rises—green in summer, gray and white in winter, and gold and crimson in fall.

The heart of all this is Parc Mont-Royal itself—nearly 500 acres of forests and meadows laid out by Frederick Law Olmsted (1822–1903), the man responsible for New York City's Central Park. He left much of the park as wild as possible, with narrow paths meandering through tall stands of maples and red oaks.

> **WORD OF MOUTH**
>
> "Speaking of food, heading north from Old Town, try to enjoy at least one evening's dinner in Little Italy in the section near Laurier Street. You'll find many good, authentic Italian restaurants (Montréal boasts a large Italian immigrant base—really!) in an area which borders an open meat and vegetable market."
>
> —zola

Just outside the park's northern boundaries are the city's two biggest cemeteries and beyond that the campus of the Université de Montréal. Not far away from the park and perched on a neighboring crest of the same mountain is the Oratoire St-Joseph, a shrine that draws millions every year. North of the oratory is the busy Côte-des-Neiges neighborhood, teeming with shops and restaurants—-Thai, Russian, Korean, Indian, Peruvian, and Filipino, to name a few. South of the oratory, on the other side of the mountain, is **Westmount,** one of the wealthiest Anglophone neighborhoods on the island. Its Francophone twin—the equally prosperous **Outremont**—skirts the mountain's northeastern slopes.

MAIN ATTRACTIONS

★ ❶ **Chalet du Mont-Royal.** The Chalet is not the only place to get an overview of the city, the river, and the countryside beyond, but it's the most spectacular. On clear days you can see not just the downtown skyscrapers, but Mont-Royal's sister mountains—Monts St-Bruno, St-Hilaire, and St-Grégoire—as well. These isolated peaks, called the Montérégies, or Mountains of the King, rise dramatically from the flat countryside. Beyond them, you might be able to see the northern reaches of the Appalachians. Be sure to take a look inside the chalet, especially at the murals depicting scenes from Canadian history. There's a snack bar in the back. ✉ *Off voie Camillien-Houde, Plateau Mont-Royal* ☎ *No phone* 🎟 *Free* ⏲ *Daily 9–5* Ⓜ *Mont-Royal.*

★ ❺ **Oratoire St-Joseph** *(St. Joseph's Oratory).* Every year two million pilgrimsvisit the world's largest shrine dedicated to Christ's earthly father (and Canada's patron saint). The most devout climb the 99 steps to its front door on their knees. The oratory and its extensive gardens dominate Mont-Royal's northwestern slope. Its dome—one of the largest in the world—can be seen from miles away in all directions. Under that dome, the interior of the main church is equally grand, but its austerity is almost frigid. The best time to visit it is for the 11 AM Sunday mass, when the sanctuary is brightly lighted and the sweet voices of Les Petits Chanteurs de Mont-Royal—the city's best boys' choir—fill the nave with music.

The crypt is shabbier than its big brother upstairs but more welcoming. In a long, narrow room behind the crypt, 10,000 votive candles glitter before a dozen carved murals extolling the virtues of St. Joseph; the walls are hung with crutches discarded by those said to have been cured. Just beyond is the simple tomb of the humble little man responsi-

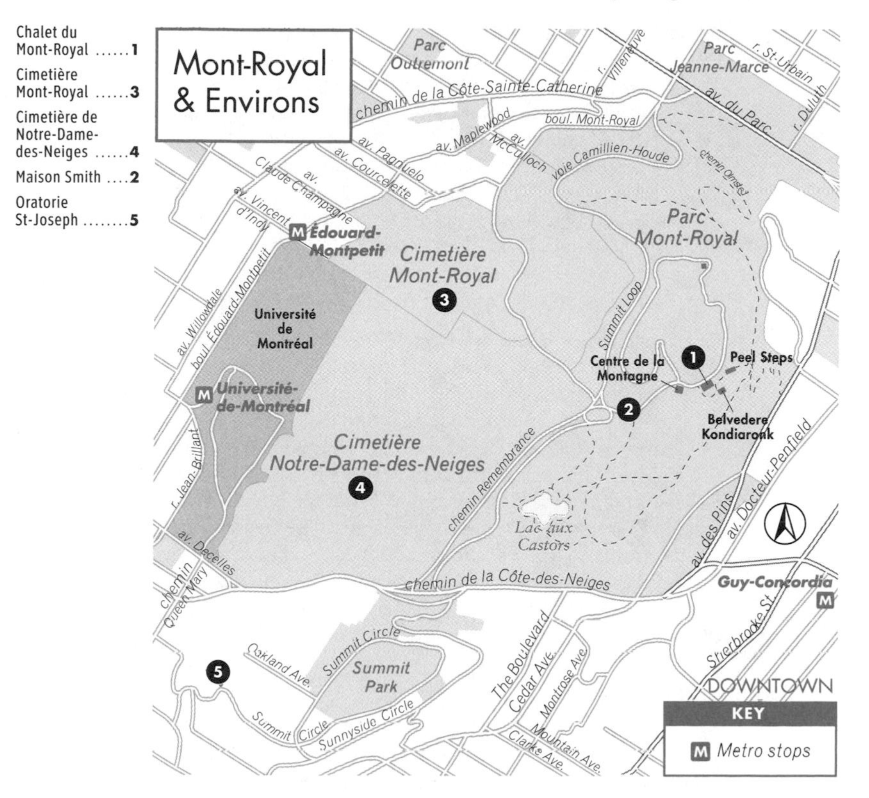

ble for building the church, Brother André Besette, a porter at the boys' school across the road who was beatified in 1982.

East of the main church, a garden commemorates the Passion of Christ, with life-size representations of the 14 traditional Stations of the Cross. To the west is Brother André's original chapel, with pressed-tin ceilings and plaster saints, which is in many ways more moving than the church that overshadows it. ✉ *3800 chemin Queen Mary, Côte-des-Neiges* ☎ *514/733–8211* 🌐 *www.saint-joseph.org* 🎟 *Free* ⏲ *Mid-Sept.–mid-May, daily 7* AM–*8:30* PM; *mid-May–mid-Sept., daily 7* AM–*9* PM Ⓜ *Côte-des-Neiges.*

AN EATING FRENZY

If you're looking for an exotic lunch, the Côte-des-Neiges neighborhood north of Mont-Royal is a maze of world-cuisine restaurants.

NEED A BREAK?

A sinfully light croissant or decadent pastry from the Duc de Lorraine (✉ *5002 Côte-des-Neiges, Côte-des-Neiges* ☎ *514/731–4128* Ⓜ *Côte-des-Neiges*) is just the antidote to the sanctity of the Oratoire St-Joseph. If it's lunchtime, try one of the Duc's meat pies or a quiche, followed by coffee and a scoop of homemade ice cream.

9

ALSO WORTH SEEING

❸ **Cimetière Mont-Royal.** If you find yourself humming *Getting to Know You* as you explore Mont-Royal Cemetery's 165 acres, blame it on the graveyard's most famous permanent guest, Anna Leonowens (1834–1915). She was the real-life model for the heroine of the musical *The King and I.* The cemetery—established in 1852 by the Anglican, Presbyterian, Unitarian, and Baptist churches—is laid out like a terraced garden with footpaths that meander between crab apple trees and past Japanese lilacs. ✉*1297 chemin de la Forêt, Côte-des-Neiges* ☎*514/279–7358* 🌐*www.mountroyalcem.com* ⏲*Mon.–Fri. 8–5, Weekends and holidays, 8–4* Ⓜ*Edouard-Montpetit.*

❹ **Cimetière de Notre-Dame-des-Neiges** *(Our Lady of the Snows Cemetery).* At 343 acres, Canada's largest cemetery is not much smaller than the neighboring **Parc Mont-Royal,** and as long as you just count the living, it's usually a lot less crowded. You don't have to be morbid to wander the graveyard's 55 km (34 mi) of tree-shaded paths and roadways past the tombs of hundreds of prominent artists, poets, intellectuals, politicians, and clerics. Among them is Calixa Lavallée (1842–91), who wrote "O Canada," the country's national anthem. Many of the monuments are the work of leading Québécois. The cemetery offers some guided tours in summer. Phone ahead for details. ✉*4601 chemin de la Côte-des-Neiges, Plateau Mont-Royal* ☎*514/735–1361* 🌐*www.cimetierenddn.org* ⏲*Daily 8–7* Ⓜ*Université-de-Montréal.*

❷ **Maison Smith.** If you need a map of Mont-Royal's extensive hiking trails or want to know about the more than 150 kinds of birds here, the old park keeper's residence is the place to go. It's also a good for getting a snack, drink, or souvenir. The pretty little stone house—built in 1858—is the headquarters of Les Amis de la Montagne (The Friends of the Mountain), an organization that offers various guided walks on the mountain and in nearby areas. ✉*1260 chemin Remembrance, Plateau Mont-Royal* ☎*514/843–8240* 🌐*www.lemontroyal.qc.ca* ⏲*Late June–early Sept., weekdays 9–6, weekends 9–8; early Sept.–late June, weekdays 9–5, weekends 9–6* Ⓜ*Mont-Royal.*

HOCHELAGA-MAISONNEUVE

The Stade Olympique that played host to the 1976 Summer Olympics and the leaning tower that supports the stadium's roof dominate the skyline of Hochelaga-Maisonneuve. But there's much more to the area than the stadium complex, including the Jardin Botanique (Botanical Garden); the Insectarium, which houses the world's largest collection of bugs; and Parc Maisonneuve, an ideal place for a stroll or a picnic. The rest of the area is largely working-class residential, but there are some good restaurants and little shops along rue Ontario Est.

Until 1918 when it was annexed by Montréal, the east-end district of Maisonneuve was a city unto itself, a booming, prosperous industrial center full of factories making everything from shoes to cheese. The neighborhood was also packed with houses for the almost entirely French-Canadian workers who kept the whole machine humming.

Maisonneuve was also the site of one of Canada's earliest experiments in urban planning, with parks and civic buildings to make working-class life more bearable.

> **WORD OF MOUTH**
>
> "If you like gardens, the Botanical Gardens are very, very beautiful and worth a visit. There's also the Biodome which you might as well visit if you're by the Botanical Gardens. It's an indoor complex with recreated ecosystems. Not really a zoo, but they have animals in different exhibits, recreating the tropical rain forest, Antarctica, etc." —Carmanah

MAIN ATTRACTIONS

Insectarium. Most of the more than 250,000 insects in the Insectarium's collection are either mounted or behind panes of glass thick enough to minimize the shudder factor—a good thing when you're looking at a tree roach the size of a wrestler's thumb. There is, however, a room full of free-flying butterflies, and in February and May the Insectarium releases thousands of butterflies and moths into the Jardin Botanique's main greenhouse. At varying times during the year the Insectarium brings in chefs to prepare such delicacies as deep-fried bumblebees and chocolate-dipped locusts—protein-rich treats that most adults seem able to resist. ✉ *4581 rue Sherbrooke Est, Hochelaga-Maisonneuve* ☎ *514/872–1400* 🌐 *www.ville.montreal.qc.ca/insectarium* *May–Oct. C$16, Nov.–Apr. C$13.50 (includes Jardin Botanique)* ⏲ *May–Aug., daily 9–6; Sept. and Oct., daily 9–9; Nov.–Apr., Tues.–Sun. 9–5* Ⓜ *Pie-IX or Viau.*

Fodor's Choice ★ **Jardin Botanique** *(Botanical Garden).* No matter how brutal it gets in January this is one corner of the city where it's always summer. With 181 acres of plantings in summer and 10 greenhouses open all year, Montréal's Jardin Botanique is the second-largest attraction of its kind in the world (after England's Kew Gardens). It grows more than 26,000 species of plants, and among its 30 thematic gardens are a rose garden, an alpine garden, and—a favorite with the kids—a poisonous-plant garden. You can attend traditional tea ceremonies in the Japanese Garden, which has one of the best bonsai collections in the West. ✉ *4101 rue Sherbrooke Est, Hochelaga-Maisonneuve* ☎ *514/872–1400* 🌐 *www.ville.montreal.qc.ca/jardin* *May–Oct. C$12.75, Nov.–Apr. C$9.75 (includes Insectarium)* ⏲ *May–Aug., daily 9–6; Sept. and Oct., daily 9–9; Nov.–Apr., Tues.–Sun. 9–5* Ⓜ *Pie-IX.*

Stade Olympique. Montrealers finished paying for their Olympic stadium in the spring of 2006—30 years after the games it was built for—but they still call it the Big Owe, and not very affectionately, either. It certainly looks dramatic, squatting like a giant flying saucer in the middle of the east end. But it's hard to heat and its retractable roof worked precisely three times. Abandoned by the baseball and football teams it was supposed to house, the stadium is now used for trade shows, motorcycle races, and monster-truck competitions. Daily guided tours of the complex in French and English leave from **Tourist Hall** (☎ *514/252–8687*) in the base of the Tour Olympique every hour on the hour between 11 and 4 from September to June and 10 and 5 from June to September. ✉ *4141 av. Pierre-de-Coubertin, Hochelaga-*

9

Maisonneuve ☎*514/252–8687* *Tour of Olympic complex C$8* *www.rio.gouv.qc.ca* Ⓜ*Pie-IX or Viau.*

Tour Olympique. The world's tallest tilting structure—eat your heart out, Pisa—is the 890-foot tower that was supposed to hold the Stade Olympique's retractable roof—an idea that never worked properly. For a great view of the city, ride one of the cable cars that slide up the outside of the tower to the observatory at the top. On a clear day you can see up to 80 km (50 mi). ✉*4141 av. Pierre-de-Coubertin, Hochelaga-Maisonneuve* ☎*514/252–4141 Ext. 5246* *Observation deck $14; Observation deck and guided tour of Olympic complex $17.75* *Mid-June–Labor Day, daily 9–7; Labor Day–mid-June, 9–5* Ⓜ*Pie-IX or Viau.*

ALSO WORTH SEEING

Biodôme. Not everyone thought it was a great idea to transform an Olympic bicycle-racing stadium into a natural-history exhibit, but the result is one of the city's most popular attractions. Four ecosystems—a boreal forest, a tropical forest, a polar landscape, and the St. Lawrence River—are under one climate-controlled dome. You follow protected pathways through each environment, observing indigenous flora and fauna. A word of warning: the tropical forest is as hot and humid as the real thing, and the Québec and arctic exhibits can be quite frigid. If you want to stay comfortable, dress in layers. ✉*4777 av. Pierre-de-Coubertin, Hochelaga-Maisonneuve* ☎*514/868–3000* *www.biodome.qc.ca* *C$16* *Late June–early Sept., daily 9–6; early Sept.–late June, Tues.–Sun. and holiday Mondays 9–5* Ⓜ*Viau.*

Château Dufresne. The adjoining homes of a pair of shoe manufacturers, Oscar and Marius Dufresne, provide a revealing glimpse into the lives of Montréal's Francophone bourgeoisie in the early 20th century. The brothers built their beaux-arts palace in 1916 along the lines of the Petit-Trianon in Paris, and lived in it with their families—Oscar in the eastern half and Marius in the western half. Worth searching out are the delicate domestic scenes on the walls of the Petit Salon, where Oscar's wife entertained her friends. Her brother-in-law relaxed with his male friends in a smoking room decked out like a Turkish lounge. ✉*2929 rue Jeanne-d'Arc, Hochelaga-Maisonneuve* ☎*514/259–9201* *www.chateaudufresne.qc.com* *C$7* *Thurs.–Sun. 10–5* Ⓜ*Viau.*

Maisonneuve. At the beginning of the 20th century, civic leaders wanted to transform this industrial center into a model city with broad boulevards, grandiose public buildings, and fine homes. World War I and the Depression killed those plans, but a few fine fragments of the grand dream survive, just three blocks south of the Olympic site. The magnificent beaux-arts public market stands at the northern end of tree-lined avenue Morgan. Monumental staircases and a heroic rooftop sculpture embellish the public baths across the street. The **Théâtre Denise Pelletier,** at the corner of rue Ste-Catherine Est and rue Morgan, has a lavish Italianate interior; **Fire Station No. 1,** at 4300 rue Notre-Dame Est, was inspired by Frank Lloyd Wright's Unity Temple in suburban Chicago; and the sumptuously decorated **Église Très-Saint-Nom-de-**

Jésus has one of the most powerful organs in North America. The 60-acre **Parc Maisonneuve**, stretching north of the botanical garden, is a lovely place for a stroll. Ⓜ *Pie-IX or Viau.*

NEED A BREAK?

If you're feeling a bit peckish and want to soak up a little neighborhood ambience, drop into the cash-only Chez Clo (✉ *3199 rue Ontario Est, Hochelaga-Maisonneuve* ☎ *514/522-5348* Ⓜ *Pie-IX or Viau*) for a bowl of the best pea soup in the city, followed—if you have the room for it—by a slab of *tourtière* (meat pie) with homemade ketchup.

THE ISLANDS

Expo '67—the World's Fair staged to celebrate the centennial of the Canadian federation—was the biggest party in Montréal's history, and it marked a defining moment in the city's evolution as a modern metropolis. That party was held on two islands in the middle of the St. Lawrence River—Île Ste-Hélène, formed by nature, and Île Notre-Dame, created with the stone rubble excavated from the construction of Montréal's Métro. Both are very accessible. You can drive to them via the Pont de la Concorde or the Pont Jacques-Cartier, or take the Métro from the Berri-UQAM station.

MAIN ATTRACTIONS

Biosphère. Nothing captures the exuberance of Expo '67 better than the geodesic dome designed by Buckminster Fuller (1895–1983) as the American Pavilion. It's only a skeleton now—the polymer panels that protected the U.S. exhibits from the elements were burned out in a fire long ago—but it's still an eye-catching sight, like something plucked from a science-fiction film. There's nothing particularly fanciful about the environmental center the federal government has built in the middle of the dome, however. Its purpose is to heighten awareness of the problems faced by the St. Lawrence River system, whose water levels have dropped dramatically in recent decades. ✉ *160 chemin Tour-de-l'Île, Île Ste-Hélène* ☎ *514/283-5000* 🌐 *www.biosphere.ec.gc.ca* 🎫 *C$10* 🕒 *June–Sept., daily 10–6; Oct.–May, Tues.–Fri. noon–5* Ⓜ *Jean-Drapeau.*

Casino de Montréal. You don't have to be a gambler to visit Montréal's government-owned casino. You can come for the bilingual cabaret theater or to sip a martini in the Cheval bar or to dine in Nuances, where the prices are almost as spectacular as the views of the city across the river. You can even come just to look at the architecture—the main building was the French pavilion at Expo '67. But if you do want to risk the family fortune, there are more than 3,200 slot machines, a keno lounge, a high-stakes gaming area, and 120 tables for playing blackjack, baccarat, roulette, craps, and various types of poker. ✉ *1 av. du Casino H3C 4W7, Île Notre-Dame* ☎ *514/392-2746 or 800/665-2274* 🌐 *www.casino-de-montreal.com* Ⓜ *Jean-Drapeau (then Bus 167).*

Fodor'sChoice ★ **Parc Jean-Drapeau.** Île Ste-Hélène and Île Notre-Dame now constitute a single park named, fittingly enough, for Jean Drapeau (1916–99), the visionary (and spendthrift) mayor who built the Métro and brought the city both the 1967 World's Fair and the 1976 Olympics. In winter you can skate on the old Olympic rowing basin or slide down iced trails on an inner tube. ☎ *514/872–6120* 🌐 *www.parcjeandrapeau.com/en* Ⓜ *Jean-Drapeau.*

ISLAND TRIP TIP

A ferry carries foot passengers and their bikes from the Bassin Jacques-Cartier in the Vieux-Port to Île Ste-Hélène—the nicest way to get to the islands.

★ **Stewart Museum at the Fort.** Each summer the grassy parade square of the Old Fort comes alive with the crackle of colonial muskets and the skirl of bagpipes. The French are represented by the Compagnie Franche de la Marine and the British by the kilted 78th Fraser Highlanders, one of the regiments that participated in the conquest of Québec in 1759. The two companies of colonial soldiers raise the flag every day at 11 AM, practice maneuvers at 1 PM, put on a combined display of precision drilling and musket fire at 3 PM, and lower the flag at 4:30 PM. Children are encouraged to take part. The fort itself, built between 1820 and 1824 to protect Montréal from an American invasion that never came, is now a museum that tells the story of colonial life in the city through displays of old firearms, maps, and uniforms. ✉ *West of Pont Jacques-Cartier, Île Ste-Hélène* ☎ *514/861–6701* 🌐 *www.stewart-museum.org* 🎫 *C$10* ⏲ *Early May–mid-Oct., daily 10–5; mid-Oct.–early May, Wed.–Mon. 10–4:30* Ⓜ *Jean-Drapeau, plus 10-min. walk.*

ALSO WORTH SEEING

Circuit Gilles Villeneuve. In July you can join the glitterati of Europe and America in the Circuit Gilles Villeneuve's grandstand to watch million-dollar Formula 1 cars shriek around the 4.3-km (2.7-mi) track—if you're lucky enough and rich enough to get a ticket, that is. This is the kind of crowd that uses Perrier water to mop up caviar stains from the refreshment tables. ✉ *Île Notre-Dame* ☎ *514/350–0000* 🌐 *www.grandprix.ca* Ⓜ *Jean-Drapeau.*

Plage de l'Île Notre-Dame *(Île Notre-Dame Beach).* In midsummer, you get the distinct impression that swimming is not uppermost on the minds of many of the scantily clad, well-oiled hordes. If you do want to swim, however, the water is filtered and closely monitored for contamination, and there are lifeguards on duty. A shop rents swimming and boating paraphernalia, and there are picnic areas and a restaurant. ✉ *West side of Île Notre-Dame, Île Notre-Dame* ☎ *514/872–4537* 🎫 *C$7.50* ⏲ *Late June–Aug., daily 10–7* Ⓜ *Jean-Drapeau.*

La Ronde. Every year, it seems, La Ronde adds some new and monstrous way to scare the living daylights (and perhaps your lunch as well) out of you. The most recent addition is the Goliath, a giant steel roller-coaster that opened in the summer of 2006. It dwarfs the previous favorites—the aptly named Vampire and Monstre—in both height and speed. But if the idea of hurtling along a narrow steel track at 110 kph (68 mph) doesn't appeal to you, you might prefer the boat rides or the Ferris wheel. The popular **International Fireworks Competition** is held here weekends and a couple of weeknights in late June and July. ✉ *Eastern end of Île Ste-Hélène, Île Ste-Hélène* ☎ *514/397–2000 or 800/361–4595* 🌐 *www.laronde.com/en* 🎫 *C$30* ⏲ *Late May, weekends 10–8; early June–late June, daily 10–8; late June–late Aug., daily 10* AM*–10:30* PM*; Sept., weekends 10–7; Oct., Fri. 5* PM*–9* PM*, Sat. noon–9, Sun. noon–8* Ⓜ *Jean-Drapeau.*

WHERE TO EAT

Good restaurants can pop up just about anywhere in Montréal, and sometimes they appear in the oddest places. Toqué!, for example, long touted as one of the city's best, is on the ground floor of an office tower in the financial district. Still, there are those certain areas—such as rue St-Denis and boulevard St-Laurent between rues Sherbrooke and Mont-Royal—that have long been the city's hottest dining strips, with everything from sandwich shops to high-price gourmet shrines.

The bring-your-own-wine craze started on rue Prince-Arthur and avenue Duluth, two lively pedestrian streets in the Plateau that still specialize in good, relatively low-cost meals. Most downtown restaurants are clustered between rues Guy and Peel on the side streets that run between boulevard René-Lévesque and rue Sherbrooke. Some interesting little cafés and restaurants have begun to spring up in the heart of the antiques district along rue Notre-Dame Ouest near avenue Atwater. Vieux-Montréal, too, has a good collection of restaurants, most of them clustered on rue St-Paul and Place Jacques-Cartier.

Wherever you go to eat, be sure to watch for such Québec specialties as veal from Charlevoix, lamb from Kamouraska, strawberries from Île d'Orléans, shrimp from Matane, lobster from the Îles-de-la-Madeleine, blueberries from Lac St-Jean, and cheese from just about everywhere.

Menus in many restaurants are bilingual, but some are only in French. If you don't understand what a dish is, don't be shy about asking; a good server will be happy to explain. If you feel brave enough to order in French, remember that in French an *entrée* is an appetizer and what Americans call an entrée is a *plat principal,* or main dish.

Dinner reservations are highly recommended for weekend dining.

WHAT IT COSTS IN CANADIAN DOLLARS					
	¢	$	$$	$$$	$$$$
AT DINNER	Under C$8	C$8–C$12	C$13–C$20	C$21–C$30	over C$30

Prices are per person for a main course at dinner.

9

VIEUX-MONTRÉAL

CAFÉS

$-$$ ★ **Claude Postel.** Fast food with style is the specialty of Claude Postel's staff, and that goes down just fine with the hordes of hungry clerks and lawyers who line up at lunchtime for such ready-made meals as braised veal and poached salmon with perhaps a vegetable and orange soup to start. Mid-afternoon hunger pangs? Stop by for a cone of intensely flavored gelato-style ice cream. The place closes at 7 PM. *75 rue Notre-Dame Ouest, Vieux-Montréal 514/844–8750 MC, V Place-d'Armes.*

FRENCH

$$$–$$$$ **Les Remparts.** The weathered piece of gray stone in the corner of the dining room might once have been part of the city's ramparts, but the food is as up to date as a skyscraper. To start, the seared foie gras with caramelized pears or the perfectly seasoned chicken-liver mousse are good choices, and for the main dish try the roasted venison or the seared duck breast. But it's not all meat. Chef Jannick Bouchard also prepares a nightly vegetarian dish. *93 rue de la Commune Est, Vieux-Montréal 514/392–1649 AE, DC, MC, V No lunch weekends Place-d'Armes.*

$$$–$$$$ ★ **Vauvert.** Black walls and twinkling lights makes Vauvert sound more like the setting for a Halloween movie or a Marilyn Manson concert than a place for a seriously romantic tête-à-tête, but somehow it all works. And there's nothing gimmicky about chef Pascal Leblond's bold takes on such classics as filet mignon with caramelized onions, bacon, and fried potatoes doused in cheddar cheese and perfectly bronzed Guinea hen. *355 rue McGill, Vieux-Montréal 514/867–2823 AE, DC, MC, V Square-Victoria.*

$$$ **Bonaparte.** Book a table in one of the front window alcoves and watch the calèches clatter by over the cobblestones as you dine. You can order à la carte, but the restaurant's best deal is the six-course tasting menu, which includes such classics as lobster bisque flavored with anise, and breast of duck cooked with maple syrup and berries. Don't be intimidated by the number of courses—portions are generally smaller than main-menu versions—and their delivery is gently paced by one of the city's most professional staffs. Upstairs is a small inn. *443 rue St-François-Xavier, Vieux-Montréal 514/844–4368 Reservations essential AE, DC, MC, V No lunch weekends Place-d'Armes.*

$$$ **Chez l'Épicier.** The name means The Grocery and, indeed, shelves stocked with such products as Hawaiian sea salt and lobster oil fill the front part of the room, along with refrigerated displays of pâtés and terrines. The menu, printed on brown paper bags, starts with appetizers such as shepherd's pie (made with snails instead of beef and spiked with roasted garlic) and a nutty parsnip soup flavored with orange and ginger. More-conservative main dishes might include poached sea bass or veal chops in sherry-vinegar sauce. *311 rue St-Paul Est, Vieux-Montréal 514/878–2232 AE, DC, MC, V No lunch weekends Place-d'Armes.*

$$ ✕**Bistro Boris.** At this huge, tree-shaded *terrasse* the French fare includes blood pudding, grilled fish, or chops, all served with salad or fries. But get there early. The outdoor tables fill up quickly. ✉*465 rue McGill, Vieux-Montréal* ☎*514/848–9575* ▭*AE, DC, MC, V* Ⓜ*Square-Victoria.*

ITALIAN

$$$–$$$$ Fodor'sChoice ★ ✕**Toqué!** The name—slang for a "little mad"— fit when chef Normand Laprise catered to the überhip in a funky storefront on rue St-Denis. But there's nothing crazy about his current gray-and-burgundy home on the ground floor of a glass tower, or about the pin-striped, expense-account crowd it attracts. Still, Laprise—the earliest champion of home-grown Québec products—hasn't lost his touch with the food. The menu changes daily, depending on what he finds at the market, but dinner could start with ravioli stuffed with braised duck followed by lamb from the Gatineau Valley. For dessert, cross your fingers and hope the almond-crusted blueberry pie is on the menu. ✉*900 pl. Jean-Paul-Riopelle, Vieux-Montréal* ☎*514/499–2084* ✍*Reservations essential* ▭*AE, DC, MC, V* ⊙*Closed Mon. No lunch* Ⓜ*Square-Victoria or Place-d'Armes.*

$$$ ✕**Da Emma.** Mama Emma's cooking is satisfying enough to drive out any lingering ghosts from the sad days when this was a women's prison. The stone walls and heavy beams make an ideal, catacomb-like setting for such Roman specialties as suckling pig roasted with garlic and rosemary and, on very special occasions, tripe Romaine. You might also want to try Mama's big juicy meatballs. ✉*777 rue de la Commune Ouest, Vieux-Montréal* ☎*514/392–1568* ▭*AE, D, DC, MC, V* ⊙*No lunch Sat.* Ⓜ*Square-Victoria.*

$$$ ✕**Méchant Boeuf.** If you have a yen for the past as it never really was, Hôtel Nelligan's casual dining room trades on nostalgia with a 1980s sound track and such comfort-food favorites as braised pork, beer-can chicken, and what might be the best hamburgers in town. The food may be humble, but the atmosphere is cheeky and chic. ✉*124 rue St-Paul Ouest, Vieux-Montréal* ☎*514/788–2040* ▭*AE, D, DC, MC, V* Ⓜ*Place-d'Armes.*

$$$ ✕**Verses.** The setting—a stone-walled room overlooking the hubbub of rue St-Paul—is the most romantic in the old city. And the food can be poetic—especially with appetizers such as grilled shrimp with mangoes and pineapple or tuna tartare with ginger, sesame oil, and wasabi. But the reason for this restaurant's name is that it's housed on the ground floor of Hôtel Nelligan, named after the Romantic Québécois poet Émile Nelligan. For a main course try the duck breast with tamarind and caramel or the beef fillet with mashed potatoes and chives. ✉*Hôtel Nelligan, 100 rue St-Paul Ouest, Vieux-Montréal* ☎*514/788–4000* ✍*Reservations essential* ▭*AE, DC, MC, V* Ⓜ*Place-d'Armes.*

$$–$$$ Fodor'sChoice ★ ✕**Club Chasse et Pêche.** The name—which means Hunting and Fishing Club—is an ironic reference to the wood-and-leather decor Chef Claude Pelletier inherited from the previous owners. He's jazzed it up, though, with some halogen lamps that make it easier for you to see the food, which looks almost as good as it tastes. The elegant setting, Pelletier's innovative style, and impeccable service has made this a favorite

with the city's serious foodies. For a different riff on an old favorite, try Pelletier's version of surf-and-turf. You get the lobster tail, but instead of steak you get a juicy lump of suckling pig, or a crispy heap of sweetbreads. ✉ *423 rue St-Claude, Vieux-Montréal* ☎ *514/861–1112* ✍ *Reservations essential* ▭ *AE, DC, MC, V* ⊙ *Closed Sun. and Mon. No lunch Sat.* Ⓜ *Champ-de-Mars.*

POLISH

$–$$ ✕ **Café Stash.** On chilly nights many Montrealers come here for sustenance—for borscht, pork chops, pierogies, or cabbage and sausage—in short, for all the hearty specialties of a Polish kitchen. Seating is on pews from a chapel and at tables from an old convent. ✉ *200 rue St-Paul Ouest, Vieux-Montréal* ☎ *514/845–6611* ▭ *AE, MC, V* Ⓜ *Place-d'Armes.*

DOWNTOWN & CHINATOWN

CHINESE

$–$$ ✕ **Maison Kam Fung.** Kam Fung is no place for a romantic tête-à-tête, but it's a great place to go with a gang of friends for a noisy dim sum feast. From 7 AM until 3 PM waiters clatter up and down the aisles between tables, pushing a parade of trolleys bearing such treats as firm dumplings stuffed with pork and chicken, stir-fried squid, barbecued chicken feet, and delicate shrimp-filled envelopes of pastry. ✉ *1111 rue St-Urbain, Chinatown* ☎ *514/878–2888* ▭ *AE, DC, MC, V* Ⓜ *Place-d'Armes.*

FRENCH

$$$$ ✕ **Guy and Dodo Morali.** In the best French tradition, Guy runs the kitchen and wife Dodo handles the front room, although Guy wanders out occasionally to chat with customers and listen to complaints and compliments. The decor's classic, too—pale yellow walls hung with impressionist prints and photos of Paris—as is the cooking. The daily table d'hôte menu is the best bet, with openers such as lobster bisque followed by sweetbreads with mushrooms or lobster poached with champagne. For dessert try the tarte tatin (apples and caramel with crème anglaise). In summer, diners spill out onto a little terrace on rue Metcalfe. ✉ *Les Cours Mont-Royal, 1444 rue Metcalfe, Downtown* ☎ *514/842–3636* ✍ *Reservations essential* ▭ *AE, DC, MC, V* ⊙ *Closed Sun.* Ⓜ *Peel.*

$$$–$$$$ Fodor'sChoice ★ ✕ **La Rapière.** The musketeer D'Artagnan, master of the rapier (or *rapière*), came from southwestern France, as do most of this elegant restaurant's specialties. Start with paper-thin slices of the house-smoked goose meat or a portion of delicately pink duck foie gras, followed by a cassoulet of duck, pork, and haricots (beans). For dessert there's nougat ice with custard, crème brûlée, or an excellent cheese plate. The room itself is soothing, with terra-cotta-color walls, tapestries, and stained-glass windows. ✉ *Sun Life Building, 1155 rue Metcalfe, Downtown* ☎ *514/871–8920* ✍ *Reservations essential* ▭ *AE, DC, MC, V* ⊙ *Closed Sun. No lunch Sat.* Ⓜ *Peel.*

$$$ ✕**Le Caveau.** Among the towers of downtown is this Victorian house where buttery sauces and creamy desserts have survived the onslaught of nouvelle cuisine. The restaurant takes its name from its warm and comfortable cellar, but if you don't like low ceilings, there's plenty of room upstairs amid the sculptures and paintings on the upper two floors. Main courses might include rabbit cooked with wine, raisins, and spices or rack of lamb crusted with bread crumbs, mustard, garlic, and herbs. A children's menu, rare in restaurants of Le Caveau's caliber, is available. ✉*2063 av. Victoria, Downtown* ☎*514/844–1624* ▭*AE, DC, MC, V* ⏲*No lunch weekends* Ⓜ*McGill.*

$$ ✕**Bistro Gourmet.** Yogi Berra's immortal line—"Nobody goes to that restaurant anymore, it's too crowded"—could easily be applied to Chef Gabriel Ohana's tiny yellow and blue room. It's usually so packed that service can be painfully slow, especially on weekends. But that's because the food is great and the prices are low enough to make it attractive even to college students. Try the duck breast in a citrus sauce or the tuna fillets in a sesame sauce. ✉*2100 rue St-Mathieu, Downtown* ☎*514/846–1553* ▭*MC, V* ⏲*No lunch weekends* Ⓜ*Guy-Concordia.*

$$ ✕**Le Paris.** Every city needs a faded bistro with big tables, age-dimmed paint, and honest, soulful French food like grilled *boudin* (blood sausage), calves' liver, and roast chicken. Le Paris is the kind of place that makes you want to take your shoes off and relax. Try the *brandade de morue*—a kind of spread made with salt cod, potatoes, garlic, and cream—spread on little pieces of toast. And to finish? How about stewed rhubarb or *île flottante* (meringue floating in a sea of custard)? ✉*1812 rue Ste-Catherine Ouest, Downtown* ☎*514/937–4898* ▭*AE, DC, MC, V* ⏲*No lunch Sun.* Ⓜ*Guy-Concordia.*

INDIAN

$$ ✕**Devi.** Devi's chefs cater to the true aficionados who know there's more to food of the Asian subcontinent than hot, hotter, and scalding—although some of their less subtly spiced dishes (the lamb vindaloo, for example) can still take your breath away. And for the romantic, the setting is classy-exotic, with jeweled lanterns and raw silk hangings. ✉*1450 rue Crescent, Downtown* ☎*514/286–0303* ▭*AE, DC, MC, V* ⏲*No lunch Sun.* Ⓜ*Guy-Concordia or Peel.*

ITALIAN

$$$ ✕**Cavalli.** The young and the beautiful like to sip cocktails by Cavalli's big front window, which in summer is open to the passing scene on busy rue Peel. The interior—a pink-and-black illuminated bar, green velvet chairs, and blond-wood paneling—makes an enticing backdrop. And the food? Italian, sort of. Seared tuna comes with bok choy and couscous, and beef carpaccio is served with Minolette cheese and slices of baby peaches preserved with white truffles. ✉*2040 rue Peel, Downtown* ☎*514/843–5100* ✍*Reservations essential* ▭*AE, DC, MC, V* ⏲*No lunch weekends* Ⓜ*Peel.*

$$$ ✕**Da Vinci.** If you're a hockey fan, you might spot Sheldon Souray or Michael Ryder of the Montréal Canadiens dropping in for roast veal tenderloin or crab-stuffed ravioli. Big, comfortable chairs, discreet ser-

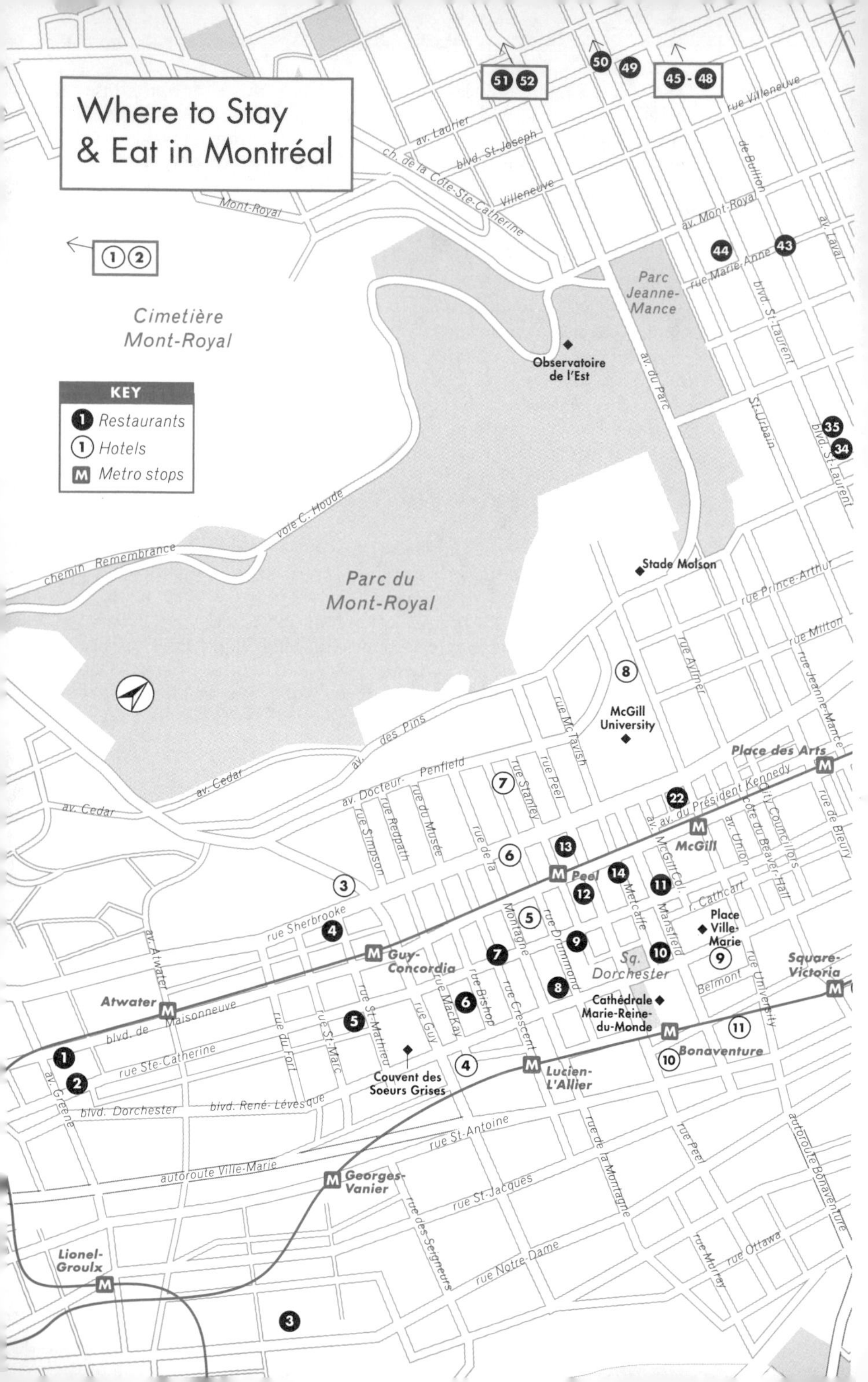
Where to Stay & Eat in Montréal
KEY
Restaurants
Hotels
Metro stops
Cimetière Mont-Royal
Parc du Mont-Royal
Parc Jeanne-Mance
Observatoire de l'Est
Stade Molson
McGill University
Place Ville-Marie
Sq. Dorchester
Cathédrale Marie-Reine-du-Monde
Couvent des Soeurs Grises
Place des Arts
McGill
Peel
Guy-Concordia
Atwater
Lucien-L'Allier
Bonaventure
Square-Victoria
Georges-Vanier
Lionel-Groulx
av. Laurier
blvd. St-Joseph
ch. de la Côte-Ste-Catherine
Villeneuve
rue Villeneuve
Mont-Royal
av. Mont-Royal
de Bullion
rue Marie-Anne
av. Laval
blvd. St-Laurent
St-Urbain
av. du Parc
voie C. Houde
chemin Remembrance
rue Prince-Arthur
rue Milton
rue Aylmer
rue Jeanne-Mance
rue McTavish
av. des Pins
av. Cedar
av. Docteur-Penfield
rue Stanley
rue Peel
rue Simpson
rue Redpath
rue du Musée
rue de la Montagne
av. du Président Kennedy
av. McGill Col.
av. Union
côte du Beaver-Hall
City Councillors
rue de Bleury
rue Sherbrooke
Metcalfe
Mansfield
r. Cathcart
rue Drummond
rue Bishop
rue Crescent
rue MacKay
rue Guy
rue St-Mathieu
rue St-Marc
rue du Fort
av. Atwater
blvd. de Maisonneuve
rue Ste-Catherine
av. Greene
blvd. Dorchester
blvd. René-Lévesque
Belmont
rue University
rue St-Antoine
autoroute Ville-Marie
rue St-Jacques
rue des Seigneurs
rue de la Montagne
rue Peel
autoroute Bonaventure
rue Notre-Dame
rue Murray
rue Ottawa

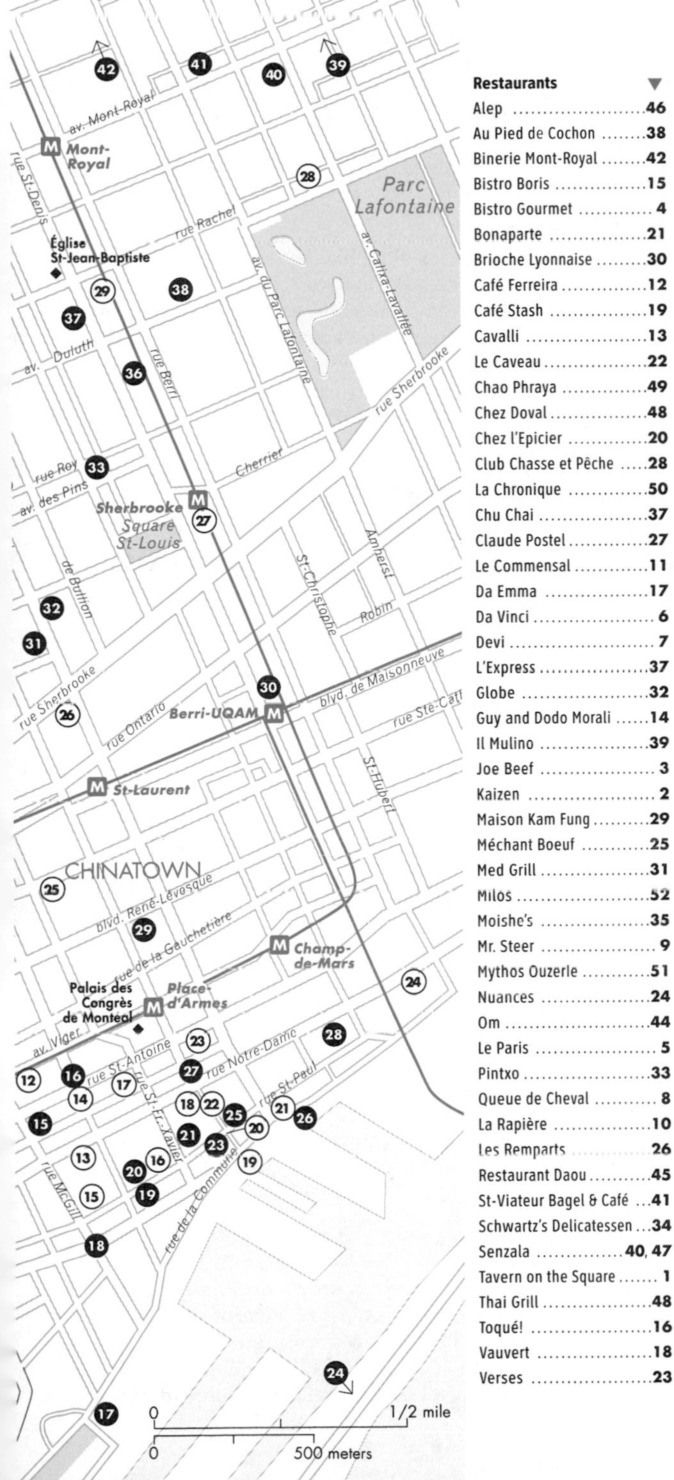

Restaurants ▼

Alep 46
Au Pied de Cochon 38
Binerie Mont-Royal 42
Bistro Boris 15
Bistro Gourmet 4
Bonaparte 21
Brioche Lyonnaise 30
Café Ferreira 12
Café Stash 19
Cavalli 13
Le Caveau 22
Chao Phraya 49
Chez Doval 48
Chez l'Epicier 20
Club Chasse et Pêche 28
La Chronique 50
Chu Chai 37
Claude Postel 27
Le Commensal 11
Da Emma 17
Da Vinci 6
Devi 7
L'Express 37
Globe 32
Guy and Dodo Morali 14
Il Mulino 39
Joe Beef 3
Kaizen 2
Maison Kam Fung 29
Méchant Boeuf 25
Med Grill 31
Milos 52
Moishe's 35
Mr. Steer 9
Mythos Ouzerie 51
Nuances 24
Om 44
Le Paris 5
Pintxo 33
Queue de Cheval 8
La Rapière 10
Les Remparts 26
Restaurant Daou 45
St-Viateur Bagel & Café ...41
Schwartz's Delicatessen ...34
Senzala 40, 47
Tavern on the Square 1
Thai Grill 48
Toqué! 16
Vauvert 18
Verses 23

Hotels ▼

Auberge Bonaparte 18
Auberge de la Fontaine ...28
Auberge de la Place Royale 19
Auberge du Vieux-Port 21
Auberge les Passants du Sans Soucy ...16
Château Versailles 3
Fairmont La Reine Elizabeth 9
Hostelling International.... 4
Hôtel Anne ma soeur Anne 29
Hôtel de l'Institut 27
Hôtel Gault 13
Hôtel Le St. James 17
Hôtel Opus 26
Hôtel Nelligan 20
Hôtel St. Paul 15
Hôtel Terrasse Royale 2
Hôtel W 12
Hyatt Regency Montréal ...25
Inter-Continental Montréal 14
Loews Hôtel Vogue 5
Manoir Ambrose 7
Le Marriott Château Champlain 10
McGill Student Apartments 8
Montréal Bonaventure 11
Pierre du Calvet AD 1725 24
Le Place d'Armes Hôtel & Suites 23
Ritz-Carlton Montréal 6
Le Saint Sulpice 22
Université de Montréal Residence 1

vice, and generous portions have made Da Vinci an after-practice and after-game favorite for decades. When ordering, however, keep in mind just how much professional hockey players earn these days. ✉ *1180 rue Bishop, Downtown* ☎ *514/874–2001* ✍ *Reservations essential* ▭ *AE, DC, MC, V* ⊗ *Closed Sun.* Ⓜ *Guy-Concordia.*

MODERN CANADIAN

$$$ Fodor's Choice ★ ✕ **Joe Beef.** Dining at Joe Beef is a little like being invited to a dinner party by a couple of friends who just happen to be top-notch chefs. David MacMillan and Frédéric Morin cook whatever they want for a bunch of diners who are more like friends than customers. There's nothing fancy or fussy about the cuisine—everything is simple and good, from the oysters to the grilled rib steak. If you're really hungry, try the cream chicken with little onions, or the spaghetti loaded with big juicy chunks of lobster. ✉ *2491 rue Notre-Dame Ouest, Downtown* ☎ *514/935–6504* ✍ *Reservations essential* ▭ *AE, DC, MC, V* ⊗ *Closed Sun. and Mon. No lunch* Ⓜ *Lionel-Groulx.*

PORTUGUESE

$$$ ★ ✕ **Café Ferreira.** A huge mural of antique pottery fragments decorates the pale-yellow walls of this high-ceiling room—an elegant setting for its "haute" version of Portuguese cuisine. The traditional *caldo verde,* a soup made with kale and sausage, shares space on the menu with grilled fresh sardines; baked salt cod topped with a tomato, onion, and pepper salsa; and *arroz di marisco,* a paella-like dish full of seafood, garlic, and onions. ✉ *1446 rue Peel, Downtown* ☎ *514/848–0988* ▭ *AE, MC, V* ⊗ *No lunch Sat.* Ⓜ *Peel.*

STEAK

$$$$ ✕ **Queue de Cheval.** The white-aproned chefs toiling away under the 20-foot-wide copper canopy look more like pagan priests engaged in some arcane ritual than cooks grilling slabs of dry-aged, prime beef on a huge open grill. The meat is sold by the pound, and all accompaniments are extra, so the crowd is pretty much limited to people whose wallets are as thick as the steaks—say, 1½ to 3½ inches. Herringbone brick walls and wide windows create an atmosphere that's half stable, half château. ✉ *1221 blvd. René-Lévesque Ouest, Downtown* ☎ *514/390–0090* ▭ *AE, D, DC, MC, V* Ⓜ *Peel.*

$ ✕ **Mr. Steer.** Brisk service, well-worn vinyl booths, and thick, juicy, almost spherical hamburgers, discreetly seasoned and served slightly *saignant* (rare) with heaps of curled french fries, are the hallmarks of this unpretentious spot in the downtown shopping district. Steak, too, is available at reasonable prices. ✉ *1198 rue Ste-Catherine Ouest, Downtown* ☎ *514/866–3233* ▭ *MC, V* Ⓜ *Peel.*

VEGETARIAN

$ ✕ **Le Commensal.** You don't have to be a vegetarian to like Le Commensal. Even members of the steak-frites crowd drop in occasionally to sample the salads, couscous, and meatless versions of such favorites as lasagna and shepherd's pie that this Montréal-grown chain dishes out. The food is served buffet style and sold by weight. There are at least seven outlets on the island, all of them big and bright with modern furniture; the nicest is on the second floor of a downtown building with windows overlooking busy, fashionable rue McGill College. ✉ *1204 rue McGill College, Downtown* ☎ *514/871–1480* ▭ *AE, DC, MC, V* Ⓜ *McGill* ✉ *1720 rue St-Denis, Quartier Latin* ☎ *514/845–2627* Ⓜ *Sherbrooke* ✉ *5199 ch. de la Côte-des-Neiges, Plateau Mont-Royal* ☎ *514/733–9755* Ⓜ *Côte-des-Neiges.*

THE PLATEAU & ENVIRONS

BASQUE

$$ ✕**Pintxo.** You don't dine at Pintxo—you graze. Pintxos (pronounced "pinchos") are the Basque version of tapas, tiny two-bite solutions to the hunger problem, best enjoyed with a good beer or a glass of chilled sherry. There are about 15 of them on the menu every night, ranging from tiny stacks of grilled vegetables to more substantial dishes, such as seared scallops with black olives and tuna fillets with ratatouille. More normal-size dishes include beef cheeks braised in wine and pan-fried fish with leeks and artichokes. ✉ *256 rue Roy Est, Plateau Mont-Royal* ☎ *514/844–0222* ✍ *Reservations essential* ▭ *AE, DC, MC, V* ⏲ *Closed Sun. No lunch Sat.–Tues.* Ⓜ *Sherbrooke.*

BRAZILIAN

$–$$ ✕**Senzala.** Two homey locations serve good Brazilian fare, including such specialties as *feijoada* (a stew of pork, black beans, cabbage, and oranges). But brunch—served Thursday to Sunday—is what the locals line up for. Familiar foods like bacon and eggs are served with a tropical touch alongside fried plantains and fruit kabobs. There's also a great selection of fruity smoothies. ✉ *177 rue Bernard Ouest, Mile-End* ☎ *514/274–1464* Ⓜ *St-Laurent* ✉ *4218 rue de la Roche, Plateau Mont-Royal* ☎ *514/521–1266* Ⓜ *Mont-Royal* ▭ *AE, MC, V* ⏲ *No lunch Mon.–Wed.*

CAFÉS

$–$$ Fodor'sChoice ★ ✕**Brioche Lyonnaise.** You'll have to go a long way to find a better butter brioche—and try saying that three times quickly—than the one at the Brioche Lyonnaise. Order one along with a steaming bowl of café-au-lait (please don't call it a latte—not here), and you've got a breakfast fit for a king. Come back in the afternoon to try one of the butter-and-cream-loaded pastries in the display case. Heartier fare is available at lunch and dinner, and the place stays open until midnight. The atrium in the back and a *terrasse* are open when the weather is nice. ✉ *1593 rue St-Denis, Quartier Latin* ☎ *514/842–7017* ▭ *AE, MC, V* Ⓜ *Berri-UQAM.*

¢ Fodor'sChoice ★ ✕**St-Viateur Bagel & Café.** Even New Yorkers have been known to prefer Montréal's light, crispy, and slightly sweet bagel to its heavier Manhattan cousin. (The secret? The dough is boiled in honey-sweetened water before baking.) St-Viateur's wood-fired brick ovens have been operating since 1959. With coffee and smoked salmon, these bagels make a great breakfast. ✉ *1127 av. Mont-Royal Est, Mile-End* ☎ *514/528–6361* ▭ *No credit cards* Ⓜ *Laurier.*

CANADIAN

$$ ✕ **Au Pied de Cochon.** Whatever you do, don't let your cardiologist see Martin Picard's menu; if he spots the pigs' feet stuffed with foie gras, he's liable to have a stroke, and he won't be too happy about the pork hocks braised in maple syrup, either, or the *oreilles-de-crisse* (literally, Christ's ears)—crispy, deep-fried crescents of pork skin that Picard serves as appetizers. But it's foie gras that Picard really loves. He lavishes the stuff on everything, including hamburgers and his own version of poutine. ✉ *536 av. Duluth, Plateau Mont-Royal* ☎ *514/281–1114* *Reservations essential* *AE, D, DC, MC, V* *Closed Mon. No lunch* Ⓜ *Sherbrooke or Mont-Royal.*

Fodor's Choice ★

$ ✕ **Binerie Mont-Royal.** That rarest of the city's culinary finds—authentic Québécois food—is the specialty at this tiny restaurant. The fare includes stews made with meatballs and pigs' feet, various kinds of tourtière, and pork and beans. It's cheap, filling, and charming. ✉ *367 av. Mont-Royal Est, Plateau Mont-Royal* ☎ *514/285–9078* *No credit cards* *No dinner weekends* Ⓜ *Mont-Royal.*

DELICATESSEN

$–$$ ✕ **Schwartz's Delicatessen.** Schwartz's has no frills. The furniture's shabby, the noise level high, and the waiters are—well, brisk would be the polite word. But its cooks do such a good job of curing, smoking, and slicing (a skill in itself) beef brisket that even when it's 20 below zero you can't see through the windows because locals line up outside to get a seat at the city's most famous deli and order a sandwich thick enough to dislocate jaws. So avoid lunch and dinner hours, and when you do get in, just order a smoked meat on rye with fries and a side order of pickles—and make it snappy. Your waiter is in a hurry. ✉ *3895 blvd. St-Laurent, Plateau Mont-Royal* ☎ *514/842–4813* *Reservations not accepted* *No credit cards* Ⓜ *Sherbrooke.*

Fodor's Choice ★

FRENCH

$ ✕ **L'Express.** Mirrored walls and noise levels that are close to painful on weekends make L'Express the closest thing Montréal (and maybe even Canada) has to a Parisian bistro. Service is fast, prices are reasonable, and the food is good, even if the tiny crowded tables barely have room to accommodate it. Steak tartare with french fries, salmon with sorrel, and calves' liver with tarragon are marvelous. Jars of gherkins, fresh baguettes, and aged cheeses make the pleasure last longer. ✉ *3927 rue St-Denis, Plateau Mont-Royal* ☎ *514/845–5333* *Reservations essential* *AE, DC, MC, V* Ⓜ *Sherbrooke.*

GREEK

$$$ ✕ **Milos.** Don't let the nets and floats hanging from the ceiling fool you: Milos is no simple taverna—a fact reflected in the prices, which some argue are exorbitant. The main dish is usually the catch of the day grilled over charcoal and seasoned with parsley, capers, and lemon juice. Fish are priced by the pound (C$23–C$32). ✉ *5357 av. du Parc, Mile-End* ☎ *514/272–3522* *Reservations essential* *AE, D, DC, MC, V* *No lunch weekends* Ⓜ *Laurier.*

$$ ✕ **Mythos Ouzerie.** Scores of fun-seeking diners come to this brick-lined semibasement every weekend to eat, drink, and be merry in a delight-

fully chaotic atmosphere. The food—moussaka, plump stuffed grape leaves, braised lamb, grilled squid—is always good, but go Thursday, Friday, or Saturday night, when the live and very infectious bouzouki music makes it impossible to remain seated. ✉ *5318 av. du Parc, Mile-End* ☎ *514/270–0235* ▭ *AE, DC, MC, V* Ⓜ *Laurier.*

ITALIAN

$$$ ✕ **Il Mulino.** Nothing about the decor or the location of this family-run restaurant in Little Italy hints at the good things inside. The antipasti alone—grilled mushrooms, stuffed eggplant, broiled scallops—are worth the trip. The pasta is excellent, especially the *agnolotti* (crescent-shape stuffed pasta) and the gnocchi. Main dishes include simply prepared lamb chops, veal, and excellent fish. ✉ *236 rue St-Zotique Est, Little Italy* ☎ *514/273–5776* ✍ *Reservations essential* ▭ *AE, DC, MC, V* ⏲ *Closed Sun. and Mon.* Ⓜ *Beaubien.*

MODERN CANADIAN

$$$ ✕ **La Chronique.** Without fuss or fanfare, chef Marc de Canck has been cranking out the city's most adventurous dishes ever since he opened his 36-seat restaurant in 1995. Incapable of compromise or playing safe, de Cranc seamlessly blends lightened French fare with Japanese, Chinese, and Creole touches. Starters like sashimi salmon rubbed with coarsely ground pepper, coriander, and mustard seed might precede veal sweetbreads with chorizo or panfried mahimahi with thin slices of eggplant filled with goat cheese. Weekend dinners are prix-fixe only—four courses are C$68, and six courses are C$95. ✉ *99 rue Laurier Ouest, Mile-End* ☎ *514/271–3095* ✍ *Reservations essential* ▭ *AE, DC, MC, V* ⏲ *Closed Mon. No lunch* Ⓜ *Laurier.*

$$$ ★ ✕ **Globe.** There's a persistent rumor that some people actually go to the Globe for the food, that they don't just order up braised venison or wild chinook salmon or raspberry tart so they'll have an excuse to sit at a table in one of Montréal's liveliest restaurants for a couple of hours and ogle the other slickly dressed patrons (or be ogled by them). ✉ *3455 blvd. St-Laurent, Plateau Mont-Royal* ☎ *514/284–3823* ▭ *AE, DC, MC, V* ⏲ *No lunch* Ⓜ *Sherbrooke.*

$$$ ✕ **Med Grill.** Dining in the Med Grill is a little like dining in a fishbowl, which might not appeal to everyone. But if you want to see and be seen, it's pretty hard to beat a set of floor-to-ceiling windows big enough for an automobile showroom. (Tip: to look your best, dress to match the cherry-red walls.) But the Med's not all show and no eat. The food—pepper-crusted tuna with sweetbreads, for example, and a spectacular molten-chocolate cake—looks as delectable as the crowd. ✉ *3500 blvd. St-Laurent, Plateau Mont-Royal* ☎ *514/844–0027* ✍ *Reservations essential* ▭ *AE, MC, V* ⏲ *No lunch* Ⓜ *Sherbrooke.*

MIDDLE EASTERN

$$ ✕ **Alep.** Graze on *mouhamara* (pomegranate and walnuts), *sabanegh* (spinach and onions), *fattouche* (salad with pita and mint), and *yalanti* (vine leaves stuffed with rice, chickpeas, walnuts, and tomatoes) in a pleasant, stone-walled room draped with ivy. Kebabs dominate the main courses. ✉ *199 rue Jean-Talon Est, Little Italy* ☎ *514/270–6396* ▭ *MC, V* ⏲ *Closed Sun. and Mon.* Ⓜ *Jean-Talon or de Castelnau.*

$$ ✕ **Restaurant Daou.** Heaven knows that singer Céline Dion could afford to fly her lunch in from Beirut on a chartered jet, but when she and hubby René Angelil—whose parents were both Syrians—are in town, this is where they come to get Lebanese food. The decor is nothing to write home about, but the hummus with ground meat, stuffed grape leaves, and delicately seasoned kebabs attract plenty of Middle Eastern expatriates and native-born Montrealers. ✉*519 rue Faillon, Villeray* ☎*514/276–8310* ▭*AE, DC, MC, V* ⏲*Closed Mon.* Ⓜ*Parc.*

PORTUGUESE

$ ✕ **Chez Doval.** Chez Doval is a neighborhood restaurant with a split personality. If you're looking for a little intimacy, book a table in the softly lighted dining room on one side of the building; if you're looking for something a little more raucous—guitar music, maybe a friendly argument about sports or politics—try the tavern on the other side. Foodwise it doesn't really matter where you sit. The chicken, sardines, grouper, and squid—all broiled à-la-Portugaise on an open grill behind the bar—are succulent, simple, and good. ✉*150 rue Marie-Anne Est, Plateau Mont-Royal* ☎*514/843–3390* ▭*AE, MC, V* Ⓜ*Mont-Royal.*

STEAK

$$$ ✕ **Moishe's.** The motto says it all: "There is absolutely nothing trendy about Moishe's." And that would include the patrons, most of whom look like they would be more comfortable wearing fedoras. But if you're looking for a thick, marbled steak, perfectly grilled—preceded perhaps by a slug of premium single-malt Scotch—this is the place to come. ✉*3961 blvd. St-Laurent, Plateau Mont-Royal* ☎*514/845–3509* ▭*AE, DC, MC, V* Ⓜ*St-Laurent.*

THAI

$$ ✕ **Chao Phraya.** The huge front window of this bright, airy restaurant decorated with subtle Asian accents overlooks fashionable rue Laurier. Customers come for such classics as crunchy *poe pia* (tightly wrapped spring rolls), *pha koung* (grilled-shrimp salad), and fried halibut in a red curry sauce with lime juice. ✉*50 rue Laurier Ouest, Laurier* ☎*514/272–5339* ✍*Reservations essential* ▭*AE, DC, MC, V* ⏲*No lunch* Ⓜ*Laurier.*

$$ ✕ **Thai Grill.** Dishes range from the fiery—mussaman curry with beef, sautéed chicken with cashews, onions, and dried red peppers—to such fragrantly mild delicacies as *gai hor bai toey* (chicken wrapped in pandanus leaves and served with a black-bean sauce). Pale-yellow walls, rich wood trim, and traditional Thai masks decorate the elegant dining room. ✉*5101 blvd. St-Laurent, Plateau Mont-Royal* ☎*514/270–5566* ▭*AE, DC, MC, V* Ⓜ*Laurier.*

TIBETAN

$ ✕ **Om.** Be careful; stepping into Om's saffron scented calm from the noise and tumult of boulevard St-Laurent can be startling enough to give you the bends. Walls the color of the Dalai Lama's robes provide the backdrop for such traditional Tibetan dishes as *momos* (beef, chicken, or vegetarian dumplings), *churu* (soup with cheese and lamb), and the fiery and sweet chicken chili. There's also an extensive list of Indian dishes. ✉ *4382 blvd. St-Laurent, Plateau Mont-Royal* ☎ *514/287–3553* ▭ *AE, MC, V* ⊙ *Closed Mon.* Ⓜ *Mont-Royal.*

VEGETARIAN

$$ ✕ **Chu Chai.** Chefs at the rigorously vegan Chu Chai prepare meatless versions of such classics as duck salad with pepper and mint leaves, fish with three hot sauces, and beef with yellow curry and coconut milk, substituting soy and *seitan* (a firm, chewy meat substitute made from wheat gluten) for the real thing. ✉ *4088 rue St-Denis, Plateau Mont-Royal* ☎ *514/843–4194* ✍ *Reservations essential* ▭ *AE, DC, MC, V* Ⓜ *Sherbrooke or Mont-Royal.*

MONT-ROYAL & ENVIRONS

JAPANESE

$$$ ✕ **Kaizen.** If you like a little drama with your sushi, Kaizen's black-clad hostesses, floor-to-ceiling red curtains, and glassed-in wine cellar certainly add a dash of theater to dinner. It's a buzz place that attracts the kind of well-dressed patrons who can't bear to leave their cell phone and Blackberry at home. The sushi, maki, lambas, sashimi, and seafood soups are all well above average, and the Kobe beef is just daring enough to be interesting without being intimidating. Try the oysters Tri Afeller, mixed with spinach and shallots. ✉ *4075 rue Ste-Catherine Ouest, Westmount* ☎ *514/932–5654* ✍ *Reservations essential* ▭ *AE, DC, MC, V* ⊙ *No lunch weekends* Ⓜ *Atwater.*

MODERN CANADIAN

$$ ✕ **Tavern on the Square.** The business crowd sips martinis at the bar, young Westmount matrons entertain their toddlers on the *terrasse*, and a mixed crowd of visitors and locals—all dressed casual chic—munch on crispy shrimp and seared tuna. The Tavern's the kind of easygoing place you can take your family, your date, or your business acquaintance. ✉ *1 Westmount Sq., Westmount* ☎ *514/989–9779* ▭ *AE, DC, MC, V* ⊙ *Closed Sun. No lunch weekends* Ⓜ *Atwater.*

9

THE ISLANDS

FRENCH

$$$$ ✕ **Nuances.** If you hit the jackpot on one of the slot machines downstairs or strike it rich at the baccarat table, you'll have no trouble paying the bill at the Casino de Montréal's premier restaurant. Otherwise, check the credit limit on your plastic before booking a table. And if you go ahead, make sure you get a table next to one of the windows so you can enjoy the million-dollar view of the river and Montréal's twinkling skyline while you. ✉ *1 av. du Casino, Île Notre-Dame* ☎ *514/392–2708* ✍ *Reservations essential* ▭ *AE, DC, MC, V* ⊙ *No lunch* Ⓜ *Jean-Drapeau.*

WHERE TO STAY

Montréal has a wide variety of accommodations, from the big chain hotels you'll find in every city to historic inns, boutique hotels, and bargain-rate hostels. You can sleep in the room where Liz Taylor and Richard Burton got married or book a bed in an 18th-century stone inn where George Washington didn't sleep, but Benjamin Franklin did.

Keep in mind that during peak season (May through August), finding a bed without making reservations can be difficult. From mid-November to early April, rates often drop, and throughout the year many hotels have two-night, three-day, double-occupancy packages at substantial discounts.

Most of the major hotels are in the downtown area, which makes them ideal for those who want all the facilities along with easy access to shopping, nightlife, and museums. If you want something a little more historic, the dozen or so boutique hotels that occupy the centuries-old buildings lining the cobbled streets of Vieux-Montréal offer all the conveniences along with the added charm of stone walls, casement windows, and period-style furnishings.

If, however, your plans include shopping expeditions to avenue Mont-Royal and rue Laurier, then the place to bed down is in one of the Plateau Mont-Royal's small but comfortable hotels. Room rates in the area tend to be quite reasonable, but the hotels right in the middle of the action—on rue St-Denis for example—can be a little noisy.

WHAT IT COSTS IN CANADIAN DOLLARS

	¢	$	$$	$$$	$$$$
HOTELS	Under C$75	C$75–C$125	C$126–C$175	C$176–C$250	over C$250

Prices are for two people in a standard double room in high season, excluding tax.

VIEUX-MONTRÉAL

$$$$ Fodor's Choice ★ **Hôtel Nelligan.** Verses by Émile Nelligan, Québec's most passionate poet, decorate the stone and brick walls of this ultraromantic hotel on fashionable rue St-Paul. The hotel, just a block south of the Basilique Notre-Dame-de-Montréal, was dramatically expanded in 2007 and now occupies four adjoining buildings from the 1850s. Some suites have terraces with views of the river; others overlook the four-story, brick-walled atrium. Complimentary wine and cheese are served every afternoon. **Pros:** Rooftop lounge and restaurant have great views of the old city; lively bar right on rue St-Paul; romantic ambience. **Cons:** Rooms on rue St-Paul can be noisy at night. ✉ *106 rue St-Paul Ouest, Vieux-Montréal, H2Y 1Z3* ☎ *514/788–2040 or 877/788–2040* 🌐 *www.hotelnelligan.com* *105 rooms, 28 suites, penthouse* *In-room: safe, ethernet. In-hotel: 2 restaurants, room service, bar, gym, concierge, laundry service, parking (fee), no-smoking building* ▭ *AE, D, DC, MC, V* 🍽 *CP* Ⓜ *Place-d'Armes.*

$$$$ ★ **Hôtel Le St. James.** When the Stones rolled into town in 2003, Mick and the boys took over this lavishly furnished luxury hotel. It was once the Mercantile Bank of Canada, which is why a former boardroom has 20-foot ceilings and lovingly restored murals of hydroelectric dams and waterfalls. Guest rooms include large marble bathrooms with separate tubs and showers and have Bang & Olufsen sound systems; some rooms have gas fireplaces. The hotel restaurant XO is in what used to be the main banking hall. **Pros:** Great, in-room sound systems; decadently luxurious bathrooms; stateliest lobby in the city. **Con:** Rue St-Jacques is a very quiet street after 6 pm. *355 rue St-Jacques, Vieux-Montréal, H2Y 1N9 514/841–3111 or 866/841–3111 www.hotellestjames.com 23 rooms, 38 suites, 1 apartment In-room: Wi-Fi. In-hotel: restaurant, room service, bar, gym, spa, concierge, laundry service, parking (fee), some pets allowed AE, D, DC, MC, V EP Square-Victoria.*

$$$$ **Hôtel St. Paul.** Stark white walls and huge shuttered windows give the "sky rooms" in this converted 19th-century office building on the western edge of Vieux-Montréal a light, ethereal feel. The "earth rooms" are decorated in richer, darker colors. All have separate sitting areas with sleek leather furniture. **Pro:** Decorators delight. **Con:** Poor location for shopping and night life. *355 rue McGill, Vieux-Montréal, H2Y 2E8 514/380–2222 or 866/380–2202 www.hotelstpaul.com 96 rooms, 24 suites In-room: ethernet, dial-up. In-hotel: restaurant, room service, bar, gym, concierge, laundry service, parking (fee), no-smoking rooms, refrigerator AE, D, DC, MC, V BP Square-Victoria.*

$$$$ Fodor's Choice ★ **Hôtel W.** This ultrachic, ultraluxurious chain took a risk opening its first Canadian hotel in a city whose major language is almost devoid of the letter "w." The famed "whatever, whenever service," for example, becomes "service top désirs." Not as alliterative, but the idea is the same. Want rose petals in your bathtub at 3 AM? Just call. The hotel is housed in the old Bank of Canada building, but you'd never know it once you walk through those whooshing sliding doors into the modern lobby. The bright, airy guest rooms are decorated in various shades of gray highlighted with electric-blue pinstripes. **Pros:** Huge bathtubs; fastest room service in town. **Cons:** Slightly out of the way of major sites. *901 Square Victoria, Vieux-Montréal, H2Z 1R1 514/395–3100 www.whotels.com/montreal 152 rooms, 30 suites In-room: safe, DVD, dial-up, Wi-Fi. In-hotel: restaurant, room service, 2 bars, gym, spa, concierge, some pets allowed, minibar AE, D, DC, MC, V EP Square-Victoria.*

$$$$ **Pierre du Calvet AD 1725.** Merchant Pierre du Calvet—a notorious republican and Freemason—entertained Benjamin Franklin behind the stone walls of this elegant 18th-century home in Vieux-Montréal. Today it's a B&B luxuriously decorated with antique furnishings and Oriental rugs. Its Filles du Roy restaurant specializes in such traditional Québécois dishes as tourtière (meat pie) and braised venison, while the Le Calvet dining room celebrates classic French cuisine. The glassed-in garden, filled with flowers and potted plants, is a great place for breakfast. **Pros:** Garden setting for breakfast; opulent antiques. **Con:**

Not the best choice if you're traveling with kids. ✉405 *rue Bonsecours, Vieux-Montréal, H2Y 3C3* ☎*514/282–1725 or 866/282–1725* 🌐*www.pierreducalvet.ca* *1 room, 8 suites* *In-room: no TV, Wi-Fi. In-hotel: restaurants, laundry service, parking (fee), no-smoking rooms, no elevator* *AE, D, DC, MC, V* *BP* Ⓜ*Champ-de-Mars.*

$$$$ ★ **Le Saint-Sulpice.** The Basilique Notre-Dame-de-Montréal is next door, and the comfortable lobby lounge and bar open onto a courtyard garden that's one of the rare green spots in Vieux-Montréal's stony landscape. The lodgings—huge suites with queen-size beds piled high with feather duvets, leather armchairs, and casement windows that actually open—are in a structure built in 2002 to blend in with the rest of the neighborhood; the gym and business center are in an adjoining 19th-century building. Some suites have fireplaces and balconies. **Pros:** Private garden; easy access to the Basilique Notre-Dame-de-Montréal. **Cons:** Church bells on Sunday morning. ✉*414 rue St-Sulpice, Vieux-Montréal, H2Y 2V5* ☎*514/288–1000 or 877/785–7423* 🌐*www.lesaintsulpice.com* *108 suites* *In-room: safe, kitchen, high-speed Internet. In-hotel: restaurant, room service, spa, concierge, laundry service, parking (fee), no-smoking rooms, some pets allowed (fee), minibar* *AE, MC, V* *BP* Ⓜ*Place-d'Armes.*

$$$–$$$$ ★ **Auberge du Vieux-Port.** Rumor has it that it was here that Suzanne took Leonard Cohen to her loft by the river and fed him oranges and tea that came "all the way from China"—a tidbit to keep in mind if you're coming to Montréal for a romantic weekend. Suzanne—actually dancer Suzanne Verdal—is long gone, but the Auberge's stone and brick walls, brass beds, and exposed beams will almost certainly please your sweetheart. On warm summer nights you can sip white wine on the rooftop terrace and watch the fireworks competitions. Warning: make sure that your room is in the main building and not in the St. Paul annex. **Pros:** Rooftop terrace has perfect views of the harbor, as well as easy access to Vieux-Port and rue St-Paul. **Cons:** Cramped elevator and noisy rooms on rue St-Paul side. ✉*97 rue de la Commune Est, Vieux-Montréal, H2Y 1J1* ☎*514/876–0081 or 888/660–7678* 🌐*www.aubergeduvieuxport.com* *27 rooms* *In-room: safe, Wi-Fi. In-hotel: restaurant, room service, concierge, laundry service, parking (fee), no-smoking rooms, some pets allowed (fee)* *AE, DC, MC, V* *BP* Ⓜ*Place-d'Armes or Champ-de-Mars.*

$$$–$$$$ ★ **Hôtel Gault.** The street is lined with gaslights and the facade dates from the 1800s, but the loft-style rooms in this boutique hotel look like something out of a modern-design magazine. Each is different: some have tile-and-concrete floors brightened by boldly patterned geometric rugs; others have sleek, blond-wood furnishings and contrasting rough-brick walls. All have CD and DVD players. Bathrooms have freestanding modern tubs and heated tile floors. **Pros:** Very large rooms. **Cons:** A bit off the beaten path. ✉*449 rue Ste-Hélène, Vieux-Montréal, H2V 2K9* ☎*514/904–1616 or 866/904–1616* 🌐*www.hotelgault.com* *30 rooms, 8 suites* *In-room: safe, DVD, ethernet, dial-up. In-hotel: room service, bar, gym, laundry service, parking (fee), no-smoking rooms, some pets allowed, minibar* *AE, D, MC, V* *CP* Ⓜ*Square-Victoria.*

$$$–$$$$ **Inter-Continental Montréal.** On the edge of Vieux-Montréal, this modern luxury hotel is part of the Montréal World Trade Center, a block-long retail and office complex. The 26-story brick tower is softened a bit with fanciful turrets and pointed roofs. Rooms are large, with lush carpets, pastel walls, and heavy drapes that pull back to reveal floor-to-ceiling windows overlooking downtown or Vieux-Montréal and the waterfront. Bathrooms have separate marble tubs and showers. **Pros:** Easy underground access to shopping and nightlife. **Cons:** Business oriented (the convention centre is across the street) and a bit stuffy. ✉ *360 rue St-Antoine Ouest, Vieux-Montréal, H2Y 3X4* ☎ *514/987–9900 or 800/361–3600* 🌐 *www.montreal.interconti.com* *334 rooms, 23 suites* *In-room: ethernet, dial-up. In-hotel: 2 restaurants, room service, bar, pool, gym, concierge, laundry service, parking (fee), minibar* *AE, D, DC, MC, V* *EP* Ⓜ *Square-Victoria or Place-d'Armes.*

$$$–$$$$ Fodor'sChoice ★ **Le Place d'Armes Hôtel & Suites.** The high-ceiling guest rooms—some with exposed brick or stone walls—combine old-fashioned grandeur with sleek modern furnishings. The large bathrooms are tiled in black granite and white marble. The 2,000-square-foot spa includes the city's first *hammam,* or Middle Eastern–style steam bath. **Pros:** Houses the best spa in town and has easy access to the sights of Vieux-Montréal. **Cons:** Rooms are small for the price, and the noontime Angelus bells at the Basilique Notre-Dame-de-Montréal across the square can make sleeping late difficult. ✉ *55 rue St-Jacques, Vieux-Montréal, H2Y 3X2* ☎ *514/842–1887 or 888/450–1887* 🌐 *www.hotelplacedarmes.com* *83 rooms, 52 suites* *In-room: safe, Wi-Fi. In-hotel: 2 restaurants, room service, 2 bars, gym, spa, concierge, laundry service, parking (fee), minibar* *AE, DC, MC, V* *BP* Ⓜ *Place-d'Armes.*

$$$ Fodor'sChoice ★ **Auberge les Passants du Sans Soucy.** Daniel Soucy and Michael Banks, two of the friendliest and most urbane hosts you're likely to run into, will go out of their way to make you feel like a house guest rather than a customer—if you're lucky enough to snag one of their 10 rooms, that is. The hotel lobby doubles as an art gallery and the rooms have brass beds, stone walls, exposed beams, whirlpool baths, and lots of fresh-cut flowers. For breakfast there are selections such as salmon omelets and French toast, all served in front of a fireplace that's full of flowers in summer and crackling logs in winter. **Pros:** Exquisitely personal service and easy access to Vieux-Montréal's best museums. **Cons:** Rooms need to be booked far in advance and parking is a hassle. ✉ *171 rue St-Paul Ouest, Vieux-Montréal, H2Y 1Z5* ☎ *514/842–2634* 🌐 *www.lesanssoucy.com* *8 rooms, 1 suite* *In-hotel: laundry service, no-smoking building, no elevator* *AE, MC, V* *BP* Ⓜ *Square-Victoria or Place-d'Armes.*

9

$$–$$$ **Auberge Bonaparte.** One of the finest restaurants in Vieux-Montréal, Auberge Bonaparte has converted the upper floors of its 19th-century building into an inn. Wrought-iron or Louis Philippe–style furnishings fill the guest rooms, some of which have double whirlpool baths. The rooms in the rear (some with balconies) have views over the private gardens of the Basilique Notre-Dame-de-Montréal. Breakfast is served in your room. **Pros:** Quiet location, perfect for theatre lovers—the Centaur Theatre is next door. **Cons:** Downstairs restaurant can

be noisy on weekends. ✉*447 rue St-François-Xavier, Vieux-Montréal, H2Y 2T1* ☎*514/844–1448* 🌐*www.bonaparte.ca* *30 rooms, 1 suite* *In-room: high-speed Internet. In-hotel: restaurant, room service, bar, concierge, parking (fee), no-smoking building* *AE, D, DC, MC, V* *BP* Ⓜ*Place-d'Armes.*

$$ ★ **Auberge de la Place Royale.** What was once a 19th-century rooming house is now a waterfront B&B overlooking the Vieux-Port. A magnificent wood staircase links the floors of this stone building. Antiques and reproductions furnish the spacious guest rooms, some of which have whirlpool tubs. A full breakfast is served either on a sidewalk terrace on warm sunny days or in a dining room when it cold or wet. The service is very attentive. **Pros:** Wonderful views of the Vieux-Port; attentive service; pleasant sidewalk restaurant. **Cons:** Parking is very difficult. ✉*115 rue de la Commune Ouest, Vieux-Montréal, H2Y 2C7* ☎*514/287–0522* 🌐*www.aubergeplaceroyale.com* *6 rooms, 6 suites* *In-room: dial-up. In-hotel: restaurant, laundry service, parking (fee), no-smoking rooms, no elevator* *AE, MC, V* *BP* Ⓜ*Place-d'Armes.*

DOWNTOWN & CHINATOWN

$$$$ **Le Marriott Château Champlain.** At the southern end of Place du Canada stands this 36-floor skyscraper with distinctive half-moon windows that give it a Moorish look (although some argue that it resembles a cheese grater). Those oddly shaped windows give the rooms wonderful views of Mont-Royal to the north and the St. Lawrence River to the south and east. **Pros:** Good views and parkside location. **Cons:** A favorite for parties and receptions—especially with the high-school-prom crowd in the spring. ✉*1050 rue de la Gauchetière Ouest, Downtown, H3B 4C9* ☎*514/878–9000 or 800/200–5909* 🌐*www.marriott.com* *611 rooms, 33 suites* *In-room: Wi-Fi. In-hotel: restaurant, room service, bar, pool, gym, concierge, laundry service, parking (fee), no-smoking building, minibar* *AE, DC, MC, V* *BP* Ⓜ*Bonaventure.*

$$$$ ★ **Ritz-Carlton Montreal.** Montréal's grandest hotel successfully blends Edwardian style—all rooms have marble baths, and some suites have working fireplaces—with modern amenities. Your shoes are shined, there's fresh fruit in your room, and everyone greets you by name, which is probably why guests have included such luminaries as Elizabeth Taylor and Richard Burton, who were married here in 1964. The lovely garden in the courtyard is a favorite spot for afternoon tea. **Pros:** Lives up to Ritz standards of luxury and service; great shopping within a five-minute walk. **Cons:** Poor Métro access and less-than-perfect soundproofing. ✉*1228 rue Sherbrooke Ouest, Square Mile, H3G 1H6* ☎*514/842–4212 or 800/363–0366* 🌐*www.ritzmontreal.com* *419 rooms, 47 suites* *In-room: safe, dial-up. In-hotel: restaurant, room service, bar, gym, concierge, laundry service, parking (fee), some pets allowed (fee), minibar* *AE, DC, MC, V* *EP* Ⓜ*Peel or Guy-Concordia.*

$$$–$$$$ **Fairmont Le Reine Elizabeth.** John Lennon and Yoko Ono staged their "bed in for peace" in Room 1742 of this hotel in 1969. Rooms are modern, spacious, and spotless, with lush carpeting and richly colored fabrics. The suite-level floors—20 and 21—have business services, and the Gold floors—18 and 19—have their own elevator, check-in, and concierge. **Pros:** Easy access to trains, Métro, and the Underground City; excellent afternoon tea. **Con:** Lobby is as busy as a train station. *900 blvd. René-Lévesque Ouest, Downtown, H3B 4A5 514/861–3511 or 800/441–1414 www.fairmont.com 939 rooms, 100 suites In-room: minibar, refrigerator (some), high-speed Internet. In-hotel: 2 restaurants, tea salon, room service, 3 bars, pool, gym, concierge, laundry service, executive floor, parking (fee), no-smoking rooms, some pets allowed (fee) AE, D, DC, MC, V EP Bonaventure.*

$$$–$$$$ **Hilton Montréal Bonaventure.** The 2½ acres of rooftop gardens and the open-air year-round swimming pool make the Bonaventure a great place to take the family. The location on top of the Place Bonaventure exhibition center gives it easy access to the Métro and the Underground City. **Pros:** Spectacular rooftop garden and swimming pool. **Cons:** Confusing layout, full of conventioneers. *900 rue de la Gauchetière, Downtown, H5A 1E4 514/878–2332 or 800/267–2575 www.hilton.com 395 rooms, 15 suites In-room: ethernet. In-hotel: restaurant, room service, bar, pool, gym, concierge, laundry service, parking (fee), no-smoking rooms, some pets allowed, minibar AE, D, DC, MC, V EP Bonaventure.*

$$$–$$$$ **Hyatt Regency Montréal.** The Hyatt is *the* place to stay during the International Jazz Festival in July—if you're a fan, that is. The 12-story hotel at the northern end of Complexe Desjardins shopping mall overlooks the Place des Arts plaza where most of the festival's free concerts are staged. The Musée d'Art Contemporain is across the street and Chinatown is a block away (you can walk to both via the Underground City if it's raining). **Pros:** Great location for shoppers and concert-lovers, and good access to the Underground City. **Cons:** Tired decor; lackluster service. *1255 rue Jeanne-Mance, Downtown, H5B 1E5 514/982–1234 or 800/361–8234 www.montreal.hyatt.com/property 605 rooms, 30 suites In-room: dial-up, Wi-Fi. In-hotel: restaurant, bar, pool, gym, spa, laundry service, parking (fee), no-smoking floors, minibar AE, D, DC, MC, V EP Place-des Arts or Place-d'Armes.*

$$$–$$$$ Fodor's Choice ★ **Loews Hôtel Vogue.** This is where such stars as George Clooney, Julia Roberts, and Matt Damon come to stay and play. The lobby bar with its big bay window overlooking rue de la Montagne is a favorite for martinis after work, but for something a little quieter you can sip your predinner drinks by the big fireplace in the lobby lounge. Guest rooms are luxurious, with striped silk upholstered furniture and beds draped with lacy duvets. Canopy beds give many rooms a romantic touch. The bathrooms have whirlpool baths, televisions, and phones. **Pros:** Cocktails with a view in the lobby bar; Holt Renfrew and Ogilvy's is a five-minute walk away; good celebrity spotting. **Cons:** Standard rooms are small, considering the price. *1425 rue de la Montagne, Downtown, H3G 1Z3 514/285–5555 or 800/465–6654 www.loewshotels.*

com ⇆ *126 rooms, 16 suites* ☝ *In-room: dial-up. In-hotel: restaurant, room service, bar, gym, concierge, children's programs (ages 1–18), laundry service, parking (fee), some pets allowed, minibar* ▭ *AE, D, DC, MC, V* 🍴 *EP* Ⓜ *Peel.*

$$–$$$ **Château Versailles.** The two elegant mansions that make up this luxury hotel were built at the turn of the 20th century, and have high ceilings and plaster moldings. The sumptuous furnishings throughout reflect the beaux-arts architecture. The marble fireplaces in many of the guest rooms and public rooms still work—a treat on chilly evenings. **Pros**: Huge rooms with fireplaces; easy access to museum district. **Cons**: Located at busy intersection; has no in-hotel Métro access; not much night life nearby. ✉ *1659 rue Sherbrooke Ouest, Square Mile, H3H 1E3* ☎ *514/933–3611 or 888/933–8111* 🌐 *www.versailleshotels.com* ⇆ *63 rooms, 2 suites* ☝ *In-room: safe. In-hotel: room service, bar, Wi-Fi, gym, concierge, laundry service, parking (fee), no-smoking rooms, minibar* ▭ *AE, DC, MC, V* 🍴 *CP* Ⓜ *Guy-Concordia.*

$–$$ **Manoir Ambrose.** Staying at the Manoir Ambrose is like staying with an eccentric relative who just happens to have a couple of mansions halfway up the southern slope of Mont-Royal and just a few hundred yards from some of the best shopping in Canada. Despite its grand past, the Manoir is more homey than luxurious, like a comfortable pair of slippers. Within a few hours, manager Lucie Gagnon and her staff will have you feeling as if you've lived in the Golden Square Mile all your life. The two-room family suite is a great deal at C$150 a night. **Pros**: Homey atmosphere and Golden Square Mile location for a fair price. **Cons**: Parking can be very difficult. ✉ *3422 rue Stanley, Square Mile, H3A 1R8* ☎ *514/288–6922* 🌐 *www.manoirambrose.com* ⇆ *22 rooms, 20 with private bath, 2 with shared bath* ☝ *In-room: all air-conditioned. In-hotel: laundry service, Wi-Fi, no-smoking building, no elevator* ▭ *AE, MC, V* 🍴 *CP* Ⓜ *McGill.*

¢–$ **McGill Student Apartments.** From mid-May to mid-August, while McGill students are on summer recess, you can stay in the school's dorms on the grassy, quiet campus in the heart of the city. You can use the campus swimming pool and gym facilities for a fee. The university cafeteria is open during the week, serving breakfast and lunch. Be sure to book early. **Pros**: Inexpensive, big rooms (some halfway up Mont-Royal); access to McGill's extensive athletic facilities. **Cons**: Shared baths, institutional decor, and a somewhat battered look. ✉ *3935 rue University, Square Mile, H3A 2B4* ☎ *514/398–6367* 🌐 *www.mcgill.ca/residences* ⇆ *1,000 rooms without bath* ☝ *In-room: kitchen (some). Access to cafeteria, pool (fee), gym (fee). In-hotel: restaurant, pool, gym* ▭ *MC, V* ⏲ *Closed mid-Aug.–mid-May* 🍴 *CP* Ⓜ *McGill.*

¢ **Hostelling International.** With its red awnings and friendly café-bar, Hostelling International's Montréal branch resembles a small European hotel. Its same-sex dorms sleep 4, 6, or 10 people and its private rooms are suitable for couples or small groups. Non-Canadians must have a Hostelling International membership to stay (C$35 for two years). Reserve early for summer lodging. **Pro**: Sweet price for a downtown location near the Centre Bell and the nightlife of rue Crescent. **Con**: Noisy. ✉ *1030 rue Mackay, Downtown, H3G 2H1* ☎ *514/843—3317,*

866/843–3317 🌐www.hostellingmontreal.com 243 beds In-room: no a/c (some), no TV. In-hotel: restaurant, laundry facilities, no-smoking rooms ▭AE, DC, MC, V EP Ⓜ Lucien-L'Allier.

THE PLATEAU & ENVIRONS

$$$–$$$$ Fodor's Choice ★ **Hôtel Opus.** When the Vancouver-based Opus group took over the Hôtel Godin in 2007, it was already one of the chicest and sleekest hotels on St-Laurent, with such hot spots as The Globe and the Med Grill just across the street. Opus has stuck with the uncompromisingly modern interior—exposed concrete ceilings, tile floors, stainless-steel furnishings—but has added some splashes of vibrant reds, greens, and oranges. The result could be called minimalist-plus. The exterior is just as striking—one half is an art-nouveau classic from 1915; the other is a brick-and-concrete contemporary completed in 2004. In the evening, the mirror-walled breakfast room opening onto St-Laurent slips into evening attire and becomes a popular lounge dispensing cocktails and tapas. **Pros:** Classic art-deco building; luxury rooms; hot location for nightlife. **Cons:** Congested street and iffy parking. *✉10 rue Sherbrooke Ouest, Quartier Latin, H2X 4C9 ☎514/843–6000 or 866/744–6346 🌐www.opusmontreal.com 122 rooms, 14 suites In-room: high-speed Internet, minibar. In-hotel: Wi-Fi, room service, gym, hair salon, sauna, bar, concierge, dry cleaning, laundry service, parking (fee), no-smoking rooms, some pets allowed. ▭AE, DC, MC, V CP Ⓜ St-Laurent.*

$$–$$$ ★ **Auberge de la Fontaine.** If you're a cyclist, the Auberge de la Fontaine is an ideal place to park your bike (and yourself). Housed in two adjoining turn-of-the-20th-century residences, the hotel overlooks Parc Lafontaine and one of the city's major bicycle trails. And although it looks a little staid on the outside, the interior is what Montrealers would call *branché*—or just a little zany. One wall of your room might be bare brick, for example, another purple, and the ceiling might be green. But somehow it all works. Some rooms have whirlpool baths, and a few have private balconies with views of the park. A copious Continental breakfast is served in the dining room, and you are free to use the little ground-floor kitchen and help yourself to snacks from the refrigerator. **Pros:** Parkside location on a bicycle trail; some of the city's trendiest restaurants and night spots are nearby. **Con:** Some rooms are quite small and not very well soundproofed. *✉1301 rue Rachel Est, Plateau Mont-Royal, H2J 2K1 ☎514/597–0166 or 800/597–0597 🌐www.aubergedelafontaine.com 18 rooms, 3 suites In-room: Wi-Fi. In-hotel: guests' kitchen, parking (no fee), no-smoking rooms, no elevator ▭AE, DC, MC, V CP Ⓜ Mont-Royal.*

$$ **Hôtel de l'Institut.** People rave about the unbeatable location on Square St-Louis and the great views of the St. Lawrence River from the balconies, but what sets this hotel apart is the charming service. It occupies two floors of the Institut de Tourisme et d'Hôtellerie du Québec, an internationally known school that trains students seeking careers in the hospitality industry. As a result you're cared for by squads of smiling, eager-to-please young people in crisp uniforms. **Pros:** Rooms with

balconies; earnest, friendly service. **Con**: Earnest doesn't always mean polished. ✉*3535 rue St-Denis, Quartier Latin, H2X 3P1* ☎*514/282–5120 or 800/361–5111 Ext. 5120* 🌐*www.ithq.qc.ca* *40 rooms, 2 suites* *In-room: Wi-Fi. In-hotel: restaurant, bar, concierge, parking (fee), no-smoking rooms* *AE, DC, MC, V* *BP* Ⓜ*Sherbrooke.*

$ **Hôtel Anne ma soeur Anne.** Staying at Anne ma soeur Anne is a little like having your own *pied-à-terre* in the Plateau Mont-Royal, especially if you book a back room with a view over the little tree-shaded garden (worth every penny of the extra cost). The built-in furniture adds to the effect: tip up your Murphy bed and you have a living room right on rue St-Denis. The rooms all have coffeemakers, microwaves, and toaster ovens, but every morning Anne or one of her staff delivers fresh coffee and a croissant to your room. **Pros**: Great croissants, friendly staff, lovely garden—all in the heart of Plateau Mont-Royal's nightlife. **Cons**: A sometimes noisy street scene right outside. ✉*4119 rue St-Denis, Plateau Mont-Royal, H2W 2M7* ☎*514/281–3187 or 877/281–3187* 🌐*www.annemasoeuranne.com* *17 rooms* *In-room: Wi-Fi. In-hotel: no elevator* *AE, MC, V* *CP* Ⓜ*Mont-Royal.*

MONT-ROYAL & ENVIRONS

$ **Hôtel Terrasse Royale.** At first blush, the location looks remote. But the Oratoire St-Joseph and Parc Mont-Royal are just a walk away and the busy local neighborhood—Côte-des-Neiges—is full of little markets and ethnic restaurants where you can dine cheaply and well. Getting downtown is no problem, either: the Côte-des-Neiges Métro is just across the street. The hotel itself is clean and comfortable, and the rooms all have kitchen facilities. **Pros**: Practical kitchens; lively, multilingual neighborhood; easy access to Métro. **Cons**: Noisy, grubby lobby. ✉*5225 chemin de la Côte-des-Neiges, Mont-Royal, H3T 1Y1* ☎*524/739–6391 or 800/567–0804* 🌐*www.terrasse-royale.com* *56 rooms* *In-room: kitchen. In-hotel: parking (fee)* *AE, D, DC, MC, V* *EP* Ⓜ*Côte-des-Neiges.*

¢–$ **Université de Montréal Residence.** The university's student housing accepts visitors from early May to mid-August. Rooms are simple but clean and well maintained. It's on the opposite side of Mont-Royal from downtown and Vieux-Montréal, but next to the Edouard-Montpetit Métro station. You have access to the university's extensive pool and gym facilities for C$7 a day. **Pros**: Great athletic facilities for a nominal fee; easy access to Mont-Royal and the Oratoire St-Joseph; good opportunity to practice French. **Cons**: Spartan rooms; remote from downtown; largely French unilingual staff. ✉*2350 blvd. Edouard-Montpetit, Mont-Royal, H3T 1J4* ☎*514/343–6531* 🌐*www.resid.umontreal.ca* *800 rooms, 200 with bath* *In-room: refrigerator. In-hotel: pool, gym, laundry facilities, parking (fee)* *MC, V* *Closed late Aug.–early May* *EP* Ⓜ*Université-de-Montréal or Edouard-Monpetit.*

NIGHTLIFE & THE ARTS

The "Friday Preview" section of the *Gazette* (*www.montrealgazette.com*), the English-language daily paper, has a thorough list of events at the city's concert halls, theaters, clubs, dance spaces, and movie houses. Nightlife Magazine offers a city-centric guide to the various goings-on about town, MAG33 is also worth a look. *Le Mirror* (*www.montrealmirror.com*) and French-language *Le Voir* (*www.voir.ca*) also list events and are distributed free at restaurants and other public places. Have a look at the following Web sites for comprehensive information about Montréal's nightlife scene: www.montreal.tv, www.montrealclubs.com, www.madeinmtl.com, and www.toutmontreal.com

For tickets to major pop and rock concerts, shows, festivals, and hockey, soccer, and football games, you can go to the individual box offices or contact **Admission** (*514/790–1245 or 800/361–4595* *www.admission.com*). Tickets to Théâtre St-Denis and other venues are available through **Ticketmaster** (*514/790–1111* *www.ticketmaster.ca*)

THE ARTS

It's hardly surprising that North America's largest French-speaking metropolis should be the continent's capital of French theater, with nearly a dozen professional companies and several important theater schools. But the city also has a lively English-language theater scene and one of the few Yiddish theaters in North America. Add a couple of world-renowned orchestras and some bold dance companies to the mix and you have a rich cultural stew that has something to appeal to everyone.

CIRCUS

Fodor's Choice ★ **Cirque du Soleil.** The Cirque—founded in 1984 by a pair of street performers—has revolutionized the ancient art of circus. Its shows, now an international phenomenon, use no lions, tigers, or animals of any kind. Instead, colorful acrobatics flirt with the absurd through the use of music, humor, dance, and glorious (and often risqué) costumes, The cirque has four resident companies in Las Vegas, one in Orlando, but none in Montréal. However, every couple of years—usually odd-numbered ones—one of its touring companies sets up the familiar blue-and-yellow tent in the Vieux-Port for a summer of sold-out shows. *514/790–1245 or 800/361–4595* *www.cirquedusoleil.com.*

CLASSICAL MUSIC

★ **I Musici de Montréal.** Arguably the best chamber orchestra in Canada, I Musici performs at Place des Arts and Pollack Hall, but its music is best suited to Tudor Hall atop the Ogilvy department store. *934 rue Ste-Catherine Est* *514/982—6037, tickets 514/982-6038* *www.imusici.com.*

Orchestre Métropolitain du Grand Montréal. During their regular season, October–April, the Orchestre Métropolitain performs at Place des Arts with a focus on the promotion of Canadian talent. *486 rue Ste-Catherine Ouest* *514/598–0870* *www.orchestremetropolitain.com.*

9

Fodor'sChoice ★ **Orchestre Symphonique de Montréal.** When not on tour or in the recording studio, Montréal's internationally renowned symphony orchestra plays at the Salle Wilfrid-Pelletier at Place des Arts. The orchestra also gives holiday and summer concerts in Basilique Notre-Dame-de-Montréal and pop concerts at the Arena Maurice Richard. For their free summertime concerts, check the *Gazette* listings. ☎*514/842–9951* 🌐*www.osm.ca.*

DANCE

Traditional and contemporary dance companies thrive in Montréal, though many take to the road or are on hiatus in summer.

Les Ballets Jazz de Montréal. Les Ballets Jazz has done much to popularize modern dance through its free performances at the open-air Théâtre de Verdure in Parc Lafontaine. Performances are also held at Place des Arts and Agora de la Danse. ☎*514/982–6771* 🌐*www.bjmdanse.ca.*

Les Grands Ballets Canadiens. Québec's premier ballet company performs at Place des Arts. Its seasonal offerings mix such classics as *Romeo and Juliet* and *The Nutcracker* with more-contemporary fare. The company also hosts performances by visiting international troupes. ☎*514/849–8681* 🌐*www.grandsballets.qc.ca.*

LaLaLa Human Steps. Casablanca-born choreographer Édouard Lock founded LaLaLa to explore the boundaries of modern dance. The popular troupe has a heavy international schedule but also performs at Place des Arts and at Montréal festivals. ☎*514/277–9090* 🌐*www.lalalahumansteps.com.*

Montréal Danse. Lavish sets and dazzlingly sensual choreography have helped make Montréal Danse one of Canada's most popular contemporary repertory companies. They have a busy touring schedule but also regularly perform at Place des Arts, Agora de la Danse, Théâtre de Verdure, and elsewhere. ☎*514/871–4005* 🌐*www.montrealdanse.com.*

FILM

Ex-Centris. Cinema buffs looking for the best in independent productions—both Canadian and foreign—head for Ex-Centris. A pleasant 15-minute walk from the Mont-Royal Métro station, it's worth a visit if only to see the huge rotating clock in the lobby and its bathrooms with their reflective metal walls. Its three comfortable theaters are equipped to screen digital works. ✉*3536 blvd. St-Laurent, Plateau Mont-Royal* ☎*514/847–2206* 🌐*www.ex-centris.com* Ⓜ*Sherbrooke.*

OPERA

L'Opéra de Montréal. L'Opéra de Montréal stages five productions a year at Place des Arts and features opera workshops as well as an annual benefit performance. ☎*514/985–2258* 🌐*www.operademontreal.com.*

THEATER

There are at least 10 major French-language theater companies in town, some of which enjoy international reputations. The choices for Anglophones are more limited.

CLOSE UP

Montreal Festivals

Teams from around the world compete in the **Concours d'Art International Pyrotechnique** (*International Fireworks Competition* ☎ *514/397–2000, 514/790–1245, 800/361–4595 in Canada, 800/678–5440 in the U.S.* 🌐 *www.montrealfeux.com*), held in late June and July (mostly on weekends). Their launch site is La Ronde, on Île Ste-Hélène. A ticket includes an amusement-park pass and a reserved seat with a view, but thousands fill the Jacques-Cartier Bridge to watch the show for free, and hundreds more head to the Vieux-Port.

International stars show up for the **Festival International des Films du Monde** (*World Film Festival* ☎ *514/848–3883* 🌐 *www.ffm-montreal.org*), from late August to early September, which usually screens about 400 films in a dozen venues.

The **Festival International de Jazz de Montréal** (*Montréal International Jazz Festival* ☎ *514/790–1245, 800/361–4595 in Canada, 800/678–5440 in the U.S.* 🌐 *www.montreal-jazzfest.com*) brings together more than 1,000 musicians for more than 400 concerts over a period of nearly two weeks, from the end of June to the beginning of July. Past stars have included Count Basie, Ella Fitzgerald, Lauryn Hill, Wynton Marsalis, Chick Corea, Dave Brubeck, and Canada's most famed singer-pianist, Diana Krall. About three-fourths of the concerts are presented free on outdoor stages. You can also hear blues, Latin rhythms, gospel, Cajun, and world music. Contact **Bell Info-Jazz** (☎ *514/871–1881 or 888/515–0515*) for information about the festival and travel packages.

FrancoFolies (☎ *514/876–8989* 🌐 *www.francofolies.com*) celebrates the art of French songwriting. Such major French stars as Isabelle Boulay, Paul Piché, and Michel Rivard play at packed concert halls, while lesser-known artists play free outdoor concerts. More than 1,000 musicians perform in dozens of styles, including rock, hip-hop, jazz, funk, and Latin. The festival usually starts in late July and lasts through early August.

Montréal en Lumière (*Montréal Highlights* ☎ *514/288–9955 or 888/477–9955* 🌐 *www.montrealenlumiere.com*) brightens the bleak days of February. For every event, experts artfully illuminate a few historic buildings. Such leading chefs as Paul Bocuse of France come to town to give demonstrations and to take over the kitchens of leading restaurants. Concerts, ice-sculpture displays, plays, dance recitals, and other cultural events take place during the festival.

9

★ **Centaur Theatre.** Montréal's best-known English-language theater company stages everything from frothy musical revues to serious works by Eugène Ionesco and prominently features works by local playwrights. Its home is in the former stock-exchange building in Vieux-Montréal. ✉ *453 rue St-François-Xavier, Vieux-Montréal* ☎ *514/288–3161 or 514/288–1229* 🌐 *www.centaurtheatre.com* Ⓜ *Place-d'Armes.*

Leanor and Alvin Segal Theatre. English-language classics like The Odd Couple or the Diary of Anne Frank can be seen at this center for the arts both for Montréal as a whole and for the Jewish community in particular. ✉ *5170 chemin de la Côte Ste-Catherine, Côte-des-Nei-*

ges ☎*514/739–2301 or 514/739–7944* ⊕*www.saidyebronfman.org* Ⓜ *Côte-Ste-Catherine.*

Monument-National. The National Theatre School of Canada—or the École Nationale de Théâtre du Canada—supplies world stages with a steady stream of well-trained actors and directors. Graduating classes perform professional-level plays in both French and English in a glorious old theater that has played host to such luminaries as Édith Piaf and Emma Albani. The theater also plays host to an assortment of touring plays, musicals, and concerts. ✉*1182 blvd. St-Laurent, Downtown* ☎*514/871–2224 or 800/361–4595* ⊕*www.monument-national.qc.ca* Ⓜ *St-Laurent.*

Théâtre Denise Pelletier. The Pelletier, with an objective to introduce younger audiences to theater, puts on French-language productions in a beautifully restored Italianate hall. It's is a 15-minute walk from the Métro station. ✉*4353 rue Ste-Catherine Est, Hochelaga-Maisonneuve* ☎*514/253–8974* ⊕*www.denise-pelletier.qc.ca* Ⓜ *Joliette.*

Théâtre de Quat'Sous. This cerebral theater puts on modern and experimental plays in French. ✉*100 av. des Pins Est, Downtown* ☎*514/845–7277* ⊕*www.quatsous.com* Ⓜ *Sherbrooke.*

Fodor's Choice ★ **Théâtre du Nouveau Monde.** In this North American temple of French and stage classics, a season's offerings can include works by locals Michel Tremblay and Robert Lepage as well as works by Shakespeare, Molière, Camus, Ibsen, Chekhov, and Arthur Miller. ✉*84 rue Ste-Catherine Ouest, Downtown* ☎*514/866–8667* ⊕*www.tnm.qc.ca* Ⓜ *St-Laurent.*

Théâtre du Rideau Vert. A modern French repertoire is the specialty at this theater. ✉*4664 rue St-Denis, Plateau Mont-Royal* ☎*514/844–1793* ⊕*www.rideauvert.qc.ca* Ⓜ *Mont-Royal.*

NIGHTLIFE

Hot spots are peppered throughout the city, with compact clusters along rue Crescent, blvd St-Laurent, boulevard Mont-Royal, and rue St-Denis. Prominent rue Ste-Catherine plows through town connecting most of these nighttime niches, and farther east, near Beaudry Métro station, it becomes the main drag for the Gay Village. The Old Port is Montreal's upcoming neighborhood with a steady stream of venues opening all the time in this cobblestone district. Most Montréal bars stop serving around 3 AM and close shortly thereafter (with the exception of sanctioned "after hour" haunts.).

BARS & LOUNGES

There's certainly no shortage of places to go drinking in Montreal. Over the last few years, a sleek hybrid has evolved known as the resto-bar: a savvy combination of gourmet recipes, trendy decor and designer cocktails. During the warmer months, local watering holes spill onto the street and outdoor terraces.

Barfly. Fans of blues, punk rock, country, and bluegrass jam into this tiny but tasteful hole-in-the-wall. ✉*4062A blvd. St-Laurent, Plateau Mont-Royal* ☎*514/284–6665* Ⓜ *Sherbrooke.*

Bifteck. Once the center of the indie music scene and a choice location for those looking to mingle with visiting rock stars, the Bif is not as vibrant as it was in its heyday, but it still packs 'em in most nights with university students and local rock musicians. ✉ *3702 blvd. St-Laurent, Plateau Mont-Royal* ☎ *514/844–6211* Ⓜ *Sherbrooke or St-Laurent.*

Boa. The self-proclaimed "tavern moderne" doubles as a swank art space attracting gallerinas from around town. The Asian-inspired "Boa," a tangy blend of vodka, sake, lychee liqueur, and cranberry juice, is the choice beverage. ✉ *5301 blvd St-Laurent, Mile End* ☎ *514/270–3262* Ⓜ *Laurier or Rosemont.*

Bu. The hip wine bar, drenched in lushious green, offers over 500 types of wine and the melodious clang of trumpet jazz. ✉ *5245 blvd. St-Laurent, Mile End* ☎ *514/276–0249* Ⓜ *Laurier.*

Café des Eclusiers. When spring rolls around there's no better place to get a tan and a buzz before dinner. Perched along the water in the picturesque Old Port district, the ambience is so enjoyable that regulars easily forgive the use of plastic cups. ✉ *400 rue de la Commune, Ouest, Old Port* ☎ *514/496–0109* Ⓜ *Place d'Armes.*

Casa del Popolo. Both local and visiting musicians make this scruffy bar one of the city's top venues for indie rock music. While you enjoy the music, take a look at the original art and sample some of the tasty, reasonably priced grub. ✉ *4873 blvd. St-Laurent, Plateau Mont-Royal* ☎ *514/284–0122* Ⓜ *Mont-Royal.*

Foufounes Electriques. The oldest alternative rock venue in the city has hosted everyone from Nirvana to the Dickies. The name translates as "electric buttocks." ✉ *87 rue Ste-Catherine Est, Downtown* ☎ *514/844–5539* Ⓜ *St-Laurent.*

★ **Gogo Lounge.** Funky, colorful decor and a retro-café feel attract twenty- and thirtysomethings to sip kitschy-named martinis like Hello Kitty, and Yellow Submarine. ✉ *3682 blvd. St-Laurent, Plateau Mont-Royal* ☎ *514/286–0882* Ⓜ *Sherbrooke.*

Hurley's Irish Pub. A sprawling Irish pub with dangling antique lamps and a stage for live music. ✉ *1225 rue Crescent, Downtown* ☎ *514/861–4111* Ⓜ *Guy-Concordia.*

Mile-End Bar. Although the days as the toast of the town are somewhat fading, the Mile-End remains a favorite spot for lunchtime drinks and late-night romps under the lavish chandelier on the second floor. ✉ *5322 blvd. St-Laurent, Mile-End* ☎ *514/279–0200* Ⓜ *Laurier.*

Le Sainte-Elisabeth. A stone's throw from the heart of the city's traditional red-light district, this bar has one of the nicest backyard terraces in town. Friendly service and a good selection of domestic and imported beers attract francophone twentysomethings and students from the nearby UQAM campus. Great patio. ✉ *1412 rue Ste-Elisabeth, Downtown* ☎ *514/286–4302* Ⓜ *St-Laurent.*

Le Social. Set in an old manse, the stone turret, darkwood paneling, and Gothic stained-glass window make this house of hooch a new favorite among young professionals seeking classier digs. ✉ *1445 rue Bishop, Downtown* ☎ *514/849–8585* Ⓜ *Guy-Concordia.*

Stogie's Lounge. If the surprisingly swish interior and views of rue Crescent below aren't reason enough to swing by, then check out the conspicuous glass humidor housing a seemingly infinite supply of imported cigars. ✉*2015 rue Crescent, Downtown* ☎*514/848–0069* Ⓜ*Guy-Concordia.*

Suite 701. Come drop the big bucks with sundry young professionals who slide through the enormous glass doors for hand-crafted cocktails. ✉*701 Côte de la Place d'Armes, Old Port* ☎*514/904–1201* Ⓜ*Place d'Armes.*

Whiskey Café. Sip one of the 70 kinds of Scotch at the granite countertop and absorb the decidedly adult atmosphere amid imported artifacts like a stone Romanesque horse head. ✉*5800 blvd St-Laurent, Plateau Mont-Royal* ☎*514/278–2646* Ⓜ*Rosemont.*

Winnie. Relax among a sea of red leather chairs and enjoy the second floor's old-school redbrick interior. Note the obligatory portrait of Sir Winston Churchill, for whom the bar is named. ✉*1455 rue Crescent, Downtown* ☎*514/288–3814* Ⓜ*Guy-Concordia.*

CASINO

On Île Notre-Dame, only a few minutes by car, bicycle, or Métro from the city's downtown core, is the **Casino de Montréal.** There are some quirks here for those used to Vegas-style gambling: no drinking on the floor, and no tipping the croupiers. Winners may want to spend some of their gains at Nuances or one of the casino's three other restaurants. The Cabaret de Casino offers some of the best shows in town. To get to the casino, which is open around the clock, you can take a C$10 cab ride from downtown, drive (parking is free), or take the Métro to the Jean-Drapeau station and then board Bus 167, which will deliver you right to the doorstep. ✉*1 av. du Casino, Île Notre-Dame* ☎*514/392–2746 or 800/665–2274* 🌐*www.casino-de-montreal.com* Ⓜ*Jean-Drapeau.*

COMEDY

The Montréal Just For Laughs comedy festival, which takes place every July, has been the largest such festival in the world since its inception back in 1983. But Montrealers don't have to wait until summer every year to get their comedy fix, as there are several downtown clubs catering exclusively to all-things-funny.

Comedy Nest. Established Canadian and international comedians share the stage of this unassuming club with some of the city's funniest up-and-comers. Dinner-and-show packages are available. ✉*Pepsi Forum, 2313 rue Ste-Catherine Ouest, 3rd fl., Downtown* ☎*514/932–6378* 🌐*www.thecomedynest.com* Ⓜ*Atwater.*

Comedyworks. Comedyworks is a popular room at the back of an Irish pub that books both amateur and established comics and has a reputation for offering fairly risqué fare on occasion. ✉*1238 rue Bishop, Downtown* ☎*514/398–9661* 🌐*www.comedyworks.com* Ⓜ*Guy-Concordia.*

CLUBS

At the height of the disco era in the 1970s, Montréal was considered one of the top five cities in the world for both its trendsetting dance music and its sheer number of clubs. The legacy continues today, with an impressive armada of local DJs and frequent visits from artists on the international circuit. Club covers can range from $4 to $20 depending on the night of the week and the notoriety of the DJ.

Aria. Take a disco nap in the afternoon because its worth staying up late to check out Montréal's most established after-hours club, which caters to an urban crowd with local and international DJs. Doors open at 1:30 AM on weekends. ✉*1280 rue St-Denis, Quartier Latin* ☎*514/987–6712* Ⓜ*Berri-UQAM.*

Cactus. Thursday through Saturday, the dance floor is always packed with patrons enjoying the rigorously authentic Latin music. ✉*4461 rue St-Denis, Plateau Mont-Royal* ☎*514/849–0349* Ⓜ*Mont-Royal.*

Club 737. A sweeping panoramic view and a rooftop terrace are two of the outstanding features of this multilevel dance club. It also does the weekend disco thing and is very popular with the mid-twenties to mid-thirties office crowd. ✉*1 pl. Ville-Marie, Downtown* ☎*514/397–0737* Ⓜ*Bonaventure.*

Newtown. The tri-level supper club, named for Formula 1 racer Jacques Villeneuve, is easy on the eyes and ears. Super-sleek window treatments, and a smooth wooden interior have converted this older mansion into one of the chicest spots in town. Reserve early for the private tables outside on the terrace. ✉*2145 rue Crescent, Downtown* ☎*514/284–9119* Ⓜ*Guy-Concordia.*

Salsathèque. If you can get past the blinking lights at the entrance without having a seizure, you'll find a kitschy Latin paradise decked with beach paraphernalia. Check out the old-school salsa competitions on Friday nights, or enjoy raggaeton, Latin, and top 40 beats on other evenings. ✉*1220 rue Peel, Downtown* ☎*514/875–0016* Ⓜ*Peel.*

GAY BARS & NIGHTCLUBS

Colorful drag theatres, brilliant discotheques, and steaming bathhouses fill up the one-time warehouses around the Beaudry Métro station. Gay or straight, a night in the "Gay Village" will surely be a memorable one. All of the clubs with dance floors charge a cover fee ranging from $4 to $20, depending on the night of the week and the notoriety of the DJ

Agora. Agora is usually quiet and perfect for intimate conversation—apart, of course, from Saturday karaoke nights. ✉*1160 rue Mackay, Downtown* ☎*514/934–1428* Ⓜ*Guy-Concordia.*

Cabaret Mado. Pass Madame Simone and her drag-tastic hats to enter the quirky cabaret-theme club where drag queen extraordinaire Mado holds court and encourages patrons to get involved in the weekly karaoke and improv nights. ✉*1115 rue Ste-Catherine Est, Village* ☎*514/525–7566* 🌐*www.mado.qc.ca* Ⓜ*Beaudry.*

Club Bolo. Country-and-western dancing and ambience attract both men and women to this Village club staffed partly by country-lovin' volunteers. ✉*960 rue Amherst, Village* ☎*514/849–4777* Ⓜ*Berri-UQAM.*

Le Drugstore. Although the factory-like complex of dance floors and billiard rooms teems with crowds of all kinds, it's most popular with lesbians. ✉*1360 rue Ste-Catherine Est, Village* ☎*514/524–1960* Ⓜ*Beaudry.*

Sky Pub/Sky Club. The second-story dance floor and the rooftop deck with hot tub and city views make the Sky complex a favorite with 20-something gays. ✉*1474 rue Ste-Catherine Est, Village* ☎*514/529–6969* Ⓜ*Beaudry.*

JAZZ & BLUES

House of Jazz. This is a great spot to catch live performances and chow down on some tasty ribs and chicken, too. ✉*2060 rue Aylmer, Downtown* ☎*514/842–8656* Ⓜ*McGill.*

Upstairs Jazz Club. Local and imported jazz musicians take the stage seven nights a week and frequent jam sessions. ✉*1254 rue Mackay, Downtown* ☎*514/931–6808* 🌐*www.upstairsjazz.com* Ⓜ*Guy-Concordia.*

SPORTS & THE OUTDOORS

AUTO RACING

Grand Prix du Canada. One of only two venues in North America where Formula 1 racing can be witnessed, the Canadian Grand Prix takes place in late June at the Circuit Gilles Villeneuve on Île Notre-Dame, consistently inspiring Montréal's busiest tourist weekend. ☎*514/350–4731, 514/350–0000 tickets* 🌐*www.grandprix.ca.*

BIKING

More than 350 km (217 mi) of cycling paths crisscross the metropolitan area, and bikes are welcome on the first car of Métro trains during off-peak hours. Ferries at the Vieux-Port take cyclists to Île Ste-Hélène and the south shore of the St. Lawrence River, where riders can connect to hundreds of miles of trails in the Montérégie region.

★ **Lachine Canal.** The most popular cycling trail on the island begins at the Vieux-Port and wends its way to the shores of Lac St-Louis in Lachine.

Le Pôle des Rapides. This network of 100 km (62 mi) of bicycle trails follows lakefronts, canals, and aqueducts. ☎*514/364–4490* 🌐*www.poledesrapides.com.*

Vélo Montréal. The closest place to rent bicycles for a tour of Parc Maisonneuve, the Botanical Gardens, and the site of the 1976 summer Olympics is this east-end shop. ✉*3880 rue Rachel Est, Rosemont* ☎*514/236–8356 or 514/259–7272* 🌐*www.velomontreal.com* Ⓜ*Pie- IX.*

BOATING

In Montréal you can climb aboard a boat at a downtown wharf and be crashing through Class V white water minutes later.

Lachine Rapids Tours. For an hour-long voyage up the river in a big aluminum jet boat, Lachine Rapids Tours offers daily departures (every two hours) from May through October at a cost of C$60 per person with all gear included. ✉*Clock Tower Pier (for jet-boating) and Jacques Cartier Pier (for speedboating), located at the Old Port of Montréal, Vieux-Montréal* ☎*514/284–9607* 🌐*www.jetboatingmontreal.com* Ⓜ*Champ-de-Mars.*

FOOTBALL

Montréal Alouettes. The "Als" play the Canadian version of the game—bigger field, just three downs, and a more wide-open style—under open skies at McGill University's Molson Stadium from June through October. *☎514/871–2266 information, 514/871–2255 tickets 🌐www.montrealalouettes.com.*

HOCKEY

Although variations of ice hockey are said to have been played in other U.S. and Canadian cities as early as 1800, the first organized game was played in Montréal in 1875, and the first official team, the McGill University Hockey Club, was founded in Montréal in 1880. Ever since, the sport has been more a religion than a game for the city's ardent fans.

Montréal Canadiens. The oldest team in the National Hockey League plays at the Centre Bell from October through April (and even later if it makes the play-offs). The club is one of the most successful teams in North American sports, with 24 Stanley Cups to its credit. Although it hasn't won one since 1993, tickets for home games are still a hot commodity. Most non-season-ticket holders rely on scalpers to get a seat. *✉1260 rue de la Gauchetière Ouest, Downtown ☎514/932–2582 🌐www.canadiens.com Ⓜ Lucien-L'Allier or Peel.*

ICE-SKATING

Access Montréal has information on the numerous ice-skating rinks (at least 195 outdoor and 21 indoor) in the city. It's best to call or check the Web sites listed. Outdoor rinks are open from January until mid-March, and admission is free. The rinks on Île Ste-Hélène and at the Vieux-Port (C4$ admission) are especially large. *☎514/872–1111 🌐www.ville.montreal.qc.ca.*

Atrium le Mille de la Gauchetière has skating year-round in the atrium of a downtown skyscraper with disco skating Friday and Saturday nights from October to April. Skate rental is C$5.75 per day. *✉1000 rue de la Gauchetière, Downtown ☎514/395–1000 or 514/395–0555 🌐www.le1000.com Ⓜ Bonaventure.*

SKIING & SNOWBOARDING

Tourisme Québec. The "Ski-Québec" brochure available from the tourism office has a wealth of information about skiing in and around the city. *☎514/873–2015 or 800/363–7777 🌐www.bonjourquebec.com.*

CROSS-COUNTRY

Cap-St-Jacques Regional Park. Cross-country trails crisscross most city parks, including Parcs des Îles, Maisonneuve, Mont-Royal, and the 900-acre Cap-St-Jacques park in the city's west end, about a half-hour drive from downtown. *✉20099 blvd. Gouin Ouest, Pierrefonds ☎514/280–6784 or 514/280–6871 Ⓜ Henri-Bourassa (Bus 69 west).*

DOWNHILL

Mont-Bromont. About a 45-minute drive from downtown Montréal, Mont-Bromont (72 trails, 6 lifts) is the closest Appalachian hill, with a 1,329-foot vertical drop. It's in the Eastern Townships, southeast of the city. *☎450/534–2200.*

Mont-St-Sauveur. With a vertical drop of 700 feet, Mont-St-Sauveur (38 trails, 8 lifts) is the closest decent-size ski area in the Laurentian Mountains, the winter and summer playground for Montrealers. It's about an hour's drive northwest of Montréal. ☎*514/871–0101*.

SHOPPING

Montrealers *magasinent* (shop) with a vengeance, so it's no surprise that the city has 160 multifaceted retail areas encompassing some 7,000 stores. The law allows shops to stay open weekdays 9–9 and weekends 9–5. However, many merchants close evenings Monday through Wednesday and on Sunday. Many specialty service shops are closed Monday as well. Just about all stores accept major credit cards. Most purchases are subject to a federal goods-and-services tax (GST) of 5% as well as a provincial tax of 7.5%.

Montréal is one of the fur capitals of the world. If you think you might be buying fur, check with your country's customs officials to find out which animals are considered endangered and cannot be imported. The same caveat applies Inuit ivory carvings, which cannot be imported into the United States or other countries. If you do buy Inuit art, look for the government of Canada's igloo symbol, which attests to the piece's authenticity.

SHOPPING DISTRICTS

FodorśChoice ★ **Avenue Laurier Ouest.** Shops and boutiques along the eight blocks between boulevard St-Laurent and chemin de la Côte-Ste-Catherine sell high-end fashions, home furnishings, decorative items, artwork, books, kitchenware, toys and children's items, and gourmet food. There are plenty of restaurants, bars, and cafés in which to rest your feet and check your purchases. The street is about a 15-minute walk from the Laurier Métro station.

★ **Boulevard St-Laurent.** Affectionately known as the Main, St-Laurent has restaurants, boutiques, and nightclubs that cater mostly to an upscale clientele. Still, the area has managed to retain its working-class immigrant roots and vitality to some degree: high-fashion shops are interspersed with ethnic-food stores, secondhand bookshops, and hardware stores. Indeed, a trip up this street takes you from Chinatown to Little Italy. Shoppers flock to the two blocks of avenue Mont-Royal just east of boulevard St-Laurent for secondhand clothing. The street is a 10-minute walk west of the Mont-Royal Métro station.

Downtown. Montréal's largest retail district takes in rues Sherbrooke and Ste-Catherine, boulevard de Maisonneuve, and the side streets between them. Because of the proximity and diversity of the stores, it's the best shopping bet if you're in town overnight or for a weekend. The area bounded by rues Sherbrooke, Ste-Catherine, de la Montagne, and Crescent has antiques and art galleries in addition to designer salons. Fashion boutiques and art and antiques galleries line rue Sherbrooke. Rue Crescent holds a tempting blend of antiques, fashions, and jewelry displayed beneath colorful awnings. To get here, take the Métro to the Peel, McGill, or Guy-Concordia station.

Rue Amherst. Antiques shops began springing up in the Village in the early 1990s, most of them on rue Amherst between rues Ste-Catherine and Ontario. The area used to be less expensive than rue Notre-Dame, but it's not always the case these days. Use the Beaudry Métro station.

Rue Chabanel. The eight-block stretch of Chabanel just west of boulevard St-Laurent is the heart of the city's garment district. The goods seem to get more stylish and more expensive the farther west you go. For really inexpensive leather goods, sportswear, children's togs, and linens, try the shops at 99 rue Chabanel. Many of the city's furriers have also moved into the area. A few places on Chabanel accept credit cards, but bring cash anyway. If you pay in cash, the price will often include the tax. From the Crémazie Métro station, take Bus 53 north.

Rue Notre-Dame Ouest. The fashionable place for antiquing is a formerly run-down five-block strip of Notre-Dame between rue Guy and avenue Atwater. Most of the action is at the western end of the strip, as are many of the restaurants and cafés that have sprung up to cater to shoppers. The Lionel-Groulx Métro station is the closest.

Vieux-Montréal. The old part of the city has more than its share of garish souvenir shops, but fashion boutiques and shoe stores with low to moderate prices line rues Notre-Dame and St-Jacques, from rue McGill to Place Jacques-Cartier. The area is also rich in art galleries and crafts shops, especially along rue St-Paul. Use the Place-d'Armes or Champ-de-Mars Métro station.

DEPARTMENT STORES

La Baie. The Bay is a descendant of the Hudson's Bay Company, the great 17th-century fur trading company that played a pivotal role in Canada's development. La Baie has been a department store since 1891. In addition to selling typical department-store goods, it's known for its duffel coats and signature red, green, and white striped blankets. ✉ *585 rue Ste-Catherine Ouest, Downtown* ☎ *514/281–4422* Ⓜ *McGill.*

Fodor'sChoice ★ **Holt Renfrew.** This high-end department store is Canada's answer to Saks Fifth Avenue, with labels such as Theory, Catherine Malandrino, Marc Jacobs, and Vince. Each designer has its own miniboutique. ✉ *1300 rue Sherbrooke Ouest, Downtown* ☎ *514/842–5111* Ⓜ *Peel or Guy-Concordia.*

★ **Ogilvy.** Founded in 1865, Ogilvy still stocks items by high-end retailers such as Burberry, Louis Vuitton, and Lalique. The store is divided into individual designer boutiques. A kilted piper regales shoppers each day at noon. ✉ *1307 rue Ste-Catherine Ouest, Downtown* ☎ *514/842–7711* Ⓜ *Peel.*

Simons. This youth-oriented department store in elegant 19th-century digs specializes in high-quality clothes for men and women, including its own highly respected house label. Its sales are excellent. ✉ *977 rue Ste-Catherine Ouest, Downtown* ☎ *514/282–1840* Ⓜ *Peel.*

SHOPPING CENTERS & MALLS

> **FOR SERIOUS SHOPPERS ONLY**
>
> Bargain-hunter alert: twice a year—in mid-June and at the end of August—the Main Madness street sale transforms boulevard St-Laurent into an open-air bazaar.

Le Centre Eaton. Eaton Center has a youthful edge, with a huge Levi's outlet and some trendy sporting-goods stores. The five-story mall, the largest in the downtown core, has 175 boutiques and shops and is linked to the McGill Métro station. ✉*705 rue Ste-Catherine Ouest, Downtown* ☎*514/288–3708* Ⓜ*McGill.*

Le Complexe Les Ailes. The Les Ailes flagship store in this complex attached to Le Centre Eaton sells women's clothing and accessories; the other 60 retailers include Tommy Hilfiger and Archambault, a music store. ✉*677 rue Ste-Catherine Ouest, Downtown* ☎*514/285–1080* Ⓜ*McGill.*

Les Cours Mont-Royal. This elegant mall caters to expensive tastes, but even bargain hunters find it an intriguing spot for window-shopping. The more than 80 shops include DKNY and Harry Rosen. Beware: the interior layout can be disorienting. ✉*1455 rue Peel, Downtown* ☎*514/842–7777* Ⓜ*Peel.*

Marché Bonsecours. Inaugurated in the 1840s as the city's principal public market, this neoclassical building now houses boutiques that showcase Québécois, Canadian, and First Nations artwork, clothing, and furniture. The Institut de Design Montréal Gallery boutique is full of intriguing office and home gadgets that make unique gifts. ✉*350 rue St-Paul Est, Vieux-Montréal* ☎*514/872–7730* Ⓜ*Champ-de-Mars.*

Marché Central. You can buy everything from fish to electronic gear, from pasta to high fashion, and from canoes to prescription glasses at this sprawling, million-square-foot outlet complex in the north end of the city. It's hard to get to by public transit but there are acres of free parking and it's an easy 10-minute drive from downtown. ✉*615 rue du Marché Central, North End* ☎*514/381–8804* Ⓜ*Crémazie and Bus 100 or 146.*

Place Ville-Marie. Place Ville-Marie is where weatherproof indoor shopping first came to Montréal in 1962. It was also the start of the underground shopping network that Montréal now enjoys. Stylish shoppers head to the 100-plus retail outlets for lunchtime sprees. ✉*Blvd. René-Lévesque and rue University, Downtown* ☎*514/866–6666* Ⓜ*McGill or Bonaventure.*

Les Promenades de la Cathédrale. There are more than 50 shops at this complex directly beneath Christ Church Cathedral, including Canada's largest Linen Chest outlet, with hundreds of bedspreads and duvets, plus aisles of china, crystal, linen, and silver. The Anglican Church's Diocesan Book Room sells an unusually good and ecumenical selection of books as well as religious objects. ✉*625 rue Ste-Catherine Ouest, Downtown* ☎*514/845–8230* Ⓜ*McGill.*

SPECIALTY SHOPS

ANTIQUES

L'Antiquaire Joyal. Art deco furnishings and decorations have top billing at this modest little shop. ✉ *1751 rue Amherst, Village* ☎ *514/524–0057* Ⓜ *Beaudry.*

Antiquités Curiosités. This shop carries well-priced Victorian-era tables and tallboys, as well as lamps and lighting fixtures. The merchandise is crammed into three rooms spread over two floors. ✉ *1769 rue Amherst, Village* ☎ *514/525–8772* Ⓜ *Beaudry.*

Antiquités Pour La Table. As the name suggests, this store specializes in making your table look perfect. There's an extensive selection of antique porcelain, crystal, and linens—all impeccably preserved and beautifully displayed. Don't bother coming here to replace missing or broken pieces, though, since most of what's on display is complete sets. ✉ *902 rue Lenoir, St-Henri* ☎ *514/989–8945* Ⓜ *St-Henri.*

Cité Déco. Nostalgic for the good old days? This is just the place to pick up a chrome-and-Arborite dining-room set and an RCA tube radio. It also has art deco furnishings and accessories from the '30s, '60s, and '70s, as well as Danish teak and rosewood furniture. ✉ *1761 rue Amherst, Village* ☎ *514/528–0659* Ⓜ *Beaudry.*

Ruth Stalker. She made her reputation finding and salvaging fine pieces of early-Canadian pine furniture, but Ruth Stalker has also developed a good instinct for such folk art as exquisitely carved hunting decoys, weather vanes, and pottery. ✉ *4447 rue Ste-Catherine Ouest, Westmount* ☎ *514/931–0822* Ⓜ *Atwater.*

Viva Gallery. Asian antique furniture and art take center stage at Viva, where you'll find a wide selection of carved tables, benches, and armoires. ✉ *1970 rue Notre-Dame Ouest, St-Henri* ☎ *514/932–3200* Ⓜ *Lucien-L'Allier.*

ART

Montréal brims with art galleries that present work by local luminaries as well as international artists. The downtown area has a wide choice; Vieux-Montréal is also rich in galleries, most of which specialize in Québécois and First Nations work.

★ **Edifice Belgo.** In a nondescript building, Edifice Belgo is in essence a mall of roughly 20 art galleries showing both established and emerging artists. Galerie Roger Bellemare is one of the best galleries in which to look for contemporary art. Galerie Trois Points showcases the work of Montréal and Québec artists. Both galleries are on the fifth floor. ✉ *372 rue Ste-Catherine Ouest, Downtown* ☎ *514/393–9969 Galerie René Blouin, 514/866–8008 Galerie Trois Points* Ⓜ *Place-des-Arts.*

Galerie Art & Culture. Canadian landscapes from the 19th and 20th centuries are the specialty here. ✉ *227 rue St-Paul Ouest, Vieux-Montréal* ☎ *514/843–5980* Ⓜ *Place-d'Armes.*

Galerie de Bellefeuille. This Westmount gallery has a knack for discovering important new talents. It represents many of Canada's top contemporary artists as well as some international ones. Its 5,000 square feet hold a good selection of sculptures, paintings, and limited-edition prints. ✉ *1367 av. Greene, Westmount* ☎ *514/933–4406* Ⓜ *Atwater.*

Galerie de Chariot. This gallery claims to have the largest collection of Inuit soapstone and ivory carvings in Canada. It also has a wide selection of drawings and beadwork, all of which is government authenticated. ✉*446 pl. Jacques-Cartier, Vieux-Montréal* ☎*514/875–6134* Ⓜ*Champ-de-Mars.*

★ **Galerie Walter Klinkhoff.** Brothers Alan and Eric Klinkhoff specialize in Canadian historical and contemporary art. ✉*1200 rue Sherbrooke Ouest, Square Mile* ☎*514/288–7306* Ⓜ*Peel.*

★ **La Guilde Graphique.** The Graphic Guild has an exceptional selection of original prints, engravings, and etchings. ✉*9 rue St-Paul Ouest, Vieux-Montréal* ☎*514/844–3438* Ⓜ*Champ-de-Mars.*

CLOTHING

Aime Com Moi. Québécois designers create the exclusive women's clothing sold at this shop. ✉*150 av. Mont-Royal Est, Plateau Mont-Royal* ☎*514/982–0088* Ⓜ*Mont-Royal.*

BCBG MAX AZRIA. Max Azria's super-stylish clothing, shoes, and handbags all make a statement. ✉*1300 rue Ste-Catherine Ouest, Downtown* ☎*514/398–9130* Ⓜ*Peel.*

Bedo. If you want to look fashionable without going broke, this is the place to shop for men's and women's casual wear. ✉*1256 rue Ste-Catherine Ouest, Downtown* ☎*514/866–4962* Ⓜ*Peel.*

Bovet. If you're looking for the biggest selection of middle-of-the-road fashions the city has to offer at reasonable prices, head for this local chain's North End branch on boulevard Métropolitain. ✉*4475 blvd. Métropolitain Est, North End* ☎*514/374–4551* Ⓜ*Viau.*

Buffalo David Bitton. Buffalo jeans—and the billboards advertising them—are deliberately and daringly sexy, even for this day and age. But their fans claim they're also comfortable and they certainly go well with the belts, T-shirts, shoes, and other accessories Montrealer David Bitton designs. ✉*1223 rue Ste-Catherine Ouest, Downtown* ☎*514/845–1816* Ⓜ*Peel.*

Le Château. This Québec chain designs its own line of reasonably priced trendy fashions for men and women. Its flagship store is on rue Ste-Catherine, but it also has a factory outlet at the Marché Central. ✉*1310 rue Ste-Catherine Ouest, Downtown* ☎*514/866–2481* Ⓜ*Peel.* ✉*Marché Central, 1007B1A rue Marché Central, North End* ☎*514/382–4220* Ⓜ*Crémazie and Bus 100 or 146.*

Cuir Danier. Leather fashions for men and women are the specialty of this Toronto-based chain, which designs and manufactures it own lines of jackets, skirts, pants, hats, purses, etc. It has a downtown branch in Place Ville-Marie and a warehouse outlet at Marché Central. ✉ *1 Place Ville-Marie, Downtown* ☎*514/874–0472* Ⓜ*McGill or Bonaventure* ✉*Marché Central, 999 rue Marché Central, North End* ☎*514/382–4220* Ⓜ*Crémazie and Bus 100 or 146.*

Diffusion Griff 3000. This is Anne de Shalla's showcase for leading Québécois fashion designers. ✉*350 rue St-Paul Est, Vieux-Montréal* ☎*514/398–0761* Ⓜ*Champ-de-Mars.*

General 54. Stores like this are what give Mile-End its rep for cutting edge. The clothes—many by local designers—are very feminine and whimsical. ✉*54 rue St-Viateur Ouest, Mile-End* ☎*514/271–2129* Ⓜ*Laurier.*

Harricana. Yesterday's old fur coats and stoles are transformed into everything from car coats and ski jackets to baby wraps and cushion covers by the artisans of this Québec City–based company named for one of the province's great northern rivers. The fashions are sold at dozens of shops, but the best place to see what's available is this combination atelier and boutique. ✉ *3000 rue St-Antoine Ouest, Downtown* ☎ *877/894–9919* Ⓜ *Lionel-Groulx.*

Harry Rosen. Harry and Lou Rosen's 16-store chain supplies some of the country's best-dressed men with high-end shirts, suits, jackets, and slacks. ✉ *Cours Mont-Royal, 1445 rue Peel, Downtown* ☎ *514/284–3315* Ⓜ *Peel.*

Henri Henri. Simply the best men's hat store in Canada, Henri Henri has a huge stock of Homburgs, Borsalinos, fedoras, top hats, and derbies, as well as cloth caps and other accessories. Hat prices range from about C$60 to well over C$1,000 for a top-of-the-line Homburg or Panama. ✉ *189 rue Ste-Catherine Est, Downtown* ☎ *514/288–0109 or 888/388–0109* Ⓜ *St-Laurent.*

Indigo. As the name suggests, the main product here is jeans, but this is Westmount, so you know your choices won't be cheap. ✉ *4920 rue Sherbrooke Ouest, Westmount* ☎ *514/486–4420* Ⓜ *Vendôme.*

Jacob. Fashionable professional women shop at Jacob for office-appropriate clothes—as well as some slightly daring lingerie. ✉ *1220 rue Ste-Catherine Ouest, Downtown* ☎ *514/861–9346* Ⓜ *Peel.*

Kamkyl. Yvonne and Douglas Mandel design silky sweaters, beautifully cut jackets, patterned shirts for men who are serious about fashion. ✉ *CXN 439 rue St-Pierre, Vieux-Montréal* ☎ *514/281–8221 or 877/281–8221* Ⓜ *Place-d'Armes.*

Kanuk. This company's owl trademark has become something of a status symbol among the shivering urban masses. Its layered coats aren't just elegant; they could keep an Arctic explorer warm and dry. ✉ *485 rue Rachel Est, Plateau Mont-Royal* ☎ *514/527–4494* Ⓜ *Mont-Royal.*

Lola & Emily. The perfect boutique for the undecided woman: Lola's side specializes in the fun and frilly, Emily's in everything in basic black or beige. ✉ *3475 blvd. St-Laurent, Plateau Mont-Royal* ☎ *514/288–7598* Ⓜ *Mont-Royal.*

Mains Folles. You'll find tropical-print dresses, skirts, and blouses imported from Bali at this store. ✉ *4427 rue St-Denis, Plateau Mont-Royal* ☎ *514/284–6854* Ⓜ *Mont-Royal.*

Parasuco. Montrealer Salvatore Parasuco—inventor of "ergonomic jeans"—has been making history in denim ever since he opened his first store in 1975 at the age of 19. He has since spread across the country and into the United States, but his flagship shop—completely refurbished in 2006—is in Montréal. ✉ *1414 rue Crescent, Downtown* ☎ *514/284–2288* Ⓜ *Guy-Concordia.*

Revenge. Nearly 40 Canadian and Québécois designers create Revenge's well-crafted original fashions for women. ✉ *3852 rue St-Denis, Plateau Mont-Royal* ☎ *514/843–4379* Ⓜ *Sherbrooke.*

Roots. Quality materials and an approachable, sometimes retro look have made Roots a fashion favorite for the casual, outdoorsy look.

Good leather wear. ✉ *1025 rue Ste-Catherine Ouest, Downtown* ☎ *514/845–7995* Ⓜ *Peel.*

Scandale. The cutting-edge fashions sold here are all originals created on-site by Québécois designer Georges Lévesque. In keeping with the name, the window displays are always a bit lurid. ✉ *3639 blvd. St-Laurent, Plateau Mont-Royal* ☎ *514/842–4707* Ⓜ *Sherbooke.*

Space FB. The initials stand for François Beauregard, a Montréal designer whose snug tank tops and hip-hugging pants are much loved by the younger crowd. ✉ *3632 blvd. St-Laurent, Plateau Mont-Royal* ☎ *514/282–1991* Ⓜ *Mont-Royal.*

Tilley Endurables. The famous Canadian-designed Tilley hat is sold here, along with other easy-care travel wear. ✉ *1050 rue Laurier Ouest, Outremont* ☎ *514/272–7791* Ⓜ *Laurier.*

Tristan & America. This chain sells sleek modern fashions that appeal to the just-out-of-university set. ✉ *1001 rue Laurier Ouest, Outremont* ☎ *514/271–7787* Ⓜ *Laurier.*

L'Uomo. L'Uomo bills itself as the "finest men's store in Canada," and it does, indeed, stock some of the finest European labels—Prada, Bottega Veneta, Loro Piana, Avon Celli, and Borelli, to name a few. ✉ *1452 rue Peel, Downtown* ☎ *514/844–1008 or 877/844–1008* Ⓜ *Peel.*

Winners. This discount clothing store has turned shopping into a sport. And now that it carries housewares, leaving empty-handed is even more difficult. Its downtown outlet is on the lowest level of Place Montréal Trust. ✉ *1500 av. McGill College, Downtown* ☎ *514/788–4949* Ⓜ *McGill.*

CHILDREN'S

Oink Oink. This piggy store carries fashions as well as toys and books for infants and children. It also stocks clothes for teenagers. It's fun to hear the staff answer the phone. ✉ *1343 av. Greene, Westmount* ☎ *514/939–2634* Ⓜ *Atwater.*

FURS

Close to 90% of Canada's fur manufacturers are based in Montréal, as are many of their retail outlets. Most stores are clustered along rue Mayor and boulevard de Maisonneuve between rues de Bleury and Aylmer.

Alexandor. Alexandor caters to downtown shoppers. It sells fur-lined cloth coats as well as coats in mink, fox, chinchilla, and beaver. ✉ *2055 rue Peel, Downtown* ☎ *514/288–1119* Ⓜ *Peel.*

Holt Renfrew. The fur showroom here is perhaps the most exclusive in the city, with prices to match. When Queen Elizabeth II got married in 1947, Holt gave her a priceless Labrador mink. ✉ *1300 rue Sherbrooke Ouest, Downtown* ☎ *514/842–5111* Ⓜ *Peel or Guy-Concordia.*

McComber Grosvenor. Two of Montréal's biggest fur merchants merged to create this showroom filled with beautiful mink coats and jackets. ✉ *9250 ave du Parc (near Chanabel), Mile End* ☎ *514/288–1255* Ⓜ *Bleury.*

LINGERIE

Collange. Lacy goods of the designer variety are sold here. ✉ *1 Westmount Sq., Westmount* ☎ *514/933–4634* Ⓜ *Atwater.*

Deuxième Peau. As its name suggests, Second Skin sells lingerie so fine you don't notice you're wearing it. While you're feeling brave and beautiful, kill two birds with one stone and try on a bathing suit. ✉ *4457 rue St-Denis, Plateau Mont-Royal* ☎ *514/842–0811* Ⓜ *Mont-Royal.*

Lyla. Lyla carries seductively lacy lingerie. ✉ *400 rue Laurier Ouest, Outremont* ☎ *514/271–0763* Ⓜ *Laurier.*

VINTAGE **Boutique Encore.** Although best known for its nearly new women's fashions, it also includes the big names for men. ✉ *2165 rue Crescent, Downtown* ☎ *514/849–0092* Ⓜ *Peel or Guy-Concordia.*

Eva B. If your fantasy is being a flapper, or if you want to revive the pillbox hat, turn back the clock and perk up your wardrobe with an item from the vast collection sold here. ✉ *2015 blvd. St-Laurent, Downtown* ☎ *514/849–8246* Ⓜ *St-Laurent.*

FOOD

Marché Atwater. The venerable Atwater Market is a favorite with downtowners looking for fresh produce, specialty meats and sausages, fresh fish, and Québec cheese. The main produce market is outdoors under shelters. Restaurants and shops inside a two-story complex are perfect for rainy-day browsing. ✉ *138 av. Atwater, Downtown* ☎ *514/937–7754* Ⓜ *Lionel-Groulx.*

Fodor'sChoice ★ **Marché Jean-Talon.** This is the biggest and liveliest of the city's public markets. On weekends in summer and fall, crowds swarm the half acre or so of outdoor produce stalls, looking for the fattest tomatoes, sweetest melons, and juiciest strawberries. Its shops also sell meat, fish, cheese, sausage, bread, pastries, and other delicacies. The market is in the northern end of the city but is easy to get to by Métro. ✉ *7070 rue Henri-Julien, Little Italy* ☎ *514/937–7754* Ⓜ *Jean-Talon.*

Milano. One of the largest cheese selections in the city as well as fresh pastas of all kinds are the highlights of this market. An entire wall is devoted to olive oils and vinegars; there's also a butcher and a sizeable produce section. ✉ *6862 blvd. St-Laurent, Little Italy* ☎ *514/273–8558* Ⓜ *Jean-Talon.*

JEWELRY

Birks. Since 1879 Birks has been helping shoppers mark special occasions, whether engagements, weddings, or retirements. ✉ *1240 Phillips Sq., Downtown* ☎ *514/397–2511* Ⓜ *McGill.*

★ **Kaufmann de Suisse.** Expert craftspeople create the fine jewelry sold here. ✉ *2195 rue Crescent, Downtown* ☎ *514/848–0595* Ⓜ *Guy-Concordia.*

SHOES

Browns. This local institution stocks fashion footwear and accessories for men and women. As well as the store's own label, it carries DKNY, Costume National, Dolce & Gabbana, Christian Dior, and Tods. ✉ *1191 rue Ste-Catherine Ouest, Downtown* ☎ *514/987–1206* Ⓜ *Peel.*

Mona Moore. Pale-pink walls and glass shelves create the backdrop for one of the city's best selections of women's shoes, featuring such names as Marc Jacobs, Chloé, and Pierre Hardy. ✉ *1446 rue Sherbrooke Ouest, Downtown* ☎ *514/842–0662* Ⓜ *Guy-Concordia.*

Tony's. Dedicated to the finely shod foot, Tony's places stylish imports beside elegantly sensible domestic footwear for men and women. ✉ *1346 av. Greene, Westmount* ☎ *514/935–2993* Ⓜ *Atwater.*

TOYS & GAMES

★ **Cerf Volanterie.** Claude Thibaudeau makes the sturdy, gloriously colored kites sold here. He signs each of his creations and guarantees them for three years. ✉ *4019 rue Ste-Catherine Est, Hochelaga-Maisonneuve* ☎ *514/845–7613* Ⓜ *Pie-IX.*

Jouets Choo-Choo. This shop 20 minutes from downtown sells quality European toys and educational games. ✉ *940 blvd. St-Jean, Pointe-Claire* ☎ *514/697–7550.*

MONTRÉAL ESSENTIALS

TRANSPORTATION

BY AIR

Montréal–Trudeau International Airport (still commonly called Dorval), 22½ km (14 mi) west of the city, handles all passenger flights.

A taxi from Trudeau International to downtown costs about C$35. La Québécoise shuttles are a much cheaper alternative. They leave the Montréal Central Bus Station every 20 minutes and pick up and drop off passengers at the downtown train station, as well as at major hotels. Fares are C$14 one-way, C$24 round-trip.

Airports **Aéroports de Montréal** (✉ *1100 René-Lévesque blvd. Ouest, Suite 2100* ☎ *514/394–7200* 🌐 *www.admtl.com*). **Montréal–Pierre Elliott Trudeau International Airport** (✉ *975 Roméo-Vachon blvd. Nord, Dorval* ☎ *514/394–7377*). **La Québécoise** (☎ *514/842–2281* 🌐 *www.autobus.qc.ca*).

BY BUS

All inter-city bus lines servicing Montréal arrive at and depart from the city's downtown bus terminal, the Station Centrale d'Autobus Montréal, which is built on top of the Berri-UQAM Métro station. The staff has schedule and fare information for all bus companies at the station.

Within the city, Société de Transport de Montréal (STM) administers municipal buses as well as the Métro; the same tickets and transfers are valid on either service.

Bus Stations **Central Bus Station** (✉ *505 blvd. de Maisonneuve Est, Quartier Latin* ☎ *514/842–2281* Ⓜ *Berri-UQAM*). **Greyhound** (☎ *800/231–2222, 800/661–8747 in Canada* 🌐 *www.greyhound.ca*). **Orléans Express** (☎ *514/395–4000* 🌐 *www.orleansexpress.com*). **La Québécoise** (☎ *514/842–2281* 🌐 *www.autobus.qc.ca*).

BY CAR

Montréal is accessible from the rest of Canada via the Trans-Canada Highway, which crosses the southern part of the island as Route 20, with Route 720 leading into downtown. Route 40 parallels Route 20 to the north; exits to downtown include St-Laurent and St-Denis. From

New York, take I–87 north until it becomes Route 15 at the Canadian border; continue for another 47 km (29 mi) to the outskirts of Montréal. You can also follow U.S. I–89 north until it becomes two-lane Route 133, which eventually joins Route 10, an east–west highway that leads west across the Champlain Bridge and right into downtown. From I–91 through Massachusetts via New Hampshire and Vermont, you can take Route 55 to Route 10. Again, turn west to reach Montréal. At the border you must clear Canadian Customs, so be prepared with proof of citizenship (with photo ID) and your vehicle's ownership papers. On holidays and during the peak summer season, expect to wait a half hour or more at the major crossings.

Finding your way around Montréal by car is not difficult, since the streets are laid out in a fairly straightforward grid and one-way streets are clearly marked. Parking isn't easy, however, and the narrow cobbled streets of Vieux-Montréal can be a trial. It's much easier to park near a Métro station and use public transit.

In winter, remember that your car may not start on extra-cold mornings unless it has been kept in a heated garage.

PARKING A parking ticket costs between C$42 and C$100. If your car is towed after being illegally parked, it will cost an additional C$62 to C$88 to retrieve it. Be especially alert in winter: Montréal's street plowers are ruthless in dealing with parked cars in their way. If they don't tow them, they'll bury them. When parking in residential neighborhoods, beware of the alternate-side-of-the-street-parking rules.

BY MÉTRO

The Montréal Métro, the city's clean, quiet subway system runs on rubber wheels. Warm in winter and cool in summer, it's also very safe, but as in any metropolitan area you should be alert and attentive to personal property such as purses and wallets. The Métro is connected to the more than 30 km (19 mi) of the Underground City, meaning that you can go shopping around the city and never come above ground.

Free maps are available at Métro ticket booths. Try to get the *Carte Réseau* (System Map); it's the most complete. Each Métro station connects with one or more bus routes, which cover the rest of the island. Transfers (correspondences in French) from Métro to buses are available from the dispenser just beyond the ticket booth inside the station. Bus-to-bus and bus-to-Métro transfers may be obtained from the bus driver.

FARES & SCHEDULES Métro hours on the Orange, Green, Blue, and Yellow lines are weekdays 5:30 AM to 12:30 AM and weekends 5:30 AM to 12:30, 1, or 1:30 AM (it varies by line). Trains run as often as every three minutes on the most crowded lines—Orange and Green—at rush hours.

Tickets and transfers are valid on any bus or the subway line. You should be able to get within a few blocks of anywhere in the city on one fare. Rates are C$2.75 for a single ticket, C$11.75 for six tickets, C$19 for a weeklong pass, and C$65 for a monthly pass. Transfers—correspondences in French—are free. You can buy a day pass for C$9 or a three-day pass for C$17. Various bus passes can be obtained at many of the larger hotels, at the Berri-UQAM Métro station, and at some other downtown stations.

The Société de Transport de Montréal (STM) operates an automated phone line for information on bus and Métro schedules, but it's only in French. The STM Web site, however, is in French and English and is a particularly good resource, with excellent maps and route planners.

Contact **Société de Transport de Montréal** (*STM* ☎ *514/288–6287 or 514/786–4636* 🌐 *www.stm.info/*).

BY TAXI

Taxis in Montréal all run on the same rate: $3.15 minimum and C$1.45 per kilometer (½ mi). Taxis are usually easy to hail on the street or find at a rank outside train stations, in shopping areas, and at major hotels, although finding one on a rainy night after the Métro has closed can be difficult. If the cab's rooftop light is lit, the driver is ready to take passengers. You can also call a dispatcher to send a driver to pick you up at no extra cost (you'll usually have to wait about 15 minutes). Taxis are administered by the Bureau du Taxi et Remorquage, a city agency. If you have a complaint about fares, safety, or cleanliness, phone 514/180–6600.

Taxi Companies **Atlas Taxi** (☎ *514/485–8585*). **Champlain Taxi** (☎ *514/273–2435*). **Co-op Taxi** (☎ *514/725–9885*). **Diamond Taxi** (☎ *514/274–6331*). **Unitaxi** (☎ *514/482–3000*).

BY TRAIN

Gare Centrale (Central Station), on rue de la Gauchetière between rues University and Mansfield (behind Le Reine Elizabeth), is the rail terminus for all trains from the U.S. and from other Canadian provinces. The Amtrak *Adirondack* leaves New York's Penn Station every morning for the 10½-hour trip through upstate New York to Montréal. VIA Rail connects Montréal with all the major cities of Canada, including Québec City, Halifax, Ottawa, Toronto, Winnipeg, Edmonton, and Vancouver.

Train Lines **Amtrak** (☎ *800/872–7245* 🌐 *www.amtrak.com*). **VIA Rail** (☎ *514/989–2626 or 888/842–7245* 🌐 *www.viarail.ca*).

CONTACT & RESOURCES

EMERGENCIES

The U.S. Consulate maintains a list of medical specialists in the Montréal area. There's a dental clinic on avenue Van Horne that's open 24 hours; Sunday appointments are for emergencies only.

Many pharmacies stay open until midnight, including Jean Coutu and Pharmaprix stores. Some are open around the clock, including the Pharmaprix on chemin de la Côte-des-Neiges.

Dentists **Dental clinic** (✉ *3546 av. Van Horne, Côte-des-Neiges* ☎ *514/342–4444* Ⓜ *Plamondon*).

Emergency Services **Ambulance, fire, police** (☎ *911*). **Québec Poison Control Centre** (☎ *800/463–5060*). **U.S. Consulate** (☎ *514/398–9695, 514/981–5059 emergencies*).

Hospital **Montréal General Hospital (McGill University Health Centre)** (✉ *1650 av. Cedar, Downtown* ☎ *514/934–1934* Ⓜ *Guy-Concordia*).

Late-Night Pharmacies **Jean Coutu** (✉ *501 rue Mont-Royal Est, Plateau Mont-Royal* ☎ *514/521–1058* Ⓜ *Mont-Royal* ✉ *5510 chemin de la Côte-des-Neiges, Côte-des-Neiges* ☎ *514/344–8338* Ⓜ *Côte-des-Neiges*). **Pharmaprix** (✉ *1500 rue Ste-Catherine Ouest, Downtown* ☎ *514/933–4744* Ⓜ *Guy-Concordia* ✉ *5038 Sherbrooke Ouest, Notre-Dame-de-Grace* ☎ *514/484–3531* Ⓜ *Vendôme* ✉ *901 rue Ste-Catherine Est, Village* ☎ *514/842–4915* Ⓜ *Berri-UQAM* ✉ *5122 chemin de la Côte-des-Neiges, Côte-des-Neiges* ☎ *514/738-8464* Ⓜ *Côte-des-Neiges*).

TOURS

BOAT TOURS From May through October, Amphi Tour sells a unique one-hour tour of Vieux-Montréal and the Vieux-Port on both land and water in an amphibious bus. Bateau-Mouche runs four harbor excursions and an evening supper cruise daily from May through October. Boats leave from the Jacques Cartier Pier at the foot of Place Jacques-Cartier in the Vieux-Port.

Contacts **Amphi Tour** (☎ *514/849–5181* 🌐 *www.montreal-amphibus-tour.com*). **Bateau-Mouche** (☎ *514/849–9952 or 800/361–9952* 🌐 *www.bateau-mouche.com*).

BUS TOURS Gray Line has nine different types of tours of Montréal from June through October and one tour the rest of the year. There are also day trips to Ottawa and Québec City. The company offers pickup service at the major hotels and at Info-Touriste (1001 Square Dorchester).

Gray Lines also owns Imperial Tours, whose double-decker buses follow a nine-stop circuit of the city. You can get off and on as often as you like and stay at each stop as long as you like. There's pickup service at major hotels.

Contacts **Imperial Tours** (☎ *877/348–5599 or 514/348–5599*). **Gray Line** (☎ *800/461–1223 or 514/934–1222* 🌐 *www.coachcanada.com*).

CALÈCHE RIDES Open horse-drawn carriages (fleece-lined in winter) leave from Place Jacques-Cartier, Square Dorchester, Place d'Armes, and rue de la Commune. A one- to two-hour ride costs about C$65, although slow days mean you have a better chance of bargaining.

WALKING TOURS Guidatour offers walking tours of Vieux-Montréal, the red-light district, and the Golden Square Mile.

From mid-April to mid-November, Circuit des Fantômes du Vieux-Montréal has walking tours through the old city where a host of spirits are said to still haunt the streets. Kaleidoscope has a wide selection of guided walking tours through Montréal's many culturally diverse neighborhoods.

Contacts **Circuit des Fantômes du Vieux-Montréal** (*Old Montréal Ghost Trail* ✉ *469 rue St-François-Xavier, Vieux-Montréal* ☎ *514/868-0303 or 877/868-0303* 🌐 *www.fantommontreal.com* Ⓜ *Champ-de-Mars*). **Guidatour** (✉ *477 rue St-François-Xavier, Suite 300, Vieux-Montréal* ☎ *514/844-4021 or 800/363-4021* 🌐 *www.guidatour.qc.ca* Ⓜ *Place-d'Armes*). **Kaleidoscope** (✉ *6592 Châteaubriand, Villeray* ☎ *514/990-1872* 📠 *514/277-4630* 🌐 *www.tourskaleidoscope.com* Ⓜ *Beaubien*)

VISITOR INFORMATION

Centre Info-Touriste, on Square Dorchester, has extensive tourist information on Montréal and the rest of the province of Québec, as well as a currency-exchange service and Internet café. It's open June through early September, daily 8:30–7:30, and early September through May, daily 9–6. The Vieux-Montréal branch is open daily 9–7 between June and September and is otherwise opened Wednesday–Sunday 9–5 with a one-hour lunch break 1–2.

Tourist Information **Centre Info-Touriste** (✉ *1001 Square Dorchester, Downtown* ☎ *514/873-2015 or 877/266-5687* 🌐 *www.bonjourquebec.com* Ⓜ *Peel or Bonaventure* ✉ *174 rue Notre-Dame Est, at pl. Jacques-Cartier, Vieux-Montréal* Ⓜ *Champ-de-Mars*). **Tourisme-Montréal** (☎ *877/266-5687* 🌐 *www.tourisme-montreal.org*). The city tourist office doesn't operate an information service for the public, but its Web site has a wealth of well-organized information..

Québec City

WORD OF MOUTH

"Montréal is lively and exciting . . . but Québec City wins hands-down for me . . . Seeing it is like traveling to any beautiful old European city, right here in the heart of North America. The city is very walkable. I saw it all by foot myself, and loved discovering all the hidden treasures . . . And oh my, the food!"

—westcoasthoney8

"The paved cobblestone streets will fool you into believing you've been transported to France during a bygone age. As you look north along the river from the patio that borders the famous Hotel Frontenac . . . you'll be able to see where the St. Lawrence grows wider, providing a panorama of luscious beauty against the mountains which dot the horizon."

—zola

www.fodors.com/forums

Updated by Paul Waters

NO TRIP TO FRENCH-SPEAKING CANADA is complete without a visit to romantic Québec City. There's a definite European sensibility here and you'll feel farther from home then you are, walking down cobblestone streets and stopping in small shops selling everything from pastries and local cheese to antiques and art. For 2008, the city has invited the world to help celebrate its 400th anniversary, and it's sure to be the biggest party north of Montréal.

The heart of the city is Vieux-Québec (Old Québec), which is divided between the Haute-Ville (Upper Town) and the Basse-Ville (Lower Town). Surrounded by walkable stone ramparts that once protected the city, Old Québec is today a small, dense, well-maintained neighborhood steeped in four centuries of French, English, and Canadian history and tradition. The city's finest 17th- and 18th-century buildings are here, as are its best parks and monuments. Because of the fortified city's immaculate preservation, Old Québec was designated a UNESCO World Heritage Site in 1985. But the Old City is just a part of the Québec City experience.

EXPLORING QUÉBEC CITY

By far the best way—and in some places the only way—to explore Québec City is on foot. Top sights, restaurants, and hotels are within or near Vieux-Québec, which takes up only 11 square km (4 square mi). Helpful city maps are available at visitor-information offices, the best of which is on the public square in front of the Château Frontenac.

Although summer here is the most popular time to visit, the city shows its true colors in winter. Locals don't hole up once the weather gets cold—they revel it in, all bundled in their parkas, ready to go out on the town.

UPPER TOWN

Home to many of the city's most famous sites, Upper Town also offers a dramatic view of the St. Lawrence River and the surrounding countryside. It's where you'll find historic institutions and, of course, rue St-Jean's bars, cafés, and shops, along with hotels and bed-and-breakfasts.

Like the Citadel, most of the many elegant homes that line the narrow streets in Upper Town are made of granite cut from nearby quarries in the 1800s. The stone walls, copper roofs, and heavy wooden doors on the government buildings and high-steepled churches in the area also reflect the Upper Town's place as the political, educational, and religious nerve center of both the province and the country during much of the past four centuries.

No other place in Canada has so much history squeezed into such a small spot. The Upper Town was a barren, windswept cape when Champlain built a fort here almost 400 years ago. Now, of course, it's a major tourist destination surrounded by cannon-studded stone ramparts.

TOP REASONS TO GO

VISIT CHÂTEAU FRONTENAC
Even if you're not staying at this historic château, make sure to pop in to see the lobby, check out the shops, and take a tour.

STROLL AROUND VIEUX-QUÉBEC
Spend at least a day exploring the streets of the Old City—and don't miss a ride on the funicular for fabulous views of the St. Lawrence.

EXPLORE LA CITADELLE
You don't have to be a history buff to enjoy standing atop Québec City's highest perch, which is the largest fortified base in North America.

MAIN ATTRACTIONS

⓬ **Basilique Notre-Dame-de-Québec** *(Our Lady of Québec Basilica)*. The somber, ornate interior of Québec City's Catholic cathedral includes a canopy dais over the episcopal throne, a ceiling of painted clouds decorated with gold leaf, richly colored stained-glass windows, and a chancel lamp that was a gift from Louis XIV. More than 900 bodies are interred in the crypt, including 20 bishops and four governors of New France. Samuel de Champlain may be buried near the basilica: archaeologists have been searching for his tomb since 1950. Information panels and guided tours are available. ✉*16 rue de Buade, Upper Town* ☎*418/692–2533 church* 🌐*www.patrimoine-religieux.com* 🎫*Basilica free, guided tour C$2, crypt C$2* 🕒*Mid-Oct.–Apr., daily 7:30–4; May–mid-Oct., weekdays 7:30–4, weekends 7:30–5.*

❺ **Couvent des Ursulines** *(Ursuline Convent)*. North America's oldest teaching institution for girls, is still a private school. Founded in 1639 by French nun Marie de l'Incarnation and laywoman Madame de la Peltrie, the convent has many of its original walls intact and houses a little chapel and a museum. The **Chapelle des Ursulines** (*Ursuline Chapel* ✉*10 rue Donnacona, Haute-Ville* ☎*No phone* 🎫*Free* 🕒*Chapel May–Oct., Tues.–Sat. 10–11:30 and 1:30–4:30; Sun. 1:30–4:30*) is where French general Louis-Joseph Montcalm was buried after he died in the 1759 battle that decided the fate of New France. In 2001 Montcalm's remains were transferred to rest with those of his soldiers at the Hôpital Général de Québec's cemetery, at 260 boulevard Langelier. The chapel's exterior was rebuilt in 1902, but the interior, which took sculptor Pierre-Noël Levasseur from 1726 to 1736 to complete, is unchanged. The sanctuary lamp was lighted in 1717 and has never been extinguished. The **Musée des Ursulines** (✉*12 rue Donnacona, Upper Town* ☎*418/694–0694* 🎫*C$6* 🕒*Museum May–Sept., Tues.–Sat. 10–noon and 1–5, Sun. 1–5; Oct., Nov., and Feb.–Apr., Tues.–Sun. 1–4:30*) once the residence of Madame de la Peltrie, provides an informative perspective on 120 years of the Ursulines' life under the French regime, from 1639 to 1759. It took an Ursuline nun nine years of training to attain the level of a professional embroiderer; the museum contains magnificent pieces of ornate embroidery, such as altar frontals with gold and silver threads intertwined with semiprecious jewels. In the lobby of

rue St-Paul
rue Ste-Marguerite
175
rue Ste-Madeleine
rue St-Olivier
côte d'Abraham
autoroute Dufferin-Montmorency
rue des Prairies
ru de l'Éperon
rue Vallière
Train and Bus Station
21
rue Richelieu
côte Ste-Geneviève
rue Saint-Augustin
rue d'Aiguillon
440
rue St-Olivier
rue St-Nicolas
rue Lacroix
rue St-Paul
rue Abraham Martin
rue de l'Arsenal
rue St-Jean
rue Richelieu
rue d'Youville
rue des Glacis
Parc de l'Artillerie
Rue Carleton
Rue de l'Arsenal
rue St-Vallier
côte Dinan
rue des Remparts
rue St-Joachim
avenue Honoré-Mercier
8
rue McMahon
rue St-Simon
rue St-Patrick
rue Elgin
rue McWilliam
Place d'Youville
Porte St-Jean
Convention Center
côte du Palais
9
rue Charlevoix
rue Collins
rue Ste-Angèle
rue St-Stanislas
rue St-Jean
côte Kent
boulevard René Levêsque Est
rue Joly de Lotbinière
Porte Kent
rue Dauphine
rue Hamel
rue Christie
rue St-Flavien
rue Garneau
côte de la Fabrique
rue Pierre-Olivier Chauveau
Chassée des Écossais
rue Cook
rue Ferland
Place de l'Hôtel-de-Ville
rue Ste-Famille
de la Merlagerie
Parliament Buildings
rus des Parlementaires
Dufferin
7
rue d'Auteuil
rue Ste-Ursule
rue des Jardins
11
12
Grande Allée Est
av.
Porte St-Louis
Parc de l'Esplanade
5
rue Donnacona
rue du Parloir
6
rue Ste-Anne
rue du Trésor
rue de Buade
av. Laurier
côte de la Citadelle
rue St-Louis
rue du Fort
1
Parc Montmorency
rue Haldimand
13
Escalier Frontenac
Porte Prescott
av. Ste-Geneviève
rue Mont-Carmel
2
rue de Brébeuf
rue des Grissons
rue de la Porte
4
rue des Carrières
Funiculaire
14
Sous-le-Fort
15
av. St-Denis
Terrasse Dufferin
rue du Petit-Champlain
rue du Marché-Champlain
rue Champlain
3
16
Av. du Cap-Diamants
Citadelle
QUARTIER PETIT-CHAMPLAIN
blvd Champlain
Promenade des Gouverneurs
0
1/4 mile
0
400 meters

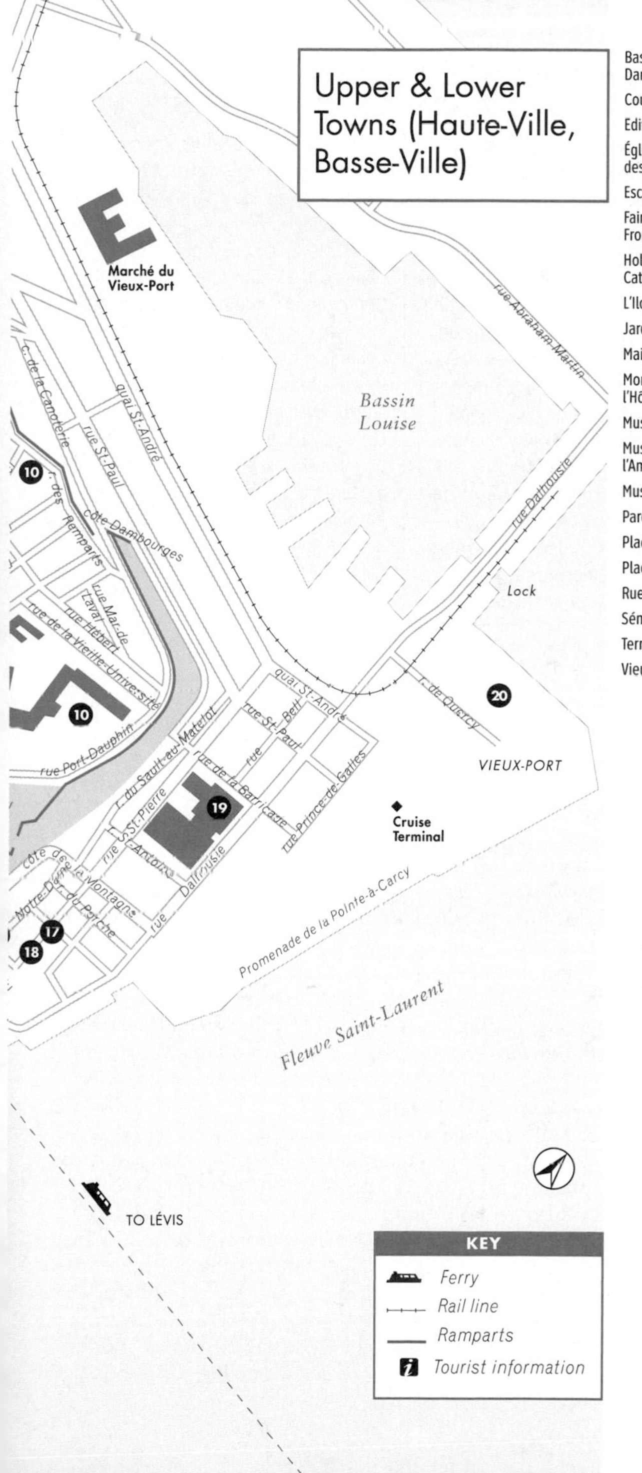

Basilique Notre-Dame-de-Québec **12**
Couvent des Ursulines **5**
Edifice Price **7**
Église Notre-Dame-des-Victoires **18**
Escalier Casse-Cou **15**
Fairmont Le Château Frontenac **2**
Holy Trinity Anglican Cathedral **6**
L'Ilot des Palais **21**
Jardin des Gouverneurs **4**
Maison Louis-Jolliet **14**
Monastère des Augustines de l'Hôtel-Dieu de Québec **9**
Musée de la Civilisation **19**
Musée de l'Amérique Française **11**
Musée du Fort **13**
Parc de l'Artillerie **8**
Place d'Armes **1**
Place Royale **17**
Rue du Petit-Champlain **16**
Séminaire du Québec **10**
Terrasse Dufferin **3**
Vieux-Port de Québec **20**

GREAT ITINERARIES

IF YOU HAVE 2 DAYS
With only a couple of days, you should devote one day to Lower Town, which is the earliest site of French civilization in North America, and the second day to Upper Town. On Day 1, stroll the narrow streets of the Quartier Petit-Champlain, visiting the Maison Chevalier and browsing at the many handicraft stores. Moving on to Place Royale, head for the Église Notre-Dame-des-Victoires; in summer there's almost always entertainment in the square. On Day 2, view the St. Lawrence River from Terrasse Dufferin and visit the impressive buildings of Upper Town, where 17th- and 18th-century religious and educational institutions predominate.

IF YOU HAVE 4 DAYS
Four days will give you some time to explore outside the walls of the Old City as well as the countryside. Follow the itinerary above for a two-day trip. On Day 3, plan a picnic on the Plains of Abraham, site of the battle that ended France's colonial dreams in North America and marked the beginning of British rule in Canada. In the afternoon check out the Musée National des Beaux-Arts du Québec or the Musée de la Civilisation. On Day 4, head out of town to explore the Côte de Beaupré, including the colossal Basilique Ste-Anne-de-Beaupré, or see Montmorency Falls and Île d'Orléans.

the museum is the **Centre Marie-de-l'Incarnation** (✉*10 rue Donnacona, Upper Town* ☎*418/694–0413* ⏲*May–Oct., Tues.–Sat. 10–11:30 and 1:30–4:30, Sun. 1:30–4:30; Feb.–Apr., Tues.–Sun. 1:30–4:30*), a center with an exhibit and books for sale on Marie de l'Incarnation's life.

❷ Fodor'sChoice ★ **Fairmont Le Château Frontenac.** Québec City's most celebrated landmark, this imposing green-turreted castle with a copper roof stands on the site of what was the administrative and military headquarters of New France. It owes its name to the Comte de Frontenac, governor of the French colony between 1672 and 1698. Considering the magnificence of the château's location overlooking the St. Lawrence River, you can see why Frontenac said, "For me, there is no site more beautiful nor more grandiose than that of Québec City." Samuel de Champlain was responsible for Château St-Louis, the first structure to appear on the site of the Frontenac; it was built between 1620 and 1624 as a residence for colonial governors. In 1784 Château Haldimand was constructed here, but it was demolished in 1892 to make way for Château Frontenac, built as a hotel a year later. The Frontenac was remarkably luxurious at that time: guest rooms contained fireplaces, bathrooms, and marble fixtures, and a special commissioner purchased antiques for the establishment. The hotel was designed by New York architect Bruce Price, who also worked on Québec City's Gare du Palais (rail station) and other Canadian landmarks. The addition of a 20-story central tower in 1925 completed the hotel. Its star-studded guest roster includes Queen Elizabeth and Ronald Reagan. Franklin Roosevelt and Winston Churchill met here in 1943 and 1944 for two wartime conferences. Guides dressed in 19th-century-style costumes conduct tours of the luxurious interior. ✉*1 rue des Carrières, Upper Town*

☎418/691–2166 🌐www.fairmont.com 🎫Tours C$8 ⏲Tours May–mid-Oct., daily 10–6 on the hr; mid-Oct.–Apr., weekends noon–5 or on demand. Reservations essential.

★ ❻ **Holy Trinity Anglican Cathedral.** This stone church was one of the first Anglican cathedrals built outside the British Isles. Built in 1804, its simple, dignified facade is reminiscent of London's St. Martin-in-the-Fields. The Récollet fathers (Franciscan friars from France) made their church available to Anglicans when Québec came under British rule. Later, King George III of England ordered construction of the present cathedral, and to this day, a portion of the north balcony still is reserved exclusively for the use of the reigning sovereign or his or her representative. The cathedral's impressive organ has 3,058 pipes. The bells—restored for the city's 400th-birthday celebrations in 2008—ring traditional English "changes" on Sunday mornings. *✉31 rue des Jardins, Upper Town ☎418/692–2193 🎫Free ⏲Mid-May–June, daily 9–6; July and Aug., daily 9–8; Sept.–mid-Oct., weekdays 10–4; mid-Oct.–mid-May, services only; morning services year-round in English daily at 8:30, and Sun. also at 11 AM, in French at 9:30 AM.*

❹ Fodor's Choice ★ **Jardin des Gouverneurs** *(Governors' Park).* In this small park just south of the Château Frontenac stands the **Wolfe-Montcalm Monument,** a 50-foot-tall obelisk that is unique because it pays tribute to both a winning (English) and a losing (French) general. The monument recalls the 1759 battle on the Plains of Abraham, which ended French rule here. British general James Wolfe lived only long enough to hear of his victory; French general Louis-Joseph Montcalm died shortly after Wolfe with the knowledge that the city was lost. On the south side of the park is **avenue Ste-Geneviève,** lined with well-preserved Victorian houses dating from 1850 to 1900. Several have been converted to inns.

★ ❽ **Parc de l'Artillerie** *(Artillery Park).* This national historic park includes four buildings—all that remains of several structures situated to guard the St. Charles River and the Old Port. The oldest buildings, dating to the early 1700s, served as headquarters for the French garrison. When they were overtaken by the British in 1759 they were used as barracks for British troops—30 years earlier than the first barracks used in England. In 1765 the Royal Artillery Regiment was stationed here, giving the fortress its name. From 1882 until 1964 the area served as an industrial complex, providing ammunition for the Canadian army. The **Dauphin Redoubt,** completed in 1748, served as a barracks for the French and then the English garrisons until 1784–85, when it became an officers' mess for the Royal Artillery Regiment. The **Officers' Quarters,** a dwelling for Royal Artillery officers until the British army's departure in 1871, illustrates military family life during the British regime. In July and August you may be able to sample bread baked in the outdoor oven and, in the afternoon, watch a French soldier reenactor demonstrate shooting with a flintlock musket. *✉2 rue d'Auteuil, Upper Town ☎418/648–4205 🌐www.parkscanada.gc.ca 🎫C$4 ⏲Apr., Wed.–Sun. 10–5; May–mid-Oct., daily 10–5.*

CLOSE UP

Québec City History

French explorer Jacques Cartier arrived in Québec in 1535, but it was Champlain who founded "New France" some 70 years later. In 1608, he built a fort on the banks of the St. Lawrence on a spot that is today called Place Royale.

The British were persistent in their efforts to dislodge the French from North America, but the colonists of New France built forts and other military structures, such as a wooden palisade (defensive fence) that reinforced their position on top of the cliff. It was Britain's naval supremacy that ultimately led to New France's demise. After capturing all French forts east of Québec, General James Wolfe led a British army to Québec City in the summer of 1759.

After a months-long siege, thousands of mostly Scots soldiers scaled the heights along a narrow cow path on a moonless night. Surprised to see British soldiers massed on a farmer's field so near the city, French General Louis-Joseph Montcalm rushed out to meet the British in what became known as the Battle of the Plains of Abraham. The French were routed in the violent 20-minute conflict, which claimed the lives of both Wolfe and Montcalm. The battle marked the death of New France and the birth of British Canada.

Under British rule, Québec City's fishing, fur-trading, shipbuilding, and timber industries expanded rapidly, and the quality of people's lives also greatly improved.

Wary of invasion from its former American colonies, the British also expanded the city's fortifications. They replaced the wooden palisades with a massive cut-stone wall and built a star-shaped fortress. Both works are still prominent in the city's urban landscape.

The constitution of 1791 established Québec City as the capital of Lower Canada, a position it held until 1840, when the Act of Union united Upper and Lower Canada and made Montréal the capital. When the British North America Act united four colonial provinces (Québec, Ontario, New Brunswick, and Nova Scotia) in the Dominion of Canada, Québec City became the province's capital city, a role it continues to play. The Québec government officially calls the city *"la capitale Nationale,"* a reflection of the nationalist sentiments that have marked Québec politics for the past 40 years.

❶ **Place d'Armes.** For centuries, this square atop a cliff has been used for parades and military events. Upper Town's most central location, the plaza is bordered by government buildings; at its west side stands the majestic **Palais de Justice** (Courthouse), a Renaissance-style building from 1887. The Gothic-style **fountain** at the center of Place d'Armes pays tribute to their arrival in 1615 of the Récollet Franciscan missionaries, the first order of priests to come to new France. They once had a church and convent on the land now occupied by the plaza. ✉ *Rues St-Louis and du Fort, Upper Town.*

❸ **Terrasse Dufferin.** This wide boardwalk with an intricate wrought-iron guardrail has a panoramic view of the St. Lawrence River, the town of Lévis on the opposite shore, Île d'Orléans, and the Laurentian Mountains. It was named for Lord Dufferin, governor of Canada between 1872 and 1878, who had this walkway constructed in 1878. Dufferin Terrace is currently a dig site, scheduled to be completed by 2008, as archaeologists from Parks Canada work to uncover the remains of the château, which was home to the governors from 1626 to 1834, when it was destroyed by fire, and Fort St-Louis. There are 90-minute tours of the fortifications that leave from here. The **Promenade des Gouverneurs** begins at the boardwalk's western end; the path skirts the cliff and leads up to Québec's highest point, Cap Diamant, and also to the Citadelle.

ALSO WORTH SEEING

7 **Edifice Price.** Styled after the Empire State Building, the 15-story, art deco structure was the city's first skyscraper. Built in 1929, it served as headquarters of the Price Brothers Company, a lumber firm founded by Sir William Price. Don't miss the interior: exquisite copper plaques depict scenes of the company's early pulp and paper activities, and the two maple-wood elevators are '30s classics. ✉ *65 rue Ste-Anne, Upper Town.*

9 **Monastère des Augustines de l'Hôtel-Dieu de Québec** *(Augustinian Monastery).* Augustinian nuns arrived from Dieppe, France, in 1639 with a mission to care for the sick in the new colony. They established the first hospital north of Mexico, the **Hôtel-Dieu,** the large building west of the monastery. Upon request the Augustinians offer free guided tours of the 1800 **chapel** and the cellars used by the nuns as a shelter, beginning in 1695, during bombardments by the British. During World War II the cellars hid national treasures that had been smuggled out of Poland for safekeeping. The monastery will likely begin long-awaited renovations in 2008. ✉ *32 rue Charlevoix, Upper Town* ☎ *418/692–2492 tours* 🎫 *Free* ⏲ *Tues.–Sat. 9:30–noon and 1:30–5, Sun. 1:30–5.*

11 **Musée de l'Amérique Française.** A former student residence of the Séminaire de Québec at Université Laval houses this museum that focuses on the history of the French in North America. You can view about 20 of the museum's 400 landscape and still-life paintings, some from as early as the 15th century, along with French colonial money and scientific instruments. Don't miss the 26-minute film (English subtitles) about Francophones and the accompanying exhibit that details their journey across North America. ✉ *2 côte de la Fabrique, Upper Town* ☎ *418/692–2843* 🌐 *www.mcq.org* 🎫 *C$5, free Tues. Nov.–May* ⏲ *June 24–early Sept., daily 9:30–5; early Sept.–June 23, Tues.–Sun. 10–5.*

13 **Musée du Fort.** A sound-and-light show reenacts the area's important battles, including the Battle of the Plains of Abraham and the 1775 attack by American generals Arnold and Montgomery. Three permanent expositions on the history of New France—including weapons, uniforms, and military insignia—were recently added. In 2006, the model of the city—complete with ships, cannons, and soldiers lined up for battle—was cleaned and repainted to celebrate its 40th anniversary. A tribute to the museum's founder, Anthony Price, provides insight into this labor of love. ✉ *10 rue Ste-Anne, Upper Town* ☎ *418/692–*

1759 🌐www.museedufort.com 🎫C$7.50 ⏲Feb. and Mar., Thurs.–Sun. 11–4; Apr.–Oct., daily 10–5; Nov.–Jan., by appointment.

STROLLING ON ST-JEAN

Rue St-Jean becomes a pedestrian street for summer at Place d'Youville—that means you'll have to leave your car behind at the public parking lot and walk.

⓾ **Séminaire de Québec.** Behind these gates lies a tranquil courtyard surrounded by austere stone buildings with rising steeples; these structures have housed classrooms and student residences since 1663. François de Montmorency Laval, the first bishop of New France, founded the seminary to train priests in the new colony. In 1852 the seminary became Université Laval, the first Catholic university in North America. In 1946 the university moved to a larger campus in suburban Ste-Foy. Today priests live on the premises, and Laval's architecture school occupies part of the building. The on-site **Musée de l'Amérique Française** gives tours of the seminary grounds and the interior in summer. Tours start from the museum, located at 2 côte de la Fabrique. The small Second Empire–style **Chapelle Extérieure,** at the west entrance of the seminary, was built in 1888 after fire destroyed the 1750 original. ✉*1 côte de la Fabrique, Upper Town* ☎*418/692–3981* 🎫*C$5* ⏲*Tours weekends mid-June–early Sept.; call for tour times.*

LOWER TOWN

Basse-Ville's once-dilapidated warehouses now house boutique hotels, trendy shops, chic art galleries, and popular restaurants and bars, serving everyone from politicos and businesspeople to tourists and hip youngsters. After exploring Place Royale and its cobblestone streets, you can walk along the edge of the St. Lawrence River and watch the sailboats and ships go by, shop at the market, or kick back on a *terrasse* with a Kir Royal. Rue Petit-Champlain also has charming places to stop and listen to street musicians.

In 1608 Champlain chose this narrow, U-shaped spit of land as the site for his settlement. Champlain later abandoned the fortified *abitation* (residence) at the foot of Cap Diamant and relocated to the more easily defendable Upper Town.

MAIN ATTRACTIONS

⓲ **Église Notre-Dame-des-Victoires** *(Our Lady of Victory Church).* The oldest church in Québec was built in 1688 and has been restored twice. It was named for two French victories against the British: one in 1690 against Admiral William Phipps and another in 1711 against Sir Hovendon Walker. Suitably, its altar is shaped like a fort, and a scale model of Le Brezé, the ship that transported soldiers to New France in 1664, hangs from the ceiling. ✉*Place Royale, Lower Town* ☎*418/692–1650* 🎫*Free, C$2 for guided tours* ⏲*Early May–late Oct., daily 9–5; late Oct.–early May, daily 10–4; closed to visitors during mass (Sun. at 10:30 and noon), marriages, and funerals.*

CLOSE UP

Québec City's 400th Birthday

It's a big year for this little city on the banks of the St-Lawrence, as 2008 marks Québec City's 400th birthday. The celebration begins on New Year's Eve, and various programs, exhibits, and festivals marking the anniversary continue through October.

The big bash, however, takes place from July 3–6, which coincides with the annual Québec City Summer Festival, when music, arts, and other cultural performances extend well into the evening. And, in typical Québécois fashion, festivities on the 6th will end with the *Chemin qui marche*, a spectacle that combines fire, water, dance, and other audiovisual treats, as well as an all-night party on the banks of the St-Lawrence that's sure to last until dawn.

For more information on the 400th anniversary, visit the city's official Web site, 🌐www.ville.quebec.qc.ca.

⓯ **Escalier Casse-Cou.** The steepness of the city's first iron stairway, an ambitious 1893 design by city architect and engineer Charles Baillairgé, is ample evidence of how it got its name: Breakneck Steps. The 170 steps were built on the site of the original 17th-century stairway that linked the Upper Town and Lower Town. There are shops and restaurants at various levels.

⓮ **Maison Louis-Jolliet.** The first settlers of New France used this 1683 house as a base for further westward explorations. Today it's the lower station of the funicular. A monument commemorating French explorer Louis Jolliet's 1672 discovery of the Mississippi River stands in the park next to the house. The **Escalier Casse-Cou** is at the north side of the house. ✉*16 rue du Petit-Champlain, Lower Town.*

NEED A BREAK?

Beer has been brewed in Québec since the early 1600s, and L'Inox (✉*37 quai St-André, Lower Town* ☎*418/692–2877*) carries on the tradition with a combination brewpub and museum. Cherry-red columns and a stainless-steel bar contrast with exposed stone and brick walls, blending the old with the new. A large, sunny terrace is open in summer. L'Inox serves many of its own beers, as well as other beverages, alcoholic and not. Food is limited to plates of Québec cheeses or European-style hot dogs served in baguettes. Tours of the brewery are available for groups of eight or more.

★ ⓳ **Musée de la Civilisation** *(Museum of Civilization).* Architect Moshe Safdie designed the striking limestone-and-glass facade of this spacious museum to blend into the old city with a campanile that echoes the shape of the city's church steeples. Two excellent permanent exhibits examine Québec's history. People of Québec uses artifacts and original films to synthesize 400 years of social and political history. It's a great introduction to the issues that face the province today. The Nous, les Premières Nations (Encounter with the First Nations) exhibit looks at Québec's 11 aboriginal nations. Imaginative artwork, video screens, computers, and sound, appeal to both adults and children. ✉*85 rue Dalhousie, Lower Town* ☎*418/643–2158* 🌐*www.mcq.org* 🎫*C$8,*

10

free Tues. Nov.–May ⏲Late June–early Sept., daily 9:30–6:30; early Sept.–mid-June, Tues.–Sun. 10–5.

17 Fodor'sChoice ★ **Place Royale.** Once the homes of wealthy merchants, houses with steep Normandy-style roofs, dormer windows, and chimneys encircle this cobblestone square. Until 1686 the area was called Place du Marché, but its name changed when a bust of Louis XIV was placed at its center. After the French colony fell to British rule in 1759, Place Royale flourished with shipbuilding, logging, fishing, and fur trading. The *Fresque des Québécois,* a 4,665-square-foot trompe-l'oeil mural depicting 400 years of Québec's history, is to the east of the square, at the corner of rue Notre-Dame and côte de la Montagne. An information center, the **Centre d'Interprétation de Place Royale** (*✉27 rue Notre-Dame, Lower Town ☎418/646–3167*) includes exhibits and a Discovery Hall with a replica of a 19th-century home, where children can try on period costumes. A clever multimedia presentation, good for kids, offers a brief history of Québec. Admission is C$4, but it's free on Tuesday from November to May. It's open daily 9:30–5 from June 24 to early September; the rest of the year it's open Tuesday–Sunday 10–5.

OFF THE BEATEN PATH

Québec–Lévis Ferry. For a striking view of the Québec City skyline, it's hard to beat a short voyage on the cross-river ferry to the city of Lévis. The view is even more impressive at night. Ferries generally run every half hour from 6 AM until 6 PM, and then hourly until 2:20 AM; there are additional ferries from April through November. From late June to August you can combine a Québec–Lévis ferry ride with a bus tour of Lévis. *✉Rue Dalhousie, 1 block south of Place de Paris, Lower Town ☎418/644–3704 or 877/787–7483 🌐www.traversiers.gouv.qc.ca 🎫June–Sept. C$2.50, Oct.–May C$2.60.*

16 **Rue du Petit-Champlain.** The oldest street in the city is now lined with pleasant boutiques and cafés. In summer, it's packed with tourists shopping for good buys in weaving, Inuit carvings, hand-painted silks, and enameled copper.

NEED A BREAK?

For a respite from the shoppers on rue du Petit-Champlain, take a table outdoors at Bistrot Le Pape Georges (*✉8 rue du Cul-de-Sac, Lower Town ☎418/692–1320 🌐www.papegeorges.com*) and cool off with a drink and creamy, tangy local cheeses and fruit. This stone-and-wood wine bar is also nice indoors; there's folk and chanson music from Thursday to Sunday nights.

20 **Vieux-Port de Québec** *(Old Port of Québec).* If you're looking for nightlife, this is where to find it. But during the day you can stroll along the riverside promenade, where merchant and cruise ships dock. The old harbor dates from the 17th century, when ships brought supplies and settlers to the new colony. At one time this port was among the busiest on the continent: between 1797 and 1897, Québec shipyards turned out more than 2,500 ships, many of which passed the 1,000-ton mark. In the northwest section of the port, the **Old Port of Québec Interpretation Center** (*✉100 quai St-André, Lower Town ☎418/648–3300*) presents the history of the port in relation to the lumber trade and shipbuilding.

ALSO WORTH SEEING

21 **L'Îlot des Palais** *(The Palace Block)*. More than 300 years of history are laid bare at this archaeological museum on the site of the first two official residences of New France's colonial officials. The basement vaults of one of them houses an exceptional archaeology exhibit and a multimedia display. ☒*8 rue Vallière, Lower Town* ☎*418/691–6092* *C$3* *June 24–early Sept., daily 10–5.*

THE FORTIFICATIONS

Declared a Canadian historical monument in 1957, the 4½-km-long (3-mi-long) wall began as a series of earthworks and wooden palisades built by French military engineers to protect the Upper Town from an inland attack following the siege of the city by Admiral Phipps in 1690. Two of the city's three sides have the natural protection of the 295-foot-high facade of Cap Diamant, so the cape itself was studded with cannon batteries overlooking the river.

Over the next century, the French expended much time, energy, and money to strengthen the city's fortifications. Dauphine Redoubt, built in 1712, it is the only one of 11 such buildings that remains, and is fully restored and open to the public. After the fall of New France, the British built an earth-and-wood citadel atop Cap Diamant, and added four martello towers during the Napoleonic Wars. Of the three that remain, two are open to the public. The British also slowly replaced the wooden palisades with a massive cut-stone wall. After the War of 1812, the British built the Citadel, a star-shaped stone fortress with two cannon-lined sides facing the river. It earned Québec City its 19th-century nickname "North America's Gibraltar."

MAIN ATTRACTIONS

2 **La Citadelle** *(The Citadel)*. Built at the city's highest point, on Cap Diamant, the Citadel is the largest fortified base in North America still occupied by troops. It was intended to protect the port from American invasion and provide a refuge in case of an attack. By the time it was completed in 1832, all threats to British rule had evaporated. Since 1920 the Citadel has served as a base for the French-speaking Royal 22e Régiment, whose story is told in the regimental museum in the former powder magazine, built in 1720. In summer the changing-of-the-guard and retreat ceremonies, featuring soldiers resplendent in scarlet tunics and bearskin hats, are not to be missed. ☒*1 côte de la Citadelle, Upper Town* ☎*418/694–2815* *www.lacitadelle.qc.ca* *C$8* *Apr.–mid-May, daily 10–4; mid-May–June, daily 9–5; July–Labor Day, daily 9–6; early Sept.–end Sept., daily 9–4; Oct., daily 10–3; Nov.–Mar., groups only (reservations required). Changing of the guard June 24–Labor Day, daily at 10* AM*. Retreat ceremony July and Aug., Fri.–Sun. at 7* PM*.*

Fodor's Choice ★

1 **Fortifications of Québec National Historic Site.** In the early 19th century this was a clear space surrounded by a picket fence and poplar trees. What's here now is the **Poudrière de l'Esplanade** (☒*100 rue St-Louis, Upper Town* ☎*418/648–7016* *www.parkscanada.gc.ca* *C$3.50*

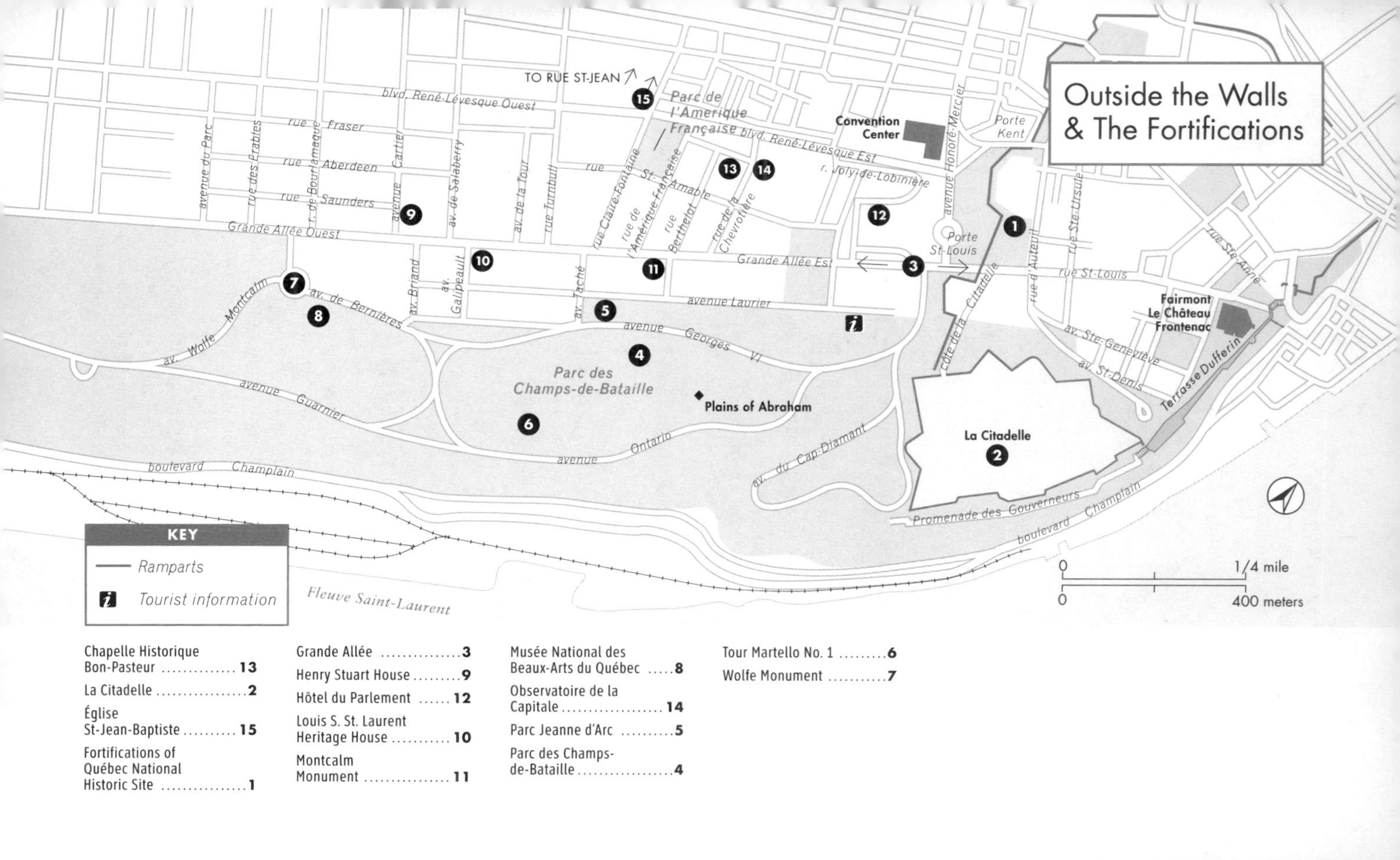

Chapelle Historique Bon-Pasteur **13**
La Citadelle **2**
Église St-Jean-Baptiste **15**
Fortifications of Québec National Historic Site **1**
Grande Allée **3**
Henry Stuart House **9**
Hôtel du Parlement **12**
Louis S. St. Laurent Heritage House **10**
Montcalm Monument **11**
Musée National des Beaux-Arts du Québec **8**
Observatoire de la Capitale **14**
Parc Jeanne d'Arc **5**
Parc des Champs-de-Bataille **4**
Tour Martello No. 1 .... **6**
Wolfe Monument **7**

May–early Oct., daily 10–5), the powder magazine (used to store gunpowder) that the British constructed in 1820, and an interpretation center with a multimedia video and a model depicting the evolution of the wall surrounding Vieux-Québec. From June 1 to early October, the park can also be the starting point for walking the city's 4½ km (3 mi) of walls. There are two guided tours (C$10 each); one starts at the interpretation center and the other begins at Terrasse Dufferin.

WORD OF MOUTH

"You should try to visit La Citadelle, the historic fort that dominates the Upper Town. There are guided tours, and in summer, the Royal 22e Régiment performs the changing of the guard every morning, and on weekends, the beating of retreat ceremony in the evening. The views from the ramparts are outstanding."

—laverendrye

10 **Louis S. St. Laurent Heritage House.** A costumed maid or chauffeur greets you when you visit this elegant Grande Allée house, the former home of Louis S. St. Laurent, prime minister of Canada from 1948 to 1957. Period furnishings and multimedia touches tell St. Laurent's story and illustrate the lifestyle of upper-crust families in 1950s Québec City. *201 Grande Allée Est, Montcalm 418/648–4071 C$10, including house, nearby martello tower, and minibus tour of Plains of Abraham June 24–Labor Day, daily 1–5; early Sept.–June 23, group visits by reservation only.*

11 **Montcalm Monument.** France and Canada jointly erected this monument honoring Louis-Joseph Montcalm, the French general who won four major battles in North America but is most famous for losing Québec City to the British on September 13, 1759. Montcalm was north of Québec City at Beauport when he learned that the British attack was imminent. He quickly assembled his troops to meet the enemy. Wounded in the ensuing battle, Montcalm died the next day. The monument depicts the standing figure of Montcalm, with an angel over his shoulder. *Place Montcalm, Montcalm.*

★ 8 **Musée National des Beaux-Arts du Québec** *(National Museum of Fine Arts of Québec)*. More than 22,000 traditional and contemporary pieces of Québec art fill this neoclassical showcase, including works by Jean-Paul Riopelle (1923–2002), Jean-Paul Lemieux (1904–1990), and Horatio Walker (1858–1938). In 2006, the museum unveiled the Brousseau Inuit Art Collection, containing 150 objects from the past three centuries. The museum's dignified building incorporates part of an abandoned prison dating from 1867. A hallway of cells, with the iron bars and courtyard, has been preserved as part of a permanent exhibition. *1 av. Wolfe-Montcalm, Montcalm 418/643–2150 www.mnba.qc.ca Free, special exhibits C$12 Sept.–May, Tues. and Thurs.–Sun. 10–5, Wed. 10–9; June–Aug., Thurs.–Tues. 10–6, Wed. 10–9.*

10

5 **Parc Jeanne d'Arc.** An equestrian statue of Joan of Arc is the focus of this park, which is bright with colorful flowers in summer. in the statue is a tribute to the heroes of 1759. The Canadian national anthem, "O Canada"was played here for the first time on June 24, 1880. ✉*Avs. Laurier and Taché, Montcalm.*

> **WORD OF MOUTH**
>
> "I loved Québec City; very old world European feel."
>
> —Aunt Annie

4 Fodor's Choice ★ **Parc des Champs-de-Bataille** *(Battlefields Park).* The 250 acres of grassland and trees overlooking the St. Lawrence River is a peaceful haven today, a refuge where harried urbanites can stroll or cycle in summer or cross-country ski in winter. But it was here, on the Plains of Abraham (named for river-pilot Abraham Martin), where General James Wolfe defeated the French in 1759 and sealed the fate of new France. The park celebrates its 100th anniversary in 2008 and in August 2009, 2,000 "soldiers" will re-enact the fateful clash of 1759. In summer a bus driven by a guide portraying Abraham Martin provides an entertaining tour—with commentary in French and English—around the park. At the **Discovery Pavilion of the Plains of Abraham** you can take in the multimedia display, Odyssey: A Journey Through History on the Plains of Abraham, which depicts 400 years of Canada's history. ✉*Discovery Pavilion of the Plains of Abraham, 835 av. Wilfrid-Laurier, Level 0 (next to Drill Hall), Montcalm* ☎*418/648–4071 for Discovery Pavilion and bus-tour information* 🌐*www.ccbn-nbc.gc.ca* *Discovery Pavilion C$8 for 1-day pass, bus tour included* ⏲*Discovery Pavilion June 24–Labor Day, daily 8:30–5:30; Labor Day–June 23, weekdays 8:30–5, Sat. 9–5, Sun. 10–5.*

7 **Wolfe Monument.** This tall monument marks the place where the British general James Wolfe died in 1759. Wolfe landed his troops about 3 km (2 mi) from the city's walls; 4,500 mostly Scottish soldiers scaled the cliff and began fighting on the Plains of Abraham. Wolfe was mortally wounded in battle and was carried behind the lines to this spot. ✉*Rue de Bernières and av. Wolfe-Montcalm, Montcalm.*

ALSO WORTH SEEING

9 **Henry Stuart House.** If you want to get a firsthand look at how the well-to-do English residents of Québec City lived in a bygone era, this Regency-style cottage built in 1849 is the place. Guided tours of the house and garden start on the hour and include a cup of tea. ✉*82 Grande Allée Ouest, Montcalm* ☎*418/647–4347* *C$5* ⏲*June 24–Labor Day, daily 11–4; day after Labor Day–June 23, Sun. 1–5.*

NEED A BREAK?

Halles Petit-Cartier (✉*1191 av. Cartier, Montcalm* ☎*418/688–1635*), a small but busy food and shopping mall just a few steps north of the Henry Stuart House on avenue Cartier, has restaurants and shops that sell flowers, local cheeses, pastries, breads, vegetables, and candies. Bite into a submarine sandwich or relax over coffee or tea and watch the world go by or pick up the makings of a picnic and head for the Plains of Abraham.

❻ **Tour Martello No. 1** *(Martello Tower No. 1)*. Of the 16 martello towers in Canada, 4 were built in Québec City, because the British government feared an invasion after the American Revolution. Tour Martello No. 1, which exhibits the history of the four structures, was built between 1802 and 1810. ✉ *South end of Parc Jeanne d'Arc, Montcalm* ☎ *418/648–4071 for information on towers and for Tour No. 2 mystery dinner show* 🎫 *C$10 for day pass to tower and Discovery Pavilion on Plains of Abraham* ⏲ *Daily 10–5* PM.

OUTSIDE THE WALLS

Unique boutiques, snazzy restaurants and historic churches make rue St-Jean one of the city's trendiest neighborhoods. Also growing in popularity is the St-Roch district, where high-tech businesses share blocks with artists' studios, galleries, cafés, and boutiques

Farther west, rue St-Jean turns into chemin Ste-Foy, which runs all the way out to the Université Laval campus and the leafy streets and shopping malls of suburban Ste-Foy.

MAIN ATTRACTIONS

⓭ **Chapelle Historique Bon-Pasteur** *(Historic Chapel of the Good Shepherd)*. Charles Baillairgé designed this slender church with a steep sloping roof in 1868 for the Soeurs du Bon-Pasteur. Carved-wood designs elaborately highlighted in gold leaf decorate the baroque interior, along with 32 religious paintings created by the nuns of the community. In addition to the regular weekday hours below, the chapel is also open Sunday between 10 and 1, before and after a musical artists' mass, which begins at 10:45; call ahead on weekdays if you want to visit during this time. ✉ *1080 rue de la Chevrotière, Montcalm* ☎ *418/522–6221* 🎫 *C$2 for tour of chapel; C$15 for classical choral concerts* ⏲ *Weekdays 9–5, weekends by reservation only.*

★ ⓯ **Église St-Jean-Baptiste** *(St. John the Baptist Church)*. Architect Joseph-Ferdinand Peachy's crowning glory rivals Our Lady of Québec Basilica in beauty and size. Seven varieties of Italian marble were used in its soaring columns, statues, and pulpit. Its 36 stained-glass windows consist of 30 sections each, and the organ, like the church, is classified as a historic monument. From October 1 to June 23 and outside regular opening hours, knock at the **presbytery** at 490 rue St-Jean to see the church. ✉ *410 rue St-Jean, St-Jean-Baptiste* ☎ *418/525–7188* ⏲ *June 24–Sept., weekdays 10–4:30, Sun. 9–4.*

★ ⓬ **Hôtel du Parlement** (Parliament Buildings). Québec's provincial legislature—the Assemblée Nationale—meets in these Renaissance-style buildings designed by architect Eugène-Étienne Taché and completed in 1884. A 30-minute tour (in English, French, or Spanish) takes in the Speaker's Gallery, the Parlementaire restaurant, the Legislative Council Chamber, and the National Assembly Chamber. Tours may be restricted during legislative sessions. ✉ *Av. Honoré-Mercier and Grande Allée, Door 3, Montcalm* ☎ *418/643–7239* 🌐 *www.assnat.qc.ca* 🎫 *Free*

Guided tours weekdays 9–4:30; late June–early Sept. also open for tours weekends 10–4:30.

DID YOU KNOW?

One of Québec City's early 400th birthday presents comes from the Simons family, owners of Simons department stores. The Fontaine de Tourny, which once stood in Bordeaux, France, now graces the green space in front of the Assemblée Nationale.

14 **Observatoire de la Capitale.** This observation gallery is atop Edifice Marie-Guyart, Québec City's tallest office building. The gray, modern concrete tower, 31 stories tall, has by far the best view of the city and the surrounding area. Take in the permanent and temporary exhibits and enjoy a coffee while you're there. *1037 rue de la Chevrotière, Montcalm 418/644–9841 www.observatoirecapitale.org C$5 Late June–mid-Oct., daily 10–5; mid-Oct.–late June, Tues.–Sun. 10–5.*

ALSO WORTH SEEING

3 **Grande Allée.** One of the city's oldest streets, Grande Allée's neo-Gothic and Queen Anne–style mansions now house trendy cafés, clubs, and restaurants. The street actually has four names: inside the city walls it's rue St-Louis; outside the walls, Grande Allée; farther west, chemin St-Louis; and farther still, boulevard Laurier.

OFF THE BEATEN PATH

Ice Hotel. At this hotel—the first of its kind in North America—constructed completely of ice and snow, you can tour the art galleries of ice sculptures, get married in the chapel, lounge in the hot tub, have a drink at the bar made of ice, dance in the ice club, then nestle into a bed lined with deerskin. The hotel is open from mid-January to March 31. A night's stay, a four-course supper, breakfast, and a welcome cocktail cost around C$250 per person. *Duchesnay Ecotourism Station, 143 Rte. Duchesnay, Ste-Catherine-de-Jacques-Cartier about 20 mins west of Québec City 418/875–4522 or 877/505–0423 www.icehotel-canada.com.*

WHERE TO EAT

Most restaurants here have a selection of dishes available à la carte, but more-creative (and often cheaper) specialties are found on the table d'hôte, a two- to four-course meal chosen daily by the chef. At dinner many restaurants will offer a *menu dégustation* (tasting menu), a five- to seven-course dinner of the chef's finest creations. In French-speaking Québec City, an *entrée,* as the name suggests, is an appetizer. It is followed by a *plat principal,* the main dish. Lunch generally costs about 30% less than dinner, and many of the same dishes are available. Lunch is usually served 11:30 to 2:30, dinner 6:30 until about 11. Tip at least 15% of the bill.

Reservations are necessary for most restaurants during peak season, May through September, as well as on holidays and during Winter Carnival. In summer, do as the locals do and dine alfresco.

Québec City restaurants and bars, along with any public buildings, became smoke-free in June 2006. Some may have protected smoking sections, but chances are that folks looking to light up may have to do so outdoors.

WHAT IT COSTS IN CANADIAN DOLLARS					
	¢	$	$$	$$$	$$$$
AT DINNER	under C$8	C$8–C$12	C$13–C$20	C$21–C$30	under C$30

Prices are per person for a main course at dinner.

UPPER TOWN

CAFÉS

¢–$ ✕**Brulerie Tatum.** Piles of coffee beans and an old coffee grinder in the window signal this lively café's specialty, and the smell of coffee roasting permeates the brightly colored main floor and mezzanine. The Brulerie is a favorite with students and shoppers, who come for their daily fix as well as for soup, sandwiches, salads, and desserts. It's also popular at breakfast for its omelets, crêpes, and such dishes as egg in phyllo pastry with hollandaise sauce and potatoes and fruit. About 40 different types each of coffee and tea are sold here. ✉*1084 rue St-Jean, Upper Town* ☎*418/692–3900* ▭*AE, D, MC, V.*

¢–$ ★ ✕**Casse-Crêpe Breton.** Generously-sized crêpes filled with everything from chocolate to ham and cheese are served in this busy café-style restaurant. Many tables surround four round griddles at which you watch your creations being made. This place is popular with tourists and locals alike, and there can be lines to get in at peak hours and seasons. ✉*1136 rue St-Jean, Upper Town* ☎*418/692–0438* ✍*Reservations not accepted* ▭*MC, V.*

¢ ✕**Le Temporel.** At this small, crowded (but no longer smoky) café, struggling writers and musicians, join bureaucrats and businessmen to enjoy the city's best coffee and feast on *croque monsieurs* (French-bread topped with ham, tomato, and broiled cheese), chili, and soups. Good, modestly priced beer and wine are also served. Some patrons start their day here with croissants and coffee at 7 AM and are still here when the place closes at 1:30 AM (an hour later on Friday and Saturday). ✉*25 rue Couillard, Upper Town* ☎*418/694–1813* ✍*Reservations not accepted* ▭*V.*

CANADIAN

$$ ✕**Aux Anciens Canadiens.** People come to this 17th-century house for authentic French-Canadian cooking; hearty specialties include duck in a maple glaze, Lac St-Jean meat pie, and maple-syrup pie with fresh cream. Enjoy a triple treat of filet mignon—caribou, bison, and deer—served with a cognac pink-pepper sauce, or wapiti with a mustard sauce. One of the best deals is a three-course meal for C$14.75, served from noon until 5:45. ✉*34 rue St-Louis, Upper Town* ☎*418/692–1627* ✍*Reservations essential* ▭*AE, DC, MC, V.*

CHINESE

$ ✕ **L'Elysée Mandarin.** A 19th-century home has been transformed into an elegant Chinese mandarin's garden where you can sip jasmine tea to the strains of soothing Asian music. Among the restaurant's Szechuan specialties are beef fillets with orange flavoring and crispy chicken in ginger sauce. The crispy duck with five spices is delicious. ✉ *65 rue d'Auteuil, Upper Town* ☎ *418/692–0909* ▭ *AE, DC, MC, V.*

CONTINENTAL

$$$ ✕ **Le Continental.** If Québec City had a dining hall of fame, Le Continental would be there among the best. House specialties include orange duckling and filet mignon, flambéed right at your table. Try the appetizer with foie gras, sweetbreads, scampi, and snow crab delicately served on a square glass plate. A house staple is the tender, velvety filet mignon "en boîte," flambéed in a cognac sauce at the table and covered in a gravy seasoned with mustard and sage. ✉ *26 rue St-Louis, Upper Town* ☎ *418/694–9995* ▭ *AE, D, DC, MC, V.*

FRENCH

$$$–$$$$ ✕ **Le Saint-Amour.** Light spills in through an airy atrium at one of the city's most romantic restaurants. Chef and co-owner Jean-Luc Boulay entices diners with such creations as caribou steak grilled with a wildberry and peppercorn sauce, and filet mignon with port wine and local blue cheese. Sauces are generally light, with no flour or butter. The C$95 menu has nine courses; the C$48 table d'hôte has five. ✉ *48 rue Ste-Ursule, Upper Town* ☎ *418/694–0667* ⊕ *www.saint-amour.com* ✍ *Reservations essential* ▭ *AE, DC, MC, V.*

$$ ✕ **Les Frères de la Côte.** A favorite among politicians and the journalists who cover them, this busy bistro serves such specialties as osso buco and a tender leg of lamb. ✉ *1190 rue St-Jean, Upper Town* ☎ *418/692–5445* ▭ *AE, D, MC, V.*

ITALIAN

$$ ✕ **Portofino Bistro Italiano.** Owner James Monti joined two 18th-century houses to create an Italian bistro with burnt-sienna walls and a wood-burning pizza oven. Don't miss the thin-crust pizza and its accompaniment of oils flavored with pepper and oregano. Guillermo Saldana performs music to eat to each weeknight. ✉ *54 rue Couillard, Upper Town* ☎ *418/692–8888* ⊕ *www.portofino.qc.ca* ▭ *AE, D, DC, MC, V.*

LOWER TOWN

CAFÉ

$$ ✕ **Le Cochon Dingue.** The café fare at this cheerful chain, whose name translates into the Crazy Pig, includes delicious mussels, *steak-frites* (steak with french fries), thick soups, and apple pie with maple cream. At the boulevard Champlain location, sidewalk tables and indoor dining rooms artfully blend the chic and the antique; black-and-white checkerboard floors contrast with ancient stone walls. ✉ *46 blvd. Champlain, Lower Town* ☎ *418/692–2013* ✉ *6 rue Cul-de-Sac, Lower Town* ☎ *418/694–0303* ▭ *AE, DC, MC, V.*

CANADIAN

$ ✕ **Le Buffet de L'Antiquaire.** Hearty home cooking, generous portions, and rock-bottom prices have made this no-frills, diner-style eatery a Lower Town institution. As the name suggests, it's in the heart of the antiques district. The traditional Québécois dishes such as *tourtière* (meat pie) are outstanding. Desserts, such as the triple-layer orange cake, are homemade and delicious. ✉ *95 rue St-Paul, Lower Town* ☎ *418/692–2661* ▭ *AE, MC, V.*

FRENCH

$$$$ ✕ **Panache.** Wooden floors and exposed beams make a perfect setting for chef François Blais's modern take on traditional French-Canadian cuisine. The menus change with the seasons, but spit-roasted duck is always available. ✉ *10 rue St-Antoine, Lower Town* ☎ *418/692–1022* ▭ *AE, DC, MC, V.*

$$$–$$$$ ✕ **L'Initiale.** Widely spaced tables and a warm brown-and-cream decor place L'Initiale in the upper echelon of restaurants in this city. Chef Yvan Lebrun, whose menu changes with the seasons, favors spit-roasted meats, especially lamb. There's also a C$89 eight-course menu dégustation. For dessert, many small treats are arranged attractively on a single plate. ✉ *54 rue St-Pierre, Lower Town* ☎ *418/694–1818* ▭ *AE, DC, MC, V* ⊙ *Closed Sun. and early Jan.*

Fodor's Choice ★

$$$–$$$$ ✕ **Le Toast!** Very chic and very intimate, Le Toast!'s eclectic menu lists such exotic dishes as vegetable and red curry imperial rolls and poached eggs with Sir Laurier cheese and ham. For Sunday brunch try the goat cheese and salmon. ✉ *17 rue Sault-au-Matelot, Lower Town* ☎ *418/692–1334* 🌐 *www.restauranttoast.com* ▭ *AE, DC, MC, V* ⊙ *No lunch weekends; no dinner Mon.*

$$$ ✕ **Largo.** The food is Mediterranean, Moroccan, and Spanish, the music is live jazz, and the original art on the wall is for sale (proceeds go to help local artists through the Fondation Largo pour les Arts). Specialties include a bouillabaisse Marseillaise and tartares. Plan to shell out C$25 for the show, and get there an hour before it starts. ✉ *643 rue St-Joseph Est, St-Roch* ☎ *418/529–3111* 🌐 *www.largorestoclub.com* ✍ *Reservations essential* ▭ *AE, MC, V.*

$$$ ✕ **L'Echaudé.** A chic beige-and-green bistro, L'Echaudé attracts a mix of businesspeople and tourists because of its location between the financial and antiques districts. Lunch offerings include duck confit with fries and fresh salad. Highlights of the three-course brunch are eggs Benedict and tantalizing desserts. The decor is modern, with hardwood floors, a mirrored wall, and a stainless-steel bar where you can dine atop a high stool. ✉ *73 rue Sault-au-Matelot, Lower Town* ☎ *418/692–1299* ▭ *AE, DC, MC, V* ⊙ *No Sun. brunch mid-Oct.–mid-May.*

$$$ ✕ **L'Utopie.** Sixteen-foot ceilings and the tall potted trees used as table dividers create a calm, modern atmosphere. Fine wines, expert service, and French cuisine with a Mediterranean flair complete the picture. The "menu architecture," inspired by architect Pierre Bouvier, designer of this utopian space, runs C$109, wine included. ✉ *226½ rue St-Joseph Est, St-Roch* ☎ *418/523–7878* 🖷 *418/523–2349* ▭ *AE, DC, MC, V* ⊙ *Closed Mon. No lunch weekends.*

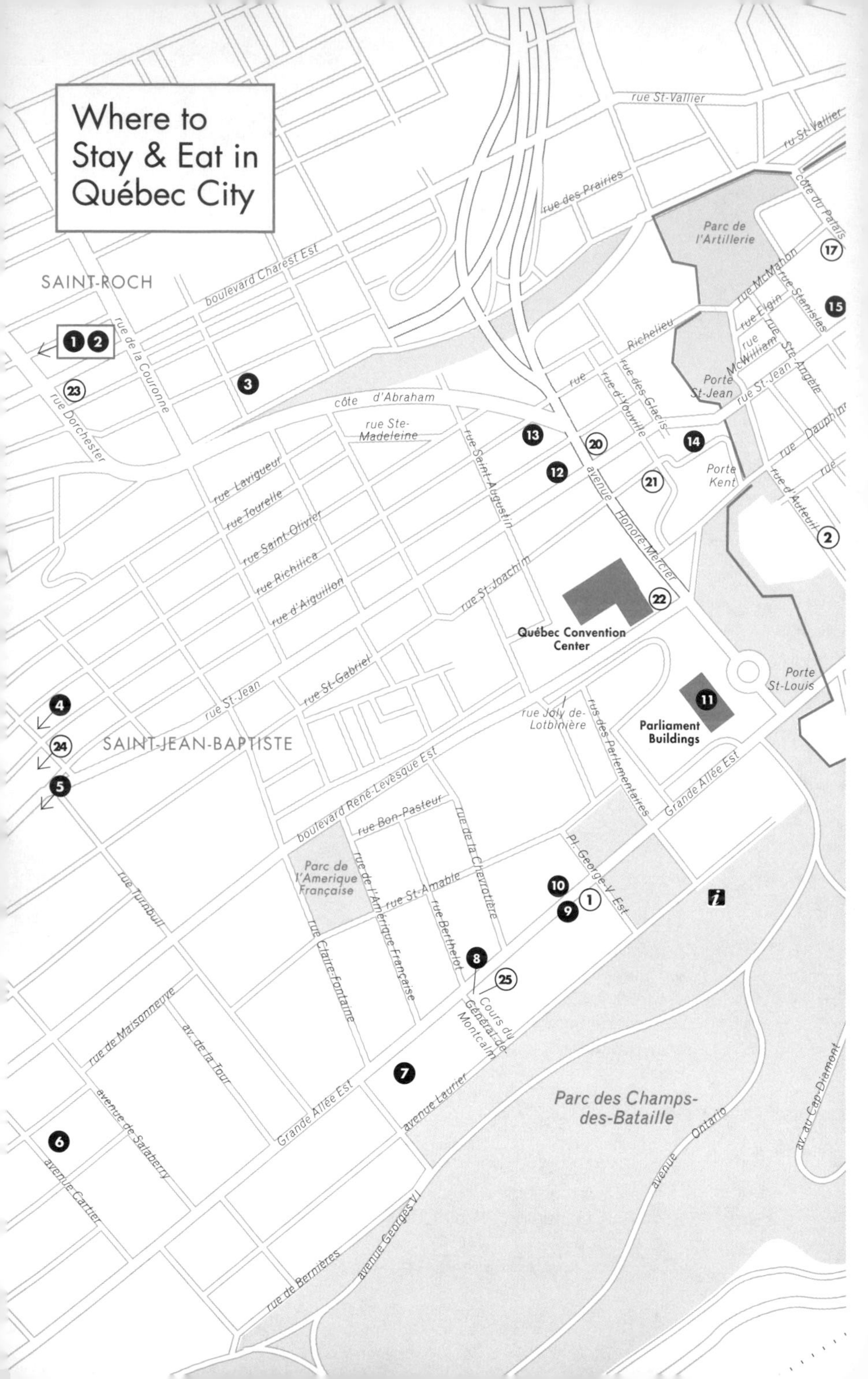

Where to Stay & Eat in Québec City
SAINT-ROCH
SAINT-JEAN-BAPTISTE
rue St-Vallier
ru St-Vallier
rue des Prairies
boulevard Charest Est
côte du Palais
Parc de l'Artillerie
rue McMahon
rue Stanislas
rue Elgin
rue McWilliam
rue Ste-Angèle
Richelieu
rue de la Couronne
rue Dorchester
côte d'Abraham
rue Ste-Madeleine
rue
rue d'Youville
rue des Glacis
Porte St-Jean
rue St-Jean
rue Dauphine
Porte Kent
rue d'Auteuil
avenue Honoré-Mercier
rue Saint-Augustin
rue Lavigueur
rue Tourelle
rue Saint-Olivier
rue Richilica
rue d'Aiguillon
rue St-Joachim
Québec Convention Center
Porte St-Louis
rue St-Gabriel
rue St-Jean
rue Joly de-Lotbinière
rus des Parlementaires
Parliament Buildings
boulevard René-Levesque Est
Grande Allée Est
rue Bon-Pasteur
rue de la Chevrotière
pl. George-V Est
Parc de l'Amerique Française
rue de l'Amérique Française
rue St-Amable
rue Berthelot
rue Turnbull
rue Claire-Fontaine
Cours du Général-de Montcalm
rue de Maisonneuve
av. de la Tour
Grande Allée Est
avenue Laurier
Parc des Champs-des-Bataille
avenue de Salaberry
avenue Cartier
avenue Ontario
av. au Cap-Diamant
avenue Georges VI
rue de Bernières

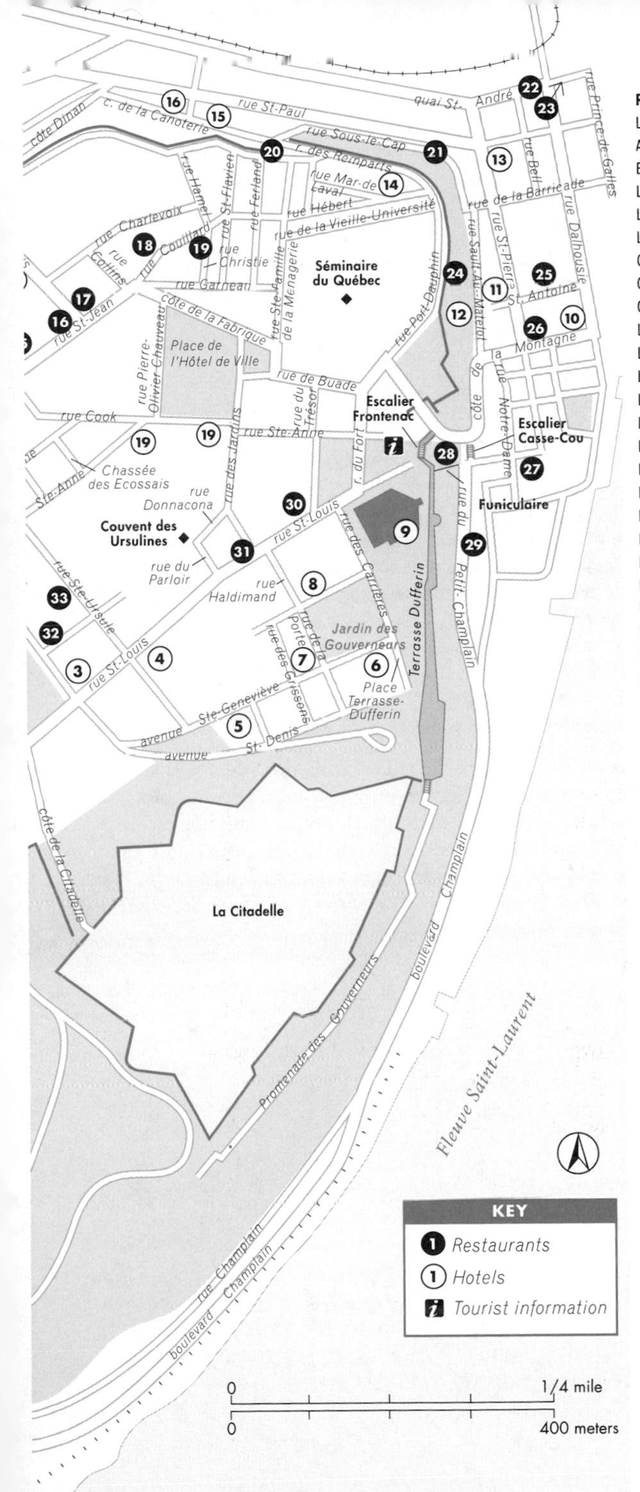

Restaurants

- L'Astral ... 8
- Aux Anciens Canadiens ... 31
- Brulerie Tatum ... 15
- Le Buffet de L'Antiquaire ... 21
- Le Café du Monde ... 23
- Le Café Krieghoff ... 6
- Casse-Crêpe Breton ... 16
- Chez Cora ... 3
- Chez Victor ... 5
- La Closerie ... 9
- Le Cochon Dingue ... 27, 29
- Le Commensal ... 12
- Le Continental ... 33
- L'Echaudé ... 24
- L'Elysée Mandarin ... 32
- Les Frères de la Côte ... 17
- L'Initiale ... 26
- Largo ... 2
- Laurie Raphaël ... 22
- Louis Hébert ... 10
- Le Marie Clarisse ... 28
- Panache ... 25
- Le Parlementaire ... 11
- La Pointe des Amériques ... 4, 14
- Portofino Bistro Italiano ... 18
- Ristorante Michelangelo ... 7
- Le Saint-Amour ... 30
- Le Temporel ... 19
- Le Toast! ... 20
- Thang Long ... 13
- L'Utopie ... 1

Hotels

- Au Jardin du Gouverneur ... 8
- Auberge St-Antoine ... 10
- L'Autre Jardin Average ... 23
- Château Bonne Entente ... 24
- Courtyard by Marriott Québec ... 21
- Fairmont Le Château Frontenac ... 9
- Hilton Québec ... 22
- Hôtel Belley ... 15
- Hôtel Cap Diamant ... 5
- Hôtel Château Bellevue ... 7
- Hôtel Château Laurier ... 1
- Hôtel Clarendon ... 19
- Hôtel Dominion 1912 ... 13
- Hôtel Le Clos St-Louis ... 4
- Hôtel Le Priori ... 12
- Hôtel Le St-Paul ... 16
- Hôtel Loews Le Concorde ... 25
- Hôtel Manoir de l'Esplanade ... 3
- Hôtel Manoir des Remparts ... 14
- Hôtel Manoir Victoria ... 17
- Hôtel Marie Rollet ... 18
- Hôtel Palace Royal ... 20
- Hôtel 71 ... 11
- Manoir d'Auteuil ... 2
- Manoir Sur le Cap ... 6

CLOSE UP

A Québec City Cheese Primer

It used to be that all good cheese in Québec City was imported from France—but not anymore. During the last several years, there's been a cheese movement, and regional cheese makers have begun producing award-winning aged cheddar and *lait cru* (unpasteurized) cheeses that you won't want to go home without sampling.

Luckily, there are enough cheese shops to keep you cheese-shop-hopping all afternoon. Stop by the **Épicerie Européenne** (✉ *560 rue St-Jean* ☎ *418/529-4847*) in the St-Jean-Baptiste quarter to try some of the lait cru that everyone is raving about. Along the same street, wander through **Épicerie J. A. Moisan** (✉ *699 rue St-Jean* ☎ *418/522-0685*), another well-known, well-stocked market, or visit **Aux Petits Délices** (✉ *1191 av. Cartier* ☎ *418/522-5154*) in the market at Les Halles du Petit Quartier for a large selection of specialty cheeses, along with fruit, breads, crackers, and wine for a picnic on the Plains.

Some good cheeses to watch out for at these shops and others include Bleu Bénédictin from the St-Benoît Abbey, the Île aux-Grues four-year-old cheddar, Portneuf Camembert, or the same region's La Sauvagine, a 2006 top prize winner. There's also a *chèvre noire*, a raw, semifirm goat cheese by Fromagerie Tournevant—wrapped in black wax—that's not to be missed, and the fresh goat cheese La Biquette. If Gouda is your thing, try a piece from Fromagerie Bergeron.

$$ **Le Café du Monde.** With a terrace overlooking the St. Lawrence River and an atrium overlooking l'Agora amphitheater and the old stone Customs House, the view here matches the food. Etched-glass dividers, wicker chairs, and palm trees complement the bistro-style menu, which includes such classics as duck confit accompanied by garlic-fried. ✉ *84 rue Dalhousie, Lower Town* ☎ *418/692-4455* *Reservations essential* *AE, DC, MC, V.*

MODERN CANADIAN

$$$–$$$$ Fodor's Choice ★ **Laurie Raphaël Restaurant-Atelier-Boutique.** Chef Daniel Vézina uses local and regional products to create such dishes as duck foie gras with cranberry juice and port, and smoked with English cucumbers, curry oil, and a maple glaze. The seven-course menu dégustation is C$89, but if you're adventurous, try the C$56 Chef Chef menu—a surprise meal will be delivered to your table. Vézina also offers cooking classes Wednesday evening and Saturday at noon. ✉ *117 rue Dalhousie, Lower Town, G1K 9C8* ☎ *418/692-4555* *www.laurieraphael.com* *AE, D, DC, MC, V* *Closed Sun., Mon., and Jan. 1–15.*

SEAFOOD

$$$ **Le Marie Clarisse.** Named for a schooner, it's no wonder this restaurant at the bottom of Escalier Casse-Cou specializes in such seafood dishes as halibut with nuts and honey and scallops with port and paprika, but it also features venison and other game. ✉ *12 rue du Petit-Champlain, Lower Town* ☎ *418/692-0857* *Reservations essential* *AE, DC, MC, V* *No lunch weekends Oct.–Apr.*

OUTSIDE THE WALLS

ASIAN

$$ ✕ **Thang Long.** Low prices and some of the best Asian food in the city ensure this restaurant's popularity. The simple menu of Vietnamese, Chinese, Thai, and Japanese dishes has a few surprises. *Chakis,* for example, is a tasty fried appetizer of four wrappers filled with shrimp, onions, and sugared potatoes. Bring your own wine or beer. ✉ *869 côte d'Abraham, St-Jean-Baptiste* ☎ *418/524–0572* *Reservations essential* *MC, V* *BYOB* *No lunch weekends.*

CAFÉ

¢–$ ✕ **Le Café Krieghoff.** Modeled after a typical Paris bistro café and named for a Canadian painter who lived just up the street (and whose prints hang on the walls), this busy, noisy restaurant with patios in front and back is a popular place with the locals. Open every day from 7 AM to midnight, Krieghoff serves specialties that include croissants, "la Toulouse" (big French sausage with sauerkraut), steak with french fries, spinach pie, *boudin* (pig-blood sausage), and "la Bavette" (a French-style minute steak). This place is a big local literary hangout, with great coffee, tea, and desserts. ✉ *1089 rue Cartier, Montcalm* ☎ *418/522–3711* *DC, MC, V.*

ECLECTIC

¢–$ ✕ **Chez Cora.** Spectacular breakfasts with mounds of fresh fruit are the specialty at this sunny chain restaurant. Try the Eggs Ben et Dictine, which has smoked salmon, or the Gargantua—two eggs, sausage, ham, pancakes, *cretons* (pâtés), and baked beans. Kids love the Banana Surprise, a banana wrapped in a pancake with chocolate or peanut butter and honey. The restaurant also serves light lunch fare, such as salads and sandwiches. ✉ *545 rue de l'Église, St-Roch* ☎ *418/524–3232* *AE, DC, MC, V* *No dinner.*

FAST FOOD

¢–$ ✕ **Chez Victor.** Brick and stone walls and hearty burgers topped with onions, mushrooms, pickles, hot mustard, mayonnaise, and a choice of cheeses attract an arty crowd. French fries are served with a dollop of mayonnaise and poppy seeds. ✉ *145 rue St-Jean, St-Jean-Baptiste* ☎ *418/529–7702* *MC, V.*

FRENCH

$$$ ✕ **Louis Hébert.** Fine French cuisine, a location near the Hôtel du Parlement, and discreet meeting rooms have made Louis Hébert a favorite with Québec's decision makers. In summer, though, most guest try to snag a table on the front terrace where they can keep an eye on the bustling scene on Grande Allée. In winter, chef Hervé Toussaint's roast lamb in a nut crust with Stilton and port is a favorite. In summer, seafood dishes such as lobster and fresh pasta with a lobster sauce and asparagus are popular. ✉ *668 Grande Allée Est, Montcalm* ☎ *418/525–7812* *AE, D, DC, MC, V* *No lunch weekends Oct.–Apr.*

$$–$$$ ✕ **La Closerie.** There are really two Closeris, both in the Hôtel Laurier. In the more-elegant Grande Table dining room, rich sauces enhance such dishes as *magret de canard aux cerises séchées* (duck breast with

dried-cherry sauce). In the slightly less-expensive French bistro, dishes include artichoke-heart pizza and salmon fillet. ✉ *1220 pl. Georges V Ouest, Montcalm* ☎ *418/523–9975* ▭ *AE, DC, MC, V.*

ITALIAN

$$$–$$$$ ✕ **Ristorante Michelangelo.** Don't be put off by the funeral-home appearance; this is one of the few restaurants outside Italy recognized as authentically Italian by the Italian government—a distinction earned by homemade pasta, succulent veal dishes, and an 18,000-bottle wine cellar. ✉ *3111 chemin St-Louis, Ste-Foy* ☎ *418/651–6262* ▭ *AE, DC, MC, V* ⊙ *Closed Sun. No lunch Sat.*

MODERN CANADIAN

$$$ ✕ **L'Astral.** The pork in soy sauce and the Barbary duck with honey and Szechuan pepper are good, but most people come to this revolving restaurant atop Hôtel Loews LeConcord for the spectacular view of the city and the river. L'Astral offers a three-course table d'hôte and a C$40 nightly buffet but no à la carte menu. ✉ *1225 Cours du Général-de Montcalm, Montcalm* ☎ *418/647–2222* ▭ *AE, D, DC, MC, V.*

$$ ✕ **Le Parlementaire.** Despite its magnificent beaux-arts interior and its reasonable prices, the National Assembly's restaurant remains one of the best-kept secrets in town. In summer the three-course lunch menu includes everything from mini-fondues made with Charlevoix cheese to ravioli made from lobster caught in the Gaspé. Call ahead. ✉ *Av. Honoré-Mercier and Grande Allée Est, Door 3, Montcalm* ☎ *418/643–6640* ▭ *AE, MC, V* ⊙ *Closed weekends June 24–Labor Day; closed Sat.–Mon. Labor Day–June 23. Usually no dinner.*

PIZZA

$$ ✕ **La Pointe des Amériques.** Adventurous pizza lovers can try toppings like alligator, smoked Gouda, Cajun sauce, and hot peppers, but there's plenty for more-timid diners in this century-old building just outside the St-Jean gate. ✉ *964 rue St-Jean, Carré d'Youville* ☎ *418/694–1199* ✉ *2815 blvd. Laurier, Ste-Foy* ☎ *418/658–2583* ▭ *AE, DC, MC, V.*

VEGETARIAN

$ ✕ **Le Commensal.** Brick walls and potted plans add a touch of class to this meatless cafeteria. Plates are weighed to determine the price. ✉ *860 rue St-Jean, St-Jean-Baptiste* ☎ *418/647–3733* ▭ *AE, DC, MC, V* 🍷 *BYOB.*

WHERE TO STAY

More than 35 hotels are within Québec City's walls, and there is also an abundance of family-run bed-and-breakfasts. Landmark hotels are as prominent as the city's most historic sights; modern high-rises outside the ramparts have spectacular views of the Old City. Another choice is to immerse yourself in the city's historic charm by staying in an old-fashioned inn, where no two rooms are alike.

Be sure to make a reservation if you visit during peak season (May through September) or during the Winter Carnival, in January and/or February.

During especially busy times, hotel rates usually rise 30%. From November through April, many lodgings offer weekend discounts and other promotions.

Hotels are bound to be packed during this year's 400th anniversary celebrations, which officially run through October, so the sooner you book, the better.

WHAT IT COSTS IN CANADIAN DOLLARS					
	¢	$	$$	$$$	$$$$
HOTELS	under C$75	C$75–C$125	C$126–C$175	C$176–C$250	over C$250

Prices are for two people in a standard double room in high season; excluding tax.

UPPER TOWN

$$$$ Fodor'sChoice ★ **Fairmont Le Château Frontenac.** Towering above the St. Lawrence River, the Château Frontenac is a Québec City landmark. Its public rooms—from the intimate piano bar to the 700-seat ballroom reminiscent of the Hall of Mirrors at Versailles—are all opulent. Rooms are elegantly furnished, but some are small; some have views of the river. At Le Champlain, classic French cuisine is served by waitstaff in traditional French costumes. This hotel is a tourist attraction in its own right, so the lobby can be quite busy. Reserve well in advance, especially for late June to mid-October. ✉ *1 rue des Carrières, Upper Town* ☎ *418/692–3861 or 800/441–1414* 📠 *418/692–1751* 🌐 *www.fairmont.com* *585 rooms, 33 suites* *In-room: high-speed Internet. In-hotel: public Wi-Fi, 2 restaurants, room service, bar, pool, gym, concierge, laundry service, executive floor, parking (fee), some pets allowed* 💳 *AE, D, DC, MC, V* *EP.*

$$$ **Hôtel Manoir Victoria.** A discreet, old-fashioned entrance leads you into this European-style hotel with in-house spa. Rooms are decorated simply but elegantly with wood-accented standard hotel furnishings. Three rooms and three suites have whirlpool baths and electric fireplaces. You can't beat its location. ✉ *44 côte du Palais, Upper Town, G1R 4H8* ☎ *418/692–1030 or 800/463–6283* 📠 *418/692–3822* 🌐 *www.manoir-victoria.com* *156 rooms, 3 suites* *In-room: ethernet, Wi-Fi, safe (some). In-hotel: public Wi-Fi, 2 restaurants, room service, pool, gym, spa, concierge, laundry service, parking (fee), no-smoking rooms* 💳 *AE, D, DC, MC, V* *EP.*

$$$ **Hôtel Château Bellevue.** Behind the Château Frontenac, this 1898 hotel has comfortable accommodations at reasonable prices in a good location. Guest rooms are modern, with standard hotel furnishings; many have a view of the St. Lawrence River. The rooms vary considerably in size (many are a bit cramped), and package deals are available. ✉ *16 rue de la Porte, Upper Town, G1R 4M9*

☎418/692–2573 or 800/463–2617 ⎙418/692–4876 ⊕*www.oldquebec.com/bellevue* ⇨*58 rooms* ♁*In-room: Wi-Fi, refrigerator (if requested). In-hotel: public Wi-Fi, bar, laundry service, parking (fee)* ▭*AE, D, DC, MC, V* ⫯◎⫯*EP.*

$$$ **Hôtel Clarendon.** Built in 1866, the Clarendon is the oldest operating hotel in Québec City, and now it's been refurbished in art deco and art nouveau styles, most notably in the public areas. Some guest rooms have period touches, and some are more modern. Half the rooms have excellent views of Old Québec; the others overlook a courtyard. The new loungy Le Charles-Baillairgé is more contemporary in terms of décor and cuisine than its predecessor, L'Emprise, which was *the* jazz bar in Québec City. ✉*57 rue Ste-Anne, Upper Town,* ☎*418/692–2480 or 888/554–6001* ⎙*418/692–4652* ⊕*www.hotelclarendon.com* ⇨*138 rooms, 5 suites* ♁*In-room: dial-up, Wi-Fi. In-hotel: restaurant, room service, bar, parking (fee)* ▭*AE, D, DC, MC, V* ⫯◎⫯*EP.*

$$$ ★ **Hôtel Le Clos St-Louis.** Winding staircases and crystal chandeliers add to the Victorian elegance of this central inn made up of two 1845-era houses. All rooms have antiques or reproductions; some have romantic four-poster or sleigh beds; eight have decorative fireplaces. If you stay on the main floor you can avoid having to climb the steep stairs. ✉*69 rue St-Louis, Upper Town, G1R 3Z2* ☎*418/694–1311 or 800/461–1311* ⎙*418/694–9411* ⊕*www.clossaintlouis.com* ⇨*16 rooms, 2 suites* ♁*In-room: Wi-Fi. In-hotel: parking (fee), no-smoking rooms, no elevator* ▭*AE, MC, V* ⫯◎⫯*CP.*

$$$ **Manoir d'Auteuil.** An ornate sculpted iron banister wraps up through four floors (note that there is no elevator), and guest rooms blend modern design with the art deco structure. Each room is different; one was once a chapel, and two have a tiny staircase leading to their bathrooms. Two rooms have showers with seven showerheads. Rooms on the fourth floor are smaller but are less expensive and come with great views of the Hôtel du Parlement. One room is named for singer Édith Piaf who used to frequent the hotel. ✉*49 rue d'Auteuil, Upper Town, G1R 4C2* ☎*418/694–1173* ⎙*418/694–0081* ⊕*www.manoirdauteuil.com* ⇨*14 rooms, 2 suites* ♁*In-room: Wi-Fi. In-hotel: public Wi-Fi, laundry service, parking (fee), no-smoking rooms, no elevator* ▭*AE, D, MC, V* ⫯◎⫯*CP.*

$$ ★ **Hôtel Cap Diamant.** Vintage furniture with ecclesiastical accents—stained glass, a confessional door, even the odd angel—complement the marble fireplaces, stone walls, and hardwood floors at this hotel made up of two adjacent 1826 houses. Stairs to third-floor rooms are a bit steep, but there is a baggage lift. ✉*39 av. Ste-Geneviève, Upper Town, G1R 4B3* ☎*418/694–0313* ⎙*418/692–1375* ⊕*www.hcapdiamant.qc.ca* ⇨*12 rooms* ♁*In-room: no phone, refrigerator, Wi-Fi. In-hotel: laundry service, no-smoking rooms, no elevator* ▭*MC, V* ⫯◎⫯*CP.*

$$ **Hôtel Manoir de l'Esplanade.** The four 1845 stone houses at the corner of rues d'Auteuil and St-Louis conceal one of the city's good deals: a charming hotel with well-appointed rooms and breakfast included. Rooms have an antique feel with either rich dark-wood furniture or more-modern light-wood furniture, and colors and fabrics vary as well. Some rooms have exposed brick walls, a fireplace, and a glass chan-

delier. The front rooms, facing St-Louis Gate, are the most spacious. Those on the fourth floor are right under the eaves. ✉ *83 rue d'Auteuil, Upper Town, G1R 4C3* ☎ *418/694–0834* 🖷 *418/692–0456* 🌐 *www.manoiresplanade.ca* *36 rooms* *In-room: refrigerator (some), Wi-Fi. In-hotel: public Wi-Fi and public Internet, laundry service, no-smoking rooms, no elevator* ▭ *AE, MC, V* *EP.*

$$ ★ **Hôtel Marie Rollet.** In the heart of Vieux-Québec, this intimate little inn built in 1876 by the Ursuline Order has warm woodwork and antique charm to match its surroundings. Two rooms have working fireplaces. Some bathrooms are so tiny the sink is in the bedroom. Steep stairs lead to a rooftop terrace with a garden view. ✉ *81 rue Ste-Anne, Upper Town, G1R 3X4* ☎ *418/694–9271 or 800/275–0338* 🌐 *www.hotelmarierollet.com* *10 rooms* *In-room: no phone. In-hotel: parking (fee), no-smoking rooms, no elevator* ▭ *AE, MC, V* *EP.*

$$ **Manoir Sur le Cap.** No two rooms are alike in this elegant 19th-century inn with beautiful views of Governors' Park and the St. Lawrence RiverRooms are light and airy, with antiques and hardwood floors. Some have brass beds, brick walls, or small balconies. Note that some bathrooms have only showers and no tubs, and that one room is in the basement. There's no elevator. ✉ *9 av. Ste-Geneviève, Upper Town, G1R 4A7* ☎ *418/694–1987 or 866/694–1987* 🖷 *418/627–7405* 🌐 *www.manoir-sur-le-cap.com* *11 rooms, 3 suites, 1 apartment* *In-room: no a/c (some), no phone (some), refrigerator (some), dial-up (some), Wi-Fi (some). In-hotel: public Wi-Fi, no-smoking rooms, no elevator* ▭ *AE, MC, V* *EP.*

$ **Au Jardin du Gouverneur.** This cream-color stone house with windows trimmed in dark blue is an inexpensive, unpretentious hotel behind the Château Frontenac. ✉ *16 rue Mont-Carmel, Upper Town, G1R 4A3* ☎ *418/692–1704 or 877/692–1704* 🖷 *418/692–1713* 🌐 *www.quebecweb.com/hjg* *16 rooms, 1 suite* *In-room: no phone, refrigerator (some). In-hotel: no-smoking rooms, no elevator* ▭ *AE, MC, V* *CP.*

$ **Hôtel Manoir des Remparts.** A home away from home every May for Mississippi State University students studying French, this hotel's basic but cheery rooms and inexpensive rates that also attract many Europeans. The two 1830 houses forming this hotel arc opposite the wall enclosing Haute-Ville and have a view of the port. The 10 fourth-floor rooms share bathrooms and a TV. ✉ *3½ rue des Remparts, Upper Town, G1R 3R4* ☎ *418/692–2056, 866/692–2056 in Canada* 🖷 *418/692–1125* *manoirdesremparts@sympatico.ca* 🌐 *www.manoirdesremparts.com* *34 rooms, 24 with bath* *In-room: no a/c (some), no phone, kitchen (some), refrigerator (some), no TV (some), dial-up. In-hotel: public Wi-Fi, no-smoking rooms, no elevator* ▭ *AE, DC, MC, V* *CP.*

10

LOWER TOWN

$$$$ Fodor's Choice ★ **Auberge St-Antoine.** A member of the Relais & Châteaux chain, the auberge incorporates the stone walls of a 19th-century maritime warehouse. Antiques and contemporary pieces fill the bedrooms, some with fireplaces, hot tubs, large terraces, or river views. In the Cinéma St-Antoine, two classic movies are shown each night, one in English and one in French, both subtitled, at 6 and 8 PM. ✉ *8 rue St-Antoine, Lower Town* ☎ *418/692–2211 or 888/692–2211* 📠 *418/692–1177* 🌐 *www.saint-antoine.com* *82 rooms, 12 suites* *In-room: ethernet, dial-up, refrigerator. In-hotel: restaurant, room service, bar, concierge, laundry service, public Wi-Fi, parking (fee), no-smoking rooms* 💳 *AE, DC, MC, V* 🍽 *EP, BP.*

$$$–$$$$ Fodor's Choice ★ **Hôtel Dominion 1912.** Sophistication and attention to the smallest detail prevail in the modern rooms of this four-star boutique hotel—from the custom-designed swing-out night tables to the white goose-down duvets and custom umbrellas. Built in 1912 as a warehouse, the hotel has rooms on higher floors with views of either the St. Lawrence River or the Old City. ✉ *126 rue St-Pierre, Lower Town, G1K 4A8* ☎ *418/692–2224 or 888/833–5253* 📠 *418/692–4403* 🌐 *www.hotel-dominion.com* *60 rooms* *In-room: ethernet, refrigerator, Wi-Fi. In-hotel: public Wi-Fi, gym, concierge, laundry service, parking (fee), some pets allowed* 💳 *AE, DC, MC, V* 🍽 *CP.*

$$$–$$$$ **Hôtel 71.** This four-star luxury hotel is located in the founding building of the National Bank of Canada. Owners Patrick and Sonia Gilbert also own the neighboring Auberge Saint-Pierre. Lots of natural light has been worked into the decor in rooms with 12-foot-high ceilings, functional yet contemporary design by local artists, and stunning views of Old Québec and its river, or both settings from a corner suite. Rain-forest showers and surround-sound systems are in every room. ✉ *71 rue St-Pierre, Lower Town, G1K 4A4* ☎ *418/692–1171 or 888/692–1171* 📠 *418/692–0669* 🌐 *www.hotel71.ca* *34 rooms, 6 suites* *In-room: safe, Wi-Fi. In-hotel: public Wi-Fi, restaurant, bar, gym, concierge, laundry service, parking (fee), no-smoking rooms* 💳 *AE, MC, V* 🍽 *CP.*

$$$ **Hôtel Le Priori.** A modern, four-star boutique hotel, Le Priori is nestled in the Lower Town. Suites have fabulous names such as Roméo and Juliette, Diva, and Rolf Benz, and are over 1,000 square feet. Some have kitchens and working fireplaces. Le Priori is a member of Epoque hotels. ✉ *15 rue Sault-au-Matelot, Lower Town, G1K 3YZ* ☎ *418/692–3992 or 800/351–3992* 📠 *418/692–0883* 🌐 *www.hotel-lepriori.com* *20 rooms, 6 suites* *In-room: refrigerator (some), Wi-Fi. In-hotel: public Wi-Fi, restaurant, laundry service, parking (fee), no-smoking rooms* 💳 *AE, D, DC, MC, V* 🍽 *BP.*

$$ **Hôtel Belley.** Works by local artists are everywhere in this modest little hotel above Belley Tavern, a stone's throw from the train station and the antiques district. Built as a private home around 1842, the hotel opened in 1987. Rooms are simple, with exposed brick walls and beamed ceilings. Bathrooms have showers but no tubs. Five apartments are also available in a separate building. ✉ *249 rue St-Paul, Lower Town, G1K 3W5* ☎ *418/692–1694 or 888/692–1694* 📠 *418/692–*

1696 www.oricom.ca/belley 8 rooms, 5 apartments In-room: refrigerator (some), Wi-Fi. In-hotel: public Wi-Fi, restaurant, laundry service, parking (fee), no elevator AE, D, MC, V EP.

$$ **Hôtel Le Saint-Paul.** Perched at the edge of the antiques district, this basic hotel in a 19th-century office building is near art galleries and the train station. Rooms have hunter-green carpeting and bedspreads with a Renaissance motif of characters in period dress. Some rooms have exposed brick walls. *229 rue St-Paul, Lower Town, G1K 3W3 418/694–4414 or 888/794–4414 418/694–0889 www.lesaintpaul.qc.ca 23 rooms, 3 suites In-room: refrigerator (some), dial-up, Wi-Fi. In-hotel: public Wi-Fi, restaurant, laundry service, no-smoking rooms AE, DC, MC, V BP.*

OUTSIDE THE WALLS

$$$$ Fodor's Choice ★ **Château Bonne Entente.** Now a member of Leading Hotels of the World, the Château Bonne Entente's classic rooms were redone in 2006 with white duvets, marble bathrooms, and refinished wood furniture. Urbania—a boutique hotel within the château—offers guests tall ceilings, leather headboards, plasma-screen TVs, and bathrooms right out of a design magazine. Guests can tee off at nearby La Tempête, and Amerispa runs the luxurious spa. The hotel is 20 minutes from downtown, with free shuttle service June through mid-September. *3400 chemin Ste-Foy, Ste-Foy, G1X 1S6 418/653–5221 or 800/463–4390 418/653–3098 www.chateaubonneentente.com 120 rooms, 45 suites In-room: safe, ethernet, Wi-Fi, refrigerator. In-hotel: public Wi-Fi, 2 restaurants, bar, pool, gym, spa, concierge, laundry service, airport shuttle (summer), parking (no fee), no-smoking rooms AE, DC, MC, V EP.*

$$$ Fodor's Choice ★ **L'Autre Jardin Auberge.** A nonprofit organization owns and operates this modern, pleasant inn in the St Roch district. It caters to academics, high-tech entrepreneurs, and others who visit the many new office and administrative buildings that surround it. The breakfast buffet, includes fair-trade coffee, a variety of breads, fresh croissants, and local cheeses. A fair-trade shop sells foods and other items from developing countries. *365 blvd. Charest Est, St-Roch, G1K 3H4 418/523–1790 or 877/747–0447 418/523–9735 www.autrejardin.com 24 rooms, 3 suites In-room: ethernet, Wi-Fi. In-hotel: public Wi-Fi, parking (fee), no-smoking rooms, no elevator AE, D, DC, MC, V BP.*

$$$ **Courtyard by Marriott Québec.** Stained-glass windows, two fireplaces, and a tiny lobby bar give this former office building a touch of elegance. Wood furniture fills the blue and beige rooms. The washing machine and dryer are a rarity in downtown Québec hotels. *850 pl. d'Youville, Carré d'Youville, G1R 3P6 418/694–4004 or 866/694–4004 418/694–4007 www.marriott-quebec.com 102 rooms, 9 suites In-room: dial-up. In-hotel: restaurant, room service, bar, laundry facilities, laundry service, public Wi-Fi, parking (fee), no-smoking rooms AE, DC, MC, V EP.*

$$$ **Hilton Québec.** Just opposite the Assemblèe Nationale and connected to the city's convention center by tunnel, the Hilton's lobby and lobby bar and restaurant are often busy. Rooms on the upper floors have fine views of Vieux-Québec. Rates for rooms on the executive floors include a Continental breakfast and an open bar from 5 PM to 10:30 PM. *1100 blvd. René-Lévesque Est, Montcalm, G1K 7K7 418/647–2411, 800/447–2411 in Canada 418/647–3737 www.hiltonquebec.com 529 rooms, 42 suites In-room: refrigerator, Wi-Fi. In-hotel: public Wi-Fi, restaurant, room service, bar, pool, gym, concierge, laundry service, parking (fee), no-smoking rooms, some pets allowed AE, D, DC, MC, V EP.*

$$$ **Hôtel Château Laurier.** Brown leather sofas and easy chairs and wrought-iron and wood chandeliers fill the spacious lobby of this former private house in the heart of the bustling Grande-Allèe district. All rooms have sleigh beds with bedspreads in green, beige, or blue. Deluxe rooms have fireplaces and double whirlpool baths. Some rooms look out on the Plains of Abraham. In 2007, 92 rooms were added—with urban plasma screens, white linen, and warm wood. *1220 pl. Georges V Ouest, Montcalm, G1R 5B8 418/522–8108 or 800/463–4453 418/524–8768 www.oldquebec.com/laurier 291 rooms, 3 suites In-room: dial-up, Wi-Fi, safe. In-hotel: public Wi-Fi, restaurant, room service, bar, pool, laundry service, parking (fee), no-smoking rooms AE, D, DC, MC, V EP.*

$$$ ★ **Hôtel Loews Le Concorde.** An excellent location on Grand Allée overlooking Battlefields Park has made Le Concorde a popular spot with guests ranging from the Rolling Stones to President George W. Bush. *1225 Cours du Général-de Montcalm, Montcalm, G1R 4W6 418/647–2222 or 800/463–5256 418/647–4710 www.loewshotels.com 388 rooms, 16 suites In-room: refrigerator, dial-up, Wi-Fi. In-hotel: public Wi-Fi, 2 restaurants, room service, bar, pool, gym, concierge, laundry service, parking (fee), some pets allowed AE, D, DC, MC, V EP.*

$$$ ★ **Hôtel Palace Royal.** A soaring indoor atrium with balconies overlooking a tropical garden, swimming pool, and hot tub lends a sense of drama to this luxury hotel. Its eclectic design makes use of everything from Asian styles to art deco. Rooms have views of either the Old City or the atrium. *775 av. Honoré-Mercier, Carré d'Youville, G1R 6A5 418/694–2000 or 800/567–5276 418/380–2553 www.jaro.qc.ca 67 rooms, 167 suites In-room: refrigerator, Wi-Fi. In-hotel: public Wi-Fi, restaurant, room service, bar, pool, gym, concierge, parking (fee) AE, D, DC, MC, V EP.*

NIGHTLIFE & THE ARTS

Québec City's cultural offerings include several good theater companies, a lively music scene, a variety of major festivals, and the oldest symphony orchestra in Canada. Tickets for most shows are sold at **Billetech** (*Bibliothèque Gabrielle-Roy, 350 rue St-Joseph Est, St-Roch 418/691–7400 Colisée Pepsi, Parc de l'Expocité, 250 blvd. Wilfrid-Hamel, Limoilou 418/691–7211 Grand Théâtre de*

Québec, 269 blvd. René-Lévesque Est, Montcalm ☎*418/643–8131 or 877/643–8131* ✉*Salle Albert-Rousseau, 2410 chemin Ste-Foy, Ste-Foy* ☎*418/659–6710* ✉*Théâtre Capitole, 972 rue St-Jean, Carré d'Youville* ☎*418/694–4444* 🌐*www.billetech.com*).

THE ARTS

Fodor's Choice ★ **Grande Théâtre de Québec.** This is Québec City's main theater, with two stages for concerts, plays, dance performances, and touring companies of all sorts. A three-wall mural by Québec sculptor Jordi Bonet depicts Death, Life, and Liberty. Bonet wrote "La Liberté" on one wall to bring attention to the Québécois struggle for freedom and cultural distinction. ✉*269 blvd. René-Lévesque Est, Montcalm* ☎*418/643–8131* 🌐*www.grandtheatre.qc.ca.*

DANCE

Grand Théâtre de Québec. Dancers appear at the Bibliothèque Gabrielle-Roy, Salle Albert-Rousseau, and Complexe Méduse. The Grand Théâtre presents a dance series with Canadian and international companies. ✉*269 blvd. René-Lévesque Est, Montcalm* ☎*418/643–8131* 🌐*www.grandtheatre.qc.ca.*

FILM

Cineplex Odeon Ste-Foy. This multiplex offers all the new releases, including English-language ones. ✉*1200 blvd. Duplessis, Ste-Foy* ☎*418/871–1550* 🌐*www.cineplex.com.*

IMAX theater. If the weather turns, this is a great place to bring the kids. It features educational fare on scientific, historical, and adventure topics. Translation headsets are available. ✉*Galeries de la Capitale, 5401 blvd. des Galeries, Lebourgneuf* ☎*418/624–4629.*

MUSIC

Bibliothèque Gabrielle-Roy. This branch of the Québec City library network hosts plenty of concerts in its **Joseph Lavergne Auditorium** and art exhibits in a space beside it. Tickets may be bought in advance, but are also sold at the door. ✉*350 rue St-Joseph Est, St-Roch* ☎*418/691–7400.*

Colisée Pepsi. Popular music concerts are often booked here. ✉*Parc de l'Expocité, 250 blvd. Wilfrid-Hamel, Limoilou* ☎*418/691–7211.*

Maison de la Chanson. This intimate theater is ideal for contemporary Francophone music during the year and plays in summer. ✉*Théâtre Petit Champlain, 68 rue du Petit-Champlain, Lower Town* ☎*418/692–4744.*

Fodor's Choice ★ **Orchestre Symphonique de Québec** *(Québec Symphony Orchestra).* Canada's oldest symphony orchestra, renowned for its musicians and conductor Yoav Talmi, performs at Louis-Frechette Hall in the Grand Théâtre de Québec. ✉*269 blvd. René-Lévesque Est, Montcalm* ☎*418/643–8131.*

THEATER

Most theater productions are in French. The theaters listed below schedule shows from September to April.

In summer, open-air concerts are presented at Place d'Youville (just outside St-Jean Gate) and on the Plains of Abraham.

Carrefour International de Théâtre de Québec. This international theatrical adventure takes over several spaces during the month of May: Salle Albert-Rousseau, Grand Théâtre de Québec, Théâtre Périscope (near avenue Cartier), and Complexe Méduse. There are usually at least one or two productions in English or with English subtitles. ☎*418/692–3131 or 888/529–1996* 🌐*www.carrefourtheatre.qc.ca.*

Complexe Méduse. This multidisciplinary arts center is the hub for local artists. Have coffee or a light meal at Café-Bistrot l'Abraham-Martin. ✉*541 St-Vallier Est, St-Roch* ☎*418/640–9218* 🌐*www.meduse.org.*

Grand Théâtre de Québec. Classic and contemporary plays are staged here by the leading local company, le Théâtre du Trident. ✉*269 blvd. René-Lévesque Est, Montcalm* ☎*418/643–8131.*

Salle Albert-Rousseau. A diverse repertoire, from classic to comedy, is staged here. ✉*2410 chemin Ste-Foy, Ste-Foy* ☎*418/659–6710.*

Théâtre Capitole. This restored cabaret-style theater schedules pop music and musical comedy shows. It has been home to Elvis Story and to Night Fever, a musical presentation, complete with dance floors, of music from the disco generation. ✉*972 rue St-Jean, Carré d'Youville* ☎*418/694–4444.*

NIGHTLIFE

Québec City nightlife centers on the clubs and cafés of rue St-Jean, avenue Cartier, and Grande Allée. In winter, evening activity grows livelier as the week nears its end, beginning on Wednesday. As warmer temperatures set in, the café-terrace crowd emerges, and bars are active seven days a week. Most bars and clubs stay open until 3 AM.

BARS & LOUNGES

Bar St-Laurent. One of the city's most romantic spots is in the Château Frontenac's bar, with its soft lights, a panoramic view of the St. Lawrence, and a fireplace. ✉*1 rue des Carrières, Upper Town* ☎*418/692–3861.*

Bar Les Voûtes Napoléon. The brick walls and wine cellar–like atmosphere help make Les Voûtes a popular place to listen to Québécois music and sample beer from local microbreweries. ✉*680 Grande Allée Est, Montcalm* ☎*418/640–9388.*

Le Boudoir. A hot spot for singles and younger couples, Le Boudoir features live bands on Wednesday, guest DJs on Friday, Latin rhythms on Saturday, and cabaret on Sunday. ✉*441 rue du Parvis, St-Roch* ☎*418/524–2777.*

Chez Maurice. Named for former premier Maurice Duplessis, Chez Maurice's racy, sexually charged atmosphere draws a young crowd. ✉*575 Grande Allée Est, 2nd fl., Montcalm* ☎*418/647–2000.*

★ **Le Pub Saint-Alexandre.** This popular English-style pub serves 40 kinds of single-malt scotch and 200 kinds of beer, 25 of which are on tap. ✉*1087 rue St-Jean, Upper Town* ☎*418/694–0015.*

Les Salons d'Edgar. Les Salons d'Edgar thirty-somethings with its eclectic music—everything from salsa beats and tango to jazz and techno.

CLOSE UP

Québec City Festivals

Festival d'Été International de Québec *(Québec City Summer Festival).* An exuberant, 11-day music festival with rock, folk, hip-hop, and more, the main concerts take place each evening on three outdoor stages. A button (C$30; C$20 if purchased in advance) admits you to all events. Don't worry if you don't know the performers; this is a chance to expand your musical horizons. At night, rue St-Jean near the city gate turns into a free street theater, with drummers, dancers, and skits. Book lodging several months in advance if you plan to attend this popular event. ☎ *418/523–4540 or 888/992–5200* 🌐 *www.infofestival.com.*

Festival OFF. This is a sidekick of the Festival d'Été. Most of the shows are free and take place in offbeat spaces—in front of Église St-Jean-Baptiste, Bar Le Sacrilèe, and the Musée de l'Amérique Française, just to name a few. Folk, alternative, experimental, and everything in between is what you'll find. The Festival OFF takes to the stage in July at the same time as its big brother. ☎ *418/692–1008* 🌐 *www.quebecoff.org.*

Fêtes de la Nouvelle France *(New France Festival).* The streets of the Lower Town are transported back in time during this five-day festival in early to mid-August. People dress in period costume are everywhere and events range from an old-time farmers' market to games, music, demonstrations, and spontaneous skits. ☎ *418/694–3311* 🌐 *www.nouvelle-france.qc.ca.*

Québec City International Festival of Military Bands. During the festival held in mid-August, the streets of Old Québec resound with military airs. Bands from several countries participate in the four-day festival, which includes a gala parade. Shows—most of them free—are held in Vieux-Québec or just outside the walls. ☎ *418/694–5757.*

It's closed in July and August. ✉ *263 rue St-Vallier Est, St-Roch* ☎ *418/523–7811.*

CLUBS

Beaugarte. Named for Humphrey Bogart, this restaurant-bar-discothèque is for dancing, being seen, drinking, and eating. Supper is served from 4 to 11 PM. There's free indoor parking. ✉ *2600 blvd. Laurier, Ste-Foy* ☎ *418/659–2442.*

Chez Dagobert. There's a little bit of everything—from rock bands to loud disco—here in this large, popular club. Local bands also perform downstairs some nights. ✉ *600 Grande Allée Est, Montcalm* ☎ *418/522–0393.*

Le Sonar. Electronic music and a trendy vibe have made Le Sonar one of the hottest dance clubs in town. ✉ *1147 av. Cartier, Montcalm* ☎ *418/640–7333.*

FOLK, JAZZ & BLUES

Bar Le Sacrilèe. Le Sacrilèe has folk music on Thursday and some Friday nights in room furnished with church pews and decorated with icons. ✉ *447 rue St-Jean, Montcalm* ☎ *418/649–1985.*

Chez Son Père. You can sing along to popular Québécois folk songs every night on the second floor of an old building in the Latin Quarter. ✉*24 rue St-Stanislas, Upper Town* ☎*418/692–5308.*

SPORTS & THE OUTDOORS

Scenic rivers and nearby mountains (no more than 30 minutes away by car) make Québec City a great place for the sporting life. For information about sports and fitness, contact **Québec City Tourist Information** (✉*835 av. Wilfrid-Laurier, Montcalm, G1R 2L3* ☎*418/641–6290* 🌐*www.quebecregion.com/eice*). The **Québec City Bureau of Recreation and Community Life** (✉*160, 76th rue E, 4e, St-Roch, G1K 6G7* ☎*418/641–6224* 🌐*www.ville.quebec.qc.ca*) has information about municipal facilities.

Tickets for events can be bought at **Colisée Pepsi** (✉*Parc de l'Expocité, 250 blvd. Wilfrid-Hamel, Limoilou* ☎*418/691–7211*). You can order tickets for many events through **Billetech** (🌐*www.billetech.com*).

BIKING

There are 64 km (40 mi) of fairly flat, well-maintained bike paths on Québec City's side of the St. Lawrence River and an equal amount on the south shore. Detailed route maps are available through tourism offices. The best and most scenic path is a 10-km (6-mi) route that follows the old railway in Lévis. Take the Québec–Lévis ferry to get there. It is now part of the Route Verte, a government-funded, province-wide system that boasts 4,000 km (2,500 mi) of bike paths and road routes.

Corridor des Cheminots. Ambitious cyclists appreciate the 22-km-long (14-mi-long) trail which runs from Limoilou near Vieux-Québec to the town of Shannon.
Côte de Beaupré. The scenic trail along the coast to Montmorency Falls begins northeast of the city at rue de la Verandrye and boulevard Montmorency or rue Abraham-Martin and Pont Samson.
Mont-Ste-Anne. Québec City's main ski resort has 150 km (93 mi) of mountain-bike trails and an extreme-mountain-biking park.

BOATING

Parc Nautique de Cap-Rouge. Located at the western tip of Québec City, on the St. Lawrence River, here you can rent canoes and pedal boats. ✉*4155 chemin de la plage Jacques-Cartier, Cap-Rouge* ☎*418/641–6148.*

DOGSLEDDING

Aventures Nord-Bec Stoneham. A half day spent here, just 30 minutes from the city, will initiate you in the art of making the huskies run. Overnight camping trips, snowmobiling, snowshoeing, and ice fishing are also available. ✉*4 ch. des Anémones, Stoneham* ☎*418/848–3732* 🌐*www.traineaux-chiens.com.*

FISHING

Most sporting-goods stores and all Wal-Mart and Canadian Tire stores sell the necessary permits. The fee for nonresidents is C$10.25 for one day, C$22.75 for three, $35 for seven, and $52 for the season. That covers all sport fish except Atlantic salmon.

Gesti-faune. For C$300 to C$500 a day, Gesti-faune's guides organize summer trout-fishing trips that include food and lodging in wilderness retreats within easy driving distance of Québec City. ☎*418/848–5424* 🌐*www.gestifaune.com.*

Réserve Faunique des Laurentides. A wildlife reserve with good lakes for fishing, it is approximately 48 km (30 mi) north of Québec City via Route 73. Reserve a boat 48 hours in advance by phone. ☎*418/528–6868, 800/665–6527 fishing reservations* 🌐*www.sepaq.com.*

HIKING & JOGGING

Bois-de-Coulonge Park. Along with Battlefields Park, Bois-de-Coulonge is one of the most popular places for jogging. ✉*1215 chemin St-Louis, Sillery* ☎*418/528–0773.*

Cartier-Brébeuf National Historic Site. North of the Old City, along the banks of the St. Charles River, you'll be able to keep going along about 13 km (8 mi) of hiking and biking trails. This historic site also has a small museum and a reconstruction of a Native Canadian longhouse. ✉*175 rue de l'Espinay, Limoilou* ☎*418/648–4038.*

ICE-SKATING

The ice-skating season is usually December through March.

Patinoire de la Terrasse. Try the terrace ice rink, adjacent to the Château Frontenac and open November–April, daily 11–11; it costs C$5 to skate with skate rental included, and C$2 to skate if you have your own. ☎*418/828–9898.*

Place d'Youville. This well-known outdoor rink just outside St-Jean Gate is open daily November through the end of March, from 8 AM to 10 PM. Skate rental is C$5, and skating itself is free. A locker will run you C$1. ☎*418/641–6256.*

RAFTING

Excursions et Mechoui Jacques Cartier. The Jacques Cartier River, about 48 km (30 mi) northwest of Québec City, has good rafting from May through October. Tours originate from Tewkesbury, a half-hour drive from Québec City. A half-day tour costs C$50 on weekdays. ✉*978 av. Jacques-Cartier Nord, Tewkesbury* ☎*418/848–7238.*

Village Vacances Valcartier. This center runs rafting excursions on the Jacques Cartier River from May through September. A three-hour excursion costs C$50, plus C$16 to rent a wet suit. Quieter family tours are also available. ✉*1860 blvd. Valcartier, St-Gabriel-de-Valcartier* ☎*418/844–2200.*

SKIING

Brochures offering general information about ski centers in Québec are available from the **Québec Tourism and Convention Bureau** (☎*877/266–5687* 🌐*www.bonjourquebec.com*). Thirty-seven cross-country ski centers in the Québec area have 2,000 km (1,240 mi) of groomed trails and heated shelters between them; for information, contact the **Regroupement des Stations de Ski de Fond** (☎*418/653–5875* 🌐*www.rssfrq.qc.ca*). The **Hiver Express** (☎*418/525–5191*) winter shuttle runs between major hotels in Vieux-Québec and ski centers. It leaves hotels in Vieux-Québec at 8 and 10 AM for the ski hills and returns at 2:30 and 4:30 PM. The cost is C$23; reserve and pay in advance at hotels.

CROSS-COUNTRY

Le Centre de Randonnée à Skis de Duchesnay. Located north of Québec City, this center has 150 km (93 mi) of marked trails. ✉*143 Rte. de Duchesnay, St-Catherine-de-Jacques-Cartier* ☎*418/875–2711.*

Mont-Ste-Anne. The training ground for Olympic-level athletes from across the continent, Mont-Ste-Anne has 359 km (223 mi) of trails. It's about 40 km (25 mi) northeast of the city. ✉*2000 blvd. du Beaupré, Beaupré* ☎*418/827–4561.*

Parc des Champs-de-Bataille *(Battlefields Park).* You can reach the park from Place Montcalm. It has more than 10 km (6 mi) of scenic, marked, cross-country skiing trails.

DOWNHILL

Mont-Ste-Anne. Just 40 minutes east of Québec City, Mont-Ste-Anne has a vertical drop of 2,050 feet, 56 downhill trails, a half-pipe for snowboarders, and 13 lifts. It also has the longest system of lighted night-ski runs in Canada. ✉*2000 blvd. du Beaupré, Beaupré* ☎*418/827–4561, 800/463–1568 lodging.*

Station Touristique Stoneham. Stoneham, just 20 minutes north of the city, has a vertical drop of 1,380 feet and is known for its long, easy slopes. ✉*1420 av. du Hibou, Stoneham* ☎*418/848–2411.*

SNOW SLIDES

Glissades de la Terrasse. A wooden toboggan takes you down a 700-foot snow slide that's adjacent to the Château Frontenac. The cost is C$2 per ride per adult and C$1.25 for children under six. ☎*418/829–9898.*

Village Vacances Valcartier. Use inner tubes or carpets on any of 42 snow slides here. Rafting and sliding cost C$23 per day, C$25 with skating. Trails open daily at 10 AM; closing times vary. ✉*1860 blvd. Valcartier, St-Gabriel-de-Valcartier* ☎*418/844–2200* 🌐*www.valcartier.com.*

SNOWMOBILING

Québec is the birthplace of the snowmobile, and with 32,000 km (19,840 mi) of trails, it's one of the best places in the world for the sport.

SM Sport. These folks will pick you up from several downtown hotels at prices starting at C$20 per person. Snowmobile rentals begin at C$45 per hour, or C$135 per day, plus tax, C$15 insurance, and the cost of gas. ✉*113 blvd. Valcartier, Loretteville* ☎*418/842–2703.*

WATER PARKS

Village Vacances Valcartier. This is the largest water park in Canada, with a wave pool, a 1-km (½-mi) tropical-river adventure called the Amazon, 35 waterslides, and a 100-foot accelerating slide on which bathers reach a speed of up to 80 kph (50 mph). Admission is C$26.33 a day for those at least 52 inches tall, C$20.18 for those under 52 inches. ✉*1860 blvd. Valcartier, St-Gabriel-de-Valcartier* ☎*418/844–2200.*

WINTER CARNIVAL

Fodor's Choice ★ **Carnaval de Québec.** The whirl of activities over three weekends in January and/or February includes night parades, a snow-sculpture competition, and a canoe race across the St. Lawrence River. You can participate in or watch just about every snow activity imaginable, from dogsledding to ice climbing. ✉ *290 rue Joly, Québec City* 🌐 *www.carnaval.qc.ca.*

SHOPPING

On the fashionable streets of Old Québec shopping has a European tinge. The boutiques and specialty shops clustered along narrow streets such as rue du Petit-Champlain, and rues de Buade and St-Jean in the Latin Quarter, are like trips back in time.

Stores are generally open Monday–Wednesday 9:30–5:30, Thursday and Friday until 9, Saturday until 5, and Sunday noon–5. In summer most shops have later evening hours.

DEPARTMENT STORES

Large department stores can be found in the malls of suburban Ste-Foy.

La Baie. Part of the historic Hudson's Bay Company conglomerate, La Baie carries clothing for the entire family, as well as household wares. ✉ *Place Laurier, Ste-Foy* ☎ *418/627–5959.*

Holt Renfrew. One of the country's more expensive stores, Holt Renfrew carries furs in winter, perfume, and tailored designer collections for men and women. ✉ *Place Ste-Foy, Ste-Foy* ☎ *418/656–6783.*

Simons. An old Québec City store, Simons used to be the city's only source for fine British woolens and tweeds. Now the store also carries designer clothing, linens, and other household items. ✉ *20 côte de la Fabrique, Upper Town* ☎ *418/692–3630* ✉ *Place Ste-Foy, Ste-Foy* ☎ *418/692–3630.*

10

SHOPPING MALLS

Galeries de la Capitale. An indoor amusement park with a roller coaster and an IMAX theater attracts families to this 250-store mall. It's about a 20-minute drive from Vieux-Québec. ✉ *5401 blvd. des Galeries, Lebourgneuf* ☎ *418/627–5800.*

Place de la Cité. There are more than 150 boutiques, services, and restaurants at this shopping center. ✉ *2600 blvd. Laurier, Ste-Foy* ☎ *418/657–6920.*

Les Promenades du Vieux-Québec. You'll find high-end items—clothing, perfume, and art—great for packaging as gifts or tucking away as souvenirs of this unique little shopping corner's boutiques. There's also a restaurant and a change bureau. ✉ *43 rue de Buade, Upper Town* ☎ *418/692–6000.*

Fodor's Choice ★ **Quartier Petit-Champlain.** A pedestrian mall in Lower Town, surrounded by rues Champlain and du Marché-Champlain, Quartier Petit-Champlain has some 50 boutiques, local businesses, and restaurants. This popular district is the best area for native Québec wood sculptures, weavings, ceramics, and jewelry. ☎*418/692–2613.*

SPECIALTY STORES

ANTIQUES

French-Canadian, Victorian, and art deco furniture, along with clocks, silverware, and porcelain, are some of the rare collectibles found here. Authentic Québec pine furniture, characterized by simple forms and lines, is rare—and costly.

Antiquités Marcel Bolduc. The largest antiques store on rue St-Paul features furniture, household items, old paintings, and knickknacks. ✉*74 rue St-Paul, Lower Town* ☎*418/694–9558* 🌐*www.marcelbolduc.com.*

Argus Livres Anciens. Antique books, most of them in French, draw bibliophiles to this store. ✉*160 rue St-Paul, Lower Town* ☎*418/694–2122.*

Gérard Bourguet Antiquaire. You're not likely to find any bargains here, but this shop has a very good selection of authentic 18th- and 19th-century Québec pine furniture. ✉*97 rue St-Paul, Lower Town* ☎*418/694–0896* 🌐*www.gerardbourguet.com.*

L'Héritage Antiquité. This is probably the best place in the antiques district to find good Québécois furniture, clocks, oil lamps, porcelain, and ceramics. ✉*109 rue St-Paul, Lower Town* ☎*418/692–1681.*

ART

Aux Multiples Collections. Inuit art and antique wood collectibles are sold here. ✉*69 rue Ste-Anne, Upper Town* ☎*418/692–1230.*

★ **Galerie Brousseau et Brousseau.** High-quality Inuit art is the specialty of this large, well-known gallery. ✉*35 rue St-Louis, Upper Town* ☎*418/694–1828* 🌐*www.sculpture.artinuit.ca.*

Galerie Madeleine Lacerte. Head to this gallery in an old car-repair garage for contemporary art and sculpture. ✉*1 côte Dinan, Lower Town* ☎*418/692–1566* 🌐*www.galerielacerte.com.*

CLOTHING

Bedo. A popular chain with trendy, well-priced items to round out your work wardrobe, Bedo also has great sales racks to sort through at the end of seasons. ✉*1161 rue St-Jean, Upper Town* ☎*418/692–0761.*

Le Blanc Mouton. Locally designed creations for women, including accessories and jewelry, fill this boutique in Quartier Petit-Champlain. ✉*51 Sous le Fort, Lower Town* ☎*418/692–2880.*

Boutique Flirt. The name of the game is pleasure at this brightly colored boutique where lingerie for men and women cohabit, and fun meets femme fatale. Flirt specializes in hard-to-find sizes. They carry Cristina, Iaia, Parah, Argento Vivo, Simone Perèle, Le Jaby, Prima Donna, and Empreinte. ✉*525 rue St-Joseph Est, St-Roch* ☎*418/529–5221.*

François Côté Collection. This chic boutique sells fashions for men. ✉*1200 Germain des Prés, Ste-Foy* ☎*418/657–1760.*

Jacob. A popular chain, this Montréal-based store sells tops and bottoms that are going-out and work appropriate. ✉*1160–1170 rue St-Jean, Upper Town* ☎*418/694–0580.*

Louis Laflamme. A large selection of stylish men's clothes is available here. ✉*1192 rue St-Jean, Upper Town* ☎*418/692–3774.*

La Maison Darlington. Head here for well-made woolens, dresses, and other items for men, women, and children by fine names in couture. ✉*7 rue de Buade, Upper Town* ☎*418/692–2268.*

CRAFTS

Les Trois Colombes. Handmade items, including clothing made from handwoven fabric, native and Inuit carvings, furs, and ceramics, are available. ✉*46 rue St-Louis, Upper Town* ☎*418/694–1114.*

FOOD

de Blanchet Pâtisserie, Épicerie Fine. Breads, meats, pastries, and a few shelves stocked with hard-to-find specialty items fill this spacious shop. ✉*435 St-Joseph Est, St-Roch* ☎*418/525–9779* 🖷*418/525–7337.*

La Boîte à Pain. Baker Patrick Nisot offers a selection of baguettes, multigrain breads (pumpernickel, rye), special flavors (olive, tomato and pesto, Sicilian), and dessert breads. Closed Monday. No credit cards are accepted. ✉*289 St-Joseph Est, St-Roch* ☎*418/647–3666.*

Camellia Sinensis Maison de Thé. This modest space stock 150 different teas from China, Japan, Africa, and beyond. Sign up for a tea-tasting session on Saturday at 11 AM. Open Tuesday–Sunday. ✉*624 St-Joseph Est, St-Roch* ☎*418/525–0247* 🌐*www.camellia-sinensis.com.*

Choco-Musée Érico. Chocolatier Éric Normand will craft whatever you like out of chocolate within a few days. ✉*634 rue St-Jean, St-Jean-Baptiste* ☎*418/524–2122.*

FUR

The fur trade has been an important industry here for centuries. Québec City is a good place to purchase high-quality furs at fairly reasonable prices.

Fourrures Richard Robitaille. An on-site workshop produces custom designs. ✉*329 rue St-Paul, Lower Town* ☎*418/692–9699.*

J. B. Laliberté. In business since 1867, Laliberté carries men's and women's furs and accessories. ✉*595 rue St-Joseph Est, St-Roch* ☎*418/525–4841.*

GIFTS

Collection Lazuli. This store carries unusual art objects and jewelry from around the world. ✉*Place de la Cité, 2600 blvd. Laurier, Ste-Foy* ☎*418/652–3732.*

★ **Point d'Exclamation!** Handcrafted bags, jewelry, hair accessories, paper, notebooks, cards, and paintings by 140 Québécois artisans fill Diane Bergeron's two rue St-Jean shops. ✉*387 rue St-Jean, St-Jean-Baptiste* ☎*418/523–9091* ✉*762 rue St-Jean, St-Jean-Baptiste* ☎*418/525–8053.*

10

JEWELRY

Joaillier Louis Perrier. Louis Perrier sells Québec-made gold and silver jewelry. ✉*48 rue du Petit-Champlain, Lower Town* ☎*418/692–4633.*

Zimmermann. Exclusive handmade jewelry can be found at this Upper Town shop. ✉*46 côte de la Fabrique, Upper Town* ☎*418/692–2672.*

QUÉBEC CITY ESSENTIALS

TRANSPORTATION

BY AIR

Canada's national airline, Air Canada, offers direct flights daily to Québec City from Toronto and Ottawa. Discount carriers Jazz (an Air Canada subsidiary) and Québecair have, respectively, 15 and 3 daily flights to Québec City from Montréal. Two U.S. carriers also offer direct flights to Québec City: Continental has four from Newark and one from Cleveland; Northwest has two from Detroit.

Jean Lesage International Airport is about 19 km (12 mi) northwest of downtown. Major renovations are underway, so be patient.

If you're driving from the airport into town, take Route 540 (Autoroute Duplessis) to Route 175 (boulevard Laurier), which becomes Grande Allée and leads right to Vieux-Québec. The ride takes about 30 minutes and may be slightly longer (45 minutes or so) during rush hours (7:30–8:30 AM into town and 4–5:30 PM leaving town).

Private limo service is expensive, starting at C$65 for the ride from the airport into Québec City. Taxis are available immediately outside the airport exit near the baggage-claim area. A ride into the city costs about C$30. Two local taxi firms are Taxi Coop de Québec, the largest company in the city, and Taxi Québec.

Information **Jean Lesage International Airport** (✉*500 rue Principale, Ste-Foy* ☎*418/640–2600* 🌐*www.aeroportdequebec.com*). **Taxi Coop de Québec** (✉*496 2e av., Limoilou* ☎*418/525–5191*). **Taxi Québec** (✉*975 8e av., Limoilou* ☎*418/522–2001*).

BY BOAT & FERRY

The Québec–Lévis ferry crosses the St. Lawrence River to the town of Lévis and gives you a magnificent panorama of Old Québec. Although the crossing takes 15 minutes, waiting time can increase the trip to an hour. The cost is C$2.65. The first ferry from Québec City leaves daily at 6:30 AM from the pier at rue Dalhousie, opposite Place Royale. Crossings run every half hour from 7:30 AM until 6:30 PM, then hourly until 2:30 AM. From April through November the ferry adds extra service every 10 to 20 minutes during rush hours (7–10 AM and 3–6:45 PM). Schedules can change, so be sure to check the ferry Web site or call ahead.

Boat & Ferry Information **Québec–Lévis ferry** (☎ *418/644–3704 Québec City, 418/837–2408 Lévis, 418/837–2408 bilingual service 8:30–4:30 daily* 🌐 *www.traversiers.gouv.qc.ca*).

BY BUS

Orléans Express provides daily service between Montréal and Québec City. The trip takes three hours.

Buses from Montréal to Québec City depart daily on the half hour from 5:30 AM to 10:30 PM. Buses run from 6:30 AM to 10 PM on Sunday. A one-way ticket costs about C$50.14, round-trip costs C$77.49. Tickets can be purchased only at terminals.

Within Québec City, the city's transit system, the Réseau de Transport de la Capitale, runs buses approximately every 10 minutes stopping at major points around town. The cost is C$2.50, and you must have exact change. For a discount on your fare, buy bus tickets at magazine shops and some grocery stores for C$2.30 (C$5.95 for a day pass, which can be used by two people on the weekend). The terminals are in Lower Town at Place Jacques-Cartier and outside St-Jean Gate at Place d'Youville in Upper Town. Timetables are available at some visitor information offices and at Place Jacques-Cartier.

Bus Line **Orléans Express** (☎ *418/525–3000*).

Terminals **Québec City Terminal** (✉ *320 rue Abraham-Martin, Lower Town* ☎ *418/525–3000*). **Ste-Foy Terminal** (✉ *3001 chemin Quatre Bourgeois, Ste-Foy* ☎ *418/650–0087*). **Voyageur Terminal** (✉ *505 blvd. de Maisonneuve Est, Downtown, Montréal* ☎ *514/842–2281*).

Information **Réseau de Transport de la Capitale** (☎ *418/627–2511* 🌐 *www.stcuq.qc.ca*).

BY CAR

Walking is the best way to see the city, and a car is necessary only if you plan to visit outlying areas.

Montréal and Québec City are linked by Autoroute 20 on the south shore of the St. Lawrence River and by Autoroute 40 on the north shore. On both highways, the ride between the two cities is about 240 km (149 mi) and takes about three hours. U.S. I–87 in New York, U.S. I–89 in Vermont, and U.S. I–91 in New Hampshire connect with Autoroute 20, as does Highway 401 from Toronto.

Driving northeast from Montréal on Autoroute 20, follow signs for Pont Pierre-Laporte (Pierre Laporte Bridge) as you approach Québec City. After you've crossed the bridge, turn right onto boulevard Laurier (Route 175), which becomes the Grande Allée.

Keep in mind that street signs are in French. It's useful to know the following terms: *droit* (right), *gauche* (left), *nord* (north), *sud* (south), *est* (east), and *ouest* (west).

The narrow streets of the Old City leave few two-hour metered parking spaces available. However, several parking garages at central locations charge about C$12 a day on weekdays or C$7 for 12 hours on weekends. Main garages are at Hôtel de Ville (City Hall), Place d'Youville, Edifice Marie-Guyart, Place Québec, Château Frontenac, rue St-Paul, and the Old Port.

BY TAXI

Taxis are stationed in front of major hotels and the Hôtel de Ville (City Hall), along rue des Jardins, and at Place d'Youville outside St-Jean Gate. You're charged an initial C$3.15, plus C$1.45 for each kilometer (½ mi). For radio-dispatched cars, try Taxi Coop de Québec or Taxi Québec.

Groupe Limousine A-1 has 24-hour limousine service.

Contacts Groupe Limousine A-1 (✉ *361 rue des Commissaires Est, St-Roch* ☎ *418/523-5059*). **Taxi Coop de Québec** (☎ *418/525-5191*). **Taxi Québec** (☎ *418/522-2001*).

BY TRAIN

VIA Rail, Canada's passenger rail service, has service between Montréal and Québec City. The train arrives at the 19th-century Gare du Palais in Lower Town. Trains from Montréal to Québec City and from Québec City to Montréal run four times daily on weekdays, three times daily on weekends. The trip takes less than three hours, with a stop in Ste-Foy. Tickets can be purchased in advance at VIA Rail offices, at the station prior to departure, through a travel agent, or online. The basic one-way fare, including taxes, is C$76.35.

First-class service costs C$142.44 each way and includes early boarding, seat selection, and a three-course meal with wine. One of the best deals, subject to availability, is the round-trip ticket bought 10 days in advance for C$112.81.

Train Information Gare du Palais (✉ *450 rue de la Gare du Palais, Lower Town* ☎ *No phone*). **VIA Rail** (☎ *888/842-7245 in the U.S and in Canada* 🌐 *www.viarail.ca*).

CONTACTS & RESOURCES

TOUR OPTIONS

Tours can include Montmorency Falls, whale-watching, and Ste-Anne-de-Beaupré in addition to sights in Québec City. Combination city and harbor-cruise tours are also available. Québec City tours operate year-round; excursions to outlying areas may operate only in summer.

BOAT TOURS Croisières AML has day and evening cruises, some of which include dinner, on the St. Lawrence River aboard the MV *Louis-Jolliet*. The 1½- to 3-hour cruises run from May through mid-October and start at C$33 plus tax.

Contact Croisières AML (✉ *Pier Chouinard, 10 rue Dalhousie, beside the Québec–Lévis ferry terminal, Lower Town* ☎ *418/692–1159 or 800/563–4643* 🌐 *www.croisieresaml.com*).

BUS TOURS Autocar Dupont-Gray Line bus tours of Québec City depart across the square from the Hôtel Château Laurier (1230 place Georges V); you can purchase tickets at most major hotels. The company also runs guided tours in a minibus as well as tours of Côte de Beaupré and Île d'Orléans, and for whale-watching. Tours run year-round and cost C$34–C$125. Call for a reservation and the company will pick you up at your hotel.

Contact Autocar Dupont-Gray Line (☎ *418/649–9226 or 888/558–7668*).

CALÈCHE TOURS You can hire a calèche, a horse-drawn carriage, at Place d'Armes near the Château Frontenac, at the St-Louis Gate, or on rue d'Auteuil between the St-Louis and Kent gates. Balades en Les Calèches de la Nouvelle-France, Les Calèches Royales du Vieux-Québec, and Les Calèches du Vieux-Québec are three calèche companies. If you call ahead, some companies can also pick you up at your hotel. Some drivers talk about Québec's history and others don't; if you want a storyteller, ask for one in advance. The cost is about C$80 including all taxes for a 40-minute tour of Vieux-Québec.

Contacts Les Calèches de La Nouvelle-France (☎ *418/692–0068*). **Les Calèches Royales du Vieux-Québec** (☎ *418/687–6653*). **Les Calèches du Vieux-Québec** (☎ *418/683–9222*).

WALKING TOURS Les Tours Voir Québec leads English-language walking tours of the Old City through the narrow streets that buses cannot enter. A two-hour tour costs C$19.50.

Ghost Tours of Québec gives ghoulish 90-minute evening tours of Québec City murders, executions, and ghost sightings. Costumed actors lead the C$17.50 tours, in English or French, from May through October. Ghost Tours now offers Witchcraft on Tour as well, which is a reenactment of a trial in English, held indoors.

Le Promenade des Écrivains (Writers' Walk) takes you through the Old City, where guide Marc Rochette, a local writer, stops to read passages about Québec City from the works of famous writers that include Melville, Thoreau, Camus, Ferron, and others. The two-hour tours cost C$15 and are given Wednesday and Saturday.

La Compagnie des Six-Associés gives several historical theme-driven walking tours year-round, starting at C$12. A tour-ending drink is included. The themes cover such timeless topics as "Killers and Beggars," "The Lily and the Lion," and "Lust and Drunkenness."

Contacts La Compagnie des Six-Associés (✉ *381 des Franciscains, Upper Town* ☎ *418/692–3033* 🌐 *www.sixassocies.com*). **Ghost Tours of Québec** (✉ *85 rue St-Louis, Upper Town* ☎ *418/692–9770* 🌐 *www.ghosttoursofquebec.com*). **Le Promenade des Écrivains** (✉ *1588 av. Bergemont, Upper Town* ☎ *418/264–2772*). **Les Tours Voir Québec** (✉ *12 rue St-Anne, Upper Town* ☎ *418/694–2001* 🌐 *www.toursvoirquebec.com*).

VISITOR INFORMATION

The Québec City Region Tourism and Convention Bureau's visitor information centers in Montcalm and Ste-Foy are open June 24–early September, daily 8:30–7:30; early September–mid-October, daily 8:30–6:30; and mid-October–June 23, Monday–Thursday and Saturday 9–5, Friday 9–6, and Sunday 10–4. A mobile information service operates between mid-June and September 7 (look for the mopeds marked with a big question mark).

The Québec government tourism department, Tourisme Québec, has a center open September 3–March, daily 9–6; and April–September 2, daily 8:30–7:30.

Tourist Information Québec City Tourist Information (✉ *835 av. Laurier, Montcalm, G1R 2L3* ☎ *418/641–6290* 🌐 *www.quebecregion.com*). **Ste-Foy information center** (✉ *3300 av. des Hôtels, Ste-Foy G1W 5A8* ☎ *418/651–2891*). **Tourisme Québec** (✉ *12 rue Ste-Anne, Place d'Armes, Upper Town* ☎ *877/266–5687* 🌐 *www.bonjourquebec.com*).

Side Trips in Québec Province

WORD OF MOUTH

"I just got back from a quick trip up to the Laurentians just north of Montréal. The ride is quite pretty with pine-filled hills and rocky contours . . . The houses located on the sides of mountains really were a sight to behold."

—Daniel_Williams

"In the Charlevoix region, the town of La Malbaie would be a good spot. The views of the St. Lawrence River are terrific, and there are several activities such as whale watching, visiting art galleries or playing golf. The food in the region is terrific."

—MF

www.fodors.com/forums

Updated by Paul Waters

QUÉBEC IS VAST ENOUGH TO INTIMIDATE even the most intrepid travelers. In fact, France would fit quite comfortably into its former North American possession three times with plenty of land left over. Much of the landscape, however, is wilderness—a tangle of lakes, bush, rivers, muskeg, and mountains that stretches from the St. Lawrence River to the northern tundra. Save for a few mining towns, a couple of huge hydroelectric projects, and a scattering of Native Canadian settlements, this enormous backcountry is virtually uninhabited.

More than half the province's 6 million people live in the major urban centers of Montréal and Québec City. Most of the rest live close to the shores of the St. Lawrence River, a waterway that is central to Québec's history and identity.

French explorer Jacques Cartier sailed up the St. Lawrence in 1534, looking for gold and a route to China. He found neither. His countryman, Samuel de Champlain, had no more luck in that regard when he arrived in what is now Québec in 1603. He did, however, found the first French settlements and opened what was to be the new colony's most lucrative industry, the fur trade. In 1663 Louis XIV proclaimed the colony New France.

But at the end of the Seven Years' War in 1763, France ceded virtually all its vast North American holdings to Britain. The "French fact" however survived, even prospered. The British made no changes to the seigneurial system of aristocratic landholders and tenant farmers, and it left the Catholic Church untouched. In fact, in 1774, with the American colonies on the brink of rebellion, the British Parliament assured the loyalty of its French-speaking subjects by passing the Québec Act, which basically guaranteed the colony would remain both French and Catholic.

In 1867 Québec—then known as Lower Canada—was one of the four original provinces to form the Dominion of Canada. However, tensions between French- and English-speaking Canada continued throughout the 20th century, and in 1974 the province proclaimed French its sole official language, in much the same way that the provinces of Manitoba and Alberta took steps earlier in the century to make English their sole official language.

The ability to speak French can make a visit to the province more pleasant—many locals, at least in rural areas, don't speak English. If you don't speak French, arm yourself with a phrase book or at least some knowledge of basic phrases.

EXPLORING QUÉBEC

Many of the most interesting parts of the province are within easy striking distance of Montréal or Québec City. Stressed-out Montrealers, for example, have two quite different playgrounds on their urban doorstep—the rugged pre-Cambrian landscapes of the Laurentians to the north and the more pastoral beauty of the Eastern Townships and the Appalachian Mountains to the southeast. For their part, weary Québec City residents can find solace and excitement by driving east to Charle-

TOP REASONS TO GO

FISHING

More than 20 outfitters (some of whom are also innkeepers) work in the northern Laurentians area, where provincial parks and game sanctuaries abound. Pike, walleye, and lake and speckled trout are plentiful. Open year-round in most cases, the lodging facilities range from luxurious, first-class resorts to log cabins.

SKIING

The Laurentians are well-known internationally as a downhill destination. The Eastern Townships have more than 1,000 km (620 mi) of cross-country trails; the area is also popular as a downhill ski center, with ski hills on four mountains that dwarf anything the Laurentians have to offer, with the exception of Mont-Tremblant. Charlevoix has three main ski areas, with excellent facilities for both downhill and cross-country skiers.

SUGAR SHACKS

In late March and early April the combination of sunny days and cold nights causes the sap to run in the maple trees. Cabanes à sucre (sugar shacks) go into operation, boiling the sap collected from the trees in buckets (at some places, complicated tubing and vats now do the job). The many commercial enterprises scattered over the area host "sugaring offs" and tours of the process, including tapping the maple trees, boiling the sap in vats, and tire sur la neige—pouring hot syrup over cold snow to give it a taffy consistency just right for "pulling" and eating.

voix, a region of charming villages, precipitous cliffs, and fast-flowing rivers that cling to the north shore of the St. Lawrence.

ABOUT THE RESTAURANTS & HOTELS

Nearly all Québecers take dining seriously, and even the smallest towns have at least one or two good restaurants. Traditional country cooking tends to be hearty, featuring such favorites as cassoulets, creamy pea soups, game pies, and rich dessert puddings. Maple syrup, much of it produced locally, is a mainstay of Québécois dishes. Cloves, nutmeg, cinnamon, and pepper—spices used by the first settlers—haven't gone out of style.

But it's certainly not all rustic dining. The haute cuisine of many inns and restaurants in the Laurentians, the Townships, Charlevoix, and the Gaspé can match anything you can find in Montréal (or New York, for that matter). Reservations are essential. Many restaurants are closed Monday, but Tuesday isn't too soon to book weekend tables at the best provincial restaurants.

Accommodations in the province range from resort hotels and elegant Relais & Châteaux properties to mom-and-pop motels. Many establishments operate on the Modified American Plan, which means that breakfast and dinner are included in the cost of a night's stay. Be sure to ask what's included. Off-season prices are often lower, but keep in mind that the Laurentians, the Townships, and, to a lesser extent, Charlevoix are popular all year round, thanks to skiing and snowmobiling in winter, hiking, swimming, golf and canoeing in summer, and leaf-peeping in fall.

	WHAT IT COSTS IN CANADIAN DOLLARS				
	¢	$	$$	$$$	$$$$
RESTAURANTS	Under C$8	C$8–C$12	C$13–C$20	C$21–C$30	over C$30
HOTELS	under C$75	C$75–C$125	C$126–C$175	C$176–C$250	over C$250

Restaurant prices are for a main course at dinner. Hotel prices are for two people in a standard double room in high season, excluding tax.

TIMING

The Laurentians are a big skiing destination in winter, but the other seasons all have their own charms: you can drive up from Montréal to enjoy the fall foliage; to hike, bike, or play golf; or to engage in spring skiing—and still get back to the city before dark. The only slow periods are early November, when there isn't much to do, and June, when the area has plenty to do but is also plagued by blackflies. Control programs have improved the situation somewhat.

The Eastern Townships are best in fall, when the foliage is at its peak; the region borders Vermont and has the same dramatic colors. It's possible to visit wineries at this time, but you should call ahead, since harvest is a busy time. Charlevoix is lovely in fall, but winter is particularly magical—although the steep and narrow roads can be challenging. In summer the silvery light, born of the mountains and the proximity to the sea, attracts many painters.

THE LAURENTIANS

The Laurentian Mountains (les Laurentides) that cover much of Québec north of the St. Lawrence River are among the oldest in the world. Formed 540 million years ago, they've been worn down by time and the glaciers of several ice ages. The peaks in the resort area north of Montréal seldom rise more than 300 metres (1,000 feet) above the Laurentian plateau, but what they lack in grandeur they make up in rugged charm.

The main resort area starts at St-Sauveur-des-Monts, 60 km (35 mi) north of the city on Autoroute 15 (Exit 60), and extends 70 km (42 mi) north to Mont-Tremblant. This region—a pleasant hodgepodge of villages, lakes, and mountains—became a popular recreational destination almost by accident. In 1909 the Canadian Pacific Railway, prodded by church and government leaders, completed a 200-km (124-mi) railway north from St-Jérôme to Mont-Laurier to encourage settlement in the largely empty territory. But as thin soil made commercial farming impractical, many families discovered they could make a better living catering to the hordes of city-dwellers who used "le P'tit train du Nord" to escape to the Laurentians' lakes in summer and its slopes in winter. As a result, the Laurentians boast some of North America's oldest ski resorts.

ST-SAUVEUR-DES-MONTS

25 km (16 mi) north of St-Jérôme, 63 km (39 mi) north of Montréal.

A sleepy Laurentian hamlet until the 1980s, St-Sauveur-des-Monts is now a bustling resort with one of the liveliest après-ski scenes anywhere in Québec. Dozens of bars, nightclubs, boutiques, and restaurants serving everything from sandwiches to steaks draw hundreds of visitors to the town all year long. On weekends, rue Principale is so choked with cars and shoppers that locals have taken to calling it the Rue Crescent of the North after Montréal's famous nightclub strip.

The ski hills around St-Sauveur aren't very big—the highest has a drop of no more than 700 feet—but there are hundreds of trails—most of them lighted at night—and dozens of high-speed lifts to keep the traffic moving. With the city only 45 minutes away, the resort is a favorite with day-trippers and overnighters alike. Blue signs on Route 117 and Autoroute 15 indicate where the ski hills are.

WHAT TO SEE

The historic railway line that opened the Laurentians to development is now the Parc Linéaire le P'tit Train du Nord, a hugely popular trail used by cyclists in summer and snowmobilers and cross-country skiers in winter. It runs 200 km (124 mi) from St-Jérôme to Mont Laurier, and has plenty of markers to help users track their distance. Many of the old railway stations and historic landmarks along the route have been converted into places where vélo-touristes (bike tourists) can stop for a snack.

Mont-St-Sauveur Water Park. Mont-St-Sauveur Water Park keeps children occupied with slides, a giant wave pool, a wading pool, and snack bars. The rafting river attracts an older, braver crowd; the nine-minute ride follows the natural contours of steep hills. On the tandem slides, plumes of water flow through figure-eight tubes. *350 rue St-Denis 450/227–4671 or 800/363–2426 www.mssi.ca Full day C$31, after 3* PM *C$26, after 5* PM *C$19 Early June–mid-June and late Aug.–early Sept., daily 10–5; mid-June–mid-Aug., daily 10–7.*

WHERE TO STAY & EAT

$$ **Le Bifthèque.** This is a branch of a popular local chain that specializes in perfectly aged steaks and roast beef, as well as such other hearty fare as lamb loin with Dijon mustard and trout stuffed with crab and shrimp. Pick up steaks to go at the meat counter if you're staying where you can grill your own. *86 rue de la Gare 450/227–2442 AE, MC, V No lunch Mon.–Thurs.*

$$$ **Relais St-Denis.** The dormer windows and steeply sloping roof are typical of traditional Québécois architecture, but it's the fireplace in every room that makes this cozy inn special. For more luxury, the junior suites all have whirlpool baths. Treille de Bacchus dining room emphasizes regional cuisine. *61 rue St-Denis, J0R 1R4 450/227–4766 or 888/997–4766 www.relaisstdenis.com 22 rooms, 22 suites In-room: refrigerator, dial-up. In-hotel: restaurant, bar, pool, no-smoking rooms, some pets allowed AE, D, MC, V CP, MAP.*

The Laurentians (les Laurentides)
Reservoir Taureau
Lac Anicet
Lac du Diable
Lac Forbes
Parc du Mont-Tremblant
TO MONT-LAURIER
St-Donat
Lac Archambault
Lac Ouareau
Lac Tremblant
Mont-Tremblant
Mont-Tremblant
St-Jovite
Lac des Iles
Estérel
Ste-Agathe-des-Monts
Val David
Ste-Marguerite-Estérel
Ste-Adolphe d'Howard
Ste-Adèle
St-Sauveur-des-Monts
Morin Heights
Ville des Laurentides
St-Jérôme
Brownsburg Chatham
Lachute
Mirabel
Ste-Scholastique
TRANS-CANADA HWY.
Ottowa River
MONTRÉAL
St-Joseph-du-Lac
Abbaye Cistercienne d'Oka
Oka Calvary
Oka
Lac des Deux-Montagnes
ONTARIO
QUÉBEC
Lac St-Louis
Lac St-François
0
20 miles
0
30 km
131
347
343
348
343
125
158
335
117
329
125
323
327
364
364
327
25
640
15
158
117
148
25
40
344
40
40
20
20
138
15

SPORTS & THE OUTDOORS

La Vallée de St-Sauveur. This is the collective name for the ski hills that surround St-Sauveur-des-Monts. The area is especially well known for its night skiing.

Mont-Avila. This mountain has 12 trails (2 rated for beginners, 3 at an intermediate level, and 7 for experts), three lifts, and a 615-foot vertical drop. ✉ *500 chemin Avila, Piedmont* ☎ *450/227–4671 or 514/871–0101* 🌐 *www.mssi.ca.*

Mont-St-Sauveur. Mont-St-Sauveur has 38 trails (17 for beginning and intermediate-level skiers, 16 for experts, and 5 that are extremely difficult), eight lifts, and a vertical drop of 700 feet. ✉ *350 rue St-Denis, St-Sauveur* ☎ *450/227–4671, 514/871–0101, or 800/363–2426* 🌐 *www.mssi.ca.*

SHOPPING

Fodor's Choice ★ **Factoreries St-Sauveur.** Canadian, American, and European manufacturers sell goods, from designer clothing to household items, at this emporium at reduced prices. The factory-outlet mall has more than 25 stores and sells labels such as Guess, Nike, Jones New York, and Reebok. ✉ *100 rue Guindon, Autoroute 15, Exit 60.*

Rue Principale. Fashion boutiques and gift shops, adorned with bright awnings and flowers line this popular shopping street.

STE-ADÈLE

12 km (7 mi) north of Morin Heights, 85 km (53 mi) north of Montréal.

With a permanent population of more than 10,000, Ste-Adèle is one of the largest communities in the Laurentians, with government offices, shopping malls, and cinemas. Of interest are the sports shops, boutiques, restaurants, family-oriented amusements, and, if you understand French, its summer theater.

WHAT TO SEE

Au Pays des Merveilles. Snow White, Little Red Riding Hood, and Alice in Wonderland wander the grounds, playing games with children. Small fry may also enjoy the petting zoo, amusement rides, wading pool, and puppet theater. The park's 49 activities are enough to keep the two-to-nine-year-old set amused for at least half a day. Check the Web site for discount coupons. The theme park is 100% accessible to wheelchairs. ✉ *3795 rue de la Savane* ☎ *450/229–3141* 🌐 *www.paysmerveilles.com* *C$15* ⏲ *Early June–mid-June, weekends 10–6; mid-June–late Aug., daily 10–6.*

WHERE TO STAY & EAT

$$$ ✕ **La Clef des Champs.** The French food served at this romantic restaurant includes such game dishes of roasted ostrich in a port, grilled venison, and caribou in red-currant marinade. Desserts include *gâteaux aux deux chocolats* (two-chocolate cake) and crème brûlée. Or you can sample a bit of everything with the C$75 *menu dégustation* (tasting menu). ✉ *875 chemin Pierre-Péladeau* ☎ *450/229–2857* ▭ *AE, DC, MC, V* ⏲ *Closed Mon. No lunch.*

$$$$ Fodor's Choice ★ **L'Eau à la Bouche.** Superb service, stunning rooms awash with color, a Nordic spa, and a terrace with a flower garden are highlights of this charming inn. Skiing is literally at your door, since the inn faces Le Chantecler's slopes. The restaurant here interprets nouvelle cuisine with regional ingredients. Owner-chef Anne Desjardins' menu changes with the seasons, but it has included foie gras with apple-cider sauce, breast of Barbary duck, and red-wine-marinated venison *3003 blvd. Ste-Adèle, J8B 2N6 450/229–2991 or 888/828–2991 www.leau-alabouche.com 21 rooms, 1 suite In-room: Wi-Fi. In-hotel: restaurant, bar, pool, no elevator, laundry service, no-smoking rooms AE, DC, MC, V EP.*

$$$ **Hôtel Mont-Gabriel.** This 1,200-acre resort began with a simple log structure built by Josephine Hartford Bryce, whose grandfather founded the A&P grocery chain. You can relax in a contemporary room with a valley view or commune with nature in a rustic-style cabin with a fireplace. In winter you can ski out from many rooms. The French cuisine is good, with entrées such as salmon with braised leeks, and pork with ginger and orange. *1699 chemin du Mont-Gabriel (Autoroute 15, Exit 64), J8B 1A5 450/229–3547, 800/668–5253, or 450/229–3547 450/229–7034 www.montgabriel.com 129 rooms, 1 suite, 2 chalets In-room: Wi-Fi. In-hotel: restaurant, room service, bar, golf course, tennis courts, pools, gym, spa, no-smoking rooms AE, DC, MC, V EP.*

$$ **Le Chantecler.** Nestled beside Lac Ste-Adèle, Le Chantecler's rooms and chalets, furnished with Canadian pine, have a rustic appeal. Activities ranging from snowshoeing to cycling races make Le Chantecler perfect for high-energy guests. *1474 chemin Chantecler, J0B 1A2 450/229–3555 or 888/916–1616 www.lechantecler.com 186 rooms, 29 suites, 7 chalets In-room: no a/c (some), kitchen (some), refrigerator, Wi-Fi. In-hotel: restaurant, room service, bar, golf course, tennis courts, pool, gym, spa, beachfront, bicycles, concierge, children's programs (ages 6 and older), laundry service, no-smoking rooms AE, D, DC, MC, V EP.*

SPORTS & THE OUTDOORS

GOLF **Club de Golf Chantecler.** This par-72, 18-hole (6,215 yards) course is off Exit 67 of Autoroute 15. Green fees range from C$30.72 on weekdays to C$39.49 on weekends. *2520 chemin du Club 450/476–1339 or 450/229–3742 www.golflechantecler.com.*

SKIING **Ski Mont-Gabriel.** About 19 km (12 mi) northeast of Ste-Adèle, Mont-Gabriel has 18 downhill trails, primarily for intermediate and advanced skiers, and seven lifts. The vertical drop is 656 feet. *31501 chemin du Mont-Gabriel, Ste-Adèle 450/227–1100 or 800/363–2426 www.skimontgabriel.com.*

VAL DAVID

18 km (11 mi) west of Estérel, 82 km (51 mi) north of Montréal.

Val David is a premier destination for mountain climbers, hikers, and campers. But it also has its gentler side. Many Québec artists and artisans have made their homes in the village, and the main street has several enticing little galleries and shops.

WHAT TO SEE

Village du Père Noël *(Santa Claus Village)*. At Santa Claus's summer residence kids can sit on his knee and speak to him in French or English. The grounds contain bumper boats, a petting zoo (with goats, sheep, horses, and colorful birds), games, and a large outdoor pool. There's a snack bar, but visitors are encouraged to bring their own food (there are numerous picnic tables). ✉*987 rue Morin* ☎*819/322–2146 or 800/287–6635* *www.noel.qc.ca* *C$10.50* *Early June–late Aug., daily 10–6; Dec. 22–Jan. 6, daily 11–5.*

WHERE TO STAY & EAT

$$–$$$ ★ **Hôtel La Sapinière.** This homey, wood-frame hotel overlooks a lake surrounded by fir trees (*sapins* in French). Rooms have country-style furnishings and pastel floral accents. Some have romantic four-poster beds and fireplaces. The property is renowned for its French nouvelle cuisine: salmon smoked on the premises comes with black-olive tapenade, and bison is cooked in a red-wine sauce with shiitake mushrooms. For dessert, try the mascarpone cheese mousse with berries and a spicy fruit terrine. ✉*1244 chemin de la Sapinière, J0T 2N0* ☎*819/322–2020 or 800/567–6635* *www.sapiniere.com* *44 rooms, 25 suites* *In-room: refrigerator (some), dial-up, Wi-Fi. In-hotel: restaurant, room service, bar, tennis courts, pool, gym, bicycles, no elevator, laundry service, no-smoking rooms, no elevator* *AE, DC, MC, V* *MAP.*

SPORTS & THE OUTDOORS

Mont-Alta. This ski resort has 22 downhill trails—about 40% of them for advanced skiers—and one lift. The vertical drop is 600 feet. ✉*2114 Rte. 117* ☎*819/322–3206* *www.mont-alta.com.*

SHOPPING

1001 Pots. This boutique showcases the Japanese-style pottery of Kinya Ishikawa, as well as pieces by some 110 other ceramists. The exhibition takes place from mid-July through mid-August. Ishikawa's studio also displays work by his wife, Marie-Andrée Benoît, who makes fish-shaped bowls with a texture derived from pressing canvas on the clay. ✉*L'Atelier du Potier, 2435 rue de l'Église* ☎*819/322–6868* *www.1001pots.com* *Daily 10–6 (summer); call for hrs in other seasons.*

Atelier Bernard Chaudron, Inc. Atelier Bernard Chaudron sells hand-forged, lead-free pewter objects d'art such as oil lamps, plus hammered-silver beer mugs, pitchers, and candleholders, as well as some crystal. ✉*2449 chemin de l'Île* ☎*819/322–3944 or 888/322–3944.*

La Verdure. Everything from wood walking sticks to duck decoys and gold, platinum, and silver jewelry is made by the owner, Paul Simard. ✉*1310 Dion* ☎*819/322–2919.*

MONT-TREMBLANT

Fodor'sChoice ★ *25 km (16 mi) north of Ste-Agathe-des-Monts, 135 km (85 mi) north of Montréal.*

At more than 3,000 feet, Mont-Tremblant is the highest peak in the Laurentians and the site of one of the best and most extensive ski resorts in eastern North America. It's also the name of a nearby village. The resort area at the foot of the mountain (called simply Tremblant) is spread around 14-km-long (9-mi-long) Lac Tremblant. The hub of the resort is a pedestrians-only village like Québec City as Walt Disney would have designed it. The buildings are constructed in the style of New France, with dormer windows and steep roofs, but they're thoroughly modern and house restaurants, pubs, boutiques, movie theaters, condominiums, and hotels.

WHAT TO SEE

Fodor'sChoice ★ **Parc National du Mont-Tremblant.** Created in 1894, the park was the home of the Algonquins, who called this area Manitonga Soutana, meaning "mountain of the spirits." Today it's a vast wildlife sanctuary of more than 400 lakes and rivers holding nearly 200 species of birds and animals, including moose, bear, and beaver. In winter its trails are used by cross-country skiers, snowshoers, and snowmobilers. Camping and canoeing are the main summer activities. Entrance to the park is C$3.50; the main entry point is through the town of St-Donat, about 45 minutes north of Mont-Tremblant, via routes 329 and 125. ☎*819/688–2281* 🌐*www.sepaq.com.*

WHERE TO STAY & EAT

$$$ ✕ **Restaurant Le Cheval de Jade.** The Jade Horse's elegant dining room has lace curtains, white linens, and ivory china. The food is the real thing—local ingredients and organic produce are used to create classic French fare such as rack of lamb, bouillabaisse, and shrimp flambéed with black pepper-sauce and green tea. ✉*688 rue de St-Jovite, Mont-Tremblant* ☎*819/425–5233* 🌐*www.chevaldejade.com* ✍*Reservations essential* ▭*AE, DC, V* ⏲*Closed Wed. No lunch.*

$$ ✕ **Auberge du Coq de Montagne.** Friendly hosts Nino and Kay serve such Italian favorites as veal marsala and veal fiorentina in a comfortable dining room five minutes from the slopes. ✉*2151 chemin du Village* ☎*819/425–3380 or 800/895–3380* ✍*Reservations essential* ▭*AE, MC, V.*

$$$$ ★ 🏨 **Fairmont Tremblant.** Wood paneling, stained glass, and stone fireplaces give the Tremblant resort's classy centerpiece the look of one of Canada's historic railroad castles. Guests on the Gold Floor receive complimentary breakfast, evening appetizers, and Internet access. Skiers can zoom off the mountain right into the ground-level deli, near the full-service spa. Elaborate theme buffets are the draw at the Windigo restaurant. ✉*3045 chemin de la Chapelle, Box 100, J8E 1E1* ☎*819/681–7000 or 800/441–1414* 🌐*www.fairmont.com/tremblant* 🛏*314 rooms, 61 suites* 👍*In-room: kitchen (some), dial-up, ethernet. In-hotel: restaurant, room service, bar, pools, gym, spa, concierge, laundry service, public Wi-Fi, no-smoking rooms* ▭*AE, DC, MC, V* 🍽*BP.*

$$$$ **Hotel Club Tremblant.** Built in the early 1900s, this building was a rooming house, brothel, and private club before it became a hotel. The original log-built is rustic but comfortable. Its outstanding French restaurant's Saturday-night buffet includes a wide selection of seafood. Rooms in the lodge and the newer condominium complex have fireplaces, private balconies, kitchenettes, and magnificent views of Mont-Tremblant. A complimentary shuttle takes you to the ski hills. *✉121 rue Cuttle, J8E 1B9 ☎819/425–2731 or 800/567–8341 ⊕www.clubtremblant.com 122 suites In-room: no a/c (some), kitchen, dial-up. In-hotel: restaurant, bar, tennis court, pool, gym, spa, beachfront, no elevator, concierge, children's programs (ages 4–16), no-smoking rooms, no elevator ▭AE, DC, MC, V MAP.*

THE GO-TO FOR SPA LOVERS

Relax at the **Spa Nature Le Scandinave Mont-Tremblant** (*✉4280 Montée Ryan, Mont-Tremblant ☎819/425–5524 or 888/537–2263 ⊕www.scandinave.com*) by spending a few hours in their Finnish sauna, Norwegian steam bath, or by taking a dip in one of their several outdoor pools. Swedish massage is available, the grounds are delightful, and admission fees are refreshingly reasonable.

$$$$ ★ **Quintessence.** This quiet hotel is on 3 acres along the shore of Lac Tremblant and near the ski slopes. Each suite has a king-size bed, a balcony or patio with lake views, a wood-burning fireplace, a stereo, and a bathroom with a heated marble floor and Jacuzzi. Service, including a ski shuttle and a concierge who can provide firewood, is an emphasis here. *✉3004 chemin de la Chapelle, J8E 1E1 ☎819/425–3400 or 866/425–3400 ⊕www.hotelquintessence.com 30 suites, 1 cabin In-room: safe, refrigerator, VCR, Wi-Fi. In-hotel: restaurant, room service, bar, pool, gym, spa, concierge, laundry service, no-smoking rooms, some pets allowed ▭AE, DC, MC, V CP.*

$$$ **Le Grand Lodge.** This Scandinavian-style log cabin hotel is on 13½ acres on Lac Ouimet. Accommodations, from studios to two-bedroom suites, are spacious, with kitchenettes, stone fireplaces, and balconies that overlook the water. The indoor-outdoor café, which serves light dishes, also looks out on the lake. The more-formal Chez Borivage, which has a good wine cellar, specializes in French cuisine. Although the resort attracts a sizable number of business travelers here for conferences, it caters to families as well, with day-care facilities, a game room for teens, and activities that include making summer bonfires on the beach and taffy on the winter snow. *✉2396 rue Labelle, J8E 1T8 ☎819/425–2734 or 800/567–6763 ⊕www.legrandlodge.com 11 rooms, 101 suites In-room: kitchen, dial-up, Wi-Fi. In-hotel: restaurant, bar, 4 tennis courts, pool, gym, spa, bicycles, concierge, laundry service, no-smoking rooms ▭AE, D, DC, MC, V EP.*

SPORTS & THE OUTDOORS

Mont-Tremblant. Its 2,131-foot vertical drop and 610 acres of skiable terrain makes Mont-Tremblant the largest ski resorts in Québec. And with 13 lifts (one of them a heated gondola), 94 downhill trails, and 110 km

(68 mi) of cross-country trails, it has something for skiers of all levels. ☎*800/461–8711 or 819/681–3000* 🌐*www.tremblant.ca.*

THE EASTERN TOWNSHIPS

It's no surprise that the Eastern Townships—Cantons de l'Est in French—more closely resemble New England than New France because of the brick and clapboard villages, covered bridges, and country inns. The first Europeans to settle in the valleys of the northern Appalachians were Empire Loyalists fleeing first the Revolutionary War and, later, the newly created United States of America to live under the British crown.

BROMONT

78 km (48 mi) east of Montréal.

Boating, camping, golf, horseback riding, swimming, tennis, biking, canoeing, fishing, hiking, cross-country and downhill skiing, and snowshoeing are available here—all within an hour's drive of Montréal

WHAT TO SEE

Bromont Aquatic Park. This water park has more than 23 rides and games, including the Corkscrew and the Elephant's Trunk (where kids shoot out of a model of an elephant's head). Slides are divided into four degrees of difficulty, from easy to extreme (recommended for adults and older children only). Admission includes a chairlift ride to the top of the ski hill. From September through late October it's open only for mountain biking. ✉*Autoroute 10, Exit 78* ☎*450/534–2200* 🌐*www.skibromont.com* *C$15* *June–late Aug., daily 10–5.*

WHERE TO STAY & EAT

$$$ **Hôtel Château Bromont.** Massages, "electropuncture," algae wraps, aromatherapy, and a Turkish-style steam room are just a few of the services at this European-style resort. Rooms are large and comfortable, with contemporary furniture. Greenery and patio furniture surround the swimming pool in the middle of the atrium. Restaurant Les Quatres Canards—with chef Jacques Poulin at the helm—serves regional cuisine, much of which features duck, an area specialty. The dining room has a panoramic view. For an additional fee, you may choose a meal plan that includes breakfast and dinner. ✉*90 rue Stanstead, J2L 1K6* ☎*450/534–3433 or 800/304–3433* 🌐*www.chateaubromont.com* *164 rooms, 8 suites* *In-hotel: 2 restaurants, bar, pools, spa, public Wi-Fi, no-smoking rooms* *AE, D, DC, MC, V* *EP.*

SPORTS & THE OUTDOORS

Station de Ski Bromont. With 46 trails for downhill skiing (20 of which are lighted for night skiing), Ski Bromont was the site of the 1986 World Cup Slalom. The vertical drop is 1,336 feet, and there are three lifts. Hiking and mountain biking are popular here in summer and early fall. ✉*150 rue Champlain* ☎*450/534–2200 or 866/276–6668* *450/534–4617* 🌐*www.skibromont.com.*

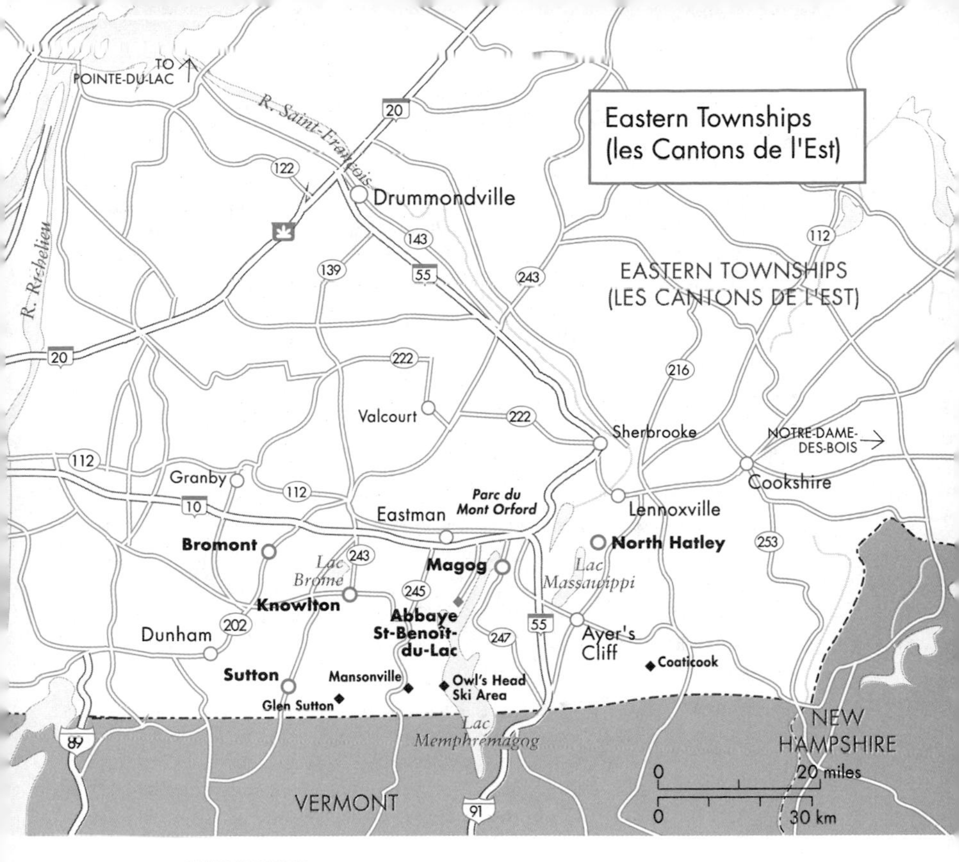

SHOPPING

FodorśChoice ★ **Bromont Five-Star Flea Market.** The gigantic sign on Autoroute 10 is hard to miss. More than 1,000 vendors sell their wares here—everything from T-shirts to household gadgets—each weekend from May to the end of October, 10 AM–6 PM. Shoppers come from Montréal as well as Vermont, just over the border.

SUTTON

106 km (66 mi) southeast of Montréal.

Sutton is a sporty community with crafts shops, welcoming eateries, and bars. Surrounded by mountains, the town is best explored on foot; a circuit of 12 heritage sites makes an interesting self-guided walk past the boutiques and the houses built by Loyalists. For a route map with a description of each building and its history, go to the tourist office in the City Hall building at 11B rue Principale.

WHERE TO STAY & EAT

$$ **Au Diable Vert.** On 200 acres overlooking the Missisquoi River, Au Diable Vert hosts a wide variety of outdoor activities, including hiking, guided moonlight kayak excursions along the Missisquoi, and horseback-riding lessons. It's also home to the hosts' Scottish High-

CLOSE UP

A Winery Driving Tour

Almost a dozen wineries along the Route des Vins (Wine Route) in and around the town of Dunham, about 20 km (12 mi) south of Bromont on Route 202, offer tastings and tours. Call for business hours, which can be erratic, especially in autumn, when harvesting is under way. **Vignoble Domaine Côtes d'Ardoise** (✉ *879 rue Bruce, Rte. 202, Dunham* ☎ *450/295–2020* 🌐 *www.cotesdardoise.com*) was one of the first wineries to set up shop in the area, back in 1980. **Vignoble de l'Orpailleur** (✉ *1086 Rte. 202, Dunham* ☎ *450/295–2763* 🌐 *www.orpailleur.ca*). Before walking through the vineyard here be sure to stop by the ecomuseum to learn about the production of wine. There's a gift shop, patio restaurant, and daily tastings. **Vignoble Les Trois Clochers** (✉ *341 chemin Bruce, Rte. 202, Dunham* ☎ *450/295–2034*). This lovely winery produces a dry, fruity white from Seyval grapes as well as several other white, ice, and red wines.

land cattle, which are raised free-range for meat. Dogs are allowed at Au Diable Vert and guests are encouraged to bring them. ✉ *169 chemin Staines, J0E 2K0* ☎ *450/538–5639* 🌐 *www.audiablevert.qc.ca* *4 rooms, 1 with bath; 1 suite, 2 cabins, 30 campsites* *In-hotel: no elevator* *AE, MC, V* *EP.*

SPORTS & THE OUTDOORS

GOLF **Les Rochers Bleus.** You'll need a reservation to golf at this 6,230-yard, par-72, 18-hole course. Its narrow fairways, surrounded by mountains, can be a challenge. Green fees are C$15–C$49 plus an additional C$26 to rent a cart. ✉ *550 Rte. 139* ☎ *450/538–2324 or 800/361–2468* 🌐 *www.lesrochersbleus.com.*

SKIING **Mont-Sutton.** Known for some of the best snowboarding hills in Québec, Mont-Sutton has 53 downhill trails, a vertical drop of 1,518 feet, and nine lifts. This ski area, one of the region's largest, attracts a die-hard crowd of skiers and snowboarders from Québec. Trails plunge and meander through pine, maple, and birch trees. ✉ *671 Maple St. (Rte. 139 Sud)* ☎ *450/538–2339, 450/538–2545, or 866/538–2545* 🌐 *www.montsutton.com.*

KNOWLTON (LAC BROME)

101 km (63 mi) southeast of Montréal.

Knowlton is a good stop for antiques, clothes, and gifts. The village is full of high-quality boutiques, art galleries, and interesting little restaurants that have taken residence in renovated clapboard buildings painted every shade of the rainbow. The town also has several factory outlets. The area's most famous product is the Brome Lake duck, bred and fattened on a farm just outside town and regarded by many chefs as the nec-plus-ultra of ducks. You can pick up a self-guided walking-tour map at the reception area of Auberge Knowlton.

WHERE TO STAY & EAT

$$ Fodor's Choice ★ **Auberge Knowlton.** The 12-room inn has been a local landmark since 1849, when it was a stagecoach stop. The inn attracts businesspeople, as well as vacationers and locals who like coming to the old, familiar hotel for special occasions. Bistro Le Relais serves local wines and cheeses and has a wide range of duck dishes, including warm duck salad served with gizzards and confit *de canard.* ✉*286 chemin Knowlton, Lac Brom, J0E 1V0* ☎*450/242–6886* *450/242–1055* *www.aubergeknowlton.ca* *12 rooms* *In-room: no a/c (some), dial-up, Wi-Fi. In-hotel: restaurant, no-smoking rooms, some pets allowed, no elevator* *AE, MC, V* *EP.*

NIGHTLIFE & THE ARTS

Fodor's Choice ★ **Arts Knowlton.** This local theater company stages plays, musicals, and productions of classic Broadway and West End hits. It hosts professional and amateur English-language productions but has also dabbled in bilingual productions and some new Canadian works. The 175-seat, air-conditioned theater is behind the Knowlton Pub. ✉*9 Mount Echo Rd.* ☎*450/242–2270 or 450/242–1395* *450/242–2320* *www.theatrelacbrome.ca.*

SPORTS & THE OUTDOORS

Golf Inverness. Not far from Knowlton is this 18-hole, par-71 course (6,326 yards) with an elegant clubhouse that dates back to 1915. Green fees are C$35–C$45 plus an additional C$30 to rent a cart. ✉*511 chemin Bondville, Rte. 215* ☎*450/242–1595 or 800/468–1595* *www.golf-inverness.com.*

SHOPPING

Agnes & Grace. Agnes & Grace is a unique clothing line designed by Jodi Mallinson, a former Elite model. With five boutiques in the United States, Jodi Mallinson chose only two Canadian locations to showcase her creations, which have been described as "elegant" and "timeless," one in Montréal and the other in the idyllic hamlet of Knowlton. ✉*3 chemin du Mt. Echo* ☎*450/243–1000* *www.agnesandgrace.com* *Daily 10–5:30.*

Fodor's Choice ★ **Station Knowlton.** Inside an old wrought-iron workshop, colorful Station Knowlton carries locally made gift items, including its own line of homemade soaps and bath salts. The comfortable café here attracts a mix of tourists and locals. ✉*7 chemin du Mont-Echo* ☎*450/242–5862* *www.stationknowlton.com* *Weekdays 11–6.*

Township Toy Trains. Big and small kids visit this delightful shop to check out its stock of trains and dollhouse miniatures. ✉*5 chemin du Mont-Echo* ☎*450/243–1881* *www.townshiptoytrains.com* *Thurs.–Sun. 10–5.*

MAGOG

118 km (74 mi) east of Montréal.

This bustling town is at the northern tip of Lac Memphrémagog, a large body of water that reaches into northern Vermont. Its sandy beaches are a draw, and it's also a good place for boating, bird-watching, sailboarding, horseback riding, dogsledding, in-line skating, golfing, and snowmobiling. You might even see Memphré, the lake's sea dragon, on one of the many lake cruises—there have been more than 100 sightings since 1816.

WHAT TO SEE

Le Cep d'Argent. The sparkling white wine is particularly good, and the dessert wine, which is similar to a port and flavored with a little maple syrup, goes well with the local cheese. The winery plays a leading role in the annual wine festival that's held in Magog (late August and early September). The guided visit and tasting of four different wines for C$7 is available only from May to December. ✉ *1257 chemin de la Rivière* ☎ *819/864–4441 or 877/864–4441* 📠 *819/864–7534* 🌐 *www.cepdargent.com* ⏲ *Daily 10–5.*

Abbaye St-Benoît-du-Lac. Some 60 Benedictine monks live, work, and pray in this magnificent but peaceful abbey on the shores of Lac Memphrèmagog. They make cheese and sparkling cider, which they sell in the monastery shop, and spend several hours a day in the starkly beautiful abbey church chanting the traditional hours of the Roman Catholic office. Dress modestly if you plan to attend Sunday mass or vespers. If you wish to experience a few days of retreat, reserve well in advance (a contribution of C$40 per night, which includes meals, is suggested). To get to the abbey from Magog, take Route 112 and follow the signs for the side road (Rural Route 2, or rue des Pères) to the abbey. ✉ *R.R. 2, St-Benoît-du-Lac* ☎ *819/843–4080* 🌐 *www.st-benoit-du-lac.com* ⏲ *Daily 10–5.*

OFF THE BEATEN PATH

Sucrerie des Normand. One of the oldest, most traditional maple-syrup operations in the Eastern Townships is in Eastman, about 15 km (9 mi) west of Magog. You can tour the farm's 250 acres of wooded land on a horse-drawn wagon and watch the whole production process—from the tapping of trees to the rendering down of the sweet liquid into syrup and sugar. After the tour, owners Richard and Marlene Normand serve traditional Québécois food in a wood cabin. ✉ *426 chemin Georges Bonnalie, Eastman* ☎ *450/297–2659 or 866/297–2659* 🌐 *www.hautboisnormand.ca* ⏲ *Dec.–Apr., daily 10–3.*

WHERE TO STAY & EAT

$$ **Spa Eastman.** The oldest spa in Québec sits on 350 acres of rolling, wooded land 15 km (9 mi) west of Magog. Some bedrooms have fireplaces, large balconies, and views of Mont-Orford. Vegetarian dishes, prepared with produce from the chef's garden, dominate menu. Fish, rabbit, and chicken courses accompanied by interesting herbs and sauces are also served from time to time. ✉ *895 chemin des Diligences, Eastman, J0E 1P0* ☎ *450/297–3009 or 800/665–5272* 🌐 *www.spa-eastman.com* *44 rooms* *In-room: no a/c (some), no TV. In-hotel: restaurant, pool, spa, no kids under 16* 💳 *AE, MC, V* *MAP.*

$ **Auberge l'Étoile Sur-le-Lac.** The rooms at this popular inn on Magog's waterfront are modern and have fresh furnishings; some have water views or whirlpools and fireplaces. Large windows overlooking mountain-ringed Lac Memphrémagog make the restaurant—which specializes in French cuisine—bright and airy. In summer you can eat outside. *⊠1200 rue Principale Ouest, Magog, J1X 2B8 ☎819/843–6521 or 800/567–2727 ⊕www.etoile-sur-le-lac.com ⇨51 rooms, 2 suites In-room: Wi-Fi (some), dial-up. In-hotel: restaurant, spa, bicycles, no elevator ▭AE, DC, MC, V ¶CP, MAP.*

NIGHTLIFE & THE ARTS

In recent years this formerly depressed textile town has enjoyed something of an economic and cultural rebirth, largely thanks to the tourism industry, but also partially due to the substantial number of artists who have chosen to relocate to this welcoming, and relatively inexpensive, region of the province.

NIGHTLIFE **Auberge Orford.** A patio bar overlooks the Magog River (you can moor your boat alongside it). Sometimes there's live entertainment, but when musicians aren't around to keep them at bay, flocks of ducks line up alongside the café to beg crumbs from patrons' plates—an entertaining sight in itself. *⊠20 rue Merry Sud ☎819/843–9361.*

Microbrasserie La Memphré. Named for the monster said to lurk in Lake Memphrémagog, La Memphré brews its own beer and serves fondue, sausages with sauerkraut, and paninis. *⊠12 rue Merry Sud ☎819/843–3405.*

SPORTS & THE OUTDOORS

GOLF **Golf Owl's Head.** Laid out with undulating fairways, bent-grass greens, and 64 sand bunkers, the 6,705-yard, 18-hole course (par 72), is surrounded by mountain scenery. The timber-and-fieldstone clubhouse is a favorite watering hole for locals and visitors alike. Green fees are C$35–C$55; cart rental costs C$30. *⊠181 chemin du Mont-Owl's Head, Mansonville ☎450/292–3666 or 800/363–3342 ⊕www.owlshead.com.*

Orford Le Golf. This venerable course—it was laid out in 1939—is an 18-hole, par-70, 6,287-yard course that winds around forested land. Green fees are C$15–C$36. *⊠3074 chemin du Parc ☎819/843–5688 ⊕www.mt-orford.com.*

SKIING **Owl's Head Ski Area.** Owl's Head is great for skiers seeking sparser crowds and great views. It has eight lifts, a 1,782-foot vertical drop, and 43 trails, including a 4-km (2½-mi) intermediate run. *⊠40 chemin de Mont-Owl's Head, Rte. 243 Sud; Autoroute 10, Exit 106 ☎450/292–3342 or 800/363–3342 ⊕www.owlshead.com.*

NORTH HATLEY

134 km (83 mi) east of Montréal.

After the American Civil War, North Hatley became a favorite with rich Southerners looking for a Yankee-free summer retreat. As a result many of the homes in this village on the shores of Lac Massawippi have a genteel antebellum air. The village also has a theater and some excellent inns and restaurants.

WHERE TO STAY & EAT

$$$ ★ **Manoir Hovey.** No, you're not hallucinating: this lakeside manor was, indeed, modeled on George Washington's Mount Vernon estate. Built in 1900 many of the manor's rooms have fireplaces and private balconies overlooking the lake. The restaurant serves such specialties as roasted loin of caribou and pan-seared bass with Scottish sauce and lardons. The posh afternoon tea features scones, clotted cream, jam, and more than 40 teas. ✉ *575 chemin Hovey, J0B 2C0* ☎ *819/842–2421 or 800/661–2421* 🌐 *www.manoirhovey.com* *40 rooms, 3 suites, 1 4-bedroom cottage* *In-room: Wi-Fi. In-hotel: restaurant, bars, tennis court, pool, beachfront, bicycles, public Internet, no-smoking rooms, no elevator* *AE, DC, MC, V* *MAP.*

$$$ **Ripplecove Inn.** The accommodations, service, and food at the Ripplecove in Ayer's Cliff at the southern end of Lac Massawippi are excellent. The rooms, some with lake views, are furnished with antiques. The chef assembles Eastern Townships menus that might consist of pheasant with wild-mushroom sauce, braised leg of rabbit, panfried local trout with a white-wine-and-watercress emulsion, and crème brûlée with a crust of local maple syrup for C$85 a person. There's also a spa with a variety of treatments. ✉ *700 rue Ripplecove, Ayer's Cliff, J0B 1C0* ☎ *819/838–4296 or 800/668–4296* 🌐 *www.ripplecove.com* *34 rooms, 5 suites, 3 cottages* *In-room: no TV (some), Wi-Fi. In-hotel: restaurant, pool, beachfront, water sports, public Internet, no-smoking rooms, no elevator* *AE, MC, V* *MAP.*

NIGHTLIFE & THE ARTS

Fodor's Choice ★ **Piggery.** A theater that was once a pig barn reigns supreme in the Townships' cultural life. The venue, which has an on-site restaurant, often presents new plays by Canadian writers and experiments with bilingual productions. The season runs July through mid-September. ✉ *215 chemin Simard, off Rte. 108* ☎ *819/842–2431* 🌐 *www.piggery.com.*

CHARLEVOIX

Bordered by the Laurentian Mountains to the north, the Saguenay River to the east, and the wide and tidal waters of the St. Lawrence River to the south, the Charlevoix region is famous for awe-inspiring vistas and kaleidoscopes of color that change throughout the day. French explorer Jacques Cartier is believed to have landed in the area in 1535. More certain is a visit 73 years later by Samuel de Champlain.

French settlers began arriving in the early 1700s. Among other things, they developed a small shipbuilding industry that specialized in sturdy schooners called *goélettes,* which were used to haul everything from logs to lobsters up and down the coast in the days before rail and paved roads. In the 19th century, as steamships plied the St. Lawrence, Charlevoix, named for New France's first historian, the Jesuit priest François-Xavier de Charlevoix (pronounced sharle-*vwah*), became a popular tourist destination for well-to-do English Canadians and British colonial administrators from Montréal and Québec City. Since then, tourism—and hospitality—has become Charlevoix's trademark.

The region has attracted and inspired generations of painters, poets, writers, and musicians from across Québec and Canada, and became a UNESCO World Biosphere Reserve in 1989. In summer hiking, fishing, picnicking, sightseeing, and whale-watching are the area's main attractions. Winter activities include downhill and cross-country skiing, ski-dooing (or snowmobiling), ice fishing, dogsledding, and snowshoeing.

BAIE-ST-PAUL

120 km (72 mi) northeast of Québec City.

Baie-St-Paul, one of the oldest towns in the province, is popular with craftspeople and artists. With its centuries-old mansard-roof houses, the village is on the banks of a winding river on a wide plain encircled by high hills. Boutiques and a handful of commercial galleries line the historic narrow streets in the town center; most have original artwork and crafts for sale.

WHAT TO SEE

Centre d'Art Baie-St-Paul. Adjacent to the city's main church, this center displays a diverse collection of works by more than 20 Charlevoix artists. In the tapestry atelier, weavers create traditional and contemporary pieces and demonstrate techniques. ✉ *4 rue Ambroise-Fafard* ☎ *418/435–3681* 🎫 *Free* ⏲ *Apr.–mid-June, Tues.–Sun. 10–5; late June–early Sept., Tues.–Sun. 10–6; early Sept.–mid-Nov., Tues.–Sun. 10–5; mid-Nov.–Mar., Fri.–Sun. 10–5.*

Centre d'Exposition de Baie-St-Paul. The mandate of the exhibition center is to promote modern and contemporary art created by Charlevoix artists from 1920 to 1970. The center is in a modern building that was awarded a provincial architectural prize in 1992. ✉ *23 rue Ambroise-Fafard* ☎ *418/435–3681* 🌐 *www.centredart-bsp.qc.ca.* 🎫 *C$4* ⏲ *June 24–early Sept., Tues. and Wed. 10–6, Thurs.–Sun. noon–8; Sept.–June, Tues.–Sun. 11–5*

Maison René Richard. Jean-Paul Lemieux, Clarence Gagnon, and many more of Québec's greatest landscape artists have depicted the area. Some of these works are for sale at this gallery, which also houses Gagnon's old studio. ✉ *58 rue St-Jean-Baptiste* ☎ *418/435–5571* ⏲ *Daily 10–6.*

WHERE TO STAY & EAT

$$$$ ★ **Auberge la Maison Otis.** Three buildings in the village center house the calm, romantic accommodations of this inn. Some guest rooms, decorated in traditional or country styles, have whirlpools, fireplaces, and antique furnishings. The restaurant, in an elegant, Norman-style house that dates to the mid-1850s, serves creative, regionally oriented French cuisine, such as *pintade,* a local fowl, lamb, or Angus beef. Dinner is a five-course, fixed-price affair, but you can also order à la carte. At the Café des Artistes you can find espresso coffee and Guinness on tap. Food includes European-style pizzas, pasta, and soup. It's a popular spot. ✉ *23 rue St-Jean-Baptiste, G3Z 1M2* ☎ *418/435–2255 or 800/267–2254* 🌐 *www.maisonotis.com* *29 rooms, 4 suites, 3 apartments* *In-room:*

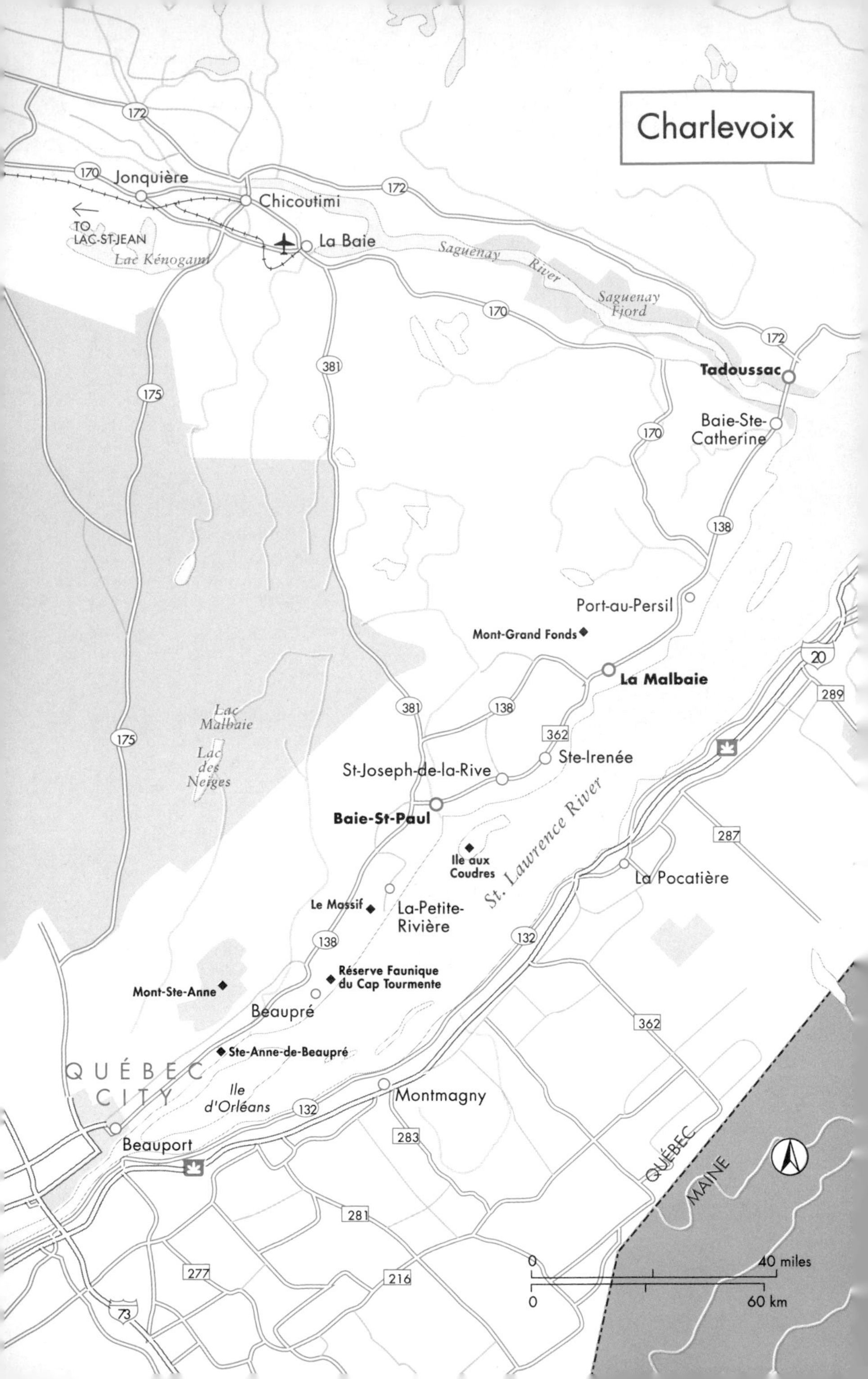
Charlevoix
Jonquière
Chicoutimi
TO LAC-ST-JEAN
La Baie
Lac Kénogami
Saguenay River
Saguenay Fjord
Tadoussac
Baie-Ste-Catherine
Port-au-Persil
Mont-Grand Fonds
La Malbaie
Lac Malbaie
Lac des Neiges
Ste-Irenée
St-Joseph-de-la-Rive
Baie-St-Paul
Ile aux Coudres
St. Lawrence River
La Pocatière
Le Massif
La-Petite-Rivière
Réserve Faunique du Cap Tourmente
Mont-Ste-Anne
Beaupré
Ste-Anne-de-Beaupré
QUÉBEC CITY
Ile d'Orléans
Montmagny
Beauport
QUÉBEC
MAINE
0
40 miles
0
60 km
172
170
175
381
138
362
20
289
287
132
283
281
277
216
73

no a/c (some), dial-up, Wi-Fi. In-hotel: restaurant, bar, pool, no elevator, public Wi-Fi, spa, some pets allowed ☰*MC, V* 🍽*MAP.*

SPORTS & THE OUTDOORS

Le Massif. This magnificent ski resort with soaring views over the St. Lawrence River and the coastal mountains has the longest vertical drop in eastern Canada—770 meters or 2,526 feet. Its 43 trails range from long, well-groomed steeps to rugged powder runs. The hill gets an average of 600 centimeters (20 feet) of snow a year. The resort is in the village of Petite-Rivière-St-François 20 km (12 mi) west of Baie-St-Paul. ☎*877/536–2774 or 418/632–5876* 🌐*www.lemassif.com.*

EN ROUTE

From Baie-St-Paul, instead of the faster Route 138 to La Malbaie, drivers can choose the open, scenic coastal drive on **Route 362.** This section of road has memorable views of rolling hills—green, white, or ablaze with fiery hues, depending on the season—meeting the broad expanse of the "sea," as the locals like to call the St. Lawrence estuary.

LA MALBAIE

35 km (22 mi) northeast of St-Joseph-de-la-Rive.

La Malbaie, one of the province's most elegant and historically interesting resort towns, was known as Murray Bay when wealthy Anglophones summered here. The area became popular with American and Canadian politicians in the late 1800s, when Ottawa Liberals and Washington Republicans partied decorously all summer with members of the Québec judiciary. William Howard Taft built the "summer White House," the first of three summer residences, in 1894, when he was the American civil governor of the Philippines. He became the 27th president of the United States in 1908.

Many Taft-era homes now serve as handsome inns, offering old-fashioned coddling with such extras as breakfast in bed, whirlpool baths, and free shuttles to the ski areas in winter. Many of the homes serve lunch and dinner to nonresidents, so you can tour the area going from one gourmet delight to the next. The cuisine, as elsewhere in Québec, is genuine French or regional fare.

WHAT TO SEE

Casino de Charlevoix. The casino is the smallest of Québec's three government-owned gaming halls, but it still draws more than 1 million visitors a year—some of whom stay at the Fairmont Le Manoir Richelieu, which is connected to the casino by a tunnel. There are 20 gaming tables and more than 800 slot machines. The minimum gambling age is 18. Photo ID is required to enter the casino. ✉*183 rue Richelieu, Pointe-au-Pic* ☎*418/665–5300 or 800/665–2274* 🌐*www.casino-de-charlevoix.com* 🕓*Mid-June–Aug., Sun.–Thurs. 10* AM*–2* AM*, Fri. and Sat. 10* AM*–3* AM*; Sept.–mid-June, Sun.–Thurs. 11* AM*–midnight, Fri. and Sat. 11* AM*–3* AM.

Musée de Charlevoix. A major permanent exhibit called Appartenances (Belonging), installed in 2003, uses folk art, paintings, and artifacts to recount the region's past, starting with the French, then the Scottish settlers, and the area's evolution into a vacation spot and artists' haven. ✉ *10 chemin du Havre, Pointe-au-Pic* ☎ *418/665–4411* *C$4* *Late June–early Sept., daily 10–6; early Sept.–late June, Tues.–Fri. 10–5, weekends 1–5.*

WHERE TO STAY & EAT

$$$$ ★ **Auberge la Pinsonnière.** Country luxury prevails at this Relais & Châteaux inn. All the rooms have fireplaces and whirlpools, most have king-size beds, and some have glass-walled balconies overlooking the bay. With a 25-foot window and balcony, you'll feel like you're sleeping on the river! The restaurant has one of the region's best kitchens and one of the largest wine cellars in North America, housing 12,000 bottles. The haute cuisine doesn't come cheap; appetizers like foie gras with pear confit, duck ravioli, and braised sweetbreads, cost as much as the entrées in other area establishments, but the dining experience is worth the money. ✉ *124 rue St-Raphaël, Cap-à-l'Aigle, G5A 1X9* ☎ *418/665–4431 or 800/387–4431* *www.lapinsonniere.com* *18 rooms* *In-room: safe, refrigerator, Wi-Fi. In-hotel: restaurant, bar, tennis court, pool, spa, beachfront, no elevator, no-smoking rooms* *AE, MC, V.*

$$$ ★ **Fairmont Le Manoir Richelieu.** Constructed in 1929, this castlelike building and its sweeping grounds underwent a C$100 million restoration in the late 1990s. The restaurants offer a wide range of food, from family fare to haute cuisine. At the clubby after-dinner lounge you can smoke a cigar and sip a single malt or vintage port. The full-service spa has 22 treatment rooms, and the links-style golf course overlooks the St. Lawrence. A tunnel connects the hotel with the Casino de Charlevoix. A sports facility—including two heated pools and a Jacuzzi outside, and a pool, hot tub, and steam bath indoors—is great for all ages. ✉ *181 rue Richelieu, Pointe-au-Pic, G5A 1X7* ☎ *418/665–3703 or 800/463–2613* *www.fairmont.com* *390 rooms, 15 suites* *In-room: safe, refrigerator, Wi-Fi. In-hotel: 3 restaurants, room service, bars, public Wi-Fi, golf course, tennis courts, pool, gym, spa, bicycles, concierge, children's programs (ages 4–12), laundry service, executive floor, no-smoking rooms, some pets allowed* *AE, DC, MC, V* *BP.*

THE ARTS

Domaine Forget (✉ *5 St-Antoine, Ste-Irenée* ☎ *418/452–3535 or 888/336–7438* *www.domaineforget.com*) is a music and dance academy that has a 604-seat hall in Ste-Irenée, 15 km (9 mi) south of La Malbaie. Fine musicians from around the world, many of whom teach or study at the school, perform during its International Festival. The festival, which runs from mid-June to late August, includes Sunday musical brunches with a variety of music, a buffet lunch, and a view of the St. Lawrence.

SPORTS & THE OUTDOORS

Club de Golf de Manoir Richelieu (✉ *595 côte Bellevue, Pointe-au-Pic* ☎ *418/665–2526 or 800/463–2613* *www.fairmont.com*) is a par-71, 6,225-yard, links-style course with 18 holes. Green fees start at C$135. The resort also has a 9-hole course.

TADOUSSAC

71 km (44 mi) north of La Malbaie.

Strictly speaking, the little town of Tadoussac, a short ferry ride across the Saguenay Fjord from Baie Ste-Catherine, is part of the Côte-Nord (North Shore), not Charlevoix. But don't let that deter you. It would be a shame to come this far without visiting this historic coastal community at the confluence of two of Canada's great rivers.

Tadoussac is probably one of Canada's oldest trading centers. Native Canadians from many nations had been meeting here to barter and parlay for centuries before Jacques Cartier arrived in 1535. The fur traders who followed in the French explorer's wake in 1600 simply took advantage of this long trading tradition and set up shop there themselves.

The glory days of the fur trade are long gone, but another natural resource draws thousands of visitors to Tadoussac every summer—whales. The meeting of the freshwater Saguenay and the saltwater St. Lawrence has created a marine environment rich in plankton, and every summer several species of whales—minkes, pilots, finbacks, and even the occasional blue—feed in the waters off Tadoussac. The Saguenay Fjord is home to a permanent, but sadly dwindling, population of white beluga whales. Whale-watching cruises are a thriving local industry.

WHAT TO SEE

Centre d'Interprétation des Mammifères Marins. You can learn more about the whales and their habitat at this interpretation center run by members of a locally based research team. They're only too glad to answer questions. In addition, explanatory videos and exhibits (including a collection of whale skeletons) tell you everything there is to know about the mighty cetaceans. ✉*108 rue de la Cale-Sèche* ☎*418/235–4701* 🌐*www.whales-online.net* *C$8* ⏱*Mid-May–mid-June and mid-Sept.–mid-Oct., daily noon–5; mid-June–mid-Sept., daily 9–8.*

Parc Marine du Saguenay–St-Laurent. The 800-square-km (309-square-mi) marine park, at the confluence of the Saguenay and St. Lawrence rivers, has been created to protect the latter's fragile ecosystem. ✉*Park office: 182 rue de l'Église* ☎*418/235–4703 or 800/463–6769.*

WHERE TO STAY

$$$ **Hôtel Tadoussac.** If the rambling white Victorian-style hotel with a red mansard roof looks familiar, it might be because it played the role of the Hotel New Hampshire in the 1984 movie with Jodie Foster and Rob Lowe. The spacious lobby of the 1942 has a stone fireplace and sofas for relaxing. Long corridors lead to country-furnished rooms, half of them overlooking the bay. ✉*165 rue Bord d'Eau, G0T 4A0* ☎*418/235–4421 or 800/561–0718* *418/235–4607* 🌐*www.hotel-tadoussac.com* *149 rooms* *In-room: no a/c. In-hotel: 3 restaurants, bar, tennis court, pool, spa, no-smoking rooms, public Wi-Fi* *AE, D, DC, MC, V* ⏱*Closed late Oct.–late May* *EP.*

SPORTS & THE OUTDOORS

The best months for seeing whales are August and September, although some operators extend the season at either end if whales are around. **Croisières AML** (☎*418/692–1159 or 800/463–1292* 🌐*www.croisieresaml.com*) offers two- to three-hour whale-watching tours for C$52–C$62. The tours, in Zodiacs or larger boats, depart from Baie-Ste-Catherine and Tadoussac. Fjord tours are also available.

WORD OF MOUTH

"Many varieties of whales can be seen in the St. Lawrence from May to the end of September, and the mouth of the Saguenay at Tadoussac is one of the best places to see them. There will be lots to see at the end of June. The drive from Québec City through the Charlevoix region is quite beautiful, and although you could do it in a day, it would be best to plan an overnight stay at Tadoussac."

—laverendrye

Croisières Dufour (☎*800/463–5250* 🌐*www.dufour.ca*) offers daylong cruises combined with whale-watching from Québec City as well as 2¼- and 3-hour whale-watching cruises (C$57) from Baie-Ste-Catherine and Tadoussac. Tours, some of which cruise up the Saguenay Fjord, use Zodiacs or larger boats.

THE GASPÉ PENINSULA

The Gaspé Peninsula (Gaspésie in French) juts into the Gulf of St. Lawrence like the prow of a ship. Its sheer cliffs tower above broad beaches, and tiny coastal fishing communities cling to the shoreline. Inland the Chic-Chocs rise, eastern Canada's highest mountains and the realm of bears, deer, moose, and caribou.

The Gaspé was on Jacques Cartier's itinerary—his first step in North America was here in 1534—but Vikings, Basques, and Portuguese fishermen had come before. Acadians, displaced by the British from New Brunswick in 1755, settled Bonaventure; Paspébiac still has a gunpowder shed that was built in the 1770s to help defend the peninsula from American ships; and Empire Loyalists settled New Carlisle in 1784. Townspeople in some areas speak mainly English.

Today the area still seems unspoiled and timeless, a blessing for anyone driving along the spectacular coastal highways or venturing on river-valley roads to the interior. A vast, mainly uninhabited forest covers the mountainous hinterland.

PERCÉ

767 km (477 mi) east of Québec City.

Percé Rock, an 88-meter-high (290 feet) slab of limestone a few hundred yards offshore from this coastal village, is one of the quintessential landmarks of Québec, as familiar to calendar-buyers as the Château Frontenac and the Montréal skyline. What sets it apart is the 15-meter-high (50 feet) hole that pieces—hence the name—its seaward end, creating one of the world's grandest natural arches. The little fishing village that takes its name from the rock is one of Québec's prettiest seaside resorts.

WHERE TO STAY & EAT

$$$ ✕ **Maison du Pécheur.** The wharf where the local boats land is a stone's throw away, so the fish is fresh, and the lobster comes from the restaurant's own tanks. For something really decadent, try the Trudent, lobster cooked in a Cointreau sauce, with scallops dipped in melted local goat cheese, and salmon coated with maple syrup. ✉ *155 Place du Quai* ☎ *418/782–5331* *Reservations essential* *AE, MC, V* *Oct.–May.*

$$ **Hôtel Le Mirage.** This hilltop hotel has the best views of Percé Rock and Bonaventure Island. All 68 rooms face the water and have private balconies. Breakfast is the only meal served in the dining room, which also has splendid water views. ✉ *288 Rte. 132 Ouest, G0C 2L0* ☎ *800/463–9011 or 418/782–5151* *www.hotelmirage.com* *67 rooms* *Restaurant, cable TV, tennis court, pool, babysitting, laundry facilities, no-smoking rooms, no a/c in some rooms* *AE, MC, V* *Closed Nov.–mid-May.*

$$ **Hôtel La Normandie.** All but eight rooms here face the ocean and have views of both Percé Rock and Bonaventure Island. Third-floor rooms are the most spacious. A boardwalk gives you access to the beach. The views also get top billing in the restaurant, which is romantic and serves fine French and regional fare. Shops and activities are within walking distance. ✉ *221 Rte. 132 Ouest, G0C 2L0* ☎ *800/463–0820 or 418/782–2112* *www.normandieperce.com* *45 rooms* *Restaurant, cable TV, in-room broadband, lounge, meeting rooms, some pets allowed; no a/c, no smoking rooms* *MC, V* *Closed Nov–mid-May.*

$$ **Hôtel Le Mirage.** This hilltop hotel has the best views of Percé Rock and Bonaventure Island. All 68 rooms face the water and have private balconies. Breakfast is the only meal served in the dining room, which also has splendid water views. ✉ *288 Rte. 132 Ouest, G0C 2L0* ☎ *800/463–9011 or 418/782–5151* *www.hotelmirage.com* *67 rooms* *Restaurant, cable TV, tennis court, pool, babysitting, laundry facilities, no-smoking rooms, no a/c in some rooms* *AE, MC, V* *Closed Nov.–mid-May.*

STE-ANNE-DES-MONTS

282 km (175 mi) northwest of Percé.

The name, which means St. Anne of the Mountains, is certainly appropriate. This little town of 7,000 people on the Gaspé's northern coast is the gateway to the peninsula's rugged interior. Just a few miles south are the Chic-Choc Mountains, a name that means "impassable" in the native Mi'kmaq language. This is the highest range in eastern Canada, and more than 25 of its peaks are higher than 1,000 meters (3,200 feet). Route 299, which runs south from Ste-Anne-des-Monts to New Richmond on the south coast, is probably the most spectacular mountain drive in Québec.

Gaspé Peninsula (Gaspésie)
TO GODBOUT
TO BAIE COMEAU
St. Lawrence River
Cap-Chat
Ste-Anne-des-Monts
Réserve Faunique des Chic-Choc
Gros Morne
Murdochville
Dartmouth R.
Rivière-au-Renard
Parc Nat. de Forillon
Gaspé
Baie de Gaspé
Parc Prov. de la Gaspésie
CHIC-CHOC MOUNTAINS
Matane
TO STE-FLAVIE
Réserve Faunique de Matane
Réserve Faunique de Baldwin
Lac Matapédia
Amqui
Causapscal
Bonaventure Island
Percé
Grande-Rivière
Chandler
Pabos Mills
PARC PORT DANIEL
Daniel R.
Bonaventure River
Gulf of St. Lawrence
Parc National de Miguasha
Carleton
Bonaventure
New Carlisle
Paspébiac
Miscou Island
Campbellton
Dalhousie
Matapédia
Baie des Chaleurs
NEW BRUNSWICK
0
40 miles
0
60 km
132
195
198
197
299
17
11

WHAT TO SEE

Parc de la Gaspésie. With more than 140 km (84 mi) of trails and two of the highest mountains in the east—Mont Albert and Mont Jacques-Cartier—makes this provincially run park a paradise for hikers, climbers, cross-country skiers, telemark skiers, anglers, and canoeists. The park's permanent residents include wolves, moose, and the southernmost herd of caribou in the world. Accommodation ranges from primitive campsites and Spartan cabins to the luxurious Gîte du Mont-Albert agency. ✉ *Rte. 299 Ouest* ☎ *866/727–2427 or 418/763–3301* 🌐 *www.sepaq.com*

WHERE TO STAY

$$–$$$ ★ **Gîte du Mont-Albert.** After a day of hiking, canoeing, or climbing in the wilderness of the Parc de la Gaspésie, you can retreat to this luxurious hotel at the foot of Mont Albert to pamper yourself with a gourmet dinner and a long, hot soak in a well-appointed modern room. Or if you prefer you can rent a two-bedroom cottage with a stone fireplace. ✉ *Parc de la Gaspésie, 2001 Rte. du Parc, G4V 2E4* ☎ *888/270–4483 or 418/762–2288* 🌐 *www.sepaq.com* *65* rooms *Restaurant, pool, sauna, bar, meeting rooms, guide service, no a/c in some rooms, no TV is some rooms* *AE, DC, MC, V* *Closed Nov.–mid-May.*

SIDE TRIPS IN QUÉBEC PROVINCE ESSENTIALS

TRANSPORTATION

BY AIR

Montréal is the gateway city to explore the Laurentians and the Eastern Townships—both beginning only a short drive from the Pierre Elliot Trudeau (P.E.T.) International airport.

There are no regional airports of note in either the Laurentians or Eastern Townships. Still, they are both easily accessible by car, with the foothills of the Laurentian Mountains less than a half-hour drive north of the airport along Highway 30, and the Townships region beginning an hour's drive southeast of the airport along Highway 20 and Highway 10.

There are several car-rental outlets operating out of P.E.T., so finding a vehicle to explore these areas shouldn't present much of a problem.

Québec City's Jean-Lesage Airport is the gateway to the Charlevoix region, which begins about an hour's drive west of the city on Highway 138.

Two regional airports serve the more remote Gaspé region—one at Mont-Joli at the western end of the peninsula, and the other in the town of Gaspé at the eastern end. Both are served by Air Canada's subsidiary, Jazz.

BY BIKE

Québec is in the process of developing the Route Verte, or the Green Route, a 3,600-km (2,230-mi) network of bike trails covering the southern half of the province, which will eventually link with trails in New England and New York. More than half of the marked trails are already open, and when the project is completed, it will comprise 4,300 km (more than 2,600 mi) of bikeways. For information and a map, contact Vélo Québec.

Contact **Vélo Québec** (*☎514/521–8356 or 800/567–8356 ⊕www.routeverte.com*)

BY BUS

A patchwork of independent companies service the outlying regions of Québec, among them Orléans Express, Limocar, and Intercar. Services, however, are fairly well integrated, and tickets and passes for all lines can be purchased at the central bus terminals in Montréal and Québec City.

In summer the Rout-Pass allows you unlimited travel on all provincial lines for 7, 14, or 28 days. The Rout-Pass is available at the Montréal and Québec City terminals.

Contacts **Gare du Palais** (*Québec bus terminal ✉320 rue Abraham-Martin, Québec City ☎418/525–3000*).

Station Centrale d'Autobus Montréal (*✉505 blvd. de Maisonneuve Est, Montréal ☎514/842–2281*)

BY CAR

Major entry points are Ottawa/Hull; U.S. 87 from New York State south of Montréal; U.S. 91 and U.S. 89 from Vermont into the Eastern Townships area; and the Trans-Canada Highway (Highway 40 to the west of Montréal, Highway 20 to the east).

Québec roads do not seem to bear the ravages of winter as well as those in neighboring New England. Even the major four-lane highways can be badly pitted by frost and wear. The province, however, excels at snow clearing, and driving in winter is relatively carefree.

The main route to the Laurentians is the Autoroute 15, aka the Laurentian Autoroute or the Autoroute des Laurentides. It stops at Ste-Agathe-des-Monts, but Highway 117 continues to Mont-Trembland and Mont-Laurier. The main route to the Eastern Townships is Autoroute 10, aka the eastern Townships Autoroute or the Autoroute des cantons de l'Est. It runs from Montréal to Sherbrooke, the largest city in the Townships. But if you're driving, get off the main highways (exits are called sorties) and explore the many beautiful side roads and back roads of both regions.

If you're entering Canada from New England, Interstate 91 takes you right into the heart of the Townships and links up with the eastern end of Autoroute 10.

Route 138, a two-lane highway, links Québec City to Charlevoix and points east. It's the only road link to such lower St. Lawrence centers as Baie-Comeau and Sept-Îles, and can be busy. When you get to Baie-St-Paul, turn off the main road and follow Route 362 along the coast to La Malbaie.

To get to the Gaspé from either Montréal or Québec City, follow Autoroute 20, a four-lane, limited access highway, to Rivière-du-Loup. From there, continue east on Route 132, which loops the entire peninsula.

BY TRAIN

Sadly, there is no train service to the Laurentians, the Eastern Townships, or Charlevoix. However, Via Rail, Canada's national passenger service, runs a full-service train with sleeping accommodations from Montreal to the Gaspé three times a week. The run along the Baie des Chaleurs through Percé to the town of Gaspé is a favorite with train buffs.

Contacts Via Rail (☎ *888/842–7245 toll-free in Canada* 🌐 *www.viarail.ca).*

CONTACTS & RESOURCES

EMERGENCIES

Hospitals Centre Hospitalier de Charlevoix (✉ *74 blvd. Ambroise Fafard, Baie-St-Paul.***Centre Hospitalier de Gaspé Centre** (✉ *215 boul York Ouest, Gaspé* ☎ *418/368–3301).* **Hospitalier Universitaire de Sherbrooke (CHUS)** (*CUSE* ✉ *580 rue Bowen Sud, Sherbrooke* ☎ *819/346–1110).* **CSSS des Sommets** (✉ *234 rue St-Vincent, Ste-Agathe-des-Monts* ☎ *819/324–4000).*

TOURS

The Zoological Society of Montréal is a nature-oriented group that runs lectures, field trips, and weekend excursions. Tours include whale-watching in the St. Lawrence estuary and hiking and bird-watching in national parks throughout Québec, Canada, and the northern United States.

Contact Zoological Society of Montréal (☎ *514/845–8317* 🌐 *www.zoological-societymtl.org).*

FISHING

The Fédération des Pourvoiries du Québec (Québec Outfitters Federation) has a list of outfitters (in French) that is available through tourist offices. Fishing requires a permit, available from the regional offices of the Ministère de l'Environnement et de la Faune (Ministry of the Environment and Wildlife), or at regional sporting-goods stores displaying an "authorized agent" sticker. The Gaspé region, in particular, is famous for fishing. Anglers can fish for a variety of species from wharves, fish for trout and salmon in rivers, or take deep-sea fishing excursions.

Contacts Déstinations Saumon Gaspésie (✉ *504 Rte. 299, Cascapédia-Saint-Jules G0C 1T0* ☎ *418/392–6768* 🌐 *www.gaspesalmon.com).* **Fédération des Pourvoiries du Québec** (✉ *237 blvd. Hamel, Bureau 270, Québec City G2E 2H2* ☎ *418/877–5191* 🌐 *www.fpq.com)***Ministère de l'Environment et de la Faune** (✉ *674 blvd. René-Lévesque Est, Québec City G1R 5V7* ☎ *800/561–1616 or 418/521–3830* 🌐 *www.fpq.com).*

MOUNTAIN CLIMBING

The Fédération Québécoise de la Montagne et de l'Escalade (Québec Mountain-Climbing Federation) has information about climbing, as do the province's tourist offices.

Contacts **Fédération Québécoise de la Montagne et de l'Escalade** (✉ *4545 av. Pierre-de-Coubertin, C.P. 1000, Succursale M, Montréal, H1V 3R2* ☎ *514/252-3004* 🌐 *www.fqme.qc.ca*).

RAFTING

Aventure en Eau Vive and New World River Expeditions—specializing in white-water rafting at Rivière Rouge—are on-site at a departure point near Calumet. All offer four- to five-hour rafting trips and provide transportation to and from the river site, as well as guides, helmets, life jackets, and, at the end of the trip, a much-anticipated meal. Most have facilities on-site or nearby for dining, drinking, camping, bathing, swimming, hiking, and horseback riding.

Contacts **Aventure Eau en Vie** (☎ *800/567-6881*).**New World River Expeditions** (☎ *800/361-5033 or 819/242-7238* 🌐 *www.newworld.ca*).

SKIING

Lift tickets range from C$20 to C$72. The Association des Stations de Ski du Québec's Web site has information on just about every downhill ski hill in the province with links to their Web sites. For information about cross-country ski conditions, call Tourisme Québec and ask for the ski report.

Contacts **Association des Stations de Ski du Québec** (☎ *514/493-1810* 🌐 *www.quebecskisurf.com*).**Tourisme Québec** (☎ *800/363-7777* 🌐 *www.bonjourquebec.com*).

SNOWMOBILING

Regional tourist offices have information about snowmobiling, snowmobile maps, and lists of services. Snowmobilers who use trails in Québec must obtain an access pass or day user's pass for the trails, which are regulated by the Québec Federation of Snowmobiling Clubs.

Contacts **Québec Federation of Snowmobiling Clubs** (☎ *514/252-3076* 🌐 *www.fcmq.qc.ca*).

VISITOR INFORMATION

In the Laurentians the major tourist office is the Association Touristique des Laurentides, just off Autoroute des Laurentides 15 Nord at Exit 39. Mont-Tremblant, Piedmont/St-Sauveur, Ste-Adèle, St-Adolphe-d'Howard, Ste-Agathe-des-Monts, St-Eustache, St-Jovite, and Val-David have regional tourist offices that are open year-round. Seasonal tourist offices (open mid-June–early September) are in Ferme Neuve, Grenville, Labelle, Lac-du-Cerf, Lachute, Nominique, Notre-Dame-du-Laus, Oka, St-Jérôme, Ste-Marguerite-Estérel, and St-Sauveur.

In the Eastern Townships, year-round provincial tourist offices are in Bromont, Coaticook, Granby, Lac-Mégantic, Magog-Orford, Sherbrooke, and Sutton. Seasonal tourist offices (open June–early September) are in Birchton, Danville, Dudswell, Dunham, Eastman, Frelighsburg, Lac-Brome (Foster), Lambton, Masonsville, Pike River, Ulverton, and Waterloo. The schedules of seasonal bureaus are irregular, so contact the Association Touristique des Cantons de l'Est before visiting. This association also provides lodging information.

In Charlevoix there are year-round information offices in Baie-St-Paul and La Malbaie, as well as a season office open from late June to early September in Isle-aux-Coudres and St-Siméon.

In the Gaspé region there are year-round tourism offices in four towns: Sainte-Flavie, Sainte-Anne-des-Monts, Murdochville, and Gaspé. There are two dozen seasonal offices. The best way to see the Gaspé is by taking Highway 132 along the north and eastern shores of the region, then either Highway 199 north at Bonaventure or Highway 132 at Matapédia and the New Brunswick border. The 199 is the most scenic route, traveling through the majestic Cascapédia River valley.

Tourist Information **Association Touristique des Cantons de l'Est** (✉ *20 rue Don Bosco Sud, Sherbrooke J1L 1W4* ☎ *819/820–2020 or 800/355–5755* 📠 *819/566–4445* 🌐 *www.cantonsdelest.com*). **Tourisme Charlevoix** (✉ *405 blvd. de Comporté, La Malbaie G5A 3G3* ☎ *800/667–2276 or 418/665–4454* 📠 *418/665–3811* 🌐 *www.tourismecharlevoix.com*). **Tourisme Gaspésie** (✉ *357 Rte. de la Mer, Ste-Flavie G0J 2L0* ☎ *800/463–0323 or 418/775–2223* 📠 *418/775–2234* 🌐 *www.tourisme-gaspesie.com*). **Association Touristique des Laurentides** ✉ *14142 rue de la Chapelle, Mirabel J7J 2C8* ☎ *450/224–7007, 450/436–8532, 800/561–6673, 514/990–5625 in Montréal* 📠 *450/436–5309* 🌐 *www.laurentides.com*).

Tourisme Québec ✉ *1001 rue du Square-Dorchester, No. 100, C.P. 979, Montréal H3C 2W3* ☎ *800/363–7777* 🌐 *www.bonjourquebec.com*).

New Brunswick

WORD OF MOUTH

"The Fundy Tides are an extraordinary site at both Fundy National Park (or the adjacent village of Alma) and Hopewell Rocks, but are most dramatic if you are in one place long enough to witness the contrast between high and low tide. Staying somewhere like Moncton overnight would allow you to daytrip both spots."

—mat106

www.fodors.com/forums

Updated by Sandra Phinney

THE GREAT CANADIAN FOREST MEETS the sea in New Brunswick, where it is sliced by sweeping river valleys and modern highways. Near Moncton, for instance, wild strawberries perfume the air of the grassy slopes of Fort Beauséjour. The dual heritage of New Brunswick (33% of its population is Acadian French) provides added spice. Come where cultures meet.

For every gesture as grand as the giant rock formations carved by the Bay of Fundy tides, there is one as subtle as the gifted touch of a sculptor in a studio.

New Brunswick's forest, which covers 85% of the province's entire area, drives the economy, defines the landscape, and delights hikers, anglers, campers, and bird-watchers. New Brunswick's soul is the sea. The warm waters of the Baie des Chaleurs, Gulf of St. Lawrence, and Northumberland Strait lure swimmers to sandy beaches, and the chilly Bay of Fundy, with its monumental tides, draws breaching whales, whale-watchers, and kayakers.

EXPLORING NEW BRUNSWICK

Rivers and ocean are the original highways of New Brunswick. A well-designed and marked system of provincial scenic drives takes you to most of the places you want to go. Highways, marked with various logos, take you from the Bay of Fundy, through forests, along gentle coastlines, and into the Appalachians.

ABOUT THE HOTELS & RESTAURANTS

Among its more interesting options, New Brunswick has a number of officially designated Heritage Inns. These historically significant establishments run the gamut from elegant to homey; many have antique china and furnishings. Cottage clusters are springing up in coastal communities, and Saint John, Moncton, and Fredericton each have a link in first-rate hotel chains. Accommodations are at a premium in summer, so reserve ahead. Air-conditioning is unnecessary at most coastal properties, especially along the Bay of Fundy. New Brunswick is also a smoke-free province, and smoking is not allowed in public places, including shopping malls, pubs, and bars. Although some larger properties still have smoking rooms and floors, most smaller ones are no-smoking.

Good things often come in small packages in this province. Watch for little restaurants, where the owner is apt to be the chef or waiter or even both. These places are closely tied to the community.

WHAT IT COSTS IN CANADIAN DOLLARS

	¢	$	$$	$$$	$$$$
RESTAURANTS	under C$8	C$8–C$12	C$13–C$20	C$21–C$30	over C$30
HOTELS	under C$75	C$75–C$125	C$126–C$175	C$176–C$250	over C$250

Restaurant prices are per person for a main course at dinner. Hotel prices are for two people in a standard double room in high season, excluding tax.

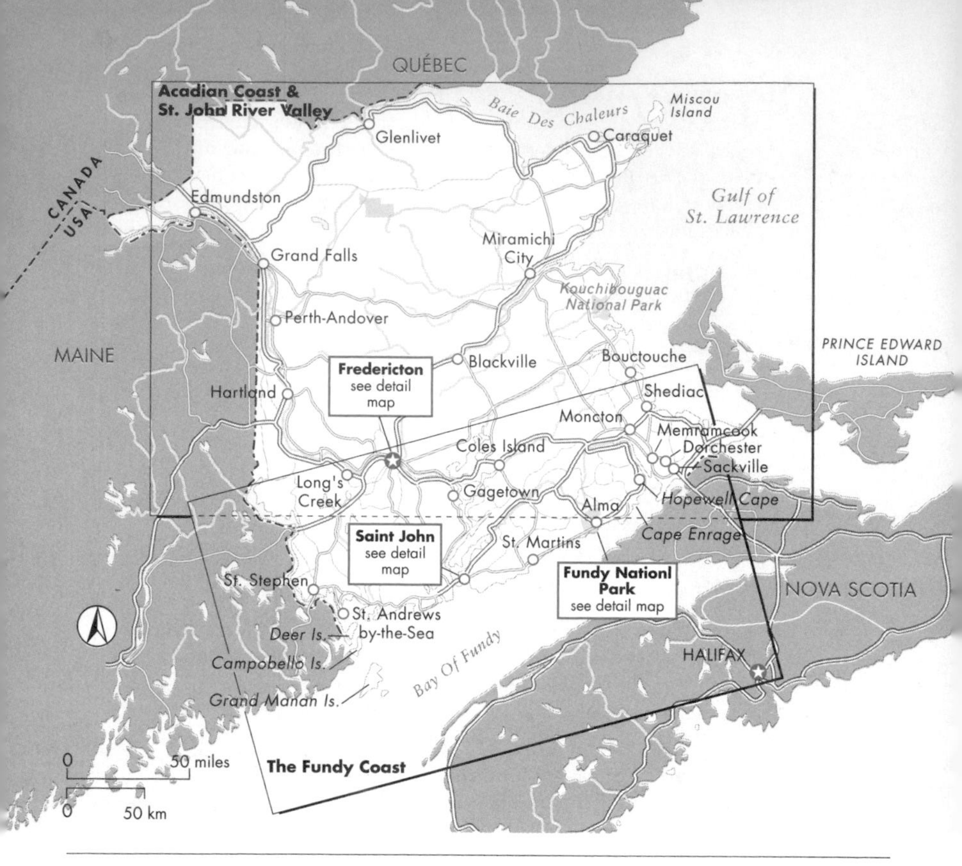

SAINT JOHN

Aboriginal people welcomed Samuel de Champlain and Sieur de Monts when they landed here on St. John the Baptist Day in 1604. Nearly two centuries later, in May 1783, 3,000 British Loyalists poured off a fleet of ships to make a home here. After the Napoleonic Wars in 1815, thousands ofIrish workers found their way to Saint John. However, the potato famine spawned the largest influx of Irish immigrants, and their descendants make Saint John Canada's most Irish city.

Industry and salt air have combined to give parts of this city a weather-beaten quality, but you also find lovingly restored 19th-century wooden and redbrick homes as well as modern office buildings, hotels, and shops.

DOWNTOWN SAINT JOHN

An urban-renewal program in the early 1980s spruced up the waterfront and converted old warehouses into trendy spots. An underground and overhead walkway known as the "Inside Connection" links guest rooms, attractions, and shops.

TOP REASONS TO GO

WHALE WATCHING
There are licensed tour operators in St. Andrews, Blacks Harbour, Grand Manan, and Campobello Island.

ACADIAN CULTURE
Must-see attractions include Le Pays de la Sagouine and Acadian Historical Village.

SALMON, SALMON, SALMON
Have it served to you at least two dozen ways, or cast your line and catch your own—you'll find professional outfitters in the Miramichi area.

TAKE A HIKE
The 13 provincial and national parks have amazing trails. Sit on a mountaintop and meditate. Watch birds from an ocean cliff.

GO FOR A SWIM
With 34 beaches you can choose from nippy to warm, fresh to salty, expansive spaces to intimate coves.

WHAT TO SEE

3 **Barbour's General Store.** This 19th-century shop, now a museum, is filled with the aromas of tobacco, peppermint, and dulse. ✉ *Market Slip* ☎ *506/658–2939* *Free* *Mid-June–mid-Sept., daily 9–6.*

1 **King Street.** The steepest, shortest main street in Canada, lined with solid Victorian redbrick buildings, is filled with a variety of shops.

8 **King's Square.** Laid out in a Union Jack pattern, this green refuge has a two-story bandstand and a number of monuments. ✉ *Between Charlotte and Sydney Sts.*

5 **Loyalist House.** This imposing Georgian structure, built in 1810, is distinguished by its authentic period furniture and eight fireplaces. ✉ *120 Union St.* ☎ *506/652–3590* *$3* *June, weekdays 10–5; July and Aug., daily 10–5; Sept.–May, by appointment.*

9 **Loyalist Burial Ground.** This Loyalist cemetery, now a landscaped park, is like a history book published in stone. ✉ *Sydney St., between King and E. Union Sts.* *Free* *Daily 24 hrs.*

2 **Market Slip.** The waterfront area at the foot of King Street is the site of Market Square, the Hilton Saint John Hotel, and restaurants. A floating wharf accommodates boating visitors to the city and those waiting for the tides to be right to sail up the St. John River.

4 ★ **New Brunswick Museum.** Delilah, a suspended, full-size young right-whale skeleton, is on display at this fine museum. Exhibits trace the province's industrial, social, and artistic history, and outstanding artwork hangs in the galleries. The Family Discovery Gallery has fun and educational games. ✉ *Market Sq.* ☎ *506/643–2300* *http://website.nbm-mnb.ca/english/00aa.html* *$6* *Weekdays 9–5, Thurs. 9–9, Sat. 10–5, Sun. noon–5; Closed Mon. mid-Nov.–mid-May.*

10 **Old Courthouse.** This 1829 neoclassical building has a three-story spiral staircase built of tons of unsupported stones. ✉ *King St. E and Sydney St.* *Free* *Weekdays 9–5.*

GREAT ITINERARIES

IF YOU HAVE 4 DAYS

If here for a short time, concentrate on one region, such as the Fundy Coast. Art, history, nature, and seafood abound in the resort community of **St. Andrews by-the-Sea**. Just an hour's drive east is the city of **Saint John**. It's steeped in English and Irish traditions, rich in history and art. Spend a day and a night here, then take Route 1 past Sussex to Route 114 and **Fundy National Park**. Route 915 above the park hugs the coast. Watch for **Cape Enrage**, which is as dramatic as it sounds. There are lots of things to do around **Riverside-Albert** and **Hopewell Cape**. Finish the trip with **Moncton**, a microcosm of New Brunswick culture and less than an hour's drive from Riverside-Albert.

IF YOU HAVE 7 DAYS

Head north from **Moncton** and explore the area around **Shediac**, famous for its lobsters and Parlee Beach. **Bouctouche** is just beyond, with wonderful dunes. Another 50 km (31 mi) north is unspoiled **Kouchibouguac National Park**, which protects beaches, forests, and peat bogs. The coastal drive from Kouchibouguac Park to **Miramichi City**, about 75 km (47 mi), passes through several fishing villages. A stopover here positions you perfectly to begin your exploration of the Acadian Peninsula beginning in **Caraquet**, about 120 km (74 mi) from Miramichi City. The Acadian Historical Village is a careful re-creation of the traditional Acadian way of life. Add this to the four-day trip above.

IF YOU HAVE 10 DAYS

Follow the seven-day itinerary above. From **Caraquet** plan at least a half day to drive across the top of New Brunswick to the St. John River valley. Begin your explorations among the flowers and the music of the New Brunswick Botanical Gardens in St-Jacques, just outside **Edmundston**. The drive from here to Fredericton is about 275 km (171 mi) of panoramic pastoral and river scenery, including a dramatic gorge and waterfall at **Grand Falls** and the longest covered bridge in the world at Hartland. **Kings Landing Historical Settlement**, near Fredericton, provides a faithful depiction of life on the river in the 19th century. With its Gothic cathedral and Victorian architecture, **Fredericton** is a beautiful, historic, and cultural stopping place. The drive from Fredericton to Saint John on Route 102 is just over 100 km (62 mi); about halfway between the two is the village of **Gagetown**, a must-see for art and history buffs.

⓬ **Prince William Street.** This street is full of historic bank and business buildings that now hold shops, galleries, and restaurants.

❼ **Saint John City Market.** The 1876 inverted ship's-hull ceiling of Canada's oldest charter market occupies a city block. Its temptations include live and fresh-cooked lobsters, great cheeses, dulse, and tasty, inexpensive snacks, along with plenty of souvenir and crafts items. ✉ *47 Charlotte St.* ☎ *506/658–2820* ⏲ *Weekdays 7:30–6, Sat. 7:30–5.*

❻ **Stone Church.** The first stone church in the city was built for the garrison posted at nearby Fort Howe. ✉ *87 Carleton St.* ☎ *506/634–1474* 🎟 *By donation* ⏲ *July and Aug., Tues., Wed., and Fri. 8:30–3:30.*

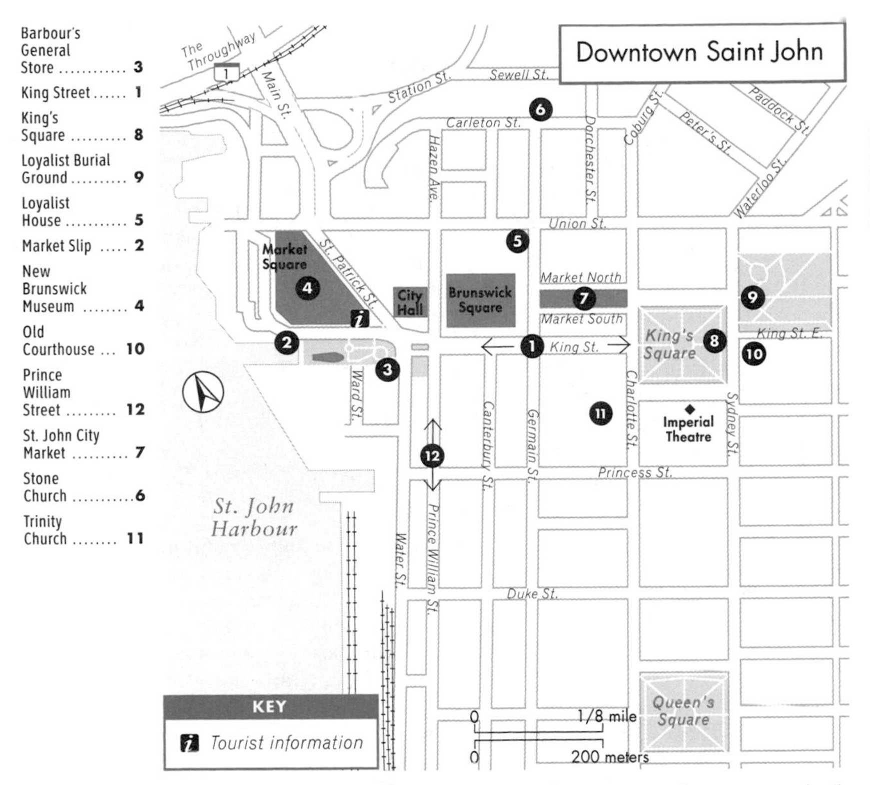

Trinity Church. The present church dates from 1880, when it was rebuilt after the Great Fire. Inside, over the west door, there's a coat of arms—a symbol of the monarchy—rescued from the council chamber in Boston by a British colonel during the American Revolution. It was deemed a worthy refugee and given a place of honor in the church. ✉ *115 Charlotte St.* ☎ *506/693–8558* 🎫 *Free* ⏲ *Hrs vary; call ahead.*

GREATER SAINT JOHN

The St. John River, its Reversing Falls, and St. John Harbour divide the city into eastern and western districts. The historic downtown area is on the east side. On the lower west side, painted-wood homes with flat roofs—characteristic of Atlantic Canadian seaports—slope to the harbor. Industrial activity is prominent on the west side, which has stately older homes on huge lots.

WHAT TO SEE

Carleton Martello Tower. The tower, a great place from which to survey the harbor and Partridge Island, was built during the War of 1812 as a precaution against an American attack. ✉ *Whipple St. at Fundy Dr.* ☎ *506/636–4011* 🎫 *$3.95* ⏲ *June–early Oct., daily 10–5:30.*

Cherry Brook Zoo. This is a small zoo with exotic beasts, pleasant woodland trails, a monkey house, and extinct-animal exhibits. *901 Foster Thurston Dr. 506/634–1440 $8 Daily, year-round 10 AM. Closing varies from 4:30 to 7 depending on the season.*

> **WORD OF MOUTH**
>
> "I went back to see the Reversing Falls at low tide. I agree that the falls are not that impressive, but it is kind of neat to go there twice and see the difference between high and low tides if the times are convenient and you are interested in that sort of thing."
>
> —just wandering

Irving Nature Park. A lovely 600-acre park on a peninsula close to downtown. Roads and eight walking trails make bird- and nature-watching easy. Many shorebirds breed here, and it's a staging site on the flight path of shorebirds migrating to and from the Arctic and South America. *Sand Cove Rd., from downtown take Rte. 1 west to Exit 119A (Catherwood Rd.) south; follow Sand Cove Rd. 4½ km (3 mi) 506/632–7777 Free May–mid-Nov., daily dawn–dusk; vehicles permitted 8–8.*

★ **Reversing Falls.** The strong Fundy tides rise higher than the water level of the river, so twice daily, at the Reversing Falls rapids, the tide water pushes the river water back upstream. When the tide ebbs, the river once again pours over the rock ledges and the rapids appear to reverse themselves. There are two restaurants here. A pulp mill on the bank is not so scenic, but multimillion dollar upgrades have eliminated any unpleasant odors. *Rte. 100, Reversing Falls Bridge 506/658–2937 Free Daily dawn–dusk; jet-boat tours June–mid-Oct., daily 10 AM–dusk.*

Rockwood Park. Encompassing 2,200 acres, this is one of the largest in-city parks in Canada. Among other things, there are hiking trails, lakes, sandy beaches, horseback riding, and a unique play park geared for everyone. *Main entrance off Crown St. 506/658–2883 Free Daily 8 AM–dusk.*

WHERE TO STAY & EAT

$$–$$$$ **Billy's Seafood Company.** It's a restaurant, it's an oyster bar, it's a fish market. The fresh fish selection is impressive and everything is cooked to perfection. Huge pesto scallops are always a hit, as is the grilled halibut with blueberry balsamic vinegar. This is where "cedar planked salmon" originated. *Saint John City Market, Charlotte St. entrance 506/672–3474 or 888/933–3474 AE, DC, MC, V.*

$$$ ★ **Beatty and the Beastro.** This quirky place hops at lunchtime and during pretheater dinners. The frequently changing menu, with its distinctive European accent, takes advantage of local and seasonal meat, seafood, and produce. Breads and soups are specialties. *60 Charlotte St., at King's Sq. 506/652–3888 AE, DC, MC, V Closed Sun.*

$$–$$$ **Lemongrass Thai Fare.** Phad Yum, a traditional red curry with seafood and lime leaves, is the house specialty, but you could make a meal of appetizers such as *satay gai* (chicken, beef, or pork), *hoy op* (mussels),

and *tod mun pla* (fish cakes). At this intimate restaurant, you call the shots when it comes to the spices, so your meal is as hot (or not) as you like. There's even a limited "un-Thai'ed" menu. ✉*42 Princess St.* ☎*506/657–8424* ▭*AE, MC, V* ⊗*No lunch weekends.*

$$ ✕ **Opera Bistro.** This hip place is also fun and unpretentious. The food features local ingredients with international flavor. The "Operetta-small plates" are popular, and include Atlantic crab cakes served with apple and caper salsa. A bonus: homemade Gelato ice cream. ✉*60 Prince William St.* ☎*506/642–2822* ▭*AE, MC, V.*

¢–$$ ✕ **Taco Pica.** This modest place is a slice of home for the former Guatemalan refugees, now proud Canadian citizens, who run it as a worker's co-op. The atmosphere is colorful, and the recipes are authentic: seasoned with garlic, mint, coriander seeds, and cilantro. A guitarist often entertains on Friday and Saturday evenings. ✉*96 Germain St.* ☎*506/633–8492* ▭*AE, DC, MC, V* ⊗*Closed Sun.*

$$–$$$ ✕ **Delta Brunswick Hotel.** This hotel has rooms that are large, modern, and comfortable. Shucker's Restaurant ($$–$$$) specializes in dishes made with local seafood, fiddleheads, and blueberries. ✉*39 King St., E2L 4W3* ☎*506/648–1981* 🖷*506/658–0914* 🌐*www.deltahotels.ca* *254 rooms* *In-room: Wi-Fi. In-hotel: restaurant, bar, pool, gym, laundry facilities, parking (fee), some pets allowed, no-smoking rooms* ▭*AE, D, DC, MC, V.*

$$–$$$ ✕ **Dufferin Inn & Suites.** An elegant, upscale, and renovated four-room inn that's more than 100 years old. Dinners are a special occasion in the San Martello Dining Room. For a vacation with a difference, check out the cooking classes with the inn's chef—they include lunch or dinner. ✉*357 Dufferin Row* ☎*506/642–2822* 🌐*www.dufferininn.com* *4 rooms* *In-room: Wi-Fi, no a/c. In-hotel: restaurant, bar, laundry service, parking (fee), no-smoking rooms* ▭*AE, MC, V* 🍽*BP.*

$–$$$ ★ ✕ **Shadow Lawn Inn.** In an affluent suburb with tree-lined streets, palatial homes, tennis, golf, and a yacht club, this inn fits right in. Some rooms have fireplaces. The chefs' creative ideas are reflected in the dining room's ($$–$$$$) Continental and seafood dishes. ✉*3180 Rothesay Rd., 12 km (7 mi) northeast of Saint John, Rothesay E2E 5V7* ☎*506/847–7539 or 800/561–4166* 🖷*506/849–9238* 🌐*www.shadowlawninn.com* *9 rooms, 2 suites* *In-room: Wi-Fi. In-hotel: restaurant, laundry service, parking (no fee), no-smoking rooms, some pets allowed no elevator* ▭*AE, DC, MC, V* 🍽*CP.*

$$–$$$ **Inn on the Cove & Spa.** With its back lawn terraced down to the ocean, this inn near Irving Nature Park has character. Bedrooms are furnished with local antiques, and several have balconies overlooking the ocean. A four-course dinner (reservations essential) is served in a dining room with a view of the Bay of Fundy. Guests and nonguests can, with reservations, get treatments at the spa. ✉*1371 Sand Cove Rd., E2M 4Z9* ☎*506/672–7799 or 877/257–8080* 🌐*www.innonthecove.com* *8 rooms, 1 apartment* *In-room: DVD, Wi-Fi. In-hotel: spa, parking (no fee), no-smoking rooms, some pets allowed, no elevator* ▭*AE, MC, V* 🍽*BP.*

$–$$ **Homeport Historic Bed & Breakfast Inn.** Graceful arches, fine antiques, Italian marble fireplaces, Oriental carpets, and a Maritime theme are at home in these 19th-century twin mansions. There are stunning harbor views. Each oversize room is elegant, unique, and equipped with modern amenities. Harbor breezes usually make air-conditioning unnecessary, but it is available if needed. Breakfasts are hearty. ✉*60–80 Douglas Ave., E2K 1E4* ☎*506/672–7255 or 888/678–7678* 🖷*506/672–7250* 🌐*www.homeport.nb.ca* *6 rooms, 4 suites* *In-room: refrigerator (some), VCR, Wi-Fi. In-hotel: parking (no fee), no-smoking rooms, some pets allowed, no elevator* *AE, MC, V* *BP.*

> **WORD OF MOUTH**
>
> "Personally, (and I live in Saint John), a trip to the City Market, and a walk through the Loyalist Burial Ground are a must (sounds morbid, but a very popular thing to do and a beautiful green space in the city)." —sar_gil

SPORTS & THE OUTDOORS

The **Reversing Falls Jet Boat** (✉*Fallsview Park off Fallsview Dr.* ☎*506/634–8987 or 888/634–8987* 🌐*www.jetboatrides.com* ⏲*June–mid-Oct.*) has 20-minute thrill rides in the heart of the Reversing Falls ($30). Be prepared for a wild ride and don't think for a second that the yellow slickers they supply will keep you dry—having a change of clothes in your car is an excellent idea. There is also the even more extreme option of bouncing down the river in a "bubble" contraption ($95). Age and size restrictions apply to the jet boat and bubble, and times depend on the tides. The company also offers more sedate sightseeing tours ($30) along the falls and up the river departing from Market Square June to mid-October, 10 AM to dusk.

SHOPPING

★ **Brunswick Square** (✉*King and Germain Sts.* ☎*506/658–1000*), a vertical mall, has many top-quality boutiques. **Peter Buckland Gallery** (✉*80 Prince William St.* ☎*506/693–9721*), open Tuesday through Saturday or by appointment, carries prints, photos, paintings, drawings, and sculpture by Canadian artists. **Tim Isaac Antiques** (✉*97 Prince William St.* ☎*506/652–3222*) has fine furniture, glass, china, and Oriental rugs. **Trinity Galleries** (✉*128 Germain St.* ☎*506/634–1611*) represents fine Maritime and Canadian artists.

THE FUNDY COAST

Bordering the chilly and powerful tidal Bay of Fundy is some of New Brunswick's most dramatic coastline. This area extends from the border town of St. Stephen and the lovely resort village of St. Andrews, through Saint John, and on to Fundy National Park. The Fundy Isles—Grand Manan Island, Deer Island, and Campobello—are havens of peace that have lured harried vacationers for generations.

The **Fundy Trail Parkway** (*www.fundytrailparkway.com*) is 11 km (7 mi) of coastal roadway with a 16-km (10-mi) network of walking, hiking, and biking trails that lead to an interpretive center and suspension bridge at Big Salmon River. On the other side of the bridge is the Fundy Footpath for serious hikers. *506/833–2019* *$3* *Mid-May–mid-Oct.*

ST. STEPHEN

107 km (66 mi) west of Saint John.

The chocolate bar was invented in St. Stephen, across the St. Croix River from Calais, Maine, and the small town is a mecca for chocoholics. An elegant factory-outlet chocolate-candy store dominates the main street and in early August "Choctails," chocolate puddings, cakes, and even complete chocolate meals, are served during the Chocolate Festival. The provincial **visitor information center** (*5 King St.* *506/466–7390*) has details.

ST. ANDREWS BY-THE-SEA

29 km (18 mi) southeast of St. Stephen.

St. Andrews by-the-Sea, a designated National Historic District on Passamaquoddy Bay, is one of North America's prettiest resort towns. It has long been a summer retreat of the affluent (mansions ring the town). Of the town's 550 buildings, 280 were erected before 1880, and 14 of those have survived from the 1700s. Some Loyalists even brought their homes with them piece by piece from Castine, Maine, across the bay, when the American Revolution didn't go their way. For a self-guided tour, pick up a walking-tour map at the visitor information center at 46 Reed Avenue and follow it through the pleasant streets. Water Street, by the harbor, has eateries, gift and crafts shops, and artists' studios.

Greenock Church (*Montague and Edward Sts.* *No phone*) owes its existence to a remark someone made at an 1822 dinner party about the "poor" Presbyterians not having a church of their own. Captain Christopher Scott, who took exception to the slur, spared no expense on the building, which is decorated with a carving of a green oak tree in honor of Scott's birthplace, Greenock, Scotland.

Fodor's Choice ★

Nearly 2,500 varieties of trees, shrubs, and plants cover the 27 acres of woodland trails and many theme gardens at the **Kingsbrae Horticultural Garden.** One of the gardens is specially designed for touch and smell; other themed gardens are a rose garden, a bird and butterfly garden, and a gravel garden, just to name a few. A children's fantasy garden offers child-centered activities and there are daily kids programs from 1:30 to 2:30. Kingsbrae also has an art gallery and a café. *220 King St.* *506/529–3335* *www.kingsbraegarden.com* *$9* *mid-May–mid-Oct., daily 9–6.*

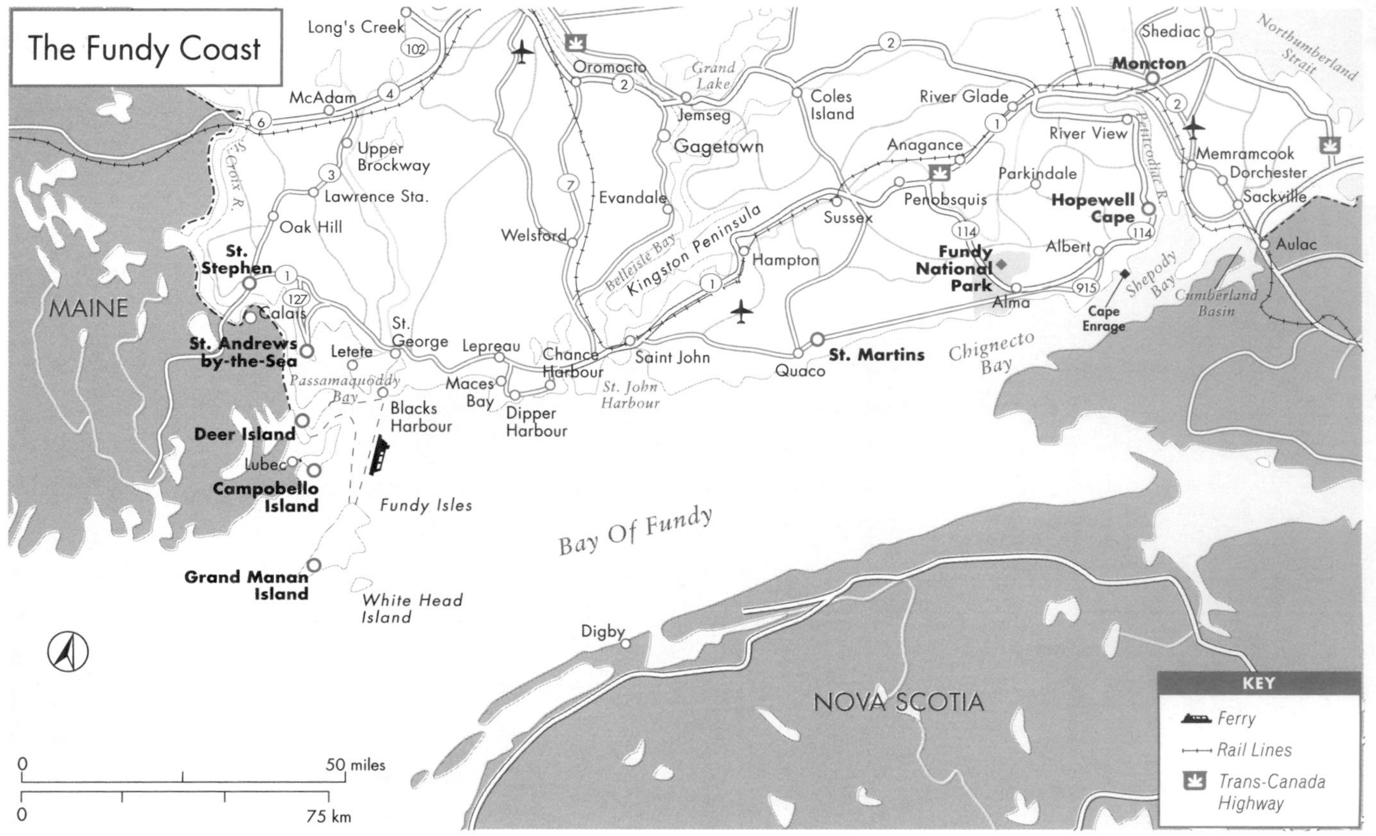
The Fundy Coast
Long's Creek
McAdam
Upper Brockway
Lawrence Sta.
Oak Hill
St. Croix R.
St. Stephen
Calais
MAINE
St. Andrews by-the-Sea
Letete
St. George
Lepreau
Passamaquoddy Bay
Blacks Harbour
Maces Bay
Dipper Harbour
Chance Harbour
Deer Island
Lubec
Campobello Island
Fundy Isles
Grand Manan Island
White Head Island
Oromocto
Grand Lake
Jemseg
Gagetown
Evandale
Welsford
Belleisle Bay
Kingston Peninsula
Hampton
Saint John
St. John Harbour
Coles Island
Sussex
Quaco
St. Martins
River Glade
Anagance
Penobsquis
Parkindale
Fundy National Park
Alma
Chignecto Bay
Albert
Hopewell Cape
Cape Enrage
Shepody Bay
Cumberland Basin
River View
Petitcodiac R.
Moncton
Shediac
Memramcook
Dorchester
Sackville
Aulac
Northumberland Strait
Bay Of Fundy
Digby
NOVA SCOTIA
KEY
Ferry
Rail Lines
Trans-Canada Highway
0
50 miles
0
75 km

The Huntsman Marine Science Centre provides educational displays at its **Huntsman Aquarium and Museum.** Marine life includes a teeming touch tank and seals that are fed at 11 and 4 daily. There is a new live-shark and giant-sturgeon exhibit, too. *1 Lower Campus Rd. 506/529-1202 www.huntsmanmarine.ca $7.50 May–Sept., daily 10–5.*

WHERE TO STAY & EAT

¢–$$ **Ossie's Seafood Take-Out.** The gaudy billboard outside this unassuming take-out joint reads THE BEST SEAFOOD IN NORTH AMERICA and those who have tried it tend to agree. Ossie's seafood is deep-fried and served with a famous house tartar sauce. Other than the fried seafood, though, Ossie's also turns out fish chowder, turkey soup, rolls, and pies and other desserts. There is no dining room, but there are lots of picnic tables. *3222 Hwy. 1, Bethel 506/755-2758 No credit cards Closed late Oct.–early Apr.*

¢–$ **Sweet Harvest Market.** Known for its natural products and made-on-site breads, cookies, cakes, cheesecakes, and preserves, this casual bakery-deli-restaurant is always experimenting. Try the salmon mousse or the house-made roast beef. *182 Water St. 506/529-6249 V.*

$–$$ **Rossmount Inn Hotel Restaurant & Bar.** This inn is set on 87 acres at the base of Chamcook Mountain. The rooms are understated; the handsome dining room features crystal chandeliers and dark mahagony furniture, which sets the scene for fine dining ($$–$$$) at its best. Local seafood and organic produce (much of it plucked from the inn's organic garden minutes before a meal) are featured daily. The vanilla poached "naked" lobster with sweet-pea reduction is a masterpiece. *4599 Rte. 127, St. Andrews by-the-Sea 506/529-3351 Reservations essential for dining room www.rossmountinn.com 18 rooms In-room: Wi-Fi, no phone, no TV, no a/c. In-hotel: restaurant, bar, pool, no-smoking rooms AE, MC, V Closed Jan.–Easter.*

$$$$ ★ **Fairmont Algonquin.** The bellhops wear kilts and dinner is served on the wraparound veranda in fine weather. The rooms have an air of relaxed refinement; those in the newer Prince of Wales wing are especially comfortable. The Passamaquoddy Dining Room, open for breakfast and dinner (summer only), is noted for its seafood and regional dishes. Other options are the casual Right Whale Pub and the cozy Library Lounge and Bistro. *184 Adolphus St., E5B 1T7 506/529-8823 506/529-7162 www.fairmont.com/algonquin 234 rooms In-room: refrigerator (some), WiFi. In-hotel: 3 restaurants, room service, bars, golf course, tennis courts, pool, gym, spa, beachfront, bicycles, laundry service, some pets allowed, no-smoking rooms AE, DC, MC, V.*

$$$$ Fodor's Choice ★ **Kingsbrae Arms.** This restored 1897 estate is an experience. Eclectic antiques fill the rooms, and pampering touches are plentiful—roses, Belgian chocolates, plush robes, a pantry stocked with biscotti, and daily afternoon tea. The two-story carriage house has a private entrance, patio, and balcony, plus a kitchen (minus stove). Fine dining here reaches new heights with a "menuless" approach. The chef prepares a daily degustation using the finest and freshest ingredients—perhaps a fresh catch from the fishmonger or a last minute delivery of wild boar. *219 King St., E5B 1Y1 506/529-4558 506/529-1197 www.*

kingsbrae.com 6 *suites, 2 rooms In-room: DVD, VCR, dial-up. In-hotel: pool, laundry service, no-smoking rooms, some pets allowed, minibar (some), no elevator* ▭*AE, MC, V* *MAP.*

$$$–$$$$ ★ **Pansy Patch.** A visit to this bed-and-breakfast is a bit like a close encounter with landed gentry who are patrons of the arts and who like their gardens as rich and formal as their meals. Four rooms are in the Corey Cottage next door. Afternoon tea and cookies are served wherever you like—in the breakfast room, in your room, in the garden, or on the deck overlooking the water. ✉*59 Carleton St., E5B 1M8* ☎*506/529–3834 or 888/726–7972* *506/529–9042* *www.pansypatch.com* *9 rooms In-room: no TV (some), In-hotel: ethernet, no elevator, no-smoking rooms* ▭*AE, MC, V* *Closed mid-Oct.–mid-May* *BP.*

SPORTS & THE OUTDOORS

St. Andrews Creative Playground (✉*168 Frederick St.*) is an amazing wooden structure for climbing, swinging, performing, making music, and playing games.

GOLF The **Algonquin Golf Club** (✉*Off Rte. 127* ☎*506/529–8165* *www.algonquingolf.com*) has a beautifully landscaped 18-hole, par-71 signature course, designed by Thomas McBroom.

WATER SPORTS Whale and nature cruises and kayak tours all begin at the **Day Adventure Centre** at the town wharf. **Fundy Tide Runners** (☎*506/529–4481* *www.fundytiderunners.com*) uses a 24-foot Zodiac to search for whales, seals, and marine birds. **Tall Ship Whale Adventures** (☎*506/529–8116*) operates the *Cory*, an elegant vessel for whale-watching.

SHOPPING

The **Crocker Hill Store/Steven Smith Designs** (✉*45 King St.* ☎*506/529–4303*) has art and other items for those who love gardens and birds. **Garden by the Sea (NB)** (✉*217 Water St.* ☎*506/529–8905*) is an aromatic shop with fabulous flowers, soaps, and teas. They specialize in all-natural body products including Bay of Fundy sea salts and ecoflowers.

★ The **Seacoast Gallery** (✉*174 Water St.* ☎*506/529–0005*) carries fine arts and crafts. **Serendipin' Art** (✉*168 Water St.* ☎*506/529–3327*) sells handblown glass, hand-painted silks, jewelry, and other crafts by New Brunswick artists.

GRAND MANAN ISLAND

35 km (22 mi) east of St. Andrews by-the-Sea to Black's Harbour, 1½ hrs by car ferry from Black's Harbour.

Grand Manan (population 2,700), the largest of the three Fundy Islands, is also the farthest from the mainland. Circular herring weirs dot the island's coastal waters, and fish sheds and smokehouses lie beside long wharfs that reach out to bobbing fishing boats. It's easy to get around; only about 32 km (20 mi) of road lead from the lighthouse at Southern Head to the one at North Head. John James Audubon visited the island in 1831, attracted by the more than 240 species of seabirds that nest here. The puffin may be the island's symbol, but whales are the stars. Giant finbacks, right whales, minkes, and humpbacks feed in the rich waters. Plan to be at the ferry early as it operates on a first-come, first-served basis.

Ferry service, provided by **Coastal Transport** (☎*506/662–3724* *Cars are $30 payable on return passage from Grand Manan; adults are $10.35, children 5 to 12 years old are $5.50, under 5 free*), leaves the mainland from Black's Harbour, off Route 1, and docks at North Head on Grand Manan Island.

WHERE TO STAY & EAT

$–$$ **Inn at Whale Cove.** This is a secluded waterfront compound where rustic surroundings join with elegant furnishings. Full breakfast is included for guests staying at the inn (not in the cottages). The dining room ($$–$$$) features fresh seasonal choices. Cottages are available by the week only. ✉*26 Whale Cove Cottage Rd., E5G 2B5* ☎*506/662–3181* 🌐*www.holidayjunction.com/whalecove* *3 rooms, 3 cottages* *In-room: no a/c (some), no phone, no TV. In-hotel: beachfront, no-smoking rooms, some pets allowed, no elevator* *MC, V* *Closed Nov.–Apr.*

$ **Marathon Inn.** This mansion built by a sea captain overlooks the harbor. It has been an inn since 1871, and many of its original furnishings can still be found in the guest rooms. Seafood is featured in the dining room; lunch is not served, but guests can request packed lunches. ✉*19 Marathon La., Grand Manan E5G 3A4* ☎*506/662–8488* 🌐*www.marathoninn.com* *24 rooms* *In-room: no a/c, no TV (some). In-hotel: restaurant, bar, some pets allowed, no-smoking rooms, no elevator* *MC, V.*

SPORTS & THE OUTDOORS

WHALE WATCHING A whale-watching cruise from Grand Manan takes you well out into the bay. Dress warmly; some boats have winter jackets, hats, and mittens on board for those who don't heed this advice. Most operators give refunds if no whales are sighted. Interpreters on **Sea Watch Tours** (☎*877/662–8552* 🌐*www.seawatchtours.com*) are very knowledgeable about the birds you might encounter on your cruise, as well as the whales. Trips ($55) are four to five hours, July through September.

For complete information on bird-watching, nature photography, hiking, cycling, horseback riding, sea kayaking, and whale-watching, contact **Tourism New Brunswick** (*Box 12345, Fredericton E3B 5C3* ☎*800/561–0123* 🌐*www.tourismnbcanada.com*).

DEER ISLAND

50 km (31 mi) east of St. Andrews by-the-Sea to Letete, 40 mins by free ferry from Letete.

Exploring the island takes only a few hours; it's 12 km (7 mi) long, varying in width from almost 5 km (3 mi) to a few hundred feet at some points.

At **Deer Point,** walk through a small nature park while waiting for the ferry to Campobello Island. If you listen carefully, you may be able to hear the sighing and snorting of the **Old Sow,** the second-largest whirlpool in the world. If you can't hear it, you'll be able to see it, just a few feet offshore in the Western Passage off Point Park.

WHERE TO STAY & EAT

¢–$$$ **45th Parallel Restaurant.** Their lobster roll is reknowned, but other popular menu items include fresh panfried haddock or scallops. Old-fashioned chicken dinners—baked chicken, stuffing, real gravy, mashed potatoes, veggies, and cranberry sauce—still exist here, too. *941 Hwy. 772, Fairhaven 506/747–2222 year-round, 506/747–2231 May–Oct. AE, MC, V Closed weekdays Nov.–Mar.*

¢–$ **Sunset Beach Cottage & Suites.** A modern property surrounded by natural beauty, this complex is right on a secluded cove. Watch the porpoises and bald eagles during the day, and in the evening enjoy a rare east-coast treat—an ocean sunset in the newly installed hot tub. *21 Cedar Grove Rd., Fairhaven E5V 1N3 506/747–2972 or 888/576–9990 www.cottageandsuites.com 5 suites, 1 cottage In-room: no a/c (some), VCR. In-hotel: pool, no-smoking rooms, no elevator V.*

SPORTS & THE OUTDOORS

Lambert's Outer Island Tours (*Lord's Cove Wharf 506/747–2426 or 866/694–2537 www.outerislandtours.com*) offers whale-watching and eco@tours ($50 tax, included). The captain is a ninth-generation Deer Islander.

CAMPOBELLO ISLAND

★ *40 mins by ferry (June to September) Campobello to Deer Island departs on the hour, every hour; 90 km (56 mi) southeast of St. Stephen via bridge from Lubec, Maine.*

The 34-room rustic summer cottage of the family of President Franklin Delano Roosevelt is now part of a nature preserve, **Roosevelt Campobello International Park,** a joint project of the Canadian and U.S. governments. The miles of trails here make for pleasant strolling. *Roosevelt Park Rd. 506/752–2922 Free House late May–mid-Oct., daily 10–5:45 grounds daily year-round.*

The island's **Herring Cove Provincial Park** (*Welshpool 506/752–7010*) has camping facilities, a restaurant, a 9-hole, par-36 Geoffrey Cornish golf course, a sandy beach, and miles of hiking trails.

WHERE TO STAY & EAT

¢–$$$$ **Lupine Lodge.** Originally a vacation home built by the Adams family (friends of the Roosevelts) in the early 1900s, these three attractive log cabins on a bluff overlooking the Bay of Fundy are now a modern guest lodge. Two of the cabins contain the guest rooms, which are rustic, with modern furniture and homemade quilts. The third cabin houses the dining room ($–$$), which specializes in simple but well-prepared local seafood. *610 Rte. 774, Welshpool E5E 1A5 506/752–2555 or 888/912–8880 www.lupinelodge.com 11 rooms In-room:*

no a/c, no phone, no TV. In-hotel: restaurant, bar, no-smoking rooms, no elevator ▭*MC, V.*

ST. MARTINS

45 km (28 mi) east of Saint John.

The fishing village of St. Martins has a rich shipbuilding heritage, whispering caves, miles of lovely beaches, spectacular tides, and a cluster of covered bridges. It's also the gateway to the Fundy Trail Parkway.

The scenic drive portion of the linear **Fundy Trail Parkway** extends to an interpretive center at Salmon River. ☎*506/833–2019* ⊕*www.fundytrailparkway.com* *$3.*

WORD OF MOUTH

"From Saint John to Alma, the secondary road which will take you through St. Martins is a nice drive. St. Martins is a lovely spot but you don't need to spend a lot of time. Good picture opportunity with covered bridges, etc. Not at all like Hopewell Rocks. Your other option would be to stop at Fundy (Alma) for the night giving you time to explore the National Park and the next day visit Cape Enrage (in my opinion, more spectacular than Hopewell Rocks) and then the Rocks on your way to PEI." —Tanya

WHERE TO STAY & EAT

$$–$$$ ✕**Broadway Café.** On a quiet and colorful street in "downtown" Sussex, this charming café sits across from a defunct but well-maintained train station, now an ice-cream parlor and tourist center. Sandwiches, pizzas, and salads fill the lunch menu; eclectic dinner choices include curries, rack of lamb, and seafood. ✉*73 Broad St., 60 km (37 mi) northeast of St. Martins, Sussex* ☎*506/433–5414* ▭*MC, V* ⊗*Closed Sun. No dinner Mon. and Tues.*

$–$$ ✕**Quaco Inn.** The elegant guest rooms are furnished with antiques but have contemporary luxuries like whirlpool spa baths. The dining room serves delectable land and sea dishes ($$$): try the Quaco Duck, a breast of duck with a poached pear and a Port reduction. ✉*16 Beach St., E5R 1C7* ☎*506/833–4772* ⊕ *www.quacoinn.com/index.htm* *12 rooms* *In-room: Wi-Fi. In-hotel: restaurant, laundry service, free parking, no smoking, no pets* ▭*MC, V.*

$–$$ ✕**St. Martins Country Inn.** This restored sea captain's home is furnished with Victorian antiques. The adjacent carriage house has four rooms. Formal dinners ($$–$$$) in the Candlelight Dining Room are excellent. Coquille St. Martins, a rich medley of lobster, scallops, shrimp, and crab in a creamy wine sauce, is the house specialty. Children are welcome to stay in the carriage house, though not in the main inn. ✉*303 Main St., E5R 1C1* ☎*506/833–4534 or 800/565–5257* *506/833–4725* ⊕*www.stmartinscountryinn.com* *16 rooms* *In-room: VCR. In-hotel: restaurant, bar, laundry service, no-smoking rooms, no elevator* ▭*MC, V.*

$ ✕**Weslan Inn.** Fireplaces, antiques, and lots of floral prints give the rooms in this Heritage Inn an English country feel. Breakfast is served in your room. The relaxed dining room (¢–$; reservations essential) specializes in seafood. ✉*45 Main St., E5R 1B4* ☎*506/833–2351* *www.weslaninn.com 4 rooms In-room: DVD, VCR. In-hotel: restaurant, laundry service; Wi-Fi, no elevator MC, V BP.*

SPORTS & THE OUTDOORS

SKIING **Poley Mountain Resort** (*Waterford Rd., 10 km [6 mi] southeast of Sussex 506/433–7653 www.poleymountain.com*) has 23 trails, a snowboard park, a 660-foot vertical drop, night skiing, and half-pipe snowboarding.

FUNDY NATIONAL PARK

Fodor'sChoice ★ *135 km (84 mi) northeast of Saint John.*

Fundy National Park is an awesome 206-square-km (80-square-mi) microcosm of New Brunswick's inland and coastal climates. Park naturalists offer several programs each day, including beach walks and hikes to explore the park's unique climatic conditions and the fascinating biological evolution evident in the forests. The park has 100 km (60 mi) of varied hiking and mountain-biking trails, year-round camping, golf, tennis, a heated Bay of Fundy saltwater pool, a playground, and a restaurant. In the evening there are interactive programs in the amphitheater and campfires. Its more than 600 campsites range from full service to wilderness. *Rte. 114, Alma E4H 1B4 506/887–6000 www.pc.gc.ca $6.90.*

The small seaside town of **Alma** services Fundy National Park with motels, restaurants that serve good lobster, and a bakery that sells sublime sticky buns. Around this area, much of it in Albert County, there's plenty to do outdoors—from bird-watching to spelunking.

WHERE TO STAY

$–$$ **Parkland Village Inn.** Right on the water and in the heart of the bustling village, this rambling inn with an original section and a modern addition has a large dining room ($–$$$) where the hummingbird feeders in the windows are frequently visited. Lobster and scallops are popular menu selections. *8601 Main St., E4H 1N6 506/887–2313 506/887–2315 www.parklandvillageinn.com 10 rooms, 5 suites In-room: refrigerator (some), Wi-Fi, no a/c. In-hotel: restaurant, bar, beachfront, laundry service, no-smoking rooms, no elevator MC, V Closed Nov.–Apr. BP.*

SPORTS & THE OUTDOORS

BIRD-WATCHING The bit of shoreline at **Marys Point** (*Follow signs off Rte. 915*) draws tens of thousands of migrating birds, including semipalmated sandpipers and other shorebirds, each summer. The area, now a bird sanctuary and interpretive center, is near Riverside-Albert.

GOLF The **Fundy National Park Golf Club** (*Fundy National Park near the Alma entrance 506/887–2970*) is near cliffs overlooking the restless Bay of Fundy; it's one of the province's most beautiful and challenging 9-hole courses.

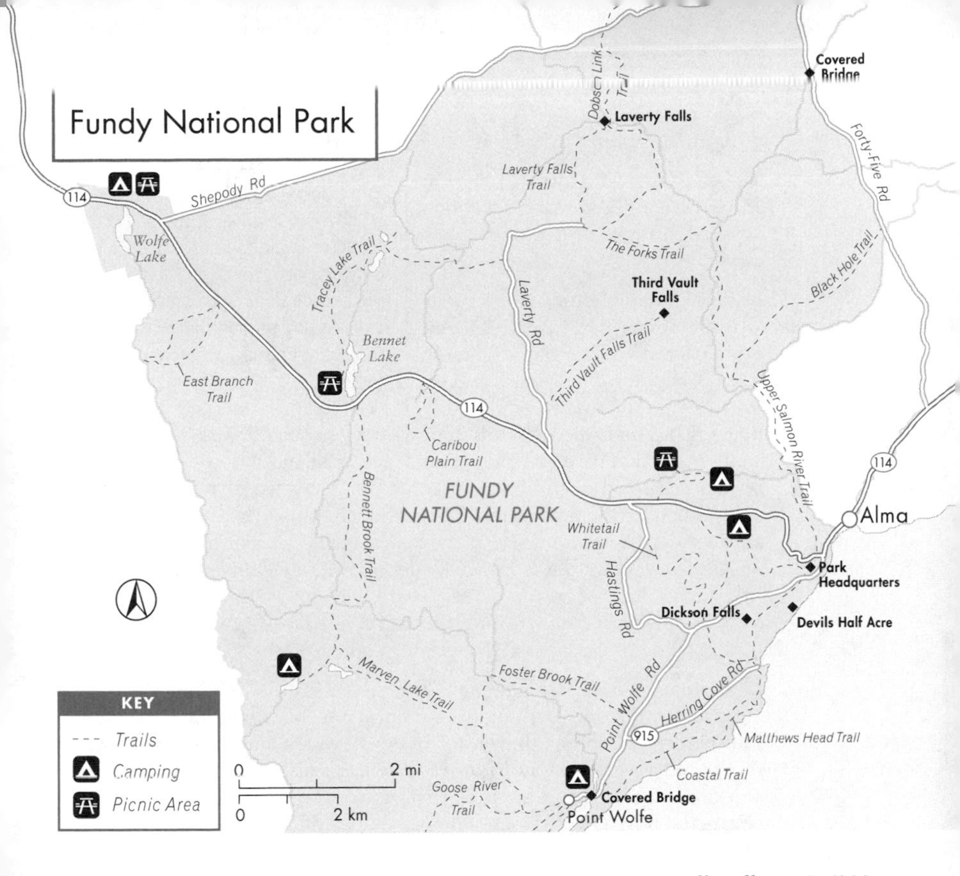

HORSEBACK RIDING **Broadleaf Guest Ranch** (✉ *5526 Rte. 114, Hopewell Hill* ☎ *506/882–2349 or 800/226–5405* 🌐 *www.broadleafranch.com*) can provide an overnight adventure in the forest or a short trail ride through lowland marshes or along a beach. The Ranch Restaurant has themed evenings—for example, line dancing or roping instruction; reservations are required. Stay a while in a two-bedroom log cottage with all the comforts of home for $150 a night (5 people or less); $200 (6 people or more).

SEA KAYAKING **FreshAir Adventure** (✉ *16 Fundy View Dr., Alma* ☎ *506/887–2249 or 800/545–0020* 🌐 *www.freshairadventure.com*) conducts Bay of Fundy sea-kayaking excursions that last from two hours to three days. Guides, instruction, and equipment are provided.

SPELUNKING **Baymount Outdoor Adventures** (✉ *Hillsborough* ☎ *506/734–2660* 🌐 *www.baymountadventures.com*) has interpreters who lead expeditions into the White Caves near the Bay of Fundy. Caving is fun—it requires crawling on cave floors and slithering through narrow openings. Baymount also arranges hikes, biking, and sea kayaking at Hopewell Rocks. Make reservations for all activities.

HOPEWELL CAPE

40 km (25 mi) north of Alma.

The coastal road (Route 114) from Alma to Moncton winds through covered bridges and along rocky coasts.

> **WORD OF MOUTH**
>
> "The Hopewell Rocks are amazing to see—you can watch the tide go in and out, and there is a good visitor center explaining the phenomenon. I don't think you need a whole day or night there, however. Look up the tides before you go and you can get some idea of when to arrive. Definitely try to arrive so you can walk down on the 'ocean floor.' " —nkh

Fodor'sChoice ★ **Hopewell Rocks** is home to the famous Giant Flowerpots—rock formations carved by the Bay of Fundy tides. They're topped with vegetation and are uncovered only at low tide, when you can climb down for a closer study. There are trails, two restaurants, and a children's play area, amng other attractions. Be careful, though—there are big cliffs at low tide, and you must exit the beach quickly when the tide comes in. ✉*131 Discovery Rd.* ☎*877/734–3429* 🌐*www.thehopewellrocks.ca* *$8* ⏲*Late May–June, Sept., and Oct., daily 9–5; July and Aug., daily 8–8; closing hrs vary slightly, so call ahead.*

WHERE TO STAY

$–$$ **Florentine Manor Heritage Inn.** With silver candlesticks on the dining-room table and handmade quilts on the beds, this restored old shipbuilder's house is a haven for honeymooners and romantics. Two rooms have fireplaces and two have whirlpool baths. Picnic lunches and candlelight dinners are prepared by request. ✉*356 Rte. 915, Harvey on the Bay E4H 2M2* ☎*506/882–2271 or 800/665–2271* 🌐*www.florentinemanor.com* *9 rooms* *In-room: no a/c, no phone, no TV. In-hotel: bicycles, laundry service, no kids under 8, no-smoking rooms, no elevator* *MC, V* *BP.*

MONCTON

80 km (50 mi) north of Alma.

Canada's first officially bilingual city, Moncton is often called the Gateway to Acadia because of its cultural mix and proximity to the Acadian shore. The greater Moncton area is considered the shopping mecca of Atlantic Canada. A water-theme park and nearby beaches make Moncton a cool summer spot, and the World Wine Festival in November and HubCap Comedy Festival in February warm up winter.

Before the harbor mouth filled with silt, the **Tidal Bore** was an incredible sight, a high wall of water that surged in through the narrow opening of the river to fill red mud banks to the brim. It still moves up the river, and is worth seeing, but it's no longer a raging torrent.

Magnetic Hill creates a bizarre optical illusion. If you park your car in neutral at the designated spot, you seem to be coasting uphill without power. Shops, a restaurant, an award-winning zoo, a golf course, and a small railroad are part of the larger complex here; there are extra charges for the attractions. ✉ *North of Moncton off Trans-Canada Hwy. Exit 450 from Trans Canada Highway; watch for signs* 🎟 *$5* ⏲ *May–early Sept., daily 8–8.*

An excellent water-theme park, **Magic Mountain** is adjacent to Magnetic Hill. ✉ *Off Trans-Canada Hwy. Exit 450 on the outskirts of Moncton* ☎ *506/857–9283, 800/331–9283 in Canada* 🎟 *$22.50* ⏲ *Mid–late June and mid-Aug.–early Sept., daily 10–6; July–mid-Aug., daily 10–8.*

The **Magnetic Hill Zoo,** the largest zoo in Atlantic Canada, has no shortage of exotic species, including lemurs, lions, and muntjacs (a type of small deer). A tropical house has reptiles, amphibians, birds, and primates, and at Old MacDonald's Barnyard, children can pet domestic animals or ride a pony in summer. ✉ *Off Trans-Canada Hwy. Exit 450 on the outskirts of Moncton* ☎ *506/384–0303* 🎟 *$8.50* ⏲ *Apr.–Oct.; hours vary.*

★ A restored 1920s vaudeville stage, the opulent **Capitol Theatre** is a beautiful attraction in itself as well as a venue for plays, musicals, ballets, and concerts. Free tours are given when guides are available. ✉ *811 Main St.* ☎ *506/856–4379, 800/567–1922 in Canada* ⏲ *Tour times vary according to performances and availability; call ahead.*

The Atlantic Ballet Theatre of Canada is a professional touring company of high artistic standard. It just moved into the old Moncton YMCA building, a community landmark since 1870. The company features a number of classically trained, soloist ballet dancers from around the world. ✉ *68 Highfield St., 2nd fl.* ☎ *506/ 383–5951.*

Comprehensive exhibits trace the city's history from the days of the Mi'Kmaq people to the present at the **Moncton Museum.** ✉ *20 Mountain Rd.* ☎ *506/856–4383* 🎟 *By donation* ⏲ *Mon.–Sat. 9–4:30, Sun. 1–5.*

The halls of the **Aberdeen Cultural Centre,** a converted schoolhouse, ring with music and chatter. This is home to theater and dance companies, a framing shop, and several galleries. **Galerie 12** represents leading contemporary Acadian artists. **Galerie Sans Nom** is an artist-run co-op supporting avant-garde artists from throughout Canada. The artist-run **IMAGO Inc.** is the only print-production shop in the province. Guided tours are available by appointment. ✉ *140 Botsford St.* ☎ *506/857–9597* 🎟 *Free* ⏲ *Weekdays 10–4.*

WHERE TO STAY & EAT

$$$–$$$$ ★ ✕ **Little Louis's Oyster Bar.** "Intimate" and "interesting" are good words to describe this second-floor restaurant where you can make a meal of oysters, though a great wine list, steaks, and other specialties such as osso buco steal some of the limelight from the excellent seafood. ✉ *245 Collishaw St.* ☎ *506/855–2022* 💳 *AE, DC, MC, V* ⏲ *No lunch July and Aug.*

$$–$$$ ✕ **Pisces by Gaston.** It didn't take long for this new kid on the block to develop a reputation for good food: the menu is creative, locally inspired, and ranges from inspired shellfish dishes to tender steaks. The decor is impressive and elegant, but the atmosphere is casual. Lunch is

a particularly good option, with a spectacular seafood buffet. ✉300 Main St. ☎506/854–0444 ▭AE, MC, V.

¢–$$ ★ ✕ **Pump House Brewery.** The fare here goes above and beyond standard pub grub, with wood-fired pizzas—the veggie version is particularly hearty—and vegetable quesadillas sharing the menu with burgers, steaks, club sandwiches, and snack food. Beer is brewed on-site; the root beer and cream soda soda, made in-house, are also delish. ✉*5 Orange La.* ☎*506/855–2337* ▭*AE, MC, V.*

$$–$$$ ★ ✕ **Delta Beauséjour.** Moncton's finest hotel is located downtown, and has had a facelift. L'Auberge, the main restaurant ($–$$$$), has a distinct Acadian flavor, while the more formal Windjammer dining room ($$$$, reservations essential) is modeled after the luxury liners of the early 1900s, with a sea-inspired menu featuring local lobsters and oysters. Try the chateaubriand buffalo for a tableside treat. ✉*750 Main St. E1C 1E6* ☎*506/854–4344* *506/858–0957* *www.deltahotels.com* *290 rooms, 6 suites* *In-room: ethernet. In-hotel: 2 restaurants, pool, gym, laundry service, parking (no fee), no-smoking rooms, some pets allowed* ▭*AE, D, DC, MC, V.*

$$–$$$ **Ramada Plaza Crystal Palace.** Part of an amusement complex, this hotel features theme rooms devoted to rock and roll, the Victorian era, and more. There are also movie theaters, a giant bookstore, an indoor pool, and an indoor amusement park. Champlain Mall is just across the parking lot. Note that the hotel is technically in Dieppe, but the two cities are seamless and it is right on the border with Moncton. ✉*499 Paul St., Dieppe E1A 6S5* ☎*506/858–8584 or 800/561–7108* *506/858–5486* *www.crystalpalacehotel.com* *92 rooms, 23 suites* *In-room: Wi-Fi, In-hotel: restaurant, pool, gym, room service, laundry services, no-smoking rooms* ▭*AE, D, DC, MC, V.*

NIGHTLIFE & THE ARTS

Fodor's Choice ★ Top musicians and other big acts appear at the **Coliseum Arena Complex** (✉*377 Killam Dr.* ☎*506/857–4100* *www.monctoncoliseum.com*). **Studio 700** (✉*700 Main St.* ☎*506/857–9117*) is open Wednesday through Sunday for rock, jazz, or blues, and dancing. There's live jazz on Friday; other live bands play Sunday. **The Old Triangle Irish Alehouse** (✉*751 Main St.* ☎*506/384–7474* *www.oldtriangle.com.*), a creation of three Irishmen, has three lively rooms: the Snug, the Pourhouse, and Tigh An Cheoil (house of music)—they symbolize food for the body, drink for the spirit, and music for the soul. **Voodoo** (✉*938 Mountain Rd.* ☎*506/858–8844*) has lots of room for dancing and caters to the 25-plus crowd.

SPORTS & THE OUTDOORS

Fox Creek Golf Club (✉*200 Golf St.* ☎*506/859–4653* *www.foxcreekgolfclub.ca*), inaugurated in 2005, offers an exceptional 6,900 yard course, 9,000 square foot clubhouse. It's fast becoming famous for the architectural and natural beauty of the course. **Royal Oaks Golf Club** (✉*1746 Elmwood Dr.* ☎*506/388–6257, 866/769–6257 in Canada* *www.royaloaks.ca*) is an 18-hole, par-72 PGA Championship course, the first Canadian course designed by Rees Jones.

The **All World Super Play Park** (✉ *Cleveland Ave., Riverview*), across the river from Moncton, is a giant wooden structure with plenty of room for children to exercise their bodies and imaginations. **Supersplash Water Park** (✉ *City Centre, St. George Blvd.*) is a state of the art outdoor water playground located in the rear of Moncton at Centennial Park. The big perk is that admission is free.

SHOPPING

The **Dieppe Market** (✉ *333 Acadie Ave.* ☎ *506/382–5750*) brims with fresh produce, baked goods, ethnic cuisine, and crafts every Saturday from 7 to 1. There's also a buzzing scene at **Moncton Market** (✉ *120 Westmorland St.* ☎ *506/389–5969*), also open 7 to 1 on Saturday. Ethnic vendors serve delicious lunches Wednesday through Saturday.

THE ACADIAN COAST & ST. JOHN RIVER VALLEY

History and nature meet on the Tantramar salt marshes east of Moncton. Bounded by the upper reaches of the Bay of Fundy, the province of Nova Scotia, and the Northumberland Strait, the region is rich in history and culture and is teeming with birds. The marshes provide a highly productive wetland habitat, and this region is along one of North America's major migratory bird routes.

The white sands and gentle tides of the Northumberland Strait and Baie des Chaleurs are as different from the rocky cliffs and powerful tides of the Bay of Fundy as the Acadians are from the Loyalists. Along the Acadian Coast the water is warm, the sand is fine, and the accent is French—except in the middle. Where the Miramichi River meets the sea, there is an island of First Nations, English, Irish, and Scottish tradition that is unto itself, rich in folklore and legend. Many people here find their livelihood in the forests, in the mines, and on the sea. In the Acadian Peninsula, fishing boats and churches define the land where a French-language culture survives. You're not likely to run into any language barriers in stores, restaurants, and attractions along the beaten path, but down the side roads it's a different story altogether.

SACKVILLE

22 km (14 mi) southeast of Dorchester and Memramcook.

Sackville is a university town complete with a swan-filled pond, and stately homes shaded by venerable trees.

The **Sackville Waterfowl Park,** in the heart of the town, has more than 3 km (2 mi) of boardwalk and trails through 55 acres of wetlands. Viewing areas and interpretive signs reveal the rare waterfowl species that nest here. There's an interpretive center, and guided tours ($5) are available in French and English mid-June through mid-September. ✉ *Main St.* ☎ *506/364–4967 (June–Aug.)* 🌐 *www.sackville.com/visit/waterfowl* 🎫 *Free* 🕑 *Daily dawn–dusk.*

The sophisticated **Owens Art Gallery** is on the Mt. Allison University campus. One of the oldest and largest university art galleries in the country, it houses 19th- and 20th-century European, American, and Canadian artwork. ✉*61 York St.* ☎*506/364–2574* 🌐*www.mta.ca/owens* *Free* *Weekdays 10–5, weekends 1–5.*

WHERE TO STAY & EAT

$ ★ **Marshlands Inn.** In this white clapboard inn with a carriage-house annex, a double parlor with fireplace sets the comfortable country atmosphere. Bedrooms are furnished with sleigh beds or four-posters. The chefs offer traditional and modern dishes; seafood, pork, and lamb are specialties ($$–$$$). In summer some of the herbs, vegetables, and flowers used in the kitchen and dining room come from the property's own lovely gardens. ✉*55 Bridge St., E4L 3N8* ☎*506/536–0170 or 800/561–1266* *506/536–0721* 🌐*www.marshlands.nb.ca* *20 rooms* *In-room: no a/c (some), no TV (some), Wi-Fi (some). In-hotel: restaurant, no-smoking rooms, some pets allowed, no elevator* *MC, V* *EP.*

SPORTS & THE OUTDOORS

Without a doubt, bird-watching is the pastime of choice in this region. For information, contact the **Canadian Wildlife Service** (✉*17 Waterfowl La.* ☎*506/364–5044*). **Cape Jourimain Nature Centre** (✉*Exit 51 off Rte. 16 at the foot of Confederation Bridge, Bayfield* ☎*866/538–2220 or 506/538–2220* 🌐*www.capejourimain.ca*), at the Cape Jourimain National Wildlife Area, covers 1,800 acres of salt and brackish marshes. Large numbers of waterfowl, shorebirds, and other species can be seen here. The outstanding interpretive center includes a restaurant specializing in local fare and a boutique with nature art and fine crafts. **Goodwin's Pond** (✉*Off Rte. 970*), near the Red-Wing Blackbird Trail in Baie Verte, allows for easy viewing of wetland birds and has more birds per acre than anywhere else in the province. The **Port Elgin Rotary Pond and Fort Gaspereaux Trail** (✉*30 km [19 mi] northeast of Sackville via Rte. 16*) have diverse coastal landscapes that attract migrating waterfowl, bald eagles, and osprey. The **Tintamarre National Wildlife Area** (✉*Goose Lake Rd. off High Marsh Rd.* ☎*506/364–5044*) consists of 5,000 acres of protected land ideal for sighting several species of ducks, rails, pied-billed grebes, and American bittern.

SHOPPING

Fog Forest Gallery (✉*14 Bridge St.* ☎*506/536–9000* 🌐*www.fogforestgallery.ca*) is a small, friendly, and reputable commercial gallery representing Atlantic Canadian artists.

SHEDIAC

25 km (16 mi) east of Moncton.

Beautiful Parlee Beach is what draws people to this fishing village–resort town.

★ A 3-km (2-mi) stretch of glistening sand, **Parlee Beach** has been named the best beach in Canada by several surveys. It is a popular vacation

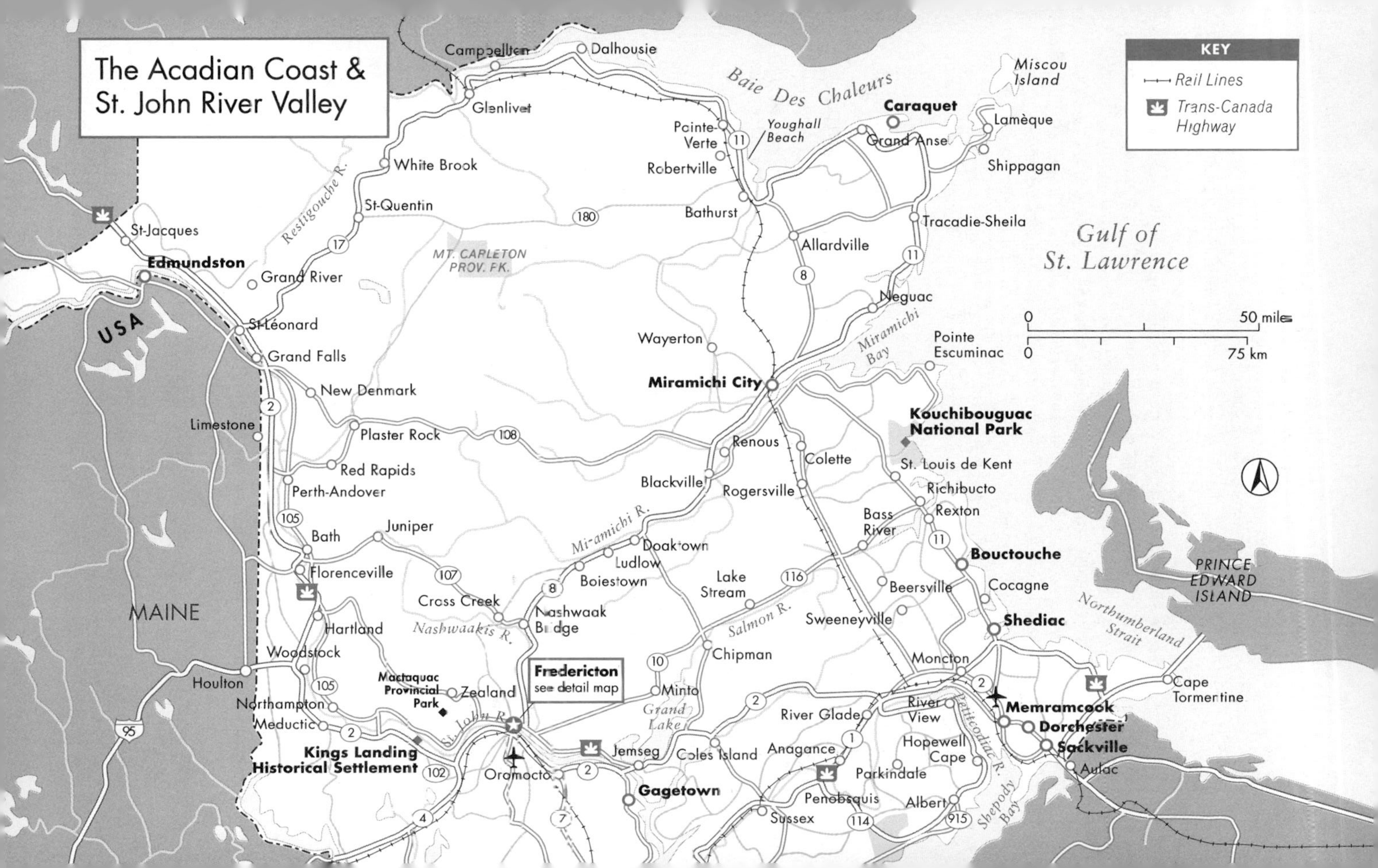
The Acadian Coast &
St. John River Valley
KEY
Rail Lines
Trans-Canada Highway
Gulf of St. Lawrence
Baie Des Chaleurs
Miscou Island
Caraquet
Lamèque
Shippagan
Grand Anse
Youghall Beach
Pointe-Verte
Robertville
Bathurst
Tracadie-Sheila
Allardville
Neguac
Miramichi Bay
Pointe Escuminac
0
50 miles
0
75 km
Campbellton
Dalhousie
Glenlivet
White Brook
St-Quentin
Restigouche R.
St-Jacques
Edmundston
Grand River
St-Léonard
Grand Falls
USA
MT. CARLETON PROV. PK.
Wayerton
Miramichi City
New Denmark
Limestone
Plaster Rock
Red Rapids
Perth-Andover
Kouchibouguac National Park
Renous
Colette
St. Louis de Kent
Blackville
Rogersville
Richibucto
Rexton
Bass River
Bath
Juniper
Mi-amichi R.
Doaktown
Ludlow
Boiestown
Lake Stream
Bouctouche
Cocagne
PRINCE EDWARD ISLAND
Florenceville
Cross Creek
Nashwaak Bridge
Beersville
Sweeneyville
Shediac
Northumberland Strait
MAINE
Hartland
Nashwaakis R.
Salmon R.
Woodstock
Chipman
Moncton
Houlton
Fredericton
see detail map
Minto
Cape Tormentine
Mactaquac Provincial Park
Zealand
Northampton
Meductic
St. John R.
Grand Lake
River Glade
River View
Memramcook
Dorchester
Sackville
Petitcodiac R.
Hopewell Cape
Kings Landing Historical Settlement
Jemseg
Coles Island
Anagance
Parkindale
Aulac
Oromocto
Gagetown
Penobsquis
Albert
Sussex
Shepody Bay
180
17
11
8
2
108
105
107
116
10
102
4
7
1
114
915
95

spot for families and plays host to beach-volleyball and touch-football tournaments; an annual sand-sculpture contest and a triathlon are held here as well. Services include canteens and a restaurant. ✉*Exit 37 off Rte. 133* ☎*506/533–3363* *$9 per vehicle* *Mid-May–mid-Sept., Daily 7* AM*–9* PM.

Parc de l'Aboiteau, on the western end of Cap-Pelé, has a fine, sandy beach as well as a boardwalk that runs through salt marshes where waterfowl nest. The beach complex includes a restaurant and lounge with live music in the evening. Cottages are available for rent year-round. ✉*Exit 53 off Rte. 15* ☎*506/577–2080, for cottage information, 506/577–2005* *$4 per vehicle* *Beach June–Sept., daily dawn–dusk.*

WHERE TO STAY & EAT

$$–$$$$ ✕ **The Green House on Main Restaurant.** Loaded with charm, artwork, and antiques, this upbeat restaurant is trendy despite the building from the 19th century. You can eat outside on the heated patio or upstairs in the intimate dining room. The tiger prawns and Thai shrimp are faultless. ✉*406 Main St.* ☎*506/533–7097* *AE, MC, V.*

$–$$ Fodor's Choice ★ ✕ **Little Shemogue Country Inn.** The unusual name (pronounced shim-o-*gwee*) is Mi'Kmaq for "good feed for geese." The main inn is a beautifully restored country home. A three-story wall of windows in the common area of the modern Log Point annex overlooks the ocean; the rooms here are large and have ocean views and whirlpool tubs. The 200-acre property has its own white-sand beach, canoes, and trails along a salt marsh. There is an exquisite five-course, prix-fixe dinner ($$$$) served in four intimate dining rooms, Everything here is pure delight and exceptional value. ✉*2361 Rte. 955, 40 km (25 mi) east of Shediac, Little Shemogue E4M 3K4* ☎*506/538–2320* *506/538–7494* *www.little-inn.nb.ca* *9 rooms* *In-room: Wi-Fi, no a/c (some). In-hotel: spa, beachfront, bicycles, no kids under 10, no-smoking rooms, no elevator* *AE, MC, V.*

$$$–$$$$ **Tait House.** This elegant and stately historic mansion was built back in 1911. The rooms have fireplaces, canopy beds, and Jacuzzis, and the on-site restaurant features contemporary cuisine as well as another menu that specializes in fondues—cheese, meat, fish, and dessert fondues—and seafood. ✉*293 Main St.* ☎*506/532–4233* *AE, MC, V* *www.maisontaithouse.com* *9 rooms* *In-room: Wi-Fi. In-hotel: restaurant, no-smoking rooms.*

BOUCTOUCHE

35 km (22 mi) north of Shediac.

This bustling town on the sandy shores of Bouctouche Bay is famous as the home of K.C. Irving, patriarch of the New Brunswick Irving industrial dynasty. The area's great dune is one of the few remaining on this coast of North America.

★ **Irving Eco-Centre: La Dune de Bouctouche** is a superb example of a coastal ecosystem that protects the exceptionally fertile oyster beds in Bouctouche Bay. Hiking trails and boardwalks to the beach make it possible to explore sensitive areas without disrupting the environment of one of the few remaining great dunes on the northwest coast of the Atlantic Ocean. Swimming is allowed. ✉ *1932 Rte. 475* ☎ *888/640–3300 or 506/743–2600* 🌐 *www.irvingecocentre.com* 🎟 *Free* ⏲ *Hiking trails and boardwalk daily dawn–dusk. Visitor center July and Aug., daily 10–8; call ahead for reduced hrs in May, June, Sept., and Oct.*

About 10 km (6 mi) up the coast from Bouctouche in Sainte-Anne-de-Kent is **The Olivier Soapery.** There's a skin-care art gallery and, naturally, plenty of soap for sale. By far the best attraction, however, is the soap-making demonstration, five times a day. ✉ *831 Rte. 505* ☎ *506/743–8938 or 800/775–5550* 🌐 *www.oliviersoaps.com* 🎟 *Free* ⏲ *June–early Sept., Sun.–Fri., 9–5; Closed Mon., Sept.–May by appointment.*

WHERE TO STAY & EAT

$$$ **Auberge le Vieux Presbytère de Bouctouche.** This inn is brimming with atmosphere. The restaurant, "Le Tire Bouchon" ($$–$$$) serves seafood and Acadian fare. The terraced café is lovely for lunch. ✉ *157 chemin du Couvent, E4S 3B8* ☎ *506/743–5568* 🖷 *506/743–5566* 🌐 *www.vieuxpresbytere.nb.ca* *17 rooms, 2 suites* *In-room: no a/c (some). In-hotel: restaurant, bicycles, no-smoking rooms* 💳 *AE, MC, V* ⏲ *Closed Oct.–May* *BP.*

KOUCHIBOUGUAC NATIONAL PARK

★ *40 km (25 mi) north of Bouctouche, 100 km (62 mi) north of Moncton.*

The park's white, dune-edged beaches, some of the finest on the continent, are preserved here. Kellys Beach is supervised and has facilities. The cycling is great, with more than 35 km (22 mi) of virtually flat biking trails. In winter the trails are ideal for cross-country skiing, snowshoeing, snow walking, and kick sledding. The park also protects forests and peat bogs, which can be explored along its 10 nature trails. There are lots of nature-interpretation programs, and you can canoe, kayak, and picnic, too. Bikes and boats can be rented. Reserve ahead for one of the 311 campsites. ✉ *186 Rte. 117, Kouchibouguac* ☎ *506/876–2443* 🌐 *www.pc.gc.ca* 🎟 *$6.90 late May–mid-Sept.; free mid-Sept.–late May.*

MIRAMICHI

40 km (25 mi) north of Kouchibouguac, 150 km (93 mi) north of Moncton.

Celebrated for salmon rivers that reach into some of the province's richest forests, and the ebullient nature of its residents, this is a land of lumber kings, ghost stories, folklore, and festivals. Sturdy wood homes dot the banks of Miramichi Bay. The city of Miramichi incorporates the former towns of Chatham and Newcastle and several small villages.

Ritchie Wharf Park has a nautical-theme playground complete with a "Splash Pad" that sprays water from below and dumps it from buckets above. Shops sell local crafts, and there are several restaurants and docking facilities. *Norton's La., Newcastle waterfront off King George Hwy.* *Free* *Park daily dawn–dusk. Shops June–early Sept., daily 9–9.*

The **Central New Brunswick Woodmen's Museum** has a 100-year-old trapper's cabin, blacksmith shop, wheelwright shop, cookhouse-bunkhouse-dingle, and other exhibits pertaining to the woodman's way of life at this fabulous historic site. A popular 10-passenger amusement train ($2) is a 1½-km (1-mi) woodland adventure. *6342 Rte. 8, 110 km (68 mi) southwest of Miramichi City, Boiestown* *506/369–7214* *www.woodsmenmuseum.com* *$5* *May–mid-Oct., daily 9:30–5.*

WHERE TO STAY & EAT

$–$$ **Cunard Restaurant.** Miramichi is an unlikely place to find a great Chinese restaurant. The Cunard, however, has what it takes to make it anywhere. It is renowned for its Szechuan chicken and hot orange beef. *32 Cunard St.* *506/773–7107* *AE, DC, MC, V.*

$$ **Rodd Miramichi River.** This grand riverside hotel, with warm natural wood and earth-tone interior, manages to feel like a fishing lodge. The rooms are comfortable, with lots of outdoorsy prints on the walls. The Angler's Reel Restaurant ($$–$$$) features 20 different fresh salmon dishes. *1809 Water St., E1N 1B2* *506/773–3111* *506/773–3110* *www.rodd-hotels.ca* *76 rooms, 4 suites* *In-room: dial-up. In-hotel: restaurant, bar, pool, gym, pets allowed* *AE, DC, MC, V.*

$ **Metepenagiag Lodge.** About a 20-minute drive from Miramichi on Route 420 West, in a community called Red Bank, the Metepenagiag Lodge is on the Little Southwest Miramichi River and specializes in outdoor and cultural adventures. Rooms are comfortable, and much of the food served incorporates items that have sustained the Mi'kmaq people for centuries. Lumberjack-sized breakfasts are $6, lunches $10, and three-course dinners are $15. Fully air-conditioned, all 10 rooms have exits to a screened-in porch. *2202 MicMac Rd., Red Bank E9E 2P3* *506/836–6128* *506/836–6188* *www.metepenagiaglodge.com* *10 rooms* *In-room: no TV (some). In-hotel: Wi-Fi, restaurant, no-smoking rooms* *DC, MC, V.*

CARAQUET

40 km (25 mi) west of Shippagan.

Perched along the Baie des Chaleurs, Caraquet is rich in French flavor and is the acknowledged Acadian capital.

The two-week **Acadian Festival** (*506/727–2787*), held here in August, includes the Tintamarre, in which costumed participants noisily parade through the streets, and the Blessing of the Fleet, a colorful and moving ceremony that eloquently expresses the importance of fishing to the Acadian economy and way of life.

★ A highlight of the Acadian Peninsula is **Acadian Historical Village.** The more than 40 restored buildings re-create Acadian communities between 1770 and 1939. There are modest homes, a church, a school, and a village shop, as well as an industrial area that includes a working hotel, a bar and restaurant, a lobster hatchery, a cooper, and tinsmith shops. ✉ *Rte. 11, 10 km (6 mi) west of Caraquet* ☎ *506/726–2600 or 877/721–2200* 🌐 *www.villagehistoriqueacadien.com* 🎫 *$15* ⏲ *June–early Sept., daily 10–6; mid-Sept., daily 10–5 with only 6 homes open; late Sept.–mid-Oct., daily 10–5.*

WHERE TO STAY & EAT

$$–$$$$ ✕ **La Fine Grobe-Sur-Mer.** North of Bathurst in Nigadoo, about 80 km (50 mi) outside of Caraquet, is one of New Brunswick's finest restaurants. The French cuisine, seafood, and wine are outstanding. The chef-owner grows his own herbs and greens, and bakes his baguettes in an outside oven. Lobster, lamb, and *lapin* (domestic rabbit) are all on the menu. The dining room is small but has three walls of windows overlooking the ocean. ✉ *289 rue Principal, Nigadoo* ☎ *506/783–3138* 🌐 *www.finegrobe.com* 💳 *AE, DC, MC, V* ⏲ *Lunch by special arrangement only.*

$$$–$$$$ ★ ✕🏨 **Hotel Paulin.** Caraquet is famous not only for lobsters, oysters, artisans, and festivals—but also for Hotel Paulin. A classic Victorian hotel built in 1891, it is now a historical boutique-style hotel on the Bay of Chaleur. Still owned and operated by the Paulin family, it offers more than a place to stay and dine. The nightly three- or four-course meals depend on guest preferences and what is fresh (local foods like a superb goat cheese are used, and seafood comes straight from the bay). Excellence is everywhere. ✉ *143 blvd. St-Pierre W, E1W 1B6* ☎ *506/727–9981 or 866/727–9981* 📠 *506/727–4808* 🌐 *www.hotel-paulin.com* 🛏 *6 rooms, 6 suites* 🛎 *In-room: DVD, VCR, Wi-Fi. In-hotel: restaurant, room service, beachfront, bicycles, laundry service, no-smoking rooms, some pets allowed, no elevator* 💳 *MC, V* 🍽 *BP.*

ST. JOHN RIVER VALLEY

The St. John River valley scenery is panoramic—gently rolling hills and sweeping forests, with just enough rocky gorges to keep it interesting. The native peoples—French, English, Scots, and Danes who live along the river—ensure that its culture is equally intriguing. Gentle hills of rich farmland and the blue sweep of the water make this a lovely area in which to drive.

EDMUNDSTON

275 km (171 mi) northwest of Fredericton.

Edmundston has always depended on the wealth of the deep forest around it—the legend of Paul Bunyan was born in these woods. Even today the town looks to the Fraser Papers pulp mills as the major source of employment.

The annual **Foire Brayonne** (☎*506/739–6608*), held in Edmundston over the long weekend surrounding New Brunswick Day (starts on Wednesday before the first Monday in August), is one of the largest Francophone festivals outside of Québec.

At the **New Brunswick Botanical Garden** roses, rhododendrons, alpine flowers, and dozens of other annuals and perennials bloom in eight gardens. Two arboretums have coniferous and deciduous trees and shrubs. Mosaiculture plantings on metal frames placed throughout the gardens illustrate legends and cultural themes. Children enjoy the insectarium and candle-making workshops. ✉*Main St., St-Jacques* ☎*506/737–5383* 🌐*www.umce.ca/jardin* *$14* *June and Sept., daily 9–6; July and Aug., daily 9–8.*

WHERE TO STAY & EAT

$–$$ **Auberge les Jardins Inn.** Fine French cuisine ($$–$$$$) is the major attraction at this modern inn. Some rooms have whirlpool baths and others have fireplaces. There's lovely terrace dining in summer, a walking trail runs past the front door, and the New Brunswick Botanical Garden is nearby. The restaurant serves breakfast and dinner. ✉*60 rue Principal, St-Jacques E7V 1B7* ☎*506/739–5514 or 800/630–8011* 🌐*www.auberge-lesjardins-inn.com* *30 rooms, 10 cottages* *In-room: VCR, Ethernet. In-hotel: restaurant, pool, bicycle rentals, laundry facilities, laundry service, no-smoking rooms, no elevator* *AE, DC, MC, V.*

KINGS LANDING HISTORICAL SETTLEMENT

Fodor'sChoice ★

210 km (130 mi) south of Grand Falls, 30 km (19 mi) west of Fredericton.

The Kings Landing Historical Settlement was built by moving period buildings to a new shore. To best appreciate the museum, plan to spend at least half a day.

This excellent outdoor living-history museum on the St. John River evokes the sights, sounds, and society of rural New Brunswick between 1790 and 1900. The winding country lanes and meticulously restored homes pull you back a century or more, and programs are available to let you "process" wool "from sheep to shawl" and prepare herbal remedies from the plants in the lanes and gardens. Hearty meals are served at the Kings Head Inn. ✉*Exit 253 off Trans-Canada Hwy., near Prince William* ☎*506/363–4999* 🌐*www.kingslanding.nb.ca* *$15* *June–mid-Oct., daily 10–5.*

FREDERICTON

The small inland city of Fredericton spreads itself on a broad point of land jutting into the St. John River. Its predecessor, the early French settlement of St. Anne's Point, was established in 1642. Settled by Loyalists and named for Frederick, second son of George III, the city serves as the seat of government for New Brunswick's 753,000 residents.

Fredericton is the first city in Canada to offer free Wi-Fi. Called Fred-eZone, it allows free access to the Internet with Wi-Fi-enabled laptops or PDAs in many Fredericton public areas. To learn more check out 🌐*www.fred-ezone.ca.*

EXPLORING FREDERICTON

Downtown Queen Street runs parallel with the river, and has several historic sights and attractions. Most major sights are within walking distance of one another. An excursion to Kings Landing Historical Settlement, a reconstructed village, can bring alive the province's history.

WHAT TO SEE

3 ★ **Beaverbrook Art Gallery.** A lasting gift of the late Lord Beaverbrook, this gallery could hold its head high in the company of some smaller European galleries. Salvador Dalí's gigantic *Santiago el Grande* has always been the star, but a rotation of avant-garde Canadian paintings now shares pride of place. The McCain "gallery-within-a-gallery" is devoted to the finest Atlantic Canadian artists. ✉*703 Queen St.* ☎*506/458–8545* 🎫*$5* ⏲*Fri.–Wed. 9–5:30, Thurs. 9–9.*

7 **Boyce Farmers' Market.** It's hard to miss this Saturday-morning market because of the crowds. There are lots of local meat and produce, cheeses, baked goods, and crafts. The market sells good ready-to-eat food, from German sausages to tasty samosas. ✉*Bounded by Regent, Brunswick, and George Sts.*

4 ★ **Christ Church Cathedral.** This gray stone building, completed in 1853, is an excellent example of decorated neo-Gothic architecture. The cathedral's design was based on an actual medieval prototype in England, and it became a model for many American churches. Inside is a clock known as "Big Ben's little brother," the test run for London's famous timepiece, designed by Lord Grimthorpe. ✉*Church St.* ☎*506/450–8500* 🎫*Free* ⏲*Self-guided tours daily 9–4, except during services. Guided tours July and Aug., weekdays 9–6, Sat. 10–5, Sun. 1–5.*

1 **Historic Garrison District.** The restored buildings of this British and Canadian post, which extends two blocks along Queen Street, include soldiers' barracks, a guardhouse, and a cell block. This is a National Historic Site and one of New Brunswick's top attractions. Local artisans operate studios in the casemates below the soldiers' barracks in Barracks Square. In July and August free guided tours run throughout the day, and there are outdoor concerts in Officers' Square Tuesday and Thursday evenings. Sunday evenings in July and August, free classic movies are shown under the stars in Barracks Square at dusk. ✉*Queen St. at Carleton St.* ☎*506/460–2129* 🎫*Free* ⏲*Daily 24 hrs.*

9 **Old Government House.** This imposing 1828 Palladian mansion has been restored as the official seat of office for the province's lieutenant governor. A hands-on interpretive center spans 12,000 years of history. The 11-acre grounds include a 17th-century Acadian settlement and border an early Maliseet burial ground. ✉*51 Woodstock Rd.* ☎*506/453–2505* 🎫*Free* ⏲*Mon.–Sat., 10 AM to 5 PM; Sun. noon–5.*

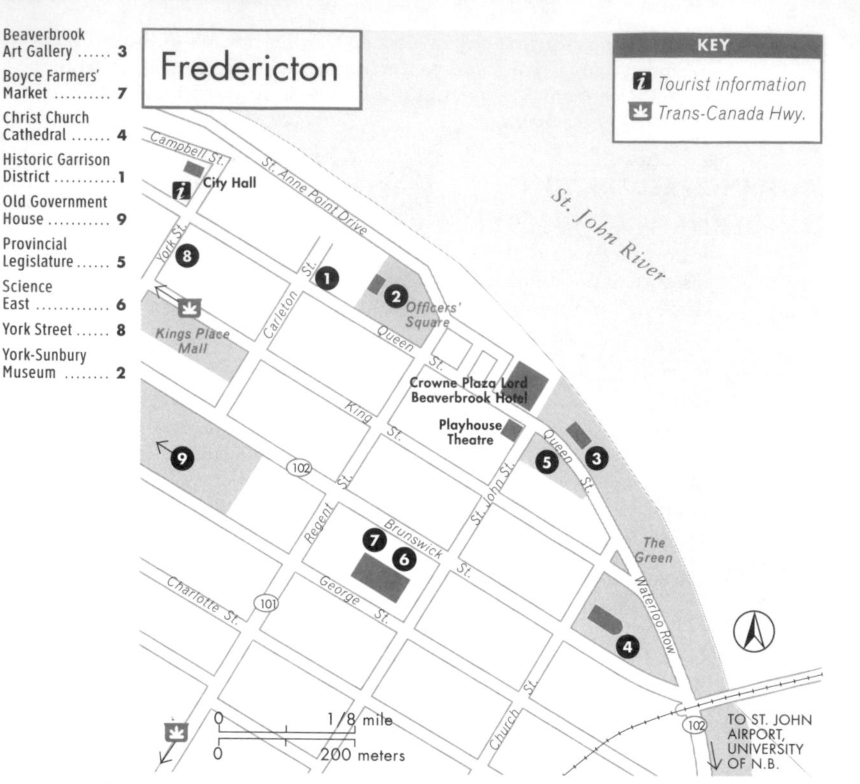

❺ **Provincial Legislature.** The interior chamber of the legislature, where the premier and elected members govern the province, reflects the taste of the late Victorians. There's a freestanding circular staircase, and a volume of Audubon's *Birds of America* is on display. ✉ *Queen St.* ☎ *506/453–2527* 🎫 *Free* 🕒 *Legislature tours late May to late Aug., daily 9–7 (last tour at 6:30); Sept.–late May, weekdays 9–4. Library weekdays 8:15–5.*

❻ **Science East.** This hands-on science center, in the former York County Jail, has family fun locked up with over 130 hands-on exhibits. Walk into a giant kaleidoscope, see a pattern-making laser beam, create a minitornado, and explore the museum in the dungeon. ✉ *668 Brunswick St.* ☎ *506/457–2340* 🌐 *www.scienceeast.nb.ca* 🎫 *$5* 🕒 *June–Sept., Mon.–Sat. 10–5, Sun. 1–4; Oct.–May, Tues.–Fri. noon–5, Sat. 10–5.*

❽ **York Street.** This is the city's high-fashion block, with designer shops,

WORD OF MOUTH

"St. Andrew's is a lovely little town, fairly touristy..and your drive along the coast is probably around the same. Fredericton, on the other hand is really beautiful, the downtown area is on a river, and I just love it..I am a little biased, as I am from F'ton, but I think it is more worth a visit then Saint John or Moncton." —LissaJ

an incense boutique, a general store with an eclectic assortment of gifts and housewares, and a newsstand–cigar store. At the middle of the upriver side of the block is Mazucca's Alley, the gateway to more shops and the pubs and restaurants in Piper's Lane.

York-Sunbury Museum. The Officers' Quarters in the Historic Garrison District houses a museum that offers a living picture of the community from the time when only First Nations peoples inhabited the area, through the Acadian and Loyalist days, to the immediate past. *Officers' Sq., Queen St. 506/455–6041 $3 June–Labor Day, Mon.–Sat. 10–5, Sun. 1–5; off-season by appointment.*

WHERE TO STAY & EAT

$$–$$$ **Amici.** This new restaurant has developed a fabulous reputation in no time flat, with its authentic Italian dishes that are mouthwatering and delicious. You can match your favorite pasta with your favorite sauce, or order from "land-and-sea" fare that includes veal osso buco and a shrimp-stuffed sole. Indulge yourself—try the white-chocolate cheesecake ravioli. *426 Queen St. 506/455–0300 AE, MC, V.*

$$–$$$ **The Blue Door.** This is upscale global cuisine, with a particularly Asian (Thai) bent. The food is inventive and consistently excellent. There's seafood with a twist, such as maple-chili salmon and Athenian haddock. Lots of local fine art adds a nice touch. *100 Regent St., at King St. 506/455–2583 AE, MC, V.*

$$–$$$ ★ **The Palate Restaurant & Café.** The kitchen is open, the atmosphere is intimate, and the art is local (and available for sale). The chef leans toward Mediterranean and Western European dishes, but isn't afraid to experiment. Even lunches, which are a real bargain, are creative. *462 Queen St. 506/450–7911 AE, MC, V Closed Sun.*

¢–$$ **Trinitea's Cup.** Superb lunches, light dinners of hearty soups and sandwiches, and an astonishing array of tea—over 70 varieties, including bubble tea—are available. High tea (by reservation) includes finger sandwiches, savories, assorted fruit, fancy squares and scones. *87 Regent St. 506/458–8327 AE, MC, V.*

$$$ **Delta Fredericton Hotel.** This stately riverside property is a pleasant walk to the downtown core. The elegant country decor is almost as delightful as the sunset views over the river from the patio restaurant and many of the modern rooms. The restaurant, Bruno's, serves legendary Sunday brunch buffets. *225 Woodstock Rd., E3B 2H8 506/457–7000 506/457–4000 www.deltahotels.com 208 rooms, 14 suites In-room: Eethernet. In-hotel: 3 restaurants, bar, pools, gym, spa, laundry service, some pets allowed, no smoking rooms AE, DC, MC, V.*

$$$ **Holiday Inn Hotel and Resort Fredericton.** This modern hotel has a luxurious look, but a relaxed, country atmosphere. There's a fireplace in the lobby, and the suites have electric fireplaces. Some of the rooms with water views have cathedral ceilings. The cottages are ideal for boating and skiing families. *35 Mactaquac Rd., off Rte. 102, 20 km (12 mi) west of Fredericton, E3E 1L2 506/363–5111 or 800/561–5111 506/363–3000 www.holidayinnfredericton.com 82 rooms, 4*

suites, 6 cottages ♨In-room: dial-up. In-hotel: Wi-Fi, bar, tennis court, pool, gym, laundry facilities, laundry service, pets allowed, no-smoking rooms ▭AE, D, DC, MC, V.

$–$$ **The Very Best: A Victorian B&B.** This elegant home, with its fine antiques and original artwork, is in the downtown Heritage Preservation Area. Some rooms have fireplaces. ✉*806 George St., E3B 1K7* ☎*506/451–1499* 📠*506/454–1454* 🌐*www.bbcanada.com/2330.html* *5 rooms* *In-room: DVD, Wi-Fi. In-hotel: pool, bicycles, laundry facilities, no-smoking rooms, A/C, no elevator* ▭*AE, MC, V* 🍽*BP.*

$ **Carriage House Inn.** The lovely bedrooms in this venerable mansion are furnished with Victorian antiques. Breakfasts, served in the ballroom, are legendary. ✉*230 University Ave., E3B 4H7* ☎*506/452–9924 or 800/267–6068* 📠*506/452–2770* 🌐*www.carriagehouse-inn.net* *10 rooms* *In-room: Wi-Fi. In-hotel: no-smoking rooms, no elevator* ▭*AE, DC, MC, V* 🍽*BP.*

SPORTS & THE OUTDOORS

CANOEING & KAYAKING

Shells, canoes, and kayaks can be rented by the hour or day at the **Small Craft Aquatic Center** (✉*Behind Victoria Health Centre where Brunswick St. becomes Woodstock Rd.* ☎*506/460–2260*), which also arranges guided tours and instruction.

GOLF

The **Kingswood** (✉*31 Kingswood Park* ☎*506/443–3333 or 800/423–5969*) features an 18-hole, par-72 championship course and a 9-hole executive course designed by Cooke-Huxham International.

WALKING

Fredericton has a fine network of walking trails, one of which follows the river from the Green, past the Victorian mansions on Waterloo Row, behind the Beaverbrook Art Gallery, and along the riverbank to the Sheraton. The **visitor information center** (✉*City Hall, Queen St. at York St.* ☎*506/460–2129*) has a trail map.

SHOPPING

Indoor mammoth crafts markets are held in the fall and a Labor Day–weekend outdoor crafts fair (the New Brunswick Fine Crafts Festival) is held in Officers' Square.

★ **Aitkens Pewter** (✉*408 Queen St.* ☎*506/453–9474*) makes its own pewter goblets, belt buckles, candlesticks, and jewelry. **Gallery 78** (✉*976 Queen St.* ☎*506/454–5192*) has original works by Atlantic Canadian artists. **String Fever Textiles** (✉*Queen St., at the York Sunbury Museum in the Historic Garrison District* ☎*506/443–9119*) is a unique retail gallery featuring works by top textile artists from throughout the province. **Think Play** (✉*59 York St.* ☎*506/472–7529*) has funky toys and games that appeal to all ages.

12

GAGETOWN

50 km (31 mi) southeast of Fredericton. Rte. 2 is fast and direct; Rte. 102 from Fredericton is scenic.

Historic Gagetown bustles in summer, when artists welcome visitors, many of whom arrive by boat and tie up at the marina, to their studios and galleries.

The **Queens County Museum** is growing by leaps and bounds. Its original building, **Tilley House** (a National Historic Site) was the birthplace of Sir Leonard Tilley, one of the Fathers of Confederation. It displays Loyalist and First Nations artifacts, early-20th-century medical equipment, Victorian glassware, and more. The nearby old **Queens County Courthouse** (✉*Courthouse Rd.* ☎*506/488–2483*) is part of the museum and has archival material and courthouse furniture, as well as changing exhibits. ✉*Front St.* ☎*506/488–2483* *$2 for one building, $3 for both buildings* ⏲*Mid-June–mid-Sept., daily 10–5.*

WHERE TO STAY

¢–$ **Step-Aside B&B.** This waterfront heritage B&B in the heart of the village overlooks the marina. There are some lovely antiques, and the rooms are bright and cheerful. Two of them are in the original house, and two more are in a modern addition. ✉*58 Front St., E5M 1A1* ☎*506/488–1808* 🌐*www.bbcanada.com/6860.html* *4 rooms* *In-room: no a/c, no TV. In-hotel: no-smoking rooms, no elevator* *V* ⏲*Closed Jan.–Apr.* *BP.*

SHOPPING

Grimross Crafts (✉*17 Mill Rd.* ☎*506/488–2832*) represents 25 area craftspeople. **Flo Grieg's** (✉*36 Front St.* ☎*506/488–2074*) carries superior pottery made on the premises. **Juggler's Cove** (✉*27 Front St.* ☎*506/488–2574*) is a studio-gallery featuring pottery, paintings, and woodwork. **Loomcrofters** (✉*23 Loomcroft La., an extension of Tilly Rd.* ☎*506/488–2400*) is a good choice for handwoven items.

NEW BRUNSWICK ESSENTIALS

To research prices, get advice from other travelers, and book travel arrangements, visit www.fodors.com.

TRANSPORTATION

BY AIR

Airports in Saint John, Moncton, and Fredericton are served by Air Canada and Air Canada's Jazz. Moncton is also served by WestJet, and Lufthansa; Fredericton also has Delta service to and from Boston.

New Brunswick has three major airports. Saint John Airport is about 15 minutes east of downtown. Moncton Airport is about 10 minutes east of downtown. Fredericton Airport is 10 minutes east of downtown.

Contacts Fredericton Airport (✉ *Lincoln Rd., Lincoln* ☎ *506/460–0920* 🌐 *www.frederictonairport.ca*). **Moncton Airport** (✉ *Champlain Rd., Dieppe* ☎ *506/856–5444* 🌐 *www.gma.ca*). **Saint John Airport** (✉ *Loch Lomond Rd.* ☎ *506/638–5555* 🌐 *www.saintjohnairport.com*).

BY BOAT & FERRY

Bay Ferries Ltd. runs from Saint John, New Brunswick, to Digby, Nova Scotia, return, once or twice a day, depending on the season. The ferry *Princess of Acadia* has been tastefully refurbished with a library, the cozy Sea Breeze lounge, and the "Little Mates Quarters" play station for kids. Passenger fares are $30 for an adult; it's $80 for a car, plus $20 fuel surcharge for the three-hour, one-way trip July through September. Off season rates are cheaper.

Deer Island Ferries run from Deer Island, New Brunswick, to Campobello, New Brunswick, and Eastport, Maine.

Coastal Transport has up to seven crossings per day from Black's Harbour to Grand Manan in July and August. Round-trip fares, payable on the Grand Manan side, are $31.40 for a car and $10.50 for an adult. A one-way crossing takes about 1½ hours. The half-hour ferry crossing from Letete to Deer Island is free. The July and August crossing from Deer Island to Campobello takes about 40 minutes. The car and driver fare is $13; passenger fares are $2.

Contacts Bay Ferries Ltd. (☎ *902/245–2116 or 888/249–7245* 🌐 *www.nfl-bay.com*). **Deer Island Ferries** (☎ *506/747–2159 or 877/747–2159* 🌐 *www.deerisland.nb.ca/ferries.htm*). **Coastal Transport** (☎ *506/662–3724 Ext. 1* 🌐 *www.coastaltransport.ca*).

BY BUS

Acadian Lines runs buses within the province and connects with most major bus lines.

Contacts Acadian Lines (☎ *506/870–4852 or 800/567–5151* 🌐 *www.acadianbus.com*).

BY CAR

Several car-rental agencies serve New Brunswick; call or visit the Web sites to search for pick-up and drop-off locations throughout the province.

From Québec, the Trans-Canada Highway (Route 2) enters New Brunswick at St-Jacques and follows the St. John River through Fredericton and on to Moncton and the Nova Scotia border. From Maine, Interstate 95 crosses at Houlton to Woodstock, New Brunswick, where it connects with the Trans-Canada Highway. Those traveling up the coast of Maine on Route 1 cross at Calais to St. Stephen, New Brunswick. New Brunswick's Route 1 extends through Saint John and Sussex to join the Trans-Canada Highway near Moncton.

New Brunswick has an excellent highway system with numerous facilities. The Trans-Canada Highway, marked by a maple leaf, is the same as Route 2. Route 7 joins Saint John and Fredericton. Fredericton is connected to Miramichi City by Route 8. Route 15 links

Moncton to the eastern coast and to Route 11, which follows the coast to Miramichi City, around the Acadian Peninsula, and up to Campbellton. Get a good map at a visitor information center. Tourism New Brunswick has mapped five scenic routes: the Fundy Coastal Drive, the River Valley Scenic Drive, the Acadian Coastal Drive, the Miramichi River Route, and the Appalachian Range.

BY TRAIN

VIA Rail offers passenger service every day but Tuesday from Campbellton, Newcastle, and Moncton to Montréal and Halifax.

CONTACTS & RESOURCES

EMERGENCIES

Emergency Services **Ambulance, fire, police** (☎ *911*).

Hospitals **Campbellton Regional Hospital** (✉ *189 Lilly Lake Rd., Campbellton* ☎ *506/789–5000*). **Chaleur Regional Hospital** (✉ *1750 Sunset Dr., Bathurst* ☎ *506/548–8961*). **Dr. Everett Chalmers Hospital** (✉ *Priestman St., Fredericton* ☎ *506/452–5400*). **Dr. Georges Dumont Hospital** (✉ *330 Archibald St., Moncton* ☎ *506/862–4000*). **Edmundston Regional Hospital** (✉ *275 Hébert Blvd., Edmundston* ☎ *506/739–2200*). **Miramichi Regional Hospital** (✉ *500 Water St., Miramichi City* ☎ *506/623–3000*). **Moncton City Hospital** (✉ *135 MacBeath Ave., Moncton* ☎ *506/857–5111*). **Saint John Regional Hospital** (✉ *Tucker Park Rd., Saint John* ☎ *506/648–6000*).

SPORTS & OUTDOORS

Whale-watching, sea kayaking, bird-watching, scuba diving, garden touring, river cruising, and fishing are just a few of the province's great experiences. Contact Tourism New Brunswick for details.

Information **Tourism New Brunswick** (☎ *800/561–0123* 🌐 *www.tourismnewbrunswick.ca*).

BICYCLING B&Bs frequently have bicycles for rent. Tourism New Brunswick has listings and free cycling maps. Baymount Outdoor Adventures operates bicycle tours for large groups along the Fundy shore near Hopewell Cape.

Contacts **Baymount Outdoor Adventures** (✉ *17 Elwin Jay Dr., Hillsborough* ☎ *506/734–2660*). **Tourism New Brunswick** (☎ *800/561–0123* 🌐 *www.tourismnewbrunswick.ca*).

FISHING New Brunswick Fish and Wildlife has information on sporting licenses and can tell you where the fish are.

Contact **New Brunswick Fish and Wildlife** (☎ *506/453–2440*).

GOLF The most up-to-date information about new courses and upgrades to existing courses is available at the New Brunswick Golf Association.

Contact **New Brunswick Golf Association** (☎ *506/451–1349 or 877/833–4662* 🌐 *www.golfnb.com*).

HIKING The New Brunswick Trails Council has complete information on the province's burgeoning trail system.

Contact New Brunswick Trails Council (☎ *506/459–1931 or 800/526–7070* 🌐 *www.sentiernbtrail.com*).

TOURS

City of Saint John visitor information centers have brochures for three good self-guided walking tours. Rockwood Park Stables in Saint John has 4-passenger horse-drawn carriages ($65/hour) and 14-passenger trollies ($184/hour) for rent, and offers rides anywhere in the city.

Contacts City of St. John (☎ *506/658–2855*). **Rockwood Park Stables** (☎ *506/633–7659*).

VISITOR INFORMATION

Tourism New Brunswick can provide information on day adventures, scenic driving routes, accommodations, and the seven provincial tourist bureaus. Also helpful are the information services in large centers like Bathurst, Edmundston, St-Jacques, Fredericton, Grand Falls, Moncton, St. Andrews, Saint John, and St. Stephen.

Contacts City of Bathurst (☎ *506/548–0400* 🌐 *www.bathurst.ca*). **Edmundston–St-Jacques Tourism** (☎ *506/735–2747*). **Fredericton Tourism** (☎ *506/460–2041, 506/460–2129, or 888/888–4768*). **Go Moncton** (☎ *800/363–4558* 🌐 *www.gomoncton.com*). **St. Andrews Chamber of Commerce** (✉ *46 Reed Ave., St. Andrews* ☎ *506/529–3555, 506/529–3556, or 800/563–7397*). **Tourism New Brunswick** (📫 *Box 12345, Fredericton E3B 5C3* ☎ *800/561–0123* 🌐 *www.tourismnbcanada.com*). **Tourism Saint John** (☎ *506/658–2990 or 866/463–8639* 🌐 *www.tourismsaintjohn.com*). **Town of Grand Falls** (🌐 *www.grandfalls.com*). **Town of St. Stephen** (✉ *34 Milltown Blvd., St. Stephen* ☎ *506/466–7700* 🌐 *www.town.ststephen.nb.ca*).

Prince Edward Island

WORD OF MOUTH

"You must see the Anne of Green Gables 'home' [Green Gables, in Cavendish] . . . I believe it is illegal to go to PEI and NOT visit."

—LJ 09/07

www.fodors.com/forums

Updated by Jeff Bursey

AN ENCHANTING MEDLEY OF RICH COLOR, Prince Edward Island is a unique landmass with verdant patchwork fields that stretch out beneath an endless cobalt sky to meet the surrounding sea. At just 195 km (121 mi) long and 61¼ km (38 mi) wide, the accessible size is part of the Island's appeal. Warm hospitality welcomes you, and the laid-back, slow-paced Island lifestyle entices visitors back year after year. Almost every attraction and property is family-owned and -operated.

The Confederation Bridge, linking Prince Edward Island's Borden-Carleton with New Brunswick's Cape Jourimain, physically seals the Island's connection with the mainland. To create this engineering marvel, massive concrete pillars—65 feet across and 180 feet high—were sunk into waters more than 110 feet deep to cope with traffic that now brings more than 1 million visitors annually. When the bridge first opened in 1997, some residents feared the loss of the Island's tranquility, and as you explore the villages and fishing ports, it's not hard to understand why. Outside the tourist mecca of Cavendish, otherwise known as Anne's Land, the Island seems like an oasis of peace in an increasingly busy world. Fears have diminished a lot over the years, and the bridge has moved into its second decade, still an engineering marvel and a great boon to travel, commerce, and culture. An influx of visitors, and the greater ability for islanders to visit other places, has increased the cross-pollination of ideas and made Prince Edward Island more easily accessible.

EXPLORING PRINCE EDWARD ISLAND

A car, motorcycle, or moped is essential, as there is little public transport across the Island, though there is now municipal bus service in Charlottetown. If your plan is to set up camp in Charlottetown, renting a car after flying in is a good option. In the summer, bicyclists can enjoy the scenery, and it can be quite enjoyable to tour the Island that way. If you are touring Atlantic Canada, you can bring your car with you, you can cross by ferry from Caribou, Nova Scotia, to Wood Islands in Kings County, or by the Confederation Bridge, from Cape Jourimain in New Brunswick, to Borden-Carleton in Queens County.

ABOUT THE HOTELS & RESTAURANTS

Full-service resorts, luxury hotels, family-run farms, and moderately priced motels, cottages, and lodges are just some of your choices in PEI. Book three to six months in advance for July and August.

Dining in one of PEI's restaurants is always a casual, relaxed experience even in fine dining establishments. All restaurants, cafés, and pubs are non-smoking. Water views are not hard to come by.

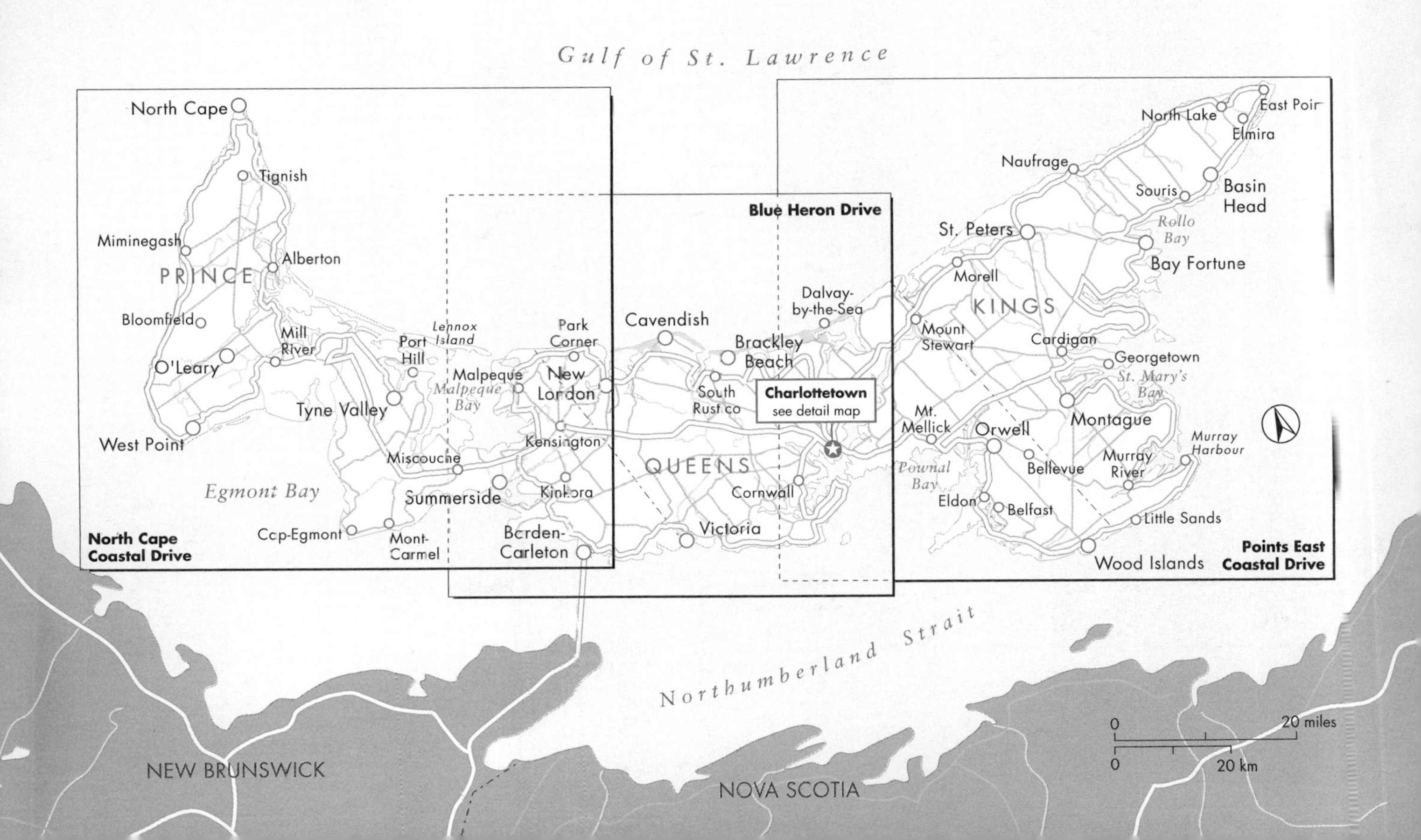
Gulf of St. Lawrence
North Cape
Tignish
Miminegash
Alberton
PRINCE
Bloomfield
Mill River
O'Leary
West Point
Tyne Valley
Port Hill
Lennox Island
Egmont Bay
Ccp-Egmont
Mont-Carmel
Miscouche
Summerside
Malpeque
Malpeque Bay
North Cape Coastal Drive
Park Corner
New London
Kensington
Kinkora
Borden-Carleton
Blue Heron Drive
Cavendish
Brackley Beach
South Rustico
Dalvay-by-the-Sea
Charlottetown
see detail map
QUEENS
Cornwall
Victoria
St. Peters
Naufrage
North Lake
East Poir
Elmira
Souris
Basin Head
Rollo Bay
Bay Fortune
Morell
KINGS
Mount Stewart
Cardigan
Georgetown
St. Mary's Bay
Montague
Mt. Mellick
Orwell
Pownal Bay
Bellevue
Murray River
Murray Harbour
Eldon
Belfast
Little Sands
Wood Islands
Points East Coastal Drive
Northumberland Strait
NEW BRUNSWICK
NOVA SCOTIA
0
20 miles
0
20 km

TOP REASONS TO GO

BEACH, OCEAN, PEACE
Endless sandy beaches; walk, wade, or bodysurf in the ocean, then settle in under the sun.

GREEN GRASS, RED CLAY, BLUE SKY
Admire the colorful fields, or a sky that looks like it was painted that morning.

SEAFOOD THAT STILL TASTES LIKE THE SEA
Fresh from the nets, this is nothing like the frozen-fish sticks of your childhood.

ANNE OF GREEN GABLES
The orphan that nobody wanted has been adopted by the world; she's at conferences, festivals, and in musicals.

GET PHYSICAL
Water to kayak, paths to hike, and trails to bike; reconnect with Mother Nature.

WHAT IT COSTS IN CANADIAN DOLLARS

	¢	$	$$	$$$	$$$$
RESTAURANTS	under C$8	C$8–C$12	C$13–C$20	C$21–C$30	over C$30
HOTELS	under C$75	C$75–C$125	C$126–C$175	C$176–C$250	over C$250

Restaurant prices are per person for a main course at dinner. Hotel prices are for two people in a standard double room in high season, excluding tax.

CHARLOTTETOWN

Prince Edward Island's oldest city is peppered with gingerbread-clad Victorian houses and tree-shaded squares. The population is 33,000.

While suburbs were springing up, the city core remained unchanged, and the waterfront has been restored to recapture an earlier flavor. Visit Peake's Wharf and Confederation Landing Park, with their informal restaurants and shops, as well as a walking path leading visitors through some of the most interesting historical areas of the Old City.

EXPLORING CHARLOTTETOWN

Walking is the best way to explore Charlottetown's historic homes and churches. Walk & Sea Charlottetown *www.walkandseacharlottetown.com* has developed activity packages of varying length that include theater shows, bicycling, and dining, among other activities. Pick up *Take a Jaunt* brochure at a visitor center or when you get settled in your room.

WHAT TO SEE

9  **Beaconsfield Historic House.** Built in 1877, this Victorian home is one of the Island's finest. You can tour the first and second floors and enjoy views of the garden and Charlottetown Harbour. A carriage house on

GREAT ITINERARIES

IF YOU HAVE 1 DAY

Leaving **Charlottetown** on Route 2 west, take Route 15 north to **Brackley Beach**. This puts you onto a 137-km-long (85-mi-long) scenic drive. Blue Heron Drive (Route 20) takes you to the Anne of Green Gables Museum in Park Corner. Go south on Route 20 to Route 2 south (at Kensington) and turn onto Route 1A east (at Travellers Rest). Follow the Trans-Canada Highway (Route 1) east back to Charlottetown. At seaside **Victoria**, enjoy this village's restaurants and crafts shops.

IF YOU HAVE 3 DAYS

Explore the historic sites of **Summerside** before following North Cape Coastal Drive through Acadian country to Miscouche. Leave midafternoon and take Route 12 to the scenic and peaceful **Tyne Valley**. From here, visit the Mi'Kmaq community at Lennox Island. On Day 3, make your way to **North Cape** and explore its reef and the Atlantic Wind Test Site and Interpretive Centre. Plan to arrive early in the afternoon at **West Point**, where you can enjoy walking trails and visit the lighthouse.

IF YOU HAVE 7 DAYS

After shopping in **Charlottetown**, take Route 10 to **Victoria**. Enjoy lunch at one of this tiny village's three restaurants, then visit the chocolate shop. Continue to the restored stone train station at Kensington. The next day, drive north to Woodleigh Replicas in Burlington. Head east for lunch and fun in **Cavendish**. Start Day 3 at Green Gables and end at scenic **Prince Edward Island National Park**. On Day 4, visit the Anne of Green Gables Museum in Park Corner. Then follow Blue Heron Drive to **Summerside** for a performance at the Jubilee Theatre. The next day, take North Cape Coastal Drive (Route 11) to Cap-Egmont to view the bottle houses. Continue on to Route 178 and **Tyne Valley**. In nearby **Port Hill**, wander through the Shipbuilding Museum. Don't miss the Mi'Kmaq handicrafts on Lennox Island, off Route 12 on Route 163. End the day at **North Cape**, overlooking one of the world's longest natural rock reefs. On Day 6, hike or bike along the Confederation Trail, which begins at Mile 0 in Tignish. Complete your tour at **West Point**, whose lighthouse-museum has guest rooms.

the grounds has a children's festival on weekday mornings during July and August **Beaconsfield Children's Festival** in July and August (call for exact times and price). ✉ *2 Kent St.* ☎ *902/368–6603* 🌐 *www.peimuseum.com* 🎟 *$4.25* ⏲ *Sept.–June, call for hours; July and Aug., daily 10–5.*

⑩ **Charlottetown Driving Park Entertainment Centre.** Since 1880 this track has been the home of harness racing. The Centre also features Texas Hold'em Poker and a simulcast theater. August features **Old Home Week,** when eastern Canada's best converge for 15 races in eight days. Old Home Week also brings the provincial agricultural exhibition and an entertainment midway to the Park. ✉ *21 Exhibition Dr.* ☎ *902/620–4222* 🌐 *www.cdpec.ca* 🎟 *Free* ⏲ *Races Apr.–Jan., schedule varies. Old Home Week, mid-Aug., Mon.–Sat. twice daily.*

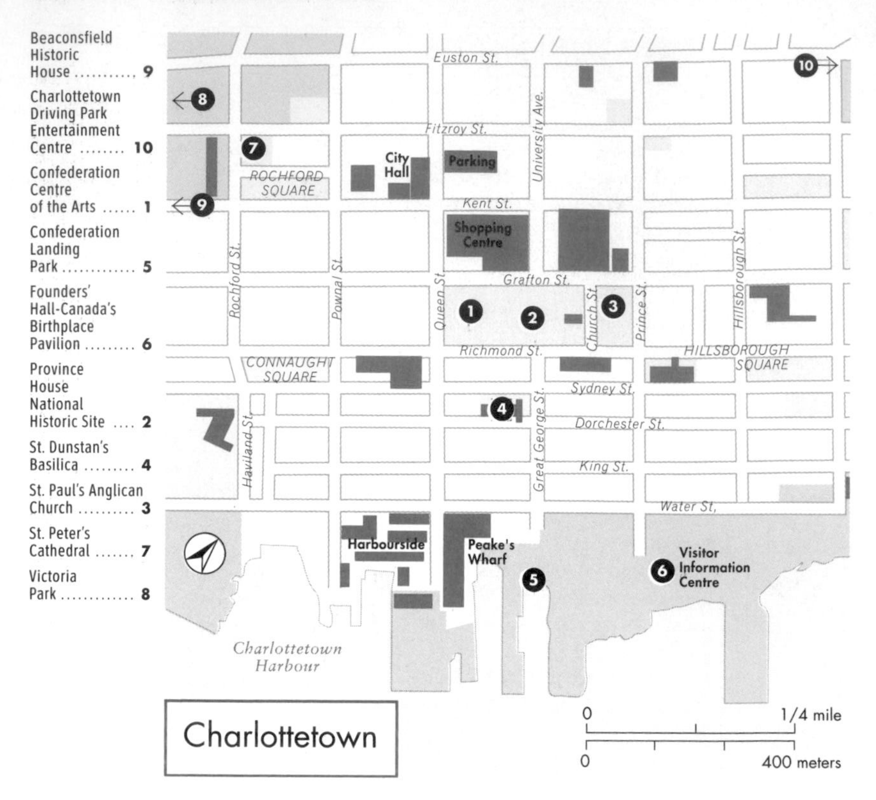

❶ **Confederation Centre of the Arts.** The Confederation Centre of the Arts houses a 1,102-seat main-stage theater, a 1,000-seat outdoor amphitheater, and a 190-seat second-stage theater off-site. The Centre is most famous for the **Charlottetown Festival,** which runs from mid-June to September, with concerts, comedy performances, and musical-theater productions, including *Anne of Green Gables—The Musical*™. During fall and winter, the Centre presents touring and local productions, while the art gallery has a year-round exhibition program showcasing contemporary and historical Canadian art. ✉ *145 Richmond St.* ☎ *902/566–1267 or 800/565–0278* 🌐 *www.confederationcentre.com* ⏲ *Oct.–May, daily 8–10; hrs extended June–Sept.*

❺ **Confederation Landing Park.** This waterfront recreation area at the bottom of Great George Street marks the site of the historic landing of the Fathers of Confederation in 1864. Walkways and park benches offer vantage points to survey the activity of the harbor, with the added attraction of banks of fragrant wild rose bushes. **Peake's Wharf,** right next to the park, has casual restaurants, bars, souvenir and crafts shops, and a marina where boat tours may be arranged. ✉ *Water St. between Queen and Hillsborough Sts.* 🎟 *Free* ⏲ *Daily dawn–dusk.*

St. Dunstan's Basilica. St. Dunstan's is the seat of the Roman Catholic diocese on the Island and is known for its fine Italian carvings and twin Gothic spires. *Great George St. 902/894–3486 www.stdunstans.pe.ca.*

WORD OF MOUTH

"[Confederation Centre of the Arts] is only a few minutes' walk up to Province House and the Confederation Centre. The art gallery at the centre has some really well curated and interesting exhibits, surprising for such a small venue. The craft shop is nice too with lots of local products." —lucyp

Founders' Hall—Canada's Birthplace Pavilion. State-of-the-art displays at this 21,000-square-foot interpretive center merge high-tech with history in the "Time Travel Tunnel" that transports visitors back to the Charlottetown Conference of 1864. The Charlottetown Visitor Information Centre dispenses maps, brochures, and advice; you can also purchase dinner reservations and theater tickets there. *Historic Charlottetown Waterfront, 6 Price St. 902/368–1864 or 800/955–1864 www.foundershall.ca $7 Feb.–Apr., weekdays 10–3; early–mid-May, Tues.–Sat. 9–3:30; mid-May–mid-Oct., daily 8:30–4 or later in summer; mid-Oct.–Nov., Tues.–Fri. 9–3 Closed Dec. and Jan.*

NEED A BREAK?

Cows Ice Cream (*Queen St. 902/892–6969 www.cows.ca Peake's Wharf 902/566–4886*) is the most famous ice cream on the Island. Fresh milk from Prince Edward Island cows is carefully combined with other natural ingredients to create over 30 delightful flavors. Buy some of their humorously captioned cow-embellished T-shirts. Cows Ice Cream can also be found at Cavendish (on Rte. 6), in Summerside (Water St., across from Spinnaker's Landing), in PEI Factory Shops in North River, in Gateway Village at the approach to the Confederation Bridge, and on board the PEI–Nova Scotia passenger ferry, The Confederation.

St. Paul's Anglican Church. Large sandstone blocks give it a heavy exterior, but the interior soars, largely because of the vaulted ceilings. It seats only 450, but appears much larger. Some of the stained glass dates back to the 19th century. *101 Prince St. 902/892–1691 www.stpaulschurch.ca Weekdays 9–5.*

St. Peter's Cathedral. Inside it is **All Souls' Chapel,** a true gem that's attached to the side of the cathedral. It may be open for viewing by chance; if not, inquire inside the cathedral. *Rochford St. 902/566–2102 Weekdays 9–5.*

Province House National Historic Site. This three-story sandstone building, completed in 1847 to house the colonial government and now the seat of the Provincial Legislature, has been restored to its mid-19th-century Victorian appearance, including the historic Confederation Chamber, where representatives of the 19th-century British colonies met. A short historic film explains the significance of the meeting. Visitors to the public gallery of the Legislature are always welcome, and you might even see local politicians in debate. *Richmond St.*

LOCAL DINING & LODGING

Full-service resorts, luxury hotels, family-run farms, and moderately priced motels, cottages, and lodges are just some of the choices in Prince Edward Island. Due to the sandy composition of the land elevators are few, but accommodations' staff are always ready to help with luggage. Book camp and hotel accommodations three to six months in advance for July and August.

In the last few years, new restaurants have opened up in Charlottetown. You can eat Indian, Italian, French, Lebanese, or Canadian with a contemporary twist. English pubs are close to Asian teahouses. It's a casual, relaxed experience for diners, even in the finest places. All restaurants, cafés, and pubs are nonsmoking.

☎ *902/566–7626* *By donation* ⏲ *Mid-Oct.–May, weekdays 9–5; June–mid-Oct., daily 8:30–5.*

8 **Victoria Park.** At the southern tip of the city and overlooking Charlottetown Harbour are 40 beautiful acres in which to wander, picnic, or watch a baseball game. Next to the park, on a hill between groves of white birches, is the white colonial **Government House.** Built in 1832 as the official residence for the province's lieutenant governors, it's open weekdays 10 to 4, with entry by donation. There is a playground, a pool, and a water-play area at the northwest entrance to the park. Runners or walkers can take advantage of the boardwalk that edges the harbor. ✉ *Lower Kent St.* ⏲ *Daily sunrise–sunset.*

WHERE TO STAY & EAT

$$–$$$ ★ ✕ **Claddagh Oyster House.** Urban meets rural in this upscale restaurant. Seafood is a speciality—the mussels and whitefish are particularly good—and there's also beef, chicken, and pork dishes. Upstairs, the Olde Dublin Pub showcases live musical entertainment from mid-June to mid-September. ✉ *131 Sydney St.* ☎ *902/892–6992* ▭ *AE, DC, MC, V.*

$$–$$$ ✕ **Sims Corner Steakhouse and Wine Bar.** This new restaurant provides a wide selection of choice Canadian AAA beef as well as an impressive all-Island oyster bar. They use fresh local produce, and the menu contains celiac-friendly items. Wander into the wine bar to select a nightcap from perhaps the Island's biggest selection of Old and New World wines. ✉ *86 Queen St.* ☎ *902/894–7467* ▭ *AE, DC, MC, V* ⏲ *No lunch.*

$–$$$ ✕ **Merchantman Pub.** Located in a 19th-century building with original brick and open-beam ceilings, this pub has all the traditional favorites. The dinner menu is contemporary and contains Island products from land and sea, including seafood and beef. Local and imported draft beer is on tap. ✉ *Queen and Water Sts.* ☎ *902/892–9150* ▭ *AE, MC, V.*

$–$$$ ★ ✕ **Sirenella Ristorante.** Specializing in northern Italian cuisine, this restaurant has no local equal. The menu changes twice a year. Owner Italo Marzari is behind each delightful dish—using Island vegetables, beef, pork, and seafood extensively—and he handpicks the Italian wines. ✉ *83 Water St.* ☎ *902/628–2271* ▭ *AE, DC, MC, V* ⊗ *Closed Jan.*

¢ ★ ✕ **Interlude Café.** This cozy restaurant has a devoted clientele who love the combination of Asian spiced meat, seafood, and tofu with fruit and Island potatoes. They're all homemade by Ally, and served with black, green, and bubble teas direct from Taiwan. Fruit chillers and yogurt drinks are better than most places' desserts. The unique decor includes 150-year-old windows and an 800-year-old bench that was once the root system of a tree. ✉ *223 University Ave.* ☎ *902/367–3055* ▭ *No credit cards* ⊗ *Closed weekends.*

13

$–$$$ ✕ **Dundee Arms Inn.** Depending on your mood, you can choose to stay in either a 1960s motel or a 1903 Queen Anne–style inn. The motel is modern and neat; the inn is homey. All suites have double Jacuzzis; two have working fireplaces. The Dundee Arms is located downtown. The Griffon Dining Room ($$–$$$$) serves French Continental cuisine; the Hearth and Cricket Pub ($–$$) serves hearty British fare and a good assortment of beers. ✉ *200 Pownal St., C1A 3W8* ☎ *902/892–2496 or 877/638–6333* 🖷 *902/368–8532* 🌐 *www.dundeearms.com* *18 rooms, 34 suites* *In-room: dial-up, Wi-Fi. In-hotel: 2 restaurants, bar, no-smoking rooms* ▭ *AE, MC, V.*

$$–$$$$ **Delta Prince Edward Hotel.** Located next to Peake's Wharf, this hotel is ideally located for exploration of the historic downtown areas. It has the comforts and luxuries familiar to Delta hotels. The restaurant has an international menu. Recreation facilities include an indoor pool, indoor and outdoor hot tubs, and a tanning booth. Two-thirds of the guest rooms in the 10-story hotel have waterfront views. ✉ *18 Queen St., Box 2170, C1A 8B9* ☎ *902/566–2222 or 866/894–1203* 🖷 *902/566–1745* 🌐 *www.deltaprinceedward.pe.ca* *211 rooms, 33 suites* *In-room: dial-up. In-hotel: restaurant, room service, bar, pool, gym, spa, laundry facilities, laundry service, concierge, public Wi-Fi, parking (fee), no-smoking rooms, some pets allowed (fee)* ▭ *AE, DC, MC, V.*

$$–$$$$ Fodor's Choice ★ **Fairholm National Historic Inn.** Fairholm has seven spaciously elegant rooms that include fireplaces; some rooms have whirlpool tubs. Enhanced with inlaid-hardwood floors, antiques, Island art, and wallpaper imported from England, this inn joins together British roots and Island hospitality. It's close to the waterfront, shopping, restaurants, and theater. ✉ *230 Prince St., C1A 4S1* ☎ *902/892–5022 or 888/573–5022* 🖷 *902/892–5060* 🌐 *www.fairholm.pe.ca* *7 rooms* *In room: DVDs, Wi-Fi. In hotel: no-smoking rooms* ▭ *AE, MC, V* *BP.*

$$–$$$$ ★ **The Great George.** This complex includes historic 1800s structures: the 24-room Pavilion, the 5-room Wellington/Carriage House, and two romantic hideaway suites. A Continental breakfast buffet is presented in the Pavilion reception area. The town houses can accommodate families or groups; the Charlotte Club is a floor dedicated to women business travelers. Breadth of room choice makes this a luxurious, must-stay destination. ✉ *58 Great George St., C1A 4K3* ☎ *902/892–0606 or 800/361–1118* 🖷 *902/628–2079* 🌐 *www.thegreatgeorge.com* *25 rooms, 20 suites, 10 houses* *In-room: Dial up In-hotel: gym, public Wi-Fi, no-smoking rooms* ▭ *AE, DC, MC, V* *CP.*

¢–$ **Sherwood Motel.** Don't be daunted by the Sherwood's proximity to the airport—very little traffic passes in front of this property. There are 28 motel rooms in the main building and 18 units in the newer motor inn behind the motel. ✉*281 Brackley Point Rd.–Rte. 15, 5 km (3 mi) north of downtown Charlottetown, C1E 2A3* ☎*902/892–1622 or 800/567–1622* 🌐*www.canadaselect.com* *46 rooms* *In-room: kitchen (some), Wi-Fi (some). In-hotel: some pets allowed, no-smoking rooms* ▭*MC, V.*

NIGHTLIFE & THE ARTS

★ For complete and current listings of entertainment events pick up a free copy of *The Buzz,* available at most hotels and restaurants, and in many newstands. For a quiet drink try **Mavor's** (✉*Grafton St.* ☎*902/628–6107*), in Confederation Centre. Escape summer heat in the outdoor courtyard or retreat to the suave interior for a Starbucks coffee.

SPORTS & THE OUTDOORS

BICYCLING

There are several companies in Charlottetown that offer bicycle repairs and rentals as well as offer helpful suggestions on good city bicycle tours, among them **Smooth Cycle** (✉*308 Queen St.* ☎*902/566–5530*).

GOLF

The 27-hole **Dog River Golf Links** (✉*472 Clyde River Road RR #2, off Route 1, Clyde River* ☎*902/675–2585, 902/675–4602 off-season*) is 13 km (8 mi) from town. The only 27-hole course on the Island is divided into a linked course of 18 (par 71) and a separate 9 (par 35). The course, its clubhouse and its restaurant, are open from mid-April to the end of October.

The 18-hole **Fox Meadow Golf and Country Club** (✉*167 Kinlock Rd., Stratford* ☎*902/569–4653*) is 5 km (3 mi) from town. The challenging par-72 championship course was designed by Rob Heaslip and overlooks the community of Stratford and Charlottetown Harbour.

WATER SPORTS

You can arrange pick-up service from your hotel for north shore sea kayaking. A good way to discover the area's natural beauty is to contact **Outside Expeditions** (✉*370 Harbourview Dr., 8 km [5 mi] east of Cavendish, North Rustico* ☎*902/963–3366 or 800/207–3899* 🌐*www.getoutside.com*).

SHOPPING

The most interesting shops are on Peake's Wharf, along Victoria Row (the section of Richmond Street between Queen and Great George streets), and on Water Street.

The **Charlottetown Farmer's Market** (✉*100 Belvedere Ave.* ☎*902/626–3733*), held Saturday year-round and also Wednesday during the sum-

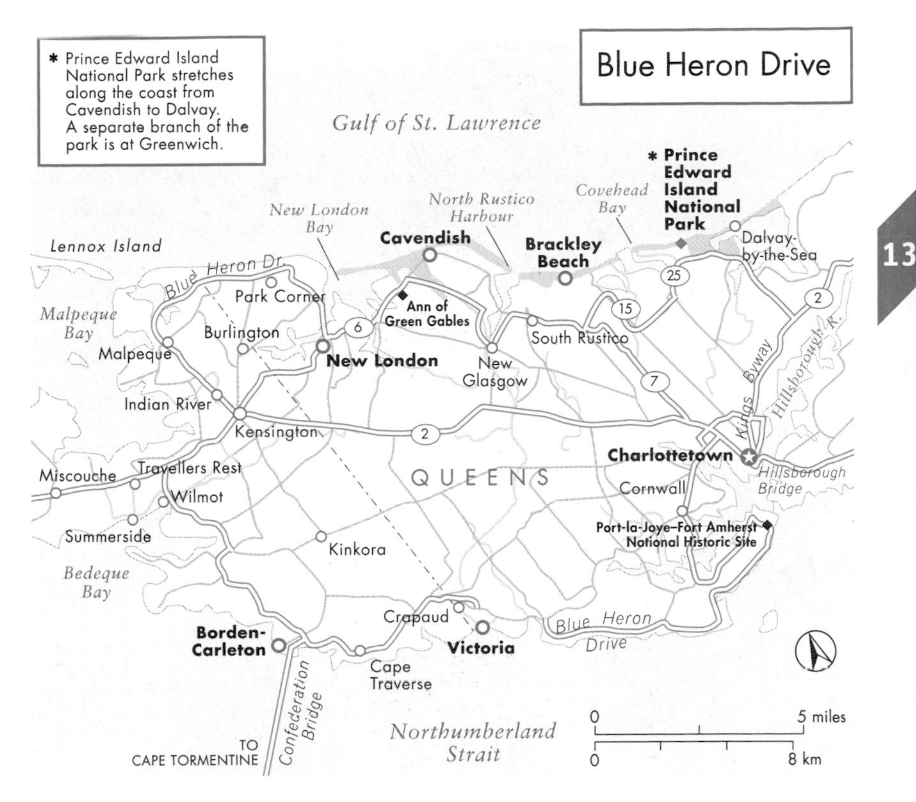

mer months, offers Island-made crafts, along with ethnic foods and local produce. At **Just Us Girls** (✉ *100 Queen St.* ☎ *902/566–1285*) you'll find international clothing, gourmet food in the café, and Italian gelato. Next door, **Best of PEI** (✉ *156 Richmond St.* ☎ *902/368–8835*) is your one stop for Island-made pottery, woodwork, crafts and glassware. **Moonsnail Soapworks and Aromatherapy** (✉ *85 Water St.* ☎ *902/892–7627 or 888/771–7627*) produces handmade soaps and a full line of natural body-care products that contain herbs, spices, and pure essential oils for scent. **Firehorse Studios** (✉ *89 Water St.* ☎ *902/368–3378*) features fused, custom, and stained glass from local artists, as well as paintings.

BLUE HERON DRIVE

The Blue Heron Drive follows Route 15 north to the north shore, then winds along Route 6 through Anne of Green Gables country. The northern section around the Green Gables farmhouse is cluttered with commercial tourist operations, but unspoiled beauty still exists in the magnificent sunsets, refreshing open spaces, and everchanging sculpted coastline.

PRINCE EDWARD ISLAND NATIONAL PARK

Fodor's Choice ★ *24 km (15 mi) north of Charlottetown.*

Prince Edward Island National Park is where sky and sea meet long stretches of sand. The national park stretches more than 40 km (25 mi) along the north shore of the Island, from Cavendish to Tracadie Bay, plus a separate extension, about 24 km (15 mi) farther east at Greenwich.

Cavendish Grove, off Route 6, occupies the former home of a 16-hectare amusement park, which Parks Canada bought in 2005. Park here and you have a pleasant 25-minute tree-lined walk to the beach. Picnic in the grove and listen to songbirds. Call Parks Canada in spring and summer for rates and schedules if you are planning a camping trip. The national park has two campgrounds, Cavendish and Stanhope, which are in walking distance of beaches. Fees and seasons vary. For campground reservations, visit www.pccamping.ca or call 877/737–3783. ☎*902/672–6350* ⊕*www.pc.gc.ca* *$7, $17 for family* *Daily dawn–dusk.*

WHERE TO STAY & EAT

$$–$$$$ Fodor's Choice ★ ✕ **Dayboat.** Sean Furlong is a young chef with a budding master's eye for texture, design, and layout, combined with an appreciation for fresh produce, much of which comes off Island farms or out of the nearby waters. The menu is surprising and the portions are generous. Steak, seafood, fresh vegetables—they're all treated with care and imagination. The desserts are scrumptious. An added bonus is the view up the Wheatley River; in fine weather you can dine on the large deck. ✉*Rte. 6, Oyster Bed Bridge* *5033 Rustico Rd., Hunter River R.R.3, C0A 1N0* ☎*902/963–3833* *AE, MC, V* *Oct.–May.*

$$$–$$$$ **Dalvay-by-the-Sea.** This Victorian house was built in 1895. Rooms are furnished with antiques and reproductions. Sip cocktails or tea on the porch while admiring the inn's gardens or Dalvay Lake. In addition to the inn's rooms, Dalvay also has eight upscale overnight cottages. There are no TVs in the rooms, and ocean breezes provide the air-conditioning. Park entrance fees apply. ✉*Rte. 6, near Dalvay Beach* *Box 8, PEI National Park, Grand Tracadie C0A 1P0* ☎*902/672–2048 or 888-366–2955* ⊕*www.dalvaybythesea.com* *26 rooms, 8 cottages* *In-room: no a/c, no TV. In-hotel: restaurant, bar, tennis court, bicycles, no-smoking rooms* *AE, DC, MC, V* *Closed mid-Oct.–early June* *MAP.*

$$–$$$$ **Blue Heron Hideaways Beach Houses.** Blue Heron comprises one six-bedroom beach house (sleeps 10) and one studio cottage, both on Point DeRoche's 10 km (6 mi) of white-ocean beach, a private beach. Two other beach houses, located about 5 km (3 mi) away at Blooming Point on Tracadie Bay, have views of the bay. One sleeps up to 9, the other up to 12. From mid-June to mid-September, both properties are rented by the week only; off-season, rentals as short as three days will be considered. ✉*Rte. 218, Point DeRoche C0A 1H0* ☎*902/566–2427* *902/368–3798* ⊕*www.blueheronhideaways.com* *3 houses, 1 cot-*

tage *In-room: no a/c, kitchen, refrigerator, VCR* *No credit cards* *Closed mid-Oct.–early June.*

> **WORD OF MOUTH**
>
> "[What are my top 6 things to do in PEI?] Three lobster dinners, two lobster lunches, and one lobster breakfast would be a good start. Each in a different location, of course." —BAK

CAMPING **Prince Edward Island National Park.** The park is on the north shore of PEI, running from Cavendish to Dalvay, and along part of the Greenwich Peninsula. Parks Canada runs two campsites at Cavendish and Stanhope. Some sites are serviced with kitchen shelters, electricity, and water and sewer. National park fees apply. Both sites feature hiking trails, playgrounds, and park activities on natural and cultural history. *902/672–6350* *Flush toilets, guest laundry, showers, play area* *www.pc.gc.ca* *AE, MC, V* *Closed late Aug.–mid-June.*

SPORTS & THE OUTDOORS

The **Links at Crowbush Cove** (*Off Rte. 2 on Rte. 350, Lakeside* *902/961–7306 or 800/235–8909*), an 18-hole, par-72 Scottish-style course with ocean views, is about 40 km (25 mi) east of the national park. The 18 holes of the links-style, par-72 course at **Stanhope Golf and Country Club** (*Off Rte. 6, Stanhope* *902/672–2842*) are among the most challenging and scenic on the Island. The course is a couple of miles west of Dalvay, along Covehead Bay.

BRACKLEY BEACH

15 km (9 mi) north of Charlottetown.

Brackley Beach offers a variety of country-style accommodations and eating establishments.

WHERE TO STAY & EAT

$$–$$$ Fodor's Choice ★ **Dunes Café.** A pottery studio and art gallery, with an annex housing clothing, furniture, and more, share space with this stunning café that offers an eclectic and delightful mix of seafood, lamb, beef, and vegetables. A full menu is offered in the lounge and on the patio overlooking the gardens with their amusing statuary. *Rte. 15, 1 km (½ mi) south of the national park, The Dunes, R.R.#9, Brackley Beach C1E 1Z3* *902/672–2586 for the café, 902/672–2586 for the gallery* *AE, MC, V* *Closed early Oct.–late May.*

$$$ ★ **Shaw's Hotel and Cottages.** This 1860s hotel has country elegance. Shaw's is one of only two remaining hotels on the Island that have been operating for more than a century. The hotel and cottages have bay vistas. Half the cottages have fireplaces; all have televisions. The restaurant ($$–$$$) has four-course menus of seafood, meats, and pastas. Seafood is served at the Sunday-evening buffet ($$$$). *Rte. 15, Brackley Beach C1E 1Z3* *902/672–2022* *902/672–3000* *www.shawshotel.ca* *14 rooms, 3 suites, 25 cottages* *In-room: no a/c, no TV (some). In-hotel: restaurant, bar, beachfront, bicycles, children's program (ages 3–12), no-smoking rooms* *AE, MC, V* *Closed early Oct.–May; 6 cottages open year-round* *MAP.*

CLOSE UP

Who Is Anne, Anyway?

Well, the first thing to remember is that it's Anne, spelled with an "e"—not Ann.

In Lucy Maud Montgomery's classic novel, first published in 1908, Marilla Cuthbert and her brother Matthew live on a farm in Prince Edward Island. They're getting on in years and decide to adopt an orphan boy to help out with the chores. It's with some surprise, then, that Matthew comes back from the train station with a feisty, eleven-year-old, redheaded girl, but it's not long before Anne—and her adventures and mishaps and friends—becomes an essential part of their lives.

Anne of Green Gables was made into a two-part television movie in 1985, starring Megan Follows. It was a huge success, airing first on the CBC in Canada, and then on PBS in the United States. It was followed by a television series which ran from 1990 to 1996.

SPORTS & THE OUTDOORS

Northshore Rentals (☒*Rte. 15 at Shaw's Hotel* ☏*902/672–2022*) rents canoes, river kayaks, peddleboats, and bicycles.

SHOPPING

The Dunes Studio Gallery (☒*Rte. 15 south of the national park* ☏*902/672–2586*), owned and run by Peter Jansons and his partner Nash, is a peaceful setting where you can buy clothing by Nash, with its Indonesian stylishness; pottery and furniture by Peter; works by acclaimed local artists; and the products of craftspeople from around the world.

CAVENDISH

21 km (13 mi) west of Brackley Beach.

Cavendish is the most-visited Island community outside Charlottetown because of the heavy influx of visitors to Green Gables and Prince Edward Island National Park. In 1908, Lucy Maud Montgomery (1874–1942) entered immortality as a beloved Canadian writer of fiction. Her novel *Anne of Green Gables* is enjoyed today by more fans than ever.

The **Site of Lucy Maud Montgomery's Cavendish Home** is where the writer lived with her maternal grandparents after the death of her mother. Though the foundation and surrounding white-picket fence of the home where Montgomery wrote *Anne of Green Gables* are all that remain, the homestead's fields and old apple-tree gardens provide lovely walking grounds. A bookstore and museum are operated by descendants of the family. This is a National Historic Site of Canada. ☒*Rte. 6, just east of Green Gables* ☏*902/963–2969* 🌐*www.peisland.com/lmm* 🎟*$4* ⏲*Mid-May–mid-Oct., daily 9–5.*

★ **Green Gables,** ½ km (¼ mi) west of Lucy Maud Montgomery's Cavendish homesite, is the green-and-white farmhouse that served as the setting for

Anne of Green Gables. It belonged to Montgomery's grandfather's cousins. The buildings and property re-create some of the settings found in the book, as do posted walking trails of the Haunted Wood (1 km [½ mi]) and Balsam Hollow (1 km [½ mi]). Check out The Butter Churn Café. The site has been part of Prince Edward Island National Park since 1937. ✉*Rte. 6, west of Rte. 13* ☎*902/963–7874* 🌐*www.pc.gc.ca/lhn-nhs/pe/greengables/index_E.asp* *$5.50* ⏲*May–late June, Sept., and Oct., daily 9–5; late June–Aug., daily 9–6; Oct. 31–Apr., call for hrs.*

WORD OF MOUTH

"Our favorite part of our trip was PEI. We stayed at Kindred Spirits Inn in Cavendish and I loved it. They treated us like royalty. Ask for the romance package as they give you extras such as a chowder supper and picnic for the beach. The room was heavenly and breakfasts out of this world. They are the nicest people!" —Dorris

New Glasgow Country Gardens, about 10 km (6 mi) south of Cavendish, overlooks a beautiful river valley. The garden is 12 acres, with 2 km (1 mi) of walking trails past fountains and groomed garden beds. ✉*Rte. 224, New Glasgow* ☎*902/964–4300* 🌐*www.preservecompany.com* *By donation* ⏲*Call for hrs.*

13

WHERE TO STAY & EAT

Accommodations in the Cavendish area are often booked a year in advance for July and most of August. Hotels in Charlottetown and elsewhere in the central region are still within easy driving distance.

$–$$$$ ✕ **New Glasgow Lobster Suppers.** New Glasgow Lobster Suppers brings fresh lobster to your plate. Scallops, roast beef, and ham are other choices. Bar service is also available, and there's a children's menu. The dining area can seat up to 500 guests at one time, and it often fills up, but since turnover is fast, there isn't usually a long wait. ✉*Rtes. 604 and 258 at New Glasgow* ☎*902/964–2870* *902/964–3116* 🌐*www.peilobstersuppers.com* *AE, MC, V* ⏲*No lunch. Closed mid-Oct.–late May.*

$–$$$ ✕ **Prince Edward Island Preserve Company.** This restaurant serves breakfast, lunch, and dinner. Notable items include the potato pie with maple-bacon cream and raspberry cream-cheese pie. The ice cream is homemade. Two walls of windows look over a peaceful winding river valley with its abundant bird life. ✉*Rtes. 224 and 258, New Glasgow* ☎*902/964–4300 or 800/565–5267* 🌐*www.preservecompany.com* *AE, DC, MC, V* ⏲*Closed early Oct.–late May.*

$–$$$ **Kindred Spirits Country Inn and Cottages.** It's a short walk from here to Green Gables House and Golf Course. Relax by the parlor fireplace or in a large room or suite, decorated with local antiques. Twenty large cottages range from economy to luxury (the upper-end cottages have fireplaces and hot tubs). All cottages are fully equipped for cooking; some have dishwashers and all have barbecues. ✉*Memory La. off Rte. 6, C0A 1N0* ☎*902/963–2434 or 800/461–1755* *902/963–2619* 🌐*www.kindredspirits.ca* *25 rooms, 20 cottages* *In-room: kitchen (some), VCR (some), Wi-Fi. In-hotel: pool, gym, no-smoking rooms* *AE, MC, V* ⏲*Closed mid-Oct.–mid-May* *BP.*

$ **Bay Vista Motor Inn and Cottage.** This motel caters to families. The outdoor deck allows a panoramic view of New London Bay while keeping an eye on the children in the large playground. Beaches, a hiking trail, and area attractions are nearby. A three-bedroom cedar cottage is available for weekly rental. *Rte. 6 9517 Cavendish Rd. W, Bayview C0A 1E0 902/963–2225 or 800/846–0601 www.bayvistamotorinn.com 28 rooms, 2 apartments, 1 cottage In-room: refrigerator, ethernet. In-hotel: pool, laundry facilities, public Wi-Fi, no-smoking rooms, some pets allowed AE, MC, V Closed late Sept.–mid-June CP.*

CAMPING **Marco Polo Land Campground.** The private campground has supervised activities, including hayrides. The serviced lots are often reserved well in advance for July and August. A beach is a 2-km (1-mi) walk or a 4-km (2½-mi) drive away. Some tent sites have electricity and water. *Rte. 13 902/963–2352 or 800/665–2352 902/963–2384 www.marcopololand.com 243 tent sites, 263 RV sites Flush toilets, full hookups, partial hookups, dump station, guest laundry, showers, fire pits, picnic tables, food service, general store, play area, swimming (2 pools) Reservations essential MC, V Closed late May–late Sept.*

SPORTS & THE OUTDOORS

SEA KAYAKING Trips with **Outside Expeditions** (*370 Harbourview Dr., off Rte. 242, 8 km [5 mi] east of Cavendish, Rustico 902/963–3366 or 800/207–3899 www.getoutside.com*), in North Rustico Harbour, can be geared to suit beginning or experienced paddlers. Tours include food from light snacks to full-fledged meals, depending on the expedition.

NEW LONDON

11 km (7 mi) southwest of Cavendish.

This tiny picturesque fishing village overlooking New London Harbour is the birthplace of Lucy Maud Montgomery. There are many seasonalshops in the area.

The **Lucy Maud Montgomery Birthplace** is a modest white-and-green house overlooking New London Harbour; the author was born here in 1874. The interior of the house has been furnished with Victorian antiques to re-create the era. Among memorabilia on display are a replica of Montgomery's wedding dress, and personal scrapbooks filled with many of her poems and stories. *Rtes. 6 and 20 902/886–2099 or 902/436–7329 $3 Mid-May–June and Sept.–mid-Oct., daily 9–5; July and Aug., daily 9–5.*

WHERE TO EAT

¢–$$$ **Carr's Oyster Bar.** Sit on the deck, look down the Stanley River to the dunes of the national park, and after the first few oysters you may never want to leave. The pub-style menu also includes swimming fish as well as chicken, burgers, fries, and steak. Also on the premises is a small aquarium (admission $6.50). *Rte. 6, Stanley Bridge 902/886–3355 MC, V Closed Nov.–mid-May.*

NORTHWEST CORNER

Blue Heron Dr. begins 12 km (7 mi) west of New London, and extends 66 km (41 mi) to Borden-Carleton.

As the drive follows the north shore coastline south to the other side of the Island, it passes fetile farmland and the shores of that blue jewel, Malpeque Bay

Woodleigh Replicas & Gardens is a 45-acre park with scale replicas of Great Britain's best-known architecture, including the Tower of London and Dunvegan Castle. Some models are large enough to enter. A medieval maze and 10 acres of English country gardens are also on the grounds, as is a picnic area, a children's playground, and a snack bar. *Rte. 234, Burlington 902/836-3401 www.woodleighreplicas.com $10 June, Sept., and Oct., daily 9–5; July and Aug., daily 9–7.*

The **Anne of Green Gables Museum at Silver Bush** was once the home of Lucy Maud Montgomery's aunt and uncle. Montgomery herself lived here for a time and was married in the parlor in 1911. Inside the house, which is still owned by descendants of Montgomery, are mementos such as photographs and a quilt worked on by the writer. One of the highlights of a visit to Silver Bush is a ride in Matthew's carriage. *Rte. 20, Park Corner 902/886-2884 www.annesociety.org/anne $3 Late May, daily 11–4; June and Sept., daily 10–4; July and Aug., daily 9–5; Oct., 1–4, days vary.*

WHERE TO STAY

$–$$$ **Stanley Bridge Country Resort & Conference Centre.** This centrally located collection of cottages, lodge rooms, and inn rooms is an ideal base for exploring the province. The cottages are available in several price ranges, with or without kitchens and with one to three bedrooms. Lodge rooms have kitchenettes. *Rte. 6, Stanley Bridge Box 8203, Kensington C0B 1M0 902/886-2882 or 800/361-2882 902/886-2940 www.stanleybridgeresort.com 16 cottages, 10 lodge rooms, 28 inn rooms In-room: kitchen (some). In-hotel: restaurant bar, pool, gym, laundry facilities, public Internet, Wi-Fi (inn), no-smoking rooms AE, MC, V Closed late Oct.–early May EP; complimentary CP for inn.*

BORDEN-CARLETON

35 km (22 mi) south of New London.

Borden-Carleton is linked to the mainland via the Confederation Bridge. The 13-km (8-mi) bridge spans the Northumberland Strait and ends in Cape Jourimain, New Brunswick.

The **Gateway Village** complex (*Foot of Confederation Bridge, near tollbooths 902/437-8539 or 888/437-6565, info center: 902/437-8570*) has shops and food outlets, plus a visitor information center.

VICTORIA

22 km (14 mi) east of Borden-Carleton.

Victoria-by-the-Sea, as this community is known locally, is a fishing village filled with art galleries, charming shops, and eateries, owned by local people.

WHERE TO STAY & EAT

$–$$$ ✕ **Landmark Café.** This quirky eatery has its own speciality—Eugene's Cajun-style shrimp and scallops. Finish with the walnut-filled brownie for dessert. You can count on great service, too. *✉12 Main St. ☎902/658–2286 ▭MC, V ⊙Closed Oct.–May.*

$ ★ **Orient Hotel.** One of two hotels on Prince Edward Island that have been in continuous operation for more than a century, this B&B has cozy guest rooms and suites. The rooms have been decorated with a fine eye for style and colors. Breakfast is served in the downstairs breakfast room, "Mrs. Profitt's Tea Room." There you can also get a snack Tuesday to Sunday from 11:30 to 4. It's worth the trip to Victoria just for the scones with clotted cream, or the English trifle parfait. *✉34 Main St., Box 55, C0A 2G0 ☎902/658–2503 or 800/565–6743 ⊕www.theorienthotel.com ⇨5 rooms, 3 suites ♿In-room: no a/c. In hotel: restaurant, bicycles, no kids under 12, no-smoking rooms ▭MC, V ⊙Closed mid-Oct.–mid-May ¶BP.*

NIGHTLIFE & THE ARTS

From late June through September the historic **Victoria Playhouse** (*✉Howard and Main Sts. ☎902/658–2025 or 800/925–2025 ⊕www.victoriaplayhouse.com*), which seats 150 and has excellent acoustics, presents a diverse selection of plays. The world premiere of *Anne and Gilbert*, a musical covering the two L.M. Montgomery books that followed *Anne of Green Gables,* was held here in 2005.

POINTS EAST COASTAL DRIVE

For 375 km (233 mi), the Points East Coastal Drive traces the coastline of Kings, meandering through wooded areas, fishing villages, and beaches.

MONTAGUE

44 km (25 mi) east of Charlottetown.

Montague is a lovely little town that straddles the Montague River and serves as a departure point for seal-watching boat tours.

WHERE TO STAY

$–$$ **Roseneath Bed & Breakfast.** This heritage home, built in 1868, faces Brudenell River. You can golf at the adjacent Brudenell and Dundarave courses, walk or bike the Confederation Trail (which crosses the property), or explore the 90 acres of woodlands. All rooms have views of the river or the property's extensive gardens. Morning brings coffee delivered to your room and a home-cooked breakfast downstairs. *✉R.R. 6, Cardigan C0A 1G0 ☎902/838–4590 or 800/823–8933*

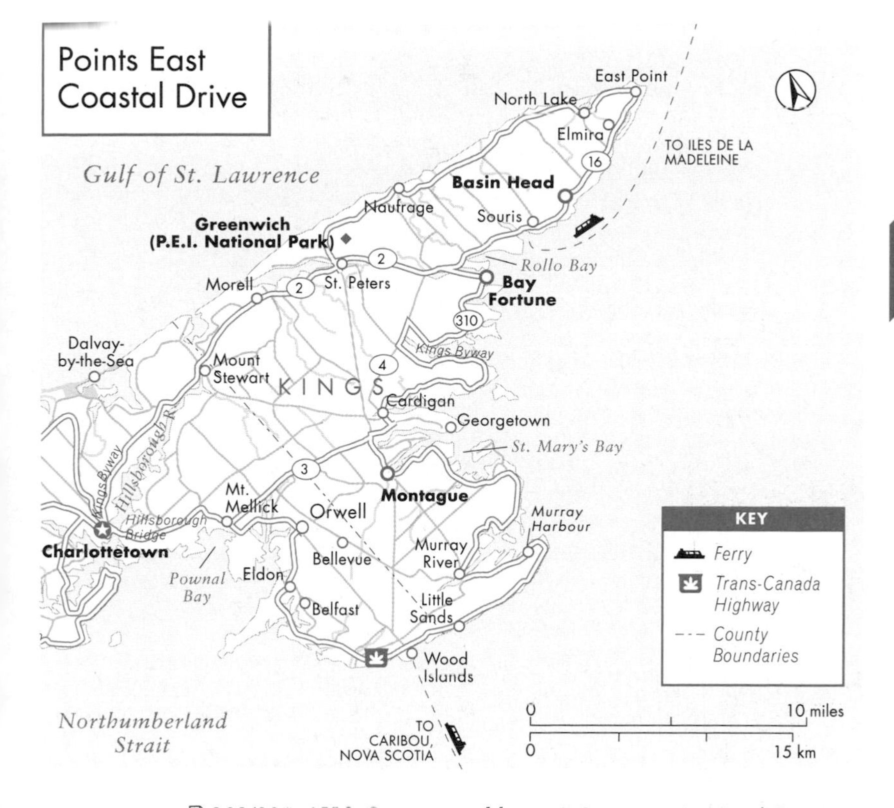

902/838–4590 www.rosebb.ca 3 rooms, 1 suite In-room: no a/c, no TV, Wi-Fi. In-hotel: bicycles MC, V Closed Nov.–Apr.; open off-season by reservation BP.

BAY FORTUNE

23 km (14 mi) north of Montague.

Bay Fortune, site of a large harbor, is an out-of-the-way place that some people regard as their secret sweet spot for relaxing. It has varied and gorgeous scenery.

WHERE TO STAY & EAT

$$–$$$$ ★ **Inn at Bay Fortune.** The inn overlooks Fortune Harbour and the Northumberland Strait. Many of the rooms have fireplace sitting areas; some have a balcony. Local fresh-caught and fresh-harvested ingredients are served in an old-time ambience at the restaurant ($$$–$$$$), where guests can dine on the wrap-around veranda that provides breathtaking water views, or in the kitchen at the chef's table. Many of the herbs and fruits come from the Inn's extensive gardens. *Rte. 310 off Rte. 2, C0A 2B0 902/687–3745, 860/563–6090 off-season www.innat-bayfortune.com 17 rooms, 2 houses In-room: kitchen (some).*

In-hotel: restaurant, public Internet, public Wi-Fi, no-smoking rooms ☰AE, MC, V ⏲Closed late Oct.–mid-May *BP.*

$$–$$$$ Fodor'sChoice ★ **Inn at Spry Point.** The sister property of the Inn at Bay Fortune, this luxury retreat hugs the end of a 110-acre peninsula. In addition to 4 km (2½ mi) of shoreline walking trails, the serene property has a 1-km (½-mi) sandy beach. Each rooms has a king bed. Scallops, halibut, and salmon, with fresh produce, are served in the restaurant for lunch ($$$–$$$$). Guests go to the Inn at Bay Fortune *(see above)* for dinner. ✉*Spry Point Rd.* ☎*902/583–2400, 860/563–6090 off-season* 🖷*902/583–2176* 🌐*www.innatsprypoint.com* *15 rooms* *In-room: no TV. In-hotel: reestaurant, bicycle, public Wi-Fi, no-smoking rooms* ☰*AE, MC, V* ⏲*Closed early Oct.–late May* *BP.*

$ **Rollo Bay Inn.** This roadside inn, open year-round, is done up in a Queen Anne style, and has spacious rooms. The local beach is a five-minute drive away, and the breakfast room has a picturesque view of the bay. The lone suite has a kitchenette. ✉*Rte. 2, 4 km west of Souris, Rollo Bay C0A 2B0* ☎*902/687–3350* 🖷*902/687–3570* 🌐*www.peisland.com/rollobayinn* *19 rooms, 1 suite* *In-room: Wi-Fi. In-hotel: no-smoking rooms* ☰*AE, MC, V.*

BASIN HEAD

13 km (8 mi) north of Souris.

The beach is noted for exquisite silvery sand that stretches northeast for miles, backed by high grassy dunes. Known locally as "singing sand," it is a phenomenon found in only a few locations worldwide. The high silica content helps produce the sound.

GREENWICH (P.E.I. NATIONAL PARK)

19 km (12 mi) southwest of Basin Head.

The western portion of the Greenwich peninsula became part of Prince Edward Island National Park in 1998. To get to the national park, follow Route 16 to St. Peters Bay and Route 313 to Greenwich. The road ends at an interpretive center (open mid-May to mid-September). Because of the rather delicate nature of the dune system, visitors must stay on the trails and refrain from touching the flora. ✉*Rte. 313, 6 km (4 mi) north of St. Peters Bay* ☎*902/672–6350* 🌐*www.pc.gc.ca* *$7, $17 for family* ⏲*Daily dawn–dusk.*

WHERE TO STAY & EAT

¢–$ **Rick's Fish and Chips.** The chips are fresh cut and the fish is fresh caught. The menu includes grilled salmon, quiche, and pizza. There are picnic tables outside, too. ✉*Rte. 2, St. Peters* ☎*902/961–3438* *Reservations not accepted* ☰*MC, V* ⏲*Closed early Oct.–early May.*

$$$$ ★ **The Inn at St. Peters.** Overlooking the serene waters of St. Peters Bay, this inn is the only four-star property in the eastern part of the island. It's situated on 13 acres filled with more than 25,000 flowers, near the beaches and sand dunes of Greenwich. All suites have a working fireplace, a rocking chair, and a deck facing the bay. Walkers and

bicyclist can explore the nearby Confederation Trail, and owner Karen Davey will help arrange golf packages at area courses. Rates include breakfast and dinner in the top-notch McCulloch Room ($$$–$$$$), where you are treated to Continental cuisine with a contemporary flair as you enjoy the beautiful sunsets. ✉*1668 Greenwich Rd., St. Peters Bay C0A 2A0* ☎*902/961–2135 or 800/818–0925* 🌐*www.innatstpeters.com* *16 suites* *In-room: refrigerator, VCR, Wi-Fi. In-hotel: restaurant, bicycles, some pets allowed (fee), no-smoking rooms* ▭*MC, V* ⏲*Mid-Oct.–late May* *MAP.*

WORD OF MOUTH

"I love to hike and bike. The Confederation Trail on PEI is ideal for either. The beaches are gorgeous. The fresh seafood is wonderful."
—cmcfong

NORTH CAPE COASTAL DRIVE

The North Cape Coastal Drive winds along Prince County's coast through very old and very small villages that adhere to tradition. Acadians, descendants of the original French settlers, inhabit many of these hamlets.

SUMMERSIDE

71 km (44 mi) west of Charlottetown.

Summerside, the second-largest city on the Island, has an attractive waterfront area with a beach and boardwalk. It takes about a half hour to drive by car from Summerside to major attractions such as Cavendish in the central region of Prince Edward Island.

Spinnakers' Landing, a boardwalk along the water's edge, has a good blend of shopping, history, and entertainment. The re-created lighthouse may be climbed for panoramic views of Bedeque Bay and the city. In summer, weather permitting, there's often free evening entertainment (usually at 7 PM) on the outdoor stage over the water. ✉*150 Harbour Dr.* ☎*902/436–6692 or 902/888–8364* 🌐*www.spinnakerslanding.com.*

Many descendants of the Island's early French settlers live in the Miscouche area, 10 km (6 mi) northwest of Summerside, and the **Acadian Museum** *(Musée Acadien)*, a National Historic Site, commemorates their history. It also has a genealogical center and an Acadian gift shop. ✉*23 Main Dr. E (Rte. 2), Miscouche* ☎*902/432–2880* 🌐*www.peimuseum.com* *$4.50* ⏲*July and Aug., daily 9:30–7; reduced hrs off-season.*

WHERE TO STAY & EAT

$–$$ ✕**The Deckhouse Pub & Eatery.** Seafood is the specialty at this spot on the historic waterfront, but the menu includes beef, chicken, and other dishes, so there are plenty of choices. Dining on the deck offers a superb water view and the summer breeze. The friendly staff does their best to accommodate substitutions. ✉*150 Harbour Dr.* ☎*902/436–0660* ▭*AE, MC, V.*

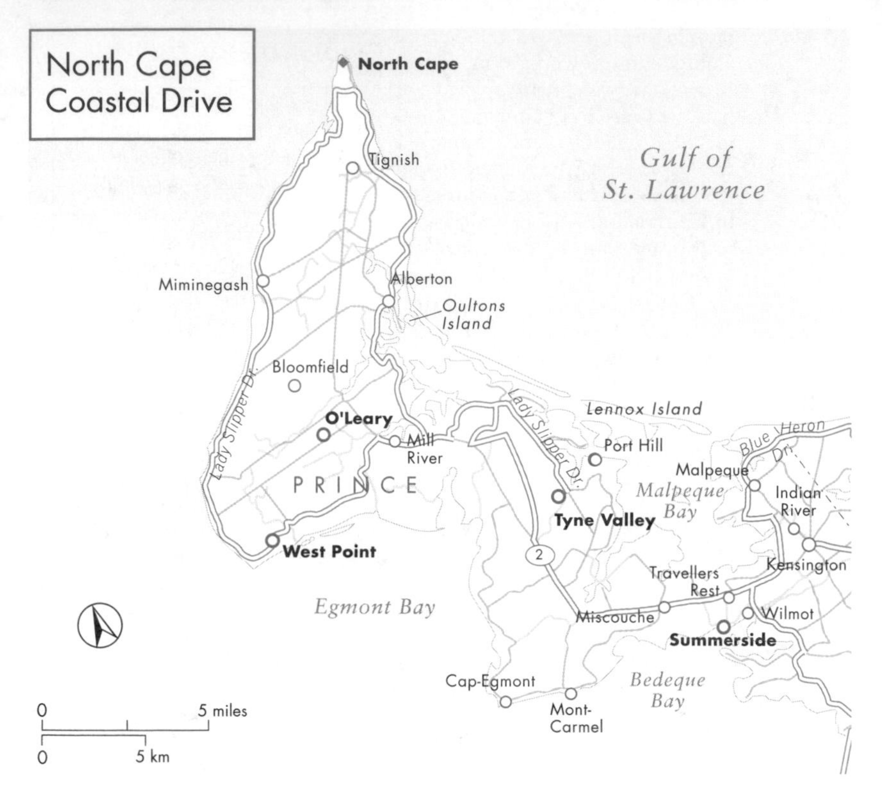

$$ ★ **Loyalist Country Inn–A Lakeview Resort.** The Loyalist combines the atmosphere of a country inn with the professionalism of a large hotel. The property overlooks the city waterfront, a yacht club, and a marina, while the rear faces the main downtown area, the former railway station, and the Confederation Trail—good for biking. The Prince William Dining Room's menu contains seafood, steaks, and Island delicacies. Ask for one of the many light-filled rooms facing the harbor, so you can wake up to blue water, green land, and blue sky. ✉ *195 Harbour Dr., C1N 5R1* ☎ *902/436–3333 or 800/361–2668* 📠 *902/436–4304* 🌐 *www.lakeviewhotels.com/summerside* *100 rooms, 3 suites* *In-hotel: restaurant, bar, pool, gym, public Wi-Fi, no-smoking rooms* 💳 *AE, DC, MC, V.*

TYNE VALLEY

8 km (5 mi) south of Port Hill.

Tyne Valley is a charming community. Watch for fisherfolk standing in flat boats wielding rakes to harvest the famous Malpeque oysters. A gentle river flows through the middle of the village, with lush green lawns and sweeping trees edging the water.

SHOPPING

Lennox Island has one of the largest communities of Mi'Kmaq, the First Nations people who came to Malpeque Bay nearly 10,000 years ago, in the province. Take Route 12 west to Route 163 and follow the road over the causeway leading to a large island projecting into Malpeque Bay. **Indian Art & Craft of North America** (✉*Rte. 163* ☎*902/831–2653*) specializes in Mi'Kmaq ash-split baskets as well as jewelry, carvings, and beadwork. Call for hours.

WORD OF MOUTH

"I took lots of pictures, but PEI was pretty in a way that defied my ability to photograph it. It wasn't dramatically pretty the way mountains and forests are pretty. It was all rolling green fields, acres of yellow flowers, bright blue skies, and little churches with their white steeples shining in the sun. It was those incredible red dirt roads through potato fields and woods, leading directly into the turquoise ocean. Can you tell that I liked it a lot, and I want to go back?" —china_cat

O'LEARY

37 km (23 mi) northeast of Tyne Valley.

Farmers driving their tractors through fields of rich, red soil, and colorful lobster boats braving the seas are common scenes in this area. This region is well known for its magnificent red cliffs, majestic lighthouses, and glistening sunsets. Woodstock, north of O'Leary, has a resort where opportunities for outdoor activities abound.

WHERE TO STAY & EAT

$–$$$ **Rodd Mill River—A Rodd Signature Resort.** With activities ranging from night skiing to golfing, canoeing, and kayaking, this is truly an all-season resort. Every table at the restaurant ($$–$$$) has a view of the golf course (see below). Menu items include planked salmon and a lobster platter, plus pastas, steak, and chicken. The heated pool has a 90-foot slide. ✉*Rte. 136, 5 km (3 mi) east of O'Leary, Box 399, Woodstock C0B 1V0* ☎*902/859–3555 or 800/565–7633* 🖷*902/859–2486* 🌐*www.roddvacations.com* *80 rooms, 10 suites* *In-room: dial-up. In-hotel: restaurant, bar, golf course, tennis court, pool, gym, spa, water sports, spa, bicycles public Wi-Fi, some pets allowed, no-smoking rooms* 💳*AE, DC, MC, V* ⏲*Closed Nov.–Jan. and Apr.*

SPORTS & THE OUTDOORS

Among the most scenic and challenging courses in eastern Canada is the 18-hole, par-72 **Mill River Provincial Golf Course** (✉*Mill River Provincial Park, Rte. 136, Woodstock* ☎*902/859–3920 or 800/235–8909* ⏲*Closed late Oct.–early May*). It is ranked among the country's top 50 courses and has been the site of several championship tournaments. Book in advance.

NORTH CAPE

27 km (17 mi) north of O'Leary.

In the northwest, the Island narrows to a north-pointing arrow of land, at the tip of which is North Cape with its imposing lighthouse. At low tide, one of the longest reefs in the world gives way to tidal pools teeming with marine life. Here you'll see the wind turbines at the Atlantic Wind Test Site.

The **Irish Moss Interpretive Centre,** in the tiny ocean-side town of Miminegash, tells you about Irish moss, the fan-shape red alga found in abundance on this coast and used as a thickening agent in foods and other products. "Seaweed pie," made with Irish moss, is served at the adjacent Seaweed Pie Café. ✉ *Rte. 14; 20 km (12 mi) south of North Cape* ☎ *902/882–4313* *$2* *Early June–Sept., daily 10–7.*

WHERE TO STAY & EAT

$–$$$ **Wind & Reef Restaurant.** This restaurant serves Island clams, mussels, and lobster, as well as steaks, prime rib, and chicken. There's a fine view of the Gulf of St. Lawrence and the Northumberland Strait. ✉ *End of Rte. 12, North Cape* ☎ *902/882–3535* *MC, V* *Closed Oct.–May.*

$ **Tignish Heritage Inn.** Originally built as a convent in 1868, this large inn is close to North Cape, Mile 0 of the Confederation Trail, and the facilities offered in the town of Tignish. Rooms range in size from cozy to spacious. Each room has a view of the grounds, which include a quiet pathway weaving through tall maple trees. Some of the bathrooms have cast-iron, claw-foot tubs. The peaceful gardens are dotted with a gazebo, a fountain, and flowers. ✉ *Maple St. behind St. Simon and St. Jude Church, Box 398, Tignish C0B 2B0* ☎ *902/882–2491 or 877/882–2491* *902/882–2500* *www.tignish.com/heritageinn* *17 rooms, 1 suite* *In-room: no a/c. In-hotel: laundry facilities, public Wi-Fi, no-smoking rooms* *AE, DC, MC, V* *Closed mid-Oct.–mid-May, except for groups by reservation only* *CP.*

WEST POINT

35 km (22 mi) south of Miminegash.

At the southern tip of the western shore, West Point has a tiny fishing harbor, campsites, and a supervised beach.

Fodor's Choice ★ **West Point Lighthouse,** built in 1875, is the tallest lighthouse on the Island. It's open daily, late May through late September, from 9 to 9; Admission is $2.50.

WHERE TO STAY & EAT

$–$$ Fodor's Choice ★ **West Point Lighthouse.** Few people can say they've actually spent a night in a lighthouse, but here's your chance to do just that. This one was first lit in 1876. Rooms, most with ocean views, are pleasantly furnished with local antiques and cheerful handmade quilts. The restaurant ($–$$$) serves fresh lobster, scallops, mussels, chowder, and other seafood. Climb the 72 steps to the top of the lighthouse museum for a spectacular view of the Northumberland Strait, and the exercise. Make your reservations early. ✉ *Rte. 14* ☐ *O'Leary R.R. 2, C0B 1V0* ☎ *902/859–3605 or 800/764–6854* 📠 *902/859–1510* 🌐 *www.westpointlighthouse.com* *10 rooms* *In-hotel: restaurant, beachfront, no-smoking rooms* 💳 *AE, DC, MC, V* ⊗ *Closed Oct.–May.*

PRINCE EDWARD ISLAND ESSENTIALS

To research prices, get advice from other travelers, and book travel arrangements, visit www.fodors.com.

TRANSPORTATION

BY AIR

Air Canada and its regional carriers offer daily nonstop service from Charlottetown to Halifax and Toronto, both of which have connections to the rest of Canada, the United States, and beyond. WestJet offers summer service to Toronto. Northwest flies directly from Detroit to Charlottetown during the summer season. Delta flies direct from Boston. Sunwing flies in from Toronto. Prince Edward Air is available for private charters.

Charlottetown Airport is 5 km (3 mi) north of town.

Contacts **Charlottetown Airport** (☎ *902/566–7997*). **Prince Edward Air** (☎ *902/566–4488* 🌐 *www.peair.com*). **Sunwing** (☎ *800/761–1711* 🌐 *www.sunwing.ca*).

BY BOAT & FERRY

Northumberland Ferries sails between Wood Islands and Caribou, Nova Scotia, from May to mid-December. The crossing takes about 75 minutes, and the round-trip costs approximately $60 per vehicle, $80 for a recreational vehicle; foot passengers pay $14 (you pay only when leaving the Island). A fuel surcharge is added. Ask about this when booking. There are 18 crossings per day in summer.

Contacts **Northumberland Ferries** (☎ *888/249–7245* 🌐 *www.nfl-bay.com*).

BY CAR

The 13-km-long (8-mi-long) Confederation Bridge connects Cape Jourimain, in New Brunswick, with Borden-Carleton, Prince Edward Island. The crossing takes about 13 minutes. The toll is about $41 per car, $47 for a recreational vehicle; it's collected when you leave the Island. The lack of public transportation on the Island (except for buses in Charlottetown) makes having your own vehicle a necessity. There are more than 3,700 km (2,300 mi) of paved road in the province, including the three scenic coastal drives: North Cape Coastal Drive, Blue Heron Drive, and Points East Coastal Drive. A helpful highway map of the province is available from Tourism PEI and at visitor centers on the Island.

Designated Heritage Roads are surfaced with red clay, the local soil base. The unpaved roads take in rural and undeveloped areas, where you're likely to see lots of wildflowers and birds. A four-wheel-drive vehicle is not necessary, but in the fall and spring, and when there's inclement weather, the mud can get quite deep and the narrow roads become impassable. Keep an eye open for bicycles, motorcycles, and pedestrians.

Contacts Tourism PEI (☎ *888/734–7529 or 902/368–4444*).

CONTACTS & RESOURCES

EMERGENCIES

Emergency Services Ambulance, fire, police (☎ *911 or 0*).

Hospitals Prince County Hospital (✉ *65 Roy Boates Ave., Summerside* ☎ *902/438–4200*). **Queen Elizabeth Hospital** (✉ *60 Riverside Dr., Charlottetown* ☎ *902/894–2200 or 902/894–2095*).

SPORTS & THE OUTOORS

BICYCLING The Island is popular with bicyclists for its moderately hilly roads and stunning scenery, yet there are plenty of level areas, especially west of Summerside to Tignish and along the north shore. A 9-km (5½-mi) path near Cavendish Campground loops around marsh, woods, and farmland. The Confederation Trail allows people to cycle from one end of the Island to the other. Shoulderless, narrow secondary roads in some areas and summer car traffic can be challenging. Several tour companies rent bicycles and provide custom-made tours. Trailside Adventures in Mt. Stewart provides five suggested tours with maps (2 to 52 km [1 to 32 mi]) and will make suggestions for longer trips. A two-sided map and information sheet is available from Tourism PEI.

Contacts Tourism PEI (☎ *800/463–4734 or 902/368–4444*). **Trailside Adventures** (☎ *888/704–6595* 🌐 *www.trailside.ca*).

FISHING Deep-sea fishing boats are available along the eastern end of the Island as well as in the north-shore region. Although some boats can be chartered for fishing bluefin tuna, most operators offer excursions to fish for mackerel. Freshwater sportfishing for trout or salmon is also an option. A nonresident three-day fishing license is the shortest one you can get. It costs $27. The season license costs $40. They can be purchased at many businesses (hardware, tackle, convenience stores) throughout Prince Edward Island. A few operations rent fishing tackle and offer "no license required" fishing on private ponds. The Government of Prince Edward Island Web site lists businesses that sell fishing licenses.

Contacts Government of Prince Edward Island (🌐 *www.gov.pe.ca/egovernment*).

GOLF More than two dozen 9- and 18-hole courses are open to the public. Several of the more beautiful ones have scenic ocean vistas, and almost all have hassle-free golfing, with easily booked tee times, inexpensive rates, and uncrowded courses, particularly in fall. For a publication listing golf courses in Prince Edward Island, and to book online, contact Tourism PEI. Most courses may be booked directly or by contacting Golf PEI.

Contacts Golf PEI (☎ *866/465–3734* 🌐 *www.golfpei.com*). **Tourism PEI** (☎ *800/463–4734 or 902/368–4444 information, 800/235–8909 booking* 🌐 *www.golflinkspei.com*).

SEA KAYAKING With its quiet coves and cozy bays, Prince Edward Island has become a haven for those who enjoy sea kayaking. Outside Expeditions provides rentals and tours designed for all levels of expertise.

Contacts Outside Expeditions (☎ *902/963–3366 or 800/207–3899* 🌐 *www.getoutside.com*).

13

SHOPPING For information on crafts outlets around Prince Edward Island, contact the Prince Edward Island Crafts Council.

Contacts Prince Edward Island Crafts Council (☎ *902/892–5152*).

TOURS

The Island has about 20 sightseeing tours, including double-decker bus tours, taxi tours, cycling tours, harbor cruises, and walking tours. Most tour companies are based in Charlottetown and offer excursions around the city and to the beaches.

DRIVING TOURS Yellow Cab can be booked for tours by the hour or day.

Contacts Yellow Cab (☎ *902/892–6561*).

WALKING TOURS Island Nature Trust sells a nature-trail map of the Island. Tourism PEI has maps of the 350-km (217-mi) multiuse Confederation Trail.

Contacts Island Nature Trust (☎ *902/892–7513* 🌐 *www.islandnaturetrust.ca*). **Tourism PEI** (☎ *800/463–4734 or 902/368–4444* 📠 *902/566–4336* 🌐 *www.peiplay.com*).

VISITOR INFORMATION

Tourism PEI publishes an informative annual guide for visitors and maintains eight visitor information centers (VICs) on the Island. It also produces a map of the 350-km (217-mi) Confederation Trail. The main visitor information center is in Charlottetown and is open early-May to October daily and November to mid-May weekdays.

Contacts Tourism PEI (☎ *800/463–4734 or 902/368–4444* 📠 *902/368–6613* 🌐 *www.peiplay.com*). **Visitor Information Center** (☎ *902/888–8364 in summer*).

Nova Scotia

WORD OF MOUTH

"Peggy's Cove is not really a town, it's a very small village. I think of it as an essential "scenic stop"— the tiny cove itself is ringed with wooden buildings and colourful fishing vessels, and the shoreline of the bordering open ocean is composed of exposed granite bedrock with the waves crashing against it. Very dramatic. But personally I would consider a lunch stop in another town along the coast, like Mahone Bay or Lunenburg, after (or before) an hour or so taking photos in Peggy's Cove."

—mat106

www.fodors.com/forums

Updated by
Amy Pugsley
Fraser

NOVA SCOTIA PACKS AN IMPOSSIBLE VARIETY of cultures and landscapes into an area half the size of Ohio. Fifty-six kilometers (35 mi) is the farthest you can get from the sea anywhere in the province.

Within the convoluted coastline of Nova Scotia you'll find highlands, fjords, farmland; and rivers, ponds, and lakes. Over time, pounding waves and grinding ice have sculpted the coastal rocks and reduced sandstone cliffs to stretches of sandy beach. Inland, the fertile fields of the Annapolis Valley yield peaches, corn, apples, and plums, and in spring and summer a succession of wildflowers covers the roadside with blankets of color. Bogs, dry barrens, tidal wetlands, open fields, dense spruce woods, and hardwood forests—each habitat has its own distinctive plant life. Wildlife abounds: ospreys and bald eagles, moose and deer, whales off Cape Breton and Brier Island.

The Mi'Kmaqs have been here for 10,000 years; eventually, waves of European immigrants filled the province. The result: there are Gaelic signs in Mabou and Iona, German sausage and sauerkraut in Lunenburg, and Greek-music festivals in Halifax. The Acadians fly their tricolor flag with pride and Scots step dance to antique fiddle airs. The fragrance of burning sweet grass mingles with the prayers of the Mi'Kmaqs' Catholic mass, the old blending with the new.

EXPLORING NOVA SCOTIA

The wild Atlantic Ocean crashes against rocky outcrops, eddies into sheltered coves, or flows placidly over expanses of white sand. In the Bay of Fundy, which has the highest tides in the world, the receding sea reveals stretches of red-mud flats. There are dense forests, and rolling farms. In Cape Breton, rugged mountains plunge to meet the waves.

If arriving in Nova Scotia from New Brunswick via the Trans-Canada Highway (Highway 104), there are three ways to proceed into the province. Amherst is the first community after the border and from here Highway 104 takes you toward Halifax, a two-hour drive away. You can opt for the northern drive, via Highway 6, which follows the shore of the Northumberland Strait; farther east is Cape Breton. Highway 2, to the south, is a less-traveled road and a favorite because of nearby fossil-studded shores. Branch roads lead to the Annapolis Valley and other points south. Drivers should be aware that the sharply curving rural roads warrant careful attention.

ABOUT THE RESTAURANTS

Helping travelers discover for themselves the best tastes of the province, the Nova Scotian culinary industry has formed an organization called the Taste of Nova Scotia. It pulls together the producers and the preparers, setting quality standards to ensure that patrons at member restaurants receive authentic Nova Scotian food. Look for their symbol: a golden oval porthole framing food and a ship.

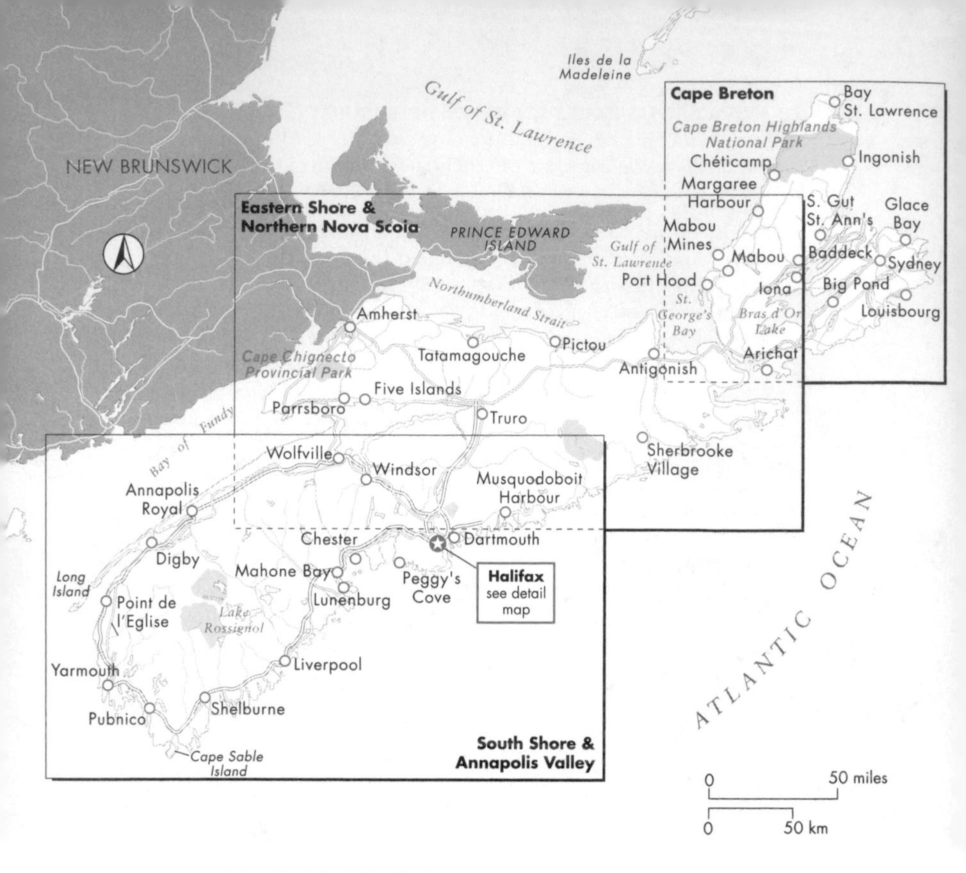

ABOUT THE HOTELS

Nova Scotia's strength lies in a sprinkling of first-class resorts that have retained a traditional feel, top country inns with a dedication to fine dining and high-level accommodation, and a few superior corporate hotels. Bed-and-breakfasts, particularly those in smaller towns, are often exceptional. Most resorts and many B&Bs are seasonal, closing during the winter. Expect to pay considerably more in Halifax and Dartmouth than elsewhere. Air-conditioning is the norm in most city hotels, whereas inns and B&Bs, especially along the vast coastline, rely more on the ocean breezes to cool you down.

WHAT IT COSTS IN CANADIAN DOLLARS

	¢	$	$$	$$$	$$$$
RESTAURANTS	under C$8	C$8–C$12	C$13–C$20	C$21–C$30	over C$30
HOTELS	under C$75	C$75–C$125	C$126–C$175	C$176–C$250	over C$250

Restaurant prices are per person for a main course at dinner. Hotel prices are for two people in a standard double room in high season, excluding tax.

TOP REASONS TO GO

GO COASTAL
The coastline is never more than 55 km (35 mi) away, with fishing villages and sandy beaches.

STEP INTO THE PAST
At Fortress Louisbourg on Cape Breton Island, experience life in the 1740s while walking through this reconstructed town.

MUSIC
Traditional Celtic and Acadian music share the stage with rock, hip-hop, and jazz.

GET WET
Five-thousand miles of seacoast and thousands of lakes, rivers, and brooks make a paradise for kayaking, sailing, swimming, whale-watching, and fishing.

SEAFOOD
Nova Scotia is shaped liked a lobster claw, and the lobster here is delicious; scallops, mussels, and salmon are also plentiful.

HALIFAX & DARTMOUTH

The cities of Halifax and Dartmouth gaze upon each other across Halifax Harbor. Once the point of entry to Canada for refugees and immigrants, the port remains a busy shipping center. Pleasure boats and yachts tie up alongside weathered schooners at the Historic Properties Wharf, and pubs, shops, museums, and parks welcome visitors and locals. In summer, jazz concerts and buskers, music festivals and sports events enliven the outdoor atmosphere. The film *Titanic* brought fresh attention to part of Halifax's history; some 150 victims of the disaster are buried in three cemeteries here, and the Maritime Museum of the Atlantic has a *Titanic* display.

HALIFAX

1,137 km (705 mi) northeast of Boston; 275 km (171 mi) southeast of Moncton, New Brunswick.

Halifax is an intimate city that's large enough to have the trappings of a capital city, yet small enough that many of its sights can be seen on a pleasant walk downtown.

WHAT TO SEE

9 **Art Gallery of Nova Scotia.** Within this 1867 building is an extensive permanent collection of more than 4,000 works, including an internationally recognized collection of Maritime and folk art. Also here is the actual home of the late folk painter Maude Lewis. The collection of contemporary art has major works by Christopher Pratt, Alex Colville, John Nesbitt, and Dawn McNutt. ✉ *1723 Hollis St.* ☎ *902/424–5280* 🌐 *www.agns.gov.ns.ca* 🎟 *$12* 🕐 *June–Aug., Mon.–Wed. and Fri.–Sun., 10–5, Thurs. 10–9; Sept.–May, Tues.–Fri. 10–5, weekends noon–5.*

 **Anna Leonowens Gallery.** Named for the Victorian governess in the employ of the King of Siam, and whose memoirs served as inspira-

GREAT ITINERARIES

IF YOU HAVE 3 DAYS

Start in **Halifax**, then head for **Peggy's Cove**, a fishing village perched on sea-washed granite. Explore the crafts shops of **Mahone Bay** and travel on to **Lunenburg** and the Fisheries Museum. Continue to **Shelburne** on Day 2. Visit **Yarmouth** and travel on to **Digby** to try its famous scallops. **Annapolis Royal** is a lovely spot to spend an afternoon. Travel on to the elm-lined streets of **Wolfville** and explore nearby Grand Pré National Historic Site. On Day 3, check tide times and drive to Minas Basin, where the tides are the highest in the world. A leisurely drive puts you back in Halifax by late afternoon.

IF YOU HAVE 5 DAYS

Spend a day or two in **Halifax** before exploring the Eastern Shore along Highway 7. **Musquodoboit Harbour** is a haven for fishing enthusiasts. Nearby is Martinique Beach, one of Nova Scotia's best. Spend time in **Sherbrooke Village**. Continue on Highway 7 toward **Antigonish** on the Sunrise Trail. Visit Hector Heritage Quay in **Pictou**, where the Scots landed in 1773. From Pictou, Highway 6 runs beside a string of beaches. Turn right to **Malagash** and Jost Vineyards. A half-hour drive takes you to **Amherst**. Continue on to **Joggins** and search for souvenirs in its sandstone cliffs. For more fossils, head to **Parrsboro**.

IF YOU HAVE 7 DAYS

Cape Breton Island is the perfect place for a leisurely 7-day tour. Overnight in **Mabou**, the heart of the island's rich musical tradition. From a base in **Margaree Harbour**, take a day or more to explore the Cabot Trail and Cape Breton Highlands National Park, and then on to **Baddeck.** Spend the night in **Iona**. A day or two in **Sydney** positions you for an excursion to the Cape Breton Miners' Museum in **Glace Bay** and a daylong visit to Fortress of Louisbourg National Historic Park and the town of **Louisbourg**. Take Highway 4 back to Canso Causeway through **Big Pond**, and spend a day wandering the colorful Acadian villages of Isle Madame, such as **Arichat**.

tion for Rodgers and Hammerstein's *The King and I.* Three exhibition spaces serve as a showcase for the college faculty and students; the displays focus on contemporary studio and media art. ✉*1891 Granville St.* ☎*902/494–8223* *Free* ⏲*Tues.–Fri. 11–5, Sat. noon–4.*

⓭ The **Brewery Market.** This sprawling stone complex ,where Alexander Keith once brewed the beer that still bears his name, has been better known as a Saturday farmers' market, but it also hosts several excellent eateries and a bakery (Cheelin, City Deli, Mary's Bread Basket) as well as gift shops. At this writing, the market was scheduled to move to a seven-day operation called the Farmers' Seaport Market, in a brand new, green energy building at Pier 20, 1061 Marginal Road. ✉*1496 Lower Water Sts.* ☎*902/423–2279* ⏲*Sat. 7–1.*

⓮ **Government House.** Built between 1799 and 1805, for some time this house has been the official residence of the province's lieutenant governor. It's North America's oldest consecutively occupied government

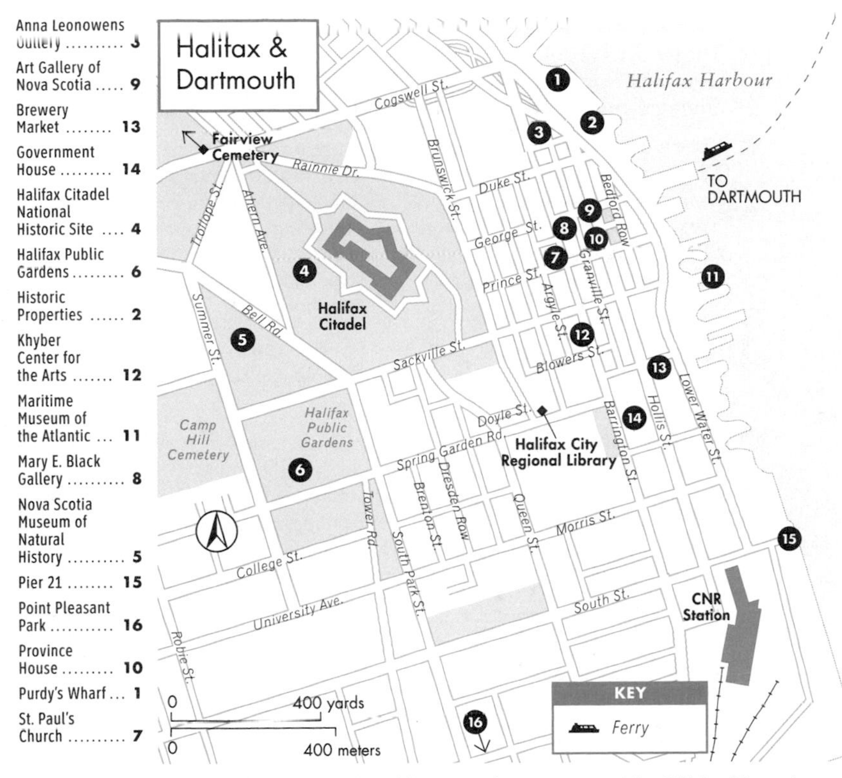

residence, because the older President's House (the White House) was evacuated and burned during the War of 1812. The house, which has been restored to its original elegance, isn't open to the public. ✉ *1451 Barrington St.*

❹ ★ **Halifax Citadel National Historic Site.** The Citadel, erected between 1826 and 1856, was the heart of the city's fortifications and was linked to smaller forts and gun emplacements on the harbor islands and on the bluffs above the harbor entrance. Kilted soldiers drill in front of the **Army Museum,** and a cannon is fired every day at noon—a tradition since 1749. Before leaving, take in the view from the Citadel: the spiky downtown crowded between the hilltop and the harbor; the wooded islands at the harbor's mouth; and the naval dockyard. The handsome, four-sided **Town Clock** on Citadel Hill was given to Halifax by Prince Edward, Duke of Kent, military commander from 1794 to 1800. ✉ *Citadel Hill* ☎ *902/426–5080* 🌐 *www.parkscanada.gc.ca* 🎟 *June–mid-Sept. $10.90; May 7–31 and mid-Sept.–Oct. $7.15; rest of yr free* ⏲ *May 7–June 30, Sept., and Oct., daily 9–5; July and Aug., daily 9–6.*

❻  **Halifax Public Gardens.** This oasis had its start in 1753 as a private garden. Gravel paths wind among ponds, trees, and flower beds, revealing an astonishing variety of plants from all over the world. The centerpiece is a gazebo erected in 1887 for Queen Victoria's Golden Jubilee. The gardens are closed in winter but you can still take a pleasant walk along the cast-iron fence of the perimeter. ⊠*Bounded by Sackville, Summer, and S. Park Sts. and Spring Garden Rd.*

❷ **Historic Properties.** These waterfront warehouses date from the early 19th century. They were built by such raffish characters as Enos Collins, whose vessels defied Napoléon's blockade to bring American supplies to the Duke of Wellington. The buildings have since been taken over by high-quality shops, chic offices, and restaurants. ⊠*Lower Water and Hollis Sts.*

⓬ **Khyber Center for the Arts.** Primarily a gallery for young and emerging artists, the Khyber is home to works in numerous genres, including performance art. ⊠*1588 Barrington St.* ☎*902/422–9668* *Free* *Tues.–Sat. noon–5.*

⓫ **Maritime Museum of the Atlantic.** The exhibits in this restored chandlery and warehouse on the waterfront include small boats once used around the coast, as well as displays describing Nova Scotia's proud sailing heritage, from the days when the province, on its own, was one of the world's foremost shipbuilding and trading nations. Other exhibits explore the Halifax Explosion of 1917, shipwrecks, and lifesaving.

The museum has a permanent exhibit about the *Titanic* disaster. The display includes the only surviving deck chair; a section of wall paneling; a balustrade molding and part of a newel from the dual curving staircase; and the log kept by a wireless operator at Cape Race, Newfoundland, on the fateful night. ⊠*1675 Lower Water St.* ☎*902/424–7490 or 902/424–7491* *museum.gov.ns.ca/mma* *$8.50* *May–Oct., Mon. and Wed.–Sat. 9:30–5:30, Tues. 9:30–8; May and Oct., Sun. 1–5:30; June–Sept., Sun. 9:30–5:30; Nov.–Apr., Wed.–Sat. 9:30–5, Tues. 9:30–8, Sun. 1–5.*

❽ **Mary E. Black Gallery.** The exhibit space for the Nova Scotia Centre for Craft and Design presents rotating shows of high-quality crafts. ⊠*1061 Marginal Rd.* ☎*902/492–2522* *Free* *Mon.–Wed. and Fri. 11–5, Thurs. 11–8, Sat. 10–5, Sun. 1–5.*

❺ **Nova Scotia Museum of Natural History.** Easily recognized by the huge fiberglass model of the tiny northern spring peeper (a frog) that "clings" to the side of the building May through October. The Nature Centre is home to live snakes, frogs, insects, and other creatures; the Butterfly Pavilion is filled with species from around the world. ⊠*1747 Summer St.* ☎*902/424–7353* *nature.museum.gov.ns.ca* *$8; free Wed. 5–8* *Mid-May–mid-Oct., Mon., Tues., and Thurs.–Sat 9:30–5:30, Wed. 9:30–8, Sun. 1–5; Nov.–mid-May, Tues. and Thurs.–Sat. 9:30–5, Wed. 9:30–8, Sun. 1–5.*

⓯ **Pier 21.** From 1928 until 1971, refugees, returning troop ships, war brides, and more than a million immigrants arrived on Canadian soil through Pier 21, the front door to Canada. It's now a museum where the immigrant experience is re-created through live performances, multimedia presentations, and displays of photographs, documents, and artifacts. ✉1055 *Marginal Rd.* ☎*902/425–7770* 🌐*www.pier21.ca* 🎫*$8.50* 🕐*May–Nov., daily 9:30–5:30; Dec.–Mar., Tues.–Sat. 10–5; Apr., Mon.–Sat. 10–5.*

WORD OF MOUTH

"Halifax is a lovely city, urban with a small town feel... LOL, people actually still make eye contact there and will stop to offer assistance if they see you looking at a map." —Retired_teacher 02/07

16 **Point Pleasant Park.** This public park encompasses 186 wooded acres with walking trails and seafront paths. In September 2003, Hurricane Juan tore through it, uprooting or damaging 57,000 (about 70%) of the century-old trees in a matter of hours, leaving present-day park goers the same harbor views that must have inspired its use as a military command post in the first place. ✉*About 12 blocks down S. Park St. from Spring Garden Rd.*

10 **Province House.** Erected in 1819 to house Britain's first overseas self-government, the sandstone building serves as the meeting place for the provincial legislature. ✉*1726 Hollis St.* ☎*902/424–4661* 🎫*Free* 🕐*July and Aug., weekdays 9–5, weekends 10–4; Sept.–June, weekdays 9–4.*

1 **Purdy's Wharf.** The wharf is composed of a pier and twin office towers that stand right in the harbor. The buildings actually use ocean water to generate air-conditioning. ✉*Upper Water St.*

7 **St. Paul's Church.** Opened in 1750, this is Canada's oldest Protestant church and the burial site of many colonial notables. Embedded in an inside wall is a fragment of the *Mont Blanc*, one of the two ships whose collision caused the Halifax Explosion of December 6, 1917. ✉*1749 Argyle St.* ☎*902/429–2240* 🕐*Sept.–May, weekdays 9–4:30; June–Aug., Mon.–Sat. 9–4:30.*

WHERE TO STAY & EAT

$$$ Fodor's Choice ★ ✕ **Da Maurizio Dining Room.** At this Italian restaurant, Chef Maurizio's creativity and attention to detail create meals that have made him a local legend. The excellent seared foie gras is always on the menu, as are scampi crowned with a garlic-and-cognac sauce. For dessert, have the zabaglione. ✉*1496 Lower Water St.,* ☎*902/423–0859* 💳*AE, MC, V* 🕐*Closed Sun. No lunch.*

$$$ ✕ **Press Gang.** One of the hippest upscale establishments in Halifax. The Oyster bar offers the delicacy on the half-shell or Rockefeller-style, and for dinner, try the blackened-scallop chowder, citrus cumin–crab cakes, or the lavender-glazed rack of lamb. Thick, cold stone walls testify to the building's era—it was built in 1759—but the restaurant is warmed by comfortable seating and intimate lighting. ✉*5218 Prince St.* ☎*902/423–8816* ✍*Reservations recommended* 💳*AE, DC, MC, V.*

$$$ ★ ✕ **Salty's on the Waterfront.** Overlooking Privateer's Wharf and the entire harbor, this restaurant gets the prize for best location in the city. Huge bowls of steaming mussels and an excellent surf and turf crown a menu sure to satisfy any seafood lover. Save room for the famous dessert, chocolate mousse over praline crust. The Bar & Grill ($$), on the ground level, is less expensive and serves lunch outside on the wharf in

LOCAL FOOD & LODGING

Seafood, fresh apples, blueberries, and corn. Umm. If you're serious about discovering Nova Scotian meals, try Hodge Podge—fresh beans, peas, carrots, and baby potatoes, cooked in cream. Seek out local favorites like Solomon Gundy (a pickled-herring pâté), and blueberry grunt (a steamed pudding featuring Nova Scotia's finest berries).

In terms of accommodation, Nova Scotia offers a sprinkling of first-class resorts, top country inns, a few superior corporate hotels, and some exceptional bed-and-breakfasts. Most resorts and many B&Bs are seasonal, closing after Thanksgiving. You'll pay considerably more in Halifax and Dartmouth than elsewhere. Inns and B&Bs rely on ocean breezes for air-conditioning. Nova Scotia's computerized system Check In (☎902/425-5781 or 800/565-0000 🌐www.checkinnovascotia.com) provides information about and makes reservations with more than 700 hotels, motels, inns, campgrounds, and car-rental agencies.

summer (be warned: it can be very windy). ✉*1869 Upper Water St.* ☎*902/423-6818* *Reservations recommended for upstairs* ▭*AE, D, DC, MC, V.*

$$–$$$ ★ ✕**Bish World Cuisine.** Flavors from different parts of the world come together at this restaurant bordered on three sides by large windows overlooking Halifax Harbor. Try the Madras lamb or the rare seared tuna with lemon grass and basmati rice. ✉*1475 Lower Water St.* ☎*902/425-7993* ▭*AE, MC, V* ⊙*Closed Sun. No lunch.*

$$–$$$ ★ ✕**Chives Canadian Bistro.** The two chef-owners are wizards at defining eclectic Canadian cuisine, with a few French, German, and Asian influences thrown in for good measure. The large, casual restaurant with planked-wood floors and cozy lighting also offers an intimate table for four in their wine "vault" (the restaurant used to be a bank). The menu adapts to what's fresh and seasonal at the fishmongers and the farmers' market. ✉*1537 Barrington St.* ☎*902/420-9626* ▭*AE, DC, MC, V.*

$$–$$$ ✕**The Wooden Monkey.** This restaurant has a menu with a conscience and attracts diners with its locally grown macrobiotic and organic food, fair-trade organic coffee, and locally brewed beers and wines. Even if you don't enter for your health, stay for your taste buds: with starters such as julienne vegetable rolls and entrées like blackened haddock with homemade salsa, you'll soon be a convert. ✉*1685 Argyle St.* ☎*902/444-3844* ▭*AE, DC, MC, V.*

$–$$$ ✕**Dharma Sushi.** Tidy sushi, fresh sashimi, and feather-light tempura are artfully presented here and although the service is fast paced, the food doesn't suffer as a result. The daily lunch specials—including California rolls, vegetable tempura, and a popular chicken teriyaki—are a real deal and ready fast. ✉*1576 Argyle St.* ☎*902/425-7785* ▭*AE, MC, V* ⊙*Closed Sun. No lunch Sat.*

$–$$ ✕**Cheelin Restaurant.** Fresh and flavorful dishes are prepared in the open kitchen at this informal Chinese restaurant. Each dish receives individual attention and care, and the chef-owner personally checks with diners to make sure they are satisfied. If you're looking for something different, try the amazing stuffed eggplant in Yu Xiang (dark Szechuan) sauce. ✉*Brewery Market, 1496 Lower Water St.* ☎*902/422–2252* ▭*AE, MC, V* ⏲*No dinner Mon. No lunch Sun.*

$–$$ ✕**Il Mercato Ristorante.** Enter this Italian eatery at your own risk: the gleaming display cases of antipasti and desserts are sure to tempt. In the heart of the downtown shopping district, Il Mercato is an ideal lunch stop but come early for dinner, because this hopping place does not take reservations. ✉*5650 Spring Garden Rd.* ☎*902/422–2866* *Reservations not accepted* ▭*AE, MC, V.*

¢–$$ ✕**The Harbourside Market.** This casual cluster of restaraunt boutiques is perfect for families. There are six restaurants to choose from—kids can have pizza or burgers, and there's seafood or wonderful Greek dishes for the grown-ups. Seating is inside (with full windows overlooking neighboring Dartmouth) or outside. ✉*1869 Upper Water St.* ☎*902/422–3077* 🌐*www.historicproperties.ca/merch_1.htm* ▭*AE, MC, V.*

14

¢–$$ ✕**Satisfaction Feast.** This small vegetarian restaurant is informal, friendly, and usually packed at lunchtime. The food is wholesome, with lots of ethnic influences—think fresh whole-wheat bread and curries. Sweet, sharp ginger beer is brewed on the premises and is wonderful cold, with soda water, or hot, as a tea. Enjoy an organic coffee with one of the fine cakes or desserts. ✉*1581 Grafton St.* ☎*902/422–3540* ▭*MC, V.*

$$$–$$$$ ★ **Prince George Hotel.** A luxurious and understated business-oriented hotel. Gio Restaurant ($$) serves eclectic cuisine in a casual setting. The hotel is connected by underground tunnel to the World Trade and Convention Centre; walkways provide access to shops, offices, and entertainment, including the harborside casino. ✉*1725 Market St., B3J 3N9* ☎*902/425–1986, 800/565–1567 in Canada* 🌐*www.princegeorgehotel.com* *189 rooms, 14 suites* *In-room: Wi-Fi. In-hotel: restaurant, bar, pool, gym, concierge, parking (fee)* ▭*AE, DC, MC, V.*

$$–$$$$ **Cambridge Suites.** Besides the convenience of being able to prepare your own food, the best feature of this all-suites hotel is its location near downtown Halifax and Citadel Hill. It's four blocks (albeit up a steep hill) from the waterfront hub and one block from Spring Garden Road's fabulous shopping and people-watching. ✉*1583 Brunswick St., B3J 3P5* ☎*902/420–0555 or 800/565–1263* *902/420–9379* 🌐*www.cambridgesuiteshalifax.com* *200 suites* *In-room: kitchen, Wi-Fi. In-hotel: restaurant, room service, bar, fitness center, hot tub, sauna* ▭*AE, D, DC, MC, V* *CP.*

$$–$$$$ **Halifax Marriott Harbourfront.** This waterfront hotel varies in appearance from others in the chain. Its convenient location in the Historic Properties area contributes to its elegance. Rooms are fairly spacious; all have desks and sitting areas. ✉*1919 Upper Water St., B3J 3J5* ☎*902/421–1700* *902/422–5805* 🌐*www.marriott.com* *335 rooms, 19 suites* *In-room: Wi-Fi. In-hotel: restaurant, coffee shop, room service, bar, pool, gym, hair salon, spa, concierge, laundry service, parking (fee), no-smoking rooms* ▭*AE, DC, MC, V.*

$$–$$$$ **The Halliburton.** Period antiques and goose-down duvets await you in the comfortable (but dark) rooms. Suites have fireplaces, and there's a lovely garden. The rates here vary, with some topping $300. Local

game and Atlantic seafood are served in a small but elegant dining room, Stories ($$–$$$$). ✉ *5184 Morris St., B3J 1B3* ☎ *902/420–0658* 📠 *902/423–2324* 🌐 *www.thehalliburton.com* *25 rooms, 4 suites* *In-hotel: restaurant, parking (no fee), no elevator* 💳 *AE, DC, MC, V* *CP.*

$$–$$$$ **Westin Nova Scotian.** This grand hotel, which had renovations in 2004, sits solidly in downtown Halifax with the harbor behind it. All rooms have the chain's signature "heavenly beds" with duvet and five pillows, and are outfitted with ergonomic chairs and a desk. The restaurant serves fresh fish and shellfish dishes as well as pastas and meatier fare. ✉ *1181 Hollis St., B3H 2P6* ☎ *902/421–1000 or 877/993–7846* 📠 *902/422–9465* 🌐 *www.westin.ns.ca* *297 rooms, 13 suites* *In-room: dial-up. In-hotel: restaurant, bar, tennis court, pool, gym, laundry service, no-smoking rooms, minibar* 💳 *AE, DC, MC, V.*

$$–$$$ **Inn on the Lake.** A great value in a quiet location, this small country club–style hotel sits on 5 acres of parkland on the edge of a Fall River lake, 30 minutes from Halifax and 10 minutes from the airport. Rooms are spacious and have balconies, and many have whirlpool tubs. ✉ *3009 Highway 2, Fall River B2T 1J5* ☎ *902/861–3480 or 800/463–6465* 📠 *902/861–4883* 🌐 *www.innonthelake.com* *20 rooms, 20 suites* *In-room: Wi-Fi. In-hotel: restaurant, bar, tennis courts, pool, beachfront, airport shuttle, parking (no fee), no elevator* 💳 *AE, MC, V.*

$ **Garden View Bed & Breakfast.** This lovely Victorian home sits on a quiet residential street near the Halifax Commons and you can relax in the living room in front of the fire. The garden is especially charming. The living room has cable TV and DVD. Breakfast is served in the dining room. Only one room has a private bathroom. ✉ *6052 Williams St., B3K 1E9* ☎ *902/423–2943 or 888/737–0778* 📠 *902/423–4355* 🌐 *www.interdesign.ca/gardenview* *3 rooms, 1 with bath* *In-room: no a/c, no phone (some), no TV (some). In-hotel: no-smoking rooms, no elevator* 💳 *MC, V* *BP.*

NIGHTLIFE & THE ARTS

THEATER The **Neptune Theatre** (✉ *1593 Argyle St.* ☎ *902/429–7300, 800/565–7345 information, 902/429–7070 box office* 🌐 *www.neptunetheatre.com*), Canada's oldest professional repertory playhouse, has a main stage and studio theater under one roof. It stages year-round performances ranging from classics to comedy and contemporary Canadian drama. In July and August, **Shakespeare by the Sea** (☎ *902/422–0295* 🌐 *www.shakespearebythesea.ca*) performs the Bard's works Thursday through Sunday evenings at 7 PM, and weekends at 1 PM in Point Pleasant Park, at the southern end of the Halifax peninsula. No tickets are required—just show up and contribute to the bucket ($10 is suggested).

SPORTS & THE OUTDOORS

GOLF Within an easy drive of downtown Halifax is **Granite Springs Golf Club** (✉ *4441 Prospect Rd.* ☎ *902/852–4653*), an 18-hole, par-72, semi-private course open to greens-fee play. **Glen Arbour** (✉ *40 Clubhouse Lane, Hammonds Plains* ☎ *902/835–4944*) has two courses (18 holes and 9 holes) in this residential/golf community that are open to transient players after 10 AM during the week and after 11 AM on the weekends—but if you book four days in advance, you can start earlier. Green fees vary with the months of the summer.

SHOPPING

The **Art Gallery of Nova Scotia Shop** (⊠*1741 Hollis St.* ☎*902/424–7542*) carries a good selection of arts and crafts; it also has a wonderful café decorated with colorful regional art. **Attica** (⊠*1566 Barrington St.* ☎*902/423–2557*) sells furniture, objets d'art, and housewares by Canadian and international designers. You can find fine crafts in the stores within the large **Barrington Inn Complex** (⊠*1875 Barrington St.*).

Nova Scotian Crystal Ltd. (⊠*George and Lower Water Sts.* ☎*902/492–0416*) is the place to watch Waterford master craftspeople blowing glass into graceful decanters and bowls, which can be purchased in the showroom. **Pete's Frootique** (⊠*1515 Dresden Row*) is the brainchild of British greengrocer (and Canadian TV personality) Pete Luckett. Stop in at the vast gourmet food–and-produce store for a quick bite in the café or a ready-made gourmet sandwich for a picnic at the nearby Public Gardens.

DARTMOUTH

Immediately north of Halifax via the A. Murray Mackay and Angus L. Macdonald bridges.

You can drive, or take the ferry from Halifax to Dartmouth—the two cities are closely connected, and only about a 20-minute ferry ride away. If you take the ferry (its $2 fare is the cheapest Halifax Harbor cruise and it's only about a 20–minute ride), be sure to check out the sculptures by artist Dawn McNutt in the courtyard just outside the Dartmouth terminal.

If you'd rather walk to Dartmouth, try the Angus L. Macdonald Bridge, which has a walkway and a bicycle path—the bridge is 2 km (1 mi) long, so estimate a 20-minute walk from stem to stern.

The **Black Cultural Centre for Nova Scotia,** in Westphal (a neighborhood of Dartmouth), is in the heart of the oldest black community in the area. The museum, library, and educational complex are dedicated to the preservation of the history and culture of African Americans in Nova Scotia, who first arrived here in the 1600s. ⊠*Hwy. 7 and Cherrybrook Rd.* ☎*902/434–6223* *$5* *June–Sept., weekdays 9–5, Sat. 10–5.*

WHERE TO STAY & EAT

$$–$$$ ✕**La Perla.** The rich food at this northern Italian restaurant overlooking the harbor is consistently excellent. Servings are hearty. Calamari tossed with chilies and tomato has never been so tender; snails swim in a heady Gorgonzola cream sauce. For dessert, try the homemade ice cream or sorbettis. ⊠*73 Alderney Dr.* ☎*902/469–3241* 🌐*www.laperla.ca* *AE, MC, V.*

$–$$$ **Park Place Ramada Renaissance.** In Dartmouth's Burnside Industrial Park, this luxury hotel caters to business travelers and families. There is a 108-foot indoor waterslide. *240 Brownlow Ave., B3B 1X6 902/468–8888, 800/561–3733 in Canada 902/468–8765 www.ramadans.com 178 rooms, 30 suites In-hotel: restaurant, room service, bar, pool, gym, parking (no fee), Wi-Fi AE, DC, MC, V.*

SOUTH SHORE & ANNAPOLIS VALLEY

The South Shore is rocky coast, island-dotted bays, fishing villages, and shipyards; the Annapolis Valley is lumberyards, farms, vineyards, and orchards. The South Shore is German, French, and Yankee; the valley is British.

Highway 103, Highway 3, and various secondary roads form the province's designated Lighthouse Route, which leads southwest from Halifax down the South Shore. It ends in Yarmouth, where the Evangeline Trail begins, winding along the shore of St. Mary's Bay through a succession of Acadian villages that blend into each other—a charming mosaic of culture.

The Annapolis Valley runs northeast, sheltered on both sides by the North and South mountains. Like the South Shore, the valley is punctuated with pleasant small towns, each with a generous supply of extravagant Victorian homes and churches.

PEGGY'S COVE

48 km (30 mi) southwest of Halifax.

Peggy's Cove, on Highway 333, marks the entrance to St. Margaret's Bay, which has been guarded for years by its famous octagonal lighthouse. Don't be tempted to venture too close to the lighthouse—many an unwary visitor has been swept away by the mighty surf that sometimes breaks here. Park in the spacious public lot and enjoy the village's shops and services during the three-minute walk up to the lighthouse.

WHERE TO STAY & EAT

$–$$$ **Sou'wester Restaurant.** Sou'wester, at the base of the Peggy's Cove lighthouse, serves home-style fare, including a wide range of Maritime specialties—try the *Solomon Gundy* (herring and onion with sour cream)—and fish-and-chips. There's also a large souvenir shop. *178 Peggy's Point Rd., off Hwy. 333 902/823–2561 AE, DC, MC, V.*

$–$$$ ★ **Havenside B&B.** At this luxurious home, multilevel decks overlook a delightful seascape near Peggy's Cove. A serene gathering room with fireplace, a games room with a pool table, and a "breakfast that makes lunch redundant"—fresh homemade muffins, pancakes, French toast, eggs—enhance the package. *225 Boutillier's Cove Rd., Hackett's Cove B3Z 3J6 902/823–9322 or 800/641–8272 902/823–9322 www.havenside.com 3 rooms, 1 suite In-room: no a/c, no phone, no TV, Wi-Fi. In-hotel: no-smoking rooms, no elevator MC, V BP.*

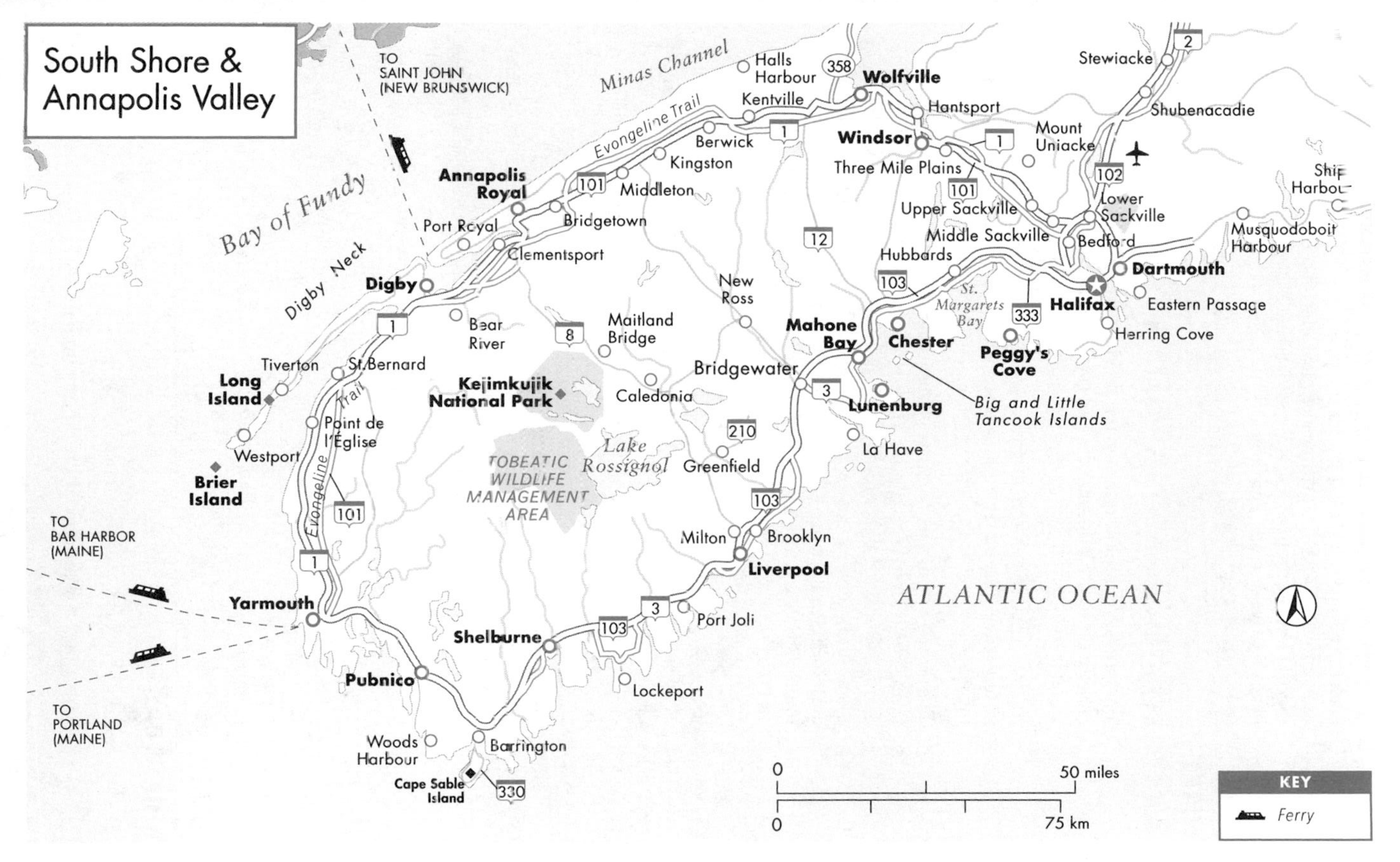
South Shore & Annapolis Valley
TO SAINT JOHN (NEW BRUNSWICK)
Minas Channel
Halls Harbour
358
Wolfville
Kentville
Hantsport
Evangeline Trail
Berwick
1
Windsor
Mount Uniacke
Stewiacke
2
Shubenacadie
Kingston
Three Mile Plains
101
102
Annapolis Royal
Middleton
Lower Sackville
Bay of Fundy
Port Royal
Bridgetown
Upper Sackville
Middle Sackville
Bedford
Musquodoboit Harbour
12
Hubbards
Clementsport
Dartmouth
Digby Neck
Digby
New Ross
103
St. Margarets Bay
Halifax
Eastern Passage
Bear River
8
Maitland Bridge
Mahone Bay
Chester
333
Herring Cove
Tiverton
St. Bernard
Peggy's Cove
Long Island
Kejimkujik National Park
Caledonia
Bridgewater
3
Lunenburg
Big and Little Tancook Islands
Point de l'Église
210
La Have
Westport
Lake Rossignol
Greenfield
TOBEATIC WILDLIFE MANAGEMENT AREA
Brier Island
TO BAR HARBOR (MAINE)
Milton
Brooklyn
Liverpool
ATLANTIC OCEAN
Yarmouth
Port Joli
Shelburne
Pubnico
Lockeport
TO PORTLAND (MAINE)
Woods Harbour
Barrington
Cape Sable Island
330
0
50 miles
0
75 km
KEY
Ferry

SHOPPING

Beales' Bailiwick (✉ *124 Peggy's Point Rd.* ☎ *902/823–2099*) carries outstanding crafts—Maritime-designed clothing, pewter, jewelry, and more. The adjoining coffee shop affords the best photo opportunity for Peggy's Cove and the lighthouse.

CHESTER

64 km (40 mi) west of Peggy's Cove.

Chester is a popular summer retreat for an established population of Americans and Haligonians whose splendid homes and yachts rim the waterfront.

In fact, yachting is the town's principal summer occupation, culminating each August in **Chester Race Week,** Atlantic Canada's largest regatta.

★ The **Ross Farm Living Museum of Agriculture,** a restored 19th-century farm, illustrates the evolution of agriculture from 1600 to 1925. The animals here are those found on a farm of the 1800s—draft horses, oxen, and older breeds or types of animals. Blacksmithing and other crafts are demonstrated. The Pedlar's Shop sells items made in the community. ✉ *Hwy. 12, 29 km (18 mi) inland from Chester, New Ross* ☎ *902/689–2210 or 877/689–2210* *$6* *May–Oct., daily 9:30–5:30; Nov.–Apr., Wed.–Sun. 9:30–4:30, hrs vary; call ahead.*

WHERE TO STAY & EAT

¢–$ Fodor's Choice ★ **Julien's Pastry Shop & Bakery.** Grab a few delectable goodies to go along with the deluxe sandwiches from this fabulous French bakery and then take a picnic along Chester's scenic waterfront. Julien's is open from 8 AM to 5 PM. ✉ *43 Queen St.* ☎ *902/275–2324* *MC, V* *Closed Mon. mid-Sept.–mid-June.*

$–$$$ **Dauphinee Inn.** This charming country inn has first-class accommodations and an excellent restaurant ($$–$$$), the Hot Rocks: it's a social-dining concept where you are invited to cook fresh vegetables, seafood, beef, or chicken on a hot slab of granite. Opportunities abound for bicycling, bird-watching, and deep-sea fishing, and six golf courses are within a half-hour drive. The spacious rooms have antique beds with old-fashioned quilts and newer touches such as whirlpool tubs and CD players. ✉ *167 Shore Club Rd., Box 640, Exit 6 off Hwy. 103, 19 km (12 mi) east of Chester, Hubbards Cove B0J 1T0* ☎ *902/857–1790 or 800/567–1790* *902/857–9555* *www.dauphineeinn.com* *6 rooms* *In-room: no a/c, no phone, Wi-Fi. In-hotel: restaurant, bar, no-smoking rooms, no elevator* *AE, D, DC, MC, V* *Closed Nov.–Apr.* *BP.*

MAHONE BAY

24 km (15 mi) west of Chester.

This quiet town perched on the idyllic bay of the same name comes alive each summer.

WHERE TO STAY & EAT

$-$$ **Innlet Café.** A pleasant restaurant with a fine view of the town across the bay, whose broad Canadian-style menu features poultry, meats, seafood, and a few vegetarian options. The Heavenly Chicken has been a delicious mainstay at the café for years. *249 Edgewater St. 902/624–6363 MC, V.*

$ **Amber Rose Inn.** All the creature comforts are available at this 1875 inn. Each of the large suites has a whirlpool tub and handsome antiques. It's not unusual to hear your bilingual hosts chatting in Spanish around the table in the morning, where the lavish breakfast might include Sky-High Pie (spinach and cheese) or strata (asparagus and egg). *319 Main St., Box 450, B0J 2E0 902/624–1060 902/624–0997 www.amberroseinn.com 3 suites In-room: refrigerator. In-hotel: parking (no fee), no-smoking rooms, no elevator AE, MC, V BP.*

SHOPPING

The work of fine Atlantic Canada artists and artisans is for sale at **Moorings Gallery & Shop** (*575 Main St. 902/624–6208*). **Suttles and Seawinds** (*466 Main St. 902/624–6177*) has a worldwide reputation for their distinctively designed, high-quality quilts. An adjacent carriage house is a gallery for stunning quilts and fabrics.

LUNENBURG

9 km (6 mi) south of Mahone Bay.

Victorian-era architecture, wooden boats, historic inns, and good restaurants—Lunenburg delights all the senses. The center of town, known as Old Town, is a UNESCO World Heritage Site, and the fantastic old school on the hilltop is the region's finest remaining example of Second Empire architecture.

★ Lunenburg is home port to the *Bluenose II* (*866/579–4909 www.schoonerbluenose2.ca*), a tall-ship ambassador for Canada. She's a replica of the first *Bluenose*, the great racing schooner depicted on the back of the Canadian dime that was the winner of four international races and the pride of Canada. When in port, the *Bluenose II* is open for tours through the Fisheries Museum of the Atlantic. Two-hour harbor sailings in summer cost $35.

Fodor's Choice ★ The **Fisheries Museum of the Atlantic**, on the Lunenburg waterfront, gives a comprehensive overview of Nova Scotia fisheries with demonstrations such as sail making, dory building, boat launching, and fish splitting. A touch tank with starfish, shellfish, and anemones; participatory demonstrations of rug hooking and quilting; and a daylong schedule of films at the theater make visiting here a busy but rich experience. *68 Bluenose Dr. 902/634–4794 museum.gov.ns.ca/fma $9 May–Oct., free Nov.–Apr. July and Aug., 9:30–7; May, June, Sept., and Oct., daily 9:30–5:30; Nov.–Apr., weekdays 9–4 or by appointment.*

WHERE TO STAY & EAT

$–$$$ ✕ **Grand Banker Seafood Bar & Grill.** A wide variety of seafood at modest prices is the mainstay at this bustling, big-menu establishment. You can dine on scallops, shrimp, or lobster in season, or, for those with hearty appetites, the seafood platter with a combination. ✉ *82 Montague St.* ☎ *902/634–3300* 💳 *AE, D, DC, MC, V.*

$–$$ ★ ✕ **Magnolia's Grill.** This kitschy 1950s diner is as famous for its key lime pie as for its creole peanut soup. Full of vintage collectibles, the popular and always-packed grill also serves local fare such as cod cheeks and pulled pork. ✉ *128 Montague St.* ☎ *902/634–3287* 💳 *AE, MC, V* ⏲ *Closed Dec. and Jan.*

$$ 🏨 **Lunenburg Inn.** The two suites and five rooms with private baths are spacious and furnished with fine antiques. An elegant main-floor parlor adjoins the bright blue-and-white dining room; a computer with wireless Internet access in the sitting room adds a modern touch. The top-floor 775-square-foot suite has a tiny kitchenette. ✉ *26 Dufferin St., B0J 2C0* ☎ *902/634–3963 or 800/565–3963* 🖷 *902/634–9419* 🌐 *www.lunenburginn.com* *5 rooms, 2 suites* *In-room: no a/c (some), kitchenette (some), VCRs and DVDs (some). In-hotel: no-smoking rooms, public Internet, no elevator* 💳 *DC, MC, V* *BP.*

$–$$ 🏨 **Arbor View Inn.** Leaded and stained-glass windows, wood trim, and antiques enhance every room of this early-20th-century house, and spacious grounds invite strolls. The top-floor suite has a queen-size canopy bed, a two-person whirlpool tub, and a deck. ✉ *216 Dufferin St., B0J 2C0* ☎ *800/890–6650 or 902/634–3658* 🌐 *www.arborview.ca* *2 rooms, 2 suites* *In-room: no a/c, no phone, no TV. In-hotel: no-smoking rooms, no elevator* 💳 *MC, V* *BP.*

$ 🏨 **1826 Maple Bird House B&B.** This B&B has a huge garden overlooking the harbor and a golf course. The piano in the drawing room sets the relaxing mood that characterizes this home, and the hosts know a thing or two about breakfast—crepes, omelets, cereals, and fruits appear in ample amounts. ✉ *36 Pelham St., Box 278, B0J 2C0* ☎ *902/634–3863 or 888/395–3863* 🌐 *www.maplebirdhouse.ca* *4 rooms* *In-room: no a/c, no phone, no TV. In-hotel: pool, no-smoking rooms, no elevator* 💳 *MC, V* *BP.*

SPORTS & THE OUTDOORS

June through October **Lunenburg Whale-Watching** (☎ *902/527–7175*) has three-hour trips daily at 8:30, 11:30, 2:30, and 5:30, seven days a week, from the Fisheries Museum Wharf for $45. You can also arrange for bird-watching excursions and tours of Lunenburg Harbour.

SHOPPING

The **Lunenburg Forge & Metalworks Gallery** (✉ *146 Bluenose Dr.* ☎ *902/634–7125*) is a traditional artist-blacksmith shop on the waterfront. One-of-a-kind handcrafted wrought-iron items and custom orders, including time-honored designs and whimsical creations, are available.

LIVERPOOL

46 km (29 mi) south of Bridgewater.

Settled around 1760 by New Englanders, and a privateering centre during the War of 1812, Liverpool is now a fishing and paper-milling town.

In a renovated Canadian National railway station, the **Hank Snow Country Music Centre Museum** commemorates the great country singer whose childhood home is nearby. A country-music archive and library, and memorabilia of the singer's career are on view. A new memorabilia gallery highlights new Canadian country-music stars. ✉*148 Bristol Ave., off Hwy. 103* ☎*902/354–4675 or 888/450–5525* 🎟*$3* ⏲*Mid-May–mid-Oct., Mon.–Sat. 9–5, Sun. noon–5.*

★ **Rossignol Cultural Centre.** This is an eclectic mix of two galleries and five museums, including a trapper's cabin, an early-20th-century drugstore, 50 stuffed-wildlife exhibits, an outhouse museum, and a complete oval wood-paneled drawing room brought over from an English manor house. ✉*205 Church St.* ☎*902/354–3067* 🌐*www.rossignolculturalcentre.com* 🎟*$4* ⏲*Mon.–Sat. 10–5:30; July and Aug., also Sun. noon–5:30.*

Fort Point Lighthouse Park, on the site where explorers Samuel de Champlain and Sieur de Monts landed in 1604, overlooks Liverpool Harbour. Interpretive displays and models in the 1855 lighthouse recall the area's privateering and shipbuilding heritage. ✉*End of Main St. off Hwy. 103* ☎*902/354–5260* 🎟*By donation* ⏲*May, June, Sept., and Oct., daily 10–6; July and Aug., daily 9–7.*

The **Simeon Perkins House,** built in 1766 by ships' carpenters, the house gives the illusion of standing in the upside-down hull of a ship. ✉*105 Main St.* ☎*902/354–4058* 🎟*$2* ⏲*June–mid-Oct., Mon.–Sat. 9:30–5:30, Sun. 1–5:30.*

Kejimkujik Seaside Adjunct has isolated coves, broad white beaches, and imposing headlands and is protected by Kejimkujik National Park. A hike along the 6-km (4-mi) trail reveals a pristine coastline that is home to harbor seals, eider ducks, and many other species. To protect nesting areas of the endangered piping plover, parts of the St. Catherine's River beach (the main beach) are closed to the public from late April to early August. ✉*Off Hwy. 103, 25 km (16 mi) southwest of Liverpool, Port Joli* ☎*902/682–2772* 🎟*$4 May 15–Oct. 14* ⏲*Daily 24 hrs.*

WHERE TO STAY & EAT

$–$$$ ✕**Quarterdeck Grill.** Enjoy spectacular views of surf and sand while relishing this landmark restaurant's use of seasonal fresh ingredients. It's well known for its steamed lobster and grilled-fish dishes. ✉*7499 Hwy. 3, 15 km (10 mi) west of Liverpool* ☎*902/683–2998 or 800/565–1119* 💳*AE, DC, MC, V.*

$–$$$ ✕🏨**Lane's Privateer Inn.** This 200-year-old inn has comfortable guest rooms, a restaurant serving Canadian fare ($–$$$), a pub, a bookstore-café, and a specialty-food shop. Most of the 27 rooms have views overlooking the Mersey River or harbor. Nearby, there's windsurfing, golfing, deep-sea fishing, and five spectacular beaches. ✉ *27 Bristol Ave., B0T 1K0* ☎ *902/354–3456 or 800/794–3332* 📠 *902/354–7220* 🌐 *www.lanesprivateerinn.com* *27 with bath* *In-room: Wi-Fi. In-hotel: bar, no-smoking rooms, no elevator* 💳 *AE, MC, V* *CP.*

KEJIMKUJIK NATIONAL PARK

67 km (42 mi) northwest of Liverpool.

The gentle waterways of this 381-square-km (147-square-mi) park have been the canoe routes of the Mi'Kmaq for thousands of years. Today the routes and land trails are well marked and mapped, permitting canoeists, hikers, and campers to explore, swim in the warm lake, and glimpse white-tailed deer, beaver, owls, loons, and other wildlife. Canoes and camping equipment can be rented. ✉ *Hwy. 8, between Liverpool and Annapolis Royal, Maitland Bridge* ☎ *902/682–2772* 🌐 *www.pc.gc.ca* *$5.50* ⏲ *Daily 24 hrs.*

WHERE TO STAY

$$–$$$$ ★ **White Point Beach Resort.** Activities like kayaking, birding, and walking nature trails make for dynamic holidays at this resort. On-site is a beachfront grill restaurant with outdoor buffets and barbecues. Choose a room outfitted with pine furniture in one of the lodges or a one- to three-bedroom cottage with a living room and fireplace, along the beach or nestled amid mature trees. ✉ *Exit 20A off Hwy. 103, White Point B0T 1G0* ☎ *902/354–2711 or 800/565–5068* 📠 *902/354–7278* 🌐 *www.whitepoint.com* *77 rooms, 44 cottages* *In-room: no a/c (some), refrigerator. In-hotel: golf course, tennis courts, pool, spa, beachfront, bicycles, no-smoking rooms* 💳 *AE, MC, V.*

$–$$ ★ **Mersey River Chalets.** Yoga, swimming in the lake, bonfires, and outdoor sports fill the agenda at this 375-acre wilderness resort. Seven two-bedroom chalets are nestled in dense forest and you can see river and waterfall scenery from the nearly 2-km-long (1-mi-long) boardwalk. There are even tepees built on platforms on the shore of Lake Harry. ✉ *Off Hwy. 8, General Delivery, Caledonia B0T 1B0* ☎ *902/682–2443* 📠 *902/682–2332* 🌐 *www.merseyriverchalets.com* *7 chalets, 5 tepees* *In-room: no a/c, no TV. In-hotel: seasonal restaurant, tennis court, no elevator* 💳 *MC, V.*

SHELBURNE

69 km (43 mi) south of Liverpool.

Shelburne is a fishing and shipbuilding town at the mouth of the Roseway River.

Tours of some of Shelburne's historic homes are offered during periodic fund-raising endeavors; **Shelburne Visitor Information** (☎ *902/875–4547*) has details.

WHERE TO STAY & EAT

$$–$$$ Fodor'sChoice ★ **Charlotte Lane Café.** Swiss specialties, along with seafood, meats, and salads, are served in this beautifully restored building which dates to the mid-1800s. Try the rack of lamb. The café has a pleasant garden patio and a shop selling local crafts. *13 Charlotte La. 902/875–3314 MC, V Closed Sun. and Mon. and mid-Dec.–early May.*

$–$$$ **Cooper's Inn.** One of the last cooperages in North America is also a unique inn on Shelburne's historic waterfront, which was the site of a major Loyalist landing in 1783. Inside the elegant 1784 inn are antiques and fine art. *36 Dock St., B0T 1W0 902/875–4656 or 800/688–2011 902/875–4447 www.thecoopersinn.com 7 rooms, 1 suite In-room: Wi-Fi, no a/c, off-street parking (no fee). In-hotel: no elevator AE, MC, V Closed Nov.–Mar. BP.*

PUBNICO

48 km (30 mi) northwest of Barrington.

Pubnico marks the beginning of the Acadian milieu; from here to Digby the communities are mostly French-speaking.

WHERE TO EAT

$–$$ **Red Cap Restaurant.** This venerable 1946 establishment, which seats 140, overlooks Pubnico Harbour and includes a six-unit motel and a café that serves an acclaimed version of rappie pie (chicken stew with dried shredded potatoes). The menu also contains seafood, and bread pudding. *Exit 31 off Rte. 335 S, Middle West Pubnico B0W 2M0 902/762–2112 902/762–2887 www.redcapmotel-rest.com AE, MC, V.*

YARMOUTH

41 km (25 mi) north of Pubnico.

Yarmouth has attracted visitors for nearly three centuries. The town's status as a large port city and its proximity to New England accounted for its early prosperity, and its great shipping heritage is reflected in its fine harbor, two marinas, and museums.

The **Yarmouth County Museum & Archives** has one of the largest collections of ship paintings in Canada; artifacts associated with the *Titanic*; exhibits of household items displayed in period rooms; musical instruments, including rare mechanical pianos and music boxes; and items that richly evoke centuries past. *22 Collins St. 902/742–5539 yarmouthcountymuseum.ednet.ns.ca Museum $3, museum and Pelton-Fuller House $4, archives $5 Museum June–mid-Oct., Mon.–Sat. 9–5, Sun. 2–5; mid-Oct.–May, Tues.–Sun. 2–5. Pelton-Fuller House June–mid-Oct., Mon.–Sat. 9–5.*

The **Firefighters Museum of Nova Scotia** recounts Nova Scotia's fire-fighting history through photographs and artifacts, including vintage pumpers, hose wagons, ladder trucks, and an 1863 Amoskeag Steamer. Kids can don a fire helmet and take the wheel of a 1933 Bickle Pumper.

✉451 Main St. ☎902/742–5525 $3 ⊙June and Sept., Mon.–Sat. 9–5; July and Aug., Mon.–Sat. 9–9, Sun. 10–5; Oct.–May, weekdays 9–4, Sat. 1–4.

WHERE TO STAY & EAT

$$–$$$ ✕ **Chez Bruno Cafe Bistro.** It might be surprising to find a Mediterannean bistro in Yarmouth, but don't be surprised by how good it is. They serve everything from fresh seafood to sandwich wraps to homemade Belgian waffles. *✉278 Main St. ☎902/742–0031 ▭AE, V ⊙Closed Sun.*

$$–$$$ ★ **Charles C. Richards House Historic Bed & Breakfast.** One of Nova Scotia's most distinctive B&Bs, a Queen Anne–style structure built in 1893. In 1999 it was lovingly restored: the spacious rooms are well outfitted, with scrupulously polished antiques. A tropical conservatory opens onto a wide veranda and a patio. Breakfast is an elegant affair. *✉17 Collins St., B5A 3C7 ☎902/742–0042 or 866/798–0929 🖷902/742–0326 ⊕www.charlesrichardshouse.ns.ca 3 rooms In-room: no a/c. In-hotel: no-smoking rooms, no elevator ▭AE, MC, V BP.*

$–$$ **Harbour's Edge Bed & Breakfast.** This serene 1864 home has a spectacular view of Yarmouth Harbour. Ornate wrought-iron fireplaces dominate the parlor and dining room, which open onto a veranda overlooking the harbor. At high tide the water laps against the lawn; at low tide myriad birds pay frequent visits. Harbour's Edge was reclaimed by new owners in 1990, and they are landscaping the vast 2-acre garden, with its century-old rhododendrons, quince, laburnum, and Japanese cherry trees. *✉12 Vancouver St., B5A 2N8 ☎902/742–2387 ⊕www.harboursedge.ns.ca 4 rooms In-room: Wi-Fi, no a/c, no phone, no TV. In-hotel: no-smoking rooms, no elevator ▭MC, V BP.*

$ **Murray Manor Bed & Breakfast.** The distinctive, pointed windows of this handsome 1825 Gothic-style house are reminiscent of a church. Century-old rhododendrons bloom in the garden and decorate the long dining room table, where guests share a hearty breakfast of fresh fruit, eggs, and maple sausages. The ferry terminal is a block away. The rooms share one bathroom. *✉225 Main St., B5A 1C6 ☎902/742–9625 or 877/742–9629 ⊕www.murraymanor.com 3 rooms without bath In-room: Wi-Fi, no a/c, no phone. In-hotel: no-smoking rooms, no elevator ▭MC, V BP.*

DIGBY

35 km (22 mi) northeast of Point de l'Église.

Digby has a rich history that dates to the arrival in 1783 of Loyalist refugees from New England; a famous scallop fleet that anchors in colorful profusion at the waterfront; and the plump, sweet scallops that are served everywhere. You can buy ultrafresh halibut, cod, scallops, and lobster—some merchants will even cook them up for you on the spot.

Digby Scallop Days is a four-day festival replete with parades, fireworks, and food in early August.

WHERE TO STAY & EAT

$$–$$$ ★ **Digby Pines Golf Resort and Spa.** Complete with fireplaces, sitting rooms, walking trails, and a view of the Annapolis Basin, this casually elegant property contains a Norman château–style hotel, 31 cottages, and lavish gardens. Local seafood with a French touch is served daily in the restaurant ($$$–$$$$). A 2,500-square-foot Aveda spa opened in 2005 and its poolside facility is a relaxing spot after a round of golf on the par-71, 18-hole course. *103 Shore Rd., Box 70, B0V 1A0 902/245–2511 or 800/667–4637 902/245–6133 www.digbypines.ca 84 rooms, 6 suites, 31 cottages In-hotel: restaurant, bar, golf course, tennis courts, pool, gym, no-smoking rooms AE, D, DC, MC Closed mid-Oct.–May.*

ANNAPOLIS ROYAL

29 km (18 mi) northeast of Digby.

One of Canada's oldest settlements, Annapolis Royal was founded as Port Royal by the French in 1605, destroyed by the British in 1613, rebuilt by the French as the main town of French Acadia, and fought over for a century. Finally, in 1710, New England colonists claimed the town and renamed it in honor of Queen Anne.

A lively **market** with fresh produce, home baking, local artists, and street musicians takes place every Saturday mid-May through mid-October on St. George Street, next to Ye Olde Town Pub.

★ **Fort Anne National Historic Site,** first fortified in 1629, holds the remains of the fourth fort to be erected here and garrisoned by the British as late as 1854. Earthwork fortifications, an early-18th-century gunpowder magazine, and officers' quarters have been preserved. *323 St. George St. 902/532–2397 or 902/532–2321 www.parkscanada.gc.ca Grounds free, museum $4 Mid-May–mid-Oct., daily 9–5:30; mid-Oct.–mid-May, by appointment.*

The **Annapolis Royal Historic Gardens** are 10 acres of magnificent, historically themed gardens, including a Victorian garden and a knot garden, a typical Acadian house with garden, and a 2,000-bush rose collection. *441 Upper St., George St. 902/532–7018 $8.50 Mid-May–June and Sept.–mid-Oct., daily 9–5; July and Aug., daily 8–dusk.*

WHERE TO STAY & EAT

$–$$ **Charlie's Place.** Fresh local seafood as well as meat and vegetarian fare are prepared in Cantonese style at this pleasant restaurant on the edge of town. *38 Prince Albert Rd. (Hwy. 1) 902/532–2111 AE, MC, V.*

¢–$ **German Bakery and Garden Cafe.** As the name suggests, there are plenty of Germanic influences at this soup and sandwich café, including schnitzel, sauerkraut, and sausages. All are served in a garden that overlooks the Annapolis Royal Historic Gardens. *441 St. George St. 902/532–1990 MC, V Closed Oct.–May. No dinner.*

¢–$$ **Garrison House Inn.** Opened in 1854, this inn facing Fort Anne has been carefully restored with period furniture and Victorian-era touches.

Three intimate private dining rooms ($$$–$$$$) and a dining deck are the settings for dinners that favor fresh seafood, especially scallops and salmon. Breakfast is included in the room rate during summer. ✉ *350 St. George St., B0S 1A0* ☎ *902/532–5750* 📠 *902/532–5501* 🌐 *www.garrisonhouse.ca* *7 rooms, 1 suite* *In-hotel: restaurant, no elevator* 💳 *AE, MC, V* ⏲ *Closed Jan.–Mar.*

$$ ★ **The Bailey House.** This relative newcomer to Annapolis Royal (it opened in 2005) does everything right and is the only B&B in town located on the water. The Georgian-style house, dating to 1770, has been immmaculately restored. Wood moldings, painted pine floors, and even the oddly-shaped front door with its massive wrought-iron hinges are all original. Each room has a fireplace, an en-suite bathroom, and views of the Annapolis Bay. Afternoon refreshments are included in the room rate, as is a large breakfast. ✉ *150 St. George St., B0S 1A0* ☎ *877/532–1285 or 902/532–1285* 🌐 *www.baileyhouse.ca* *2 rooms* 💳 *MC, V* *BP.*

$–$$ ★ **Bread and Roses Inn.** This Queen Anne–style inn is replete with exquisite architectural details and trim made from mahogany, black walnut, black cherry, and other woods. A traditional fountain is on the front lawn, and the garden invites sitting and strolling. Lavish breakfasts may include homemade scones or muffins, and quiche. ✉ *82 Victoria St., B0S 1A0* ☎ *902/532–5727 or 888/899–0551* 🌐 *www.breadandroses.ns.ca* *9 rooms* *In-room: no a/c (some), some satellite TV, Wi-Fi. In-hotel: no-smoking rooms, no elevator* 💳 *AE, MC, V* *BP.*

$–$$ **Hillsdale House Inn.** This historic 1849 property is furnished with antiques and paintings and surrounded by 12 acres of lawns and gardens. The renovated coach house has added two bright and spacious rooms to the original 11 bedrooms. The large breakfast includes homemade breads and jams. ✉ *519 George St., Box 148, B0S 1A0* ☎ *902/532–2345 or 877/839–2821* 📠 *905/532–2345* 🌐 *www.hillsdalehouseinn.ca* *13 rooms* 💳 *MC, V* *BP.*

LONG ISLAND & BRIER ISLAND

Tiverton, Long Island, is a 5-min ferry ride from East Ferry at the end of Digby Neck. Brier Island is an 8-min ferry ride from Freeport, Long Island.

Digby Neck is extended seaward by two narrow islands, Long Island and Brier Island, and because the surrounding waters are rich in plankton, the islands attract a variety of whales, including finbacks, humpbacks, minkes, and right whales, as well as harbor porpoises. The islands are also an excellent spot for bird-watching.

Brier Island Ferry (☎ *902/839–2302*) links the islands. Ferries must scuttle sideways to fight the ferocious Fundy tidal streams coursing through the narrow gaps. They operate hourly, at a cost of $5 return for car and passengers.

WHERE TO STAY & EAT

$-$$ **Brier Island Lodge and Restaurant.** This rustic lodge commands a panoramic view of the Bay of Fundy. Most rooms have ocean and lighthouse views. Fish chowder, fish cakes, and scallops are dinner specialties in the attractive restaurant ($$), which also serves breakfast and packs box lunches for day-trippers. ✉ *Water St., Brier Island, Westport B0V 1H0* ☎ *902/839–2300 or 800/662–8355* 📠 *902/839–2006* 🌐 *www.brierisland.com* *39 rooms* *In-room: no a/c. In-hotel: restaurant, bar, no-smoking rooms* 💳 *AE, DC, MC, V* *Closed Nov.–Apr.*

SPORTS & THE OUTDOORS

WHALE WATCHING **Brier Island Whale and Seabird Cruises** (☎ *902/839–2995 or 800/656–3660* 🌐 *www.brierislandwhalewatch.com*) offers whale-watching and seabird tours May through October. Onboard researchers and naturalists collect data for international research organizations. The fare is $48, and a portion of the fee is used to fund the research.

14

WOLFVILLE

60 km (37 mi) east of Annapolis Royal.

Settled in the 1760s by New Englanders, Wolfville is a college town with stately trees and ornate Victorian homes. Dikes, built by the Acadians in the early 1700s to reclaim fertile land from the unusually high tides, can still be viewed in Wolfville at the harbor and along many of the area's back roads.

The **Grand Pré National Historic Site** commemorates the expulsion of the Acadians by the British in 1755. This tragic story is retold in an innovative multimedia presentation featuring holograms and a film at the visitor center. ✉ *Hwy. 1, 5 km (3 mi) east of Wolfville, Grand Pré* ☎ *902/542–3631* *$7.15* *May–Oct., daily 9–6.*

WHERE TO STAY & EAT

$$–$$$$ ★ **Tempest.** Ethnic food and world-fusion cuisine fill the lunch and dinner menu at this trendy, upscale restaurant. Their seafood chowder isn't how your mother made it: they use finnan haddie (smoked haddock) and chorizo sausage instead of haddock and bacon. Nova Scotia arctic char is accompanied by local sauerkraut. Between courses, there's sorbet, and the Chocolate Duet provides a smooth ending. ✉ *117 Front St.* ☎ *902/542–0588* 💳 *AE, MC, V* *No lunch Mon.*

$–$$$$ ★ **Blomidon Inn.** Ramble through this inn's 3-acre English country garden, with its fish-stocked ponds, roses, and rhododendrons, and a terraced vegetable garden that also serves as a restaurant when the weather is fine. Intimate meals are expertly prepared in the main dining room ($$–$$$$; reservations essential), where fresh Atlantic salmon—grilled, steamed or plank—is a specialty. It's a family affair at the inn: the owners' sons are the chef and sommelier. ✉ *195 Main St. B4P 1C3* ☎ *902/542–2291 or 800/565–2291* 📠 *902/542–7461* 🌐 *www.blomidon.ns.ca* *28 rooms* *In-hotel: restaurant, tennis court, no elevator* 💳 *MC, V* *CP.*

$–$$ Fodor'sChoice ★ **Farmhouse Inn Bed and Breakfast.** This 1860 B&B has cozy accommodations, most with a two-person whirlpool tub and/or propane fireplace. Afternoon tea is complimentary, as is the pre-breakfast room service of coffee, tea, and muffins, and breakfast itself. *9757 Main St., 15 km (10 mi) north of Wolfville 902/582–7900 or 800/928–4346 www.farmhouseinn.ns.ca 2 rooms, 4 suites In-room: VCR. In-hotel: no elevator AE, MC, V BP.*

SPORTS & THE OUTDOORS

★ A popular series of **hiking trails** (*25 km [16 mi]) north of Wolfville*) leads from the end of Highway 358 to the dramatic cliffs of Cape Split, a 13-km (8-mi) round-trip.

WINDSOR

25 km (16 mi) southeast of Wolfville.

Windsor's history dates to 1703 when it was settled as an Acadian community.

Fort Edward, an assembly point for the Acadian expulsion, is the only remaining colonial blockhouse in Nova Scotia. *Exit 6 off Hwy. 1; take the 1st left at King St., then another left up street facing fire station No phone www.glinx.com/~whhs/ftedward.html Free Mid-June–early Sept., Tues.–Sat., 10–6.*

The **Mermaid Theatre of Nova Scotia** uses puppets and performers to retell traditional and contemporary children's classics. The troupe performs all over the world, but you can see the props and puppets on display right here. *132 Gerrish St. 902/798–5841 www.mermaidtheatre.ns.ca By donation Jan.–Nov., weekdays 9–4:30.*

WHERE TO EAT

¢–$ Fodor'sChoice ★ **Rose Arbour Café.** True to its name, the Rose Arbour has a flowery, bright interior, with posy-covered plates, cups, and saucers hung on the walls. Tasty food and reasonable prices make this a pleasant find. Try the fish-and-chips or fresh clams in season, and one of their homemade desserts, such as the popular rice pudding or cheesecake. *109 Gerrish St., 902/798–2322 AE, MC, V.*

THE EASTERN SHORE & NORTHERN NOVA SCOTIA

The road toward Cape Breton meanders past fishing villages, forests, and remote cranberry barrens, whereas the Northumberland Strait is bordered by sandy beaches and hiking trails. The Bay of Fundy has spectacular scenery—dense forests and steep cliffs that harbor prehistoric fossils and semiprecious stones.

The Sunrise Trail Heritage Tour takes you from the Tantramar Marsh in Amherst to the still-active St. Augustine Monastery. The Fundy

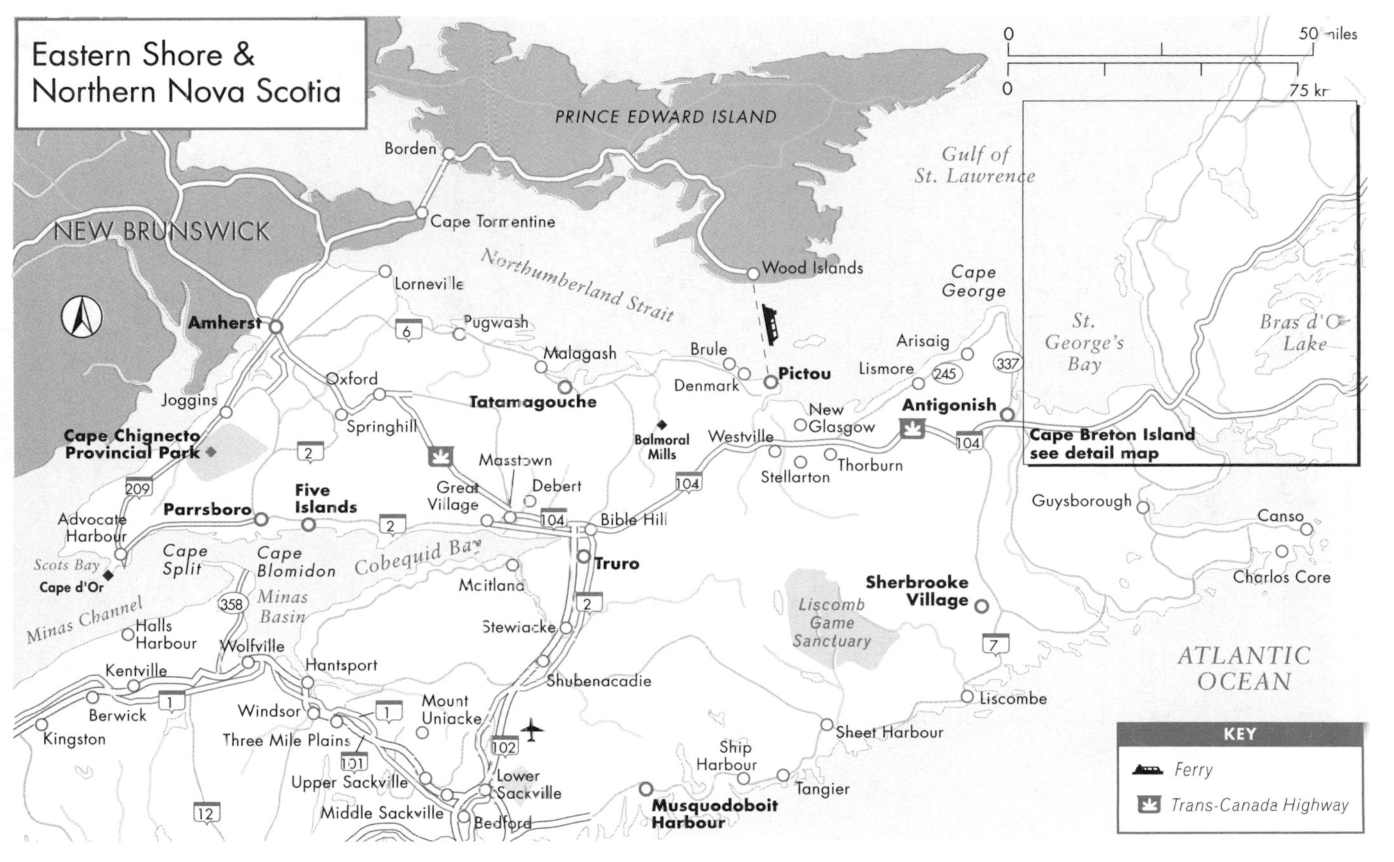

Eastern Shore & Northern Nova Scotia
0
50 miles
0
75 km
PRINCE EDWARD ISLAND
NEW BRUNSWICK
Gulf of St. Lawrence
Northumberland Strait
St. George's Bay
Bras d'Or Lake
Cape Breton Island see detail map
Borden
Cape Tormentine
Wood Islands
Lorneville
Amherst
Pugwash
Malagash
Brule
Denmark
Pictou
Cape George
Arisaig
Lismore
Antigonish
Oxford
Joggins
Springhill
Tatamagouche
Balmoral Mills
Westville
New Glasgow
Stellarton
Thorburn
Cape Chignecto Provincial Park
Masstown
Debert
Great Village
Five Islands
Parrsboro
Advocate Harbour
Bible Hill
Truro
Guysborough
Canso
Charlos Core
Scots Bay
Cape d'Or
Cape Split
Cape Blomidon
Cobequid Bay
Maitland
Minas Basin
Minas Channel
Halls Harbour
Wolfville
Stewiacke
Sherbrooke Village
Liscomb Game Sanctuary
ATLANTIC OCEAN
Kentville
Hantsport
Shubenacadie
Liscombe
Berwick
Kingston
Windsor
Three Mile Plains
Mount Uniacke
Sheet Harbour
Ship Harbour
Upper Sackville
Middle Sackville
Lower Sackville
Bedford
Musquodoboit Harbour
Tangier
KEY
Ferry
Trans-Canada Highway
6
2
209
104
337
245
358
7
1
101
102
12

Shore Ecotour traces 100 million years of geology, the legends of the Mi'Kmaq, the Acadians, and the shipbuilders.

This region takes in parts of three of the official Scenic Trails, including the 315-km (195-mi) Marine Drive, the 316-km (196-mi) Sunrise Trail, and the 365-km (226-mi) Glooscap Trail. Any one leg of the routes could be done comfortably as an overnight trip from Halifax.

MUSQUODOBOIT HARBOUR

45 km (28 mi) east of Dartmouth.

Musquodoboit Harbour (locals pronounce it *must*-go-*dob*-bit) is a substantial village with about 2,500 residents. Musquodoboit River offers good trout fishing.

One of the province's best beaches, **Martinique Beach,** is about 12 km (7 mi) south of Musquodoboit Harbour, at the end of East Petpeswick Road. Clam Bay and Clam Harbour (where there is a spectacularly popular sand-castle competition every August), several miles east of Martinique, are also fine, if occasionally foggy, beaches.

WHERE TO STAY & EAT

$–$$ **Salmon River House Country Inn.** Views of the water and countryside are glorious from the inn's guest rooms and cottages. One cottage on the ocean is intended for stays of a week or more. Some rooms have whirlpool tubs, and the cottage allows pets in the winter. At the inn, you can fish from the floating dock, hike the trails of the 30-acre property, or make use of the canoe, kayak, or rowboat. The Lobster Shack restaurant ($–$$$) serves lunch, dinner, and a breakfast buffet on its screened deck. *9931 Hwy. 7, 10 km (6 mi) east of Musquodoboit Harbour, Salmon River Bridge, Jeddore B0J 1P0 902/889–3353 or 800/565–3353 902/889–3653 www.salmonriverhouse.com 7 rooms, 1 cottage In-room: no a/c, some DVDs. In-hotel: restaurant, no elevator, no-smoking rooms AE, DC, MC, V.*

SHERBROOKE VILLAGE

Fodor's Choice ★

166 km (103 mi) northeast of Musquodoboit Harbour.

A living-history museum set within the contemporary town of Sherbrooke, Sherbrooke Village contains 30 restored 19th-century buildings that re-create life during the town's heyday, from 1860 to 1914. Back then, this was a prime shipbuilding, lumbering, and gold-rush center. Artisans demonstrate weaving, wood turning, and pottery-, candle-, and soap making daily. *Hwy. 7, Sherbrooke 902/522–2400 or 888/743–7845 www.sherbrookevillage.ca $9 June–mid-Oct., daily 9:30–5.*

WHERE TO STAY & EAT

$ **Sherbrooke Village Inn & Cabins.** This comfy hostelry with rooms and woodsy cabins is a five-minute walk from St. Mary's River (open for trout and sometimes salmon fishing). Take part in nature walks and enjoy a spectacular view. The pleasant dining room ($$–$$$) serves homemade meals—full Canadian breakfasts, lunches, and dinners heavy on the seafood. The restaurant is closed from November to mid-April. ✉ *7975 Hwy. 7, Box 40, Sherbrooke B0J 3C0* ☎ *902/522–2235 or 866/522–3818* 📠 *902/522–2716* 🌐 *www.sherbrookevillageinn.ca* *15 rooms, 3 cabins* *In-room: no a/c, phones, Internet access. In-hotel: no-smoking rooms, no elevator* 💳 *AE, DC, MC, V.*

ANTIGONISH

85 km (53 mi) northwest of Canso.

Antigonish is on the main route to Cape Breton Island.

The biggest and oldest **Highland Games** (☎ *902/863–4275* 🌐 *www.antigonishhighlandgames.com*) outside of Scotland are held here each July, complete with caber tossing, Highland flinging, and pipe skirling.

WHERE TO STAY & EAT

$$–$$$$ Fodor's Choice ★ ✕ **Gabrieau's Bistro.** Gabrieau's has earned a place in Antigonish hearts with its pleasant interior and epicurean yet affordable menu of continental cuisine. Seafood, gourmet pizzas, luscious desserts, and several vegetarian selections are available. ✉ *350 Main St.* ☎ *902/863–1925* 🌐 *www.gabrieaus.com* 💳 *AE, D, MC, V* ⏲ *Closed Sun.*

$–$$ ✕ **Maritime Inn.** The Main Street Café ($$–$$$) at this inn serves breakfast, lunch, and a tempting dinner menu with lots of seafood. Try the tropical-glazed haddock and shrimp or the baby back ribs. One of five in a Maritime chain, this property has two sizes of rooms and one two-bedroom suite with a whirlpool bath. ✉ *158 Main St., B2G 2B7* ☎ *902/863–4001 or 888/662–7484* 📠 *902/863–2672* 🌐 *www.maritimeinns.com* *31 rooms, 1 suite* *In-room: VCR (some), Wi-Fi. In-hotel: restaurant, room service, no-smoking rooms, some small pets allowed, no elevator* 💳 *AE, D, DC, MC, V.*

PICTOU

20 km (12 mi) north of Stellarton.

Pictou was first settled by the Mi'Kmaqs. In 1773, the Hector arrived, bearing the first Scottish Highlanders.

The **Hector Heritage Quay,** where the new 110-foot fully rigged *Hector* can be toured, recounts the story of the hardy Scottish pioneers and the flood of Scots who followed them. ✉ *33 Caladh Ave.* ☎ *902/485–4371 or 877/574–2868* *$5* ⏲ *Mid-May–late Oct., Mon.–Sat. 9–5, Sun. 10–5.*

Melmerby Beach, one of the warmest beaches in the province, is about 23 km (14 mi) east of Pictou. To get here, follow the shore road from Highway 104.

WHERE TO STAY & EAT

¢–$$ **Braeside Country Inn.** This handsome 1938 inn is perched on a 5-acre hillside. You can stroll to the historic waterfront or watch ships come into Pictou Harbour from the picture window in the dining room ($$–$$$$), where prime rib and seafood are specialties. *126 Front St., Box 1810, B0K 1H0 902/485–5046 or 800/613–7701 902/485–1701 www.braesideinn.com 18 rooms In-room: refrigerator (some), VCR (some), Wi-Fi. In-hotel: restaurant, no-smoking rooms, no elevator AE, DC, MC, V BP.*

$–$$$ Fodor's Choice ★ **Stonehame Lodge & Chalets.** Handmade quilts and welcoming jars of homemade jam await at these log chalets and lodge rooms atop Fitzpatrick Mountain. In season, you can swim in the heated outdoor pool, hike or ski nearby woodland trails, visit a neighboring dairy farm, take a sleigh ride, see crop harvesting, or just relax before the chalet's woodstove or in the outdoor hot tub. *R.R. 3, 12 km (7½ mi) west of Pictou, Exit 19 or 21 off TCH 104, Scotsburn B0K 1R0 902/485–3468 or 877/646–3468 www.stonehamechalets.com 5 rooms, 10 chalets In-room: no a/c (some), kitchen (some), kitchenette (some), VCR, DVD. In-hotel: some pets allowed, bicycles, no elevator AE, DC, MC, V.*

TATAMAGOUCHE

50 km (31 mi) west of Pictou.

Despite the size of its population (700), Tatamagouche (a Mi'Kmaq name meaning "meeting place of the waters") bustles. Canada's second-largest Oktoberfest and a major quilt show are held here each fall, and summer brings strawberry and blueberry festivals, lobster and chowder suppers, and a lively farmers' market on Saturday mornings.

The **Sunrise Trail Museum** traces the town's Mi'Kmaq, Acadian, French, and Scottish roots and its shipbuilding heritage. *216 Main St. 902/657–2689 $2 Late June–early Sept., daily 9–5.*

WHERE TO STAY & EAT

¢–$$ **Big Al's Acadian Restaurant and Lounge.** Here, there are murals, and wooden statues, depicting the village's history. Overlooking Tatamagouche Bay, Big Al's serves steaks, seafood, and chicken wings, as well as pizza from Papa Al's Pizza, which is in the same building. *9 Station Rd. 902/657–0335 902/657–3341 AE, V.*

$$$$ **Fox Harb'r Golf Resort & Spa.** Manor-style houses have suites with views of the Northumberland Strait, plus luxuries such as heated-marble–bathroom floors, propane fireplaces, and terrace access at this 1,000-acre gated complex with a manicured garden. A sprawling, 18-hole traditional Scottish golf course on the jagged ocean coastline is the resort's crown jewel—a round of golf is $200. The cuisine ($$$$) is classic French and European, and frequent options are lobster, lamb, and filet mignon. Guests arrive by car, private plane, or boat. *1337 Fox Harbour Rd., 22 km (13½ mi) west of Tatamagouche and 8 km (5 mi) north of Wallace, B0K 1Y0 902/257–1801 or 866/257–1801 902/257–1852 www.foxharbr.com 72 suites In-room:*

kitchen, Wi-Fi. In-hotel: 2 restaurants, golf course, tennis courts, pool, spa, no-smoking rooms, minibars, no elevator ▭*AE, D, DC, MC, V* ⊙*Closed late Oct.–May.*

$–$$ ★ **Train Station Inn.** This unique inn has B&B accommodations in a century-old station and in seven cabooses parked nearby. The station-master's quarters include three rooms, a guest parlor, and a kitchen and laundry for guest use. Downstairs is a main-floor café where tasty breakfasts are served. The caboose suites have all the comforts, plus touches of railroad life—signal switches and elevated conductors' cupolas with their revolving chairs. Land and sea dinners are served in the dining car ($$–$$$). ✉*21 Station Rd., B0K 1V0* ☎*902/657–3222 or 888/724–5233* 🌐*www.trainstation.ca* *3 rooms, 7 suites* *In-room: no TV (some), Wi-Fi. In-hotel: laundry facilities, no elevator* ▭*AE, DC, MC, V* *CP.*

SHOPPING

At **Sara Bonnyman Pottery** (✉*Hwy. 246, 1½ km [1 mi] uphill from post office* ☎*902/657–3215* 🌐*www.sarabonnymanpottery.com*), watch the well-known potter at work each morning, producing handsome stoneware pieces bearing sunflower and blueberry motifs, and her one-of-a-kind plates and bowls.

AMHERST

28 km (17 mi) northwest of Springhill.

This now-quiet town was a center of industry and influence from the mid-1800s to the early 1900s. Four of Canada's Fathers of Confederation hailed from Amherst, including Sir Charles Tupper, who later became prime minister.

In contrast with tame Amherst is the **Tantramar Marsh,** alive with incredible birds and wildlife. It was originally called Tintamarre (literally "din," in French) because of the racket made by vast flocks of wildfowl. Said to be the world's largest marsh, the Tantramar is a migratory route for hundreds of thousands of birds, and a breeding ground for more than 100 species.

WHERE TO STAY & EAT

$–$$ ★ **Amherst Shore Country Inn.** This seaside country inn, with a beautiful view of Northumberland, has rooms, suites, and a cottage fronting 600 feet of private beach. Some suites have double whirlpool baths, propane fireplaces, and small decks. The two-bedroom rustic seaside cottage has kitchen facilities. Well-prepared four-course, prix-fixe dinners incorporating homegrown produce are served at one daily seating ($$$$; reservations essential). ✉*Hwy. 366, 32 km (20 mi) northeast of Amherst, Lorneville B4H 3X9* ☎*800/661–2724* ☎*902/661–4800* 🌐*www.ascinn.ns.ca* *4 rooms, 4 suites, 1 cottage* *In-hotel: restaurant, beachfront, no-smoking rooms, no elevator* ▭*AE, MC, V* ⊙*Closed weekdays Nov.–Apr.*

CAPE CHIGNECTO & CAPE D'OR

70 km (43 mi) southwest of Joggins.

Two imposing promontories—Cape Chignecto and Cape d'Or—reach into the Bay of Fundy near Chignecto Bay.

Fodor'sChoice ★ The newest provincial park, **Cape Chignecto Provincial Park**, opened officially in 1998. It's an untouched wilderness with 10,000 acres of old-growth forest harboring deer, moose, and eagles circumnavigated by a 51-km (31-mi) hiking trail along rugged cliffs that rise to 600 feet above the bay. Wilderness cabins and campsites are available. ✉*1108 West Advocate Rd., off Hwy. 209, West Advocate* ☎*902/392–2085* 🌐*www.capechignecto.net* 🎟*$3.20* ⏲*Early May–Mid-Nov., Mon.–Sat. 8–8; Sun. 8–5.*

Fodor'sChoice ★ South of Cape Chignecto is **Cape d'Or** *(Cape of Gold)*, named by Samuel de Champlain for its glittering veins of copper. The region was actively mined a century ago; at nearby Horseshoe Cove you may still find nuggets of almost pure copper on the beach as well as amethysts and other semiprecious stones. Hiking trails border the cliff edge above the Dory Rips, a turbulent meeting of currents.

A delightful beach walk at **Advocate Harbour** follows the top of an Acadian dike that was built by settlers in the 1700s to reclaim farmland from the sea. Advocate Beach, noted for its tide-cast driftwood, stretches 5 km (3 mi) from Cape Chignecto to Cape d'Or.

The **Age of Sail Museum Heritage Centre** traces the history of the area's shipbuilding and lumbering industries. You can also see a restored 1857 Methodist church, a blacksmith shop, and a lighthouse. ✉*Hwy. 209, Port Greville* ☎*902/348–2030* 🎟*$3* ⏲*July and Aug., daily 10–6; June and Sept., Thurs.–Mon. 10–6.*

WHERE TO STAY & EAT

¢–$ ✕ **Fundy Tides Campground Restaurant.** This small restaurant is large on hospitality. In the campground's main building, the 20-seat restaurant serves diner-type food that ranges from hamburgers to seafood. Everything is made from scratch, from the fries to the fish batter. You can eat-in or take-out. ✉*95 Mills Rd., Advocate Harbour* ☎*902/392–2584 or 888/392–2584* 💳*No credit cards* ⏲*Closed mid-Oct.–mid-May.*

$$ 🏨 **Driftwood Park Retreat.** Five mist-blue cottages face the Fundy shore. Four of the two-story, two-bedroom units have pine floors, gas fireplaces, well-equipped kitchens, and upstairs living rooms with fine views of the bay. The fifth cottage is an open-plan ranch unit with living room, dining room, and kitchen area. The living room has a propane fireplace. The cottages are close to a driftwood beach, hiking trails, and clam-digging and mineral-hunting areas. ✉*47 Driftwood La., West Advocate B0M 1A0* ☎*902/392–2008 or 866/810–0110* 📠*902/392–2041* 🌐*www.driftwoodparkretreat.com* *5 cottages* *In-room: no a/c, kitchen, no TV. In-hotel: laundry service, no-smoking rooms, no elevator* 💳*MC, V.*

$ 🏨 **The Lighthouse on Cape d'Or.** Two light keepers used to man the crucial light on the rocky Cape d'Or shore. Their cottages have been transformed: one to an excellent restaurant, the other to a small inn with a comfortable lounge and picture windows overlooking the Minas Basin. Enjoy hiking, bird-watching, seal sightings, outdoor lobster boils and clambakes, and gourmet cooking. A common area has a breakfast bar, books and games, and a small refrigerator. ✉*Cape d'Or off Hwy. 209* *Box 122, Advocate B0M 1A0* ☎*902/670–0534* *www.capedor.ca* *4 rooms, 2 with bath* *In-room: no a/c, no TV. In-hotel: restaurant, no-smoking rooms, no elevator* *No credit cards* *Closed late Oct.–mid-May.*

WORD OF MOUTH

"A little known B&B in Nova Scotia and one of the highlights of our trip is the Cape D'Or Lighthouse B&B, overlooking the Bay of Fundy. It only has 4-rooms and some might think it rustic, but if you want a unique experience and a great view, this is the place."
—mcmouse 09/07

PARRSBORO

55 km (34 mi) east of Cape d'Or.

A center for rock hounds and fossil hunters, Parrsboro holds the **Nova Scotia Gem and Mineral Show** every third weekend of August.

Semiprecious stones such as amethyst, quartz, and stilbite can be found at **Partridge Island,** 1 km (½ mi) offshore and connected to the mainland by an isthmus.

The **Fundy Geological Museum** isn't far from the Minas Basin area, where some of the oldest dinosaur fossils in Canada have been found. Two-hundred-million-year-old dinosaur fossils are showcased here alongside other mineral, plant, and animal relics. ✉*162 Two Island Rd.* ☎*902/254–3814* *www.fundygeo.museum.gov.ns.ca* *$6.25* *June–mid-Oct., daily 9:30–5:30; mid-Oct.–May, Tues.–Sat., hrs vary, call ahead.*

This harbor town was also a major shipping and shipbuilding port, and its history is described at the **Ottawa House Museum-by-the-Sea.** ✉*1155 Whitehall Rd., 3 km (2 mi) east of downtown* ☎*902/254–2376* *$2* *Mid-June–mid Sept., daily 10–6.*

WHERE TO STAY & EAT

$–$$ ✕**Harbour View Restaurant.** Fresh scallops and lobster, along with clams, flounder, and other seafood, are menu staples at this beachfront restaurant. The dining room, with windows overlooking the water and the lighthouse, displays paintings and photos of Parrsboro's past. Breakfast is also served all day. ✉*476 Pier Rd.* ☎*902/254–3507* *AE, MC, V* *Closed mid-Oct.–Apr.*

$$$$ **Beach House on Hatfield Road.** Fourteen picture windows provide panoramic views of the Bay of Fundy and a saltwater marsh. The two-story house can sleep six to eight and is on two beaches and close to all the attractions of the Glooscap Trail. Fully equipped, from beach towels to wireless Internet, fondue pots to a fireplace, it includes two bedrooms, two bathrooms, a sunroom, balconies, a dining room, and

a sitting room with fireplace. The house is rented in one-week increments for summer and shorter breaks in winter. *19 km (12 mi) west of Parrsboro, Fox River Reservations: 96 Sherwood Ave., Toronto, ON M4P 2A7 416/481–4096 416/487–4048 www.novascotia-beachhouse.com 1 house In-room: no a/c, kitchen. In-hotel: beachfront, laundry facilities, no-smoking rooms, some pets allowed, Wi-Fi, no elevator No credit cards.*

$ **Gillespie House Inn.** Wild roses border the driveway leading up to this handsome home. A lavish vegetarian breakfast and tons of visitor information are part of the service. Antique furnishings, hardwood floors, and fireplaces take you back in time in this 1890s home. *358 Main St., B0M 1S0 902/254–3196 or 877/901–3196 www.gillespie-houseinn.com 7 rooms In-room: no a/c, no TV. In-hotel: bicycles, Wi-Fi, no elevator AE, MC, V Closed Nov.–Apr. BP.*

FIVE ISLANDS

24 km (15 mi) east of Parrsboro.

Five Islands Provincial Park, on the shore of Minas Basin, has a campground ($19.22 a night), a beach, and hiking trails. Interpretive displays reveal the area's interesting geology: semiprecious stones, Jurassic-age dinosaur bones, and fossils. The Five Islands Lighthouse, at Sand Point Campground, has access to good swimming and clamming. *Hwy. 2, 32 km (20 mi) east of Parrsboro and 57 km (35 mi) west of Truro 902/254–2980 Free Mid-May–Aug., daily dawn–dusk.*

Cobequid Interpretation Centre highlights the geology, history, and culture of the area with pictures, videos, and interpretive panels. Get a sweeping view of the countryside and the impressive tides from the World War II observation tower. The center is home base for **Kenomee Hiking and Walking Trails,** which allow you to explore the area's varied landscapes—the coast itself plus cliffs, waterfalls, and forested valleys. *3246–3248 Hwy. 2, Central Economy 902/647–2600 By donation June and Sept.–mid-Oct., daily 9–5; July and Aug., daily 9–6.*

WHERE TO STAY

$ **Gemstow Bed and Breakfast.** Breakfast is served in an airy sun porch that overlooks flowery perennial beds and has a fine vista of Five Islands and beyond. Inside, the rooms and the lounge are tastefully furnished. Your host—who has a cat and a dog on-site—leads hikes to a hidden waterfall or clamming on the shore. *463 Hwy. 2, 20 km (12 mi) east of Parrsboro, Lower Five Islands B0M 1N0 902/254–2924 www3.ns.sympatico.ca/gemstow 2 rooms In-room: no a/c, no phone, no TV, no elevator MC, V BP.*

TRURO

67 km (42 mi) east of Five Islands.

Throughout Truro, watch for the Truro Tree Sculptures—a creative tribute to trees killed by the dreaded Dutch Elm disease. Artists Albert Deveau, Ralph Bigney, and Bruce Wood have been transforming the dead trees into sculptures of historical figures, wildlife, and cultural icons. Truro's central location places it on many travelers' routes.

Truro's least-known asset is also its biggest—the 1,000-acre **Victoria Park,** where, smack in the middle of town, you can find hiking trails, a winding stream flowing through a deep gorge with a 200-step climb to the top, and two waterfalls. *Park Rd. 902/893–6078 Free Daily dawn–dusk.*

WHERE TO STAY & EAT

$–$$ **Frank & Gino's Grill and Pasta House.** Each of this restaurant's corners is filled with memorabilia focusing on one of four themes: Marilyn Monroe, antique sports, local lore, or traveling ships. Enjoy the popular pasta or ribs, along with a full menu. Portions are generous—pasta includes salad and bread—so Frank & Gino's Teeny Weeny Cheesecake is just the right size for a taste-of-heaven dessert. *286 Robie St. 902/895–2165 www.frankandginos.com AE, DC, MC, V.*

¢–$ Fodor's Choice ★ **Sugar Moon Farm Maple Products & Pancake House.** Nova Scotia's only year-round maple destination is this log sugar camp and pancake house nestled in the Cobequid Mountains about 30 km (19 mi) north of Truro. Enjoy whole-grain buttermilk pancakes and waffles, maple syrup, local sausage, fresh biscuits, maple baked beans, and organic coffee. One night each month, a guest chef prepares a gourmet meal ($69). *Alex MacDonald Rd., Earltown 902/657–3348 or 866/816–2753 www.sugarmoon.ca MC, V Closed weekdays Sept.–June.*

$$ ★ **John Stanfield Inn.** The John Stanfield Inn has been beautifully restored to its original Queen Anne style, with delicate wood carvings, elaborate fireplaces, bow windows, and fine antique furniture. The restaurant ($$–$$$$) serves unusual seafood specialties and desserts such as berries Romanoff. *437 Prince St., B2N 1E6 902/895–1505, 902/895–1651, 800/561–7666 902/893–4427 www.johnstanfieldinn.com 10 rooms In-room: kitchen (some), Wi-Fi. In-hotel: restaurant, bar, laundry service, no-smoking rooms, no elevator AE, D, DC, MC, V CP.*

$ **Suncatcher Bed and Breakfast.** Call this modest B&B 10 minutes outside of Truro a glass act: stained glass adorns every available window, wall, and cranny. On the nonglass front, the breakfast menu includes homemade breads, jams, muffins, fruits (in season), bacon or sausage, and eggs. The four rooms share two bathrooms. *25 Wile Crest Ave.–R.R. 6, B2N 5B4 877/203–6032 902/893–7169 www.bbcanada.com/1853.html 2 rooms with ensuites In-room: no a/c. In-hotel: no-smoking rooms, no elevator AE, V BP.*

SPORTS & THE OUTDOORS

Riding the rushing tide aboard a 16-foot self-bailing Zodiac with **Shubenacadie River Runners** (✉ *8681 Hwy. 215, Maitland* ☎ *902/261–2770 or 800/856–5061* 🌐 *www.tidalborerafting.com*) is an adventure you won't soon forget. Tide conditions and time of day let you choose a mildly turbulent ride or an ultrawild one. A 3½-hour excursion costs $75 (with a barbecue), and a two-hour trip is $55 (with a snack). Gear included in both.

CAPE BRETON ISLAND

The highways and byways of the Island of Cape Breton, including those on the **Cabot Trail,** make up one of the most spectacular drives in North America. As you wind through the rugged coastal headlands of Cape Breton Highlands National Park, you can climb mountains and plunge back down to the sea in a matter of minutes. Every May the rugged but beautiful terrain plays host to **The Cabot Trail Relay Race,** a 17-stage run over almost 300 km (185 mi).

Fodor'sChoice ★

The Margaree River is a cultural dividing line: south of the river the settlements are Scottish, up the river they are largely Irish, and north of the river they are Acadian French. Maritime cultural heritage is alive and vibrant and ancient dialects can still be heard in the villages.

Bras d'Or Lake, a vast, warm, almost landlocked inlet of the sea, occupies the entire center of Cape Breton. The coastline of the lake is more than 967 km (600 mi) long, and people sail yachts from all over the world to cruise its serene, unspoiled coves and islands. Bald eagles have become so plentiful around the lake that they are exported to the United States to restock natural habitats. Four of the largest communities along the shore are native Mi'Kmaq communities.

MABOU

13 km (8 mi) northeast of Port Hood on Hwy. 19.

The pretty village of Mabou is very Scottish, with its Gaelic signs and most Saturday nights offer a helping of local culture in the form of a dance or "kitchen party."

WHERE TO STAY & EAT

$–$$$ ✕🏨 **Duncreigan Country Inn.** Though they were built in the 1990s, these buildings on the shore of Mabou Harbour suggest the early 1900s in design and furnishings. Several decks afford beautiful views and are ideal for relaxing, reading, and leaving your cares behind. A full breakfast buffet is included in the room rate in summer. The inn's restaurant, **Mull Café & Deli** ($–$$$), draws diners for its pasta, seafood chowder, steaks, and homemade desserts. The restaurant is open for dinner from July to mid-October; it has a deli counter and is fully licensed. The café closes at 8 PM in summer and 7 PM in winter. ✉ *11409–11411 Rte. 19, B0E 1X0* ☎ *902/945–2207, 800/840–2207 for reservations* 📠 *902/945–2206* 🌐 *www.duncreigan.ca* 🛏 *7 rooms, 1 suite* ♿ *In-*

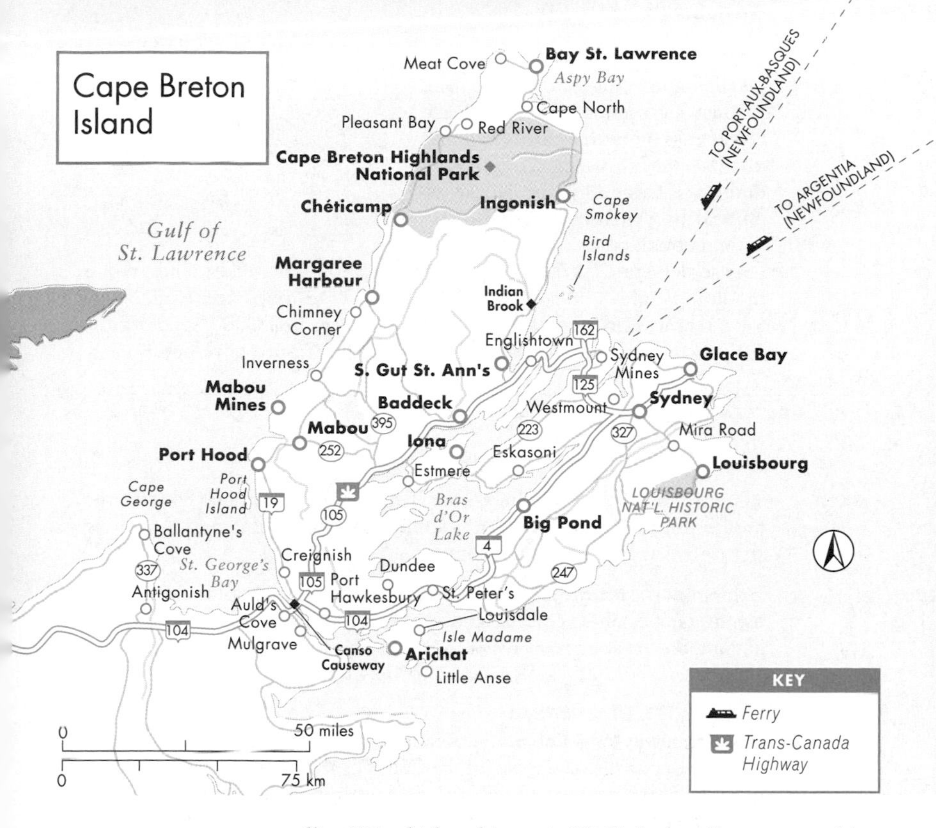

room: satellite TV, whirlpool (some), Wi-Fi, In-hotel: restaurant, bicycles, no elevator ▭*MC, V.*

$–$$$ **Glenora Inn & Distillery.** North America's first and Canada's only single-malt-whiskey distillery adjoins this friendly inn. Here you can sample a "wee dram" of the inn's own whiskey—Glen Breton Rare. Take a tour of the distillery and museum, enjoy fine cuisine and traditional Cape Breton music, and tour the courtyard gardens. Rooms in the inn overlook the courtyard; chalets have two-person whirlpool baths, woodstoves, and kitchens. ✉*Hwy. 19, Box 181, Glenville B0E 1X0* ☎*902/258–2662 or 800/839–0491* 📠*902/258–3572* 🌐*www.glenora-distillery.com* *9 rooms, 6 chalets* *In-room: no a/c (some), kitchen (some), satellite TV. In-hotel: restaurant, bar, gift shop, no elevator* ▭*AE, D, MC, V* ⏲*Closed Nov.–May.*

MABOU MINES

10 km (6 mi) northwest of Mabou.

This quiet area is a place so hauntingly exquisite that you expect to meet the *sidhe,* the Scottish fairies, capering on the hillsides. Within the hills of Mabou Mines is some of the finest hiking in the province, and above the land fly bald eagles, plentiful in this region.

OUTDOORS & SPORTS

> **WORD OF MOUTH**
>
> "Hiking in Cape Breton is as good as it gets. Once you get to Cape Breton, you may not want to leave." —fewglow 08/09

★ Gaelic and English names on wooden signs mark the way for 15 **hiking trails** on more than 20 square km (8 square mi) of coastal wilderness in Cape Mabou. All are as natural as possible. Some follow old cart tracks that connected pioneer settlements. It's a region of plunging cliffs, isolated beaches, rising mountains, glens, meadows, and forests. Trail maps are available at local retailers or by mail from the **Cape Mabou Trail Club** (✉*Inverness, B0E 1N0*). Include $2 and a self-addressed, stamped envelope.

MARGAREE HARBOUR

33 km (20 mi) north of Mabou.

The Ceilidh Trail joins the Cabot Trail at Margaree Harbour at the mouth of the Margaree River, a famous salmon-fishing and fly-fishing stream and a favorite canoe route.

Exhibits at the **Margaree Salmon Museum,** in a former schoolhouse, include fishing tackle, photographs, and other memorabilia related to salmon angling on the Margaree River. ✉*60 E. Big Intervale Rd., North East Margaree* ☎*902/248–2848* *$2* ⏲*Mid-June–mid-Oct., daily 9–5.*

WHERE TO STAY & EAT

$–$$$ ✕ **Normaway Inn & Cabins.** Nestled on 250 acres in the hills of the Margaree Valley at the beginning of the Cabot Trail, this secluded 1920s inn has distinctive rooms and cabins, most with woodstoves and screened porches. The restaurant ($$$$) is known for its country cuisine, particularly the vegetable chowders and fresh seafood ragout. Cabins and the dining room are available off-season by arrangement. ✉*691 Egypt Rd., Box 101, 3 km (2 mi) off Cabot Trail, B0E 2C0* ☎*902/248–2987 or 800/565–9463* *902/248–2600* *www.normaway.com* *12 rooms, 17 cabins* *In-room: no a/c, no TV. In-hotel: restaurant, tennis court, no elevator* *MC, V* ⏲*Closed mid-Oct.–mid-June.*

CHÉTICAMP

26 km (16 mi) north of Margaree Harbour.

After 200 years of history, Chéticamp's Acadian culture and traditions are very much a way of life in the region. The community offers the pride, traditions, and warmth of Acadian hospitality. Its tall silver steeple towers over the village, which stands exposed on a wide lip of flat land below a range of hills. The area is known for its *suêtes,* strong southeast winds of 120 to 130 kph (75 to 80 mph) that may develop into a force of up to 200 kph (125 mph): they've been known to blow the roofs off buildings.

Chéticamp is famous for its hooked rugs, available at many local gift shops.

The **Dr. Elizabeth LeFort Gallery and Museum: Les Trois Pignons** displays artifacts, fine hooked rugs, and tapestries. LeFort, born in 1914, created more than 300 tapestries, some of which have been hung in the Vatican, the White House, and Buckingham Palace. ✉ *15584 Cabot Trail, Box 430, B0E 1H0* ☎ *902/224–2642* 🖷 *902/224–1579* 🌐 *www.lestroispignons.com* 🎟 *$5* ⏲ *July and Aug., daily 9–7; May, June, Sept., and Oct., daily 9–5.*

WORD OF MOUTH

"The Cabot Trail is terrific... especially if it is nice weather. It takes about 2-3 hours to go around the Cape Breton Highlands national park, which is the best part of the Cabot Trail. I suggest that you go clockwise when doing it because a lot of the scenery will be in front of you (i.e., go from Cheticamp-Ingonish)." —moise 08/06

WHERE TO STAY & EAT

$$–$$$ ✕ **Le Gabriel.** You can't miss Le Gabriel, with its large lighthouse entranceway. The casual tavern offers simple but good fresh fish dinners and traditional Acadian dishes, such as meat pie, fish cakes, or *fricot* (stew with potatoes, pork bits, chives, and beef or chicken). Snow crab and lobster specials are available in season. ✉ *15424 Cabot Trail* ☎ *902/224–3685* 🌐 *www.legabriel.com* 💳 *AE, MC, V* ⏲ *Dining room closed late Oct.–Apr.*

$$–$$$$ **Cabot Trail Sea & Golf Chalets.** Next to Le Portage Golf Course and overlooking the ocean, these chalets are ideal for families and golfers. One- and two-bedroom units have covered decks with gas barbecues, and some have fireplaces. The three-bedroom country suite has a washer, dryer, and dishwasher. ✉ *71 Fraser Doucet La., Box 324, B0E 1H0* ☎ *902/224–1777 or 877/224–1777* 🖷 *902/224–1999* 🌐 *www.seagolfchalets.com* *12 chalets, 1 suite* *In-room: no a/c, kitchen (some). In-hotel: golf course, no elevator* 💳 *AE, D, MC, V* ⏲ *Closed mid-Oct.–mid-May.*

¢–$ **Chéticamp Outfitters' Inn Bed & Breakfast.** Rooms at this homey inn overlook the ocean, mountains, and valley. The furniture includes homemade wooden pieces, paintings by the innkeeper, and quilts. Fantastic blueberry muffins are a highlight of the home-cooked breakfast. ✉ *13938 Cabot Trail, B0E 1H0* ☎🖷 *902/224–2776* 🌐 *www.cheticampns.com/cheticampoutfitters* *6 rooms, 1 chalet* *In-room: no a/c, refrigerator (some), VCR (some), satellite TV (some), no elevator* 💳 *AE, MC, V* ⏲ *Closed Dec.–Apr. 15* *BP.*

SPORTS & THE OUTDOORS

WHALE WATCHING

Chéticamp is known for its whale-watching cruises, which depart from the government wharf twice daily in May, three times daily June through August. **Captain Zodiac Whale Cruise** (☎ *902/224–1088 or 877/232–2522* 🌐 *www.wesleyswhalewatch.com*) guarantees whale sightings on a two-hour Zodiac tour ($39). **Whale Cruisers Ltd.** (☎ *902/224–3376 or 800/813–3376*) is a reliable charter company, and was the first whale-watching company in Nova Scotia. Tours run two or three times daily, May 15 through October 15, and are $25. Expect to see minke, pilot, and finback whales in their natural environment; seabird and bald-eagle sightings are also common.

CAPE BRETON HIGHLANDS NATIONAL PARK

Fodor'sChoice ★ *5 km (3 mi) north of Chéticamp; 108 km (67 mi) north of Ingonish.*

A 950-square-km (366-square-mi) wilderness of wooded valleys, plateau barrens, and steep cliffs, this park stretches across northern Cape Breton from the gulf shore to the Atlantic. The Cabot Trail highway through the park rises to the tops of the coastal mountains and descends through scenic switchbacks to the sea. Good brakes and attentive driving are advised. For wildlife watchers there's much to see, including moose, eagles, deer, bears, foxes, and bobcats—your chances of seeing wildlife are better if you venture off the main road and hike one of the trails at dusk or dawn. Note that it is illegal to feed or approach any animal in the park. Always take care to observe the animals from a safe distance; in particular, exercise caution driving in the moose zones, marked by signs on the highway. Hitting one can be damaging to both you and the animal.

High-altitude bogs are home to delightful wild orchids and other unique flora and fauna. If you plan to hike or camp in the park, stop at the Chéticamp Information Centre for advice and necessary permits. A park permit or pass is required for sightseeing along sections of the Cabot Trail highway when within the National Park and for use of the facilities such as exhibits, hiking trails, and picnic areas; there are additional fees for camping, fishing, and golf. ✉*Entrances on Cabot Trail near Chéticamp and Ingonish* ☎*902/224–2306, 902/224–3814 bookstore* 🌐*www.pc.gc.ca* 🎟*$6.90* ⏲*Year-round, daily dawn–dusk.*

For those who prefer to stay on dry land to observe sea life, stop by the **Whale Interpretive Centre.** Using zoom scopes on the whale-spotting deck, you may catch a close-up glimpse of many different species of whales that are often frolicking just offshore from the center. Inside the modern structure, exhibits and models explain the unique world of whales. ✉*104 Harbour Rd., Pleasant Bay* ☎*902/224–1411* 📠*902/224–1751* 🌐*www.whalecentre.ca* 🎟*$4.50* ⏲*Mid-June–early Sept., daily 9–8; mid-May–mid-June and early Sept.–Oct., daily 9–6.*

SPORTS & THE OUTDOORS

WHALE WATCHING

All whale-watching tours have a money-back guarantee if you don't see a whale.

You may see pilot, finback, humpback, or minke whales on **Captain Mark's Whale & Seal Cruise** (☎*902/224–1316 or 888/754–5112* 🌐*www.whaleandsealcruise.com*). An underwater video camera adds to the experience. Cruises allow for exploration of sea caves, waterfalls, and rock and cliff formations along a remote stretch of unspoiled Cape Breton coastline. Tours are May 15 through October 15 and cost $25 to $44. **Wesley's Whale Watching** (☎*902/224–1919 or 866/999–4253*) leads two-hour trips in Cape Island boats May 15 through October 15 to see whales, dolphins, seals, and scenery. Tours are $25.

BAY ST. LAWRENCE

76 km (47 mi) north of Chéticamp.

Bay St. Lawrence restsled in a bowl-shaped valley around a harbor pond. You can hike along the shore to the east and the Money Point Lighthouse, or find a quiet corner of the shoreline for contemplation.

Cabot's Landing Provincial Park (✉*Bay St. Lawrence Rd., 2 km [1 mi] north of Four Mile Beach Inn* ☎*No phone*) is a must-visit for views, walking, and a sandy beach enclosed by rugged mountains. It's a perfect spot for a picnic. Admission to the park is free, and it's open daily 9 to 9 mid-May through mid-October. A National Historic Site cairn of Italian explorer John Cabot is on-site.

WHERE TO STAY

$–$$ Fodor'sChoice ★ **Four Mile Beach Inn.** The view of Aspy Bay and the ridge of the highland mountains is fantastic from this large white 19th-century house near Cabot's Landing. Canoeing and kayaking are possible from the small dock on the property, and bike rentals are available. Rooms are clean and have a country look. The suites have a private entrance and a deck. ✉*R.R. 1, Aspy Bay, Cape North B0C 1G0* ☎*902/383–2282 or 888/503–5551* 🌐*www.fourmilebeachinn.com* *3 rooms, 5 suites* *In-room: a/c (some), kitchen (some), no TV. In-hotel: bicycles, public Internet, no elevator* 💳*AE, MC, V* ⏲*Closed mid-Oct.–June* *CP.*

INGONISH

113 km (70 mi) northeast of Chéticamp; 37 km (23 mi) south of Bay St. Lawrence.

> **WORD OF MOUTH**
>
> "You will love Ingonish!... Be sure and go all the way to Meat Cove via White Point when you have a clear day." —smcgown 09/07

Ingonish, one of the leading vacation destinations on the island, is actually several villages—Ingonish Centre, Ingonish Beach, South Ingonish Harbour, and Ingonish Ferry—on two bays, divided by a long narrow peninsula called Middle Head. Each bay has a sandy beach.

WHERE TO STAY & EAT

$$$$ Fodor'sChoice ★ **Keltic Lodge.** Spread across cliffs overlooking the ocean, the provincially owned Keltic Lodge in Cape Breton Highlands National Park has stunning views of Cape Smokey and the surrounding highlands. Rooms in the main lodge have charm and character; rooms at the Inn at Keltic are larger and air-conditioned. Cottages and suites are also available. Activities include golfing and guided hikes. Freshwater and saltwater beaches are within walking distance, and nightly entertainment is offered in the Highland Sitting Room. Seafood stars in the Purple Thistle Dining Room ($$$$). The 5,000-square-foot Spa at Keltic opened on the property in 2005, taking full advantage of the cliffside view. ✉*Middle Head Peninsula, Ingonish Beach* ☎*902/285–2880 or 800/565–0444* 🌐*www.signatureresorts.com* *72 rooms, 2 suites, 11 cottages* *In-room: no a/c (some). In-hotel: 2 restaurants, pool, beachfront, bicycles, laundry service* 💳*AE, D, DC, MC, V* ⏲*Closed late Oct.–mid-May* *MAP.*

$-$$$$ **Glenghorm Beach Resort.** Swim in the ocean, and hike or bike from the motor inn, cottages, or beach-house suites. *36743 Cabot Trail, Box 39, B0C 1K0 902/285–2049 or 800/565–5660 902/285–2395 www.capebretonresorts.com 54 rooms, 10 suites, 10 cottages In-room: no a/c (some). In-hotel: restaurant, bar, pool, exercise room, beachfront, laundry facilities, no elevator AE, D, DC, MC, V Closed Nov.–mid-May.*

$$–$$$ **Lantern Hill & Hollow.** The six cottages are just steps from a 3-km (2-mi) beach: perfect for lazy summer days, a quick dip, and nightly bonfires. Bonfire wood is supplied, as are beach toys. Five cottages have two bedrooms, and the sixth is a one-bedroom unit with a corner whirlpool tub. Each comes fully equipped, including patio furniture and barbecue, and have covered verandas. *36845 Cabot Trail, B0C 1L0 902/285–2010 or 888/663–0225 902/285–2001 www.lanternhillandhollow.com 3 suites, 6 cottages In-room: no a/c, kitchen (some), mini-refrigerator, no elevator MC, V mid-Oct.–late May.*

$–$$ **Castle Rock Country Inn.** Surrounded by an idyllic setting of mountains and ocean, this Georgian-style inn provides an excellent environment for contemplation and relaxation. The spacious guest rooms have queen beds, and most have an additional sofa bed; some have ocean views. *39339 Cabot Trail, B0C 1L0 902/285–2700 or 888/884–7625 902/285–2525 www.ingonish.com/castlerock 16 rooms In-room: no a/c, satellite TV, no elevator AE, MC, V.*

SPORTS & THE OUTDOORS

Perennially ranked as one of Canada's top courses, **Highlands Links** (*Cape Breton Highlands National Park 902/285–2600 or 800/441–1118 www.highlandslinksgolf.com*) has abundant natural scenery in the form of mountains and sea, not to mention great golfing. It's open daily, from mid-May until the end of October, dawn until dusk, weather permitting. A round of 18 holes is $88.

SOUTH GUT ST. ANN'S

10 km (6 mi) west of Englishtown.

The **Great Hall of the Clans** depicts Scottish history and has an account of the Great Migration, the exodus of Scottish people for the new world in the late 18th and early 19th centuries. Gaelic College offers courses in Gaelic language and literature, Scottish music and dancing, weaving, and other Scottish arts. There's also a Scottish gift shop. *Gaelic College, 51779 Cabot Trail, Exit 11 off Hwy. 105 902/295–3411 www.gaeliccollege.edu $7 Mid-June–mid-Sept., daily 9–5.*

WHERE TO STAY

$–$$ **English Country Garden Bed & Breakfast.** A peaceful, lakefront setting greets you at this 1940 home, 12 km (7½ mi) from South Gut St. Ann's; there are three guest suites and a B&B cottage. The African Room, the Conservatory, the Russian Room, and the barrier-free Rose Cottage are richly decorated. With advance notice, an evening meal ($80 per couple) is available for in-house guests; a full English breakfast is included.

There's snowshoeing on the property in winter. TVs and DVDs are available on request. ✉45478 Cabot Trail, Indian Brook B0C 1H0 ☎866/929–2721 🌐www.capebretongarden.com 3 suites, 1 cottage In-room: no a/c, Internet, no phone, no elevator ▭MC, V BP.

BADDECK

20 km (12 mi) south of South Gut St. Ann's.

Baddeck, the most highly developed tourist center on Cape Breton, has more than 1,000 motel beds, a golf course, fine gift shops, and many restaurants. This was also the summer home of Alexander Graham Bell until he died here at the age of 75. The annual **regatta** of the Bras d'Or Yacht Club is held the first week of August. Sailing tours and charters are available, as are bus tours along the Cabot Trail.

14

The **Celtic Colours International Festival** (☎*902/562–6700 or 877/285–2321* 🌐*www.celtic-colours.com*) takes place during 10 days spanning the second and third weekends in October. It draws the world's best Celtic performers at the height of autumn splendor. International artists travel from Celtic countries around the world, and homegrown talent shines in 44-plus performances in more than 38 communities scattered around the island. The cost for each performance is $20 to $90.

★ The **Alexander Graham Bell National Historic Site of Canada** explores Bell's inventions. Experiments, kite making, and other hands-on activities are designed for children. From films, artifacts, and photographs, you learn what ideas led Bell to create man-carrying kites, airplanes, and a record-setting hydrofoil boat. ✉*559 Chebucto St.* ☎*902/295–2069* 🌐*www.parkscanada.ca* *$7.15* *July–mid-Oct., daily 8:30–6; mid-Oct.–May, daily 9–5; June, daily 9–6.*

At the **Wagmatcook Culture & Heritage Centre** the ancient history and rich traditions of the native Mi'Kmaq are demonstrated on request. Mi'Kmaq guides provide interpretations and cultural entertainment. The on-site restaurant highlights traditional foods such as moose and eel dishes, as well as more contemporary choices. The crafts shop has products by local native people. ✉*Wagmatcook First Nation, Rte. 105, 16 km (10 mi) west of Baddeck* ☎*902/295–2999* 🌐*www.wagmatcook.com* *Free* *Year-round.*

WHERE TO STAY & EAT

$$–$$$ **Baddeck Lobster Suppers.** For super-fresh lobsters, try this restaurant in a former legion hall. During busy times, you may have to wait for a table. Entrées come with mussels, chowder, dessert, beverage, and homemade buns and biscuits. At lunch, the menu is considerably cheaper and options include a lobster-roll platter, chowder, mussels, and homemade beef soup. There's a bar and a gift shop. ✉*17 Ross St.* ☎*902/295–3307* *902/295–3424* ▭*MC, V* *Closed mid-Oct.–mid-June.*

$$–$$$$ **Inverary Resort.** On the shores of the magnificent Bras d'Or Lake, this resort has stunning views and lots of activities. You can choose from cottage suites, modern hotel units, or the elegant 100-year-old

main lodge; some rooms have fireplaces. There's boating on the premises and swimming close to the village. Dine at the elegant main dining room ($$–$$$) where a bounty of seafood—smoked salmon, scallops, and lobster—joins dishes like New Zealand lamb. ✉ *Hwy. 205 and Shore Rd., Box 190, B0E 1B0* ☎ *902/295–3500 or 800/565–5660* 📠 *902/295–3527* 🌐 *www.capebretonresorts.com/inverary.asp* *129 rooms, 9 cottages* *In-room: Wi-Fi. In-hotel: restaurant, bar, tennis courts, pool, gym, spa, water sports, bicycles, no elevator* 💳 *AE, D, DC, MC, V.*

$$–$$$$ **Auberge Gisele's Inn.** This inn and motel share lovely landscaped flower gardens and overlook the Bras d'Or Lake. Some rooms have fireplaces. The chef prepares breakfast and dinner. The executive suites have whirlpool tubs and gas fireplaces. Rooms are modern and deluxe. ✉ *387 Shore Rd., B0E 1B0* ☎ *902/295–2849* 📠 *902/295–2033* 🌐 *www.giseles.com* *75 rooms, 3 suites* *In-room: dial-up. In-hotel: laundry facilities* 💳 *AE, D, MC, V* *Closed late Oct.–early May.*

¢–$ **Bain's Heritage House B&B.** This lovely heritage home (1850s) is in the center of Baddeck. On cooler evenings, relax in front of the fire in the sitting room. ✉ *121 Twining St., B0E 1B0* ☎ *902/295–1069* *3 rooms, 1 with bath* *In-room: no a/c, no elevator* 💳 *MC, V* *BP.*

IONA

56 km (35 mi) south of Baddeck.

To get here from Baddeck, take Trans-Canada Highway 105 to Exit 6, which leads to Little Narrows, where you can take a ferry to the Washabuck Peninsula.

Fodor'sChoice ★ The **Highland Village Museum** is set high on a mountainside, with a spectacular view of Bras d'Or Lake and the narrow Barra Strait. The village's 11 historical buildings were assembled from all over Cape Breton to depict the Highland Scots' way of life from their origins in the Hebrides to the present day. ✉ *4119 Hwy. 223* ☎ *902/725–2272* 🌐 *www.highlandvillage.museum.gov.ns.ca* *$9* *June–mid-Oct., daily 9:30–5:30.*

WHERE TO STAY & EAT

$–$$ **Highland Heights Inn.** Enjoy rural surroundings and Scottish home-style cooking, with a view of the lake. The inn overlooks Iona. The salmon (or any fish in season), fresh-baked oatcakes, and homemade desserts at the restaurant ($–$$$) are good choices. ✉ *4115 Hwy. 223, B2C 1A3* ☎ *902/725–2360 or 800/660–8122* 📠 *902/725–2800* 🌐 *www.highlandheightsinn.ca* *32 rooms* *In-room: no a/c. In-hotel: restaurant, no-smoking rooms, no elevator* 💳 *D, MC, V* *Closed mid-Oct.–mid-May.*

SYDNEY

60 km (37 mi) northeast of Iona.

This city encompasses villages, unorganized districts, and a half dozen towns. These are warmhearted, interesting communities with a diverse ethnic population that includes Ukrainians, Welsh, Poles, Lebanese, West Indians, and Italians.

Sydney is also a departure point. Fast ferries leave from North Sydney for Newfoundland, and scheduled air service to Newfoundland and the French islands of St-Pierre and Miquelon departs from Sydney Airport. Cruise ships have been a familiar sight since 1962 and dock at the big violin scultpure on the waterfront.

14

WHERE TO STAY & EAT

$–$$$ ✕**Governor's Pub and Eastery.** This Victorian home was built in the late 1800s. The restaurant, with hardwood floors, a fireplace, and high ceilings, is known for its seafood and steaks, though it has a full menu. Both the restaurant and the pub upstairs have two large patios that overlook Sydney Harbour. Desserts are homemade. ✉*233 Esplanade B1P 1A6* ☎*902/562–7646* ▭*AE, D, MC, V.*

$$–$$$$ ★ ✕**Gowrie House.** This unexpected find between North Sydney and Sydney Mines, minutes from the Newfoundland ferry, is shaded by towering trees on grounds filled with gardens and flowering shrubs. Cherry trees supply the main ingredient for chilled black-cherry soup in the restaurant ($$$$). The main house has six rooms; the secluded garden house four more; and the caretaker's cottage provides deluxe private accommodation. Dinner reservations are essential. ✉*840 Shore Rd., Sydney Mines B1V 1A6* ☎*902/544–1050 or 800/372–1115* ⊕*www.gowriehouse.com* *10 rooms, 1 cottage* *In-hotel: restaurant, no elevator* ▭*AE, MC, V* *BP.*

$$–$$$ **Cambridge Suites Hotel.** Put yourself in the center of the action on the Sydney waterfront by staying at this comfortable all-suites hotel. Some of the spacious rooms directly overlook the harbour. ✉*380 Esplanade, B1P 1B1* ☎*902/562–6500 or 800/565–9466* ⊕*www.cambridgesuitessydney.com* *147 rooms* *In-room: kitchen, dial-up In-hotel: restaurant, lounge, fitness center, no-smoking rooms* ▭*AE, D, DC, MC, V* *CP.*

$$–$$$ **Delta Sydney.** This hotel is on the harbor, beside the yacht club and close to the center of town. Guest rooms are pleasant and have harbor views. The restaurant ($$) specializes in seafood and pasta. The 50-foot waterslide makes it fun for kids, too. ✉*300 Esplanade, B1P 1A7* ☎*902/562–7500 or 800/565–1001* *902/562–3023* ⊕*www.deltahotels.com* *152 rooms* *In-hotel: restaurant, bar, hot tub, pool, gym, Wi-Fi* ▭*AE, DC, MC, V.*

GLACE BAY

21 km (13 mi) east of Sydney.

A coal-mining town and fishing port, Glace Bay has a rich history of industrial struggle.

★ The **Cape Breton Miners' Museum** houses exhibits and artifacts illustrating the hard life of early miners in Cape Breton's undersea collieries. Former miners guide you down into the damp recesses of the mine and tell stories of working all day where the sun never shines. ✉*42 Birkley St., Quarry Point* ☎*902/849–4522* 🌐*www.minersmuseum.com* 🎟*Museum $5, museum and mine tour $10* ⏲*June 1–Sept. 1, daily 10–6, until 7 on Tues.; Sept. 2–Oct. 30, daily 9–4; Oct. 31–June 1, weekdays 9–4.*

> **WORD OF MOUTH**
>
> "I recommend the Miners Museum in Glace Bay. Retired coal miners take you on tours of the coal mines located beneath the ocean surface. The mines are interesting and the museum has some good exhibits, but the miners' stories are even more interesting."
>
> —just_wandering

The **Marconi National Historic Site of Canada** commemorates the site at Table Head, where in 1902 Guglielmo Marconi built four tall wooden towers and beamed the first official wireless messages across the Atlantic Ocean. An interpretive trail leads to the foundations of the original towers and transmitter buildings. The visitor center has large models of the towers as well as artifacts and photographs chronicling the radio pioneer's life and work. ✉*Timmerman St. (Hwy. 255)* ☎*902/842–2530* 🌐*www.parkscanada.ca* 🎟*Free* ⏲*June–mid-Sept., daily 10–6.*

LOUISBOURG

55 km (34 mi) south of Glace Bay.

Though best known as the home of the largest historical reconstruction in North America, Louisbourg is also an important fishing community with a lovely harbor front.

★ The **Fortress of Louisbourg National Historic Site of Canada** may be the most remarkable site in Cape Breton. After the French were forced out of mainland Nova Scotia in 1713, they established their headquarters here in a walled and fortified town on a low point of land at the mouth of Louisbourg Harbour. The fortress was twice captured, once by New Englanders and once by the British; after the second siege, in 1758, it was razed. A quarter of the original town has been rebuilt on its foundations, just as it was in 1744, before the first siege. Watch a military drill, see nails and lace being made, and eat food prepared from 18th-century recipes in the town's three inns. Louisbourg's chilly, so pack warm. ✉*259 Parks Service Rd.* ☎*902/733–2280 or 888/773–8888* 🌐*www.parkscanada.ca* 🎟*$16.35* ⏲*June and Sept., daily 9:30–5; July and Aug., daily 9–5:30; Oct. 1–15, daily 9:30–5; Oct. 15–31, by guided tour only. English tours at 11 and 2, French tour at 1.*

WHERE TO STAY & EAT

$–$$$ ✕ **Grubstake Restaurant.** Coquilles St. Jacques, chateaubriand, and stuffed sole are popular menu items at this 120-seat restaurant where elegant, family, and country cuisine come together. Desserts are made on-site *7499 Main St., B1C 1H8* *902/733–2308* *www.c-level.com/grubstake* *AE, MC, V* *Closed Nov.–mid-June.*

$–$$$$ **Point of View Suites.** The only Louisbourg property on the water offers views of Fortress Louisbourg and the ocean. The suites have balconies, and most have cooking areas with utensils; the luxury apartments each have three queen-size beds, a full kitchen, and a hot tub. The casual beach-house restaurant ($$–$$$) specializes in lobster and crab boils, cooked nightly in season on their private beach and served in the dining room. *15 Commercial St. Ext., B1C 2J4* *902/733–2080 or 888/374–8439* *902/733–2638* *www.louisbourgpointofview.com* *5 rooms, 15 suites* *In-room: kitchen (some). In-hotel: restaurant, beachfront, laundry facilities, no-smoking rooms, no elevator* *MC, V* *Closed Nov.–mid-May.*

$–$$$ **Louisbourg Heritage House Bed & Breakfast.** Built in 1886, this former Victorian rectory opened as a B&B in 2002. Original wood floors, high ceilings, and private balconies in each room add charm. The inn is tucked between two churches and is close to restaurants and the Louisbourg Playhouse. Some rooms have views of Fortress Louisbourg or the harbor. *7544 Main St., B1C 1J5* *902/733–3222 or 888/888–8466* *www.louisbourgheritagehouse.com* *6 rooms* *In-room: no a/c, refrigerator (some), no elevator* *AE, MC, V* *Closed Nov.–June* *BP.*

$–$$ **Cranberry Cove Inn.** This fully renovated home from the early 1900s is within walking distance of the Fortress of Louisbourg National Historic Park. Each room has a different theme, ranging from the captain's den to the secret garden. Rooms are available off season by arrangement. High-end evening dining is available to guests and the public from mid-June through September ($$–$$$). *12 Wolfe St., B1C 2J2* *902/733–2171 or 800/929–0222* *902/733–2171* *www.cranberrycoveinn.com* *7 rooms* *In-room: no a/c, Wi-Fi. In-hotel: no-smoking rooms, no elevator* *AE, MC, V* *BP* *Open May–Oct.*

BIG POND

50 km (31 mi) west of Louisbourg.

This little town is made up of only a few houses, and one of them is the former home of singer-songwriter Rita MacNeil, who operates **Rita's Tea Room.** Originally a one-room schoolhouse, the building has been expanded to accommodate the multitude of visitors who come to sample Rita's Tea Room Blend Tea, which is served along with a fine selection of sandwiches and baked goods. You can visit a display room of Rita's awards and photographs and browse through her gift shop. *Hwy. 4* *902/828–2667* *www.ritamacneil.com* *Gift shop, June–Oct., daily 10–6; Tea room, July–mid-Oct.*

ARICHAT

62 km (38 mi) southwest of Big Pond.

The principal town of Isle Madame, Arichat is a 27-square-km (10-square-mi) island named for Madame de Maintenon, second wife of

Louis XIV. Known today for its friendly Acadian culture and many secluded coves and inlets, the town was an important shipbuilding and trading center during the 19th century, and some fine old houses from that period still remain. The two cannons overlooking the harbor were installed after the town was sacked by John Paul Jones during the American Revolution.

To get here from Big Pond, take Route 4 to Highway 320, which leads through Poulamon and D'Escousse and overlooks Lennox Passage. Highway 206 meanders through the low hills to a maze of land and water at West Arichat. Together, the two routes encircle the island, meeting at Arichat. The island lends itself to biking, as most roads glide gently along the shore. A good half-day hike leads to Gros Nez, the "large nose" that juts into the sea.

One of the best ways to experience Isle Madame is by foot. Try Cape Auguet Eco-Trail, an 8-km (5-mi) hiking trail that extends from Boudreauville to Mackerel Cove on Isle Madame and follows the rocky coastline overlooking Chedabucto Bay.

Arichat was once the seat of the local Catholic diocese. **Notre Dame de l'Assumption** church, built in 1837, still retains the grandeur of its former cathedral status. Its bishop's palace is now a law office. ✉*2316 Hwy. 206* ☎*902/226–2109* *Free* ⏲*Dawn–dusk. Mass, June–Sept., Sat. 7* PM *and Sun. 9:30* AM.

NOVA SCOTIA ESSENTIALS

To research prices, get advice from other travelers, and book travel arrangements, visit www.fodors.com.

TRANSPORTATION

BY AIR

Westjet, Air Canada, and Air Canada Jazz provide service to Halifax and Sydney from various cities. Air travel within the area is very limited. Air Canada provides regional service to other provinces and to Sydney, Nova Scotia. Provincial Airlines, a regional Air Canada carrier, flies between Newfoundland, Labrador, and Halifax. Porter airlines provides service to Ottawa, Montréal, and Toronto, whereas Sunwing flies daily to Toronto. United Airlines flies to Chicago from June through October, and offers daily nonstop service to Washington. American Eagle flies daily to New York (Laguardia and JFK). Halifax is also served by Continental (from Newark), and Northwest (from Detroit and Newark). Delta (through SkyWest) offers a weekly roundtrip from Atlanta and Zoom Airlines now services four seasonal European gateways nonstop from Halifax (London, Glasgow, Belfast, and Paris). Icelandair travels three times a week to Reykjavík.

The Halifax International Airport is 40 km (25 mi) northeast of downtown Halifax. Sydney Airport is 13 km (8 mi) east of Sydney.

Limousine and taxi services, as well as car rentals, are available at Halifax and Sydney airports. Airport bus service to Halifax and Dartmouth hotels from Halifax International Airport costs $36 round-trip, $18 one-way. Airbus has regular bus service from the Halifax airport to most major hotels in Halifax. Regular taxi and limo fares to Halifax from Halifax International are $53 each way. If you book ahead with Share-A-Cab, the fare is $28, but you must share your car with another passenger. The trip takes 30 to 40 minutes.

Contacts Airbus (☎ *902/873–2091*). **Halifax Robert L. Stanfield International Airport** (☎ *902/873–1223*). **Provincial Airlines** (☎ *709/576–1666, 800/563–2800 in Atlantic Canada* 🌐 *www.provair.com*). **Share-A-Cab** (☎ *902/429–5555*). **Sydney Airport** (☎ *902/564–7720*). **Zoom** (☎ *866/359–9666* 🌐 *www.flyzoom.com*).

BY BOAT & FERRY

Car ferries connect Nova Scotia with Maine and New Brunswick: Bay Ferries Ltd. sails from Bar Harbor and Portland Maine to Yarmouth, and from Saint John, New Brunswick, to Digby, Nova Scotia, two to three times daily. July through August and once daily May to June and September to October. Bay Ferries' Bar Harbor–Yarmouth and Portland–Yarmouth service uses a high-speed catamaran, which makes the crossings in 3 hours and 5½ hours, respectively. Known as *The Cat,* this catamaran is very popular for both its convenience and speed, so reserve ahead.

Weather permitting, from May through December, Northumberland Ferries operates between Caribou, Nova Scotia, and Wood Islands, Prince Edward Island, making the trip several times a day. Marine Atlantic operates regular, year-round between North Sydney and Port aux Basques, on the west coast of Newfoundland, and a three-times-a-week service between North Sydney and Argentia, on Newfoundland's east coast, runs from mid June through September.

Metro Transit runs passenger ferries from the Halifax ferry terminal at Lower Water Street to Alderney Gate in downtown Dartmouth and to Woodside Terminal (near Dartmouth Hospital) on the hour and half hour from 6:30 AM to 11:45 PM. Ferries are more frequent during weekday rush hours; they also operate on Sunday in summer (10 to 6, June through September). Free transfers are available from the ferry to the bus system (and vice versa). A single crossing costs $2 and is worth it for the up-close view of both waterfronts.

Contacts Bay Ferries Ltd. (☎ *902/566–3838 or 888/249–7245* 🌐 *www.nfl-bay.com*). **Marine Atlantic** (☎ *902/794–5254 or 800/341–7981* 🌐 *www.marine-atlantic.ca*). **Metro Transit** (☎ *902/490–6614 or 902/490–4000*). **Northumberland Ferries** (☎ *902/566–3838 or 800/565–0201*).

BY BUS

Because of conflicting schedules, getting to Nova Scotia by bus can be problematic. Greyhound Lines from New York and Montréal, connect with Acadian through New Brunswick. Acadian also provides service between urban centers within Nova Scotia. Airbus runs between the Halifax International Airport and major hotels in Halifax and Dartmouth. Shuttle van services with convenient transportation between Halifax and Sydney include Cape Shuttle Service and Scotia Shuttle Service.

There are a number of small, regional bus services; however, connections are not always convenient. Outside of Halifax there are no inner-city bus services. For information, call Nova Scotia Tourism.

Metro Transit provides bus service throughout Halifax and Dartmouth, the town of Bedford, and (to an increasingly broader extent) the outlying areas around Halifax. The fare is $2; only exact change is accepted.

Contacts **Acadian** (☎ *800/567–5151* 🌐 *www.smtbus.com*). **Airbus** (☎ *902/873–2091*). **Cape Shuttle Service** (☎ *800/349–1698*). **Metro Transit** (☎ *902/490–6614 or 902/490–4000* 🌐 *www.halifax.ca/metrotransit*). **Nova Scotia Tourism** (☎ *902/425–5781 or 800/565–0000* 🌐 *www.novascotia.com*). **Scotia Shuttle Service** (☎ *902/435–9686 or 800/898–5883* 🌐 *www.atyp.com/scotiashuttle*).

BY CAR

Halifax is the most convenient place from which to begin a driving tour of Nova Scotia or Atlantic Canada.

Most highways in the province lead to Halifax and Dartmouth. Highways 3/103, 7, 2/102, and 1/101 terminate in the twin cities. Many of the roads in rural Nova Scotia require attentive driving, as they are not well signed, are narrow, and do not always have a paved shoulder. But they are generally well surfaced and offer exquisite scenery.

Motorists can enter Nova Scotia through the narrow neck of land that connects the province to New Brunswick and the mainland. The Trans-Canada Highway (Highway 2 in New Brunswick) becomes Highway 104 on crossing the Nova Scotia border at Amherst. It is possible to drive over the Confederation Bridge from Prince Edward Island into New Brunswick near the Nova Scotia border. Otherwise, car ferries dock at Yarmouth (from Maine), Digby (from New Brunswick), Caribou (from Prince Edward Island), and North Sydney (from Newfoundland).

ROAD MAPS The province has 11 designated "Scenic Travelways," 5 in Cape Breton and 6 on the mainland, which are identified by roadside signs with icons that correspond with trail names. These lovely routes are also shown on tourist literature from Nova Scotia Tourism and on maps, which are available at gas stations and tourist information centers.

RULES OF THE ROAD Highways numbered from 100 to 199 are all-weather, limited-access roads, with 100-kph to 110-kph (62-mph to 68-mph) speed limits. The last two digits usually match the number of an older trunk highway along the same route, numbered from 1 to 99. Thus, Highway 102, between Halifax and Truro, matches the older Highway 2, between the same towns. Roads numbered from 200 to 399 are secondary roads that usually link villages. Unless otherwise posted, the speed limit on these and any roads other than the 100-series highways is 80 kph (50 mph).

BY TAXI

In Halifax, rates begin at about $3 and increase based on mileage and time. A crosstown trip should cost $7 or $8, depending on traffic. There are taxi stands at major hotels and shopping malls or you can usually hail a cab in the downtown area. Most Haligonians simply phone for taxi service.

Taxi Companies **Casino Taxi** (☎ *902/429–6666 or 902/425–6666*). **Yellow Cab** (☎ *902/420–0000 or 902/422–1551*).

CONTACTS & RESOURCES

EMERGENCIES

Emergency Services **Ambulance, fire, or police** (☎ *911*).

Hospitals **Cape Breton Regional Hospital** (✉ *1482 George St., Sydney* ☎ *902/567–8000*). **IWK Health Centre (for Women and Children)** (✉ *5850 University Ave.,Halifax* ☎ *902/470–8888 switchboard*). **Queen Elizabeth II Health Sciences Centre** (✉ *1796 Summer St., Halifax* ☎ *902/473–2700 switchboard*). **South Shore Regional Hospital** (✉ *90 Glen Allan Dr., Bridgewater* ☎ *902/543–4603 switchboard*).

SPORTS & THE OUTDOORS

BICYCLING *Nova Scotia By Bicycle* ($13.95) is published by Bicycle Nova Scotia; it's available at Mountain Equipment Co-op, Cyclesmith, and The Book Room. Atlantic Canada Cycling can provide information on tours and rentals.

Contacts **Atlantic Canada Cycling** (☎ *902/423–2453 or 888/879–2453* ⊕ *www.atl-canadacycling.com*). **Bicycle Nova Scotia** (✉ *5516 Spring Garden Rd., Box 3010, Halifax B3J 3G6* ☎ *902/425–5450* ⊕ *www.bicycle.ns.ca*). **The Book Room** (✉ *1546 Barrinton St., Halifax* ☎ *902/423–8271*). **Cyclesmith** (✉ *6112 Quinpool Rd., Halifax* ☎ *902/425–1756*). **Mountain Equipment Co-op** (✉ *1550 Granville St., Halifax* ☎ *902/421–2667* ⊕ *www.mec.ca*).

BIRD-WATCHING Nova Scotia is on the Atlantic flyway and is an important staging point for migratory species. A fine illustrated book, *Birds of Nova Scotia,* by Robie Tufts is a must on every ornithologist's reading list. The Nova Scotia Museum of Natural History organizes walks and lectures for people interested in viewing local bird life in the Halifax area.

Contacts **Nova Scotia Bird Society** (☎ *902/445–2922* ⊕ *nsbs.chebucto.org*). **Halifax Field Naturalists** (⊕ *hfn.chebucto.org/fieldnat.html*). **Nova Scotia Museum of Natural History** (☎ *902/424–7353*).

CANOEING There are wonderful canoe routes in Kejimkujik National Park. Canoeing information is available from Canoe NS. The provincial department of Service Nova Scotia offers canoe route maps for sale online, by mail, or in person through the Nova Scotia Geomatics Centre in Amherst. The publication *Canoe Routes of Nova Scotia* has good information, and so does the Web site for Canoe/Kayak Nova Scotia, which lists a Waterway Index and locations to purchase local maps.

Contacts **Canoe/Kayak Nova Scotia** (*902/425–5450 Ext. 316 ckns.homestead.com*). **Nova Scotia Geomatics Centre** (*902/667–7231 or 800/798–0706 [Nova Scotia only]*). **Service Nova Scotia** (*www.gov.ns.ca/snsmr/maps*)

FISHING You are required by law to have a valid Nova Scotia fishing license for inland lakes and rivers. A seven-day nonresident license costs $32.02; or by the day, $12.57. A guidebook, The Nova Scotia Anglers Handbook, is included in the price of the license and outlines where you can fish as well as opening and closing dates for the seasons. You do not need a license to fish in tidal or saltwater in Nova Scotia. However, you must respect Canadian federal fishing seasons and bag limits. For information about obtaining licenses, contact Service Nova Scotia. For specific information on sport fishing in Nova Scotia, contact the Inland Fisheries Division of the Department of Fisheries.

Contacts **Service Nova Scotia** (*902/424–4467 or 902/424–4821*). **Nova Scotia Department of Fisheries and Aquaculture, Inland Fisheries Division** (*902/485–5056*).

GOLF The province offers golfers many well-manicured courses that are both panoramic and challenging. Contact Golf Nova Scotia for information on individual courses and tournaments. Tourism Nova Scotia also has information on golf packages.

Contacts **Golf Nova Scotia** (*877/777–1117*). **Tourism Nova Scotia** (*800/565–0000 www.golfnovascotia.com*).

HIKING Nova Scotia has a wide variety of trails along the rugged coastline and inland through forest glades, which enable you to experience otherwise inaccessible scenery, wildlife, and vegetation. *Hiking Trails of Nova Scotia,* published by Gooselane Editions, is available at most local bookstores. There are a number of Web sites that provide extensive information on routes and trails.

Contacts **Gooselane Editions** (*469 King St., Fredericton, NB E3R 1E5 506/450–4251*). **NovaTrails** (*www.novatrails.com*). **Trails Nova Scotia** (*www.trails.gov.ns.ca*). **Hiking in Nova Scotia** (*www.canadatrails.ca/hiking/hike_ns.html*).

SKIING There are four alpine ski hills and hundreds of trails for cross-country skiing in Nova Scotia.

Contacts **Cross Country Ski Nova Scotia** (*www.crosscountryskins.homestead.com/crosscountryskins.html*). **Ski Ben Eoin** (*902/828–2804 www.skibeneoin.com*). **Ski Martock** (*902/798—9501 www.martock.com*). **Ski Wentworth** (*902/548–2089 www.skiwentworth.ca*). **Ski Cape Smokey** (*902/285–2760 www.skicapesmokey.com*).

TOURS

BOAT TOURS Boat tours have become very popular in all regions of the province. Murphy's on the Water sails various vessels: *Harbour Queen I,* a paddle wheeler; *Haligonian III,* an enclosed motor launch; and *Mar,* a 75-foot sailing ketch. All operate from mid-May to late October from berths at 1751 Lower Water Street on Cable Wharf next to the Historic Properties in Halifax. Some tours include lunch, dinner, or entertainment. A cash bar may also be available. Costs vary, but a basic tour of the Halifax Harbour ranges from $17.99 to $44.99. Tours vary from one to four hours.

Harbour Hopper Tours offers a unique amphibious tour of historic downtown Halifax and the Halifax Harbour. Tours are approximately one-hour long (half on land, half on water) and run hourly from the early morning until late evening. The cost is $24.99 for adults or $70.99 for a family of four.

Contacts **Harbour Hopper Tours** (☎ *902/490–8687*). **Murphy's on the Water** (☎ *902/420–1015*).

BUS & RICKSHAW TOURS

Ambassatours Gray Line Sightseeing and Cabana Tours run coach tours through Halifax, Dartmouth, and Peggy's Cove. Halifax Double Decker Tours offers two-hour tours on double-decker buses that leave daily from the Historic Properties in Halifax. Virtually every cab company in Halifax gives custom tours. Cab tours to locations such as Wolfville or Peggy's Cove are possible with prior arrangement. Prices vary, but be sure to set a fee with the tour guide before you begin. Rickshaw tours can be found on the waterfront.

Contacts **Cabana Tours** (☎ *902/455–8111*). **Ambassatours Gray Line Sightseeing** (☎ *902/423–6242*). **Halifax Double Decker Tours** (☎ *902/420–1155*). **Casino Cab** (☎ *902/425–6666 or 902/429–6666*). **Yellow Cab** (☎ *902/420–0000 or 902/422–1551*).

WALKING TOURS

Explore Halifax's rich tradition of stories of pirates, haunted houses, buried treasure, and ghosts with a ghoulish ghost walk. Tours begin at the Old Town Clock at 7:30 PM Wednesday through Sunday, May through October.

Contacts **Ghost Walk of Historic Halifax** (☎ *902/494–0525* ⊕ *www.tattletours.ca*). **Historical Walking Tour** (☎ *902/494–0525*).

VISITOR INFORMATION

Nova Scotia Tourism publishes a wide range of literature, including an annual (free) travel guide called the *Nova Scotia Doers and Dreamers Guide*. Call to have it mailed to you, or stop in at one of the visitor information centers for an in-person query.

Contacts **Nova Scotia Tourism** (☎ *902/425–5781 or 800/565–0000* ⊕ *www.novascotia.com*). **Nova Scotia Tourism** (☎ *902/424–4248*). **Tourism Cape Breton** (☎ *902/563–4636* ⊕ *www.cbisland.com*). **Tourism Halifax** (☎ *902/490–5946* ⊕ *www.halifaxinfo.com*).

Newfoundland & Labrador

15

WORD OF MOUTH

"Coastal Newfoundland has its charms in all seasons but for whales and puffins late June through mid August is the best time."

—gannetmusic 1/06

www.fodors.com/forums

Updated by [illegible] Bates

ALONG NEWFOUNDLAND AND LABRADOR'S NEARLY 17,699 km (11,000 mi) of coastline, humpback whales feed near shore, millions of seabirds nest, and 10,000-year-old icebergs drift by fishing villages.

The first European settlement in North America was established by Vikings more than 1,000 years ago. They settled in what is now a National Historic Site at L'Anse aux Meadows, calling their new home Vinland. They were preceded by people who lived in the region 9,000 years ago. A 7,500-year-old burial ground in southern Labrador is the oldest-known cemetery in North America.

When explorer John Cabot arrived at Bonavista from England in 1497, he reported an ocean so full of fish they could be caught in a basket lowered over the side of a boat. Soon, fishing boats from France, England, Spain, and Portugal vied to catch Newfoundland cod, the fish that helped shape the province's history.

In 1949, Newfoundland and Labrador joined Confederation, bringing into the country a half-hour time difference and a unique lifestyle. Visitors will straddle time zones and Irish, French, and English dialects found throughout the province.

Wherever you travel in the province, you're sure to meet some of the warmest, humorous people in North America. Strangers have always been welcome in Newfoundland. Your first task is to master the name of the island portion of the province—it's New-fun-*land,* and it rhymes with understand.

EXPLORING NEWFOUNDLAND & LABRADOR

A leisurely drive around the province is the best way to absorb its culture and beauty. Most tourists fly in to St. John's; major car-rental agencies have kiosks at the airport. Newfoundland has become a popular tourist destination, so you book at least your first night's accommodation and your car rental in advance. If you don't have a car, St. John's has Metrobus for travel in the capital city region, and DRL Coachlines travels across the island from St. John's to Port aux Basques, stopping at major towns on Route 1 (also known as the Trans-Canada Highway). Ferry services connect to Labrador as well as to Nova Scotia, and smaller ferries run to smaller island communities around the coast.

ABOUT THE HOTELS & RESTAURANTS

Lodgings in Newfoundland and Labrador range from modestly priced bed-and-breakfasts, which you can find through local tourist offices, to luxury accommodations. In remote areas, be prepared to find very basic lodgings, though some of the best lodging in the province can be found in rural areas. Great hospitality often makes up for a lack of amenities.

Generally only the large urban centers, especially St. John's and Corner Brook, have sophisticated restaurants. Fish is a safe dish just about everywhere. Excellent, home-cooked meals are offered in the province's network of B&Bs.

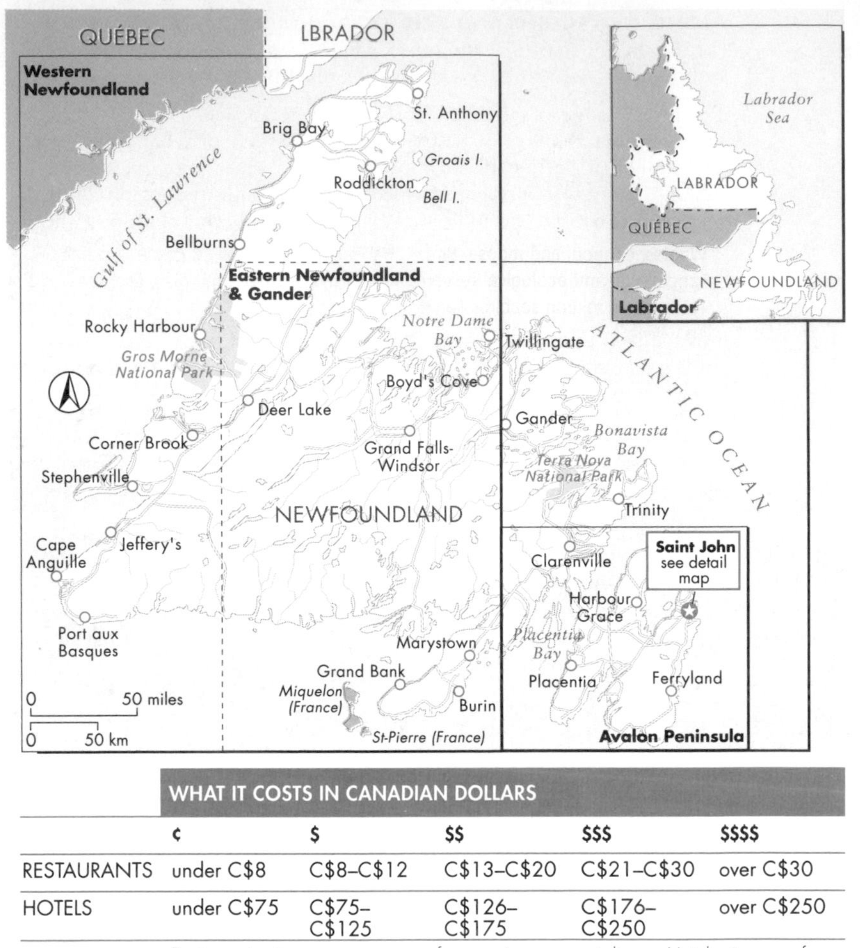

WHAT IT COSTS IN CANADIAN DOLLARS					
	¢	$	$$	$$$	$$$$
RESTAURANTS	under C$8	C$8–C$12	C$13–C$20	C$21–C$30	over C$30
HOTELS	under C$75	C$75–C$125	C$126–C$175	C$176–C$250	over C$250

Restaurant prices are per person for a main course at dinner. Hotel prices are for two people in a standard double room in high season, excluding tax.

ST. JOHN'S, NEWFOUNDLAND

When Sir Humphrey Gilbert sailed into St. John's to establish British colonial rule for Queen Elizabeth in 1583, he found Spanish, French, and Portuguese fishermen already fighting for a spot in the lucrative cod fishery. For centuries, Newfoundland was the largest supplier of salt cod in the world, with St. John's Harbour the center of the trade. Today the province's capital (population 100,646) is a modern as they come yet retains something of its original nature—office buildings are surrounded by heritage shops and colorful row houses. English and Irish influences, Victorian architecture and modern convenience, and

TOP REASONS TO GO	
THE RUGGED BEAUTY Magnificent mountains, wooden houses perched on rocky seacliffs, sweeping vistas, hidden fjords, and the deep blue ocean.	**THE CULTURE** Be entertained by storytelling, Irish music, plays, festivals, writers, and comedians.
WILDLIFE Whales, caribou, and moose. Bird sanctuaries and ecological reserves. Thirty-three million seabirds can't be wrong.	**AMAZING FISH DISHES** Crab cakes, chowder, capelin, shrimp—and cod au gratin, pan-fried, or in the traditional dish, fish and brewis.

traditional music and rock and roll, make a heady brew—a lively city with a relaxed pace.

EXPLORING ST. JOHN'S

The city encircles St. John's Harbour, expanding past the hilly, narrow streets of old St. John's. Much of the row housing dates back to the Great Fire of 1892. Heritage houses on Waterford Bridge Road, Rennies Mill Road, and Circular Road were originally the homes of sea captains and merchants. Duckworth Street and Water Street, running parallel to the harbor, are filled with shops and restaurants. A walk downtown takes in many historic buildings, but a car is needed to explore some farther-flung sights.

WHAT TO SEE

Anglican Cathedral of St. John the Baptist. A fine example of Gothic Revival architecture, this church was first completed in the mid-1800s; it was rebuilt after the 1892 fire. Every Wednesday, there's a free lunchtime organ recital from 1:15 to 1:45. Women of the parish operate a tearoom in the crypt 2:30 to 4:30 daily in July and August, from 2 PM on Wednesday ($8). ✉*22 Church Hill* ☎*709/726–5677* 🌐*www.infonet.st-johns.nf.ca/cathedral* *Free* ⏲*Tours June–Sept., weekdays 10–noon and 2–4, Sat. 10–noon, Sun., after 11 AM service.*

Basilica Cathedral of St. John the Baptist. This 1855 Roman Catholic cathedral in the Romanesque style has a commanding position above Military Road. A religious museum is next door. ✉*200 Military Rd.* ☎*709/726–3660* 🌐*www.stjohnsarchdiocese.nf.ca* *Museum $2* ⏲*Museum June–mid-Sept., Mon.–Sat. 10–4, Sun. 11–4.*

Circular Road. This street contains some very fine Victorian houses and shady trees.

Colonial Building. This columned building (erected 1847–50) was the seat of the Newfoundland government from the 1850s until 1960, when the legislature moved to its current home, the Confederation Building, in the north end of the city. ✉*Military and Bannerman Rds.*

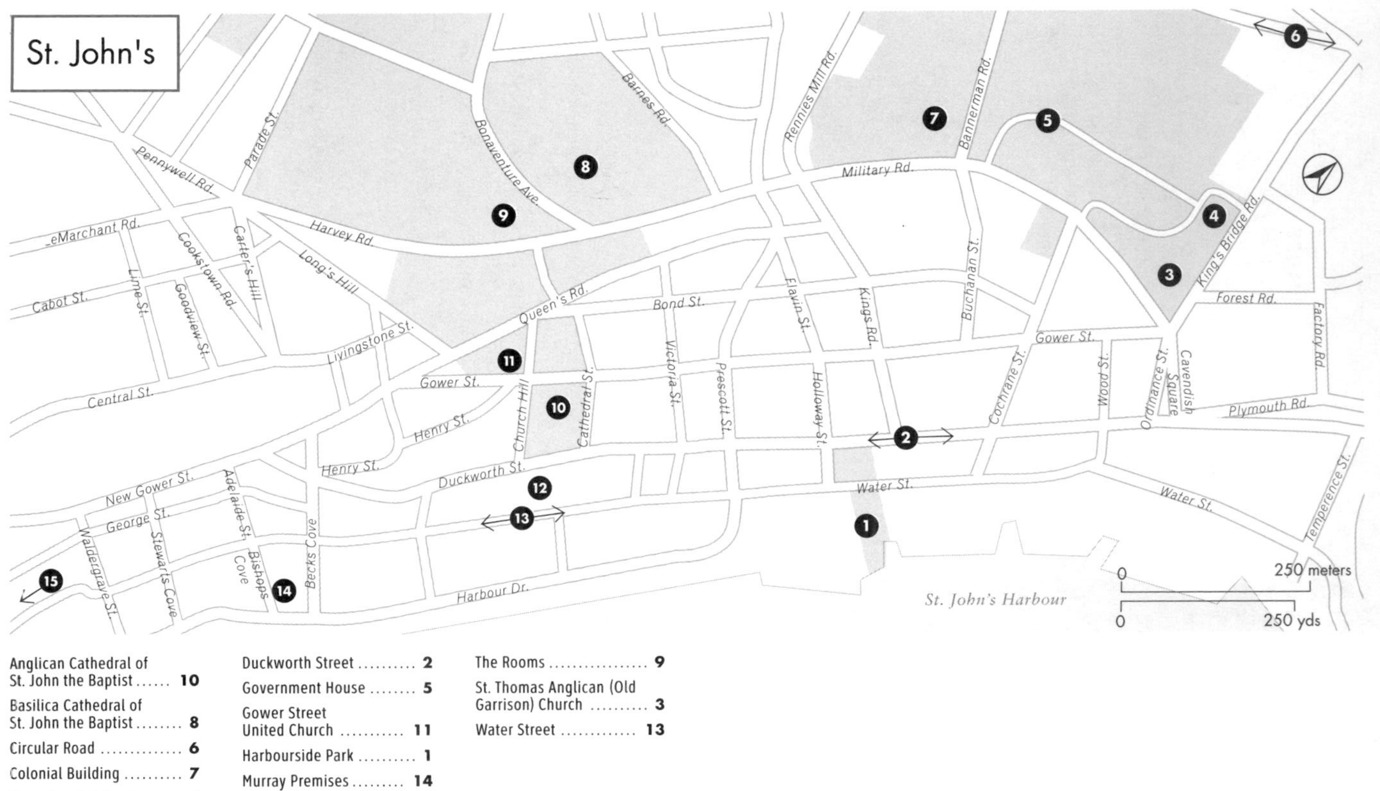
St. John's
Pennywell Rd.
Parade St.
Bonaventure Ave.
Barnes Rd.
Rennies Mill Rd.
Bannerman Rd.
Military Rd.
King's Bridge Rd.
Forest Rd.
Factory Rd.
LeMarchant Rd.
Cookstown Rd.
Carter's Hill
Harvey Rd.
Long's Hill
Cabot St.
Lime St.
Goodview St.
Queen's Rd.
Bond St.
Flavin St.
Kings Rd.
Buchanan St.
Gower St.
Livingstone St.
Victoria St.
Prescott St.
Holloway St.
Cochrane St.
Wood St.
Ordinance St.
Cavendish Square
Plymouth Rd.
Central St.
Church Hill
Cathedral St.
Henry St.
Duckworth St.
Water St.
Temperence St.
New Gower St.
George St.
Adelaide St.
Waldergrave St.
Stewarts Cove
Bishops Cove
Becks Cove
Harbour Dr.
St. John's Harbour
0
250 meters
0
250 yds
Anglican Cathedral of St. John the Baptist 10
Basilica Cathedral of St. John the Baptist 8
Circular Road 6
Colonial Building 7
Commissariat House 4
Court House 12
Duckworth Street 2
Government House 5
Gower Street United Church 11
Harbourside Park 1
Murray Premises 14
Newman Wine Vaults 15
The Rooms 9
St. Thomas Anglican (Old Garrison) Church 3
Water Street 13

GREAT ITINERARIES

IF YOU HAVE 3 DAYS

On the west coast, after arriving by ferry at **Port aux Basques**, drive through the Codroy Valley, heading north to **Gros Morne National Park**, and overnight in nearby Rocky Harbour. The next day, visit **L'Anse aux Meadows National Historic Site**, where the Vikings built a village a thousand years ago. Spend the night in **St. Anthony** or nearby.

On the east coast, the ferry docks at Argentia. Explore the Avalon Peninsula, beginning in **St. John's**. The next day visit **Cape Spear,** the most easterly point in North America, and the **Witless Bay Ecological Reserve**, where you can see whales, seabirds, and icebergs. Drive through **Placentia** and spend your third day at **Cape St. Mary's Ecological Reserve**, known for its gannets and dramatic coastal scenery.

IF YOU HAVE 6 DAYS

On Newfoundland's west coast, add southern Labrador to your trip. A ferry takes you from St. Barbe to Blanc Sablon on the Québec–Labrador border. Drive 96 km (60 mi) to **Red Bay** to explore the remains of a 17th-century Basque whaling station; then head to **L'Anse Amour** to see Canada's second-tallest lighthouse. Overnight at **L'Anse au Clair**. Return through Gros Morne National Park and explore **Corner Brook**. The next day, explore the Port au Port Peninsula, home of Newfoundland's French-speaking population.

On the east coast add **Trinity** to your must-see list, and spend the night there or in **Clarenville**. The north shore of Conception Bay is home to many picturesque villages, including **Cupids** and **Harbour Grace**. Several half-day, full-day, and two-day excursions are possible from St. John's, and in each direction a different personality of the region unfolds.

IF YOU HAVE 9 DAYS

In addition to the places already mentioned on the west coast, drive into central Newfoundland and visit Notre Dame Bay. Overnight in **Twillingate**. Catch a ferry to **Fogo** or the **Change Islands.** Accommodations are available on both islands, but book ahead.

On the east coast, add a trip to France to your itinerary. You can reach the French territory of **St-Pierre and Miquelon** by passenger ferry from Fortune. Explore romantic **Grand Bank**, named for the famous fishing area just offshore, and climb Cook's Lookout in **Burin**, where Captain James Cook kept watch for smugglers from St-Pierre.

15

4 **Commissariat House.** The residence and office of the British garrison's supply officer in the 1830s has been restored to reflect that era. ✉*King's Bridge Rd.* ☎*709/729–6730 or 709/729–0592* 🌐*www.tcr.gov.nl.ca/tcr/historicsites* 🎟*$3* ⏲*Mid-May–Sept., daily 10–5:30.*

12 **Court House.** The late-19th-century courthouse has an eccentric appearance: each of its four turrets is a different style. ✉*Duckworth St. at bottom of Church Hill.*

2 **Duckworth Street.** This has been St. John's "second street" for centuries. (Water Street is the main street.) Stretching from the bottom of Signal

Hill in the east to near City Hall in the west, Duckworth Street is home to restaurants, bars, and shops.

5 **Government House.** This is the residence of the lieutenant governor, the queen's representative in Newfoundland. It has a moat, which was designed to allow more light into the basement rooms. Built in the 1830s, the house is not open for tours, but it has a marvelous garden you can explore. ✉ *Military Rd.* ☎ *709/729–4494* 🌐 *www.mun.ca/govhouse* *Free* ⏲ *Garden daily dawn–dusk.*

11 **Gower Street United Church.** This 1896 church has 50 stained-glass windows and a massive pipe organ. ✉ *99 Gower St., at Queen's Rd.* ☎ *709/753–7286* 🌐 *www.gowerunited.ca* *Free* ⏲ *Sept.–May, weekdays 9–3; July and Aug., weekdays 9–12; tours available year-round during office hours.*

1 **Harbourside Park.** This small park is a good vantage point to watch the boats come and go and rest from your walk, but the larger parks have more green space and are better for picnics. ✉ *Water St. E.*

14 **Murray Premises.** One of the oldest buildings in St. John's, the Murray Premises dates from 1846. This restored warehouse houses shops, restaurants, and a hotel. The **Newfoundland Science Centre** (☎ *709/754–0823*), open daily, with hands-on exhibits and special demonstrations, is within the Murray Premises. ✉ *Water St. and Harbour Dr., at Beck's Cove* ☎ *709/754–0823* 🌐 *www.nlsciencecentre.com* *$6* ⏲ *Weekdays 10–5, Sat. 10–6, Sun. noon–6.*

15 **Newman Wine Vaults.** This 200-year-old building with stone barrel vaults is where the renowned Newman's Port was aged. This is a provincial historic site with guides who interpret Newfoundland's long and unique association with port. You can purchase more than 20 different brands here. ✉ *436 Water St.* ☎ *709/739–7870* 🌐 *www.historictrust.com* *Donations accepted* ⏲ *June–Aug., daily 10–4:30 or by appointment.*

9 **The Rooms.** Provincial archives, a museum, and an art gallery are housed in The Rooms. The design was inspired by traditional "fishing rooms," tracts of land by the waterside where fishing activity took place. The views of St. John's from the third and fourth levels are awe inspiring. The two floors of galleries hold a collection of more than 7,000 contemporary works of art. A fourth-floor restaurant ($–$$) serves tasty seafood dishes and desserts like Newfoundland Berry Cobbler and Sticky Toffee Pudding with Crème Anglaise. ✉ *9 Bonaventure Ave.* ☎ *709/757–8000* *$5, free Wed. 6–9 PM and first Sat. of each month; special exhibits $12* ⏲ *June–mid-Oct., Mon., Tues., Fri., and Sat. 10–5, Wed. and Thurs. 10–9, Sun. noon–5; mid-Oct.–May, Tues., Fri., and Sat. 10–5, Wed. and Thurs. 10–9, Sun. noon–5. Archives closed Sun.*

Fodor's Choice ★

3 **St. Thomas Anglican (Old Garrison) Church.** English soldiers used to worship at this black wooden church, the oldest in the city, during the early and mid-1800s. ✉ *8 Military Rd.* ☎ *709/576–6632* *Free* ⏲ *Late June–Aug., daily 9:30–5:30; call for off-season hrs.*

13 **Water Street.** Originally called the Lower Path, Water Street has been the site of businesses since at least the 1620s. The older architecture resembles that of seaports in southwest England and Ireland.

GREATER ST. JOHN'S

A number of must-see attractions can be found a short drive from the downtown core. Plan to spend a full day exploring Greater St. John's to give yourself some time at each spot.

> **WORD OF MOUTH**
>
> "Be sure to go out to Cape Spear (eastern most point on the NA continent) where you might want to take in a sunrise and watch the whales at play from the lighthouse point. Signal Hill is also a must and you would probably enjoy the challenging hiking trails there as well as the magnificent view from Cabot Tower."
>
> —Retired_teacher 07/06

WHAT TO SEE

The Battery. This tiny fishing village perches precariously at the base of steep cliffs between Signal Hill and St. John's Harbour. Narrow lanes snake around the houses, which empty directly onto the street, making this a good place to walk.

Cabot Tower. This tower at the summit of Signal Hill was constructed in 1897 to commemorate the 400th anniversary of Cabot's landing in Newfoundland. The ride here along Signal Hill Road affords fine harbor, ocean, and city views, as does the tower. ✉*Signal Hill Rd.* ☎*709/772–5367* 🌐*www.pc.gc.ca* *Free* *Apr.–Dec., daily 9–5, mid-May–Labor Day, daily 8:30* AM*–9* PM.

★ **Cape Spear National Historic Site.** At the easternmost point of land on the continent, songbirds begin chirping in the dim light of dawn, and whales (in early summer) feed directly below the cliffs, providing an unforgettable start to the day. From April through July, you may see icebergs floating by. **Cape Spear Lighthouse,** Newfoundland's oldest such beacon, has been restored to its original form and furnishings. ✉*Rte. 11* ☎*709/772–5367* 🌐*www.pc.gc.ca* *Site free, lighthouse $3.95* *Site daily dawn–dusk; lighthouse mid-May–mid-Oct., daily 10–6; Visitor Interpretation Centre and Heritage Gift Shop mid-May–Labor Day, daily 9:30–8, after Labor Day–Oct. 15, daily 10–6.*

The Fluvarium. At the only public facility of its kind in North America, you can observe (in season) spawning brown and brook trout in their natural habitat through underwater windows. Feeding time for the fish, frogs, and eels is 4 PM daily. ✉*5 Nagle's Pl., C.A. Pippy Park* ☎*709/754–3474* 🌐*www.fluvarium.ca* *$5.50* *May–Labor Day, daily 9–5; Labor Day–Apr., weekdays 9–4:30, weekends 9–5.*

Johnson GEO CENTRE. Built deep into the earth with only the entryway protruding aboveground, this geological shrine is literally embedded in Signal Hill. Kids five and up love the theater with sounds of thunder and lightning, and kids under five love squirting water at the rocks and seeing the different rock formations. ✉*175 Signal Hill Rd.* ☎*709/737–7880 or 866/868–7625* *709/737–7885* 🌐*www.geocentre.ca* *$10.25*

⌚Mid-May–mid-Oct., Mon.–Sat. 9:30–5, Sun. 1–5; mid-Oct.–mid-May, Tues.–Sat. 9:30–5, Sun. 1–5.

★ **Memorial University Botanical Garden.** This 110-acre natural area includes rock gardens and scree, a Newfoundland historic-plants bed, peat and woodland beds, an alpine house, a medicinal garden, and native-plant collections. There are four pleasant walking trails. See the varieties of rhododendron, as well as many kinds of butterflies and the rare hummingbird hawkmoth. *✉C.A. Pippy Park, Oxen Pond, 306 Mt. Scio Rd. ☎709/737–8590 🌐www.mun.ca/botgarden 🎟$3.50 ⌚May–Nov., daily 10–5; Dec.–Apr., daily 10–4.*

DAY AT THE RACES

If you are in St. John's on the first Wednesday of August, head down to Quidi Vidi Lake and experience the Royal St. John's Regatta (🌐 *www.stjohnsregatta.org*), the oldest continuous sporting event in North America. The fixed-seat rowing shells hold a crew of six and the coxswain. This garden party/reunion/sporting event draws more than 30,000 people.

Quidi Vidi. No one knows the origin of the name of this fishing village, one of the oldest parts of St. John's. The town is best explored on foot, as the narrow roads make driving difficult. The inlet, called the Gut is a traditional outport in the middle of a modern city. *✉Take the first right off Kings Bridge Rd. (left of the Fairmont Hotel) onto Forest Rd., which heads into the village.*

Quidi Vidi Battery. This small redoubt has been restored to the way it appeared in 1812 when soldiers stood guard to fight off a possible American attack during the War of 1812–14. *✉Off Cuckold's Cove Rd. ☎709/729–2977 or 709/729–0592 🎟$3 ⌚Mid-May–Sept., daily 10–5:30.*

Fodor's Choice ★ **Signal Hill National Historic Site.** Throughout the 1600s and 1700s Signal Hill changed hands between the French, English, and Dutch forces. In 1762, this was the site of the final battle between the French and British in the Seven Years' War (called the French and Indian War in the United States). In 1901 Guglielmo Marconi received the first transatlantic-wire transmission near **Cabot Tower** at the top of Signal Hill—visit the Marconi Exhibit on the top floor. From the top of the hill it's a 500-foot drop to the narrow harbor entrance below; views are excellent. Walking trails take you to the base of the hill and closer to the ocean. Be careful, and dress warmly. *✉Signal Hill Rd. ☎709/772–5367 🌐www.pc.gc.ca 🎟Site free; visitor center $3.95 ⌚Site daily dawn–dusk. Visitor Centre mid-June–Labor Day, daily 8:30–8; Labor Day–Oct. and May–mid-June, daily 8:30–4:30; Nov.–Apr., weekdays 8:30–4:30.*

WHERE TO STAY & EAT

$$–$$$$ ✕**The Cellar.** This classy restaurant's menu features lamb, pork, chicken, beef, and delicious local seafood dishes. *✉189 Water St. ☎709/579–8900 ▭AE, MC, V ⌚No lunch weekends.*

$-$$$ ✕**The Casbah** A bright red exterior welcomes you into this trendy, tropical-looking spot. The menu includes soups, salads, panini sandwiches, meats, and seafood. It's the weekend brunch that's truly special. For your money, you get a big feed of steak and eggs, potatoes, grilled vegetables, baked beans, and home-style toast. ✉*2 Cathedral St.* ☎*709/738–5293* ✍*Reservations essential* ▭*MC, V.*

LOCAL FOOD

Seafood is an excellent value here. Cod is panfried, baked, or poached; cold-water shrimp, snow crab, and lobster are delicious choices. Many restaurants offer seasonal specialties with a wide variety of traditional wild and cultured species, such as steelhead trout, salmon, mussels, and sea scallops.

¢–$$ ✕**Pasta Plus Café.** Pasta is the specialty here, but the local chain also serves curries, salads, and pizza. Try a curry dish served with banana-date chutney, or a crepe stuffed with seasonally available seafood. Desserts are scumptious. ✉*233 Duckworth St.* ☎*709/739–6676* ✉*Avalon Mall, Thorburn Rd.* ☎*709/722–6006* ✉*Churchill Sq., Elizabeth Ave.* ☎*709/739–5818* ✉*The Village Shopping Centre* ☎*709/368–3481* ▭*AE, DC, MC, V.*

15

¢–$ Fodor'sChoice ★ ✕**Ches's.** Since the 1950s, this restaurant has been serving fish-and-chips to a steady stream of customers from noon until after midnight. It's strictly laminated tabletops and plastic chairs, but the fish is hot and fresh. ✉*9 Freshwater Rd.* ☎*709/722–4083* ✉*655 Topsail Rd.* ☎*709/368–9473* ✉*29–33 Commonwealth Ave., Mount Pearl* ☎*709/364–6837* ✉*8 Highland Dr.* ☎*709/738–5022* ▭*MC, V.*

¢–$ ✕**The Sprout.** On the walls, local artists and craftspeople display their work, but the real works of art arrive at your table in the form of salads, soups, and sandwiches (the Bravocado is cheese, avocado, and sprouts on homemade grain bread). It's great vegetarian fare; the vegan chocolate mousse is decadent. You can sit at tables or one of the four booths. ✉*364 Duckworth St.* ☎*709/579–5485* ✍*No reservations* ▭*AE, DC, MC, V* ⏲*Closed Mon. No lunch Sun.*

$$$–$$$$ ★ ✕🏨**Fairmont Newfoundland.** Charming rooms overlook the harbor at this nine-story hotel. Ask for a south-facing room for a great view of Signal Hill and the Narrows. The hotel is noted for its Sunday and evening buffets in the Bonavista restaurant ($$–$$$), and the fine cuisine at the Cabot Club ($$$–$$$$). An indoor garden atrium overlooks the Narrows and is an ideal spot for breakfast or afternoon tea. ✉*115 Cavendish Sq., Box 5637, A1C 5W8* ☎*709/726–4980* 🖷*709/725–2025* 🌐*www.fairmont.com* *301 rooms, 14 suites* *In-room: refrigerator (some), dial-up. In-hotel: 2 restaurants, room service, bar, pool, gym, spa, laundry service, concierge, executive floor, parking (no fee), no-smoking rooms, some pets allowed* ▭*AE, DC, MC, V.*

$$$ ✕🏨**Blue on Water.** Natural flavors and a simplistic approach to organic fare is what this trendy restaurant (reservations essential; $$$–$$$$) is all about. Try the carrot ginger soup, and if you want your fish fresh, this is the place. Above is a modern boutique hotel with turquoise-colored walls and wide-screen flat-panel TVs. If you leave the windows open, you can catch a fresh whiff of the Atlantic Ocean. ✉*319 Water St., A1C 1B9*

709/754–2583 www.blueonwater.com 7 rooms In-room: DVD, ethernet. In-hotel: restaurant, room service, no elevator, no-smoking rooms D, DC, MC, V.

LOCAL LODGING

One night in a bed-and-breakfast and you'll experience Newfoundland's renowned hospitality. All you may want is a place to lay down your head; you'll probably leave feeling like family.

$$–$$$ **Delta St. John's.** Rooms in this popular convention hotel in downtown St. John's are standard, but they overlook the harbor and the city. Rooms facing New Gower Street have the best views. The restaurant, Quinn's Plate ($$–$$$$), serves steak and seafood, but restaurants of all types are in abundance nearby. *120 New Gower St., A1C 6K4 709/739–6404 or 800/563–3838 709/570–1622 www.deltahotels.com 404 rooms, 30 suites In-room: refrigerator (some), dial-up. In-hotel: restaurant, room service, bar, pool, gym, laundry service, parking (fee), no-smoking rooms, some pets allowed AE, DC, MC, V.*

$$–$$$ **Murray Premises Hotel.** Set under original beamed ceilings, columns, and timber-slanted roofs, this boutique hotel abounds in luxurious extras. All rooms feature custom maple furniture and a bed adorned with a beautiful, warm duvet and high-quality linens. Large marble bathrooms have oversize Jacuzzis and towel warmers. *5 Becks Cove, A1C 6H1 709/738–7773 or 866/738–7773 709/738–7775 www.murraypremiseshotel.com 28 rooms In-room: DVD, refrigerator, ethernet. In-hotel: laundry service, parking (no fee), no-smoking rooms AE, DC, MC, V CP.*

$–$$$ ★ **Elizabeth Manor Bed & Breakfast.** Local artwork decorates the walls of this 1894 Victorian, one of the city's most established and popular B&Bs. The inn tastefully blends the new and the old, and is central to shops and downtown attractions. *21 Military Rd., A1C 2C3 709/753–7733 or 888/263–3786 709/753–6036 www.elizabethmanor.nl.ca 8 rooms, 2 with shared bath In-room: no a/c, Wi-Fi, kitchen. In-hotel: no elevator, no-smoking rooms AE, MC, V BP.*

$$ Fodor'sChoice ★ **Angel House Heritage Inn.** When William Hurt was in town filming a movie, he rented out this 1878 home, which sits on an acre of land and is set back from the road for privacy. The house is impeccable, as is its park-like garden. A generous breakfast is served in the dining room or outside on the patio. *146 Hamilton Ave., Box 2463, Stn. C, A1C 6E7 709/739–4223 or 866/719–4223 709/576–3367 www.angelhousebb.com 4 rooms In-room: DVD, Wi-Fi. In-hotel: no-smoking rooms AE, MC, V BP.*

$$ Fodor'sChoice ★ **Everton House.** Five-star luxury is everywhere in this grand heritage home built in 1891. Its 12-foot-high ceilings, yellow kitchen with glass-door cupboards, and huge windows make it warm and welcoming. The rooms are carpeted and very elegantly decorated. *25 Kingsbridge Rd., A1C 3K4 709/739–1616 or 877/739–1616 709/739–8726 www.evertonhouse.com 4 rooms, 1 suite In-room: DVD, VCR, Wi-Fi. In-hotel: bar, no elevator, laundry service, parking (no fee), no-smoking rooms AE, DC, MC, V BP.*

$$ **Holiday Inn.** This chain hotel is next to walking trails that meander around small lakes and link into the Grand Concourse. Pippy Park, which has two golf courses, is directly across the street, and a miniature golf course is nearby. The in-house restaurant, East Side Mario's, serves Italian food and burgers. *180 Portugal Cove Rd., A1B 2N2 709/722–0506 709/722–9756 www.holidayinnstjohns.com 250 rooms In-room: refrigerator (some), dial-up. In-hotel: restaurant, bar, pool, gym, laundry service, parking (no fee), no-smoking rooms, some pets allowed AE, D, DC, MC, V.*

$–$$ **Park House Inn, Bed and Breakfast.** Three Newfoundland prime ministers lived at this house built in the late 1870s. It sits next to Colonial House, the former seat of government, a great base for exploring downtown St. John's. The grand foyer has 5-foot-high wainscoting and a circular mahogany staircase. A large white deck embraces the back of the house, and the rooms—with queen-size sleigh beds and fireplaces—are luxurious, warm, and inviting. *112 Military Rd., A1C 2C9 709/576–2265 or 866/303–0565 709/576–2268 www.newfoundlandbedandbreakfast.nl.ca 4 rooms In-room: DVD, dial-up. In-hotel: no elevator, laundry facilities, parking (no fee), no-smoking rooms AE, MC, V BP.*

15

SPORTS & THE OUTDOORS

GOLF

The par-71, 18-hole Admiral's Green and the par-35, 9-hole Captain's Hill are adjacent public courses in **C.A. Pippy Park** (*460 Allandale Rd. 709/753–7110 www.pippyparkgolf.com*) that overlook St. John's. **Clovelley** (*Off Stavanger Dr. 709/722–7170 www.clovellygolf.com*) has two 18-hole courses: the 72-par Osprey and the 62-par Black Duck, in the east end of St. John's. Like anywhere else, call several days in advance to book a tee time.

HIKING

A well developed, marked trail system, the **Grand Concourse** (*709/737–1077 www.grandconcourse.ca*), crisscrosses the city of St. John's, covering more than 120 km (70 mi). Some trails traverse river valleys, parks, and other open areas, and others are sidewalk routes. Well-maintained trails encircle several lakes, including Long Pond and Quidi Vidi Lake, both of which are great for bird-watching. Detailed maps are available at tourist information centers and many hotels.

SCUBA DIVING

Ocean Quest (*Foxtrap Marina, Foxtrap 709/834–7234 or 866/623–2664 www.oceanquestcharters.com*) offers classes for beginners as well as leads ocean tours aboard Zodiacs and a 38-foot custom boat to popular scuba-diving sites, including the WWII shipwrecks off Bell Island and Conception Harbor whaling wrecks.

WHALE-WATCHING

The east coast of Newfoundland, including the area around St. John's, provides spectacular whale-watching opportunities with up to 22 species of dolphins and whales visible along the coast. Huge humpback whales weighing up to 30 tons come close to shore to feed in late spring and early summer. You may be able to spot icebergs and large flocks of nesting seabirds in addition to whales on many boat tours. For tour times and rates, visit the tour company booths at harborside in summer, near Pier 7, or inquire at your hotel.

SHOPPING

Christina Parker Gallery (⊠*7 Plank Rd.* ☎*709/753–0580* 🌐*www.christinaparkergallery.com*) carries mainly the work of local artists in all media, including paintings (Barbara, Christopher, and Mary Pratt), sculpture, drawing, and prints. **Fred's Records** (⊠*198 Duckworth St.* ☎*709/753–9191* 🌐*www.freds.nf.ca*) has the best selection of local recordings, as well as other music. **Livyers** (⊠*202 Duckworth St.* ☎*709/726–5650*) has a little of everything, from furniture and books to maps and prints.The **Newfoundland Weavery** (⊠*177 Water St.* ☎*709/753–0496*) sells rugs, prints, lamps, books, crafts, and other gift items.

AVALON PENINSULA

On the southern half of the peninsula, hamlets are separated by stretches of wilderness. At the intersection of Routes 90 and 91 in Salmonier, you can head west and then south to Route 100 to Cape St. Mary's Ecological Reserve, or head north toward Salmonier Nature Park and on to the towns on Conception Bay. Both take about three hours.

WITLESS BAY ECOLOGICAL RESERVE

29 km (18 mi) south of St. John's.

Four small islands and the ocean make up the reserve, summer home of millions of puffins, murres, kittiwakes, razorbills, and guillemots. Those seabirds, and the humpback and minke whales that linger here before moving north to the summer grounds in the Arctic, feed on capelin that swarm inshore to spawn. ⊠*Rte. 10; take Pitts Memorial Dr. (Rte. 2) from downtown St. John's and turn right onto Goulds off-ramp, then left onto Rte. 10.*

SPORTS & THE OUTDOORS

From mid-May to mid-October, **Gatherall's Puffin and Whale Watch** (☎*709/334–2887 or 800/419–4253* 🌐*www.gatheralls.com*) leads six 90-minute trips per day into the reserve on a high-speed catamaran. The catamaran is quite stable in rough seas, so if you get queasy that might be the way to go. Shuttle service is available from St. John's hotels. **O'Brien's Whale and Bird Tours** (☎*709/753–4850 or 877/639–4253* 🌐*www.obriensboattours.com*) offers two-hour excursions in a 46-passenger boat to view whales, icebergs, and seabirds. They also lead sea kayak and Zodiac Coastal Explorer tours. Dress warmly.

CLOSE UP

Newfoundland English

Newfoundland English is made up from words that came here centuries ago when fertile fishing grounds brought sailors from all over Europe and the British Isles to these shores. Then in the late 16th century, colonies of people were brought here to settle, with very little—except, of course, for their culture in the form of words, sayings, and songs. Because of the province's relative isolation, accents remained strong and these archaic words took root to become Newfoundland English.

There are words for everything, from food words such as scoff (a big meal), touton (fried bread dough), and duff (a pudding), to words to describe the fickle weather, such as leeward (a threatening storm), airsome (bracing cold), and mauzy (foggy and damp). "The sun is splitting the rocks!" is something you might hear on a fine day.

There are words that relate to the fishery: a flake is where you dry fish, perhaps after having caught them on your dory, a small rowboat. A bedlamer is a young seal. And, of course, there are plenty of words to describe all manner of people: a gatcher is a show-off and a cuffer tells tall tales.

A drung is a narrow road, a scuff is a dance, to coopy means to crouch down, and if you are going for a twack, you're window-shopping. If you're from Upalong, that means you're not from here.

To help develop an ear for the provincial dialects, pick up a copy of the Dictionary of Newfoundland English (www.heritage.nf.ca/dictionary). The dictionary was first published in 1982; it's now in its second edition and has more than 5,000 words.

15

FERRYLAND

43½ km (27 mi) south of Witless Bay Ecological Reserve.

The major ongoing **Colony of Avalon** archaeological dig at Ferryland has uncovered the early-17th-century colony of Lord Baltimore, who abandoned the area after a decade. The site includes an archaeology laboratory, exhibit center and museum, period gardens, and a reconstructed 17th-century kitchen. Guided tours are available. *Rte. 10, Ferryland 709/432–3200 or 877/326–5669 www.heritage.nf.ca/avalon $8 includes tour Mid-May–Oct., daily 10–5; late June–Labor Day, daily 9–7.*

Ferryland Lighthouse. This historic lighthouse, built in 1871, now signals the spot for breathtaking views, worry-free picnics, and great food, such as crab cakes, green salads, and gooseberry fools. You bring the appetite, they pack everything else—even the blanket. Bread is baked daily in the lighthouse. Check the Web site for menus (which vary day to day) and a list of events. Picnics start at $15 per person. *Ferryland Lighthouse 709/363–7456 www.lighthousepicnics.ca June–Sept., Tues.–Sun. 11:30–6; call for off-season arrangements.*

HARBOUR GRACE

21 km (13 mi) north of Cupids.

Beginning in 1919, Harbour Grace was the departure point for many attempts to fly the Atlantic. Amelia Earhart left from here in 1932 to become the first woman to fly solo across the Atlantic. The town has two fine churches and several registered historic houses.

SHOPPING

You can't miss **Victoria Manor Shoppes & Gallery** (*✉25 Victoria St. ☎709/596–8111 ⏲Tues.–Sat. 10–5, Sun. noon–5, or by appointment*), a bright yellow heritage home–turned–antiques store trimmed in red. Funky knitted woolens are just one of the one-of-kind limited-edition crafts. If you're feeling bookish, have a gander at their used and antique bookstore. There's also a fine-art gallery with exhibits by emerging local artists. Well worth the stop.

WHERE TO STAY

$ **Rothesay House Inn Bed & Breakfast.** This Provincial Heritage Site B&B was built in 1855 in Brigus, then dismantled, transported, and reconstructed in the Queen Anne style in Harbour Grace in 1906. The front of the house has a lovely porch, and the greens, yellows, and reds of the exterior are echoed in the room colors. ✉34 Water St., Box 577, A0A 2M0 ☎709/596–2268 📠709/596–0317 🌐www.rothesay.com 4 rooms In-room: no a/c, no TV. In-hotel: restaurant, no elevator, no-smoking rooms 💳MC, V 🍽BP.

PLACENTIA

48 km (30 mi) south of Rte. 1.

Placentia was first settled by 16th-century Basque fishermen, then became the French capital of Newfoundland in the 1600s.

WHERE TO STAY

$ **Rosedale Manor Bed & Breakfast.** Wake up to the smell of home-baked bread and pastries prepared by the chef/host of this 1893 waterfront heritage home in the Second Empire style. Rooms are bright and cheery, and the grounds are filled with flowers. Rosedale is well-located: 1 km (½ mi) from Argentia Ferry, 50 km (31 mi) from Cape St. Mary's, and 1½ hours from St. John's. *✉40 Orcan Dr., Box 329, A0B 2Y0 ☎709/227–3613 or 877/999–3613 🌐www.rosedalemanor.ca 5 rooms In-room: no a/c, no phone, no TV, Wi-Fi. In-hotel: no elevator, no-smoking rooms 💳MC, V 🍽BP.*

15

CAPE ST. MARY'S ECOLOGICAL RESERVE

★ *65 km (40 mi) south of Placentia.*

Cape St. Mary's Ecological Reserve is the third-largest nesting colony of gannets in North America and the most accessible seabird colony on the continent. You can visit the interpretation center—guides are on site in summer—and then walk to within 100 feet of the colony of nesting gannets, murres, black-billed kittiwakes, and razorbills. Most birds are March through August visitors. This reserve has incredibly dramatic coastal scenery and is a good place to spot whales. *✉Off Rte. 100 ☎709/227–1666, 709/635–4520, 709/337–2473 weather line 🌐www.gov.nl.ca/parks&reserves Site free, center $5 Mid-May–June and Sept.–mid-Oct., daily 9–5; July–Sept., daily 8–7.*

> **WORD OF MOUTH**
>
> "Cape St. Mary's [Ecological Reserve] is an absolute must-see. Their Interpretive Centre is excellent, the scenery is superb, and the seabird colony—especially the 11,000 Northern Gannets—is awe-inspiring.... We are returning for the eighth time this summer—drawn back by the landscapes, incredible wildlife, the music, and especially by the wonderful people."
>
> —gannetmusic

WHERE TO STAY

¢–$ **Bird Island Resort.** This pleasant lodging is a half-hour drive from Cape St. Mary's. The motel units are standard, but cottages are carpeted, have decks and kitchens, and overlook the water. *✉Off Rte. 100, St. Bride's A0B 2Z0 ☎709/337–2450 or 888/337–2450 📠709/337–2903* *www.birdislandresort.com 5 rooms, 15 cottages In-room: no a/c, kitchen (some). In-hotel: gym, no elevator, laundry facilities, no-smoking rooms AE, MC, V.*

EASTERN NEWFOUNDLAND

Clarenville, about two hours northwest of St. John's via the Trans-Canada Highway (Route 1), is the departure point for several different excursions: the Bonavista Peninsula, Terra Nova National Park, and the Burin Peninsula.

CLARENVILLE

189 km (117 mi) northwest of St. John's.

★ If history and quaint towns appeal to you, follow the **Discovery Trail,** which begins in Clarenville on Route 230A. The trail includes two gems: the old town of Trinity, famed for its architecture and theater festival, and Bonavista, one of John Cabot's reputed landing spots.

WHERE TO STAY

$ **Clarenville Inn.** This hotel on the Trans-Canada Highway has a fabulous view of Random Sound. Rooms are standard. A convenient base for tourists looking to take trips along the Discovery Trail, down the Burin Peninsula, or to the Avalon region. Popular with families because children under 10 eat free in July and August, and there's a heated swimming pool. *134 Transcanada Hwy., A5A 1Y3 709/466–7911 or 877/466–7911 709/466–3854 www.clarenvilleinn.ca 62 rooms, 1 suite In-room: no a/c, ethernet. In-hotel: restaurant, room service, bar, pool, no elevator, laundry facilities, no-smoking rooms AE, DC, MC, V.*

TERRA NOVA NATIONAL PARK

24 km (15 mi) northwest of Clarenville.

Terra Nova Park boasts natural beauty, a dramatic coastline, and rugged woods, as well as moose, black bear, and other wildlife. Pods of whales play within sight of the shores, and many species of birds inhabit the cliffs and shores encompassed by the 396-square-km (153-square-mi) park.

There are golf, sea kayaking, fishing, camping, nature walks, whale-watching tours, and a snack bar–cafeteria. Eight backcountry camping areas are accessible by trail or canoe. *Trans-Canada Hwy., Glovertown A0G 2L0 709/533–2801 or 709/533–2942 www.pc.gc.ca $5.45 mid-May–mid-Oct., free mid-Oct.–mid-May Site daily dawn–dusk; center July and Aug., daily 9–8; May, June, Sept., and Oct., daily 10–5.*

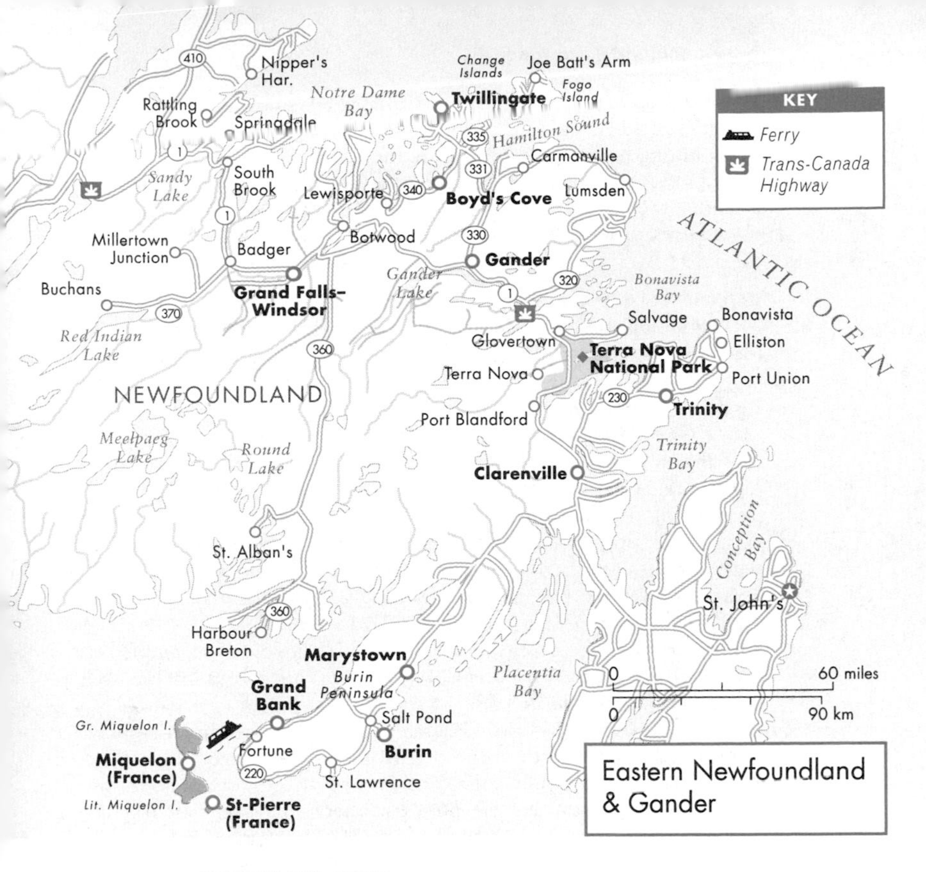

WHERE TO STAY

$–$$ **Terra Nova Golf Resort.** The 18-hole Twin Rivers course, traversed by two salmon rivers, and the 9-hole Eagle Creek impress golfers with their beauty. The high-end lodgings combine hotel luxury and country inn charm. Rooms are large and bright with spectacular views. There's lots to do, from hiking and swimming to an array of recreational activities. It's smart to book tee-times two to three months ahead. Kids under 12 stay free, and there are children's programs in July and August. *Rte. 1, Box 160, Port Blandford A0C 2G0 709/543–2525, 709/543–2626 golf reservations 709/543–2201 www.terranova-golf.com 83 rooms, 6 suites In-room: refrigerator (some), dial-up. In-hotel: 3 restaurants, room service, bar, golf course, tennis court, pool, children's programs July and Aug. (ages 6 and up), no-smoking rooms AE, D, MC, V.*

TRINITY

71 km (44 mi) northeast of Clarenville.

Trinity's ocean views, winding lanes, and snug houses are the main attractions. Several homes have been turned into museums and inns. To get here, take Route 230 to Route 239.

The **Lester-Garland Premises Provincial Historic Site** takes you back over a century ago when merchant families ruled tiny communities. Next door the counting house has been restored to the 1820s, the retail store to the 1900s. An interpretation center traces the history of the town, once a mercantile center. ✉ *West St.* ☎ *709/464–2042 or 800/563–6353* 🌐 *www.tcr.gov.nl.ca/tcr/historicsites* *$3* *Mid-May–Sept., daily 10–5:30.*

WHERE TO STAY & EAT

¢–$$$ ★ **Dock Restaurant.** This restaurant is in a restored 300-year-old fish merchant's headquarters. Its menu includes Newfoundland meals and seafood as well as the standard Canadian fare: burgers, chicken, and steak. Upstairs is an art gallery and crafts shop. ✉ *Trinity Waterfront* ☎ *709/464–2133* *AE, DC, MC, V* *Closed Nov.–Apr.*

$ **Eriksen Premises.** This two-story mansard-style building was built in the late 1800s as a general store and tearoom. It's been restored to its original elegance and character. The rooms here are larger than at its sister property, Bishop White Manor. They're also furnished with antiques and have views of the bay. The restaurant ($–$$; reservations essential) is known for its fish. ✉ *West St., Box 58, Trinity Bay A0C 2S0* ☎ *709/464–3698 or 877/464–3698* *709/464–2104* 🌐 *www.trinityexperience.com* *7 rooms* *In-room: no phone, no TV. In-hotel: restaurant, no elevator, no-smoking rooms* *AE, MC, V* *Closed Nov.–Apr.* *BP.*

$–$$$ **Campbell House B&B–Artisan House.** The mid-19th-century Campbell House is decorated with antiques and has low-ceilinged, light-filled rooms and a two-bedroom suite. The Twine Loft Restaurant offers fine dining by reservation. No elevator, but there's a wheelchair friendly ground-floor apartment. ✉ *49 High St., A0C 2S0* ☎ *877/464–7700* ☎ *709/464–3377* 🌐 *www.trinityvacations.com* *4 rooms, 1 suites, 1 studio* *In-room: no a/c, kitchen (some), ethernet. In-hotel: restaurant, no elevator, laundry service, no-smoking rooms* *AE, DC, MC, V* *Closed Nov.–Apr.* *BP.*

¢–$ **Sherwood Suites.** The cottages here are spacious and have living rooms and private patios. Opt for a cottage if you plan to do your own cooking. Motel rooms are large and bright with private entrances. ✉ *Rocky Hill Rd., Box 2, Port Rexton A0C 2H0* ☎ *709/464–2130 or 877/464–2133* 🌐 *www.sherwoodsuites.com* *4 rooms, 12 cottages* *In-room: no a/c, kitchen (some). In-hotel: no elevator, laundry facilities, no-smoking rooms, some pets allowed* *AE, DC, MC, V* *Closed Oct.–late May.*

NIGHTLIFE & THE ARTS

Shakespeare productions, dinner theater, and local dramas and comedies run throughout July and August at the Summer in the Bight festival at the **Rising Tide Theatre** (✉ *Rte. 230 to Rte. 239, then left onto road into Trinity* ☎ *709/464–3232 or 888/464–3377* 🌐 *www.risingtidetheatre.com*). Check out the Web site for show information, dates, and times. The theater, on the waterfront, is styled like an old mercantile warehouse.

BONAVISTA

28 km (17 mi) north of Trinity.

No one knows exactly where explorer John Cabot landed when he came to Atlantic Canada in 1497, but many believe it was Bonavista.

The **Ryan Premises National Historic Site** on the waterfront depicts the almost-500-year history of the commercial cod fishery in a restored fish merchant's property. *✉Off Rte. 230 ☎709/468–1600 🌐www.pc.gc.ca $3.95 ⏲Mid-May–Oct., daily 10–6.*

WORD OF MOUTH

"I can not begin to tell you of a place more beautiful, with people as beautiful, as warm, as giving—if there is such a thing as peace on earth, I suspect it is Newfoundland! I posted our trip on this site, you may want to read more—go, go go, take photos, keep a journal—enjoy this magnificant place!" —jtp 1/07

15

The **Mockbeggar Plantation** teaches about the life of an outport merchant in the years immediately before Confederation. See the 18th-century fish store, carpentry shop, and cod-liver-oil factory. *✉Off Rte. 230 ☎709/468–7300 or 800/563–6353 $3, includes Cape Bonavista Lighthouse ⏲Mid-May–Sept., daily 10–5:30.*

WHERE TO STAY & EAT

$$ **The Harbour Quarters.** Built in the 1920s and overlooking Bonavista harbour, it's a fabulous place to drop anchor. The rooms are comfortable. Skipper's restaurant has delicious seafood dishes and a priceless view of the harbour. *✉42 Campbell St., Box 399, Bonavista A0C 2S0 ☎709/468–7982 or 866/468–7982 📠709/468–7945 🌐www.harbourquarters.com 11 rooms In-room: ethernet. In-hotel: restaurant AE, DC,MC, V CP.*

MARYSTOWN

283 km (175 mi) south of Bonavista.

Marystown, on the Burin Peninsula, is built around beautiful Mortier Bay, so big it was considered large enough for the entire British fleet during the early days of World War II.

WHERE TO STAY

$ **Hotel Marystown.** This is the largest hotel on the Burin Peninsula; rooms are standard but comfortable. Rooms on the upper floors are a bit brighter. In the chain restaurant, P. J. Billington's, the peninsula's history of rum smuggling and connection to gangster Al Capone is told in photographs on the wall. *✉76 Ville Marie Dr., A0E 2M0 ☎709/279–1600 or 866/612–6800 📠709/279–4088 🌐www.cityhotels.ca 131 rooms In-room: no a/c (some), kitchen (some), Wi-Fi. In-hotel: restaurant, room service, bar, gym, no elevator, laundry service, some pets allowed AE, DC, MC, V.*

BURIN

17 km (11 mi) south of Marystown.

When Captain James Cook was stationed here to chart the coast in the 1760s, one of his duties was to watch for smugglers bringing in rum from the island of St-Pierre. Cook's Lookout, a hill overlooking Burin, is where he kept watch.

WHERE TO STAY

¢–$ **Sound of the Sea Bed and Breakfast.** The sound of waves crashing on the shore drifts into this three-story B&B. The owners restored this 70-year-old merchant's house and have decorated it with antiques from the area. *11A Seaview Dr. Rte. 221, A0E 1E0 709/891–2115 or 866/891–2115 709/891–2377 3 rooms In-room: no a/c. In-hotel: no elevator, laundry facilities, public Internet, no-smoking rooms MC, V BP.*

GRAND BANK

62 km (38 mi) west of Burin.

Grand Bank has a fascinating history as an important fishing center. Because of trading patterns, the architecture here was influenced more by Halifax, Boston, and Bar Harbor, Maine, than by the rest of Newfoundland.

WHERE TO STAY

$ Fodor'sChoice ★ **Thorndyke Bed & Breakfast.** This 1917 Queen Anne–style mansion, a former sea captain's house, is a designated historic structure. The blown-glass objects, colored panels, and sunporch have been part of the house since it was first built. The dining room walls are painted warm red, and a licensed dinner is available by prebooking. The ferry to St-Pierre is a five-minute drive away. *33 Water St., A0E 1W0 709/832–0820 or 866/882–0820 www.thethorndyke.com 5 rooms In-room: no a/c, DVD. In-hotel: no elevator, no-smoking rooms AE, D, DC, MC, V Closed mid-Sept.–Apr. BP.*

ST-PIERRE & MIQUELON

70-min ferry ride from Fortune, which is 10 km (6 mi) south of Grand Bank.

The islands of St-Pierre and Miquelon, France's only territory in North America, are a ferry ride away. Bakeries open early, so there's always piping-hot fresh bread for breakfast. Bargain hunters can find reasonably priced French wines. Visitors must carry proof of citizenship—U.S. citizens must have a passport, and Canadians should have a passport or a government-issued photo ID. Because of the ferry schedule, a trip to St-Pierre means an overnight stay in a hotel or a pension, the French equivalent of a B&B.

Call the **St-Pierre Tourist Board** (*011/50841–02–00 or 800/565–5118 for information about accommodations*).

A passenger ferry operated by **St-Pierre Tours** (☎*709/832–2006, 709/722–4103, or 800/563–2006*) leaves Fortune (south of Grand Bank) daily from mid-June to late September; the crossing takes a little over an hour. Call for schedule and rates.

WHERE TO STAY

$$ **Hotel Robert.** Al Capone stayed here. Rooms are spacious, but be warned—smoke lingers in the air. The owner is fluently bilingual and eager to educate tourists. The hotel, a short walk from where the boat docks, is popular because of its tour packages. If you book your reservation through St-Pierre Tours, listed above, you'll get a deal that includes transportation and a cheaper room rate than if you book with the hotel directly. ✉*Rue du 11 Novembre, St-Pierre 97500* ☎*508/41–2879, 709/832–2006, 800/563–2006 reservations, 011/50841–2879* *43 rooms* *In-room: no a/c, no phone. In-hotel: restaurant, no elevator, laundry facilities* *MC, V* *CP.*

GANDER & AROUND

Gander, in east-central Newfoundland, is known for its aviation history. North of it is Notre Dame Bay, an area of rugged coastline and equally rugged islands that were once the domain of the now extinct Beothuk tribe. Before English settlers moved into the area in the late 18th and early 19th centuries, it was seasonally occupied by French fisherfolk. The bay is swept by the cool Labrador Current that carries icebergs south through Iceberg Alley.

GANDER

367 km (228 mi) north of Grand Bank.

A busy town, Gander (population 9,651) has many lodgings and makes a good base for travel in this part of Newfoundland. **Gander International Airport** (✉*James Blvd.* ☎*709/256–6677* *www.ganderairport.com*) is a major air-traffic control center.

The **North Atlantic Aviation Museum** gives an expansive view of Gander's and Newfoundland's roles in aviation. You can climb into the cockpit of a real DC-3 parked outside next to a World War II Hudson bomber and a Canadian jet fighter. ✉*135 Trans Canada Hwy. (Rte. 1), between hospital and visitor information center* ☎*709/256–2923* *www.naam.ca* *$4* *June–Sept., daily 9–9; Oct.–May, weekdays 9–5.*

WHERE TO STAY

$ **Hotel Gander.** The view at this hotel is unremarkable, but rooms are spacious, modern, and clean. The largest hotel in Gander, it has a decent restaurant that serves standard Canadian fare. Children under 12 stay and eat for free. ✉*100 Trans-Canada Hwy., A1V 1P5* ☎*709/256–3931 or 800/563–2988* *709/651–2641* *www.hotelgander.com* *152 rooms, 4 suites* *In-room: no a/c (some), dial-up. In-hotel: restaurant, room service, bar, pool, laundry facilities, no-smoking rooms* *AE, DC, MC, V.*

BOYD'S COVE

66 km (41 mi) north of Gander.

The **Boyd's Cove Beothuk Interpretation Centre** provides a fresh look into the Beothuks, an extinct First Nations people who succumbed in the early 19th century to a combination of disease and battle with European settlers. It adjoins an archaeological site that was inhabited from about 1650 to 1720, when pressure from settlers drove the Beothuks from this part of the coast. ✉ *Rte. 340* ☎ *709/656–3114 or 800/563–6353* 🌐 *www.tcr.gov.nl.ca/tcr/historicsites* *$3* *Mid-May–Sept., daily 10–5:30.*

TWILLINGATE

31 km (19 mi) north of Boyd's Cove.

The inhabitants of this fishing village have made their living from the sea for nearly two centuries. It's considered one of the best places on the island to see icebergs. These majestic and dangerous mountains of ice are awe inspiring to see when they're grounded in early summer.

WHERE TO STAY

$ **Toulinguet Inn Bed & Breakfast.** In this 1920s-era home on the harbor front, rooms are old-fashioned, bright, and airy. Each room has two windows, and two of the rooms have views of the harbor. A second-story balcony looks out over the Atlantic Ocean. You can wind down in the living room or den and admire the antiques and original character of the heritage house. ✉ *56 Main St., A0G 4M0* ☎ *709/884–2080 or 888/447–8687* *709/884–1274* 🌐 *www.bbcanada.com/9127.html* *3 rooms* *In-room: no a/c. In-hotel: no elevator, laundry facilities, public Internet, some pets allowed, no-smoking rooms* *V* *Closed Oct.–Apr.* *CP.*

SPORTS & THE OUTDOORS

Twillingate Island Boat Tours/Iceberg Craft Shop (☎ *709/884–2242 or 800/611–2374* 🌐 *www.icebergtours.ca*) offers two-hour cruises to see whales, icebergs, and birds. Iceberg photography is the company's specialty, and there are tours that take amateur photographers out to get that perfect shot. Tours are $30 plus tax.

GRAND FALLS–WINDSOR

95 km (59 mi) west of Gander.

This central Newfoundland town is an amalgamation of two towns that were joined in 1991. Grand Falls is the quintessential company town, founded by British newspaper barons early in the 20th century. Windsor was once an important stop on the railway. Only the paper mill still functions.

Mary March Provincial Museum. Mary March was the European name given to Demasduit, one of the last Beothuks. Displays trace the lives and customs of aboriginal cultures in Newfoundland and Labrador. *16 St. Catherine's St. 709/292–4522 www.therooms.ca/museum/prov_museums.asp $2.50, includes A Logger's Life Museum May–late Oct., daily 9:30–4:45.*

WHERE TO STAY

$ **Mount Peyton Hotel.** This lodging establishment has hotel and motel rooms, apartments with kitchenettes, and a good steak house. The hotel rooms have more services than the motel rooms, and easy access to the restaurant and bar. The motel rooms are across a divided highway from the hotel, making accessing the bar and restaurants tricky. *214 Lincoln Rd., A2A 1P8 709/489–2251 or 800/563–4894 709/489–6365 www.mountpeyton.com 150 rooms, 16 housekeeping units, 4 suites In-room: kitchen (some), Wi-Fi. In-hotel: 2 restaurants, bar, no elevator, laundry service, some pets allowed, no-smoking rooms AE, DC, MC, V Motel rooms closed Sept.–Mar.*

WESTERN NEWFOUNDLAND

The Great Northern Peninsula is the northernmost visible extension of the Appalachian Mountains. The Viking Trail snakes along its western coast through fjords and sand dunes. The Vikings established the first European settlement in North America a thousand years ago at the tip of the peninsula. Thousands of years before them, the area was home to native peoples.

Western Newfoundland is known for Atlantic salmon fishing and papermaking. This area includes Corner Brook. To the south, the Port au Port Peninsula west of Stephenville shows the French influence in Newfoundland, distinct from the farming valleys of the southwest, which were settled by Scots. A ferry from Nova Scotia docks at Port aux Basques in the far southwest corner.

DEER LAKE

208 km (129 mi) west of Grand Falls–Windsor.

The opening of Gros Morne National Park in the early 1970s, and the construction of Route 430—a first-class paved highway passing right through to St. Anthony—as well as an airport makes Deer Lake a good starting point for a fly–drive vacation.

The **Newfoundland Insectarium** holds an intriguing collection of live and preserved insects, spiders, scorpions, and the like. A big attraction is the greenhouse, with live tropical butterflies. The gift shop sometimes sells chocolate-covered crickets to eat. *Rte. 430, Reidville 709/635–4545 or 866/635–5454 www.nfinsectarium.com $10 Mid-Apr.–June and Sept.–mid-Oct., Tues.–Fri. 9–5, weekends 10–5; July and Aug., daily 9–9.*

WHERE TO STAY & EAT

¢–$ ✕ **Deer Lake Irving Big Stop.** Good home-cooking and clean washrooms make this chain a welcome pit stop. Standard burgers and fries are available, but you can also get pita pockets and grilled-chicken burgers. ✉ *Rte. 1, Deer Lake* ☎ *709/635–2129* ▭ *No credit cards.*

$$ **Deer Lake Motel.** The motel is clean and comfortable, but request a room in the back, because the front rooms face the highway. ✉ *15 Trans-Canada Hwy., A8A 2E5* ☎ *709/635–2108, 800/563–2144 in Newfoundland* 📠 *709/635–3842* 🌐 *www.deerlakemotel.com* *54 rooms, 2 suites* *In-room: ethernet. In-hotel: 2 restaurants, room service, bar, no elevator, laundry service, parking (no fee), no-smoking rooms* ▭ *AE, MC, V.*

GROS MORNE NATIONAL PARK

Fodor'sChoice ★ *46 km (29 mi) north of Deer Lake on Rte. 430.*

Because of its geological uniqueness and immense splendor, this park has been named a UNESCO World Heritage Site. Among the more breathtaking visions are the expanses of wild orchids in springtime. Camping and hiking are popular recreations, and boat tours are available. To see Gros Morne properly, allow yourself at least three days.

The **Tablelands,** rising behind Norris Point, is a unique rock massif that was raised from the earth's mantle through tectonic upheaval. Its rocks are toxic to most plant life, and Ice Age conditions linger in the form of persistent snow and moving rock glaciers.

Head to the northern side of the park to visit **Rocky Harbour** with its range of restaurants, lodgings, and a luxurious indoor public pool and large hot tub—the perfect place to soothe tired limbs after a strenuous day.

A very popular attraction is the boat tour of **Western Brook Pond.** Hikers in good shape can tackle the 16-km (10-mi) hike up **Gros Morne Mountain,** at 2,644 feet the second-highest peak in Newfoundland. The park's **northern coast** has an unusual mix of sand beaches, rock pools, and trails through tangled dwarf forests. ✉ *Viking Trail (Rte. 430) from Deer Lake* ☎ *709/458–2417* 📠 *709/458–2059* 🌐 *www.pc.gc.ca* *$8.90* ⏲ *Mid-May–mid-Oct., daily 10–5:30.*

WHERE TO STAY & EAT

$–$$$ ✕ **Seaside Restaurant.** Fresh seafood in traditional Newfoundland style—try the scallops and shrimp sautéed or in a stir-fry, or choose from a wide selection of seafood dinners, including catfish and cod tongue. ✉ *Main St., Trout River* ☎ *709/451–3461* ▭ *MC, V* ⏲ *Closed Nov.–late May.*

$–$$ ✕ **Fisherman's Landing.** The good food ranges from seafood dishes (in season) to standard Canadian fare, such as club and hot turkey sandwiches or pork chops and steak. ✉ *Main St., Rocky Harbour* ☎ *709/458–2060* ▭ *AE, MC, V.*

$–$$ Fodor'sChoice ★ ✕ **Java Jack's.** The coffee is strong and freshly brewed. This is a great place to pick up a take-away bag lunch, such as shredded pork with partridgeberry-honey mustard for the boat trip to Western Brook Pond. Or dine in and enjoy a great view of the harbor. For dinner, try their

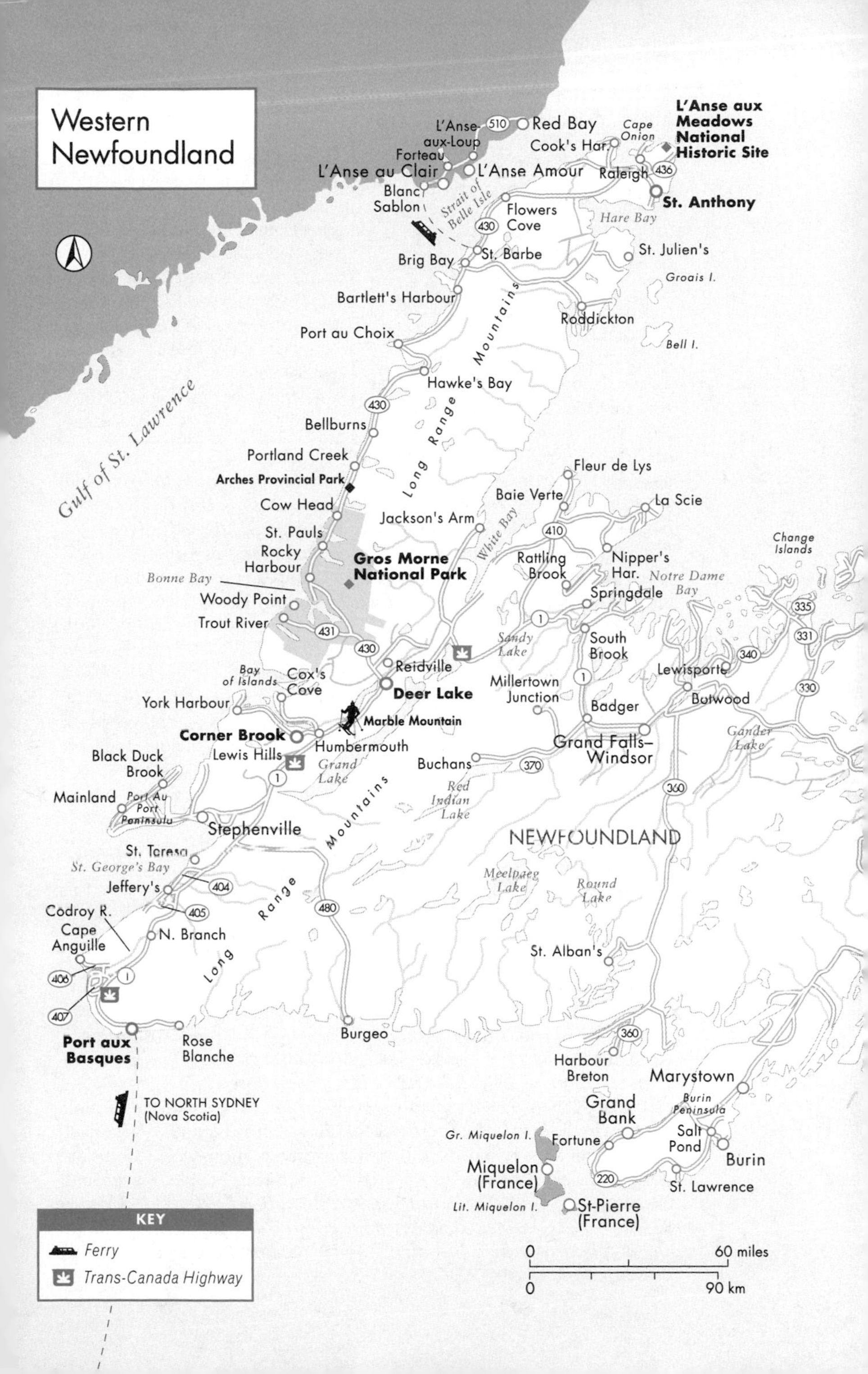

Western Newfoundland
Red Bay
L'Anse-aux-Loup
Forteau
L'Anse au Clair
L'Anse Amour
Blanc Sablon
Strait of Belle Isle
Cape Onion
Cook's Har.
L'Anse aux Meadows National Historic Site
Raleigh
St. Anthony
Flowers Cove
Hare Bay
St. Barbe
Brig Bay
St. Julien's
Groais I.
Bartlett's Harbour
Roddickton
Port au Choix
Bell I.
Hawke's Bay
Long Range Mountains
Gulf of St. Lawrence
Bellburns
Portland Creek
Arches Provincial Park
Fleur de Lys
Cow Head
Baie Verte
La Scie
Jackson's Arm
White Bay
St. Pauls
Rocky Harbour
Gros Morne National Park
Rattling Brook
Nipper's Har.
Notre Dame Bay
Change Islands
Bonne Bay
Woody Point
Springdale
Trout River
Sandy Lake
South Brook
Reidville
Bay of Islands
Cox's Cove
Deer Lake
Millertown Junction
Lewisporte
Botwood
York Harbour
Badger
Marble Mountain
Corner Brook
Humbermouth
Grand Falls–Windsor
Gander Lake
Black Duck Brook
Lewis Hills
Grand Lake
Buchans
Red Indian Lake
Mainland
Port Au Port Peninsula
Stephenville
NEWFOUNDLAND
St. Teresa
St. George's Bay
Meelpaeg Lake
Round Lake
Jeffery's
Codroy R.
Cape Anguille
N. Branch
St. Alban's
Port aux Basques
Rose Blanche
Burgeo
Harbour Breton
Marystown
TO NORTH SYDNEY (Nova Scotia)
Grand Bank
Burin Peninsula
Gr. Miquelon I.
Fortune
Salt Pond
Burin
Miquelon (France)
St. Lawrence
Lit. Miquelon I.
St-Pierre (France)
KEY
Ferry
Trans-Canada Highway
0
60 miles
0
90 km

seafood bubbly bake, with seasonal fish in a cream sauce. ✉*88 Main St. N, Rocky Harbour* ☎*709/458–3004* 💳*AE, MC, V* ⏲*Closed mid-Oct.–mid-May.*

WORD OF MOUTH

"When I started planning my trip to Newfoundland two years ago, I started reading about Gros Morne National Park, with people describing its beauty with words normally used for places like Yosemite. I was EXTREMELY skeptical—and even MORE wrong. This place is like Yosemite and Big Sur combined. As I said to my wife, this place has a lot of 'OMG!' moments." —PaulRabe

$$ **Fisherman's Landing Inn.** The rooms are spacious and bright and have private outside entrances. They're set up like modern hotel rooms, with a country charm. In the coffee shop–bar you can get three meals a day, and linger for a few drinks. Kids 16 and under stay for free. ✉*West Link Rd., off Rte. 430, Box 124, Rocky Harbour A0K 4N0* ☎*709/458–2711 or 866/458–2711* 📠*709/458–2168* 🌐*www.fishermanslandinginn.com* *40 rooms* *In-room: dial-up. In-hotel: Restaurant, room service, bar, laundry facilities, no-smoking rooms* 💳*AE, DC, MC, V.*

$–$$ **Gros Morne Cabins.** These modern log chalets on the Gulf of St. Lawrence are near restaurants and stores in Rocky Harbour. Cabins have hardwood floors, log walls, and a tremendous ocean view. They can accommodate up to four people. ✉*Main St., Rocky Harbour A0K 4N0* ☎*709/458–2020 or 888/603–2020* 📠*709/458–2882* 🌐*www.grosmornecabins.com* *22 cabins* *In-room: no a/c, kitchen, Wi-Fi. In-hotel: laundry facilities, no-smoking rooms* 💳*AE, DC, MC, V.*

$–$$ **Gros Morne Resort.** Rooms in the front ovelook the ocean; those in the rear face the Long Range mountains. The rooms are spacious and have private balconies or patios. Some suites have whirlpool tubs. Guests can choose from a restaurant serving traditional meals or fine dining. ✉*Rte. 430, Box 100, St. Pauls A0K 4Y0* ☎*709/243–2606 or 888/243–2644* 📠*709/243–2615* *8 rooms, 12 suites* *In-hotel: 2 restaurants, bar, refrigerator (some), no-smoking rooms* 💳*AE, DC, MC, V.*

$–$$ **Sugar Hill Inn.** Vince McCarthy's culinary talents have earned this inn a reputation for fine wining and dining. There's only one sitting, at 7:30 PM, for the three-course meal in the dining room. Afterward, sit under the vaulted cedar ceiling of the common room, or relax in the cedar-lined hot-tub room with attached sauna. ✉*115–129 Sexton Rd., Box 100, Norris Point A0K 3V0* ☎*709/458–2147 or 888/299–2147* 📠*709/458–2166* 🌐*www.sugarhillinn.nf.ca* *3 rooms, 3 suites, 1 cottage* *In-hotel: room service, no elevator, laundry facilities, no-smoking rooms* 🍽*CP, BP* 💳*AE, MC, V* ⏲*Closed Nov.–Feb.*

$ **Crocker Cabins.** These spacious two-bedroom cabins with two double beds are in the quieter southern part of Gros Morne National Park. Each building contains two cabins, which share a common deck. Rooms are standard, clean, and can accommodate up to four people. Playground on-site. ✉*57 Duke St., Trout River A0K 5P0* ☎📠*709/451–3236 or 877/951–3236* 🌐*www.crockercabins.com* *4 cabins* *In-room: no a/c, no phone, kitchen. In-hotel: laundry facilities, some pets allowed, no-smoking rooms* 💳*AE, MC, V.*

CAMPING To make reservations at Gros Morne campgrounds listed below, contact **Parks Canada at Gros Morne** (☎*877/737–3783* 🖷*709/458–2059* 🌐*www.pccamping.ca*). For more info on the various campsites, go to www.pc.gc.ca. The campsite prices are in addition to the $8.90 park admission fee.

Berry Hill Campground. These wooded sites are near the recreation complex, visitor center, and Lobster Cove Head Lighthouse. If you like hikes, there are three trails from the campground. *Flush toilets, dump station, showers, fire pits, play area 146 drive-in, 6 walk-in sites ✉Rte. 430, 10 km (6 mi) north of Rocky Harbour, AE, MC, V ⊙Closed mid-Sept.–mid-June.*

Shallow Bay Campground. The campsites themselves may be a little too close together, but with a long stretch of sandy beach, and washrooms, showers, and dishwashing facilities nearby, Shallow Bay is a great place to camp nonetheless. It's also close to Western Brook Pond. *Flush toilets, dump station, showers, picnic tables, play area, fireplaces 62 drive-in sites ✉Rte. 430, near Cow Head AE, MC, V ⊙Closed mid-Sept.–early June.*

15

SPORTS & THE OUTDOORS

Gros Morne Adventures (☎*709/458–2722 or 800/685–4624* 🌐*www.grosmorneadventures.com*) has sea kayaking up the fjords and landlocked ponds of Gros Morne National Park, as well as a variety of hikes and adventures in the area.

L'ANSE AUX MEADOWS NATIONAL HISTORIC SITE

Fodor's Choice ★ *210 km (130 mi) northeast of Arches Provincial Park.*

Around 1000 AD, Vikings from Greenland and Iceland founded the first European settlement in North America near the northern tip of Newfoundland. They stayed only a few years and were forgotten for centuries. In 1960 the Norwegian team of Helge and Anne Stine Ingstad discovered the remains of the Viking settlement's long sod huts. Today, L'Anse aux Meadows is a UNESCO World Heritage Site. Parks Canada has a fine visitor center and has reconstructed some of the huts. ✉*Rte. 436* ☎*709/623–2608* 🖷*709/623–2028 summer only* 🌐*www.pc.gc.ca/lhn-nhs/nl/meadows* *$10.40* ⊙*June–early Oct., daily 9–6.*

Two kilometers (1 mi) east of L'Anse aux Meadows is a Viking attraction, **Norstead.** This reconstruction of an 11th-century Viking port has a chieftain's hall, church, and ax-throwing arena. It's aimed at kids, but the Viking boatbuilding course is designed for all ages. ✉*Rte. 436* ☎*709/623–2828 or 877/620–2828* 🌐*www.norstead.com* *$8* ⊙*June–late-Sept., daily 9–6.*

WHERE TO STAY & EAT

$$–$$$$ Fodor's Choice ★ **Norseman Restaurant.** This restaurant on the harbor front allows you to pick your own lobster. An extensive wine list accompanies a menu ranging from seafood and pasta to caribou tenderloins. ✉*Turn right at end of Rte. 436; Box 265, L'Anse aux Meadows* ☎*877/623–2018* *DC, MC, V.*

¢–$$$ ✕ **Fisherman's Galley.** Don't let the modest facade fool you—inside, huge windows frame a magnificent view of a shallow harbor protected by an island dotted with grazing sheep. Seabirds circle overhead. Try the cod chowder or halibut. The attached store sells crafts and books. *✉Rte. 436, St. Lunaire–Griquet ☎709/623–2431 ▭AE, DC, MC, V ⊗Closed Oct.–Apr.*

$ **Valhalla Lodge Bed & Breakfast.** The Valhalla, positioned on a hill, is 8 km (5 mi) from L'Anse aux Meadows. Some fossils are part of the rock fireplace in the common room. Rooms are quiet, with large windows, pine Scandinavian furniture, and handmade quilts. The lodge includes two homes in which E, Annie Proulx lived. The "Quoyle's" is a three-bedroom A-frame house with a view of the ocean; "Wavey's" is a two-bedroom low-ceilinged Newfoundland Saltbox. *✉Box 10, Gunner's Cove, St. Lunaire–Griquet A0K 2X0 ☎709/623–2018, 877/623–2018, 709/754–3105 off-season 🖷709/623–2144 ⊕www.valhalla-lodge.com 5 rooms In-room: no a/c, DVD, VCR. In-hotel: no elevator, laundry facilities, public Internet, no-smoking rooms ▭DC, MC, V BP ⊗Closed mid-Oct.–early May.*

Fodor'sChoice ★

¢–$ **Viking Nest/Viking Village Bed & Breakfast.** Only one of the four rooms at the Viking Nest has a private bathroom. The Viking Village is a five-room inn, with doors opening onto a fenced patio. Rooms here have spruce walls and Scandinavian furniture. Room phones are available only by request. It's 1 km (½ mi) from L'Anse aux Meadows. *Box 127, Hay Cove A0K 2X0 ☎877/858–2238 ☎🖷709/623–2238 ⊕www.vikingvillage.ca and www.bbcanada.com/vikingnest 9 rooms, 6 with bath In-room: no phone, no TV. In-hotel: no elevator, laundry service, airport shuttle, ▭AE, MC, V BP.*

ST. ANTHONY

16 km (10 mi) south of L'Anse aux Meadows.

St. Anthony is built around a natural harbor on the eastern side of the Great Northern Peninsula. If you take a trip out to the lighthouse, you may see an iceberg float by.

WHERE TO STAY & EAT

¢–$$ ✕ **The Light Keeper's Seafood Restaurant.** Good seafood and solid Canadian fare are served in this former lighthouse keeper's home overlooking the ocean. Halibut, shrimp, and cod are usually good bets, as is the seafood chowder. *✉Fishing Point Rd. ☎709/454–4900 ▭MC, V ⊗Closed Nov.—Apr.*

$–$$ **Tuckamore Lodge & Country Inn.** The Scandinavian-style cedar lodge with a lofty ceiling provides a luxurious base from which to explore the area. Lunch and dinner (corn chowder, cod fondue, chocolate macaroon pie, etc.) are offered for an additional price. There are eight rooms in the lodge, which is for guests on package tours, and four rooms in the pine A-frame country inn. In both lodges, meals are served at big communal tables. *✉ 1 Southwest Pond Rd., Box 100, Main Brook A0K 3N0 ☎709/865–6361 or 888/865–6361 🖷709/865–2112 ⊕www.tuckamorelodge.com 9 rooms, 3 suites In-room: no a/c,* *no TV, Wi-Fi. In-hotel: laundry service, airport shuttle, no-smoking rooms* ▭*AE, DC, MC, V* 🍽*BP.*

$ **Vinland Motel.** These are standard rooms, but the motel is in the center of town, so what it lacks in a view it makes up for in convenience. Two rooms and the suite have whirlpool baths. ✉*19 West St., A0K 4S0* ☎*709/454–8843 or 800/563–7578* 📠*709/454–8468* ✉*vinlandmotel@nf.sympatico.ca* *43 rooms, 1 suite* *In-hotel: restaurant, bar, gym, laundry facilities, some pets allowed, no-smoking rooms* ▭*AE, DC, MC, V.*

SPORTS & THE OUTDOORS

Northland Discovery Boat Tours (✉*Behind the Grenfell Interpretation Centre off West St.* ☎*709/454–3092 or 877/632–3747* 🌐*www.discovernorthland.com*) leads specialized trips to see whales, icebergs, and seabirds, as well as salmon-fishing excursions.

15

CORNER BROOK

50 km (31 mi) southwest of Deer Lake.

Mountains fringe three sides of the city, which has beautiful views of the harbor and the Bay of Islands. Corner Brook is a convenient hub and point of departure for exploring the west coast. It's only a three-hour drive (allowing for traffic) from the Port aux Basques ferry from Nova Scotia. The nearby Humber River is the best-known salmon river in the province.

The north and south shores of the Bay of Islands have fine paved roads—Route 440 on the north shore and Route 450 on the south—and both are a half-day drive from Corner Brook. On both roads, farming and fishing communities exist side by side.

WHERE TO STAY & EAT

$$–$$$$ ★ ✕**13 West.** Start your meal off with oysters and chase them down with one of the wonderful salmon specials: strawberry salmon, mango salmon, blackened salmon, or salmon with rosemary and peppercorns. For those not interested in seafood, the rack of lamb and pork tenderloin are good choices. ✉*13 West St.* ☎*709/634–1300* ▭*AE, D, DC, MC, V* ⊙*No lunch weekends.*

$$$–$$$$ ✕**Strawberry Hill Resort.** This resort has Newfoundland's finest salmon fishing, hiking, skiing, and snowmobiling. The property consists of a main house and eight luxury 3-bedroom chalets. Fish along the Humber River, or go golfing or hiking; winter doesn't slow down, with skiing and snowmobiling. At the end of the day, relax in the hot tub or sauna. Some rooms in the manor house have fireplaces and sitting areas; all come with a Continental breakfast. Chalets ($$$–$$$$), which sleep up to seven, have all the conveniences of home, with washers and dryers, kitchens, several bedrooms, and full-size living rooms. The resort has boat, helicopter, and snowmobile tours of the area, plus guided fishing, sea-kayaking, hiking, and spelunking trips. The dining room menu in the main house changes daily and the salmon dishes are delectable. ✉*Rte. 1, Box 2200, 12 km (7 mi) east of Corner*

Brook, Little Rapids A2H 2N2 ☎709/634–0066 or 877/434–0066 📠709/639–7604 🌐www.strawberryhill.net ⇒Manor House has 6 bedrooms, 8 chalets ♿In-room: Wi-Fi, no a/c, no pets, no elevator. In-chalet: kitchen, refrigerator, Wi-Fi, VCR, laundry facilities, no elevator, no pets, no a/c, no-smoking rooms 💳*AE, MC, V* 🍽*CP.*

$ ★ **Glynmill Inn.** This Tudor-style inn has cozy rooms, and the dining room serves basic and well-prepared Newfoundland seafood, soups, and specialty desserts. There's also a popular steak house ($$–$$$) in the basement. ✉*1B Cobb La., Box 550, A2H 6E6 ☎709/634–5181, 800/563–4400 in Canada 📠709/634–5106 🌐www.glynmillinn.ca ⇒58 rooms, 23 suites ♿In-hotel: 2 restaurants, bar, Wi-Fi, gym, no-smoking rooms, some pets allowed* 💳*AE, DC, MC, V.*

SPORTS & THE OUTDOORS

The growing **Marble Mountain Resort** (✉*Rte. 1, 5 km [3 mi] east of Corner Brook, Steady Brook ☎709/637–7600 or 888/462–7253 🌐www.skimarble.com*) has 35 downhill runs and four lifts capable of moving 6,500 skiers an hour, as well as a large day lodge, ski shop, day-care center, and restaurant. The vertical drop is 1,700 feet. A full-day lift ticket is $45.

PORT AUX BASQUES

166 km (103 mi) south of Stephenville.

Port aux Basques was a Basque port along Newfoundland's west coast during the 1500s and early 1600s and was given its name by the town's French successors. It's now the main ferry port connecting the island to Nova Scotia.

WHERE TO STAY

$–$$ **St. Christopher's Hotel.** This clean, comfortable two-story hotel is minutes from the ferry and has good food. The quiet rooms are bright and modern; the suites are spacious, with hardwood flooring and fireplaces. ✉*146 High St., Box 2049, A0M 1C0 ☎709/695–7034 or 800/563–4779 📠709/695–9841 🌐www.stchrishotel.com ⇒83 rooms ♿In-room: ethernet (some). In-hotel: restaurant, room service, bar, gym, laundry facilities, public Internet, some pets allowed, no-smoking rooms* 💳*AE, DC, MC, V.*

$ **Hotel Port aux Basques.** This is a good choice for families because children stay free. The restaurant offers a choice of good local dishes. This modern hotel is closer to the ferry than any other in town. Suites have whirlpool baths. ✉*1 Grand Bay Rd., A0M 1C0 ☎709/695–2171 or 877/695–2171 📠709/695–2250 🌐www.hotelpab.com ⇒47 rooms 3 suites ♿In-room: kitchen (some), Wi-Fi. In-hotel: restaurant, room service, bar, no elevator, some pets allowed, no-smoking rooms* 💳*AE, DC, MC, V.*

LABRADOR

The Straits in southeastern Labrador were a rich hunting-and-gathering ground for the area's earliest peoples, the Maritime Archaic tribes. The oldest industrial site in the New World is here—the 16th-century Basque whaling station at Red Bay. Along the southern coast, most villages are inhabited by descendants of Europeans, whereas farther north they are mostly Inuit and Innu. In summer the ice retreats and a coastal steamer delivers goods, but in winter small airplanes and snowmobiles are the only ways in and out. Labrador West's subarctic landscape is challenging and unforgettable. The area has the largest iron ore deposits in the world.

L'ANSE AU CLAIR

5 km (3 mi) from Blanc Sablon, Québec (ferry from St. Barbe, Newfoundland docks in Blanc Sablon).

In L'Anse au Clair—French for "clear water cove"—anglers can try their luck for trout and salmon on the scenic Forteau and Pinware rivers. The French place-name dates from the early 1700s when this area was settled by French speakers from Québec.

WHERE TO STAY

$–$$ **Northern Light Inn.** Loads of bus-tour passengers make this a stop in summer because it's the only accommodation of any size along Route 510. Pretty ordinary, but breakfasts, lunches, and dinners are decent, the rooms spacious, and the furnishings of good quality. *58 Main St. (Rte. 510), A0K 3K0 709/931–2332 or 800/563–3188 709/931–2708 www.northernlightinn.com 54 rooms, 5 cottages In-room: kitchen (some). In-hotel: restaurant, bar, laundry facilities, no elevator, no-smoking rooms AE, DC, MC, V.*

L'ANSE AMOUR

19 km (12 mi) east of L'Anse au Clair.

The elaborate **Maritime Archaic Indian burial site** (*Rte. 510*), discovered near L'Anse Amour, is 7,500 years old. A plaque marks a site that is the oldest-known aboriginal–funeral monument in North America.

COASTAL LABRADOR

To get to the south coast of Labrador, you can catch the ferry (July to December) at St. Barbe on Route 430 in Newfoundland to Blanc Sablon, Québec. From here you can drive to Mary's Harbour, and on to Cartwright, along Route 510. **Tourism Newfoundland and Labrador** (*800/563–6353*) has information about ferry schedules.

A coastal boat takes passengers into a number of small communities. For information and schedules, call **Coastal Labrador Marine Services** (*866/535–2567*) or visit the government Web site at www.gov.nl.ca/ferryservices.

BATTLE HARBOUR NATIONAL HISTORIC SITE

★ *12 km (7 mi) by boat from Mary's Harbour.*

This near-shore island site has the only remaining intact outport fishing merchant's premises in the province. Settled in the 18th century, Battle Harbour was the main fishing port in Labrador until the first half of the 20th century. After fires destroyed some of the community, the people moved to nearby Mary's Harbour. The Battle Harbour Historic Trust has restored the community with historical structures and artifacts. You can stay overnight on the island at accommodations that range from individual cottages to a hostel-type bunkhouse. There is a restaurant on the Battle Harbour site. Information is available from the **Battle Harbour Historic Trust** (☎*709/921–6677* ⊕*www.battleharbour.com*). To get to the site, go to Government Wharf in Mary's Harbour and board the **MV** *Trinity Pride,* which leaves daily at 11 AM and 7 PM for the one-hour trip from Mary's Harbour. The boat returns from Battle Harbour at 9 AM and 4 PM daily. Tickets are $40 round-trip, and can be purchased at the wharf. There's no need to buy tickets in advance; space is not an issue. ✉*Southern Labrador coast, accessible by boat from Mary's Harbour* ☎📠*709/921–6325* ⊕*www.battleharbour.com* 🎫*$8 includes optional guided tour* ⏲*Mid-June–mid-Sept., daily 8–5.*

WHERE TO STAY

$ **Battle Harbour Inn.** Perched on a hilltop with a view of the Labrador Straits from every window, this fully restored two-story house overlooks the merchant premises and Great Caribou Island. The rooms share two baths. The house is furnished with antiques and has a sunporch in which to soak up the view. The inn doesn't have a phone or television, but there is a phone at the general store. ✉*Battle Harbour Historic Site, Box 140, Mary's Harbour A0K 3P0* ☎*709/921–6216* ☎📠*709/921–6325* 🌐*www.battleharbour.com* *5 rooms without bath, 3 cottages* *In-room: no a/c, no phone, no TV. In-hotel: no-smoking rooms, no elevator* 💳*MC, V* ⏲*Closed mid-Sept.–mid-June.*

HAPPY VALLEY–GOOSE BAY

525 km (326 mi) east of Labrador City.

Happy Valley–Goose Bay is the chief service center for coastal Labrador. The town is used as a low-level flying training base by the British, Dutch, and German air forces.

WHERE TO STAY

$–$$ **Hotel North.** Rooms at this newly renovated hotel, though basic, are the best of the limited selection here. All are clean and comfortable, and the hotel is a two-minute drive from the airport. ✉*25 Loring Dr., A0P 1C0* ☎*709/896–9301 or 877/996–9301* 📠*709/896–9302* 🌐*www.atyp.com/hotelnorth* *54 rooms, 3 suites* *In-room: refrigerator, Wi-Fi. In-hotel: restaurant, laundry facilities, no-smoking rooms, no elevator* 💳*AE, DC, MC, V* *CP.*

WABUSH

525 km (326 mi) west of Happy Valley–Goose Bay.

The modern town of Wabush has all the amenities of larger centers, including accommodations, sports and recreational facilities, and shopping. Labrador City and Wabush exist because of the rich iron-ore deposits, and the Iron Ore Company of Canada offers tours of the IOCC mine. Another highly recommended tour is the one for Churchill Falls, one of the world's largest underground hydro-generating stations. Both tours take place July and August on Wednesday and Sunday at 1:30 PM, and cost $11.50 each.

SPORTS & THE OUTDOORS

The **Smokey Mountain Ski Club** (✉*Rte. 500* ☎*709/944–2129* 🌐*www.smokeymountain.ca*), west of Wabush, is open mid-November to late April and has 18 groomed runs to accommodate beginners and advanced skiers. The vertical drop is 1,000 feet. A full-day lift ticket is about $30.

LABRADOR CITY

525 km (326 mi) west of Happy Valley–Goose Bay.

Labrador City has all the facilities of nearby Wabush, but more of them. At just fewer than 10,000 people, the city has more than three times the population of Wabush.

NEWFOUNDLAND & LABRADOR ESSENTIALS

To research prices, get advice from other travelers, and book travel arrangements, visit www.fodors.com.

TRANSPORTATION

BY AIR

Air Canada flies into St. John's. Regional connectors are Air Canada Jazz (Québec to Wabush), Air Labrador, and Provincial Airlines. WestJet has flights into the province as well. Continental Airlines has direct flights from Newark to St. John's. Air Transat operates some charter flights. At this writing, the reliability of air travel to cities around Newfoundland—other than to St. John's—is in a state of flux, so call airlines for up-to-date information.

The province's main airport is St. John's International Airport, though another international airport is at Gander, farther north. Domestic airports in Newfoundland are at Stephenville, Deer Lake, and St. Anthony. Airports in Labrador are in Happy Valley–Goose Bay, Wabush, and Churchill Falls.

Contacts **Air Labrador** (☎ *800/563–3042* 🌐 *www.airlabrador.com*). **Churchill Falls Airport** (☎ *709/925–3405*). **Deer Lake Regional Airport** (☎ *709/635–3601*). **Gander International Airport** (☎ *709/256–6677* 🌐 *www.ganderairport.com*). **Goose Bay Airport** (☎ *709/896–5445*). **Provincial Airlines** (☎ *709/576–1666, 800/563–2800 in Atlantic Canada* 🌐 *www.provincialairlines.com*). **St. John's International Airport** (☎ *709/758–8515* 🌐 *www.stjohnsairport.com*). **Stephenville Airport** (☎ *709/643–8444* 🌐 *www.cyjt.com*). **Wabush Airport** (☎ *709/282–5412*).

BY BOAT & FERRY

Marine Atlantic operates a car ferry from North Sydney, Nova Scotia, to Port aux Basques, Newfoundland (crossing time is 6 hours), and, from June through September, from North Sydney to Argentia, three times a week (crossing time 12 to 14 hours). In all cases, reservations are required. To explore the south coast of Labrador, catch the ferry at St. Barbe on Route 430 in Newfoundland to Blanc Sablon, Québec. From here you can drive to Cartwright along Route 510. Tourism Newfoundland and Labrador has information about ferry schedules. Canadian Sailing Expeditions offers weeklong sailing trips aboard tall ships up the Northern Peninsula. Coastal Labrador Marine Services takes passengers to smaller communities in Labrador.

Contacts **Canadian Sailing Expeditions** (*902/429–1474 or 877/429–9463 www.canadiansailingexpeditions.com*). **Coastal Labrador Marine Services** (*866/535–2567 www.tw.gov.nl.ca/ferryservices*). **Marine Atlantic** (*800/341–7981, 902/794–8109 TTY www.marine-atlantic.ca*). **Tourism Newfoundland and Labrador** (*800/563–6353 www.newfoundlandandlabrador.com*).

BY BUS

DRL Coachlines runs a trans-island bus service in Newfoundland. Buses leave daily at 8 AM from St. John's and Port aux Basques. Outport taxis connect the major centers with surrounding communities.

Contacts **DRL Coachlines** (*888/263–1854 www.drlgroup.com*).

BY CAR

In winter, some highways close during and after severe snowstorms. The Government of Newfoundland and Labrador's Department of Transportation & Works Web site has up-to-date information on road conditions and closures. Newfoundland and Labrador Tourism can help with any travel-related problems.

Newfoundland has an excellent highway system, and all but a handful of secondary roads are paved. The province's roads are generally uncrowded. Travel time along the Trans-Canada Highway (Route 1) from Port aux Basques to St. John's is about 13 hours, with time out for a meal. The trip from Corner Brook to St. Anthony at the northernmost tip of the island is about five hours. The drive from St. John's to Grand Bank on the Burin Peninsula takes about four hours. If you're heading for the southern coast of the Avalon Peninsula, pick up Route 10 just south of St. John's and follow it toward Trepassey.

The southeastern coast of Labrador is becoming more accessible by car. Route 510 now goes all the way to Cartwright. Route 500 links Labrador City with Happy Valley–Goose Bay via Churchill Falls. Conditions on this 526-km (326-mi) wilderness road are best from June through October. Labrador's road system is being extended and upgraded. If you plan to do extensive driving in Labrador, contact Newfoundland and Labrador Tourism for advice on the best routes and road conditions.

Contacts **Newfoundland and Labrador Tourism** (*709/729–2830, 800/563–6353 in North America www.newfoundlandandlabrador.com*). **Department of Transportation & Works** (*709/635–4144 in Deer Lake, 709/292–4444 in Grand Falls–Windsor and Central Newfoundland, 709/466–4160 in Clarenville, 709/729–7669 in St. John's, 709/896–7888 in Happy Valley–Goose Bay www.roads.gov.nl.ca*).

CONTACTS & RESOURCES

EMERGENCIES

Emergency Services **Ambulance, fire, police** (☎ *911 or 0*).

Hospitals **Captain William Jackman Hospital** (✉ *410 Booth Ave., Labrador City* ☎ *709/944–2632*). **Charles S. Curtis Memorial Hospital** (✉ *West St., St. Anthony* ☎ *709/454–3333*). **General Hospital** (✉ *300 Prince Philip Dr., St. John's* ☎ *709/777–6300*). **George B. Cross Hospital** (✉ *Manitoba Dr., Clarenville* ☎ *709/466–3411*). **James Paton Memorial Hospital** (✉ *125 Trans-Canada Hwy., Gander* ☎ *709/651–2500*). **St. Clare's Mercy Hospital** (✉ *154 Le Marchant Rd., St. John's* ☎ *709/777–5000*). **Western Memorial Regional Hospital** (✉ *Brookfield Ave., Corner Brook* ☎ *709/637–5000*).

SPORTS & THE OUTDOORS

FISHING Newfoundland has more than 200 salmon rivers and thousands of trout streams, and fishing these unpolluted waters is an angler's dream. The Atlantic salmon is king of the game fish. Top salmon rivers in Newfoundland include the Gander, Humber, and Exploits, and Labrador's top-producing waters are the Sandhill, Michaels, Flowers, and Eagle rivers. Lake trout, brook trout, and landlocked salmon are other favorite species. In Labrador, northern pike and arctic char can be added to that list. Seasonal and regulatory fishing information can be obtained from Newfoundland and Labrador Tourism. Nonresidents must hire a guide or outfitter for anything other than roadside angling. Big River Camps operates two remote fishing lodges in Labrador open during July and August; Eureka Outdoors has a salmon fishing lodge on the Humber River in Newfoundland.

Outfitter **Big River Camps** (☎ *709/686–2242* 🌐 *www.bigrivercamps.ca*). **Eureka Outdoors** (☎ *709/785–1992* 🌐 *www.eurekaoutdoors.nf.ca*).

HIKING The island portion of the province is a hiker's paradise, with a vast network of trails, some of which cut through resettled communities. Many provincial parks and both of the national parks have hiking and nature trails, and coastal and forest trails radiate out from most small communities. The East Coast Trail on the Avalon Peninsula covers 540 km (336 mi) of coastline; the trail stretches from Fort Amherst, in St. John's, to Cappahayden, on the beautiful southern shore. The trail begins in Conception Bay South and moves north to Cape St. Francis and then south all the way down to Trepassey. It passes through two dozen communities and along cliff tops that provide ideal lookouts for icebergs and seabirds. Call individual parks or the tourist information line for specifics. East Coast Trail Association helps hikers navigate the 540 km (336 mi) East Coast Trails, which hug the coastline of the Avalon Peninsula. Gros Morne Adventures runs guided day hikes and a six-day hiking adventure in Gros Morne National Park.

Outfitter **East Coast Trail Association** (☎ *709/738–4453* 🌐 *www.eastcoasttrail.com*). **Gros Morne Adventures** (☎ *709/458–2722* 🌐 *www.grosmorneadventures.com/hiking.html*).

TOURS

ADVENTURE TOURS

Local operators offer sea kayaking, ocean diving, canoeing, wildlife viewing, mountain biking, white-water rafting, heli-hiking, and interpretive walks in summer. In winter, snowmobiling and caribou- and seal-watching expeditions are popular. In spring and early summer, a favored activity is iceberg-watching.

Eastern Edge Kayak Adventures leads east-coast sea-kayaking tours and gives white-water kayaking instruction. Maxxim Vacations in St. John's organizes packaged adventure and cultural tours. Tuckamore Lodge, in Main Brook, uses its luxurious lodge on the Great Northern Peninsula as a base for viewing caribou, seabird colonies, whales, and icebergs, and for winter snowmobile excursions. Wildland Tours in St. John's has three weeklong guided tours that view wildlife and visit historically and culturally significant sites across Newfoundland.

Contacts **Eastern Edge Outfitters Ltd.** (☎ *709/ 773-2201 or 866/782-5925* ⊕ *www.kayakjim.com*). **Maxxim Vacations** (☎ *709/754-6666 or 800/567-6666* ⊕ *www.maxximvacations.com*). **Newfoundland and Labrador Tourism** (☎ *709/729-2830, 800/563-6353 in North America* ⊕ *www.newfoundlandandlabrador.com*). **Tuckamore Lodge** (☎ *709/865-6361 or 888/865-6361* ⊕ *www.tuckamorelodge.com*). **Wildland Tours** (☎ *709/722-3123, 888/615-8279* ⊕ *www.wildlands.com*).

BUS TOURS

Local tours are available for Port aux Basques, the Codroy Valley, Corner Brook, the Bay of Islands, Gros Morne National Park, the Great Northern Peninsula, and St. John's. Local information chalets—provincially run tourist centers located strategically along the Trans-Canada Highway—have contact names and numbers. Newfoundland and Labrador Tourism can help out here as well. McCarthy's Party in St. John's has guided bus tours across Newfoundland, learning vacations, and charter services. Wildland Tours also offers charters and learning vacations, including whale-study weeks and culinary tours of the island.

Contacts **McCarthy's Party** (☎ *709/579-4444 or 888/660-6060* ⊕ *www.mccarthysparty.com*). **Newfoundland and Labrador Tourism** (☎ *709/729-2830, 800/563-6353 in North America* ⊕ *www.newfoundlandandlabrador.com*). **Wildland Tours** (☎ *709/722-3123, 888/615-8279* ⊕ *www.wildlands.com*).

WALKING TOURS

On the St. John's Haunted Hike, the Reverend Thomas Wickam Jarvis (actor Dale Jarvis) leads several different and very popular walking tours of the city's haunted sites and urban legends on summer evenings; tours begin at the west entrance of the Anglican Cathedral on Church Hill. Look for the crowd of people standing in the dark.

Contacts **St. John's Haunted Hike** (☎ *709/576-2087 or 709/685-3444* ⊕ *www.hauntedhike.com*).

15

VISITOR INFORMATION

Newfoundland and Labrador Tourism distributes brochures from its offices. The province maintains a 24-hour tourist-information line year-round that can help with accommodations and reservations.

From June until Labor Day, a network of visitor information centers, open daily 9 to 9, dot the province. These centers have information on events, accommodations, shopping, and crafts stores in their areas. The airports in Gander and St. John's operate in-season visitor-information booths. The city of St. John's operates an information center in a restored railway carriage next to the harbor.

Tourist Information **City of St. John's Economic Development, Tourism & Culture** (☎ *709/576–8106* 🌐 *www.stjohns.ca/visitors/index.jsp*).

Newfoundland and Labrador Tourism (☎ *709/729–2830, 800/563–6353 in North America* 🌐 *www.newfoundlandandlabrador.com*).

Wilderness Canada

THE YUKON, THE NORTHWEST TERRITORIES & NUNAVUT

WORD OF MOUTH

"The Yukon really does have a great deal to offer during the summer months. Top of the list is Dawson City, home of the Klondike Gold Rush. It's a wonderful tourist place with restored 1890's buildings, saloons, and Canada's oldest Gambling Hall, Diamond Tooth Gertie's. Whitehorse is a 'big' city, for the North anyhow, but it doesn't have nearly the tourist appeal of Dawson City. For outdoor-types Yukon is wonderful, especially for canoeing and fishing. In June and July there are over 20 hours of daylight . . . for a real adventure you can take the Dempster Highway (virtually all gravel) from Dawson City to Canada's Arctic metropolis–Inuvik NWT, which is well north of the Arctic Circle. "

—gary

www.fodors.com/forums

Updated by Teresa Earle and Hélèna Katz

THE WORLD NORTH OF THE 60TH PARALLEL—the latitudinal line separating Canada's provinces from the Yukon, the Northwest Territories, and Nunavut—is vast, rugged, and thinly populated. Landscapes range from glacier-capped mountains to low-lying wetlands, from dense forest to treeless barrenlands. And then there's all that water, including two of the continent's biggest lakes and most powerful pristine rivers.

In midsummer sunrise and sunset merge, and north of the Arctic Circle they don't occur at all. Summer is so short wildflowers don't finish blooming before the foliage picks up its fall colors. In autumn and winter steadily longer nights arrive along with the mystical northern lights.

This is wilderness, and the wildlife loves it. People are profoundly outnumbered by bears (black, grizzly, polar), mountain sheep, wolves, moose, and bison. A caribou herd exceeding 80,000 is not uncommon, and that's a number to keep in perspective: it matches the entire human census of the region.

Highways thread together huge portions of the Yukon and Northwest Territories. Yet many hamlets cannot be reached by road except in winter, when highways are built of hard-packed snow over frozen rivers and lakes. In Nunavut there are no roads between communities at all. And no roads link the territory to the rest of Canada. Bush planes are called "the taxis of the North," since they're everyday lifelines for people who live enormous distances from one another.

Northern First Nations, who make up about half the population, sustain traditional cultures, but also fully participate in regional business and government. The main native groups are the Dene (or Athapaskan-speaking) peoples of the Yukon and the Northwest Territories; the Inland Tlingit of the Yukon; the Métis, Inuvialuit (western Inuit) peoples of the Mackenzie River valley; and the Inuit of the Arctic coast and Nunavut.

A visit to the Far North requires commitment and preparation. Lodging for less than C$100 a night is rare, unless you camp or book yourself into one of the growing number of bed-and-breakfasts. Relying on planes to get from one place to another raises travel costs even more. Guides and outfitters can be expensive, too, but their fees aren't out of line with the general cost of living in the Far North, and their travel packages often end up saving you money.

You must be willing to abide possible discomforts and inconveniences. Mosquitoes and blackflies rule the North in summer and early fall, and anyone without insect repellent is in for big trouble. Packing gloves and insulated clothing for a visit in August might seem excessive, but such are the necessities of traveling in a world where it's not uncommon for summer temperatures to drop in a day from above 21°C (70°F) to below freezing.

Visiting the Far North can be daunting, difficult, frightening, and even dangerous. But for those who prepare themselves for the challenge, it can be nothing short of exhilarating.

TOP REASONS TO GO

AURORA BOREALIS
Few spectacles on the planet rival the aurora borealis, also known as the northern lights, which fills the subarctic heavens on clear nights from September through March. In Yellowknife, there's a chance of seeing the aurora on 243 nights in a year. Can't beat those odds!

SPORTS & THE OUTDOORS
In warmer months you can hike, bike, fish, take a rafting or canoeing trip, or venture on wildlife-watching field trips. During the colder months you can cross-country ski, snowmobile, and even go on a dogsled adventure.

FIRST NATIONS' ARTS & CRAFTS
You'll find the most compelling buys in the Far North. Prices are best when buying directly from artists, craftspeople, or shops in local communities. But galleries and stores in the cities carry a wider selection of works from many regions.

EXPLORING WILDERNESS CANADA

The Yukon, the Northwest Territories, and Nunavut make up 3,787,800 square km (1,462,470 square mi), almost three times the size of Alaska and half the size of the rest of the United States. There are small cities—Whitehorse in the Yukon and Yellowknife in the Northwest Territories—but there are many more communities that are accessible only by plane.

It would be nearly impossible to explore all of Canada's Far North in a single trip—comparable to trying to visit Florida, New England, and the Rocky Mountains on the same vacation, only with far fewer roads. Size is only one problem; expense is another. Food, gas, and lodging are typically priced higher than in other parts of Canada, but the biggest cost is transportation, especially in those vast, roadless areas where you'll need to depend on air travel. This isn't to say it's difficult to get from one place to another. The large number of charter-plane operators and expert bush pilots makes getting around easier than you might think. But as we mentioned, the cost of traveling by small planes can be dizzying.

The best strategy for exploring the Far North is to focus on a specific area (such as Baffin Island, the Nahanni region, Dawson City) or activity (fishing, wildlife viewing). Planning ahead can save hundreds, even thousands, of dollars. The choices fall roughly into four categories: visits to main cities (Dawson City, Whitehorse, Yellowknife, Inuvik, and Iqaluit), excursions from the main cities, rambling in the backcountry wilderness, and adventures in the Arctic North.

ABOUT THE RESTAURANTS

Cuisine in the Far North rarely reaches grand epicurean standards, but it can have a distinctive character. In some places and at certain times of year, a caribou steak or a moose burger may be easier to find than a fresh salad. Outside the main cities, the dining room of your hotel or lodge may well be your only choice. But if the Far North is not neces-

GREAT ITINERARIES

IF YOU HAVE 4 DAYS

Start your tour in **Whitehorse**. The S.S. *Klondike*, the MacBride Museum, and Miles Canyon all hold a bit of character from the gold-rush era and are a good way to learn about the Yukon's colorful history. On Day 2 drive two hours east on the Alaska Highway towards Whitehorse and then five hours north on the Klondike Highway to **Dawson City**. There are some delightful highway stops for lunch and coffee on this route.

On your third day drive down Bonanza Creek Road to Dredge No. 4 and the original claim where gold was discovered in 1896. Spend Day 4 visiting Robert Service Cabin, Diamond Tooth Gertie's Gambling Hall, and other sights in Dawson City.

IF YOU HAVE 10 DAYS

A 10-day itinerary allows adequate time to explore the Yukon wilds. An extended stay at a fly-in wilderness lodge provides you with a base camp from which to set off for several backcountry adventures. Once you reach the lodge, your hosts help arrange hiking, boating, and fishing excursions, and they'll point you in the direction of the best wildlife-viewing areas.

A 10-day Klondike Gold Rush itinerary could include a canoe trip down the Yukon River plus a visit to **Dawson City**.

Some of the planet's best hiking is possible in **Kluane National Park**. A 10-day itinerary could take you as far back as the Donjek Glacier or allow you to make multiple three-day trips in a variety of different landforms, using backpack, paddle, or bike.

Finally, you could venture up the Dempster Highway, past the Arctic Circle to **Inuvik**, just over the Yukon border in the Northwest Territories, an adventurous add-on to the itinerary above.

sarily a gastronomic paradise, it is surprising and certainly admirable given what some chefs are able to concoct with limited ingredients.

ABOUT THE HOTELS

Lodging prices in the Far North have come down in the past decade—a reflection of the steady increase in tourism here. Still, in some communities a single lodge or co-op hotel may be your only option, so if you don't like the price or the room, you don't have much choice. In addition, the brief tourism season forces lodging proprietors to try to make ends meet in two or three months of active vacation business. Although you might think you're paying a good chunk of change for ordinary accommodations, consider the lack of quality building materials in many areas and the prohibitive costs of construction. In months other than July and August, expect better deals—room prices reduced by 50% or more—but fewer choices, because many places are closed from September through June.

Wilderness lodges offer a once-in-a-lifetime experience in some of the most remote and beautiful areas of the region. A one-week stay allows you to explore the wilds during the day and then return to the comfort of a cabin and home-cooked meal in the evening. You generally have to fly in to the lodges; the airfare is often covered in the lodging price.

In the Yukon, Whitehorse serves as a departure point for those heading to lodges farther north. Sports lovers planning a trip to the Northwest Territories can set out from Yellowknife for backcountry lodges on the shores of Great Slave Lake or on one of the thousands of smaller lakes that, along with their barren rock underpinnings and scrub growth, are the principal geological features of the Far North's interior.

Territorial, or public, campgrounds are found along all roads in the North and are open from the spring thaw until the fall freeze. Visitor information centers throughout the region can provide details on specific campground locations and facilities as well as permits. Note: it's advisable to boil or filter all water, even water that has been designated as "drinking water," at a campground.

WHAT IT COSTS IN CANADIAN DOLLARS

	¢	$	$$	$$$	$$$$
RESTAURANTS	under C$8	C$8–C$12	C$13–C$20	C$21–C$30	over C$30
HOTELS	under C$75	C$75–C$125	C$126–C$175	C$176–C$250	over C$250

Restaurant prices are for a main course at dinner. Hotel prices are for two people in a standard double room in high season, excluding tax.

TIMING

June through August is peak season in the Far North. For the remaining nine months of the year, many businesses and outfitters close, as much for lack of business as the length of winter. However, many northerners say that March and April, when daylight lengthens and the weather is perfect for such snow sports as skiing and dogsledding, are the best times to visit. September is another choice month, when the autumn colors are brilliant and ducks, geese, and caribou begin their migrations. And as harsh—and dark—as other months are, they can be prime time for visitors fascinated by the spectral displays of the northern lights.

THE YUKON

The stories and events surrounding the Klondike Gold Rush of 1896 draw many visitors to the Yukon. The gold rush attracted stampeders from all across America and as far away as Europe and Australia to the remote Yukon. Every year, people come to find long-lost relatives, or relive the excitement of a bygone era. Gold continues to be actively mined in the Yukon, and grizzled miners still find ample nuggets on a Dawson claim.

If backcountry adventure is more your style, consider taking a guided hiking or canoeing trip, which might run anywhere from 6 to 14 days. The Yukon is one of the premier wilderness adventure destinations in the world. A combination of hiking, biking, canoeing, rafting, and wildlife viewing ventures could keep you occupied for months. However, be advised that the Yukon's wilderness is truly wild. If you're an inexperienced hiker (or canoeist or snowmobiler), it's best to take a guided excursion into the backcountry. Even a hike over the Chilkoot Trail, which is monitored by the U.S. and Canadian park services, is extremely rigorous.

A network of well-maintained roads crisscrosses the Yukon, making it much more accessible than the more remote Northwest Territories and Nunavut. The Yukon ranks with Alaska as one of the great road-touring regions of North America, and in summer you'll share the road with RV and bus traffic. All Yukon highway signs are marked in kilometers. The Alaska Highway, however, has white posts that count off the 2,430 km (1,507 mi) from Dawson Creek, British Columbia, to Delta Junction, Alaska. The bush pilot tradition is still strong in the Yukon—often the best fly-fishing, hiking, sightseeing, and lodges are accessible by air.

WHITEHORSE

2,400 km (1,488 mi) north of Vancouver.

Begun as an encampment near the White Horse Rapids of the Yukon River, Whitehorse was a logical layover for gold rushers in the late 1890s heading north from Skagway, Alaska, over the Chilkoot Trail to seek their fortune in Dawson. Today's city of 24,000 residents is the Yukon's center of commerce, communications, and transportation and is the seat of the territorial government. Though there's enough in the city to keep you occupied for a day or two, it's best to regard Whitehorse as a base camp from which to venture out and explore other parts of the Yukon.

The **Whitehorse Visitor Information Centre** is the best place to pick up information on the Yukon and local lodgings, restaurants, shops, attractions, and special events. It's also the place to look into adventure travel: the center has information on the hundreds of tour and guide companies in the territory. A free 15-minute film provides a wonderful introduction to the Yukon's stunning scenery. ✉*2nd Ave. and Hanson St.* ☎*867/667–3084* 🌐*www.travelyukon.com* ⏲*Mid-May–late-Sept., daily 8–8; late-Sept.–mid-May, weekdays 8:30–noon and 1–5, Sat. 10–2.*

The scenic **Waterfront Walkway,** just east of the Yukon Visitor Information Centre, runs along the Yukon River. Head downstream (north) to see the old White Pass & Yukon Route building on Main Street. Erected in 1900, the building today marks the start or finish (depending on the year) of the Yukon Quest International Sled Dog Race. Walk upstream (south) on the **Millenium Trail,** a 5-km (3-mi) paved loop trail that winds along the river's edge to a bridge just below the dam.

The **MacBride Museum** encompasses more than 6,500 square feet of artifacts, natural-history specimens, historic photographs, maps, and diagrams covering prehistory to the present. Exhibits provide a historical overview of the Yukon, from the earliest exploration through the trapping era and the gold rush. Sam McGee's cabin is a main attrac-

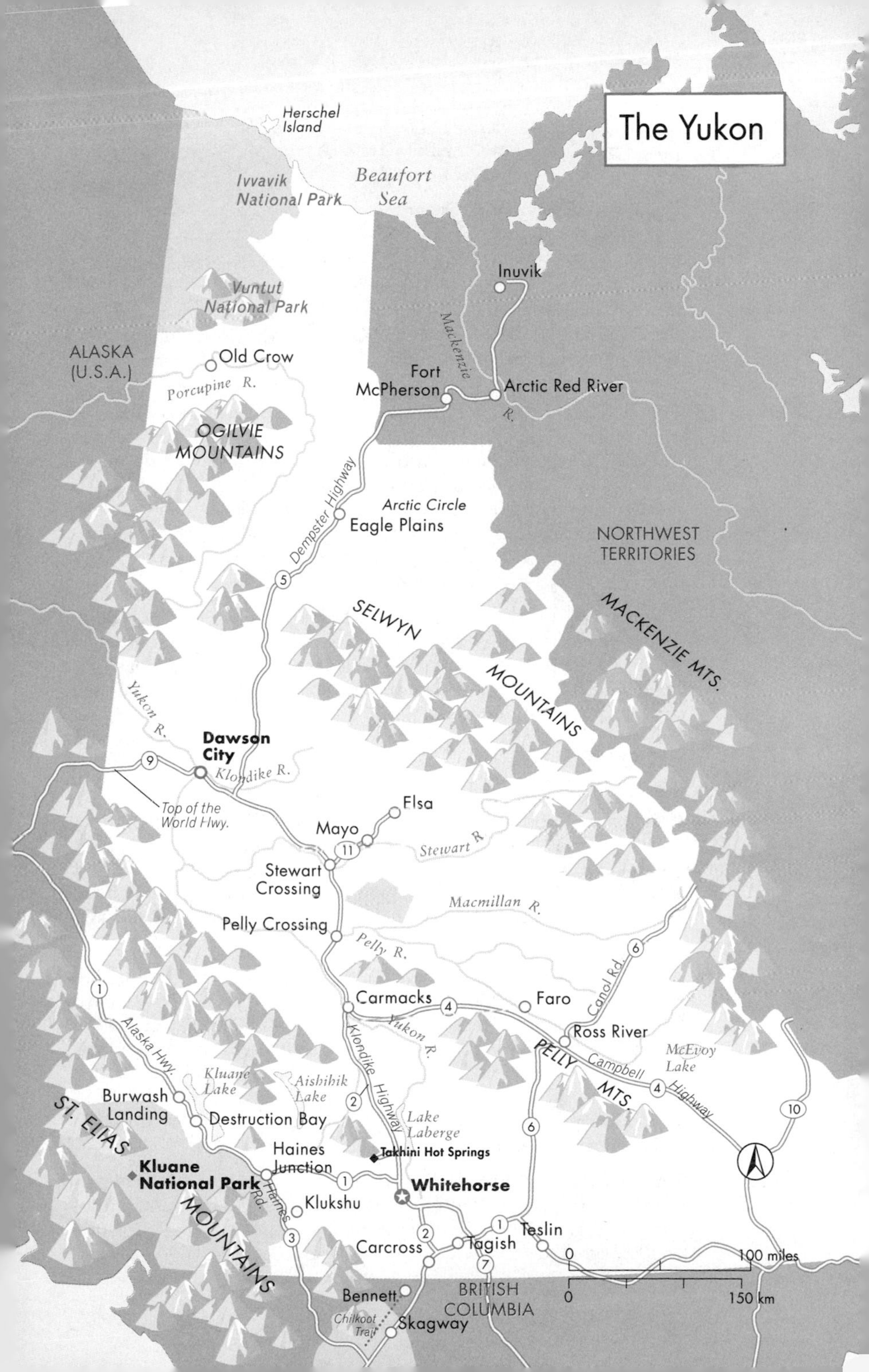

The Yukon
Herschel Island
Ivvavik National Park
Beaufort Sea
Inuvik
Vuntut National Park
Mackenzie R.
ALASKA (U.S.A.)
Old Crow
Porcupine R.
Fort McPherson
Arctic Red River
OGILVIE MOUNTAINS
Dempster Highway
Arctic Circle
Eagle Plains
NORTHWEST TERRITORIES
SELWYN MOUNTAINS
MACKENZIE MTS.
Yukon R.
Dawson City
Klondike R.
Top of the World Hwy.
Elsa
Mayo
Stewart R.
Stewart Crossing
Macmillan R.
Pelly Crossing
Pelly R.
Canol Rd.
Carmacks
Faro
Klondike Highway
Yukon R.
Ross River
Alaska Hwy.
PELLY MTS.
Campbell Highway
McEvoy Lake
Kluane Lake
Aishihik Lake
Burwash Landing
Destruction Bay
Lake Laberge
ST. ELIAS MOUNTAINS
Haines Junction
Takhini Hot Springs
Kluane National Park
Haines Rd.
Whitehorse
Klukshu
Teslin
Carcross
Tagish
0
100 miles
BRITISH COLUMBIA
0
150 km
Bennett
Chilkoot Trail
Skagway

tion, and the new Modern History Gallery showcases Yukon's development from 1880 to 1953. ✉ *1st Ave. and Wood St.* ☎ *867/667–2709* 🌐 *www.macbridemuseum.com* 🎫 *C$7* ⏲ *Mid-May–Aug., daily 9–6; Sept.–mid-May, Tues.–Sat. noon–4.*

★ The **SS *Klondike* National Historic Site,** a 210-foot stern-wheeler built in 1929, was the largest boat plying the Yukon River back in the days when the river was the only transportation link between Whitehorse and Dawson. Though the boat sank in 1936 it was rebuilt a year later and, after successive restorations, is now dry-docked in its 1930s glory. ✉ *Robert Service Way and 2nd Ave.* ☎ *867/667–3910 year-round, 867/667–4511 in summer, 800/661–0486* 🌐 *www.pc.gc.ca* 🎫 *C$6.15* ⏲ *Mid-May–Sept., daily 9–6.*

The best time to visit the **Whitehorse Rapids Dam and Fish Ladder** is in August, during the longest chinook (king) salmon migration in the world. From the viewing platform overlooking the river you might spot salmon as they use the ladder to bypass the dam. Plan to go in the evening, when the temperature drops a few degrees and the fish swim about more freely. Interpretive displays explain the phenomenon. ✉ *End of Nisutlin Dr.* ☎ *867/633–5965* 🌐 *www.yukonfga.ca* 🎫 *By donation* ⏲ *June–Aug., daily 9–9.*

A two-hour cruise aboard the **MV *Schwatka*** lets you experience the Miles Canyon section of the Yukon River as Jack London did when he was a pilot on its turbulent waters. The evening cruise, available mid-June through mid-August, includes a complimentary buffet and a cash bar. ✉ *Schwatka Lake, 3 km (2 mi) south of downtown Whitehorse on Miles Canyon Rd.* ☎ *867/668–4716* 🌐 *www.yukon-wings.com* 🎫 *C$25* ⏲ *Cruises early June–mid-June and mid-Aug.–early Sept., daily at 2; mid-June–mid-Aug., daily at 2 and 6.*

Miles Canyon (✉ *Miles Canyon Rd.*), 2 km (1 mi) south of Schwatka Lake, where the MV *Schwatka* is moored, is a public park laced with hiking trails of varying difficulty. A 20-minute trail leads to Canyon City, where gold-rush stampeders stopped before heading through the treacherous canyon and the White Horse Rapids. Contact the Yukon Visitor Information Centre for information on trails.

At the **Yukon Beringia Interpretive Centre** paleontological exhibits and interactive computer kiosks tell the story of the Yukon's ice-age past. The ancient remains of woolly mammoths, giant steppe bison, 400-pound beavers, primeval horses, giant short-faced bears, scimitar cats, and American lions are among the center's holdings. ✉ *Mile 914, Alaska Hwy., next to the Whitehorse Airport* ☎ *867/667–8855* 🌐 *www.beringia.com* 🎫 *C$6* ⏲ *May–Sept., daily 9–6; Oct.–Apr., Sun. 1–5 and by appointment.*

The **Yukon Transportation Museum,** north of the Yukon Beringia Interpretive Centre, displays artifacts and exhibits on the Yukon's unusual transportation legacy, from snowshoes and dogsleds to cars and airplanes. ✉ *30 Electra Crescent, next to Whitehorse Airport* ☎ *867/668–4792* *www.yukontransportationmuseum.ca* *C$6* *Mid-May–Aug., daily 10–6.*

Takhini Hot Springs, 25 minutes north of Whitehorse on Takhini Hot Springs Road, has swimming in the 40°C (104°F) mineral-spring pool (suits and towels are available for rental), horseback riding, cross-country skiing, a climbing tower, restaurant, campground, and areas for picnicking. *Km 9.6 on Takhini Hot Springs Rd., 10 km (6 mi) north of Whitehorse* *867/–456–8000* *takhinihotsprings.yk.ca* *C$9.50* *Mid-June–mid-Sept., daily 8 AM–10 PM; call for hrs rest of yr (usually Thurs.–Fri. 4 PM–10 PM, weekends 10 AM–10 PM).*

The **Yukon Wildlife Preserve** offers a foolproof way of photographing rarely spotted animals in a natural setting. You might see elk, caribou, mountain goats, musk ox, bison, moose, and mule deer as well as Dall, mountain, and stone sheep on the 700-acre preserve. In summer 1½-hour guided tours depart at 10 AM, noon, 2, and 4 every day; an 8 AM tour is available by appointment only. *Mile 5 (Km 8) Takhini Hotsprings Rd., Box 20191, Whitehorse, YT, Y1A 7A2* *867/633–2922* *www.yukonwildlife.ca* *C$22* *Daily tours mid-June–Aug.; Sept.–June, by appointment.*

WHERE TO STAY & EAT

$$$ ★ **Giorgio's Cuccina.** In winter this place is packed with Yukoners who, starved for summer, appreciate its oasislike surroundings—terra-cotta walls lined with giant palms. In addition to Mediterranean-inspired creations such as spinach-stuffed cannelloni, Giorgio's serves local foods like halibut, salmon, king crab, and arctic char. The hearty salads—such as the smoked-salmon Caesar—make use of both traditional and unique ingredients. When you get tired of eating moose jerky, try the delectable marinated octopus appetizer. Steaks, ostrich, pasta, and thin-crust pizza round out the menu. *206 Jarvis St.* *867/668–4050* *MC, V.*

$–$$ ★ **Sanchez Mexican Cantina.** Owner Otelina Sanchez lives many, many miles away from her hometown of Veracruz, Mexico. Fortunately for the Yukon she has her family recipes with her. Everything at the Cantina is homemade, even the tortilla chips and salsa. The always-intriguing specials range from seafood paella to chicken mole. From the menu, the fresh fish seviche and enchiladas go well with the selection of perfectly chilled Mexican beers. *211 Hanson St.* *867/668–5858* *MC, V.*

$$ **Klondike Rib and Salmon BBQ.** The first thing you notice about Klondike Rib and Salmon is the line out the door. The next thing is the rustic wall tent construction—it's the oldest operating building in Whitehorse. But the wait is worthwhile, and the atmosphere is authentic Yukon. Dona and Trevor's hallmark is exceptionally friendly service and tasty northern fare—fresh wild local salmon, arctic char, halibut, bison, caribou, and musk ox. *2116 2nd Ave.* *867/667–7554* *V* *Closed Sept.–May.*

¢–$ **The Alpine Bakery.** This store and lunch spot serves vegetarian soups, sushi, and savory pizzas. Everything is organic: including chocolates, milk, tea, eggs, breads, nut butters, hummus, and yogurt. This is also an excellent place to find baked items for backpacking or canoeing trips—the expedition bread and fruitcake are pack-friendly, healthy, and really delicious. ✉ *5th Ave. and Alexander St.* ☎ *867/668–6871* ▭ *AE, MC, V* ⏲ *Closed Sun. and Mon. No dinner.*

¢–$ ✕ **Baked Café.** World cuisine made with the freshest organic ingredients will give you an idea of what Main Street café is all about. At lunch the blackboard specials usually include a chunky, fragrant soup and a savory dish like quesadillas or Moroccan curry served with organic greens. The local Bean North Coffee is fair trade, and it's the only place in town for gelato. Sunny, streetside seating tops off the long list of reasons why Baked is a popular local haunt. ✉ *1st Ave. and Main St.* ☎ *867/633–6291* ▭ *V* ⏲ *No dinner.*

¢–$ ★ ✕ **Chocolate Claim.** In addition to handmade chocolates, truffles, and cakes, the chefs at the Claim turn out Thai soups and homespun surprises like pumpkin cheesecake. The company is always interesting, the panini and sandwiches are highly recommended, and the local art on the wall is for sale. ✉ *305 Strickland St.* ☎ *867/667–2202* ▭ *V* ⏲ *No dinner.*

¢–$ ✕ **Zola's Café Doré.** You won't find a full-course meal here, but you can enjoy the best coffee and people-watching in the Yukon. The marvelous baked goods include a zesty lemon-cranberry muffin and a fragrant Morning Glory muffin made with carrots and spices. Sandwiches, wraps, and sinfully rich desserts round out the snacking options. Midnight Sun Coffee Roasters also has take-out locations at the Canada Games Centre and Icycle Sports. ✉ *305 Main St., in the Hougen Centre* ☎ *867/668–5780* ▭ *V* ⏲ *No dinner.*

$$ **Edgewater Hotel.** On a quiet end of Main Street, this small hotel is a good alternative if you want to avoid the tour-bus bustle. The lobby is small and the passageway to the rooms is a bit narrow and awkward, but the rooms are large, with modern furnishings. The Cellar is a somewhat elegant dining choice, with Alaska king crab, prime rib, and tapas on the menu. The casual Gallery, upstairs in the hotel, serves breakfast and lunch (burgers, sandwiches, and seafood). ✉ *101 Main St., Y1A 2A7* ☎ *867/667–2572 or 877/484–3334* 📠 *867/668–3014* 🌐 *www.edgewaterhotel.yk.ca* *30 rooms, 2 suites* *In-room: ethernet. In-hotel: 2 restaurants, bar, no elevator* ▭ *AE, DC, MC, V.*

$$ **Westmark Whitehorse Hotel.** A favorite of business travelers as well as Holland America tourists, the Westmark can be a bustling place in summer when tour buses fill the parking lot and the accompanying busloads of luggage fill the lobby. The rooms are new, modern, and restful, and include hair dryers and coffeemakers. The hotel even has its own vaudeville show, *Frantic Follies,* a revue playing heavily on gold-rush themes. The hotel's restaurant can get crowded; the menu includes everything from traditional grilled halibut to a portobello mushroom Reuben. A gift shop and a travel agency are on the premises. ✉ *2nd Ave. and Wood St., Box 4250, Y1A 3T3* ☎ *867/393–9700 or 800/544–0970* 📠 *867/668–2789* 🌐 *www.westmarkhotels.com* *180 rooms, 8 suites* *In-room: ethernet. In-hotel: restaurant, bar, spa, public Internet.* ▭ *AE, DC, MC, V.*

$–$$ **High Country Inn.** This comfortable inn near the SS *Klondike* is a great value. The rooms are clean, well maintained, and nicely decorated in light pastel colors. With hot tubs, fireplaces, and canopy beds, the suites are exceptional. The lobby, restaurant, and lounge are cozy, and the Yukon Mining Company saloon on the outdoor deck is a favorite Friday-night gathering spot. *4051 4th Ave., Y1A 1H1* *867/667–4471 or 800/554–4471* *867/667–6457* *www.highcountryinn.yk.ca* *84 rooms, 30 suites* *In-room: Internet, Wi-Fi* *AE, DC, MC, V.*

FLY-IN WILDERNESS LODGES

$$$$ **Inconnu Lodge.** Inconnu is a statement in relative luxury. This fly-in lodge on the shores of McEvoy Lake, about 300 km (186 mi) northeast of Whitehorse, provides accommodations in modern log cabins. The principal activities are fishing and heli-hiking, but the lodge also arranges canoe trips on nearby rivers. Wildlife is plentiful, as attested by the taxidermy displayed in the main lodge's living room. The lodge also serves as a jumping-off point for canoe and climbing trips into Nahanni National Park. Rates for five-day packages, including transportation to and from Whitehorse, are about US$5,995 per person. *Box 29008, OK Mission RPO, Kelowna, BC V1W 4A7* *250/860–4187* *250/860–8894* *www.inconnulodge.com* *5 duplex cabins* *In-hotel: no elevator* *MC, V* *FAP.*

$$$$ **Tincup Lake Lodge.** When this luxurious lodge was built in 1991, no expense was spared—an amazing fact considering that all of the materials had to be flown in to the remote site. The main lodge is surrounded by cozy log guest cabins with woodstoves, covered verandas, and private bathrooms. This was originally a fishing lodge, but activities now include kayaking, canoeing, and wildlife-viewing excursions. You can even take a cooking class. A seven-day package, including the round-trip flight from Whitehorse, an hour away by plane, is about US$4,495 per person. *Box 30049, Whitehorse, YT Y1A 3M2* *604/762–0382 autumn–spring, 600/700–0654 summer* *www.tincup-lodge.com* *3 duplex cabins* *In-hotel: laundry service, no elevator* *V* *FAP.*

THE ARTS

Tourism Yukon publishes "Art Adventures on Yukon Time," which is available at the Yukon Visitor Information Centre. Many artists work from their homes, but welcome visitors to view their wares by prior appointment. Some of the most beautiful First Nations artwork (including masks, carvings, mukluks, and clothing) is best purchased through commission or special order.

More than 35 Yukon artists are represented at **Yukon Artists at Work** (*867/393–4848*), an artist-run gallery and studio overlooking the Yukon River valley. The complex is a five-minute drive south of Whitehorse in the McCrae Industrial Park off the Alaska Highway (address is 3B Glacier Road, but watch for "gallery" signs on the left side of the highway as you drive south from Whitehorse). The gallery is open daily in summer from noon until 5.

16

Arts in the Park (*867/667–4080 for schedule information*) is a delightful way to spend a sunny lunch hour in Whitehorse. Every weekday from mid-June through late August, between 11 and 2, a visual artist and a performing artist set up in LePage Park on the corner of 3rd Avenue and Wood Street. The events are free.

SPORTS & THE OUTDOORS

CANOEING

A canoe trip down the Thirty-Mile section of the Yukon River lets you observe wildlife and stunning river scenery; **Kanoe People** (*Box 5152, Y1A 4S3 www.kanoepeople.com 867/668–4899*) will rent you the gear, or they can arrange trips on a variety of rivers, guided and unguided, from 3 hours to 20 days in duration. In summer **Up North Adventures** (*103 Strickland St., Y1A 2J6 www.upnorth.yk.ca 867/667–7035*) offers guided and self-guided daylong and multiday canoe trips on the Yukon River.

DOGSLEDDING

If you're visiting in winter, don't miss the chance to experience firsthand one of the most beautiful and graceful ways to traverse the backcountry: dogsledding. Local tour operators don't expect most clients to have any experience, so don't be shy. If you aren't visiting in winter, a trip to a local dogsled kennel is still worthwhile and a fun experience—instead of a sled, the dogs pull a wheeled buggy. You'll likely be entertained by the stories—dog mushers are legendary spinners of yarns—and by the husky puppies clamoring for attention. **Muktuk Kennels** (*Km 1442.5, Alaska Highway, Y1A 7A2 www.muktuk.com 867/668–3647*), owned and operated by Frank Turner, a 25-year mushing veteran and a former winner of the Yukon Quest, offers dog yard tours (year-round), day trips, and longer expeditions. Known to deliver just the right amount of pampering at their elegant Homestead and yurts, Rod and Martha Taylor of **Uncommon Journeys** (*Box 20621, Y1A 7A2 867/668–2255 www.uncommonyukon.com*) offer one-week and longer dogsledding adventures.

SNOWMOBILING

The Yukon Visitor Information Centre has maps, produced by the Klondike Snowmobile Association, of local snowmobiling trails. You can rent snowmobiles at **Yukon Honda** (*1 Chilkoot Way, Y1A 6T6 867/668–4451*). If you're not an experienced snowmobiler, you should opt for a guided tour. **Up North Adventures** (*103 Strickland St., Y1A 2J6 867/667–7035*) arranges guided trips that last anywhere from one hour to five days; some are geared toward beginners.

SHOPPING

Aroma Borealis Herb Shop (*504B Main St. 867/667–4372*) is a treat for the senses, filled with Yukon-made herbal creams, aromatherapy facial products, healing salves, soaps, teas, and even natural mosquito repellent. The revolving exhibits at the **Arts Underground** (*Downstairs at 305 Main St. 867/667–6058*) showcase the sculpture, paintings, photography, and crafts of both emerging and established northern artists. **Coast Mountain Sports** (*Corner of 4th Ave and Main St. 867/667–4074*) sells clothing, footwear, and gear for outdoor pursuits. **Mac's Fireweed Books** (*203 Main St. 867/668–2434*) boasts one of the best magazine stands in North America plus northern books, maps, and souvenirs. First Nations–made clothing, local artwork, and indigenous crafts ranging from moose-hair tuftings to beadwork are available at the **Indian Craft Shop** (✉*504 Main St.* ☎*867/667–7216*).

Midnight Sun Gallery & Gifts (✉*205 Main St.* ☎*867/668–4350*) sells affordable Yukon and Canadian arts and crafts. **Murdoch's Gem Shop** (✉*207 Main St.* ☎*867/668–7867*) is the Yukon's largest manufacturer of gold-nugget jewelry. The **North End Gallery** (✉*1st Ave. and Steele St.* ☎*867/393–3590*) carries a large selection of exceptional northern art; it ships anywhere in the world. The **Whitehorse General Store** (✉*205 Main St.* ☎*867/393–8203*) has a folksy atmosphere and sells antiques and collectibles. The **Yukon Brewing Company** (✉*102A Copper Rd.* ☎*867/668–4183*) sells T-shirts, hats, and glassware. You can also take a free brewery tour and sample the brews. **Yukon Gallery** (✉*2054 2nd Ave.* ☎*867/667–2391*) specializes in original works by Yukon artists.

KLUANE NATIONAL PARK

Fodor'sChoice ★

160 km (99 mi) west of Whitehorse.

16

Kluane National Park, neighboring Wrangell–St. Elias National Park and Glacier Bay National Park in Alaska, and Tatshenshini Provincial Park in British Columbia form the largest expanse of contiguous national-park land in the world and a UNESCO World Heritage Site. Glaciers up to 100 km (62 mi) long stretch from the huge ice fields of the interior, constituting the largest nonpolar ice mass in the world. Canada's highest mountain, Mt. Logan (19,550 feet), is another of Kluane's natural wonders. Few visitors other than experienced mountaineers (who must receive authorization from the park superintendent) get a full sense of Kluane's most extraordinary terrain, as neither roads nor trails lead into the interior. A helicopter or fixed-wing flight over the Kluane ice fields is well worth the price on a clear day. Expect to pay more than C$150 per person for helicopter rides; fixed-wing flights are slightly cheaper. Many people are content with exploring the front ranges, which have impressive mountains with abundant wildlife—Dall sheep, black bears, and grizzly bears are the most noteworthy species.

The front-country trail system of Kluane National Park is the most extensive in the Far North, where you can experience everything from half-day hikes to multiday backpacking excursions. It's possible to make a five-day backpacking trip on marked trails, with opportunities for off-trail scrambling on mountaintops. Most marked hiking trails are relatively easy to negotiate. Keep in mind that this is bear country, and all bear precautions—especially storing food in canisters—must be taken. You might also consider buying a can of capsicum (pepper-spray) bear repellent, available in sporting-goods stores.

The town of Haines Junction marks the junction of the Haines and Alaska highways and is the headquarters of the **Kluane National Park Reserve** (✉*Mile 1016, Alaska Hwy.* ☎*867/634–7250* 🌐*www.pc.gc.ca*), a visitor center and the most logical place to begin your excursion into the park. A free 25-minute slide presentation provides an excellent introduction to the region's geology, flora, and fauna, and the amiable staff is well armed with valuable information concerning the condition of the many hiking trails—including any recent bear sightings. Day hikers should check in for a summer schedule of guided hikes. The center can provide information on companies that run helicopter and fixed-wing flights over the park. You can also pick up an overnight camping permit (C$10 per person per day) and free food-storage canisters here. You'll find one of Kluane's gems about 20 minutes (27 km/17 mi) south of Haines Junction nestled at the foot of the Kluane Front Range. **Kathleen Lake** is a stunning place to spend a day in a canoe or explore the pebble beach, boardwalks, and nearby trails. More-ambitious hikers can backpack from the **Tachal Dhal (Sheep Mountain) Visitor Center** (✉ *Mile 1019, Alaska Hwy.* ☎ *867/634–2251*) up the Slims River valley to the toe of the Kaskawulsh Glacier, a 27-km (17-mi) jaunt. This visitor center, which is open from mid-May through mid-September, is an outpost of Kluane headquarters within the park's borders.

AROUND KLUANE NATIONAL PARK

Once you've explored the rugged wonders of Kluane National Park, you may want to venture south of Haines Junction on Haines Road, which hugs the park and connects a few sights worth seeing.

Rock Glacier Trail is on the west side of Dezadeash Lake at Km 45. This 1½-km (1-mi) trail on the outskirts of Kluane National Park is well maintained and suitable for people of all ages and abilities. The trail passes over one of Kluane's thousands of glacierlike tongues of fragmented rock that have accumulated over deep layers of ice. The trail also affords a beautiful view of the Dezadeash Valley.

The village of **Klukshu,** on the small Klukshu River, is an important site of Southern Tutchone and Tlingit culture. For centuries First Nations people have been coming here from late July until September to fish for salmon. Interpretive displays along the banks of the river explain how fish were caught over the years. Smokehouses are still used to preserve the fish. A small crafts shop sells moccasins and wood and antler carvings, and on occasion you might catch one of the elders telling stories related to the area. From Haines Road the turnoff to the village is 80 km (50 mi) south of Haines Junction.

The spectacular **Million Dollar Falls,** fed by the Takhanne River, are 25 km (16 mi) south of Klukshu on Haines Road. Two trails, one 1 km (½ mi) long and the other 2½ km (1½ mi) long, lead down to the falls. They're steep but well maintained, and in season you can spot salmon in the clear waters. In winter you can put on skis or snowshoes and see how the falls transform into fantastic ice sculptures.

WHERE TO STAY & EAT

$$ ★ **Raven Hotel & Gourmet Dining.** The food at Haines Junction's finest dining and lodging establishment is so good that Whitehorse residents often make the two-hour drive to dine here. The menu changes every few days, depending on what seafood or produce is freshly available. Past choices have included fresh local salmon and lake trout, homemade pasta, and juicy steaks, all topped with homegrown herbs and

served at tables with views of Kluane's front ranges. Hardwood furniture fills the tasteful rooms. *Alaska Hwy., Box 5470, Haines Junction, Y0B 1L0 867/634–2500 867/634–2517 www.yukonweb.com/tourism/raven 12 rooms In-room: dial-up. In-hotel: restaurant, room service, no-smoking rooms, no elevator AE, MC, V Closed Nov.–Apr. CP.*

$ **Alcan Motor Inn.** This motel has a rustic chalet appeal, with pine furniture and multicolor bedspreads that decorate the airy and spacious rooms; those on the second floor have balconies with spectacular views of Kluane's front ranges. Some of the rooms have Jacuzzis and kitchenettes. *Alaska Hwy. and Haines Rd., Box 5460, Haines Junction, Y0B 1L0 867/634–2371 or 888/265–1018 867/634–2833 www.yukonweb.com/tourism/alcan 22 rooms In-room: kitchen (some), dial-up. In-hotel: laundry facilities, some pets allowed, no elevator AE, MC, V CP.*

¢ **Cozy Corner.** This small motel is a throwback to the days when weary Alaska Highway travelers would pull in for the night, park their cars in front of their rooms, and head to the restaurant for the comforts of a home-style meal. Rooms are unusually large—big enough for a bed and sofa bed—but the bathrooms are small. Some rooms have views of the front ranges of Kluane National Park. *Alaska Hwy. and Haines Rd., Box 5406, Haines Junction, Y0B 1L0 867/634–2511 867/634–2119 12 rooms In-hotel: restaurant, no elevator AE, DC, MC, V.*

16

DAWSON CITY

Fodor's Choice ★ *536 km (332 mi) north of Whitehorse.*

At the turn of the 20th century, Dawson City was the epicenter of gold fever. Preservationists have done an admirable job restoring many of the city's historic buildings and enforcing a zoning code that requires new structures to adopt facades conforming to the way the town would have looked in its Klondike Gold Rush heyday.

Covering everything from historical minutiae to lodging availability, the **Dawson City Visitor Information Centre** is the place to get your bearings. With so many impressive attractions and things to do in the Klondike, center staff can help you plan your days. *Front and King Sts. 867/993–5566 www.travelyukon.com Mid-May–mid-Sept., daily 8–8.*

Part opera house and part dance hall, the **Palace Grand Theatre** is the ticket headquarters for all Parks Canada tours and attractions in the Klondike. Parks Canada is a major presence in Dawson, owning more than 35 historical properties plus SS Keno and Dredge #4. A Parks Canada walking tour is generally the best way to start exploring Dawson—costumed interpreters lead visitors along dusty boardwalks, telling stories about the painstakingly restored buildings that give Dawson City its special character. Parks Canada passes are great value. Ask at the Palace Grand about free programs, special performances, and tours of the stately theater. ✉*King and 3rd Sts.* ☎*867/993–7200* ⏲*Late-May–mid-Sept., daily 9–5.*

The **Danoja Zho Cultural Centre** hosts daily tours that highlight Tr'ondek Hwech'in culture and history. The Hammerstone Gallery presents a hundred years of First Nations culture, and audiovisual presentations and performances of traditional songs, dances, and customs share a rich heritage. The center is a testament to the resilient culture of these people, who endured great hardship during and after the gold rush. ✉*Front and King Sts.* ☎*867/993–6768 or 867/993–5385* 🌐*www.trondek.com* 🎟*C$5* ⏲*May–Sept., daily 10–6; Oct.–Apr. by appointment.*

The **Dawson City Museum** chronicles the Klondike Gold Rush and includes exhibits on the material culture of the local Han people, steam locomotives, and the paleontology of the region. There's a genealogical library if you're trying to trace relatives who traveled to Dawson during the gold rush. The visible storage exhibit showcases scores of fascinating artifacts that would otherwise be stored away. ✉*5th Ave. between Mission and Turner Sts.* ☎*867/993–5291* 🌐*www.dawsonmuseum.ca* 🎟*C$9* ⏲*Mid-May–mid-Sept., daily 10–6; by appointment rest of yr.*

Works such as *The Call of the Wild* and *White Fang* were inspired by the time Jack London spent in the Yukon wilds. At the **Jack London Cabin and Interpretive Centre** you can visit the cabin in which the writer entertained miners with his knowledge of the classics during the winter of 1897. The interpretive center houses an exhibit of historic photographs chronicling London's life. ✉*8th Ave. and 1st St.* ☎*867/993–5575* 🌐*www.dawsoncity.org* 🎟*C$2* ⏲*Late May–mid-Sept., daily 10–6.*

Robert Service, primarily a poet, has been dubbed "the Bard of the Klondike." Originally from England, Service came to the Yukon in the early 1900s, well after the gold rush was over. Before coming to Dawson, Service worked in Whitehorse at the Canadian Imperial Bank of Commerce where he wrote "The Shooting of Dan McGrew," his most famous poem. The small **Robert Service Cabin** is a good representation of what many Dawson cabins looked like during and after the Klondike Gold Rush. The sod roof even bears raspberries in summer. ✉*8th Ave. and Hanson St.* ☎*867/993–7200* 🎟*C$6* ⏲*Mid-May–mid-Sept., daily 10–4.*

If you want a firsthand experience of river travel, board the *Yukon Queen II*, a 110-passenger vessel docked along Front Street that makes the downstream 173-km (107-mi) trip westward to Eagle, Alaska, in approximately four hours, and the upstream trip back to Dawson in approximately six hours. In between arrival and departure, you'll have about two hours to stroll around scenic Eagle. The boat trip is fully narrated and there is meal service on board. Reserve early as trips tend to sell out. Tickets can be bought in advance through **Gray Line Yukon** (📫*208G Steele St., Whitehorse YT Y1A 2C4* ☎*867/668–3225 or 800/544–2206*). ✉*Front St.* ☎*867/993–5599* 🌐*www.hollandamer-*

ica.com 🎫 *C$110 one-way, C$220 round trip* ⏲ *Departures mid-May–mid-Sept., daily at 9* AM; *approximate arrival back in Dawson is 8* PM.

Dawson really got its start at the gold-mining sites east of town. Huge mounds of rock and slag along the roadside attest to the considerable amount of earth turned over in search of the precious metal. The most famous mining site is **Bonanza Creek,** 1 km (½ mi) south of Dawson City on Bonanza Creek Road, which produced several million-dollar claims in the days when gold went for $16 an ounce. A brass plaque on Bonanza Creek Road marks the **Discovery Claim,** staked by George Carmack in August 1896, when he and his companions Skookum Jim and Dawson Charlie discovered the gold that sparked the great Klondike Gold Rush. The creek is so rich in minerals that it's still being mined today.

If you want to try your luck at gold panning, head out to **Claim No. 6** (✉ *Mile 9, Bonanza Creek Rd.*). Gold panning is free on this open claim, and you can keep all the gold you find. You can purchase the necessary pan, which makes a fabulous souvenir, at **Dawson Hardware** (✉ *2nd Ave. near King St.* ☎ *867/993–5433*).

Rent the necessary gold-panning gear for C$5 at **Claim No. 33.** You're guaranteed some gold, but don't expect to strike it rich. ✉ *Mile 7, Bonanza Creek Rd.* ☎ *867/993–5804* ⏲ *Daily 9–5.*

Dredge No. 4 was used to dig up the creek bed and sift gold from gravel during the height of Bonanza Creek's largesse. In summer, daily tours are conducted through the dredge, which is approximately 15 minutes by car up Bonanza Creek Road from its intersection with the Klondike Highway. ✉ *Mile 7.8, Bonanza Creek Rd.* ☎ *867/993–7228* 🎫 *C$6* ⏲ *June–mid-Sept., daily 10–4 (tours on the hr).*

WHERE TO STAY & EAT

$–$$$ ✕ **Backalley Pizzeria.** The pizza—including a wonderful Greek vegetarian pizza—is excellent, as are the Greek salad, spanakopita, and homemade lasagna. In winter it's takeout only, but there are many local pubs that allow you to bring your own eats. In warmer weather you can dine on the outdoor patio. The name of this place suits it—the pizzeria is literally in the back alley behind CIBC Bank. ✉ *Alley between 2nd and 3rd Aves.* ☎ *867/993–5800* 💳 *MC, V.*

$ ✕ **Riverwest Cappuccino & Bistro.** Riverwest is a favorite morning destination of Dawson locals grabbing a custom coffee and breakfast before bustling off to work. On the menu are healthful muffins, cookies, freshly made soups, vegetarian fare, wraps, and hearty sandwiches. The seating area is an airy mix of booths and pine tables, perfect for relaxing and nibbling. ✉ *Front and Queen Sts.* ☎ *867/993–6339* 💳 *MC, V.*

$$$ Fodor's Choice ★ **Bombay Peggy's Inn & Lounge.** Yukon's only restored brothel revels in its past: rooms have names like "Purple Palace" and "Lipstick Room." Each of the four main rooms and two suites is decorated differently, but all have deep claw-foot tubs, velvet bed linens, and antique furnishings. Peggy's also has four "snugs," rooms with shared bath, starting at C$99 a night. ✉ *2nd Ave. and Princess St., Box 411, Y0B 1G0* ☎ *867/993–6969* 📠 *867/993–6199* 🌐 *www.bombaypeggys.com* ⇨ *8*

16

rooms, 4 with bath; 2 suites In-room: VCR, Wi-Fi. In-hotel: Wi-Fi, bar, airport shuttle, no-smoking rooms, no elevator MC, V.

> **WORD OF MOUTH**
>
> "...hop on Air North from Fairbanks to Dawson City (Yukon, Canada) and get a real feel for the Klondike gold rush and all the stories associated. Have a flutter at the tables at Diamond Tooth Gertie's, or try the Sour Toe Cocktail at the Downtown hotel (alledgedly a human toe in the booze bottle.) Dawson is a fascinating destination." —Gardyloo

$$–$$$ **Aurora Inn.** Rooms at the Aurora are spacious and have queen-size beds and contemporary pine furniture. Suites have king-size beds and hot tubs. You can mingle with other guests or relax and watch TV in the large sitting room. The restaurant serves excellent Swiss-style cuisine. *5th Ave. and Harper St., Box 1748, Y0B 1G0 867/993–6860 867/993–5689 www.aurorainn.ca 20 rooms, 2 suites In-room: dial-up, Wi-Fi. In-hotel: Wi-Fi, restaurant, no-smoking rooms, no elevator MC, V.*

$–$$$ ★ **Klondike Kate's Cabins & Restaurant.** The line at Klondike Kate's can sometimes get a little intimidating, but the food is extremely good and the restaurant has an extensive martini menu to boot. Mexican and Middle Eastern dishes are often featured, but the real standout is the local king salmon. In summer meals are served on a large, covered outdoor deck, where the main decorative statement is a big map of the world onto which guests are invited to stick pins marking their hometowns. Fifteen well-appointed log cabins are scattered on the property. Reservations are recommended, or check at the restaurant for vacancies. *3rd Ave. and King St. 867/993–6527 MC, V Closed Oct.–Apr.*

$ **Downtown Hotel.** The red facade of the Downtown Hotel reigns over the dusty intersection at 2nd and Queen. Saunter through the swinging saloon doors, and you really know you're in the Klondike. Locals and tourists alike line the bar, and some even partake in a Downtown specialty, the Sour Toe Cocktail. The hotel features gold rush antiques and interesting local artwork, and the Jack London Grill evokes an early-1900s men's club. The main building has 34 guest rooms and is open all year; the annex across the street has 25 rooms and is open only in summer. *2nd Ave. and Queen St., Box 780, Y0B 1G0 867/993–5346 or 800/661–0514 867/993–5076 www.downtownhotel.ca 59 rooms in summer, 34 rooms rest of yr In-room: dial-up, Wi-Fi. In-hotel: Wi-Fi, restaurant, bar, public Internet, airport shuttle, no elevator AE, DC, MC, V.*

¢–$ **Dawson City Bunkhouse.** For budget-minded travelers, this is the best deal in town. Although the rooms here are spare, they're comfortable and clean. Some have private baths, phone, and cable TV; others do not. *Front and Prince Sts., Bag 4040, Y0B 1G0 867/993–6164 867/993–6051 32 rooms, 5 with bath In-room: no phone (some). In-hotel: airport shuttle, no-smoking rooms, no elevator MC, V Closed early Sept.–May.*

NIGHTLIFE & THE ARTS

THE ARTS The **Dawson City Music Festival** (*Dawson City Music Festival Association, Box 456, Y0B 1G0* ☎*867/993–5584* *www.dcmf.com*), which presents mainly Canadian musicians as well as a smattering of local and international performers, is held each July. It's one of the most popular events in the north, so tickets can be extremely difficult to get. Write to the Festival Association in spring to request tickets. The festival's Web site posts information on ticket availability.

NIGHTLIFE **Diamond Tooth Gertie's Gambling Hall** offers a glimpse of the frolicking times of the gold rush. "Gertie" and her cancan dancers put on three shows nightly while grizzled miners sit at the poker table. Gamblers can try their luck at slot machines, blackjack, red dog, and roulette. Note: no minors are admitted. ✉*4th Ave. and Queen St.* ☎*867/993–5575* *www.dawsoncity.ca* *C$6* *Mid-May–mid-Sept., daily 7* PM–2 AM.

SHOPPING

Klondike Nugget and Ivory Shop (✉*Front and Queen Sts.* ☎*867/993–5432*) sells a large selection of gold-nugget and mammoth-tusk ivory jewelry.

The **Fashion Nugget** (✉*5057 2nd Ave.* ☎*867/993–6101*) is a funky boutique featuring the work of local designer, Megan Waterman. The **No Gold Gallery** on Front Street carries local art, crafts, and collectibles. (✉*Front and Queen Sts.* ☎*867/993–5203*). A couple doors away, **Maximilian's Gold Rush Emporium** (✉*Front and Queen Sts.* ☎*867/993–5486*) has a bit of everything, with a strong emphasis on northern books and souvenirs.

16

SIDE TRIPS FROM DAWSON CITY

The 108-km (67-mi) trip west of Dawson City along the **Top of the World Highway** to the Yukon–Alaska border exposes you to beautiful, expansive vistas. The road partially lives up to its name, set as it is along ridge lines and high-mountain shoulders, but the dirt-and-gravel surface can hardly be called a highway. The northernmost border crossing on land between Canada and the United States is along this route; the U.S. side is Poker Creek, Alaska—population: 2.

Fodor's Choice ★ The **Dempster Highway's** arctic tundra and mountain scenery are always beautiful, but are most spectacular in late August. Autumn comes early to the tundra and colors the landscape in vivid reds and yellows.

The 766-km (475-mi) journey north on the Dempster Highway to the town of Inuvik, in the Northwest Territories, is a much more adventurous and ambitious undertaking than driving the Top of the World Highway. The only public highway in Canada to cross the Arctic Circle, the Dempster passes through a tundra landscape that is delicate, mountainous, and ever-changing.

Near its southern end, the highway passes through **Tombstone Territorial Park** and the alluring ranges of the Ogilvie Mountains. Guides at the Tombstone Interpretive Centre lead daily nature walks and can answer just about any question pertaining to the natural or cultural history of the area. You can find Tombstone's rolling subarctic tundra and mountain ridges have some of the most splendid hiking in the North. The area is rich with wildlife and birds—cameras and binoculars are essential. Even if you only make it to Tombstone for the day before returning to Dawson, the diversion is well worth it. Many travelers stay at the lovely campground at Tombstone before venturing farther north up the Dempster.

The route crosses Eagle Plains (approximately halfway between Dawson and Inuvik and a good stopping point for gas and supplies) before reaching the Arctic Circle, marked by a sign. From here the highway passes through the Richardson Mountains and enters the flatlands surrounding the Mackenzie River delta before reaching Inuvik. This is certainly one of *the* great wilderness drives in North America, but because there are no services for 370 km (229 mi) between the junction of the Dempster and Klondike highways and Eagle Plains, you should be prepared to cope with possible emergencies. Be sure to carry a minimum of two spare tires.

WHERE TO STAY

Eagle Plains Hotel. Thirty-five kilometers from the Arctic Circle, this hotel is an outpost in the wilderness. The complex includes a gift shop, RV park, restaurant, service station, and large lounge with a shuffle board and pool table. The hotel is "home" to the highway workers who patrol the road every day—you'll likely spot them in the lounge relaxing after work. ✉*Km 371, Dempster Hwy., Bag Service 2735, Whitehorse, YT Y1A 3V5* ☎*867/993–2453* *32 rooms* *MC, V.*

THE NORTHWEST TERRITORIES

The Northwest Territories cover an area of 1,171,918 square km (452,476 square mi)—about the size of Texas or Alaska. This huge chunk of Canada sprawls north from the 60th parallel to the coast and islands of the western Arctic. To the west lie the northern Rockies and the Yukon. Running from Great Slave Lake to the Beaufort Sea, the great Mackenzie Valley, with its majestic river systems and vast lakes, is the Northwest Territories' heartland. The rugged Barrenlands begin east of the valley and stretch to the border of Nunavut. Very few people live in this dramatic landscape, rock-strewn treeless tundra. The Northwest Territories' 42,000 citizens are governed by a multicultural, multilingual legislature whose elected members converge at Yellowknife's Legislative Assembly.

Aside from Yellowknife and Inuvik—the regional centers used as bases for travelers—the communities in the Northwest Territories are extremely small. Some families here still support themselves by hunting, fishing, and trapping, although modern technology is becoming increasingly widespread. There are many opportunities to learn about the rich history and traditional ways of the Dene, Métis, Inuit, and Inuvialuit communities, where native languages are spoken on a par with English and French. You'll be welcome at all the local festivals and ceremonies that take place throughout the year.

YELLOWKNIFE

2,595 km (1,613 mi) northeast of Vancouver, 1,508 km (937 mi) north of Edmonton.

Back in 1934, when gold was discovered on the North Arm of Great Slave Lake, Yellowknife began as a rough-and-tumble mining camp. The town is named after the local Dene who started trading furs with Europeans in the surrounding region in the late 18th century. The fur-company explorers called these Dene "Yellowknives" because, unlike other Dene groups, they carried knives made of "yellow" copper, obtained on hunting journeys to the Arctic coast.

Yellowknife, which has been a center of government since the 1960s, once had several gold mines, but the last of these has closed down. During the 1990s diamond mining brought new prosperity to the town. Lac de Gras, 350 km (217 mi) northwest of town, is the site of Ekati Mine, the Western Hemisphere's first diamond producer. Two more diamond mines have since begun operations. New diamond-cutting factories are an important spin-off. Additionally, exploration and drilling for oil and gas in the Mackenzie Valley and Beaufort Sea are booming. All this activity has fueled a building surge and a buoyant outlook in the Northwest Territories' capital city, whose population has grown from 12,000 in 1991 to nearly 20,000 today.

Much of Yellowknife stands on ancient Precambrian bedrock overlooking Great Slave Lake. The hilly topography bordering the lake, also known as the Big Lake, rises to a flat area chosen by pioneering councilmen in the late 1940s to be the "New Town," now the city's commercial center (also known as downtown) dominated by a cluster of hotels, office and apartment buildings, stores, and restaurants. At the heart of all this lies scenic Frame Lake, with a 9-km (5½-mi) trail loop that winds through woods and rocky shoreline and takes you past City Hall, the Prince of Wales Northern Heritage Centre, and the Legislative Assembly of the Northwest Territories.

★ The **Prince of Wales Northern Heritage Centre,** a few minutes northwest of the city center, houses extensive displays of such northern artifacts as the only mooseskin boat to be preserved. The aviation section documents the north's history of flight. The Beaufort-Delta and subarctic galleries feature changing exhibits about life in those regions of the Northwest Territories such as traditional clothing and the beluga whale hunt. Special interactive areas are designed to involve children. The museum's Heritage Café serves lovely soups, salads, and sandwiches from 11:30 AM to 2 PM weekdays. Main courses are C$11–C$16. ✉ *On the shore of Frame Lake opposite City Hall* ☎ *867/873–7551* 🌐 *www.pwnhc.ca* *Free* ⏲ *June–Aug., daily 10:30–5:30; Sept.–May, weekdays 10:30–5, weekends noon–5.*

The Northwest Territories & Nunavut
ARCTIC OCEAN
NORTHWEST TERRITORIES
NUNAVUT
Ellef Rignes Island
North Magnetic Pole
Prince Patrick Island
Beaufort Sea
Bathurst Island National Park (Tuktusiuqvialuk)
Melville Island
Aulavik National Park
Bathurst Island
Herschel Island
Viscount Melville Sound
Banks Island
Sachs Harbour
Tuktoyaktuk
Amundsen Gulf
Prince of Wales Island
Inuvik
Fort McPherson
REINDEER GRAZING RESERVE
Holman
Tsiigehtchic
Paulatuk
Tuktut Nogait National Park
Victoria Island
McClintock Channel
TREE LINE (Approximate northern limit of trees)
MACKENZIE
PEEL RIVER PRESERVE
Fort Good Hope
Cambridge Bay
King William Island
Kugluktuk
Norman Wells
Umingmaktok
Queen Maud Gulf
Coppermine
Great Bear Lake
Bathurst Inlet
Tulita
Deline
Queen Maud Bird Sanctuary
MTS.
Mackenzie River
NORTHWEST TERRITORIES
River
Garry Lake
Wrigley
Thelon Wildlife Sanctuary
Nahanni National Park
Thelon River
Fort Simpson
Yellowknife
Baker Lake
Liard R.
Blachford Lake
Nahanni Butte
Fort Providence
Lutsel K'e
Great Slave Lake
Fort Liard
Dubawnt Lake
Hay River
Fort Resolution
Alexandra Falls
Fort Smith
Wood Buffalo National Park
Slave River
BRITISH COLUMBIA
60th Parallel
Nueltin Lake
Peace River
Uranium City
Lake Athabasca
ALBERTA
SASKATCHEWAN

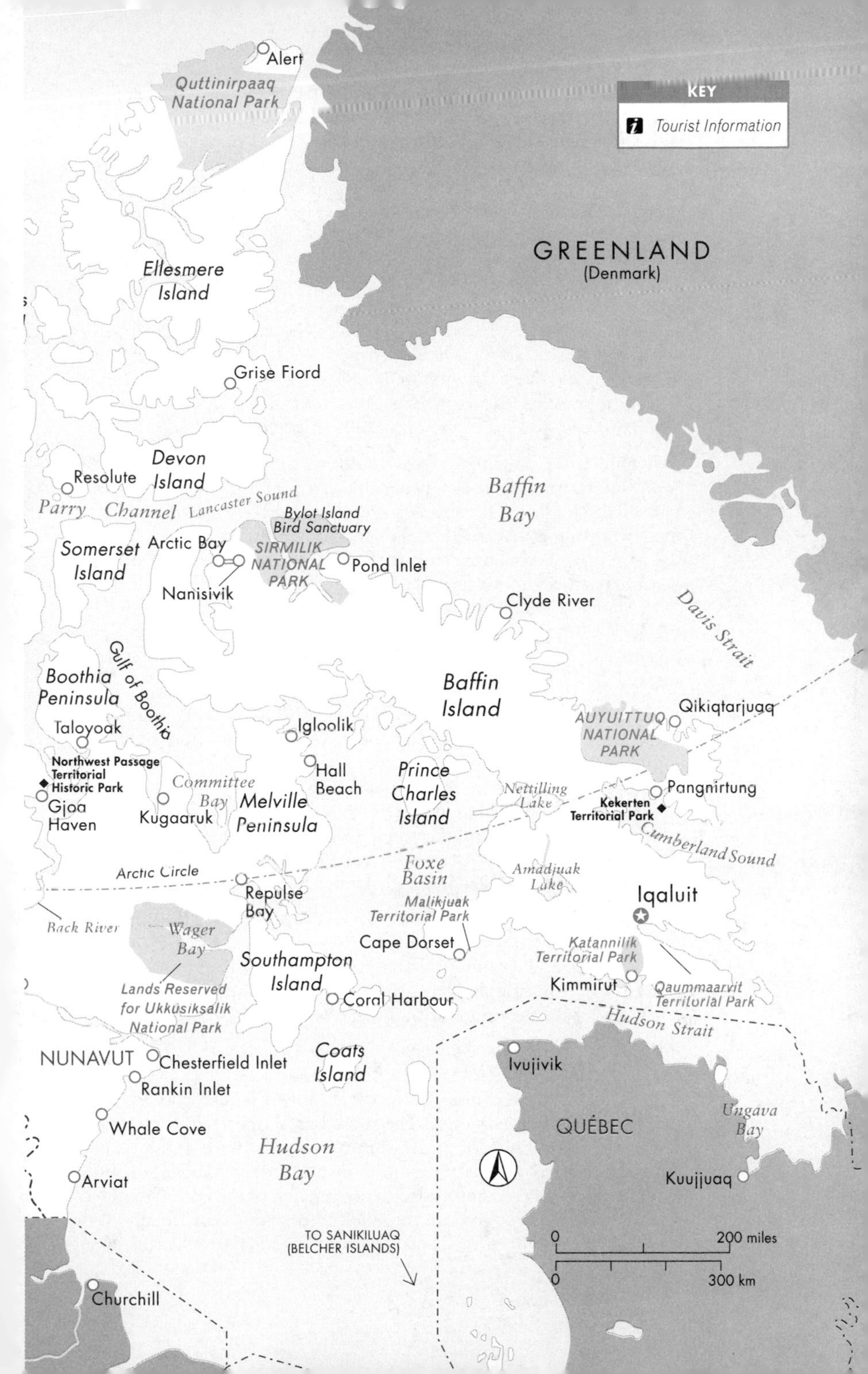

KEY
Tourist Information
Alert
Quttinirpaaq National Park
GREENLAND
(Denmark)
Ellesmere Island
Grise Fiord
Devon Island
Resolute
Parry Channel
Lancaster Sound
Bylot Island Bird Sanctuary
Baffin Bay
Somerset Island
Arctic Bay
SIRMILIK NATIONAL PARK
Pond Inlet
Nanisivik
Clyde River
Davis Strait
Gulf of Boothia
Boothia Peninsula
Baffin Island
Taloyoak
Igloolik
AUYUITTUQ NATIONAL PARK
Qikiqtarjuaq
Northwest Passage Territorial Historic Park
Hall Beach
Prince Charles Island
Committee Bay
Melville Peninsula
Nettilling Lake
Pangnirtung
Gjoa Haven
Kugaaruk
Kekerten Territorial Park
Cumberland Sound
Arctic Circle
Foxe Basin
Amadjuak Lake
Iqaluit
Repulse Bay
Malikjuak Territorial Park
Back River
Wager Bay
Cape Dorset
Katannilik Territorial Park
Southampton Island
Kimmirut
Lands Reserved for Ukkusiksalik National Park
Coral Harbour
Qaummaarvit Territorial Park
Hudson Strait
NUNAVUT
Chesterfield Inlet
Coats Island
Ivujivik
Rankin Inlet
Whale Cove
QUÉBEC
Ungava Bay
Hudson Bay
Arviat
Kuujjuaq
TO SANIKILUAQ (BELCHER ISLANDS)
0
200 miles
0
300 km
Churchill

The glass-domed **Legislative Assembly of the Northwest Territories** rises above the boreal forest. Free one-hour tours guide you through the splendid building in summer. You can visit the council chamber and see the translation booths that permit debates to be carried out in nine official languages. The legislature houses the ceremonial mace, a symbol of government. Made in 2000 of intricately engraved and decorated gold, silver, and bronze, it's the world's only "talking" mace. The designers filled it with tiny pebbles collected in the Northwest Territories' 33 communities. When the mace is moved, the pebbles create a musical sound that is intended to represent the voices of the people. The building lies a few hundred yards west of the Prince of Wales Northern Heritage Centre, a short taxi ride or 10-minute walk from the city center. ✉ *Turn left off Hwy. 3, northwest of town* ☎ *867/669–2230 or 800/661–0784* 🌐 *www.assembly.gov.nt.ca* 🎫 *Free* ⏲ *June–Aug., tours weekdays at 10:30, 1:30, and 3:30; Sun. at 1:30. Sept.–May, tours weekdays at 10:30.*

Downhill from downtown Yellowknife is the mostly residential **Old Town,** built around a rocky peninsula that juts into Yellowknife Bay, part of Great Slave Lake. You can reach it from downtown in 15 minutes by strolling toward the lake along Franklin Avenue; or you can drive, perhaps taking time to turn off and explore the winding streets of historic neighborhoods first settled in the area in the 1930s and 1940s. One of these neighborhoods is called the **Woodyard.** Once a thriving fuel depot run by a pioneer businessman, it's now known for its eccentric cabins, log dwellings, and Yellowknife's most famous street, **Ragged Ass Road,** named after hard-luck prospectors.

If you proceed north on Franklin Avenue, it becomes McDonald Drive. From McDonald Drive turn left onto Weaver Road and right onto Ingraham Drive, which travels over **The Rock** a steep Precambrian outcropping where miners first pitched their tents in the mid-1930s. The wooden stairs at Ingraham Drive's highest point lead to the **Pilot's Monument,** a hilltop marker built in honor of the bush flyers who opened up the North. The climb is worth it: there's a 360-degree view of Great Slave Lake, neighboring islands, and Yellowknife itself.

To continue exploring the Old Town, head back down to McDonald Drive and follow it around the Rock. Watch for the **Float Plane Base,** heavy with traffic coming in from and going out to mining-exploration camps. You can also cross the causeway to **Latham Island,** where a handful of B&Bs mingle with upscale housing.

It's hard to overstress the beauty of **Great Slave Lake,** the fifth-largest freshwater lake in North America, at 28,568 square km (11,030 square mi). Clean, cold, and deep, it dwarfs Yellowknife and the few other communities along its shores. The lake's East Arm, a two- to three-day sail from Yellowknife, is prime cruising country, with dramatic cliffs rising from narrow bays. For those unsure of their navigation skills, hiring a skipper is recommended because many of the lake's small bays are uncharted. Excursions on the lake can be arranged with any of the local operators who provide sail and motorboat charters, cruises, and sightseeing trips.

GREAT ITINERARIES

IF YOU HAVE 3 DAYS

You can jet north from Edmonton or Calgary across the Arctic Circle to the Northwest Territories' **Inuvik** to see the amazing Mackenzie Delta, **Tuktoyaktuk**, and the Beaufort Sea. Two nights in Inuvik also give you time for a flying tour over the giant estuary (where belugas romp in summer) to **Herschel Island**, a haunt of 19th-century whalers.

IF YOU HAVE 5 DAYS

Fly to **Yellowknife** and spend your first day exploring the Old Town and the cultural attractions downtown. The focus of Day 2 could be an outdoor activity, such as a dogsled ride or a cruise on Great Slave Lake. With its good choice of dining and lodging options, Yellowknife is a fine base from which to head out and explore **Nahanni National Park.** It's best to book a scheduled flight to Fort Simpson, where several plane and helicopter services offer flightseeing trips to the park's breathtaking Virginia Falls. (You can also drive to Nahanni, but the trip will take up all of Day 3.) If you choose to fly to Nahanni, spend two days at the park or use one day to tour Fort Simpson, long a Dene meeting place, where you can tour heritage buildings and go bird-watching along the banks of the Mackenzie River.

Wood Buffalo National Park is another possible road excursion from Yellowknife, though the drive will take up most of Day 3. On the fourth day explore the park's front-country trails; be on the lookout for bison and bald eagles. Whether you choose to drive to Nahanni National Park or to Wood Buffalo National Park, reserve Day 5 for the trip back to Yellowknife.

Alternatively, five days is a good amount of time to explore the Northwest Territories, basing yourself in **Iqaluit**, on Baffin Island, the capital of Nunavut. You can fly directly to Iqaluit from Ottawa, Montréal, or Edmonton, via Yellowknife. Here, you can explore several territorial and national parks, including **Auyyittuq National Park**, with one of the recommended outfitters in this chapter.

16

WHERE TO STAY & EAT

$$$$ Fodor'sChoice ★ ✕ **L'Héritage Restaurant Français.** Stepping inside L'Héritage, especially in darkest winter, is like being transported to some warm city in southern Europe. White tablecloths are matched with comfortable press-back chairs, and candlelight gleams on polished wood. Northern specialties are served with a French twist: musk-ox tenderloin with a fruit and brandy sauce, for example, and bison strip loin with bourbon-steeped figs and berries. Deer and elk are also adorned with clever sauces, and everything comes nestled in crisp vegetables. The wine list is excellent. ✉ *5019 49th St., Box 775, Yellowknife, NT* ☎ *867/873-9561* 🌐 *www.lefrolic.com* *Reservations essential* 💳 *AE, DC, MC, V* ⊗ *No lunch.*

$$$ ✕ **Le Frolic Bistro/Bar.** Wine lovers favor this lively downtown bistro, which shares a highly regarded wine cellar with the more formal restaurant, L'Héritage Restaurant Français, upstairs. Also available to drink are 27 single-malt whiskeys and seven beers on tap. The appetizers range from imaginative salads and antipasti to curried prawns. The

truly hungry may want to order a buffalo burger, wild game fondue, succulent rack of lamb, or fresh panfried Great Slave Lake pickerel. For Saturday brunch you can order just about any kind of eggs, including eggs *Arctique* (with smoked char), plus reliable burgers, sandwiches, and salads. ✉ *5019 49th St.* ☎ *867/669–9852* 🌐 *www.lefrolic.com* 💳 *AE, MC, V* ⏲ *Closed Sun.*

$$$ ✕ **Old Town Landing.** Open March–October, this sociable and spacious waterside restaurant is a favorite on long summer evenings, when guests can dine on one of two outdoor decks with unobstructed views of passing sailboats and floatplanes. Popular northern food stars here: the Caribou French Rack is roasted in a sauce of locally harvested wild berries, while arctic char is served grilled with herbed cream cheese, or smoked over linguine with dill sauce. Delicate Great Slave Lake whitefish is topped with a creamy peach cider sauce. Eight-ounce steaks, chicken, and pork tenderloin round out the ambitious menu. ✉ *3506 Wiley Rd.* ☎ *867/920–4473* 🌐 *www.oldtownlanding.com* 💳 *AE, MC, V.*

$$–$$$ ✕ **Bullock's Bistro.** Old Town's atmospheric and popular eatery is warm, friendly, and rustic, with only a dozen or so tables from which you can join the lively banter in the open kitchen. Bullock's specializes in succulent fish, fried to order in batter or straight in the pan. The fries are hand cut, and the catch of the day is fresh from Great Slave Lake. ✉ *3534 Weaver Dr.* ☎ *867/873–3474* 💳 *MC, V.*

$$ ✕ **Wildcat Café.** An institution as much as a restaurant, the Wildcat has been around since 1937. The low-slung log structure and split-log tables and benches inside evoke life at the frontier's edge. This is a place where strangers are expected to share tables. The food, ranging from fresh fish and vegetarian chili to caribou medallions in a tangy horseradish-Dijon sauce, is excellent. Many people drop in at the Wildcat for coffee and desserts—including their delectable bannock bread pudding. ✉ *3904 Wiley Rd.* ☎ *867/873–4004* 💳 *MC, V* ⏲ *Closed Oct.–late May.*

¢–$ ✕ **Javaroma Gourmet Coffee.** On the main floor of the telephone company's downtown office tower, Javaroma is a friendly meeting place where you can order good soups, fresh bagel sandwiches (including Santa Fe chicken, and turkey with cranberry sauce), wraps, and healthful salads. There's a changing roster of muffins and Italianate specialty coffees as well as straightforward java brews from around the world. ✉ *5201 50th Ave.* ☎ *867/669–0725* 💳 *MC, V.*

$$$ 🏨 **Chateau Nova.** This hotel on the fringe of the commercial area, overlooking the Old Town, is sleek and urban, yet one wall in the lobby is solid Precambrian rock, and framed vintage photographs of Yellowknife's early years hang at well-spaced intervals. In the rooms, subtle creams and pastels contrast with wood furniture and plush, earth-tone carpeting and bedspreads. The hotel's Millwright Restaurant has gained a reputation for intriguing interpretations of northern staples—caribou escallop with a port-wine and chutney reduction, or smoked arctic char with pear poached in wine, stuffed with lemon cream cheese and drizzled with blueberry-maple vinaigrette. ✉ *4401 50th Ave., X1A 2N2* ☎ *867/873–9700 or 877/839–1236* 📠 *867/873–*

9702 @www.chateaunova.com 60 rooms In-room: ethernet, dial-up. In-hotel: restaurant, bar, gym, public Internet, airport shuttle, A/C. AE, DC, MC, V.

$$$ **Explorer Hotel.** The city's largest hotel underwent a massive facelift in 2005. The woodsy new color theme, beginning with the high-rise exterior and carried through the reconfigured lobby and dining room, blends subtle tones of green, gray, and beige. In the guest rooms (all with renovated baths), rich russet-beige fabrics combine with dark wood furniture. The **Trader's Grill** is more of a steak house whereas the **Trapline Lounge** offers varied pub-style fare. *4825 49th Ave., Postal Service 7000, X1A 2R3 867/873–3531, 800/661–0892 in Canada 867/873–2789 www.explorerhotel.ca 187 rooms In-room: Wi-Fi. In-hotel: 2 restaurants, bar, gym, laundry service, public Internet, airport shuttle, no-smoking rooms, a/c AE, DC, MC, V CP.*

$$ **Yellowknife Inn.** The city's oldest hotel first opened its doors in 1947, but don't expect vintage architecture. The inn has been reinvented and rebuilt several times. Today's lavish marble lobby is a far cry from the first frame structure that stood in this spot. The lobby opens onto the Centre Square shopping mall, which in addition to shops, has the hotel's casual bistro-style restaurant, L'atitudes. The Mackenzie Lounge is a nice place to meet for a drink before dinner. Basic pastels and cheery print bedspreads decorate the comfortable guest rooms. *5010 49th St., Box 490, X1A 2N4 867/873–2601 or 800/661–0580 867/873–2602 www.yellowknifeinn.com 126 rooms In-room: Wi-Fi. In-hotel: restaurant, bar, airport shuttle, no smoking rooms, a/c (some) AE, DC, MC, V CP.*

$–$$ **Embleton House.** A great B&B choice if you'd like to be close to shopping, entertainment, and the city's business center—yet escape traffic and noise. Embleton House, surrounded by award-winning gardens, is two blocks from downtown. Accommodations range from cozily appointed doubles with shared baths to suites with private baths and skylights—great for watching the aurora, which you can also view from the deck. Guests are welcome to use the barbecue and garden. Embleton House is run by lifelong Yellowknifers with inside knowledge of the city's attractions. *5203–52nd St., X1A 1T8 867/873–2892 or 866/873–2066 867/873–4927 www.bbcanada.com/embletonhouse 7 rooms In-room: no a/c, DVD, VCR. In-hotel: public Internet, no-smoking rooms, no elevator AE, MC, V CP.*

¢–$ **Blue Raven.** Thanks to its attractive location on a high bluff at the edge of the Old Town and overlooking Great Slave Lake, the Blue Raven is among the best of Yellowknife's B&Bs. A full breakfast is served in a common room with a fireplace and a superb view of the lake. There's also a deck for enjoying summer days. The rooms are small, modern, clean, and quiet, set apart from one another by the home's three-story configuration. *37 Otto Dr., X1A 2T9 867/873–6328 tmacfoto@arcticdata.ca 867/766–3214 3 rooms without bath In-room: no a/c. In-hotel: no-smoking rooms, no elevator. MC, V CP.*

16

FLY-IN WILDERNESS LODGES

$$$$ ★ **Blachford Lake Lodge.** Overlooking a small lake southeast of Yellowknife, Blachford is more than just a fishing lodge. Depending on the season, you can canoe, hike, cross-country ski, ice fish, or go snowshoeing or dogsledding. Prices for three-, six-, and eight-day packages vary depending on whether you stay in the main lodge, with all meals included, or opt for self-catering in a log cabin (cabins sleep five). If you elect to bring and prepare your own food, bedding, and fishing tackle, the cost can be kept to about C$300 per person per day (including round-trip flights from Yellowknife and use of lodge boats, but not guiding services)—modest by fly-in standards. *Box 1568, Yellowknife NTX1A 2P2 867/873–3303 867/920–4013 www.blachfordlakelodge.com 5 rooms in main lodge, 5 cabins In-room: no a/c, no TV. In-hotel: bar, no elevator MC, V EP, FAP.*

$$$$ **Frontier Fishing Lodge.** On the East Arm of Great Slave Lake near the Dene community of Lutsel K'e, the Frontier is typical of a full-service fishing lodge. You can stay in the two main lodges, in outlying log cabins (which sleep four to six people), or in comfortable rooms attached to the conference and recreation building. Wherever you stay, you'll have to share bathrooms with other guests. Breakfast and dinner are served daily around a big table in the main lodge. Guides take you to the best fishing waters on Great Slave as well as adjoining rivers and lakes; lake trout exceeding 25 pounds are landed regularly. Packages, including flights to and from Yellowknife, begin at around US$600 per person per day. *Box 32008, Edmonton, AB T6K 4C2 780/465–6843 780/466–3874 www.frontierfishinglodge.com 6 rooms, 7 cabins; all with shared bath In-room: no a/c, no TV MC, V Closed mid-Sept.–mid-June MAP.*

$$$$ **Treeline Lodge.** Treeline, affiliated with the highly regarded Bathurst Inlet Lodge, is an oasis in the rugged transition zone between the boreal forest and the open tundra that rolls east to Nunavut. The full-service lodge is a refurbished mine complex where guests share small, dormlike rooms and dining facilities. About 16 km (10 mi) of roads are ideal for hiking and wildlife viewing from a vehicle or mountain bike. Explore Matthews Lake aboard a pontoon boat, go paddling, or fish for lake trout, northern pike, and arctic grayling. Packages, including the round-trip flight from Yellowknife, start at C$300 per person per day. *Box 820, Yellowknife, NT X1A 2N6 867/873–2595 867/920–4263 www.treelinelodge.com 17 rooms In-room: no a/c, no phone, no TV. In-hotel: bicycles MC, V Closed Oct.–May MAP.*

NIGHTLIFE & THE ARTS

Locals gather in the **Black Knight Pub** (*4910 49th St. 867/920–4041*) for the large selection of beers on tap, 49 different kinds of Scotch, and sports programs on the large-screen TVs. The decent pub snacks include wings and burgers with fries.

Folk on the Rocks (*Box 326, X1A 2N3 867/920–7806 www.folkontherocks.com*), a lakeside music festival held in mid-July, attracts musicians from throughout North America and the circumpolar world, including Dene and Inuit performers.

Raven Mad Daze (✉*Yellowknife Chamber of Commerce, #21, 4910 50th Ave., X1A 3S5* ☎*867/920–4944*) takes place during summer solstice (the third week in June), when the sun is still out at midnight. Sidewalk sales, street vendors, concerts, and dances are part of the fun.

SPORTS & THE OUTDOORS

CRUISES

The **MS *Norweta*** (✉*#8–8 Riverview Circle, Cochrane, AB T4C 1X1* ☎*403/932–7590 or 866/667–9382* 🌐*www.norweta.com*) operates several summer cruises along the Mackenzie River. Most voyagers travel one way: northward, beginning in Yellowknife and crossing Great Slave Lake to the river's mouth, then on to the Arctic; or southbound, starting from Inuvik as the *Norweta* reverses her route. Each trip lasts eight or nine days.

Aurora World Corporation (✉*Box 2435, Yellowknife, NT X1A 2P8* ☎*867/873–4776* 🌐*www.auroraworld.ca*) operates two-hour cruises on Yellowknife Bay.

Sail North (📭*Box 2497, X1A 2P4* ☎*867/873–8019*) rents boats (including houseboats) for cruises on Great Slave Lake.

HIKING

Ecologist and author Jamie Bastedo of **Cygnus Ecotours** (📭*Box 682, X1A 2N5* ☎*867/873–4782* ✍*cygnus@theedge.ca*) leads entertaining, enlightening, and nontechnical natural-history hikes in the backwoods and along lakeshores near Yellowknife.

SHOPPING

Northern Images (✉*4801 50th Ave.* ☎*867/873–5944* 🌐*www.northernimages.ca*) sells Inuit and Dene crafts and artwork, from sculpture to moose-hair tuftings to clothing. It's one of four galleries owned by a Dene and Inuit artists co-op, with other northern branches in Churchill, Winnipeg, and Inuvik. With a good selection and fair prices, **Gallery of the Midnight Sun** (✉*5005 Bryson Dr.* ☎*867/873–8064* 🌐*www.gallerymidnightsun.com*) sells Inuit art and sculptures, northern clothing, Dene crafts from moose-hair tuftings to birchbark baskets and smaller gifts.

DEPARTURES FROM YELLOWKNIFE

Yellowknife is a transportation hub for outlying areas in the western Arctic. For driving excursions from Yellowknife, you can pass through Wood Buffalo National Park and Fort Smith to the south and through Fort Liard to the west. These are not, generally speaking, rousing scenic drives. Long stretches of road cutting through the low-lying subarctic bush are highlighted by occasional waterfalls or the sight of wildlife on or near the highway.

ALEXANDRA FALLS

537 km (333 mi) south of Yellowknife.

Of the scenic waterfalls along the road between Yellowknife and the Alberta border, the most dramatic is Alexandra Falls, where the Hay River drops 108 feet over limestone cliffs. The falls are a few miles south of the town of Hay River, on Route 1 at the junction of Routes 1 and 2.

WOOD BUFFALO NATIONAL PARK

330 km (205 mi) southwest of Alexandra Falls, 599 km (371 mi) south of Yellowknife.

The area where you're most likely to spot wildlife in the southern Northwest Territories is Wood Buffalo National Park, which straddles the Alberta–Northwest Territories border, off Route 5. Covering 44,807 square km (17,300 square mi), this is the largest national park in Canada, home to the world's largest free-roaming bison herd (about 5,600 total), as well as wolves, bears, and moose. It's also a summer nesting ground for many bird species, including bald eagles and the rare whooping crane. Much of the terrain—a flat land of bogs, swamps, salt plains, sinkholes, and meandering streams and rivers—at this UNESCO World Heritage Site is essentially inaccessible to visitors, but a few front-country trails allow exploration. One campground has 15 sites with picnic tables, firewood, running water, and playgrounds. *Superintendent, Wood Buffalo National Park, Box 750, Fort Smith, X0E 0P0 867/872–7900 www.pc.gc.ca/pn-np/nt/woodbuffalo Free; camping C$15 per person per night.*

NAHANNI NATIONAL PARK

Fodor's Choice ★ *608 km (377 mi) west of Yellowknife.*

The principal reason to head west from Yellowknife is to visit Nahanni National Park (C$25 for a day-use pass). The Mackenzie and Liard rivers, which join at the town of Fort Simpson, are the region's approximate geographical dividers, separating the low-lying bush of the east and the mountains to the west. Access to Nahanni National Park is possible only by floatplane; inside the park, canoes and rafts are the principal means of travel. Well-maintained park campsites near the Virginia Falls facilitate overnight excursions. The park season is from June to September 15. The **Nahanni National Park Reserve** (*Box 348, Fort Simpson X0E 0N0 867/695–3151 www.pc.gc.ca/pn-np/nt/nahanni*) can provide a list of air services to Nahanni National Park. Perhaps the most impressive feature in Nahanni National Park is **Virginia Falls,** more than 410 feet high and about 656 feet wide—a thunderous wall of white water cascading around a central spire of rock. Several plane and helicopter services offer flights over the falls.

The spectacular **Cirque of the Unclimbables,** a breathtaking cathedral of rock towers rising as much as 3,000 vertical feet, does not live entirely up to its name, but the few who have made successful ascents here can be counted among the most proficient rock climbers in the world. Perhaps the biggest problem posed by the Cirque is that it is nearly as unreachable as it is unclimbable.

The **South Nahanni,** with its stunning scenery, is among the loveliest rivers in the Far North. Two-week canoe trips start from Rabbit Kettle Lake at the park's northwestern extreme but require portage around Virginia Falls. Various 8- to 12-day canoe or raft trips begin below

Virginia Falls. (Reservations are required for all paddling trips on the South Nahanni.) White water along the way is minimal, so previous canoeing or rafting experience isn't essential. Paddlers on multiday trips should buy an annual parks pass ($149), also good for admission to other northern national parks.

SPORTS & THE OUTDOORS

Nahanni River Adventures (*Box 31203, Whitehorse, YT Y1A 5P7 867/668–3180 or 800/297–6927 www.nahanni.com*) provides reliable guided river trips. **Nahanni Wilderness Adventures** (*969A Lawrence Grassi Ridge, Canmore, AB T1W 3C3 403/678–3374 or 888/897–5223 www.nahanniwild.com*) specializes in canoeing and rafting adventures in Nahanni National Park.

Simpson Air (*Box 260, Fort Simpson, NT X0E 0N0 867/695–2505 and 866/995–2505 www.simpson-air.com*) shuttles climbers to the Cirque of the Unclimbables from Fort Simpson.

INUVIK

1,086 air km (673 air mi) northwest of Yellowknife.

Inuvik is the one and only town you can reach by road in the Canadian Arctic—via the Dempster Highway, which runs 766 km (475 mi) northeast from Dawson City, Yukon, to this small town. Many adventurous drivers enjoy the challenge of passing through the mountains, across the sweeping tundra of the northern interior, all the way to the huge Mackenzie Delta, where the Mackenzie River (*Deh Cho* to the Dene people of this region) meets the Beaufort Sea. However, it's not necessary to drive to get here: daily air service connects Inuvik to Yellowknife; Edmonton, Alberta; and the Yukon.

This Arctic town, the northernmost settlement of its size anywhere in the world, is the busy gateway of tours of the Mackenzie Delta, the western Arctic islands, and the Arctic coast. It's also a good place to spot rare wildlife and experience vibrant northern cultures. The town's population of 3,500 mixes major northern identities: Gwich'in Dene, Inuvialuit, Métis, and settlers from southern Canada. Various arts festivals and seasonal celebrations blend traditional and modern life throughout the year.

You can meet First Nations people and experience their culture on guided tours to fishing and whaling camps with **Arctic Nature Tours** (*Box 1190, Inuvik, NT X0E 0T0 867/777–3300 www.arcticnaturetours.com*).

WHERE TO STAY & EAT

$$$–$$$$ **Tominoes.** This restaurant is in the Mackenzie Hotel across from the Igloo Church. A fireplace is the centerpiece of the dining room, which also features a waterfall. The restaurant offers standard fare steaks, burgers, pasta, Friday lunch special of fish-and-chips and prime rib on Friday night. Also open for breakfast and lunch. *185 Mackenzie Rd. 867/777–4900 867/777–4906 AE, MC, V.*

$$$ **Capital Suites.** On Mackenzie Road near the colorful houses known as Smartie houses for their resemblance to the chocolate candies, the Capital Suites is a new, modern building. The studio, one- and two-bedroom suites have kitchens where you can prepare your own meals, and daily housekeeping. Coffee is in the lobby weekday mornings. *Box 2096, 198 Mackenzie Rd., X0E 0T0 867/678–6300 867/678–6309 www.capitalsuites.ca/inuvik.htm 82 rooms In-room: no a/c, Wi-Fi. In-hotel: gym, laundry, public Internet, no-smoking rooms AE, MC, V.*

DEPARTURES FROM INUVIK

You don't "tour" the Northwest Territories in the usual sense of the word. Here a tour is more of an expedition. Inuvik serves as a base camp from which to make day trips or extended side trips in the Mackenzie Delta, along the coast, or north to the islands of the western Arctic Archipelago.

Using regional airlines, you can take a short flight to the village of **Tuktoyaktuk,** overlooking the Beaufort Sea, where you can visit strange ice-cored hills called pingos and experience a bit of Inuvialuit culture.

From Tuktoyaktuk it's a short hop by plane to the coastal village of Paulatuk and **Tuktut Nogait National Park,** a wilderness park without any development that was set aside to protect caribou calving grounds. (*Box 91, Paulatuk X0E 1N0 867/580–3233 C$25 day use, C$148 season).*

Inuvik operators will also arrange trips to **Banks Island,** 523 air km (324 air mi) northeast of Inuvik, where once-endangered musk oxen find sanctuary in **Aulavik National Park** (*Box 29, Sachs Harbour X0E 0Z0 867/690–3904 C$25 day use, C$148 season*).

Although it's a Yukon Territorial Park, **Herschel Island** in the Beaufort Sea is usually accessed by air excursions from Inuvik. A 19th-century whaling station, it's now home to Arctic birds, wildflowers, and weathering relics that date back 100 years.

Lodging and transportation in the Arctic North tend to be expensive even by high-end northern standards, so having a well-defined travel plan is critical to staying within a budget. Trip organizers and outfitters can be particularly helpful in tailoring a travel program to meet particular interests and budgets. Keep in mind that the prime Arctic travel season is very short: many visitor services and tour organizers operate only in July and August. *(⇨ For more information, see listings in Wilderness Canada Essentials, under Tours/Northwest Territories.)*

CLOSE UP

Nunavut

There are no roads to Nunavut. This fact alone makes the Arctic territory a unique travel destination. But consider its other amazements: no forests grow here—Nunavut lies almost entirely above the tree line. In winter, night can last around the clock. In summer, the sun never sets. It's a land of glaciers and looming peaks, where caribou outnumber people.

At 2,121,012 square km (818,923 square mi), Nunavut is the largest political entity in North America. Only about 27,000 people live in all this vastness, many of them in isolated settlements where hunting and fishing are still the main activities. Nunavut's communities, 28 in all, are linked to one another by modern communications, and all are served by regional airlines. Yet they are among the world's most remote places to live. You won't find tidy suburban gardens or paved roads here. Instead of neatly trimmed hedges, drying caribou hides and dismantled snowmobiles flank many a front door.

Nunavut's warm heart is its people, the Inuit of Canada's Far North, to whom its name means "our land." Inuktitut is the main language, and you'll hear it and see its written syllabics everywhere you go. This isn't a barrier to visitors: English and French are also official languages and most Nunavimiut are bilingual.

Experiencing the Arctic is still an adventure relatively few travelers undertake. Without roads, getting around within the territory by air tends to be both time-consuming and expensive. Amenities can be very basic. Still, there are countless wonders to be found. If you opt for the services of the local and international outfitters who sell packages that range from comfortable Arctic cruises to outdoor adventures or cultural tours in the villages—sometimes combining all of these—you can often cut costs. For more information contact

Nunavut Tourism (*Box 1450, Iqaluit, NU X0A 0H0 867/979-6551 or 866/686-2888 www.nunavut-tourism.com*).

RECOMMENDED OUTFITTERS:
Bathurst Inlet Lodge is among Canada's foremost naturalist desinations. (*867/873-2595 www.bathurstinletlodge.com*).

Central Arctic Tours and Outfitters runs dogsled tours along the south coast of Victoria Island. (*867/983-2024*).

Northwinds Arctic Adventures specializes in naturalist tours and expeditions to the high Arctic. (*867/979-0551 or 800/549-0551 www.northwinds-arctic.com*).

Nuna Tours offers trips to Kekerten Territorial Park, Auyuittuq National Park, and Cumberland Sound, with opportunities to watch birds, whales, and other sea mammals. (*867/473-8692*).

Qimuk Adventure Tours arranges aurora-viewing trips and cultural adventures from Iqaluit by snowmobile, boat, and dog team. (*867/979-2777 pooka.nunanet.com/~qimuk*).

WILDERNESS CANADA ESSENTIALS

TRANSPORTATION

BY AIR TO & AROUND WILDERNESS CANADA

Whitehorse International Airport, 5 km (3 mi) from downtown Whitehorse, is the Yukon's major airport. Yellowknife Airport, the main facility for the Northwest Territories, is 5 km (3 mi) northwest of Yellowknife's city center. Iqaluit Airport is Nunavut's main hub, with connections to regional centers; some flights to the region also fly through Rankin Inlet Airport.

Information **Iqaluit Airport** (☎ *867/979–5224*). **Rankin Inlet Airport** (☎ *867/645–3838*). **Whitehorse International Airport** (☎ *867/667–8440*). **Yellowknife Airport** (☎ *867/873–4049*).

Once you're outside the Yukon and the southwest section of the Northwest Territories, flying is pretty much the only way to get around in wilderness Canada. Air Nunavut, Canadian North, First Air, and Kivalliq Air have regularly scheduled service within the Northwest Territories and Nunavut. Air North, Air Tindi, Alkan Air, Buffalo Airways, Calm Air, and North-Wright Airways all also offer charter air service, an option worth considering for groups of four or more and usually the only option for getting to and from remote wilderness areas. Check with regional tourist offices for other charter services operating locally and regionally.

Pilots visiting the Northwest Territories can order a copy of the *Air Tourist's Information* brochure by contacting NWT Arctic Tourism.

Note that there is restricted access in some parts of the Northwest Territories and Nunavut, though you can sometimes obtain a permit to visit these areas. Contact NWT Arctic Tourism or Nunavut Tourism for more information. If you travel with a licensed operator, permits will be included in your package.

YUKON Contacts **Air North** (☎ *867/668–2228 or 800/661–0407* 🌐 *www.flyairnorth.com*). **Alkan Air** (☎ *867/668–2107 or 800/661–0432* 🌐 *www.alkanair.com*).

NORTHWEST TERRITORIES Contacts **Air Tindi** (☎ *867/669–8200 or 888/545–6794* 🌐 *www.airtindi.com*). **Buffalo Airways** (☎ *867/873–6112* 🌐 *www.buffaloairways.com*). **Calm Air** (☎ *800/839–2256* 🌐 *www.calmair.com*). **North-Wright Airways** (☎ *867/587–2288* 🌐 *www.north-wrightairways.com*). **NWT Arctic Tourism** (✉ *4916 47th St., 3rd fl., Yellowknife, NT X1A 1L7* 📫 *Box 610, Yellowknife, NT X1A 2N5* ☎ *867/873–5007 or 800/661–0788* 🌐 *www.explorenwt.com*).

NUNAVUT Contacts **Air Nunavut** (☎ *867/979–4018* 🌐 *inuit.pail.ca/air-nunavut.htm*). **Kivalliq Air** (☎ *867/645–2992 or 877/855–1500* 🌐 *www.kivalliqair.com*). **Nunavut Tourism** (📫 *Box 1450, Iqaluit, NU X0A 0H0* ☎ *867/979–6551 or 866/686–2888* 🌐 *www.nunavuttourism.com*).

BY BUS

Greyhound Canada Transportation has service from Edmonton to Hay River and Yellowknife, Northwest Territories. Greyhound also has service from Edmonton and Vancouver to Whitehorse in the Yukon.

In the Yukon, Alaska Direct Transport and Bus Line has scheduled service from Whitehorse to Haines Junction, Dawson City, Burwash Landing, and Beaver Creek, as well as many Alaskan communities. Alaskon Express has service from Whitehorse to cities in Alaska from mid-May to mid-September. Frontier Coachlines connects the Northwest Territories' towns of Fort Smith, Fort Providence, Hay River, and Yellowknife. Summer bus service between Dawson and Inuvik is offered by Gold City Tours.

Information **Alaska Direct Transport and Bus Line** (✉ *Corner of 5th Ave. and Ogilvie St., Whitehorse, YT Y1A 1H1* ☎ *867/668–4833*). **Alaskon Express** (✉ *208-G Steele St., Whitehorse, YT Y1A 2C4* ☎ *867/668–3225 or 800/544–2206*). **Dawson City Courier** (✉ *4230 4th Ave., Suite J, Whitehorse, YT Y1A 1K1* ☎ *867/393–3334*). **Frontier Coachlines** (✉ *16-102 St., Hay River, NT X0E 0R9* ☎ *867/874–2566* ✉ *113 Kam Lake Rd., Yellowknife, NT X1A 3T3* ☎ *867/873–4892*). **Gold City Tours** (📫 *Box 960, Dawson City, YT Y0B 1G0* ☎ *867/993–5175*). **Greyhound Canada Transportation** (☎ *800/661–8747* 🌐 *www.greyhound.com*).

BY CAR

It hardly needs to be said that getting to the Yukon or the Northwest Territories by car calls for a good deal of driving. The best route into the region is the Alaska Highway (Route 97 in British Columbia), accessible from Edmonton via routes 43, 34, and 2 and from Vancouver via Route 1. After Fort Nelson, British Columbia, routes 7, 1, and 3 lead to Yellowknife; the Alaska Highway (also known as Route 1 in the Yukon) continues on to Whitehorse. The good news is that with so few roads in the region it's difficult to make a wrong turn. With relatively little lodging along the way, you might want to embark on the trip in a camper or recreational vehicle. There are no roads to Nunavut.

In general, exploring by car is a more sensible idea in the Yukon than in the Northwest Territories. Many highways in the Yukon are paved, the scenery along the way considerable, and roadside services more extensive. The only part of the Northwest Territories with any kind of highway network is the southwest, where the Mackenzie Highway is paved from the Alberta border to Yellowknife. Farther north and west, roads are hard-packed gravel. And there are no roads connecting the hamlets of Nunavut.

If you're traveling by car in the Far North, take precautions. At least one good spare tire is essential, and many residents of the region carry more, especially when traveling long distances. It's also advisable to carry extra parts (air filter, fan belt) and fluids. Another common practice is to cover headlights, grills, and even windshields with plastic shields or wire mesh to protect against flying gravel. Be sure your vehicle has good suspension, even if you plan to stick to the major highways; shifting permafrost regularly damages paved roads, and ruts and washboard occasionally appear on unpaved roads, especially after periods of bad weather.

Winter driving requires extra precautionary measures. Many a Far North resident can tell you a tale about overnighting on the road and waiting out fierce weather. Take along emergency survival gear, including an ax, shovel, flashlight, plenty of matches, kindling (paper or wood) to start a fire, sleeping bag, rugged outerwear, and food. Also, you should have a properly winterized car, with light engine oil and transmission fluid, a block heater, tire chains, and good antifreeze.

GASOLINE As you drive farther north, gas stations are few and gas is very expensive. Distances from one service area to the next typically exceed 160 km (100 mi), so be sure to monitor your fuel gauge.

ROAD CONDITIONS Several river crossings in the Northwest Territories don't have real bridges. In summer you ride a free car ferry; in winter you cross on ice bridges. However, there are the seasons known as "freeze-up" and "break-up," in fall and spring, respectively, when ice bridges aren't solid but rivers are too frozen for ferries to run. Call for daily ferry reports, available late May to late October for the south Mackenzie region, and June to late October for areas farther north.

Information about winter road conditions and the Yukon Highway also are available.

Contacts **Ferry crossings and road conditions** (☎*800/661–0750 in Northwest Territories, 867/456–7623, 877/456–7623 in Yukon* 🌐*www.gov.yk.ca/roadreport*).

CONTACTS & RESOURCES

EMERGENCIES

It's a good idea when traveling in the Far North—especially in remote wilderness areas and if unescorted by a guide or outfitter—to give a detailed itinerary to someone at home or to the police to facilitate emergency rescue.

For emergency services in the Yukon, the Northwest Territories, and Nunavut, dial 0 for the operator and explain the nature of the emergency. You will then be connected with the police, fire department, or medical service, as needed. In Whitehorse dial 911 for emergencies.

Medical services, with staff on call 24 hours a day, are available at Baffin Regional Hospital in Iqaluit, Fort Smith Health Services, H.H. Williams Memorial Hospital in Hay River, Inuvik Regional Hospital, Stanton Yellowknife Hospital, and Whitehorse General Hospital. You may also call a Royal Canadian Mounted Police toll-free number for medical assistance from anywhere in the Yukon.

Pharmacies can be found in major settlements of the Yukon, the Northwest Territories, and Nunavut, but late-night service is rare; after hours contact the nearest hospital or nursing station. If you have a preexisting medical condition that requires special medication, be sure you are well supplied before your trip, as getting unusual prescriptions filled can be difficult or impossible.

Doctors **Fort Smith Health Services** (✉ *Byrant St., Fort Smith* ☎ *867/872–6200*). **Great Slave Medical House** (✉ *Yellowknife* ☎ *867/920–4211*).

Emergency Services **Royal Canadian Mounted Police** (☎ *867/669–1111 in Yellowknife, 867/667–5555 toll-free emergency number in Whitehorse, 867/667–3333 for medical assistance*).

Hospitals **Baffin Regional Hospital** (✉ *Northern section of town, Iqaluit* ☎ *867/979–7300*). **H. H. Williams Memorial Hospital** (✉ *3 Gaetz Dr., Hay River* ☎ *867/874–6512*). **Inuvik Regional Hospital** (✉ *185 Mackenzie Rd., Inuvik* ☎ *867/777–8000*). **Stanton Yellowknife Hospital** (✉ *550 Byrne Rd., Yellowknife* ☎ *867/669–4111*). **Whitehorse General Hospital** (✉ *5 Hospital Rd., Whitehorse* ☎ *867/393–8700*).

TOURS

THE YUKON

The best way to find a Yukon tour that suits your style, budget, and interests is to visit the Yukon Wild Web site or pick up a brochure at the Whitehorse Visitor Information Centre. Yukon Wild represents all of the established wilderness tour operators in the Yukon, offering everything from aurora viewing, cabin rentals, dogsledding, and sea kayaking to van tours.

Canadian River Expeditions/Nahanni River Adventures conducts guided wilderness trips on the Tatshenshini, Alsek, Yukon, Nahanni, Firth, and other northern rivers. Walden's Guiding & Outfitting offers guided canoeing trips in the Peel River watershed (Snake, Wind, and Hart rivers) as well as the Tesline, Yukon, and Beaver rivers.

Kanoe People arranges guided and unguided canoe trips, from a half day to two weeks, on several rivers. Up North Adventures offers canoeing, kayaking, and fishing trips in the Yukon, Teslin, Big Salmon, Nisutlin, and Takhini rivers; in winter you can join snowmobiling excursions. Uncommon Journeys and Muktuk Adventures offer dogsledding excursions.

Holland America Westours organizes bus tours through the Yukon and Alaska as well as combined cruise ship–bus tours that link in Skagway, Alaska. Gray Line Yukon conducts package tours to Dawson City and Alaska as well as Yukon River cruises.

Contacts **Yukon Wild** (🌐 *www.yukonwild.com*). **Gray Line Yukon** (✉ *208-G Steele St., Box 4157, Whitehorse, YT Y1A 2C4* ☎ *867/668–3225*). **Holland America Westours** (✉ *300 Elliott Ave. W, Seattle, WA 98119* ☎ *206/281–3535 or 888/252–7524* 🌐 *www.hollandamerica.com*). **Kanoe People** (📫 *Box 5152, Whitehorse, YT Y1A 4S3* ☎ *867/668–4899* 🌐 *www.kanoepeople.com*). **Muktuk Adventures** (📫 *Box 20716, Whitehorse, YT Y1A 7A2* ☎ *867/668–3647* 🌐 *www.muktuk.com*). **Nahanni River Adventures/Canadian River Expeditions** (📫 *Box 31203, Whitehorse, YT Y1A 5P7* ☎ *867/668–3180 or 800/297–6927* 🌐 *www.nahanni.com*). **Uncommon Journeys** (📫 *Box 20621, Whitehorse, YT Y1A 7A2* ☎ *867/668–2255* 🌐 *www.uncommonyukon.com*). **Up North Adventures** (✉ *103 Strickland St., Whitehorse, YT Y1A 2J6* ☎ *867/667–7035* 🌐 *www.upnorth.yk.ca*).

Walden's Guiding and Outfitting (*Box 10402, Whitehorse, YT Y1A 7A1 867/667-7040 www.waldensguiding.com*).

NORTHWEST TERRITORIES Aurora-viewing and river tours are available through Arctic Nature Tours, which also runs trips to Banks and Herschel islands. One of the largest adventure-travel companies in Canada, Black Feather Wilderness Adventures leads canoeing and hiking trips in Nahanni National Park, the Mackenzie Mountains, and the central Arctic. The N.W.T. Marine Group offers a 1,600-km (992-mi) 8- to 9-day cruise along the Mackenzie River from Yellowknife to Inuvik aboard the MS *Norweta*. Raven Tours conducts tours of Yellowknife and the Great Slave Lake area, including aurora-viewing tours in winter. Simpson Air runs flightseeing trips over Nahanni National Park, including a half-day excursion that takes in Virginia Falls. The Taiga Tour Company operates various naturalist tours—including snowmobiling, dogsledding, wildlife-watching, and van tours—of 3 to 10 days in Wood Buffalo National Park.

Contacts **Arctic Nature Tours** (*Box 1530, Inuvik, NT X0E 0T0 867/777-3300 www.arcticnaturetours.com*). **Black Feather Wilderness Adventures** (*R. R. 3, Parry Sound, ON P2A 2W9 705/746-1372 or 888/849-7668 www.blackfeather.com*). **N.W.T. Marine Group** (*4-66 Woodland Dr., Hay River, NT X0E 1G1 877/874-6001 www.norweta.com*). **Raven Tours** (*Box 2435, Yellowknife, NT X1A 2P8 867/873-4776 www.raventours.yk.com*). **Simpson Air** (*Box 260, Fort Simpson, NT X0E 0N0 867/695-2505 www.simpsonair.ca*). **Taiga Tour Company** (*Box 852, Fort Smith, NT X0E 0P0 867/872-2060 www.taigatour.com*).

VISITOR INFORMATION

YUKON Tourism Yukon is the central source of information for the entire area. It also operates six regional information centers, open mid-May to mid-September, in Beaver Creek, Carcross, Dawson City, Haines Junction, Watson Lake, and Whitehorse.

Information **Beaver Creek** (*Km 1,934, or Mi 1,202, on Alaska Hwy. 867/862-7321*). **Carcross** (*Old Train Depot 867/821-4431*). **Dawson City** (*Front and King Sts. 867/993-5566*). **Haines Junction** (*Kluane National Park Visitor Centre 867/634-2345*). **Tourism Yukon** (*Box 2703, Whitehorse Y1A 2C6 867/667-5340 www.travelyukon.com*). **Watson Lake** (*Rtes. 1 and 4 867/536-7469*). **Whitehorse** (*100 Hanson St., at 2nd Ave. 867/667-3084*).

NORTHWEST TERRITORIES For general information and a copy of the Northwest Territories "Explorers' Guide," contact NWT Arctic Tourism. The Northern Frontier Visitors Centre has information about Yellowknife and its environs. Some smaller communities, notably Hay River, Fort Simpson, and Fort Smith, have their own local visitor centers. Highway stop-offs include the 60th Parallel Visitor Information Centre (at the Alberta/NWT border) and the Visitor Information Centre, 80 km (50 mi) farther north at Enterprise. For the Far Northwest, contact the Western Arctic Regional Visitors Centre.

Contacts NWT Arctic Tourism (✉ *4916 47th St., 3rd fl., Yellowknife X1A 1L7* 📫 *Box 610, Yellowknife X1A 2N5* ☎ *867/873-5007 or 800/661-0788* 🌐 *www.explorenwt.com*). **Northern Frontier Visitors Centre** (✉ *4807 49th St., Box 1107, Yellowknife X1A 3T5* ☎ *867/873-4262 or 877/881-4262* 🌐 *www.discovernorth.ca*). **Checkpoint Visitor Information Centre** (✉ *Intersection of NWT Hwys. 1 and 7* ☎ *867/695-2953*). **Fort Simpson Visitor Information Centre** (📫 *Box 438, Fort Simpson X0E 0N0* ☎ *867/695-3555 or 867/695-3182*). **Hay River Tourist Information Centre** (✉ *73 Woodland Dr., Hay River X0E 1G1* ☎ *867/874-6522 or 867/874-3180*). **Town of Fort Smith Visitor Information Centre** (✉ *108 King St., Box 147, Fort Smith X0E 0P0* ☎ *867/872-3065*). **Western Arctic Regional Visitors Centre** (📫 *Parks and Tourism, Bag Service No. 1, Inuvik X0E 0T0* ☎ *867/777-4727 or 867/777-7237* 🌐 *www.iti.gov.nt.ca*).

Canada Essentials

PLANNING TOOLS, EXPERT INSIGHT, GREAT CONTACTS

There are planners and there are those who, excuse the pun, fly by the seat of their pants. We happily place ourselves among the planners. Our writers and editors try to anticipate all the issues you may face before and during any journey, and then they do their research. This section is the product of their efforts. Use it to get excited about your trip to Canada, to inform your travel planning, or to guide you on the road should the seat of your pants start to feel threadbare.

STARTED

oud of our Web site: s a great place to begin any can Travel Wire for suggested es, travel deals, restaurant and openings, and other up-to-the-minute info. Check out Booking to research prices and book plane tickets, hotel rooms, rental cars, and vacation packages. Head to Talk for on-the-ground pointers from travelers who frequent our message boards. You can also link to loads of other travel-related resources.

RESOURCES

ONLINE TRAVEL TOOLS

Currency Conversion **Google** (www.google.com) does currency conversion. Just type in the amount you want to convert and an explanation of how you want it converted (e.g., "14 Swiss francs in dollars"), and then voilà. **Oanda.com** (www.oanda.com) also allows you to print out a handy table with the current day's conversion rates. **XE.com** (www.xe.com) is a good currency conversion Web site.

Safety **Transportation Security Administration** (TSA; www.tsa.gov).

Time Zones **Timeanddate.com** (www.timeanddate.com/worldclock) can help you figure out the correct time anywhere.

Weather **Accuweather.com** (www.accuweather.com) is an independent weather-forecasting service with good coverage of hurricanes. **Weather.com** (www.weather.com) is the Web site for the Weather Channel.

Other Resources **CIA World Factbook** (www.odci.gov/cia/publications/factbook/index.html) has profiles of every country in the world. It's a good source if you need some quick facts and figures.

VISITOR INFORMATION

Contacts **Canadian Tourism Commission** (613/946–1000 www.travelcanada.ca).

WORD OF MOUTH

After your trip, be sure to rate the places you visited and share your experiences and travel tips with us and other Fodorites in Travel Ratings and Talk on www.fodors.com.

THINGS TO CONSIDER

GOVERNMENT ADVISORIES

As different countries have different world views, look at travel advisories from a range of governments to get more of a sense of what's going on out there. And be sure to parse the language carefully. For example, a warning to "avoid all travel" carries more weight than one urging you to "avoid nonessential travel," and both are much stronger than a plea to "exercise caution." A U.S. government travel warning is more permanent (though not necessarily more serious) than a so-called public announcement, which carries an expiration date.

TIP→ **Consider registering online with the State Department (https://travelregistration.state.gov/ibrs), so the government will know to look for you should a crisis occur in the country you're visiting.**

The U.S. Department of State's Web site has more than just travel warnings and advisories. The consular information sheets issued for every country have general safety tips, entry requirements (though be sure to verify these with the country's embassy), and other useful details.

General Information & Warnings **Australian Department of Foreign Affairs & Trade** (www.smartraveller.gov.au). **Consular Affairs Bureau of Canada** (www.voyage.gc.ca). **U.K. Foreign & Commonwealth Office** (www.fco.gov.uk/travel). **U.S. Department of State** (www.travel.state.gov).

GEAR

The weather in many parts of Canada can change without warning, so it's always best to wear layers that you can peel off. If you plan on camping or hiking in the deep woods in summer, particularly in northern Canada, always carry insect repellent, especially in June, which is blackfly season.

SHIPPING LUGGAGE AHEAD

Imagine globe-trotting with only a carry-on in tow. Shipping your luggage in advance via an air-freight service is a great way to cut down on backaches, hassles, and stress—especially if your packing list includes strollers, car seats, etc. There are some things to be aware of, though.

First, research carry-on restrictions; if you absolutely need something that isn't practical to ship and isn't allowed in carry-ons, this strategy isn't for you. Second, plan to send your bags several days in advance to U.S. destinations and as much as two weeks in advance to some international destinations. Third, plan to spend some money: it will cost at least $100 to send a small piece of luggage, a golf bag, or a pair of skis to a domestic destination, much more to places overseas.

Some people use Federal Express to ship their bags, but this can cost even more than air-freight services. All these services insure your bag (for most, the limit is $1,000, but you should verify that amount); you can, however, purchase additional insurance for about $1 per $100 of value.

Contacts **Luggage Concierge** (☎800/288-9818 🌐www.luggageconcierge.com). **Luggage Express** (☎866/744-7224 🌐www.usxpluggageexpress.com). **Luggage Free** (☎800/361-6871 🌐www.luggagefree.com). **Sports Express** (☎800/357-4174 🌐www.sportsexpress.com) specializes in shipping golf clubs and other sports equipment. **Virtual Bellhop** (☎877/235-5467 🌐www.virtualbellhop.com).

PASSPORTS

Citizens and legal residents of the United States do not need a passport or a visa to enter Canada, but proof of citizenship (a birth certificate or valid passport) and some form of photo identification will be requested. Naturalized U.S. residents should carry their naturalization certificate. Permanent residents who are not citizens should carry their green cards. U.S. residents entering Canada from a third country must have a valid passport, naturalization certificate, or green card.

PASSPORTS

A passport verifies both your identity and nationality—a great reason to have one. Another reason is that you need a passport now more than ever. At this writing, U.S. citizens must have a passport when traveling by air between the United States and several destinations for which other forms of identification (e.g., a driver's license and a birth certificate) were once sufficient. These destinations include Mexico, Canada, Bermuda, and all countries in Central America and the Caribbean (except the territories of Puerto Rico and the U.S. Virgin Islands). Soon enough you'll need a passport when traveling between the United States and such destinations by land and sea, too.

U.S. passports are valid for 10 years. You must apply in person if you're getting a passport for the first time; if your previous passport was lost, stolen, or damaged; or if your previous passport has expired and was issued more than 15 years ago or when you were under 16. All children under 18 must appear in person to apply for or renew a passport. Both parents must accompany any child under 14 (or send a notarized statement with their permission) and provide proof of their relationship to the child.

■ TIP→ Before your trip, make two copies of your passport's data page (one for someone at home and another for you to carry separately). Or scan the page and e-mail it to someone at home and/or yourself.

There are 13 regional passport offices, as well as 7,000 passport acceptance facilities in post offices, public libraries, and other governmental offices. If you're renewing a passport, you can do so by mail. Forms are available at passport acceptance facilities and online.

The cost to apply for a new passport is $97 for adults, $82 for children under 16; renewals are $67. Allow six weeks for processing, both for first-time passports and renewals. For an expediting fee of $60 you can reduce this time to about two weeks. If your trip is less than two weeks away, you can get a passport even more rapidly by going to a passport office with the necessary documentation. Private expediters can get things done in as little as 48 hours, but charge hefty fees for their services.

U.S. Passport Information **U.S. Department of State** (☎877/487–2778 🌐http://travel.state.gov/passport).

U.S. Passport Expediters **A. Briggs Passport & Visa Expeditors** (☎800/806–0581 or 202/338–0111 🌐www.abriggs.com). **American Passport Express** (☎800/455–5166 🌐www.americanpassport.com). **Passport Express** (☎800/362–8196 🌐www.passportexpress.com). **Travel Document Systems** (☎800/874–5100 or 202/638–3800 🌐www.traveldocs.com). **Travel the World Visas** (☎866/886–8472 or 202/223–8822 🌐www.world-visa.com).

SHOTS & MEDICATIONS

There are no specific shots necessary for visitors to Canada, but the U.S. Centers for Disease Control and Prevention recommend that you be up-to-date with your measles/mumps/rubella and diphtheria/pertussis/tetanus vaccinations.

For more information see Health under On the Ground in Canada, below.

TIP→ If you travel a lot internationally—particularly to developing nations—refer to the CDC's *Health Information for International Travel* (aka Traveler's Health Yellow Book). Info from it is posted on the CDC Web site (🌐wwwn.cdc.gov/travel/contentYellowBook.aspx), or you can buy a copy from your local bookstore for $24.95.

Health Warnings **National Centers for Disease Control & Prevention** (CDC ☎877/394–8747 international travelers' health line 🌐www.cdc.gov/travel). **World Health Organization** (WHO 🌐www.who.int).

TRIP INSURANCE

What kind of coverage do you honestly need? Do you even need trip insurance at all? Take a deep breath and read on.

We believe that comprehensive trip insurance is especially valuable if you're booking a very expensive or complicated trip (particularly to an isolated region) or if you're booking far in advance. Who knows what could happen six months down the road? But whether or not you get insurance has more to do with how comfortable you are assuming all that risk yourself.

Comprehensive travel policies typically cover trip-cancellation and interruption, letting you cancel or cut your trip short because of a personal emergency, illness, or, in some cases, acts of terrorism in your destination. Such policies also cover evacuation and medical care. Some also cover you for trip delays because of bad weather or mechanical problems as well as for lost or delayed baggage. Another type of coverage to look for is financial default—that is, when your trip is disrupted because a tour operator, airline, or cruise line goes out of business. Generally you must buy this when you book your trip or shortly thereafter, and it's only available to you if your operator isn't on a list of excluded companies.

If you're going abroad, consider buying medical-only coverage at the very least. Neither Medicare nor some private insurers cover medical expenses anywhere outside of the United States (including time aboard a cruise ship, even if it leaves from a U.S. port). Medical-only policies

Trip Insurance Resources		
INSURANCE COMPARISON SITES		
Insure My Trip.com	800/487-4722	www.insuremytrip.com
Square Mouth.com	800/240-0369	www.quotetravelinsurance.com
COMPREHENSIVE TRAVEL INSURERS		
Access America	866/807-3982	www.accessamerica.com
CSA Travel Protection	800/873-9855	www.csatravelprotection.com
HTH Worldwide	610/254-8700 or 888/243-2358	www.hthworldwide.com
Travelex Insurance	888/457-4602	www.travelex-insurance.com
Travel Guard International	715/345-0505 or 800/826-4919	www.travelguard.com
Travel Insured International	800/243-3174	www.travelinsured.com
MEDICAL-ONLY INSURERS		
International Medical Group	800/628-4664	www.imglobal.com
International SOS	215/942-8000 or 713/521-7611	www.internationalsos.com
Wallach & Company	800/237-6615 or 504/687-3166	www.wallach.com

typically reimburse you for medical care (excluding that related to pre-existing conditions) and hospitalization abroad, and provide for evacuation. You still have to pay the bills and await reimbursement from the insurer, though.

Expect comprehensive travel insurance policies to cost about 4% to 7% or 8% of the total price of your trip (it's more like 8%–12% if you're over age 70). A medical-only policy may or may not be cheaper than a comprehensive policy. Always read the fine print of your policy to make sure that you are covered for the risks that are of most concern to you. Compare several policies to make sure you're getting the best price and range of coverage available.

BOOKING YOUR TRIP

Unless your cousin is a travel agent, you're probably among the millions of people who make most of their travel arrangements online.

But have you ever wondered just what the differences are between an online travel agent (a Web site through which you make reservations instead of going directly to the airline, hotel, or car-rental company), a discounter (a firm that does a high volume of business with a hotel chain or airline and accordingly gets good prices), a wholesaler (one that makes cheap reservations in bulk and then resells them to people like you), and an aggregator (one that compares all the offerings so you don't have to)?

Is it truly better to book directly on an airline or hotel Web site? And when does a real live travel agent come in handy?

ONLINE

You really have to shop around. A travel wholesaler such as HotelClub.net or Hotels.com can be a source of good rates, as can discounters such as Hotwire or Priceline, particularly if you can bid for your hotel room or airfare. Indeed, such sites sometimes have deals that are unavailable elsewhere. They do, however, tend to work only with hotel chains (which makes them just plain useless for getting hotel reservations outside of major cities) or big airlines (so that often leaves out upstarts like jetBlue and some foreign carriers like Air India).

Also, with discounters and wholesalers you must generally prepay, and everything is nonrefundable. And before you fork over the dough, be sure to check the terms and conditions, so you know what a given company will do for you if there's a problem and what you'll have to deal with on your own.

■TIP→To be absolutely sure everything was processed correctly, confirm reservations made through online travel agents, discounters, and wholesalers directly with your hotel before leaving home.

Booking engines like Expedia, Travelocity, and Orbitz are actually travel agents, albeit high-volume, online ones. And airline travel packagers like American Airlines Vacations and Virgin Vacations—well, they're travel agents, too. But they may still not work with all the world's hotels.

An aggregator site will search many sites and pull the best prices for airfares, hotels, and rental cars from them. Most aggregators compare the major travel-booking sites such as Expedia, Travelocity, and Orbitz; some also look at airline Web sites, though rarely the sites of smaller budget airlines. Some aggregators also compare other travel products, including complex packages—a good thing, as you can sometimes get the best overall deal by booking an air-and-hotel package.

WITH A TRAVEL AGENT

If you use an agent—brick-and-mortar or virtual—you'll pay a fee for the service. And know that the service you get from some online agents isn't comprehensive. For example Expedia and Travelocity don't search for prices on budget airlines like jetBlue, Southwest, or small foreign carriers. That said, some agents (online or not) *do* have access to fares that are difficult to find otherwise, and the savings can more than make up for any surcharge.

A knowledgeable brick-and-mortar travel agent can be a godsend if you're booking a cruise, a package trip that's not available to you directly, an air pass, or a complicated itinerary including several overseas flights. What's more, travel agents that specialize in a destination may have exclusive access to certain deals and insider information on things such as charter flights. Agents who specialize in types of travelers (senior citizens, gays and lesbians, naturists) or types of trips (cruises, luxury travel, safaris) can also be invaluable.

■ TIP➔Remember that Expedia, Travelocity, and Orbitz are travel agents, not just booking engines. To resolve any problems with a reservation made through these companies, contact them first.

A top-notch agent planning your trip to Russia will make sure you get the correct visa application and complete it on time; the one booking your cruise may get you a cabin upgrade or arrange to have bottle of champagne chilling in your cabin when you embark. And complain about the surcharges all you like, but when things don't work out the way you'd hoped, it's nice to have an agent to put things right.

Agent Resources **American Society of Travel Agents** (☎703/739–2782 ⊕www.travelsense.org).

ACCOMMODATIONS

Canada doesn't have a national government rating system for hotels, but many provinces do rate their accommodations. For example, in British Columbia and Alberta, a blue Approved Accommodation decal on the window or door of a hotel or motel indicates that it has met provincial hotel-association standards for courtesy, comfort, and cleanliness. Ontario's voluntary rating system includes about 1,000 Ontario properties. Québec's tourism ministry rates the province's hotels; the stars are more a reflection of the number of facilities than of the hotel's overall atmosphere.

Expect accommodations to cost more in summer than in the off-season (except for places such as ski resorts, where winter is high season). When making reservations, ask about special deals and packages. Big city hotels that cater to business travelers often offer weekend packages, and many city hotels discount prices by as much as 50% in winter. If you're planning to visit a major city or resort area in high season, book well in advance. Also be aware of any special events or festivals that may coincide with your visit and fill every room for miles around.

The lodgings we list are the cream of the crop in each price category. We always list the facilities that are available—but we don't specify whether they cost extra; when pricing accommodations, always ask what's included and what costs extra. Properties indicated by ✕🏨 are lodging establishments whose restaurant warrants a special trip. *For price charts, see the beginning of individual chapters.*

CATEGORY	COST
$$$$	over C$250
$$$	C$176–C$250
$$	C$126–C$175
$	C$75–C$125
¢	under C$75

All prices are for a standard double room in high season

Most hotels and other lodgings require you to give your credit-card details before they will confirm your reservation. If you don't feel comfortable e-mailing this information, ask if you can fax it (some places even prefer faxes). However you book, get confirmation in writing and have a copy of it handy when you check in.

Be sure you understand the hotel's cancellation policy. Some places allow you to cancel without any kind of penalty—even if you prepaid to secure a discounted rate—if you cancel at least 24 hours in advance. Others require you to cancel a week in advance or penalize you the cost of one night. Small inns and B&Bs are most likely to require you to cancel far in advance. Most hotels allow children

Online Booking Resources

AGGREGATORS		
Kayak	www.kayak.com	also looks at cruises and vacation packages.
Mobissimo	www.mobissimo.com	also looks at car rental rates and activities.
Qixo	www.qixo.com	also compares cruises, vacation packages, and even travel insurance.
Sidestep	www.sidestep.com	also compares vacation packages and lists travel deals.
Travelgrove	www.travelgrove.com	also compares cruises and packages.
BOOKING ENGINES		
Cheap Tickets	www.cheaptickets.com	a discounter.
Expedia	www.expedia.com	a large online agency that charges a booking fee for airline tickets.
Hotwire	www.hotwire.com	a discounter.
lastminute.com	www.lastminute.com	specializes in last-minute travel; the main site is for the U.K., but it has a link to a U.S. site.
Luxury Link	www.luxurylink.com	has auctions (surprisingly good deals) as well as offers on the high-end side of travel.
Onetravel.com	www.onetravel.com	a discounter for hotels, car rentals, airfares, and packages.
Orbitz	www.orbitz.com	charges a booking fee for airline tickets, but gives a clear breakdown of fees and taxes before you book.
Priceline.com	www.priceline.com	a discounter that also allows bidding.
Travel.com	www.travel.com	allows you to compare its rates with those of other booking engines.
Travelocity	www.travelocity.com	charges a booking fee for airline tickets, but promises good problem resolution.
ONLINE ACCOMMODATIONS		
Hotelbook.com	www.hotelbook.com	focuses on independent hotels worldwide.
Hotel Club	www.hotelclub.net	good for major cities worldwide.
Hotels.com	www.hotels.com	a big Expedia-owned wholesaler that offers rooms in hotels all over the world.
Quikbook	www.quikbook.com	offers "pay when you stay" reservations that let you settle your bill at checkout, not when you book.
OTHER RESOURCES		
Bidding For Travel	www.biddingfortravel.com	a good place to figure out what you can get and for how much before you start bidding on, say, Priceline.

under a certain age to stay in their parents' room at no extra charge, but others charge for them as extra adults; find out the cutoff age for discounts.

■ TIP→ Assume that hotels operate on the European Plan (EP, no meals) unless we specify that they use the Breakfast Plan (BP, with full breakfast), Continental Plan (CP, Continental breakfast), Full American Plan (FAP, all meals), Modified American Plan (MAP, breakfast and dinner) or are all-inclusive (AI, all meals and most activities).

APARTMENT & HOUSE RENTALS

You can find apartments and houses to rent in all Canadian cities. Mont Tremblant, Muskoka (Ontario), Whistler, and other resort areas usually have agencies or a tourism office handling a variety of rental properties.

CONTACTS

Interhome (☎954/791–8282 or 800/882–6864 ⊕www.interhome.us). **Vacation Home Rentals Worldwide** (☎201/767–9393 or 800/633–3284 ⊕www.vhrww.com). **Villas International** (☎415/499–9490 or 800/221–2260 ⊕www.villasintl.com).

ONLINE BOOKING RESOURCES

International Agents **CottageLINK** (☎519/746–1959 or 800/734–3992 ⊕www.cottagelink.com). **Mont Tremblant Resort** (☎514/876–7273 or 888/738–1777 ⊕www.tremblant.ca). **Whistler Tourism** (☎604/932–3928 or 800/9447–8537 ⊕www.tourism-whistler.com).

BED & BREAKFASTS

B&Bs can be found in both the country and the cities. For assistance in booking a room, contact the appropriate provincial tourist board, which either has a listing of B&Bs or can refer you to an association that can help you secure reservations. Be sure to check out the B&B's Web site, which may have useful information, although you should also find out how up-to-date it is. Room quality varies from house to house as well, so you may want to ask to see a room before making a choice if possible.

WORD OF MOUTH

Did the resort look as good in real life as it did in the photos? Did you sleep like a baby, or were the walls paper thin? Did you get your money's worth? Rate hotels and write your own reviews in Travel Ratings or start a discussion about your favorite places in Travel Talk on www.fodors.com. Your comments might even appear in our books. Yes, you, too, can be a correspondent!

Reservation Services **Bed & Breakfast.com** (☎512/322–2710 or 800/462–2632 ⊕www.bedandbreakfast.com) also sends out an online newsletter. **Bed & Breakfast Inns Online** (☎310/280–4363 or 800/215–7365 ⊕www.bbonline.com). **BnB Finder.com** (☎212/432–7693 or 888/547–8226 ⊕www.bnbfinder.com).

HOME EXCHANGES

With a direct home exchange you stay in someone else's home while they stay in yours. Some outfits also deal with vacation homes, so you're not actually staying in someone's full-time residence, just their vacant weekend place.

Exchange Clubs **Home Exchange.com** (☎800/877–8723 ⊕www.homeexchange.com); $99.95 for a 1-year online listing. **HomeLink International** (☎800/638–3841 ⊕www.homelink.org); $90 yearly for Web-only membership; $140 includes Web access and two catalogs. **Intervac U.S.** (☎800/756–4663 ⊕www.intervacus.com); $95 for Web-only membership; $150 includes Web access and a catalog.

HOSTELS

Hostels offer bare-bones lodging at low, low prices—often in shared dorm rooms with shared baths—to people of all ages, though the primary market is young travelers, especially students. Most hostels serve breakfast; dinner and/or shared cooking facilities may also be available. In some hostels you aren't allowed to be in your room during the day, and there may be a curfew at night. Nevertheless, hostels provide a sense of community, with public rooms where travelers often gather to share stories. Many hostels are affiliated with Hostelling International (HI), an umbrella group of hostel associations with some 4,500 member properties in more than 70 countries. Other hostels are completely independent and may be nothing more than a really cheap hotel.

Membership in any HI association, open to travelers of all ages, allows you to stay in HI-affiliated hostels at member rates. One-year membership is about $28 for adults; hostels charge about $10–$30 per night. Members have priority if the hostel is full; they're also eligible for discounts around the world, even on rail and bus travel in some countries.

Information **Hostelling International—USA** (☎301/495-1240 🌐www.hiusa.org).

AIRLINE TICKETS

Most domestic airline tickets are electronic; international tickets may be either electronic or paper. With an e-ticket the only thing you receive is an e-mailed receipt citing your itinerary and reservation and ticket numbers.

The greatest advantage of an e-ticket is that if you lose your receipt, you can simply print out another copy or ask the airline to do it for you at check-in. You usually pay a surcharge (up to $50) to get a paper ticket, if you can get one at all.

The sole advantage of a paper ticket is that it may be easier to endorse over to another airline if your flight is canceled and the airline with which you booked can't accommodate you on another flight.

TIP→ Discount air passes that let you travel economically in a country or region must often be purchased before you leave home. In some cases you can only get them through a travel agent.

The least expensive airfares to Canada are often priced for round-trip travel and must usually be purchased in advance. Airlines generally allow you to change your return date for a fee; most low-fare tickets, however, are nonrefundable.

Air Pass Info **Air Canada Flight Passes** (☎800/247-2262 🌐www.aircanada.com).

CHARTER FLIGHTS

Charter companies rent aircraft and offer regularly scheduled flights (usually nonstops). Charter flights are generally cheaper than flights on regular airlines, and they often leave from and travel to a wider variety of airports. For example, you could have a nonstop flight from Columbus, Ohio, to Punta Cana, Dominican Republic, or from Chicago to Dubrovnik, Croatia.

You don't, however, have the same protections as with regular airlines. If a charter can't take off for mechanical or other reasons, there usually isn't another plane to take its place. If not enough seats are sold, the flight may be canceled. And if a company goes out of business, you're out of luck (unless, of course, you have insurance with financial default coverage; ⇨*Trip Insurance under Things to Consider in Getting Started, above*).

RENTAL CARS

When you reserve a car, ask about cancellation penalties, taxes, drop-off charges (if you're planning to pick up the car in one city and leave it in another), and surcharges (for being under or over a certain age, for additional drivers, or for driving across state or country borders or beyond a specific distance from your point of rental). All these things can add substantially to your costs. Request car seats and extras such as GPS when you book.

Rates are sometimes—but not always—better if you book in advance or reserve through a rental agency's Web site. There are other reasons to book ahead, though:

Car Rental Resources

AUTOMOBILE ASSOCIATIONS		
American Automobile Association	315/797-5000	www.aaa.com; most contact with the organization is through state and regional members.
National Automobile Club	650/294-7000	www.thenac.com; membership open to CA residents only.
MAJOR AGENCIES		
Alamo	800/462-5266	www.alamo.com
Avis	800/230-4898 or 0870/606-0100 in U.K.	www.avis.com
Budget	800/527-0700	www.budget.com
Hertz	800/654-3131 or 0870/844-8844 in U.K.	www.hertz.com
National Car Rental	800/227-7368	www.nationalcar.com

for popular destinations, during busy times of the year, or to ensure that you get certain types of cars (vans, SUVs, exotic sports cars).

■TIP→ Make sure that a confirmed reservation guarantees you a car. Agencies sometimes overbook, particularly for busy weekends and holiday periods.

Rates in Montréal begin at C$36 a day and C$312 a week for an economy car with air-conditioning and unlimited free kilometers. Rates begin at C$32 a day and C$289 a week in Toronto, and C$90 a day and C$267 a week in Vancouver. These prices include taxes.

In Canada a U.S. driver's license is acceptable. Some provinces have age restrictions on younger drivers. In Ontario, for example, drivers must be 21; in Québec, drivers under 25 often have to pay a surcharge of C$5 a day. Rental-car companies have not set an upper age limit. There are sometimes other restrictions; for example, some rental agencies in Newfoundland prohibit taking their cars over to Labrador.

Your driver's license may not be recognized outside your home country. You may not be able to rent a car without an International Driving Permit (IDP), which can be used only in conjunction with a valid driver's license and which translates your license into 10 languages. Check the AAA Web site for more info as well as for IDPs ($15) themselves.

CAR-RENTAL INSURANCE

Everyone who rents a car wonders whether the insurance that the rental companies offer is worth the expense. No one—including us—has a simple answer. It all depends on how much regular insurance you have, how comfortable you are with risk, and whether or not money is an issue.

If you own a car, your personal auto insurance may cover a rental to some degree, though not all policies protect you abroad; always read your policy's fine print. If you don't have auto insurance, then seriously consider buying the collision- or loss-damage waiver (CDW or LDW) from the car-rental company, which eliminates your liability for damage to the car. Some credit cards offer CDW coverage, but it's usually supplemental to your own insurance and rarely covers SUVs, minivans, luxury models, and the like. If your coverage is secondary, you may still be liable for loss-of-use costs from the car-rental company. But no credit-card insurance is valid unless you use that card for *all* transactions, from reserving to paying the final bill. All companies exclude car rental in some countries, so be sure to find out about the destination to which you are traveling.

■ TIP→ Diners Club offers primary CDW coverage on all rentals reserved and paid for with the card. This means that Diners Club's company—not your own car insurance—pays in case of an accident. It *doesn't* mean your car-insurance company won't raise your rates once it discovers you had an accident.

Some rental agencies require you to purchase CDW coverage; many will even include it in quoted rates. All will strongly encourage you to buy CDW—possibly implying that it's required—so be sure to ask about such things before renting. In most cases it's cheaper to add a supplemental CDW plan to your comprehensive travel-insurance policy *(⇨ Trip Insurance under Things to Consider in Getting Started, above)* than to purchase it from a rental company. That said, you don't want to pay for a supplement if you're required to buy insurance from the rental company.

Drivers must carry owner registration and proof of insurance coverage, which is compulsory in Canada. The Canadian Non-Resident Inter-Provincial Motor Vehicle Liability Insurance Card, available from any U.S. insurance company, is accepted as evidence of financial responsibility in Canada. The minimum liability coverage in Canada is C$200,000, except in Québec, where the minimum is C$50,000. If you're driving a car that is not registered in your name, carry a letter from the owner that authorizes your use of the vehicle.

■ TIP→ You can decline the insurance from the rental company and purchase it through a third-party provider such as Travel Guard (www.travelguard.com)—$9 per day for $35,000 of coverage. That's sometimes just under half the price of the CDW offered by some car-rental companies.

Insurance Information **Insurance Bureau of Canada** (☎416/362–2031, 800/387–2880 in Canada 🌐www.ibc.ca).

VACATION PACKAGES

Packages *are not* guided excursions. Packages combine airfare, accommodations, and perhaps a rental car or other extras (theater tickets, guided excursions, boat trips, reserved entry to popular museums, transit passes), but they let you do your own thing. During busy periods packages may be your only option, as flights and rooms may be sold out otherwise.

Packages will definitely save you time. They can also save you money, particularly in peak seasons, but—and this is a really big "but"—you should price each part of the package separately to be sure. And be aware that prices advertised on Web sites and in newspapers rarely include service charges or taxes, which can up your costs by hundreds of dollars.

■ TIP→ Some packages and cruises are sold only through travel agents. Don't always assume that you can get the best deal by booking everything yourself.

Each year consumers are stranded or lose their money when packagers—even large ones with excellent reputations—go out of business. How can you protect yourself?

First, always pay with a credit card; if you have a problem, your credit-card company may help you resolve it. Second, buy trip insurance that covers default. Third, choose a company that belongs to the United States Tour Operators Association, whose members must set aside funds to cover defaults. Finally, choose a company that also participates in the Tour Operator Program of the American Society of Travel Agents (ASTA), which will act as mediator in any disputes.

You can also check on the tour operator's reputation among travelers by posting an inquiry on one of the Fodors.com forums.

Organizations **American Society of Travel Agents** (ASTA ☎703/739–2782 or 800/965–2782 🌐www.astanet.com). **United States Tour Operators Association** (USTOA ☎212/599–6599 🌐www.ustoa.com).

■ TIP→ Local tourism boards can provide information about lesser-known and small-niche operators that sell packages to only a few destinations.

GUIDED TOURS

Guided tours are a good option when you don't want to do it all yourself. You travel along with a group (sometimes large, sometimes small), stay in prebooked hotels, eat with your fellow travelers (the cost of meals sometimes included in the price of your tour, sometimes not), and follow a schedule.

But not all guided tours are an if-it's-Tuesday-this-must-be-Belgium experience. A knowledgeable guide can take you places that you might never discover on your own, and you may be pushed to see more than you would have otherwise. Tours aren't for everyone, but they can be just the thing for trips to places where making travel arrangements is difficult or time-consuming (particularly when you don't speak the language).

Whenever you book a guided tour, find out what's included and what isn't. A "land-only" tour includes all your travel (by bus, in most cases) in the destination, but not necessarily your flights to and from or even within it. Also, in most cases prices in tour brochures don't include fees and taxes. And remember that you'll be expected to tip your guide (in cash) at the end of the tour.

SPECIAL-INTEREST TOURS

The companies listed below offer multi-day tours in Canada. Additional local or regionally based companies that have different-length trips with these themes are listed in each chapter, either with information about the town or in the Essentials section that concludes the chapter.

ADVENTURE

Contacts **Ecosummer Expeditions** (☎250/674–0102 or 800/465–8884 🌐www.ecosummer.com). **The Great Canadian Adventure Company** (☎708/414–1676 or 888/285–1676 🌐www.adventures.ca). **Mountain Travel Sobek** (☎510/594–6000 or 888/687–6235 🌐www.mtsobek.com). **Nahanni River Adventures** (☎867/668–3180 or 800/297–6927 🌐www.nahanni.com). **O.A.R.S** (☎209/736–4677 or 800/346–6277 🌐www.oars.com). **Trek America** (☎973/983–1144 or 800/221–0596 🌐www.trekamerica.com).

BIKING

■ TIP→ Most airlines accommodate bikes as luggage, provided they're dismantled and boxed.

Contacts **Backroads** (☎510/527–1555 or 800/462–2848 🌐www.backroads.com). **Bicycle Adventures** (☎360/786–0989 or 800/443–6060 🌐www.bicycleadventures.com). **Bike Rider Tours** (☎617/723–2354 or 800/473–7040 🌐www.bikeriderstours.com). **Butterfield & Robinson** (☎416/864–1354 or 866/551–9090 🌐www.butterfield.com). **Easy Rider Tours** (☎978/463–6955 or 800/488–8332 🌐www.easyridertours.com). **Rocky Mountain Worldwide Cycle Tours** (☎604/898–8488 or 800/661–2453 🌐www.rockymountaincycle.com). **Timberline Adventures** (☎303/368–4481 or 800/417–2453 🌐www.timbertours.com). **Vermont Bicycle Touring** (☎802/453–4811 or 800/245–3868 🌐www.vbt.com). **Voyages du Tour de l'Île** (☎514/521–8356 or 800/567–8356 🌐www.velo.qc.ca).

DUDE RANCHES

Contacts **The Great Canadian Adventure Company** (☎780/414–1676 or 888/285–1676 🌐www.adventures.ca).

FISHING

Contacts **Fishing International** (☎707/542–4242 or 800/950–4242 🌐www.fishinginternational.com). **Rod & Reel Adventures** (☎541/349–0777 or 800/356–6982 🌐www.rodreeladventures.com).

PHOTOGRAPHY

Contacts **Newfoundland PhotoTours** (☎902/425–6070 or 416/807–7575 🌐www.nfldphototours.com).

SKIING

Contacts **Canadian Mountain Holidays** (☎403/762–7100 or 800/661–0252 🌐www.cmhhike.com). **Selkirk Tangiers Helicopter Skiing** (☎250/837–5378 or 800/663–7080 🌐www.selkirk-tangiers.com). **Skican** (☎416/488–1169, 888/475–4226, or 800/363–3009 🌐www.skican.com). **Whistler Heli-Skiing** (☎604/932–4105 or 888/435–4754 🌐www.whistlerheliskiing.com).

WALKING–HIKING

Walking is a popular pastime for Candians of all ages. Walking the World specializes in tours for people 50 and older.

Contacts **Backroads** (☎510/527–1555 or 800/462–2848 🌐www.backroads.com). **Butterfield & Robinson** (☎416/864–1354 or 866/551–9090 🌐www.butterfield.com). **Canadian Mountain Holidays** (☎403/762–7100 or 800/661–0252 🌐www.cmhhike.com). **Country Walkers** (☎802/244–1387 or 800/464–9255 🌐www.countrywalkers.com). **New England Hiking Holidays** (☎603/356–9696 or 800/869–0949 🌐www.nehikingholidays.com). **Timberline Adventures** (☎303/368–4418 or 800/417–2453 🌐www.timbertours.com). **Walking the World** (☎970/498–0500 or 800/340–9255 🌐www.walkingtheworld.com).

TRANSPORTATION

BY AIR

Flying time to Montréal is 1½ hours from New York, 2 hours from Chicago, 6 hours from Los Angeles, and 6½ hours from London. Toronto is 1½ hours from New York and Chicago, 4½ hours from Los Angeles, and 6½ hours from London. Vancouver is 6½ hours from Montréal, 4 hours from Chicago, and 2½ hours from Los Angeles.

With airport security increasing worldwide, carrying a valid passport is the easiest way to ensure you have the correct documentation when dealing with airline and customs officials.

U.S. Customs and Immigration maintains offices at the airports in Calgary, Edmonton, Montréal, Ottawa, Toronto, Vancouver, and Winnipeg; U.S.-bound passengers should arrive early enough to clear customs before their flight.

Security measures at Canadian airports are similar to those in the United States. Be sure you're not carrying anything that could be construed as a weapon: a letter opener, a Swiss Army knife, or a toy weapon, for example. Arriving passengers from overseas flights might find a beagle in a green coat sniffing their luggage; he's looking for forbidden agricultural and food products.

TIP→ Ask the local tourist board about hotel and local transportation packages that include tickets to major museum exhibits or other special events.

Airlines & Airports **Airline and Airport Links.com** (www.airlineandairportlinks.com) has links to many of the world's airlines and airports.

Airline Security Issues **Transportation Security Administration** (www.tsa.gov) has answers for almost every question that might come up.

AIRPORTS

Canada's major airports are Montréal's Pierre Elliott Trudeau International Airport (also known by its previous name, Dorval Airport; airport code YUL), Toronto's Lester B. Pearson International Airport (YYZ), and Vancouver International Airport (YVR). *For airports in other provinces and territories, see the Essentials section in each chapter.*

TIP→ Long layovers don't have to be only about sitting around or shopping. These days they can be about burning off vacation calories. Check out www.airportgyms.com for lists of health clubs that are in or near many U.S. and Canadian airports.

Airport Information **Lester B. Pearson International Airport** (866/207–1690 www.gtaa.com). **Pierre Elliott Trudeau International Airport** (800/465–1213 www.admtl.com). **Vancouver International Airport** (604/207–7077 www.yvr.ca).

GROUND TRANSPORTATION

The most reasonably priced option to and from the airport is a shuttle bus. At Toronto's Pearson International, the Toronto Airport Express to downtown hotels and the bus terminal departs every 20 minutes in rush hour and 30 minutes off-peak and costs C$16.95 one-way, C$29.95 round-trip. The trip takes 1½ to 2 hours, depending on traffic. Taxis take about 30 minutes and cost C$40 to C$50.

At Pierre Trudeau International Airport in Montréal, L'Aérobus departs for downtown destinations every 25 minutes. The 40-minute cost is C$14 one-way, C$24 round-trip. The fixed rate for a taxi is $35.

At Vancouver International Airport, the Airporter departs every 20 minutes, takes about 45 minutes, and costs C$13.50 one-way, C$21 round-trip. Getting to

Vancouver by taxi costs C$23 and takes approximately 30 minutes.

Contacts Toronto Airport Express (☎905/564-3232 or 800/387-6787 🌐www.torontoairportexpress.com). **L'Aérobus** (☎514/394-7377 or 800/465-1213 🌐www.laerobus.qc.ca). **Airporter** (☎604/946-8866 or 800/668-3141 🌐www.yvrairporter.com).

FLIGHTS

From the U.S. airlines, Continental flies to Calgary, Halifax, Moncton, Montréal, Ottawa, Québec City, St. John's.

Toronto, and Vancouver. Delta serves Calgary, Charlottetown, Fredericton, Halifax, Montréal, Ottawa, Québec City, Toronto, Vancouver, and Victoria. Northwest flies to Calgary, Edmonton, Kitchener, London, Montréal, Ottawa, Québec City, Regina, Saskatoon, Thunder Bay, Toronto, Vancouver, and Winnipeg. US Airways flies to Calgary, Edmonton, Montréal, Ottawa, Toronto, and Vancouver. United serves Calgary, Edmonton, Halifax, Ottawa, Toronto, Vancouver, and Winnipeg, and also has a code-sharing agreement with Air Canada that enables U.S. passengers to reach many more Canadian destinations on a United ticket.

Among smaller carriers, Alaska Airlines flies to Calgary and Vancouver from many western U.S. cities, and Horizon Air serves Calgary, Edmonton, Kelowna, Kamloops, Vancouver, and Victoria.

Within Canada, regularly scheduled flights to every major city and to most smaller cities are available on Air Canada and its subsidiaries. Air Canada has a no-frills carrier called Jazz that flies to 80 destinations across Canada and the U.S. WestJet serves many destinations throughout Canada. Smaller regional airlines—Air North, Canadian North, and First Air—service communities in Alberta, the Yukon, Nunavut, and the Northwest Territories. Air Labrador offers service in the Atlantic region. Bearskin Airlines offers flights to communities in Northern Ontario, Manitoba, Ottawa, and Kitchener. Porter Airlines, a carrier known for its service, flies between Toronto, Ottawa, Montréal, and Halifax.

Airline Contacts Air Canada (☎888/712-7786 🌐www.aircanada.ca). **Alaska Airlines** (☎800/252-7522 or 206/433-3100 🌐www.alaskaair.com). **American Airlines** (☎800/433-7300 🌐www.aa.com). **Continental Airlines** (☎800/523—3273 for U.S. and Mexico reservations, 800/231-0856 for international reservations 🌐www.continental.com). **Delta Airlines** (☎800/221-1212 for U.S. reservations, 800/241-4141 for international reservations 🌐www.delta.com). **Horizon Air** (☎800/547-9308 🌐www.horizonair.com). **Northwest Airlines** (☎800/225-2525 🌐www.nwa.com). **United Airlines** (☎800/864-8331 for U.S. reservations, 800/538-2929 for international reservations 🌐www.united.com). **US Airways** (☎800/428-4322 for U.S. and Canada reservations, 800/622-1015 for international reservations 🌐www.usairways.com).

Within Canada Air Canada (☎888/247-2262 🌐www.aircanada.ca). **Air Labrador** (☎800/563-3042 🌐www.airlabrador.com). **Air North** (☎800/661-0407 🌐www.flyairnorth.com). **Air Transat** (☎866/847-1112 🌐www.airtransat.com). **Bearskin Airlines** (☎807/475-0006 🌐www.bearskinairlines.com). **Canadian North** (☎800/661-1505 🌐www.canadiannorth.com). **First Air** (☎800/267-1247 🌐www.firstair.ca). **Porter Airlines** (☎888/619-8622 🌐www.flyporter.com). **WestJet Airlines** (☎800/538-5696 🌐www.westjet.com).

BY BOAT

Car ferries provide essential transportation on both the eastern and western coasts of Canada and in Ontario and Québec. Ferries also operate between the U.S. state of Washington and British Columbia's Vancouver Island, and between the state of Maine and the province of Nova Scotia.

For additional information about regional ferry service, see individual chapters.

Information BC Ferries (☎888/223-3779 ⊕www.bcferries.com). **Marine Atlantic** (☎800/341-7981 ⊕www.marine-atlantic.ca). **Northumberland and Bay Ferries Ltd.** (☎888/249-7245 ⊕www.nfl-bay.com).

BY BUS

The bus is an essential form of transportation in Canada, especially if you want to visit out-of-the-way towns that do not have airports or train stations. Except in winter, when snow or ice storms can delay travels, buses are dependable. There's no smoking on buses, a policy that's enforced. Greyhound Lines and Voyageur provide interprovincial service. Acadian Lines operates bus service throughout Atlantic Canada.

The major bus lines have only one class of service—economy—on intercity routes; private or charter carriers may offer additional levels of service.

Greyhound's Coach Pass provides unlimited bus travel for 7, 15, 30, or 60 days; a 7-day pass is C$352, though you can sometimes find special deals. The company also has a Companion Fare pass: buy a regular-fare ticket and get up to 75% off your companion's ticket. Children under 4 ride free, but they can only occupy a seat if one is available; otherwise, they pay half-price, the same as kids ages 5 to 11. Passengers over 60 receive a 10% discount. You can purchase the passes at any Greyhound terminal in Canada or through Greyhound's Web site prior to your arrival.

Bus terminals in major cities and even in many smaller ones are usually efficient operations with service all week and plenty of agents on hand to handle ticket sales. In villages and some smaller towns the bus station is simply a counter in a local convenience store, gas station, or snack bar. Getting information on schedules beyond the local ones is sometimes difficult in these places. In rural Québec it's advisable to bring along a French–English dictionary, although most merchants and clerks can handle a simple ticket sale in English.

In major bus terminals, most bus lines accept at least some of the major credit cards. Some smaller lines require cash or take only Visa or MasterCard. All accept traveler's checks in U.S. or Canadian currency, with suitable identification, but it's advisable to exchange foreign currency (including U.S. currency) at a bank or exchange office. To buy a ticket in really small centers, it's best to use cash.

Most smaller bus lines do not accept reservations. You should plan on picking up your tickets at least 45 minutes before the bus's scheduled departure time.

Bus Information Acadian Lines (☎800/567-5151 ⊕www.acadianbus.com). **Greyhound Lines** (☎800/661-8747 in Canada, 800/231-2222 in U.S. ⊕www.greyhound.ca). **Voyageur** (☎514/842-2281 ⊕www.greyhound.ca).

BY CAR

International driving permits (IDPs) are not required by American citizens holding valid licenses from their state of residence; visitors from other countries should check with their local automobile association for specific information. IDPs are available from the American and Canadian automobile associations and, in the United Kingdom, from the Automobile Association and Royal Automobile Club. These international permits, valid only in conjunction with your regular driver's license, are universally recognized; having one may save you a problem with local authorities.

Canada's highway system is excellent. It includes the Trans-Canada Highway, which uses several numbers and is the longest highway in the world—running about 8,000 km (5,000 mi) from Victoria, British Columbia, to St. John's, Newfoundland, using ferries to bridge coastal waters at each end. The second-longest Canadian highway, the Yellowhead Highway (Highway 16), runs from the Pacific coast and over the Rockies to the prairies. North of the population centers, roads become fewer and less developed.

Note that distances are always shown in kilometers, and that road signs in the province of Québec are only posted in French (though they're designed for everyone to understand them). Keep in mind the following terms: *gauche* (left), *droit* (right), *ouest* (west), *est* (east), *nord* (north), *sud* (south).

GASOLINE

In Canada, gasoline is always sold in liters (a gallon contains 3.8 liters). Gas prices vary by province and city; at this writing, the per-liter price of gasoline was between 90¢ and C$1.20. Even within the same city, gas prices can vary by as much as 10¢ per liter. Gasoline tends to be least expensive in Alberta, the heart of Canada's petroleum industry, and most expensive in places such as Newfoundland, where transport costs and high provincial taxes boost the price. Diesel is cheaper than unleaded gas. Many gas stations are self-serve. At full-service stations, attendants do not expect tips. Major credit cards are universally accepted.

FROM THE U.S.

The U.S. Interstate Highway System leads directly into Canada: I–95 from Maine to New Brunswick; I–91 and I–89 from Vermont to Québec; I–87 from New York to Québec; I–81 and a spur off I–90 from New York to Ontario; I–94, I–96, and I–75 from Michigan to Ontario; I–29 from North Dakota to Manitoba; I–15 from Montana to Alberta; and I–5 from Washington state to British Columbia. Most of these connections hook up with the Trans-Canada Highway within a few miles. There are many smaller highway crossings between the two countries as well. From Alaska, take the Alaska Highway (from Fairbanks), the Klondike Highway (from Skagway), and the Top of the World Highway (to Dawson City).

ROAD CONDITIONS

Canadian highways and roads are generally in good shape, as is the highway signage. There tends to be a lot of road repair work in summer, especially in cities, where the winters and heavy traffic create potholes.

RULES OF THE ROAD

By law, you're required to wear seat belts and to use infant seats. Some provinces have a statutory requirement to drive with vehicle headlights on for extended periods after dawn and before sunset. In the Yukon, the law requires that you drive with your headlights on when using territory highways. Right turns are permitted on red signals in all provinces, but not within Montréal. Radar-detection devices are illegal in many provinces, and their presence in a car, even if they're not in operation, is illegal in the provinces of Ontario and Québec. Speed limits, given in kilometers, vary from province to province, but they're usually within the 90 kph–110 kph (55 mph–68 mph) range outside the cities. Drunk driving laws are strictly enforced. The legal limit is 80 mg of alcohol per 100 milliliters of blood (0.08).

BY TRAIN

Amtrak has service from New York to Montréal, New York and Buffalo to Toronto, Chicago to Toronto, and Seattle to Vancouver, providing connections between Amtrak's countrywide network and VIA Rail's Canadian routes. VIA Rail Canada provides transcontinental rail service. Rocky Mountaineer Vacations runs several spectacular all-daylight rail trips through the Canadian Rockies from the west coast.

If you're planning to travel a lot by train, look into buying a rail pass. The Canrail pass allows 12 days of coach-class travel within a 30-day period; sleeping cars are available at an extra cost, but they sell out very early and must be reserved at least a month in advance from June to mid-October. The standard Canrail pass costs C$873 (with discounts for youths and senior citizens) in high season; off-season rates are C$523. If you only want to travel in southern Québec and southern Ontario, the Corridorpass gives you 10 days of travel within a 30-day period anywhere between Québec City and Windsor, including Niagara Falls. Prices are C$299 (discounts for youths and seniors) for coach and C$714 for first class. For more information and reservations, contact a travel agent in the United States.

The 30-day North American RailPass, offered jointly by Amtrak and VIA Rail, allows unlimited coach travel in the United States and Canada. If you wish, you can reserve your seats in advance when purchasing the pass. The cost is C$1,149 from late May to mid-October, C$815 at other times.

Information **Amtrak** (☎800/872–7245 🌐www.amtrak.com). **Rocky Mountaineer Vacations** (☎877/460–3200 🌐www.rkymtnrail.com). **VIA Rail Canada** (☎888/842–7245 🌐www.viarail.com).

ON THE GROUND

COMMUNICATIONS

INTERNET

Contacts **Cybercafes** (www.cybercafes.com) lists over 4,000 Internet cafés worldwide.

PHONES

The good news is that you can now make a direct-dial telephone call from virtually any point on earth. The bad news? You can't always do so cheaply. Calling from a hotel is almost always the most expensive option; hotels usually add huge surcharges to all calls, particularly international ones. In some countries you can phone from call centers or even the post office. Calling cards usually keep costs to a minimum, but only if you purchase them locally. And then there are mobile phones (⇨below), which are sometimes more prevalent—particularly in the developing world—than land lines; as expensive as mobile phone calls can be, they are still usually a much cheaper option than calling from your hotel.

CALLING OUTSIDE CANADA

The country code for the United States is 1.

To call home, just dial the same digits you would from the U.S.

MOBILE PHONES

If you have a multiband phone (some countries use different frequencies from what's used in the United States) and your service provider uses the world-standard GSM network (as do T-Mobile, Cingular, and Verizon), you can probably use your phone abroad. Roaming fees can be steep, however: 99¢ a minute is considered reasonable. And overseas you normally pay the toll charges for incoming calls. It's almost always cheaper to send a text message than to make a call, since text messages have a very low set fee (often less than 5¢).

If you just want to make local calls, consider buying a new SIM card (note that your provider may have to unlock your phone for you to use a different SIM card) and a prepaid service plan in the destination. You'll then have a local number and can make local calls at local rates. If your trip is extensive, you could also simply buy a new cell phone in your destination, as the initial cost will be offset over time.

TIP→ If you travel internationally frequently, save one of your old mobile phones or buy a cheap one on the Internet; ask your cell phone company to unlock it for you, and take it with you as a travel phone, buying a new SIM card with pay-as-you-go service in each destination.

Contacts **Cellular Abroad** (☎800/287–5072 www.cellularabroad.com) rents and sells GMS phones and sells SIM cards that work in many countries. **Mobal** (☎888/888–9162 www.mobalrental.com) rents mobiles and sells GSM phones (starting at $49) that will operate in 140 countries. Per-call rates vary throughout the world. **Planet Fone** (☎888/988–4777 www.planetfone.com) rents cell phones, but the per-minute rates are expensive.

CUSTOMS & DUTIES

You're always allowed to bring goods of a certain value back home without having to pay any duty or import tax. But there's a limit on the amount of tobacco and liquor you can bring back duty-free, and some countries have separate limits for perfumes; for exact figures, check with your customs department. The values of so-called "duty-free" goods are included in these amounts. When you shop abroad, save all your receipts, as customs inspectors may ask to see them as well as the items you purchased. If the total value of your goods is more than the duty-free limit, you'll have to pay a tax (most often a flat percentage) on the value of everything beyond that limit.

U.S. Customs and Immigration has preclearance services at international airports in Calgary, Edmonton, Montréal, Ottawa, Toronto, Vancouver, and Winnipeg. This allows U.S.-bound air passengers to depart their airplane directly on arrival at their U.S. destination without further inspection or delay.

American and British visitors may bring in the following items duty-free: 200 cigarettes, 50 cigars, and 7 ounces of tobacco; 1 bottle (1.14 liters or 40 imperial ounces) of liquor or wine, or 24 355-ml (12-ounce) bottles or cans of beer for personal consumption. Any alcohol and tobacco products in excess of these amounts are subject to duty, provincial fees, and taxes. You can also bring in gifts up to a total value of C$750.

A deposit is sometimes required for trailers (refunded upon return). Cats and dogs must have a certificate issued by a licensed veterinarian that clearly identifies the animal and certifies that it has been vaccinated against rabies during the preceding 36 months. Guide dogs are allowed into Canada without restriction. Plant material must be declared and inspected. There may be restrictions on some live plants, bulbs, and seeds. With certain restrictions or prohibitions on some fruits and vegetables, visitors may bring food with them for their own use, providing the quantity is consistent with the duration of the visit.

Canada's firearms laws are significantly stricter than those in the United States. All handguns and semiautomatic and fully automatic weapons are prohibited and cannot be brought into the country. Sporting rifles and shotguns may be brought into the country provided they are to be used for sporting, hunting, or competition while in Canada. All firearms must be declared to Canada Customs at the first point of entry. Failure to declare firearms will result in their seizure, and criminal charges may be made. Regulations require visitors to have a confirmed "Firearms Declaration" to bring any guns into Canada; a fee of C$25 applies, good for one year. For more information, contact the Canadian Firearms Centre.

Information in Canada Canada Customs and Revenue Agency (☎204/983–3500, 506/636–5064, 800/461–9999 in Canada 🌐www.ccra.gc.ca). **Canadian Firearms Centre** (☎800/731–4000 🌐www.cfc-cafc.gc.ca).

U.S. Information U.S. Customs and Border Protection (🌐www.cbp.gov).

EATING OUT

The restaurants we list are the cream of the crop in each price category. *Information about regional dining, including a price chart, is included at the beginning of each chapter.*

MEALS & MEALTIMES

Unless otherwise noted, the restaurants listed in this guide are open daily for lunch and dinner.

PAYING

For guidelines on tipping see Tipping below.

CATEGORY	COST
$$$$	Over C$30
$$$	C$21–C$30
$$	C$13–C$20
$	C$8–C$12
¢	Under C$8

All prices are per person for a main course at dinner.

RESERVATIONS & DRESS

Regardless of where you are, it's a good idea to make a reservation if you can. In some places (Hong Kong, for example), it's expected. We only mention them specifically when reservations are essential (there's no other way you'll ever get a table) or when they are not accepted. For popular restaurants, book as far ahead as you can (often 30 days), and reconfirm as soon as you arrive. (Large parties should always call ahead to check the reservations policy.) We mention dress only when men are required to wear a jacket or a jacket and tie.

Online reservation services make it easy to book a table before you even leave home. OpenTable covers most states, including 20 major cities, and has limited listings in Canada, Mexico, the United Kingdom, and elsewhere. DinnerBroker has restaurants throughout the United States as well as a few in Canada.

Contacts OpenTable (www.opentable.com). **DinnerBroker** (www.dinnerbroker.com).

ELECTRICITY

Consider making a small investment in a universal adapter, which has several types of plugs in one lightweight, compact unit. Most laptops and mobile phone chargers are dual voltage (i.e., they operate equally well on 110 and 220 volts), so require only an adapter. These days the same is true of small appliances such as hair dryers. Always check labels and manufacturer instructions to be sure. Don't use 110-volt outlets marked FOR SHAVERS ONLY for high-wattage appliances such as hair-dryers.

Contacts Steve Kropla's Help for World Traveler's (www.kropla.com) has information on electrical and telephone plugs around the world. **Walkabout Travel Gear** (www.walkabouttravelgear.com) has a good coverage of electricity under "adapters."

EMERGENCIES

All embassies are in Ottawa; there are consulates in some major cities. Emergency information is given in the Essentials section at the end of each chapter.

WORD OF MOUTH

Was the service stellar or not up to snuff? Did the food give you shivers of delight or leave you cold? Did the prices and portions make you happy or sad? Rate restaurants and write your own reviews in Travel Ratings or start a discussion about your favorite places in Travel Talk on www.fodors.com. Your comments might even appear in our books. Yes, you, too, can be a correspondent!

Embassies U.S. Embassy (490 Sussex Dr., Ottawa 613/238–5335).

HEALTH

Infectious diseases can be airborne or passed via mosquitoes and ticks and through direct or indirect physical contact with animals or people. Some, including Norwalk-like viruses that affect your digestive tract, can be passed along through contaminated food. If you are traveling in an area where malaria is prevalent, use a repellant containing DEET and take malaria-prevention medication before, during, and after your trip as directed by your physician. Condoms can help prevent most sexually transmitted diseases, but they aren't absolutely reliable and their quality varies from country to country. Speak with your physician or check the CDC or World Health Organization Web sites for health alerts, particularly if you're pregnant, traveling with children, or have a chronic illness.

For information on travel insurance, shots and medications, and medical-assistance companies see Shots & Medications under Things to Consider in Before You Go, above.

HOURS OF OPERATION

Most banks in Canada are open Monday–Thursday 10–4 and Friday 10–5 or 6. Some banks are open longer hours and also on Saturday morning. All banks are closed on national holidays. Most banks (and some gas stations) have automatic teller machines (ATMs) that are accessible around the clock.

Most highway and city gas stations in Canada are open daily (although there's rarely a mechanic on duty Sunday) and some are open around the clock. In small towns, gas stations are often closed on Sunday, although they may take turns staying open.

Hours at museums vary, but most open at 10 or 11 and close in the evening. Some smaller museums close for lunch. Many museums are closed on Monday; some make up for it by staying open late on Wednesday or Thursday, often waiving admission.

The days when churches were always open are gone; vandalism, theft, and the drop in general piety have seen to that. But the major churches in big cities—the Basilique Notre-Dame-de-Montréal, for example—are open daily, usually about 9–6.

Pharmacies in big cities are often open daily until 11 PM, and major cities like Montréal, Ottawa, Toronto, and Vancouver usually have some 24-hour pharmacies. Pharmacies in less populated areas usually keep regular business hours (9 to 5 or 6) during the week, and may have reduced hours on weekends.

Stores, shops, and supermarkets are usually open Monday–Saturday 9–6, although in major cities, supermarkets are often open 7:30 AM–9 PM, and some food stores are open around the clock. Blue laws are in effect in much of Canada, but in a growing number of provinces, stores—even liquor stores—have limited Sunday hours, usually noon–5. Shops in areas highly frequented by tourists are usually open Sunday. Stores often stay open Thursday and Friday evenings, most shopping malls until 9 PM. Drugstores in major cities are often open until 11 PM, and convenience stores tend to be open 24 hours a day, seven days a week.

HOLIDAYS

Canadian national holidays are as follows: New Year's Day (January 1), Good Friday, Easter Monday, Victoria Day (Monday preceding May 25), Canada Day (July 1), Labour Day (first Monday in September), Thanksgiving (second Monday in October), Remembrance Day (November 11), Christmas, and Boxing Day (December 26).

MAIL

If you're sending mail to or within Canada, be sure to include the postal code (six digits and letters). Note that the suite number often appears before the street number in an address, followed by a hyphen.

Following are postal abbreviations for provinces and territories: Alberta, AB; British Columbia, BC; Manitoba, MB; New Brunswick, NB; Newfoundland and Labrador, NF; Northwest Territories, NT; Nova Scotia, NS; Nunavut, NU; Ontario, ON; Prince Edward Island, PE; Québec, QC; Saskatchewan, SK; Yukon, YT.

Within Canada, postcards and letters up to 30 grams cost 52¢; between 31 grams and 50 grams, the cost is 93¢; and between 51 grams and 100 grams, the cost is C$1.10.

Most mail sent out of Canada goes by air. Letters and postcards to the United States cost 93¢ for up to 30 grams, C$1.10 for 31 grams to 50 grams, and C$1.86 for 51 grams to 100 grams.

International mail and postcards run C$1.55 for up to 30 grams, C$2.20 for 31 grams to 50 grams, and C$3.60 for 51 grams to 100 grams.

You may have mail sent to you in care of General Delivery in the town you're visiting for pickup in person within 15 days, after which it will be returned to the sender.

SHIPPING PACKAGES

For parcels to the U.S., Canada Post offers numerous shipping options: next-day delivery, delivery within 5 to 10 business days, or 6 to 12 business days. The cheapest service, if you're sending up to 1 kg/2.2 lbs, is surface small package delivery. For shipping to most other countries, you have a choice of delivery within 2 to 3 business days, 6 to 10 business days, or by surface mail, 4 to 6 weeks. You can buy envelopes and shipping boxes at any post office.

MONEY

Throughout this book, unless otherwise stated, all prices, including dining and lodging, are given in Canadian dollars, indicated by C$; prices in this Smart Travel Tips section are listed in U.S. dollars ($) or Canadian dollars (C$), depending on the context.

ITEM	AVERAGE COST
Cup of Coffee	C$1.50–C$2.50
Glass of Beer	C$3.50–C$6.50
Sandwich	C$3.50–C$8.50
One-Mile Taxi Ride in Capital City	C$5–C$7.50
Museum Admission	C$5–C$10

Prices throughout this guide are given for adults. Substantially reduced fees are almost always available for children, students, and senior citizens.

TIP→ Banks never have every foreign currency on hand, and it may take as long as a week to order. If you're planning to exchange funds before leaving home, don't wait till the last minute.

ATMS & BANKS

Your own bank will probably charge a fee for using ATMs abroad; the foreign bank you use may also charge a fee. Nevertheless, you'll usually get a better rate of exchange at an ATM than you will at a currency-exchange office or even when changing money in a bank. And extracting funds as you need them is a safer option than carrying around a large amount of cash.

TIP→ PIN numbers with more than four digits are not recognized at ATMs in many countries. If yours has five or more, remember to change it before you leave.

ATMs are available in most bank, trust-company, and credit-union branches across the country, as well as in most convenience stores, malls, and gas stations.

CREDIT CARDS

Throughout this guide, the following abbreviations are used: **AE,** American Express; **D,** Discover; **DC,** Diners Club; **MC,** MasterCard; and **V,** Visa.

It's a good idea to inform your credit-card company before you travel, especially if you're going abroad and don't travel internationally very often. Otherwise, the credit-card company might put a hold on your card owing to unusual activity—not a good thing halfway through your trip. Record all your credit-card numbers—as well as the phone numbers to call if your cards are lost or stolen—in a safe place, so you're prepared should something go wrong. Both MasterCard and Visa have general numbers you can call (collect if you're abroad) if your card is lost, but you're better off calling the number of your issuing bank, since MasterCard and Visa usually just transfer you to your bank; your bank's number is usually printed on your card.

If you plan to use your credit card for cash advances, you'll need to apply for a PIN at least two weeks before your trip. Although it's usually cheaper (and safer) to use a credit card abroad for large purchases (so you can cancel payments or be reimbursed if there's a problem), note that some credit-card companies *and* the banks that issue them add substantial percentages to all foreign transactions, whether they're in a foreign currency or not. Check on these fees before leaving home, so there won't be any surprises when you get the bill.

TIP→ Before you charge something, ask the merchant whether or not he or she plans to do a dynamic currency conversion (DCC). In such a transaction the credit-card *processor* (shop, restaurant, or hotel, not Visa or MasterCard) converts the currency and charges you in dollars. In most cases you'll pay the merchant a 3% fee for this service in addition to any credit-card company and issuing-bank foreign-transaction surcharges.

Dynamic currency conversion programs are becoming increasingly widespread. Merchants who participate in them are supposed to ask whether you want to be charged in dollars or the local currency, but they don't always do so. And even if they do offer you a choice, they may well avoid mentioning the additional surcharges. The good news is that you *do* have a choice. And if this practice really gets your goat, you can avoid it entirely thanks to American Express; with its cards, DCC simply isn't an option.

Reporting Lost Cards **American Express** (☎800/528–4800 in U.S., 336/393–1111 collect from abroad 🌐www.americanexpress.com). **Diners Club** (☎800/234–6377 in U.S., 303/799–1504 collect from abroad 🌐www.dinersclub.com). **Discover** (☎800/347–2683 in U.S., 801/902–3100 collect from abroad 🌐www.discovercard.com). **MasterCard** (☎800/627–8372 in U.S., 636/722–7111 collect from abroad 🌐www.mastercard.com). **Visa** (☎800/847–2911 in U.S., 410/581–9994 collect from abroad 🌐www.visa.com).

CURRENCY & EXCHANGE

U.S. dollars are accepted in much of Canada (especially in communities near the border). However, to get the most favorable exchange rate, exchange at least some of your money into Canadian funds at a bank or other financial institution. Traveler's checks (some are available in Canadian dollars) and major U.S. credit cards are accepted in most areas.

The units of currency in Canada are the Canadian dollar (C$) and the cent, in almost the same denominations as U.S. currency (C$5, C$10, C$20, 1¢, 5¢, 10¢, 25¢, etc.). The C$1 and C$2 bill are no longer used; they have been replaced by C$1 and C$2 coins (known as a "loonie," because of the loon that appears on the coin, and a "toonie," respectively). At this writing the exchange rate was dead even: US$1 to C$1.

TIP→ Even if a currency-exchange booth has a sign promising no commission, rest assured that there's some kind of huge, hidden fee. (Oh . . . that's right. The sign didn't say no *fee*.) And as for rates, you're almost always better off getting foreign currency at an ATM or exchanging money at a bank.

TRAVELER'S CHECKS & CARDS

Some consider this the currency of the cave man, and it's true that fewer establishments accept traveler's checks these days. Nevertheless, they're a cheap and secure way to carry extra money, particularly on trips to urban areas. Both Citibank (under the Visa brand) and American Express issue traveler's checks in the United States, but Amex is better known and more widely accepted; you can also avoid hefty surcharges by cashing Amex checks at Amex offices. Whatever you do, keep track of all the serial numbers in case the checks are lost or stolen.

Contacts **American Express** (☎888/412–6945 in U.S., 801/945–9450 collect outside of U.S. to add value or speak to customer service 🌐www.americanexpress.com).

RESTROOMS

Find a Loo The Bathroom Diaries (www.thebathroomdiaries.com) is flush with unsanitized info on restrooms the world over—each one located, reviewed, and rated.

SAFETY

TIP→ Distribute your cash, credit cards, IDs, and other valuables between a deep front pocket, an inside jacket or vest pocket, and a hidden money pouch. Don't reach for the money pouch once you're in public.

TAXES

A goods and services tax (GST) of 6% applies to virtually every transaction in Canada except for the purchase of basic groceries.

In addition to imposing the GST, all provinces except Alberta, the Northwest Territories, and the Yukon levy a sales tax from 5% to 8% on most items purchased in shops, on restaurant meals, and sometimes on hotel rooms. In Newfoundland, Prince Edward Island, Nova Scotia, and New Brunswick, the single harmonized sales tax (HST) of 14% is used.

Ontario offers a sales-tax rebate system. The 8% Provincial Sales Tax (PST) is refunded on purchases with a retail value of at least $625. The tax is not refundable on consumer goods, accommodation, transportation, service, and rentals. Most provinces do not tax goods shipped directly by the vendor to the visitor's home address.

Information Ontario Ministry of Revenue (905/432-3431 or 800/263-7965 www.rev.gov.on.ca/english/refund/visitor).

TIME

Canada spans six time zones (relation to Greenwich mean time in parentheses): Pacific (-8 hours), Mountain (-7), Central (-6), Eastern (-5), Atlantic (-4), and Newfoundland (-4½).

Daylight saving time is observed in summer. Traditionally agricultural Saskatchewan observes Central time in winter and Mountain time in summer.

TIPPING

Tips and service charges are not usually added to the bill in Canada. In general, tip 15% of the total bill. This goes for servers, barbers and hairdressers, and taxi drivers. Porters and doormen should get about C$2 a bag. For maid service, leave at least C$2 per person per day (C$3 in luxury hotels).

INDEX

G

H

N

O

P

Q

R

S

V

W

PHOTO CREDITS

10, *P. Narayan/age fotostock.* 11 (left), *Wolfgang Kaehler/Alamy.* 11 (right), *Douglas Williams/age fotostock.* 12, *Josh McCulloch/age fotostock.* 13 (left), *Tony Pleavin/Alamy.* 13 (right), *Luis Orteo/Hemis.fr/Aurora Photos.* 14, *Bruno Perousse/age fotostock.* 15, *Barrett & MacKay/age fotostock.* 16, *Marek Slusarczyk.* 17, *Ray Stubblebine/Icon Sports Media.* 18, *Randy Lincks/age fotostock.* 19 (left), *Bill Brooks/Alamy.* 19 (right), *Atlantide S.N.C./age fotostock.* **Chapter 4: Banff National Park:** *198–201, Travel Alberta.* **Chapter 5: Jasper National Park:** *228–29, Travel Alberta.*

NOTES

NOTES

NOTES

NOTES

NOTES

NOTES

NOTES

NOTES

NOTES

NOTES

Shannon Kelly, a freelance writer and editor, has contributed to many Fodor's guides, including San Francisco, Brazil, and New York City. A serial mover, she lives, for now, in Toronto's Little Italy.

Vancouver-born freelance writer **Sue Kernaghan** has written about British Columbia for dozens of publications throughout North America and the United Kingdom. A fourth-generation British Columbian, she has contributed to several editions of *Fodor's Vancouver & British Columbia,* as well as to *Fodor's Alaska, Great Canadian Vacations, Healthy Escapes,* and *Escape to Nature Without Roughing It*. She lives on Salt Spring Island with her partner and small son.

An award-winning, freelance travel writer, **Chris McBeath's** more than 25 years in tourism have given her an insider's eye as to what makes a great vacation experience. Whether routing through backcountry, or discovering a hidden-away inn, Chris has combined history, insight, and anecdotes into her research for this book, and of her home, British Columbia. Many of her articles can be found at www.greatestgetaways.com.

After a decade living in L.A., **Celeste Moure** recently traded traffic and smog for a slice of Vancouver heaven: crisp mountain air, fresh powder, and old-growth forests. Her work has appeared in *Condé Nast Traveler, Outside, Spin,* and various other publications. She updated the Whistler Excursion and covered the Nightlife and the Arts chapter of Vancouver.

Debbie Olsen is an Alberta-based freelance travel writer who spends much of her time exploring national parks with her husband and four children. She writes travel columns for the *Red Deer Advocate* and the *Calgary Herald* and freelance travel articles for other publications.

Sandra Phinney writes from her perch in Yarmouth, Nova Scotia where she's penned two books and hundreds of articles in over 60 publications. She's happiest when meeting people and exploring off-the-beaten-track places in Atlantic Canada.

Pat Rediger, a city entertainment and lifestyle magazine. An author of 18 books, he has also served as editor of *Saskatchewan Business* and *Alberta Business* magazines and written articles for numerous publications.

Sarah Richards was delighted to settle in Toronto, what she touts as the world's most multicultural city, after wandering about Asia and Europe for five years. She updated the Toronto sections for this edition. She has also contributed to past editions of *Fodor's Japan* and *Fodor's Great Britain*.

Amy Rosen is a Toronto-based food and travel writer who has also authored two cookbooks. She pens and illustrates a weekly "Dish" column in the *National Post* newspaper, and is a contributing editor for *enRoute* magazine. Amy, a James Beard Award nominee, is currently working on a culinary work of fiction.

A travel writer who's lived in France, Mexico, the U.S. and various Canadian cities, **Mary Ann Simpkins** always returns to her first love, Ottawa. Besides writing for the *Ottawa Citizen, Montreal Gazette* and others, she wrote *Travel Bug Canada* and co-authored *Ottawa Stories*.

Paul Waters, a journalist and veteran travel writer, is on the editorial board of the *Montréal Gazette*. His wife and travel-writing partner, **Julie Waters**, writes for several trade publications.

ABOUT OUR WRITERS

Alison Appelbe is a Vancouver-based freelance writer and photographer. She frequently writes about her native city of Vancouver and the province of British Columbia, where favorite haunts include Tofino, covered in this guide, and the Okanagan Valley. Her work appears in mostly print publications in Canada, the United States, Australia, and occasionally Europe.

Wanita Bates has lived in five different Canadian provinces but, since 1992, has become a self-proclaimed "NBC'er"—a Newfoundlander By Choice—and loves it. Based in St. John's and the Southern Shore, Wanita spends her time traveling around the easternmost province telling people's stories, in words, photographs and on radio. Her work has appeared in *Canadian Geographic, Chatelaine, Today's Parent,* and *Border Crossings.*

Bruce Bishop has been updating Fodor's guides from Singapore to the Caribbean to Denmark to his native Canada since 1998. He lived and worked for 25 years in Toronto, and considers it his second home. Bruce currently resides in Nova Scotia, where he continues to write for a variety of international travel magazines and newspapers, and is enjoying his second career as a media-relations consultant with his company, brucebishop.com.

Jeff Bursey has only ever lived on islands, including PEI and Newfoundland and Labrador. He's written tourism pieces on PEI for national and international vacationers. His fiction, book reviews, and articles have appeared throughout North America and England.

Teresa Earle writes for Tourism Yukon and her travel articles have appeared in the *Globe and Mail, Canadian Geographic Travel* and *Up Here.* A resident of Whitehorse, she's spent the past decade exploring the parks, mountains, and rivers of Yukon's vast wilderness.

Amy Pugsley Fraser, a reporter at the *Halifax Herald,* updated the Nova Scotia Essentials and the Nova Scotia and Atlantic Canada Essentials sections for this edition. Her writing has been published in local books such as *Hurricane Juan: The Story of a Storm* and *Halifax Street Names,* as well as in *Canadian House & Home* and other national magazines. Amy lives in Halifax with her husband and two young sons.

Carolyn B. Heller, who updated the Vancouver Dining and Okanagan Excursion chapters, has been enthusiastically exploring—and eating—her way across her adopted city of Vancouver since she relocated here in 2003. Her travel and food articles have appeared in publications ranging from the *Boston Globe* and the *Los Angeles Times,* to *FamilyFun* magazine and *Travelers' Tales Paris,* and she's contributed to more than 25 Fodor's guides for destinations from New England to New Zealand.

Homegrown Manitoba freelance writer **Christine Hanlon** is passionate about her province, through which she has traveled extensively. She's also had the privilege to cover its vibrant culture, people and places through such magazines as Style Manitoba, Western Living and Going Places, publication of the Canadian Automobile Association.

Hélèna Katz has been a travel journalist for 10 years and her work has appeared in a variety of magazines and newspapers including *Canadian Geographic, Outdoor Canada, Montréal Gazette, Above & Beyond, More Magazine* and *Up Here.* From caribou and northern agriculture to ice roads and the Mackenzie River, she covers the Canadian North for various publications. Hélèna lives in Fort Smith, Northwest Territories on the edge of Wood Buffalo National Park.